TOP OF
THE CHARTS

TOP OF
THE CHARTS

THE MOST COMPLETE LISTING EVER

Nelson George

New Century Publishers, Inc.

To my mother, my sister, and little Ebony

Charts are the courtesy of Record World Publishing Company, Inc.

Printing Code
11   12   13   14   15   16

Library of Congress Cataloging in Publication Data

George, Nelson.
Top of the charts.

1. Music, Popular (Songs, etc.)—United States—Discography. 2. Music, Popular (Songs, etc.)—United States—Chronology. I. Title.
ML156.4.P6G46   1983   789.9′1245′00973   83-8108
ISBN 0-8329-0260-8

CONTENTS

ACKNOWLEDGMENTS

Many people contributed valuable time and effort to the writing and compilation of the material in this book, often exceeding the call of duty. For those extra efforts I'm particularly grateful to: Heidi Smith, Marcia Belle, Dawn Lewis, Robin Downes, Kerry Reagen, Lance Kirwan, Jim Mendiola, Andrea George and Elaine Wapples. My thanks also to my agent, Robert Cornfield; to my special consultants, Robert Ford Jr. and Robert Christgau; to my friends, Brian Chin, Jared McAlister, Ellen Ford, Russell Simmons, Von Alexander, Dr. Dionne Cooke, and Sheila Eldridge; and to all the others forced to listen to my endless moaning. A bow to Mike Sigman for his invaluable assistance and for giving me the information which made this work possible and my thanks to Sheryl Hilliard for all the advice and all the sweetness.

FOREWORD

What we have here, ladies and gentlemen, is the popular music of the 1970s and early 1980s in words, pictures, and charts. To some this must seem a useless exercise since they consider 1970s music, and the decade in general, a wasteland preceded by the wonderful, liberating, exhilarating, innovative ten years known as the 1960s. All those free-loving baby boomers who came of age in 1968, 1966, or even 1963, have become as narrow-minded and parochial as they claimed their parents were. I have nothing against nostalgia—it is an inevitable and pleasant part of life, but I worry that memories of the 1960s are stifling the children of the 1970s. I fear that the events of the '70s will be smothered under the myths of the '60s, our nostalgia ridiculed or undervalued by folks whose eyes still mist over at the mention of Haight-Ashbury, the Chicago convention or—give me a break—acid trips.

Yes, this sounds a touch melodramatic. But there is a cultural elitism, superiority complex, and just plain snobbery about the 1960s that is truly irksome. When I see 17-year-olds wearing Grateful Dead T-shirts, buying biographies of Jim Morrison, and buying out rock clubs to see James Brown, I see kids seduced into revering the myths of another age. They have been persuaded that their generation has no identity.

Yet the 1970s left much to savor. The Eagles; Michael Jackson; Bruce Springsteen; The Cars; Earth, Wind and Fire; Chic; Al Green; Steely Dan; Bob Marley; Weather Report; Eddie Rabbitt; The Clash; Prince; The Police; Peabo Bryson; Lynyrd Skynyrd; Elton John; and Rick James all debuted in the 1970s. At the same time Billy Joel, Kenny Gamble and Leon Huff, The Bee Gees, Fleetwood Mac, Pink Floyd, Neil Young, Paul Simon, Isaac Hayes, and Willie Nelson were doing their best work. Miles Davis and Stevie Wonder utilized the unprecedented growth of studio technology to expand the palate of contemporary music and founded new genres, fusion- and synthesizer-pop.

In fact, there was a growth in the number of musical genres in pop in the 1970s. Since the birth of rock 'n' roll in about 1955, American popular music was defined with broad, all-encompassing terms like rock, mainstream pop, MOR (middle of the road), soul/R&B (rhythm and blues),

country, and jazz. During the 1970s it became clear that these terms were too vague to describe the variety of musical styles and audiences contemporary music reached.

Out of soul/R&B came disco (for self-consciously trendy urban gays, blacks, and Latins), funk (founded in the industrial Midwest and South among working-class blacks), black pop (for whites as well as blacks), and rap (black inner-city youth music). From rock came heavy metal (for white suburban youth), pop rock (a mix of pop melodies with the musical trappings of heavy metal made for mass appeal), punk (nihilistic music that charmed a cult following in America and a mass audience in Great Britain), and new wave (a nostalgic return to the basic rock 'n' roll of the 1950s). From jazz came fusion (an electrified mating of a jazz sensibility and electronics that entertained bored rock fans), pop jazz (laid-back, cocaine-mellow sound for those who craved jazz's sensitivity but not its complexity), and avant-garde (experimental music followed by dedicated aficionados).

Like paintings on ancient walls, you can learn a lot from the charts contained herein. The trends in country music are a good example. The emergence of "outlaw" country stars Willie Nelson and Waylon Jennings in the mid-'70s, their preference for Western imagery and clothing, and dominance of the country charts into the 1980s laid the groundwork for the country "chic" that *Urban Cowboy* (film and soundtrack) capitalized upon. That Americans elected a president who favors Western garb at the height of Waylon and Willie's popularity (when even inner-city blacks wore ten-gallon hats) and Miles Davis wrote a tune called "Willie Nelson" is perhaps no accident. President Reagan's identification with the simple Americana of country music (visually if not morally), along with his boots, may have meant as much to voters as supply-side economics.

Because of their sequential nature these charts lend themselves to interpretation and story telling. The durability of The Rolling Stones, Marvin Gaye's occasional brilliance, the death of Memphis soul, the mediocrity of Paul McCartney, the surrender of adventurous fusion into safe pop-jazz are just five trends to be observed.

The charts, themselves, have a story. At the beginning of

the 1970s there was no black-album chart, since black music fans weren't considered album buyers. It wasn't until Sly and the Family Stone's *Stand* in late 1969 that black musicians realized the possibilities of the album as an creative expression. By the time *Record World* introduced the black chart in 1971, Marvin Gaye, the Norman Whitfield-produced Temptations, and Isaac Hayes had established the album as a powerful commercial and artistic tool in black music.

Hayes is also a central figure in the decline of sales-based jazz charts as a meaningful chronicle of new trends in improvisational music. With *Shaft*, *The Isaac Hayes Movement*, and other early 1970s efforts, Hayes topped both the black (then R&B) and jazz charts, though his music bore the most superficial relationship to jazz. Hayes excelled at mellow mood music and by the 1980s George Benson, Grover Washington Jr., and a long list of ex-jazzmen were making cocaine-mellow music for a large, loyal audience. Only rarely did a Miles Davis or Weather Report strike a commercial blow for more ambitious composing.

Also noteworthy is the evolution of heavy metal. Led Zeppelin made music of a bluesy intensity and pastoral splendor rock had rarely seen. R.E.O. Speedwagon began its career, as did so many young Midwestern "head-banger" bands of the 1970s, emulating many of Led Zep's ideas. But R.E.O. didn't make big money until they smoothed out the rough edges into melodic curves that Elton John must envy these days. R.E.O. found, as did Boston, Styx, Journey, and Kansas, that the 1970s demanded craft, calculation, and maturity if they were to survive the uncertain economics of the late 1970s.

The bottom fell out of the record industry after 1978. The recession, bad business practices, and the cassette replacement of albums and singles as the dominant format for enjoying music racked the industry with uncertainty. People love music. Just look at the ratings of FM music stations and sales of cassettes and tape players. The record industry, with characteristic foresight, wasn't ready for the change and adopted a siege mentality that continues to this day. As with the national economic scene, a total rethinking of how the record industry does business is now essential and inevitable.

This volume contains the top 10 pop, black, jazz, and country records for every week from 1970 to 1981 as listed in *Record World* magazine. Any inconsistencies (for example, a jazz chart missing in November 1971) is because it wasn't printed and doesn't exist. Now fans of lists, it's all yours.

NELSON GEORGE
Jamaica, New York

TOP OF
THE CHARTS

1970

The first year of the decade was more an end than a beginning. The bands, the sounds, and the movements of the 1960s still held center stage at the start of Richard Nixon's second full year in office. However, by December, three of the era's greatest artists had been claimed by disintegration or by death.

The Beatles fragmented into four pieces that would never match their collective achievements. Following the band's demise, the *Let It Be* album and film was released. The music in *Let It Be* captured the emotional and musical simplicity of their early years, highlighted by two enduring performances: the rocking "Get Back" with Billy Preston on keyboards and Paul McCartney's Phil Spector-ized ballad, "The Long and Winding Road." The film is a fascinating account of The Beatles' internal conflicts, particularly the tension between John Lennon, Yoko Ono, and Paul McCartney. George Harrison's philosophical *All Things Must Pass* was, to the surprise of many, the best of the immediate post-Beatles albums. His songwriting, previously stifled by McCartney and Lennon's hegemony finally was given free reign.

Drugs were glorified by the flower children, symbolic of the 1960s youth culture, and the inspiration for so much music. But drugs were no plaything, a lesson many learned much too late. Heroin claimed Janis Joplin—a sad end for a woman-child who lusted after experience with vigor, but poor judgment. Stories are legend about her adventures in the realm of sex and drugs. Thankfully, everything you need to know about Joplin came through her voice—a raspy, vital, strained, thrilling, screaming instrument that was as flamboyant as her life—which set standards for emotional honesty that no subsequent female rock singer would match.

Jimi Hendrix, the man who had recreated the electric guitar with his unmatched virtuosity, suffocated on his own vomit after downing too many sleeping pills in a London flat. Prior to his death, Hendrix was moving away from the narrow confines of heavy metal—a style he had defined—and expressed interest in playing jazz compositions and utilizing R&B rhythms. In fact, *Band of Gypsys* was recorded with black musicians: drummer Buddy Miles and bassist Billy Cox. Not surprisingly, it became the forerunner of black rock, a sound the Isley Brothers, among others, would later adopt.

Hendrix also played an important part in both the film and record of the mammoth 1969 Woodstock festival. Though there were exhilarating performances by The Who, Joe Cocker, and Sly and the Family Stone, it was Hendrix who put the final cap on the previous decade's last gasps. As Hendrix warped "The Star-Spangled Banner," and the camera panned over a dirty, half-awake crowd and garbage-covered field, one couldn't help but feel that his guitar was a bell chiming the end, not just to another concert, but to the utopian visions of a disappointed generation.

ALBUMS: Grand Funk Railroad's (guitarist-vocalist Mark Farmer, drummer Don Brewer, bassist Mel Schacher) spectacular sales were matched by savage critical attacks, establishing a pattern of commercial acceptance and critical contempt for Midwestern bands. On *Grand Funk, Closer to Home*, and the double album *Grand Funk Live*, this Michigan-based power trio bastardized the innovations of Cream and the Jimi Hendrix Experience into a slick, easy-to-package format. Unlike their inspirations, Grand Funk Railroad wasn't dangerous or unpredictable, which offended the critical community, who felt both were essential to rock 'n' roll. In contrast, Grand Funk Railroad's fans, mostly young people who identified intensely with their rock heroes, found that predictability quite appealing.

Chicago also would suffer critical attacks throughout the decade and, like Grand Funk Railroad, prosper. Where Grand Funk Railroad's rise (and subsequent fall) was meteoric, Chicago's hallmark was consistency. During the 1970s Chicago's initial big-band style would come to embrace the entire spectrum of pop music. The *Chicago II* album, for example, contained the ballad "Make Me Smile," the blistering rocker "25 or 6 to 4," and a composition in six movements called "Ballet for a Girl in Buchanan."

Simon and Garfunkel's *Bridge Over Troubled Water* was the most successful and, sadly, their last LP of the decade. It reached #1 on the charts, with the title track becoming one of pop's most recorded songs. But by the end of the recording sessions, it was clear that Paul Simon and Art Garfunkel were going in different directions.

Sly and the Family Stone's *Stand* was the most brilliant album of this great band's career. The songs were joyous (the title song, "Everybody Is A Star"), the musicianship superb ("Sex Machine"), and the lyrics committed ("Don't Call Me Nigger, Whitey"). Sly Stone's music would never be this happy or invigorating again.

Traffic's *John Barleycorn Must Die* possessed a unique mix of folk, rock, and jazz molded by the exceptional musician-vocalist Steve Winwood. The shifting textures and jam session atmosphere of "Freedom Rider" and the title song are as fascinating today as when the LP was released.

Of all the music released in 1970, Miles Davis's *Bitches Brew* was among the most influential. The masterful jazz trumpeter plugged his horn into an amplifier and recorded with electric instruments. The result was called jazz-rock. Musicians, fans, and writers debated its validity, its musicality, its commerciality: Davis just played it. On this album he introduced guitarist John McLaughlin, plus keyboard players Herbie Hancock and Chick Corea to the rock community. The three best electric jazz bands of the 1970s—Weather Report, Return to Forever, and The Mahavishnu Orchestra—were offshoots of *Bitches Brew*.

The country albums of the year all came from that music's most unlikely star, Charley Pride. Tall, handsome black men were not supposed to appeal to the white working-class folks who fancy country's tales of loves lost and lonesome highways. Yet Pride's reassuring croon made *The Best of Charley Pride, Just Plain Charley*, and *Charley Pride's 10th Album* huge sellers.

Pretty pop songs made for humming along with were plentiful. The Carpenters' "Close to You," B.J. Thomas's "Raindrops Keep Falling on My Head," Marvin Gaye and Tammi Terrell's "Ain't No Mountain High Enough," Ray

Stevens's "Everything is Beautiful," Bread's "Make It With You," and The Hollies' "He Ain't Heavy (He's My Brother)" have all become standards, played by bar mitzvah bands, heard in elevators, and sung at high school talent shows.

The Motown sound, modified with funk and supporting some new faces, continued to prosper. The young Jackson 5 led the way with "ABC," "The Love You Save," and "I Want You Back"—the most explosive first three singles by any group in pop history. The Temptations' "Ball of Confusion," Stevie Wonder's "Signed, Sealed, Delivered," Edwin Starr's "War," and the Spinners' "It's A Shame," were all strong records that attracted whites and blacks. The original shapers of the Motown sound, producers Brian Holland, Lamont Dozier, and Eddie Holland, scored impressively with two songs on their Invictus label: "Band of Gold" by Freda Payne and "Give Me Just A Little More Time" by Chairmen of the Board.

1970 was also a great year for one-hit groups. All those summer bands you'd never heard of before and never would again provided the catchiest music. "Hitchin' A Ride" by Vanity Fare, "Signs" by the Five Man Electrical Band, "Chick-A-Boom" by Daddy Dewdrop, "Sweet City Woman" by the Stampeders, "Right On the Tip of My Tongue" by Brenda and the Tabulations, and the unforgettable "Groove Me" by King Floyd were aural cotton candy of the most addictive sort.

The literature of pop music was enhanced greatly by Charlie Gillet's *Sound of the City*. Gillet provided an exhaustive (and occasionally exhausting) history of rock 'n' roll keyed to the regional styles and the small independent companies that supported the music during its formative years. Today *Sound* is still considered the best narrative history of American popular music's post-World War II development.

George Harrison

Charley Pride

Chicago

The Carpenters

The Jackson 5

JANUARY 3, 1970

POP SINGLES

1. RAINDROPS KEEP FALLIN' ON MY HEAD
   (B.J. Thomas)
2. SOMEDAY WE'LL BE TOGETHER
   (The Supremes)
3. LEAVING ON A JET PLANE
   (Peter, Paul, and Mary)
4. HOLLY HOLY
   (Neil Diamond)
5. WHOLE LOTTA LOVE
   (Led Zeppelin)
6. JAM UP AND JELLY TIGHT
   (Tommy Roe)
7. VENUS
   (Shocking Blue)
8. JINGLE JANGLE
   (The Archies)
9. I WANT YOU BACK
   (The Jackson 5)
10. LA LA LA (IF I HAD YOU)
    (Bobby Sherman)

POP ALBUMS

1. ABBEY ROAD
   (The Beatles)
2. LED ZEPPELIN II
   (Led Zeppelin)
3. LET IT BLEED
   (The Rolling Stones)
4. WILLIE AND THE POOR BOYS
   (Creedence Clearwater Revival)
5. TOM JONES LIVE IN LAS VEGAS
   (Tom Jones)
6. ENGELBERT HUMPERDINCK
   (Engelbert Humperdinck)
7. CAPTURED LIVE AT THE FORUM
   (Three Dog Night)
8. BLOOD, SWEAT AND TEARS
   (Blood, Sweat and Tears)
9. CROSBY, STILLS AND NASH
   (Crosby, Stills and Nash)
10. JOE COCKER!
    (Joe Cocker)

BLACK SINGLES

1. I WANT YOU BACK
   (The Jackson 5)
2. SOMEDAY WE'LL BE TOGETHER
   (Diana Ross and the Supremes)
3. TO BE YOUNG, GIFTED AND BLACK
   (Nina Simone)
4. IS IT BECAUSE I'M BLACK
   (Syl Johnson)
5. AIN'T IT FUNKY
   (James Brown)
6. THESE EYES
   (Junior Walker and the All Stars)
7. I LOVE YOU
   (Otis Leavill)
8. ANYWAY THAT YOU WANT ME
   (Walter Jackson)
9. HOW I MISS YOU BABY
   (Bobby Womack)
10. HELLO SUNSHINE
    (Maceo Woods)

JAZZ ALBUMS

1. MEMPHIS UNDERGROUND
   (Herbie Mann)
2. HOT BUTTERED SOUL
   (Isaac Hayes)
3. SWISS MOVEMENT
   (Les McCann and Eddie Harris)
4. WALKING IN SPACE
   (Quincy Jones)
5. HIGH VOLTAGE
   (Eddie Harris)
6. BUDDY AND SOUL
   (Buddy Rich Big Band)
7. SELFLESSNESS
   (John Coltrane)
8. CRYSTAL ILLUSIONS
   (Sergio Mendes and Brasil '66)
9. LIGHTHOUSE '69
   (Jazz Crusaders)
10. IN A SILENT WAY
    (Miles Davis)

COUNTRY SINGLES

1. BABY BABY
   (David Houston)
2. IF IT'S ALL THE SAME TO YOU
   (Bill Anderson and Jan Howard)
3. WISH I DIDN'T HAVE TO MISS YOU
   (Jack Greene and Jeannie Seely)
4. BIG IN VEGAS
   (Buck Owens)
5. YOU AND YOUR SWEET LOVE
   (Connie Smith)
6. BLISTERED/SEE RUBY FALL
   (Johnny Cash)
7. I'M SO AFRAID OF LOSING YOU AGAIN
   (Charley Pride)
8. NO BLUES IS GOOD NEWS/SHE'S MINE
   (George Jones)
9. WINGS UPON YOUR HORNS
   (Loretta Lynn)
10. CAMELIA
    (Marty Robbins)

COUNTRY ALBUMS

1. BEST OF CHARLEY PRIDE
   (Charley Pride)
2. JOHNNY CASH AT SAN QUENTIN
   (Johnny Cash)
3. LIVE AT COBO HALL, DETROIT
   (Hank Williams Jr.)
4. THE ASTRODOME PRESENTS SONNY JAMES IN PERSON
   (Sonny James)
5. MY BLUE RIDGE MOUNTAIN BOY
   (Dolly Parton)
6. PORTRAIT OF MERLE HAGGARD
   (Merle Haggard)
7. ORIGINAL GOLDEN HITS VOLS. I AND II
   (Johnny Cash)
8. TALL DARK STRANGER
   (Buck Owens)
9. WARMTH OF EDDY
   (Eddy Arnold)
10. STORY SONGS OF THE TRAINS AND RIVERS
    (Johnny Cash and The Tennessee Two)

JANUARY 10, 1970

POP SINGLES

1. RAINDROPS KEEP FALLIN' ON MY HEAD
   (B.J. Thomas)
2. SOMEDAY WE'LL BE TOGETHER
   (The Supremes)
3. I WANT YOU BACK
   (The Jackson 5)
4. VENUS
   (Shocking Blue)
5. WHOLE LOTTA LOVE
   (Led Zeppelin)
6. JAM UP AND JELLY TIGHT
   (Tommy Roe)
7. JINGLE JANGLE
   (The Archies)
8. HOLLY HOLY
   (Neil Diamond)
9. LA LA LA (IF I HAD YOU)
   (Bobby Sherman)
10. MIDNIGHT COWBOY
    (Ferrante and Teicher)

POP ALBUMS

1. LED ZEPPELIN II
   (Led Zeppelin)
2. ABBEY ROAD
   (The Beatles)
3. LET IT BLEED
   (The Rolling Stones)
4. TOM JONES LIVE IN LAS VEGAS
   (Tom Jones)
5. WILLIE AND THE POOR BOYS
   (Creedence Clearwater Revival)
6. CAPTURED LIVE AT THE FORUM
   (Three Dog Night)
7. CROSBY, STILLS AND NASH
   (Crosby, Stills and Nash)
8. BLOOD, SWEAT AND TEARS
   (Blood, Sweat and Tears)
9. FROM MEMPHIS TO VEGAS
   (Elvis Presley)
10. MONSTER
    (Steppenwolf)

BLACK SINGLES

1. I WANT YOU BACK
   (The Jackson 5)
2. IS IT BECAUSE I'M BLACK
   (Syl Johnson)
3. TO BE YOUNG, GIFTED AND BLACK
   (Nina Simone)
4. SOMEDAY WE'LL BE TOGETHER
   (Diana Ross and the Supremes)
5. I LOVE YOU
   (Otis Leavill)
6. AIN'T IT FUNKY
   (James Brown)
7. YOU KEEP ME HANGIN' ON
   (Wilson Pickett)
8. THESE EYES
   (Junior Walker and the All Stars)
9. LOVE BONES
   (Johnnie Taylor)
10. POINT IT OUT
    (The Miracles)

JAZZ ALBUMS

1. HOT BUTTERED SOUL
   (Isaac Hayes)
2. MEMPHIS UNDERGROUND
   (Herbie Mann)
3. WALKING IN SPACE
   (Quincy Jones)
4. SWISS MOVEMENT
   (Les McCann and Eddie Harris)
5. CRYSTAL ILLUSIONS
   (Sergio Mendes and Brasil '66)
6. HIGH VOLTAGE
   (Eddie Harris)
7. BUDDY AND SOUL
   (Buddy Rich Big Band)
8. SELFLESSNESS
   (John Coltrane)
9. LIGHTHOUSE '69
   (Jazz Crusaders)
10. HERBIE MANN LIVE AT THE WHISKEY A GO GO
    (Herbie Mann)

COUNTRY SINGLES

1. BIG IN VEGAS
   (Buck Owens)
2. IF IT'S ALL THE SAME TO YOU
   (Bill Anderson and Jan Howard)

3. WISH I DIDN'T HAVE TO MISS YOU
   (*Jack Greene and Jeannie Seely*)
4. BABY BABY
   (*David Houston*)
5. WINGS UPON YOUR HORNS
   (*Loretta Lynn*)
6. YOU AND YOUR SWEET LOVE
   (*Connie Smith*)
7. NO BLUES IS GOOD NEWS/SHE'S MINE
   (*George Jones*)
8. I'M SO AFRAID OF LOSING YOU AGAIN
   (*Charley Pride*)
9. BLISTERED/SEE RUBY FALL
   (*Johnny Cash*)
10. CAMELIA
    (*Marty Robbins*)

COUNTRY ALBUMS

1. BEST OF CHARLEY PRIDE
   (*Charley Pride*)
2. JOHNNY CASH AT SAN QUENTIN
   (*Johnny Cash*)
3. LIVE AT COBO HALL, DETROIT
   (*Hank Williams Jr.*)
4. PORTRAIT OF MERLE HAGGARD
   (*Merle Haggard*)
5. THE ASTRODOME PRESENTS SONNY
   JAMES IN PERSON
   (*Sonny James*)
6. TALL DARK STRANGER
   (*Buck Owens*)
7. MY BLUE RIDGE MOUNTAIN BOY
   (*Dolly Parton*)
8. ORIGINAL GOLDEN HITS VOLS. I AND II
   (*Johnny Cash*)
9. SONGS THAT MADE COUNTRY GIRLS
   FAMOUS
   (*Lynn Anderson*)
10. STORY SONGS OF THE TRAINS AND RIVERS
    (*Johnny Cash and The Tennessee Two*)

JANUARY 17, 1970

POP SINGLES

1. RAINDROPS KEEP FALLIN' ON MY HEAD
   (*B.J. Thomas*)
2. I WANT YOU BACK
   (*The Jackson 5*)
3. VENUS
   (*Shocking Blue*)
4. WHOLE LOTTA LOVE
   (*Led Zeppelin*)
5. JAM UP AND JELLY TIGHT
   (*Tommy Roe*)
6. SOMEDAY WE'LL BE TOGETHER
   (*Diana Ross and the Supremes*)
7. JINGLE JANGLE
   (*The Archies*)
8. LA LA LA (IF I HAD YOU)
   (*Bobby Sherman*)
9. DON'T CRY DADDY/RUBBERNECKIN'
   (*Elvis Presley*)
10. EARLY IN THE MORNING
    (*Vanity Fare*)

POP ALBUMS

1. ABBEY ROAD
   (*The Beatles*)
2. LED ZEPPELIN II
   (*Led Zeppelin*)
3. TOM JONES LIVE IN LAS VEGAS
   (*Tom Jones*)
4. LET IT BLEED
   (*The Rolling Stones*)
5. WILLIE AND THE POOR BOYS
   (*Creedence Clearwater Revival*)
6. CAPTURED LIVE AT THE FORUM
   (*Three Dog Night*)

7. BLOOD, SWEAT AND TEARS
   (*Blood, Sweat and Tears*)
8. CROSBY, STILLS AND NASH
   (*Crosby, Stills and Nash*)
9. ENGELBERT HUMPERDINCK
   (*Engelbert Humperdinck*)
10. MONSTER
    (*Steppenwolf*)

BLACK SINGLES

1. TO BE YOUNG, GIFTED AND BLACK
   (*Nina Simone*)
2. IS IT BECAUSE I'M BLACK
   (*Syl Johnson*)
3. I WANT YOU BACK
   (*The Jackson 5*)
4. YOU KEEP ME HANGIN' ON
   (*Wilson Pickett*)
5. I LOVE YOU
   (*Otis Leavill*)
6. LOVE BONES
   (*Johnnie Taylor*)
7. SOMEDAY WE'LL BE TOGETHER
   (*Diana Ross and the Supremes*)
8. AIN'T IT FUNKY
   (*James Brown*)
9. THE TOUCH OF YOU
   (*Brenda and the Tabulations*)
10. POINT IT OUT
    (*The Miracles*)

JAZZ ALBUMS

1. HOT BUTTERED SOUL
   (*Isaac Hayes*)
2. WALKING IN SPACE
   (*Quincy Jones*)
3. MEMPHIS UNDERGROUND
   (*Herbie Mann*)
4. SWISS MOVEMENT
   (*Les McCann and Eddie Harris*)
5. HERBIE MANN LIVE AT THE WHISKEY A
   GO GO
   (*Herbie Mann*)
6. CRYSTAL ILLUSIONS
   (*Sergio Mendes and Brasil '66*)
7. HIGH VOLTAGE
   (*Eddie Harris*)
8. YE ME LE
   (*Sergio Mendes and Brasil '66*)
9. BUDDY AND SOUL
   (*Buddy Rich Big Band*)
10. SELFLESSNESS
    (*John Coltrane*)

COUNTRY SINGLES

1. IF IT'S ALL THE SAME TO YOU
   (*Bill Anderson and Jan Howard*)
2. WISH I DIDN'T HAVE TO MISS YOU
   (*Jack Greene and Jeannie Seely*)
3. WINGS UPON YOUR HORNS
   (*Loretta Lynn*)
4. BIG IN VEGAS
   (*Buck Owens*)
5. BABY BABY
   (*David Houston*)
6. NO BLUES IS GOOD NEWS/SHE'S MINE
   (*George Jones*)
7. YOU AND YOUR SWEET LOVE
   (*Connie Smith*)
8. BROWN-EYED HANDSOME MAN
   (*Waylon Jennings*)
9. ONE MINUTE PAST ETERNITY
   (*Jerry Lee Lewis*)
10. I'M SO AFRAID OF LOSING YOU AGAIN
    (*Charley Pride*)

COUNTRY ALBUMS

1. BEST OF CHARLEY PRIDE
   (*Charley Pride*)

2. PORTRAIT OF MERLE HAGGARD
   (*Merle Haggard*)
3. THE ASTRODOME PRESENTS SONNY
   JAMES IN PERSON
   (*Sonny James*)
4. TALL DARK STRANGER
   (*Buck Owens*)
5. JOHNNY CASH AT SAN QUENTIN
   (*Johnny Cash*)
6. LIVE AT COBO HALL, DETROIT
   (*Hank Williams Jr.*)
7. STORY SONGS OF THE TRAINS AND RIVERS
   (*Johnny Cash and The Tennessee Two*)
8. SONGS THAT MADE COUNTRY GIRLS
   FAMOUS
   (*Lynn Anderson*)
9. MY BLUE RIDGE MOUNTAIN BOY
   (*Dolly Parton*)
10. LIVE
    (*Glen Campbell*)

JANUARY 24, 1970

POP SINGLES

1. VENUS
   (*Shocking Blue*)
2. I WANT YOU BACK
   (*The Jackson 5*)
3. RAINDROPS KEEP FALLIN' ON MY HEAD
   (*B.J. Thomas*)
4. JINGLE JANGLE
   (*The Archies*)
5. DON'T CRY DADDY/RUBBERNECKIN'
   (*Elvis Presley*)
6. WITHOUT LOVE (THERE'S NOTHING)
   (*Tom Jones*)
7. JAM UP AND JELLY TIGHT
   (*Tommy Roe*)
8. THANK YOU/EVERYBODY IS A STAR
   (*Sly and the Family Stone*)
9. EARLY IN THE MORNING
   (*Vanity Fare*)
10. I'LL NEVER FALL IN LOVE AGAIN
    (*Dionne Warwick*)

POP ALBUMS

1. ABBEY ROAD
   (*The Beatles*)
2. LED ZEPPELIN II
   (*Led Zeppelin*)
3. LET IT BLEED
   (*The Rolling Stones*)
4. WILLIE AND THE POOR BOYS
   (*Creedence Clearwater Revival*)
5. TOM JONES LIVE IN LAS VEGAS
   (*Tom Jones*)
6. ENGELBERT HUMPERDINCK
   (*Engelbert Humperdinck*)
7. CAPTURED LIVE AT THE FORUM
   (*Three Dog Night*)
8. BLOOD, SWEAT AND TEARS
   (*Blood, Sweat and Tears*)
9. CROSBY, STILLS AND NASH
   (*Crosby, Stills and Nash*)
10. JOE COCKER!
    (*Joe Cocker*)

BLACK SINGLES

1. THANK YOU/EVERYBODY IS A STAR
   (*Sly and the Family Stone*)
2. IS IT BECAUSE I'M BLACK
   (*Syl Johnson*)
3. LOVE BONES
   (*Johnnie Taylor*)
4. THE TOUCH OF YOU
   (*Brenda and the Tabulations*)

5. TO BE YOUNG, GIFTED AND BLACK
   (Nina Simone)
6. I WANT YOU BACK
   (The Jackson 5)
7. IF WALLS COULD TALK
   (Little Milton)
8. I LOVE YOU
   (Otis Leavill)
9. POINT IT OUT
   (The Miracles)
10. SOMEDAY WE'LL BE TOGETHER
    (Diana Ross and the Supremes)

JAZZ ALBUMS

1. HOT BUTTERED SOUL
   (Isaac Hayes)
2. SWISS MOVEMENT
   (Les McCann and Eddie Harris)
3. WALKING IN SPACE
   (Quincy Jones)
4. MEMPHIS UNDERGROUND
   (Herbie Mann)
5. YE ME LE
   (Sergio Mendes and Brasil '66)
6. HERBIE MANN LIVE AT THE WHISKEY A
   GO GO
   (Herbie Mann)
7. CRYSTAL ILLUSIONS
   (Sergio Mendes and Brasil '66)
8. LIGHTHOUSE '69
   (Jazz Crusaders)
9. HIGH VOLTAGE
   (Eddie Harris)
10. IN A SILENT WAY
    (Miles Davis)

COUNTRY SINGLES

1. WISH I DIDN'T HAVE TO MISS YOU
   (Jack Greene and Jeannie Seely)
2. IF IT'S ALL THE SAME TO YOU
   (Bill Anderson and Jan Howard)
3. WINGS UPON YOUR HORNS
   (Loretta Lynn)
4. NO BLUES IS GOOD NEWS/SHE'S MINE
   (George Jones)
5. BROWN-EYED HANDSOME MAN
   (Waylon Jennings)
6. ONE MINUTE PAST ETERNITY
   (Jerry Lee Lewis)
7. BABY BABY
   (David Houston)
8. BIG IN VEGAS
   (Buck Owens)
9. HE'D STILL LOVE ME
   (Lynn Anderson)
10. YOU AND YOUR SWEET LOVE
    (Connie Smith)

COUNTRY ALBUMS

1. BEST OF CHARLEY PRIDE
   (Charley Pride)
2. TALL DARK STRANGER
   (Buck Owens)
3. PORTRAIT OF MERLE HAGGARD
   (Merle Haggard)
4. THE ASTRODOME PRESENTS SONNY
   JAMES IN PERSON
   (Sonny James)
5. JOHNNY CASH AT SAN QUENTIN
   (Johnny Cash)
6. LIVE AT COBO HALL, DETROIT
   (Hank Williams Jr.)
7. STORY SONGS OF THE TRAINS AND RIVERS
   (Johnny Cash and The Tennessee Two)
8. LIVE
   (Glen Campbell)
9. SONGS THAT MADE COUNTRY GIRLS
   FAMOUS
   (Lynn Anderson)
10. MY BLUE RIDGE MOUNTAIN BOY
    (Dolly Parton)

JANUARY 31, 1970

POP SINGLES

1. VENUS
   (Shocking Blue)
2. I WANT YOU BACK
   (The Jackson 5)
3. RAINDROPS KEEP FALLIN' ON MY HEAD
   (B.J. Thomas)
4. JAM UP AND JELLY TIGHT
   (Tommy Roe)
5. DON'T CRY DADDY/RUBBERNECKIN'
   (Elvis Presley)
6. JINGLE JANGLE
   (The Archies)
7. WHOLE LOTTA LOVE
   (Led Zeppelin)
8. WITHOUT LOVE (THERE'S NOTHING)
   (Tom Jones)
9. EARLY IN THE MORNING
   (Vanity Fare)
10. SOMEDAY WE'LL BE TOGETHER
    (Diana Ross and the Supremes)

POP ALBUMS

1. ABBEY ROAD
   (The Beatles)
2. LED ZEPPELIN II
   (Led Zeppelin)
3. LET IT BLEED
   (The Rolling Stones)
4. WILLIE AND THE POOR BOYS
   (Creedence Clearwater Revival)
5. ENGELBERT HUMPERDINCK
   (Engelbert Humperdinck)
6. TOM JONES LIVE IN LAS VEGAS
   (Tom Jones)
7. CAPTURED LIVE AT THE FORUM
   (Three Dog Night)
8. JOE COCKER!
   (Joe Cocker)
9. CROSBY, STILLS AND NASH
   (Crosby, Stills and Nash)
10. BLOOD, SWEAT AND TEARS
    (Blood, Sweat and Tears)

BLACK SINGLES

1. THANK YOU/EVERYBODY IS A STAR
   (Sly and the Family Stone)
2. LOVE BONES
   (Johnnie Taylor)
3. THE TOUCH OF YOU
   (Brenda and the Tabulations)
4. IF WALLS COULD TALK
   (Little Milton)
5. POINT IT OUT
   (The Miracles)
6. HEY THERE LONELY GIRL
   (Eddie Holman)
7. THE THRILL IS GONE
   (B.B. King)
8. I WANT YOU BACK
   (The Jackson 5)
9. LET A MAN COME IN AND DO THE
   POPCORN (PART 2)
   (James Brown)
10. PSYCHEDELIC SHACK
    (Temptations)

JAZZ ALBUMS

1. HOT BUTTERED SOUL
   (Isaac Hayes)
2. SWISS MOVEMENT
   (Les McCann and Eddie Harris)
3. MEMPHIS UNDERGROUND
   (Herbie Mann)

4. WALKING IN SPACE
   (Quincy Jones)
5. CRYSTAL ILLUSIONS
   (Sergio Mendes and Brasil '66)
6. HERBIE MANN LIVE AT THE WHISKEY A
   GO GO
   (Herbie Mann)
7. IN A SILENT WAY
   (Miles Davis)
8. HOT DOG
   (Lou Donaldson)
9. YE ME LE
   (Sergio Mendes and Brasil '66)
10. HIGH VOLTAGE
    (Eddie Harris)

COUNTRY SINGLES

1. WINGS UPON YOUR HORNS
   (Loretta Lynn)
2. BROWN-EYED HANDSOME MAN
   (Waylon Jennings)
3. WISH I DIDN'T HAVE TO MISS YOU
   (Jack Greene and Jeannie Seely)
4. NO BLUES IS GOOD NEWS/SHE'S MINE
   (George Jones)
5. ONE MINUTE PAST ETERNITY
   (Jerry Lee Lewis)
6. SIX WHITE HORSES
   (Tommy Cash)
7. IF IT'S ALL THE SAME TO YOU
   (Bill Anderson and Jan Howard)
8. BABY BABY
   (David Houston)
9. NOBODY'S FOOL
   (Jim Reeves)
10. A WEEK IN A COUNTRY JAIL
    (Tom T. Hall)

COUNTRY ALBUMS

1. BEST OF CHARLEY PRIDE
   (Charley Pride)
2. TALL DARK STRANGER
   (Buck Owens)
3. JOHNNY CASH AT SAN QUENTIN
   (Johnny Cash)
4. PORTRAIT OF MERLE HAGGARD
   (Merle Haggard)
5. LIVE AT COBO HALL, DETROIT
   (Hank Williams Jr.)
6. STORY SONGS OF THE TRAINS AND RIVERS
   (Johnny Cash and The Tennessee Two)
7. THE ASTRODOME PRESENTS SONNY
   JAMES IN PERSON
   (Sonny James)
8. LIVE
   (Glen Campbell)
9. MY BLUE RIDGE MOUNTAIN BOY
   (Dolly Parton)
10. TAMMY WYNETTE'S GREATEST HITS
    (Tammy Wynette)

FEBRUARY 7, 1970

POP SINGLES

1. VENUS
   (Shocking Blue)
2. I WANT YOU BACK
   (The Jackson 5)
3. THANK YOU/EVERYBODY IS A STAR
   (Sly and the Family Stone)
4. WITHOUT LOVE (THERE'S NOTHING)
   (Tom Jones)
5. DON'T CRY DADDY/RUBBERNECKIN'
   (Elvis Presley)
6. RAINDROPS KEEP FALLIN' ON MY HEAD
   (B.J. Thomas)
7. NO TIME
   (The Guess Who)

8. HEY THERE LONELY GIRL
   (Eddie Holman)
9. I'LL NEVER FALL IN LOVE AGAIN
   (Dionne Warwick)
10. EARLY IN THE MORNING
    (Vanity Fare)

POP ALBUMS

1. LED ZEPPELIN II
   (Led Zeppelin)
2. ABBEY ROAD
   (The Beatles)
3. LET IT BLEED
   (The Rolling Stones)
4. TOM JONES LIVE IN LAS VEGAS
   (Tom Jones)
5. WILLIE AND THE POOR BOYS
   (Creedence Clearwater Revival)
6. CAPTURED LIVE AT THE FORUM
   (Three Dog Night)
7. JOE COCKER!
   (Joe Cocker)
8. ENGELBERT HUMPERDINCK
   (Engelbert Humperdinck)
9. BLOOD, SWEAT AND TEARS
   (Blood, Sweat and Tears)
10. CROSBY, STILLS AND NASH
    (Crosby, Stills and Nash)

BLACK SINGLES

1. THANK YOU/EVERYBODY IS A STAR
   (Sly and the Family Stone)
2. LOVE BONES
   (Johnnie Taylor)
3. PSYCHEDELIC SHACK
   (Temptations)
4. IF WALLS COULD TALK
   (Little Milton)
5. HEY THERE LONELY GIRL
   (Eddie Holman)
6. THE THRILL IS GONE
   (B.B. King)
7. POINT IT OUT
   (The Miracles)
8. THE TOUCH OF YOU
   (Brenda and the Tabulations)
9. GUESS WHO
   (Ruby Winters)
10. I WANT YOU BACK
    (The Jackson 5)

JAZZ ALBUMS

1. HOT BUTTERED SOUL
   (Isaac Hayes)
2. SWISS MOVEMENT
   (Les McCann and Eddie Harris)
3. MEMPHIS UNDERGROUND
   (Herbie Mann)
4. WALKING IN SPACE
   (Quincy Jones)
5. CRYSTAL ILLUSIONS
   (Sergio Mendes and Brasil '66)
6. YE ME LE
   (Sergio Mendes and Brasil '66)
7. HERBIE MANN LIVE AT THE WHISKEY A
   GO GO
   (Herbie Mann)
8. FANCY FREE
   (Donald Byrd)
9. IN A SILENT WAY
   (Miles Davis)
10. HIGH VOLTAGE
    (Eddie Harris)

COUNTRY SINGLES

1. BROWN-EYED HANDSOME MAN
   (Waylon Jennings)
2. ONE MINUTE PAST ETERNITY
   (Jerry Lee Lewis)

3. A WEEK IN A COUNTRY JAIL
   (Tom T. Hall)
4. WINGS UPON YOUR HORNS
   (Loretta Lynn)
5. SIX WHITE HORSES
   (Tommy Cash)
6. THAT'S WHEN SHE STARTED TO STOP
   LOVING YOU
   (Conway Twitty)
7. NOBODY'S FOOL
   (Jim Reeves)
8. WISH I DIDN'T HAVE TO MISS YOU
   (Jack Greene and Jeannie Seely)
9. DON'T CRY DADDY/RUBBERNECKIN'
   (Elvis Presley)
10. IT'S JUST A MATTER OF TIME
    (Sonny James)

COUNTRY ALBUMS

1. BEST OF CHARLEY PRIDE
   (Charley Pride)
2. TALL DARK STRANGER
   (Buck Owens)
3. STORY SONGS OF THE TRAINS AND RIVERS
   (Johnny Cash and The Tennessee Two)
4. PORTRAIT OF MERLE HAGGARD
   (Merle Haggard)
5. JOHNNY CASH AT SAN QUENTIN
   (Johnny Cash)
6. LIVE
   (Glen Campbell)
7. TAMMY WYNETTE'S GREATEST HITS
   (Tammy Wynette)
8. MY BLUE RIDGE MOUNTAIN BOY
   (Dolly Parton)
9. LIVE AT COBO HALL, DETROIT
   (Hank Williams Jr.)
10. TOGETHER
    (Jerry Lee Lewis and Linda Gail Lewis)

FEBRUARY 14, 1970

POP SINGLES

1. THANK YOU/EVERYBODY IS A STAR
   (Sly and the Family Stone)
2. VENUS
   (Shocking Blue)
3. WITHOUT LOVE (THERE'S NOTHING)
   (Tom Jones)
4. HEY THERE LONELY GIRL
   (Eddie Holman)
5. NO TIME
   (The Guess Who)
6. I WANT YOU BACK
   (The Jackson 5)
7. I'LL NEVER FALL IN LOVE AGAIN
   (Dionne Warwick)
8. PSYCHEDELIC SHACK
   (Temptations)
9. RAINDROPS KEEP FALLIN' ON MY HEAD
   (B.J. Thomas)
10. WALKIN' IN THE RAIN
    (Jay and the Americans)

POP ALBUMS

1. LED ZEPPELIN II
   (Led Zeppelin)
2. ABBEY ROAD
   (The Beatles)
3. TOM JONES LIVE IN LAS VEGAS
   (Tom Jones)
4. WILLIE AND THE POOR BOYS
   (Creedence Clearwater Revival)
5. CAPTURED LIVE AT THE FORUM
   (Three Dog Night)
6. LET IT BLEED
   (The Rolling Stones)
7. ENGELBERT HUMPERDINCK
   (Engelbert Humperdinck)

8. JOE COCKER!
   (Joe Cocker)
9. SANTANA
   (Santana)
10. EASY RIDER
    (Original Soundtrack)

BLACK SINGLES

1. THANK YOU/EVERYBODY IS A STAR
   (Sly and the Family Stone)
2. PSYCHEDELIC SHACK
   (Temptations)
3. HEY THERE LONELY GIRL
   (Eddie Holman)
4. DIDN'T I BLOW YOUR MIND THIS TIME
   (The Delfonics)
5. THE THRILL IS GONE
   (B.B. King)
6. RAINY NIGHT IN GEORGIA
   (Brook Benton)
7. LOVE BONES
   (Johnnie Taylor)
8. IF WALLS COULD TALK
   (Little Milton)
9. LOVELY WAY SHE LOVES
   (The Moments)
10. GIVE ME JUST A LITTLE MORE TIME
    (Chairmen of the Board)

JAZZ ALBUMS

1. SWISS MOVEMENT
   (Les McCann and Eddie Harris)
2. HOT BUTTERED SOUL
   (Isaac Hayes)
3. WALKING IN SPACE
   (Quincy Jones)
4. MEMPHIS UNDERGROUND
   (Herbie Mann)
5. YE ME LE
   (Sergio Mendes and Brasil '66)
6. HERBIE MANN LIVE AT THE WHISKEY A
   GO GO
   (Herbie Mann)
7. FANCY FREE
   (Donald Byrd)
8. CRYSTAL ILLUSIONS
   (Sergio Mendes and Brasil '66)
9. IN A SILENT WAY
   (Miles Davis)
10. INSIDE
    (Paul Horn)

COUNTRY SINGLES

1. THAT'S WHEN SHE STARTED TO STOP
   LOVING YOU
   (Conway Twitty)
2. IT'S JUST A MATTER OF TIME
   (Sonny James)
3. A WEEK IN A COUNTRY JAIL
   (Tom T. Hall)
4. ONE MINUTE PAST ETERNITY
   (Jerry Lee Lewis)
5. HONEY COME BACK
   (Glen Campbell)
6. NOBODY'S FOOL
   (Jim Reeves)
7. WELFARE CADILLAC
   (Guy Drake)
8. TAKE A LETTER MARIA
   (Anthony Armstrong Jones)
9. HELLO I'M A JUKE BOX
   (George Kent)
10. THINKING ABOUT YOU BABE
    (Billy Walker)

COUNTRY ALBUMS

1. BEST OF CHARLEY PRIDE
   (Charley Pride)

2. STORY SONGS OF THE TRAINS AND RIVERS
   (Johnny Cash and The Tennessee Two)
3. TALL DARK STRANGER
   (Buck Owens)
4. PORTRAIT OF MERLE HAGGARD
   (Merle Haggard)
5. TAMMY WYNETTE'S GREATEST HITS
   (Tammy Wynette)
6. OKIE FROM MUSKOGEE
   (Merle Haggard)
7. JOHNNY CASH AT SAN QUENTIN
   (Johnny Cash)
8. LIVE
   (Glen Campbell)
9. SONGS THAT MADE COUNTRY GIRLS FAMOUS
   (Lynn Anderson)
10. TOGETHER
    (Jerry Lee Lewis and Linda Gail Lewis)

FEBRUARY 28, 1970

POP SINGLES

1. BRIDGE OVER TROUBLED WATER
   (Simon and Garfunkel)
2. HEY THERE LONELY GIRL
   (Eddie Holman)
3. TRAVELING BAND/WHO'LL STOP THE RAIN
   (Creedence Clearwater Revival)
4. THANK YOU/EVERYBODY IS A STAR
   (Sly and the Family Stone)
5. RAINY NIGHT IN GEORGIA
   (Brook Benton)
6. PSYCHEDELIC SHACK
   (Temptations)
7. NO TIME
   (The Guess Who)
8. MA BELLE AMIE
   (The Tee Set)
9. ARIZONA
   (Mark Lindsay)
10. HONEY COME BACK
    (Glen Campbell)

POP ALBUMS

1. LED ZEPPELIN II
   (Led Zeppelin)
2. ABBEY ROAD
   (The Beatles)
3. WILLIE AND THE POOR BOYS
   (Creedence Clearwater Revival)
4. TOM JONES LIVE IN LAS VEGAS
   (Tom Jones)
5. ENGELBERT HUMPERDINCK
   (Engelbert Humperdinck)
6. BRIDGE OVER TROUBLED WATER
   (Simon and Garfunkel)
7. LET IT BLEED
   (The Rolling Stones)
8. I WANT YOU BACK
   (The Jackson 5)
9. SANTANA
   (Santana)
10. CAPTURED LIVE AT THE FORUM
    (Three Dog Night)

BLACK SINGLES

1. THANK YOU/EVERYBODY IS A STAR
   (Sly and the Family Stone)
2. PSYCHEDELIC SHACK
   (Temptations)
3. RAINY NIGHT IN GEORGIA
   (Brook Benton)
4. DO THE FUNKY CHICKEN
   (Rufus Thomas)
5. CALL ME
   (Aretha Franklin)

6. GIVE ME JUST A LITTLE MORE TIME
   (Chairmen of the Board)
7. DIDN'T I (BLOW YOUR MIND THIS TIME)
   (The Delfonics)
8. I'M JUST A PRISONER
   (Candi Staton)
9. NEVER HAD A DREAM COME TRUE
   (Stevie Wonder)
10. THE BELLS
    (The Originals)

JAZZ ALBUMS

1. SWISS MOVEMENT
   (Les McCann and Eddie Harris)
2. WALKING IN SPACE
   (Quincy Jones)
3. MEMPHIS UNDERGROUND
   (Herbie Mann)
4. YE ME LE
   (Sergio Mendes and Brasil '66)
5. HOT BUTTERED SOUL
   (Isaac Hayes)
6. FANCY FREE
   (Donald Byrd)
7. HERBIE MANN LIVE AT THE WHISKEY A GO GO
   (Herbie Mann)
8. IN A SILENT WAY
   (Miles Davis)
9. CONCERTO GROSSO IN D BLUES
   (Herbie Mann)
10. CRYSTAL ILLUSIONS
    (Sergio Mendes and Brasil '66)

COUNTRY SINGLES

1. HONEY COME BACK
   (Glen Campbell)
2. IT'S JUST A MATTER OF TIME
   (Sonny James)
3. FIGHTIN' SIDE OF ME
   (Merle Haggard)
4. WELFARE CADILLAC
   (Guy Drake)
5. I'LL SEE HIM THROUGH
   (Tammy Wynette)
6. THEN HE TOUCHED ME
   (Jean Shepard)
7. IF I WERE A CARPENTER
   (Johnny Cash and June Carter)
8. THAT'S WHEN SHE STARTED TO STOP LOVIN' YOU
   (Conway Twitty)
9. SHE'LL BE HANGIN' ROUND SOMEWHERE
   (Mel Tillis)
10. HELLO I'M A JUKE BOX
    (George Kent)

COUNTRY ALBUMS

1. BEST OF CHARLEY PRIDE
   (Charley Pride)
2. STORY SONGS OF THE TRAINS AND RIVERS
   (Johnny Cash and The Tennessee Two)
3. OKIE FROM MUSKOGEE
   (Merle Haggard)
4. FROM MEMPHIS TO VEGAS
   (Elvis Presley)
5. TALL DARK STRANGER
   (Buck Owens)
6. JOHNNY CASH AT SAN QUENTIN
   (Johnny Cash)
7. TRY A LITTLE KINDNESS
   (Glen Campbell)
8. TAMMY WYNETTE'S GREATEST HITS
   (Tammy Wynette)
9. THE EVERLOVIN' SOUL OF ROY CLARK
   (Roy Clark)
10. HELLO, I'M JOHNNY CASH
    (Johnny Cash)

MARCH 7, 1970

POP SINGLES

1. BRIDGE OVER TROUBLED WATER
   (Simon and Garfunkel)
2. TRAVELING BAND/WHO'LL STOP THE RAIN
   (Creedence Clearwater Revival)
3. HEY THERE LONELY GIRL
   (Eddie Holman)
4. RAINY NIGHT IN GEORGIA
   (Brook Benton)
5. MA BELLE AMIE
   (The Tee Set)
6. PSYCHEDELIC SHACK
   (Temptations)
7. THANK YOU/EVERYBODY IS A STAR
   (Sly and the Family Stone)
8. NO TIME
   (The Guess Who)
9. THE RAPPER
   (Jaggerz)
10. ARIZONA
    (Mark Lindsay)

POP ALBUMS

1. BRIDGE OVER TROUBLED WATER
   (Simon and Garfunkel)
2. LED ZEPPELIN II
   (Led Zeppelin)
3. ABBEY ROAD
   (The Beatles)
4. WILLIE AND THE POOR BOYS
   (Creedence Clearwater Revival)
5. TOM JONES LIVE IN LAS VEGAS
   (Tom Jones)
6. I WANT YOU BACK
   (The Jackson 5)
7. SANTANA
   (Santana)
8. LET IT BLEED
   (The Rolling Stones)
9. CHICAGO
   (Chicago)
10. RAINDROPS KEEP FALLIN' ON MY HEAD
    (B.J. Thomas)

BLACK SINGLES

1. RAINY NIGHT IN GEORGIA
   (Brook Benton)
2. CALL ME
   (Aretha Franklin)
3. THANK YOU/EVERYBODY IS A STAR
   (Sly and the Family Stone)
4. DO THE FUNKY CHICKEN
   (Rufus Thomas)
5. THE BELLS
   (The Originals)
6. GIVE ME JUST A LITTLE MORE TIME
   (Chairmen of the Board)
7. NEVER HAD A DREAM COME TRUE
   (Stevie Wonder)
8. IT'S A NEW DAY
   (James Brown)
9. GOOD GUYS ONLY WIN IN THE MOVIES
   (Mel and Tim)
10. PSYCHEDELIC SHACK
    (Temptations)

JAZZ ALBUMS

1. SWISS MOVEMENT
   (Les McCann and Eddie Harris)
2. WALKING IN SPACE
   (Quincy Jones)
3. MEMPHIS UNDERGROUND
   (Herbie Mann)

4. YE ME LE
   (Sergio Mendes and Brasil '66)
5. HOT BUTTERED SOUL
   (Isaac Hayes)
6. FANCY FREE
   (Donald Byrd)
7. IN A SILENT WAY
   (Miles Davis)
8. HERBIE MANN LIVE AT THE WHISKEY A
   GO GO
   (Herbie Mann)
9. CONCERTO GROSSO IN D BLUES
   (Herbie Mann)
10. CRYSTAL ILLUSIONS
    (Sergio Mendes and Brasil '66)

COUNTRY SINGLES

1. HONEY COME BACK
   (Glen Campbell)
2. IT'S JUST A MATTER OF TIME
   (Sonny James)
3. FIGHTIN' SIDE OF ME
   (Merle Haggard)
4. WELFARE CADILLAC
   (Guy Drake)
5. I'LL SEE HIM THROUGH
   (Tammy Wynette)
6. THEN HE TOUCHED ME
   (Jean Shepard)
7. IF I WERE A CARPENTER
   (Johnny Cash and June Carter)
8. THAT'S WHEN SHE STARTED TO STOP
   LOVIN' YOU
   (Conway Twitty)
9. SHE'LL BE HANGING AROUND
   (Mel Tillis)
10. HELLO I'M A JUKE BOX
    (George Kent)

COUNTRY ALBUMS

1. BEST OF CHARLEY PRIDE
   (Charley Pride)
2. STORY SONGS OF THE TRAINS AND RIVERS
   (Johnny Cash and The Tennessee Two)
3. OKIE FROM MUSKOGEE
   (Merle Haggard)
4. FROM MEMPHIS TO VEGAS
   (Elvis Presley)
5. TALL DARK STRANGER
   (Buck Owens)
6. JOHNNY CASH AT SAN QUENTIN
   (Johnny Cash)
7. TRY A LITTLE TENDERNESS
   (Glen Campbell)
8. TAMMY WYNETTE'S GREATEST HITS
   (Tammy Wynette)
9. THE EVERLOVIN' SOUL OF ROY CLARK
   (Roy Clark)
10. HELLO, I'M JOHNNY CASH
    (Johnny Cash)

MARCH 14, 1970

POP SINGLES

1. BRIDGE OVER TROUBLED WATER
   (Simon and Garfunkel)
2. TRAVELING BAND/WHO'LL STOP THE
   RAIN
   (Creedence Clearwater Revival)
3. RAINY NIGHT IN GEORGIA
   (Brook Benton)
4. THE RAPPER
   (Jaggerz)
5. MA BELLE AMIE
   (The Tee Set)
6. HEY THERE LONELY GIRL
   (Eddie Holman)

7. THANK YOU/EVERYBODY IS A STAR
   (Sly and the Family Stone)
8. GIVE ME JUST A LITTLE MORE TIME
   (Chairmen of the Board)
9. DIDN'T I BLOW YOUR MIND THIS TIME
   (The Delfonics)
10. HOUSE OF THE RISING SUN
    (Frijid Pink)

POP ALBUMS

1. BRIDGE OVER TROUBLED WATER
   (Simon and Garfunkel)
2. LED ZEPPELIN II
   (Led Zeppelin)
3. ABBEY ROAD
   (The Beatles)
4. WILLIE AND THE POOR BOYS
   (Creedence Clearwater Revival)
5. I WANT YOU BACK
   (The Jackson 5)
6. CHICAGO
   (Chicago)
7. SANTANA
   (Santana)
8. LET IT BE
   (The Beatles)
9. TOM JONES LIVE IN LAS VEGAS
   (Tom Jones)
10. HELLO, I'M JOHNNY CASH
    (Johnny Cash)

BLACK SINGLES

1. CALL ME
   (Aretha Franklin)
2. IT'S A NEW DAY
   (James Brown)
3. THE BELLS
   (The Originals)
4. RAINY NIGHT IN GEORGIA
   (Brook Benton)
5. GOTTA HOLD ON TO THIS FEELING
   (Junior Walker and the All Stars)
6. TO THE OTHER WOMAN
   (Doris Duke)
7. YOU'RE THE ONE
   (Little Sister)
8. THANK YOU/EVERYBODY IS A STAR
   (Sly and the Family Stone)
9. NEVER HAD A DREAM COME TRUE
   (Stevie Wonder)
10. TAKE IT OFF HIM AND PUT IT ON ME
    (Clarence Carter)

JAZZ ALBUMS

1. SWISS MOVEMENT
   (Les McCann and Eddie Harris)
2. MEMPHIS UNDERGROUND
   (Herbie Mann)
3. WALKING IN SPACE
   (Quincy Jones)
4. YE ME LE
   (Sergio Mendes and Brasil '66)
5. HOT BUTTERED SOUL
   (Isaac Hayes)
6. IN A SILENT WAY
   (Miles Davis)
7. CRYSTAL ILLUSIONS
   (Sergio Mendes and Brasil '66)
8. HERBIE MANN LIVE AT THE WHISKEY A
   GO GO
   (Herbie Mann)
9. BUDDY AND SOUL
   (Buddy Rich)
10. FANCY FREE
    (Donald Byrd)

COUNTRY SINGLES

1. FIGHTIN' SIDE OF ME
   (Merle Haggard)

2. IT'S JUST A MATTER OF TIME
   (Sonny James)
3. HONEY COME BACK
   (Glen Campbell)
4. I'LL SEE HIM THROUGH
   (Tammy Wynette)
5. IF I WERE A CARPENTER
   (Johnny Cash and June Carter)
6. WELFARE CADILLAC
   (Guy Drake)
7. TENNESSEE BIRDWALK
   (Jack Blanchard and Misty Morgan)
8. THEN HE TOUCHED ME
   (Jean Shepard)
9. OCCASIONAL WIFE
   (Faron Young)
10. COUNTRY GIRL
    (Jeannie C. Riley)

COUNTRY ALBUMS

1. BEST OF CHARLEY PRIDE
   (Charley Pride)
2. OKIE FROM MUSKOGEE
   (Merle Haggard)
3. TRY A LITTLE KINDNESS
   (Glen Campbell)
4. FROM MEMPHIS TO VEGAS
   (Elvis Presley)
5. HELLO, I'M JOHNNY CASH
   (Johnny Cash)
6. JOHNNY CASH AT SAN QUENTIN
   (Johnny Cash)
7. TAMMY WYNETTE'S GREATEST HITS
   (Tammy Wynette)
8. WAYS TO LOVE A MAN
   (Tammy Wynette)
9. WINGS UPON YOUR HORNS
   (Loretta Lynn)
10. STORY SONGS OF THE TRAINS AND RIVERS
    (Johnny Cash and The Tennessee Two)

MARCH 21, 1970

POP SINGLES

1. THE RAPPER
   (Jaggerz)
2. RAINY NIGHT IN GEORGIA
   (Brook Benton)
3. BRIDGE OVER TROUBLED WATER
   (Simon and Garfunkel)
4. MA BELLE AMIE
   (The Tee Set)
5. INSTANT KARMA
   (John Lennon/Yoko Ono)
6. LOVE GROWS
   (Edison Lighthouse)
7. HOUSE OF THE RISING SUN
   (Frijid Pink)
8. GIVE ME JUST A LITTLE MORE TIME
   (Chairmen of the Board)
9. DIDN'T I BLOW YOUR MIND THIS TIME
   (The Delfonics)
10. EVIL WAYS
    (Santana)

POP ALBUMS

1. BRIDGE OVER TROUBLED WATER
   (Simon and Garfunkel)
2. LED ZEPPELIN II
   (Led Zeppelin)
3. HEY JUDE
   (The Beatles)
4. MORRISON HOTEL
   (The Doors)
5. SANTANA
   (Santana)
6. CHICAGO
   (Chicago)

7. ABBEY ROAD
   (The Beatles)
8. WILLIE AND THE POOR BOYS
   (Creedence Clearwater Revival)
9. HELLO, I'M JOHNNY CASH
   (Johnny Cash)
10. EASY RIDER
    (Original Soundtrack)

BLACK SINGLES

1. CALL ME
   (Aretha Franklin)
2. IT'S A NEW DAY
   (James Brown)
3. THE BELLS
   (The Originals)
4. RAINY NIGHT IN GEORGIA
   (Brook Benton)
5. GOTTA HOLD ON TO THIS FEELING
   (Junior Walker and the All Stars)
6. TO THE OTHER WOMAN
   (Doris Duke)
7. YOU'RE THE ONE
   (Little Sister)
8. THANK YOU/EVERYBODY IS A STAR
   (Sly and the Family Stone)
9. NEVER HAD A DREAM COME TRUE
   (Stevie Wonder)
10. TAKE IT OFF HIM AND PUT IT ON ME
    (Clarence Carter)

JAZZ ALBUMS

1. SWISS MOVEMENT
   (Les McCann and Eddie Harris)
2. MEMPHIS UNDERGROUND
   (Herbie Mann)
3. WALKING IN SPACE
   (Quincy Jones)
4. YE ME LE
   (Sergio Mendes and Brasil '66)
5. HOT BUTTERED SOUL
   (Isaac Hayes)
6. BUDDY AND SOUL
   (Buddy Rich Big Band)
7. HERBIE MANN LIVE AT THE WHISKEY A GO GO
   (Herbie Mann)
8. IN A SILENT WAY
   (Miles Davis)
9. BEST OF RAMSEY
   (Ramsey Lewis)
10. BEST OF HERBIE MANN
    (Herbie Mann)

COUNTRY SINGLES

1. FIGHTIN' SIDE OF ME
   (Merle Haggard)
2. I'LL SEE HIM THROUGH
   (Tammy Wynette)
3. IF I WERE A CARPENTER
   (Johnny Cash and June Carter)
4. TENNESSEE BIRDWALK
   (Jack Blanchard and Misty Morgan)
5. IT'S JUST A MATTER OF TIME
   (Sonny James)
6. HONEY COME BACK
   (Glen Campbell)
7. ONCE MORE WITH FEELING
   (Jerry Lee Lewis)
8. OCCASIONAL WIFE
   (Faron Young)
9. NORTHEAST ARKANSAS MISSISSIPPI COUNTRY BOOTLEGGER
   (Kenny Price)
10. COUNTRY GIRL
    (Jeannie C. Riley)

COUNTRY ALBUMS

1. BEST OF CHARLEY PRIDE
   (Charley Pride)

2. OKIE FROM MUSKOGEE
   (Merle Haggard)
3. TRY A LITTLE KINDNESS
   (Glen Campbell)
4. HELLO, I'M JOHNNY CASH
   (Johnny Cash)
5. JOHNNY CASH AT SAN QUENTIN
   (Johnny Cash)
6. JUST PLAIN CHARLEY C. PRIDE
   (Charley Pride)
7. WAYS TO LOVE A MAN
   (Tammy Wynette)
8. WINGS UPON YOUR HORNS
   (Loretta Lynn)
9. BIG IN VEGAS
   (Buck Owens)
10. SHE EVEN WOKE ME UP TO SAY GOODBYE
    (Jerry Lee Lewis)

MARCH 28, 1970

POP SINGLES

1. THE RAPPER
   (Jaggerz)
2. ABC
   (The Jackson 5)
3. BRIDGE OVER TROUBLED WATER
   (Simon and Garfunkel)
4. INSTANT KARMA
   (John Lennon/Yoko Ono)
5. LOVE GROWS
   (Edison Lighthouse)
6. LET IT BE
   (The Beatles)
7. HOUSE OF THE RISING SUN
   (Frijid Pink)
8. RAINY NIGHT IN GEORGIA
   (Brook Benton)
9. HE AIN'T HEAVY, HE'S MY BROTHER
   (The Hollies)
10. DIDN'T I BLOW YOUR MIND THIS TIME
    (The Delfonics)

POP ALBUMS

1. HEY JUDE
   (The Beatles)
2. BRIDGE OVER TROUBLED WATER
   (Simon and Garfunkel)
3. MORRISON HOTEL
   (The Doors)
4. SANTANA
   (Santana)
5. LED ZEPPELIN II
   (Led Zeppelin)
6. CHICAGO
   (Chicago)
7. WILLIE AND THE POOR BOYS
   (Creedence Clearwater Revival)
8. EASY RIDER
   (Original Soundtrack)
9. ABBEY ROAD
   (The Beatles)
10. FRIJID PINK
    (Frijid Pink)

BLACK SINGLES

1. CALL ME
   (Aretha Franklin)
2. THE BELLS
   (The Originals)
3. GOTTA HOLD ON TO THIS FEELING
   (Junior Walker and the All Stars)
4. YOU'RE THE ONE
   (Little Sister)
5. TO THE OTHER WOMAN
   (Doris Duke)
6. ABC
   (The Jackson 5)

7. UP THE LADDER TO THE ROOF
   (The Supremes)
8. RAINY NIGHT IN GEORGIA
   (Brook Benton)
9. IT'S A NEW DAY
   (James Brown)
10. CRYIN' IN THE STREETS
    (George Perkins)

JAZZ ALBUMS

1. SWISS MOVEMENT
   (Les McCann and Eddie Harris)
2. WALKING IN SPACE
   (Quincy Jones)
3. HOT BUTTERED SOUL
   (Isaac Hayes)
4. MEMPHIS UNDERGROUND
   (Herbie Mann)
5. YE ME LE
   (Sergio Mendes and Brasil '66)
6. BEST OF HERBIE MANN
   (Herbie Mann)
7. BEST OF RAMSEY
   (Ramsey Lewis)
8. HERBIE MANN LIVE AT THE WHISKEY A GO GO
   (Herbie Mann)
9. IN A SILENT WAY
   (Miles Davis)
10. BUDDY AND SOUL
    (Buddy Rich Big Band)

COUNTRY SINGLES

1. TENNESSEE BIRDWALK
   (Jack Blanchard and Misty Morgan)
2. I'LL SEE HIM THROUGH
   (Tammy Wynette)
3. MY WOMAN, MY WOMAN, MY WIFE
   (Marty Robbins)
4. FIGHTIN' SIDE OF ME
   (Merle Haggard)
5. IF I WERE A CARPENTER
   (Johnny Cash and June Carter)
6. ONCE MORE WITH FEELING
   (Jerry Lee Lewis)
7. OCCASIONAL WIFE
   (Faron Young)
8. IT'S JUST A MATTER OF TIME
   (Sonny James)
9. ALL I HAVE TO DO IS DREAM
   (Glen Campbell and Bobbie Gentry)
10. IS ANYBODY GOIN' TO SAN ANTONE
    (Charley Pride)

COUNTRY ALBUMS

1. OKIE FROM MUSKOGEE
   (Merle Haggard)
2. JUST PLAIN CHARLEY C. PRIDE
   (Charley Pride)
3. BEST OF CHARLEY PRIDE
   (Charley Pride)
4. HELLO, I'M JOHNNY CASH
   (Johnny Cash)
5. TRY A LITTLE KINDNESS
   (Glen Campbell)
6. WINGS UPON YOUR HORNS
   (Loretta Lynn)
7. WAYS TO LOVE A MAN
   (Tammy Wynette)
8. JOHNNY CASH AT SAN QUENTIN
   (Johnny Cash)
9. BIG IN VEGAS
   (Buck Owens)
10. SHE EVEN WOKE ME UP TO SAY GOODBYE
    (Jerry Lee Lewis)

APRIL 4, 1970

POP SINGLES

1. ABC
   (The Jackson 5)
2. LET IT BE
   (The Beatles)
3. INSTANT KARMA
   (John Lennon/Yoko Ono)
4. LOVE GROWS
   (Edison Lighthouse)
5. BRIDGE OVER TROUBLED WATER
   (Simon and Garfunkel)
6. HOUSE OF THE RISING SUN
   (Frijid Pink)
7. SPIRIT IN THE SKY
   (Norman Greenbaum)
8. HE AIN'T HEAVY, HE'S MY BROTHER
   (The Hollies)
9. THE RAPPER
   (Jaggerz)
10. COME AND GET IT
    (Badfinger)

POP ALBUMS

1. HEY JUDE
   (The Beatles)
2. BRIDGE OVER TROUBLED WATER
   (Simon and Garfunkel)
3. MORRISON HOTEL
   (The Doors)
4. SANTANA
   (Santana)
5. CHICAGO
   (Chicago)
6. LED ZEPPELIN II
   (Led Zeppelin)
7. EASY RIDER
   (Original Soundtrack)
8. WILLIE AND THE POOR BOYS
   (Creedence Clearwater Revival)
9. FRIJID PINK
   (Frijid Pink)
10. ABBEY ROAD
    (The Beatles)

BLACK SINGLES

1. ABC
   (The Jackson 5)
2. GOTTA HOLD ON TO THIS FEELING
   (Junior Walker and the All Stars)
3. CALL ME
   (Aretha Franklin)
4. YOU'RE THE ONE
   (Little Sister)
5. THE BELLS
   (The Originals)
6. UP THE LADDER TO THE ROOF
   (The Supremes)
7. TURN BACK THE HANDS OF TIME
   (Tyrone Davis)
8. CRYIN' IN THE STREETS
   (George Perkins)
9. LOVE OR LET ME BE LONELY
   (Friends of Distinction)
10. TO THE OTHER WOMAN
    (Doris Duke)

JAZZ ALBUMS

1. SWISS MOVEMENT
   (Les McCann and Eddie Harris)
2. WALKING IN SPACE
   (Quincy Jones)
3. HOT BUTTERED SOUL
   (Isaac Hayes)
4. MEMPHIS UNDERGROUND
   (Herbie Mann)
5. BEST OF RAMSEY
   (Ramsey Lewis)
6. BEST OF HERBIE MANN
   (Herbie Mann)
7. YE ME LE
   (Sergio Mendes and Brasil '66)
8. STONE FLUTE
   (Herbie Mann)
9. HERBIE MANN LIVE AT THE WHISKEY A GO GO
   (Herbie Mann)
10. IN A SILENT WAY
    (Miles Davis)

COUNTRY SINGLES

1. MY WOMAN, MY WOMAN, MY WIFE
   (Marty Robbins)
2. ONCE MORE WITH FEELING
   (Jerry Lee Lewis)
3. TENNESSEE BIRDWALK
   (Jack Blanchard and Misty Morgan)
4. IS ANYBODY GOIN' TO SAN ANTONE
   (Charley Pride)
5. OCCASIONAL WIFE
   (Faron Young)
6. FIGHTIN' SIDE OF ME
   (Merle Haggard)
7. ALL I HAVE TO DO IS DREAM
   (Glen Campbell and Bobbie Gentry)
8. I'LL SEE HIM THROUGH
   (Tammy Wynette)
9. I KNOW HOW
   (Loretta Lynn)
10. TOMORROW IS FOREVER
    (Porter Wagoner and Dolly Parton)

COUNTRY ALBUMS

1. HELLO, I'M JOHNNY CASH
   (Johnny Cash)
2. JUST PLAIN CHARLEY C. PRIDE
   (Charley Pride)
3. WINGS UPON YOUR HORNS
   (Loretta Lynn)
4. OKIE FROM MUSKOGEE
   (Merle Haggard)
5. BEST OF CHARLEY PRIDE
   (Charley Pride)
6. WAYS TO LOVE A MAN
   (Tammy Wynette)
7. TRY A LITTLE KINDNESS
   (Glen Campbell)
8. SHE EVEN WOKE ME UP TO SAY GOODBYE
   (Jerry Lee Lewis)
9. BIG IN VEGAS
   (Buck Owens)
10. GOLDEN CREAM OF THE COUNTRY
    (Jerry Lee Lewis)

APRIL 11, 1970

POP SINGLES

1. LET IT BE
   (The Beatles)
2. ABC
   (The Jackson 5)
3. INSTANT KARMA
   (John Lennon/Yoko Ono)
4. LOVE GROWS
   (Edison Lighthouse)
5. SPIRIT IN THE SKY
   (Norman Greenbaum)
6. HOUSE OF THE RISING SUN
   (Frijid Pink)
7. COME AND GET IT
   (Badfinger)
8. EASY COME EASY GO
   (Bobby Sherman)
9. BRIDGE OVER TROUBLED WATER
   (Simon and Garfunkel)
10. UP THE LADDER TO THE ROOF
    (The Supremes)

POP ALBUMS

1. HEY JUDE
   (The Beatles)
2. BRIDGE OVER TROUBLED WATER
   (Simon and Garfunkel)
3. MORRISON HOTEL
   (The Doors)
4. CHICAGO
   (Chicago)
5. DEJA VU
   (Crosby, Stills, Nash and Young)
6. SANTANA
   (Santana)
7. FRIJID PINK
   (Frijid Pink)
8. LED ZEPPELIN II
   (Led Zeppelin)
9. EASY RIDER
   (Original Soundtrack)
10. ABBEY ROAD
    (The Beatles)

BLACK SINGLES

1. ABC
   (The Jackson 5)
2. TURN BACK THE HANDS OF TIME
   (Tyrone Davis)
3. YOU'RE THE ONE
   (Little Sister)
4. UP THE LADDER TO THE ROOF
   (The Supremes)
5. GOTTA HOLD ON TO THIS FEELING
   (Junior Walker and the All Stars)
6. CALL ME
   (Aretha Franklin)
7. CRYIN' IN THE STREETS
   (George Perkins)
8. LOVE OR LET ME BE LONELY
   (Friends of Distinction)
9. YOU NEED LOVE LIKE I DO
   (Gladys Knight and the Pips)
10. THE BELLS
    (The Originals)

JAZZ ALBUMS

1. SWISS MOVEMENT
   (Les McCann and Eddie Harris)
2. WALKING IN SPACE
   (Quincy Jones)
3. HOT BUTTERED SOUL
   (Isaac Hayes)
4. BEST OF RAMSEY
   (Ramsey Lewis)
5. BEST OF HERBIE MANN
   (Herbie Mann)
6. MEMPHIS UNDERGROUND
   (Herbie Mann)
7. STONE FLUTE
   (Herbie Mann)
8. IN A SILENT WAY
   (Miles Davis)
9. COUNTRY PREACHER
   (Cannonball Adderley Quintet)
10. YE ME LE
    (Sergio Mendes and Brasil '66)

COUNTRY SINGLES

1. ONCE MORE WITH FEELING
   (Jerry Lee Lewis)
2. MY WOMAN, MY WOMAN, MY WIFE
   (Marty Robbins)
3. IS ANYBODY GOIN' TO SAN ANTONE
   (Charley Pride)

4. TENNESSEE BIRDWALK
   (Jack Blanchard and Misty Morgan)
5. ALL I HAVE TO DO IS DREAM
   (Glen Campbell and Bobbie Gentry)
6. I KNOW HOW
   (Loretta Lynn)
7. TOMORROW IS FOREVER
   (Porter Wagoner and Dolly Parton)
8. YOU WOULDN'T KNOW LOVE
   (Ray Price)
9. THE POOL SHARK
   (Dave Dudley)
10. OCCASIONAL WIFE
    (Faron Young)

COUNTRY ALBUMS

1. HELLO, I'M JOHNNY CASH
   (Johnny Cash)
2. JUST PLAIN CHARLEY C. PRIDE
   (Charley Pride)
3. WINGS UPON YOUR HORNS
   (Loretta Lynn)
4. WAYS TO LOVE A MAN
   (Tammy Wynette)
5. OKIE FROM MUSKOGEE
   (Merle Haggard)
6. BEST OF CHARLEY PRIDE
   (Charley Pride)
7. SHE EVEN WOKE ME UP TO SAY GOODBYE
   (Jerry Lee Lewis)
8. TRY A LITTLE KINDNESS
   (Glen Campbell)
9. TO SEE MY ANGEL
   (Conway Twitty)
10. TAMMY WYNETTE'S GREATEST HITS
    (Tammy Wynette)

APRIL 18, 1970

POP SINGLES

1. LET IT BE
   (The Beatles)
2. ABC
   (The Jackson 5)
3. SPIRIT IN THE SKY
   (Norman Greenbaum)
4. LOVE GROWS
   (Edison Lighthouse)
5. HOUSE OF THE RISING SUN
   (Frijid Pink)
6. EASY COME, EASY GO
   (Bobby Sherman)
7. COME AND GET IT
   (Badfinger)
8. INSTANT KARMA
   (John Lennon/Yoko Ono)
9. UP THE LADDER TO THE ROOF
   (The Supremes)
10. AMERICAN WOMAN/NO SUGAR TONIGHT
    (The Guess Who)

POP ALBUMS

1. DEJA VU
   (Crosby, Stills, Nash and Young)
2. BRIDGE OVER TROUBLED WATER
   (Simon and Garfunkel)
3. HEY JUDE
   (The Beatles)
4. MORRISON HOTEL
   (The Doors)
5. CHICAGO
   (Chicago)
6. LED ZEPPELIN II
   (Led Zeppelin)
7. FRIJID PINK
   (Frijid Pink)
8. SANTANA
   (Santana)

9. ABBEY ROAD
   (The Beatles)
10. AMERICAN WOMAN
    (The Guess Who)

BLACK SINGLES

1. ABC
   (The Jackson 5)
2. TURN BACK THE HANDS OF TIME
   (Tyrone Davis)
3. YOU'RE THE ONE
   (Little Sister)
4. UP THE LADDER TO THE ROOF
   (The Supremes)
5. CRYIN' IN THE STREETS
   (George Perkins)
6. YOU NEED LOVE LIKE I DO
   (Gladys Knight and the Pips)
7. LOVE OR LET ME BE LONELY
   (Friends of Distinction)
8. CALL ME
   (Aretha Franklin)
9. LOVE ON A TWO WAY STREET
   (The Moments)
10. CALIFORNIA GIRL
    (Eddie Floyd)

JAZZ ALBUMS

1. SWISS MOVEMENT
   (Les McCann and Eddie Harris)
2. BEST OF RAMSEY
   (Ramsey Lewis)
3. WALKING IN SPACE
   (Quincy Jones)
4. HOT BUTTERED SOUL
   (Isaac Hayes)
5. STONE FLUTE
   (Herbie Mann)
6. MEMPHIS UNDERGROUND
   (Herbie Mann)
7. BEST OF HERBIE MANN
   (Herbie Mann)
8. COUNTRY PREACHER
   (Cannonball Adderley Quintet)
9. IN A SILENT WAY
   (Miles Davis)
10. HEAVY EXPOSURE
    (Woody Herman)

COUNTRY SINGLES

1. IS ANYBODY GOIN' TO SAN ANTONE
   (Charley Pride)
2. I KNOW HOW
   (Loretta Lynn)
3. THE POOL SHARK
   (Dave Dudley)
4. ONCE MORE WITH FEELING
   (Jerry Lee Lewis)
5. MY WOMAN, MY WOMAN, MY WIFE
   (Marty Robbins)
6. YOU WOULDN'T KNOW LOVE
   (Ray Price)
7. LOVE IS A SOMETIMES THING
   (Bill Anderson)
8. ALL I HAVE TO DO IS DREAM
   (Glen Campbell and Bobbie Gentry)
9. TENNESSEE BIRDWALK
   (Jack Blanchard and Misty Morgan)
10. I WALKED OUT ON HEAVEN
    (Hank Williams Jr.)

COUNTRY ALBUMS

1. HELLO, I'M JOHNNY CASH
   (Johnny Cash)
2. JUST PLAIN CHARLEY C. PRIDE
   (Charley Pride)
3. WINGS UPON YOUR HORNS
   (Loretta Lynn)

4. WAYS TO LOVE A MAN
   (Tammy Wynette)
5. OKIE FROM MUSKOGEE
   (Merle Haggard)
6. TAMMY WYNETTE'S GREATEST HITS
   (Tammy Wynette)
7. BEST OF CHARLEY PRIDE
   (Charley Pride)
8. TRY A LITTLE KINDNESS
   (Glen Campbell)
9. YOU GOTTA HAVE A LICENSE
   (Porter Wagoner)
10. TO SEE MY ANGEL CRY
    (Conway Twitty)

APRIL 25, 1970

POP SINGLES

1. LET IT BE
   (The Beatles)
2. ABC
   (The Jackson 5)
3. SPIRIT IN THE SKY
   (Norman Greenbaum)
4. COME AND GET IT
   (Badfinger)
5. LOVE GROWS
   (Edison Lighthouse)
6. EASY COME, EASY GO
   (Bobby Sherman)
7. AMERICAN WOMAN/NO SUGAR TONIGHT
   (The Guess Who)
8. UP THE LADDER TO THE ROOF
   (The Supremes)
9. INSTANT KARMA
   (John Lennon/Yoko Ono)
10. SOMETHING'S BURNING
    (Kenny Rogers and the First Edition)

POP ALBUMS

1. DEJA VU
   (Crosby, Stills, Nash and Young)
2. BRIDGE OVER TROUBLED WATER
   (Simon and Garfunkel)
3. HEY JUDE
   (The Beatles)
4. CHICAGO
   (Chicago)
5. SANTANA
   (Santana)
6. LED ZEPPELIN II
   (Led Zeppelin)
7. MORRISON HOTEL
   (The Doors)
8. AMERICAN WOMAN
   (The Guess Who)
9. EASY RIDER
   (Original Soundtrack)
10. ABBEY ROAD
    (The Beatles)

BLACK SINGLES

1. TURN BACK THE HANDS OF TIME
   (Tyrone Davis)
2. ABC
   (The Jackson 5)
3. LOVE ON A TWO WAY STREET
   (The Moments)
4. CRYIN' IN THE STREETS
   (George Perkins)
5. YOU NEED LOVE LIKE I DO
   (Gladys Knight and the Pips)
6. LOVE OR LET ME BE LONELY
   (Friends of Distinction)
7. UP THE LADDER TO THE ROOF
   (The Supremes)
8. YOU'RE THE ONE
   (Little Sister)

9. DEEPER (IN LOVE WITH YOU)
  (The O'Jays)
10. CALIFORNIA GIRL
  (Eddie Floyd)

JAZZ ALBUMS

1. SWISS MOVEMENT
  (Les McCann and Eddie Harris)
2. BEST OF RAMSEY
  (Ramsey Lewis)
3. HOT BUTTERED SOUL
  (Isaac Hayes)
4. MEMPHIS UNDERGROUND
  (Herbie Mann)
5. COUNTRY PREACHER
  (Cannonball Adderley Quintet)
6. WALKING IN SPACE
  (Quincy Jones)
7. GREATEST HITS
  (Wes Montgomery)
8. BEST OF HERBIE MANN
  (Herbie Mann)
9. BEST OF EDDIE HARRIS
  (Eddie Harris)
10. HEAVY EXPOSURE
  (Woody Herman)

COUNTRY SINGLES

1. IS ANYBODY GOIN' TO SAN ANTONE
  (Charley Pride)
2. I KNOW HOW
  (Loretta Lynn)
3. THE POOL SHARK
  (Dave Dudley)
4. ONCE MORE WITH FEELING
  (Jerry Lee Lewis)
5. MY WOMAN, MY WOMAN, MY WIFE
  (Marty Robbins)
6. YOU WOULDN'T KNOW LOVE
  (Ray Price)
7. LOVE IS A SOMETIMES THING
  (Bill Anderson)
8. ALL I HAVE TO DO IS DREAM
  (Glen Campbell and Bobbie Gentry)
9. TENNESSEE BIRDWALK
  (Jack Blanchard and Misty Morgan)
10. I WALKED OUT ON HEAVEN
  (Hank Williams Jr.)

COUNTRY ALBUMS

1. HELLO, I'M JOHNNY CASH
  (Johnny Cash)
2. JUST PLAIN CHARLEY C. PRIDE
  (Charley Pride)
3. WINGS UPON YOUR HORNS
  (Loretta Lynn)
4. TAMMY WYNETTE'S GREATEST HITS
  (Tammy Wynette)
5. OKIE FROM MUSKOGEE
  (Merle Haggard)
6. WAYS TO LOVE A MAN
  (Tammy Wynette)
7. TO SEE MY ANGEL CRY
  (Conway Twitty)
8. BEST OF CHARLEY PRIDE
  (Charley Pride)
9. YOU GOTTA HAVE A LICENSE
  (Porter Wagoner)
10. IT'S JUST A MATTER OF TIME
  (Sonny James)

MAY 2, 1970

POP SINGLES

1. SPIRIT IN THE SKY
  (Norman Greenbaum)

2. LET IT BE
  (The Beatles)
3. AMERICAN WOMAN/NO SUGAR TONIGHT
  (The Guess Who)
4. ABC
  (The Jackson 5)
5. LOVE GROWS
  (Edison Lighthouse)
6. COME AND GET IT
  (Badfinger)
7. TURN BACK THE HANDS OF TIME
  (Tyrone Davis)
8. SOMETHING'S BURNING
  (Kenny Rogers and the First Edition)
9. LOVE OR LET ME BE LONELY
  (Friends of Distinction)
10. WOODSTOCK
  (Crosby, Stills, Nash and Young)

POP ALBUMS

1. DEJA VU
  (Crosby, Stills, Nash and Young)
2. BRIDGE OVER TROUBLED WATER
  (Simon and Garfunkel)
3. HEY JUDE
  (The Beatles)
4. CHICAGO
  (Chicago)
5. SANTANA
  (Santana)
6. MORRISON HOTEL
  (The Doors)
7. I WANT YOU BACK
  (The Jackson 5)
8. AMERICAN WOMAN
  (The Guess Who)
9. LED ZEPPELIN II
  (Led Zeppelin)
10. ABBEY ROAD
  (The Beatles)

BLACK SINGLES

1. TURN BACK THE HANDS OF TIME
  (Tyrone Davis)
2. LOVE ON A TWO WAY STREET
  (The Moments)
3. YOU NEED LOVE LIKE I DO
  (Gladys Knight and the Pips)
4. ABC
  (The Jackson 5)
5. CRYIN' IN THE STREETS
  (George Perkins)
6. LOVE OR LET ME BE LONELY
  (Friends of Distinction)
7. CHICKEN STRUT
  (The Meters)
8. COLE, COOK AND REDDING/SUGAR SUGAR
  (Wilson Pickett)
9. UP THE LADDER TO THE ROOF
  (The Supremes)
10. YOU'RE THE ONE
  (Little Sister)

JAZZ ALBUMS

1. SWISS MOVEMENT
  (Les McCann and Eddie Harris)
2. COUNTRY PREACHER
  (Cannonball Adderley Quintet)
3. BEST OF RAMSEY
  (Ramsey Lewis)
4. WALKING IN SPACE
  (Quincy Jones)
5. MEMPHIS UNDERGROUND
  (Herbie Mann)
6. HOT BUTTERED SOUL
  (Isaac Hayes)
7. GREATEST HITS
  (Wes Montgomery)
8. BEST OF HERBIE MANN
  (Herbie Mann)

9. BEST OF EDDIE HARRIS
  (Eddie Harris)
10. JEWELS OF THOUGHT
  (Pharaoh Sanders)

COUNTRY SINGLES

1. THE POOL SHARK
  (Dave Dudley)
2. IS ANYBODY GOIN' TO SAN ANTONE
  (Charley Pride)
3. LOVE IS A SOMETIMES THING
  (Bill Anderson)
4. I KNOW HOW
  (Loretta Lynn)
5. YOU WOULDN'T KNOW LOVE
  (Ray Price)
6. ONCE MORE WITH FEELING
  (Jerry Lee Lewis)
7. MY WOMAN, MY WOMAN, MY WIFE
  (Marty Robbins)
8. I DO MY SWINGING AT HOME
  (David Houston)
9. SHOESHINE MAN
  (Tom T. Hall)
10. LOOK IS THAT ME
  (Jack Greene)

COUNTRY ALBUMS

1. JUST PLAIN CHARLEY C. PRIDE
  (Charley Pride)
2. HELLO, I'M JOHNNY CASH
  (Johnny Cash)
3. WINGS UPON YOUR HORNS
  (Loretta Lynn)
4. WAYS TO LOVE A MAN
  (Tammy Wynette)
5. OKIE FROM MUSKOGEE
  (Merle Haggard)
6. TAMMY WYNETTE'S GREATEST HITS
  (Tammy Wynette)
7. IT'S JUST A MATTER OF TIME
  (Sonny James)
8. YOU GOTTA HAVE A LICENSE
  (Porter Wagoner)
9. TO SEE MY ANGEL CRY
  (Conway Twitty)
10. BEST OF CHARLEY PRIDE
  (Charley Pride)

MAY 9, 1970

POP SINGLES

1. SPIRIT IN THE SKY
  (Norman Greenbaum)
2. AMERICAN WOMAN/NO SUGAR TONIGHT
  (The Guess Who)
3. TURN BACK THE HANDS OF TIME
  (Tyrone Davis)
4. VEHICLE
  (Ides of March)
5. LET IT BE
  (The Beatles)
6. LOVE OR LET ME BE LONELY
  (Friends of Distinction)
7. SOMETHING'S BURNING
  (Kenny Rogers and the First Edition)
8. ABC
  (The Jackson 5)
9. FOR THE LOVE OF HIM
  (Bobbi Martin)
10. WOODSTOCK
  (Crosby, Stills, Nash and Young)

POP ALBUMS

1. DEJA VU
  (Crosby, Stills, Nash and Young)

2. BRIDGE OVER TROUBLED WATER
   (Simon and Garfunkel)
3. CHICAGO
   (Chicago)
4. HEY JUDE
   (The Beatles)
5. SANTANA
   (Santana)
6. McCARTNEY
   (Paul McCartney)
7. AMERICAN WOMAN
   (The Guess Who)
8. MORRISON HOTEL
   (The Doors)
9. HERE COMES BOBBY
   (Bobby Sherman)
10. LED ZEPPELIN II
    (Led Zeppelin)

BLACK SINGLES

1. LOVE ON A TWO WAY STREET
   (The Moments)
2. TURN BACK THE HANDS OF TIME
   (Tyrone Davis)
3. OPEN UP YOUR HEART/NADINE
   (The Dells)
4. YOU NEED LOVE LIKE I DO
   (Gladys Knight and the Pips)
5. ABC
   (The Jackson 5)
6. CHICKEN STRUT
   (The Meters)
7. HEY GIRL
   (George Kerr)
8. COLE, COOK AND REDDING/SUGAR SUGAR
   (Wilson Pickett)
9. FARTHER DOWN THE ROAD
   (Joe Simon)
10. BABY I LOVE YOU
    (Little Milton)

JAZZ ALBUMS

1. SWISS MOVEMENT
   (Les McCann and Eddie Harris)
2. COUNTRY PREACHER
   (Cannonball Adderley Quintet)
3. GREATEST HITS
   (Wes Montgomery)
4. THE ISAAC HAYES MOVEMENT
   (Isaac Hayes)
5. WALKING IN SPACE
   (Quincy Jones)
6. BEST OF RAMSEY
   (Ramsey Lewis)
7. HOT BUTTERED SOUL
   (Isaac Hayes)
8. STONE FLUTE
   (Herbie Mann)
9. JEWELS OF THOUGHT
   (Pharaoh Sanders)
10. MEMPHIS UNDERGROUND
    (Herbie Mann)

COUNTRY SINGLES

1. LOVE IS A SOMETIMES THING
   (Bill Anderson)
2. THE POOL SHARK
   (Dave Dudley)
3. IS ANYBODY GOIN' TO SAN ANTONE
   (Charley Pride)
4. I DO MY SWINGING AT HOME
   (David Houston)
5. I KNOW HOW
   (Loretta Lynn)
6. YOU WOULDN'T KNOW LOVE
   (Ray Price)
7. MY LOVE
   (Sonny James)
8. SHOESHINE MAN
   (Tom T. Hall)
9. WHAT IS TRUTH
   (Johnny Cash)

10. DON'T TAKE ALL YOUR LOVING
    (Don Gibson)

COUNTRY ALBUMS

1. JUST PLAIN CHARLEY C. PRIDE
   (Charley Pride)
2. IT'S JUST A MATTER OF TIME
   (Sonny James)
3. WAYS TO LOVE A MAN
   (Tammy Wynette)
4. OKIE FROM MUSKOGEE
   (Merle Haggard)
5. YOU GOTTA HAVE A LICENSE
   (Porter Wagoner)
6. HELLO, I'M JOHNNY CASH
   (Johnny Cash)
7. WINGS UPON YOUR HORNS
   (Loretta Lynn)
8. TAMMY WYNETTE'S GREATEST HITS
   (Tammy Wynette)
9. PORTER WAYNE AND DOLLY REBECCA
   (Porter Wagoner and Dolly Parton)
10. THE FAIREST OF THEM ALL
    (Dolly Parton)

MAY 16, 1970

POP SINGLES

1. AMERICAN WOMAN/NO SUGAR TONIGHT
   (The Guess Who)
2. TURN BACK THE HANDS OF TIME
   (Tyrone Davis)
3. VEHICLE
   (Ides of March)
4. SPIRIT IN THE SKY
   (Norman Greenbaum)
5. LOVE OR LET ME BE LONELY
   (Friends of Distinction)
6. LET IT BE
   (The Beatles)
7. SOMETHING'S BURNING
   (Kenny Rogers and the First Edition)
8. REFLECTIONS OF MY LIFE
   (Marmalade)
9. FOR THE LOVE OF HIM
   (Bobbi Martin)
10. UP AROUND THE BEND/RUN THROUGH
    THE JUNGLE
    (Creedence Clearwater Revival)

POP ALBUMS

1. McCARTNEY
   (Paul McCartney)
2. BRIDGE OVER TROUBLED WATER
   (Simon and Garfunkel)
3. DEJA VU
   (Crosby, Stills, Nash and Young)
4. HEY JUDE
   (The Beatles)
5. AMERICAN WOMAN
   (The Guess Who)
6. LIVE
   (Glen Campbell)
7. HERE COMES BOBBY
   (Bobby Sherman)
8. CHICAGO
   (Chicago)
9. BAND OF GYPSYS
   (Jimi Hendrix)
10. CRICKLEWOOD GREEN
    (Ten Years After)

BLACK SINGLES

1. LOVE ON A TWO WAY STREET
   (The Moments)

2. OPEN UP YOUR HEART/NADINE
   (The Dells)
3. REACH OUT AND TOUCH
   (Diana Ross)
4. TURN BACK THE HANDS OF TIME
   (Tyrone Davis)
5. ABC
   (The Jackson 5)
6. CHICKEN STRUT
   (The Meters)
7. HEY GIRL
   (George Kerr)
8. BABY I LOVE YOU
   (Little Milton)
9. FARTHER DOWN THE ROAD
   (Joe Simon)
10. UHH
    (Dyke and the Blazers)

JAZZ ALBUMS

1. THE ISAAC HAYES MOVEMENT
   (Isaac Hayes)
2. GREATEST HITS
   (Wes Montgomery)
3. SWISS MOVEMENT
   (Les McCann and Eddie Harris)
4. BEST OF RAMSEY LEWIS
   (Ramsey Lewis)
5. COUNTRY PREACHER
   (Cannonball Adderley Quintet)
6. WALKING IN SPACE
   (Quincy Jones)
7. THE PIANO PLAYER
   (Ramsey Lewis)
8. JEWELS OF THOUGHT
   (Pharaoh Sanders)
9. HOT BUTTERED SOUL
   (Isaac Hayes)
10. STONE FLUTE
    (Herbie Mann)

COUNTRY SINGLES

1. I DO MY SWINGING AT HOME
   (David Houston)
2. LOVE IS A SOMETIMES THING
   (Bill Anderson)
3. MY LOVE
   (Sonny James)
4. THE POOL SHARK
   (Dave Dudley)
5. WHAT IS TRUTH
   (Johnny Cash)
6. IS ANYBODY GOIN' TO SAN ANTONE
   (Charley Pride)
7. SHOESHINE MAN
   (Tom T. Hall)
8. I KNOW HOW
   (Loretta Lynn)
9. HELLO DARLIN'
   (Conway Twitty)
10. RISE AND SHINE
    (Tommy Cash)

COUNTRY ALBUMS

1. JUST PLAIN CHARLEY C. PRIDE
   (Charley Pride)
2. IT'S JUST A MATTER OF TIME
   (Sonny James)
3. OKIE FROM MUSKOGEE
   (Merle Haggard)
4. WAYS TO LOVE A MAN
   (Tammy Wynette)
5. HELLO, I'M JOHNNY CASH
   (Johnny Cash)
6. YOU GOTTA HAVE A LICENSE
   (Porter Wagoner)
7. TAMMY WYNETTE'S GREATEST HITS
   (Tammy Wynette)
8. PORTER WAYNE AND DOLLY REBECCA
   (Porter Wagoner and Dolly Parton)

9. WINGS UPON YOUR HORNS
   (Loretta Lynn)
10. THE FAIREST OF THEM ALL
    (Dolly Parton)

MAY 23, 1970

POP SINGLES

1. TURN BACK THE HANDS OF TIME
   (Tyrone Davis)
2. AMERICAN WOMAN/NO SUGAR TONIGHT
   (The Guess Who)
3. VEHICLE
   (Ides of March)
4. UP AROUND THE BEND/RUN THROUGH
   THE JUNGLE
   (Creedence Clearwater Revival)
5. CECELIA
   (Simon and Garfunkel)
6. SPIRIT IN THE SKY
   (Norman Greenbaum)
7. REFLECTIONS OF MY LIFE
   (Marmalade)
8. FOR THE LOVE OF HIM
   (Bobbi Martin)
9. EVERYTHING IS BEAUTIFUL
   (Ray Stevens)
10. GET READY
    (Rare Earth)

BLACK SINGLES

1. LOVE ON A TWO WAY STREET
   (The Moments)
2. REACH OUT AND TOUCH
   (Diana Ross)
3. OPEN UP YOUR HEART/NADINE
   (The Dells)
4. COLE, COOK AND REDDING/SUGAR SUGAR
   (Wilson Pickett)
5. CALIFORNIA SOUL
   (Marvin Gaye and Tammi Terrell)
6. TURN BACK THE HANDS OF TIME
   (Tyrone Davis)
7. FARTHER DOWN THE ROAD
   (Joe Simon)
8. UHH
   (Dyke and the Blazers)
9. HEY GIRL
   (George Kerr)
10. I CAN'T LEAVE YOUR LOVE ALONE
    (Clarence Carter)

JAZZ ALBUMS

1. THE ISAAC HAYES MOVEMENT
   (Isaac Hayes)
2. GREATEST HITS
   (Wes Montgomery)
3. BEST OF RAMSEY
   (Ramsey Lewis)
4. WALKING IN SPACE
   (Quincy Lewis)
5. SWISS MOVEMENT
   (Les McCann and Eddie Harris)
6. COUNTRY PREACHER
   (Cannonball Adderley Quintet)
7. THE PIANO PLAYER
   (Ramsey Lewis)
8. JEWELS OF THOUGHT
   (Pharoah Sanders)
9. BITCHES BREW
   (Miles Davis)
10. MEMPHIS UNDERGROUND
    (Herbie Mann)

COUNTRY SINGLES

1. MY LOVE
   (Sonny James)
2. I DO MY SWINGING AT HOME
   (David Houston)
3. WHAT IS TRUTH
   (Johnny Cash)
4. LOVE IS A SOMETIMES THING
   (Bill Anderson)
5. HELLO DARLIN'
   (Conway Twitty)
6. THE POOL SHARK
   (Dave Dudley)
7. SHOESHINE MAN
   (Tom T. Hall)
8. SINGER OF SAD SONGS
   (Waylon Jennings)
9. RISE AND SHINE
   (Tommy Cash)
10. IS ANYBODY GOIN' TO SAN ANTONE
    (Charley Pride)

COUNTRY ALBUMS

1. JUST PLAIN CHARLEY C. PRIDE
   (Charley Pride)
2. IT'S JUST A MATTER OF TIME
   (Sonny James)
3. OKIE FROM MUSKOGEE
   (Merle Haggard)
4. HELLO, I'M JOHNNY CASH
   (Johnny Cash)
5. TAMMY WYNETTE'S GREATEST HITS
   (Tammy Wynette)
6. BABY BABY
   (David Houston)
7. TO SEE MY ANGEL CRY
   (Conway Twitty)
8. PORTER WAYNE AND DOLLY REBECCA
   (Porter Wagoner and Dolly Parton)
9. WAYS TO LOVE A MAN
   (Tammy Wynette)
10. YOU GOTTA HAVE A LICENSE
    (Porter Wagoner)

MAY 30, 1970

POP SINGLES

1. TURN BACK THE HANDS OF TIME
   (Tyrone Davis)
2. UP AROUND THE BEND/RUN THROUGH
   THE JUNGLE
   (Creedence Clearwater Revival)
3. VEHICLE
   (Ides of March)
4. CECELIA
   (Simon and Garfunkel)
5. AMERICAN WOMAN/NO SUGAR TONIGHT
   (The Guess Who)
6. LOVE ON A TWO WAY STREET
   (The Moments)
7. EVERYTHING IS BEAUTIFUL
   (Ray Stevens)
8. FOR THE LOVE OF HIM
   (Bobbi Martin)
9. GET READY
   (Rare Earth)
10. REACH OUT AND TOUCH
    (Diana Ross)

POP ALBUMS

1. McCARTNEY
   (Paul McCartney)
2. DEJA VU
   (Crosby, Stills, Nash and Young)
3. BRIDGE OVER TROUBLED WATER
   (Simon and Garfunkel)

4. BAND OF GYPSYS
   (Jimi Hendrix)
5. HEY JUDE
   (The Beatles)
6. CHICAGO
   (Chicago)
7. HERE COMES BOBBY
   (Bobby Sherman)
8. TOM
   (Tom Jones)
9. IT AIN'T EASY
   (Three Dog Night)
10. LIVE CREAM
    (Cream)

BLACK SINGLES

1. REACH OUT AND TOUCH
   (Diana Ross)
2. LOVE ON A TWO WAY STREET
   (The Moments)
3. COLE, COOK AND REDDING/SUGAR SUGAR
   (Wilson Pickett)
4. BROTHER RAPP
   (James Brown)
5. CALIFORNIA SOUL
   (Marvin Gaye and Tammi Terrell)
6. OPEN UP YOUR HEART/NADINE
   (The Dells)
7. FARTHER DOWN THE ROAD
   (Joe Simon)
8. MAMA'S BABY DADDY'S MAYBE
   (Swamp Dogg)
9. I CAN'T LEAVE YOUR LOVE ALONE
   (Clarence Carter)
10. CHECK OUT YOUR MIND
    (The Impressions)

JAZZ ALBUMS

1. THE ISAAC HAYES MOVEMENT
   (Isaac Hayes)
2. WALKING IN SPACE
   (Quincy Jones)
3. GREATEST HITS
   (Wes Montgomery)
4. SWISS MOVEMENT
   (Les McCann and Eddie Harris)
5. BITCHES BREW
   (Miles Davis)
6. BEST OF RAMSEY
   (Ramsey Lewis)
7. JEWELS OF THOUGHT
   (Pharoah Sanders)
8. COUNTRY PREACHER
   (Cannonball Adderley Quintet)
9. THE PIANO PLAYER
   (Ramsey Lewis)
10. HEAVY EXPOSURE
    (Woody Herman)

COUNTRY SINGLES

1. MY LOVE
   (Sonny James)
2. WHAT IS TRUTH
   (Johnny Cash)
3. I DO MY SWINGING AT HOME
   (David Houston)
4. HELLO DARLIN'
   (Conway Twitty)
5. LOVE IS A SOMETIMES THING
   (Bill Anderson)
6. SINGER OF SAD SONGS
   (Waylon Jennings)
7. THE POOL SHARK
   (Dave Dudley)
8. RISE AND SHINE
   (Tommy Cash)
9. STAY THERE TILL I GET THERE
   (Lynn Anderson)
10. STREET SINGER
    (Merle Haggard and The Strangers)

COUNTRY ALBUMS

1. JUST PLAIN CHARLEY C. PRIDE
   (Charley Pride)
2. HELLO, I'M JOHNNY CASH
   (Johnny Cash)
3. BABY BABY
   (David Houston)
4. WAYS TO LOVE A MAN
   (Tammy Wynette)
5. TO SEE MY ANGEL CRY
   (Conway Twitty)
6. OKIE FROM MUSKOGEE
   (Merle Haggard)
7. IT'S JUST A MATTER OF TIME
   (Sonny James)
8. TAMMY WYNETTE'S GREATEST HITS
   (Tammy Wynette)
9. PORTER WAYNE AND DOLLY REBECCA
   (Porter Wagoner and Dolly Parton)
10. BEST OF JERRY LEE LEWIS
    (Jerry Lee Lewis)

JUNE 6, 1970

POP SINGLES

1. CECELIA
   (Simon and Garfunkel)
2. UP AROUND THE BEND/RUN THROUGH
   THE JUNGLE
   (Creedence Clearwater Revival)
3. EVERYTHING IS BEAUTIFUL
   (Ray Stevens)
4. LOVE ON A TWO WAY STREET
   (The Moments)
5. THE LONG AND WINDING ROAD/
   FOR YOU BLUE
   (The Beatles)
6. GET READY
   (Rare Earth)
7. THE LETTER
   (Joe Cocker)
8. WHICH WAY ARE YOU GOING BILLY
   (The Poppy Family)
9. REACH OUT AND TOUCH
   (Diana Ross)
10. TURN BACK THE HANDS OF TIME
    (Tyrone Davis)

POP ALBUMS

1. McCARTNEY
   (Paul McCartney)
2. DEJA VU
   (Crosby, Stills, Nash and Young)
3. LET IT BE
   (The Beatles)
4. BAND OF GYPSYS
   (Jimi Hendrix)
5. BRIDGE OVER TROUBLED WATER
   (Simon and Garfunkel)
6. TOM
   (Tom Jones)
7. CHICAGO
   (Chicago)
8. HEY JUDE
   (The Beatles)
9. AMERICAN WOMAN
   (The Guess Who)
10. THE ISAAC HAYES MOVEMENT
    (Isaac Hayes)

BLACK SINGLES

1. BROTHER RAPP
   (James Brown)
2. LOVE ON A TWO WAY STREET
   (The Moments)

---

3. COLE, COOK AND REDDING/SUGAR SUGAR
   (Wilson Pickett)
4. CHECK OUT YOUR MIND
   (The Impressions)
5. IT'S ALL IN THE GAME
   (The Four Tops)
6. REACH OUT AND TOUCH
   (Diana Ross)
7. I CAN'T LEAVE YOUR LOVE ALONE
   (Clarence Carter)
8. THE LOVE YOU SAVE
   (The Jackson 5)
9. CALIFORNIA SOUL
   (Marvin Gaye and Tammi Terrell)
10. BALL OF CONFUSION
    (Temptations)

JAZZ ALBUMS

1. THE ISAAC HAYES MOVEMENT
   (Isaac Hayes)
2. BITCHES BREW
   (Miles Davis)
3. SWISS MOVEMENT
   (Les McCann and Eddie Harris)
4. BEST OF RAMSEY
   (Ramsey Lewis)
5. WALKING IN SPACE
   (Quincy Jones)
6. COUNTRY PREACHER
   (Cannonball Adderley Quintet)
7. JEWELS OF THOUGHT
   (Pharaoh Sanders)
8. GREATEST HITS
   (Wes Montgomery)
9. THE PIANO PLAYER
   (Ramsey Lewis)
10. MEMPHIS UNDERGROUND
    (Herbie Mann)

COUNTRY SINGLES

1. WHAT IS TRUTH
   (Johnny Cash)
2. MY LOVE
   (Sonny James)
3. HELLO DARLIN'
   (Conway Twitty)
4. SINGER OF SAD SONGS
   (Waylon Jennings)
5. I DO MY SWINGING AT HOME
   (David Houston)
6. STREET SINGER
   (Merle Haggard and The Strangers)
7. HEART OVER MIND
   (Mel Tillis)
8. LOVE IS A SOMETIMES THING
   (Bill Anderson)
9. STAY THERE TILL I GET THERE
   (Lynn Anderson)
10. LOVIN' MAN (OH PRETTY WOMAN)
    (Arlene Harden)

COUNTRY ALBUMS

1. JUST PLAIN CHARLEY C. PRIDE
   (Charley Pride)
2. HELLO, I'M JOHNNY CASH
   (Johnny Cash)
3. WAYS TO LOVE A MAN
   (Tammy Wynette)
4. IT'S JUST A MATTER OF TIME
   (Sonny James)
5. BABY BABY
   (David Houston)
6. OKIE FROM MUSKOGEE
   (Merle Haggard)
7. TAMMY WYNETTE'S GREATEST HITS
   (Tammy Wynette)
8. TO SEE MY ANGEL CRY
   (Conway Twitty)
9. BEST OF JERRY LEE LEWIS
   (Jerry Lee Lewis)
10. GREATEST HITS
    (Hank Williams Jr.)

JUNE 13, 1970

POP SINGLES

1. THE LONG AND WINDING ROAD/
   FOR YOU BLUE
   (The Beatles)
2. EVERYTHING IS BEAUTIFUL
   (Ray Stevens)
3. LOVE ON A TWO WAY STREET
   (The Moments)
4. WHICH WAY ARE YOU GOING BILLY
   (The Poppy Family)
5. GET READY
   (Rare Earth)
6. CECELIA
   (Simon and Garfunkel)
7. THE LETTER
   (Joe Cocker)
8. THE LOVE YOU SAVE
   (The Jackson 5)
9. HITCHIN' A RIDE
   (Vanity Fare)
10. DAUGHTER OF DARKNESS
    (Tom Jones)

POP ALBUMS

1. LET IT BE
   (The Beatles)
2. McCARTNEY
   (Paul McCartney)
3. BAND OF GYPSYS
   (Jimi Hendrix)
4. DEJA VU
   (Crosby, Stills, Nash and Young)
5. WOODSTOCK
   (Original Soundtrack)
6. TOM
   (Tom Jones)
7. BRIDGE OVER TROUBLED WATER
   (Simon and Garfunkel)
8. THE ISAAC HAYES MOVEMENT
   (Isaac Hayes)
9. AMERICAN WOMAN
   (The Guess Who)
10. CHICAGO
    (Chicago)

BLACK SINGLES

1. BROTHER RAPP
   (James Brown)
2. LOVE ON A TWO WAY STREET
   (The Moments)
3. CHECK OUT YOUR MIND
   (The Impressions)
4. IT'S ALL IN THE GAME
   (The Four Tops)
5. THE LOVE YOU SAVE
   (The Jackson 5)
6. COLE, COOK AND REDDING/SUGAR SUGAR
   (Wilson Pickett)
7. I CAN'T LEAVE YOUR LOVE ALONE
   (Clarence Carter)
8. BALL OF CONFUSION
   (Temptations)
9. SWEET FEELING
   (Candi Staton)
10. THE SLY, SLICK AND WICKED
    (Lost Generation)

JAZZ ALBUMS

1. THE ISAAC HAYES MOVEMENT
   (Isaac Hayes)
2. BITCHES BREW
   (Miles Davis)
3. SWISS MOVEMENT
   (Les McCann and Eddie Harris)

4. COUNTRY PREACHER
   (Cannonball Adderley Quintet)
5. WALKING IN SPACE
   (Quincy Jones)
6. GREATEST HITS
   (Wes Montgomery)
7. MEMPHIS UNDERGROUND
   (Herbie Mann)
8. COMMENT
   (Les McCann)
9. BEST OF RAMSEY
   (Ramsey Lewis)
10. JEWELS OF THOUGHT
    (Pharaoh Sanders)

COUNTRY SINGLES

1. HELLO DARLIN'
   (Conway Twitty)
2. WHAT IS TRUTH
   (Johnny Cash)
3. SINGER OF SAD SONGS
   (Waylon Jennings)
4. MY LOVE
   (Sonny James)
5. HEART OVER MIND
   (Mel Tillis)
6. STREET SINGER
   (Merle Haggard and The Strangers)
7. I DO MY SWINGING AT HOME
   (David Houston)
8. SHE'S A LITTLE BIT COUNTRY
   (George Hamilton IV)
9. LOVIN' MAN (OH PRETTY WOMAN)
   (Arlene Harden)
10. LONG LONG TEXAS ROAD
    (Roy Drusky)

COUNTRY ALBUMS

1. JUST PLAIN CHARLEY C. PRIDE
   (Charley Pride)
2. WAYS TO LOVE A MAN
   (Tammy Wynette)
3. IT'S JUST A MATTER OF TIME
   (Sonny James)
4. HELLO, I'M JOHNNY CASH
   (Johnny Cash)
5. PORTER WAYNE AND DOLLY REBECCA
   (Porter Wagoner and Dolly Parton)
6. GREATEST HITS
   (Hank Williams Jr.)
7. TAMMY WYNETTE'S GREATEST HITS
   (Tammy Wynette)
8. OKIE FROM MUSKOGEE
   (Merle Haggard)
9. WE'RE GONNA GET TOGETHER
   (Buck Owens and Susan Raye)
10. YOU GOTTA HAVE A LICENSE
    (Porter Wagoner)

JUNE 20, 1970

POP SINGLES

1. THE LONG AND WINDING ROAD/
   FOR YOU BLUE
   (The Beatles)
2. WHICH WAY ARE YOU GOING BILLY
   (The Poppy Family)
3. GET READY
   (Rare Earth)
4. EVERYTHING IS BEAUTIFUL
   (Ray Stevens)
5. HITCHIN' A RIDE
   (Vanity Fare)
6. THE LOVE YOU SAVE
   (The Jackson 5)
7. THE LETTER
   (Joe Cocker)

8. LOVE ON A TWO WAY STREET
   (The Moments)
9. LAY DOWN (CANDLES IN THE RAIN)
   (Melanie and the Edwin Hawkins Singers)
10. DAUGHTER OF DARKNESS
    (Tom Jones)

POP ALBUMS

1. LET IT BE
   (The Beatles)
2. McCARTNEY
   (Paul McCartney)
3. WOODSTOCK
   (Original Soundtrack)
4. DEJA VU
   (Crosby, Stills, Nash and Young)
5. BRIDGE OVER TROUBLED WATER
   (Simon and Garfunkel)
6. BAND OF GYPSYS
   (Jimi Hendrix)
7. TOM
   (Tom Jones)
8. THE ISAAC HAYES MOVEMENT
   (Isaac Hayes)
9. LIVE AT LEEDS
   (The Who)
10. GREATEST HITS
    (The Fifth Dimension)

BLACK SINGLES

1. THE LOVE YOU SAVE
   (The Jackson 5)
2. IT'S ALL IN THE GAME
   (The Four Tops)
3. CHECK OUT YOUR MIND
   (The Impressions)
4. LOVE ON A TWO WAY STREET
   (The Moments)
5. BROTHER RAPP
   (James Brown)
6. BALL OF CONFUSION
   (Temptations)
7. COLE, COOK AND REDDING/SUGAR SUGAR
   (Wilson Pickett)
8. SPIRIT IN THE DARK/THE THRILL IS GONE
   (Aretha Franklin)
9. SWEET FEELING
   (Candi Staton)
10. THE SLY, SLICK AND WICKED
    (Lost Generation)

JAZZ ALBUMS

1. THE ISAAC HAYES MOVEMENT
   (Isaac Hayes)
2. BITCHES BREW
   (Miles Davis)
3. SWISS MOVEMENT
   (Les McCann and Eddie Harris)
4. COUNTRY PREACHER
   (Cannonball Adderley Quintet)
5. GREATEST HITS
   (Wes Montgomery)
6. WALKING IN SPACE
   (Quincy Jones)
7. BEST OF RAMSEY
   (Ramsey Lewis)
8. MEMPHIS UNDERGROUND
   (Herbie Mann)
9. COME ON DOWN
   (Eddie Harris)
10. COMMENT
    (Les McCann)

COUNTRY SINGLES

1. HELLO DARLIN'
   (Conway Twitty)
2. HE LOVES ME ALL THE WAY
   (Tammy Wynette)

3. HEART OVER MIND
   (Mel Tillis)
4. SHE'S A LITTLE BIT COUNTRY
   (George Hamilton IV)
5. LONG LONG TEXAS ROAD
   (Roy Drusky)
6. WHAT IS TRUTH
   (Johnny Cash)
7. MY LOVE
   (Sonny James)
8. SINGER OF SAD SONGS
   (Waylon Jennings)
9. HEAVENLY SUNSHINE
   (Ferlin Husky)
10. I DO MY SWINGING AT HOME
    (David Houston)

COUNTRY ALBUMS

1. JUST PLAIN CHARLEY C. PRIDE
   (Charley Pride)
2. HELLO, I'M JOHNNY CASH
   (Johnny Cash)
3. PORTER WAYNE AND DOLLY REBECCA
   (Porter Wagoner and Dolly Parton)
4. WAYS TO LOVE A MAN
   (Tammy Wynette)
5. TAMMY'S TOUCH
   (Tammy Wynette)
6. GREATEST HITS
   (Hank Williams Jr.)
7. TAMMY WYNETTE'S GREATEST HITS
   (Tammy Wynette)
8. YOU AIN'T HEARD NOTHING YET
   (Danny Davis and the Nashville Brothers)
9. OKIE FROM MUSKOGEE
   (Merle Haggard)
10. TO SEE MY ANGEL CRY
    (Conway Twitty)

JUNE 27, 1970

POP SINGLES

1. THE LOVE YOU SAVE
   (The Jackson 5)
2. THE LONG AND WINDING ROAD/
   FOR YOU BLUE
   (The Beatles)
3. MAMA TOLD ME
   (Three Dog Night)
4. HITCHIN' A RIDE
   (Vanity Fare)
5. THE WONDER OF YOU
   (Elvis Presley)
6. WHICH WAY ARE YOU GOING BILLY
   (The Poppy Family)
7. LAY DOWN (CANDLES IN THE RAIN)
   (Melanie and the Edwin Hawkins Singers)
8. RIDE CAPTAIN RIDE
   (The Blues Image)
9. GET READY
   (Rare Earth)
10. BALL OF CONFUSION
    (Temptations)

POP ALBUMS

1. LET IT BE
   (The Beatles)
2. WOODSTOCK
   (Original Soundtrack)
3. McCARTNEY
   (Paul McCartney)
4. GREATEST HITS
   (The Fifth Dimension)
5. LIVE AT LEEDS
   (The Who)
6. DEJA VU
   (Crosby, Stills, Nash and Young)

7. BAND OF GYPSYS
   (*Jimi Hendrix*)
8. BRIDGE OVER TROUBLED WATER
   (*Simon and Garfunkel*)
9. ABC
   (*The Jackson 5*)
10. CHICAGO
    (*Chicago*)

BLACK SINGLES

1. THE LOVE YOU SAVE
   (*The Jackson 5*)
2. BALL OF CONFUSION
   (*Temptations*)
3. CHECK OUT YOUR MIND
   (*The Impressions*)
4. SPIRIT IN THE DARK/THE THRILL IS GONE
   (*Aretha Franklin*)
5. IT'S ALL IN THE GAME
   (*The Four Tops*)
6. LOVE ON A TWO WAY STREET
   (*The Moments*)
7. THE SLY, SLICK AND WICKED
   (*Lost Generation*)
8. SWEET FEELING
   (*Candi Staton*)
9. AND MY HEART SINGS
   (*Brenda and the Tabulations*)
10. STEAL AWAY
    (*Johnnie Taylor*)

JAZZ ALBUMS

1. BITCHES BREW
   (*Miles Davis*)
2. THE ISAAC HAYES MOVEMENT
   (*Isaac Hayes*)
3. WALKING IN SPACE
   (*Quincy Jones*)
4. GREATEST HITS
   (*Wes Montgomery*)
5. COUNTRY PREACHER
   (*Cannonball Adderley Quintet*)
6. SWISS MOVEMENT
   (*Les McCann and Eddie Harris*)
7. MEMPHIS UNDERGROUND
   (*Herbie Mann*)
8. BEST OF RAMSEY
   (*Ramsey Lewis*)
9. COME ON DOWN
   (*Eddie Harris*)
10. THE PIANO PLAYER
    (*Ramsey Lewis*)

COUNTRY SINGLES

1. HE LOVES ME ALL THE WAY
   (*Tammy Wynette*)
2. HEART OVER MIND
   (*Mel Tillis*)
3. HELLO DARLIN'
   (*Conway Twitty*)
4. SHE'S A LITTLE BIT COUNTRY
   (*George Hamilton IV*)
5. LONG LONG TEXAS ROAD
   (*Roy Drusky*)
6. HEAVENLY SUNSHINE
   (*Ferlin Husky*)
7. I NEVER ONCE STOPPED LOVING YOU
   (*Connie Smith*)
8. I CAN'T SEEM TO SAY GOODBYE
   (*Jerry Lee Lewis*)
9. YOU AND ME AGAINST THE WORLD
   (*Bobby Lord*)
10. I'VE JUST BEEN WASTING MY TIME
    (*John Wesley Ryles*)

COUNTRY ALBUMS

1. JUST PLAIN CHARLEY C. PRIDE
   (*Charley Pride*)

2. HELLO, I'M JOHNNY CASH
   (*Johnny Cash*)
3. PORTER WAYNE AND DOLLY REBECCA
   (*Porter Wagoner and Dolly Parton*)
4. TAMMY'S TOUCH
   (*Tammy Wynette*)
5. YOU AIN'T HEARD NOTHING YET
   (*Danny Davis and the Nashville Brothers*)
6. GREATEST HITS
   (*Hank Williams Jr.*)
7. TAMMY WYNETTE'S GREATEST HITS
   (*Tammy Wynette*)
8. TO SEE MY ANGEL CRY
   (*Conway Twitty*)
9. BIRDS OF A FEATHER
   (*Jack Blanchard and Misty Morgan*)
10. WAYS TO LOVE A MAN
    (*Tammy Wynette*)

JULY 4, 1970

POP SINGLES

1. MAMA TOLD ME
   (*Three Dog Night*)
2. THE LOVE YOU SAVE
   (*The Jackson 5*)
3. HITCHIN' A RIDE
   (*Vanity Fare*)
4. THE WONDER OF YOU
   (*Elvis Presley*)
5. LAY DOWN (CANDLES IN THE RAIN)
   (*Melanie and the Edwin Hawkins Singers*)
6. BAND OF GOLD
   (*Freda Payne*)
7. RIDE CAPTAIN RIDE
   (*The Blues Image*)
8. BALL OF CONFUSION
   (*Temptations*)
9. THE LONG AND WINDING ROAD/
   FOR YOU BLUE
   (*The Beatles*)
10. WHICH WAY ARE YOU GOING BILLY
    (*The Poppy Family*)

POP ALBUMS

1. LET IT BE
   (*The Beatles*)
2. WOODSTOCK
   (*Original Soundtrack*)
3. LIVE AT LEEDS
   (*The Who*)
4. GREATEST HITS
   (*The Fifth Dimension*)
5. McCARTNEY
   (*Paul McCartney*)
6. BRIDGE OVER TROUBLED WATER
   (*Simon and Garfunkel*)
7. ABC
   (*The Jackson 5*)
8. DEJA VU
   (*Crosby, Stills, Nash and Young*)
9. CHICAGO
   (*Chicago*)
10. THE ISAAC HAYES MOVEMENT
    (*Isaac Hayes*)

BLACK SINGLES

1. THE LOVE YOU SAVE
   (*The Jackson 5*)
2. BALL OF CONFUSION
   (*Temptations*)
3. SPIRIT IN THE DARK/THE THRILL IS GONE
   (*Aretha Franklin*)
4. STEAL AWAY
   (*Johnnie Taylor*)
5. CHECK OUT YOUR MIND
   (*The Impressions*)

6. THE SLY, SLICK AND WICKED
   (*Lost Generation*)
7. IT'S ALL IN THE GAME
   (*The Four Tops*)
8. AIN'T THAT LOVING YOU
   (*Luther Ingram*)
9. MAYBE
   (*The Three Degrees*)
10. LOVE ON A TWO WAY STREET
    (*The Moments*)

JAZZ ALBUMS

1. BITCHES BREW
   (*Miles Davis*)
2. THE ISAAC HAYES MOVEMENT
   (*Isaac Hayes*)
3. WALKING IN SPACE
   (*Quincy Jones*)
4. COUNTRY PREACHER
   (*Cannonball Adderley Quintet*)
5. SWISS MOVEMENT
   (*Les McCann and Eddie Harris*)
6. MEMPHIS UNDERGROUND
   (*Herbie Mann*)
7. GREATEST HITS
   (*Wes Montgomery*)
8. COME ON DOWN
   (*Eddie Harris*)
9. BEST OF RAMSEY
   (*Ramsey Lewis*)
10. COMMENT
    (*Les McCann*)

COUNTRY SINGLES

1. HEART OVER MIND
   (*Mel Tillis*)
2. HE LOVES ME ALL THE WAY
   (*Tammy Wynette*)
3. LONG LONG TEXAS ROAD
   (*Roy Drusky*)
4. SHE'S A LITTLE BIT COUNTRY
   (*George Hamilton IV*)
5. HEAVENLY SUNSHINE
   (*Ferlin Husky*)
6. I NEVER ONCE STOPPED LOVING YOU
   (*Connie Smith*)
7. I CAN'T SEEM TO SAY GOODBYE
   (*Jerry Lee Lewis*)
8. HELLO DARLIN'
   (*Conway Twitty*)
9. YOU AND ME AGAINST THE WORLD
   (*Bobby Lord*)
10. IF I EVER FALL IN LOVE (WITH A HONKY
    TONK GIRL)
    (*Faron Young*)

COUNTRY ALBUMS

1. JUST PLAIN CHARLEY C. PRIDE
   (*Charley Pride*)
2. TAMMY'S TOUCH
   (*Tammy Wynette*)
3. HELLO, I'M JOHNNY CASH
   (*Johnny Cash*)
4. PORTER WAYNE AND DOLLY REBECCA
   (*Porter Wagoner and Dolly Parton*)
5. GREATEST HITS
   (*Hank Williams Jr.*)
6. YOU AIN'T HEARD NOTHING YET
   (*Danny Davis and the Nashville Brothers*)
7. TAMMY WYNETTE'S GREATEST HITS
   (*Tammy Wynette*)
8. MY WOMAN, MY WOMAN, MY WIFE
   (*Marty Robbins*)
9. WE'RE GONNA GET TOGETHER
   (*Buck Owens and Susan Raye*)
10. A TASTE OF COUNTRY
    (*Jerry Lee Lewis*)

JULY 11, 1970

POP SINGLES

1. MAMA TOLD ME
   (Three Dog Night)
2. BALL OF CONFUSION
   (Temptations)
3. BAND OF GOLD
   (Freda Payne)
4. THE WONDER OF YOU
   (Elvis Presley)
5. LAY DOWN (CANDLES IN THE RAIN)
   (Melanie and the Edwin Hawkins Singers)
6. THE LOVE YOU SAVE
   (The Jackson 5)
7. RIDE CAPTAIN RIDE
   (The Blues Image)
8. HITCHIN' A RIDE
   (Vanity Fare)
9. THE LONG AND WINDING ROAD/
   FOR YOU BLUE
   (The Beatles)
10. GIMME DAT DING
    (The Pipkins)

POP ALBUMS

1. LET IT BE
   (The Beatles)
2. WOODSTOCK
   (Original Soundtrack)
3. LIVE AT LEEDS
   (The Who)
4. McCARTNEY
   (Paul McCartney)
5. ABC
   (The Jackson 5)
6. DEJA VU
   (Crosby, Stills, Nash and Young)
7. GREATEST HITS
   (The Fifth Dimension)
8. CHICAGO
   (Chicago)
9. BRIDGE OVER TROUBLED WATER
   (Simon and Garfunkel)
10. CANDLES IN THE RAIN
    (Melanie)

BLACK SINGLES

1. BALL OF CONFUSION
   (Temptations)
2. THE LOVE YOU SAVE
   (The Jackson 5)
3. SPIRIT IN THE DARK/THE THRILL IS GONE
   (Aretha Franklin)
4. STEAL AWAY
   (Johnnie Taylor)
5. AIN'T THAT LOVING YOU
   (Luther Ingram)
6. THE SLY, SLICK AND WICKED
   (Lost Generation)
7. MAYBE
   (The Three Degrees)
8. IT'S ALL IN THE GAME
   (The Four Tops)
9. THE END OF OUR ROAD
   (Marvin Gaye)
10. OOH CHILD
    (The Five Stairsteps)

JAZZ ALBUMS

1. THE ISAAC HAYES MOVEMENT
   (Isaac Hayes)
2. BITCHES BREW
   (Miles Davis)
3. WALKING IN SPACE
   (Quincy Jones)
4. SWISS MOVEMENT
   (Les McCann and Eddie Harris)
5. BEST OF RAMSEY
   (Ramsey Lewis)
6. MEMPHIS UNDERGROUND
   (Herbie Mann)
7. COUNTRY PREACHER
   (Cannonball Adderley Quintet)
8. THE PIANO PLAYER
   (Ramsey Lewis)
9. GREATEST HITS
   (Wes Montgomery)
10. LENA AND GABOR
    (Lena Hall and Gabor Szabo)

COUNTRY SINGLES

1. LONG LONG TEXAS ROAD
   (Roy Drusky)
2. HE LOVES ME ALL THE WAY
   (Tammy Wynette)
3. IF I EVER FALL IN LOVE (WITH A HONKY TONK GIRL)
   (Faron Young)
4. HEART OVER MIND
   (Mel Tillis)
5. I NEVER ONCE STOPPED LOVING YOU
   (Connie Smith)
6. WONDER COULD I LIVE THERE ANY MORE
   (Charley Pride)
7. SHE'S A LITTLE BIT COUNTRY
   (George Hamilton IV)
8. HEAVENLY SUNSHINE
   (Ferlin Husky)
9. JESUS TAKE A HOLD
   (Merle Haggard)
10. I NEVER PICKED COTTON
    (Roy Clark)

COUNTRY ALBUMS

1. JUST PLAIN CHARLEY C. PRIDE
   (Charley Pride)
2. MY WOMAN, MY WOMAN, MY WIFE
   (Marty Robbins)
3. TAMMY'S TOUCH
   (Tammy Wynette)
4. PORTER WAYNE AND DOLLY REBECCA
   (Porter Wagoner and Dolly Parton)
5. THE WORLD OF JOHNNY CASH
   (Johnny Cash)
6. HELLO, I'M JOHNNY CASH
   (Johnny Cash)
7. WORLD OF TAMMY WYNETTE
   (Tammy Wynette)
8. TAMMY WYNETTE'S GREATEST HITS
   (Tammy Wynette)
9. BABY BABY
   (David Houston)
10. BEST OF CHARLEY PRIDE
    (Charley Pride)

JULY 18, 1970

POP SINGLES

1. MAMA TOLD ME
   (Three Dog Night)
2. BAND OF GOLD
   (Freda Payne)
3. BALL OF CONFUSION
   (Temptations)
4. LAY DOWN (CANDLES IN THE RAIN)
   (Melanie and the Edwin Hawkins Singers)
5. RIDE CAPTAIN RIDE
   (Blues Image)
6. CLOSE TO YOU
   (The Carpenters)
7. THE LOVE YOU SAVE
   (The Jackson 5)

8. GIMME DAT DING
   (The Pipkins)
9. OOH CHILD
   (The Five Stairsteps)
10. MAKE IT WITH YOU
    (Bread)

POP ALBUMS

1. WOODSTOCK
   (Original Soundtrack)
2. LET IT BE
   (The Beatles)
3. LIVE AT LEEDS
   (The Who)
4. McCARTNEY
   (Paul McCartney)
5. ABC
   (The Jackson 5)
6. SELF-PORTRAIT
   (Bob Dylan)
7. DEJA VU
   (Crosby, Stills, Nash and Young)
8. CANDLES IN THE RAIN
   (Melanie)
9. CHICAGO
   (Chicago)
10. ON STAGE-FEBRUARY 1970
    (Elvis Presley)

BLACK SINGLES

1. BALL OF CONFUSION
   (Temptations)
2. STEAL AWAY
   (Johnnie Taylor)
3. MAYBE
   (The Three Degrees)
4. THE LOVE YOU SAVE
   (The Jackson 5)
5. THE END OF THE ROAD
   (Marvin Gaye)
6. SIGNED, SEALED, DELIVERED I'M YOURS
   (Stevie Wonder)
7. SPIRIT IN THE DARK/THE THRILL IS GONE
   (Aretha Franklin)
8. AIN'T THAT LOVING YOU
   (Luther Ingram)
9. WHEN WE GET MARRIED
   (Intruders)
10. OOH CHILD
    (The Five Stairsteps)

JAZZ ALBUMS

1. THE ISAAC HAYES MOVEMENT
   (Isaac Hayes)
2. BITCHES BREW
   (Miles Davis)
3. WALKING IN SPACE
   (Quincy Jones)
4. SWISS MOVEMENT
   (Les McCann and Eddie Harris)
5. MEMPHIS UNDERGROUND
   (Herbie Mann)
6. COUNTRY PREACHER
   (Cannonball Adderley Quintet)
7. GREATEST HITS
   (Wes Montgomery)
8. COME ON DOWN
   (Eddie Harris)
9. JEWELS OF THOUGHT
   (Pharaoh Sanders)
10. BEST OF RAMSEY
    (Ramsey Lewis)

COUNTRY SINGLES

1. IF I EVER FALL IN LOVE (WITH A HONKY TONK GIRL)
   (Faron Young)

2. WONDER COULD I LIVE THERE ANYMORE
   (*Charley Pride*)
3. HE LOVES ME ALL THE WAY
   (*Tammy Wynette*)
4. LONG LONG TEXAS ROAD
   (*Roy Drusky*)
5. JESUS TAKE A HOLD
   (*Merle Haggard*)
6. THE KANSAS CITY SONG
   (*Buck Owens*)
7. HEART OVER MIND
   (*Mel Tillis*)
8. I NEVER PICKED COTTON
   (*Roy Clark*)
9. SHE'S A LITTLE BIT COUNTRY
   (*George Hamilton IV*)
10. SOMEDAY WE'LL BE TOGETHER
    (*Bill Anderson and Jan Howard*)

COUNTRY ALBUMS

1. JUST PLAIN CHARLEY C. PRIDE
   (*Charley Pride*)
2. THE WORLD OF JOHNNY CASH
   (*Johnny Cash*)
3. TAMMY'S TOUCH
   (*Tammy Wynette*)
4. MY WOMAN, MY WOMAN, MY WIFE
   (*Marty Robbins*)
5. WORLD OF TAMMY WYNETTE
   (*Tammy Wynette*)
6. HELLO DARLIN'
   (*Conway Twitty*)
7. PORTER WAYNE AND DOLLY REBECCA
   (*Porter Wagoner and Dolly Parton*)
8. TAMMY WYNETTE'S GREATEST HITS
   (*Tammy Wynette*)
9. BEST OF CHARLEY PRIDE
   (*Charley Pride*)
10. BABY BABY
    (*David Hamilton*)

JULY 25, 1970

POP SINGLES

1. BAND OF GOLD
   (*Freda Payne*)
2. CLOSE TO YOU
   (*The Carpenters*)
3. MAMA TOLD ME
   (*Three Dog Night*)
4. BALL OF CONFUSION
   (*Temptations*)
5. MAKE IT WITH YOU
   (*Bread*)
6. TIGHTER TIGHTER
   (*Alive and Kicking*)
7. OOH CHILD
   (*The Five Stairsteps*)
8. GIMME DAT DING
   (*The Pipkins*)
9. RIDE CAPTAIN RIDE
   (*The Blues Image*)
10. A SONG OF JOY
    (*Miguel Rios*)

POP ALBUMS

1. SELF-PORTRAIT
   (*Bob Dylan*)
2. LET IT BE
   (*The Beatles*)
3. WOODSTOCK
   (*Original Soundtrack*)
4. LIVE AT LEEDS
   (*The Who*)
5. BLOOD, SWEAT AND TEARS
   (*Blood, Sweat and Tears*)
6. McCARTNEY
   (*Paul McCartney*)

7. CLOSER TO HOME
   (*Grand Funk Railroad*)
8. ABC
   (*The Jackson 5*)
9. DEJA VU
   (*Crosby, Stills, Nash and Young*)
10. ON STAGE-FEBRUARY 1970
    (*Elvis Presley*)

BLACK SINGLES

1. BALL OF CONFUSION
   (*Temptations*)
2. MAYBE
   (*The Three Degrees*)
3. STEAL AWAY
   (*Johnnie Taylor*)
4. SIGNED, SEALED, DELIVERED I'M YOURS
   (*Stevie Wonder*)
5. THE END OF OUR ROAD
   (*Marvin Gaye*)
6. THE SLY, SLICK AND WICKED
   (*Lost Generation*)
7. WHEN WE GET MARRIED
   (*Intruders*)
8. THE LOVE YOU SAVE
   (*The Jackson 5*)
9. TRYING TO MAKE A FOOL OUT OF ME
   (*The Delfonics*)
10. OOH CHILD
    (*The Five Stairsteps*)

JAZZ ALBUMS

1. BITCHES BREW
   (*Miles Davis*)
2. THE ISAAC HAYES MOVEMENT
   (*Isaac Hayes*)
3. WALKING IN SPACE
   (*Quincy Jones*)
4. SWISS MOVEMENT
   (*Les McCann and Eddie Harris*)
5. MEMPHIS UNDERGROUND
   (*Herbie Mann*)
6. COUNTRY PREACHER
   (*Cannonball Adderley Quintet*)
7. BEST OF RAMSEY
   (*Ramsey Lewis*)
8. GREATEST HITS
   (*Wes Montgomery*)
9. COME ON DOWN
   (*Eddie Harris*)
10. RED CLAY
    (*Freddie Hubbard*)

COUNTRY SINGLES

1. WONDER COULD I LIVE THERE ANYMORE
   (*Charley Pride*)
2. IF I EVER FALL IN LOVE (WITH A HONKY TONK GIRL)
   (*Faron Young*)
3. JESUS TAKE A HOLD
   (*Merle Haggard*)
4. THE KANSAS CITY SONG
   (*Buck Owens*)
5. HE LOVES ME ALL THE WAY
   (*Tammy Wynette*)
6. I NEVER PICKED COTTON
   (*Roy Clark*)
7. SOMEDAY WE'LL BE TOGETHER
   (*Bill Anderson and Jan Howard*)
8. FOR THE GOOD TIMES/GRAZIN' IN GREENER PASTURES
   (*Ray Price*)
9. LONG LONG TEXAS ROAD
   (*Roy Drusky*)
10. YOU WANNA GIVE ME A LIFT
    (*Loretta Lynn*)

COUNTRY ALBUMS

1. THE WORLD OF JOHNNY CASH
   (*Johnny Cash*)
2. JUST PLAIN CHARLEY C. PRIDE
   (*Charley Pride*)
3. HELLO DARLIN'
   (*Conway Twitty*)
4. WORLD OF TAMMY WYNETTE
   (*Tammy Wynette*)
5. MY WOMAN, MY WOMAN, MY WIFE
   (*Marty Robbins*)
6. TAMMY'S TOUCH
   (*Tammy Wynette*)
7. PORTER WAYNE AND DOLLY REBECCA
   (*Porter Wagoner and Dolly Parton*)
8. LOVE IS A SOMETIMES THING
   (*Bill Anderson*)
9. BEST OF CHARLEY PRIDE
   (*Charley Pride*)
10. YOU AIN'T HEARD NOTHING YET
    (*Danny Davis and the Nashville Brothers*)

AUGUST 8, 1970

POP SINGLES

1. CLOSE TO YOU
   (*The Carpenters*)
2. MAKE IT WITH YOU
   (*Bread*)
3. BAND OF GOLD
   (*Freda Payne*)
4. SIGNED, SEALED, DELIVERED, I'M YOURS
   (*Stevie Wonder*)
5. TIGHTER TIGHTER
   (*Alive and Kicking*)
6. SPILL THE WINE
   (*Eric Burdon and War*)
7. OOH CHILD
   (*The Five Stairsteps*)
8. WAR
   (*Edwin Starr*)
9. MAMA TOLD ME
   (*Three Dog Night*)
10. ARE YOU READY
    (*Pacific Gas and Electric*)

POP ALBUMS

1. BLOOD SWEAT AND TEARS 3
   (*Blood, Sweat and Tears*)
2. SELF PORTRAIT
   (*Bob Dylan*)
3. COSMO'S FACTORY
   (*Creedence Clearwater Revival*)
4. WOODSTOCK
   (*Original Soundtrack*)
5. LIVE AT LEEDS
   (*The Who*)
6. CLOSER TO HOME
   (*Grand Funk Railroad*)
7. LET IT BE
   (*The Beatles*)
8. McCARTNEY
   (*Paul McCartney*)
9. ABC
   (*The Jackson 5*)
10. ECOLOGY
    (*Rare Earth*)

BLACK SINGLES

1. SIGNED, SEALED, DELIVERED, I'M YOURS
   (*Stevie Wonder*)
2. GET UP
   (*James Brown*)
3. WAR
   (*Edwin Starr*)

4. BALL OF CONFUSION
   (Temptations)
5. GROOVY SITUATION
   (Gene Chandler)
6. STEAL AWAY
   (Johnnie Taylor)
7. STEALING IN THE NAME OF THE LORD
   (Paul Kelly)
8. DO YOU SEE MY LOVE
   (Junior Walker and the All Stars)
9. EVERYBODY'S GOT THE RIGHT TO LOVE
   (The Supremes)
10. THE SLY, SLICK AND WICKED
    (Lost Generation)

JAZZ ALBUMS

1. BITCHES BREW
   (Miles Davis)
2. THE ISAAC HAYES MOVEMENT
   (Isaac Hayes)
3. SWISS MOVEMENT
   (Les McCann and Eddie Harris)
4. WALKING IN SPACE
   (Quincy Jones)
5. GREATEST HITS
   (Wes Montgomery)
6. COUNTRY PREACHER
   (Cannonball Adderley Quintet)
7. MEMPHIS UNDERGROUND
   (Herbie Mann)
8. HOT BUTTERED SOUL
   (Isaac Hayes)
9. JEWELS OF THOUGHT
   (Pharaoh Sanders)
10. BLACK TALK
    (Charles Earland)

COUNTRY SINGLES

1. JESUS TAKE A HOLD
   (Merle Haggard)
2. WONDER COULD I LIVE THERE ANYMORE
   (Charley Pride)
3. THE KANSAS CITY SONG
   (Buck Owens)
4. FOR THE GOOD TIMES/GRAZIN' IN
   GREENER PASTURES
   (Ray Price)
5. SOMEDAY WE'LL BE TOGETHER
   (Bill Anderson and Jan Howard)
6. DON'T KEEP ME HANGIN' ON
   (Sonny James)
7. YOU WANNA GIVE ME A LIFT
   (Loretta Lynn)
8. I NEVER PICKED COTTON
   (Roy Clark)
9. HUMPHREY THE CAMEL
   (Jack Blanchard and Misty Morgan)
10. MULE SKINNER BLUES
    (Dolly Parton)

COUNTRY ALBUMS

1. HELLO DARLIN'
   (Conway Twitty)
2. THE WORLD OF JOHNNY CASH
   (Johnny Cash)
3. TAMMY'S TOUCH
   (Tammy Wynette)
4. THE FIGHTIN' SIDE OF ME
   (Merle Haggard)
5. JUST PLAIN CHARLEY C. PRIDE
   (Charley Pride)
6. CHARLEY PRIDE'S 10th ALBUM
   (Charley Pride)
7. BEST OF CHARLEY PRIDE
   (Charley Pride)
8. LOVE IS A SOMETIMES THING
   (Bill Anderson)
9. YOU WOULDN'T KNOW LOVE
   (Ray Price)
10. MY WOMAN, MY WOMAN, MY WIFE
    (Marty Robbins)

AUGUST 15, 1970

POP SINGLES

1. MAKE IT WITH YOU
   (Bread)
2. SIGNED, SEALED, DELIVERED I'M YOURS
   (Stevie Wonder)
3. TIGHTER TIGHTER
   (Alive and Kicking)
4. CLOSE TO YOU
   (The Carpenters)
5. SPILL THE WINE
   (Eric Burdon and War)
6. WAR
   (Edwin Starr)
7. IN THE SUMMERTIME
   (Mungo Jerry)
8. LAY A LITTLE LOVIN' ON ME
   (Robin MacNamara)
9. BAND OF GOLD
   (Freda Payne)
10. SLY, SLICK AND WICKED
    (Lost Generation)

POP ALBUMS

1. BLOOD, SWEAT AND TEARS 3
   (Blood, Sweat and Tears)
2. COSMO'S FACTORY
   (Creedence Clearwater Revival)
3. SELF-PORTRAIT
   (Bob Dylan)
4. WOODSTOCK
   (Original Soundtrack)
5. LIVE AT LEEDS
   (The Who)
6. CLOSER TO HOME
   (Grand Funk Railroad)
7. JOHN BARLEYCORN MUST DIE
   (Traffic)
8. OPEN ROAD
   (Donovan)
9. ERIC CLAPTON
   (Eric Clapton)
10. ECOLOGY
    (Rare Earth)

BLACK SINGLES

1. SIGNED, SEALED, DELIVERED I'M YOURS
   (Stevie Wonder)
2. GET UP
   (James Brown)
3. WAR
   (Edwin Starr)
4. GROOVY SITUATION
   (Gene Chandler)
5. DO YOU SEE MY LOVE
   (Junior Walker and the All Stars)
6. PATCHES
   (Clarence Carter)
7. STEALING IN THE NAME OF THE LORD
   (Paul Kelly)
8. EVERYBODY'S GOT THE RIGHT TO LOVE
   (The Supremes)
9. THE SLY, SLICK AND WICKED
   (Lost Generation)
10. I LIKE YOUR LOVIN' (DO YOU LIKE MINE)
    (The Chi-Lites)

JAZZ ALBUMS

1. THE ISAAC HAYES MOVEMENT
   (Isaac Hayes)
2. SWISS MOVEMENT
   (Les McCann and Eddie Harris)
3. BITCHES BREW
   (Miles Davis)
4. WALKING IN SPACE
   (Quincy Jones)

5. COUNTRY PREACHER
   (Cannonball Adderley Quintet)
6. HOT BUTTERED SOUL
   (Isaac Hayes)
7. MEMPHIS UNDERGROUND
   (Herbie Mann)
8. BLACK TALK
   (Charles Earland)
9. GREATEST HITS
   (Wes Montgomery)
10. MY KIND OF JAZZ
    (Ray Charles)

COUNTRY SINGLES

1. FOR THE GOOD TIMES/GRAZIN' IN
   GREENER PASTURES
   (Ray Price)
2. JESUS TAKE A HOLD
   (Merle Haggard)
3. DON'T KEEP ME HANGIN' ON
   (Sonny James)
4. SOMEDAY WE'LL BE TOGETHER
   (Bill Anderson and Jan Howard)
5. WONDER COULD I LIVE THERE ANYMORE
   (Charley Pride)
6. YOU WANNA GIVE ME A LIFT
   (Loretta Lynn)
7. THE KANSAS CITY SONG
   (Buck Owens)
8. HUMPHREY THE CAMEL
   (Jack Blanchard and Misty Morgan)
9. MULESKINNER BLUES
   (Dolly Parton)
10. I NEVER PICKED COTTON
    (Roy Clark)

COUNTRY ALBUMS

1. HELLO DARLIN'
   (Conway Twitty)
2. THE FIGHTIN' SIDE OF ME
   (Merle Haggard)
3. CHARLEY PRIDE'S 10th ALBUM
   (Charley Pride)
4. TAMMY'S TOUCH
   (Tammy Wynette)
5. THE WORLD OF JOHNNY CASH
   (Johnny Cash)
6. JUST PLAIN CHARLEY C. PRIDE
   (Charley Pride)
7. YOU WOULDN'T KNOW LOVE
   (Ray Price)
8. BEST OF CHARLEY PRIDE
   (Charley Pride)
9. LORETTA LYNN WRITES 'EM AND
   SINGS 'EM
   (Loretta Lynn)
10. LOVE IS A SOMETIMES THING
    (Bill Anderson)

AUGUST 22, 1970

POP SINGLES

1. SIGNED, SEALED, DELIVERED I'M YOURS
   (Stevie Wonder)
2. MAKE IT WITH YOU
   (Bread)
3. TIGHTER TIGHTER
   (Alive and Kicking)
4. SPILL THE WINE
   (Eric Burdon and War)
5. IN THE SUMMERTIME
   (Mungo Jerry)
6. WAR
   (Edwin Starr)
7. LAY A LITTLE LOVIN' ON ME
   (Robin MacNamara)
8. CLOSE TO YOU
   (The Carpenters)

9. PATCHES
   (Clarence Carter)
10. SLY, SLICK AND WICKED
    (Lost Generation)

POP ALBUMS

1. BLOOD, SWEAT AND TEARS 3
   (Blood, Sweat and Tears)
2. COSMO'S FACTORY
   (Creedence Clearwater Revival)
3. SELF-PORTRAIT
   (Bob Dylan)
4. WOODSTOCK
   (Original Soundtrack)
5. JOHN BARLEYCORN MUST DIE
   (Traffic)
6. CLOSER TO HOME
   (Grand Funk Railroad)
7. OPEN ROAD
   (Donovan)
8. ERIC CLAPTON
   (Eric Clapton)
9. LIVE AT LEEDS
   (The Who)
10. ECOLOGY
    (Rare Earth)

BLACK SINGLES

1. GET UP
   (James Brown)
2. WAR
   (Edwin Starr)
3. GROOVY SITUATION
   (Gene Chandler)
4. SIGNED, SEALED, DELIVERED I'M YOURS
   (Stevie Wonder)
5. DO YOU SEE MY LOVE
   (Junior Walker and the All Stars)
6. PATCHES
   (Clarence Carter)
7. EVERYBODY'S GOT THE RIGHT TO LOVE
   (The Supremes)
8. STEALING IN THE NAME OF THE LORD
   (Paul Kelly)
9. I LIKE YOUR LOVIN' (DO YOU LIKE MINE)
   (The Chi-Lites)
10. IT'S A SHAME
    (Spinners)

JAZZ ALBUMS

1. THE ISAAC HAYES MOVEMENT
   (Isaac Hayes)
2. BITCHES BREW
   (Miles Davis)
3. WALKING IN SPACE
   (Quincy Jones)
4. SWISS MOVEMENT
   (Les McCann and Eddie Harris)
5. HOT BUTTERED SOUL
   (Isaac Hayes)
6. COUNTRY PREACHER
   (Cannonball Adderley Quintet)
7. BLACK TALK
   (Charles Earland)
8. GREATEST HITS
   (Wes Montgomery)
9. MEMPHIS UNDERGROUND
   (Herbie Mann)
10. JEWELS OF THOUGHT
    (Pharaoh Sanders)

COUNTRY SINGLES

1. DON'T KEEP ME HANGIN' ON
   (Sonny James)
2. FOR THE GOOD TIMES/GRAZIN' IN
   GREENER PASTURES
   (Ray Price)

3. SOMEDAY WE'LL BE TOGETHER
   (Bill Anderson and Jan Howard)
4. JESUS TAKE A HOLD
   (Merle Haggard)
5. YOU WANNA GIVE ME A LIFT
   (Loretta Lynn)
6. HUMPHREY THE CAMEL
   (Jack Blanchard and Misty Morgan)
7. MULESKINNER BLUES
   (Dolly Parton)
8. WHEN A MAN LOVES A WOMAN (THE WAY
   I LOVE YOU)
   (Billy Walker)
9. EVERYTHING A MAN COULD EVER NEED
   (Glen Campbell)
10. A PERFECT MOUNTAIN
    (Don Gibson)

COUNTRY ALBUMS

1. THE FIGHTIN' SIDE OF ME
   (Merle Haggard)
2. CHARLEY PRIDE'S 10th ALBUM
   (Charley Pride)
3. HELLO DARLIN'
   (Conway Twitty)
4. THE WORLD OF JOHNNY CASH
   (Johnny Cash)
5. LORETTA LYNN WRITES 'EM AND
   SINGS 'EM
   (Loretta Lynn)
6. TAMMY'S TOUCH
   (Tammy Wynette)
7. JUST PLAIN CHARLEY C. PRIDE
   (Charley Pride)
8. MY LOVE/DON'T KEEP ME HANGIN' ON
   (Sonny James)
9. BEST OF CHARLEY PRIDE
   (Charley Pride)
10. YOU WOULDN'T KNOW LOVE
    (Ray Price)

AUGUST 29, 1970

POP SINGLES

1. SPILL THE WINE
   (Eric Burdon and War)
2. MAKE IT WITH YOU
   (Bread)
3. IN THE SUMMERTIME
   (Mungo Jerry)
4. WAR
   (Edwin Starr)
5. SIGNED, SEALED, DELIVERED I'M YOURS
   (Stevie Wonder)
6. LAY A LITTLE LOVIN' ON ME
   (Robin MacNamara)
7. PATCHES
   (Clarence Carter)
8. TIGHTER TIGHTER
   (Alive and Kicking)
9. WHY CAN'T I TOUCH YOU
   (Ronnie Dyson)
10. SLY, SLICK AND WICKED
    (Lost Generation)

POP ALBUMS

1. COSMO'S FACTORY
   (Creedence Clearwater Revival)
2. BLOOD, SWEAT AND TEARS 3
   (Blood, Sweat and Tears)
3. LIVE AT LEEDS
   (The Who)
4. WOODSTOCK
   (Original Soundtrack)
5. JOHN BARLEYCORN MUST DIE
   (Traffic)
6. CLOSER TO HOME
   (Grand Funk Railroad)

7. ERIC CLAPTON
   (Eric Clapton)
8. ABSOLUTELY LIVE
   (The Doors)
9. TOMMY
   (The Who)
10. SELF-PORTRAIT
    (Bob Dylan)

BLACK SINGLES

1. GET UP
   (James Brown)
2. WAR
   (Edwin Starr)
3. GROOVY SITUATION
   (Gene Chandler)
4. PATCHES
   (Clarence Carter)
5. DO YOU SEE MY LOVE
   (Junior Walker and the All Stars)
6. EVERYBODY'S GOT THE RIGHT TO LOVE
   (The Supremes)
7. DON'T PLAY THAT SONG
   (Aretha Franklin)
8. SIGNED, SEALED, DELIVERED I'M YOURS
   (Stevie Wonder)
9. I LIKE YOUR LOVIN' (DO YOU LIKE MINE)
   (The Chi-Lites)
10. IT'S A SHAME
    (Spinners)

JAZZ ALBUMS

1. THE ISAAC HAYES MOVEMENT
   (Isaac Hayes)
2. BITCHES BREW
   (Miles Davis)
3. WALKING IN SPACE
   (Quincy Jones)
4. HOT BUTTERED SOUL
   (Isaac Hayes)
5. SWISS MOVEMENT
   (Les McCann and Eddie Harris)
6. BLACK TALK
   (Charles Earland)
7. COUNTRY PREACHER
   (Cannonball Adderley Quintet)
8. MEMPHIS UNDERGROUND
   (Herbie Mann)
9. JEWELS OF THOUGHT
   (Pharaoh Sanders)
10. GREATEST HITS
    (Wes Montgomery)

COUNTRY SINGLES

1. DON'T KEEP ME HANGIN' ON
   (Sonny James)
2. FOR THE GOOD TIMES/GRAZIN' IN
   GREENER PASTURES
   (Ray Price)
3. MULESKINNER BLUES
   (Dolly Parton)
4. WHEN A MAN LOVES A WOMAN (THE WAY
   I LOVE YOU)
   (Billy Walker)
5. YOU WANNA GIVE ME A LIFT
   (Loretta Lynn)
6. EVERYTHING A MAN COULD EVER NEED
   (Glen Campbell)
7. SOMEDAY WE'LL BE TOGETHER
   (Bill Anderson and Jan Howard)
8. HEAVEN EVERY DAY
   (Mel Tillis)
9. SALUTE TO A SWITCHBLADE
   (Tom T. Hall)
10. THE WHOLE WORLD COMES TO ME
    (Jack Greene)

COUNTRY ALBUMS

1. THE FIGHTIN' SIDE OF ME
   (Merle Haggard)
2. CHARLEY PRIDE'S 10th ALBUM
   (Charley Pride)
3. HELLO DARLIN'
   (Conway Twitty)
4. LORETTA LYNN WRITES 'EM AND
   SINGS 'EM
   (Loretta Lynn)
5. THE WORLD OF JOHNNY CASH
   (Johnny Cash)
6. MY WOMAN, MY WOMAN, MY WIFE
   (Marty Robbins)
7. MY LOVE/DON'T KEEP ME HANGIN' ON
   (Sonny James)
8. BEST OF CHARLEY PRIDE
   (Charley Pride)
9. TAMMY'S TOUCH
   (Tammy Wynette)
10. BEST OF JERRY LEE LEWIS
    (Jerry Lee Lewis)

SEPTEMBER 5, 1970

POP SINGLES

1. WAR
   (Edwin Starr)
2. IN THE SUMMERTIME
   (Mungo Jerry)
3. MAKE IT WITH YOU
   (Bread)
4. SPILL THE WINE
   (Eric Burdon and War)
5. AIN'T NO MOUNTAIN HIGH ENOUGH
   (Diana Ross)
6. PATCHES
   (Clarence Carter)
7. WHY CAN'T I TOUCH YOU
   (Ronnie Dyson)
8. 25 OR 6 TO 4
   (Chicago)
9. LOOKIN' OUT MY BACK DOOR/LONG AS I
   CAN SEE THE LIGHT
   (Creedence Clearwater Revival)
10. HI-DE-HO
    (Blood, Sweat and Tears)

POP ALBUMS

1. COSMO'S FACTORY
   (Creedence Clearwater Revival)
2. WOODSTOCK
   (Original Soundtrack)
3. LIVE AT LEEDS
   (The Who)
4. BLOOD, SWEAT AND TEARS 3
   (Blood, Sweat and Tears)
5. JOHN BARLEYCORN MUST DIE
   (Traffic)
6. ABSOLUTELY LIVE
   (The Doors)
7. TOMMY
   (The Who)
8. ERIC CLAPTON
   (Eric Clapton)
9. ON THE WATERS
   (Bread)
10. ERIC BURDON DECLARES WAR
    (Eric Burdon)

BLACK SINGLES

1. WAR
   (Edwin Starr)
2. PATCHES
   (Clarence Carter)

3. DON'T PLAY THAT SONG
   (Aretha Franklin)
4. GET UP
   (James Brown)
5. EVERYBODY'S GOT THE RIGHT TO LOVE
   (The Supremes)
6. I LIKE YOUR LOVIN' (DO YOU LIKE MINE)
   (The Chi-Lites)
7. IT'S A SHAME
   (Spinners)
8. I'LL BE RIGHT THERE
   (Tyrone Davis)
9. AIN'T NO MOUNTAIN HIGH ENOUGH
   (Diana Ross)
10. GROOVY SITUATION
    (Gene Chandler)

JAZZ ALBUMS

1. THE ISAAC HAYES MOVEMENT
   (Isaac Hayes)
2. BITCHES BREW
   (Miles Davis)
3. SWISS MOVEMENT
   (Les McCann and Eddie Harris)
4. HOT BUTTERED SOUL
   (Isaac Hayes)
5. WALKING IN SPACE
   (Quincy Jones)
6. BLACK TALK
   (Charles Earland)
7. JEWELS OF THOUGHT
   (Pharaoh Sanders)
8. GREATEST HITS
   (Wes Montgomery)
9. MEMPHIS UNDERGROUND
   (Herbie Mann)
10. GULA MATARI
    (Quincy Jones)

COUNTRY SINGLES

1. MULESKINNER BLUES
   (Dolly Parton)
2. DON'T KEEP ME HANGIN' ON
   (Sonny James)
3. WHEN A MAN LOVES A WOMAN (THE WAY
   I LOVE YOU)
   (Billy Walker)
4. YOU WANNA GIVE ME A LIFT
   (Loretta Lynn)
5. HEAVEN EVERY DAY
   (Mel Tillis)
6. EVERYTHING A MAN COULD EVER NEED
   (Glen Campbell)
7. FOR THE GOOD TIMES/GRAZIN' IN
   GREENER PASTURES
   (Ray Price)
8. SALUTE TO A SWITCHBLADE
   (Tom T. Hall)
9. THE WHOLE WORLD COMES TO ME
   (Jack Greene)
10. ALL FOR THE LOVE OF SUNSHINE
    *(Hank Williams Jr. and The Mike Curb
    Congregation)*

COUNTRY ALBUMS

1. CHARLEY PRIDE'S 10th ALBUM
   (Charley Pride)
2. THE FIGHTIN' SIDE OF ME
   (Merle Haggard)
3. HELLO DARLIN'
   (Conway Twitty)
4. LORETTA LYNN WRITES 'EM AND
   SINGS 'EM
   (Loretta Lynn)
5. THE WORLD OF JOHNNY CASH
   (Johnny Cash)
6. MY LOVE/DON'T KEEP ME HANGIN' ON
   (Sonny James)
7. MY WOMAN, MY WOMAN, MY WIFE
   (Marty Robbins)

8. TAMMY'S TOUCH
   (Tammy Wynette)
9. BEST OF CHARLEY PRIDE
   (Charley Pride)
10. THE KANSAS CITY SONG
    (Buck Owens and the Buckaroos)

SEPTEMBER 12, 1970

POP SINGLES

1. IN THE SUMMERTIME
   (Mungo Jerry)
2. AIN'T NO MOUNTAIN HIGH ENOUGH
   (Diana Ross)
3. WAR
   (Edwin Starr)
4. PATCHES
   (Clarence Carter)
5. LOOKIN' OUT MY BACK DOOR/LONG AS I
   CAN SEE THE LIGHT
   (Creedence Clearwater Revival)
6. 25 OR 6 TO 4
   (Chicago)
7. JULIE, DO YA LOVE ME
   (Bobby Sherman)
8. HI-DE-HO
   (Blood, Sweat and Tears)
9. MAKE IT WITH YOU
   (Bread)
10. DON'T PLAY THAT SONG
    (Aretha Franklin)

POP ALBUMS

1. COSMO'S FACTORY
   (Creedence Clearwater Revival)
2. WOODSTOCK
   (Original Soundtrack)
3. LIVE AT LEEDS
   (The Who)
4. BLOOD, SWEAT AND TEARS 3
   (Blood, Sweat and Tears)
5. TOMMY
   (The Who)
6. ABSOLUTELY LIVE
   (The Doors)
7. JOHN BARLEYCORN MUST DIE
   (Traffic)
8. ON THE WATERS
   (Bread)
9. MAD DOGS AND ENGLISHMEN
   (Joe Cocker)
10. STAGE FRIGHT
    (The Band)

BLACK SINGLES

1. PATCHES
   (Clarence Carter)
2. DON'T PLAY THAT SONG
   (Aretha Franklin)
3. AIN'T NO MOUNTAIN HIGH ENOUGH
   (Diana Ross)
4. WAR
   (Edwin Starr)
5. GET UP
   (James Brown)
6. I LIKE YOUR LOVIN' (DO YOU LIKE MINE)
   (The Chi-Lites)
7. IT'S A SHAME
   (Spinners)
8. YOURS LOVE
   (Joe Simon)
9. IF I DIDN'T CARE
   (The Moments)
10. EXPRESS YOURSELF
    (The Watts 103rd Street Rhythm Band)

JAZZ ALBUMS

1. THE ISAAC HAYES MOVEMENT
   (Isaac Hayes)
2. BITCHES BREW
   (Miles Davis)
3. HOT BUTTERED SOUL
   (Isaac Hayes)
4. WALKING IN SPACE
   (Quincy Jones)
5. SWISS MOVEMENT
   (Les McCann and Eddie Harris)
6. GULA MATARI
   (Quincy Jones)
7. BLACK TALK
   (Charles Earland)
8. JEWELS OF THOUGHT
   (Pharaoh Sanders)
9. MEMPHIS UNDERGROUND
   (Herbie Mann)
10. GREATEST HITS
    (Wes Montgomery)

COUNTRY SINGLES

1. WHEN A MAN LOVES A WOMAN (THE WAY I LOVE YOU)
   (Billy Walker)
2. ALL FOR THE LOVE OF SUNSHINE
   (Hank Williams Jr. and The Mike Curb Congregation)
3. HEAVEN EVERY DAY
   (Mel Tillis)
4. EVERYTHING A MAN COULD EVER NEED
   (Glen Campbell)
5. SALUTE TO A SWITCHBLADE
   (Tom T. Hall)
6. MULESKINNER BLUES
   (Dolly Parton)
7. THE WHOLE WORLD COMES TO ME
   (Jack Greene)
8. DADDY WAS AN OLD TIME PREACHER MAN
   (Porter Wagoner and Dolly Parton)
9. BILOXI
   (Kenny Price)
10. DON'T KEEP ME HANGIN' ON
    (Sonny James)

COUNTRY ALBUMS

1. CHARLEY PRIDE'S 10th ALBUM
   (Charley Pride)
2. THE FIGHTIN' SIDE OF ME
   (Merle Haggard)
3. HELLO DARLIN'
   (Conway Twitty)
4. LORETTA LYNN WRITES 'EM AND SINGS 'EM
   (Loretta Lynn)
5. MY WOMAN, MY WOMAN, MY WIFE
   (Marty Robbins)
6. THE WORLD OF JOHNNY CASH
   (Johnny Cash)
7. TAMMY'S TOUCH
   (Tammy Wynette)
8. MY LOVE/DON'T KEEP ME HANGIN' ON
   (Sonny James)
9. THE KANSAS CITY SONG
   (Buck Owens and the Buckaroos)
10. BEST OF JERRY LEE LEWIS
    (Jerry Lee Lewis)

SEPTEMBER 19, 1970

POP SINGLES

1. AIN'T NO MOUNTAIN HIGH ENOUGH
   (Diana Ross)
2. PATCHES
   (Clarence Carter)
3. LOOKIN' OUT MY BACK DOOR/LONG AS I SEE THE LIGHT
   (Creedence Clearwater Revival)
4. JULIE, DO YA LOVE ME
   (Bobby Sherman)
5. WAR
   (Edwin Starr)
6. 25 OR 6 TO 4
   (Chicago)
7. CANDIDA
   (Dawn)
8. DON'T PLAY THAT SONG
   (Aretha Franklin)
9. SNOWBIRD
   (Anne Murray)
10. I (WHO HAVE NOTHING)
    (Tom Jones)

POP ALBUMS

1. MAD DOGS AND ENGLISHMEN
   (Joe Cocker)
2. COSMO'S FACTORY
   (Creedence Clearwater Revival)
3. WOODSTOCK
   (Original Soundtrack)
4. TOMMY
   (The Who)
5. LIVE AT LEEDS
   (The Who)
6. BLOOD, SWEAT AND TEARS 3
   (Blood, Sweat and Tears)
7. STAGE FRIGHT
   (The Band)
8. ON THE WATERS
   (Bread)
9. NEIL DIAMOND GOLD
   (Neil Diamond)
10. JOHN BARLEYCORN MUST DIE
    (Traffic)

BLACK SINGLES

1. DON'T PLAY THAT SONG
   (Aretha Franklin)
2. AIN'T NO MOUNTAIN HIGH ENOUGH
   (Diana Ross)
3. PATCHES
   (Clarence Carter)
4. EXPRESS YOURSELF
   (The Watts 103rd Street Rhythm Band)
5. IF I DIDN'T CARE
   (The Moments)
6. IT'S A SHAME
   (Spinners)
7. I LIKE YOUR LOVIN' (DO YOU LIKE MINE)
   (The Chi-Lites)
8. YOURS LOVE
   (Joe Simon)
9. WAR
   (Edwin Starr)
10. GET UP
    (James Brown)

JAZZ ALBUMS

1. THE ISAAC HAYES MOVEMENT
   (Isaac Hayes)
2. BITCHES BREW
   (Miles Davis)
3. BLACK TALK
   (Charles Earland)
4. GULA MATARI
   (Quincy Jones)
5. WALKING IN SPACE
   (Quincy Jones)
6. SWISS MOVEMENT
   (Les McCann and Eddie Harris)
7. HOT BUTTERED SOUL
   (Isaac Hayes)
8. MEMPHIS UNDERGROUND
   (Herbie Mann)
9. MUSCLE SHOALS NITTY GRITTY
   (Herbie Mann)
10. VIVA TIRADO
    (El Chicano)

COUNTRY SINGLES

1. ALL FOR THE LOVE OF SUNSHINE
   (Hank Williams Jr. and The Mike Curb Congregation)
2. HEAVEN EVERY DAY
   (Mel Tillis)
3. WHEN A MAN LOVES A WOMAN (LIKE I LOVE YOU)
   (Billy Walker)
4. DADDY WAS AN OLD TIME PREACHER MAN
   (Porter Wagoner and Dolly Parton)
5. SALUTE TO A SWITCHBLADE
   (Tom T. Hall)
6. SNOWBIRD
   (Anne Murray)
7. WONDERS OF THE WINE
   (David Houston)
8. BILOXI
   (Kenny Price)
9. MULESKINNER BLUES
   (Dolly Parton)
10. THERE MUST BE MORE TO LOVE THAN THIS
    (Jerry Lee Lewis)

COUNTRY ALBUMS

1. CHARLEY PRIDE'S 10th ALBUM
   (Charley Pride)
2. THE FIGHTIN' SIDE OF ME
   (Merle Haggard)
3. LORETTA LYNN WRITES 'EM AND SINGS 'EM
   (Loretta Lynn)
4. HELLO DARLIN'
   (Conway Twitty)
5. MY WOMAN, MY WOMAN, MY WIFE
   (Marty Robbins)
6. THE WORLD OF JOHNNY CASH
   (Johnny Cash)
7. MY LOVE/DON'T KEEP ME HANGIN' ON
   (Sonny James)
8. THE KANSAS CITY SONG
   (Buck Owens and the Buckaroos)
9. TAMMY'S TOUCH
   (Tammy Wynette)
10. BEST OF JERRY LEE LEWIS
    (Jerry Lee Lewis)

SEPTEMBER 26, 1970

POP SINGLES

1. LOOKIN' OUT MY BACK DOOR/LONG AS I CAN SEE THE LIGHT
   (Creedence Clearwater Revival)
2. PATCHES
   (Clarence Carter)
3. JULIE, DO YA LOVE ME
   (Bobby Sherman)
4. CANDIDA
   (Dawn)
5. AIN'T NO MOUNTAIN HIGH ENOUGH
   (Diana Ross)
6. CRACKLIN' ROSE
   (Neil Diamond)
7. DON'T PLAY THAT SONG
   (Aretha Franklin)
8. SNOWBIRD
   (Anne Murray)
9. WAR
   (Edwin Starr)
10. I (WHO HAVE NOTHING)
    (Tom Jones)

POP ALBUMS

1. MAD DOGS AND ENGLISHMEN
   (Joe Cocker)
2. COSMO'S FACTORY
   (Creedence Clearwater Revival)
3. WOODSTOCK
   (Original Soundtrack)
4. TOMMY
   (The Who)
5. STAGE FRIGHT
   (The Band)
6. NEIL DIAMOND GOLD
   (Neil Diamond)
7. LIVE AT LEEDS
   (The Who)
8. BLOOD, SWEAT AND TEARS 3
   (Blood, Sweat and Tears)
9. ON THE WATERS
   (Bread)
10. A QUESTION OF BALANCE
    (The Moody Blues)

BLACK SINGLES

1. AIN'T NO MOUNTAIN HIGH ENOUGH
   (Diana Ross)
2. EXPRESS YOURSELF
   (The Watts 103rd Street Rhythm Band)
3. DON'T PLAY THAT SONG
   (Aretha Franklin)
4. IF I DIDN'T CARE
   (The Moments)
5. IT'S A SHAME
   (Spinners)
6. PATCHES
   (Clarence Carter)
7. STILL WATER
   (The Four Tops)
8. SEEMS LIKE I GOTTA DO WRONG
   (Whispers)
9. I STAND ACCUSED
   (Isaac Hayes)
10. I'M LOSING YOU
    (Rare Earth)

JAZZ ALBUMS

1. GULA MATARI
   (Quincy Jones)
2. BITCHES BREW
   (Miles Davis)
3. THE ISAAC HAYES MOVEMENT
   (Isaac Hayes)
4. BLACK TALK
   (Charles Earland)
5. SWISS MOVEMENT
   (Les McCann and Eddie Harris)
6. WALKING IN SPACE
   (Quincy Jones)
7. CHAPTER TWO
   (Roberta Flack)
8. MUSCLE SHOALS NITTY GRITTY
   (Herbie Mann)
9. HOT BUTTERED SOUL
   (Isaac Hayes)
10. GREATEST HITS
    (Wes Montgomery)

COUNTRY SINGLES

1. HEAVEN EVERY DAY
   (Mel Tillis)
2. ALL FOR THE LOVE OF SUNSHINE
   (Hank Williams Jr. and The Mike Curb Congregation)
3. THERE MUST BE MORE TO LOVE THAN THIS
   (Jerry Lee Lewis)
4. DADDY WAS AN OLD TIME PREACHER MAN
   (Porter Wagoner and Dolly Parton)

5. SNOWBIRD
   (Anne Murray)
6. WONDERS OF THE WINE
   (David Houston)
7. SUNDAY MORNING COMING DOWN
   (Johnny Cash)
8. MARTY GRAY
   (Billie Jo Spears)
9. HOW I GOT TO MEMPHIS
   (Bobby Bare)
10. THE TAKER
    (Waylon Jennings)

COUNTRY ALBUMS

1. CHARLEY PRIDE'S 10th ALBUM
   (Charley Pride)
2. THE FIGHTIN' SIDE OF ME
   (Merle Haggard)
3. HELLO DARLIN'
   (Conway Twitty)
4. THE WORLD OF JOHNNY CASH
   (Johnny Cash)
5. LORETTA LYNN WRITES 'EM AND SINGS 'EM
   (Loretta Lynn)
6. MY WOMAN, MY WOMAN, MY WIFE
   (Marty Robbins)
7. FOR THE GOOD TIMES
   (Ray Price)
8. LIVE AT THE INTERNATIONAL
   (Jerry Lee Lewis)
9. MY LOVE/DON'T KEEP ME HANGIN' ON
   (Sonny James)
10. THE KANSAS CITY SONG
    (Buck Owens and the Buckaroos)

OCTOBER 3, 1970

POP SINGLES

1. JULIE, DO YA LOVE ME
   (Bobby Sherman)
2. PATCHES
   (Clarence Carter)
3. CANDIDA
   (Dawn)
4. SNOWBIRD
   (Anne Murray)
5. CRACKLIN' ROSE
   (Neil Diamond)
6. LOOKIN' OUT MY BACK DOOR/LONG AS I CAN SEE THE LIGHT
   (Creedence Clearwater Revival)
7. I'LL BE THERE
   (The Jackson 5)
8. (I KNOW) I'M LOSING YOU
   (Rare Earth)
9. AIN'T NO MOUNTAIN HIGH ENOUGH
   (Diana Ross)
10. ALL RIGHT NOW
    (Free)

POP ALBUMS

1. COSMO'S FACTORY
   (Creedence Clearwater Revival)
2. MAD DOGS AND ENGLISHMEN
   (Joe Cocker)
3. WOODSTOCK
   (Original Soundtrack)
4. TOMMY
   (The Who)
5. STAGE FRIGHT
   (The Band)
6. NEIL DIAMOND GOLD
   (Neil Diamond)
7. A QUESTION OF BALANCE
   (The Moody Blues)
8. AFTER THE GOLD RUSH
   (Neil Young)

9. LIVE AT LEEDS
   (The Who)
10. BLOOD, SWEAT AND TEARS 3
    (Blood, Sweat and Tears)

BLACK SINGLES

1. AIN'T NO MOUNTAIN HIGH ENOUGH
   (Diana Ross)
2. EXPRESS YOURSELF
   (The Watts 103rd Street Rhythm Band)
3. IF I DIDN'T CARE
   (The Moments)
4. SOMEBODY'S BEEN SLEEPING
   (100 Proof)
5. SEEMS LIKE I GOTTA DO WRONG
   (Whispers)
6. STILL WATER
   (The Four Tops)
7. DON'T PLAY THAT SONG
   (Aretha Franklin)
8. I STAND ACCUSED
   (Isaac Hayes)
9. I'LL BE THERE
   (The Jackson 5)
10. SINCE I FELL FOR YOU I'VE LEARNED TO DO WITHOUT YOU
    (Mavis Staples)

JAZZ ALBUMS

1. GULA MATARI
   (Quincy Jones)
2. BITCHES BREW
   (Miles Davis)
3. THE ISAAC HAYES MOVEMENT
   (Isaac Hayes)
4. BLACK TALK
   (Charles Earland)
5. CHAPTER TWO
   (Roberta Flack)
6. SWISS MOVEMENT
   (Les McCann and Eddie Harris)
7. MUSCLE SHOALS NITTY GRITTY
   (Herbie Mann)
8. WALKING IN SPACE
   (Quincy Jones)
9. OLD SOCKS, NEW SHOES, NEW SOCKS, OLD SHOES
   (Jazz Crusaders)
10. VIVA TIRADO
    (El Chicano)

COUNTRY SINGLES

1. THERE MUST BE MORE TO LOVE THAN THIS
   (Jerry Lee Lewis)
2. SNOWBIRD
   (Anne Murray)
3. SUNDAY MORNING COMING DOWN
   (Johnny Cash)
4. WONDERS OF THE WINE
   (David Houston)
5. THE TAKER
   (Waylon Jennings)
6. MARTY GRAY
   (Billie Jo Spears)
7. HOW I GOT TO MEMPHIS
   (Bobby Bare)
8. HEAVEN EVERY DAY
   (Mel Tillis)
9. ANGELS DON'T LIE
   (Jim Reeves)
10. ALL FOR THE LOVE OF SUNSHINE
    (Hank Williams Jr. and The Mike Curb Congregation)

COUNTRY ALBUMS

1. CHARLEY PRIDE'S 10th ALBUM
   (Charley Pride)

2. HELLO DARLIN'
   (Conway Twitty)
3. THE FIGHTIN' SIDE OF ME
   (Merle Haggard)
4. FOR THE GOOD TIMES
   (Ray Price)
5. THE WORLD OF JOHNNY CASH
   (Johnny Cash)
6. MY WOMAN, MY WOMAN, MY WIFE
   (Marty Robbins)
7. LIVE AT THE INTERNATIONAL
   (Jerry Lee Lewis)
8. LORETTA LYNN WRITES 'EM AND
   SINGS 'EM
   (Loretta Lynn)
9. MY LOVE/DON'T KEEP ME HANGIN' ON
   (Sonny James)
10. THE KANSAS CITY SONG
    (Buck Owens and the Buckaroos)

OCTOBER 10, 1970

POP SINGLES

1. CRACKLIN' ROSE
   (Neil Diamond)
2. CANDIDA
   (Dawn)
3. I'LL BE THERE
   (The Jackson 5)
4. SNOWBIRD
   (Anne Murray)
5. JULIE, DO YA LOVE ME
   (Bobby Sherman)
6. (I KNOW) I'M LOSING YOU
   (Rare Earth)
7. LOOKIN' OUT MY BACK DOOR/LONG AS I
   CAN SEE THE LIGHT
   (Creedence Clearwater Revival)
8. ALL RIGHT NOW
   (Free)
9. PATCHES
   (Clarence Carter)
10. GROOVY SITUATION
    (Gene Chandler)

POP ALBUMS

1. COSMO'S FACTORY
   (Creedence Clearwater Revival)
2. MAD DOGS AND ENGLISHMEN
   (Joe Cocker)
3. WOODSTOCK
   (Original Soundtrack)
4. STAGE FRIGHT
   (The Band)
5. A QUESTION OF BALANCE
   (The Moody Blues)
6. NEIL DIAMOND GOLD
   (Neil Diamond)
7. AFTER THE GOLD RUSH
   (Neil Young)
8. TOMMY
   (The Who)
9. THIRD ALBUM
   (The Jackson 5)
10. JIMI HENDRIX EXPERIENCE AND OTIS
    REDDING AT THE MONTEREY
    INTERNATIONAL POP FESTIVAL
    (Jimi Hendrix Experience and Otis Redding)

BLACK SINGLES

1. EXPRESS YOURSELF
   (The Watts 103rd Street Rhythm Band)
2. I'LL BE THERE
   (The Jackson 5)
3. SOMEBODY'S BEEN SLEEPING
   (100 Proof)
4. STILL WATER
   (The Four Tops)

5. SEEMS LIKE I GOTTA DO WRONG
   (Whispers)
6. AIN'T NO MOUNTAIN HIGH ENOUGH
   (Diana Ross)
7. IF I DIDN'T CARE
   (The Moments)
8. (BABY) YOU TURN ME ON
   (The Impressions)
9. STAND BY YOUR MAN
   (Candi Staton)
10. I DO TAKE YOU
    (The Three Degrees)

JAZZ ALBUMS

1. CHAPTER TWO
   (Roberta Flack)
2. BITCHES BREW
   (Miles Davis)
3. THE ISAAC HAYES MOVEMENT
   (Isaac Hayes)
4. GULA MATARI
   (Quincy Jones)
5. BLACK TALK
   (Charles Earland)
6. WALKING IN SPACE
   (Quincy Jones)
7. MUSCLE SHOALS NITTY GRITTY
   (Herbie Mann)
8. SWISS MOVEMENT
   (Les McCann and Eddie Harris)
9. VIVA TIRADO
   (El Chicano)
10. KEEP THE CUSTOMER SATISFIED
    (Buddy Rich)

COUNTRY SINGLES

1. SNOWBIRD
   (Anne Murray)
2. SUNDAY MORNING COMING DOWN
   (Johnny Cash)
3. THERE MUST BE MORE TO LOVE THAN
   THIS
   (Jerry Lee Lewis)
4. WONDERS OF THE WINE
   (David Houston)
5. THE TAKER
   (Waylon Jennings)
6. MARTY GRAY
   (Billie Jo Spears)
7. HOW I GOT TO MEMPHIS
   (Bobby Bare)
8. ANGELS DON'T LIE
   (Jim Reeves)
9. THE GREAT WHITE HORSE
   (Buck Owens and Susan Raye)
10. RUN WOMAN RUN
    (Tammy Wynette)

COUNTRY ALBUMS

1. FOR THE GOOD TIMES
   (Ray Price)
2. CHARLEY PRIDE'S 10th ALBUM
   (Charley Pride)
3. THE FIGHTIN' SIDE OF ME
   (Merle Haggard)
4. HELLO DARLIN'
   (Conway Twitty)
5. MY WOMAN, MY WOMAN, MY WIFE
   (Marty Robbins)
6. LIVE AT THE INTERNATIONAL
   (Jerry Lee Lewis)
7. THE WORLD OF JOHNNY CASH
   (Johnny Cash)
8. MY LOVE/DON'T KEEP ME HANGIN' ON
   (Sonny James)
9. LORETTA LYNN WRITES 'EM AND
   SINGS 'EM
   (Loretta Lynn)
10. TAMMY'S TOUCH
    (Tammy Wynette)

OCTOBER 17, 1970

POP SINGLES

1. I'LL BE THERE
   (The Jackson 5)
2. CRACKLIN' ROSE
   (Neil Diamond)
3. WE'VE ONLY JUST BEGUN
   (The Carpenters)
4. CANDIDA
   (Dawn)
5. ALL RIGHT NOW
   (Free)
6. GREEN-EYED LADY
   (Sugarloaf)
7. JULIE, DO YA LOVE ME
   (Bobby Sherman)
8. LOOKIN' OUT MY BACK DOOR/LONG AS I
   CAN SEE THE LIGHT
   (Creedence Clearwater Revival)
9. SNOWBIRD
   (Anne Murray)
10. LOOK WHAT THEY'VE DONE TO MY SONG,
    MA
    (The New Seekers)

POP ALBUMS

1. COSMO'S FACTORY
   (Creedence Clearwater Revival)
2. WOODSTOCK
   (Original Soundtrack)
3. MAD DOGS AND ENGLISHMEN
   (Joe Cocker)
4. A QUESTION OF BALANCE
   (The Moody Blues)
5. AFTER THE GOLD RUSH
   (Neil Young)
6. NEIL DIAMOND GOLD
   (Neil Diamond)
7. STAGE FRIGHT
   (The Band)
8. THIRD ALBUM
   (The Jackson 5)
9. JIMI HENDRIX EXPERIENCE AND OTIS
   REDDING AT THE MONTEREY
   INTERNATIONAL POP FESTIVAL
   (Jimi Hendrix Experience and Otis Redding)
10. TOMMY
    (The Who)

BLACK SINGLES

1. I'LL BE THERE
   (The Jackson 5)
2. SOMEBODY'S BEEN SLEEPING
   (100 Proof)
3. STILL WATER
   (The Four Tops)
4. EXPRESS YOURSELF
   (The Watts 103rd Street Rhythm Band)
5. SEEMS LIKE I GOTTA DO WRONG
   (Whispers)
6. (BABY) YOU TURN ME ON
   (The Impressions)
7. STAND BY YOUR MAN
   (Candi Staton)
8. CALL ME SUPER BAD
   (James Brown)
9. I DO TAKE YOU
   (The Three Degrees)
10. UNGENA ZA ULIMWENGU (UNITE THE
    WORLD)
    (Temptations)

JAZZ ALBUMS

1. CHAPTER TWO
   (Roberta Flack)

2. BITCHES BREW
   (Miles Davis)
3. THE ISAAC HAYES MOVEMENT
   (Isaac Hayes)
4. BLACK TALK
   (Charles Earland)
5. WALKING IN SPACE
   (Quincy Jones)
6. GULA MATARI
   (Quincy Jones)
7. OLD SOCKS, NEW SHOES, NEW SOCKS, OLD SHOES
   (Jazz Crusaders)
8. SWISS MOVEMENT
   (Les McCann and Eddie Harris)
9. VIVA TIRADO
   (El Chicano)
10. MUSCLE SHOALS NITTY GRITTY
    (Herbie Mann)

COUNTRY ALBUMS

1. FOR THE GOOD TIMES
   (Ray Price)
2. CHARLEY PRIDE'S 10th ALBUM
   (Charley Pride)
3. THE FIGHTIN' SIDE OF ME
   (Merle Haggard)
4. HELLO DARLIN'
   (Conway Twitty)
5. LIVE AT THE INTERNATIONAL
   (Jerry Lee Lewis)
6. MY WOMAN, MY WOMAN, MY WIFE
   (Marty Robbins)
7. I NEVER PICKED COTTON
   (Roy Clark)
8. THE WORLD OF JOHNNY CASH
   (Johnny Cash)
9. MY LOVE/DON'T KEEP ME HANGIN' ON
   (Sonny James)
10. TAMMY'S TOUCH
    (Tammy Wynette)

OCTOBER 24, 1970

POP SINGLES

1. I'LL BE THERE
   (The Jackson 5)
2. WE'VE ONLY JUST BEGUN
   (The Carpenters)
3. GREEN-EYED LADY
   (Sugarloaf)
4. ALL RIGHT NOW
   (Free)
5. CRACKLIN' ROSE
   (Neil Diamond)
6. INDIANA WANTS ME
   (R. Dean Taylor)
7. CANDIDA
   (Dawn)
8. LOOK WHAT THEY'VE DONE TO MY SONG, MA
   (The New Seekers)
9. FIRE AND RAIN
   (James Taylor)
10. LOLA
    (The Kinks)

POP ALBUMS

1. COSMO'S FACTORY
   (Creedence Clearwater Revival)
2. ABRAXAS
   (Santana)
3. MAD DOGS AND ENGLISHMEN
   (Joe Cocker)
4. AFTER THE GOLD RUSH
   (Neil Young)
5. A QUESTION OF BALANCE
   (The Moody Blues)

6. LED ZEPPELIN III
   (Led Zeppelin)
7. THIRD ALBUM
   (The Jackson 5)
8. CLOSE TO YOU
   (The Carpenters)
9. JIMI HENDRIX EXPERIENCE AND OTIS REDDING AT THE MONTEREY INTERNATIONAL POP FESTIVAL
   (Jimi Hendrix Experience and Otis Redding)
10. SWEET BABY JAMES
    (James Taylor)

BLACK SINGLES

1. I'LL BE THERE
   (The Jackson 5)
2. STAND BY YOUR MAN
   (Candi Staton)
3. STILL WATER
   (The Four Tops)
4. CALL ME SUPER BAD
   (James Brown)
5. (BABY) YOU TURN ME ON
   (The Impressions)
6. UNGENA ZA ULIMWENGU (UNITE THE WORLD)
   (Temptations)
7. I DO TAKE YOU
   (The Three Degrees)
8. ENGINE #9
   (Wilson Pickett)
9. I NEED HELP
   (Bobby Byrd)
10. DEEPER AND DEEPER
    (Freda Payne)

JAZZ ALBUMS

1. THE ISAAC HAYES MOVEMENT
   (Isaac Hayes)
2. CHAPTER TWO
   (Roberta Flack)
3. BITCHES BREW
   (Miles Davis)
4. GULA MATARI
   (Quincy Jones)
5. BLACK TALK
   (Charles Earland)
6. WALKING IN SPACE
   (Quincy Jones)
7. SWISS MOVEMENT
   (Les McCann and Eddie Harris)
8. EVERYTHING I PLAY IS FUNKY
   (Lou Donaldson)
9. VIVA TIRADO
   (El Chicano)
10. TRANSITION
    (John Coltrane)

COUNTRY SINGLES

1. THE TAKER
   (Waylon Jennings)
2. SUNDAY MORNING COMING DOWN
   (Johnny Cash)
3. RUN WOMAN RUN
   (Tammy Wynette)
4. ANGELS DON'T LIE
   (Jim Reeves)
5. IT'S ONLY MAKE BELIEVE
   (Glen Campbell)
6. SNOWBIRD
   (Anne Murray)
7. JOLIE GIRL
   (Marty Robbins)
8. THERE MUST BE MORE TO LOVE THAN THIS
   (Jerry Lee Lewis)
9. I CAN'T BELIEVE THAT YOU'VE STOPPED LOVING ME
   (Charley Pride)
10. WONDERS OF THE WINE
    (David Houston)

COUNTRY ALBUMS

1. FOR THE GOOD TIMES
   (Ray Price)
2. THE FIGHTIN' SIDE OF ME
   (Merle Haggard)
3. CHARLEY PRIDE'S 10th ALBUM
   (Charley Pride)
4. HELLO DARLIN'
   (Conway Twitty)
5. LIVE AT THE INTERNATIONAL
   (Jerry Lee Lewis)
6. I NEVER PICKED COTTON
   (Roy Clark)
7. THE GLEN CAMPBELL GOOD TIME ALBUM
   (Glen Campbell)
8. THE WORLD OF JOHNNY CASH
   (Johnny Cash)
9. MY WOMAN, MY WOMAN, MY WIFE
   (Marty Robbins)
10. MY LOVE/DON'T KEEP ME HANGIN' ON
    (Sonny James)

OCTOBER 31, 1970

POP SINGLES

1. I'LL BE THERE
   (The Jackson 5)
2. WE'VE ONLY JUST BEGUN
   (The Carpenters)
3. GREEN-EYED LADY
   (Sugarloaf)
4. ALL RIGHT NOW
   (Free)
5. INDIANA WANTS ME
   (R. Dean Taylor)
6. FIRE AND RAIN
   (James Taylor)
7. CRACKLIN' ROSE
   (Neil Diamond)
8. LOOK WHAT THEY'VE DONE TO MY SONG, MA
   (The New Seekers)
9. LOLA
   (The Kinks)
10. IT'S ONLY MAKE BELIEVE
    (Glen Campbell)

POP ALBUMS

1. ABRAXAS
   (Santana)
2. LED ZEPPELIN III
   (Led Zeppelin)
3. THIRD ALBUM
   (The Jackson 5)
4. COSMO'S FACTORY
   (Creedence Clearwater Revival)
5. GET YER YA-YA'S OUT
   (The Rolling Stones)
6. CLOSE TO YOU
   (The Carpenters)
7. AFTER THE GOLD RUSH
   (Neil Young)
8. SWEET BABY JAMES
   (James Taylor)
9. MAD DOGS AND ENGLISHMEN
   (Joe Cocker)
10. A QUESTION OF BALANCE
    (The Moody Blues)

BLACK SINGLES

1. I'LL BE THERE
   (The Jackson 5)
2. CALL ME SUPER BAD
   (James Brown)
3. STAND BY YOUR MAN
   (Candi Staton)

4. UNGENA ZA ULIMWENGU (UNITE THE
WORLD)
(Temptations)
5. ENGINE #9
(Wilson Pickett)
6. I NEED HELP
(Bobby Byrd)
7. I DO TAKE YOU
(The Three Degrees)
8. DEEPER AND DEEPER
(Freda Payne)
9. 5-10-15-20
(The Presidents)
10. STILL WATER
(The Four Tops)

JAZZ ALBUMS

1. THE ISAAC HAYES MOVEMENT
(Isaac Hayes)
2. CHAPTER TWO
(Roberta Flack)
3. BITCHES BREW
(Miles Davis)
4. GULA MATARI
(Quincy Jones)
5. BLACK TALK
(Charles Earland)
6. WALKING IN SPACE
(Quincy Jones)
7. SWISS MOVEMENT
(Les McCann and Eddie Harris)
8. EVERYTHING I PLAY IS FUNKY
(Lou Donaldson)
9. VIVA TIRADO
(El Chicano)
10. TRANSITION
(John Coltrane)

COUNTRY SINGLES

1. RUN WOMAN RUN
(Tammy Wynette)
2. THE TAKER
(Waylon Jennings)
3. SUNDAY MORNING COMING DOWN
(Johnny Cash)
4. IT'S ONLY MAKE BELIEVE
(Glen Campbell)
5. I CAN'T BELIEVE THAT YOU'VE STOPPED
LOVING ME
(Charley Pride)
6. JOLIE GIRL
(Marty Robbins)
7. ANGELS DON'T LIE
(Jim Reeves)
8. THANK GOD AND GREYHOUND
(Roy Clark)
9. THERE MUST BE MORE TO LOVE THAN
THIS
(Jerry Lee Lewis)
10. FIFTEEN YEARS AGO
(Conway Twitty)

COUNTRY ALBUMS

1. THE FIGHTIN' SIDE OF ME
(Merle Haggard)
2. FOR THE GOOD TIMES
(Ray Price)
3. CHARLEY PRIDE'S 10th ALBUM
(Charley Pride)
4. HELLO DARLIN'
(Conway Twitty)
5. THE GLEN CAMPBELL GOOD TIME ALBUM
(Glen Campbell)
6. LIVE AT THE INTERNATIONAL
(Jerry Lee Lewis)
7. I NEVER PICKED COTTON
(Roy Clark)
8. SNOWBIRD
(Anne Murray)
9. NO LOVE AT ALL
(Lynn Anderson)

10. ONCE MORE
(Porter Wagoner and Dolly Parton)

NOVEMBER 7, 1970

POP SINGLES

1. I'LL BE THERE
(The Jackson 5)
2. WE'VE ONLY JUST BEGUN
(The Carpenters)
3. FIRE AND RAIN
(James Taylor)
4. INDIANA WANTS ME
(R. Dean Taylor)
5. I THINK I LOVE YOU
(The Partridge Family)
6. ALL RIGHT NOW
(Free)
7. LOLA
(The Kinks)
8. STILL WATER (LOVE)
(The Four Tops)
9. IT'S ONLY MAKE BELIEVE
(Glen Campbell)
10. SOMEBODY'S BEEN SLEEPING
(100 Proof)

POP ALBUMS

1. ABRAXAS
(Santana)
2. LED ZEPPELIN III
(Led Zeppelin)
3. THIRD ALBUM
(The Jackson 5)
4. COSMO'S FACTORY
(Creedence Clearwater Revival)
5. GET YER YA-YA'S OUT
(The Rolling Stones)
6. CLOSE TO YOU
(The Carpenters)
7. SWEET BABY JAMES
(James Taylor)
8. AFTER THE GOLD RUSH
(Neil Young)
9. MAD DOGS AND ENGLISHMEN
(Joe Cocker)
10. A QUESTION OF BALANCE
(The Moody Blues)

BLACK SINGLES

1. I'LL BE THERE
(The Jackson 5)
2. CALL ME SUPER BAD
(James Brown)
3. ENGINE #9
(Wilson Pickett)
4. UNGENA ZA ULIMWENGU (UNITE THE
WORLD)
(Temptations)
5. STAND BY YOUR MAN
(Candi Staton)
6. I NEED HELP
(Bobby Byrd)
7. 5-10-15-20
(The Presidents)
8. DEEPER AND DEEPER
(Freda Payne)
9. I AM SOMEBODY
(Johnnie Taylor)
10. PART TIME LOVE
(Ann Peebles)

JAZZ ALBUMS

1. THE ISAAC HAYES MOVEMENT
(Isaac Hayes)

2. GULA MATARI
(Quincy Jones)
3. BITCHES BREW
(Miles Davis)
4. CHAPTER TWO
(Roberta Flack)
5. WALKING IN SPACE
(Quincy Jones)
6. BLACK TALK
(Charles Earland)
7. EVERYTHING I PLAY IS FUNKY
(Lou Donaldson)
8. SWISS MOVEMENT
(Les McCann and Eddie Harris)
9. PTAH THE EL DAOUD
(Alice Coltrane)
10. TRANSITION
(John Coltrane)

COUNTRY SINGLES

1. IT'S ONLY MAKE BELIEVE
(Glen Campbell)
2. RUN WOMAN RUN
(Tammy Wynette)
3. I CAN'T BELIEVE THAT YOU'VE STOPPED
LOVING ME
(Charley Pride)
4. THE TAKER
(Waylon Jennings)
5. THANK GOD AND GREYHOUND
(Roy Clark)
6. JOLIE GIRL
(Marty Robbins)
7. FIFTEEN YEARS AGO
(Conway Twitty)
8. SUNDAY MORNING COMING DOWN
(Johnny Cash)
9. I CAN'T BE MYSELF/SIDEWALKS OF
CHICAGO
(Merle Haggard)
10. ALL MY HARD TIMES
(Roy Drusky)

COUNTRY ALBUMS

1. THE FIGHTIN' SIDE OF ME
(Merle Haggard)
2. FOR THE GOOD TIMES
(Ray Price)
3. CHARLEY PRIDE'S 10th ALBUM
(Charley Pride)
4. THE GLEN CAMPBELL GOOD TIME ALBUM
(Glen Campbell)
5. HELLO DARLIN'
(Conway Twitty)
6. SNOWBIRD
(Anne Murray)
7. ONCE MORE
(Porter Wagoner and Dolly Parton)
8. LIVE AT THE INTERNATIONAL
(Jerry Lee Lewis)
9. I NEVER PICKED COTTON
(Roy Clark)
10. OKIE FROM MUSKOGEE
(Merle Haggard)

NOVEMBER 14, 1970

POP SINGLES

1. WE'VE ONLY JUST BEGUN
(The Carpenters)
2. INDIANA WANTS ME
(R. Dean Taylor)
3. FIRE AND RAIN
(James Taylor)
4. I THINK I LOVE YOU
(The Partridge Family)
5. I'LL BE THERE
(The Jackson 5)

6. IT DON'T MATTER TO ME
   (Bread)
7. SOMEBODY'S BEEN SLEEPING
   (100 Proof)
8. IT'S ONLY MAKE BELIEVE
   (Glen Campbell)
9. SUPER BAD
   (James Brown)
10. ALL RIGHT NOW
    (Free)

POP ALBUMS

1. LED ZEPPELIN III
   (Led Zeppelin)
2. ABRAXAS
   (Santana)
3. THIRD ALBUM
   (The Jackson 5)
4. COSMO'S FACTORY
   (Creedence Clearwater Revival)
5. CLOSE TO YOU
   (The Carpenters)
6. SWEET BABY JAMES
   (James Taylor)
7. GET YER YA-YA'S OUT
   (The Rolling Stones)
8. AFTER THE GOLD RUSH
   (Neil Young)
9. A QUESTION OF BALANCE
   (The Moody Blues)
10. SHARE THE LAND
    (The Guess Who)

BLACK SINGLES

1. CALL ME SUPER BAD
   (James Brown)
2. ENGINE #9
   (Wilson Pickett)
3. I'LL BE THERE
   (The Jackson 5)
4. 5-10-15-20
   (The Presidents)
5. I AM SOMEBODY
   (Johnnie Taylor)
6. PART TIME LOVE
   (Ann Peebles)
7. I NEED HELP
   (Bobby Byrd)
8. DEEPER AND DEEPER
   (Freda Payne)
9. HEAVEN HELP US ALL
   (Stevie Wonder)
10. THE TEARS OF A CLOWN
    (Smokey Robinson and the Miracles)

JAZZ ALBUMS

1. THE ISAAC HAYES MOVEMENT
   (Isaac Hayes)
2. CHAPTER TWO
   (Roberta Flack)
3. BITCHES BREW
   (Miles Davis)
4. GULA MATARI
   (Quincy Jones)
5. BLACK TALK
   (Charles Earland)
6. WALKING IN SPACE
   (Quincy Jones)
7. SWISS MOVEMENT
   (Les McCann and Eddie Harris)
8. PTAH THE EL DAOUD
   (Alice Coltrane)
9. HOT BUTTERED SOUL
   (Isaac Hayes)
10. TRANSITION
    (John Coltrane)

COUNTRY SINGLES

1. I CAN'T BELIEVE THAT YOU'VE STOPPED LOVING ME
   (Charley Pride)
2. FIFTEEN YEARS AGO
   (Conway Twitty)
3. THANK GOD AND GREYHOUND
   (Roy Clark)
4. IT'S ONLY MAKE BELIEVE
   (Glen Campbell)
5. I CAN'T BE MYSELF/SIDEWALKS OF CHICAGO
   (Merle Haggard)
6. RUN WOMAN RUN
   (Tammy Wynette)
7. THE TAKER
   (Waylon Jennings)
8. ALL MY HARD TIMES
   (Roy Drusky)
9. ENDLESSLY
   (Sonny James)
10. AFTER CLOSING TIME
    (David Houston and Barbara Mandrell)

COUNTRY ALBUMS

1. THE FIGHTIN' SIDE OF ME
   (Merle Haggard)
2. FOR THE GOOD TIMES
   (Ray Price)
3. THE GLEN CAMPBELL GOOD TIME ALBUM
   (Glen Campbell)
4. SNOWBIRD
   (Anne Murray)
5. CHARLEY PRIDE'S 10th ALBUM
   (Charley Pride)
6. ONCE MORE
   (Porter Wagoner and Dolly Parton)
7. HELLO DARLIN'
   (Conway Twitty)
8. LIVE AT THE INTERNATIONAL
   (Jerry Lee Lewis)
9. OKIE FROM MUSKOGEE
   (Merle Haggard)
10. I NEVER PICKED COTTON
    (Roy Clark)

NOVEMBER 21, 1970

POP SINGLES

1. I THINK I LOVE YOU
   (The Partridge Family)
2. INDIANA WANTS ME
   (R. Dean Taylor)
3. FIRE AND RAIN
   (James Taylor)
4. WE'VE ONLY JUST BEGUN
   (The Carpenters)
5. THE TEARS OF A CLOWN
   (Smokey Robinson and the Miracles)
6. SOMEBODY'S BEEN SLEEPING
   (100 Proof)
7. CRY ME A RIVER
   (Joe Cocker)
8. GYPSY WOMAN
   (Brian Hyland)
9. SUPER BAD
   (James Brown)
10. MONTEGO BAY
    (Bobby Bloom)

POP ALBUMS

1. LED ZEPPELIN III
   (Led Zeppelin)
2. ABRAXAS
   (Santana)

3. THIRD ALBUM
   (The Jackson 5)
4. CLOSE TO YOU
   (The Carpenters)
5. NEW MORNING
   (Bob Dylan)
6. SWEET BABY JAMES
   (James Taylor)
7. GET YER YA-YA'S OUT
   (The Rolling Stones)
8. AFTER THE GOLD RUSH
   (Neil Young)
9. GREATEST HITS
   (Sly and the Family Stone)
10. SHARE THE LAND
    (The Guess Who)

BLACK SINGLES

1. CALL ME SUPER BAD
   (James Brown)
2. ENGINE #9
   (Wilson Pickett)
3. 5-10-15-20
   (The Presidents)
4. I AM SOMEBODY
   (Johnnie Taylor)
5. PART TIME LOVE
   (Ann Peebles)
6. I'LL BE THERE
   (The Jackson 5)
7. HEAVEN HELP US ALL
   (Stevie Wonder)
8. THE TEARS OF A CLOWN
   (Smokey Robinson and the Miracles)
9. I NEED HELP
   (Bobby Byrd)
10. LET ME BACK IN
    (Tyrone Davis)

JAZZ ALBUMS

1. THE ISAAC HAYES MOVEMENT
   (Isaac Hayes)
2. CHAPTER TWO
   (Roberta Flack)
3. BITCHES BREW
   (Miles Davis)
4. BLACK TALK
   (Charles Earland)
5. GULA MATARI
   (Quincy Jones)
6. WALKING IN SPACE
   (Quincy Jones)
7. SWISS MOVEMENT
   (Les McCann and Eddie Harris)
8. SUMMUN BUKMUN UMYUN
   (Pharoah Sanders)
9. PTAH THE EL DAOUD
   (Alice Coltrane)
10. TRANSITION
    (John Coltrane)

COUNTRY SINGLES

1. FIFTEEN YEARS AGO
   (Conway Twitty)
2. I CAN'T BELIEVE THAT YOU'VE STOPPED LOVING ME
   (Charley Pride)
3. THANK GOD AND GREYHOUND
   (Roy Clark)
4. I CAN'T BE MYSELF/SIDEWALKS OF CHICAGO
   (Merle Haggard)
5. ENDLESSLY
   (Sonny James)
6. AFTER CLOSING TIME
   (David Houston and Barbara Mandrell)
7. GOIN' STEADY
   (Faron Young)
8. ALL MY HARD TIMES
   (Roy Drusky)

9. WHERE HAVE ALL THE HEROES GONE?
   (Bill Anderson)
10. IT'S ONLY MAKE BELIEVE
    (Glen Campbell)

COUNTRY ALBUMS

1. THE FIGHTIN' SIDE OF ME
   (Merle Haggard)
2. THE GLEN CAMPBELL GOOD TIME ALBUM
   (Glen Campbell)
3. FOR THE GOOD TIMES
   (Ray Price)
4. THE FIRST LADY
   (Tammy Wynette)
5. SNOWBIRD
   (Anne Murray)
6. HELLO DARLIN'
   (Conway Twitty)
7. CHARLEY PRIDE'S 10th ALBUM
   (Charley Pride)
8. LIVE AT THE INTERNATIONAL
   (Jerry Lee Lewis)
9. THE JOHNNY CASH SHOW
   (Johnny Cash)
10. ONCE MORE
    (Porter Wagoner and Dolly Parton)

NOVEMBER 28, 1970

POP SINGLES

1. I THINK I LOVE YOU
   (The Partridge Family)
2. THE TEARS OF A CLOWN
   (Smokey Robinson and the Miracles)
3. INDIANA WANTS ME
   (R. Dean Taylor)
4. WE'VE ONLY JUST BEGUN
   (The Carpenters)
5. GYPSY WOMAN
   (Brian Hyland)
6. FIRE AND RAIN
   (James Taylor)
7. 5-10-15-20
   (The Presidents)
8. SOMEBODY'S BEEN SLEEPING
   (100 Proof)
9. YOU DON'T HAVE TO SAY YOU LOVE
   ME/PATCH IT UP
   (Elvis Presley)
10. MONTEGO BAY
    (Bobby Bloom)

POP ALBUMS

1. LED ZEPPELIN III
   (Led Zeppelin)
2. ABRAXAS
   (Santana)
3. CLOSE TO YOU
   (The Carpenters)
4. NEW MORNING
   (Bob Dylan)
5. THIRD ALBUM
   (The Jackson 5)
6. SWEET BABY JAMES
   (James Taylor)
7. GREATEST HITS
   (Sly and the Family Stone)
8. GRAND FUNK LIVE
   (Grand Funk Railroad)
9. GET YER YA-YA'S OUT
   (The Rolling Stones)
10. WITH LOVE, BOBBY
    (Bobby Sherman)

BLACK SINGLES

1. HEAVEN HELP US ALL
   (Stevie Wonder)
2. CALL ME SUPER BAD
   (James Brown)
3. 5-10-15-20
   (The Presidents)
4. I AM SOMEBODY
   (Johnnie Taylor)
5. ENGINE #9
   (Wilson Pickett)
6. PART TIME LOVE
   (Ann Peebles)
7. THE TEARS OF A CLOWN
   (Smokey Robinson and the Miracles)
8. I'LL BE THERE
   (The Jackson 5)
9. CHAINS AND THINGS
   (B.B. King)
10. BIG-LEGGED WOMAN
    (Israel Tolbert)

JAZZ ALBUMS

1. THE ISAAC HAYES MOVEMENT
   (Isaac Hayes)
2. CHAPTER TWO
   (Roberta Flack)
3. BITCHES BREW
   (Miles Davis)
4. GULA MATARI
   (Quincy Jones)
5. WALKING IN SPACE
   (Quincy Jones)
6. SUMMUN BUKMUN UMYUN
   (Pharaoh Sanders)
7. BLACK TALK
   (Charles Earland)
8. PTAH THE EL DAOUD
   (Alice Coltrane)
9. SWISS MOVEMENT
   (Les McCann and Eddie Harris)
10. TRANSITION
    (John Coltrane)

COUNTRY SINGLES

1. I CAN'T BE MYSELF/SIDEWALKS OF
   CHICAGO
   (Merle Haggard)
2. ENDLESSLY
   (Sonny James)
3. FIFTEEN YEARS AGO
   (Conway Twitty)
4. WHERE HAVE ALL THE HEROES GONE?
   (Bill Anderson)
5. GOIN' STEADY
   (Faron Young)
6. AFTER CLOSING TIME
   (David Houston and Barbara Mandrell)
7. I CAN'T BELIEVE THAT YOU'VE STOPPED
   LOVING ME
   (Charley Pride)
8. SO SAD (TO WATCH GOOD LOVE GO BAD)
   (Hank Williams Jr.)
9. SHE GOES WALKING THROUGH MY MIND
   (Billy Walker)
10. MORNING
    (Jim Ed Brown)

COUNTRY ALBUMS

1. FOR THE GOOD TIMES
   (Ray Price)
2. THE GLEN CAMPBELL GOOD TIME ALBUM
   (Glen Campbell)
3. THE FIGHTIN' SIDE OF ME
   (Merle Haggard)
4. THE FIRST LADY
   (Tammy Wynette)
5. HELLO DARLIN'
   (Conway Twitty)

6. SNOWBIRD
   (Anne Murray)
7. THE JOHNNY CASH SHOW
   (Johnny Cash)
8. CHARLEY PRIDE'S 10th ALBUM
   (Charley Pride)
9. LIVE AT THE INTERNATIONAL
   (Jerry Lee Lewis)
10. THE GREAT WHITE HORSE
    (Buck Owens and Susan Raye)

DECEMBER 5, 1970

POP SINGLES

1. I THINK I LOVE YOU
   (The Partridge Family)
2. THE TEARS OF A CLOWN
   (Smokey Robinson and the Miracles)
3. GYPSY WOMAN
   (Brian Hyland)
4. WE'VE ONLY JUST BEGUN
   (The Carpenters)
5. INDIANA WANTS ME
   (R. Dean Taylor)
6. 5-10-15-20
   (The Presidents)
7. YOU DON'T HAVE TO SAY YOU LOVE
   ME/PATCH IT UP
   (Elvis Presley)
8. MONTEGO BAY
   (Bobby Bloom)
9. SEE ME, FEEL ME
   (The Who)
10. HEAVEN HELP US ALL
    (Stevie Wonder)

POP ALBUMS

1. GREATEST HITS
   (Sly and the Family Stone)
2. ABRAXAS
   (Santana)
3. LED ZEPPELIN III
   (Led Zeppelin)
4. NEW MORNING
   (Bob Dylan)
5. GRAND FUNK LIVE
   (Grand Funk Railroad)
6. SWEET BABY JAMES
   (James Taylor)
7. THIRD ALBUM
   (The Jackson 5)
8. CLOSE TO YOU
   (The Carpenters)
9. SHARE THE LAND
   (The Guess Who)
10. ELTON JOHN
    (Elton John)

BLACK SINGLES

1. 5-10-15-20
   (The Presidents)
2. HEAVEN HELP US ALL
   (Stevie Wonder)
3. THE TEARS OF A CLOWN
   (Smokey Robinson and the Miracles)
4. I AM SOMEBODY
   (Johnnie Taylor)
5. CHAINS AND THINGS
   (B.B. King)
6. CALL ME SUPER BAD
   (James Brown)
7. BORDER SONG
   (Aretha Franklin)
8. BIG-LEGGED WOMAN
   (Israel Tolbert)
9. I'M NOT MY BROTHER'S KEEPER
   (Flaming Ember)
10. ACE OF SPADES
    (O.V. Wright)

JAZZ ALBUMS

1. THE ISAAC HAYES MOVEMENT
   (Isaac Hayes)
2. CHAPTER TWO
   (Roberta Flack)
3. GULA MATARI
   (Quincy Jones)
4. WALKING IN SPACE
   (Quincy Jones)
5. BITCHES BREW
   (Miles Davis)
6. SUMMUN BUKMUN UMYUN
   (Pharaoh Sanders)
7. BLACK TALK
   (Charles Earland)
8. PTAH THE EL DAOUD
   (Alice Coltrane)
9. SWISS MOVEMENT
   (Les McCann and Eddie Harris)
10. TO BE CONTINUED
    (Isaac Hayes)

COUNTRY SINGLES

1. ENDLESSLY
   (Sonny James)
2. I CAN'T BE MYSELF/SIDEWALKS OF
   CHICAGO
   (Merle Haggard)
3. WHERE HAVE ALL THE HEROES GONE?
   (Bill Anderson)
4. COAL MINER'S DAUGHTER
   (Loretta Lynn)
5. GOIN' STEADY
   (Faron Young)
6. SHE GOES WALKING THROUGH MY MIND
   (Billy Walker)
7. MORNING
   (Jim Ed Brown)
8. SO SAD (TO WATCH GOOD LOVE GO BAD)
   (Hank Williams Jr.)
9. FIFTEEN YEARS AGO
   (Conway Twitty)
10. AFTER CLOSING TIME
    (Conway Twitty)

COUNTRY ALBUMS

1. THE FIRST LADY
   (Tammy Wynette)
2. FOR THE GOOD TIMES
   (Ray Price)
3. THE FIGHTIN' SIDE OF ME
   (Merle Haggard)
4. THE GLEN CAMPBELL GOOD TIME ALBUM
   (Glen Campbell)
5. THE JOHNNY CASH SHOW
   (Johnny Cash)
6. CHARLEY PRIDE'S 10th ALBUM
   (Charley Pride)
7. HELLO DARLIN'
   (Conway Twitty)
8. SNOWBIRD
   (Anne Murray)
9. LIVE AT THE INTERNATIONAL
   (Jerry Lee Lewis)
10. THE BEST OF GEORGE JONES
    (George Jones)

DECEMBER 12, 1970

POP SINGLES

1. I THINK I LOVE YOU
   (The Partridge Family)
2. THE TEARS OF A CLOWN
   (Smokey Robinson and the Miracles)
3. GYPSY WOMAN
   (Brian Hyland)
4. MY SWEET LORD/ISN'T IT A PITY
   (George Harrison)
5. ONE LESS BELL TO ANSWER
   (The Fifth Dimension)
6. 5-10-15-20
   (The Presidents)
7. NO MATTER WHAT
   (Badfinger)
8. HEAVEN HELP US ALL
   (Stevie Wonder)
9. SHARE THE LAND
   (The Guess Who)
10. DOES ANYBODY REALLY KNOW WHAT
    TIME IT IS?
    (Chicago)

POP ALBUMS

1. ABRAXAS
   (Santana)
2. GREATEST HITS
   (Sly and the Family Stone)
3. NEW MORNING
   (Bob Dylan)
4. LED ZEPPELIN III
   (Led Zeppelin)
5. GRAND FUNK LIVE
   (Grand Funk Railroad)
6. SWEET BABY JAMES
   (James Taylor)
7. THE PARTRIDGE FAMILY ALBUM
   (The Partridge Family)
8. JESUS CHRIST SUPERSTAR
   (Cast Album)
9. TAP ROOT MANUSCRIPT
   (Neil Diamond)
10. ELTON JOHN
    (Elton John)

BLACK SINGLES

1. THE TEARS OF A CLOWN
   (Smokey Robinson and the Miracles)
2. HEAVEN HELP US ALL
   (Stevie Wonder)
3. STONED LOVE
   (The Supremes)
4. CHAINS AND THINGS
   (B.B. King)
5. IF THERE'S A HELL BELOW
   (Curtis Mayfield)
6. BORDER SONG
   (Aretha Franklin)
7. 5-10-15-20
   (The Presidents)
8. I'M NOT MY BROTHER'S KEEPER
   (Flaming Ember)
9. ACE OF SPADES
   (O.V. Wright)
10. CALL ME SUPER BAD
    (James Brown)

JAZZ ALBUMS

1. THE ISAAC HAYES MOVEMENT
   (Isaac Hayes)
2. CHAPTER TWO
   (Roberta Flack)
3. BITCHES BREW
   (Miles Davis)
4. GULA MATARI
   (Quincy Jones)
5. BLACK TALK
   (Charles Earland)
6. SUMMUN BUKMUN UMYUN
   (Pharaoh Sanders)
7. WALKING IN SPACE
   (Quincy Jones)
8. MILES DAVIS AT THE FILLMORE
   (Miles Davis)
9. TO BE CONTINUED
   (Isaac Hayes)
10. PTAH THE EL DAOUD
    (Alice Coltrane)

COUNTRY SINGLES

1. WHERE HAVE ALL THE HEROES GONE?
   (Bill Anderson)
2. COAL MINER'S DAUGHTER
   (Loretta Lynn)
3. ENDLESSLY
   (Sonny James)
4. MORNING
   (Jim Ed Brown)
5. SHE GOES WALKING THROUGH MY MIND
   (Billy Walker)
6. I CAN'T BE MYSELF/SIDEWALKS OF
   CHICAGO
   (Merle Haggard)
7. ROSE GARDEN
   (Lynn Anderson)
8. GOIN' STEADY
   (Faron Young)
9. FIFTEEN YEARS AGO
   (Conway Twitty)
10. I'M ALL RIGHT
    (Lynn Anderson)

COUNTRY ALBUMS

1. THE FIRST LADY
   (Tammy Wynette)
2. FOR THE GOOD TIMES
   (Ray Price)
3. THE FIGHTIN' SIDE OF ME
   (Merle Haggard)
4. SNOWBIRD
   (Anne Murray)
5. THE JOHNNY CASH SHOW
   (Johnny Cash)
6. THE GLEN CAMPBELL GOOD TIME ALBUM
   (Glen Campbell)
7. CHARLEY PRIDE'S 10th ALBUM
   (Charley Pride)
8. HELLO DARLIN'
   (Conway Twitty)
9. LIVE AT THE INTERNATIONAL
   (Jerry Lee Lewis)
10. THE BEST OF GEORGE JONES
    (George Jones)

DECEMBER 19, 1970

POP SINGLES

1. MY SWEET LORD/ISN'T IT A PITY
   (George Harrison)
2. THE TEARS OF A CLOWN
   (Smokey Robinson and the Miracles)
3. ONE LESS BELL TO ANSWER
   (The Fifth Dimension)
4. I THINK I LOVE YOU
   (The Partridge Family)
5. NO MATTER WHAT
   (Badfinger)
6. GYPSY WOMAN
   (Brian Hyland)
7. DOES ANYBODY REALLY KNOW WHAT
   TIME IT IS?
   (Chicago)
8. BLACK MAGIC WOMAN
   (Santana)
9. SHARE THE LAND
   (The Guess Who)
10. STONED LOVE
    (The Supremes)

POP ALBUMS

1. ABRAXAS
   (Santana)
2. GREATEST HITS
   (Sly and the Family Stone)

3. LED ZEPPELIN III
(Led Zeppelin)
4. GRAND FUNK LIVE
(Grand Funk Railroad)
5. NEW MORNING
(Bob Dylan)
6. SWEET BABY JAMES
(James Taylor)
7. STEPHEN STILLS
(Stephen Stills)
8. JESUS CHRIST SUPERSTAR
(Cast Album)
9. TAP ROOT MANUSCRIPT
(Neil Diamond)
10. THE PARTRIDGE FAMILY ALBUM
(The Partridge Family)

BLACK SINGLES

1. THE TEARS OF A CLOWN
(Smokey Robinson and the Miracles)
2. STONED LOVE
(The Supremes)
3. IF THERE'S A HELL BELOW
(Curtis Mayfield)
4. BORDER SONG
(Aretha Franklin)
5. GROOVE ME
(King Floyd)
6. I'M NOT MY BROTHER'S KEEPER
(Flaming Ember)
7. HEAVEN HELP US ALL
(Stevie Wonder)
8. CHAINS AND THINGS
(B.B. King)
9. IF I WERE YOUR WOMAN
(Gladys Knight and the Pips)
10. ALL I HAVE
(The Moments)

JAZZ ALBUMS

1. THE ISAAC HAYES MOVEMENT
(Isaac Hayes)
2. CHAPTER TWO
(Roberta Flack)
3. TO BE CONTINUED
(Isaac Hayes)
4. GULA MATARI
(Quincy Jones)
5. BITCHES BREW
(Miles Davis)
6. MILES DAVIS AT THE FILLMORE
(Miles Davis)
7. BLACK TALK
(Charles Earland)
8. SUMMUN BUKMUN UMYUN
(Pharaoh Sanders)
9. INDIANOLA MISSISSIPPI SEEDS
(B.B. King)
10. WALKING IN SPACE
(Quincy Jones)

COUNTRY SINGLES

1. COAL MINER'S DAUGHTER
(Loretta Lynn)
2. NEW MORNING
(Jim Ed Brown)
3. ROSE GARDEN
(Lynn Anderson)
4. WHERE HAVE ALL THE HEROES GONE?
(Bill Anderson)
5. SHE GOES WALKING THROUGH MY MIND
(Billy Walker)
6. ENDLESSLY
(Sonny James)
7. I CAN'T BE MYSELF/SIDEWALKS OF
CHICAGO
(Merle Haggard)
8. I WOULDN'T LIVE IN N.Y.C.
(Buck Owens)
9. COMMERCIAL AFFECTION
(Mel Tillis)
10. A GOOD YEAR FOR THE ROSES
(George Jones)

COUNTRY ALBUMS

1. FOR THE GOOD TIMES
(Ray Price)
2. THE FIRST LADY
(Tammy Wynette)
3. THE JOHNNY CASH SHOW
(Johnny Cash)
4. SNOWBIRD
(Anne Murray)
5. THE FIGHTIN' SIDE OF ME
(Merle Haggard)
6. CHARLEY PRIDE'S 10th ALBUM
(Charley Pride)
7. HELLO DARLIN'
(Conway Twitty)
8. THE GLEN CAMPBELL GOOD TIME ALBUM
(Glen Campbell)
9. FIFTEEN YEARS AGO
(Conway Twitty)
10. #1
(Sonny James)

DECEMBER 26, 1970

POP SINGLES

1. MY SWEET LORD/ISN'T IT A PITY
(George Harrison)
2. ONE LESS BELL TO ANSWER
(The Fifth Dimension)
3. BLACK MAGIC WOMAN
(Santana)
4. NO MATTER WHAT
(Badfinger)
5. STONED LOVE
(The Supremes)
6. DOES ANYBODY REALLY KNOW WHAT
TIME IT IS?
(Chicago)
7. THE TEARS OF A CLOWN
(Smokey Robinson and the Miracles)
8. KNOCK THREE TIMES
(Dawn)
9. DOMINO
(Van Morrison)
10. GYPSY WOMAN
(Brian Hyland)

POP ALBUMS

1. ALL THINGS MUST PASS
(George Harrison)
2. ABRAXAS
(Santana)
3. STEPHEN STILLS
(Stephen Stills)
4. GRAND FUNK LIVE
(Grand Funk Railroad)
5. JESUS CHRIST SUPERSTAR
(Cast Album)
6. NEW MORNING
(Bob Dylan)
7. GREATEST HITS
(Sly and the Family Stone)
8. TAP ROOT MANUSCRIPT
(Neil Diamond)
9. LED ZEPPELIN III
(Led Zeppelin)
10. SWEET BABY JAMES
(James Taylor)

BLACK SINGLES

1. STONED LOVE
(The Supremes)
2. IF THERE'S A HELL BELOW
(Curtis Mayfield)
3. IF I WERE YOUR WOMAN
(Gladys Knight and the Pips)
4. BORDER SONG
(Aretha Franklin)

5. GROOVE ME
(King Floyd)
6. THE TEARS OF A CLOWN
(Smokey Robinson and the Miracles)
7. PAY TO THE PIPER
(Chairmen of the Board)
8. ARE YOU MY WOMAN
(The Chi-Lites)
9. ALL I HAVE
(The Moments)
10. RIVER DEEP, MOUNTAINS HIGH
(The Supremes and The Four Tops)

JAZZ ALBUMS

1. TO BE CONTINUED
(Isaac Hayes)
2. CHAPTER TWO
(Roberta Flack)
3. THE ISAAC HAYES MOVEMENT
(Isaac Hayes)
4. MILES DAVIS AT THE FILLMORE
(Miles Davis)
5. BITCHES BREW
(Miles Davis)
6. GULA MATARI
(Quincy Jones)
7. BLACK TALK
(Charles Earland)
8. SUMMUN BUKMUN UMYUN
(Pharaoh Sanders)
9. DON ELLIS AT FILLMORE
(Don Ellis)
10. INDIANOLA MISSISSIPPI SEEDS
(B.B. King)

COUNTRY SINGLES

1. NEW MORNING
(Jim Ed Brown)
2. ROSE GARDEN
(Lynn Anderson)
3. COAL MINER'S DAUGHTER
(Loretta Lynn)
4. A GOOD YEAR FOR THE ROSES
(George Jones)
5. COMMERCIAL AFFECTION
(Mel Tillis)
6. SHE GOES WALKING THROUGH MY MIND
(Billy Walker)
7. I WOULDN'T LIVE IN N.Y.C.
(Buck Owens)
8. WHERE HAVE ALL THE HEROES GONE?
(Bill Anderson)
9. ENDLESSLY
(Sonny James)
10. I CAN'T BE MYSELF/SIDEWALKS OF
CHICAGO
(Merle Haggard)

COUNTRY ALBUMS

1. SNOWBIRD
(Anne Murray)
2. FOR THE GOOD TIMES
(Ray Price)
3. THE JOHNNY CASH SHOW
(Johnny Cash)
4. THE FIRST LADY
(Tammy Wynette)
5. TRIBUTE TO THE BEST DAMN FIDDLE
PLAYER IN THE WORLD (OR MY SALUTE
TO BOB WILLS)
(Merle Haggard)
6. FIFTEEN YEARS AGO
(Conway Twitty)
7. #1
(Sonny James)
8. THE FIGHTIN' SIDE OF ME
(Merle Haggard)
9. DOWN HOMERS
(Danny Davis and the Nashville Brothers)
10. CHARLEY PRIDE'S 10th ALBUM
(Charley Pride)

1971

Country music has been called "redneck music" and worse for many years. Radio programmers said only hillbillies enjoyed it and record executives agreed, claiming city people didn't like it. But slowly, country was shedding its backwoods image. By decade's end, it would be chic to wear cowboy hats and boots. Signs of country's ascension were already apparent in 1971. Lynn Anderson's "Rose Garden" and Jerry Reed's "When You're Hot, You're Hot" were national hits. Two of the year's most critically acclaimed songs, "Me and Bobby McGee," recorded by the late Janis Joplin, and "Help Me Make It Through the Night," a country hit for Sammi Stewart, were composed by young country songwriter Kris Kristofferson. Merle Haggard's *Hag* and *The Fightin' Side of Me*, Johnny Cash's *Man in Black* and *I Walk the Line*, and Loretta Lynn's *Coal Miner's Daughter* were landmark albums that documented their personal trials and tragedies with the unflinching honesty typical of country music. Also enhancing the country scene were these collections: *Best of Porter Wagoner and Dolly Parton*, *Tammy Wynette's Greatest Hits, Vol. 2* and *Glen Campbell's Greatest Hits*.

ALBUMS: Santana's *Abraxas* was a pioneering merger of rock instrumentation and the flowing rhythmic pulse of Latin music. Side one is magnificent, with two cuts, "Black Magic Woman" and "Oye Como Va," becoming rock radio favorites. Carlos Santana's lyrical solos and beautiful tone were a refreshing contrast to the clichéd heavy metal riffs of his contemporaries.

James Taylor's *Mud Slide Slim and the Blue Horizon* and *Sweet Baby James* epitomized an expression just coming into popularity: *laid back*. In fact, his vocals were so casual and guitar picking so languid, Taylor seemed relaxed to the point of sleepwalking. Taylor's cover of Carole King's *You've Got a Friend* showed him as a sensitive interpreter of songs written by others, a skill he'd demonstrate often in the future.

Emerson, Lake and Palmer's self-titled debut introduced a new sound to rock's power trio format. Keith Emerson's synthesizer, instead of electric guitar, was the chief melodic instrument, giving Emerson, Lake and Palmer a conceptual range far greater than art rock predecessors like Procol Harum. And this self-consciously artsy trio took full advantage of it, at one point recording Aaron Copeland's "Fanfare for the Common Man," and, in general, taking a highbrow approach to rock shared by two other popular art rock bands, Yes and Genesis.

During the '60s Marvin Gaye was always Motown's Mr. Versatile, adding his voice to duets with Tammi Terrell and Diana Ross, Motown-sound dance records ("Hitch Hike"), and pioneering funk ("I Heard It Through the Grapevine"). However, after winning creative control from Motown, Gaye's music changed profoundly. His *What's Going On* was dense and dark with marvelously arranged vocals and overtly political lyrics that cursed the Vietnam War and pollution. *What's Going On* not only surprised everyone, but expanded the musical and lyrical ambitions of many black musicians.

The year's most popular album came from, of all places, Broadway. The rock musical *Jesus Christ Superstar* spawned a best selling LP and, later, a film. Significantly, *JCS*, unlike previous rock musicals *Hair* and *Oh Calcutta*, didn't praise the hedonistic rock life-style, but celebrated the traditional mass opiates of religion and God.

But worshipping religious figures was not on the program for everyone. Young girls were still susceptible to teen idols—pretty boys with a bit of musical talent—whose records they could buy and whose pictures they could ogle. David Cassidy, star of the insipid "Partridge Family" situation comedy, separated these adolescents from their allowances with the cute "Doesn't Somebody Want to be Wanted," *The Partridge Family* and *Up to Date*.

Later, Cassidy's teen idol popularity would prove a curse as his more mature artistic efforts (as singer and actor) couldn't overcome his bubble-gum image. Ironically, his brother Shaun would go through the same unfortunate cycle in the late '70s.

More obnoxious than Cassidy was little Donny Osmond and the Osmonds, the Mormon church's answer to The Jackson 5. The Osmonds' "One Bad Apple" and "Sweet and Innocent" were shameless (and good) Jackson 5 rip-offs, while "Go Away Little Girl" was just the pits. Still Osmond survived, grew up, did commercials, and got his own television show.

SINGLES: There were several good double-sided singles including Rod Stewart's "Maggie May/Reason to Believe," Carole King's "It's Too Late/I Feel the Earth Move," George Harrison's "My Sweet Lord/Isn't It A Pity," and Paul McCartney's "Another Day/Oh Woman." Motown producer Norman Whitfield turned in two superb singles: "Just My Imagination (Running Away With Me)" by The Temptations, an aching chronicle of unrequited love, and the paranoid "Smiling Faces Sometimes" by Undisputed Truth. Singer-songwriters Gordon Lightfoot with "If You Could Read My Mind," and Bill Withers with "Ain't No Sunshine" used these introspective hits to build durable careers.

Unfortunately for the careers of Honey Cone, Cornelius Brothers and Sister Rose, Jean Knight, Lee Michaels, The Five Man Electric Band, Grass Roots, Ocean, and Murray Head and the Trinidad Singers, their big singles: "Want Ads," "Treat Her Like A Lady," "Mr. Big Stuff," "Do You Know What I Mean," "Signs," "Temptation Eyes," "Put Your Hand In the Hand," and "Superstar" didn't lead anywhere but trivia books.

The most significant rock event of the year was George Harrison's concert at Madison Square Garden for the victims of the Bangladesh war. It was an all-star party that was filmed and recorded and generated a lot of money. A perfect benefit. Well, no. The monies intended for the starving people in Bangladesh didn't reach them until 1982 due to colossal organization blunders.

Two excellent music books were published: Tony Heilbut's *The Gospel Sound*, the best history available of that seminal American music, and Peter Guralnick's *Feel Like Going Home*, containing graceful and heartfelt profiles of American bluesmen, with beautiful chapters on Muddy Waters and Howlin' Wolfe.

Rod Stewart

Courtesy Warner Brothers Records

Isaac Hayes

Courtesy Swan Song Records

Led Zeppelin

Santana

Sly Stone

JANUARY 2, 1971

POP SINGLES

1. MY SWEET LORD/ISN'T IT A PITY
   (George Harrison)
2. ONE LESS BELL TO ANSWER
   (The Fifth Dimension)
3. BLACK MAGIC WOMAN
   (Santana)
4. KNOCK THREE TIMES
   (Dawn)
5. STONED LOVE
   (The Supremes)
6. DOES ANYBODY REALLY KNOW WHAT TIME IT IS?
   (Chicago)
7. NO MATTER WHAT
   (Badfinger)
8. DOMINO
   (Van Morrison)
9. PAY TO THE PIPER
   (Chairmen of the Board)
10. IT'S IMPOSSIBLE
    (Perry Como)

POP ALBUMS

1. ALL THINGS MUST PASS
   (George Harrison)
2. STEPHEN STILLS
   (Stephen Stills)
3. ABRAXAS
   (Santana)
4. JESUS CHRIST SUPERSTAR
   (Original Soundtrack)
5. GRAND FUNK LIVE
   (Grand Funk Railroad)
6. JOHN LENNON/PLASTIC ONO BAND
   (John Lennon and Plastic Ono)
7. GREATEST HITS
   (Sly and the Family Stone)
8. TAP ROOT MANUSCRIPT
   (Neil Diamond)
9. PENDULUM
   (Creedence Clearwater Revival)
10. NEW MORNING
    (Bob Dylan)

BLACK SINGLES

1. IF I WERE YOUR WOMAN
   (Gladys Knight and the Pips)
2. STONED LOVE
   (The Supremes)
3. GROOVE ME
   (King Floyd)
4. PAY TO THE PIPER
   (Chairmen of the Board)
5. BORDER SONG
   (Aretha Franklin)
6. RIVER DEEP, MOUNTAIN HIGH
   (The Supremes and The Four Tops)
7. PUSH AND PULL
   (Rufus Thomas)
8. ARE YOU MY WOMAN
   (The Chi-Lites)
9. ALL I HAVE
   (The Moments)
10. KEEP ON LOVING ME
    (Bobby Bland)

JAZZ ALBUMS

1. TO BE CONTINUED
   (Isaac Hayes)
2. CHAPTER TWO
   (Roberta Flack)
3. MILES DAVIS AT THE FILLMORE
   (Miles Davis)
4. DON ELLIS AT THE FILLMORE
   (Don Ellis)
5. GULA MATARI
   (Quincy Jones)
6. THE ISAAC HAYES MOVEMENT
   (Isaac Hayes)
7. BITCHES BREW
   (Miles Davis)
8. INDIANOLA MISSISSIPPI SEEDS
   (B.B. King)
9. BLACK TALK
   (Charles Earland)
10. PTAH THE EL DAOUD
    (Alice Coltrane)

COUNTRY SINGLES

1. ROSE GARDEN
   (Lynn Anderson)
2. A GOOD YEAR FOR THE ROSES
   (George Jones)
3. COMMERCIAL AFFECTION
   (Mel Tillis)
4. MORNING
   (Jim Ed Brown)
5. COAL MINER'S DAUGHTER
   (Loretta Lynn)
6. I WOULDN'T LIVE IN NEW YORK CITY
   (Buck Owens and the Buckaroos)
7. THE WONDERS YOU PERFORM
   (Tammy Wynette)
8. SHE GOES WALKING THROUGH MY MIND
   (Billy Walker)
9. WHERE HAVE ALL THE HEROES GONE
   (Bill Anderson)
10. AMOS MOSES
    (Jerry Reed)

COUNTRY ALBUMS

1. FOR THE GOOD TIMES
   (Ray Price)
2. TRIBUTE TO THE BEST DAMN FIDDLE PLAYER IN THE WORLD (OR MY TRIBUTE TO BOB WILLS)
   (Merle Haggard)
3. SNOWBIRD
   (Anne Murray)
4. THE JOHNNY CASH SHOW
   (Johnny Cash)
5. THE FIRST LADY
   (Tammy Wynette)
6. FIFTEEN YEARS AGO
   (Conway Twitty)
7. #1
   (Sonny James)
8. DOWN HOMERS
   (Danny Davis and the Nashville Brass)
9. THE FIGHTIN' SIDE OF ME
   (Merle Haggard)
10. BEST OF DOLLY PARTON
    (Dolly Parton)

JANUARY 9, 1971

POP SINGLES

1. KNOCK THREE TIMES
   (Dawn)
2. MY SWEET LORD/ISN'T IT A PITY
   (George Harrison)
3. ONE LESS BELL TO ANSWER
   (The Fifth Dimension)
4. BLACK MAGIC WOMAN
   (Santana)
5. STONED LOVE
   (The Supremes)
6. DOES ANYBODY REALLY KNOW WHAT TIME IT IS?
   (Chicago)
7. DOMINO
   (Van Morrison)
8. PAY TO THE PIPER
   (Chairmen of the Board)
9. IT'S IMPOSSIBLE
   (Perry Como)
10. IMMIGRANT SONG
    (Led Zeppelin)

POP ALBUMS

1. ALL THINGS MUST PASS
   (George Harrison)
2. STEPHEN STILLS
   (Stephen Stills)
3. JOHN LENNON/PLASTIC ONO BAND
   (John Lennon and Plastic Ono)
4. JESUS CHRIST SUPERSTAR
   (Original Soundtrack)
5. PENDULUM
   (Creedence Clearwater Revival)
6. ABRAXAS
   (Santana)
7. GRAND FUNK LIVE
   (Grand Funk Railroad)
8. GREATEST HITS
   (Sly and the Family Stone)
9. TAP ROOT MANUSCRIPT
   (Neil Diamond)
10. ELTON JOHN
    (Elton John)

BLACK SINGLES

1. IF I WERE YOUR WOMAN
   (Gladys Knight and the Pips)
2. STONED LOVE
   (The Supremes)
3. RIVER DEEP, MOUNTAIN HIGH
   (The Supremes and The Four Tops)
4. PAY TO THE PIPER
   (Chairmen of the Board)
5. GROOVE ME
   (King Floyd)
6. PUSH AND PULL
   (Rufus Thomas)
7. ARE YOU MY WOMAN
   (The Chi-Lites)
8. STOP THE WAR—NOW
   (Edwin Starr)
9. YOUR TIME TO CRY
   (Joe Simon)
10. THIS LOVE IS REAL
    (Jackie Wilson)

JAZZ ALBUMS

1. TO BE CONTINUED
   (Isaac Hayes)
2. CHAPTER TWO
   (Roberta Flack)
3. MILES DAVIS AT THE FILLMORE
   (Miles Davis)
4. BITCHES BREW
   (Miles Davis)
5. DON ELLIS AT THE FILLMORE
   (Don Ellis)
6. GULA MATARI
   (Quincy Jones)
7. THE ISAAC HAYES MOVEMENT
   (Isaac Hayes)
8. BLACK TALK
   (Charles Earland)
9. INDIANOLA MISSISSIPPI SEEDS
   (B.B. King)
10. SUMMEN BUKMUN UNYUN
    (Pharaoh Sanders)

COUNTRY SINGLES

1. A GOOD YEAR FOR THE ROSES
   (George Jones)

2. ROSE GARDEN
   (Lynn Anderson)
3. COMMERCIAL AFFECTION
   (Mel Tillis)
4. THE WONDERS YOU PERFORM
   (Tammy Wynette)
5. MORNING
   (Jim Ed Brown)
6. COAL MINER'S DAUGHTER
   (Loretta Lynn)
7. BED OF ROSES
   (The Statler Brothers)
8. I WOULDN'T LIVE IN NEW YORK CITY
   (Buck Owens and the Buckaroos)
9. DAY DRINKIN'
   (Tom T. Hall and Dave Dudley)
10. AMOS MOSES
    (Jerry Reed)

COUNTRY ALBUMS

1. TRIBUTE TO THE BEST DAMN FIDDLE PLAYER IN THE WORLD (OR MY TRIBUTE TO BOB WILLS)
   (Merle Haggard)
2. FOR THE GOOD TIMES
   (Ray Price)
3. THE FIRST LADY
   (Tammy Wynette)
4. THE JOHNNY CASH SHOW
   (Johnny Cash)
5. FIFTEEN YEARS AGO
   (Conway Twitty)
6. #1
   (Sonny James)
7. SNOWBIRD
   (Anne Murray)
8. DOWN HOMERS
   (Danny Davis and the Nashville Brass)
9. ROSE GARDEN
   (Lynn Anderson)
10. THE FIGHTIN' SIDE OF ME
    (Merle Haggard)

JANUARY 16, 1971

POP SINGLES

1. KNOCK THREE TIMES
   (Dawn)
2. MY SWEET LORD/ISN'T IT A PITY
   (George Harrison)
3. ONE LESS BELL TO ANSWER
   (The Fifth Dimension)
4. BLACK MAGIC WOMAN
   (Santana)
5. STONED LOVE
   (The Supremes)
6. DOMINO
   (Van Morrison)
7. PAY TO THE PIPER
   (Chairmen of the Board)
8. IT'S IMPOSSIBLE
   (Perry Como)
9. DOES ANYBODY REALLY KNOW WHAT TIME IT IS?
   (Chicago)
10. IMMIGRANT SONG
    (Led Zeppelin)

POP ALBUMS

1. ALL THINGS MUST PASS
   (George Harrison)
2. JOHN LENNON/PLASTIC ONO BAND
   (John Lennon and Plastic Ono)
3. STEPHEN STILLS
   (Stephen Stills)
4. PENDULUM
   (Creedence Clearwater Revival)

5. JESUS CHRIST SUPERSTAR
   (Original Soundtrack)
6. ABRAXAS
   (Santana)
7. GRAND FUNK LIVE
   (Grand Funk Railroad)
8. ELTON JOHN
   (Elton John)
9. WORST OF THE JEFFERSON AIRPLANE
   (The Jefferson Airplane)
10. GREATEST HITS
    (Sly and the Family Stone)

BLACK SINGLES

1. IF I WERE YOUR WOMAN
   (Gladys Knight and the Pips)
2. STONED LOVE
   (The Supremes)
3. RIVER DEEP, MOUNTAIN HIGH
   (The Supremes and The Four Tops)
4. GROOVE ME
   (King Floyd)
5. YOUR TIME TO CRY
   (Joe Simon)
6. PUSH AND PULL
   (Rufus Thomas)
7. STOP THE WAR—NOW
   (Edwin Starr)
8. ARE YOU MY WOMAN
   (The Chi-Lites)
9. THIS LOVE IS REAL
   (Jackie Wilson)
10. PAY TO THE PIPER
    (Chairmen of the Board)

JAZZ ALBUMS

1. TO BE CONTINUED
   (Isaac Hayes)
2. MILES DAVIS AT THE FILLMORE
   (Miles Davis)
3. CHAPTER TWO
   (Roberta Flack)
4. BITCHES BREW
   (Miles Davis)
5. DON ELLIS AT THE FILLMORE
   (Don Ellis)
6. BLACK TALK
   (Charles Earland)
7. INDIANOLA MISSISSIPPI SEEDS
   (B.B. King)
8. GULA MATARI
   (Quincy Jones)
9. SUMMEN BUKMUN UNYUN
   (Pharaoh Sanders)
10. THE ISAAC HAYES MOVEMENT
    (Isaac Hayes)

COUNTRY SINGLES

1. A GOOD YEAR FOR THE ROSES
   (George Jones)
2. ROSE GARDEN
   (Lynn Anderson)
3. THE WONDERS YOU PERFORM
   (Tammy Wynette)
4. BED OF ROSES
   (The Statler Brothers)
5. JOSHUA
   (Dolly Parton)
6. FLESH AND BLOOD
   (Johnny Cash)
7. DAY DRINKIN'
   (Tom T. Hall and Dave Dudley)
8. MORNING
   (Jim Ed Brown)
9. PADRE
   (Marty Robbins)
10. WAITIN' FOR A TRAIN
    (Jerry Lee Lewis)

COUNTRY ALBUMS

1. TRIBUTE TO THE BEST DAMN FIDDLE PLAYER IN THE WORLD (OR MY TRIBUTE TO BOB WILLS)
   (Merle Haggard)
2. FOR THE GOOD TIMES
   (Ray Price)
3. THE FIRST LADY
   (Tammy Wynette)
4. ROSE GARDEN
   (Lynn Anderson)
5. THE JOHNNY CASH SHOW
   (Johnny Cash)
6. FIFTEEN YEARS AGO
   (Conway Twitty)
7. SNOWBIRD
   (Anne Murray)
8. THE FIGHTIN' SIDE OF ME
   (Merle Haggard)
9. #1
   (Sonny James)
10. THE BEST OF GEORGE JONES
    (George Jones)

JANUARY 23, 1971

POP SINGLES

1. KNOCK THREE TIMES
   (Dawn)
2. MY SWEET LORD/ISN'T IT A PITY
   (George Harrison)
3. ONE LESS BELL TO ANSWER
   (The Fifth Dimension)
4. GROOVE ME
   (King Floyd)
5. LONELY DAYS
   (The Bee Gees)
6. STONED LOVE
   (The Supremes)
7. PAY TO THE PIPER
   (Chairmen of the Board)
8. IT'S IMPOSSIBLE
   (Perry Como)
9. YOUR SONG
   (Elton John)
10. IF I WERE YOUR WOMAN
    (Gladys Knight and the Pips)

POP ALBUMS

1. ALL THINGS MUST PASS
   (George Harrison)
2. JOHN LENNON/PLASTIC ONO BAND
   (John Lennon and Plastic Ono)
3. PENDULUM
   (Creedence Clearwater Revival)
4. JESUS CHRIST SUPERSTAR
   (Original Soundtrack)
5. STEPHEN STILLS
   (Stephen Stills)
6. ABRAXAS
   (Santana)
7. ELTON JOHN
   (Elton John)
8. GRAND FUNK LIVE
   (Grand Funk Railroad)
9. WORST OF THE JEFFERSON AIRPLANE
   (The Jefferson Airplane)
10. THE PARTRIDGE FAMILY ALBUM
    (The Partridge Family)

BLACK SINGLES

1. IF I WERE YOUR WOMAN
   (Gladys Knight and the Pips)
2. GROOVE ME
   (King Floyd)

3. RIVER DEEP, MOUNTAIN HIGH
   (The Supremes and The Four Tops)
4. YOUR TIME TO CRY
   (Joe Simon)
5. PUSH AND PULL
   (Rufus Thomas)
6. STOP THE WAR—NOW
   (Edwin Starr)
7. SOMEBODY'S WATCHING YOU
   (Little Sister)
8. ARE YOU MY WOMAN
   (The Chi-Lites)
9. THIS LOVE IS REAL
   (Jackie Wilson)
10. GET UP, GET INTO IT, GET INVOLVED
    (James Brown)

JAZZ ALBUMS

1. TO BE CONTINUED
   (Isaac Hayes)
2. MILES DAVIS AT THE FILLMORE
   (Miles Davis)
3. CHAPTER TWO
   (Roberta Flack)
4. BITCHES BREW
   (Miles Davis)
5. GULA MATARI
   (Quincy Jones)
6. DON ELLIS AT THE FILLMORE
   (Don Ellis)
7. INDIANOLA MISSISSIPPI SEEDS
   (B.B. King)
8. BLACK TALK
   (Charles Earland)
9. THE ISAAC HAYES MOVEMENT
   (Isaac Hayes)
10. SUMMEN BUKMUN UNYUN
    (Pharaoh Sanders)

COUNTRY SINGLES

1. THE WONDERS YOU PERFORM
   (Tammy Wynette)
2. ROSE GARDEN
   (Lynn Anderson)
3. FLESH AND BLOOD
   (Johnny Cash)
4. BED OF ROSES
   (The Statler Brothers)
5. JOSHUA
   (Dolly Parton)
6. A GOOD YEAR FOR THE ROSES
   (George Jones)
7. DAY DRINKIN'
   (Tom T. Hall and Dave Dudley)
8. PADRE
   (Marty Robbins)
9. HELP ME MAKE IT THROUGH THE NIGHT
   (Sammi Stewart)
10. GUESS WHO
    (Slim Whitman)

COUNTRY ALBUMS

1. ROSE GARDEN
   (Lynn Anderson)
2. THE JOHNNY CASH SHOW
   (Johnny Cash)
3. FOR THE GOOD TIMES
   (Ray Price)
4. TRIBUTE TO THE BEST DAMN FIDDLE
   PLAYER IN THE WORLD (OR MY TRIBUTE
   TO BOB WILLS)
   (Merle Haggard)
5. FIFTEEN YEARS AGO
   (Conway Twitty)
6. THE FIRST LADY
   (Tammy Wynette)
7. #1
   (Sonny James)
8. THE FIGHTIN' SIDE OF ME
   (Merle Haggard)

9. THE BEST OF GEORGE JONES
   (George Jones)
10. SNOWBIRD
    (Anne Murray)

JANUARY 30, 1971

POP SINGLES

1. KNOCK THREE TIMES
   (Dawn)
2. MY SWEET LORD/ISN'T IT A PITY
   (George Harrison)
3. LONELY DAYS
   (The Bee Gees)
4. GROOVE ME
   (King Floyd)
5. ONE LESS BELL TO ANSWER
   (The Fifth Dimension)
6. YOUR SONG
   (Elton John)
7. IT'S IMPOSSIBLE
   (Perry Como)
8. ROSE GARDEN
   (Lynn Anderson)
9. IF I WERE YOUR WOMAN
   (Gladys Knight and the Pips)
10. LOVE THE ONE YOU'RE WITH
    (Stephen Stills)

POP ALBUMS

1. ALL THINGS MUST PASS
   (George Harrison)
2. JESUS CHRIST SUPERSTAR
   (Original Soundtrack)
3. PENDULUM
   (Creedence Clearwater Revival)
4. JOHN LENNON/PLASTIC ONO BAND
   (John Lennon and Plastic Ono)
5. ABRAXAS
   (Santana)
6. THE PARTRIDGE FAMILY ALBUM
   (The Partridge Family)
7. ELTON JOHN
   (Elton John)
8. WORST OF THE JEFFERSON AIRPLANE
   (The Jefferson Airplane)
9. GRAND FUNK LIVE
   (Grand Funk Railroad)
10. STEPHEN STILLS
    (Stephen Stills)

BLACK SINGLES

1. GROOVE ME
   (King Floyd)
2. PUSH AND PULL
   (Rufus Thomas)
3. IF I WERE YOUR WOMAN
   (Gladys Knight and the Pips)
4. RIVER DEEP, MOUNTAIN HIGH
   (The Supremes and The Four Tops)
5. YOUR TIME TO CRY
   (Joe Simon)
6. STOP THE WAR—NOW
   (Edwin Starr)
7. THIS LOVE IS REAL
   (Jackie Wilson)
8. GET UP, GET INTO IT, GET INVOLVED
   (James Brown)
9. REMEMBER ME
   (Diana Ross)
10. I'M SO PROUD
    (Main Ingredient)

JAZZ ALBUMS

1. TO BE CONTINUED
   (Isaac Hayes)

2. MILES DAVIS AT THE FILLMORE
   (Miles Davis)
3. CHAPTER TWO
   (Roberta Flack)
4. BITCHES BREW
   (Miles Davis)
5. INDIANOLA MISSISSIPPI SEEDS
   (B.B. King)
6. THE ISAAC HAYES MOVEMENT
   (Isaac Hayes)
7. DON ELLIS AT THE FILLMORE
   (Don Ellis)
8. BLACK TALK
   (Charles Earland)
9. BRIDGE OVER TROUBLED WATER
   (Paul Desmond)
10. GULA MATARI
    (Quincy Jones)

COUNTRY SINGLES

1. FLESH AND BLOOD
   (Johnny Cash)
2. JOSHUA
   (Dolly Parton)
3. BED OF ROSES
   (The Statler Brothers)
4. HELP ME MAKE IT THROUGH THE NIGHT
   (Sammi Stewart)
5. RAININ' IN MY HEART
   (Hank Williams Jr.)
6. PADRE
   (Marty Robbins)
7. THE WONDERS YOU PERFORM
   (Tammy Wynette)
8. GUESS WHO
   (Slim Whitman)
9. ROSE GARDEN
   (Lynn Anderson)
10. THE PROMISED LAND
    (Freddie Weller)

COUNTRY ALBUMS

1. ROSE GARDEN
   (Lynn Anderson)
2. TRIBUTE TO THE BEST DAMN FIDDLE
   PLAYER IN THE WORLD (OR MY TRIBUTE
   TO BOB WILLS)
   (Merle Haggard)
3. FOR THE GOOD TIMES
   (Ray Price)
4. THE JOHNNY CASH SHOW
   (Johnny Cash)
5. FIFTEEN YEARS AGO
   (Conway Twitty)
6. THE FIRST LADY
   (Tammy Wynette)
7. #1
   (Sonny James)
8. CHARLEY PRIDE'S 10th ALBUM
   (Charley Pride)
9. THE FIGHTIN' SIDE OF ME
   (Merle Haggard)
10. ALL FOR THE LOVE OF SUNSHINE
    (Hank Williams Jr. and The Mike Curb
    Congregation)

FEBRUARY 6, 1971

POP SINGLES

1. LONELY DAYS
   (The Bee Gees)
2. KNOCK THREE TIMES
   (Dawn)
3. ROSE GARDEN
   (Lynn Anderson)
4. MY SWEET LORD/ISN'T IT A PITY
   (George Harrison)

5. GROOVE ME
   (King Floyd)
6. I HEAR YOU KNOCKING
   (Dave Edmunds)
7. YOUR SONG
   (Elton John)
8. IF I WERE YOUR WOMAN
   (Gladys Knight and the Pips)
9. MAMA'S PEARL
   (The Jackson 5)
10. ONE BAD APPLE
   (The Osmonds)

POP ALBUMS

1. JESUS CHRIST SUPERSTAR
   (Original Soundtrack)
2. ALL THINGS MUST PASS
   (George Harrison)
3. JOHN LENNON/PLASTIC ONO BAND
   (John Lennon and Plastic Ono)
4. PENDULUM
   (Creedence Clearwater Revival)
5. ABRAXAS
   (Santana)
6. THE PARTRIDGE FAMILY ALBUM
   (The Partridge Family)
7. ELTON JOHN
   (Elton John)
8. WORST OF THE JEFFERSON AIRPLANE
   (The Jefferson Airplane)
9. TUMBLEWEED CONNECTION
   (Elton John)
10. GREATEST HITS
   (Sly and the Family Stone)

BLACK SINGLES

1. PUSH AND PULL
   (Rufus Thomas)
2. YOUR TIME TO CRY
   (Joe Simon)
3. THIS LOVE IS REAL
   (Jackie Wilson)
4. GROOVE ME
   (King Floyd)
5. GET UP, GET INTO IT, GET INVOLVED
   (James Brown)
6. JODY GOT YOUR GIRL AND GONE
   (Johnnie Taylor)
7. REMEMBER ME
   (Diana Ross)
8. MAMA'S PEARL
   (The Jackson 5)
9. I'M SO PROUD
   (Main Ingredient)
10. DON'T LET THE GREEN GRASS FOOL YOU
   (Wilson Pickett)

JAZZ ALBUMS

1. TO BE CONTINUED
   (Isaac Hayes)
2. MILES DAVIS AT THE FILLMORE
   (Miles Davis)
3. BITCHES BREW
   (Miles Davis)
4. CHAPTER TWO
   (Roberta Flack)
5. THE ISAAC HAYES MOVEMENT
   (Isaac Hayes)
6. INDIANOLA MISSISSIPPI SEEDS
   (B.B. King)
7. BLACK TALK
   (Charles Earland)
8. BEST OF JOHN COLTRANE
   (John Coltrane)
9. BRIDGE OVER TROUBLED WATER
   (Paul Desmond)
10. THEM CHANGES
   (Ramsey Lewis)

COUNTRY SINGLES

1. JOSHUA
   (Dolly Parton)
2. HELP ME MAKE IT THROUGH THE NIGHT
   (Sammi Stewart)
3. BED OF ROSES
   (The Statler Brothers)
4. FLESH AND BLOOD
   (Johnny Cash)
5. RAININ' IN MY HEART
   (Hank Williams Jr. and The Mike Curb
   Congregation)
6. PADRE
   (Marty Robbins)
7. THE PROMISED LAND
   (Freddie Weller)
8. GUESS WHO
   (Slim Whitman)
9. COME SUNDOWN
   (Bobby Bare)
10. SHERIFF OF BOONE COUNTY
   (Kenny Price)

COUNTRY ALBUMS

1. ROSE GARDEN
   (Lynn Anderson)
2. TRIBUTE TO THE BEST DAMN FIDDLE
   PLAYER IN THE WORLD (OR MY TRIBUTE
   TO BOB WILLS)
   (Merle Haggard)
3. FOR THE GOOD TIMES
   (Ray Price)
4. FIFTEEN YEARS AGO
   (Conway Twitty)
5. THE FIRST LADY
   (Tammy Wynette)
6. ALL FOR THE LOVE OF SUNSHINE
   (Hank Williams Jr. and The Mike Curb
   Congregation)
7. CHARLEY PRIDE'S 10th ALBUM
   (Charley Pride)
8. THE JOHNNY CASH SHOW
   (Johnny Cash)
9. THE FIGHTIN' SIDE OF ME
   (Merle Haggard)
10. BED OF ROSES
   (The Statler Brothers)

FEBRUARY 13, 1971

POP SINGLES

1. ROSE GARDEN
   (Lynn Anderson)
2. ONE BAD APPLE
   (The Osmonds)
3. LONELY DAYS
   (The Bee Gees)
4. I HEAR YOU KNOCKING
   (Dave Edmunds)
5. KNOCK THREE TIMES
   (Dawn)
6. MAMA'S PEARL
   (The Jackson 5)
7. MY SWEET LORD/ISN'T IT A PITY
   (George Harrison)
8. WATCHING SCOTTY GROW
   (Bobby Goldsboro)
9. IF I WERE YOUR WOMAN
   (Gladys Knight and the Pips)
10. REMEMBER ME
   (Diana Ross)

POP ALBUMS

1. ALL THINGS MUST PASS
   (George Harrison)

2. JESUS CHRIST SUPERSTAR
   (Original Soundtrack)
3. PENDULUM
   (Creedence Clearwater Revival)
4. JOHN LENNON/PLASTIC ONO BAND
   (John Lennon and Plastic Ono)
5. ELTON JOHN
   (Elton John)
6. TUMBLEWEED CONNECTION
   (Elton John)
7. ABRAXAS
   (Santana)
8. THE PARTRIDGE FAMILY ALBUM
   (The Partridge Family)
9. LOVE STORY
   (Original Soundtrack)
10. GREATEST HITS
   (Sly and the Family Stone)

BLACK SINGLES

1. YOUR TIME TO CRY
   (Joe Simon)
2. JODY GOT YOUR GIRL AND GONE
   (Johnnie Taylor)
3. THIS LOVE IS REAL
   (Jackie Wilson)
4. PUSH AND PULL
   (Rufus Thomas)
5. GET UP, GET INTO IT, GET INVOLVED
   (James Brown)
6. MAMA'S PEARL
   (The Jackson 5)
7. REMEMBER ME
   (Diana Ross)
8. DON'T LET THE GREEN GRASS FOOL YOU
   (Wilson Pickett)
9. I'M SO PROUD
   (Main Ingredient)
10. GROOVE ME
   (King Floyd)

COUNTRY SINGLES

1. HELP ME MAKE IT THROUGH THE NIGHT
   (Sammi Stewart)
2. RAININ' IN MY HEART
   (Hank Williams Jr. and The Mike Curb
   Congregation)
3. JOSHUA
   (Dolly Parton)
4. THE PROMISED LAND
   (Freddie Weller)
5. COME SUNDOWN
   (Bobby Bare)
6. BED OF ROSES
   (The Statler Brothers)
7. GUESS WHO
   (Slim Whitman)
8. SHERIFF OF BOONE COUNTY
   (Kenny Price)
9. ONE HUNDRED CHILDREN
   (Tom T. Hall)
10. SHE WAKES ME WITH A KISS
   (Nat Stuckey)

COUNTRY ALBUMS

1. TRIBUTE TO THE BEST DAMN FIDDLE
   PLAYER IN THE WORLD (OR MY TRIBUTE
   TO BOB WILLS)
   (Merle Haggard)
2. FOR THE GOOD TIMES
   (Ray Price)
3. ROSE GARDEN
   (Lynn Anderson)
4. ALL FOR THE LOVE OF SUNSHINE
   (Hank Williams Jr. and The Mike Curb
   Congregation)
5. THE FIRST LADY
   (Tammy Wynette)
6. FIFTEEN YEARS AGO
   (Conway Twitty)

7. CHARLEY PRIDE'S 10th ALBUM
    (*Charley Pride*)
8. BED OF ROSES
    (*The Statler Brothers*)
9. THE JOHNNY CASH SHOW
    (*Johnny Cash*)
10. THAT'S THE WAY IT IS
    (*Elvis Presley*)

FEBRUARY 20, 1971

POP SINGLES

1. ONE BAD APPLE
    (*The Osmonds*)
2. ROSE GARDEN
    (*Lynn Anderson*)
3. I HEAR YOU KNOCKING
    (*Dave Edmunds*)
4. MAMA'S PEARL
    (*The Jackson 5*)
5. KNOCK THREE TIMES
    (*Dawn*)
6. WATCHING SCOTTY GROW
    (*Bobby Goldsboro*)
7. LONELY DAYS
    (*The Bee Gees*)
8. MR. BOJANGLES
    (*Nitty Gritty Dirt Band*)
9. IF YOU COULD READ MY MIND
    (*Gordon Lightfoot*)
10. REMEMBER ME
    (*Diana Ross*)

POP ALBUMS

1. ALL THINGS MUST PASS
    (*George Harrison*)
2. JESUS CHRIST SUPERSTAR
    (*Original Soundtrack*)
3. PENDULUM
    (*Creedence Clearwater Revival*)
4. CHICAGO III
    (*Chicago*)
5. TUMBLEWEED CONNECTION
    (*Elton John*)
6. LOVE STORY
    (*Original Soundtrack*)
7. ABRAXAS
    (*Santana*)
8. ELTON JOHN
    (*Elton John*)
9. PEARL
    (*Janis Joplin*)
10. JOHN LENNON/PLASTIC ONO BAND
    (*John Lennon and Plastic Ono*)

BLACK SINGLES

1. JODY GOT YOUR GIRL AND GONE
    (*Johnnie Taylor*)
2. YOUR TIME TO CRY
    (*Joe Simon*)
3. MAMA'S PEARL
    (*The Jackson 5*)
4. DON'T LET THE GREEN GRASS FOOL YOU
    (*Wilson Pickett*)
5. GET UP, GET INTO IT, GET INVOLVED
    (*James Brown*)
6. PUSH AND PULL
    (*Rufus Thomas*)
7. YOU'RE A BIG GIRL NOW
    (*The Stylistics*)
8. I'M SO PROUD
    (*Main Ingredient*)
9. I LOVE YOU FOR ALL SEASONS
    (*Fuzz*)
10. ONE BAD APPLE
    (*The Osmonds*)

JAZZ ALBUMS

1. TO BE CONTINUED
    (*Isaac Hayes*)
2. MILES DAVIS AT THE FILLMORE
    (*Miles Davis*)
3. BITCHES BREW
    (*Miles Davis*)
4. CHAPTER TWO
    (*Roberta Flack*)
5. THE ISAAC HAYES MOVEMENT
    (*Isaac Hayes*)
6. INDIANOLA MISSISSIPPI SEEDS
    (*B.B. King*)
7. DON ELLIS AT THE FILLMORE
    (*Don Ellis*)
8. BEST OF JOHN COLTRANE
    (*John Coltrane*)
9. FREE SPEECH
    (*Eddie Harris*)
10. BLACK DROPS
    (*Charles Earland*)

COUNTRY SINGLES

1. RAININ' IN MY HEART
    (*Hank Williams Jr. and The Mike Curb Congregation*)
2. HELP ME MAKE IT THROUGH THE NIGHT
    (*Sammi Stewart*)
3. COME SUNDOWN
    (*Bobby Bare*)
4. THE PROMISED LAND
    (*Freddie Weller*)
5. JOSHUA
    (*Dolly Parton*)
6. SHERIFF OF BOONE COUNTY
    (*Kenny Price*)
7. A WOMAN ALWAYS KNOWS
    (*David Houston*)
8. ONE HUNDRED CHILDREN
    (*Tom T. Hall*)
9. SHE WAKES ME WITH A KISS
    (*Nat Stuckey*)
10. WHERE IS MY CASTLE
    (*Connie Smith*)

COUNTRY ALBUMS

1. ROSE GARDEN
    (*Lynn Anderson*)
2. FOR THE GOOD TIMES
    (*Ray Price*)
3. TRIBUTE TO THE BEST DAMN FIDDLE PLAYER IN THE WORLD (OR MY TRIBUTE TO BOB WILLS)
    (*Merle Haggard*)
4. ALL FOR THE LOVE OF SUNSHINE
    (*Hank Williams Jr. and The Mike Curb Congregation*)
5. JOSHUA
    (*Dolly Parton*)
6. SHERIFF OF BOONE COUNTY
    (*Kenny Price*)
7. A WOMAN ALWAYS KNOWS
    (*David Houston*)
8. ONE HUNDRED CHILDREN
    (*Tom T. Hall*)
9. SHE WAKES ME WITH A KISS
    (*Nat Stuckey*)
10. WHERE IS MY CASTLE
    (*Connie Smith*)

FEBRUARY 27, 1971

POP SINGLES

1. ONE BAD APPLE
    (*The Osmonds*)

2. MAMA'S PEARL
    (*The Jackson 5*)
3. I HEAR YOU KNOCKING
    (*Dave Edmunds*)
4. IF YOU COULD READ MY MIND
    (*Gordon Lightfoot*)
5. SWEET MARY
    (*Wadsworth Mansion*)
6. MR. BOJANGLES
    (*Nitty Gritty Dirt Band*)
7. WATCHING SCOTTY GROW
    (*Bobby Goldsboro*)
8. HAVE YOU EVER SEEN THE RAIN/HEY TONIGHT
    (*Creedence Clearwater Revival*)
9. ROSE GARDEN
    (*Lynn Anderson*)
10. LOVE STORY
    (*Henry Mancini*)

POP ALBUMS

1. CHICAGO III
    (*Chicago*)
2. JESUS CHRIST SUPERSTAR
    (*Original Soundtrack*)
3. ALL THINGS MUST PASS
    (*George Harrison*)
4. LOVE STORY
    (*Original Soundtrack*)
5. TUMBLEWEED CONNECTION
    (*Elton John*)
6. PENDULUM
    (*Creedence Clearwater Revival*)
7. ABRAXAS
    (*Santana*)
8. PEARL
    (*Janis Joplin*)
9. ELTON JOHN
    (*Elton John*)
10. NANTUCKET SLEIGHRIDE
    (*Mountain*)

BLACK SINGLES

1. JODY GOT YOUR GIRL AND GONE
    (*Johnnie Taylor*)
2. MAMA'S PEARL
    (*The Jackson 5*)
3. DON'T LET THE GREEN GRASS FOOL YOU
    (*Wilson Pickett*)
4. ONE BAD APPLE
    (*The Osmonds*)
5. YOUR TIME TO CRY
    (*Joe Simon*)
6. GET IT, GET INTO IT, GET INVOLVED
    (*James Brown*)
7. YOU'RE A BIG GIRL NOW
    (*The Stylistics*)
8. JUST MY IMAGINATION
    (*Temptations*)
9. I LOVE YOU FOR ALL SEASONS
    (*Fuzz*)
10. PUSH AND PULL
    (*Rufus Thomas*)

JAZZ ALBUMS

1. TO BE CONTINUED
    (*Isaac Hayes*)
2. MILES DAVIS AT THE FILLMORE
    (*Miles Davis*)
3. BITCHES BREW
    (*Miles Davis*)
4. CHAPTER TWO
    (*Roberta Flack*)
5. DON ELLIS AT THE FILLMORE
    (*Don Ellis*)
6. THE ISAAC HAYES MOVEMENT
    (*Isaac Hayes*)
7. FREE SPEECH
    (*Eddie Harris*)
8. INDIANOLA MISSISSIPPI SEEDS
    (*B.B. King*)

9. BEST OF JOHN COLTRANE
   (*John Coltrane*)
10. BRIDGE OVER TROUBLED WATER
    (*Paul Desmond*)

COUNTRY SINGLES

1. COME SUNDOWN
   (*Bobby Bare*)
2. A WOMAN ALWAYS KNOWS
   (*David Houston*)
3. THE PROMISED LAND
   (*Freddie Weller*)
4. HELP ME MAKE IT THROUGH THE NIGHT
   (*Sammi Stewart*)
5. RAININ' IN MY HEART
   (*Hank Williams Jr. and The Mike Curb Congregation*)
6. SHERIFF OF BOONE COUNTY
   (*Kenny Price*)
7. THERE GOES MY EVERYTHING/I REALLY DON'T WANT TO KNOW
   (*Elvis Presley*)
8. WHERE IS MY CASTLE
   (*Connie Smith*)
9. ONE HUNDRED CHILDREN
   (*Tom T. Hall*)
10. WATCHING SCOTTY GROW
    (*Bobby Goldsboro*)

COUNTRY ALBUMS

1. ROSE GARDEN
   (*Lynn Anderson*)
2. FOR THE GOOD TIMES
   (*Ray Price*)
3. TRIBUTE TO THE BEST DAMN FIDDLE PLAYER IN THE WORLD (OR MY TRIBUTE TO BOB WILLS)
   (*Merle Haggard*)
4. FROM ME TO YOU
   (*Charley Pride*)
5. COAL MINER'S DAUGHTER
   (*Loretta Lynn*)
6. BED OF ROSES
   (*The Statler Brothers*)
7. ALL FOR THE LOVE OF SUNSHINE
   (*Hank Williams Jr. and The Mike Curb Congregation*)
8. FIFTEEN YEARS AGO
   (*Conway Twitty*)
9. THERE MUST BE MORE TO LOVE THAN THIS
   (*Jerry Lee Lewis*)
10. MORNING
    (*Jim Ed Brown*)

MARCH 6, 1971

POP SINGLES

1. ONE BAD APPLE
   (*The Osmonds*)
2. MAMA'S PEARL
   (*The Jackson 5*)
3. IF YOU COULD READ MY MIND
   (*Gordon Lightfoot*)
4. HAVE YOU EVER SEEN THE RAIN/HEY TONIGHT
   (*Creedence Clearwater Revival*)
5. SWEET MARY
   (*Wadsworth Mansion*)
6. MR. BOJANGLES
   (*Nitty Gritty Dirt Band*)
7. AMOS MOSES
   (*Jerry Reed*)
8. I HEAR YOU KNOCKING
   (*Dave Edmunds*)
9. LOVE STORY
   (*Henry Mancini*)
10. ME AND BOBBY McGEE
    (*Janis Joplin*)

POP ALBUMS

1. CHICAGO III
   (*Chicago*)
2. JESUS CHRIST SUPERSTAR
   (*Original Soundtrack*)
3. LOVE STORY
   (*Original Soundtrack*)
4. PEARL
   (*Janis Joplin*)
5. ALL THINGS MUST PASS
   (*George Harrison*)
6. PENDULUM
   (*Creedence Clearwater Revival*)
7. ABRAXAS
   (*Santana*)
8. TUMBLEWEED CONNECTION
   (*Elton John*)
9. ELTON JOHN
   (*Elton John*)
10. NANTUCKET SLEIGHRIDE
    (*Mountain*)

BLACK SINGLES

1. MAMA'S PEARL
   (*The Jackson 5*)
2. JODY GOT YOUR GIRL AND GONE
   (*Johnnie Taylor*)
3. DON'T LET THE GREEN GRASS FOOL YOU
   (*Wilson Pickett*)
4. ONE BAD APPLE
   (*The Osmonds*)
5. JUST MY IMAGINATION
   (*Temptations*)
6. YOU'RE A BIG GIRL NOW
   (*The Stylistics*)
7. YOUR TIME TO CRY
   (*Joe Simon*)
8. WHAT'S GOING ON
   (*Marvin Gaye*)
9. I LOVE YOU FOR ALL SEASONS
   (*Fuzz*)
10. GET UP, GET INTO IT, GET INVOLVED
    (*James Brown*)

JAZZ ALBUMS

1. MILES DAVIS AT THE FILLMORE
   (*Miles Davis*)
2. TO BE CONTINUED
   (*Isaac Hayes*)
3. BITCHES BREW
   (*Miles Davis*)
4. CHAPTER TWO
   (*Roberta Flack*)
5. THEM CHANGES
   (*Ramsey Lewis*)
6. THE ISAAC HAYES MOVEMENT
   (*Isaac Hayes*)
7. FREE SPEECH
   (*Eddie Harris*)
8. DON ELLIS AT THE FILLMORE
   (*Don Ellis*)
9. STRAIGHT LIFE
   (*Freddie Hubbard*)
10. THE PRICE YOU GOT TO PAY TO BE FREE
    (*Cannonball Adderley*)

COUNTRY SINGLES

1. A WOMAN ALWAYS KNOWS
   (*David Houston*)
2. THE PROMISED LAND
   (*Freddie Weller*)
3. COME SUNDOWN
   (*Bobby Bare*)
4. THERE GOES MY EVERYTHING/I REALLY DON'T WANT TO KNOW
   (*Elvis Presley*)
5. HELP ME MAKE IT THROUGH THE NIGHT
   (*Sammi Stewart*)

6. WATCHING SCOTTY GROW
   (*Bobby Goldsboro*)
7. AFTER THE FIRE IS GONE/THE ONE I CAN'T LIVE WITHOUT
   (*Conway Twitty and Loretta Lynn*)
8. WHERE IS MY CASTLE
   (*Connie Smith*)
9. I'M GONNA KEEP ON LOVING YOU
   (*Bobby Walker*)
10. I'D RATHER LOVE YOU
    (*Charley Pride*)

COUNTRY ALBUMS

1. ROSE GARDEN
   (*Lynn Anderson*)
2. FROM ME TO YOU
   (*Charley Pride*)
3. FOR THE GOOD TIMES
   (*Ray Price*)
4. COAL MINER'S DAUGHTER
   (*Loretta Lynn*)
5. TRIBUTE TO THE BEST DAMN FIDDLE PLAYER IN THE WORLD (OR MY TRIBUTE TO BOB WILLS)
   (*Merle Haggard*)
6. BED OF ROSES
   (*The Statler Brothers*)
7. THERE MUST BE MORE TO LOVE THAN THIS
   (*Jerry Lee Lewis*)
8. MORNING
   (*Jim Ed Brown*)
9. FIFTEEN YEARS AGO
   (*Conway Twitty*)
10. THE FIRST LADY
    (*Tammy Wynette*)

MARCH 13, 1971

POP SINGLES

1. ONE BAD APPLE
   (*The Osmonds*)
2. MAMA'S PEARL
   (*The Jackson 5*)
3. HAVE YOU EVER SEEN THE RAIN/HEY TONIGHT
   (*Creedence Clearwater Revival*)
4. SHE'S A LADY
   (*Tom Jones*)
5. ME AND BOBBY McGEE
   (*Janis Joplin*)
6. AMOS MOSES
   (*Jerry Reed*)
7. DOESN'T SOMEBODY WANT TO BE WANTED
   (*The Partridge Family*)
8. FOR ALL WE KNOW
   (*The Carpenters*)
9. LOVE STORY
   (*Henry Mancini*)
10. JUST MY IMAGINATION
    (*Temptations*)

POP ALBUMS

1. PEARL
   (*Janis Joplin*)
2. LOVE STORY
   (*Original Soundtrack*)
3. CHICAGO III
   (*Chicago*)
4. JESUS CHRIST SUPERSTAR
   (*Original Soundtrack*)
5. ALL THINGS MUST PASS
   (*George Harrison*)
6. TUMBLEWEED CONNECTION
   (*Elton John*)
7. PENDULUM
   (*Creedence Clearwater Revival*)

8. ABRAXAS
   (Santana)
9. ELTON JOHN
   (Elton John)
10. IF YOU COULD READ MY MIND
    (Gordon Lightfoot)

BLACK SINGLES

1. JUST MY IMAGINATION
   (Temptations)
2. MAMA'S PEARL
   (The Jackson 5)
3. DON'T LET THE GREEN GRASS FOOL YOU
   (Wilson Pickett)
4. WHAT'S GOING ON
   (Marvin Gaye)
5. PROUD MARY
   (Ike and Tina Turner)
6. YOU'RE ALL I NEED TO GET BY
   (Aretha Franklin)
7. JODY GOT YOUR GIRL AND GONE
   (Johnnie Taylor)
8. ONE BAD APPLE
   (The Osmonds)
9. I LOVE YOU FOR ALL SEASONS
   (Fuzz)
10. AIN'T GOT TIME
    (The Impressions)

JAZZ ALBUMS

1. TO BE CONTINUED
   (Isaac Hayes)
2. BITCHES BREW
   (Miles Davis)
3. MILES DAVIS AT THE FILLMORE
   (Miles Davis)
4. CHAPTER TWO
   (Roberta Flack)
5. DON ELLIS AT THE FILLMORE
   (Don Ellis)
6. THE PRICE YOU GOT TO PAY TO BE FREE
   (Cannonball Adderley)
7. STRAIGHT LIFE
   (Freddie Hubbard)
8. THEM CHANGES
   (Ramsey Lewis)
9. THE ISAAC HAYES MOVEMENT
   (Isaac Hayes)
10. FREE SPEECH
    (Eddie Harris)

COUNTRY SINGLES

1. AFTER THE FIRE IS GONE/THE ONE I CAN'T LIVE WITHOUT
   (Conway Twitty and Loretta Lynn)
2. I'D RATHER LOVE YOU
   (Charley Pride)
3. A WOMAN ALWAYS KNOWS
   (David Houston)
4. THERE GOES MY EVERYTHING/I REALLY DON'T WANT TO KNOW
   (Elvis Presley)
5. I'M GONNA KEEP ON LOVING YOU
   (Bobby Walker)
6. WATCHING SCOTTY GROW
   (Bobby Goldsboro)
7. ARMS OF A FOOL
   (Mel Tillis)
8. COME SUNDOWN
   (Bobby Bare)
9. THE PROMISED LAND
   (Freddie Weller)
10. HELP ME MAKE IT THROUGH THE NIGHT
    (Sammi Stewart)

COUNTRY ALBUMS

1. FROM ME TO YOU
   (Charley Pride)

2. ROSE GARDEN
   (Lynn Anderson)
3. COAL MINER'S DAUGHTER
   (Loretta Lynn)
4. BED OF ROSES
   (The Statler Brothers)
5. FOR THE GOOD TIMES
   (Ray Price)
6. TRIBUTE TO THE BEST DAMN FIDDLE PLAYER IN THE WORLD (OR MY TRIBUTE TO BOB WILLS)
   (Merle Haggard)
7. THERE MUST BE MORE TO LOVE THAN THIS
   (Jerry Lee Lewis)
8. MORNING
   (Jim Ed Brown)
9. WE ONLY MAKE BELIEVE
   (Conway Twitty)
10. ELVIS COUNTRY
    (Elvis Presley)

MARCH 20, 1971

POP SINGLES

1. ME AND BOBBY McGEE
   (Janis Joplin)
2. SHE'S A LADY
   (Tom Jones)
3. HAVE YOU EVER SEEN THE RAIN/HEY TONIGHT
   (Creedence Clearwater Revival)
4. ONE BAD APPLE
   (The Osmonds)
5. AMOS MOSES
   (Jerry Reed)
6. DOESN'T SOMEBODY WANT TO BE WANTED
   (The Partridge Family)
7. FOR ALL WE KNOW
   (The Carpenters)
8. JUST MY IMAGINATION
   (Temptations)
9. MAMA'S PEARL
   (The Jackson 5)
10. PROUD MARY
    (Ike and Tina Turner)

POP ALBUMS

1. PEARL
   (Janis Joplin)
2. LOVE STORY
   (Original Soundtrack)
3. JESUS CHRIST SUPERSTAR
   (Original Soundtrack)
4. LOVE STORY
   (Andy Williams)
5. TUMBLEWEED CONNECTION
   (Elton John)
6. CHICAGO III
   (Chicago)
7. CRY OF LOVE
   (Jimi Hendrix)
8. ABRAXAS
   (Santana)
9. STONEY END
   (Barbra Streisand)
10. IF YOU COULD READ MY MIND
    (Gordon Lightfoot)

BLACK SINGLES

1. WHAT'S GOING ON
   (Marvin Gaye)
2. JUST MY IMAGINATION
   (Temptations)
3. PROUD MARY
   (Ike and Tina Turner)

4. YOU'RE ALL I NEED TO GET BY
   (Aretha Franklin)
5. SOUL POWER
   (James Brown)
6. DON'T LET THE GREEN GRASS FOOL YOU
   (Wilson Pickett)
7. MAMA'S PEARL
   (The Jackson 5)
8. AIN'T GOT TIME
   (The Impressions)
9. CHAIRMEN OF THE BOARD
   (Chairmen of the Board)
10. HEAVY MAKES YOU HAPPY
    (The Staple Singers)

JAZZ ALBUMS

1. TO BE CONTINUED
   (Isaac Hayes)
2. MILES DAVIS AT THE FILLMORE
   (Miles Davis)
3. BITCHES BREW
   (Miles Davis)
4. CHAPTER TWO
   (Roberta Flack)
5. DON ELLIS AT THE FILLMORE
   (Don Ellis)
6. THE PRICE YOU GOT TO PAY TO BE FREE
   (Cannonball Adderley)
7. STRAIGHT LIFE
   (Freddie Hubbard)
8. SUGAR
   (Stanley Turrentine)
9. THE ISAAC HAYES MOVEMENT
   (Isaac Hayes)
10. OLD SOCKS, NEW SHOES, NEW SOCKS, OLD SHOES
    (Jazz Crusaders)

COUNTRY SINGLES

1. I'D RATHER LOVE YOU
   (Charley Pride)
2. AFTER THE FIRE IS GONE/THE ONE I CAN'T LIVE WITHOUT
   (Conway Twitty and Loretta Lynn)
3. ARMS OF A FOOL
   (Mel Tillis)
4. I'M GONNA KEEP ON LOVING YOU
   (Bobby Walker)
5. A WOMAN ALWAYS KNOWS
   (David Houston)
6. THERE GOES MY EVERYTHING/I REALLY DON'T WANT TO KNOW
   (Elvis Presley)
7. SOLDIER'S LAST LETTER
   (Merle Haggard)
8. KNOCK THREE TIMES
   (Bobby "Crash" Craddock)
9. WATCHING SCOTTY GROW
   (Bobby Goldsboro)
10. THE LAST ONE TO TOUCH ME
    (Porter Wagoner)

COUNTRY ALBUMS

1. FROM ME TO YOU
   (Charley Pride)
2. ROSE GARDEN
   (Lynn Anderson)
3. COAL MINER'S DAUGHTER
   (Loretta Lynn)
4. BED OF ROSES
   (The Statler Brothers)
5. WE ONLY MAKE BELIEVE
   (Conway Twitty)
6. FOR THE GOOD TIMES
   (Ray Price)
7. TRIBUTE TO THE BEST DAMN FIDDLE PLAYER IN THE WORLD (OR MY TRIBUTE TO BOB WILLS)
   (Merle Haggard)
8. HELP ME MAKE IT THROUGH THE NIGHT
   (Sammi Stewart)

9. ELVIS COUNTRY
   (Elvis Presley)
10. MORNING
    (Jim Ed Brown)

MARCH 27, 1971

POP SINGLES

1. JUST MY IMAGINATION
   (Temptations)
2. SHE'S A LADY
   (Tom Jones)
3. ME AND BOBBY McGEE
   (Janis Joplin)
4. FOR ALL WE KNOW
   (The Carpenters)
5. DOESN'T SOMEBODY WANT TO BE WANTED
   (The Partridge Family)
6. ONE BAD APPLE
   (The Osmonds)
7. PROUD MARY
   (Ike and Tina Turner)
8. HELP ME MAKE IT THROUGH THE NIGHT
   (Sammi Stewart)
9. LOVE STORY
   (Andy Williams)
10. WHAT IS LIFE/APPLE SCRUFFS
    (George Harrison)

POP ALBUMS

1. PEARL
   (Janis Joplin)
2. LOVE STORY
   (Original Soundtrack)
3. JESUS CHRIST SUPERSTAR
   (Original Soundtrack)
4. LOVE STORY
   (Andy Williams)
5. CRY OF LOVE
   (Jimi Hendrix)
6. TUMBLEWEED CONNECTION
   (Elton John)
7. CHICAGO III
   (Chicago)
8. ABRAXAS
   (Santana)
9. STONEY END
   (Barbra Streisand)
10. GOLDEN BISCUITS
    (Three Dog Night)

BLACK SINGLES

1. WHAT'S GOING ON
   (Marvin Gaye)
2. JUST MY IMAGINATION
   (Temptations)
3. PROUD MARY
   (Ike and Tina Turner)
4. YOU'RE ALL I NEED TO GET BY
   (Aretha Franklin)
5. SOUL POWER
   (James Brown)
6. DO ME RIGHT
   (Detroit Emeralds)
7. HEAVY MAKES YOU HAPPY
   (The Staple Singers)
8. AIN'T GOT TIME
   (The Impressions)
9. CHAIRMEN OF THE BOARD
   (Chairmen of the Board)
10. CHERISH WHAT IS DEAR TO YOU
    (Freda Payne)

JAZZ ALBUMS

1. TO BE CONTINUED
   (Isaac Hayes)

2. MILES DAVIS AT THE FILLMORE
   (Miles Davis)
3. BITCHES BREW
   (Miles Davis)
4. THE PRICE YOU GOT TO PAY TO BE FREE
   (Cannonball Adderley)
5. SUGAR
   (Stanley Turrentine)
6. CHAPTER TWO
   (Roberta Flack)
7. DON ELLIS AT THE FILLMORE
   (Don Ellis)
8. OLD SOCKS, NEW SHOES, NEW SOCKS, OLD SHOES
   (Jazz Crusaders)
9. B.B. KING LIVE AT COOK COUNTY JAIL
   (B.B. King)
10. THE ISAAC HAYES MOVEMENT
    (Isaac Hayes)

COUNTRY SINGLES

1. ARMS OF A FOOL
   (Mel Tillis)
2. I'D RATHER LOVE YOU
   (Charley Pride)
3. AFTER THE FIRE IS GONE/THE ONE I CAN'T LIVE WITHOUT
   (Conway Twitty and Loretta Lynn)
4. I'M GONNA KEEP ON LOVING YOU
   (Bobby Walker)
5. SOLDIER'S LAST LETTER
   (Merle Haggard)
6. KNOCK THREE TIMES
   (Billy "Crash" Craddock)
7. THE LAST ONE TO TOUCH ME
   (Porter Wagoner)
8. EMPTY ARMS
   (Sonny James)
9. A WOMAN ALWAYS KNOWS
   (David Houston)
10. HERE COME THE RATTLESNAKES
    (Wendy Bagwell)

COUNTRY ALBUMS

1. ROSE GARDEN
   (Lynn Anderson)
2. WE ONLY MAKE BELIEVE
   (Conway Twitty and Loretta Lynn)
3. FROM ME TO YOU
   (Charley Pride)
4. COAL MINER'S DAUGHTER
   (Loretta Lynn)
5. HELP ME MAKE IT THROUGH THE NIGHT
   (Sammi Stewart)
6. FOR THE GOOD TIMES
   (Ray Price)
7. BED OF ROSES
   (The Statler Brothers)
8. ELVIS COUNTRY
   (Elvis Presley)
9. GEORGE JONES WITH LOVE
   (George Jones)
10. MORNING
    (Jim Ed Brown)

APRIL 3, 1971

POP SINGLES

1. DOESN'T SOMEBODY WANT TO BE WANTED
   (The Partridge Family)
2. SHE'S A LADY
   (Tom Jones)
3. ME AND BOBBY McGEE
   (Janis Joplin)
4. FOR ALL WE KNOW
   (The Carpenters)
5. JUST MY IMAGINATION
   (Temptations)

6. PROUD MARY
   (Ike and Tina Turner)
7. LOVE STORY
   (Andy Williams)
8. HELP ME MAKE IT THROUGH THE NIGHT
   (Sammi Stewart)
9. WHAT'S GOING ON
   (Marvin Gaye)
10. WHAT IS LIFE/APPLE SCRUFFS
    (George Harrison)

POP ALBUMS

1. PEARL
   (Janis Joplin)
2. LOVE STORY
   (Original Soundtrack)
3. CRY OF LOVE
   (Jimi Hendrix)
4. JESUS CHRIST SUPERSTAR
   (Original Soundtrack)
5. LOVE STORY
   (Andy Williams)
6. TUMBLEWEED CONNECTION
   (Elton John)
7. GOLDEN BISCUITS
   (Three Dog Night)
8. ABRAXAS
   (Santana)
9. STONEY END
   (Barbra Streisand)
10. CHICAGO III
    (Chicago)

BLACK SINGLES

1. WHAT'S GOING ON
   (Marvin Gaye)
2. PROUD MARY
   (Ike and Tina Turner)
3. YOU'RE ALL I NEED TO GET BY
   (Aretha Franklin)
4. SOUL POWER
   (James Brown)
5. DO ME RIGHT
   (Detroit Emeralds)
6. HEAVY MAKES YOU HAPPY
   (The Staple Singers)
7. JUST MY IMAGINATION
   (Temptations)
8. AIN'T GOT TIME
   (The Impressions)
9. WE CAN WORK IT OUT
   (Stevie Wonder)
10. BABY LET ME KISS YOU
    (King Floyd)

JAZZ ALBUMS

1. BITCHES BREW
   (Miles Davis)
2. MILES DAVIS AT THE FILLMORE
   (Miles Davis)
3. TO BE CONTINUED
   (Isaac Hayes)
4. THE PRICE YOU GOT TO PAY TO BE FREE
   (Cannonball Adderley)
5. SUGAR
   (Stanley Turrentine)
6. CHAPTER TWO
   (Roberta Flack)
7. B.B. KING LIVE AT COOK COUNTY JAIL
   (B.B. King)
8. OLD SOCKS, NEW SHOES, NEW SOCKS, OLD SHOES
   (Jazz Crusaders)
9. GULA MATARI
   (Quincy Jones)
10. THE ISAAC HAYES MOVEMENT
    (Isaac Hayes)

COUNTRY SINGLES

1. SOLDIER'S LAST LETTER
   (Merle Haggard)
2. KNOCK THREE TIMES
   (Billy "Crash" Craddock)
3. EMPTY ARMS
   (Sonny James)
4. ARMS OF A FOOL
   (Mel Tillis)
5. I'D RATHER LOVE YOU
   (Charley Pride)
6. BETTER MOVE IT ON HOME
   (Porter Wagoner and Dolly Parton)
7. AFTER THE FIRE IS GONE/THE ONE I
   CAN'T LIVE WITHOUT
   (Conway Twitty and Loretta Lynn)
8. HERE COME THE RATTLESNAKES
   (Wendy Bagwell)
9. WE SURE CAN LOVE EACH OTHER
   (Tammy Wynette)
10. ANYWAY
    (George Hamilton IV)

COUNTRY ALBUMS

1. ROSE GARDEN
   (Lynn Anderson)
2. WE ONLY MAKE BELIEVE
   (Conway Twitty and Loretta Lynn)
3. HELP ME MAKE IT THROUGH THE NIGHT
   (Sammi Stewart)
4. FROM ME TO YOU
   (Charley Pride)
5. COAL MINER'S DAUGHTER
   (Loretta Lynn)
6. FOR THE GOOD TIMES
   (Ray Price)
7. BED OF ROSES
   (The Statler Brothers)
8. TWO OF A KIND
   (Porter Wagoner and Dolly Parton)
9. GEORGE JONES WITH LOVE
   (George Jones)
10. MORNING
    (Jim Ed Brown)

APRIL 10, 1971

POP SINGLES

1. SHE'S A LADY
   (Tom Jones)
2. WHAT'S GOING ON
   (Marvin Gaye)
3. ME AND BOBBY McGEE
   (Janis Joplin)
4. DOESN'T SOMEBODY WANT TO BE
   WANTED
   (The Partridge Family)
5. LOVE STORY
   (Andy Williams)
6. JUST MY IMAGINATION
   (Temptations)
7. HELP ME MAKE IT THROUGH THE NIGHT
   (Sammi Stewart)
8. JOY TO THE WORLD
   (Three Dog Night)
9. ANOTHER DAY/OH WOMAN, OH WHY?
   (Paul McCartney)
10. FOR ALL WE KNOW
    (The Carpenters)

POP ALBUMS

1. LOVE STORY
   (Original Soundtrack)
2. PEARL
   (Janis Joplin)

3. CRY OF LOVE
   (Jimi Hendrix)
4. JESUS CHRIST SUPERSTAR
   (Original Soundtrack)
5. LOVE STORY
   (Andy Williams)
6. GOLDEN BISCUITS
   (Three Dog Night)
7. TUMBLEWEED CONNECTION
   (Elton John)
8. ABRAXAS
   (Santana)
9. STONEY END
   (Barbra Streisand)
10. IF I COULD ONLY REMEMBER MY NAME
    (David Crosby)

BLACK SINGLES

1. WHAT'S GOING ON
   (Marvin Gaye)
2. PROUD MARY
   (Ike and Tina Turner)
3. SOUL POWER
   (James Brown)
4. DO ME RIGHT
   (Detroit Emeralds)
5. HEAVY MAKES YOU HAPPY
   (The Staple Singers)
6. YOU'RE ALL I NEED TO GET BY
   (Aretha Franklin)
7. BABY LET ME KISS YOU
   (King Floyd)
8. WE CAN WORK IT OUT
   (Stevie Wonder)
9. JUST MY IMAGINATION
   (Temptations)
10. AIN'T GOT TIME
    (The Impressions)

JAZZ ALBUMS

1. BITCHES BREW
   (Miles Davis)
2. CHAPTER TWO
   (Roberta Flack)
3. TO BE CONTINUED
   (Isaac Hayes)
4. THE PRICE YOU GOT TO PAY TO BE FREE
   (Cannonball Adderley)
5. SUGAR
   (Stanley Turrentine)
6. MILES DAVIS AT THE FILLMORE
   (Miles Davis)
7. B.B. KING LIVE AT COOK COUNTY JAIL
   (B.B. King)
8. OLD SOCKS, NEW SHOES, NEW SOCKS, OLD
   SHOES
   (Jazz Crusaders)
9. GULA MATARI
   (Quincy Jones)
10. THE ISAAC HAYES MOVEMENT
    (Isaac Hayes)

COUNTRY SINGLES

1. KNOCK THREE TIMES
   (Billy "Crash" Craddock)
2. EMPTY ARMS
   (Sonny James)
3. BETTER MOVE IT ON HOME
   (Porter Wagoner and Dolly Parton)
4. SOLDIER'S LAST LETTER
   (Merle Haggard)
5. WE SURE CAN LOVE EACH OTHER
   (Tammy Wynette)
6. I'D RATHER LOVE YOU
   (Charley Pride)
7. HERE COME THE RATTLESNAKES
   (Wendy Bagwell)
8. AFTER THE FIRE IS GONE/THE ONE I
   CAN'T LIVE WITHOUT
   (Conway Twitty and Loretta Lynn)

9. BRIDGE OVER TROUBLED WATER
   (Buck Owens)
10. L.A. INTERNATIONAL AIRPORT
    (Susan Raye)

COUNTRY ALBUMS

1. WE ONLY MAKE BELIEVE
   (Conway Twitty and Loretta Lynn)
2. HELP ME MAKE IT THROUGH THE NIGHT
   (Sammi Stewart)
3. ROSE GARDEN
   (Lynn Anderson)
4. FOR THE GOOD TIMES
   (Ray Price)
5. FROM ME TO YOU
   (Charley Pride)
6. TWO OF A KIND
   (Porter Wagoner and Dolly Parton)
7. BED OF ROSES
   (The Statler Brothers)
8. COAL MINER'S DAUGHTER
   (Loretta Lynn)
9. THE TAKER/TULSA
   (Waylon Jennings)
10. GEORGE JONES WITH LOVE
    (George Jones)

APRIL 17, 1971

POP SINGLES

1. JOY TO THE WORLD
   (Three Dog Night)
2. WHAT'S GOING ON
   (Marvin Gaye)
3. JUST MY IMAGINATION
   (Temptations)
4. SHE'S A LADY
   (Tom Jones)
5. LOVE STORY
   (Andy Williams)
6. ANOTHER DAY/OH WOMAN, OH WHY?
   (Paul McCartney)
7. DOESN'T SOMEBODY WANT TO BE
   WANTED
   (The Partridge Family)
8. HELP ME MAKE IT THROUGH THE NIGHT
   (Sammi Stewart)
9. ME AND BOBBY McGEE
   (Janis Joplin)
10. NEVER CAN SAY GOODBYE
    (The Jackson 5)

POP ALBUMS

1. LOVE STORY
   (Original Soundtrack)
2. PEARL
   (Janis Joplin)
3. JESUS CHRIST SUPERSTAR
   (Original Soundtrack)
4. CRY OF LOVE
   (Jimi Hendrix)
5. GOLDEN BISCUITS
   (Three Dog Night)
6. LOVE STORY
   (Andy Williams)
7. TUMBLEWEED CONNECTION
   (Elton John)
8. ABRAXAS
   (Santana)
9. IF I COULD ONLY REMEMBER MY NAME
   (David Crosby)
10. TEA FOR THE TILLERMAN
    (Cat Stevens)

BLACK SINGLES

1. WHAT'S GOING ON
   (Marvin Gaye)

2. PROUD MARY
(Ike and Tina Turner)
3. SOUL POWER
(James Brown)
4. DO ME RIGHT
(Detroit Emeralds)
5. BABY LET ME KISS YOU
(King Floyd)
6. HEAVY MAKES YOU HAPPY
(The Staple Singers)
7. WE CAN WORK IT OUT
(Stevie Wonder)
8. COULD I FORGET YOU
(Tyrone Davis)
9. I DON'T BLAME YOU AT ALL
(Smokey Robinson and the Miracles)
10. GIVE MORE POWER TO THE PEOPLE
(The Chi-Lites)

JAZZ ALBUMS

1. BITCHES BREW
(Miles Davis)
2. TO BE CONTINUED
(Isaac Hayes)
3. SUGAR
(Stanley Turrentine)
4. B.B. KING LIVE AT COOK COUNTY JAIL
(B.B. King)
5. CHAPTER TWO
(Roberta Flack)
6. OLD SOCKS, NEW SHOES, NEW SOCKS, OLD SHOES
(Jazz Crusaders)
7. THE PRICE YOU GOT TO PAY TO BE FREE
(Cannonball Adderley)
8. MILES DAVIS AT THE FILLMORE
(Miles Davis)
9. JOURNEY IN SATCHIDANANDA
(Alice Coltrane/Pharoah Sanders)
10. GULA MATARI
(Quincy Jones)

COUNTRY SINGLES

1. EMPTY ARMS
(Sonny James)
2. BETTER MOVE IT ON HOME
(Porter Wagoner and Dolly Parton)
3. WE SURE CAN LOVE EACH OTHER
(Tammy Wynette)
4. KNOCK THREE TIMES
(Billy "Crash" Craddock)
5. I WON'T MENTION IT AGAIN
(Ray Price)
6. L.A. INTERNATIONAL AIRPORT
(Susan Raye)
7. HERE COME THE RATTLESNAKES
(Wendy Bagwell)
8. ALWAYS REMEMBER
(Bill Anderson)
9. I LOVE THE WAY THAT YOU'VE BEEN LOVIN' ME
(Roy Drusky)
10. SOLDIER'S LAST LETTER
(Merle Haggard)

COUNTRY ALBUMS

1. HELP ME MAKE IT THROUGH THE NIGHT
(Sammi Stewart)
2. WE ONLY MAKE BELIEVE
(Conway Twitty and Loretta Lynn)
3. ROSE GARDEN
(Lynn Anderson)
4. FOR THE GOOD TIMES
(Ray Price)
5. TWO OF A KIND
(Porter Wagoner and Dolly Parton)
6. FROM ME TO YOU
(Charley Pride)
7. COAL MINER'S DAUGHTER
(Loretta Lynn)
8. THE TAKER/TULSA
(Waylon Jennings)

9. BED OF ROSES
(The Statler Brothers)
10. GEORGE JONES WITH LOVE
(George Jones)

APRIL 24, 1971

POP SINGLES

1. JOY TO THE WORLD
(Three Dog Night)
2. WHAT'S GOING ON
(Marvin Gaye)
3. JUST MY IMAGINATION
(Temptations)
4. PUT YOUR HAND IN THE HAND
(Ocean)
5. ANOTHER DAY/OH WOMAN, OH WHY?
(Paul McCartney)
6. NEVER CAN SAY GOODBYE
(The Jackson 5)
7. SHE'S A LADY
(Tom Jones)
8. I AM . . . I SAID
(Neil Diamond)
9. LOVE STORY
(Andy Williams)
10. ONE TOKE OVER THE LINE
(Brewer and Shipley)

POP ALBUMS

1. PEARL
(Janis Joplin)
2. JESUS CHRIST SUPERSTAR
(Original Soundtrack)
3. LOVE STORY
(Original Soundtrack)
4. GOLDEN BISCUITS
(Three Dog Night)
5. UP TO DATE
(The Partridge Family)
6. LOVE STORY
(Andy Williams)
7. CRY OF LOVE
(Jimi Hendrix)
8. ABRAXAS
(Santana)
9. TEA FOR THE TILLERMAN
(Cat Stevens)
10. LOVE'S LINES, ANGLES AND RHYMES
(The Fifth Dimension)

BLACK SINGLES

1. WHAT'S GOING ON
(Marvin Gaye)
2. NEVER CAN SAY GOODBYE
(The Jackson 5)
3. BABY LET ME KISS YOU
(King Floyd)
4. DO ME RIGHT
(Detroit Emeralds)
5. GIVE MORE POWER TO THE PEOPLE
(The Chi-Lites)
6. I DON'T BLAME YOU AT ALL
(Smokey Robinson and the Miracles)
7. WE CAN WORK IT OUT
(Stevie Wonder)
8. COULD I FORGET YOU
(Tyrone Davis)
9. PROUD MARY
(Ike and Tina Turner)
10. SOUL POWER
(James Brown)

JAZZ ALBUMS

1. BITCHES BREW
(Miles Davis)

2. TO BE CONTINUED
(Isaac Hayes)
3. B.B. KING LIVE AT COOK COUNTY JAIL
(B.B. King)
4. SUGAR
(Stanley Turrentine)
5. MEMPHIS TWO-STEP
(Herbie Mann)
6. OLD SOCKS, NEW SHOES, NEW SOCKS, OLD SHOES
(Jazz Crusaders)
7. THE PRICE YOU GOT TO PAY TO BE FREE
(Cannonball Adderley)
8. CHAPTER TWO
(Roberta Flack)
9. MILES DAVIS AT THE FILLMORE
(Miles Davis)
10. JOURNEY IN SATCHIDANANDA
(Alice Coltrane/Pharoah Sanders)

COUNTRY SINGLES

1. WE SURE CAN LOVE EACH OTHER
(Tammy Wynette)
2. BETTER MOVE IT ON HOME
(Porter Wagoner and Dolly Parton)
3. EMPTY ARMS
(Sonny James)
4. I WON'T MENTION IT AGAIN
(Ray Price)
5. L.A. INTERNATIONAL AIRPORT
(Susan Raye)
6. ALWAYS REMEMBER
(Bill Anderson)
7. KNOCK THREE TIMES
(Billy "Crash" Craddock)
8. I LOVE THE WAY THAT YOU'VE BEEN LOVIN' ME
(Roy Drusky)
9. HOW MUCH MORE CAN SHE STAND
(Conway Twitty)
10. DREAM BABY
(Glen Campbell)

COUNTRY ALBUMS

1. HELP ME MAKE IT THROUGH THE NIGHT
(Sammi Stewart)
2. ROSE GARDEN
(Lynn Anderson)
3. WE ONLY MAKE BELIEVE
(Conway Twitty and Loretta Lynn)
4. TWO OF A KIND
(Porter Wagoner and Dolly Parton)
5. FOR THE GOOD TIMES
(Ray Price)
6. FROM ME TO YOU
(Charley Pride)
7. COAL MINER'S DAUGHTER
(Loretta Lynn)
8. GEORGE JONES WITH LOVE
(George Jones)
9. GEORGIA SUNSHINE
(Jerry Reed)
10. THIS, THAT AND THE OTHER
(Wendy Bagwell)

MAY 1, 1971

POP SINGLES

1. JOY TO THE WORLD
(Three Dog Night)
2. NEVER CAN SAY GOODBYE
(The Jackson 5)
3. PUT YOUR HAND IN THE HAND
(Ocean)
4. I AM. . .I SAID
(Neil Diamond)
5. ANOTHER DAY/OH WOMAN, OH WHY?
(Paul McCartney)

6. WHAT'S GOING ON
   (Marvin Gaye)
7. STAY AWHILE
   (The Bells)
8. IF
   (Bread)
9. JUST MY IMAGINATION
   (Temptations)
10. SHE'S A LADY
    (Tom Jones)

POP ALBUMS

1. JESUS CHRIST SUPERSTAR
   (Original Soundtrack)
2. PEARL
   (Janis Joplin)
3. UP TO DATE
   (The Partridge Family)
4. GOLDEN BISCUITS
   (Three Dog Night)
5. LOVE STORY
   (Andy Williams)
6. LOVE STORY
   (Original Soundtrack)
7. ABRAXAS
   (Santana)
8. TEA FOR THE TILLERMAN
   (Cat Stevens)
9. CRY OF LOVE
   (Jimi Hendrix)
10. LOVE'S LINES, ANGLES AND RHYMES
    (The Fifth Dimension)

BLACK SINGLES

1. NEVER CAN SAY GOODBYE
   (The Jackson 5)
2. BABY LET ME KISS YOU
   (King Floyd)
3. GIVE MORE POWER TO THE PEOPLE
   (The Chi-Lites)
4. WE CAN WORK IT OUT
   (Stevie Wonder)
5. WHAT'S GOING ON
   (Marvin Gaye)
6. I DON'T BLAME YOU AT ALL
   (Smokey Robinson and the Miracles)
7. BRIDGE OVER TROUBLED WATER
   (Aretha Franklin)
8. WANT ADS
   (Honey Cone)
9. RIGHT ON THE TIP OF MY TONGUE
   (Brenda and the Tabulations)
10. DON'T CHANGE ON ME
    (Ray Charles)

JAZZ ALBUMS

1. BITCHES BREW
   (Miles Davis)
2. TO BE CONTINUED
   (Isaac Hayes)
3. SUGAR
   (Stanley Turrentine)
4. B.B. KING LIVE AT COOK COUNTY JAIL
   (B.B. King)
5. MEMPHIS TWO-STEP
   (Herbie Mann)
6. OLD SOCKS, NEW SHOES, NEW SOCKS, OLD
   SHOES
   (Jazz Crusaders)
7. MILES DAVIS AT THE FILLMORE
   (Miles Davis)
8. CHAPTER TWO
   (Roberta Flack)
9. THE PRICE YOU GOT TO PAY TO BE FREE
   (Cannonball Adderley)
10. STRAIGHT LIFE
    (Freddie Hubbard)

COUNTRY SINGLES

1. I WON'T MENTION IT AGAIN
   (Ray Price)

2. WE SURE CAN LOVE EACH OTHER
   (Tammy Wynette)
3. HOW MUCH MORE CAN SHE STAND
   (Conway Twitty)
4. ALWAYS REMEMBER
   (Bill Anderson)
5. DREAM BABY
   (Glen Campbell)
6. MAN IN BLACK
   (Johnny Cash)
7. I WANNA BE FREE
   (Loretta Lynn)
8. BETTER MOVE IT ON HOME
   (Porter Wagoner and Dolly Parton)
9. EMPTY ARMS
   (Sonny James)
10. TOUCHING HOME
    (Jerry Lee Lewis)

COUNTRY ALBUMS

1. ROSE GARDEN
   (Lynn Anderson)
2. HELP ME MAKE IT THROUGH THE NIGHT
   (Sammi Stewart)
3. WE ONLY MAKE BELIEVE
   (Conway Twitty and Loretta Lynn)
4. FOR THE GOOD TIMES
   (Ray Price)
5. TWO OF A KIND
   (Conway Twitty and Loretta Lynn)
6. HAG
   (Merle Haggard)
7. GEORGE JONES WITH LOVE
   (George Jones)
8. GEORGIA SUNSHINE
   (Jerry Reed)
9. THIS, THAT AND THE OTHER
   (Wendy Bagwell)
10. FROM ME TO YOU
    (Charley Pride)

MAY 8, 1971

POP SINGLES

1. JOY TO THE WORLD
   (Three Dog Night)
2. NEVER CAN SAY GOODBYE
   (The Jackson 5)
3. PUT YOUR HAND IN THE HAND
   (Ocean)
4. STAY AWHILE
   (The Bells)
5. I AM. . .I SAID
   (Neil Diamond)
6. BRIDGE OVER TROUBLED WATER
   (Aretha Franklin)
7. IF
   (Bread)
8. POWER TO THE PEOPLE
   (John Lennon/Plastic Ono Band)
9. WHAT'S GOING ON
   (Marvin Gaye)
10. CHICK-A-BOOM
    (Daddy Dewdrop)

POP ALBUMS

1. JESUS CHRIST SUPERSTAR
   (Original Soundtrack)
2. PEARL
   (Janis Joplin)
3. UP TO DATE
   (The Partridge Family)
4. GOLDEN BISCUITS
   (Three Dog Night)
5. FOUR WAY STREET
   (Crosby, Stills, Nash and Young)
6. LOVE STORY
   (Andy Williams)

7. WOODSTOCK TWO
   (Woodstock Artists)
8. LOVE STORY
   (Original Soundtrack)
9. ABRAXAS
   (Santana)
10. SURVIVAL
    (Grand Funk Railroad)

BLACK SINGLES

1. NEVER CAN SAY GOODBYE
   (The Jackson 5)
2. GIVE MORE POWER TO THE PEOPLE
   (The Chi-Lites)
3. BRIDGE OVER TROUBLED WATER
   (Aretha Franklin)
4. WE CAN WORK IT OUT
   (Stevie Wonder)
5. WANT ADS
   (Honey Cone)
6. I DON'T BLAME YOU AT ALL
   (Smokey Robinson and the Miracles)
7. WHAT'S GOING ON
   (Marvin Gaye)
8. BABY LET ME KISS YOU
   (King Floyd)
9. RIGHT ON THE TIP OF MY TONGUE
   (Brenda and the Tabulations)
10. I'LL ERASE AWAY YOUR PAIN
    (What-nauts)

JAZZ ALBUMS

1. BITCHES BREW
   (Miles Davis)
2. TO BE CONTINUED
   (Isaac Hayes)
3. MEMPHIS TWO-STEP
   (Herbie Mann)
4. B.B. KING LIVE AT COOK COUNTY JAIL
   (B.B. King)
5. JACK JOHNSON
   (Miles Davis)
6. M.F. HORN
   (Maynard Ferguson)
7. MILES DAVIS AT THE FILLMORE
   (Miles Davis)
8. CHAPTER TWO
   (Roberta Flack)
9. SUGAR
   (Stanley Turrentine)
10. OLD SOCKS, NEW SHOES, NEW SOCKS, OLD
    SHOES
    (Jazz Crusaders)

COUNTRY SINGLES

1. HOW MUCH MORE CAN SHE STAND
   (Conway Twitty)
2. I WON'T MENTION IT AGAIN
   (Ray Price)
3. MAN IN BLACK
   (Johnny Cash)
4. ALWAYS REMEMBER
   (Bill Anderson)
5. DREAM BABY
   (Glen Campbell)
6. I WANNA BE FREE
   (Loretta Lynn)
7. WE SURE CAN LOVE EACH OTHER
   (Tammy Wynette)
8. TOUCHING HOME
   (Jerry Lee Lewis)
9. SOMETIMES YOU JUST CAN'T WIN
   (George Jones)
10. NEXT TIME I FALL IN LOVE (I WON'T)
    (Hank Thompson)

COUNTRY ALBUMS

1. ROSE GARDEN
   (Lynn Anderson)

2. HELP ME MAKE IT THROUGH THE NIGHT
   (Sammi Stewart)
3. HAG
   (Merle Haggard)
4. FOR THE GOOD TIMES
   (Ray Price)
5. WE ONLY MAKE BELIEVE
   (Conway Twitty and Loretta Lynn)
6. GLEN CAMPBELL'S GREATEST HITS
   (Glen Campbell)
7. GEORGE JONES WITH LOVE
   (George Jones)
8. THIS, THAT AND THE OTHER
   (Wendy Bagwell)
9. EMPTY ARMS
   (Sonny James)
10. BEST OF ROY CLARK
    (Roy Clark)

MAY 15, 1971

POP SINGLES

1. JOY TO THE WORLD
   (Three Dog Night)
2. NEVER CAN SAY GOODBYE
   (The Jackson 5)
3. BRIDGE OVER TROUBLED WATER
   (Aretha Franklin)
4. STAY AWHILE
   (The Bells)
5. PUT YOUR HAND IN THE HAND
   (Ocean)
6. IF
   (Bread)
7. BROWN SUGAR
   (The Rolling Stones)
8. WANT ADS
   (Honey Cone)
9. CHICK-A-BOOM
   (Daddy Dewdrop)
10. LOVE HER MADLY
    (The Doors)

POP ALBUMS

1. JESUS CHRIST SUPERSTAR
   (Original Soundtrack)
2. PEARL
   (Janis Joplin)
3. UP TO DATE
   (The Partridge Family)
4. FOUR WAY STREET
   (Crosby, Stills, Nash and Young)
5. GOLDEN BISCUITS
   (Three Dog Night)
6. SURVIVAL
   (Grand Funk Railroad)
7. WOODSTOCK TWO
   (Woodstock Artists)
8. ABRAXAS
   (Santana)
9. LOVE STORY
   (Original Soundtrack)
10. TEA FOR THE TILLERMAN
    (Cat Stevens)

BLACK SINGLES

1. BRIDGE OVER TROUBLED WATER
   (Aretha Franklin)
2. GIVE MORE POWER TO THE PEOPLE
   (The Chi-Lites)
3. WANT ADS
   (Honey Cone)
4. NEVER CAN SAY GOODBYE
   (The Jackson 5)
5. WE CAN WORK IT OUT
   (Stevie Wonder)

6. I DON'T BLAME YOU AT ALL
   (Smokey Robinson and the Miracles)
7. DON'T KNOCK MY LOVE
   (Wilson Pickett)
8. RIGHT ON THE TIP OF MY TONGUE
   (Brenda and the Tabulations)
9. SHE'S NOT JUST ANOTHER WOMAN
   (8th Day)
10. I'LL ERASE AWAY YOUR PAIN
    (What-nauts)

JAZZ ALBUMS

1. BITCHES BREW
   (Miles Davis)
2. TO BE CONTINUED
   (Isaac Hayes)
3. MEMPHIS TWO-STEP
   (Herbie Mann)
4. B.B. KING LIVE AT COOK COUNTY JAIL
   (B.B. King)
5. JACK JOHNSON
   (Miles Davis)
6. SUGAR
   (Stanley Turrentine)
7. MILES DAVIS AT THE FILLMORE
   (Miles Davis)
8. CHAPTER TWO
   (Roberta Flack)
9. LIVING BLACK
   (Charles Earland)
10. M.F. HORN
    (Maynard Ferguson)

COUNTRY SINGLES

1. MAN IN BLACK
   (Johnny Cash)
2. HOW MUCH MORE CAN SHE STAND
   (Conway Twitty)
3. I WANNA BE FREE
   (Loretta Lynn)
4. TOUCHING HOME
   (Jerry Lee Lewis)
5. ALWAYS REMEMBER
   (Bill Anderson)
6. I WON'T MENTION IT AGAIN
   (Ray Price)
7. SOMETIMES YOU JUST CAN'T WIN
   (George Jones)
8. OH SINGER
   (Jeannie C. Riley)
9. STEP ASIDE
   (Faron Young)
10. DREAM BABY
    (Glen Campbell)

COUNTRY ALBUMS

1. HAG
   (Merle Haggard)
2. HELP ME MAKE IT THROUGH THE NIGHT
   (Sammi Stewart)
3. GLEN CAMPBELL'S GREATEST HITS
   (Glen Campbell)
4. ROSE GARDEN
   (Lynn Anderson)
5. WE ONLY MAKE BELIEVE
   (Conway Twitty and Loretta Lynn)
6. FOR THE GOOD TIMES
   (Ray Price)
7. DID YOU THINK TO PRAY
   (Charley Pride)
8. THIS, THAT AND THE OTHER
   (Wendy Bagwell)
9. EMPTY ARMS
   (Sonny James)
10. WHEN YOU'RE HOT, YOU'RE HOT
    (Jerry Reed)

MAY 22, 1971

POP SINGLES

1. BROWN SUGAR
   (The Rolling Stones)
2. BRIDGE OVER TROUBLED WATER
   (Aretha Franklin)
3. JOY TO THE WORLD
   (Three Dog Night)
4. STAY AWHILE
   (The Bells)
5. NEVER CAN SAY GOODBYE
   (The Jackson 5)
6. IF
   (Bread)
7. WANT ADS
   (Honey Cone)
8. ME AND YOU AND A DOG NAMED BOO
   (Lobo)
9. LOVE HER MADLY
   (The Doors)
10. I LOVE YOU FOR ALL SEASONS
    (Fuzz)

POP ALBUMS

1. FOUR WAY STREET
   (Crosby, Stills, Nash and Young)
2. JESUS CHRIST SUPERSTAR
   (Original Soundtrack)
3. UP TO DATE
   (The Partridge Family)
4. PEARL
   (Janis Joplin)
5. SURVIVAL
   (Grand Funk Railroad)
6. MUD SLIDE SLIM AND THE BLUE HORIZON
   (James Taylor)
7. STICKY FINGERS
   (The Rolling Stones)
8. GOLDEN BISCUITS
   (Three Dog Night)
9. MAYBE TOMORROW
   (The Jackson 5)
10. TAPESTRY
    (Carole King)

BLACK SINGLES

1. BRIDGE OVER TROUBLED WATER
   (Aretha Franklin)
2. WANT ADS
   (Honey Cone)
3. GIVE MORE POWER TO THE PEOPLE
   (The Chi-Lites)
4. DON'T KNOCK MY LOVE
   (Wilson Pickett)
5. SHE'S NOT JUST ANOTHER WOMAN
   (8th Day)
6. NEVER CAN SAY GOODBYE
   (The Jackson 5)
7. SPINNING AROUND
   (Main Ingredient)
8. RIGHT ON THE TIP OF MY TONGUE
   (Brenda and the Tabulations)
9. YOUR LOVE
   (Charles Wright and Watts 103rd Street Rhythm Band)
10. I'LL ERASE AWAY YOUR PAIN
    (What-nauts)

JAZZ ALBUMS

1. BITCHES BREW
   (Miles Davis)
2. TO BE CONTINUED
   (Isaac Hayes)
3. MEMPHIS TWO-STEP
   (Herbie Mann)

4. CHAPTER TWO
   (Roberta Flack)
5. B.B. KING LIVE AT COOK COUNTY JAIL
   (B.B. King)
6. SUGAR
   (Stanley Turrentine)
7. JACK JOHNSON
   (Miles Davis)
8. TJADER
   (Cal Tjader)
9. LIVING BLACK
   (Charles Earland)
10. M.F. HORN
   (Maynard Ferguson)

COUNTRY SINGLES

1. I WANNA BE FREE
   (Loretta Lynn)
2. TOUCHING HOME
   (Jerry Lee Lewis)
3. HOW MUCH MORE CAN SHE STAND
   (Conway Twitty)
4. MAN IN BLACK
   (Johnny Cash)
5. OH SINGER
   (Jeannie C. Riley)
6. STEP ASIDE
   (Faron Young)
7. I WON'T MENTION IT AGAIN
   (Ray Price)
8. MISSISSIPPI WOMAN
   (Waylon Jennings)
9. ALWAYS REMEMBER
   (Bill Anderson)
10. ANGEL'S SUNDAY
   (Jim Ed Brown)

COUNTRY ALBUMS

1. HAG
   (Merle Haggard)
2. GLEN CAMPBELL'S GREATEST HITS
   (Glen Campbell)
3. HELP ME MAKE IT THROUGH THE NIGHT
   (Sammi Stewart)
4. ROSE GARDEN
   (Lynn Anderson)
5. DID YOU THINK TO PRAY
   (Charley Pride)
6. WE ONLY MAKE BELIEVE
   (Conway Twitty and Loretta Lynn)
7. THIS, THAT AND THE OTHER
   (Wendy Bagwell)
8. WHEN YOU'RE HOT, YOU'RE HOT
   (Jerry Reed)
9. HOW MUCH MORE CAN SHE STAND
   (Conway Twitty)
10. EMPTY ARMS
   (Sonny James)

MAY 29, 1971

POP SINGLES

1. BROWN SUGAR
   (The Rolling Stones)
2. BRIDGE OVER TROUBLED WATER
   (Aretha Franklin)
3. JOY TO THE WORLD
   (Three Dog Night)
4. WANT ADS
   (Honey Cone)
5. IT DON'T COME EASY
   (Ringo Starr)
6. ME AND YOU AND A DOG NAMED BOO
   (Lobo)
7. NEVER CAN SAY GOODBYE
   (The Jackson 5)
8. LOVE HER MADLY
   (The Doors)

9. CHICK-A-BOOM
   (Daddy Dewdrop)
10. SWEET AND INNOCENT
   (Donny Osmond)

POP ALBUMS

1. STICKY FINGERS
   (The Rolling Stones)
2. JESUS CHRIST SUPERSTAR
   (Original Soundtrack)
3. MUD SLIDE SLIM AND THE BLUE HORIZON
   (James Taylor)
4. FOUR WAY STREET
   (Crosby, Stills, Nash and Young)
5. SURVIVAL
   (Grand Funk Railroad)
6. TAPESTRY
   (Carole King)
7. UP TO DATE
   (The Partridge Family)
8. L.A. WOMAN
   (The Doors)
9. MAYBE TOMORROW
   (The Jackson 5)
10. AQUALUNG
   (Jethro Tull)

BLACK SINGLES

1. WANT ADS
   (Honey Cone)
2. BRIDGE OVER TROUBLED WATER
   (Aretha Franklin)
3. DON'T KNOCK MY LOVE
   (Wilson Pickett)
4. SHE'S NOT JUST ANOTHER WOMAN
   (8th Day)
5. GIVE MORE POWER TO THE PEOPLE
   (The Chi-Lites)
6. RIGHT ON THE TIP OF MY TONGUE
   (Brenda and the Tabulations)
7. SPINNING AROUND
   (Main Ingredient)
8. FUNKY MUSIC SHO NUFF TURNS ME ON
   (Edwin Starr)
9. YOUR LOVE
   (Charles Wright and Watts 103rd Street
   Rhythm Band)
10. I'LL ERASE AWAY YOUR PAIN
   (What-nauts)

JAZZ ALBUMS

1. BITCHES BREW
   (Miles Davis)
2. TO BE CONTINUED
   (Isaac Hayes)
3. CHAPTER TWO
   (Roberta Flack)
4. JACK JOHNSON
   (Miles Davis)
5. B.B. KING LIVE AT COOK COUNTY JAIL
   (B.B. King)
6. MEMPHIS TWO-STEP
   (Herbie Mann)
7. M.F. HORN
   (Maynard Ferguson)
8. TJADER
   (Cal Tjader)
9. LIVING BLACK
   (Charles Earland)
10. DONNY HATHAWAY
   (Donny Hathaway)

COUNTRY SINGLES

1. TOUCHING HOME
   (Jerry Lee Lewis)
2. I WANNA BE FREE
   (Loretta Lynn)

3. OH SINGER
   (Jeannie C. Riley)
4. STEP ASIDE
   (Faron Young)
5. HOW MUCH MORE CAN SHE STAND
   (Conway Twitty)
6. MAN IN BLACK
   (Johnny Cash)
7. MISSISSIPPI WOMAN
   (Waylon Jennings)
8. ANGEL'S SUNDAY
   (Jim Ed Brown)
9. TOMORROW NIGHT IN BALTIMORE
   (Roger Miller)
10. COMIN' DOWN
   (Dave Dudley)

COUNTRY ALBUMS

1. HAG
   (Merle Haggard)
2. GLEN CAMPBELL'S GREATEST HITS
   (Glen Campbell)
3. DID YOU THINK TO PRAY
   (Charley Pride)
4. HELP ME MAKE IT THROUGH THE NIGHT
   (Sammi Stewart)
5. ROSE GARDEN
   (Lynn Anderson)
6. WHEN YOU'RE HOT, YOU'RE HOT
   (Jerry Reed)
7. THIS, THAT AND THE OTHER
   (Wendy Bagwell)
8. HOW MUCH MORE CAN SHE STAND
   (Conway Twitty)
9. WE ONLY MAKE BELIEVE
   (Conway Twitty and Loretta Lynn)
10. EMPTY ARMS
   (Sonny James)

JUNE 5, 1971

POP SINGLES

1. BROWN SUGAR
   (The Rolling Stones)
2. WANT ADS
   (Honey Cone)
3. IT DON'T COME EASY
   (Ringo Starr)
4. BRIDGE OVER TROUBLED WATER
   (Aretha Franklin)
5. JOY TO THE WORLD
   (Three Dog Night)
6. ME AND YOU AND A DOG NAMED BOO
   (Lobo)
7. SWEET AND INNOCENT
   (Donny Osmond)
8. RAINY DAYS AND MONDAYS
   (The Carpenters)
9. CHICK-A-BOOM
   (Daddy Dewdrop)
10. SUPERSTAR
   (Murray Head)

POP ALBUMS

1. STICKY FINGERS
   (The Rolling Stones)
2. JESUS CHRIST SUPERSTAR
   (Original Soundtrack)
3. MUD SLIDE SLIM AND THE BLUE HORIZON
   (James Taylor)
4. TAPESTRY
   (Carole King)
5. SURVIVAL
   (Grand Funk Railroad)
6. FOUR WAY STREET
   (Crosby, Stills, Nash and Young)
7. AQUALUNG
   (Jethro Tull)

8. L.A. WOMAN
   (The Doors)
9. MAYBE TOMORROW
   (The Jackson 5)
10. RAM
    (Paul and Linda McCartney)

BLACK SINGLES

1. WANT ADS
   (Honey Cone)
2. SHE'S NOT JUST ANOTHER WOMAN
   (8th Day)
3. DON'T KNOCK MY LOVE
   (Wilson Pickett)
4. BRIDGE OVER TROUBLED WATER
   (Aretha Franklin)
5. SPINNING AROUND
   (Main Ingredient)
6. RIGHT ON THE TIP OF MY TONGUE
   (Brenda and the Tabulations)
7. GIVE MORE POWER TO THE PEOPLE
   (The Chi-Lites)
8. FUNKY MUSIC SHO NUFF TURNS ME ON
   (Edwin Starr)
9. NEVER CAN SAY GOODBYE
   (The Jackson 5)
10. YOUR LOVE
    (Charles Wright and Watts 103rd Street
    Rhythm Band)

JAZZ ALBUMS

1. BITCHES BREW
   (Miles Davis)
2. TO BE CONTINUED
   (Isaac Hayes)
3. MEMPHIS TWO-STEP
   (Herbie Mann)
4. JACK JOHNSON
   (Miles Davis)
5. LIVING BLACK
   (Charles Earland)
6. CHAPTER TWO
   (Roberta Flack)
7. M.F. HORN
   (Maynard Ferguson)
8. TJADER
   (Cal Tjader)
9. B.B. KING LIVE AT COOK COUNTY JAIL
   (B.B. King)
10. PRETTY THINGS
    (Lou Donaldson)

COUNTRY SINGLES

1. OH SINGER
   (Jeannie C. Riley)
2. TOUCHING HOME
   (Jerry Lee Lewis)
3. STEP ASIDE
   (Faron Young)
4. I WANNA BE FREE
   (Loretta Lynn)
5. HOW MUCH MORE CAN SHE STAND
   (Conway Twitty)
6. TOMORROW NIGHT IN BALTIMORE
   (Roger Miller)
7. ANGEL'S SUNDAY
   (Jim Ed Brown)
8. COMIN' DOWN
   (Dave Dudley)
9. YOU'RE MY MAN
   (Lynn Anderson)
10. I'VE GOT A RIGHT TO CRY
    (Hank Williams Jr.)

COUNTRY ALBUMS

1. HAG
   (Merle Haggard)

2. DID YOU THINK TO PRAY
   (Charley Pride)
3. WHEN YOU'RE HOT, YOU'RE HOT
   (Jerry Reed)
4. GLEN CAMPBELL'S GREATEST HITS
   (Glen Campbell)
5. HOW MUCH MORE CAN SHE STAND
   (Conway Twitty)
6. THIS, THAT AND THE OTHER
   (Wendy Bagwell)
7. HELP ME MAKE IT THROUGH THE NIGHT
   (Sammi Stewart)
8. WE SURE CAN LOVE EACH OTHER
   (Conway Twitty)
9. WE ONLY MAKE BELIEVE
   (Conway Twitty and Loretta Lynn)
10. WILLY JONES
    (Susan Raye)

JUNE 12, 1971

POP SINGLES

1. WANT ADS
   (Honey Cone)
2. IT DON'T COME EASY
   (Ringo Starr)
3. BROWN SUGAR
   (The Rolling Stones)
4. RAINY DAYS AND MONDAYS
   (The Carpenters)
5. BRIDGE OVER TROUBLED WATER
   (Aretha Franklin)
6. SWEET AND INNOCENT
   (Donny Osmond)
7. JOY TO THE WORLD
   (Three Dog Night)
8. IT'S TOO LATE
   (Carole King)
9. I'LL MEET YOU HALFWAY
   (The Partridge Family)
10. SUPERSTAR
    (Murray Head)

POP ALBUMS

1. STICKY FINGERS
   (The Rolling Stones)
2. JESUS CHRIST SUPERSTAR
   (Original Soundtrack)
3. MUD SLIDE SLIM AND THE BLUE HORIZON
   (James Taylor)
4. TAPESTRY
   (Carole King)
5. SURVIVAL
   (Grand Funk Railroad)
6. RAM
   (Paul and Linda McCartney)
7. AQUALUNG
   (Jethro Tull)
8. L.A. WOMAN
   (The Doors)
9. FOUR WAY STREET
   (Crosby, Stills, Nash and Young)
10. CARPENTERS
    (The Carpenters)

BLACK SINGLES

1. WANT ADS
   (Honey Cone)
2. SHE'S NOT JUST ANOTHER WOMAN
   (8th Day)
3. DON'T KNOCK MY LOVE
   (Wilson Pickett)
4. MR. BIG STUFF
   (Jean Knight)
5. SPINNING AROUND
   (Main Ingredient)

6. NEVER CAN SAY GOODBYE
   (The Jackson 5)
7. RIGHT ON THE TIP OF MY TONGUE
   (Brenda and the Tabulations)
8. FUNKY MUSIC SHO NUFF TURNS ME ON
   (Edwin Starr)
9. BRIDGE OVER TROUBLED WATER
   (Aretha Franklin)
10. HELP ME MAKE IT THROUGH THE NIGHT
    (Joe Simon)

JAZZ ALBUMS

1. BITCHES BREW
   (Miles Davis)
2. TO BE CONTINUED
   (Isaac Hayes)
3. LIVING BLACK
   (Charles Earland)
4. CHAPTER TWO
   (Roberta Flack)
5. MEMPHIS TWO-STEP
   (Herbie Mann)
6. JACK JOHNSON
   (Miles Davis)
7. M.F. HORN
   (Maynard Ferguson)
8. BACK TO THE ROOTS
   (Ramsey Lewis)
9. TJADER
   (Cal Tjader)
10. THE ISAAC HAYES MOVEMENT
    (Isaac Hayes)

COUNTRY SINGLES

1. STEP ASIDE
   (Faron Young)
2. YOU'RE MY MAN
   (Lynn Anderson)
3. OH SINGER
   (Jeannie C. Riley)
4. TOMORROW NIGHT IN BALTIMORE
   (Roger Miller)
5. WHEN YOU'RE HOT, YOU'RE HOT
   (Jerry Reed)
6. COMIN' DOWN
   (Dave Dudley)
7. I'VE GOT A RIGHT TO CRY
   (Hank Williams Jr.)
8. RUBY
   (Buck Owens)
9. TOUCH HOME
   (Jerry Lee Lewis)
10. GWEN
    (Tommy Overstreet)

COUNTRY ALBUMS

1. WHEN YOU'RE HOT, YOU'RE HOT
   (Jerry Reed)
2. HAG
   (Merle Haggard)
3. HOW MUCH MORE CAN SHE STAND
   (Conway Twitty)
4. DID YOU THINK TO PRAY
   (Charley Pride)
5. GLEN CAMPBELL'S GREATEST HITS
   (Glen Campbell)
6. THIS, THAT AND THE OTHER
   (Wendy Bagwell)
7. MARTY'S GREATEST HITS, VOL. 3
   (Marty Robbins)
8. HELP ME MAKE IT THROUGH THE
   NIGHT
   (Sammi Stewart)
9. WILLY JONES
   (Susan Raye)
10. WE SURE CAN LOVE EACH OTHER
    (Conway Twitty)

JUNE 19, 1971

POP SINGLES

1. WANT ADS
    (Honey Cone)
2. IT DON'T COME EASY
    (Ringo Starr)
3. RAINY DAYS AND MONDAYS
    (The Carpenters)
4. IT'S TOO LATE
    (Carole King)
5. SWEET AND INNOCENT
    (Donny Osmond)
6. BROWN SUGAR
    (The Rolling Stones)
7. I'LL MEET YOU HALFWAY
    (The Partridge Family)
8. TREAT HER LIKE A LADY
    (Cornelius Brothers and Sister Rose)
9. NATHAN JONES
    (The Supremes)
10. DON'T KNOCK MY LOVE
    (Wilson Pickett)

POP ALBUMS

1. JESUS CHRIST SUPERSTAR
    (Original Soundtrack)
2. TAPESTRY
    (Carole King)
3. STICKY FINGERS
    (The Rolling Stones)
4. RAM
    (Paul and Linda McCartney)
5. MUD SLIDE SLIM AND THE BLUE HORIZON
    (James Taylor)
6. CARPENTERS
    (The Carpenters)
7. SURVIVAL
    (Grand Funk Railroad)
8. AQUALUNG
    (Jethro Tull)
9. L.A. WOMAN
    (The Doors)
10. SHE'S A LADY
    (Tom Jones)

BLACK SINGLES

1. MR. BIG STUFF
    (Jean Knight)
2. WANT ADS
    (Honey Cone)
3. DON'T KNOCK MY LOVE
    (Wilson Pickett)
4. SHE'S NOT JUST ANOTHER WOMAN
    (8th Day)
5. SPINNING AROUND
    (Main Ingredient)
6. NEVER CAN SAY GOODBYE
    (The Jackson 5)
7. FUNKY NASSAU, PART I
    (Beginning of the End)
8. I DON'T WANT TO LOSE YOU
    (Johnnie Taylor)
9. RIGHT ON THE TIP OF MY TONGUE
    (Brenda and the Tabulations)
10. I KNOW I'M IN LOVE
    (Che Che and Pepe)

JAZZ ALBUMS

1. TO BE CONTINUED
    (Isaac Hayes)
2. BITCHES BREW
    (Miles Davis)
3. CHAPTER TWO
    (Roberta Flack)
4. SECOND MOVEMENT
    (Eddie Harris and Les McCann)
5. MEMPHIS TWO-STEP
    (Herbie Mann)
6. LIVING BLACK
    (Charles Earland)
7. BACK TO THE ROOTS
    (Ramsey Lewis)
8. JACK JOHNSON
    (Miles Davis)
9. M.F. HORN
    (Maynard Ferguson)
10. THE ISAAC HAYES MOVEMENT
    (Isaac Hayes)

COUNTRY SINGLES

1. YOU'RE MY MAN
    (Lynn Anderson)
2. WHEN YOU'RE HOT, YOU'RE HOT
    (Jerry Reed)
3. TOMORROW NIGHT IN BALTIMORE
    (Roger Miller)
4. RUBY
    (Buck Owens)
5. COMIN' DOWN
    (Dave Dudley)
6. I'VE GOT A RIGHT TO CRY
    (Hank Williams Jr.)
7. STEP ASIDE
    (Faron Young)
8. GWEN
    (Tommy Overstreet)
9. JUST ONE MORE TIME
    (Connie Smith)
10. SOMETHING BEAUTIFUL TO REMEMBER
    (Slim Whitman)

COUNTRY ALBUMS

1. WHEN YOU'RE HOT, YOU'RE HOT
    (Jerry Reed)
2. HAG
    (Merle Haggard)
3. HOW MUCH MORE CAN SHE STAND
    (Conway Twitty)
4. MARTY'S GREATEST HITS, VOL. 3
    (Marty Robbins)
5. DID YOU THINK TO PRAY
    (Charley Pride)
6. WE SURE CAN LOVE EACH OTHER
    (Tammy Wynette)
7. THIS, THAT AND THE OTHER
    (Wendy Bagwell)
8. GLEN CAMPBELL'S GREATEST HITS
    (Glen Campbell)
9. WILLY JONES
    (Susan Raye)
10. HELP ME MAKE IT THROUGH THE NIGHT
    (Sammi Stewart)

JUNE 26, 1971

POP SINGLES

1. IT DON'T COME EASY
    (Ringo Starr)
2. IT'S TOO LATE
    (Carole King)
3. RAINY DAYS AND MONDAYS
    (The Carpenters)
4. I'LL MEET YOU HALFWAY
    (The Partridge Family)
5. WANT ADS
    (Honey Cone)
6. TREAT HER LIKE A LADY
    (Cornelius Brothers and Sister Rose)
7. INDIAN RESERVATION
    (The Raiders)
8. NATHAN JONES
    (The Supremes)
9. DON'T KNOCK MY LOVE
    (Wilson Pickett)
10. DOUBLE LOVIN'
    (The Osmonds)

POP ALBUMS

1. TAPESTRY
    (Carole King)
2. RAM
    (Paul and Linda McCartney)
3. JESUS CHRIST SUPERSTAR
    (Original Soundtrack)
4. CARPENTERS
    (The Carpenters)
5. MUD SLIDE SLIM AND THE BLUE HORIZON
    (James Taylor)
6. STICKY FINGERS
    (The Rolling Stones)
7. SURVIVAL
    (Grand Funk Railroad)
8. ARETHA LIVE AT FILLMORE WEST
    (Aretha Franklin)
9. 11-17-70
    (Elton John)
10. SHE'S A LADY
    (Tom Jones)

BLACK SINGLES

1. MR. BIG STUFF
    (Jean Knight)
2. WANT ADS
    (Honey Cone)
3. I DON'T WANT TO LOSE YOU
    (Johnnie Taylor)
4. DON'T KNOCK MY LOVE
    (Wilson Pickett)
5. FUNKY NASSAU, PART I
    (Beginning of the End)
6. I DON'T WANT TO DO WRONG
    (Gladys Knight and the Pips)
7. SHE'S NOT JUST ANOTHER WOMAN
    (8th Day)
8. SPINNING AROUND
    (Main Ingredient)
9. NATHAN JONES
    (The Supremes)
10. YOU'RE THE REASON WHY
    (Ebonys)

JAZZ ALBUMS

1. TO BE CONTINUED
    (Isaac Hayes)
2. BITCHES BREW
    (Miles Davis)
3. CHAPTER TWO
    (Roberta Flack)
4. SECOND CHAPTER
    (Eddie Harris and Les McCann)
5. JACK JOHNSON
    (Miles Davis)
6. LIVING BLACK
    (Charles Earland)
7. BACK TO THE ROOTS
    (Ramsey Lewis)
8. SUGAR
    (Stanley Turrentine)
9. TJADER
    (Cal Tjader)
10. THEMBI
    (Pharaoh Sanders)

COUNTRY SINGLES

1. WHEN YOU'RE HOT, YOU'RE HOT
    (Jerry Reed)
2. YOU'RE MY MAN
    (Lynn Anderson)
3. RUBY
    (Buck Owens)

4. GWEN
   (Tommy Overstreet)
5. JUST ONE TIME
   (Connie Smith)
6. I'VE GOT A RIGHT TO CRY
   (Hank Williams Jr.)
7. TOMORROW NIGHT IN BALTIMORE
   (Roger Miller)
8. SOMETHING BEAUTIFUL TO REMEMBER
   (Slim Whitman)
9. ME AND YOU AND A DOG NAMED BOO
   (Stonewall Jackson)
10. COMIN' DOWN
    (Dave Dudley)

COUNTRY ALBUMS

1. HAG
   (Merle Haggard)
2. MARTY'S GREATEST HITS, VOL. 3
   (Marty Robbins)
3. WHEN YOU'RE HOT, YOU'RE HOT
   (Jerry Reed)
4. HOW MUCH MORE CAN SHE STAND
   (Conway Twitty)
5. WE SURE CAN LOVE EACH OTHER
   (Tammy Wynette)
6. DID YOU THINK TO PRAY
   (Charley Pride)
7. I WON'T MENTION IT AGAIN
   (Ray Price)
8. I WANNA BE FREE
   (Loretta Lynn)
9. THIS, THAT AND THE OTHER
   (Wendy Bagwell)
10. ROSE GARDEN
    (Lynn Anderson)

JULY 3, 1971

POP SINGLES

1. IT'S TOO LATE
   (Carole King)
2. RAINY DAYS AND MONDAYS
   (The Carpenters)
3. INDIAN RESERVATION
   (The Raiders)
4. IT DON'T COME EASY
   (Ringo Starr)
5. TREAT HER LIKE A LADY
   (Cornelius Brothers and Sister Rose)
6. DON'T PULL YOUR LOVE
   (Hamilton, Joe Frank and Reynolds)
7. I'LL MEET YOU HALFWAY
   (The Partridge Family)
8. DON'T KNOCK MY LOVE
   (Wilson Pickett)
9. WHEN YOU'RE HOT, YOU'RE HOT
   (Jerry Reed)
10. YOU'VE GOT A FRIEND
    (James Taylor)

POP ALBUMS

1. TAPESTRY
   (Carole King)
2. RAM
   (Paul and Linda McCartney)
3. CARPENTERS
   (The Carpenters)
4. JESUS CHRIST SUPERSTAR
   (Original Soundtrack)
5. STICKY FINGERS
   (The Rolling Stones)
6. ARETHA LIVE AT FILLMORE WEST
   (Aretha Franklin)
7. MUD SLIDE SLIM AND THE BLUE HORIZON
   (James Taylor)
8. SURVIVAL
   (Grand Funk Railroad)

9. 11-17-70
   (Elton John)
10. SHE'S A LADY
    (Tom Jones)

BLACK SINGLES

1. MR. BIG STUFF
   (Jean Knight)
2. I DON'T WANT TO DO WRONG
   (Gladys Knight and the Pips)
3. I DON'T WANT TO LOSE YOU
   (Johnnie Taylor)
4. WANT ADS
   (Honey Cone)
5. DON'T KNOCK MY LOVE
   (Wilson Pickett)
6. ESCAP-ISM
   (James Brown)
7. FUNKY NASSAU, PART I
   (Beginning of the End)
8. YOU'RE THE REASON WHY
   (Ebonys)
9. STOP, LOOK, LISTEN
   (The Stylistics)
10. NATHAN JONES
    (The Supremes)

JAZZ ALBUMS

1. SECOND MOVEMENT
   (Eddie Harris and Les McCann)
2. CHAPTER TWO
   (Roberta Flack)
3. TO BE CONTINUED
   (Isaac Hayes)
4. BITCHES BREW
   (Miles Davis)
5. THEMBI
   (Pharoah Sanders)
6. JACK JOHNSON
   (Miles Davis)
7. BACK TO THE ROOTS
   (Ramsey Lewis)
8. SUGAR
   (Stanley Turrentine)
9. LIVING BLACK
   (Charles Earland)
10. STRAIGHT LIFE
    (Freddie Hubbard)

COUNTRY SINGLES

1. RUBY
   (Buck Owens)
2. WHEN YOU'RE HOT, YOU'RE HOT
   (Jerry Reed)
3. GWEN
   (Tommy Overstreet)
4. JUST ONE TIME
   (Connie Smith)
5. SOMETHING BEAUTIFUL TO REMEMBER
   (Slim Whitman)
6. YOU'RE MY MAN
   (Lynn Anderson)
7. ME AND YOU AND A DOG NAMED BOO
   (Stonewall Jackson)
8. PLEASE DON'T TELL ME HOW THE STORY ENDS
   (Bobby Bare)
9. THE CHAIR
   (Marty Robbins)
10. THEN YOU WALK IN
    (Sammi Stewart)

COUNTRY ALBUMS

1. HAG
   (Merle Haggard)
2. MARTY'S GREATEST HITS, VOL. 3
   (Marty Robbins)
3. DID YOU THINK TO PRAY
   (Charley Pride)

4. I WON'T MENTION IT AGAIN
   (Ray Price)
5. WE SURE CAN LOVE EACH OTHER
   (Tammy Wynette)
6. WHEN YOU'RE HOT, YOU'RE HOT
   (Jerry Reed)
7. I WANNA BE FREE
   (Loretta Lynn)
8. ROSE GARDEN
   (Lynn Anderson)
9. HOW MUCH MORE CAN SHE STAND
   (Conway Twitty)
10. THIS, THAT AND THE OTHER
    (Wendy Bagwell)

JULY 10, 1971

POP SINGLES

1. IT'S TOO LATE
   (Carole King)
2. INDIAN RESERVATION
   (The Raiders)
3. TREAT HER LIKE A LADY
   (Cornelius Brothers and Sister Rose)
4. DON'T PULL YOUR LOVE
   (Hamilton, Joe Frank and Reynolds)
5. RAINY DAYS AND MONDAYS
   (The Carpenters)
6. YOU'VE GOT A FRIEND
   (James Taylor)
7. MR. BIG STUFF
   (Jean Knight)
8. WHEN YOU'RE HOT, YOU'RE HOT
   (Jerry Reed)
9. SHE'S NOT JUST ANOTHER WOMAN
   (8th Day)
10. THAT'S THE WAY I'VE ALWAYS HEARD IT SHOULD BE
    (Carly Simon)

POP ALBUMS

1. TAPESTRY
   (Carole King)
2. CARPENTERS
   (The Carpenters)
3. RAM
   (Paul and Linda McCartney)
4. JESUS CHRIST SUPERSTAR
   (Original Soundtrack)
5. ARETHA LIVE AT FILLMORE WEST
   (Aretha Franklin)
6. STICKY FINGERS
   (The Rolling Stones)
7. MUD SLIDE SLIM AND THE BLUE HORIZON
   (James Taylor)
8. SURVIVAL
   (Grand Funk Railroad)
9. 11-17-70
   (Elton John)
10. LEON RUSSELL AND THE SHELTER PEOPLE
    (Shelter)

BLACK SINGLES

1. MR. BIG STUFF
   (Jean Knight)
2. I DON'T WANT TO DO WRONG
   (Gladys Knight and the Pips)
3. ESCAP-ISM
   (James Brown)
4. BRING THE BOYS HOME
   (Freda Payne)
5. STOP, LOOK, LISTEN
   (The Stylistics)
6. LOVE THE ONE YOU'RE WITH
   (Isley Brothers)
7. YOU'VE GOT A FRIEND
   (Roberta Flack and Donny Hathaway)

8. YOU'RE THE REASON WHY
   (Ebonys)
9. SHE'S NOT JUST ANOTHER WOMAN
   (8th Day)
10. DON'T KNOCK MY LOVE
    (Wilson Pickett)

JAZZ ALBUMS

1. SECOND MOVEMENT
   (Eddie Harris and Les McCann)
2. TO BE CONTINUED
   (Isaac Hayes)
3. CHAPTER TWO
   (Roberta Flack)
4. BITCHES BREW
   (Miles Davis)
5. THEMBI
   (Pharaoh Sanders)
6. LIVING BLACK
   (Charles Earland)
7. JACK JOHNSON
   (Miles Davis)
8. BACK TO THE ROOTS
   (Ramsey Lewis)
9. WEATHER REPORT
   (Weather Report)
10. MEMPHIS TWO-STEP
    (Herbie Mann)

COUNTRY SINGLES

1. GWEN
   (Tommy Overstreet)
2. JUST ONE TIME
   (Connie Smith)
3. RUBY
   (Buck Owens)
4. SOMETHING BEAUTIFUL TO REMEMBER
   (Slim Whitman)
5. ME AND YOU AND A DOG NAMED BOO
   (Stonewall Jackson)
6. PLEASE DON'T TELL ME HOW THE STORY ENDS
   (Bobby Bare)
7. THE CHAIR
   (Marty Robbins)
8. WHEN YOU'RE HOT, YOU'RE HOT
   (Jerry Reed)
9. THEN YOU WALK IN
   (Sammi Stewart)
10. YOU'RE MY MAN
    (Lynn Anderson)

COUNTRY ALBUMS

1. I WON'T MENTION IT AGAIN
   (Ray Price)
2. DID YOU THINK TO PRAY
   (Charley Pride)
3. HAG
   (Merle Haggard)
4. MARTY'S GREATEST HITS, VOL. 3
   (Marty Robbins)
5. WE SURE CAN LOVE EACH OTHER
   (Tammy Wynette)
6. I WANNA BE FREE
   (Loretta Lynn)
7. MAN IN BLACK
   (Johnny Cash)
8. WHEN YOU'RE HOT, YOU'RE HOT
   (Jerry Reed)
9. HOW MUCH MORE CAN SHE STAND
   (Conway Twitty)
10. THIS, THAT AND THE OTHER
    (Wendy Bagwell)

JULY 17, 1971

POP SINGLES

1. INDIAN RESERVATION
   (The Raiders)

2. IT'S TOO LATE
   (Carole King)
3. DON'T PULL YOUR LOVE
   (Hamilton, Joe Frank and Reynolds)
4. TREAT HER LIKE A LADY
   (Cornelius Brothers and Sister Rose)
5. YOU'VE GOT A FRIEND
   (James Taylor)
6. MR. BIG STUFF
   (Jean Knight)
7. THAT'S THE WAY I'VE ALWAYS HEARD IT SHOULD BE
   (Carly Simon)
8. SHE'S NOT JUST ANOTHER WOMAN
   (8th Day)
9. WHEN YOU'RE HOT, YOU'RE HOT
   (Jerry Reed)
10. DRAGGIN' THE LINE
    (Tommy James)

POP ALBUMS

1. TAPESTRY
   (Carole King)
2. CARPENTERS
   (The Carpenters)
3. RAM
   (Paul and Linda McCartney)
4. JESUS CHRIST SUPERSTAR
   (Original Soundtrack)
5. ARETHA LIVE AT FILLMORE WEST
   (Aretha Franklin)
6. STICKY FINGERS
   (The Rolling Stones)
7. MUD SLIDE SLIM AND THE BLUE HORIZON
   (James Taylor)
8. LEON RUSSELL AND THE SHELTER PEOPLE
   (Shelter)
9. 11-17-70
   (Elton John)
10. AQUALUNG
    (Jethro Tull)

BLACK SINGLES

1. MR. BIG STUFF
   (Jean Knight)
2. BRING THE BOYS HOME
   (Freda Payne)
3. LOVE THE ONE YOU'RE WITH
   (Isley Brothers)
4. I DON'T WANT TO DO WRONG
   (Gladys Knight and the Pips)
5. STOP, LOOK, LISTEN
   (The Stylistics)
6. ESCAP-ISM
   (James Brown)
7. YOU'VE GOT A FRIEND
   (Roberta Flack and Donny Hathaway)
8. MERCY MERCY ME (THE ECOLOGY)
   (Marvin Gaye)
9. SHE'S NOT JUST ANOTHER WOMAN
   (8th Day)
10. YOU'RE THE REASON WHY
    (Ebonys)

BLACK ALBUMS

1. WHAT'S GOING ON
   (Marvin Gaye)
2. ARETHA LIVE AT FILLMORE WEST
   (Aretha Franklin)
3. THE SKY'S THE LIMIT
   (Temptations)
4. TOUCH
   (The Supremes)
5. BEST OF WILSON PICKETT
   (Wilson Pickett)
6. MAYBE TOMORROW
   (The Jackson 5)
7. CURTIS LIVE
   (Curtis Mayfield)
8. IF I WERE YOUR WOMAN
   (Gladys Knight and the Pips)

9. DONNY HATHAWAY
   (Donny Hathaway)
10. CHAPTER TWO
    (Roberta Flack)

JAZZ ALBUMS

1. SECOND MOVEMENT
   (Eddie Harris and Les McCann)
2. TO BE CONTINUED
   (Isaac Hayes)
3. THEMBI
   (Pharaoh Sanders)
4. BACK TO THE ROOTS
   (Ramsey Lewis)
5. WEATHER REPORT
   (Weather Report)
6. CHAPTER TWO
   (Roberta Flack)
7. BITCHES BREW
   (Miles Davis)
8. LIVING BLACK
   (Charles Earland)
9. JACK JOHNSON
   (Miles Davis)
10. MEMPHIS TWO-STEP
    (Herbie Mann)

COUNTRY SINGLES

1. JUST ONE MORE TIME
   (Connie Smith)
2. GWEN
   (Tommy Overstreet)
3. PLEASE DON'T TELL ME HOW THE STORY ENDS
   (Bobby Bare)
4. ME AND YOU AND A DOG NAMED BOO
   (Stonewall Jackson)
5. THE CHAIR
   (Marty Robbins)
6. BRIGHT LIGHTS, BIG CITY
   (Sonny James)
7. SOMETHING BEAUTIFUL TO REMEMBER
   (Slim Whitman)
8. THEN YOU WALK IN
   (Sammi Stewart)
9. TAKE MY HAND
   (Mel Tillis and Sherry Bryce)
10. RUBY
    (Buck Owens)

COUNTRY ALBUMS

1. I WON'T MENTION IT AGAIN
   (Ray Price)
2. DID YOU THINK TO PRAY
   (Charley Pride)
3. HAG
   (Merle Haggard)
4. MAN IN BLACK
   (Johnny Cash)
5. I WANNA BE FREE
   (Loretta Lynn)
6. WE SURE CAN LOVE EACH OTHER
   (Tammy Wynette)
7. HOW MUCH MORE CAN SHE STAND
   (Conway Twitty)
8. WHEN YOU'RE HOT, YOU'RE HOT
   (Jerry Reed)
9. MARTY'S GREATEST HITS, VOL. 3
   (Marty Robbins)
10. ROSE GARDEN
    (Lynn Anderson)

JULY 24, 1971

POP SINGLES

1. INDIAN RESERVATION
   (The Raiders)

2. IT'S TOO LATE
   (Carole King)
3. DON'T PULL YOUR LOVE
   (Hamilton, Joe Frank and Reynolds)
4. YOU'VE GOT A FRIEND
   (James Taylor)
5. MR. BIG STUFF
   (Jean Knight)
6. DRAGGIN' THE LINE
   (Tommy James)
7. THAT'S THE WAY I'VE ALWAYS HEARD IT SHOULD BE
   (Carly Simon)
8. SHE'S NOT JUST ANOTHER WOMAN
   (8th Day)
9. HOW CAN YOU MEND A BROKEN HEART
   (The Bee Gees)
10. TREAT HER LIKE A LADY
    (Cornelius Brothers and Sister Rose)

POP ALBUMS

1. TAPESTRY
   (Carole King)
2. CARPENTERS
   (The Carpenters)
3. JESUS CHRIST SUPERSTAR
   (Original Soundtrack)
4. RAM
   (Paul and Linda McCartney)
5. STICKY FINGERS
   (The Rolling Stones)
6. WHAT'S GOING ON
   (Marvin Gaye)
7. MUD SLIDE SLIM AND THE BLUE HORIZON
   (James Taylor)
8. LEON RUSSELL AND THE SHELTER PEOPLE
   (Shelter)
9. AQUALUNG
   (Jethro Tull)
10. TARKUS
    (Emerson, Lake and Palmer)

BLACK SINGLES

1. MR. BIG STUFF
   (Jean Knight)
2. BRING THE BOYS HOME
   (Freda Payne)
3. LOVE THE ONE YOU'RE WITH
   (Isley Brothers)
4. HOT PANTS
   (James Brown)
5. YOU'VE GOT A FRIEND
   (Roberta Flack and Donny Hathaway)
6. MERCY MERCY ME (THE ECOLOGY)
   (Marvin Gaye)
7. I DON'T WANT TO DO WRONG
   (Gladys Knight and the Pips)
8. ESCAP-ISM
   (James Brown)
9. STOP, LOOK, LISTEN
   (The Stylistics)
10. HEY LOVE/OVER AND OVER
    (The Delfonics)

BLACK ALBUMS

1. WHAT'S GOING ON
   (Marvin Gaye)
2. ARETHA LIVE AT FILLMORE WEST
   (Aretha Franklin)
3. THE SKY'S THE LIMIT
   (Temptations)
4. TOUCH
   (The Supremes)
5. CURTIS LIVE
   (Curtis Mayfield)
6. IF I WERE YOUR WOMAN
   (Gladys Knight and the Pips)
7. BEST OF WILSON PICKETT
   (Wilson Pickett)

8. MAYBE TOMORROW
   (The Jackson 5)
9. DONNY HATHAWAY
   (Donny Hathaway)
10. SWEET REPLIES
    (Honey Cone)

JAZZ ALBUMS

1. SECOND MOVEMENT
   (Eddie Harris and Les McCann)
2. THEMBI
   (Pharaoh Sanders)
3. BACK TO THE ROOTS
   (Ramsey Lewis)
4. WEATHER REPORT
   (Weather Report)
5. TO BE CONTINUED
   (Isaac Hayes)
6. CHAPTER TWO
   (Roberta Flack)
7. LIVING BLACK
   (Charles Earland)
8. MEMPHIS TWO-STEP
   (Herbie Mann)
9. BITCHES BREW
   (Miles Davis)
10. EGO
    (Tony Williams Lifetime)

COUNTRY SINGLES

1. PLEASE DON'T TELL ME HOW THE STORY ENDS
   (Bobby Bare)
2. BRIGHT LIGHTS, BIG CITY
   (Sonny James)
3. JUST ONE TIME
   (Connie Smith)
4. THE CHAIR
   (Marty Robbins)
5. TAKE MY HAND
   (Mel Tillis and Sherry Bryce)
6. INDIAN LAKE
   (Freddy Weller)
7. I'M JUST ME
   (Charley Pride)
8. ME AND YOU AND A DOG NAMED BOO
   (Stonewall Jackson)
9. GWEN
   (Tommy Overstreet)
10. RIGHT WON'T TOUCH A HAND
    (George Jones)

COUNTRY ALBUMS

1. I WON'T MENTION IT AGAIN
   (Ray Price)
2. MAN IN BLACK
   (Johnny Cash)
3. HAG
   (Merle Haggard)
4. I WANNA BE FREE
   (Loretta Lynn)
5. DID YOU THINK TO PRAY
   (Charley Pride)
6. HOW MUCH MORE CAN SHE STAND
   (Conway Twitty)
7. WHEN YOU'RE HOT, YOU'RE HOT
   (Jerry Reed)
8. WE SURE CAN LOVE EACH OTHER
   (Tammy Wynette)
9. ROSE GARDEN
   (Lynn Anderson)
10. MARTY'S GREATEST HITS, VOL. 3
    (Marty Robbins)

JULY 31, 1971

POP SINGLES

1. INDIAN RESERVATION
   (The Raiders)

2. MR. BIG STUFF
   (Jean Knight)
3. DON'T PULL YOUR LOVE
   (Hamilton, Joe Frank and Reynolds)
4. YOU'VE GOT A FRIEND
   (James Taylor)
5. DRAGGIN' THE LINE
   (Tommy Taylor)
6. HOW CAN YOU MEND A BROKEN HEART
   (The Bee Gees)
7. BRING THE BOYS HOME
   (Freda Payne)
8. TAKE ME HOME, COUNTRY ROADS
   (John Denver)
9. I DON'T WANT TO DO WRONG
   (Gladys Knight and the Pips)
10. MERCY MERCY ME (THE ECOLOGY)
    (Marvin Gaye)

POP ALBUMS

1. TAPESTRY
   (Carole King)
2. CARPENTERS
   (The Carpenters)
3. WHAT'S GOING ON
   (Marvin Gaye)
4. STICKY FINGERS
   (The Rolling Stones)
5. JESUS CHRIST SUPERSTAR
   (Original Soundtrack)
6. RAM
   (Paul and Linda McCartney)
7. MUD SLIDE SLIM AND THE BLUE HORIZON
   (James Taylor)
8. AQUALUNG
   (Jethro Tull)
9. EVERY PICTURE TELLS A STORY
   (Rod Stewart)
10. TARKUS
    (Emerson, Lake and Palmer)

BLACK SINGLES

1. HOT PANTS
   (James Brown)
2. MR. BIG STUFF
   (Jean Knight)
3. LOVE THE ONE YOU'RE WITH
   (Isley Brothers)
4. MERCY MERCY ME (THE ECOLOGY)
   (Marvin Gaye)
5. YOU'VE GOT A FRIEND
   (Roberta Flack and Donny Hathaway)
6. BRING THE BOYS HOME
   (Freda Payne)
7. I DON'T WANT TO DO WRONG
   (Gladys Knight and the Pips)
8. STOP, LOOK, LISTEN
   (The Stylistics)
9. WATCHA SEE IS WATCHA GET
   (The Dramatics)
10. HEY LOVE/OVER AND OVER
    (The Delfonics)

BLACK ALBUMS

1. WHAT'S GOING ON
   (Marvin Gaye)
2. ARETHA LIVE AT FILLMORE WEST
   (Aretha Franklin)
3. THE SKY'S THE LIMIT
   (Temptations)
4. IF I WERE YOUR WOMAN
   (Gladys Knight and the Pips)
5. MAYBE TOMORROW
   (The Jackson 5)
6. TOUCH
   (The Supremes)
7. CURTIS LIVE
   (Curtis Mayfield)
8. DONNY HATHAWAY
   (Donny Hathaway)

9. JUST AS I AM
   (Bill Withers)
10. BEST OF WILSON PICKETT
    (Wilson Pickett)

JAZZ ALBUMS

1. SECOND MOVEMENT
   (Eddie Harris and Les McCann)
2. THEMBI
   (Pharaoh Sanders)
3. WEATHER REPORT
   (Weather Report)
4. BACK TO THE ROOTS
   (Ramsey Lewis)
5. CHAPTER TWO
   (Roberta Flack)
6. TO BE CONTINUED
   (Isaac Hayes)
7. LIVING BLACK
   (Charles Earland)
8. MEMPHIS TWO-STEP
   (Herbie Mann)
9. BITCHES BREW
   (Miles Davis)
10. EGO
    (Tony Williams Lifetime)

COUNTRY SINGLES

1. BRIGHT LIGHTS, BIG CITY
   (Sonny James)
2. PLEASE DON'T TELL ME HOW THE STORY
   ENDS
   (Bobby Bare)
3. INDIAN LAKE
   (Freddy Weller)
4. TAKE MY HAND
   (Mel Tillis and Sherry Bryce)
5. I'M JUST ME
   (Charley Pride)
6. JUST ONE TIME
   (Connie Smith)
7. HE'S SO FINE
   (Jody Miller)
8. RIGHT WON'T TOUCH A HAND
   (George Jones)
9. NASHVILLE
   (David Houston)
10. SOMEDAY WE'LL LOOK BACK
    (Merle Haggard)

COUNTRY ALBUMS

1. MAN IN BLACK
   (Johnny Cash)
2. I WON'T MENTION IT AGAIN
   (Ray Price)
3. HAG
   (Merle Haggard)
4. WHEN YOU'RE HOT, YOU'RE HOT
   (Jerry Reed)
5. I WANNA BE FREE
   (Loretta Lynn)
6. HOW MUCH MORE CAN SHE STAND
   (Conway Twitty)
7. DID YOU THINK TO PRAY
   (Charley Pride)
8. WE SURE CAN LOVE EACH OTHER
   (Tammy Wynette)
9. I'M JUST ME
   (Charley Pride)
10. ROSE GARDEN
    (Lynn Anderson)

AUGUST 7, 1971

POP SINGLES

1. MR. BIG STUFF
   (Jean Knight)

2. YOU'VE GOT A FRIEND
   (James Taylor)
3. DRAGGIN' THE LINE
   (Tommy James)
4. HOW CAN YOU MEND A BROKEN HEART
   (The Bee Gees)
5. BRING THE BOYS HOME
   (Freda Payne)
6. TAKE ME HOME, COUNTRY ROADS
   (John Denver)
7. INDIAN RESERVATION
   (The Raiders)
8. MERCY MERCY ME (THE ECOLOGY)
   (Marvin Gaye)
9. I DON'T WANT TO DO WRONG
   (Gladys Knight and the Pips)
10. SOONER OR LATER
    (Grass Roots)

POP ALBUMS

1. TAPESTRY
   (Carole King)
2. STICKY FINGERS
   (The Rolling Stones)
3. WHAT'S GOING ON
   (Marvin Gaye)
4. RAM
   (Paul and Linda McCartney)
5. JESUS CHRIST SUPERSTAR
   (Original Soundtrack)
6. CARPENTERS
   (The Carpenters)
7. MUD SLIDE SLIM AND THE BLUE HORIZON
   (James Taylor)
8. AQUALUNG
   (Jethro Tull)
9. EVERY PICTURE TELLS A STORY
   (Rod Stewart)
10. STEPHEN STILLS 2
    (Stephen Stills)

BLACK SINGLES

1. HOT PANTS
   (James Brown)
2. MERCY MERCY ME (THE ECOLOGY)
   (Marvin Gaye)
3. LOVE THE ONE YOU'RE WITH
   (Isley Brothers)
4. MR. BIG STUFF
   (Jean Knight)
5. YOU'VE GOT A FRIEND
   (Roberta Flack and Donny Hathaway)
6. WATCHA SEE IS WATCHA GET
   (The Dramatics)
7. BRING THE BOYS HOME
   (Freda Payne)
8. I LIKES TO DO IT
   (People's Choice)
9. MAYBE TOMORROW
   (The Jackson 5)
10. SMILING FACES SOMETIMES
    (Undisputed Truth)

BLACK ALBUMS

1. WHAT'S GOING ON
   (Marvin Gaye)
2. ARETHA LIVE AT FILLMORE WEST
   (Aretha Franklin)
3. THE SKY'S THE LIMIT
   (Temptations)
4. IF I WERE YOUR WOMAN
   (Gladys Knight and the Pips)
5. MAYBE TOMORROW
   (The Jackson 5)
6. CURTIS LIVE
   (Curtis Mayfield)
7. DONNY HATHAWAY
   (Donny Hathaway)
8. JUST AS I AM
   (Bill Withers)

9. CONTACT
   (Freda Payne)
10. WHAT YOU HEAR IS WHAT YOU GET
    (Ike and Tina Turner)

JAZZ ALBUMS

1. SECOND MOVEMENT
   (Eddie Harris and Les McCann)
2. THEMBI
   (Pharaoh Sanders)
3. WEATHER REPORT
   (Weather Report)
4. CHAPTER TWO
   (Roberta Flack)
5. TO BE CONTINUED
   (Isaac Hayes)
6. LIVING BLACK
   (Charles Earland)
7. BACK TO THE ROOTS
   (Ramsey Lewis)
8. MEMPHIS TWO-STEP
   (Herbie Mann)
9. EGO
   (Tony Williams Lifetime)
10. BITCHES BREW
    (Miles Davis)

COUNTRY SINGLES

1. I'M JUST ME
   (Charley Pride)
2. BRIGHT LIGHTS, BIG CITY
   (Sonny James)
3. INDIAN LAKE
   (Freddy Weller)
4. HE'S SO FINE
   (Jody Miller)
5. DREAM LOVER
   (Billy "Crash" Craddock)
6. SOMEDAY WE'LL LOOK BACK
   (Merle Haggard)
7. RIGHT WON'T TOUCH A HAND
   (George James)
8. NASHVILLE
   (David Houston)
9. TAKE MY HAND
   (Mel Tillis and Sherry Bryce)
10. PLEASE DON'T TELL ME HOW THE STORY
    ENDS
    (Bobby Bare)

COUNTRY ALBUMS

1. MAN IN BLACK
   (Johnny Cash)
2. I WON'T MENTION IT AGAIN
   (Ray Price)
3. I'M JUST ME
   (Charley Pride)
4. WHEN YOU'RE HOT, YOU'RE HOT
   (Jerry Reed)
5. HAG
   (Merle Haggard)
6. HOW MUCH MORE CAN SHE STAND
   (Conway Twitty)
7. WE SURE CAN LOVE EACH OTHER
   (Tammy Wynette)
8. I WANNA BE FREE
   (Loretta Lynn)
9. ROSE GARDEN
   (Lynn Anderson)
10. SOMETHING SPECIAL
    (Jim Reeves)

AUGUST 14, 1971

POP SINGLES

1. HOW CAN YOU MEND A BROKEN HEART
   (The Bee Gees)

2. DRAGGIN' THE LINE
    (Tommy James)
3. YOU'VE GOT A FRIEND
    (James Taylor)
4. TAKE ME HOME, COUNTRY ROADS
    (John Denver)
5. BRING THE BOYS HOME
    (Freda Payne)
6. MERCY MERCY ME (THE ECOLOGY)
    (Marvin Gaye)
7. MR. BIG STUFF
    (Jean Knight)
8. WHAT THE WORLD NEEDS NOW IS
    LOVE/ABRAHAM, MARTIN AND JOHN
    (Tom Clay)
9. BEGINNINGS/COLOUR MY WORLD
    (Chicago)
10. SPANISH HARLEM
    (Aretha Franklin)

POP ALBUMS

1. TAPESTRY
    (Carole King)
2. STICKY FINGERS
    (The Rolling Stones)
3. WHAT'S GOING ON
    (Marvin Gaye)
4. RAM
    (Paul and Linda McCartney)
5. MUD SLIDE SLIM AND THE BLUE HORIZON
    (James Taylor)
6. JESUS CHRIST SUPERSTAR
    (Original Soundtrack)
7. CARPENTERS
    (The Carpenters)
8. EVERY PICTURE TELLS A STORY
    (Rod Stewart)
9. STEPHEN STILLS 2
    (Stephen Stills)
10. AQUALUNG
    (Jethro Tull)

BLACK SINGLES

1. HOT PANTS
    (James Brown)
2. MERCY MERCY ME (THE ECOLOGY)
    (Marvin Gaye)
3. MAYBE TOMORROW
    (The Jackson 5)
4. I LIKES TO DO IT
    (People's Choice)
5. WATCHA SEE IS WATCHA GET
    (The Dramatics)
6. SPANISH HARLEM
    (Aretha Franklin)
7. SMILING FACES SOMETIMES
    (Undisputed Truth)
8. LOVE THE ONE YOU'RE WITH
    (Isley Brothers)
9. AIN'T NO SUNSHINE
    (Bill Withers)
10. ONE WAY TICKET
    (Tyrone Davis)

BLACK ALBUMS

1. WHAT'S GOING ON
    (Marvin Gaye)
2. ARETHA LIVE AT FILLMORE WEST
    (Aretha Franklin)
3. THE SKY'S THE LIMIT
    (Temptations)
4. IF I WERE YOUR WOMAN
    (Gladys Knight and the Pips)
5. CURTIS LIVE
    (Curtis Mayfield)
6. MAYBE TOMORROW
    (The Jackson 5)
7. JUST AS I AM
    (Bill Withers)
8. DONNY HATHAWAY
    (Donny Hathaway)

9. CONTACT
    (Freda Payne)
10. WHAT YOU HEAR IS WHAT YOU GET
    (Ike and Tina Turner)

JAZZ ALBUMS

1. SECOND MOVEMENT
    (Eddie Harris and Les McCann)
2. TO BE CONTINUED
    (Isaac Hayes)
3. CHAPTER TWO
    (Roberta Flack)
4. THEMBI
    (Pharaoh Sanders)
5. WEATHER REPORT
    (Weather Report)
6. BITCHES BREW
    (Miles Davis)
7. BACK TO THE ROOTS
    (Ramsey Lewis)
8. JACK JOHNSON
    (Miles Davis)
9. EGO
    (Tony Williams Lifetime)
10. SUGAR
    (Stanley Turrentine)

COUNTRY SINGLES

1. SOMEDAY WE'LL LOOK BACK
    (Merle Haggard)
2. I'M JUST ME
    (Charley Pride)
3. DREAM LOVER
    (Billy "Crash" Craddock)
4. HE'S SO FINE
    (Jody Miller)
5. BRIGHT LIGHTS, BIG CITY
    (Sonny James)
6. GOOD LOVIN'
    (Tammy Wynette)
7. I WONDER WHAT SHE'LL THINK ABOUT
    MY LEAVING
    (Conway Twitty)
8. NASHVILLE
    (David Houston)
9. EASY LOVIN'
    (Freddie Hart)
10. INDIAN LAKE
    (Freddy Weller)

COUNTRY ALBUMS

1. I WON'T MENTION IT AGAIN
    (Ray Price)
2. I'M JUST ME
    (Charley Pride)
3. MAN IN BLACK
    (Johnny Cash)
4. WHEN YOU'RE HOT, YOU'RE HOT
    (Jerry Reed)
5. HAG
    (Merle Haggard)
6. I WANNA BE FREE
    (Loretta Lynn)
7. POEMS, PRAYERS AND PROMISES
    (John Denver)
8. WE SURE CAN LOVE EACH OTHER
    (Tammy Wynette)
9. YOU'RE MY MAN
    (Lynn Anderson)
10. TOUCHING HOME
    (Jerry Lee Lewis)

MARCH 27, 1971

POP SINGLES

1. DRAGGIN' THE LINE
    (Tommy James)

2. TAKE ME HOME, COUNTRY ROADS
    (John Denver)
3. HOW CAN YOU MEND A BROKEN HEART
    (The Bee Gees)
4. MERCY MERCY ME (THE ECOLOGY)
    (Marvin Gaye)
5. SWEET HITCH-HIKER
    (Creedence Clearwater Revival)
6. SPANISH HARLEM
    (Aretha Franklin)
7. WHAT THE WORLD NEEDS NOW IS
    LOVE/ABRAHAM, MARTIN AND JOHN
    (Tom Clay)
8. BEGINNINGS/COLOUR MY WORLD
    (Chicago)
9. YOU'VE GOT A FRIEND
    (James Taylor)
10. SIGNS
    (Five Man Electrical Band)

POP ALBUMS

1. TAPESTRY
    (Carole King)
2. MUD SLIDE SLIM AND THE BLUE HORIZON
    (James Taylor)
3. CARPENTERS
    (The Carpenters)
4. RAM
    (Paul and Linda McCartney)
5. STICKY FINGERS
    (The Rolling Stones)
6. JESUS CHRIST SUPERSTAR
    (Original Soundtrack)
7. WHAT'S GOING ON
    (Marvin Gaye)
8. STEPHEN STILLS 2
    (Stephen Stills)
9. EVERY PICTURE TELLS A STORY
    (Rod Stewart)
10. AQUALUNG
    (Jethro Tull)

BLACK SINGLES

1. MERCY MERCY ME (THE ECOLOGY)
    (Marvin Gaye)
2. MAYBE TOMORROW
    (The Jackson 5)
3. I LIKES TO DO IT
    (People's Choice)
4. SPANISH HARLEM
    (Aretha Franklin)
5. WATCHA SEE IS WATCHA GET
    (The Dramatics)
6. SMILING FACES SOMETIMES
    (Undisputed Truth)
7. HOT PANTS
    (James Brown)
8. AIN'T NO SUNSHINE
    (Bill Withers)
9. TIRED OF BEING ALONE
    (Al Green)
10. LOVE THE ONE YOU'RE WITH
    (Isley Brothers)

JAZZ ALBUMS

1. SECOND MOVEMENT
    (Eddie Harris and Les McCann)
2. TO BE CONTINUED
    (Isaac Hayes)
3. CHAPTER TWO
    (Roberta Flack)
4. WEATHER REPORT
    (Weather Report)
5. THEMBI
    (Pharaoh Sanders)
6. BITCHES BREW
    (Miles Davis)
7. JACK JOHNSON
    (Miles Davis)
8. BACK TO THE ROOTS
    (Ramsey Lewis)

9. SUGAR
(Stanley Turrentine)
10. EGO
(Tony Williams Lifetime)

COUNTRY SINGLES

1. GOOD LOVIN'
(Tammy Wynette)
2. I WONDER WHAT SHE'LL THINK ABOUT
MY LEAVING
(Conway Twitty)
3. DREAM LOVER
(Billy "Crash" Craddock)
4. SOMEDAY WE'LL LOOK BACK
(Merle Haggard)
5. I'M JUST ME
(Charley Pride)
6. EASY LOVIN'
(Freddie Hart)
7. THE YEAR CLAYTON DELANEY DIED
(Tom T. Hall)
8. BRIGHT LIGHTS, BIG CITY
(Sonny James)
9. THE RIGHT COMBINATION
(Porter Wagoner and Dolly Parton)
10. PHILADELPHIA FILLIES
(Del Reeves)

COUNTRY ALBUMS

1. I'M JUST ME
(Charley Pride)
2. I WON'T MENTION IT AGAIN
(Ray Price)
3. WHEN YOU'RE HOT, YOU'RE HOT
(Jerry Reed)
4. MAN IN BLACK
(Johnny Cash)
5. POEMS, PRAYERS, AND PROMISES
(John Denver)
6. YOU'RE MY MAN
(Lynn Anderson)
7. I WANNA BE FREE
(Loretta Lynn)
8. HAG
(Merle Haggard)
9. THE SENSATIONAL SONNY JAMES
(Sonny James)
10. BEST OF PORTER WAGONER AND DOLLY
PARTON
(Porter Wagoner and Dolly Parton)

AUGUST 28, 1971

POP SINGLES

1. TAKE ME HOME, COUNTRY ROADS
(John Denver)
2. MERCY MERCY ME (THE ECOLOGY)
(Marvin Gaye)
3. SWEET HITCH-HIKER
(Creedence Clearwater Revival)
4. SPANISH HARLEM
(Aretha Franklin)
5. DRAGGIN' THE LINE
(Tommy James)
6. HOW CAN YOU MEND A BROKEN HEART
(The Bee Gees)
7. BEGINNINGS/COLOUR MY WORLD
(Chicago)
8. SIGNS
(Five Man Electrical Band)
9. LIAR
(Three Dog Night)
10. SMILING FACES SOMETIMES
(Undisputed Truth)

POP ALBUMS

1. TAPESTRY
(Carole King)
2. MUD SLIDE SLIM AND THE BLUE HORIZON
(James Taylor)
3. CARPENTERS
(The Carpenters)
4. RAM
(Paul and Linda McCartney)
5. STICKY FINGERS
(The Rolling Stones)
6. B. S. & T. 4
(Blood, Sweat and Tears)
7. JESUS CHRIST SUPERSTAR
(Original Soundtrack)
8. STEPHEN STILLS 2
(Stephen Stills)
9. EVERY PICTURE TELLS A STORY
(Rod Stewart)
10. AQUALUNG
(Jethro Tull)

BLACK SINGLES

1. SMILING FACES SOMETIMES
(Undisputed Truth)
2. SPANISH HARLEM
(Aretha Franklin)
3. I LIKES TO DO IT
(People's Choice)
4. MERCY MERCY ME (THE ECOLOGY)
(Marvin Gaye)
5. TIRED OF BEING ALONE
(Al Green)
6. AIN'T NO SUNSHINE
(Bill Withers)
7. WATCHA SEE IS WATCHA GET
(The Dramatics)
8. STICKUP
(Honey Cone)
9. MAYBE TOMORROW
(The Jackson 5)
10. K-JEE
(Nite-Liters)

BLACK ALBUMS

1. WHAT'S GOING ON
(Marvin Gaye)
2. ARETHA LIVE AT FILLMORE WEST
(Aretha Franklin)
3. THE SKY'S THE LIMIT
(Temptations)
4. IF I WERE YOUR WOMAN
(Gladys Knight and the Pips)
5. WHAT YOU HEAR IS WHAT YOU GET
(Ike and Tina Turner)
6. MAYBE TOMORROW
(The Jackson 5)
7. JUST AS I AM
(Bill Withers)
8. CURTIS LIVE
(Curtis Mayfield)
9. SURRENDER
(Diana Ross)
10. DONNY HATHAWAY
(Donny Hathaway)

JAZZ ALBUMS

1. SECOND MOVEMENT
(Eddie Harris and Les McCann)
2. CHAPTER TWO
(Roberta Flack)
3. TO BE CONTINUED
(Isaac Hayes)
4. WEATHER REPORT
(Weather Report)
5. THEMBI
(Pharaoh Sanders)
6. BACK TO THE ROOTS
(Ramsey Lewis)

7. BITCHES BREW
(Miles Davis)
8. SUGAR
(Stanley Turrentine)
9. JACK JOHNSON
(Miles Davis)
10. EGO
(Tony Williams Lifetime)

COUNTRY SINGLES

1. DREAM LOVER
(Billy "Crash" Craddock)
2. I WONDER WHAT SHE'LL THINK ABOUT
MY LEAVING
(Conway Twitty)
3. GOOD LOVIN'
(Tammy Wynette)
4. THE YEAR CLAYTON DELANEY DIED
(Tom T. Hall)
5. EASY LOVIN'
(Freddie Hart)
6. I'M JUST ME
(Charley Pride)
7. SOMEDAY WE'LL LOOK BACK
(Merle Haggard)
8. PHILADELPHIA FILLIES
(Del Reeves)
9. THE RIGHT COMBINATION
(Porter Wagoner and Dolly Parton)
10. GOOD ENOUGH TO BE YOUR WIFE
(Jeannie C. Riley)

COUNTRY ALBUMS

1. I'M JUST ME
(Charley Pride)
2. YOU'RE MY MAN
(Lynn Anderson)
3. I WON'T MENTION IT AGAIN
(Ray Price)
4. THE SENSATIONAL SONNY JAMES
(Sonny James)
5. POEMS, PRAYERS AND PROMISES
(John Denver)
6. MAN IN BLACK
(Johnny Cash)
7. BEST OF PORTER WAGONER AND DOLLY
PARTON
(Porter Wagoner and Dolly Parton)
8. WHEN YOU'RE HOT, YOU'RE HOT
(Jerry Reed)
9. I WANNA BE FREE
(Loretta Lynn)
10. HAG
(Merle Haggard)

SEPTEMBER 4, 1971

POP SINGLES

1. TAKE ME HOME, COUNTRY ROADS
(John Denver)
2. MERCY MERCY ME (THE ECOLOGY)
(Marvin Gaye)
3. SPANISH HARLEM
(Aretha Franklin)
4. SWEET HITCH-HIKER
(Creedence Clearwater Revival)
5. SIGNS
(Five Man Electrical Band)
6. LIAR
(Three Dog Night)
7. SMILING FACES SOMETIMES
(Undisputed Truth)
8. HOW CAN YOU MEND A BROKEN HEART
(The Bee Gees)
9. GO AWAY LITTLE GIRL
(Donny Osmond)
10. UNCLE ALBERT/ADMIRAL HALSEY
(Paul and Linda McCartney)

POP ALBUMS

1. TAPESTRY
   (Carole King)
2. RAM
   (Paul and Linda McCartney)
3. MUD SLIDE SLIM AND THE BLUE HORIZON
   (James Taylor)
4. CARPENTERS
   (The Carpenters)
5. WHO'S NEXT
   (The Who)
6. B. S. & T. 4
   (Blood, Sweat and Tears)
7. AQUALUNG
   (Jethro Tull)
8. JESUS CHRIST SUPERSTAR
   (Original Soundtrack)
9. STICKY FINGERS
   (The Rolling Stones)
10. EVERY PICTURE TELLS A STORY
    (Rod Stewart)

BLACK SINGLES

1. SPANISH HARLEM
   (Aretha Franklin)
2. SMILING FACES SOMETIMES
   (Undisputed Truth)
3. I LIKES TO DO IT
   (People's Choice)
4. TIRED OF BEING ALONE
   (Al Green)
5. AIN'T NO SUNSHINE
   (Bill Withers)
6. STICKUP
   (Honey Cone)
7. MERCY MERCY ME (THE ECOLOGY)
   (Marvin Gaye)
8. WATCHA SEE IS WATCHA GET
   (The Dramatics)
9. THE LOVE WE HAD
   (The Dells)
10. K-JEE
    (Nite-Liters)

BLACK ALBUMS

1. WHAT'S GOING ON
   (Marvin Gaye)
2. ARETHA LIVE AT FILLMORE WEST
   (Aretha Franklin)
3. IF I WERE YOUR WOMAN
   (Gladys Knight and the Pips)
4. SHAFT
   (Isaac Hayes)
5. WHAT YOU HEAR IS WHAT YOU GET
   (Ike and Tina Turner)
6. JUST AS I AM
   (Bill Withers)
7. THE SKY'S THE LIMIT
   (Temptations)
8. MR. BIG STUFF
   (Jean Knight)
9. SURRENDER
   (Diana Ross)
10. UNDISPUTED TRUTH
    (Undisputed Truth)

JAZZ ALBUMS

1. SECOND MOVEMENT
   (Eddie Harris and Les McCann)
2. CHAPTER TWO
   (Roberta Flack)
3. WEATHER REPORT
   (Weather Report)
4. TO BE CONTINUED
   (Isaac Hayes)
5. THEMBI
   (Pharaoh Sanders)
6. BACK TO THE ROOTS
   (Ramsey Lewis)

7. SUGAR
   (Stanley Turrentine)
8. BITCHES BREW
   (Miles Davis)
9. JACK JOHNSON
   (Miles Davis)
10. EGO
    (Tony Williams Lifetime)

COUNTRY SINGLES

1. I WONDER WHAT SHE'LL THINK ABOUT MY LEAVING
   (Conway Twitty)
2. THE YEAR CLAYTON DELANEY DIED
   (Tom T. Hall)
3. EASY LOVIN'
   (Freddie Hart)
4. DREAM LOVER
   (Billy "Crash" Craddock)
5. GOOD LOVIN'
   (Tammy Wynette)
6. GOOD ENOUGH TO BE YOUR WIFE
   (Jeannie C. Riley)
7. QUITS
   (Bill Anderson)
8. PHILADELPHIA FILLIES
   (Del Reeves)
9. PITTY PITTY PATTER
   (Susan Raye)
10. YOU'RE LOOKIN' AT COUNTRY
    (Loretta Lynn)

COUNTRY ALBUMS

1. YOU'RE MY MAN
   (Lynn Anderson)
2. THE SENSATIONAL SONNY JAMES
   (Sonny James)
3. I'M JUST ME
   (Charley Pride)
4. I WON'T MENTION IT AGAIN
   (Ray Price)
5. BEST OF PORTER WAGONER AND DOLLY PARTON
   (Porter Wagoner and Dolly Parton)
6. POEMS, PRAYERS AND PROMISES
   (John Denver)
7. MAN IN BLACK
   (Johnny Cash)
8. RUBY
   (Buck Owens and the Buckaroos)
9. I WANNA BE FREE
   (Loretta Lynn)
10. HAG
    (Merle Haggard)

SEPTEMBER 11, 1971

POP SINGLES

1. UNCLE ALBERT/ADMIRAL HALSEY
   (Paul and Linda McCartney)
2. SPANISH HARLEM
   (Aretha Franklin)
3. SMILING FACES SOMETIMES
   (Undisputed Truth)
4. GO AWAY LITTLE GIRL
   (Donny Osmond)
5. TAKE ME HOME, COUNTRY ROADS
   (John Denver)
6. SIGNS
   (Five Man Electrical Band)
7. AIN'T NO SUNSHINE
   (Bill Withers)
8. THE NIGHT THEY DROVE OLD DIXIE DOWN
   (Joan Baez)

9. I JUST WANT TO CELEBRATE
   (Rare Earth)
10. WATCHA SEE IS WATCHA GET
    (The Dramatics)

POP ALBUMS

1. TAPESTRY
   (Carole King)
2. RAM
   (Paul and Linda McCartney)
3. EVERY GOOD BOY DESERVES FAVOUR
   (The Moody Blues)
4. WHO'S NEXT
   (The Who)
5. MUD SLIDE SLIM AND THE BLUE HORIZON
   (James Taylor)
6. CARPENTERS
   (The Carpenters)
7. AQUALUNG
   (Jethro Tull)
8. EVERY PICTURE TELLS A STORY
   (Rod Stewart)
9. SHAFT
   (Isaac Hayes)
10. JESUS CHRIST SUPERSTAR
    (Original Soundtrack)

BLACK SINGLES

1. SPANISH HARLEM
   (Aretha Franklin)
2. AIN'T NO SUNSHINE
   (Bill Withers)
3. STICKUP
   (Honey Cone)
4. TIRED OF BEING ALONE
   (Al Green)
5. SMILING FACES SOMETIMES
   (Undisputed Truth)
6. THE BREAKDOWN
   (Rufus Thomas)
7. THE LOVE WE HAD
   (The Dells)
8. MAKE IT FUNKY, PART I
   (James Brown)
9. I LIKES TO DO IT
   (People's Choice)
10. WEAR THIS RING
    (Detroit Emeralds)

BLACK ALBUMS

1. SHAFT
   (Isaac Hayes)
2. WHAT'S GOING ON
   (Marvin Gaye)
3. ARETHA LIVE AT FILLMORE WEST
   (Aretha Franklin)
4. THE SKY'S THE LIMIT
   (Temptations)
5. JUST AS I AM
   (Bill Withers)
6. CURTIS LIVE
   (Curtis Mayfield)
7. MR. BIG STUFF
   (Jean Knight)
8. UNDISPUTED TRUTH
   (Undisputed Truth)
9. HOT PANTS
   (James Brown)
10. GIVE MORE POWER TO THE PEOPLE
    (The Chi-Lites)

JAZZ ALBUMS

1. SECOND MOVEMENT
   (Eddie Harris and Les McCann)
2. CHAPTER TWO
   (Roberta Flack)
3. TO BE CONTINUED
   (Isaac Hayes)

4. BACK TO THE ROOTS
   (Ramsey Lewis)
5. THEMBI
   (Pharaoh Sanders)
6. WEATHER REPORT
   (Weather Report)
7. SUGAR
   (Stanley Turrentine)
8. BITCHES BREW
   (Miles Davis)
9. BREAK OUT
   (Johnny Hammond)
10. SHAFT
    (Isaac Hayes)

COUNTRY SINGLES

1. THE YEAR CLAYTON DELANEY DIED
   (Tom T. Hall)
2. EASY LOVIN'
   (Freddie Hart)
3. QUITS
   (Bill Anderson)
4. I WONDER WHAT SHE'LL THINK ABOUT
   MY LEAVIN'
   (Conway Twitty)
5. GOOD ENOUGH TO BE YOUR WIFE
   (Jeannie C. Riley)
6. PITTY PITTY PATTER
   (Susan Raye)
7. YOU'RE LOOKIN' AT COUNTRY
   (Loretta Lynn)
8. WHEN HE WALKS ON YOU
   (Jerry Lee Lewis)
9. I'D RATHER BE SORRY
   (Ray Price)
10. HERE I GO AGAIN
    (Bobby Wright)

COUNTRY ALBUMS

1. YOU'RE MY MAN
   (Lynn Anderson)
2. THE SENSATIONAL SONNY JAMES
   (Sonny James)
3. I WON'T MENTION IT AGAIN
   (Ray Price)
4. I'M JUST ME
   (Charley Pride)
5. BEST OF PORTER WAGONER AND DOLLY
   PARTON
   (Porter Wagoner and Dolly Parton)
6. MAN IN BLACK
   (Johnny Cash)
7. RUBY
   (Buck Owens and the Buckaroos)
8. POEMS, PRAYERS AND PROMISES
   (John Denver)
9. THE LAST TIME I SAW HER
   (Glen Campbell)
10. THE INCREDIBLE ROY CLARK
    (Roy Clark)

SEPTEMBER 18, 1971

POP SINGLES

1. SPANISH HARLEM
   (Aretha Franklin)
2. GO AWAY LITTLE GIRL
   (Donny Osmond)
3. SMILING FACES SOMETIMES
   (Undisputed Truth)
4. THE NIGHT THEY DROVE OLD DIXIE
   DOWN
   (Joan Baez)
5. AIN'T NO SUNSHINE
   (Bill Withers)
6. UNCLE ALBERT/ADMIRAL HALSEY
   (Paul and Linda McCartney)

7. I JUST WANT TO CELEBRATE
   (Rare Earth)
8. WON'T GET FOOLED AGAIN
   (The Who)
9. MAGGIE MAY/REASON TO BELIEVE
   (Rod Stewart)
10. WATCHA SEE IS WATCHA GET
    (The Dramatics)

POP ALBUMS

1. TAPESTRY
   (Carole King)
2. EVERY GOOD BOY DESERVES FAVOUR
   (The Moody Blues)
3. WHO'S NEXT
   (The Who)
4. EVERY PICTURE TELLS A STORY
   (Rod Stewart)
5. RAM
   (Paul and Linda McCartney)
6. MUD SLIDE SLIM AND THE BLUE HORIZON
   (James Taylor)
7. CARPENTERS
   (The Carpenters)
8. SHAFT
   (Isaac Hayes)
9. AQUALUNG
   (Jethro Tull)
10. JESUS CHRIST SUPERSTAR
    (Original Soundtrack)

BLACK SINGLES

1. SPANISH HARLEM
   (Aretha Franklin)
2. AIN'T NO SUNSHINE
   (Bill Withers)
3. STICKUP
   (Honey Cone)
4. TIRED OF BEING ALONE
   (Al Green)
5. THE BREAKDOWN
   (Rufus Thomas)
6. MAKE IT FUNKY, PART I
   (James Brown)
7. THE LOVE WE HAD
   (The Dells)
8. SMILING FACES SOMETIMES
   (Undisputed Truth)
9. TRAPPED BY A THING CALLED LOVE
   (Denise LaSalle)
10. IF YOU REALLY LOVE ME
    (Stevie Wonder)

BLACK ALBUMS

1. SHAFT
   (Isaac Hayes)
2. WHAT'S GOING ON
   (Marvin Gaye)
3. ARETHA LIVE AT FILLMORE WEST
   (Aretha Franklin)
4. JUST AS I AM
   (Bill Withers)
5. CURTIS LIVE
   (Curtis Mayfield)
6. THE SKY'S THE LIMIT
   (Temptations)
7. UNDISPUTED TRUTH
   (Undisputed Truth)
8. MR. BIG STUFF
   (Jean Knight)
9. HOT PANTS
   (James Brown)
10. GIVE MORE POWER TO THE PEOPLE
    (The Chi-Lites)

JAZZ ALBUMS

1. SECOND MOVEMENT
   (Eddie Harris and Les McCann)

2. SHAFT
   (Isaac Hayes)
3. CHAPTER TWO
   (Roberta Flack)
4. TO BE CONTINUED
   (Isaac Hayes)
5. THEMBI
   (Pharaoh Sanders)
6. BACK TO THE ROOTS
   (Ramsey Lewis)
7. SUGAR
   (Stanley Turrentine)
8. WEATHER REPORT
   (Weather Report)
9. BITCHES BREW
   (Miles Davis)
10. BREAK OUT
    (Johnny Hammond)

COUNTRY SINGLES

1. EASY LOVIN'
   (Freddie Hart)
2. THE YEAR CLAYTON DELANEY DIED
   (Tom T. Hall)
3. QUITS
   (Bill Anderson)
4. PITTY PITTY PATTER
   (Susan Raye)
5. I'D RATHER BE SORRY
   (Ray Price)
6. YOU'RE LOOKIN' AT COUNTRY
   (Loretta Lynn)
7. I WONDER WHAT SHE'LL THINK ABOUT
   MY LEAVIN'
   (Conway Twitty)
8. WHEN HE WALKS ON YOU
   (Jerry Lee Lewis)
9. HERE I GO AGAIN
   (Bobby Wright)
10. LEAVIN' AND SAYIN' GOODBYE
    (Faron Young)

COUNTRY ALBUMS

1. THE SENSATIONAL SONNY JAMES
   (Sonny James)
2. YOU'RE MY MAN
   (Lynn Anderson)
3. I'M JUST ME
   (Charley Pride)
4. BEST OF PORTER WAGONER AND DOLLY
   PARTON
   (Porter Wagoner and Dolly Parton)
5. I WON'T MENTION IT AGAIN
   (Ray Price)
6. MAN IN BLACK
   (Johnny Cash)
7. THE LAST TIME I SAW HER
   (Glen Campbell)
8. RUBY
   (Buck Owens and the Buckaroos)
9. SOMEDAY WE'LL LOOK BACK
   (Merle Haggard)
10. POEMS, PRAYERS AND PROMISES
    (John Denver)

SEPTEMBER 25, 1971

POP SINGLES

1. THE NIGHT THEY DROVE OLD DIXIE
   DOWN
   (Joan Baez)
2. GO AWAY LITTLE GIRL
   (Donny Osmond)
3. AIN'T NO SUNSHINE
   (Bill Withers)
4. MAGGIE MAY/REASON TO BELIEVE
   (Rod Stewart)

5. SPANISH HARLEM
   (Aretha Franklin)
6. SUPERSTAR
   (The Carpenters)
7. I JUST WANT TO CELEBRATE
   (Rare Earth)
8. WON'T GET FOOLED AGAIN
   (The Who)
9. I WOKE UP IN LOVE THIS MORNING
   (The Partridge Family)
10. SMILING FACES SOMETIMES
    (Undisputed Truth)

POP ALBUMS

1. TAPESTRY
   (Carole King)
2. EVERY GOOD BOY DESERVES FAVOUR
   (The Moody Blues)
3. WHO'S NEXT
   (The Who)
4. EVERY PICTURE TELLS A STORY
   (Rod Stewart)
5. RAM
   (Paul and Linda McCartney)
6. CARPENTERS
   (The Carpenters)
7. SHAFT
   (Isaac Hayes)
8. MASTER OF REALITY
   (Black Sabbath)
9. THE PARTRIDGE FAMILY SOUND
   MAGAZINE
   (The Partridge Family)
10. MUD SLIDE SLIM AND THE BLUE HORIZON
    (James Taylor)

BLACK SINGLES

1. STICKUP
   (Honey Cone)
2. THE BREAKDOWN
   (Rufus Thomas)
3. MAKE IT FUNKY, PART I
   (James Brown)
4. TIRED OF BEING ALONE
   (Al Green)
5. IF YOU REALLY LOVE ME
   (Stevie Wonder)
6. THE LOVE WE HAD
   (The Dells)
7. SPANISH HARLEM
   (Aretha Franklin)
8. TRAPPED BY A THING CALLED LOVE
   (Denise LaSalle)
9. THIN LINE BETWEEN LOVE AND HATE
   (The Persuaders)
10. CALL MY NAME, I'LL BE THERE
    (Wilson Pickett)

BLACK ALBUMS

1. SHAFT
   (Isaac Hayes)
2. WHAT'S GOING ON
   (Marvin Gaye)
3. ARETHA LIVE AT FILLMORE WEST
   (Aretha Franklin)
4. FREEDOM MEANS
   (The Dells)
5. HOT PANTS
   (James Brown)
6. JUST AS I AM
   (Bill Withers)
7. GIVE MORE POWER TO THE PEOPLE
   (The Chi-Lites)
8. KING CURTIS LIVE AT THE FILLMORE
   WEST
   (King Curtis)
9. THE SKY'S THE LIMIT
   (Temptations)
10. UNDISPUTED TRUTH
    (Undisputed Truth)

JAZZ ALBUMS

1. SHAFT
   (Isaac Hayes)
2. SECOND MOVEMENT
   (Eddie Harris and Les McCann)
3. CHAPTER TWO
   (Roberta Flack)
4. TO BE CONTINUED
   (Isaac Hayes)
5. THEMBI
   (Pharaoh Sanders)
6. SUGAR
   (Stanley Turrentine)
7. BACK TO THE ROOTS
   (Ramsey Lewis)
8. BITCHES BREW
   (Miles Davis)
9. WEATHER REPORT
   (Weather Report)
10. JACK JOHNSON
    (Miles Davis)

COUNTRY SINGLES

1. QUITS
   (Bill Anderson)
2. I'D RATHER BE SORRY
   (Ray Price)
3. YOU'RE LOOKIN' AT COUNTRY
   (Loretta Lynn)
4. PITTY PITTY PATTER
   (Susan Raye)
5. EASY LOVIN'
   (Freddie Hart)
6. THE YEAR CLAYTON DELANEY DIED
   (Tom T. Hall)
7. LEAVIN' AND SAYIN' GOODBYE
   (Faron Young)
8. HOW CAN I UNLOVE YOU
   (Lynn Anderson)
9. HERE I GO AGAIN
   (Bobby Wright)
10. BRAND NEW MISTER ME
    (Mel Tillis)

COUNTRY ALBUMS

1. THE SENSATIONAL SONNY JAMES
   (Sonny James)
2. YOU'RE MY MAN
   (Lynn Anderson)
3. I'M JUST ME
   (Charley Pride)
4. I WON'T MENTION IT AGAIN
   (Ray Price)
5. SOMEDAY WE'LL LOOK BACK
   (Merle Haggard)
6. THE LAST TIME I SAW HER
   (Glenn Campbell)
7. BEST OF PORTER WAGONER AND DOLLY
   PARTON
   (Porter Wagoner and Dolly Parton)
8. RUBY
   (Buck Owens and the Buckaroos)
9. MAN IN BLACK
   (Johnny Cash)
10. I WONDER WHAT SHE'LL THINK ABOUT
    MY LEAVIN'
    (Conway Twitty)

OCTOBER 2, 1971

POP SINGLES

1. MAGGIE MAY/REASON TO BELIEVE
   (Rod Stewart)
2. SUPERSTAR
   (The Carpenters)

3. AIN'T NO SUNSHINE
   (Bill Withers)
4. GO AWAY LITTLE GIRL
   (Donny Osmond)
5. THE NIGHT THEY DROVE OLD DIXIE
   DOWN
   (Joan Baez)
6. YO-YO
   (The Osmonds)
7. SO FAR AWAY
   (Carole King)
8. IF YOU REALLY LOVE ME
   (Stevie Wonder)
9. I WOKE UP IN LOVE THIS MORNING
   (The Partridge Family)
10. SPANISH HARLEM
    (Aretha Franklin)

POP ALBUMS

1. EVERY PICTURE TELLS A STORY
   (Rod Stewart)
2. TAPESTRY
   (Carole King)
3. EVERY GOOD BOY DESERVES FAVOUR
   (The Moody Blues)
4. WHO'S NEXT
   (The Who)
5. RAM
   (Paul and Linda McCartney)
6. SHAFT
   (Original Soundtrack)
7. MASTER OF REALITY
   (Black Sabbath)
8. THE PARTRIDGE FAMILY SOUND
   MAGAZINE
   (The Partridge Family)
9. CARPENTERS
   (The Carpenters)
10. BARK
    (The Jefferson Airplane)

BLACK SINGLES

1. MAKE IT FUNKY, PART I
   (James Brown)
2. THE BREAKDOWN
   (Rufus Thomas)
3. IF YOU REALLY LOVE ME
   (Stevie Wonder)
4. TIRED OF BEING ALONE
   (Al Green)
5. THIN LINE BETWEEN LOVE AND HATE
   (The Persuaders)
6. THE LOVE WE HAD
   (The Dells)
7. STICKUP
   (Honey Cone)
8. TRAPPED BY A THING CALLED LOVE
   (Denise LaSalle)
9. CALL MY NAME, I'LL BE THERE
   (Wilson Pickett)
10. YOU SEND ME
    (Ponderosa Twins Plus One)

BLACK ALBUMS

1. SHAFT
   (Isaac Hayes)
2. WHAT'S GOING ON
   (Marvin Gaye)
3. GIVE MORE POWER TO THE PEOPLE
   (The Chi-Lites)
4. FREEDOM MEANS
   (The Dells)
5. HOT PANTS
   (James Brown)
6. ARETHA LIVE AT FILLMORE WEST
   (Aretha Franklin)
7. JUST AS I AM
   (Bill Withers)
8. KING CURTIS LIVE AT THE FILLMORE
   WEST
   (King Curtis)

9. MR. BIG STUFF
   (Jean Knight)
10. UNDISPUTED TRUTH
    (Undisputed Truth)

JAZZ ALBUMS

1. SHAFT
   (Isaac Hayes)
2. SECOND MOVEMENT
   (Eddie Harris and Les McCann)
3. CHAPTER TWO
   (Roberta Flack)
4. THEMBI
   (Pharaoh Sanders)
5. TO BE CONTINUED
   (Isaac Hayes)
6. SUGAR
   (Stanley Turrentine)
7. BACK TO THE ROOTS
   (Ramsey Lewis)
8. BITCHES BREW
   (Miles Davis)
9. JACK JOHNSON
   (Miles Davis)
10. WEATHER REPORT
    (Weather Report)

COUNTRY SINGLES

1. I'D RATHER BE SORRY
   (Ray Price)
2. YOU'RE LOOKIN' AT COUNTRY
   (Loretta Lynn)
3. QUITS
   (Bill Anderson)
4. HOW CAN I UNLOVE YOU
   (Lynn Anderson)
5. EASY LOVIN'
   (Freddie Hart)
6. LEAVIN' AND SAYIN' GOODBYE
   (Faron Young)
7. I DON'T KNOW YOU (ANYMORE)
   (Tommy Overstreet)
8. THE YEAR CLAYTON DELANEY DIED
   (Tom T. Hall)
9. BRAND NEW MISTER ME
   (Mel Tillis)
10. PITTY PITTY PATTER
    (Susan Raye)

COUNTRY ALBUMS

1. YOU'RE MY MAN
   (Lynn Anderson)
2. THE SENSATIONAL SONNY JAMES
   (Sonny James)
3. SOMEDAY WE'LL LOOK BACK
   (Merle Haggard)
4. I'M JUST ME
   (Charley Pride)
5. I WON'T MENTION IT AGAIN
   (Ray Price)
6. THE LAST TIME I SAW HER
   (Glen Campbell)
7. TAMMY'S GREATEST HITS, VOL. 2
   (Tammy Wynette)
8. I WONDER WHAT SHE'LL THINK ABOUT MY LEAVIN'
   (Conway Twitty)
9. MAN IN BLACK
   (Johnny Cash)
10. HE'S SO FINE
    (Jody Miller)

OCTOBER 9, 1971

POP SINGLES

1. SUPERSTAR
   (The Carpenters)

---

2. MAGGIE MAY/REASON TO BELIEVE
   (Rod Stewart)
3. YO-YO
   (The Osmonds)
4. GO AWAY LITTLE GIRL
   (Donny Osmond)
5. SO FAR AWAY
   (Carole King)
6. IF YOU REALLY LOVE ME
   (Stevie Wonder)
7. AIN'T NO SUNSHINE
   (Bill Withers)
8. DO YOU KNOW WHAT I MEAN
   (Lee Michaels)
9. THE NIGHT THEY DROVE OLD DIXIE DOWN
   (Joan Baez)
10. STICKUP
    (Honey Cone)

POP ALBUMS

1. EVERY PICTURE TELLS A STORY
   (Rod Stewart)
2. TAPESTRY
   (Carole King)
3. EVERY GOOD BOY DESERVES FAVOUR
   (The Moody Blues)
4. WHO'S NEXT
   (The Who)
5. SHAFT
   (Isaac Hayes)
6. RAM
   (Paul and Linda McCartney)
7. MASTER OF REALITY
   (Black Sabbath)
8. THE PARTRIDGE FAMILY SOUND MAGAZINE
   (The Partridge Family)
9. BARK
   (The Jefferson Airplane)
10. CARPENTERS
    (The Carpenters)

BLACK SINGLES

1. MAKE IT FUNKY, PART I
   (James Brown)
2. THIN LINE BETWEEN LOVE AND HATE
   (The Persuaders)
3. IF YOU REALLY LOVE ME
   (Stevie Wonder)
4. THE BREAKDOWN
   (Rufus Thomas)
5. TIRED OF BEING ALONE
   (Al Green)
6. YOU SEND ME
   (The Ponderosa Twins Plus One)
7. TRAPPED BY A THING CALLED LOVE
   (Denise LaSalle)
8. STICKUP
   (Honey Cone)
9. CALL MY NAME, I'LL BE THERE
   (Wison Pickett)
10. A NICKEL AND A NAIL
    (O.V. Wright)

BLACK ALBUMS

1. SHAFT
   (Isaac Hayes)
2. WHAT'S GOING ON
   (Marvin Gaye)
3. GIVE MORE POWER TO THE PEOPLE
   (The Chi-Lites)
4. FREEDOM MEANS
   (The Dells)
5. HOT PANTS
   (James Brown)
6. ARETHA'S GREATEST HITS
   (Aretha Franklin)
7. ARETHA LIVE AT FILLMORE WEST
   (Aretha Franklin)

---

8. JUST AS I AM
   (Bill Withers)
9. THE SKY'S THE LIMIT
   (Temptations)
10. KING CURTIS LIVE AT THE FILLMORE WEST
    (King Curtis)

JAZZ ALBUMS

1. SHAFT
   (Isaac Hayes)
2. SECOND MOVEMENT
   (Eddie Harris and Les McCann)
3. CHAPTER TWO
   (Roberta Flack)
4. THEMBI
   (Pharaoh Sanders)
5. SUGAR
   (Stanley Turrentine)
6. TO BE CONTINUED
   (Isaac Hayes)
7. BACK TO THE ROOTS
   (Ramsey Lewis)
8. BITCHES BREW
   (Miles Davis)
9. WEATHER REPORT
   (Weather Report)
10. BREAK OUT
    (Johnny Hammond)

COUNTRY SINGLES

1. YOU'RE LOOKIN' AT COUNTRY
   (Loretta Lynn)
2. HOW CAN I UNLOVE YOU
   (Lynn Anderson)
3. I'D RATHER BE SORRY
   (Ray Price)
4. I DON'T KNOW YOU (ANYMORE)
   (Tommy Overstreet)
5. LEAVIN' AND SAYIN' GOODBYE
   (Faron Young)
6. QUITS
   (Bill Anderson)
7. EASY LOVIN'
   (Freddie Hart)
8. BRAND NEW MISTER ME
   (Mel Tillis)
9. ROLLIN' IN MY SWEET BABY'S ARMS
   (Buck Owens)
10. CEDARTOWN, GEORGIA
    (Waylon Jennings)

COUNTRY ALBUMS

1. SOMEDAY WE'LL LOOK BACK
   (Merle Haggard)
2. YOU'RE MY MAN
   (Lynn Anderson)
3. THE SENSATIONAL SONNY JAMES
   (Sonny James)
4. I'M JUST ME
   (Charley Pride)
5. I WONDER WHAT SHE'LL THINK ABOUT MY LEAVIN'
   (Conway Twitty)
6. TAMMY'S GREATEST HITS, VOL. 2
   (Tammy Wynette)
7. I WON'T MENTION IT AGAIN
   (Ray Price)
8. THE LAST TIME I SAW HER
   (Glen Campbell)
9. MAN IN BLACK
   (Johnny Cash)
10. POEMS, PRAYERS AND PROMISES
    (John Denver)

OCTOBER 16, 1971

POP SINGLES

1. YO-YO
   (The Osmonds)

2. SUPERSTAR
   (The Carpenters)
3. MAGGIE MAY/REASON TO BELIEVE
   (Rod Stewart)
4. IF YOU REALLY LOVE ME
   (Stevie Wonder)
5. SO FAR AWAY
   (Carole King)
6. DO YOU KNOW WHAT I MEAN
   (Lee Michaels)
7. GO AWAY LITTLE GIRL
   (Donny Osmond)
8. AIN'T NO SUNSHINE
   (Bill Withers)
9. SWEET CITY WOMAN
   (The Stampeders)
10. THE NIGHT THEY DROVE OLD DIXIE
    DOWN
    (Joan Baez)

POP ALBUMS

1. TAPESTRY
   (Carole King)
2. EVERY PICTURE TELLS A STORY
   (Rod Stewart)
3. IMAGINE
   (John Lennon)
4. SHAFT
   (Original Soundtrack)
5. EVERY GOOD BOY DESERVES FAVOUR
   (The Moody Blues)
6. WHO'S NEXT
   (The Who)
7. RAM
   (Paul and Linda McCartney)
8. BARK
   (The Jefferson Airplane)
9. CARPENTERS
   (The Carpenters)
10. THE PARTRIDGE FAMILY SOUND
    MAGAZINE
    (The Partridge Family)

BLACK SINGLES

1. THIN LINE BETWEEN LOVE AND HATE
   (The Persuaders)
2. MAKE IT FUNKY, PART I
   (James Brown)
3. IF YOU REALLY LOVE ME
   (Stevie Wonder)
4. YOU SEND ME
   (The Ponderosa Twins Plus One)
5. THE BREAKDOWN
   (Rufus Thomas)
6. TRAPPED BY A THING CALLED LOVE
   (Denise LaSalle)
7. YOU'VE GOT TO CRAWL (BEFORE YOU
   CAN WALK)
   (8th Day)
8. TIRED OF BEING ALONE
   (Al Green)
9. STICKUP
   (Honey Cone)
10. WOMEN'S LOVE RIGHTS
    (Laura Lee)

BLACK ALBUMS

1. SHAFT
   (Isaac Hayes)
2. WHAT'S GOING ON
   (Marvin Gaye)
3. HOT PANTS
   (James Brown)
4. ARETHA'S GREATEST HITS
   (Aretha Franklin)
5. GIVE MORE POWER TO THE PEOPLE
   (The Chi-Lites)
6. ARETHA LIVE AT FILLMORE WEST
   (Aretha Franklin)

7. FREEDOM MEANS
   (The Dells)
8. JUST AS I AM
   (Bill Withers)
9. THE SKY'S THE LIMIT
   (Temptations)
10. KING CURTIS LIVE AT THE FILLMORE
    WEST
    (King Curtis)

JAZZ ALBUMS

1. SHAFT
   (Isaac Hayes)
2. SECOND MOVEMENT
   (Eddie Harris and Les McCann)
3. CHAPTER TWO
   (Roberta Flack)
4. THEMBI
   (Pharaoh Sanders)
5. TO BE CONTINUED
   (Isaac Hayes)
6. SUGAR
   (Stanley Turrentine)
7. BITCHES BREW
   (Miles Davis)
8. BACK TO THE ROOTS
   (Ramsey Lewis)
9. WEATHER REPORT
   (Weather Report)
10. BAREFOOT BOY
    (Larry Coryell)

COUNTRY SINGLES

1. HOW CAN I UNLOVE YOU
   (Lynn Anderson)
2. LEAVIN' AND SAYIN' GOODBYE
   (Faron Young)
3. I DON'T KNOW YOU (ANYMORE)
   (Tommy Overstreet)
4. YOU'RE LOOKIN' AT COUNTRY
   (Loretta Lynn)
5. I'D RATHER BE SORRY
   (Ray Price)
6. ROLLIN' IN MY SWEET BABY'S ARMS
   (Buck Owens)
7. CEDARTOWN, GEORGIA
   (Waylon Jennings)
8. FLY AWAY AGAIN
   (Dave Dudley)
9. EASY LOVIN'
   (Freddie Hart)
10. QUITS
    (Bill Anderson)

COUNTRY ALBUMS

1. SOMEDAY WE'LL LOOK BACK
   (Merle Haggard)
2. YOU'RE MY MAN
   (Lynn Anderson)
3. I'M JUST ME
   (Charley Pride)
4. I WONDER WHAT SHE'LL THINK ABOUT
   MY LEAVIN'
   (Conway Twitty)
5. TAMMY'S GREATEST HITS, VOL. 2
   (Tammy Wynette)
6. THE SENSATIONAL SONNY JAMES
   (Sonny James)
7. I WON'T MENTION IT AGAIN
   (Ray Price)
8. PITTY PITTY PATTER
   (Susan Raye)
9. TODAY
   (Marty Robbins)
10. IN SEARCH OF A SONG
    (Tom T. Hall)

OCTOBER 23, 1971

POP SINGLES

1. YO-YO
   (The Osmonds)
2. SUPERSTAR
   (The Carpenters)
3. MAGGIE MAY/REASON TO BELIEVE
   (Rod Stewart)
4. IF YOU REALLY LOVE ME
   (Stevie Wonder)
5. DO YOU KNOW WHAT I MEAN
   (Lee Michaels)
6. GYPSIES, TRAMPS AND THIEVES
   (Cher)
7. GO AWAY LITTLE GIRL
   (Donny Osmond)
8. SWEET CITY WOMAN
   (The Stampeders)
9. AIN'T NO SUNSHINE
   (Bill Withers)
10. THIN LINE BETWEEN LOVE AND HATE
    (The Persuaders)

POP ALBUMS

1. IMAGINE
   (John Lennon)
2. EVERY PICTURE TELLS A STORY
   (Rod Stewart)
3. TAPESTRY
   (Carole King)
4. SHAFT
   (Isaac Hayes)
5. EVERY GOOD BOY DESERVES FAVOUR
   (The Moody Blues)
6. SANTANA
   (Santana)
7. BARK
   (The Jefferson Airplane)
8. CARPENTERS
   (The Carpenters)
9. BLESSED ARE
   (Joan Baez)
10. TEASER AND THE FIRECAT
    (Cat Stevens)

BLACK SINGLES

1. THIN LINE BETWEEN LOVE AND HATE
   (The Persuaders)
2. TRAPPED BY A THING CALLED LOVE
   (Denise LaSalle)
3. IF YOU REALLY LOVE ME
   (Stevie Wonder)
4. YOU SEND ME
   (The Ponderosa Twins Plus One)
5. YOU'VE GOT TO CRAWL (BEFORE YOU
   CAN WALK)
   (8th Day)
6. MAKE IT FUNKY, PART I
   (James Brown)
7. THE BREAKDOWN
   (Rufus Thomas)
8. INNER CITY BLUES
   (Marvin Gaye)
9. WOMEN'S LOVE RIGHTS
   (Laura Lee)
10. TIRED OF BEING ALONE
    (Al Green)

BLACK ALBUMS

1. SHAFT
   (Isaac Hayes)
2. WHAT'S GOING ON
   (Marvin Gaye)
3. GIVE MORE POWER TO THE PEOPLE
   (The Chi-Lites)
4. ARETHA'S GREATEST HITS
   (Aretha Franklin)

5. HOT PANTS
   (James Brown)
6. ARETHA LIVE AT FILLMORE WEST
   (Aretha Franklin)
7. JUST AS I AM
   (Bill Withers)
8. FREEDOM MEANS
   (The Dells)
9. THE SKY'S THE LIMIT
   (Temptations)
10. UNDISPUTED TRUTH
    (Undisputed Truth)

JAZZ ALBUMS

1. SHAFT
   (Isaac Hayes)
2. SECOND MOVEMENT
   (Eddie Harris and Les McCann)
3. CHAPTER TWO
   (Roberta Flack)
4. THEMBI
   (Pharaoh Sanders)
5. SUGAR
   (Stanley Turrentine)
6. TO BE CONTINUED
   (Isaac Hayes)
7. BITCHES BREW
   (Miles Davis)
8. WEATHER REPORT
   (Weather Report)
9. BACK TO THE ROOTS
   (Ramsey Lewis)
10. BAREFOOT BOY
    (Larry Coryell)

COUNTRY SINGLES

1. LEAVIN' AND SAYIN' GOODBYE
   (Faron Young)
2. I DON'T KNOW YOU (ANYMORE)
   (Tommy Overstreet)
3. ROLLIN' IN MY SWEET BABY'S ARMS
   (Buck Owens)
4. HOW CAN I UNLOVE YOU
   (Lynn Anderson)
5. FLY AWAY AGAIN
   (Dave Dudley)
6. CEDARTOWN, GEORGIA
   (Waylon Jennings)
7. I'D RATHER BE SORRY
   (Ray Price)
8. RINGS
   (Glaser Brothers)
9. NO NEED TO WORRY
   (Johnny Cash and June Carter)
10. NEVER ENDING SONG OF LOVE
    (Dickey Lee)

COUNTRY ALBUMS

1. SOMEDAY WE'LL LOOK BACK
   (Merle Haggard)
2. I WONDER WHAT SHE'LL THINK ABOUT
   MY LEAVIN'
   (Conway Twitty)
3. YOU'RE MY MAN
   (Lynn Anderson)
4. TAMMY'S GREATEST HITS, VOL. 2
   (Tammy Wynette)
5. I'M JUST ME
   (Charley Pride)
6. PITTY PITTY PATTER
   (Susan Raye)
7. EASY LOVIN'
   (Freddie Hart)
8. IN SEARCH OF A SONG
   (Tom T. Hall)
9. TODAY
   (Marty Robbins)
10. KO KO JOE
    (Jerry Reed)

OCTOBER 30, 1971

POP SINGLES

1. GYPSIES, TRAMPS AND THIEVES
   (Cher)
2. YO-YO
   (The Osmonds)
3. THEME FROM SHAFT
   (Isaac Hayes)
4. MAGGIE MAY/REASON TO BELIEVE
   (Rod Stewart)
5. DO YOU KNOW WHAT I MEAN
   (Lee Michaels)
6. IMAGINE
   (John Lennon)
7. SUPERSTAR
   (The Carpenters)
8. SWEET CITY WOMAN
   (The Stampeders)
9. THIN LINE BETWEEN LOVE AND HATE
   (The Persuaders)
10. I'VE FOUND SOMEONE OF MY OWN
    (Free Movement)

POP ALBUMS

1. IMAGINE
   (John Lennon)
2. EVERY PICTURE TELLS A STORY
   (Rod Stewart)
3. SHAFT
   (Isaac Hayes)
4. SANTANA
   (Santana)
5. TAPESTRY
   (Carole King)
6. TEASER AND THE FIRECAT
   (Cat Stevens)
7. BARK
   (The Jefferson Airplane)
8. CARPENTERS
   (The Carpenters)
9. BLESSED ARE
   (Joan Baez)
10. EVERY GOOD BOY DESERVES FAVOUR
    (The Moody Blues)

BLACK SINGLES

1. HAVE YOU SEEN HER
   (The Chi-Lites)
2. THIN LINE BETWEEN LOVE AND HATE
   (The Persuaders)
3. YOU'VE GOT TO CRAWL (BEFORE YOU
   CAN WALK)
   (8th Day)
4. INNER CITY BLUES
   (Marvin Gaye)
5. THEME FROM SHAFT
   (Isaac Hayes)
6. TRAPPED BY A THING CALLED LOVE
   (Denise LaSalle)
7. YOU SEND ME
   (The Ponderosa Twins Plus One)
8. IF YOU REALLY LOVE ME
   (Stevie Wonder)
9. IT'S IMPOSSIBLE
   (New Birth)
10. SHE'S ALL I'VE GOT
    (Freddie North)

BLACK ALBUMS

1. SHAFT
   (Isaac Hayes)
2. WHAT'S GOING ON
   (Marvin Gaye)
3. GIVE MORE POWER TO THE PEOPLE
   (The Chi-Lites)

4. ARETHA'S GREATEST HITS
   (Aretha Franklin)
5. HOT PANTS
   (James Brown)
6. GOIN' BACK TO INDIANA
   (The Jackson 5)
7. JUST AS I AM
   (Bill Withers)
8. ARETHA LIVE AT FILLMORE WEST
   (Aretha Franklin)
9. SOUL TO SOUL
   (Original Soundtrack)
10. ONE WORLD
    (Rare Earth)

JAZZ ALBUMS

1. SHAFT
   (Isaac Hayes)
2. SECOND MOVEMENT
   (Eddie Harris and Les McCann)
3. CHAPTER TWO
   (Roberta Flack)
4. THEMBI
   (Pharaoh Sanders)
5. PUSH PUSH
   (Herbie Mann)
6. SUGAR
   (Stanley Turrentine)
7. TO BE CONTINUED
   (Isaac Hayes)
8. SUNSHIP
   (John Coltrane)
9. BAREFOOT BOY
   (Larry Coryell)
10. BITCHES BREW
    (Miles Davis)

COUNTRY SINGLES

1. I DON'T KNOW YOU ANYMORE
   (Tommy Overstreet)
2. ROLLIN' IN MY SWEET BABY'S ARMS
   (Buck Owens)
3. FLY AWAY AGAIN
   (Dave Dudley)
4. RINGS
   (Glaser Brothers)
5. LEAVIN' AND SAYIN' GOODBYE
   (Faron Young)
6. NEVER ENDING SONG OF LOVE
   (Dickey Lee)
7. HERE COMES HONEY AGAIN
   (Sonny James)
8. NO NEED TO WORRY
   (Johnny Cash and June Carter)
9. HOW CAN I UNLOVE YOU
   (Lynn Anderson)
10. BE A LITTLE QUIETER
    (Porter Wagoner)

COUNTRY ALBUMS

1. SOMEDAY WE'LL LOOK BACK
   (Merle Haggard)
2. I WONDER WHAT SHE'LL THINK ABOUT
   MY LEAVIN'
   (Conway Twitty)
3. TAMMY'S GREATEST HITS, VOL. 2
   (Tammy Wynette)
4. YOU'RE MY MAN
   (Lynn Anderson)
5. EASY LOVIN'
   (Freddie Hart)
6. PITTY PITTY PATTER
   (Susan Raye)
7. IN SEARCH OF A SONG
   (Tom T. Hall)
8. I'M JUST ME
   (Charley Pride)
9. KO KO JOE
   (Jerry Reed)
10. I WON'T MENTION IT AGAIN
    (Ray Price)

NOVEMBER 6, 1971

POP SINGLES

1. THEME FROM SHAFT
   (Isaac Hayes)
2. GYPSIES, TRAMPS AND THIEVES
   (Cher)
3. YO-YO
   (The Osmonds)
4. IMAGINE
   (John Lennon)
5. MAGGIE MAY/REASON TO BELIEVE
   (Rod Stewart)
6. PEACE TRAIN
   (Cat Stevens)
7. DO YOU KNOW WHAT I MEAN
   (Lee Michaels)
8. SUPERSTAR
   (The Carpenters)
9. HAVE YOU SEEN HER
   (The Chi-Lites)
10. I'VE FOUND SOMEONE OF MY OWN
    (Free Movement)

POP ALBUMS

1. IMAGINE
   (John Lennon)
2. EVERY PICTURE TELLS A STORY
   (Rod Stewart)
3. SHAFT
   (Isaac Hayes)
4. SANTANA
   (Santana)
5. TAPESTRY
   (Carole King)
6. TEASER AND THE FIRECAT
   (Cat Stevens)
7. CARPENTERS
   (The Carpenters)
8. EVERY GOOD BOY DESERVES FAVOUR
   (The Moody Blues)
9. BLESSED ARE
   (Joan Baez)
10. RAM
    (Paul and Linda McCartney)

BLACK SINGLES

1. HAVE YOU SEEN HER
   (The Chi-Lites)
2. THEME FROM SHAFT
   (Isaac Hayes)
3. YOU'VE GOT TO CRAWL (BEFORE YOU
   CAN WALK)
   (8th Day)
4. INNER CITY BLUES
   (Marvin Gaye)
5. THIN LINE BETWEEN LOVE AND HATE
   (The Persuaders)
6. TRAPPED BY A THING CALLED LOVE
   (Denise LaSalle)
7. IT'S IMPOSSIBLE
   (New Birth)
8. YOU SEND ME
   (The Ponderosa Twins Plus One)
9. IF YOU REALLY LOVE ME
   (Stevie Wonder)
10. SHE'S ALL I'VE GOT
    (Freddie North)

BLACK ALBUMS

1. SHAFT
   (Isaac Hayes)
2. WHAT'S GOING ON
   (Marvin Gaye)
3. GIVE MORE POWER TO THE PEOPLE
   (The Chi-Lites)

---

4. ARETHA'S GREATEST HITS
   (Aretha Franklin)
5. GOIN' BACK TO INDIANA
   (The Jackson 5)
6. HOT PANTS
   (James Brown)
7. JUST AS I AM
   (Bill Withers)
8. SOUL TO SOUL
   (Original Soundtrack)
9. ARETHA LIVE AT FILLMORE WEST
   (Aretha Franklin)
10. FREEDOM MEANS
    (The Dells)

JAZZ ALBUMS

1. SHAFT
   (Isaac Hayes)
2. SECOND MOVEMENT
   (Eddie Harris and Les McCann)
3. CHAPTER TWO
   (Roberta Flack)
4. THEMBI
   (Pharaoh Sanders)
5. PUSH PUSH
   (Herbie Mann)
6. TO BE CONTINUED
   (Isaac Hayes)
7. SUGAR
   (Stanley Turrentine)
8. SUNSHIP
   (John Coltrane)
9. BAREFOOT BOY
   (Larry Coryell)
10. BITCHES BREW
    (Miles Davis)

COUNTRY SINGLES

1. ROLLIN' IN MY SWEET BABY'S ARMS
   (Buck Owens)
2. RINGS
   (Glaser Brothers)
3. FLY AWAY AGAIN
   (Dave Dudley)
4. NEVER ENDING SONG OF LOVE
   (Dickey Lee)
5. HERE COMES HONEY AGAIN
   (Sonny James)
6. LEAD ME ON
   (Loretta Lynn)
7. KO KO JOE
   (Jerry Reed)
8. ANOTHER NIGHT OF LOVE
   (Freddy Weller)
9. I DON'T KNOW YOU (ANYMORE)
   (Tommy Overstreet)
10. HOW CAN I UNLOVE YOU
    (Lynn Anderson)

COUNTRY ALBUMS

1. EASY LOVIN'
   (Freddie Hart)
2. SOMEDAY WE'LL LOOK BACK
   (Merle Haggard)
3. TAMMY'S GREATEST HITS, VOL. 2
   (Tammy Wynette)
4. I WONDER WHAT SHE'LL THINK ABOUT
   MY LEAVIN'
   (Conway Twitty)
5. IN SEARCH OF A SONG
   (Tom T. Hall)
6. PITTY PITTY PATTER
   (Susan Raye)
7. YOU'RE MY MAN
   (Lynn Anderson)
8. KO KO JOE
   (Jerry Reed)
9. I'M JUST ME
   (Charley Pride)
10. SILVER-TONGUED DEVIL AND I
    (Kris Kristofferson)

NOVEMBER 13, 1971

POP SINGLES

1. THEME FROM SHAFT
   (Isaac Hayes)
2. IMAGINE
   (John Lennon)
3. GYPSIES, TRAMPS AND THIEVES
   (Cher)
4. YO-YO
   (The Osmonds)
5. PEACE TRAIN
   (Cat Stevens)
6. HAVE YOU SEEN HER
   (The Chi-Lites)
7. MAGGIE MAY/REASON TO BELIEVE
   (Rod Stewart)
8. INNER CITY BLUES
   (Marvin Gaye)
9. TRAPPED BY A THING CALLED LOVE
   (Denise LaSalle)
10. I'VE FOUND SOMEONE OF MY OWN
    (Free Movement)

POP ALBUMS

1. SHAFT
   (Isaac Hayes)
2. IMAGINE
   (John Lennon)
3. SANTANA
   (Santana)
4. EVERY PICTURE TELLS A STORY
   (Rod Stewart)
5. TEASER AND THE FIRECAT
   (Cat Stevens)
6. TAPESTRY
   (Carole King)
7. CARPENTERS
   (The Carpenters)
8. EVERY GOOD BOY DESERVES FAVOUR
   (The Moody Blues)
9. RAM
   (Paul and Linda McCartney)
10. WHO'S NEXT
    (The Who)

BLACK SINGLES

1. THEME FROM SHAFT
   (Isaac Hayes)
2. HAVE YOU SEEN HER
   (The Chi-Lites)
3. INNER CITY BLUES
   (Marvin Gaye)
4. ROCK STEADY
   (Aretha Franklin)
5. YOU'VE GOT TO CRAWL (BEFORE YOU
   CAN WALK)
   (8th Day)
6. THIN LINE BETWEEN LOVE AND HATE
   (The Persuaders)
7. WHERE DID OUR LOVE GO
   (Donny Elbert)
8. IT'S IMPOSSIBLE
   (New Birth)
9. TRAPPED BY A THING CALLED LOVE
   (Denise LaSalle)
10. GOT TO BE THERE
    (Michael Jackson)

BLACK ALBUMS

1. SHAFT
   (Isaac Hayes)
2. WHAT'S GOING ON
   (Marvin Gaye)
3. GIVE MORE POWER TO THE PEOPLE
   (The Chi-Lites)

4. ARETHA'S GREATEST HITS
   (Aretha Franklin)
5. GOIN' BACK TO INDIANA
   (The Jackson 5)
6. HOT PANTS
   (James Brown)
7. JUST AS I AM
   (Bill Withers)
8. WHAT YOU HEAR IS WHAT YOU GET
   (Ike and Tina Turner)
9. ARETHA LIVE AT FILLMORE WEST
   (Aretha Franklin)
10. SANTANA
    (Santana)

JAZZ ALBUMS

1. SHAFT
   (Isaac Hayes)
2. SECOND MOVEMENT
   (Eddie Harris and Les McCann)
3. PUSH PUSH
   (Herbie Mann)
4. CHAPTER TWO
   (Roberta Flack)
5. THEMBI
   (Pharaoh Sanders)
6. SUNSHIP
   (John Coltrane)
7. KING CURTIS LIVE AT THE FILLMORE WEST
   (King Curtis)
8. BITCHES BREW
   (Miles Davis)
9. TO BE CONTINUED
   (Isaac Hayes)
10. SUGAR
    (Stanley Turrentine)

COUNTRY SINGLES

1. RINGS
   (Glaser Brothers)
2. NEVER ENDING SONG OF LOVE
   (Dickey Lee)
3. HERE COMES HONEY AGAIN
   (Sonny James)
4. LEAD ME ON
   (Conway Twitty and Loretta Lynn)
5. ROLLIN' IN MY SWEET BABY'S ARMS
   (Buck Owens)
6. KO KO JOE
   (Jerry Reed)
7. ANOTHER NIGHT OF LOVE
   (Freddy Weller)
8. DADDY FRANK (THE GUITAR MAN)
   (Merle Haggard)
9. SHE'S ALL I GOT
   (Johnny Paycheck)
10. FLY AWAY AGAIN
    (Dave Dudley)

COUNTRY ALBUMS

1. EASY LOVIN'
   (Freddie Hart)
2. SOMEDAY WE'LL LOOK BACK
   (Merle Haggard)
3. TAMMY'S GREATEST HITS, VOL. 2
   (Tammy Wynette)
4. IN SEARCH OF A SONG
   (Tom T. Hall)
5. PITTY PITTY PATTER
   (Susan Raye)
6. I WONDER WHAT SHE'LL THINK ABOUT MY LEAVIN'
   (Conway Twitty)
7. KO KO JOE
   (Jerry Reed)
8. SILVER-TONGUED DEVIL AND I
   (Kris Kristofferson)
9. THE WORLD OF LYNN ANDERSON
   (Lynn Anderson)
10. ME AND BOBBY McGEE
    (Kris Kristofferson)

NOVEMBER 20, 1971

POP SINGLES

1. IMAGINE
   (John Lennon)
2. THEME FROM SHAFT
   (Isaac Hayes)
3. GYPSIES, TRAMPS AND THIEVES
   (Cher)
4. HAVE YOU SEEN HER
   (The Chi-Lites)
5. PEACE TRAIN
   (Cat Stevens)
6. BABY, I'M-A WANT YOU
   (Bread)
7. INNER CITY BLUES
   (Marvin Gaye)
8. MAGGIE MAY/REASON TO BELIEVE
   (Rod Stewart)
9. TRAPPED BY A THING CALLED LOVE
   (Denise LaSalle)
10. ROCK STEADY
    (Aretha Franklin)

POP ALBUMS

1. SHAFT
   (Isaac Hayes)
2. SANTANA
   (Santana)
3. IMAGINE
   (John Lennon)
4. TEASER AND THE FIRECAT
   (Cat Stevens)
5. EVERY PICTURE TELLS A STORY
   (Rod Stewart)
6. TAPESTRY
   (Carole King)
7. CARPENTERS
   (The Carpenters)
8. EVERY GOOD BOY DESERVES FAVOUR
   (The Moody Blues)
9. HARMONY
   (Three Dog Night)
10. RAM
    (Paul and Linda McCartney)

BLACK SINGLES

1. HAVE YOU SEEN HER
   (The Chi-Lites)
2. INNER CITY BLUES
   (Marvin Gaye)
3. ROCK STEADY
   (Aretha Franklin)
4. THEME FROM SHAFT
   (Isaac Hayes)
5. WHERE DID OUR LOVE GO
   (Donny Elbert)
6. GOT TO BE THERE
   (Michael Jackson)
7. RESPECT YOURSELF
   (The Staple Singers)
8. YOU'VE GOT TO CRAWL (BEFORE YOU CAN WALK)
   (8th Day)
9. THIN LINE BETWEEN LOVE AND HATE
   (The Persuaders)
10. SHE'S ALL I'VE GOT
    (Freddie North)

BLACK ALBUMS

1. SHAFT
   (Isaac Hayes)
2. WHAT'S GOING ON
   (Marvin Gaye)
3. GIVE MORE POWER TO THE PEOPLE
   (The Chi-Lites)

4. ARETHA'S GREATEST HITS
   (Aretha Franklin)
5. GOIN' BACK TO INDIANA
   (The Jackson 5)
6. HOT PANTS
   (James Brown)
7. SANTANA
   (Santana)
8. JUST AS I AM
   (Bill Withers)
9. ARETHA LIVE AT FILLMORE WEST
   (Aretha Franklin)
10. BUDDY MILES LIVE
    (Buddy Miles)

JAZZ ALBUMS

1. SHAFT
   (Isaac Hayes)
2. SECOND MOVEMENT
   (Eddie Harris and Les McCann)
3. PUSH PUSH
   (Herbie Mann)
4. CHAPTER TWO
   (Roberta Flack)
5. THEMBI
   (Pharaoh Sanders)
6. SUNSHIP
   (John Coltrane)
7. KING CURTIS LIVE AT THE FILLMORE WEST
   (King Curtis)
8. BITCHES BREW
   (Miles Davis)
9. SUGAR
   (Stanley Turrentine)
10. TO BE CONTINUED
    (Isaac Hayes)

COUNTRY SINGLES

1. NEVER ENDING SONG OF LOVE
   (Dickey Lee)
2. HERE COMES HONEY AGAIN
   (Sonny James)
3. LEAD ME ON
   (Conway Twitty and Loretta Lynn)
4. DADDY FRANK (THE GUITAR MAN)
   (Merle Haggard)
5. SHE'S ALL I GOT
   (Johnny Paycheck)
6. RINGS
   (Glaser Brothers)
7. ANOTHER NIGHT OF LOVE
   (Freddy Weller)
8. KISS AN ANGEL GOOD MORNING
   (Charley Pride)
9. ROLLIN' IN MY SWEET BABY'S ARMS
   (Buck Owens)
10. EARLY MORNING SUNSHINE
    (Marty Robbins)

COUNTRY ALBUMS

1. EASY LOVIN'
   (Freddie Hart)
2. SOMEDAY WE'LL LOOK BACK
   (Merle Haggard)
3. SILVER-TONGUED DEVIL AND I
   (Kris Kristofferson)
4. IN SEARCH OF A SONG
   (Tom T. Hall)
5. KO KO JOE
   (Jerry Reed)
6. PITTY PITTY PATTER
   (Susan Raye)
7. THE WORLD OF LYNN ANDERSON
   (Lynn Anderson)
8. ME AND BOBBY McGEE
   (Kris Kristofferson)
9. YOU'RE LOOKIN' AT COUNTRY
   (Loretta Lynn)
10. THE JOHNNY CASH COLLECTION—HIS GREATEST HITS
    (Johnny Cash)

NOVEMBER 27, 1971

POP SINGLES

1. FAMILY AFFAIR
   (Sly and the Family Stone)
2. IMAGINE
   (John Lennon)
3. HAVE YOU SEEN HER
   (The Chi-Lites)
4. BABY, I'M-A WANT YOU
   (Bread)
5. PEACE TRAIN
   (Cat Stevens)
6. SHAFT
   (Isaac Hayes)
7. ROCK STEADY
   (Aretha Franklin)
8. GOT TO BE THERE
   (Michael Jackson)
9. EVERYBODY'S EVERYTHING
   (Santana)
10. GYPSIES, TRAMPS AND THIEVES
    (Cher)

POP ALBUMS

1. SANTANA
   (Santana)
2. SHAFT
   (Isaac Hayes)
3. TEASER AND THE FIRECAT
   (Cat Stevens)
4. IMAGINE
   (John Lennon)
5. EVERY PICTURE TELLS A STORY
   (Rod Stewart)
6. TAPESTRY
   (Carole King)
7. THERE'S A RIOT GOIN' ON
   (Sly and the Family Stone)
8. HARMONY
   (Three Dog Night)
9. CARPENTERS
   (The Carpenters)
10. CHICAGO AT CARNEGIE HALL
    (Chicago)

BLACK SINGLES

1. HAVE YOU SEEN HER
   (The Chi-Lites)
2. ROCK STEADY
   (Aretha Franklin)
3. FAMILY AFFAIR
   (Sly and the Family Stone)
4. GOT TO BE THERE
   (Michael Jackson)
5. WHERE DID OUR LOVE GO
   (Donny Elbert)
6. INNER CITY BLUES
   (Marvin Gaye)
7. RESPECT YOURSELF
   (Aretha Franklin)
8. THEME FROM SHAFT
   (Isaac Hayes)
9. SHE'S ALL I'VE GOT
   (Freddie North)
10. SCORPIO
    (Dennis Coffey)

BLACK ALBUMS

1. SHAFT
   (Isaac Hayes)
2. WHAT'S GOING ON
   (Marvin Gaye)
3. SANTANA
   (Santana)
4. GIVE MORE POWER TO THE PEOPLE
   (The Chi-Lites)

---

5. ARETHA'S GREATEST HITS
   (Aretha Franklin)
6. HOT PANTS
   (James Brown)
7. THERE'S A RIOT GOIN' ON
   (Sly and the Family Stone)
8. RAINBOW BRIDGE
   (Jimi Hendrix)
9. GOIN' BACK TO INDIANA
   (The Jackson 5)
10. ROOTS
    (Curtis Mayfield)

JAZZ ALBUMS

1. SHAFT
   (Isaac Hayes)
2. SECOND MOVEMENT
   (Eddie Harris and Les McCann)
3. CHAPTER TWO
   (Roberta Flack)
4. PUSH PUSH
   (Herbie Mann)
5. THEMBI
   (Pharaoh Sanders)
6. KING CURTIS LIVE AT THE FILLMORE
   WEST
   (King Curtis)
7. SUNSHIP
   (John Coltrane)
8. BITCHES BREW
   (Miles Davis)
9. SMACKWATER JACK
   (Quincy Jones)
10. SUGAR
    (Stanley Turrentine)

COUNTRY SINGLES

1. HERE COMES HONEY AGAIN
   (Sonny James)
2. LEAD ME ON
   (Conway Twitty and Loretta Lynn)
3. DADDY FRANK (THE GUITAR MAN)
   (Merle Haggard)
4. SHE'S ALL I GOT
   (Johnny Paycheck)
5. KISS AN ANGEL GOOD MORNING
   (Charley Pride)
6. NEVER ENDING SONG OF LOVE
   (Dickey Lee)
7. DISSATISFIED
   (Bill Anderson and Jan Howard)
8. BABY, I'M YOURS
   (Jody Miller)
9. EARLY MORNING SUNSHINE
   (Marty Robbins)
10. ANOTHER NIGHT OF LOVE
    (Freddy Weller)

COUNTRY ALBUMS

1. EASY LOVIN'
   (Freddie Hart)
2. SILVER-TONGUED DEVIL AND I
   (Kris Kristofferson)
3. SOMEDAY WE'LL LOOK BACK
   (Merle Haggard)
4. THE WORLD OF LYNN ANDERSON
   (Lynn Anderson)
5. KO KO JOE
   (Jerry Reed)
6. THE JOHNNY CASH COLLECTION—HIS
   GREATEST HITS
   (Johnny Cash)
7. ME AND BOBBY McGEE
   (Kris Kristofferson)
8. YOU'RE LOOKIN' AT COUNTRY
   (Loretta Lynn)
9. IN SEARCH OF A SONG
   (Tom T. Hall)
10. PITTY PITTY PATTER
    (Susan Raye)

DECEMBER 4, 1971

POP SINGLES

1. FAMILY AFFAIR
   (Sly and the Family Stone)
2. HAVE YOU SEEN HER
   (The Chi-Lites)
3. BABY, I'M-A WANT YOU
   (Bread)
4. IMAGINE
   (John Lennon)
5. GOT TO BE THERE
   (Michael Jackson)
6. ROCK STEADY
   (Aretha Franklin)
7. PEACE TRAIN
   (Cat Stevens)
8. THEME FROM SHAFT
   (Isaac Hayes)
9. EVERYBODY'S EVERYTHING
   (Santana)
10. AN OLD-FASHIONED LOVE SONG
    (Three Dog Night)

POP ALBUMS

1. SANTANA
   (Santana)
2. SHAFT
   (Isaac Hayes)
3. TEASER AND THE FIRECAT
   (Cat Stevens)
4. THERE'S A RIOT GOIN' ON
   (Sly and the Family Stone)
5. CHICAGO AT CARNEGIE HALL
   (Chicago)
6. IMAGINE
   (John Lennon)
7. HARMONY
   (Three Dog Night)
8. TAPESTRY
   (Carole King)
9. EVERY PICTURE TELLS A STORY
   (Rod Stewart)
10. MEATY, BEATY, BIG AND BOUNCY
    (The Who)

BLACK SINGLES

1. ROCK STEADY
   (Aretha Franklin)
2. FAMILY AFFAIR
   (Sly and the Family Stone)
3. GOT TO BE THERE
   (Michael Jackson)
4. HAVE YOU SEEN HER
   (The Chi-Lites)
5. WHERE DID OUR LOVE GO
   (Donny Elbert)
6. RESPECT YOURSELF
   (The Staple Singers)
7. I'M A GREEDY MAN (PART I)
   (James Brown)
8. THEME FROM SHAFT
   (Isaac Hayes)
9. SCORPIO
   (Dennis Coffey)
10. INNER CITY BLUES
    (Marvin Gaye)

BLACK ALBUMS

1. SHAFT
   (Isaac Hayes)
2. WHAT'S GOING ON
   (Marvin Gaye)
3. SANTANA
   (Santana)
4. GIVE MORE POWER TO THE PEOPLE
   (The Chi-Lites)

5. THERE'S A RIOT GOIN' ON
(Sly and the Family Stone)
6. ARETHA'S GREATEST HITS
(Aretha Franklin)
7. GOIN' BACK TO INDIANA
(The Jackson 5)
8. RAINBOW BRIDGE
(Jimi Hendrix)
9. ROOTS
(Curtis Mayfield)
10. HOT PANTS
(James Brown)

COUNTRY SINGLES

1. LEAD ME ON
(Conway Twitty and Loretta Lynn)
2. DADDY FRANK (THE GUITAR MAN)
(Merle Haggard)
3. SHE'S ALL I GOT
(Johnny Paycheck)
4. KISS AN ANGEL GOOD MORNING
(Charley Pride)
5. HERE COMES HONEY AGAIN
(Sonny James)
6. DISSATISFIED
(Bill Anderson and Jan Howard)
7. BABY, I'M YOURS
(Jody Miller)
8. NEVER ENDING SONG OF LOVE
(Dickey Lee)
9. HOME SWEET HOME/MAIDEN'S PRAYER
(David Houston)
10. EARLY MORNING SUNSHINE
(Marty Robbins)

COUNTRY ALBUMS

1. EASY LOVIN'
(Freddie Hart)
2. SILVER-TONGUED DEVIL AND I
(Kris Kristofferson)
3. THE WORLD OF LYNN ANDERSON
(Lynn Anderson)
4. SOMEDAY WE'LL LOOK BACK
(Merle Haggard)
5. THE JOHNNY CASH COLLECTION—HIS
GREATEST HITS
(Johnny Cash)
6. WE GO TOGETHER
(George Jones and Tammy Wynette)
7. ME AND BOBBY McGEE
(Kris Kristofferson)
8. YOU'RE LOOKIN' AT COUNTRY
(Loretta Lynn)
9. I'M JUST ME
(Charley Pride)
10. IN SEARCH OF A SONG
(Tom T. Hall)

DECEMBER 11, 1971

POP SINGLES

1. HAVE YOU SEEN HER
(The Chi-Lites)
2. FAMILY AFFAIR
(Sly and the Family Stone)
3. BABY, I'M-A WANT YOU
(Bread)
4. GOT TO BE THERE
(Michael Jackson)
5. AN OLD-FASHIONED LOVE SONG
(Three Dog Night)
6. ROCK STEADY
(Aretha Franklin)
7. IMAGINE
(John Lennon)
8. CHERISH
(David Cassidy)

9. BRAND NEW KEY
(Melanie)
10. ALL I EVER NEED IS YOU
(Sonny and Cher)

POP ALBUMS

1. SANTANA
(Santana)
2. TEASER AND THE FIRECAT
(Cat Stevens)
3. THERE'S A RIOT GOIN' ON
(Sly and the Family Stone)
4. SHAFT
(Isaac Hayes)
5. CHICAGO AT CARNEGIE HALL
(Chicago)
6. LED ZEPPELIN
(Led Zeppelin)
7. TAPESTRY
(Carole King)
8. IMAGINE
(John Lennon)
9. MEATY, BEATY, BIG AND BOUNCY
(The Who)
10. EVERY PICTURE TELLS A STORY
(Rod Stewart)

BLACK SINGLES

1. FAMILY AFFAIR
(Sly and the Family Stone)
2. GOT TO BE THERE
(Michael Jackson)
3. ROCK STEADY
(Aretha Franklin)
4. HAVE YOU SEEN HER
(The Chi-Lites)
5. I'M A GREEDY MAN (PART I)
(James Brown)
6. WHERE DID OUR LOVE GO
(Donny Elbert)
7. EVERYBODY KNOWS ABOUT MY GOOD
THING (PART I)
(Little Johnnie Taylor)
8. SCORPIO
(Dennis Coffey)
9. YOU ARE EVERYTHING
(The Stylistics)
10. SUPERSTAR (REMEMBER HOW YOU GOT
WHERE YOU ARE)
(Temptations)

BLACK ALBUMS

1. SHAFT
(Isaac Hayes)
2. THERE'S A RIOT GOIN' ON
(Sly and the Family Stone)
3. WHAT'S GOING ON
(Marvin Gaye)
4. GIVE MORE POWER TO THE PEOPLE
(The Chi-Lites)
5. ROOTS
(Curtis Mayfield)
6. SANTANA
(Santana)
7. ARETHA'S GREATEST HITS
(Aretha Franklin)
8. HOT PANTS
(James Brown)
9. STEVIE WONDER'S GREATEST HITS, VOL. 2
(Stevie Wonder)
10. FIFTH DIMENSION LIVE
(The Fifth Dimension)

JAZZ ALBUMS

1. SHAFT
(Isaac Hayes)
2. SECOND MOVEMENT
(Eddie Harris and Les McCann)

3. CHAPTER TWO
(Roberta Flack)
4. THEMBI
(Pharaoh Sanders)
5. PUSH PUSH
(Herbie Mann)
6. SUNSHIP
(John Coltrane)
7. KING CURTIS LIVE AT THE FILLMORE
WEST
(King Curtis)
8. SMACKWATER JACK
(Quincy Jones)
9. SUGAR
(Stanley Turrentine)
10. BITCHES BREW
(Miles Davis)

COUNTRY SINGLES

1. DADDY FRANK (THE GUITAR MAN)
(Merle Haggard)
2. SHE'S ALL I GOT
(Johnny Paycheck)
3. KISS AN ANGEL GOOD MORNING
(Charley Pride)
4. LEAD ME ON
(Conway Twitty and Loretta Lynn)
5. DISSATISFIED
(Bill Anderson and Jan Howard)
6. WOULD YOU TAKE ANOTHER CHANCE ON
ME
(Jerry Lee Lewis)
7. HERE COMES HONEY AGAIN
(Sonny James)
8. COUNTRY GREEN
(Don Gibson)
9. HOME SWEET HOME/MAIDEN'S PRAYER
(David Houston)
10. COAT OF MANY COLORS
(Dolly Parton)

COUNTRY ALBUMS

1. EASY LOVIN'
(Freddie Hart)
2. WE GO TOGETHER
(George Jones and Tammy Wynette)
3. THE WORLD OF LYNN ANDERSON
(Lynn Anderson)
4. THE JOHNNY CASH COLLECTION—HIS
GREATEST HITS
(Johnny Cash)
5. SILVER-TONGUED DEVIL AND I
(Kris Kristofferson)
6. SOMEDAY WE'LL LOOK BACK
(Merle Haggard)
7. I'M JUST ME
(Charley Pride)
8. ME AND BOBBY McGEE
(Kris Kristofferson)
9. WOULD YOU TAKE ANOTHER CHANCE ON
ME
(Jerry Lee Lewis)
10. IN SEARCH OF A SONG
(Tom T. Hall)

DECEMBER 18, 1971

POP SINGLES

1. HAVE YOU SEEN HER
(The Chi-Lites)
2. FAMILY AFFAIR
(Sly and the Family Stone)
3. BRAND NEW KEY
(Melanie)
4. GOT TO BE THERE
(Michael Jackson)
5. AN OLD-FASHIONED LOVE SONG
(Three Dog Night)

6. BABY, I'M-A WANT YOU
   (Bread)
7. CHERISH
   (David Cassidy)
8. ALL I EVER NEED IS YOU
   (Sonny and Cher)
9. AMERICAN PIE
   (Don McLean)
10. RESPECT YOURSELF
    (The Staple Singers)

POP ALBUMS

1. THERE'S A RIOT GOIN' ON
   (Sly and the Family Stone)
2. SANTANA
   (Santana)
3. TEASER AND THE FIRECAT
   (Cat Stevens)
4. LED ZEPPELIN
   (Led Zeppelin)
5. CHICAGO AT CARNEGIE HALL
   (Chicago)
6. E PLURIBUS FUNK
   (Grand Funk)
7. SHAFT
   (Isaac Hayes)
8. IMAGINE
   (John Lennon)
9. EVERY PICTURE TELLS A STORY
   (Rod Stewart)
10. STONES
    (Neil Diamond)

BLACK SINGLES

1. FAMILY AFFAIR
   (Sly and the Family Stone)
2. GOT TO BE THERE
   (Michael Jackson)
3. CLEAN UP WOMAN
   (Betty Wright)
4. I'M A GREEDY MAN (PART I)
   (James Brown)
5. EVERYBODY KNOWS ABOUT MY GOOD
   THING (PART I)
   (Little Johnnie Taylor)
6. HAVE YOU SEEN HER
   (The Chi-Lites)
7. ONE MONKEY DON'T STOP NO SHOW
   (Honey Cone)
8. SCORPIO
   (Dennis Coffey)
9. YOU ARE EVERYTHING
   (The Stylistics)
10. SUPERSTAR (REMEMBER HOW YOU GOT
    WHERE YOU ARE)
    (Temptations)

BLACK ALBUMS

1. SHAFT
   (Isaac Hayes)
2. THERE'S A RIOT GOIN' ON
   (Sly and the Family Stone)
3. WHAT'S GOING ON
   (Marvin Gaye)
4. GIVE MORE POWER TO THE PEOPLE
   (The Chi-Lites)
5. ROOTS
   (Curtis Mayfield)
6. SANTANA
   (Santana)
7. HOT PANTS
   (James Brown)
8. ARETHA'S GREATEST HITS
   (Aretha Franklin)
9. STEVIE WONDER'S GREATEST HITS, VOL. 2
   (Stevie Wonder)
10. GOIN' BACK TO INDIANA
    (The Jackson 5)

COUNTRY SINGLES

1. SHE'S ALL I GOT
   (Johnny Paycheck)
2. KISS AN ANGEL GOOD MORNING
   (Charley Pride)
3. WOULD YOU TAKE ANOTHER CHANCE ON
   ME
   (Jerry Lee Lewis)
4. DADDY FRANK (THE GUITAR MAN)
   (Merle Haggard)
5. DISSATISFIED
   (Bill Anderson and Jan Howard)
6. COUNTRY GREEN
   (Don Gibson)
7. COAT OF MANY COLORS
   (Dolly Parton)
8. LEAD ME ON
   (Conway Twitty and Loretta Lynn)
9. HERE COMES HONEY AGAIN
   (Sonny James)
10. HITCHIN' A RIDE
    (Jack Reno)

COUNTRY ALBUMS

1. WE GO TOGETHER
   (George Jones and Tammy Wynette)
2. EASY LOVIN'
   (Freddie Hart)
3. THE WORLD OF LYNN ANDERSON
   (Lynn Anderson)
4. THE JOHNNY CASH COLLECTION—HIS
   GREATEST HITS
   (Johnny Cash)
5. SILVER-TONGUED DEVIL AND I
   (Kris Kristofferson)
6. I'M JUST ME
   (Charley Pride)
7. WOULD YOU TAKE ANOTHER CHANCE ON
   ME
   (Jerry Lee Lewis)
8. CHARLEY PRIDE SINGS HEART SONGS
   (Charley Pride)
9. IN SEARCH OF A SONG
   (Tom T. Hall)
10. THE BEST OF BUCK OWENS
    (Buck Owens)

DECEMBER 25, 1971

POP SINGLES

1. BRAND NEW ME
   (Melanie)
2. FAMILY AFFAIR
   (Sly and the Family Stone)
3. AMERICAN PIE
   (Don McLean)
4. AN OLD-FASHIONED LOVE SONG
   (Three Dog Night)
5. HAVE YOU SEEN HER
   (The Chi-Lites)
6. GOT TO BE THERE
   (Michael Jackson)
7. CHERISH
   (David Cassidy)
8. ALL I EVER NEED IS YOU
   (Sonny and Cher)
9. RESPECT YOURSELF
   (The Staple Singers)
10. STONES
    (Neil Diamond)

POP ALBUMS

1. LED ZEPPELIN
   (Led Zeppelin)
2. THERE'S A RIOT GOIN' ON
   (Sly and the Family Stone)

3. SANTANA
   (Santana)
4. E PLURIBUS FUNK
   (Grand Funk Railroad)
5. CHICAGO AT CARNEGIE HALL
   (Chicago)
6. CAROLE KING MUSIC
   (Carole King)
7. TEASER AND THE FIRECAT
   (Cat Stevens)
8. SHAFT
   (Isaac Hayes)
9. STONES
   (Neil Diamond)
10. ALL IN THE FAMILY
    (Original Cast)

BLACK SINGLES

1. FAMILY AFFAIR
   (Sly and the Family Stone)
2. CLEAN UP WOMAN
   (Betty Wright)
3. GOT TO BE THERE
   (Michael Jackson)
4. I'M A GREEDY MAN (PART I)
   (James Brown)
5. EVERYBODY KNOWS ABOUT MY GOOD
   THING (PART I)
   (Little Johnnie Taylor)
6. ONE MONKEY DON'T STOP NO SHOW
   (Honey Cone)
7. DROWNING IN THE SEA OF LOVE
   (Joe Simon)
8. SCORPIO
   (Dennis Coffey)
9. YOU ARE EVERYTHING
   (The Stylistics)
10. LET'S STAY TOGETHER
    (Al Green)

BLACK ALBUMS

1. SHAFT
   (Isaac Hayes)
2. THERE'S A RIOT GOIN' ON
   (Sly and the Family Stone)
3. WHAT'S GOING ON
   (Marvin Gaye)
4. GIVE MORE POWER TO THE PEOPLE
   (The Chi-Lites)
5. BLACK MOSES
   (Isaac Hayes)
6. ROOTS
   (Curtis Mayfield)
7. QUIET FIRE
   (Roberta Flack)
8. SANTANA
   (Santana)
9. GOIN' BACK TO INDIANA
   (The Jackson 5)
10. HOT PANTS
    (James Brown)

COUNTRY SINGLES

1. KISS AN ANGEL GOOD MORNING
   (Charley Pride)
2. WOULD YOU TAKE ANOTHER CHANCE ON
   ME
   (Jerry Lee Lewis)
3. SHE'S ALL I GOT
   (Johnny Paycheck)
4. DISSATISFIED
   (Bill Anderson and Jan Howard)
5. COAT OF MANY COLORS
   (Dolly Parton)
6. COUNTRY GREEN
   (Don Gibson)
7. (I'VE GOT A) HAPPY HEART
   (Susan Raye)
8. DADDY FRANK (THE GUITAR MAN)
   (Merle Haggard)

9. HITCHIN' A RIDE
     (Jack Reno)
10. LIVING AND LEARNING
     (Mel Tillis and Sherry Bryce)

COUNTRY ALBUMS

1. WE GO TOGETHER
     (George Jones and Tammy Wynette)
2. EASY LOVIN'
     (Freddie Hart)
3. CHARLEY PRIDE SINGS HEART SONGS
     (Charley Pride)
4. WOULD YOU TAKE ANOTHER CHANCE ON ME
     (Jerry Lee Lewis)
5. THE WORLD OF LYNN ANDERSON
     (Lynn Anderson)
6. I'M JUST ME
     (Charley Pride)
7. HERE COMES HONEY AGAIN
     (Sonny James)
8. IN SEARCH OF A SONG
     (Tom T. Hall)
9. HOW CAN I UNLOVE YOU
     (Lynn Anderson)
10. THE JOHNNY CASH COLLECTION—HIS GREATEST HITS
     (Johnny Cash)

1972

By 1972, the communal philosophy and collective activism of the last decade had given way to an overwhelming devotion to self. For some this turn inward bordered on narcissism, for others it was merely a way to survive in an increasingly technological society. Tom Wolfe dubbed the 1970s "the time of *the me generation*," an appropriate description of a population bent on hedonism and introspection.

This concern with exploring and understanding the individual was reflected in this year's most popular albums, many of which were made by solo performers who fell neatly under the "singer–songwriter" banner. Neil Young's *Harvest*, Carole King's *Tapestry* and *Music*, Don McLean's *American Pie*, Cat Stevens's *Teaser and the Firecat*, Roberta Flack's *First Take* and *Quiet Fire*, Donny Hathaway's *Live*, and Elton John's *Madman across the Water* were the products of people from varied musical and social backgrounds. Yet they were unified, as Janet Maslin wrote, by "reactionary expressions of frustrations, confusion, irony, quiet little confidences, and personal declarations of independence." The overriding quality of these albums was a sense of melancholy and reflection, as if the performers had been locked in a dark room one rainy Sunday with a note pad and the complete works of Billie Holiday.

ALBUMS: 1972 was an excellent year for rock. The Rolling Stones were represented by *Hot Rocks: 1964–71*, a two-record set encapsulating their years of greatest artistic growth, and *Exile on Main Street*, a masterwork that extended the music found on *Hot Rocks*. Robert Christgau described *Exile* as "weary and complicated, barely afloat in its own drudgery, it rocks with extra power and concentration as a result. More indecipherable than ever, submerging Mick's [Jagger] voice under layers of studio murk, it piles all the old themes—sex as power, sex as love, sex as pleasure, distance, craziness, release—on top of an obsession with time more than appropriate in people over-thirty and committed to what was once considered youth music."

Led Zeppelin's untitled fourth album would be remembered even if it didn't contain "Stairway To Heaven," a rambling mix of folk, crunching heavy metal, and mythical mumbo-jumbo that was the rock anthem of the '70s. "Black Dog" and "Rock and Roll" were more straightforward, but almost as compelling and definitely as much fun. In the 1960s a bar band had to be able to play classic R&B or blues to get work. After Led Zeppelin it was the ability to shriek like Robert Plant, thump in the style of drummer John Bonham or solo with the lyricism of guitarist Jimmy Page that was the new cutting edge.

The best American band of the young decade was the Allman Brothers, an integrated collection of Southern musicians led by vocalist–keyboardist Greg and guitarist Duane Allman. *Eat A Peach* a double album follow-up to the classic *Live at Fillmore East*, planted seeds that flowered into Southern rock. The Charlie Daniels Band, Lynyrd Skynyrd, Wet Willie, The Marshall Tucker Band, Sea Level, The Atlanta Rhythm Section, and Black Oak Arkansas all owed a debt to the Allmans' driving twin lead guitar sound. Tragically, the Allmans' band never got any better. First, Duane Allman died in a motorcycle crash in 1971 and then bassist Berry Oakley was killed in the same manner, near the same spot, in 1972. This eerie coincidence understandably ripped apart the band's heart and spirit.

Although Memphis was losing its standing as a center for black music, a glance at the black charts this year didn't indicate this. The LP and single "Let's Stay Together" made Al Green successor to Otis Redding as soul's most captivating male singer—his kittenish falsetto and sexy mid-range made everything Green sang a magical experience. With *Shaft* and *Black Moses*, Isaac Hayes broadened the commercial impact of black records. To appreciate fully his long sultry tempos, listeners had to purchase the LP, which turned black music fans from singles to album buyers. From the same Stax-Volt label as Hayes came these superior songs: the Staples Singers' "Respect Yourself," the Dramatics' "Watcha See Is Whatcha Get," Luther Ingram's "If Loving You Is Wrong (I Don't Wanna Be Right)," and Rufus Thomas's "Do the Funky Chicken."

James Brown's *Revolution of the Mind*, War's *All Day Music*, Bill Withers's *Still Bill*, Aretha Franklin and Reverend James Cleveland's *Amazing Grace*, and Stevie Wonder's *Music of My Mind* were all exceptional black albums, but none as personal or idiosyncratic as Sly and the Family Stone's *There's A Riot Goin' On*. No longer the happy warrior of hedonistic brotherhood, Sly's accumulated anguish spilled forth through murky production and sinister vocals. Neither Sly nor his audience were the same again.

SINGLES: Whimsical songs taken seriously at great personal risk did well in 1972. Gilbert O'Sullivan's "Alone Again (Naturally)," Sammy Davis Jr.'s infantile "Candy Man," Joe Tex's lecherous "I Gotcha," Michael Jackson's "Ben," Melanie's "Brand New Key," and Chuck Berry's "My Ding-a-Ling" (amazingly his first certified gold single) invited chuckles or, at least, a faint smile.

More substantial were: Roberta Flack's melodramatic "The First Time Ever I Saw Your Face"; Don McLean's epic song–poem about Buddy Holly, Elvis Presley, and the 1950s "American Pie"; the Chi-Lites' heartbreaking "Oh, Girl"; Neil Young's "Heart of Gold"; the Stylistics' "Betcha By Golly, Wow"; and the Hollies' attractive "Long Cool Woman." Charley Pride again dominated the country charts, while Donna Fargo ("The Happiest Girl In the Whole U.S.A.") and Freddie Hart ("My Hang Up Is You," "Bless Your Heart") also enjoyed profitable years.

Black films were in vogue after the commercial success of *Shaft* and *Sweet Sweetback's Badass Song* provided black musicians with unprecedented opportunities to write soundtracks. *Trouble Man* featured Marvin Gaye's moody title song. *Sounder* was a marvelous little film that was enhanced greatly by Taj Mahal's traditional blues score. *Lady Sings the Blues* documents Diana Ross's portrayal of Billie Holliday on celluloid and vinyl. But best of all was Curtis Mayfield's compositions for *Superfly*, which included two of his finest songs, "Give Me Your Love," and "Freddie's Dead."

Roberta Flack

The Rolling Stones

Marvin Gaye

Johnny Cash

JANUARY 1, 1972

POP SINGLES

1. AMERICAN PIE
   (Don McLean)
2. BRAND NEW KEY
   (Melanie)
3. FAMILY AFFAIR
   (Sly and the Family Stone)
4. AN OLD-FASHIONED LOVE SONG
   (Three Dog Night)
5. CHERISH
   (David Cassidy)
6. SCORPIO
   (Dennis Coffey)
7. GOT TO BE THERE
   (Michael Jackson)
8. ALL I EVER NEED IS YOU
   (Sonny and Cher)
9. RESPECT YOURSELF
   (The Staple Singers)
10. HEY GIRL/I KNEW YOU WHEN
    (Donny Osmond)

POP ALBUMS

1. LED ZEPPELIN
   (Led Zeppelin)
2. CAROLE KING MUSIC
   (Carole King)
3. E PLURIBUS FUNK
   (Grand Funk Railroad)
4. THERE'S A RIOT GOIN' ON
   (Sly and the Family Stone)
5. CHICAGO AT CARNEGIE HALL
   (Chicago)
6. TEASER AND THE FIRECAT
   (Cat Stevens)
7. SANTANA
   (Santana)
8. SHAFT
   (Isaac Hayes)
9. ALL IN THE FAMILY
   (Original Cast)
10. BLACK MOSES
    (Isaac Hayes)

BLACK SINGLES

1. CLEAN UP WOMAN
   (Betty Wright)
2. FAMILY AFFAIR
   (Sly and the Family Stone)
3. DROWNING IN THE SEA OF LOVE
   (Joe Simon)
4. EVERYBODY KNOWS ABOUT MY GOOD
   THING (PART I)
   (Little Johnnie Taylor)
5. ONE MONKEY DON'T STOP NO SHOW
   (Honey Cone)
6. LET'S STAY TOGETHER
   (Al Green)
7. GOT TO BE THERE
   (Michael Jackson)
8. YOU ARE EVERYTHING
   (The Stylistics)
9. SUGAR DADDY
   (The Jackson 5)
10. I'M A GREEDY MAN (PART I)
    (James Brown)

BLACK ALBUMS

1. SHAFT
   (Isaac Hayes)
2. BLACK MOSES
   (Isaac Hayes)
3. THERE'S A RIOT GOIN' ON
   (Sly and the Family Stone)

---

4. QUIET FIRE
   (Roberta Flack)
5. WHAT'S GOING ON
   (Marvin Gaye)
6. ROOTS
   (Curtis Mayfield)
7. SANTANA
   (Santana)
8. STYLISTICS
   (The Stylistics)
9. GIVE MORE POWER TO THE PEOPLE
   (The Chi-Lites)
10. GOIN' BACK TO INDIANA
    (The Jackson 5)

JAZZ ALBUMS

1. SHAFT
   (Isaac Hayes)
2. SUNSHIP
   (John Coltrane)
3. PUSH PUSH
   (Herbie Mann)
4. SMACKWATER JACK
   (Quincy Jones)
5. UNIVERSAL CONSCIOUSNESS
   (Alice Coltrane)
6. QUIET FIRE
   (Roberta Flack)
7. BLACK MOSES
   (Isaac Hayes)
8. VISIONS
   (Grant Green)
9. THEMBI
   (Pharaoh Sanders)
10. CHAPTER TWO
    (Roberta Flack)

COUNTRY SINGLES

1. WOULD YOU TAKE ANOTHER CHANCE ON
   ME
   (Jerry Lee Lewis)
2. KISS AN ANGEL GOOD MORNING
   (Charley Pride)
3. COAT OF MANY COLORS
   (Dolly Parton)
4. SHE'S ALL I GOT
   (Johnny Paycheck)
5. COUNTRY GREEN
   (Don Gibson)
6. (I'VE GOT A) HAPPY HEART
   (Susan Raye)
7. DISSATISFIED
   (Bill Anderson and Jan Howard)
8. LIVING AND LEARNING
   (Mel Tillis and Sherry Bryce)
9. BURNING THE MIDNIGHT OIL
   (Porter Wagoner and Dolly Parton)
10. YOU BETTER MOVE ON
    (Billy "Crash" Craddock)

COUNTRY ALBUMS

1. EASY LOVIN'
   (Freddie Hart)
2. CHARLEY PRIDE SINGS HEART SONGS
   (Charley Pride)
3. WOULD YOU TAKE ANOTHER CHANCE ON
   ME
   (Jerry Lee Lewis)
4. WE GO TOGETHER
   (George Jones and Tammy Wynette)
5. HERE COMES HONEY AGAIN
   (Sonny James)
6. HOW CAN I UNLOVE YOU
   (Lynn Anderson)
7. IN SEARCH OF A SONG
   (Tom T. Hall)
8. I'M JUST ME
   (Charley Pride)
9. THE WORLD OF LYNN ANDERSON
   (Lynn Anderson)

---

10. THE JOHNNY CASH COLLECTION—HIS
    GREATEST HITS
    (Johnny Cash)

JANUARY 8, 1972

POP SINGLES

1. AMERICAN PIE
   (Don McLean)
2. BRAND NEW KEY
   (Melanie)
3. FAMILY AFFAIR
   (Sly and the Family Stone)
4. LET'S STAY TOGETHER
   (Al Green)
5. CHERISH
   (David Cassidy)
6. SCORPIO
   (Dennis Coffey)
7. GOT TO BE THERE
   (Michael Jackson)
8. SUNSHINE
   (Jonathan Edwards)
9. SUGAR DADDY
   (The Jackson 5)
10. HEY GIRL/I KNEW YOU WHEN
    (Donny Osmond)

POP ALBUMS

1. CAROLE KING MUSIC
   (Carole King)
2. LED ZEPPELIN
   (Led Zeppelin)
3. E PLURIBUS FUNK
   (Grand Funk Railroad)
4. CHICAGO AT CARNEGIE HALL
   (Chicago)
5. TEASER AND THE FIRECAT
   (Cat Stevens)
6. THERE'S A RIOT GOIN' ON
   (Sly and the Family Stone)
7. AMERICAN PIE
   (Don McLean)
8. ALL IN THE FAMILY
   (Original Cast)
9. BLACK MOSES
   (Isaac Hayes)
10. WILD LIFE
    (Paul McCartney and Wings)

BLACK SINGLES

1. DROWNING IN THE SEA OF LOVE
   (Joe Simon)
2. CLEAN UP WOMAN
   (Betty Wright)
3. LET'S STAY TOGETHER
   (Al Green)
4. EVERYBODY KNOWS ABOUT MY GOOD
   THING (PART I)
   (Little Johnnie Taylor)
5. ONE MONKEY DON'T STOP NO SHOW
   (Honey Cone)
6. SUGAR DADDY
   (The Jackson 5)
7. GOT TO BE THERE
   (Michael Jackson)
8. YOU ARE EVERYTHING
   (The Stylistics)
9. FAMILY AFFAIR
   (Sly and the Family Stone)
10. AIN'T UNDERSTANDING MELLOW
    (Butler and Eager)

BLACK ALBUMS

1. BLACK MOSES
   (Isaac Hayes)

2. THERE'S A RIOT GOIN' ON
   (Sly and the Family Stone)
3. QUIET FIRE
   (Roberta Flack)
4. WHAT'S GOING ON
   (Marvin Gaye)
5. SHAFT
   (Isaac Hayes)
6. SANTANA
   (Santana)
7. STYLISTICS
   (The Stylistics)
8. GIVE MORE POWER TO THE PEOPLE
   (The Chi-Lites)
9. GOIN' BACK TO INDIANA
   (The Jackson 5)
10. REVOLUTION OF THE MIND
    (James Brown)

JAZZ ALBUMS

1. SHAFT
   (Isaac Hayes)
2. SUNSHIP
   (John Coltrane)
3. SMACKWATER JACK
   (Quincy Jones)
4. PUSH PUSH
   (Herbie Mann)
5. QUIET FIRE
   (Roberta Flack)
6. BLACK MOSES
   (Isaac Hayes)
7. UNIVERSAL CONSCIOUSNESS
   (Alice Coltrane)
8. VISIONS
   (Grant Green)
9. CHAPTER TWO
   (Roberta Flack)
10. LIVE-EVIL
    (Miles Davis)

COUNTRY SINGLES

1. COAT OF MANY COLORS
   (Dolly Parton)
2. WOULD YOU TAKE ANOTHER CHANCE ON
   ME
   (Jerry Lee Lewis)
3. KISS AN ANGEL GOOD MORNING
   (Charley Pride)
4. (I'VE GOT A) HAPPY HEART
   (Susan Raye)
5. COUNTRY GREEN
   (Don Gibson)
6. CAROLYN
   (Merle Haggard)
7. LIVING AND LEARNING
   (Mel Tillis and Sherry Bryce)
8. BURNING THE MIDNIGHT OIL
   (Porter Wagoner and Dolly Parton)
9. YOU BETTER MOVE ON
   (Billy "Crash" Craddock)
10. ONE'S ON THE WAY
    (Loretta Lynn)

COUNTRY ALBUMS

1. CHARLEY PRIDE SINGS HEART SONGS
   (Charley Pride)
2. WOULD YOU TAKE ANOTHER CHANCE ON
   ME
   (Jerry Lee Lewis)
3. EASY LOVIN'
   (Freddie Hart)
4. HOW CAN I UNLOVE YOU
   (Lynn Anderson)
5. HERE COMES HONEY AGAIN
   (Sonny James)
6. WE GO TOGETHER
   (George Jones and Tammy Wynette)
7. IN SEARCH OF A SONG
   (Tom T. Hall)

8. I'M JUST ME
   (Charley Pride)
9. THE JOHNNY CASH COLLECTION— HIS
   GREATEST HITS
   (Johnny Cash)
10. BILL ANDERSON'S GREATEST HITS
    (Bill Anderson)

JANUARY 15, 1972

POP SINGLES

1. AMERICAN PIE
   (Don McLean)
2. BRAND NEW KEY
   (Melanie)
3. LET'S STAY TOGETHER
   (Al Green)
4. SUNSHINE
   (Jonathan Edwards)
5. CHERISH
   (David Cassidy)
6. SCORPIO
   (Dennis Coffey)
7. SUGAR DADDY
   (The Jackson 5)
8. DROWNING IN THE SEA OF LOVE
   (Joe Simon)
9. I'D LIKE TO TEACH THE WORLD TO SING
   (The New Seekers)
10. I'D LIKE TO TEACH THE WORLD TO SING
    (The Hillside Singers)

POP ALBUMS

1. CAROLE KING MUSIC
   (Carole King)
2. LED ZEPPELIN
   (Led Zeppelin)
3. E PLURIBUS FUNK
   (Grand Funk Railroad)
4. CHICAGO AT CARNEGIE HALL
   (Chicago)
5. AMERICAN PIE
   (Don McLean)
6. TEASER AND THE FIRECAT
   (Cat Stevens)
7. ALL IN THE FAMILY
   (Original Cast)
8. BLACK MOSES
   (Isaac Hayes)
9. WILD LIFE
   (Paul McCartney and Wings)
10. THERE'S A RIOT GOIN' ON
    (Sly and the Family Stone)

BLACK SINGLES

1. LET'S STAY TOGETHER
   (Al Green)
2. DROWNING IN THE SEA OF LOVE
   (Joe Simon)
3. CLEAN UP WOMAN
   (Betty Wright)
4. SUGAR DADDY
   (The Jackson 5)
5. EVERYBODY KNOWS ABOUT MY GOOD
   THING (PART I)
   (Little Johnnie Taylor)
6. SHOW ME HOW
   (Emotions)
7. THAT'S THE WAY I FEEL ABOUT CHA
   (Bobby Womack)
8. ONE MONKEY DON'T STOP NO SHOW
   (Honey Cone)
9. GOT TO BE THERE
   (Michael Jackson)
10. YOU ARE EVERYTHING
    (The Stylistics)

BLACK ALBUMS

1. BLACK MOSES
   (Isaac Hayes)
2. GREATEST HITS
   (The Jackson 5)
3. THERE'S A RIOT GOIN' ON
   (Sly and the Family Stone)
4. QUIET FIRE
   (Roberta Flack)
5. WHAT'S GOING ON
   (Marvin Gaye)
6. SHAFT
   (Isaac Hayes)
7. REVOLUTION OF THE MIND
   (James Brown)
8. STYLISTICS
   (The Stylistics)
9. SANTANA
   (Santana)
10. GOIN' BACK TO INDIANA
    (The Jackson 5)

JAZZ ALBUMS

1. SHAFT
   (Isaac Hayes)
2. PUSH, PUSH
   (Herbie Mann)
3. SMACKWATER JACK
   (Quincy Jones)
4. QUIET FIRE
   (Roberta Flack)
5. VISIONS
   (Grant Green)
6. LIVE-EVIL
   (Miles Davis)
7. BLACK MOSES
   (Isaac Hayes)
8. SUNSHIP
   (John Coltrane)
9. CHAPTER TWO
   (Roberta Flack)
10. UNIVERSAL CONSCIOUSNESS
    (Alice Coltrane)

COUNTRY SINGLES

1. CAROLYN
   (Merle Haggard)
2. WOULD YOU TAKE ANOTHER CHANCE ON
   ME
   (Jerry Lee Lewis)
3. (I'VE GOT A) HAPPY HEART
   (Susan Raye)
4. KISS AN ANGEL GOOD MORNING
   (Charley Pride)
5. ONE'S ON THE WAY
   (Loretta Lynn)
6. I CAN'T SEE ME WITHOUT YOU
   (Conway Twitty)
7. COAT OF MANY COLORS
   (Dolly Parton)
8. FOUR IN THE MORNING
   (Faron Young)
9. YOU BETTER MOVE ON
   (Billy "Crash" Craddock)
10. COUNTRY GREEN
    (Don Gibson)

COUNTRY ALBUMS

1. CHARLEY PRIDE SINGS HEART SONGS
   (Charley Pride)
2. WOULD YOU TAKE ANOTHER CHANCE ON
   ME
   (Jerry Lee Lewis)
3. HOW CAN I UNLOVE YOU
   (Lynn Anderson)
4. EASY LOVIN'
   (Freddie Hart)
5. WE GO TOGETHER
   (George Jones and Tammy Wynette)

6. HERE COMES HONEY AGAIN
   (Sonny James)
7. IN SEARCH OF A SONG
   (Tom T. Hall)
8. COAT OF MANY COLORS
   (Dolly Parton)
9. ANNE MURRAY AND GLEN CAMPBELL
   (Anne Murray and Glen Campbell)
10. BILL ANDERSON'S GREATEST HITS
    (Bill Anderson)

JANUARY 22, 1972

POP SINGLES

1. AMERICAN PIE
   (Don McLean)
2. LET'S STAY TOGETHER
   (Al Green)
3. SUNSHINE
   (Jonathan Edwards)
4. BRAND NEW KEY
   (Melanie)
5. CLEAN UP WOMAN
   (Betty Wright)
6. DROWNING IN THE SEA OF LOVE
   (Joe Simon)
7. SUGAR DADDY
   (The Jackson 5)
8. I'D LIKE TO TEACH THE WORLD TO SING
   (The New Seekers)
9. DAY AFTER DAY
   (Badfinger)
10. I'D LIKE TO TEACH THE WORLD TO SING
    (The Hillside Singers)

POP ALBUMS

1. AMERICAN PIE
   (Don McLean)
2. CAROLE KING MUSIC
   (Carole King)
3. THE CONCERT FOR BANGLADESH
   (George Harrison and Friends)
4. CHICAGO AT CARNEGIE HALL
   (Chicago)
5. LED ZEPPELIN
   (Led Zeppelin)
6. ALL IN THE FAMILY
   (Original Cast)
7. BLACK MOSES
   (Isaac Hayes)
8. TEASER AND THE FIRECAT
   (Cat Stevens)
9. WILD LIFE
   (Paul McCartney and Wings)
10. THERE'S A RIOT GOIN' ON
    (Sly and the Family Stone)

BLACK SINGLES

1. LET'S STAY TOGETHER
   (Al Green)
2. DROWNING IN THE SEA OF LOVE
   (Joe Simon)
3. SUGAR DADDY
   (The Jackson 5)
4. CLEAN UP WOMAN
   (Betty Wright)
5. THAT'S THE WAY I FEEL ABOUT CHA
   (Bobby Womack)
6. SHOW ME HOW
   (Emotions)
7. EVERYBODY KNOWS ABOUT MY GOOD
   THING (PART I)
   (Little Johnnie Taylor)
8. FIRE AND WATER
   (Wilson Pickett)
9. ONE MONKEY DON'T STOP NO SHOW
   (Honey Cone)
10. DO THE FUNKY PENGUIN
    (Rufus Thomas)

BLACK ALBUMS

1. BLACK MOSES
   (Isaac Hayes)
2. GREATEST HITS
   (The Jackson 5)
3. THERE'S A RIOT GOIN' ON
   (Sly and the Family Stone)
4. QUIET FIRE
   (Roberta Flack)
5. REVOLUTION OF THE MIND
   (James Brown)
6. INNER CITY BLUES
   (Grover Washington Jr.)
7. WHAT'S GOING ON
   (Marvin Gaye)
8. STYLISTICS
   (The Stylistics)
9. SHAFT
   (Isaac Hayes)
10. WOMEN'S LOVE RIGHTS
    (Laura Lee)

JAZZ ALBUMS

1. SHAFT
   (Isaac Hayes)
2. PUSH PUSH
   (Herbie Mann)
3. SMACKWATER JACK
   (Quincy Jones)
4. QUIET FIRE
   (Roberta Flack)
5. VISIONS
   (Grant Green)
6. LIVE-EVIL
   (Miles Davis)
7. BLACK MOSES
   (Isaac Hayes)
8. SUNSHIP
   (John Coltrane)
9. CHAPTER TWO
   (Roberta Flack)
10. UNIVERSAL CONSCIOUSNESS
    (Alice Coltrane)

COUNTRY SINGLES

1. ONE'S ON THE WAY
   (Loretta Lynn)
2. CAROLYN
   (Merle Haggard)
3. I CAN'T SEE ME WITHOUT YOU
   (Conway Twitty)
4. WOULD YOU TAKE ANOTHER CHANCE ON
   ME
   (Jerry Lee Lewis)
5. FOUR IN THE MORNING
   (Faron Young)
6. KISS AN ANGEL GOOD MORNING
   (Charley Pride)
7. (I'VE GOT A) HAPPY HEART
   (Susan Raye)
8. I'M A TRUCK
   (Red Simpson)
9. COAT OF MANY COLORS
   (Dolly Parton)
10. I'VE COME AWFUL CLOSE
    (Hank Thompson)

COUNTRY ALBUMS

1. CHARLEY PRIDE SINGS HEART SONGS
   (Charley Pride)
2. HOW CAN I UNLOVE YOU
   (Lynn Anderson)
3. WOULD YOU TAKE ANOTHER CHANCE ON
   ME
   (Jerry Lee Lewis)
4. EASY LOVIN'
   (Freddie Hart)
5. WE GO TOGETHER
   (George Jones and Tammy Wynette)

6. ANNE MURRAY AND GLEN CAMPBELL
   (Anne Murray and Glen Campbell)
7. COAT OF MANY COLORS
   (Dolly Parton)
8. RANGER'S WALTZ
   (Moms and Dads)
9. BILL ANDERSON'S GREATEST HITS
   (Bill Anderson)
10. IN SEARCH OF A SONG
    (Tom T. Hall)

JANUARY 29, 1972

POP SINGLES

1. AMERICAN PIE
   (Don McLean)
2. LET'S STAY TOGETHER
   (Al Green)
3. SUNSHINE
   (Jonathan Edwards)
4. CLEAN UP WOMAN
   (Betty Wright)
5. DAY AFTER DAY
   (Badfinger)
6. DROWNING IN THE SEA OF LOVE
   (Joe Simon)
7. SUGAR DADDY
   (The Jackson 5)
8. BRAND NEW KEY
   (Melanie)
9. NEVER BEEN TO SPAIN
   (Three Dog Night)
10. YOU ARE EVERYTHING
    (The Stylistics)

POP ALBUMS

1. CONCERT FOR BANGLADESH
   (George Harrison and Friends)
2. AMERICAN PIE
   (Don McLean)
3. CAROLE KING MUSIC
   (Carole King)
4. CHICAGO AT CARNEGIE HALL
   (Chicago)
5. LED ZEPPELIN
   (Led Zeppelin)
6. TEASER AND THE FIRECAT
   (Cat Stevens)
7. WILD LIFE
   (Paul McCartney and Wings)
8. HOT ROCKS 1964–1971
   (The Rolling Stones)
9. THERE'S A RIOT GOIN' ON
   (Sly and the Family Stone)
10. A NOD IS AS GOOD AS A WINK . . . TO A
    BLIND HORSE
    (Faces)

BLACK SINGLES

1. LET'S STAY TOGETHER
   (Al Green)
2. SUGAR DADDY
   (The Jackson 5)
3. DROWNING IN THE SEA OF LOVE
   (Joe Simon)
4. THAT'S THE WAY I FEEL ABOUT CHA
   (Bobby Womack)
5. CLEAN UP WOMAN
   (Betty Wright)
6. DO THE FUNKY PENGUIN
   (Rufus Thomas)
7. FIRE AND WATER
   (Wilson Pickett)
8. SHOW ME HOW
   (Emotions)
9. EVERYBODY KNOWS ABOUT MY GOOD
   THING (PART I)
   (Little Johnnie Taylor)

10. ONE MONKEY DON'T STOP NO SHOW
    (Honey Cone)

BLACK ALBUMS

1. BLACK MOSES
   (Isaac Hayes)
2. REVOLUTION OF THE MIND
   (James Brown)
3. GREATEST HITS
   (The Jackson 5)
4. INNER CITY BLUES
   (Grover Washington Jr.)
5. THERE'S A RIOT GOIN' ON
   (Sly and the Family Stone)
6. WOMEN'S LOVE RIGHTS
   (Laura Lee)
7. QUIET FIRE
   (Roberta Flack)
8. WHAT'S GOING ON
   (Marvin Gaye)
9. SHAFT
   (Isaac Hayes)
10. STYLISTICS
    (The Stylistics)

JAZZ ALBUMS

1. SHAFT
   (Isaac Hayes)
2. BLACK MOSES
   (Isaac Hayes)
3. PUSH PUSH
   (Herbie Mann)
4. QUIET FIRE
   (Roberta Flack)
5. LIVE-EVIL
   (Miles Davis)
6. VISIONS
   (Grant Green)
7. INNER CITY BLUES
   (Grover Washington Jr.)
8. SMACKWATER JACK
   (Quincy Jones)
9. SUNSHIP
   (John Coltrane)
10. UNIVERSAL CONSCIOUSNESS
    (Alice Coltrane)

COUNTRY SINGLES

1. I CAN'T SEE ME WITHOUT YOU
   (Conway Twitty)
2. ONE'S ON THE WAY
   (Loretta Lynn)
3. FOUR IN THE MORNING
   (Faron Young)
4. CAROLYN
   (Merle Haggard)
5. I'M A TRUCK
   (Red Simpson)
6. WOULD YOU TAKE ANOTHER CHANCE ON
   ME
   (Jerry Lee Lewis)
7. KISS AN ANGEL GOOD MORNING
   (Charley Pride)
8. (I'VE GOT A) HAPPY HEART
   (Susan Raye)
9. I'VE COME AWFUL CLOSE
   (Hank Thompson)
10. MUCH OBLIGE
    (Jack Greene and Jeannie Seely)

COUNTRY ALBUMS

1. HOW CAN I UNLOVE YOU
   (Lynn Anderson)
2. CHARLEY PRIDE SINGS HEART SONGS
   (Charley Pride)
3. EASY LOVIN'
   (Freddie Hart)

4. WOULD YOU TAKE ANOTHER CHANCE ON
   ME
   (Jerry Lee Lewis)
5. ANNE MURRAY AND GLEN CAMPBELL
   (Anne Murray and Glen Campbell)
6. RANGER'S WALTZ
   (Moms and Dads)
7. COAT OF MANY COLORS
   (Dolly Parton)
8. WE GO TOGETHER
   (George Jones and Tammy Wynette)
9. BILL ANDERSON'S GREATEST HITS
   (Bill Anderson)
10. SHE'S ALL I GOT
    (Johnny Paycheck)

FEBRUARY 5, 1972

POP SINGLES

1. DAY AFTER DAY
   (Badfinger)
2. AMERICAN PIE
   (Don McLean)
3. LET'S STAY TOGETHER
   (Al Green)
4. CLEAN UP WOMAN
   (Betty Wright)
5. NEVER BEEN TO SPAIN
   (Three Dog Night)
6. DROWNING IN THE SEA OF LOVE
   (Joe Simon)
7. SUGAR DADDY
   (The Jackson 5)
8. SUNSHINE
   (Jonathan Edwards)
9. WITHOUT YOU
   (Harry Nilsson)
10. YOU ARE EVERYTHING
    (The Stylistics)

POP ALBUMS

1. CONCERT FOR BANGLADESH
   (George Harrison and Friends)
2. AMERICAN PIE
   (Don McLean)
3. CAROLE KING MUSIC
   (Carole King)
4. CHICAGO AT CARNEGIE HALL
   (Chicago)
5. LED ZEPPELIN
   (Led Zeppelin)
6. A NOD IS AS GOOD AS A WINK. . .TO A
   BLIND HORSE
   (Faces)
7. HOT ROCKS 1964–1971
   (The Rolling Stones)
8. TEASER AND THE FIRECAT
   (Cat Stevens)
9. WILD LIFE
   (Paul McCartney and Wings)
10. THERE'S A RIOT GOIN' ON
    (Sly and the Family Stone)

BLACK SINGLES

1. LET'S STAY TOGETHER
   (Al Green)
2. THAT'S THE WAY I FEEL ABOUT CHA
   (Bobby Womack)
3. SUGAR DADDY
   (The Jackson 5)
4. DO THE FUNKY PENGUIN
   (Rufus Thomas)
5. AIN'T UNDERSTANDING MELLOW
   (Butler and Eager)
6. JUNGLE FEVER
   (Chakachas)
7. SLIPPIN' INTO DARKNESS
   (War)

8. DROWNING IN THE SEA OF LOVE
   (Joe Simon)
9. SHOW ME HOW
   (Emotions)
10. FLOY JOY
    (The Supremes)

BLACK ALBUMS

1. BLACK MOSES
   (Isaac Hayes)
2. WOMEN'S LOVE RIGHTS
   (Laura Lee)
3. INNER CITY BLUES
   (Grover Washington Jr.)
4. WHATCHA SEE IS WHATCHA GET
   (The Dramatics)
5. REVOLUTION OF THE MIND
   (James Brown)
6. I'VE BEEN HERE ALL THE TIME
   (Luther Ingram)
7. GREATEST HITS
   (The Jackson 5)
8. STANDING OVATION
   (Gladys Knight and the Pips)
9. QUIET FIRE
   (Roberta Flack)
10. THERE'S A RIOT GOIN' ON
    (Sly and the Family Stone)

JAZZ ALBUMS

1. BLACK MOSES
   (Isaac Hayes)
2. SHAFT
   (Isaac Hayes)
3. INNER CITY BLUES
   (Grover Washington Jr.)
4. QUIET FIRE
   (Roberta Flack)
5. PUSH PUSH
   (Herbie Mann)
6. LIVE-EVIL
   (Miles Davis)
7. VISIONS
   (Grant Green)
8. SUNSHIP
   (John Coltrane)
9. SMACKWATER JACK
   (Quincy Jones)
10. UNIVERSAL CONSCIOUSNESS
    (Alice Coltrane)

COUNTRY SINGLES

1. FOUR IN THE MORNING
   (Faron Young)
2. I CAN'T SEE ME WITHOUT YOU
   (Conway Twitty)
3. I'M A TRUCK
   (Red Simpson)
4. ONE'S ON THE WAY
   (Loretta Lynn)
5. CAROLYN
   (Merle Haggard)
6. TAKE ME
   (Tammy Wynette and George Jones)
7. MUCH OBLIGE
   (Jack Greene and Jeannie Seely)
8. AIN'T THAT A SHAME
   (Hank Williams Jr.)
9. FORGIVE ME FOR CALLING YOU DARLING
   (Nat Stuckey)
10. TURN YOUR RADIO ON
    (Ray Stevens)

COUNTRY ALBUMS

1. HOW CAN I UNLOVE YOU
   (Lynn Anderson)
2. CHARLEY PRIDE SINGS HEART SONGS
   (Charley Pride)

3. EASY LOVIN'
   (Freddie Hart)
4. ANNE MURRAY AND GLEN CAMPBELL
   (Anne Murray and Glen Campbell)
5. RANGER'S WALTZ
   (Moms and Dads)
6. WOULD YOU TAKE ANOTHER CHANCE ON ME
   (Jerry Lee Lewis)
7. SHE'S ALL I GOT
   (Johnny Paycheck)
8. COAT OF MANY COLORS
   (Dolly Parton)
9. THE LAND OF MANY CHURCHES
   (Merle Haggard)
10. NEVER ENDING SONG OF LOVE
    (Dickey Lee)

FEBRUARY 12, 1972

POP SINGLES

1. DAY AFTER DAY
   (Badfinger)
2. AMERICAN PIE
   (Don McLean)
3. NEVER BEEN TO SPAIN
   (Three Dog Night)
4. LET'S STAY TOGETHER
   (Al Green)
5. WITHOUT YOU
   (Harry Nilsson)
6. HURTING EACH OTHER
   (The Carpenters)
7. PRECIOUS AND FEW
   (Climax)
8. CLEAN UP WOMAN
   (Betty Wright)
9. SUGAR DADDY
   (The Jackson 5)
10. DOWN BY THE LAZY RIVER
    (The Osmonds)

POP ALBUMS

1. CONCERT FOR BANGLADESH
   (George Harrison and Friends)
2. AMERICAN PIE
   (Don McLean)
3. CAROLE KING MUSIC
   (Carole King)
4. LED ZEPPELIN
   (Led Zeppelin)
5. HOT ROCKS 1964-1971
   (The Rolling Stones)
6. A NOD IS AS GOOD AS A WINK. . .TO A BLIND HORSE
   (Faces)
7. CHICAGO AT CARNEGIE HALL
   (Chicago)
8. TEASER AND THE FIRECAT
   (Cat Stevens)
9. WILD LIFE
   (Paul McCartney and Wings)
10. MADMAN ACROSS THE WATER
    (Elton John)

BLACK SINGLES

1. LET'S STAY TOGETHER
   (Al Green)
2. SUGAR DADDY
   (The Jackson 5)
3. THAT'S THE WAY I FEEL ABOUT CHA
   (Bobby Womack)
4. DO THE FUNKY PENGUIN
   (Rufus Thomas)
5. DROWNING IN THE SEA OF LOVE
   (Joe Simon)

6. CLEAN UP WOMAN
   (Betty Wright)
7. FIRE AND WATER
   (Wilson Pickett)
8. SLIPPIN' INTO DARKNESS
   (War)
9. SHOW ME HOW
   (Emotions)
10. JUNGLE FEVER
    (Chakachas)

BLACK ALBUMS

1. BLACK MOSES
   (Isaac Hayes)
2. REVOLUTION OF THE MIND
   (James Brown)
3. INNER CITY BLUES
   (Grover Washington Jr.)
4. WOMEN'S LOVE RIGHTS
   (Laura Lee)
5. GREATEST HITS
   (The Jackson 5)
6. WATCHA SEE IS WHATCHA GET
   (The Dramatics)
7. QUIET FIRE
   (Roberta Flack)
8. THERE'S A RIOT GOIN' ON
   (Sly and the Family Stone)
9. I'VE BEEN HERE ALL THE TIME
   (Luther Ingram)
10. WHAT'S GOING ON
    (Marvin Gaye)

JAZZ ALBUMS

1. BLACK MOSES
   (Isaac Hayes)
2. SHAFT
   (Isaac Hayes)
3. INNER CITY BLUES
   (Grover Washington Jr.)
4. QUIET FIRE
   (Roberta Flack)
5. SMACKWATER JACK
   (Quincy Jones)
6. PUSH PUSH
   (Herbie Mann)
7. LIVE-EVIL
   (Miles Davis)
8. SUNSHIP
   (John Coltrane)
9. VISIONS
   (Grant Green)
10. A DIFFERENT DRUMMER
    (Buddy Rich)

COUNTRY SINGLES

1. I'M A TRUCK
   (Red Simpson)
2. FOUR IN THE MORNING
   (Faron Young)
3. TAKE ME
   (Tammy Wynette and George Jones)
4. AIN'T THAT A SHAME
   (Hank Williams Jr.)
5. FORGIVE ME FOR CALLING YOU DARLING
   (Nat Stuckey)
6. ONE'S ON THE WAY
   (Loretta Lynn)
7. MUCH OBLIGE
   (Jack Greene and Jeannie Seely)
8. BEDTIME STORY
   (Tammy Wynette)
9. I CAN'T SEE ME WITHOUT YOU
   (Conway Twitty)
10. TONIGHT MY BABY'S COMING HOME
    (Barbara Mandrell)

COUNTRY ALBUMS

1. CHARLEY PRIDE SINGS HEART SONGS
   (Charley Pride)
2. HOW CAN I UNLOVE YOU
   (Lynn Anderson)
3. EASY LOVIN'
   (Freddie Hart)
4. ANNE MURRAY AND GLEN CAMPBELL
   (Anne Murray and Glen Campbell)
5. RANGER'S WALTZ
   (Moms and Dads)
6. SHE'S ALL I GOT
   (Johnny Paycheck)
7. WOULD YOU TAKE ANOTHER CHANCE ON ME
   (Jerry Lee Lewis)
8. THE LAND OF MANY CHURCHES
   (Merle Haggard)
9. NEVER ENDING SONG OF LOVE
   (Dickey Lee)
10. COAT OF MANY COLORS
    (Dolly Parton)

FEBRUARY 19, 1972

POP SINGLES

1. WITHOUT YOU
   (Harry Nilsson)
2. AMERICAN PIE
   (Don McLean)
3. NEVER BEEN TO SPAIN
   (Three Dog Night)
4. HURTING EACH OTHER
   (The Carpenters)
5. PRECIOUS AND FEW
   (Climax)
6. DAY AFTER DAY
   (Badfinger)
7. LET'S STAY TOGETHER
   (Al Green)
8. DOWN BY THE LAZY RIVER
   (The Osmonds)
9. JOY
   (Apollo)
10. THE LION SLEEPS TONIGHT
    (Robert John)

POP ALBUMS

1. CONCERT FOR BANGLADESH
   (George Harrison and Friends)
2. AMERICAN PIE
   (Don McLean)
3. CAROLE KING MUSIC
   (Carole King)
4. HOT ROCKS 1964-1971
   (The Rolling Stones)
5. LED ZEPPELIN
   (Led Zeppelin)
6. A NOD IS AS GOOD AS A WINK. . .TO A BLIND HORSE
   (Faces)
7. TEASER AND THE FIRECAT
   (Cat Stevens)
8. MADMAN ACROSS THE WATER
   (Elton John)
9. FRAGILE
   (Yes)
10. PICTURES AT AN EXHIBITION
    (Emerson, Lake and Palmer)

BLACK SINGLES

1. THAT'S THE WAY I FEEL ABOUT CHA
   (Bobby Womack)
2. LET'S STAY TOGETHER
   (Al Green)

3. AIN'T UNDERSTANDING MELLOW
   (Butler and Eager)
4. JUNGLE FEVER
   (Chakachas)
5. SUGAR DADDY
   (The Jackson 5)
6. FLOY JOY
   (The Supremes)
7. DO THE FUNKY PENGUIN
   (Rufus Thomas)
8. I GOTCHA
   (Joe Tex)
9. MR. PENGUIN, PART I
   (Lunar Funk)
10. SHOW ME HOW
    (Emotions)

BLACK ALBUMS

1. WOMEN'S LOVE RIGHTS
   (Laura Lee)
2. BLACK MOSES
   (Isaac Hayes)
3. WHATCHA SEE IS WHATCHA GET
   (The Dramatics)
4. I'VE BEEN HERE ALL THE TIME
   (Luther Ingram)
5. INNER CITY BLUES
   (Grover Washington Jr.)
6. REVOLUTION OF THE MIND
   (James Brown)
7. STANDING OVATION
   (Gladys Knight and the Pips)
8. GONNA TAKE A MIRACLE
   (Laura Nyro)
9. QUIET FIRE
   (Roberta Flack)
10. THERE'S A RIOT GOIN' ON
    (Sly and the Family Stone)

COUNTRY SINGLES

1. TAKE ME
   (Tammy Wynette and George Jones)
2. I'M A TRUCK
   (Red Simpson)
3. AIN'T THAT A SHAME
   (Hank Williams Jr.)
4. BEDTIME STORY
   (Tammy Wynette)
5. FOUR IN THE MORNING
   (Faron Young)
6. ONE'S ON THE WAY
   (Loretta Lynn)
7. ANN (DON'T GO RUNNIN')
   (Tommy Overstreet)
8. THE BEST PART OF LIVING
   (Marty Robbins)
9. ONLY LOVE CAN BREAK A HEART
   (Sonny James)
10. TONIGHT MY BABY'S COMING HOME
    (Barbara Mandrell)

COUNTRY ALBUMS

1. CHARLEY PRIDE SINGS HEART SONGS
   (Charley Pride)
2. HOW CAN I UNLOVE YOU
   (Lynn Anderson)
3. EASY LOVIN'
   (Freddie Hart)
4. SHE'S ALL I GOT
   (Johnny Paycheck)
5. RANGER'S WALTZ
   (Moms and Dads)
6. ANNE MURRAY AND GLEN CAMPBELL
   (Anne Murry and Glen Campbell)
7. NEVER ENDING SONG OF LOVE
   (Dickey Lee)
8. THE LAND OF MANY CHURCHES
   (Merle Haggard)
9. WOULD YOU TAKE ANOTHER CHANCE ON ME
   (Jerry Lee Lewis)

10. IN SEARCH OF A SONG
    (Tom T. Hall)

FEBRUARY 26, 1972

POP SINGLES

1. WITHOUT YOU
   (Harry Nilsson)
2. HURTING EACH OTHER
   (The Carpenters)
3. PRECIOUS AND FEW
   (Climax)
4. NEVER BEEN TO SPAIN
   (Three Dog Night)
5. DOWN BY THE LAZY RIVER
   (The Osmonds)
6. AMERICAN PIE
   (Don McLean)
7. LET'S STAY TOGETHER
   (Al Green)
8. THE LION SLEEPS TONIGHT
   (Robert John)
9. JOY
   (Apollo)
10. BLACK DOG
    (Led Zeppelin)

POP ALBUMS

1. CONCERT FOR BANGLADESH
   (George Harrison and Friends)
2. AMERICAN PIE
   (Don McLean)
3. CAROLE KING MUSIC
   (Carole King)
4. HOT ROCKS 1964–1971
   (The Rolling Stones)
5. LED ZEPPELIN
   (Led Zeppelin)
6. A NOD IS AS GOOD AS A WINK...TO A BLIND HORSE
   (Faces)
7. FRAGILE
   (Yes)
8. PICTURES AT AN EXHIBITION
   (Emerson, Lake and Palmer)
9. NILSSON SCHMILSSON
   (Harry Nilsson)
10. TEASER AND THE FIRECAT
    (Cat Stevens)

BLACK SINGLES

1. THAT'S THE WAY I FEEL ABOUT CHA
   (Bobby Womack)
2. AIN'T UNDERSTANDING MELLOW
   (Butler and Eager)
3. JUNGLE FEVER
   (Chakachas)
4. LET'S STAY TOGETHER
   (Al Green)
5. FLOY JOY
   (The Supremes)
6. I GOTCHA
   (Joe Tex)
7. MR. PENGUIN, PART I
   (Lunar Funk)
8. SUGAR DADDY
   (The Jackson 5)
9. GIMME SOME MORE
   (JB's)
10. TALKING LOUD AND SAYING NOTHING
    (James Brown)

BLACK ALBUMS

1. WOMEN'S LOVE RIGHTS
   (Laura Lee)

2. WHATCHA SEE IS WHATCHA GET
   (The Dramatics)
3. I'VE BEEN HERE ALL THE TIME
   (Luther Ingram)
4. BLACK MOSES
   (Isaac Hayes)
5. GONNA TAKE A MIRACLE
   (Laura Nyro)
6. REVOLUTION OF THE MIND
   (James Brown)
7. STANDING OVATION
   (Gladys Knight and the Pips)
8. INNER CITY BLUES
   (Grover Washington Jr.)
9. TRAPPED BY A THING CALLED LOVE
   (Denise LaSalle)
10. QUIET FIRE
    (Roberta Flack)

JAZZ ALBUMS

1. BLACK MOSES
   (Isaac Hayes)
2. INNER CITY BLUES
   (Grover Washington Jr.)
3. SHAFT
   (Isaac Hayes)
4. QUIET FIRE
   (Roberta Flack)
5. SMACKWATER JACK
   (Quincy Jones)
6. PUSH PUSH
   (Herbie Mann)
7. VISIONS
   (Grant Green)
8. LIVE-EVIL
   (Miles Davis)
9. A DIFFERENT DRUMMER
   (Buddy Rich)
10. SUNSHIP
    (John Coltrane)

COUNTRY SINGLES

1. BEDTIME STORY
   (Tammy Wynette)
2. TAKE ME
   (Tammy Wynette and George Jones)
3. ANN (DON'T GO RUNNIN')
   (Tommy Overstreet)
4. ONLY LOVE CAN BREAK A HEART
   (Sonny James)
5. GOOD-HEARTED WOMAN
   (Waylon Jennings)
6. THE BEST PART OF LIVING
   (Marty Robbins)
7. FOUR IN THE MORNING
   (Faron Young)
8. I'M A TRUCK
   (Red Simpson)
9. AIN'T THAT A SHAME
   (Hank Williams Jr.)
10. UNTOUCHED
    (Mel Tillis)

COUNTRY ALBUMS

1. CHARLEY PRIDE SINGS HEART SONGS
   (Charley Pride)
2. EASY LOVIN'
   (Freddie Hart)
3. HOW CAN I UNLOVE YOU
   (Lynn Anderson)
4. SHE'S ALL I GOT
   (Johnny Paycheck)
5. RANGER'S WALTZ
   (Moms and Dads)
6. NEVER ENDING SONG OF LOVE
   (Dickey Lee)
7. ANNE MURRAY AND GLEN CAMPBELL
   (Anne Murray and Glen Campbell)
8. BURNING THE MIDNIGHT OIL
   (Porter Wagoner and Dolly Parton)

9. LEAD ME ON
   (Conway Twitty and Loretta Lynn)
10. IN SEARCH OF A SONG
   (Tom T. Hall)

MARCH 4, 1972

POP SINGLES

1. HURTING EACH OTHER
   (The Carpenters)
2. PRECIOUS AND FEW
   (Climax)
3. WITHOUT YOU
   (Harry Nilsson)
4. DOWN BY THE LAZY RIVER
   (The Osmonds)
5. THE LION SLEEPS TONIGHT
   (Robert John)
6. EVERYTHING I OWN
   (Bread)
7. LET'S STAY TOGETHER
   (Al Green)
8. JOY
   (Apollo)
9. SWEET SEASONS
   (Carole King)
10. BLACK DOG
   (Led Zeppelin)

POP ALBUMS

1. AMERICAN PIE
   (Don McLean)
2. CAROLE KING MUSIC
   (Carole King)
3. CONCERT FOR BANGLADESH
   (George Harrison and Friends)
4. FRAGILE
   (Yes)
5. HOT ROCKS 1964-1971
   (The Rolling Stones)
6. A NOD IS AS GOOD AS A WINK. . .TO A
   BLIND HORSE
   (Faces)
7. PICTURES AT AN EXHIBITION
   (Emerson, Lake and Palmer)
8. NILSSON SCHMILSSON
   (Harry Nilsson)
9. LED ZEPPELIN
   (Led Zeppelin)
10. BABY, I'M A WANT YOU
   (Bread)

BLACK SINGLES

1. AIN'T UNDERSTANDING MELLOW
   (Butler and Eager)
2. THAT'S THE WAY I FEEL ABOUT CHA
   (Bobby Womack)
3. TALKING LOUD AND SAYING NOTHING
   (James Brown)
4. JUNGLE FEVER
   (Chakachas)
5. LET'S STAY TOGETHER
   (Al Green)
6. GIMME SOME MORE
   (JB's)
7. YOU WANT IT, YOU GOT IT
   (Detroit Emeralds)
8. I GOTCHA
   (Joe Tex)
9. MR. PENGUIN, PART I
   (Lunar Funk)
10. RUNNIN' AWAY
   (Sly and the Family Stone)

BLACK ALBUMS

1. WOMEN'S LOVE RIGHTS
   (Laura Lee)

2. WHATCHA SEE IS WHATCHA GET
   (The Dramatics)
3. I'VE BEEN HERE ALL THE TIME
   (Luther Ingram)
4. GONNA TAKE A MIRACLE
   (Laura Nyro)
5. BLACK MOSES
   (Isaac Hayes)
6. STANDING OVATION
   (Gladys Knight and the Pips)
7. SOLID ROCK
   (Temptations)
8. REVOLUTION OF THE MIND
   (James Brown)
9. INNER CITY BLUES
   (Grover Washington Jr.)
10. QUIET FIRE
   (Roberta Flack)

JAZZ ALBUMS

1. BLACK MOSES
   (Isaac Hayes)
2. INNER CITY BLUES
   (Grover Washington Jr.)
3. QUIET FIRE
   (Roberta Flack)
4. SHAFT
   (Isaac Hayes)
5. PUSH PUSH
   (Herbie Mann)
6. SMACKWATER JACK
   (Quincy Jones)
7. A DIFFERENT DRUMMER
   (Buddy Rich)
8. LIVE-EVIL
   (Miles Davis)
9. VISIONS
   (Grant Green)
10. SUNSHIP
   (John Coltrane)

COUNTRY SINGLES

1. ANN (DON'T GO RUNNIN')
   (Tommy Overstreet)
2. ONLY LOVE CAN BREAK A HEART
   (Sonny James)
3. GOOD-HEARTED WOMAN
   (Waylon Jennings)
4. BEDTIME STORY
   (Tammy Wynette)
5. THE BEST PART OF LIVING
   (Marty Robbins)
6. TAKE ME
   (Tammy Wynette and George Jones)
7. MY HANG UP IS YOU
   (Freddie Hart)
8. UNTOUCHED
   (Mel Tillis)
9. CRY
   (Lynn Anderson)
10. FOUR IN THE MORNING
   (Faron Young)

COUNTRY ALBUMS

1. CHARLEY PRIDE SINGS HEART SONGS
   (Charley Pride)
2. EASY LOVIN'
   (Freddie Hart)
3. SHE'S ALL I GOT
   (Johnny Paycheck)
4. HOW CAN I UNLOVE YOU
   (Lynn Anderson)
5. LEAD ME ON
   (Conway Twitty and Loretta Lynn)
6. NEVER ENDING SONG OF LOVE
   (Dickey Lee)
7. RANGER'S WALTZ
   (Moms and Dads)
8. BURNING THE MIDNIGHT OIL
   (Porter Wagoner and Dolly Parton)

9. ANNE MURRAY AND GLEN CAMPBELL
   (Anne Murray and Glen Campbell)
10. IN SEARCH OF A SONG
   (Tom T. Hall)

MARCH 11, 1972

POP SINGLES

1. PRECIOUS AND FEW
   (Climax)
2. HURTING EACH OTHER
   (The Carpenters)
3. DOWN BY THE LAZY RIVER
   (The Osmonds)
4. WITHOUT YOU
   (Harry Nilsson)
5. THE LION SLEEPS TONIGHT
   (Robert John)
6. EVERYTHING I OWN
   (Bread)
7. HEART OF GOLD
   (Neil Young)
8. MOTHER AND CHILD REUNION
   (Paul Simon)
9. SWEET SEASONS
   (Carole King)
10. BANG A GONG
   (T. Rex)

POP ALBUMS

1. AMERICAN PIE
   (Don McLean)
2. CAROLE KING MUSIC
   (Carole King)
3. CONCERT FOR BANGLADESH
   (George Harrison and Friends)
4. FRAGILE
   (Yes)
5. HOT ROCKS 1964-1971
   (The Rolling Stones)
6. NILSSON SCHMILSSON
   (Harry Nilsson)
7. PAUL SIMON
   (Paul Simon)
8. BABY, I'M A WANT YOU
   (Bread)
9. LED ZEPPELIN
   (Led Zeppelin)
10. HARVEST
   (Neil Young)

BLACK SINGLES

1. AIN'T UNDERSTANDING MELLOW
   (Butler and Eager)
2. TALKING LOUD AND SAYING NOTHING
   (James Brown)
3. THAT'S THE WAY I FEEL ABOUT CHA
   (Bobby Womack)
4. GIMME SOME MORE
   (JB's)
5. I GOTCHA
   (Joe Tex)
6. YOU WANT IT, YOU GOT IT
   (Detroit Emeralds)
7. RUNNIN' AWAY
   (Sly and the Family Stone)
8. THE DAY I FOUND MYSELF
   (Honey Cone)
9. I CAN'T HELP MYSELF
   (Donnie Elbert)
10. DO YOUR THING
   (Isaac Hayes)

BLACK ALBUMS

1. WOMEN'S LOVE RIGHTS
   (Laura Lee)

2. WHATCHA SEE IS WHATCHA GET
   (The Dramatics)
3. GONNA TAKE A MIRACLE
   (Laura Nyro)
4. I'VE BEEN HERE ALL THE TIME
   (Luther Ingram)
5. SOLID ROCK
   (Temptations)
6. STANDING OVATION
   (Gladys Knight and the Pips)
7. BLACK MOSES
   (Isaac Hayes)
8. REVOLUTION OF THE MIND
   (James Brown)
9. INNER CITY BLUES
   (Grover Washington Jr.)
10. LET'S STAY TOGETHER
    (Al Green)

JAZZ ALBUMS

1. BLACK MOSES
   (Isaac Hayes)
2. SMACKWATER JACK
   (Quincy Jones)
3. INNER CITY BLUES
   (Grover Washington Jr.)
4. QUIET FIRE
   (Roberta Flack)
5. PUSH PUSH
   (Herbie Mann)
6. SHAFT
   (Isaac Hayes)
7. A DIFFERENT DRUMMER
   (Buddy Rich)
8. VISIONS
   (Grant Green)
9. LIVE-EVIL
   (Miles Davis)
10. MY WAY
    (Gene Ammons)

COUNTRY SINGLES

1. ONLY LOVE CAN BREAK A HEART
   (Sonny James)
2. GOOD-HEARTED WOMAN
   (Waylon Jennings)
3. MY HANG UP IS YOU
   (Freddie Hart)
4. ANN (DON'T GO RUNNIN')
   (Tommy Overstreet)
5. THE BEST PART OF LIVING
   (Marty Robbins)
6. A THING CALLED LOVE
   (Johnny Cash)
7. CRY
   (Lynn Anderson)
8. BEDTIME STORY
   (Tammy Wynette)
9. TAKE ME
   (Tammy Wynette and George Jones)
10. TODAY I STARTED LOVING YOU AGAIN
    (Charlie McCoy)

COUNTRY ALBUMS

1. CHARLEY PRIDE SINGS HEART SONGS
   (Charley Pride)
2. LEAD ME ON
   (Conway Twitty and Loretta Lynn)
3. SHE'S ALL I GOT
   (Johnny Paycheck)
4. EASY LOVIN'
   (Freddie Hart)
5. NEVER ENDING SONG OF LOVE
   (Dickey Lee)
6. HOW CAN I UNLOVE YOU
   (Lynn Anderson)
7. BURNING THE MIDNIGHT OIL
   (Porter Wagoner and Dolly Parton)
8. RANGER'S WALTZ
   (Moms and Dads)

9. I'M A TRUCK
   (Red Simpson)
10. I'VE GOT A HAPPY HEART
    (Susan Raye)

MARCH 18, 1972

POP SINGLES

1. HEART OF GOLD
   (Neil Young)
2. THE LION SLEEPS TONIGHT
   (Robert John)
3. A HORSE WITH NO NAME
   (America)
4. MOTHER AND CHILD REUNION
   (Paul Simon)
5. WITHOUT YOU
   (Harry Nilsson)
6. EVERYTHING I OWN
   (Bread)
7. PRECIOUS AND FEW
   (Climax)
8. DOWN BY THE LAZY RIVER
   (The Osmonds)
9. PUPPY LOVE
   (Donny Osmond)
10. BANG A GONG
    (T. Rex)

POP ALBUMS

1. HARVEST
   (Neil Young)
2. AMERICAN PIE
   (Don McLean)
3. CONCERT FOR BANGLADESH
   (George Harrison and Friends)
4. FRAGILE
   (Yes)
5. BABY, I'M A WANT YOU
   (Bread)
6. NILSSON SCHMILSSON
   (Harry Nilsson)
7. PAUL SIMON
   (Paul Simon)
8. CAROLE KING MUSIC
   (Carole King)
9. AMERICA
   (America)
10. HOT ROCKS 1964–1971
    (The Rolling Stones)

BLACK SINGLES

1. TALKING LOUD AND SAYING NOTHING
   (James Brown)
2. AIN'T UNDERSTANDING MELLOW
   (Butler and Eager)
3. I GOTCHA
   (Joe Tex)
4. THAT'S THE WAY I FEEL ABOUT CHA
   (Bobby Womack)
5. RUNNIN' AWAY
   (Sly and the Family Stone)
6. THE DAY I FOUND MYSELF
   (Honey Cone)
7. GIMME SOME MORE
   (JB's)
8. DO YOUR THING
   (Isaac Hayes)
9. YOU WANT IT, YOU GOT IT
   (Detroit Emeralds)
10. KING HEROIN
    (James Brown)

BLACK ALBUMS

1. WOMEN'S LOVE RIGHTS
   (Laura Lee)

2. WHATCHA SEE IS WHATCHA GET
   (The Dramatics)
3. YOUNG, GIFTED AND BLACK
   (Aretha Franklin)
4. SOLID ROCK
   (Temptations)
5. GOT TO BE THERE
   (Michael Jackson)
6. GONNA TAKE A MIRACLE
   (Laura Nyro)
7. LET'S STAY TOGETHER
   (Al Green)
8. I'VE BEEN HERE ALL THE TIME
   (Luther Ingram)
9. FACE TO FACE WITH THE TRUTH
   (Undisputed Truth)
10. STANDING OVATION
    (Gladys Knight and the Pips)

JAZZ ALBUMS

1. BLACK MOSES
   (Isaac Hayes)
2. SMACKWATER JACK
   (Quincy Jones)
3. INNER CITY BLUES
   (Grover Washington Jr.)
4. PUSH PUSH
   (Herbie Mann)
5. QUIET FIRE
   (Roberta Flack)
6. A DIFFERENT DRUMMER
   (Buddy Rich)
7. SHAFT
   (Isaac Hayes)
8. LIVE-EVIL
   (Miles Davis)
9. VISIONS
   (Grant Green)
10. MY WAY
    (Gene Ammons)

COUNTRY SINGLES

1. GOOD-HEARTED WOMAN
   (Waylon Jennings)
2. MY HANG UP IS YOU
   (Freddie Hart)
3. ONLY LOVE CAN BREAK A HEART
   (Sonny James)
4. A THING CALLED LOVE
   (Johnny Cash)
5. CRY
   (Lynn Anderson)
6. ANN (DON'T GO RUNNIN')
   (Tommy Overstreet)
7. TODAY I STARTED LOVING YOU AGAIN
   (Charlie McCoy)
8. THE BEST PART OF LIVING
   (Marty Robbins)
9. WHEN YOU SAY LOVE
   (Bob Luman)
10. TO GET TO YOU
    (Jerry Wallace)

COUNTRY ALBUMS

1. LEAD ME ON
   (Conway Twitty and Loretta Lynn)
2. CHARLEY PRIDE SINGS HEART SONGS
   (Charley Pride)
3. SHE'S ALL I GOT
   (Johnny Paycheck)
4. EASY LOVIN'
   (Freddie Hart)
5. I'M A TRUCK
   (Red Simpson)
6. BURNING THE MIDNIGHT OIL
   (Porter Wagoner and Dolly Parton)
7. NEVER ENDING SONG OF LOVE
   (Dickey Lee)
8. (I'VE GOT A) HAPPY HEART
   (Susan Raye)

9. BILL AND JAN (OR JAN AND BILL)
   (Bill Anderson and Jan Howard)
10. HOW CAN I UNLOVE YOU
    (Lynn Anderson)

MARCH 25, 1972

POP SINGLES

1. A HORSE WITH NO NAME
   (America)
2. THE LION SLEEPS TONIGHT
   (Robert John)
3. HEART OF GOLD
   (Neil Young)
4. MOTHER AND CHILD REUNION
   (Paul Simon)
5. PUPPY LOVE
   (Donny Osmond)
6. WITHOUT YOU
   (Harry Nilsson)
7. EVERYTHING I OWN
   (Bread)
8. DOWN BY THE LAZY RIVER
   (The Osmonds)
9. PRECIOUS AND FEW
   (Climax)
10. JUNGLE FEVER
    (Chakachas)

POP ALBUMS

1. HARVEST
   (Neil Young)
2. AMERICA
   (America)
3. AMERICAN PIE
   (Don McLean)
4. FRAGILE
   (Yes)
5. BABY I'M A WANT YOU
   (Bread)
6. NILSSON SCHMILSSON
   (Harry Nilsson)
7. PAUL SIMON
   (Paul Simon)
8. CAROLE KING MUSIC
   (Carole King)
9. CONCERT FOR BANGLADESH
   (George Harrison and Friends)
10. HOT ROCKS 1964–1971)
    (The Rolling Stones)

BLACK SINGLES

1. I GOTCHA
   (Joe Tex)
2. TALKING LOUD AND SAYING NOTHING
   (James Brown)
3. AIN'T UNDERSTANDING MELLOW
   (Butler and Eager)
4. THAT'S THE WAY I FEEL ABOUT CHA
   (Bobby Womack)
5. KING HEROIN
   (James Brown)
6. THE DAY I FOUND MYSELF
   (Honey Cone)
7. BETCHA BY GOLLY, WOW
   (The Stylistics)
8. IN THE RAIN
   (The Dramatics)
9. DO YOUR THING
   (Isaac Hayes)
10. RUNNIN' AWAY
    (Sly and the Family Stone)

BLACK ALBUMS

1. WOMEN'S LOVE RIGHTS
   (Laura Lee)

2. YOUNG, GIFTED AND BLACK
   (Aretha Franklin)
3. WHATCHA SEE IS WHATCHA GET
   (The Dramatics)
4. SOLID ROCK
   (Temptations)
5. GOT TO BE THERE
   (Michael Jackson)
6. LET'S STAY TOGETHER
   (Al Green)
7. FACE TO FACE WITH THE TRUTH
   (Undisputed Truth)
8. GONNA TAKE A MIRACLE
   (Laura Nyro)
9. PAIN
   (Ohio Players)
10. YOU WANT IT, YOU GOT IT
    (Detroit Emeralds)

JAZZ ALBUMS

1. BLACK MOSES
   (Isaac Hayes)
2. SMACKWATER JACK
   (Quincy Jones)
3. INNER CITY BLUES
   (Grover Washington Jr.)
4. QUIET FIRE
   (Roberta Flack)
5. PUSH PUSH
   (Herbie Mann)
6. A DIFFERENT DRUMMER
   (Buddy Rich)
7. LIVE-EVIL
   (Miles Davis)
8. SHAFT
   (Isaac Hayes)
9. MY WAY
   (Gene Ammons)
10. FIRST LIGHT
    (Freddie Hubbard)

COUNTRY SINGLES

1. MY HANG UP IS YOU
   (Freddie Hart)
2. A THING CALLED LOVE
   (Johnny Cash)
3. CRY
   (Lynn Anderson)
4. GOOD-HEARTED WOMAN
   (Waylon Jennings)
5. ONLY LOVE CAN BREAK A HEART
   (Sonny James)
6. WHEN YOU SAY LOVE
   (Bob Luman)
7. TODAY I STARTED LOVING YOU AGAIN
   (Charlie McCoy)
8. I'LL STILL BE WAITING FOR YOU
   (Buck Owens)
9. ALL HIS CHILDREN
   (Charley Pride)
10. TO GET TO YOU
    (Jerry Wallace)

COUNTRY ALBUMS

1. LEAD ME ON
   (Conway Twitty and Loretta Lynn)
2. CHARLEY PRIDE SINGS HEART SONGS
   (Charley Pride)
3. I'M A TRUCK
   (Red Simpson)
4. SHE'S ALL I GOT
   (Johnny Paycheck)
5. EASY LOVIN'
   (Freddie Hart)
6. (I'VE GOT A) HAPPY HEART
   (Susan Raye)
7. BURNING THE MIDNIGHT OIL
   (Porter Wagoner and Dolly Parton)
8. BILL AND JAN (OR JAN AND BILL)
   (Bill Anderson and Jan Howard)

9. MY HANG UP IS YOU
   (Freddie Hart)
10. HOW CAN I UNLOVE YOU
    (Lynn Anderson)

APRIL 1, 1972

POP SINGLES

1. A HORSE WITH NO NAME
   (America)
2. PUPPY LOVE
   (Donny Osmond)
3. HEART OF GOLD
   (Neil Young)
4. MOTHER AND CHILD REUNION
   (Paul Simon)
5. THE LION SLEEPS TONIGHT
   (Robert John)
6. JUNGLE FEVER
   (Chakachas)
7. WITHOUT YOU
   (Harry Nilsson)
8. IN THE RAIN
   (The Dramatics)
9. ROCKIN' ROBIN
   (Michael Jackson)
10. EVERYTHING I OWN
    (Bread)

POP ALBUMS

1. AMERICA
   (America)
2. HARVEST
   (Neil Young)
3. BABY, I'M A WANT YOU
   (Bread)
4. NILSSON SCHMILSSON
   (Harry Nilsson)
5. FRAGILE
   (Yes)
6. PAUL SIMON
   (Paul Simon)
7. AMERICAN PIE
   (Don McLean)
8. CAROLE KING MUSIC
   (Carole King)
9. HOT ROCKS 1964–1971
   (The Rolling Stones)
10. LET'S STAY TOGETHER
    (Al Green)

BLACK SINGLES

1. I GOTCHA
   (Joe Tex)
2. TALKING LOUD AND SAYING NOTHING
   (James Brown)
3. KING HEROIN
   (James Brown)
4. BETCHA BY GOLLY, WOW
   (The Stylistics)
5. IN THE RAIN
   (The Dramatics)
6. AIN'T UNDERSTANDING MELLOW
   (Butler and Eager)
7. THE DAY I FOUND MYSELF
   (Honey Cone)
8. THAT'S THE WAY I FEEL ABOUT CHA
   (Bobby Womack)
9. DAY DREAMING
   (Aretha Franklin)
10. FOR YOUR PRECIOUS LOVE
    (Linda Jones)

BLACK ALBUMS

1. YOUNG, GIFTED AND BLACK
   (Aretha Franklin)

2. WOMEN'S LOVE RIGHTS
   (Laura Lee)
3. GOT TO BE THERE
   (Michael Jackson)
4. SOLID ROCK
   (Temptations)
5. WHATCHA SEE IS WHATCHA GET
   (The Dramatics)
6. LET'S STAY TOGETHER
   (Al Green)
7. YOU WANT IT, YOU GOT IT
   (Detroit Emeralds)
8. FACE TO FACE WITH THE TRUTH
   (Undisputed Truth)
9. PAIN
   (Ohio Players)
10. BEALTITUDE/RESPECT YOURSELF
    (The Staple Singers)

JAZZ ALBUMS

1. BLACK MOSES
   (Issac Hayes)
2. SMACKWATER JACK
   (Quincy Jones)
3. INNER CITY BLUES
   (Grover Washington Jr.)
4. QUIET FIRE
   (Roberta Flack)
5. PUSH PUSH
   (Herbie Mann)
6. LIVE-EVIL
   (Miles Davis)
7. A DIFFERENT DRUMMER
   (Buddy Rich)
8. MY WAY
   (Gene Ammons)
9. SHAFT
   (Isaac Hayes)
10. FIRST LIGHT
    (Freddie Hubbard)

COUNTRY SINGLES

1. A THING CALLED LOVE
   (Johnny Cash)
2. CRY
   (Lynn Anderson)
3. MY HANG UP IS YOU
   (Freddie Hart)
4. WHEN YOU SAY LOVE
   (Bob Luman)
5. ALL HIS CHILDREN
   (Charley Pride)
6. GOOD-HEARTED WOMAN
   (Waylon Jennings)
7. I'LL STILL BE WAITING FOR YOU
   (Buck Owens)
8. WE CAN MAKE IT
   (George Jones)
9. TO GET TO YOU
   (Jerry Wallace)
10. TODAY I STARTED LOVING YOU AGAIN
    (Charlie McCoy)

COUNTRY ALBUMS

1. LEAD ME ON
   (Conway Twitty and Loretta Lynn)
2. I'M A TRUCK
   (Red Simpson)
3. CHARLEY PRIDE SINGS HEART SONGS
   (Charley Pride)
4. MY HANG UP IS YOU
   (Freddie Hart)
5. EASY LOVIN'
   (Freddie Hart)
6. (I'VE GOT A) HAPPY HEART
   (Susan Raye)
7. SHE'S ALL I GOT
   (Johnny Paycheck)
8. BILL AND JAN (OR JAN AND BILL)
   (Bill Anderson and Jan Howard)

9. BURNING THE MIDNIGHT OIL
   (Porter Wagoner and Dolly Parton)
10. GOOD-HEARTED WOMAN
    (Waylon Jennings)

APRIL 8, 1972

POP SINGLES

1. A HORSE WITH NO NAME
   (America)
2. PUPPY LOVE
   (Donny Osmond)
3. HEART OF GOLD
   (Neil Young)
4. FIRST TIME EVER I SAW YOUR FACE
   (Roberta Flack)
5. JUNGLE FEVER
   (Chakachas)
6. ROCKIN' ROBIN
   (Michael Jackson)
7. IN THE RAIN
   (The Dramatics)
8. MOTHER AND CHILD REUNION
   (Paul Simon)
9. I GOTCHA
   (Joe Tex)
10. WITHOUT YOU
    (Harry Nilsson)

POP ALBUMS

1. AMERICA
   (America)
2. NILSSON SCHMILSSON
   (Harry Nilsson)
3. HARVEST
   (Neil Young)
4. BABY, I'M A WANT YOU
   (Bread)
5. FRAGILE
   (Yes)
6. PAUL SIMON
   (Paul Simon)
7. CAROLE KING MUSIC
   (Carole King)
8. EAT A PEACH
   (Allman Brothers Band)
9. LET'S STAY TOGETHER
   (Al Green)
10. HENDRIX IN THE WEST
    (Jimi Hendrix)

BLACK SINGLES

1. IN THE RAIN
   (The Dramatics)
2. KING HEROIN
   (James Brown)
3. BETCHA BY GOLLY, WOW
   (The Stylistics)
4. DAY DREAMING
   (Aretha Franklin)
5. I GOTCHA
   (Joe Tex)
6. FOR YOUR PRECIOUS LOVE
   (Linda Jones)
7. AIN'T UNDERSTANDING MELLOW
   (Butler and Eager)
8. ROCKIN' ROBIN
   (Michael Jackson)
9. TALKING LOUD AND SAYING NOTHING
   (James Brown)
10. THE DAY I FOUND MYSELF
    (Honey Cone)

BLACK ALBUMS

1. YOUNG, GIFTED AND BLACK
   (Aretha Franklin)

2. GOT TO BE THERE
   (Michael Jackson)
3. WOMEN'S LOVE RIGHTS
   (Laura Lee)
4. SOLID ROCK
   (Temptations)
5. WHATCHA SEE IS WHATCHA GET
   (The Dramatics)
6. YOU WANT IT, YOU GOT IT
   (Detroit Emeralds)
7. BEALTITUDE/RESPECT YOURSELF
   (The Staple Singers)
8. FACE TO FACE WITH THE TRUTH
   (Undisputed Truth)
9. TODAY 1005
   (Black Ivory)
10. L.A. MIDNIGHT
    (B.B. King)

JAZZ ALBUMS

1. INNER CITY BLUES
   (Grover Washington Jr.)
2. SMACKWATER JACK
   (Quincy Jones)
3. PUSH PUSH
   (Herbie Mann)
4. BLACK MOSES
   (Isaac Hayes)
5. QUIET FIRE
   (Roberta Flack)
6. LIVE-EVIL
   (Miles Davis)
7. MY WAY
   (Gene Ammons)
8. A DIFFERENT DRUMMER
   (Buddy Rich)
9. FIRST LIGHT
   (Freddie Hubbard)
10. INVITATION TO OPENNESS
    (Les McCann)

COUNTRY SINGLES

1. CRY
   (Lynn Anderson)
2. ALL HIS CHILDREN
   (Charley Pride)
3. A THING CALLED LOVE
   (Johnny Cash)
4. WHEN YOU SAY LOVE
   (Bob Luman)
5. MY HANG UP IS YOU
   (Freddie Hart)
6. WE CAN MAKE IT
   (George Jones)
7. I'LL STILL BE WAITING FOR YOU
   (Buck Owens)
8. WHAT AIN'T TO BE, JUST MIGHT HAPPEN
   (Porter Wagoner)
9. CHANTILLY LACE/THINK ABOUT IT
   DARLIN'
   (Jerry Lee Lewis)
10. GOOD-HEARTED WOMAN
    (Waylon Jennings)

COUNTRY ALBUMS

1. MY HANG UP IS YOU
   (Freddie Hart)
2. I'M A TRUCK
   (Red Simpson)
3. LEAD ME ON
   (Conway Twitty and Loretta Lynn)
4. CHARLEY PRIDE SINGS HEART SONGS
   (Charley Pride)
5. EASY LOVIN'
   (Freddie Hart)
6. THE BIGGEST HITS OF SONNY JAMES
   (Sonny James)
7. SHE'S ALL I GOT
   (Johnny Paycheck)
8. (I'VE GOT A) HAPPY HEART
   (Susan Raye)

9. GOOD-HEARTED WOMAN
    (Waylon Jennings)
10. BEST OF CHARLEY PRIDE, VOL. 2
    (Charley Pride)

APRIL 15, 1972

POP SINGLES

1. THE FIRST TIME EVER I SAW YOUR FACE
    (Roberta Flack)
2. A HORSE WITH NO NAME
    (America)
3. ROCKIN' ROBIN
    (Michael Jackson)
4. HEART OF GOLD
    (Neil Young)
5. PUPPY LOVE
    (Donny Osmond)
6. I GOTCHA
    (Joe Tex)
7. IN THE RAIN
    (The Dramatics)
8. JUNGLE FEVER
    (Chakachas)
9. BETCHA BY GOLLY, WOW
    (The Stylistics)
10. A COWBOY'S WORK IS NEVER DONE
    (Sonny and Cher)

POP ALBUMS

1. AMERICA
    (America)
2. NILSSON SCHMILSSON
    (Harry Nilsson)
3. HARVEST
    (Neil Young)
4. PAUL SIMON
    (Paul Simon)
5. FRAGILE
    (Yes)
6. EAT A PEACH
    (Allman Brothers Band)
7. FIRST TAKE
    (Roberta Flack)
8. BABY, I'M A WANT YOU
    (Bread)
9. LET'S STAY TOGETHER
    (Al Green)
10. YOUNG, GIFTED AND BLACK
    (Aretha Franklin)

BLACK SINGLES

1. IN THE RAIN
    (The Dramatics)
2. BETCHA BY GOLLY, WOW
    (The Stylistics)
3. DAY DREAMING
    (Aretha Franklin)
4. KING HEROIN
    (James Brown)
5. FOR YOUR PRECIOUS LOVE
    (Linda Jones)
6. I GOTCHA
    (Joe Tex)
7. ROCKIN' ROBIN
    (Michael Jackson)
8. THE FIRST TIME EVER I SAW YOUR FACE
    (Roberta Flack)
9. AIN'T UNDERSTANDING MELLOW
    (Butler and Eager)
10. POOL OF BAD LUCK
    (Joe Simon)

BLACK ALBUMS

1. YOUNG, GIFTED AND BLACK
    (Aretha Franklin)

2. GOT TO BE THERE
    (Michael Jackson)
3. SOLID ROCK
    (Temptations)
4. BEALTITUDE/RESPECT YOURSELF
    (The Staple Singers)
5. WOMEN'S LOVE RIGHTS
    (Laura Lee)
6. L.A. MIDNIGHT
    (B.B. King)
7. TODAY 1005
    (Black Ivory)
8. YOU WANT IT, YOU GOT IT
    (Detroit Emeralds)
9. FROM A WHISPER TO A SCREAM
    (Esther Phillips)
10. LET'S STAY TOGETHER
    (Al Green)

JAZZ ALBUMS

1. INNER CITY BLUES
    (Grover Washington Jr.)
2. SMACKWATER JACK
    (Quincy Jones)
3. PUSH PUSH
    (Herbie Mann)
4. BLACK MOSES
    (Isaac Hayes)
5. QUIET FIRE
    (Roberta Flack)
6. MY WAY
    (Gene Ammons)
7. LIVE-EVIL
    (Miles Davis)
8. INVITATION TO OPENNESS
    (Les McCann)
9. THE INNER MOUNTING FLAME
    (Mahavishnu Orchestra)
10. A DIFFERENT DRUMMER
    (Buddy Rich)

COUNTRY SINGLES

1. ALL HIS CHILDREN
    (Charley Pride)
2. CHANTILLY LACE/THINK ABOUT IT
    DARLIN'
    (Jerry Lee Lewis)
3. WHEN YOU SAY LOVE
    (Bob Luman)
4. WE CAN MAKE IT
    (George Jones)
5. CRY
    (Lynn Anderson)
6. MY HANG UP IS YOU
    (Freddie Hart)
7. WHAT AIN'T TO BE, JUST MIGHT HAPPEN
    (Porter Wagoner)
8. A THING CALLED LOVE
    (Johnny Cash)
9. DO YOU REMEMBER THESE
    (The Statler Brothers)
10. I'LL STILL BE WAITING FOR YOU
    (Buck Owens)

COUNTRY ALBUMS

1. MY HANG UP IS YOU
    (Freddie Hart)
2. LEAD ME ON
    (Conway Twitty and Loretta Lynn)
3. I'M A TRUCK
    (Red Simpson)
4. CHARLEY PRIDE SINGS HEART SONGS
    (Charley Pride)
5. BEST OF CHARLEY PRIDE, VOL. 2
    (Charley Pride)
6. THE BIGGEST HITS OF SONNY JAMES
    (Sonny James)
7. EASY LOVIN'
    (Freddie Hart)
8. GOOD-HEARTED WOMAN
    (Waylon Jennings)

9. SHE'S ALL I GOT
    (Johnny Paycheck)
10. ONE'S ON THE WAY
    (Loretta Lynn)

APRIL 22, 1972

POP SINGLES

1. THE FIRST TIME EVER I SAW YOUR FACE
    (Roberta Flack)
2. ROCKIN' ROBIN
    (Michael Jackson)
3. A HORSE WITH NO NAME
    (America)
4. I GOTCHA
    (Joe Tex)
5. HEART OF GOLD
    (Neil Young)
6. IN THE RAIN
    (The Dramatics)
7. BETCHA BY GOLLY, WOW
    (The Stylistics)
8. DAY DREAMING
    (Aretha Franklin)
9. A COWBOY'S WORK IS NEVER DONE
    (Sonny and Cher)
10. THE FAMILY OF MAN
    (Three Dog Night)

POP ALBUMS

1. AMERICA
    (America)
2. NILSSON SCHMILSSON
    (Harry Nilsson)
3. HARVEST
    (Neil Young)
4. EAT A PEACH
    (Allman Brothers Band)
5. FRAGILE
    (Yes)
6. FIRST TAKE
    (Roberta Flack)
7. PAUL SIMON
    (Paul Simon)
8. BABY, I'M A WANT YOU
    (Bread)
9. YOUNG, GIFTED AND BLACK
    (Aretha Franklin)
10. THE PARTRIDGE FAMILY SHOPPING BAG
    (The Partridge Family)

BLACK SINGLES

1. IN THE RAIN
    (The Dramatics)
2. BETCHA BY GOLLY, WOW
    (The Stylistics)
3. DAY DREAMING
    (Aretha Franklin)
4. THE FIRST TIME EVER I SAW YOUR FACE
    (Roberta Flack)
5. KING HEROIN
    (James Brown)
6. FOR YOUR PRECIOUS LOVE
    (Linda Jones)
7. POOL OF BAD LUCK
    (Joe Simon)
8. I GOTCHA
    (Joe Tex)
9. ROCKIN' ROBIN
    (Michael Jackson)
10. LOOK WHAT YOU DONE FOR ME
    (Al Green)

BLACK ALBUMS

1. YOUNG, GIFTED AND BLACK
    (Aretha Franklin)

2. GOT TO BE THERE
   (Michael Jackson)
3. BEALTITUDE/RESPECT YOURSELF
   (The Staple Singers)
4. SOLID ROCK
   (Temptations)
5. L.A. MIDNIGHT
   (B.B. King)
6. TODAY 1005
   (Black Ivory)
7. LET'S STAY TOGETHER
   (Al Green)
8. WOMEN'S LOVE RIGHTS
   (Laura Lee)
9. FROM A WHISPER TO A SCREAM
   (Esther Phillips)
10. DONNY HATHAWAY LIVE
    (Donny Hathaway)

JAZZ ALBUMS

1. INNER CITY BLUES
   (Grover Washington Jr.)
2. PUSH PUSH
   (Herbie Mann)
3. SMACKWATER JACK
   (Quincy Jones)
4. QUIET FIRE
   (Roberta Flack)
5. BLACK MOSES
   (Isaac Hayes)
6. LIVE-EVIL
   (Miles Davis)
7. MY WAY
   (Gene Ammons)
8. THE INNER MOUNTING FLAME
   (Mahavishnu Orchestra)
9. INVITATION TO OPENNESS
   (Les McCann)
10. CRUSADERS 1
    (Crusaders)

COUNTRY SINGLES

1. CHANTILLY LACE/THINK ABOUT IT DARLIN'
   (Jerry Lee Lewis)
2. ALL HIS CHILDREN
   (Charley Pride)
3. WE CAN MAKE IT
   (George Jones)
4. DO YOU REMEMBER THESE
   (The Statler Brothers)
5. SOMEONE TO GIVE MY LOVE TO
   (Johnny Paycheck)
6. MY HANG UP IS YOU
   (Freddie Hart)
7. WHAT AIN'T TO BE, JUST MIGHT HAPPEN
   (Porter Wagoner)
8. ME AND JESUS
   (Tom T. Hall)
9. WHEN YOU SAY LOVE
   (Bob Luman)
10. JUST FOR WHAT I AM
    (Connie Smith)

COUNTRY ALBUMS

1. MY HANG UP IS YOU
   (Freddie Hart)
2. BEST OF CHARLEY PRIDE, VOL. 2
   (Charley Pride)
3. LEAD ME ON
   (Conway Twitty and Loretta Lynn)
4. CHARLEY PRIDE SINGS HEART SONGS
   (Charley Pride)
5. ONE'S ON THE WAY
   (Loretta Lynn)
6. I'M A TRUCK
   (Red Simpson)
7. GOOD-HEARTED WOMAN
   (Waylon Jennings)
8. EASY LOVIN'
   (Freddie Hart)

9. IT'S FOUR IN THE MORNING
   (Faron Young)
10. SHE'S ALL I GOT
    (Johnny Paycheck)

APRIL 29, 1972

POP SINGLES

1. THE FIRST TIME EVER I SAW YOUR FACE
   (Roberta Flack)
2. ROCKIN' ROBIN
   (Michael Jackson)
3. I GOTCHA
   (Joe Tex)
4. BETCHA BY GOLLY, WOW
   (The Stylistics)
5. IN THE RAIN
   (The Dramatics)
6. DAY DREAMING
   (Aretha Franklin)
7. A HORSE WITH NO NAME
   (America)
8. THE FAMILY OF MAN
   (Three Dog Night)
9. A COWBOY'S WORK IS NEVER DONE
   (Sonny and Cher)
10. LOOK WHAT YOU DONE FOR ME
    (Al Green)

POP ALBUMS

1. AMERICA
   (America)
2. HARVEST
   (Neil Young)
3. EAT A PEACH
   (Allman Brothers Band)
4. FIRST TAKE
   (Roberta Flack)
5. NILSSON SCHMILSSON
   (Harry Nilsson)
6. FRAGILE
   (Yes)
7. PAUL SIMON
   (Paul Simon)
8. THE PARTRIDGE FAMILY SHOPPING BAG
   (The Partridge Family)
9. BABY, I'M A WANT YOU
   (Bread)
10. LET'S STAY TOGETHER
    (Al Green)

BLACK SINGLES

1. IN THE RAIN
   (The Dramatics)
2. BETCHA BY GOLLY, WOW
   (The Stylistics)
3. THE FIRST TIME EVER I SAW YOUR FACE
   (Roberta Flack)
4. DAY DREAMING
   (Aretha Franklin)
5. POOL OF BAD LUCK
   (Joe Simon)
6. LOOK WHAT YOU DONE FOR ME
   (Al Green)
7. KING HEROIN
   (James Brown)
8. OH GIRL
   (The Chi-Lites)
9. YOU AND I
   (Black Ivory)
10. FOR YOUR PRECIOUS LOVE
    (Linda Jones)

BLACK ALBUMS

1. YOUNG, GIFTED AND BLACK
   (Aretha Franklin)

2. BEALTITUDE/RESPECT YOURSELF
   (The Staple Singers)
3. GOT TO BE THERE
   (Michael Jackson)
4. SOLID ROCK
   (Temptations)
5. LET'S STAY TOGETHER
   (Al Green)
6. TODAY 1005
   (Black Ivory)
7. L.A. MIDNIGHT
   (B.B. King)
8. FROM A WHISPER TO A SCREAM
   (Esther Phillips)
9. DONNY HATHAWAY LIVE
   (Donny Hathaway)
10. DROWNING IN A SEA OF LOVE
    (Joe Simon)

JAZZ ALBUMS

1. PUSH PUSH
   (Herbie Mann)
2. INNER CITY BLUES
   (Grover Washington Jr.)
3. QUIET FIRE
   (Roberta Flack)
4. SMACKWATER JACK
   (Quincy Jones)
5. THE INNER MOUNTING FLAME
   (Mahavishnu Orchestra)
6. MY WAY
   (Gene Ammons)
7. BLACK MOSES
   (Isaac Hayes)
8. LIVE-EVIL
   (Miles Davis)
9. CRUSADERS 1
   (Crusaders)
10. INVITATION TO OPENNESS
    (Les McCann)

COUNTRY SINGLES

1. DO YOU REMEMBER THESE
   (The Statler Brothers)
2. CHANTILLY LACE/THINK ABOUT IT DARLIN'
   (Jerry Lee Lewis)
3. SOMEONE TO GIVE MY LOVE TO
   (Johnny Paycheck)
4. ME AND JESUS
   (Tom T. Hall)
5. ALL HIS CHILDREN
   (Charley Pride)
6. JUST FOR WHAT I AM
   (Connie Smith)
7. MY HANG UP IS YOU
   (Freddie Hart)
8. NEED YOU
   (David Rogers)
9. TOUCH YOUR WOMAN
   (Dolly Parton)
10. AIN'T NOTHIN' SHAKIN'
    (Billy "Crash" Craddock)

COUNTRY ALBUMS

1. BEST OF CHARLEY PRIDE, VOL. 2
   (Charley Pride)
2. MY HANG UP IS YOU
   (Freddie Hart)
3. ONE'S ON THE WAY
   (Loretta Lynn)
4. LEAD ME ON
   (Conway Twitty and Loretta Lynn)
5. CHARLEY PRIDE SINGS HEART SONGS
   (Charley Pride)
6. BORDER LORD
   (Kris Kristofferson)
7. GOOD-HEARTED WOMAN
   (Waylon Jennings)
8. IT'S FOUR IN THE MORNING
   (Faron Young)

9. LET ME TELL YOU ABOUT A SONG
   (Merle Haggard)
10. I CAN'T SEE ME WITHOUT YOU
    (Conway Twitty)

MAY 6, 1972

POP SINGLES

1. THE FIRST TIME EVER I SAW YOUR FACE
   (Roberta Flack)
2. I GOTCHA
   (Joe Tex)
3. BETCHA BY GOLLY, WOW
   (The Stylistics)
4. ROCKIN' ROBIN
   (Michael Jackson)
5. IN THE RAIN
   (The Dramatics)
6. DAY DREAMING
   (Aretha Franklin)
7. LOOK WHAT YOU DONE FOR ME
   (Al Green)
8. THE FAMILY OF MAN
   (Three Dog Night)
9. OH GIRL
   (The Chi-Lites)
10. DOCTOR MY EYES
    (Jackson Browne)

POP ALBUMS

1. FIRST TAKE
   (Roberta Flack)
2. AMERICA
   (America)
3. HARVEST
   (Neil Young)
4. EAT A PEACH
   (Allman Brothers Band)
5. FRAGILE
   (Yes)
6. NILSSON SCHMILSSON
   (Harry Nilsson)
7. PAUL SIMON
   (Paul Simon)
8. THE PARTRIDGE FAMILY SHOPPING BAG
   (The Partridge Family)
9. BABY, I'M A WANT YOU
   (Bread)
10. SMOKIN'
    (Humble Pie)

BLACK SINGLES

1. BETCHA BY GOLLY, WOW
   (The Stylistics)
2. IN THE RAIN
   (The Dramatics)
3. THE FIRST TIME EVER I SAW YOUR FACE
   (Roberta Flack)
4. POOL OF BAD LUCK
   (Joe Simon)
5. LOOK WHAT YOU DONE FOR ME
   (Al Green)
6. OH GIRL
   (The Chi-Lites)
7. DAY DREAMING
   (Aretha Franklin)
8. YOU AND I
   (Black Ivory)
9. I'LL TAKE YOU THERE
   (The Staple Singers)
10. HEARSAY
    (The Soul Children)

BLACK ALBUMS

1. BEALTITUDE/RESPECT YOURSELF
   (The Staple Singers)

2. YOUNG, GIFTED AND BLACK
   (Aretha Franklin)
3. LET'S STAY TOGETHER
   (Al Green)
4. GOT TO BE THERE
   (Michael Jackson)
5. TODAY 1005
   (Black Ivory)
6. SOLID ROCK
   (Temptations)
7. DROWNING IN A SEA OF LOVE
   (Joe Simon)
8. FROM A WHISPER TO A SCREAM
   (Esther Phillips)
9. L.A. MIDNIGHT
   (B.B. King)
10. IN THE BEGINNING
    (Isaac Hayes)

JAZZ ALBUMS

1. QUIET FIRE
   (Roberta Flack)
2. PUSH PUSH
   (Herbie Mann)
3. THE INNER MOUNTING FLAME
   (Mahavishnu Orchestra)
4. INNER CITY BLUES
   (Grover Washington Jr.)
5. SMACKWATER JACK
   (Quincy Jones)
6. LIVE-EVIL
   (Miles Davis)
7. MY WAY
   (Gene Ammons)
8. CRUSADERS 1
   (Crusaders)
9. DONNY HATHAWAY LIVE
   (Donny Hathaway)
10. BLACK MOSES
    (Isaac Hayes)

COUNTRY SINGLES

1. SOMEONE TO GIVE MY LOVE TO
   (Johnny Paycheck)
2. DO YOU REMEMBER THESE
   (The Statler Brothers)
3. ME AND JESUS
   (Tom T. Hall)
4. CHANTILLY LACE/THINK ABOUT IT DARLIN'
   (Jerry Lee Lewis)
5. JUST FOR WHAT I AM
   (Connie Smith)
6. TOUCH YOUR WOMAN
   (Dolly Parton)
7. NEED YOU
   (David Rogers)
8. AIN'T NOTHIN' SHAKIN'
   (Billy "Crash" Craddock)
9. ALL THE LONELY WOMEN IN THE WORLD
   (Bill Anderson)
10. OUR LAST DATE
    (Conway Twitty)

COUNTRY ALBUMS

1. BEST OF CHARLEY PRIDE, VOL. 2
   (Charley Pride)
2. ONE'S ON THE WAY
   (Loretta Lynn)
3. MY HANG UP IS YOU
   (Freddie Hart)
4. LET ME TELL YOU ABOUT A SONG
   (Merle Haggard)
5. BORDER LORD
   (Kris Kristofferson)
6. CHARLEY PRIDE SINGS HEART SONGS
   (Charley Pride)
7. CRY
   (Lynn Anderson)
8. IT'S FOUR IN THE MORNING
   (Faron Young)

9. I CAN'T SEE ME WITHOUT YOU
   (Conway Twitty)
10. LEAD ME ON
    (Conway Twitty and Loretta Lynn)

MAY 13, 1972

POP SINGLES

1. THE FIRST TIME EVER I SAW YOUR FACE
   (Roberta Flack)
2. GOTCHA
   (Joe Tex)
3. OH GIRL
   (The Chi-Lites)
4. I'LL TAKE YOU THERE
   (The Staple Singers)
5. LOOK WHAT YOU DONE FOR ME
   (Al Green)
6. DAY DREAMING
   (Aretha Franklin)
7. BETCHA BY GOLLY, WOW
   (The Stylistics)
8. ROCKIN' ROBIN
   (Michael Jackson)
9. BACK OFF BOOGALOO
   (Ringo Starr)
10. DOCTOR MY EYES
    (Jackson Browne)

POP ALBUMS

1. FIRST TAKE
   (Roberta Flack)
2. AMERICA
   (America)
3. HARVEST
   (Neil Young)
4. EAT A PEACH
   (Allman Brothers Band)
5. FRAGILE
   (Yes)
6. PAUL SIMON
   (Paul Simon)
7. NILSSON SCHMILSSON
   (Harry Nilsson)
8. SMOKIN'
   (Humble Pie)
9. GRAHAM NASH/DAVID CROSBY
   (Graham Nash and David Crosby)
10. MALO
    (Malo)

BLACK SINGLES

1. BETCHA BY GOLLY, WOW
   (The Stylistics)
2. IN THE RAIN
   (The Dramatics)
3. OH GIRL
   (The Chi-Lites)
4. THE FIRST TIME EVER I SAW YOUR FACE
   (Roberta Flack)
5. I'LL TAKE YOU THERE
   (The Staple Singers)
6. LOOK WHAT YOU DONE FOR ME
   (Al Green)
7. HEARSAY
   (The Soul Children)
8. POOL OF BAD LUCK
   (Joe Simon)
9. YOU AND I
   (Black Ivory)
10. DAY DREAMING)
    (Aretha Franklin)

BLACK ALBUMS

1. BEALTITUDE/RESPECT YOURSELF
   (The Staple Singers)

2. LET'S STAY TOGETHER
   (Al Green)
3. YOUNG, GIFTED AND BLACK
   (Aretha Franklin)
4. TODAY 1005
   (Black Ivory)
5. DROWNING IN A SEA OF LOVE
   (Joe Simon)
6. SOLID ROCK
   (Temptations)
7. IN THE BEGINNING
   (Isaac Hayes)
8. GOT TO BE THERE
   (Michael Jackson)
9. FROM A WHISPER TO A SCREAM
   (Esther Phillips)
10. L.A. MIDNIGHT
    (B.B. King)

JAZZ ALBUMS

1. QUIET FIRE
   (Roberta Flack)
2. THE INNER MOUNTING FLAME
   (Mahavishnu Orchestra)
3. PUSH PUSH
   (Herbie Mann)
4. INNER CITY BLUES
   (Grover Washington Jr.)
5. SMACKWATER JACK
   (Quincy Jones)
6. LIVE-EVIL
   (Miles Davis)
7. CRUSADERS 1
   (Crusaders)
8. BLACK MOSES
   (Isaac Hayes)
9. WORLD GALAXY
   (Alice Coltrane)
10. DONNY HATHAWAY LIVE
    (Donny Hathaway)

COUNTRY SINGLES

1. ME AND JESUS
   (Tom T. Hall)
2. SOMEONE TO GIVE MY LOVE TO
   (Johnny Paycheck)
3. JUST FOR WHAT I AM
   (Connie Smith)
4. OUR LAST DATE
   (Conway Twitty)
5. TOUCH YOUR WOMAN
   (Dolly Parton)
6. ALL THE LONELY WOMEN IN THE WORLD
   (Bill Anderson)
7. AIN'T NOTHIN' SHAKIN'
   (Billy "Crash" Craddock)
8. CHANTILLY LACE/THINK ABOUT IT DARLIN'
   (Jerry Lee Lewis)
9. DO YOU REMEMBER THESE
   (The Statler Brothers)
10. GRANDMA HARP
    (Merle Haggard)

COUNTRY ALBUMS

1. BEST OF CHARLEY PRIDE, VOL. 2
   (Charley Pride)
2. ONE'S ON THE WAY
   (Loretta Lynn)
3. LET ME TELL YOU ABOUT A SONG
   (Merle Haggard)
4. MY HANG UP IS YOU
   (Freddie Hart)
5. CRY
   (Lynn Anderson)
6. BORDER LORD
   (Kris Kristofferson)
7. THE REAL McCOY
   (Charlie McCoy)
8. I CAN'T SEE ME WITHOUT YOU
   (Conway Twitty)

9. BEDTIME STORY
   (Tammy Wynette)
10. CHARLEY PRIDE SINGS HEART SONGS
    (Charley Pride)

MAY 20, 1972

POP SINGLES

1. OH GIRL
   (The Chi-Lites)
2. I'LL TAKE YOU THERE
   (The Staple Singers)
3. THE FIRST TIME EVER I SAW YOUR FACE
   (Roberta Flack)
4. LOOK WHAT YOU DONE FOR ME
   (Al Green)
5. I GOTCHA
   (Joe Tex)
6. TUMBLING DICE
   (The Rolling Stones)
7. HOT ROD LINCOLN
   (Commander Cody)
8. BACK OFF BOOGALOO
   (Ringo Starr)
9. ME AND JULIO DOWN BY THE SCHOOLYARD
   (Paul Simon)
10. LITTLE BITTY PRETTY ONE
    (The Jackson 5)

POP ALBUMS

1. FIRST TAKE
   (Roberta Flack)
2. AMERICA
   (America)
3. GRAHAM NASH/DAVID CROSBY
   (Graham Nash and David Crosby)
4. HARVEST
   (Neil Young)
5. FRAGILE
   (Yes)
6. PAUL SIMON
   (Paul Simon)
7. SMOKIN'
   (Humble Pie)
8. EAT A PEACH
   (Allman Brothers Band)
9. NILSSON SCHMILSSON
   (Harry Nilsson)
10. MALO
    (Malo)

BLACK SINGLES

1. OH GIRL
   (The Chi-Lites)
2. I'LL TAKE YOU THERE
   (The Staple Singers)
3. BETCHA BY GOLLY, WOW
   (The Stylistics)
4. WALKIN' IN THE RAIN
   (Love Unlimited)
5. HEARSAY
   (The Soul Children)
6. THE FIRST TIME EVER I SAW YOUR FACE
   (Roberta Flack)
7. IN THE RAIN
   (The Dramatics)
8. OUTA SPACE
   (Billy Preston)
9. LOOK WHAT YOU DONE FOR ME
   (Al Green)
10. LITTLE BITTY PRETTY ONE
    (The Jackson 5)

BLACK ALBUMS

1. BEALTITUDE/RESPECT YOURSELF
   (The Staple Singers)

2. LET'S STAY TOGETHER
   (Al Green)
3. YOUNG, GIFTED AND BLACK
   (Aretha Franklin)
4. A LONELY MAN
   (The Chi-Lites)
5. TODAY 1005
   (Black Ivory)
6. IN THE BEGINNING
   (Isaac Hayes)
7. DROWNING IN A SEA OF LOVE
   (Joe Simon)
8. L.A. MIDNIGHT
   (B.B. Knight)
9. GOT TO BE THERE
   (Michael Jackson)
10. THIN LINE BETWEEN LOVE AND HATE
    (The Persuaders)

JAZZ ALBUMS

1. THE INNER MOUNTING FLAME
   (Mahavishnu Orchestra)
2. QUIET FIRE
   (Roberta Flack)
3. PUSH PUSH
   (Herbie Mann)
4. CRUSADERS 1
   (Crusaders)
5. INNER CITY BLUES
   (Grover Washington Jr.)
6. SMACKWATER JACK
   (Quincy Jones)
7. BLACK MOSES
   (Isaac Hayes)
8. LIVE-EVIL
   (Miles Davis)
9. WILD HORSES ROCK STEADY
   (Johnny Hammond)
10. DONNY HATHAWAY LIVE
    (Donny Hathaway)

COUNTRY SINGLES

1. OUR LAST DATE
   (Conway Twitty)
2. ME AND JESUS
   (Tom T. Hall)
3. ALL THE LONELY WOMEN IN THE WORLD
   (Bill Anderson)
4. THE HAPPIEST GIRL IN THE WHOLE U.S.A.
   (Donna Fargo)
5. GRANDMA HARP
   (Merle Haggard)
6. AIN'T NOTHIN' SHAKIN'
   (Billy "Crash" Craddock)
7. JUST FOR WHAT I AM
   (Connie Smith)
8. SOMEONE TO GIVE MY LOVE TO
   (Johnny Paycheck)
9. DO YOU REMEMBER THESE
   (The Statler Brothers)
10. CHANTILLY LACE/THINK ABOUT IT DARLIN'
    (Jerry Lee Lewis)

COUNTRY ALBUMS

1. BEST OF CHARLEY PRIDE, VOL. 2
   (Charley Pride)
2. ONE'S ON THE WAY
   (Loretta Lynn)
3. LET ME TELL YOU ABOUT A SONG
   (Merle Haggard)
4. CRY
   (Lynn Anderson)
5. THE REAL McCOY
   (Charlie McCoy)
6. BEDTIME STORY
   (Tammy Wynette)
7. THE KILLER ROCKS ON
   (Jerry Lee Lewis)
8. I CAN'T SEE ME WITHOUT YOU
   (Conway Twitty)

9. WE ALL GOT TOGETHER AND . . .
   (Tom T. Hall)
10. MY HANG UP IS YOU
    (Freddie Hart)

MAY 27, 1972

POP SINGLES

1. OH GIRL
   (The Chi-Lites)
2. I'LL TAKE YOU THERE
   (The Staple Singers)
3. LOOK WHAT YOU DONE FOR ME
   (Al Green)
4. TUMBLING DICE
   (The Rolling Stones)
5. THE FIRST TIME EVER I SAW YOUR FACE
   (Roberta Flack)
6. HOT ROD LINCOLN
   (Commander Cody)
7. LITTLE BITTY PRETTY ONE
   (The Jackson 5)
8. BACK OFF BOOGALOO
   (Ringo Starr)
9. ME AND JULIO DOWN BY THE
   SCHOOLYARD
   (Paul Simon)
10. I GOTCHA
    (Joe Tex)

POP ALBUMS

1. FIRST TAKE
   (Roberta Flack)
2. GRAHAM NASH/DAVID CROSBY
   (Graham Nash and David Crosby)
3. AMERICA
   (America)
4. HARVEST
   (Neil Young)
5. MANASSAS
   (Stephen Stills)
6. FRAGILE
   (Yes)
7. SMOKIN'
   (Humble Pie)
8. PAUL SIMON
   (Paul Simon)
9. EAT A PEACH
   (Allman Brothers Band)
10. HISTORY OF ERIC CLAPTON
    (Eric Clapton)

BLACK SINGLES

1. OH GIRL
   (The Chi-Lites)
2. I'LL TAKE YOU THERE
   (The Staple Singers)
3. WALKIN' IN THE RAIN
   (Love Unlimited)
4. BETCHA BY GOLLY, WOW
   (The Stylistics)
5. HEARSAY
   (The Soul Children)
6. OUTA SPACE
   (Billy Preston)
7. LITTLE BITTY PRETTY ONE
   (The Jackson 5)
8. THE FIRST TIME EVER I SAW YOUR FACE
   (Roberta Flack)
9. THERE IT IS
   (James Brown)
10. WOMAN'S GOTTA HAVE IT
    (Bobby Womack)

BLACK ALBUMS

1. BEALTITUDE/RESPECT YOURSELF
   (The Staple Singers)

2. A LONELY MAN
   (The Chi-Lites)
3. LET'S STAY TOGETHER
   (Al Green)
4. YOUNG, GIFTED AND BLACK
   (Aretha Franklin)
5. TODAY 1005
   (Black Ivory)
6. IN THE BEGINNING
   (Isaac Hayes)
7. L.A. MIDNIGHT
   (B.B. King)
8. THIN LINE BETWEEN LOVE AND HATE
   (The Persuaders)
9. GOIN' FOR MYSELF
   (Dennis Coffey)
10. STYLISTICS
    (The Stylistics)

JAZZ ALBUMS

1. THE INNER MOUNTING FLAME
   (Mahavishnu Orchestra)
2. QUIET FIRE
   (Roberta Flack)
3. CRUSADERS 1
   (Crusaders)
4. PUSH PUSH
   (Herbie Mann)
5. INNER CITY BLUES
   (Grover Washington Jr.)
6. SMACKWATER JACK
   (Quincy Jones)
7. BLACK MOSES
   (Isaac Hayes)
8. LIVE-EVIL
   (Miles Davis)
9. WILD HORSES ROCK STEADY
   (Johnny Hammond)
10. SHAFT
    (Isaac Hayes)

COUNTRY SINGLES

1. THE HAPPIEST GIRL IN THE WHOLE U.S.A.
   (Donna Fargo)
2. OUR LAST DATE
   (Conway Twitty)
3. ALL THE LONELY WOMEN IN THE WORLD
   (Bill Anderson)
4. GRANDMA HARP
   (Merle Haggard)
5. ME AND JESUS
   (Tom T. Hall)
6. AIN'T NOTHIN' SHAKIN'
   (Billy "Crash" Craddock)
7. MANHATTAN, KANSAS
   (Glen Campbell)
8. THE LONESOMEST LONESOME/THAT'S
   WHAT LEAVING'S ABOUT
   (Ray Price)
9. ELEVEN ROSES
   (Hank Williams Jr.)
10. CHANTILLY LACE/THINK ABOUT IT
    DARLIN'
    (Jerry Lee Lewis)

COUNTRY ALBUMS

1. BEST OF CHARLEY PRIDE, VOL. 2
   (Charley Pride)
2. ONE'S ON THE WAY
   (Loretta Lynn)
3. CRY
   (Lynn Anderson)
4. THE REAL McCOY
   (Charlie McCoy)
5. BEDTIME STORY
   (Tammy Wynette)
6. THE KILLER ROCKS ON
   (Jerry Lee Lewis)
7. WE ALL GOT TOGETHER AND. . .
   (Tom T. Hall)
8. LET ME TELL YOU ABOUT A SONG
   (Merle Haggard)

9. I CAN'T SEE ME WITHOUT YOU
   (Conway Twitty)
10. A THING CALLED LOVE
    (Johnny Cash)

JUNE 3, 1972

POP SINGLES

1. I'LL TAKE YOU THERE
   (The Staple Singers)
2. OH GIRL
   (The Chi-Lites)
3. CANDY MAN
   (Sammy Davis Jr.)
4. TUMBLING DICE
   (The Rolling Stones)
5. LOOK WHAT YOU DONE FOR ME
   (Al Green)
6. HOT ROD LINCOLN
   (Commander Cody)
7. LITTLE BITTY PRETTY ONE
   (The Jackson 5)
8. MORNING HAS BROKEN
   (Cat Stevens)
9. THE FIRST TIME EVER I SAW YOUR FACE
   (Roberta Flack)
10. SYLVIA'S MOTHER
    (Dr. Hook and the Medicine Show)

POP ALBUMS

1. FIRST TAKE
   (Roberta Flack)
2. GRAHAM NASH/DAVID CROSBY
   (Graham Nash and David Crosby)
3. THICK AS A BRICK
   (Jethro Tull)
4. HARVEST
   (Neil Young)
5. MANASSAS
   (Stephen Stills)
6. AMERICA
   (America)
7. FRAGILE
   (Yes)
8. PAUL SIMON
   (Paul Simon)
9. JOPLIN IN CONCERT
   (Janis Joplin)
10. HISTORY OF ERIC CLAPTON
    (Eric Clapton)

BLACK SINGLES

1. I'LL TAKE YOU THERE
   (The Staple Singers)
2. OH GIRL
   (The Chi-Lites)
3. WALKIN' IN THE RAIN
   (Love Unlimited)
4. OUTA SPACE
   (Billy Preston)
5. THERE IT IS
   (James Brown)
6. HEARSAY
   (The Soul Children)
7. WOMAN'S GOTTA HAVE IT
   (Bobby Womack)
8. LITTLE BITTY PRETTY ONE
   (The Jackson 5)
9. LEAN ON ME
   (Bill Withers)
10. THE FIRST TIME EVER I SAW YOUR FACE
    (Roberta Flack)

BLACK ALBUMS

1. A LONELY MAN
   (The Chi-Lites)

2. BEALTITUDE/RESPECT YOURSELF
   (The Staple Singers)
3. LET'S STAY TOGETHER
   (Al Green)
4. TODAY 1005
   (Black Ivory)
5. YOUNG, GIFTED AND BLACK
   (Aretha Franklin)
6. GOIN' FOR MYSELF
   (Dennis Coffey)
7. L.A. MIDNIGHT
   (B.B. King)
8. THIN LINE BETWEEN LOVE AND HATE
   (The Persuaders)
9. IN THE BEGINNING
   (Isaac Hayes)
10. STYLISTICS
    (The Stylistics)

JAZZ ALBUMS

1. THE INNER MOUNTING FLAME
   (Mahavishnu Orchestra)
2. CRUSADERS 1
   (Crusaders)
3. BLACK MOSES
   (Isaac Hayes)
4. PUSH PUSH
   (Herbie Mann)
5. QUIET FIRE
   (Roberta Flack)
6. SMACKWATER JACK
   (Quincy Jones)
7. INNER CITY BLUES
   (Grover Washington Jr.)
8. SHAFT
   (Isaac Hayes)
9. LIVE-EVIL
   (Miles Davis)
10. WILD HORSES ROCK STEADY
    (Johnny Hammond)

COUNTRY SINGLES

1. GRANDMA HARP
   (Merle Haggard)
2. THE HAPPIEST GIRL IN THE WHOLE U.S.A.
   (Donna Fargo)
3. OUR LAST DATE
   (Conway Twitty)
4. ALL THE LONELY WOMEN IN THE WORLD
   (Bill Anderson)
5. MANHATTAN, KANSAS
   (Glen Campbell)
6. THE LONESOMEST LONESOME/THAT'S
   WHAT LEAVING'S ABOUT
   (Ray Price)
7. ELEVEN ROSES
   (Hank Williams Jr.)
8. MADE IN JAPAN
   (Buck Owens)
9. ME AND JESUS
   (Tom T. Hall)
10. KATE
    (Johnny Cash)

COUNTRY ALBUMS

1. CRY
   (Lynn Anderson)
2. BEST OF CHARLEY PRIDE, VOL. 2
   (Charley Pride)
3. ONE'S ON THE WAY
   (Loretta Lynn)
4. THE REAL McCOY
   (Charlie McCoy)
5. BEDTIME STORY
   (Tammy Wynette)
6. THE KILLER ROCKS ON
   (Jerry Lee Lewis)
7. WE ALL GOT TOGETHER AND . . .
   (Tom T. Hall)
8. A THING CALLED LOVE
   (Johnny Cash)

9. LET ME TELL YOU ABOUT A SONG
   (Merle Haggard)
10. I CAN'T SEE ME WITHOUT YOU
    (Conway Twitty)

JUNE 10, 1972

POP SINGLES

1. CANDY MAN
   (Sammy Davis Jr.)
2. OH GIRL
   (The Chi-Lites)
3. SYLVIA'S MOTHER
   (Dr. Hook and the Medicine Show)
4. TUMBLING DICE
   (The Rolling Stones)
5. I'LL TAKE YOU THERE
   (The Staple Singers)
6. NICE TO BE WITH YOU
   (The Gallery)
7. SONG SUNG BLUE
   (Neil Diamond)
8. MORNING HAS BROKEN
   (Cat Stevens)
9. WALKIN' IN THE RAIN
   (Love Unlimited)
10. (LAST NIGHT) I DIDN'T GET TO SLEEP
    AT ALL
    (The Fifth Dimension)

POP ALBUMS

1. THICK AS A BRICK
   (Jethro Tull)
2. GRAHAM NASH/DAVID CROSBY
   (Graham Nash and David Crosby)
3. FIRST TAKE
   (Roberta Flack)
4. MANASSAS
   (Stephen Stills)
5. HARVEST
   (Neil Young)
6. JOPLIN IN CONCERT
   (Janis Joplin)
7. AMERICA
   (America)
8. A LONELY MAN
   (The Chi-Lites)
9. ROBERTA FLACK AND DONNY HATHAWAY
   (Roberta Flack and Donny Hathaway)
10. HISTORY OF ERIC CLAPTON
    (Eric Clapton)

BLACK SINGLES

1. I'LL TAKE YOU THERE
   (The Staple Singers)
2. OH GIRL
   (The Chi-Lites)
3. OUTA SPACE
   (Billy Preston)
4. THERE IT IS
   (James Brown)
5. WOMAN'S GOTTA HAVE IT
   (Bobby Womack)
6. LEAN ON ME
   (Bill Withers)
7. WALKIN' IN THE RAIN
   (Love Unlimited)
8. HEARSAY
   (The Soul Children)
9. GOTTA BE FUNKY
   (Monk Higgins)
10. TROGLODYTE
    (Jimmy Castor Bunch)

BLACK ALBUMS

1. A LONELY MAN
   (The Chi-Lites)

2. BEALTITUDE/RESPECT YOURSELF
   (The Staple Singers)
3. MUSIC OF MY MIND
   (Stevie Wonder)
4. LET'S STAY TOGETHER
   (Al Green)
5. TODAY 1005
   (Black Ivory)
6. GOIN' FOR MYSELF
   (Dennis Coffey)
7. L.A. MIDNIGHT
   (B.B. King)
8. YOUNG, GIFTED AND BLACK
   (Aretha Franklin)
9. IN THE BEGINNING
   (Isaac Hayes)
10. IT'S JUST BEGUN
    (Jimmy Castor Bunch)

JAZZ ALBUMS

1. THE INNER MOUNTING FLAME
   (Mahavishnu Orchestra)
2. CRUSADERS 1
   (Crusaders)
3. BLACK MOSES
   (Isaac Hayes)
4. SHAFT
   (Isaac Hayes)
5. PUSH PUSH
   (Herbie Mann)
6. SMACKWATER JACK
   (Quincy Jones)
7. QUIET FIRE
   (Roberta Flack)
8. HELP ME MAKE IT THROUGH THE NIGHT
   (Hank Crawford)
9. INNER CITY BLUES
   (Grover Washington Jr.)
10. LIVE-EVIL
    (Miles Davis)

COUNTRY SINGLES

1. THE HAPPIEST GIRL IN THE WHOLE U.S.A.
   (Donna Fargo)
2. THE LONESOMEST LONESOME/THAT'S
   WHAT LEAVING'S ABOUT
   (Ray Price)
3. GRANDMA HARP
   (Merle Haggard)
4. ELEVEN ROSES
   (Hank Williams Jr.)
5. MANHATTAN, KANSAS
   (Glen Campbell)
6. MADE IN JAPAN
   (Buck Owens)
7. KATE
   (Johnny Cash)
8. OUR LAST DATE
   (Conway Twitty)
9. ALL THE LONELY WOMEN IN THE WORLD
   (Bill Anderson)
10. LOST FOREVER IN YOUR KISS
    (Porter Wagoner and Dolly Parton)

COUNTRY ALBUMS

1. CRY
   (Lynn Anderson)
2. BEST OF CHARLEY PRIDE, VOL. 2
   (Charley Pride)
3. A THING CALLED LOVE
   (Johnny Cash)
4. THE REAL McCOY
   (Charlie McCoy)
5. ONE'S ON THE WAY
   (Loretta Lynn)
6. THE KILLER ROCKS ON
   (Jerry Lee Lewis)
7. WE ALL GOT TOGETHER AND. . .
   (Tom T. Hall)
8. BEDTIME STORY
   (Tammy Wynette)

9. BUCK OWENS LIVE AT THE NUGGET
   (Buck Owens)
10. LET ME TELL YOU ABOUT A SONG
    (Merle Haggard)

JUNE 17, 1972

POP SINGLES

1. CANDY MAN
   (Sammy Davis Jr.)
2. SYLVIA'S MOTHER
   (Dr. Hook and the Medicine Show)
3. SONG SUNG BLUE
   (Neil Diamond)
4. OH GIRL
   (The Chi-Lites)
5. NICE TO BE WITH YOU
   (The Gallery)
6. I'LL TAKE YOU THERE
   (The Staple Singers)
7. TUMBLING DICE
   (The Rolling Stones)
8. (LAST NIGHT) I DIDN'T GET TO SLEEP AT ALL
   (The Fifth Dimension)
9. WALKIN' IN THE RAIN
   (Love Unlimited)
10. TROGLODYTE
    (Jimmy Castor Bunch)

POP ALBUMS

1. EXILE ON MAIN STREET
   (The Rolling Stones)
2. THICK AS A BRICK
   (Jethro Tull)
3. GRAHAM NASH/DAVID CROSBY
   (Graham Nash and David Crosby)
4. FIRST TAKE
   (Roberta Flack)
5. MANASSAS
   (Stephen Stills)
6. JOPLIN IN CONCERT
   (Janis Joplin)
7. HARVEST
   (Neil Young)
8. A LONELY MAN
   (The Chi-Lites)
9. ROBERTA FLACK AND DONNY HATHAWAY
   (Roberta Flack and Donny Hathaway)
10. HISTORY OF ERIC CLAPTON
    (Eric Clapton)

BLACK SINGLES

1. I'LL TAKE YOU THERE
   (The Staple Singers)
2. OUTA SPACE
   (Billy Preston)
3. LEAN ON ME
   (Bill Withers)
4. WOMAN'S GOTTA HAVE IT
   (Bobby Womack)
5. OH GIRL
   (The Chi-Lites)
6. TROGLODYTE
   (Jimmy Castor Bunch)
7. GOTTA BE FUNKY
   (Monk Higgins)
8. THERE IT IS
   (James Brown)
9. THAT'S THE WAY IT'S GOT TO BE (BODY AND SOUL)
   (The Soul Generation)
10. WALKIN' IN THE RAIN
    (Love Unlimited)

BLACK ALBUMS

1. A LONELY MAN
   (The Chi-Lites)
2. BEALTITUDE/RESPECT YOURSELF
   (The Staple Singers)
3. MUSIC OF MY MIND
   (Stevie Wonder)
4. LET'S STAY TOGETHER
   (Al Green)
5. L.A. MIDNIGHT
   (B.B. King)
6. GOIN' FOR MYSELF
   (Dennis Coffey)
7. TODAY 1005
   (Black Ivory)
8. IT'S JUST BEGUN
   (Jimmy Castor Bunch)
9. YOUNG, GIFTED AND BLACK
   (Aretha Franklin)
10. INSTRUMENTAL DIRECTIONS
    (Nite-Liters)

JAZZ ALBUMS

1. THE INNER MOUNTING FLAME
   (Mahavishnu Orchestra)
2. CRUSADERS 1
   (Crusaders)
3. SHAFT
   (Isaac Hayes)
4. BLACK MOSES
   (Isaac Hayes)
5. PUSH PUSH
   (Herbie Mann)
6. SMACKWATER JACK
   (Quincy Jones)
7. HELP ME MAKE IT THROUGH THE NIGHT
   (Hank Crawford)
8. QUIET FIRE
   (Roberta Flack)
9. FROM A WHISPER TO A SCREAM
   (Esther Phillips)
10. LIVE-EVIL
    (Miles Davis)

COUNTRY SINGLES

1. THE LONESOMEST LONESOME/THAT'S WHAT LEAVING'S ABOUT
   (Ray Price)
2. THE HAPPIEST GIRL IN THE WHOLE U.S.A.
   (Donna Fargo)
3. ELEVEN ROSES
   (Hank Williams Jr.)
4. MADE IN JAPAN
   (Buck Owens)
5. KATE
   (Johnny Cash)
6. THAT'S WHY I LOVE YOU LIKE I DO
   (Sonny James)
7. I'VE FOUND SOMEONE ON MY OWN
   (Cal Smith)
8. GRANDMA HARP
   (Merle Haggard)
9. LOST FOREVER IN YOUR KISS
   (Porter Wagoner and Dolly Parton)
10. OUR LAST DATE
    (Conway Twitty)

COUNTRY ALBUMS

1. A THING CALLED LOVE
   (Johnny Cash)
2. CRY
   (Lynn Anderson)
3. BEST OF CHARLEY PRIDE, VOL. 2
   (Charley Pride)
4. THE KILLER ROCKS ON
   (Jerry Lee Lewis)
5. ONE'S ON THE WAY
   (Loretta Lynn)

6. THE REAL McCOY
   (Charlie McCoy)
7. BUCK OWENS LIVE AT THE NUGGET
   (Buck Owens)
8. WE ALL GOT TOGETHER AND. . .
   (Tom T. Hall)
9. LET ME TELL YOU ABOUT A SONG
   (Merle Haggard)
10. THIS IS JERRY WALLACE
    (Jerry Wallace)

JUNE 24, 1972

POP SINGLES

1. SONG SUNG BLUE
   (Neil Diamond)
2. SYLVIA'S MOTHER
   (Dr. Hook and the Medicine Show)
3. CANDY MAN
   (Sammy Davis Jr.)
4. NICE TO BE WITH YOU
   (The Gallery)
5. OUTA SPACE
   (Billy Preston)
6. TROGLODYTE
   (Jimmy Castor Bunch)
7. (LAST NIGHT) I DIDN'T GET TO SLEEP AT ALL
   (The Fifth Dimension)
8. I'LL TAKE YOU THERE
   (The Staple Singers)
9. OH GIRL
   (The Chi-Lites)
10. TOO LATE TO TURN BACK NOW
    (Cornelius Brothers and Sister Rose)

POP ALBUMS

1. EXILE ON MAIN STREET
   (The Rolling Stones)
2. THICK AS A BRICK
   (Jethro Tull)
3. FIRST TAKE
   (Roberta Flack)
4. JOPLIN IN CONCERT
   (Janis Joplin)
5. MANASSAS
   (Stephen Stills)
6. GRAHAM NASH/DAVID CROSBY
   (Graham Nash and David Crosby)
7. A LONELY MAN
   (The Chi-Lites)
8. ROBERTA FLACK AND DONNY HATHAWAY
   (Roberta Flack and Donny Hathaway)
9. HISTORY OF ERIC CLAPTON
   (Eric Clapton)
10. HARVEST
    (Neil Young)

BLACK SINGLES

1. LEAN ON ME
   (Bill Withers)
2. I'LL TAKE YOU THERE
   (The Staple Singers)
3. OUTA SPACE
   (Billy Preston)
4. TROGLODYTE
   (Jimmy Castor Bunch)
5. WOMAN'S GOTTA HAVE IT
   (Bobby Womack)
6. PEOPLE MAKE THE WORLD GO ROUND
   (The Stylistics)
7. OH GIRL
   (The Chi-Lites)
8. GOTTA BE FUNKY
   (Monk Higgins)
9. IF LOVING YOU IS WRONG
   (Luther Ingram)
10. SUPERWOMAN
    (Stevie Wonder)

BLACK ALBUMS

1. A LONELY MAN
   (The Chi-Lites)
2. BEALTITUDE/RESPECT YOURSELF
   (The Staple Singers)
3. STILL BILL
   (Bill Withers)
4. L.A. MIDNIGHT
   (B.B. King)
5. LET'S STAY TOGETHER
   (Al Green)
6. MUSIC OF MY MIND
   (Stevie Wonder)
7. IT'S JUST BEGUN
   (Jimmy Castor Bunch)
8. GOIN' FOR MYSELF
   (Dennis Coffey)
9. TODAY 1005
   (Black Ivory)
10. INSTRUMENTAL DIRECTIONS
   (Nite-Liters)

JAZZ ALBUMS

1. THE INNER MOUNTING FLAME
   (Mahavishnu Orchestra)
2. CRUSADERS 1
   (Crusaders)
3. PUSH PUSH
   (Herbie Mann)
4. SMACKWATER JACK
   (Quincy Jones)
5. SHAFT
   (Isaac Hayes)
6. BLACK MOSES
   (Isaac Hayes)
7. WHITE RABBIT
   (George Benson)
8. LIVE-EVIL
   (Miles Davis)
9. WILD HORSES ROCK STEADY
   (Johnny Hammond)
10. FROM A WHISPER TO A SCREAM
   (Esther Phillips)

COUNTRY SINGLES

1. ELEVEN ROSES
   (Hank Williams Jr.)
2. MADE IN JAPAN
   (Buck Owens)
3. KATE
   (Johnny Cash)
4. THAT'S WHY I LOVE YOU LIKE I DO
   (Sonny James)
5. I'VE FOUND SOMEONE OF MY OWN
   (Cal Smith)
6. THE LONESOMEST LONESOME/THAT'S
   WHAT LEAVING'S ABOUT
   (Ray Price)
7. THE HAPPIEST GIRL IN THE WHOLE U.S.A.
   (Donna Fargo)
8. REACH OUT YOUR HAND
   (Tammy Wynette)
9. LOST FOREVER IN YOUR KISS
   (Porter Wagoner and Dolly Parton)
10. I'LL BE THERE
   (Johnny Bush)

COUNTRY ALBUMS

1. A THING CALLED LOVE
   (Johnny Cash)
2. THE KILLER ROCKS ON
   (Jerry Lee Lewis)
3. BEST OF CHARLEY PRIDE, VOL. 2
   (Charley Pride)
4. CRY
   (Lynn Anderson)
5. ONE'S ON THE WAY
   (Loretta Lynn)

6. BUCK OWENS LIVE AT THE NUGGET
   (Buck Owens)
7. THE REAL McCOY
   (Charlie McCoy)
8. THIS IS JERRY WALLACE
   (Jerry Wallace)
9. LET ME TELL YOU ABOUT A SONG
   (Merle Haggard)
10. WE ALL GOT TOGETHER AND . . .
   (Tom T. Hall)

JULY 1, 1972

POP SINGLES

1. SONG SUNG BLUE
   (Neil Diamond)
2. OUTA SPACE
   (Billy Preston)
3. TOO LATE TO TURN BACK NOW
   (Cornelius Brothers and Sister Rose)
4. LEAN ON ME
   (Bill Withers)
5. TROGLODYTE
   (Jimmy Castor Bunch)
6. NICE TO BE WITH YOU
   (The Gallery)
7. CANDY MAN
   (Sammy Davis Jr.)
8. SYLVIA'S MOTHER
   (Dr. Hook and the Medicine Show)
9. I NEED YOU
   (America)
10. IF LOVING YOU IS WRONG
   (Luther Ingram)

POP ALBUMS

1. EXILE ON MAIN STREET
   (The Rolling Stones)
2. THICK AS A BRICK
   (Jethro Tull)
3. FIRST TAKE
   (Roberta Flack)
4. JOPLIN IN CONCERT
   (Janis Joplin)
5. ROBERTA FLACK AND DONNY HATHAWAY
   (Roberta Flack and Donny Hathaway)
6. A LONELY MAN
   (The Chi-Lites)
7. PROCOL HARUM LIVE IN CONCERT
   (Procol Harum)
8. HISTORY OF ERIC CLAPTON
   (Eric Clapton)
9. MANASSAS
   (Stephen Stills)
10. PORTRAIT OF DONNY
   (Donny Osmond)

BLACK SINGLES

1. LEAN ON ME
   (Bill Withers)
2. TROGLODYTE
   (Jimmy Castor Bunch)
3. PEOPLE MAKE THE WORLD GO ROUND
   (The Stylistics)
4. OUTA SPACE
   (Billy Preston)
5. IF LOVING YOU IS WRONG
   (Luther Ingram)
6. I'LL TAKE YOU THERE
   (The Staple Singers)
7. I WANNA BE WHERE YOU ARE
   (Michael Jackson)
8. WOMAN'S GOTTA HAVE IT
   (Bobby Womack)
9. ALL THE KING'S HORSES
   (Aretha Franklin)
10. SUPERWOMAN
   (Stevie Wonder)

BLACK ALBUMS

1. A LONELY MAN
   (The Chi-Lites)
2. STILL BILL
   (Bill Withers)
3. L.A. MIDNIGHT
   (B.B. King)
4. BEALTITUDE/RESPECT YOURSELF
   (The Staple Singers)
5. IT'S JUST BEGUN
   (Jimmy Castor Bunch)
6. MUSIC OF MY MIND
   (Stevie Wonder)
7. I WROTE A SIMPLE SONG
   (Billy Preston)
8. LET'S STAY TOGETHER
   (Al Green)
9. GOIN' FOR MYSELF
   (Dennis Coffey)
10. SHAFT
   (Isaac Hayes)

JAZZ ALBUMS

1. THE INNER MOUNTING FLAME
   (Mahavishnu Orchestra)
2. CRUSADERS 1
   (Crusaders)
3. WHITE RABBIT
   (George Benson)
4. PUSH PUSH
   (Herbie Mann)
5. SMACKWATER JACK
   (Quincy Jones)
6. LIVE-EVIL
   (Miles Davis)
7. INNER CITY BLUES
   (Grover Washington Jr.)
8. INSTANT DEATH
   (Eddie Harris)
9. WILD HORSES ROCK STEADY
   (Johnny Hammond)
10. BUDDY RICH IN LONDON
   (Buddy Rich)

COUNTRY SINGLES

1. MADE IN JAPAN
   (Buck Owens)
2. KATE
   (Johnny Cash)
3. THAT'S WHY I LOVE YOU LIKE I DO
   (Sonny James)
4. I'VE FOUND SOMEONE OF MY OWN
   (Cal Smith)
5. ELEVEN ROSES
   (Hank Williams Jr.)
6. REACH OUT YOUR HAND
   (Tammy Wynette)
7. THE HAPPIEST GIRL IN THE WHOLE U.S.A.
   (Donna Fargo)
8. DELTA DAWN
   (Tanya Tucker)
9. LOVING YOU COULD NEVER BE BETTER
   (George Jones)
10. IT'S GONNA TAKE A LITTLE BIT LONGER
   (Charley Pride)

COUNTRY ALBUMS

1. THE KILLER ROCKS ON
   (Jerry Lee Lewis)
2. A THING CALLED LOVE
   (Johnny Cash)
3. BEST OF CHARLEY PRIDE, VOL. 2
   (Charley Pride)
4. CRY
   (Lynn Anderson)
5. THIS IS JERRY WALLACE
   (Jerry Wallace)
6. BUCK OWENS LIVE AT THE NUGGET
   (Buck Owens)

7. THE REAL McCOY
   (Charlie McCoy)
8. ONE'S ON THE WAY
   (Loretta Lynn)
9. THAT'S WHY I LOVE YOU LIKE I DO
   (Sonny James)
10. LET ME TELL YOU ABOUT A SONG
    (Merle Haggard)

JULY 8, 1972

POP SINGLES

1. OUTA SPACE
   (Billy Preston)
2. TOO LATE TO TURN BACK NOW
   (Cornelius Brothers and Sister Rose)
3. LEAN ON ME
   (Bill Withers)
4. SONG SUNG BLUE
   (Neil Diamond)
5. TROGLODYTE
   (Jimmy Castor Bunch)
6. DADDY DON'T YOU WALK SO FAST
   (Wayne Newton)
7. IF LOVING YOU IS WRONG
   (Luther Ingram)
8. I NEED YOU
   (America)
9. ROCKET MAN
   (Elton John)
10. AMAZING GRACE
    (Royal Scots Dragoon Guards)

POP ALBUMS

1. EXILE ON MAIN STREET
   (The Rolling Stones)
2. THICK AS A BRICK
   (Jethro Tull)
3. FIRST TAKE
   (Roberta Flack)
4. JOPLIN IN CONCERT
   (Janis Joplin)
5. ROBERTA FLACK AND DONNY HATHAWAY
   (Roberta Flack and Donny Hathaway)
6. HONKY CHATEAU
   (Elton John)
7. PROCOL HARUM LIVE IN CONCERT
   (Procol Harum)
8. HISTORY OF ERIC CLAPTON
   (Eric Clapton)
9. PORTRAIT OF DONNY
   (Donny Osmond)
10. LOOKIN' THROUGH THE WINDOWS
    (The Jackson 5)

BLACK SINGLES

1. IF LOVING YOU IS WRONG
   (Luther Ingram)
2. LEAN ON ME
   (Bill Withers)
3. PEOPLE MAKE THE WORLD GO ROUND
   (The Stylistics)
4. TROGLODYTE
   (Jimmy Castor Bunch)
5. I WANNA BE WHERE YOU ARE
   (Michael Jackson)
6. OUTA SPACE
   (Billy Preston)
7. ALL THE KING'S HORSES
   (Aretha Franklin)
8. I'LL TAKE YOU THERE
   (The Staple Singers)
9. BABY LET ME TAKE YOU
   (Detroit Emeralds)
10. WOMAN'S GOTTA HAVE IT
    (Bobby Womack)

BLACK ALBUMS

1. A LONELY MAN
   (The Chi-Lites)
2. STILL BILL
   (Bill Withers)
3. L.A. MIDNIGHT
   (B.B. King)
4. IT'S JUST BEGUN
   (Jimmy Castor Bunch)
5. I WROTE A SIMPLE SONG
   (Billy Preston)
6. MUSIC OF MY MIND
   (Stevie Wonder)
7. BEALTITUDE/RESPECT YOURSELF
   (The Staple Singers)
8. LOOKIN' THROUGH THE WINDOWS
   (The Jackson 5)
9. LET'S STAY TOGETHER
   (Al Green)
10. SHAFT
    (Isaac Hayes)

JAZZ ALBUMS

1. CRUSADERS 1
   (Crusaders)
2. THE INNER MOUNTING FLAME
   (Mahavishnu Orchestra)
3. WHITE RABBIT
   (George Benson)
4. SMACKWATER JACK
   (Quincy Jones)
5. BUDDY RICH IN LONDON
   (Buddy Rich)
6. THE GREAT CONCERT
   (Charles Mingus)
7. PUSH PUSH
   (Herbie Mann)
8. INSTANT DEATH
   (Eddie Harris)
9. FUNK INC.
   (Funk Inc.)
10. SHADES OF GREEN
    (Grant Green)

COUNTRY SINGLES

1. KATE
   (Johnny Cash)
2. THAT'S WHY I LOVE YOU LIKE I DO
   (Sonny James)
3. I'VE FOUND SOMEONE OF MY OWN
   (Cal Smith)
4. MADE IN JAPAN
   (Buck Owens)
5. REACH OUT YOUR HAND
   (Tammy Wynette)
6. ELEVEN ROSES
   (Hank Williams Jr.)
7. DELTA DAWN
   (Tanya Tucker)
8. LOVING YOU COULD NEVER BE BETTER
   (George Jones)
9. IT'S GONNA TAKE A LITTLE BIT LONGER
   (Charley Pride)
10. THE LONESOMEST LONESOME/THAT'S
    WHAT LEAVING'S ABOUT
    (Ray Price)

COUNTRY ALBUMS

1. THE KILLER ROCKS ON
   (Jerry Lee Lewis)
2. A THING CALLED LOVE
   (Johnny Cash)
3. BEST OF CHARLEY PRIDE, VOL. 2
   (Charley Pride)
4. THIS IS JERRY WALLACE
   (Jerry Wallace)
5. THAT'S WHY I LOVE YOU LIKE I DO
   (Sonny James)

6. BUCK OWENS LIVE AT THE NUGGET
   (Buck Owens)
7. CRY
   (Lynn Anderson)
8. THE REAL McCOY
   (Charlie McCoy)
9. ONE'S ON THE WAY
   (Loretta Lynn)
10. LET ME TELL YOU ABOUT A SONG
    (Merle Haggard)

JULY 15, 1972

POP SINGLES

1. LEAN ON ME
   (Bill Withers)
2. TOO LATE TO TURN BACK NOW
   (Cornelius Brothers and Sister Rose)
3. OUTA SPACE
   (Billy Preston)
4. DADDY DON'T YOU WALK SO FAST
   (Wayne Newton)
5. IF LOVING YOU IS WRONG
   (Luther Ingram)
6. TROGLODYTE
   (Jimmy Castor Bunch)
7. ROCKET MAN
   (Elton John)
8. I NEED YOU
   (America)
9. TAKE IT EASY
   (The Eagles)
10. SONG SUNG BLUE
    (Neil Diamond)

POP ALBUMS

1. EXILE ON MAIN STREET
   (The Rolling Stones)
2. THICK AS A BRICK
   (Jethro Tull)
3. HONKY CHATEAU
   (Elton John)
4. ROBERTA FLACK AND DONNY HATHAWAY
   (Roberta Flack and Donny Hathaway)
5. JOPLIN IN CONCERT
   (Janis Joplin)
6. PROCOL HARUM IN CONCERT
   (Procol Harum)
7. HISTORY OF ERIC CLAPTON
   (Eric Clapton)
8. PORTRAIT OF DONNY
   (Donny Osmond)
9. LOOKIN' THROUGH THE WINDOWS
   (The Jackson 5)
10. FIRST TAKE
    (Roberta Flack)

BLACK SINGLES

1. IF LOVING YOU IS WRONG
   (Luther Ingram)
2. I WANNA BE WHERE YOU ARE
   (Michael Jackson)
3. LEAN ON ME
   (Bill Withers)
4. RIP OFF
   (Laura Lee)
5. PEOPLE MAKE THE WORLD GO ROUND
   (The Stylistics)
6. BABY LET ME TAKE YOU
   (Detroit Emeralds)
7. TROGLODYTE
   (Jimmy Castor Bunch)
8. WHERE IS THE LOVE
   (Roberta Flack and Donny Hathaway)
9. ALL THE KING'S HORSES
   (Aretha Franklin)
10. TOO LATE TO TURN BACK NOW
    (Cornelius Brothers and Sister Rose)

BLACK ALBUMS

1. A LONELY MAN
   (The Chi-Lites)
2. STILL BILL
   (Bill Withers)
3. IT'S JUST BEGUN
   (Jimmy Castor Bunch)
4. L.A. MIDNIGHT
   (B.B. King)
5. I WROTE A SIMPLE SONG
   (Billy Preston)
6. MUSIC OF MY MIND
   (Stevie Wonder)
7. LOOKIN' THROUGH THE WINDOWS
   (The Jackson 5)
8. BEALTITUDE/RESPECT YOURSELF
   (The Staple Singers)
9. SHAFT
   (Isaac Hayes)
10. LET'S STAY TOGETHER
    (Al Green)

JAZZ ALBUMS

1. CRUSADERS 1
   (Crusaders)
2. WHITE RABBIT
   (George Benson)
3. THE INNER MOUNTING FLAME
   (Mahavishnu Orchestra)
4. SMACKWATER JACK
   (Quincy Jones)
5. BUDDY RICH IN LONDON
   (Buddy Rich)
6. THE GREAT CONCERT
   (Charles Mingus)
7. SHADES OF GREEN
   (Grant Green)
8. FUNK INC.
   (Funk Inc.)
9. PUSH PUSH
   (Herbie Mann)
10. INSTANT DEATH
    (Eddie Harris)

COUNTRY SINGLES

1. THAT'S WHY I LOVE YOU LIKE I DO
   (Sonny James)
2. I'VE FOUND SOMEONE OF MY OWN
   (Cal Smith)
3. KATE
   (Johnny Cash)
4. REACH OUT YOUR HAND
   (Tammy Wynette)
5. IT'S GONNA TAKE A LITTLE BIT LONGER
   (Charley Pride)
6. DELTA DAWN
   (Tanya Tucker)
7. LOVING YOU COULD NEVER BE BETTER
   (George Jones)
8. BORROWED ANGEL
   (Mel Street)
9. MADE IN JAPAN
   (Buck Owens)
10. ELEVEN ROSES
    (Hank Williams Jr.)

COUNTRY ALBUMS

1. BEST OF CHARLEY PRIDE, VOL. 2
   (Charley Pride)
2. THE KILLER ROCKS ON
   (Jerry Lee Lewis)
3. THIS IS JERRY WALLACE
   (Jerry Wallace)
4. THAT'S WHY I LOVE YOU LIKE I DO
   (Sonny James)
5. A THING CALLED LOVE
   (Johnny Cash)
6. THE REAL McCOY
   (Charlie McCoy)

---

7. BUCK OWENS LIVE AT THE NUGGET
   (Buck Owens)
8. CRY
   (Lynn Anderson)
9. ONE'S ON THE WAY
   (Loretta Lynn)
10. GREATEST HITS, VOL. 2
    (Hank Williams Jr.)

JULY 22, 1972

POP SINGLES

1. TOO LATE TO TURN BACK NOW
   (Cornelius Brothers and Sister Rose)
2. LEAN ON ME
   (Bill Withers)
3. DADDY DON'T YOU WALK SO FAST
   (Wayne Newton)
4. IF LOVING YOU IS WRONG
   (Luther Ingram)
5. BRANDY
   (The Looking Glass)
6. ROCKET MAN
   (Elton John)
7. TAKE IT EASY
   (The Eagles)
8. OUTA SPACE
   (Billy Preston)
9. ALONE AGAIN (NATURALLY)
   (Gilbert O'Sullivan)
10. I WANNA BE WHERE YOU ARE
    (Michael Jackson)

POP ALBUMS

1. EXILE ON MAIN STREET
   (The Rolling Stones)
2. HONKY CHATEAU
   (Elton John)
3. ROBERTA FLACK AND DONNY HATHAWAY
   (Roberta Flack and Donny Hathaway)
4. THICK AS A BRICK
   (Jethro Tull)
5. JOPLIN IN CONCERT
   (Janis Joplin)
6. PROCOL HARUM LIVE IN CONCERT
   (Procol Harum)
7. STILL BILL
   (Bill Withers)
8. PORTRAIT OF DONNY
   (Donny Osmond)
9. LOOKIN' THROUGH THE WINDOWS
   (The Jackson 5)
10. AMAZING GRACE
    (Aretha Franklin)

BLACK SINGLES

1. IF LOVING YOU IS WRONG
   (Luther Ingram)
2. I WANNA BE WHERE YOU ARE
   (Michael Jackson)
3. LEAN ON ME
   (Bill Withers)
4. RIP OFF
   (Laura Lee)
5. WHERE IS THE LOVE
   (Roberta Flack and Donny Hathaway)
6. BABY LET ME TAKE YOU
   (Detroit Emeralds)
7. TOO LATE TO TURN BACK NOW
   (Cornelius Brothers and Sister Rose)
8. I MISS YOU
   (Harold Melvin and the Blue Notes)
9. PEOPLE MAKE THE WORLD GO ROUND
   (The Stylistics)
10. TROGLODYTE
    (Jimmy Castor Bunch)

BLACK ALBUMS

1. A LONELY MAN
   (The Chi-Lites)
2. STILL BILL
   (Bill Withers)
3. LOOKIN' THROUGH THE WINDOWS
   (The Jackson 5)
4. IT'S JUST BEGUN
   (Jimmy Castor Bunch)
5. L.A. MIDNIGHT
   (B.B. King)
6. MUSIC OF MY MIND
   (Stevie Wonder)
7. I WROTE A SIMPLE SONG
   (Billy Preston)
8. SHAFT
   (Isaac Hayes)
9. GOIN' EAST
   (Billy Paul)
10. BEALTITUDE/RESPECT YOURSELF
    (The Staple Singers)

JAZZ ALBUMS

1. CRUSADERS 1
   (Crusaders)
2. WHITE RABBIT
   (George Benson)
3. THE INNER MOUNTING FLAME
   (Mahavishnu Orchestra)
4. SMACKWATER JACK
   (Quincy Jones)
5. BUDDY RICH IN LONDON
   (Buddy Rich)
6. THE GREAT CONCERT
   (Charles Mingus)
7. SHADES OF GREEN
   (Grant Green)
8. FUNK INC.
   (Funk Inc.)
9. INTENSITY
   (Charles Earland)
10. ETHIOPIAN NIGHTS
    (Donald Byrd)

COUNTRY SINGLES

1. IT'S GONNA TAKE A LITTLE IT LONGER
   (Charley Pride)
2. I'VE FOUND SOMEONE OF MY OWN
   (Cal Smith)
3. REACH OUT YOUR HAND
   (Tammy Wynette)
4. DELTA DAWN
   (Tanya Tucker)
5. LOVING YOU COULD NEVER BE BETTER
   (George Jones)
6. BORROWED ANGEL
   (Mel Street)
7. THAT'S WHY I LOVE YOU LIKE I DO
   (Sonny James)
8. LISTEN TO A COUNTRY SONG
   (Lynn Anderson)
9. KATE
   (Johnny Cash)
10. SWEET DREAM WOMAN
    (Waylon Jennings)

COUNTRY ALBUMS

1. BEST OF CHARLEY PRIDE, VOL. 2
   (Charley Pride)
2. THIS IS JERRY WALLACE
   (Jerry Wallace)
3. THAT'S WHY I LOVE YOU LIKE I DO
   (Sonny James)
4. THE KILLER ROCKS ON
   (Jerry Lee Lewis)
5. THE REAL McCOY
   (Charlie McCoy)
6. A THING CALLED LOVE
   (Johnny Cash)

7. BUCK OWENS LIVE AT THE NUGGET
   (Buck Owens)
8. GREATEST HITS, VOL. 2
   (Hank Williams Jr.)
9. CRY
   (Lynn Anderson)
10. GEORGE JONES
    (George Jones)

JULY 29, 1972

POP SINGLES

1. DADDY DON'T YOU WALK SO FAST
   (Wayne Newton)
2. TOO LATE TO TURN BACK NOW
   (Cornelius Brothers and Sister Rose)
3. IF LOVING YOU IS WRONG
   (Luther Ingram)
4. BRANDY
   (The Looking Glass)
5. ALONE AGAIN (NATURALLY)
   (Gilbert O'Sullivan)
6. TAKE IT EASY
   (The Eagles)
7. LEAN ON ME
   (Bill Withers)
8. WHERE IS THE LOVE
   (Roberta Flack and Donny Hathaway)
9. HOW DO YOU DO
   (Mouth and MacNeal)
10. I WANNA BE WHERE YOU ARE
    (Michael Jackson)

POP ALBUMS

1. EXILE ON MAIN STREET
   (The Rolling Stones)
2. HONKY CHATEAU
   (Elton John)
3. ROBERTA FLACK AND DONNY HATHAWAY
   (Roberta Flack and Donny Hathaway)
4. STILL BILL
   (Bill Withers)
5. PORTRAIT OF DONNY
   (Donny Osmond)
6. PROCOL HARUM LIVE IN CONCERT
   (Procol Harum)
7. LOOKIN' THROUGH THE WINDOWS
   (The Jackson 5)
8. AMAZING GRACE
   (Aretha Franklin)
9. SIMON AND GARFUNKEL'S GREATEST HITS
   (Simon and Garfunkel)
10. JOPLIN IN CONCERT
    (Janis Joplin)

BLACK SINGLES

1. I WANNA BE WHERE YOU ARE
   (Michael Jackson)
2. IF LOVING YOU IS WRONG
   (Luther Ingram)
3. WHERE IS THE LOVE
   (Roberta Flack and Donny Hathaway)
4. TOO LATE TO TURN BACK NOW
   (Cornelius Brothers and Sister Rose)
5. LEAN ON ME
   (Bill Withers)
6. I MISS YOU
   (Harold Melvin and the Blue Notes)
7. BABY LET ME TAKE YOU
   (Detroit Emeralds)
8. RIP OFF
   (Laura Lee)
9. WE'VE COME TOO FAR TO END IT NOW
   (Smokey Robinson and the Miracles)
10. BED AND BOARD
    (Barbara Mason)

BLACK ALBUMS

1. STILL BILL
   (Bill Withers)
2. A LONELY MAN
   (The Chi-Lites)
3. LOOKIN' THROUGH THE WINDOWS
   (The Jackson 5)
4. IT'S JUST BEGUN
   (Jimmy Castor Bunch)
5. MUSIC OF MY MIND
   (Stevie Wonder)
6. L.A. MIDNIGHT
   (B.B. King)
7. SHAFT
   (Isaac Hayes)
8. I WROTE A SIMPLE SONG
   (Billy Preston)
9. GOIN' EAST
   (Billy Paul)
10. AMAZING GRACE
    (Aretha Franklin)

JAZZ ALBUMS

1. WHITE RABBIT
   (George Benson)
2. CRUSADERS 1
   (Crusaders)
3. THE INNER MOUNTING FLAME
   (Mahavishnu Orchestra)
4. SMACKWATER JACK
   (Quincy Jones)
5. THE GREAT CONCERT
   (Charles Mingus)
6. SHADES OF GREEN
   (Grant Green)
7. FUNK INC.
   (Funk Inc.)
8. INTENSITY
   (Charles Earland)
9. ETHIOPIAN NIGHTS
   (Donald Byrd)
10. BUDDY RICH IN LONDON
    (Buddy Rich)

COUNTRY SINGLES

1. DELTA DAWN
   (Tanya Tucker)
2. IT'S GONNA TAKE A LITTLE BIT LONGER
   (Charley Pride)
3. REACH OUT YOUR HAND
   (Tammy Wynette)
4. BORROWED ANGEL
   (Mel Street)
5. LOVING YOU COULD NEVER BE BETTER
   (George Jones)
6. LISTEN TO A COUNTRY SONG
   (Lynn Anderson)
7. WOMAN (SENSUOUS WOMAN)
   (Don Gibson)
8. SWEET DREAM WOMAN
   (Waylon Jennings)
9. I'VE FOUND SOMEONE OF MY OWN
   (Cal Smith)
10. MY HEART HAS A MIND OF IT'S OWN
    (Susan Raye)

COUNTRY ALBUMS

1. THAT'S WHY I LOVE YOU LIKE I DO
   (Sonny James)
2. THIS IS JERRY WALLACE
   (Jerry Wallace)
3. BEST OF CHARLEY PRIDE, VOL. 2
   (Charley Pride)
4. THE REAL McCOY
   (Charley McCoy)
5. THE KILLER ROCKS ON
   (Jerry Lee Lewis)
6. A THING CALLED LOVE
   (Johnny Cash)

7. GREATEST HITS, VOL. 2
   (Hank Williams Jr.)
8. BEST OF JERRY REED
   (Jerry Reed)
9. SOMEONE TO GIVE MY LOVE TO
   (Johnny Paycheck)
10. GEORGE JONES
    (George Jones)

AUGUST 5, 1972

POP SINGLES

1. DADDY DON'T YOU WALK SO FAST
   (Wayne Newton)
2. ALONE AGAIN (NATURALLY)
   (Gilbert O'Sullivan)
3. BRANDY
   (The Looking Glass)
4. IF LOVING YOU IS WRONG
   (Luther Ingram)
5. WHERE IS THE LOVE
   (Roberta Flack and Donny Hathaway)
6. TAKE IT EASY
   (The Eagles)
7. TOO LATE TO TURN BACK NOW
   (Cornelius Brothers and Sister Rose)
8. SCHOOL'S OUT
   (Alice Cooper)
9. HOW DO YOU DO
   (Mouth and MacNeal)
10. LONG COOL WOMAN
    (The Hollies)

POP ALBUMS

1. EXILE ON MAIN STREET
   (The Rolling Stones)
2. HONKY CHATEAU
   (Elton John)
3. SCHOOL'S OUT
   (Alice Cooper)
4. STILL BILL
   (Bill Withers)
5. SIMON AND GARFUNKEL'S GREATEST HITS
   (Simon and Garfunkel)
6. PORTRAIT OF DONNY
   (Donny Osmond)
7. LOOKIN' THROUGH THE WINDOWS
   (The Jackson 5)
8. AMAZING GRACE
   (Aretha Franklin)
9. A SONG FOR YOU
   (The Carpenters)
10. ROBERTA FLACK AND DONNY HATHAWAY
    (Roberta Flack and Donny Hathaway)

BLACK SINGLES

1. I WANNA BE WHERE YOU ARE
   (Michael Jackson)
2. WHERE IS THE LOVE
   (Roberta Flack and Donny Hathaway)
3. TOO LATE TO TURN BACK NOW
   (Cornelius Brothers and Sister Rose)
4. IF LOVING YOU IS WRONG
   (Luther Ingram)
5. I MISS YOU
   (Harold Melvin and the Blue Notes)
6. LEAN ON ME
   (Bill Withers)
7. BABY LET ME TAKE YOU
   (Detroit Emeralds)
8. WE'VE COME TOO FAR TO END IT NOW
   (Smokey Robinson and the Miracles)
9. RIP OFF
   (Laura Lee)
10. THE COLDEST DAYS OF MY LIFE
    (The Chi-Lites)

BLACK ALBUMS

1. STILL BILL
   (Bill Withers)
2. A LONELY MAN
   (The Chi-Lites)
3. MUSIC OF MY MIND
   (Stevie Wonder)
4. AMAZING GRACE
   (Aretha Franklin)
5. LOOKIN' THROUGH THE WINDOWS
   (The Jackson 5)
6. IT'S JUST BEGUN
   (Jimmy Castor Bunch)
7. SHAFT
   (Isaac Hayes)
8. I WROTE A SIMPLE SONG
   (Billy Preston)
9. L.A. MIDNIGHT
   (B.B. King)
10. GOIN' EAST
    (Billy Paul)

JAZZ ALBUMS

1. WHITE RABBIT
   (George Benson)
2. THE GREATEST CONCERT
   (Charles Mingus)
3. FUNK INC.
   (Funk Inc.)
4. SHADES OF GREEN
   (Grant Green)
5. INTENSITY
   (Charles Earland)
6. CRUSADERS 1
   (Crusaders)
7. ETHIOPIAN NIGHTS
   (Donald Byrd)
8. MISSISSIPPI GAMBLER
   (Herbie Mann)
9. THE INNER MOUNTING FLAME
   (Mahavishnu Orchestra)
10. CROSSINGS
    (Herbie Hancock)

COUNTRY SINGLES

1. REACH OUT YOUR HAND
   (Tammy Wynette)
2. LOVING YOU COULD NEVER BE BETTER
   (George Jones)
3. LISTEN TO A COUNTRY SONG
   (Lynn Anderson)
4. BORROWED ANGEL
   (Mel Street)
5. WOMAN (SENSUOUS WOMAN)
   (Don Gibson)
6. DELTA DAWN
   (Tanya Tucker)
7. IT'S GONNA TAKE A LITTLE BIT LONGER
   (Charley Pride)
8. SWEET DREAM WOMAN
   (Waylon Jennings)
9. SOFT, SWEET AND WARM
   (David Houston)
10. MY HEART HAS A MIND OF ITS OWN
    (Susan Raye)

COUNTRY ALBUMS

1. THAT'S WHY I LOVE YOU LIKE I DO
   (Sonny James)
2. THE REAL McCOY
   (Charlie McCoy)
3. BEST OF CHARLEY PRIDE, VOL. 2
   (Charley Pride)
4. THIS IS JERRY WALLACE
   (Jerry Wallace)
5. A THING CALLED LOVE
   (Johnny Cash)
6. GREATEST HITS, VOL. 2
   (Hank Williams Jr.)

7. BEST OF JERRY REED
   (Jerry Reed)
8. SOMEONE TO GIVE MY LOVE TO
   (Johnny Paycheck)
9. THE KILLER ROCKS ON
   (Jerry Lee Lewis)
10. BLESS YOUR HART
    (Freddie Hart)

AUGUST 12, 1972

POP SINGLES

1. ALONE AGAIN (NATURALLY)
   (Gilbert O'Sullivan)
2. BRANDY
   (The Looking Glass)
3. DADDY DON'T YOU WALK SO FAST
   (Wayne Newton)
4. IF LOVING YOU IS WRONG
   (Luther Ingram)
5. WHERE IS THE LOVE
   (Roberta Flack and Donny Hathaway)
6. LONG COOL WOMAN
   (The Hollies)
7. SCHOOL'S OUT
   (Alice Cooper)
8. I'M STILL IN LOVE WITH YOU
   (Al Green)
9. HOW DO YOU DO
   (Mouth and MacNeal)
10. HOLD HER TIGHT
    (The Osmonds)

POP ALBUMS

1. HONKY CHATEAU
   (Elton John)
2. SCHOOL'S OUT
   (Alice Cooper)
3. EXILE ON MAIN STREET
   (The Rolling Stones)
4. SIMON AND GARFUNKEL'S GREATEST HITS
   (Simon and Garfunkel)
5. STILL BILL
   (Bill Withers)
6. A SONG FOR YOU
   (The Carpenters)
7. LOOKIN' THROUGH THE WINDOWS
   (The Jackson 5)
8. MOODS
   (Neil Diamond)
9. BIG BAMBU
   (Cheech and Chong)
10. CHICAGO V
    (Chicago)

BLACK SINGLES

1. WHERE IS THE LOVE
   (Roberta Flack and Donny Hathaway)
2. I WANNA BE WHERE YOU ARE
   (Michael Jackson)
3. I MISS YOU
   (Harold Melvin and the Blue Notes)
4. TOO LATE TO TURN BACK NOW
   (Cornelius Brothers and Sister Rose)
5. I'M STILL IN LOVE WITH YOU
   (Al Green)
6. IF LOVING YOU IS WRONG
   (Luther Ingram)
7. BACK STABBERS
   (The O'Jays)
8. THE COLDEST DAYS OF MY LIFE
   (The Chi-Lites)
9. POWER OF LOVE
   (Joe Simon)
10. POP THAT THANG
    (Isley Brothers)

BLACK ALBUMS

1. STILL BILL
   (Bill Withers)
2. A LONELY MAN
   (The Chi-Lites)
3. AMAZING GRACE
   (Aretha Franklin)
4. MUSIC OF MY MIND
   (Stevie Wonder)
5. LOOKIN' THROUGH THE WINDOWS
   (The Jackson 5)
6. UNDERSTANDING
   (Bobby Womack)
7. IT'S JUST BEGUN
   (Jimmy Castor Bunch)
8. I WROTE A SIMPLE SONG
   (Billy Preston)
9. SHAFT
   (Isaac Hayes)
10. GOIN' EAST
    (Billy Paul)

JAZZ ALBUMS

1. WHITE RABBIT
   (George Benson)
2. FUNK INC.
   (Funk Inc.)
3. SHADES OF GREEN
   (Grant Green)
4. INTENSITY
   (Charles Earland)
5. CRUSADERS 1
   (Crusaders)
6. THE GREAT CONCERT
   (Charles Mingus)
7. ETHIOPIAN NIGHTS
   (Donald Byrd)
8. MISSISSIPPI GAMBLER
   (Herbie Mann)
9. BLUE MOSES
   (Randy Weston)
10. RAMADAN
    (Jason Lindh)

COUNTRY SINGLES

1. LOVING YOU COULD NEVER BE BETTER
   (George Jones)
2. LISTEN TO A COUNTRY SONG
   (Lynn Anderson)
3. WOMAN (SENSUOUS WOMAN)
   (Don Gibson)
4. REACH OUT YOUR HAND
   (Tammy Wynette)
5. BORROWED ANGEL
   (Mel Street)
6. SOFT, SWEET AND WARM
   (David Houston)
7. IT'S GONNA TAKE A LITTLE BIT LONGER
   (Charley Pride)
8. BLESS YOUR HEART
   (Freddie Hart)
9. DELTA DAWN
   (Tanya Tucker)
10. A SEED BEFORE THE ROSE
    (Tommy Overstreet)

COUNTRY ALBUMS

1. THE REAL McCOY
   (Charlie McCoy)
2. THAT'S WHY I LOVE YOU LIKE I DO
   (Sonny James)
3. GREATEST HITS, VOL. 2
   (Hank Williams Jr.)
4. BEST OF JERRY REED
   (Jerry Reed)
5. A THING CALLED LOVE
   (Johnny Cash)
6. SOMEONE TO GIVE MY LOVE TO
   (Johnny Paycheck)

7. BEST OF CHARLEY PRIDE, VOL. 2
   (Charley Pride)
8. BLESS YOUR HEART
   (Freddie Hart)
9. THIS IS JERRY WALLACE
   (Jerry Wallace)
10. TO GET TO YOU
    (Jerry Wallace)

AUGUST 19, 1972

POP SINGLES

1. ALONE AGAIN (NATURALLY)
   (Gilbert O'Sullivan)
2. BRANDY
   (The Looking Glass)
3. LONG COOL WOMAN
   (The Hollies)
4. IF LOVING YOU IS WRONG
   (Luther Ingram)
5. I'M STILL IN LOVE WITH YOU
   (Al Green)
6. DADDY DON'T YOU WALK SO FAST
   (Wayne Newton)
7. WHERE IS THE LOVE
   (Roberta Flack and Donny Hathaway)
8. HOW DO YOU DO
   (Mouth and MacNeal)
9. THE HAPPIEST GIRL IN THE WHOLE U.S.A.
   (Donna Fargo)
10. HOLD HER TIGHT
    (The Osmonds)

POP ALBUMS

1. HONKY CHATEAU
   (Elton John)
2. SCHOOL'S OUT
   (Alice Cooper)
3. CHICAGO V
   (Chicago)
4. SIMON AND GARFUNKEL'S GREATEST HITS
   (Simon and Garfunkel)
5. A SONG FOR YOU
   (The Carpenters)
6. EXILE ON MAIN STREET
   (The Rolling Stones)
7. MOODS
   (Neil Diamond)
8. BIG BAMBU
   (Cheech and Chong)
9. ELVIS RECORDED AT MADISON SQUARE
   GARDEN
   (Elvis Presley)
10. STILL BILL
    (Bill Withers)

BLACK SINGLES

1. WHERE IS THE LOVE
   (Roberta Flack and Donny Hathaway)
2. I MISS YOU
   (Harold Melvin and the Blue Notes)
3. I'M STILL IN LOVE WITH YOU
   (Al Green)
4. I WANNA BE WHERE YOU ARE
   (Michael Jackson)
5. BACK STABBERS
   (The O'Jays)
6. TOO LATE TO TURN BACK NOW
   (Cornelius Brothers and Sister Rose)
7. THE COLDEST DAYS OF MY LIFE
   (The Chi-Lites)
8. POWER OF LOVE
   (Joe Simon)
9. IF LOVING YOU IS WRONG
   (Luther Ingram)
10. POP THAT THANG
    (Isley Brothers)

BLACK ALBUMS

1. STILL BILL
   (Bill Withers)
2. AMAZING GRACE
   (Aretha Franklin)
3. A LONELY MAN
   (The Chi-Lites)
4. UNDERSTANDING
   (Bobby Womack)
5. MUSIC OF MY MIND
   (Stevie Wonder)
6. TWO SIDES OF LAURA LEE
   (Laura Lee)
7. LOOKIN' THROUGH THE WINDOWS
   (The Jackson 5)
8. IT'S JUST BEGUN
   (Jimmy Castor Bunch)
9. I WROTE A SIMPLE SONG
   (Billy Preston)
10. BITTER SWEET
    (Main Ingredient)

JAZZ ALBUMS

1. WHITE RABBIT
   (George Benson)
2. FUNK INC.
   (Funk Inc.)
3. SHADES OF GREEN
   (Grant Green)
4. INTENSITY
   (Charles Earland)
5. CRUSADERS 1
   (Crusaders)
6. BLUE MOSES
   (Randy Weston)
7. ETHIOPIAN NIGHTS
   (Donald Byrd)
8. MISSISSIPPI GAMBLER
   (Herbie Mann)
9. THE GREAT CONCERT
   (Charles Mingus)
10. RAMADAN
    (Jason Lindh)

COUNTRY SINGLES

1. WOMAN (SENSUOUS WOMAN)
   (Don Gibson)
2. LISTEN TO A COUNTRY SONG
   (Lynn Anderson)
3. BLESS YOUR HEART
   (Freddie Hart)
4. LOVING YOU COULD NEVER BE BETTER
   (George Jones)
5. SOFT, SWEET AND WARM
   (David Houston)
6. THERE'S A PARTY GOING ON
   (Jody Miller)
7. HERE I AM AGAIN
   (Loretta Lynn)
8. BORROWED ANGEL
   (Mel Street)
9. IT'S GONNA TAKE A LITTLE LONGER
   (Charley Pride)
10. I'VE GOT TO HAVE YOU
    (Sammi Stewart)

COUNTRY ALBUMS

1. THE REAL McCOY
   (Charlie McCoy)
2. BEST OF JERRY REED
   (Jerry Reed)
3. GREATEST HITS, VOL. 2
   (Hank Williams Jr.)
4. THAT'S WHY I LOVE YOU LIKE I DO
   (Sonny James)
5. THE HAPPIEST GIRL IN THE WHOLE U.S.A.
   (Donna Fargo)
6. SOMEONE TO GIVE MY LOVE TO
   (Johnny Paycheck)

7. BLESS YOUR HEART
   (Freddie Hart)
8. TO GET TO YOU
   (Jerry Wallace)
9. BEST OF CHARLEY PRIDE, VOL. 2
   (Charley Pride)
10. GREATEST HITS, VOL. 1
    (Conway Twitty)

AUGUST 26, 1972

POP SINGLES

1. ALONE AGAIN (NATURALLY)
   (Gilbert O'Sullivan)
2. LONG COOL WOMAN
   (The Hollies)
3. I'M STILL IN LOVE WITH YOU
   (Al Green)
4. BRANDY
   (The Looking Glass)
5. IF LOVING YOU IS WRONG
   (Luther Ingram)
6. HOLD YOUR HEAD UP
   (Argent)
7. HAPPIEST GIRL IN THE WHOLE U.S.A.
   (Donna Fargo)
8. DADDY DON'T YOU WALK SO FAST
   (Wayne Newton)
9. GOODBYE TO LOVE
   (Roberta Flack and Donny Hathaway)
10. YOU DON'T MESS AROUND WITH JIM
    (Jim Croce)

POP ALBUMS

1. CHICAGO V
   (Chicago)
2. SIMON AND GARFUNKEL'S GREATEST HITS
   (Simon and Garfunkel)
3. A SONG FOR YOU
   (The Carpenters)
4. HONKY CHATEAU
   (Elton John)
5. SCHOOL'S OUT
   (Alice Cooper)
6. BIB BAMBU
   (Cheech and Chong)
7. MOODS
   (Neil Diamond)
8. CARLOS SANTANA AND BUDDY MILES
   LIVE
   (Carlos Santana and Buddy Miles)
9. ELVIS RECORDED AT MADISON SQUARE
   GARDEN
   (Elvis Presley)
10. CARNEY
    (Leon Russell)

BLACK SINGLES

1. I'M STILL IN LOVE WITH YOU
   (Al Green)
2. I MISS YOU
   (Harold Melvin and the Blue Notes)
3. WHERE IS THE LOVE
   (Roberta Flack and Donny Hathaway)
4. BACK STABBERS
   (The O'Jays)
5. POWER OF LOVE
   (Joe Simon)
6. THE COLDEST DAYS OF MY LIFE
   (The Chi-Lites)
7. TOO LATE TO TURN BACK NOW
   (Cornelius Brothers and Sister Rose)
8. THINK
   (Lynn Collins)
9. THIS WORLD
   (The Staple Singers)
10. I WANNA BE WHERE YOU ARE
    (Michael Jackson)

BLACK ALBUMS

1. STILL BILL
   (Bill Withers)
2. AMAZING GRACE
   (Aretha Franklin)
3. UNDERSTANDING
   (Bobby Womack)
4. TWO SIDES OF LAURA LEE
   (Laura Lee)
5. A LONELY MAN
   (The Chi-Lites)
6. BITTER SWEET
   (Main Ingredient)
7. MUSIC OF MY MIND
   (Stevie Wonder)
8. IT'S JUST BEGUN
   (Jimmy Castor Bunch)
9. LOOKIN' THROUGH THE WINDOWS
   (The Jackson 5)
10. CARLOS SANTANA AND BUDDY MILES LIVE
    (Carlos Santana and Buddy Miles)

JAZZ ALBUMS

1. FUNK INC.
   (Funk Inc.)
2. SHADES OF GREEN
   (Grant Green)
3. WHITE RABBIT
   (George Benson)
4. INTENSITY
   (Charles Earland)
5. BLUE MOSES
   (Randy Weston)
6. ETHIOPIAN NIGHTS
   (Donald Byrd)
7. MISSISSIPPI GAMBLER
   (Herbie Mann)
8. CRUSADERS 1
   (Crusaders)
9. RAMADAN
   (Jason Lindh)
10. I SING THE BODY ELECTRIC
    (Weather Report)

COUNTRY SINGLES

1. BLESS YOUR HEART
   (Freddie Hart)
2. HERE I AM AGAIN
   (Loretta Lynn)
3. WOMAN (SENSUOUS WOMAN)
   (Don Gibson)
4. THERE'S A PARTY GOING ON
   (Jody Miller)
5. IF YOU LEAVE ME TONIGHT I'LL CRY
   (Jerry Wallace)
6. I'M GONNA KNOCK ON YOUR DOOR
   (Billy "Cash" Craddock)
7. SOFT, SWEET AND WARM
   (David Houston)
8. LISTEN TO A COUNTRY SONG
   (Lynn Anderson)
9. I'VE GOT TO HAVE YOU
   (Sammi Stewart)
10. IF YOU TOUCH ME
    (Joe Stampley)

COUNTRY ALBUMS

1. THE HAPPIEST GIRL IN THE WHOLE U.S.A.
   (Donna Fargo)
2. BEST OF JERRY REED
   (Jerry Reed)
3. THE REAL McCOY
   (Charlie McCoy)
4. BLESS YOUR HEART
   (Freddie Hart)
5. TO GET TO YOU
   (Jerry Wallace)

6. GREATEST HITS, VOL. 2
   (Hank Williams Jr.)
7. THAT'S WHY I LOVE YOU LIKE I DO
   (Sonny James)
8. GREATEST HITS, VOL. 1
   (Conway Twitty)
9. BEST OF CHARLEY PRIDE, VOL. 2
   (Charley Pride)
10. ASHES OF LOVE
    (Dickey Lee)

SEPTEMBER 2, 1972

POP SINGLES

1. ALONE AGAIN (NATURALLY)
   (Gilbert O'Sullivan)
2. LONG COOL WOMAN
   (The Hollies)
3. I'M STILL IN LOVE WITH YOU
   (Al Green)
4. BRANDY
   (The Looking Glass)
5. HOLD YOUR HEAD UP
   (Argent)
6. GOODBYE TO LOVE
   (The Carpenters)
7. THE HAPPIEST GIRL IN THE WHOLE U.S.A.
   (Donna Fargo)
8. YOU DON'T MESS AROUND WITH JIM
   (Jim Croce)
9. BABY DON'T GET HOOKED ON ME
   (Mac Davis)
10. ROCK AND ROLL, PART 2
    (Gary Glitter)

POP ALBUMS

1. CHICAGO V
   (Chicago)
2. SIMON AND GARFUNKEL'S GREATEST HITS
   (Simon and Garfunkel)
3. BIG BAMBU
   (Cheech and Chong)
4. HONKY CHATEAU
   (Elton John)
5. A SONG FOR YOU
   (The Carpenters)
6. MOODS
   (Neil Diamond)
7. CARLOS SANTANA AND BUDDY MILES LIVE
   (Carlos Santana and Buddy Miles)
8. ELVIS RECORDED AT MADISON SQUARE GARDEN
   (Elvis Presley)
9. CARNEY
   (Leon Russell)
10. TRILOGY
    (Emerson, Lake and Palmer)

BLACK SINGLES

1. BACK STABBERS
   (The O'Jays)
2. I'M STILL IN LOVE WITH YOU
   (Al Green)
3. POWER OF LOVE
   (Joe Simon)
4. I MISS YOU
   (Harold Melvin and the Blue Notes)
5. THE COLDEST DAYS OF MY LIFE
   (The Chi-Lites)
6. THIS WORLD
   (The Staple Singers)
7. THINK
   (Lynn Collins)
8. MY MAN, A SWEET MAN
   (Millie Jackson)

9. EVERYBODY PLAYS THE FOOL
   (Main Ingredient)
10. WHERE IS THE LOVE
    (Roberta Flack and Donny Hathaway)

BLACK ALBUMS

1. STILL BILL
   (Bill Withers)
2. AMAZING GRACE
   (Aretha Franklin)
3. UNDERSTANDING
   (Bobby Womack)
4. TWO SIDES OF LAURA LEE
   (Laura Lee)
5. BITTER SWEET
   (Main Ingredient)
6. A LONELY MAN
   (The Chi-Lites)
7. CARLOS SANTANA AND BUDDY MILES LIVE
   (Carlos Santana and Buddy Miles)
8. THERE IT IS
   (James Brown)
9. IT'S JUST BEGUN
   (Jimmy Castor Bunch)
10. MUSIC OF MY MIND
    (Stevie Wonder)

JAZZ ALBUMS

1. FUNK INC.
   (Funk Inc.)
2. SHADES OF GREEN
   (Grant Green)
3. INTENSITY
   (Charles Earland)
4. ETHIOPIAN NIGHTS
   (Donald Byrd)
5. BLUE MOSES
   (Randy Weston)
6. RAMADAN
   (Jason Lindh)
7. MISSISSIPPI GAMBLER
   (Herbie Mann)
8. WHITE RABBIT
   (George Benson)
9. I SING THE BODY ELECTRIC
   (Weather Report)
10. UPENDO MI PAMOJA
    (Ramsey Lewis Trio)

COUNTRY SINGLES

1. HERE I AM AGAIN
   (Loretta Lynn)
2. IF YOU LEAVE ME TONIGHT, I'LL CRY
   (Jerry Wallace)
3. BLESS YOUR HEART
   (Freddie Hart)
4. THERE'S A PARTY GOING ON
   (Jody Miller)
5. I'M GONNA KNOCK ON YOUR DOOR
   (Billy "Crash" Craddock)
6. WHEN THE SNOW IS ON THE ROSES
   (Sonny James)
7. THE CEREMONY
   (Tammy Wynette and George Jones)
8. IF YOU TOUCH ME
   (Joe Stampley)
9. I'VE GOT TO HAVE YOU
   (Sammi Stewart)
10. WOMAN (SENSUOUS WOMAN)
    (Don Gibson)

COUNTRY ALBUMS

1. THE HAPPIEST GIRL IN THE WHOLE U.S.A.
   (Donna Fargo)
2. TO GET TO YOU
   (Jerry Wallace)

3. BLESS YOUR HEART
   (Freddie Hart)
4. BEST OF JERRY REED
   (Jerry Reed)
5. THE REAL McCOY
   (Charlie McCoy)
6. GREATEST HITS, VOL. 2
   (Hank Williams Jr.)
7. GREATEST HITS, VOL. 1
   (Conway Twitty)
8. THE LONESOMEST LONESOME
   (Ray Price)
9. CAB DRIVER
   (Hank Thompson)
10. ASHES OF LOVE
    (Dickey Lee)

SEPTEMBER 9, 1972

POP SINGLES

1. LONG COOL WOMAN
   (The Hollies)
2. I'M STILL IN LOVE WITH YOU
   (Al Green)
3. ALONE AGAIN (NATURALLY)
   (Gilbert O'Sullivan)
4. HOLD YOUR HEAD UP
   (Argent)
5. BABY DON'T GET HOOKED ON ME
   (Mac Davis)
6. GOODBYE TO LOVE
   (The Carpenters)
7. YOU DON'T MESS AROUND WITH JIM
   (Joe Croce)
8. ROCK AND ROLL, PART 2
   (Gary Glitter)
9. THE GUITAR MAN
   (Bread)
10. BACK STABBERS
    (The O'Jays)

POP ALBUMS

1. CHICAGO V
   (Chicago)
2. BIG BAMBU
   (Cheech and Chong)
3. NEVER A DULL MOMENT
   (Rod Stewart)
4. MOODS
   (Neil Diamond)
5. SIMON AND GARFUNKEL'S GREATEST HITS
   (Simon and Garfunkel)
6. CARLOS SANTANA AND BUDDY MILES
   LIVE
   (Carlos Santana and Buddy Miles)
7. CARNEY
   (Leon Russell)
8. ELVIS RECORDED AT MADISON SQUARE
   GARDEN
   (Elvis Presley)
9. TRILOGY
   (Emerson, Lake and Palmer)
10. SON OF SCHMILSSON
    (Harry Nilsson)

BLACK SINGLES

1. POWER OF LOVE
   (Joe Simon)
2. BACK STABBERS
   (The O'Jays)
3. I'M STILL IN LOVE WITH YOU
   (Al Green)
4. EVERYBODY PLAYS THE FOOL
   (Main Ingredient)
5. THINK
   (Lynn Collins)
6. THIS WORLD
   (The Staple Singers)

7. MY MAN, A SWEET MAN
   (Millie Jackson)
8. GOOD FOOT, PART 1
   (James Brown)
9. I MISS YOU
   (Harold Melvin and the Blue Notes)
10. STARTING ALL OVER AGAIN
    (Mel and Tim)

BLACK ALBUMS

1. AMAZING GRACE
   (Aretha Franklin)
2. UNDERSTANDING
   (Bobby Womack)
3. STILL BILL
   (Bill Withers)
4. TWO SIDES OF LAURA LEE
   (Laura Lee)
5. BITTER SWEET
   (Main Ingredient)
6. CARLOS SANTANA AND BUDDY MILES
   LIVE
   (Carlos Santana and Buddy Miles)
7. THERE IT IS
   (James Brown)
8. SUPERFLY
   (Curtis Mayfield)
9. CANNONBALL ADDERLEY PRESENTS SOUL
   ZODIAC
   (Cannonball Adderley)
10. IT'S JUST BEGUN
    (Jimmy Castor Bunch)

JAZZ ALBUMS

1. FUNK INC.
   (Funk Inc.)
2. INTENSITY
   (Charles Earland)
3. ETHIOPIAN NIGHTS
   (Donald Byrd)
4. BLUE MOSES
   (Randy Weston)
5. RAMADAN
   (Jason Lindh)
6. MISSISSIPPI GAMBLER
   (Herbie Mann)
7. SHADES OF GREEN
   (Grant Green)
8. I SING THE BODY ELECTRIC
   (Weather Report)
9. UPENDO MI PAMOJA
   (Ramsey Lewis)
10. WHITE RABBIT
    (George Benson)

COUNTRY SINGLES

1. IF YOU LEAVE ME TONIGHT, I'LL CRY
   (Jerry Wallace)
2. HERE I AM AGAIN
   (Loretta Lynn)
3. WHEN THE SNOW IS ON THE ROSES
   (Sonny James)
4. I'M GONNA KNOCK ON YOUR DOOR
   (Billy "Crash" Craddock)
5. I CAN'T STOP LOVING YOU
   (Conway Twitty)
6. THE CEREMONY
   (Tammy Wynette and George Jones)
7. IF YOU TOUCH ME
   (Joe Stampley)
8. BLESS YOUR HEART
   (Freddie Hart)
9. THERE'S A PARTY GOING ON
   (Jody Miller)
10. WOMAN (SENSUOUS WOMAN)
    (Don Gibson)

COUNTRY ALBUMS

1. THE HAPPIEST GIRL IN THE WHOLE U.S.A.
   (Donna Fargo)
2. TO GET TO YOU
   (Jerry Wallace)
3. BLESS YOUR HEART
   (Freddie Hart)
4. THE LONESOMEST LONESOME
   (Ray Price)
5. GREATEST HITS, VOL. 1
   (Conway Twitty)
6. BEST OF JERRY REED
   (Jerry Reed)
7. A SUNSHINY DAY
   (Charley Pride)
8. CAB DRIVER
   (Hank Thompson)
9. THE REAL McCOY
   (Charlie McCoy)
10. ASHES OF LOVE
    (Dickey Lee)

SEPTEMBER 16, 1972

POP SINGLES

1. I'M STILL IN LOVE WITH YOU
   (Al Green)
2. LONG COOL WOMAN
   (The Hollies)
3. BACK STABBERS
   (The O'Jays)
4. BABY DON'T GET HOOKED ON ME
   (Mac Davis)
5. ALONE AGAIN (NATURALLY)
   (Gilbert O'Sullivan)
6. ROCK AND ROLL, PART 2
   (Gary Glitter)
7. YOU DON'T MESS AROUND WITH JIM
   (Jim Croce)
8. BLACK AND WHITE
   (Three Dog Night)
9. THE GUITAR MAN
   (Bread)
10. SATURDAY IN THE PARK
    (Chicago)

POP ALBUMS

1. NEVER A DULL MOMENT
   (Rod Stewart)
2. BIG BAMBU
   (Cheech and Chong)
3. CHICAGO V
   (Chicago)
4. MOODS
   (Neil Diamond)
5. CARNEY
   (Leon Russell)
6. CARLOS SANTANA AND BUDDY MILES
   LIVE
   (Carlos Santana and Buddy Miles)
7. TRILOGY
   (Emerson, Lake and Palmer)
8. SEVEN SEPARATE FOOLS
   (Three Dog Night)
9. HIMSELF
   (Gilbert O'Sullivan)
10. SUPERFLY
    (Curtis Mayfield)

BLACK SINGLES

1. POWER OF LOVE
   (Joe Simon)
2. EVERYBODY PLAYS THE FOOL
   (Main Ingredient)

3. MY MAN, A SWEET MAN
   (Millie Jackson)
4. THINK
   (Lynn Collins)
5. GOOD FOOT, PART 1
   (James Brown)
6. THIS WORLD
   (The Staple Singers)
7. BACK STABBERS
   (The O'Jays)
8. STARTING ALL OVER AGAIN
   (Mel and Tim)
9. I'M STILL IN LOVE WITH YOU
   (Al Green)
10. I'LL BE AROUND
    (Spinners)

JAZZ ALBUMS

1. INTENSITY
   (Charles Earland)
2. ETHIOPIAN NIGHTS
   (Donald Byrd)
3. BLUE ROSES
   (Randy Weston)
4. FUNK INC.
   (Funk Inc.)
5. RAMADAN
   (Jason Lindh)
6. MISSISSIPPI GAMBLER
   (Herbie Mann)
7. UPENDO MI PAMOJA
   (Ramsey Lewis Trio)
8. I SING THE BODY ELECTRIC
   (Weather Report)
9. ATTICA BLUES
   (Archie Shepp)
10. SHADES OF GREEN
    (Grant Green)

COUNTRY SINGLES

1. WHEN THE SNOW IS ON THE ROSES
   (Sonny James)
2. IF YOU LEAVE ME TONIGHT, I'LL CRY
   (Jerry Wallace)
3. I CAN'T STOP LOVIN' YOU
   (Conway Twitty)
4. I'M GONNA KNOCK ON YOUR DOOR
   (Billy "Crash" Craddock)
5. THE CEREMONY
   (Tammy Wynette and George Jones)
6. IF YOU TOUCH ME
   (Joe Stampley)
7. HERE I AM AGAIN
   (Loretta Lynn)
8. IF IT AIN'T LOVE
   (Connie Smith)
9. THIS LITTLE GIRL OF MINE
   (Faron Young)
10. WHISKEY RIVER
    (Johnny Bush)

COUNTRY ALBUMS

1. THE HAPPIEST GIRL IN THE WHOLE U.S.A.
   (Donna Fargo)
2. TO GET TO YOU
   (Jerry Wallace)
3. A SUNSHINY DAY
   (Charley Pride)
4. THE LONESOMEST LONESOME
   (Ray Price)
5. GREATEST HITS, VOL. 1
   (Conway Twitty)
6. BLESS YOUR HEART
   (Freddie Hart)
7. BEST OF JERRY REED
   (Jerry Reed)
8. CAB DRIVER
   (Hank Thompson)
9. THE REAL McCOY
   (Charlie McCoy)
10. ROY CLARK COUNTRY
    (Roy Clark)

SEPTEMBER 23, 1972

POP SINGLES

1. BABY DON'T GET HOOKED ON ME
   (Mac Davis)
2. BACK STABBERS
   (The O'Jays)
3. I'M STILL IN LOVE WITH YOU
   (Al Green)
4. BLACK AND WHITE
   (Three Dog Night)
5. SATURDAY IN THE PARK
   (Chicago)
6. ROCK AND ROLL, PART 2
   (Gary Glitter)
7. HONKY CAT
   (Elton John)
8. POWER OF LOVE
   (Joe Simon)
9. GO ALL THE WAY
   (The Raspberries)
10. EVERYBODY PLAYS THE FOOL
    (Main Ingredient)

POP ALBUMS

1. NEVER A DULL MOMENT
   (Rod Stewart)
2. BIG BAMBU
   (Cheech and Chong)
3. CARNEY
   (Leon Russell)
4. TRILOGY
   (Emerson, Lake and Palmer)
5. CHICAGO V
   (Chicago)
6. SEVEN SEPARATE FOOLS
   (Three Dog Night)
7. MOODS
   (Neil Diamond)
8. HIMSELF
   (Gilbert O'Sullivan)
9. SUPERFLY
   (Curtis Mayfield)
10. CARLOS SANTANA AND BUDDY MILES LIVE
    (Carlos Santana and Buddy Miles)

BLACK SINGLES

1. EVERYBODY PLAYS THE FOOL
   (Main Ingredient)
2. GOOD FOOT, PART 1
   (James Brown)
3. MY MAN, A SWEET MAN
   (Millie Jackson)
4. THINK
   (Lynn Collins)
5. POWER OF LOVE
   (Joe Simpson)
6. I'LL BE AROUND
   (Spinners)
7. STARTING ALL OVER AGAIN
   (Mel and Tim)
8. FREDDIE'S DEAD
   (Curtis Mayfield)
9. MY DING-A-LING
   (Chuck Berry)
10. THIS WORLD
    (The Staple Singers)

JAZZ ALBUMS

1. ETHIOPIAN NIGHTS
   (Donald Byrd)
2. BLUE MOSES
   (Randy Weston)
3. RAMADAN
   (Jason Lindh)

4. INTENSITY
   (Charles Earland)
5. MISSISSIPPI GAMBLER
   (Herbie Mann)
6. UPENDO MI PAMOJA
   (Ramsey Lewis Trio)
7. ATTICA BLUES
   (Archie Shepp)
8. I SING THE BODY ELECTRIC
   (Weather Report)
9. HEATING SYSTEM
   (Jack McDuff)
10. FLUTE-IN
    (Bobbi Humphrey)

COUNTRY SINGLES

1. I CAN'T STOP LOVING YOU
   (Conway Twitty)
2. WHEN THE SNOW IS ON THE ROSES
   (Sonny James)
3. IF YOU LEAVE ME TONIGHT, I'LL CRY
   (Jerry Wallace)
4. THE CEREMONY
   (Tammy Wynette and George Jones)
5. IF IT AIN'T LOVE
   (Connie Smith)
6. IF YOU TOUCH ME
   (Joe Stampley)
7. THIS LITTLE GIRL OF MINE
   (Faron Young)
8. I'M GONNA KNOCK ON YOUR DOOR
   (Billy "Crash" Craddock)
9. WHISKEY RIVER
   (Johnny Bush)
10. I AIN'T NEVER
    (Mel Tillis)

COUNTRY ALBUMS

1. A SUNSHINY DAY
   (Charley Pride)
2. THE HAPPIEST GIRL IN THE WHOLE U.S.A.
   (Donna Fargo)
3. TO GET TO YOU
   (Jerry Wallace)
4. THE LONESOMEST LONESOME
   (Ray Price)
5. BLESS YOUR HEART
   (Freddie Hart)
6. GREATEST HITS, VOL. 1
   (Conway Twitty)
7. BEST OF JERRY REED
   (Jerry Reed)
8. ROY CLARK COUNTRY
   (Roy Clark)
9. AMERICA
   (Johnny Cash)
10. LISTEN TO A COUNTRY SONG
    (Lynn Anderson)

SEPTEMBER 30, 1972

POP SINGLES

1. BLACK AND WHITE
   (Three Dog Night)
2. BACK STABBERS
   (The O'Jays)
3. BABY DON'T GET HOOKED ON ME
   (Mac Davis)
4. SATURDAY IN THE PARK
   (Chicago)
5. EVERYBODY PLAYS THE FOOL
   (Main Ingredient)
6. POWER OF LOVE
   (Joe Simon)
7. HONKY CAT
   (Elton John)
8. GO ALL THE WAY
   (The Raspberries)

9. RUN TO ME
   (The Bee Gees)
10. POPCORN
    (Hot Butter)

POP ALBUMS

1. NEVER A DULL MOMENT
   (Rod Stewart)
2. BIG BAMBU
   (Cheech and Chong)
3. CARNEY
   (Leon Russell)
4. TRILOGY
   (Emerson, Lake and Palmer)
5. CHICAGO V
   (Chicago)
6. SEVEN SEPARATE FOOLS
   (Three Dog Night)
7. HIMSELF
   (Gilbert O'Sullivan)
8. SUPERFLY
   (Curtis Mayfield)
9. LONG JOHN SILVER
   (The Jefferson Airplane)
10. MOODS
    (Neil Diamond)

BLACK SINGLES

1. GOOD FOOT, PART 1
   (James Brown)
2. MY DING-A-LING
   (Chuck Berry)
3. I'LL BE AROUND
   (Spinners)
4. THINK
   (Lynn Collins)
5. FREDDIE'S DEAD
   (Curtis Mayfield)
6. EVERYBODY PLAYS THE FOOL
   (Main Ingredient)
7. USE ME
   (Bill Withers)
8. BEN
   (Michael Jackson)
9. MY MAN, A SWEET MAN
   (Millie Jackson)
10. (WIN, PLACE OR SHOW) SHE'S A WINNER
    (Intruders)

JAZZ ALBUMS

1. ETHIOPIAN NIGHTS
   (Donald Byrd)
2. BLUE MOSES
   (Randy Weston)
3. RAMADAN
   (Jason Lindh)
4. MISSISSIPPI GAMBLER
   (Herbie Mann)
5. UPENDO MI PAMOJA
   (Ramsey Lewis Trio)
6. I SING THE BODY ELECTRIC
   (Weather Report)
7. ATTICA BLUES
   (Archie Shepp)
8. HEATING SYSTEM
   (Jack McDuff)
9. THE AGE OF STEAM
   (Jerry Milligan)
10. FLUTE-IN
    (Bobbi Humphrey)

COUNTRY SINGLES

1. I AIN'T NEVER
   (Mel Tillis)
2. I CAN'T STOP LOVING YOU
   (Conway Twitty)
3. IF IT AIN'T LOVE
   (Connie Smith)

4. IF YOU LEAVE ME TONIGHT I'LL CRY
   (Jerry Wallace)
5. THIS LITTLE GIRL OF MINE
   (Faron Young)
6. ONEY
   (Johnny Cash)
7. MISSING YOU
   (Jim Reeves)
8. WHEN THE SNOW IS ON THE ROSES
   (Sonny James)
9. WHISKEY RIVER
   (Johnny Bush)
10. THE CLASS OF '57
    (The Statler Brothers)

COUNTRY ALBUMS

1. A SUNSHINY DAY
   (Charley Pride)
2. THE HAPPIEST GIRL IN THE WHOLE U.S.A.
   (Donna Fargo)
3. THE LONESOMEST LONESOME
   (Ray Price)
4. TO GET TO YOU
   (Jerry Wallace)
5. AMERICA
   (Johnny Cash)
6. LISTEN TO A COUNTRY SONG
   (Lynn Anderson)
7. BLESS YOUR HEART
   (Freddie Hart)
8. ROY CLARK COUNTRY
   (Roy Clark)
9. ME AND THE FIRST LADY
   (George Jones and Tammy Wynette)
10. GREATEST HITS, VOL. 1
    (Conway Twitty)

OCTOBER 7, 1972

POP SINGLES

1. BLACK AND WHITE
   (Three Dog Night)
2. BACK STABBERS
   (The O'Jays)
3. SATURDAY IN THE PARK
   (Chicago)
4. EVERYBODY PLAYS THE FOOL
   (Main Ingredient)
5. MY DING-A-LING
   (Chuck Berry)
6. POWER OF LOVE
   (Joe Simon)
7. GO ALL THE WAY
   (The Raspberries)
8. BEN
   (Michael Jackson)
9. POPCORN
   (Hot Butter)
10. RUN TO ME
    (The Bee Gees)

POP ALBUMS

1. NEVER A DULL MOMENT
   (Rod Stewart)
2. BIG BAMBU
   (Cheech and Chong)
3. CARNEY
   (Leon Russell)
4. SUPERFLY
   (Curtis Mayfield)
5. SEVEN SEPARATE FOOLS
   (Three Dog Night)
6. TRILOGY
   (Emerson, Lake and Palmer)
7. HIMSELF
   (Gilbert O'Sullivan)
8. CHICAGO V
   (Chicago)

9. LONG JOHN SILVER
   (The Jefferson Airplane)
10. ALL DIRECTIONS
    (Temptations)

BLACK SINGLES

1. MY DING-A-LING
   (Chuck Berry)
2. GOOD FOOT, PART 1
   (James Brown)
3. I'LL BE AROUND
   (Spinners)
4. FREDDIE'S DEAD
   (Curtis Mayfield)
5. USE ME
   (Bill Withers)
6. BEN
   (Michael Jackson)
7. THINK
   (Lynn Collins)
8. (WIN, PLACE OR SHOW) SHE'S A WINNER
   (Intruders)
9. WOMAN DON'T GO ASTRAY
   (King Floyd)
10. OPEN HOUSE AT MY HOUSE
    (Little Johnnie Taylor)

JAZZ ALBUMS

1. BLUE MOSES
   (Randy Weston)
2. RAMADAN
   (Jason Lindh)
3. MISSISSIPPI GAMBLER
   (Herbie Mann)
4. I SING THE BODY ELECTRIC
   (Weather Report)
5. UPENDO MI PAMOJA
   (Ramsey Lewis Trio)
6. ATTICA BLUES
   (Archie Shepp)
7. HEATING SYSTEM
   (Jack McDuff)
8. ETHIOPIAN NIGHTS
   (Donald Byrd)
9. THE AGE OF STEAM
   (Gerry Milligan)
10. FLUTE-IN
    (Bobbi Humphrey)

COUNTRY SINGLES

1. ONEY
   (Johnny Cash)
2. I AIN'T NEVER
   (Mel Tillis)
3. IF IT AIN'T LOVE
   (Connie Smith)
4. THIS LITTLE GIRL OF MINE
   (Faron Young)
5. FUNNY FACE
   (Donna Fargo)
6. WHISKEY RIVER
   (Johnny Bush)
7. MISSING YOU
   (Jim Reeve)
8. I CAN'T STOP LOVING YOU
   (Conway Twitty)
9. THE CLASS OF '57
   (The Statler Brothers)
10. BABY DON'T GET HOOKED ON ME
    (Mac Davis)

COUNTRY ALBUMS

1. A SUNSHINY DAY
   (Charley Pride)
2. THE HAPPIEST GIRL IN THE WHOLE U.S.A.
   (Donna Fargo)
3. AMERICA
   (Johnny Cash)

4. LISTEN TO A COUNTRY SONG
   (Lynn Anderson)
5. THE LONESOMEST LONESOME
   (Ray Price)
6. TO GET TO YOU
   (Jerry Wallace)
7. ME AND THE FIRST LADY
   (George Jones and Tammy Wynette)
8. ROY CLARK COUNTRY
   (Roy Clark)
9. WHEN THE SNOW IS ON THE ROSES
   (Sonny James)
10. RAY PRICE'S ALL TIME GREATEST HITS
    (Ray Price)

OCTOBER 14, 1972

POP SINGLES

1. EVERYBODY PLAYS THE FOOL
   (Main Ingredient)
2. BACK STABBERS
   (The O'Jays)
3. MY DING-A-LING
   (Chuck Berry)
4. GO ALL THE WAY
   (The Raspberries)
5. BEN
   (Michael Jackson)
6. BLACK AND WHITE
   (Three Dog Night)
7. USE ME
   (Bill Withers)
8. POPCORN
   (Hot Butter)
9. GOOD FOOT, PART 1
   (James Brown)
10. NIGHTS IN WHITE SATIN
    (The Moody Blues)

POP ALBUMS

1. NEVER A DULL MOMENT
   (Rod Stewart)
2. CARNEY
   (Leon Russell)
3. SUPERFLY
   (Curtis Mayfield)
4. SEVEN SEPARATE FOOLS
   (Three Dog Night)
5. BIG BAMBU
   (Cheech and Chong)
6. ALL DIRECTIONS
   (Temptations)
7. HIMSELF
   (Gilbert O'Sullivan)
8. CHICAGO V
   (Chicago)
9. LONG JOHN SILVER
   (The Jefferson Airplane)
10. THE LONDON CHUCK BERRY SESSIONS
    (Chuck Berry)

BLACK SINGLES

1. MY DING-A-LING
   (Chuck Berry)
2. I'LL BE AROUND
   (Spinners)
3. FREDDIE'S DEAD
   (Curtis Mayfield)
4. USE ME
   (Bill Withers)
5. BEN
   (Michael Jackson)
6. GOOD FOOT, PART 1
   (James Brown)
7. USE ME
   (Bill Withers)
8. WOMAN DON'T GO ASTRAY
   (King Floyd)

9. HONEY I STILL LOVE YOU
   (Mark IV)
10. OPEN HOUSE AT MY HOUSE
    (Little Johnnie Taylor)

JAZZ ALBUMS

1. BLUE MOSES
   (Randy Weston)
2. MISSISSIPPI GAMBLER
   (Herbie Mann)
3. I SING THE BODY ELECTRIC
   (Weather Report)
4. UPENDO MI PAMOJA
   (Ramsey Lewis Trio)
5. ATTICA BLUES
   (Archie Shepp)
6. RAMADAN
   (Jason Lindh)
7. HEATING SYSTEM
   (Jack McDuff)
8. THE AGE OF STEAM
   (Gerry Milligan)
9. FLUTE-IN
   (Bobbi Humphrey)
10. SOUL ZODIAC
    (Cannonball Adderley)

COUNTRY SINGLES

1. THIS LITTLE GIRL OF MINE
   (Faron Young)
2. FUNNY FACE
   (Donna Fargo)
3. IF IT AIN'T LOVE
   (Connie Smith)
4. ONEY
   (Johnny Cash)
5. WHISKEY RIVER
   (Johnny Bush)
6. IT'S NOT LOVE
   (Merle Haggard)
7. BABY DON'T GET HOOKED ON ME
   (Mac Davis)
8. THE CLASS OF '57
   (The Statler Brothers)
9. I AIN'T NEVER
   (Mel Tillis)
10. I CAN'T STOP LOVING YOU
    (Conway Twitty)

COUNTRY ALBUMS

1. A SUNSHINY DAY
   (Charley Pride)
2. AMERICA
   (Johnny Cash)
3. LISTEN TO A COUNTRY SONG
   (Lynn Anderson)
4. THE HAPPIEST GIRL IN THE WHOLE U.S.A.
   (Donna Fargo)
5. ME AND THE FIRST LADY
   (George Jones and Tammy Wynette)
6. THE LONESOMEST LONESOME
   (Ray Price)
7. WHEN THE SNOW IS ON THE ROSES
   (Sonny James)
8. RAY PRICE'S ALL TIME GREATEST HITS
   (Ray Price)
9. TO GET TO YOU
   (Jerry Wallace)
10. THE STORYTELLER
    (Tom T. Hall)

OCTOBER 21, 1972

POP SINGLES

1. MY DING-A-LING
   (Chuck Berry)

2. EVERYBODY PLAYS THE FOOL
   (Main Ingredient)
3. GO ALL THE WAY
   (The Raspberries)
4. BEN
   (Michael Jackson)
5. USE ME
   (Bill Withers)
6. NIGHTS IN WHITE SATIN
   (The Moody Blues)
7. POPCORN
   (Hot Butter)
8. BURNING LOVE
   (Elvis Presley)
9. GOOD FOOT, PART 1
   (James Brown)
10. TIGHT ROPE
    (Leon Russell)

POP ALBUMS

1. SUPERFLY
   (Curtis Mayfield)
2. CARNEY
   (Leon Russell)
3. NEVER A DULL MOMENT
   (Rod Stewart)
4. SEVEN SEPARATE FOOLS
   (Three Dog Night)
5. ALL DIRECTIONS
   (Temptations)
6. BIG BAMBU
   (Cheech and Chong)
7. THE LONDON CHUCK BERRY SESSIONS
   (Chuck Berry)
8. CHICAGO V
   (Chicago)
9. LONG JOHN SILVER
   (The Jefferson Airplane)
10. ROCK OF AGES
    (The Band)

BLACK SINGLES

1. I'LL BE AROUND
   (Spinners)
2. FREDDIE'S DEAD
   (Curtis Mayfield)
3. USE ME
   (Bill Withers)
4. BEN
   (Michael Jackson)
5. MY DING-A-LING
   (Chuck Berry)
6. (WIN, PLACE OR SHOW) SHE'S A WINNER
   (Intruders)
7. WOMAN DON'T GO ASTRAY
   (King Floyd)
8. HONEY I STILL LOVE YOU
   (Mark IV)
9. ONE LIFE TO LIVE
   (The Manhattans)
10. WHY CAN'T WE BE LOVERS
    (Holland and Dozier)

JAZZ ALBUMS

1. I SING THE BODY ELECTRIC
   (Weather Report)
2. UPENDO MI PAMOJA
   (Ramsey Lewis Trio)
3. ATTICA BLUES
   (Archie Shepp)
4. HEATING SYSTEM
   (Jack McDuff)
5. THE AGE OF STEAM
   (Gerry Milligan)
6. BLUE MOSES
   (Randy Weston)
7. FLUTE-IN
   (Bobbi Humphrey)
8. MISSISSIPPI GAMBLER
   (Herbie Mann)

9. SOUL ZODIAC
   (Cannonball Adderley)
10. CHERRY
    (Stanley Turrentine)

COUNTRY SINGLES

1. FUNNY FACE
   (Donna Fargo)
2. IT'S NOT LOVE
   (Merle Haggard)
3. THIS LITTLE GIRL OF MINE
   (Faron Young)
4. BABY DON'T GET HOOKED ON ME
   (Mac Davis)
5. THE CLASS OF '57
   (The Statler Brothers)
6. IF IT AIN'T LOVE
   (Connie Smith)
7. MY MAN
   (Tammy Wynette)
8. ONEY
   (Johnny Cash)
9. DON'T SHE LOOK GOOD
   (Bill Anderson)
10. WHISKEY RIVER
    (Johnny Bush)

COUNTRY ALBUMS

1. AMERICA
   (Jonny Cash)
2. A SUNSHINY DAY
   (Charley Pride)
3. LISTEN TO A COUNTRY SONG
   (Lynn Anderson)
4. ME AND THE FIRST LADY
   (George Jones and Tammy Wynette)
5. WHEN THE SNOW IS ON THE ROSES
   (Sonny James)
6. RAY PRICE'S ALL TIME GREATEST HITS
   (Ray Price)
7. THE HAPPIEST GIRL IN THE WHOLE U.S.A.
   (Donna Fargo)
8. THE STORYTELLER
   (Tom T. Hall)
9. COUNTRY MUSIC THEN AND NOW
   (The Statler Brothers)
10. THE BEST OF THE BEST OF MERLE
    HAGGARD
    (Merle Haggard)

OCTOBER 28, 1972

POP SINGLES

1. MY DING-A-LING
   (Chuck Berry)
2. BEN
   (Michael Jackson)
3. USE ME
   (Bill Withers)
4. BURNING LOVE
   (Elvis Presley)
5. NIGHTS IN WHITE SATIN
   (The Moody Blues)
6. GARDEN PARTY
   (Rick Nelson)
7. POPCORN
   (Hot Butter)
8. EVERYBODY PLAYS THE FOOL
   (Main Ingredient)
9. TIGHT ROPE
   (Leon Russell)
10. FREDDIE'S DEAD
    (Curtis Mayfield)

POP ALBUMS

1. SUPERFLY
   (Curtis Mayfield)
2. CARNEY
   (Leon Russell)
3. DAYS OF FUTURE PASSED
   (The Moody Blues)
4. ALL DIRECTIONS
   (Temptations)
5. BIG BAMBU
   (Cheech and Chong)
6. THE LONDON CHUCK BERRY SESSIONS
   (Chuck Berry)
7. ROCK OF AGES
   (The Band)
8. CHICAGO V
   (Chicago)
9. SEVEN SEPARATE FOOLS
   (Three Dog Night)
10. NEVER A DULL MOMENT
    (Rod Stewart)

BLACK SINGLES

1. I'LL BE AROUND
   (Spinners)
2. FREDDIE'S DEAD
   (Curtis Mayfield)
3. USE ME
   (Bill Withers)
4. BEN
   (Michael Jackson)
5. (WIN, PLACE OR SHOW) SHE'S A WINNER
   (Intruders)
6. WOMAN DON'T GO ASTRAY
   (King Floyd)
7. HONEY I STILL LOVE YOU
   (Mark IV)
8. ONE LIFE TO LIVE
   (The Manhattans)
9. WHY CAN'T WE BE LOVERS
   (Holland and Dozier)
10. MY DING-A-LING
    (Chuck Berry)

JAZZ ALBUMS

1. I SING THE BODY ELECTRIC
   (Weather Report)
2. HEATING SYSTEM
   (Jack McDuff)
3. THE AGE OF STEAM
   (Gerry Milligan)
4. FLUTE-IN
   (Bobbi Humphrey)
5. CHERRY
   (Stanley Turrentine)
6. UPENDO MI PAMOJA
   (Ramsey Lewis Trio)
7. ATTICA BLUES
   (Archie Shepp)
8. ALL THE KING'S HORSES
   (Grover Washington Jr.)
9. SOUL ZODIAC
   (Cannonball Adderley)
10. CHICKEN LICKIN'
    (Funk Inc.)

COUNTRY SINGLES

1. IT'S NOT LOVE
   (Merle Haggard)
2. FUNNY FACE
   (Donna Fargo)
3. MY MAN
   (Tammy Wynette)
4. BABY DON'T GET HOOKED ON ME
   (Mac Davis)
5. THE CLASS OF '57
   (The Statler Brothers)
6. DON'T SHE LOOK GOOD
   (Bill Anderson)

7. TOGETHER ALWAYS
   (Porter Wagoner and Dolly Parton)
8. THIS LITTLE GIRL OF MINE
   (Faron Young)
9. THE LAWRENCE WELK-HEE HAW
   COUNTER REVOLUTION POLKA
   (Roy Clark)
10. ONEY
    (Johnny Cash)

COUNTRY ALBUMS

1. AMERICA
   (Johnny Cash)
2. A SUNSHINY DAY
   (Charley Pride)
3. ME AND THE FIRST LADY
   (George Jones and Tammy Wynette)
4. WHEN THE SNOW IS ON THE ROSES
   (Sonny James)
5. RAY PRICE'S ALL TIME GREATEST HITS
   (Ray Price)
6. LISTEN TO A COUNTRY SONG
   (Lynn Anderson)
7. THE STORYTELLER
   (Tom T. Hall)
8. COUNTRY MUSIC THEN AND NOW
   (The Statler Brothers)
9. THE BEST OF THE BEST OF MERLE
   HAGGARD
   (Merle Haggard)
10. THE HAPPIEST GIRL IN THE WHOLE U.S.A.
    (Donna Fargo)

NOVEMBER 4, 1972

POP SINGLES

1. NIGHTS IN WHITE SATIN
   (The Moody Blues)
2. BURNING LOVE
   (Elvis Presley)
3. MY DING-A-LING
   (Chuck Berry)
4. GARDEN PARTY
   (Rick Nelson)
5. FREDDIE'S DEAD
   (Curtis Mayfield)
6. I CAN SEE CLEARLY NOW
   (Johnny Nash)
7. BEN
   (Michael Jackson)
8. GOOD TIME CHARLIE'S GOT THE BLUES
   (Danny O'Keefe)
9. TIGHT ROPE
   (Leon Russell)
10. I'LL BE AROUND
    (Spinners)

POP ALBUMS

1. DAYS OF FUTURE PASSED
   (The Moody Blues)
2. SUPERFLY
   (Curtis Mayfield)
3. ALL DIRECTIONS
   (Temptations)
4. CATCH BULL AT FOUR
   (Cat Stevens)
5. THE LONDON CHUCK BERRY SESSIONS
   (Chuck Berry)
6. ROCK OF AGES
   (The Band)
7. CARNEY
   (Leon Russell)
8. CLOSE TO THE EDGE
   (Yes)
9. BIG BAMBU
   (Cheech and Chong)
10. BEN
    (Michael Jackson)

BLACK SINGLES

1. FREDDIE'S DEAD
   (Curtis Mayfield)
2. I'LL BE AROUND
   (Spinners)
3. USE ME
   (Bill Withers)
4. BEN
   (Michael Jackson)
5. HONEY I STILL LOVE YOU
   (Mark IV)
6. WOMAN DON'T GO ASTRAY
   (King Floyd)
7. ONE LIFE TO LIVE
   (The Manhattans)
8. WHY CAN'T WE BE LOVERS
   (Holland and Dozier)
9. (WIN, PLACE OR SHOW) SHE'S A WINNER
   (Intruders)
10. THE BABYSITTER
    (Betty Wright)

JAZZ ALBUMS

1. HEATING SYSTEM
   (Jack McDuff)
2. THE AGE OF STEAM
   (Gerry Milligan)
3. I SING THE BODY ELECTRIC
   (Weather Report)
4. ALL THE KING'S MEN
   (Grover Washington Jr.)
5. CHICKEN LICKIN'
   (Funk Inc.)
6. CHERRY
   (Stanley Turrentine)
7. TALK TO THE PEOPLE
   (Les McCann)
8. SOUL ZODIAC
   (Cannonball Adderley)
9. FLUTE-IN
   (Bobbi Humphrey)
10. ATTICA BLUES
    (Archie Shepp)

COUNTRY SINGLES

1. MY MAN
   (Tammy Wynette)
2. IT'S NOT LOVE
   (Merle Haggard)
3. FUNNY FACE
   (Donna Fargo)
4. THE CLASS OF '57
   (The Statler Brothers)
5. DON'T SHE LOOK GOOD
   (Bill Anderson)
6. TOGETHER ALWAYS
   (Porter Wagoner and Dolly Parton)
7. THE LAWRENCE WELK-HEE HAW COUNTER REVOLUTION POLKA
   (Roy Clark)
8. PRIDE'S NOT HARD TO SWALLOW
   (Hank Williams Jr.)
9. I TAKE IT ON HOME
   (Charlie Rich)
10. ONEY
    (Johnny Cash)

COUNTRY ALBUMS

1. A SUNSHINY DAY
   (Charley Pride)
2. AMERICA
   (Johnny Cash)
3. WHEN THE SNOW IS ON THE ROSES
   (Sonny James)
4. RAY PRICE'S ALL TIME GREATEST HITS
   (Ray Price)
5. THE BEST OF THE BEST OF MERLE HAGGARD
   (Merle Haggard)

6. THE STORYTELLER
   (Tom T. Hall)
7. COUNTRY MUSIC THEN AND NOW
   (The Statler Brothers)
8. THE HAPPIEST GIRL IN THE WHOLE U.S.A.
   (Donna Fargo)
9. I CAN'T STOP LOVING YOU
   (Conway Twitty)
10. ME AND THE FIRST LADY
    (George Jones and Tammy Wynette)

NOVEMBER 11, 1972

POP SINGLES

1. NIGHTS IN WHITE SATIN
   (The Moody Blues)
2. BURNING LOVE
   (Elvis Presley)
3. I CAN SEE CLEARLY NOW
   (Johnny Nash)
4. GARDEN PARTY
   (Rick Nelson)
5. FREDDIE'S DEAD
   (Curtis Mayfield)
6. I'LL BE AROUND
   (Spinners)
7. I'D LOVE YOU TO WANT ME
   (Lobo)
8. GOOD TIME CHARLIE'S GOT THE BLUES
   (Danny O'Keefe)
9. I AM WOMAN
   (Helen Reddy)
10. LISTEN TO THE MUSIC
    (The Doobie Brothers)

POP ALBUMS

1. CATCH BULL AT FOUR
   (Cat Stevens)
2. SUPERFLY
   (Curtis Mayfield)
3. ALL DIRECTIONS
   (Temptations)
4. DAYS OF FUTURE PASSED
   (The Moody Blues)
5. THE LONDON CHUCK BERRY SESSIONS
   (Chuck Berry)
6. ROCK OF AGES
   (The Band)
7. CLOSE TO THE EDGE
   (Yes)
8. PHOENIX
   (Grand Funk Railroad)
9. BEN
   (Michael Jackson)
10. CARNEY
    (Leon Russell)

BLACK SINGLES

1. FREDDIE'S DEAD
   (Curtis Mayfield)
2. I'LL BE AROUND
   (Spinners)
3. ONE LIFE TO LIVE
   (The Manhattans)
4. IF YOU DON'T KNOW ME BY NOW
   (Harold Melvin and the Blue Notes)
5. HONEY I STILL LOVE YOU
   (Mark IV)
6. WOMAN DON'T GO ASTRAY
   (King Floyd)
7. THE BABYSITTER
   (Betty Wright)
8. WHY CAN'T WE BE LOVERS
   (Holland and Dozier)

9. MAN-SIZED JOB
   (Denise LaSalle)
10. SLOW MOTION
    (John Williams)

JAZZ ALBUMS

1. TALK TO THE PEOPLE
   (Les McCann)
2. ALL THE KING'S HORSES
   (Grover Washington Jr.)
3. I SING THE BODY ELECTRIC
   (Weather Report)
4. CHICKEN LICKIN'
   (Funk Inc.)
5. OFFERING
   (Larry Coryell)
6. THE AGE OF STEAM
   (Gerry Milligan)
7. HEATING SYSTEM
   (Jack McDuff)
8. SOUL ZODIAC
   (Cannonball Adderley)
9. CHERRY
   (Stanley Turrentine)
10. FREE AGAIN
    (Gene Ammons)

COUNTRY SINGLES

1. DON'T SHE LOOK GOOD
   (Bill Anderson)
2. MY MAN
   (Tammy Wynette)
3. IT'S NOT LOVE
   (Merle Haggard)
4. THE CLASS OF '57
   (The Statler Brothers)
5. PRIDE'S NOT HARD TO SWALLOW
   (Hank Williams Jr.)
6. FUNNY FACE
   (Donna Fargo)
7. I TAKE IT ON HOME
   (Charlie Rich)
8. THIS MUCH A MAN
   (Marty Robbins)
9. THE LAWRENCE WELK-HEE HAW COUNTER REVOLUTION POLKA
   (Roy Clark)
10. LONELY WOMEN MAKE GOOD LOVERS
    (Bob Luman)

COUNTRY ALBUMS

1. A SUNSHINY DAY
   (Charley Pride)
2. THE BEST OF THE BEST OF MERLE HAGGARD
   (Merle Haggard)
3. AMERICA
   (Johnny Cash)
4. WHEN THE SNOW IS ON THE ROSES
   (Sonny James)
5. I CAN'T STOP LOVING YOU
   (Conway Twitty)
6. THE HAPPIEST GIRL IN THE WHOLE U.S.A.
   (Donna Fargo)
7. THE STORYTELLER
   (Tom T. Hall)
8. COUNTRY MUSIC THEN AND NOW
   (The Statler Brothers)
9. RAY PRICE'S ALL TIME GREATEST HITS
   (Ray Price)
10. MISSING YOU
    (Jim Reeves)

NOVEMBER 18, 1972

POP SINGLES

1. I CAN SEE CLEARLY NOW
   (Johnny Nash)

2. I'LL BE AROUND
   (Spinners)
3. I'D LOVE YOU TO WANT ME
   (Lobo)
4. NIGHTS IN WHITE SATIN
   (The Moody Blues)
5. BURNING LOVE
   (Elvis Presley)
6. I AM WOMAN
   (Helen Reddy)
7. IF YOU DON'T KNOW ME BY NOW
   (Harold Melvin and the Blue Notes)
8. GARDEN PARTY
   (Rick Nelson)
9. WITCHY WOMAN
   (The Eagles)
10. IF I COULD REACH YOU
    (The Fifth Dimension)

POP ALBUMS

1. CATCH BULL AT FOUR
   (Cat Stevens)
2. SUPERFLY
   (Curtis Mayfield)
3. ALL DIRECTIONS
   (Temptations)
4. DAYS OF FUTURE PASSED
   (The Moody Blues)
5. RHYMES AND REASONS
   (Carole King)
6. CLOSE TO THE EDGE
   (Yes)
7. PHOENIX
   (Grand Funk Railroad)
8. BEN
   (Michael Jackson)
9. CARAVANSERAI
   (Santana)
10. ROCK OF AGES
    (The Band)

BLACK SINGLES

1. IF YOU DON'T KNOW ME BY NOW
   (Harold Melvin and the Blue Notes)
2. ONE LIFE TO LIVE
   (The Manhattans)
3. FREDDIE'S DEAD
   (Curtis Mayfield)
4. PAPA WAS A ROLLING STONE
   (Temptations)
5. I'M STILL IN LOVE WITH YOU
   (The Stylistics)
6. MAN-SIZED JOB
   (Denise LaSalle)
7. THE BABYSITTER
   (Betty Wright)
8. I'LL BE AROUND
   (Spinners)
9. SLOW MOTION
   (Johnny Williams)
10. HONEY I STILL LOVE YOU
    (Mark IV)

JAZZ ALBUMS

1. TALK TO THE PEOPLE
   (Les McCann)
2. ALL THE KING'S HORSES
   (Grover Washington Jr.)
3. CHICKEN LICKIN'
   (Funk Inc.)
4. FREE AGAIN
   (Gene Ammons)
5. OFFERING
   (Larry Coryell)
6. WORLDS AROUND THE SUN
   (Bayete/Todd Cochran)
7. I SING THE BODY ELECTRIC
   (Weather Report)
8. THE HUB OF HUBBARD
   (Freddie Hubbard)

9. THE AGE OF STEAM
   (Gerry Milligan)
10. THE ICEMAN'S BAND
    (Jerry Butler)

COUNTRY SINGLES

1. PRIDE'S NOT HARD TO SWALLOW
   (Hank Williams Jr.)
2. DON'T SHE LOOK GOOD
   (Bill Anderson)
3. MY MAN
   (Tammy Wynette)
4. IT'S NOT LOVE
   (Merle Haggard)
5. SHE'S TOO GOOD TO BE TRUE
   (Charley Pride)
6. LONELY WOMAN MAKE GOOD LOVERS
   (Bob Luman)
7. I TAKE IT ON HOME
   (Charlie Rich)
8. THIS MUCH A MAN
   (Marty Robbins)
9. GOT THE ALL OVERS FOR YOU
   (Freddie Hart)
10. HEAVEN IS MY WOMAN'S LOVE
    (Tommy Overstreet)

COUNTRY ALBUMS

1. THE BEST OF THE BEST OF MERLE
   HAGGARD
   (Merle Haggard)
2. A SUNSHINY DAY
   (Charley Pride)
3. I CAN'T STOP LOVING YOU
   (Conway Twitty)
4. AMERICA
   (Johnny Cash)
5. THE HAPPIEST GIRL IN THE WHOLE U.S.A.
   (Donna Fargo)
6. WHEN THE SNOW IS ON THE ROSES
   (Sonny James)
7. THE STORYTELLER
   (Tom T. Hall)
8. TOGETHER ALWAYS
   (Dolly Parton and Porter Wagoner)
9. MISSING YOU
   (Jim Reeves)
10. LADIES LOVE OUTLAWS
    (Waylon Jennings)

NOVEMBER 25, 1972

POP SINGLES

1. I'LL BE AROUND
   (Spinners)
2. I'D LOVE YOU TO WANT ME
   (Lobo)
3. I AM WOMAN
   (Helen Reddy)
4. I CAN SEE CLEARLY NOW
   (Johnny Nash)
5. IF YOU DON'T KNOW ME BY NOW
   (Harold Melvin and the Blue Notes)
6. PAPA WAS A ROLLING STONE
   (Temptations)
7. NIGHTS IN WHITE SATIN
   (The Moody Blues)
8. WITCHY WOMAN
   (The Eagles)
9. IF I COULD REACH YOU
   (The Fifth Dimension)
10. BURNING LOVE
    (Elvis Presley)

POP ALBUMS

1. CATCH BULL AT FOUR
   (Cat Stevens)
2. SUPERFLY
   (Curtis Mayfield)
3. ALL DIRECTIONS
   (Temptations)
4. RHYMES AND REASONS
   (Carole King)
5. DAYS OF FUTURE PASSED
   (The Moody Blues)
6. CLOSE TO THE EDGE
   (Yes)
7. PHOENIX
   (Grand Funk Railroad)
8. BEN
   (Michael Jackson)
9. CARAVANSERAI
   (Santana)
10. I'M STILL IN LOVE WITH YOU
    (Al Green)

BLACK SINGLES

1. IF YOU DON'T KNOW ME BY NOW
   (Harold Melvin and the Blue Notes)
2. ONE LIFE TO LIVE
   (The Manhattans)
3. PAPA WAS A ROLLING STONE
   (Temptations)
4. I'M STONE IN LOVE WITH YOU
   (The Stylistics)
5. MAN-SIZED JOB
   (Denise LaSalle)
6. YOU OUGHT TO BE WITH ME
   (Al Green)
7. ME AND MRS. JONES
   (Billy Paul)
8. FREDDIE'S DEAD
   (Curtis Mayfield)
9. THE BABYSITTER
   (Betty Wright)
10. I LOVE YOU MORE THAN YOU'LL EVER
    KNOW
    (Donny Hathaway)

JAZZ ALBUMS

1. ALL THE KING'S HORSES
   (Grover Washington Jr.)
2. CHICKEN LICKIN'
   (Funk Inc.)
3. LORD OF LORDS
   (Alice Coltrane)
4. TALK TO THE PEOPLE
   (Les McCann)
5. WORLDS AROUND THE SUN
   (Bayete/Todd Cochran)
6. OFFERING
   (Larry Coryell)
7. FREE AGAIN
   (Gene Ammons)
8. THE HUB OF HUBBARD
   (Freddie Hubbard)
9. I SING THE BODY ELECTRIC
   (Weather Report)
10. THE ICEMAN'S BAND
    (Jerry Butler)

COUNTRY SINGLES

1. SHE'S TOO GOOD TO BE TRUE
   (Charley Pride)
2. PRIDE'S NOT HARD TO SWALLOW
   (Hank Williams Jr.)
3. MY MAN
   (Tammy Wynette)
4. GOT THE ALL OVERS FOR YOU
   (Freddie Hart)
5. LONELY WOMEN MAKE GOOD LOVERS
   (Bob Luman)

6. IT'S NOT LOVE
(Merle Haggard)
7. THIS MUCH A MAN
(Marty Robbins)
8. HEAVEN IS MY WOMAN'S LOVE
(Tommy Overstreet)
9. DON'T SHE LOOK GOOD
(Bill Anderson)
10. SING ME A LOVE SONG TO BABY
(Billy Walker)

COUNTRY ALBUMS

1. THE BEST OF THE BEST OF MERLE
HAGGARD
(Merle Haggard)
2. A SUNSHINY DAY
(Charley Pride)
3. I CAN'T STOP LOVING YOU
(Conway Twitty)
4. TOGETHER ALWAYS
(Porter Wagoner and Dolly Parton)
5. THE HAPPIEST GIRL IN THE WHOLE U.S.A.
(Donna Fargo)
6. AMERICA
(Johnny Cash)
7. HERE I AM AGAIN
(Loretta Lynn)
8. LADIES LOVE OUTLAWS
(Waylon Jennings)
9. MISSING YOU
(Jim Reeves)
10. THE STORYTELLER
(Tom T. Hall)

DECEMBER 2, 1972

POP SINGLES

1. I'D LOVE YOU TO WANT ME
(Lobo)
2. I AM A WOMAN
(Helen Reddy)
3. IF YOU DON'T KNOW ME BY NOW
(Harold Melvin and the Blue Notes)
4. PAPA WAS A ROLLING STONE
(Temptations)
5. I'LL BE AROUND
(Spinners)
6. YOU OUGHT TO BE WITH ME
(Al Green)
7. I CAN SEE CLEARLY NOW
(Johnny Nash)
8. SUMMER BREEZE
(Seals and Croft)
9. IF I COULD REACH YOU
(The Fifth Dimension)
10. CLAIR
(Gilbert O'Sullivan)

POP ALBUMS

1. CATCH BULL AT FOUR
(Cat Stevens)
2. RHYMES AND REASONS
(Carole King)
3. ALL DIRECTIONS
(Temptations)
4. SUPERFLY
(Curtis Mayfield)
5. CLOSE TO THE EDGE
(Yes)
6. PHOENIX
(Grand Funk Railroad)
7. BEN
(Michael Jackson)
8. I'M STILL IN LOVE WITH YOU
(Al Green)
9. CARAVANSERAI
(Santana)

10. BABY DON'T GET HOOKED ON ME
(Mac Davis)

BLACK SINGLES

1. PAPA WAS A ROLLING STONE
(Temptations)
2. YOU OUGHT TO BE WITH ME
(Al Green)
3. I'M STONE IN LOVE WITH YOU
(The Stylistics)
4. ME AND MRS. JONES
(Billy Paul)
5. MAN-SIZED JOB
(Denise LaSalle)
6. IF YOU DON'T KNOW ME BY NOW
(Harold Melvin and the Blue Notes)
7. ONE LIFE TO LIVE
(The Manhattans)
8. CORNER OF THE SKY
(The Jackson 5)
9. PEACE IN THE VALLEY OF LOVE
(The Persuaders)
10. I LOVE YOU MORE THAN YOU'LL
EVER KNOW
(Donny Hathaway)

JAZZ ALBUMS

1. ALL THE KING'S HORSES
(Grover Washington Jr.)
2. CHICKEN LICKIN'
(Funk Inc.)
3. TALK TO THE PEOPLE
(Les McCann)
4. LORD OF LORDS
(Alice Coltrane)
5. WORLDS AROUND THE SUN
(Bayete/Todd Cochran)
6. FREE AGAIN
(Gene Ammons)
7. THE ICEMAN'S BAND
(Jerry Butler)
8. THE HUB OF HUBBARD
(Freddie Hubbard)
9. OFFERING
(Larry Coryell)
10. LEAN ON ME
(Shirley Scott)

COUNTRY SINGLES

1. SHE'S TOO GOOD TO BE TRUE
(Charley Pride)
2. GOT THE ALL OVERS FOR YOU
(Freddie Hart)
3. PRIDE'S NOT HARD TO SWALLOW
(Hank Williams Jr.)
4. HEAVEN IS MY WOMAN'S LOVE
(Tommy Overstreet)
5. LONELY WOMEN MAKE GOOD LOVERS
(Bob Luman)
6. SING ME A LOVE SONG TO BABY
(Billy Walker)
7. THIS MUCH A MAN
(Marty Robbins)
8. MY MAN
(Tammy Wynette)
9. FOOL ME
(Lynn Anderson)
10. IT'S NOT LOVE
(Merle Haggard)

COUNTRY ALBUMS

1. THE BEST OF THE BEST OF MERLE
HAGGARD
(Merle Haggard)
2. I CAN'T STOP LOVING YOU
(Conway Twitty)
3. TOGETHER ALWAYS
(Porter Wagoner and Dolly Parton)

4. A SUNSHINY DAY
(Charley Pride)
5. THE HAPPIEST GIRL IN THE WHOLE U.S.A.
(Donna Fargo)
6. HERE I AM AGAIN
(Loretta Lynn)
7. AMERICA
(Johnny Cash)
8. LADIES LOVE OUTLAWS
(Waylon Jennings)
9. MISSING YOU
(Jim Reeves)
10. LIVE AT THE WHITE HOUSE
(Buck Owens)

DECEMBER 9, 1972

POP SINGLES

1. I AM WOMAN
(Helen Reddy)
2. IF YOU DON'T KNOW ME BY NOW
(Harold Melvin and the Blue Notes)
3. PAPA WAS A ROLLING STONE
(Temptations)
4. YOU OUGHT TO BE WITH ME
(Al Green)
5. I'D LOVE YOU TO WANT ME
(Lobo)
6. CLAIR
(Gilbert O'Sullivan)
7. SUMMER BREEZE
(Seals and Croft)
8. I'LL BE AROUND
(Spinners)
9. VENTURA HIGHWAY
(America)
10. OPERATOR
(Jim Croce)

POP ALBUMS

1. RHYMES AND REASONS
(Carole King)
2. CATCH BULL AT FOUR
(Cat Stevens)
3. ALL DIRECTIONS
(Temptations)
4. SEVENTH SOJOURN
(The Moody Blues)
5. CLOSE TO THE EDGE
(Yes)
6. PHOENIX
(Grand Funk Railroad)
7. I'M STILL IN LOVE WITH YOU
(Al Green)
8. CARAVANSERAI
(Santana)
9. SUPERFLY
(Curtis Mayfield)
10. BLACK SABBATH VOL. 4
(Black Sabbath)

BLACK SINGLES

1. YOU OUGHT TO BE WITH ME
(Al Green)
2. I'M STONE IN LOVE WITH YOU
(The Stylistics)
3. ME AND MRS. JONES
(Billy Paul)
4. PAPA WAS A ROLLING STONE
(Temptations)
5. MAN-SIZED JOB
(Denise LaSalle)
6. IF YOU DON'T KNOW ME BY NOW
(Harold Melvin and the Blue Notes)
7. CORNER OF THE SKY
(The Jackson 5)
8. PEACE IN THE VALLEY OF LOVE
(The Persuaders)

9. KEEPER OF THE CASTLE
   (The Four Tops)
10. I GOT A BAG OF MY OWN
    (James Brown)

JAZZ ALBUMS

1. CHICKEN LICKIN'
   (Funk Inc.)
2. WORLDS AROUND THE SUN
   (Bayete/Todd Cochran)
3. TALK TO THE PEOPLE
   (Les McCann)
4. LORD OF LORDS
   (Alice Coltrane)
5. FREE AGAIN
   (Gene Ammons)
6. THE ICEMAN'S BAND
   (Jerry Butler)
7. ON THE CORNER
   (Miles Davis)
8. ALL THE KING'S HORSES
   (Grover Washington Jr.)
9. THE HUB OF HUBBARD
   (Freddie Hubbard)
10. LEAN ON ME
    (Shirley Scott)

COUNTRY SINGLES

1. GOT THE ALL OVERS FOR YOU
   (Freddie Hart)
2. HEAVEN IS MY WOMAN'S LOVE
   (Tommy Overstreet)
3. SHE'S TOO GOOD TO BE TRUE
   (Charley Pride)
4. SING ME A LOVE SONG TO BABY
   (Bill Walker)
5. FOOL ME
   (Lynn Anderson)
6. LONELY WOMEN MAKE GOOD LOVERS
   (Bob Luman)
7. PRIDE'S NOT HARD TO SWALLOW
   (Hank Williams Jr.)
8. WHITE SILVER SANDS
   (Sonny James)
9. MY MAN
   (Tammy Wynette)
10. PRETEND I NEVER HAPPENED
    (Waylon Jennings)

COUNTRY ALBUMS

1. THE BEST OF THE BEST OF MERLE
   HAGGARD
   (Merle Haggard)
2. I CAN'T STOP LOVING YOU
   (Conway Twitty)
3. TOGETHER ALWAYS
   (Porter Wagoner and Dolly Parton)
4. HERE I AM AGAIN
   (Loretta Lynn)
5. A SUNSHINY DAY
   (Charley Pride)
6. THE HAPPIEST GIRL IN THE WHOLE U.S.A.
   (Donna Fargo)
7. GOT THE ALL OVERS FOR YOU
   (Freddie Hart)
8. LADIES LOVE OUTLAWS
   (Waylon Jennings)
9. LIVE AT THE WHITE HOUSE
   (Buck Owens)
10. IF YOU TOUCH ME
    (Joe Stampley)

DECEMBER 16, 1972

POP SINGLES

1. I AM WOMAN
   (Helen Reddy)

2. ME AND MRS. JONES
   (Billy Paul)
3. YOU OUGHT TO BE WITH ME
   (Al Green)
4. PAPA WAS A ROLLING STONE
   (Temptations)
5. CLAIR
   (Gilbert O'Sullivan)
6. IF YOU DON'T KNOW ME BY NOW
   (Harold Melvin and the Blue Notes)
7. VENTURA HIGHWAY
   (America)
8. IT NEVER RAINS IN SOUTHERN
   CALIFORNIA
   (Albert Hammond)
9. ROCKIN' PNEUMONIA AND THE BOOGIE
   WOOGIE FLU
   (Johnny River)
10. I'M STONE IN LOVE WITH YOU
    (The Stylistics)

POP ALBUMS

1. RHYMES AND REASONS
   (Carole King)
2. SEVENTH SOJOURN
   (The Moody Blues)
3. ALL DIRECTIONS
   (Temptations)
4. CATCH BULL AT FOUR
   (Cat Stevens)
5. I'M STILL IN LOVE WITH YOU
   (Al Green)
6. PHOENIX
   (Grand Funk Railroad)
7. CLOSE TO THE EDGE
   (Yes)
8. CARAVANSERAI
   (Santana)
9. BLACK SABBATH VOL. 4
   (Black Sabbath)
10. SUMMER BREEZE
    (Seals and Crofts)

BLACK SINGLES

1. ME AND MRS. JONES
   (Billy Paul)
2. YOU OUGHT TO BE WITH ME
   (Al Green)
3. I'M STONE IN LOVE WITH YOU
   (The Stylistics)
4. PAPA WAS A ROLLING STONE
   (Temptations)
5. I GOT A BAG OF MY OWN
   (James Brown)
6. KEEPER OF THE CASTLE
   (The Four Tops)
7. CORNER OF THE SKY
   (The Jackson 5)
8. PEACE IN THE VALLEY OF LOVE
   (The Persuaders)
9. LOVE JONES
   (Brighter Side of Darkness)
10. TROUBLE IN MY HOME
    (Joe Simon)

JAZZ ALBUMS

1. CHICKEN LICKIN'
   (Funk Inc.)
2. WORLDS AROUND THE SUN
   (Bayete/Todd Cochran)
3. THE ICEMAN'S BAND
   (Jerry Butler)
4. TALK TO THE PEOPLE
   (Les McCann)
5. ON THE CORNER
   (Miles Davis)
6. LORD OF LORDS
   (Alice Coltrane)
7. THE HUB OF HUBBARD
   (Freddie Hubbard)

8. LEAN ON ME
   (Shirley Scott)
9. FREE AGAIN
   (Gene Ammons)
10. COOL COOKIN'
    (Kenny Burrell)

COUNTRY SINGLES

1. HEAVEN IS MY WOMAN'S LOVE
   (Tommy Overstreet)
2. GOT THE ALL OVERS FOR YOU
   (Freddie Hart)
3. SING ME A LOVE SONG TO BABY
   (Billy Walker)
4. FOOL ME
   (Lynn Anderson)
5. A PICTURE OF ME (WITHOUT YOU)
   (George Jones)
6. WHITE SILVER SANDS
   (Sonny James)
7. PRETEND I NEVER HAPPENED
   (Waylon Jennings)
8. SHE'S TOO GOOD TO BE TRUE
   (Charley Pride)
9. LONELY WOMEN MAKE GOOD LOVERS
   (Bob Luman)
10. PRIDE'S NOT HARD TO SWALLOW
    (Hank Williams Jr.)

COUNTRY ALBUMS

1. THE BEST OF THE BEST OF MERLE
   HAGGARD
   (Merle Haggard)
2. HERE I AM AGAIN
   (Loretta Lynn)
3. I CAN'T STOP LOVING YOU
   (Conway Twitty)
4. GOT THE ALL OVERS FOR YOU
   (Freddie Hart)
5. A SUNSHINY DAY
   (Charley Pride)
6. THE HAPPIEST GIRL IN THE WHOLE U.S.A.
   (Donna Fargo)
7. LADIES LOVE OUTLAWS
   (Waylon Jennings)
8. TOGETHER ALWAYS
   (Porter Wagoner and Dolly Parton)
9. MY MAN
   (Tammy Wynette)
10. LYNN ANDERSON'S GREATEST HITS
    (Lynn Anderson)

DECEMBER 23, 1972

POP SINGLES

1. ME AND MRS. JONES
   (Billy Paul)
2. YOU OUGHT TO BE WITH ME
   (Al Green)
3. IT NEVER RAINS IN SOUTHERN
   CALIFORNIA
   (Albert Hammond)
4. CLAIR
   (Gilbert O'Sullivan)
5. I AM WOMAN
   (Helen Reddy)
6. ROCKIN' PNEUMONIA AND THE BOOGIE
   WOOGIE FLU
   (Johnny Rivers)
7. PAPA WAS A ROLLING STONE
   (Temptations)
8. I WANNA BE WITH YOU
   (The Raspberries)
9. SOMETHING'S WRONG WITH ME
   (Austin Roberts)
10. I'M STONE IN LOVE WITH YOU
    (The Stylistics)

POP ALBUMS

1. SEVENTH SOJOURN
   (The Moody Blues)
2. RHYMES AND REASONS
   (Carole King)
3. I'M STILL IN LOVE WITH YOU
   (Al Green)
4. LIVING IN THE PAST
   (Jethro Tull)
5. CATCH BULL AT FOUR
   (Cat Stevens)
6. SUMMER BREEZE
   (Seals and Crofts)
7. CARAVANSERAI
   (Santana)
8. BLACK SABBATH VOL. 4
   (Black Sabbath)
9. ALL DIRECTIONS
   (Temptations)
10. PHOENIX
    (Grand Funk Railroad)

BLACK SINGLES

1. ME AND MRS. JONES
   (Billy Paul)
2. YOU OUGHT TO BE WITH ME
   (Al Green)
3. KEEPER OF THE CASTLE
   (The Four Tops)
4. I GOT A BAG OF MY OWN
   (James Brown)
5. I'M STONE IN LOVE WITH YOU
   (The Stylistics)
6. LOVE JONES
   (Brighter Side of Darkness)
7. CORNER OF THE SKY
   (The Jackson 5)
8. SUPERFLY
   (Curtis Mayfield)
9. SUPERSTITION
   (Stevie Wonder)
10. TROUBLE IN MY HOME
    (Joe Simon)

JAZZ ALBUMS

1. WORLDS AROUND THE SUN
   (Bayete/Todd Cochran)
2. ON THE CORNER
   (Miles Davis)
3. TALK TO THE PEOPLE
   (Les McCann)
4. THE ICEMAN'S BAND
   (Jerry Butler)
5. CHICKEN LICKIN'
   (Funk Inc.)
6. THE HUB OF HUBBARD
   (Freddie Hubbard)
7. LEAN ON ME
   (Shirley Scott)
8. ALL THE KING'S HORSES
   (Grover Washington Jr.)
9. FLY DUDE
   (Jimmy McGriff)
10. INFINITY
    (John Coltrane)

COUNTRY SINGLES

1. SING ME A LOVE SONG TO BABY
   (Billy Walker)
2. FOOL ME
   (Lynn Anderson)
3. A PICTURE OF ME (WITHOUT YOU)
   (George Jones)
4. GOT THE ALL OVERS FOR YOU
   (Freddie Hart)
5. WHITE SILVER SANDS
   (Sonny James)
6. PRETEND I NEVER HAPPENED
   (Waylon Jennings)
7. HEAVEN IS MY WOMAN'S LOVE
   (Tommy Overstreet)
8. SHE'S GOT TO BE A SAINT
   (Ray Price)
9. LOVIN' ON BACK STREETS
   (Mel Street)
10. SHE'S TOO GOOD TO BE TRUE
    (Charley Pride)

COUNTRY ALBUMS

1. HERE I AM AGAIN
   (Loretta Lynn)
2. THE BEST OF THE BEST OF MERLE HAGGARD
   (Merle Haggard)
3. GOT THE ALL OVERS FOR YOU
   (Freddie Hart)
4. A SUNSHINY DAY
   (Charley Pride)
5. THE HAPPIEST GIRL IN THE WHOLE U.S.A.
   (Donna Fargo)
6. MY MAN
   (Tammy Wynette)
7. LYNN ANDERSON'S GREATEST HITS
   (Lynn Anderson)
8. I CAN'T STOP LOVING YOU
   (Conway Twitty)
9. CHARLIE McCOY
   (Charlie McCoy)
10. LADIES LOVE OUTLAWS
    (Waylon Jennings)

DECEMBER 30, 1972

POP SINGLES

1. YOU OUGHT TO BE WITH ME
   (Al Green)
2. CLAIR
   (Gilbert O'Sullivan)
3. ME AND MRS. JONES
   (Billy Paul)
4. ROCKIN' PNEUMONIA AND THE BOOGIE WOOGIE FLU
   (Johnny Rivers)
5. IT NEVER RAINS IN SOUTHERN CALIFORNIA
   (Albert Hammond)
6. I AM WOMAN
   (Helen Reddy)
7. YOU'RE SO VAIN
   (Carly Simon)
8. I WANNA BE WITH YOU
   (The Raspberries)
9. FUNNY FACE
   (Donna Fargo)
10. SOMETHING'S WRONG WITH ME
    (Austin Roberts)

POP ALBUMS

1. SEVENTH SOJOURN
   (The Moody Blues)
2. RHYMES AND REASONS
   (Carole King)
3. I'M STILL IN LOVE WITH YOU
   (Al Green)
4. LIVING IN THE PAST
   (Jethro Tull)
5. CATCH BULL AT FOUR
   (Cat Stevens)
6. SUMMER BREEZE
   (Seals and Crofts)
7. CARAVANSERAI
   (Santana)
8. ONE MAN DOG
   (James Taylor)
9. BLACK SABBATH VOL. 4
   (Black Sabbath)
10. GUITAR MAN
    (Bread)

BLACK SINGLES

1. SUPERSTITION
   (Stevie Wonder)
2. KEEPER OF THE CASTLE
   (The Four Tops)
3. WHY CAN'T WE LIVE TOGETHER
   (Timmy Thomas)
4. I GOT A BAG OF MY OWN
   (James Brown)
5. LOVE JONES
   (Brighter Side of Darkness)
6. ME AND MRS. JONES
   (Billy Paul)
7. SUPERFLY
   (Curtis Mayfield)
8. CORNER OF THE SKY
   (The Jackson 5)
9. TROUBLE IN MY HOME
   (Joe Simon)
10. YOU OUGHT TO BE WITH ME
    (Al Green)

JAZZ ALBUMS

1. ON THE CORNER
   (Miles Davis)
2. THE ICEMAN'S BAND
   (Jerry Butler)
3. CHICKEN LICKIN'
   (Funk Inc.)
4. WORLDS AROUND THE SUN
   (Bayete/Todd Cochran)
5. LEAN ON ME
   (Shirley Scott)
6. TALK TO THE PEOPLE
   (Les McCann)
7. ALL THE KING'S HORSES
   (Grover Washington Jr.)
8. ENERGY ESSENTIALS
   (Various Artists)
9. INFINITY
   (John Coltrane)
10. LORD OF LORDS
    (Alice Coltrane)

COUNTRY SINGLES

1. FOOL ME
   (Lynn Anderson)
2. A PICTURE OF ME (WITHOUT YOU)
   (George Jones)
3. SHE'S GOT TO BE A SAINT
   (Ray Price)
4. WHITE SILVER SANDS
   (Sonny James)
5. PRETEND I NEVER HAPPENED
   (Waylon Jennings)
6. LOVIN' ON BACK STREETS
   (Mel Street)
7. SOUL SONG
   (Joe Stampley)
8. SING ME A LOVE SONG TO BABY
   (Billy Walker)
9. GOT THE ALL OVERS FOR YOU
   (Freddie Hart)
10. HEAVEN IS MY WOMAN'S LOVE
    (Tommy Overstreet)

COUNTRY ALBUMS

1. HERE I AM AGAIN
   (Loretta Lynn)
2. GOT THE ALL OVERS FOR YOU
   (Freddie Hart)
3. THE BEST OF THE BEST OF MERLE HAGGARD
   (Merle Haggard)
4. A SUNSHINY DAY
   (Charley Pride)

5. MY MAN
       (Tammy Wynette)
6. LYNN ANDERSON'S GREATEST HITS
       (Lynn Anderson)
7. THE HAPPIEST GIRL IN THE WHOLE U.S.A.
       (Donna Fargo)
8. CHARLIE McCOY
       (Charlie McCoy)
9. I CAN'T STOP LOVING YOU
       (Conway Twitty)
10. WHEEL OF FORTUNE
       (Susan Raye)

1973

With *Music of My Mind*, Stevie Wonder began changing the general public's perception of him as merely a cute, gifted little blind boy. Stevie was 23 years old now and after some legal wrangling with Motown, he, like Marvin Gaye, finally assumed control of his recordings. If *Music of My Mind* was his first tentative step in individuality, the next two albums, *Talking Book* and *Innervisions*, proved he was an Olympic runner, perhaps the class of his generation. He wrote Tin Pan Alley pop ("The Sunshine of My Life"), crunching rock 'n' roll ("Superstition"), inspirational R&B ("Higher Ground"), and apocalyptic epics of inner-city life ("Living for the City"), displaying a remarkable singing voice. Other musicians can match Wonder for talent. Few have been able to harness raw talent into music as memorable as his.

Four days after the release of *Innervisions*, his most satisfying album, he was involved in a serious auto accident. While riding through North Carolina, a log from a truck smashed through the car windshield, striking Wonder in the forehead. Miraculously, he wasn't killed, but his sense of smell was severely impaired. Despite this tragedy, he continued solidifying his unique place in contemporary pop.

It's rare that number one albums are as bleak, or Latin-influenced as War's *The World Is a Ghetto*, yet it was the year's most popular album, which says something about how the country was responding to President Nixon's reign and the lost chess match in southeast Asia. "Four-Cornered Room," "Cisco Kid," the title song, and previous hit single "Slippin' into Darkness" were dark, moody pieces layered with Lee Oskar's harmonica, slinky polyrhythms, and chanting ensemble vocals. Hardly the stuff of your typical pop band, yet with this mix War managed music that reflected a certain evil mood that pervaded America.

From the rock side, Pink Floyd's *Dark Side of the Moon* accomplished the same thing. Aided by engineer Alan Parsons, Pink Floyd's members made a sumptuous-sounding album about life, death, and lunacy (a theme suggested by the crack-up of original leader Syd Barrett) that firmly established them as the last great psychedelic band. Pink Floyd's somber lyrics and oppressive music certainly differed from War, but struck the same discordant tones. On tour that summer, Pink Floyd ushered in the era of the multi-million-dollar rock extravaganza. Airplane crashes, fiery gongs, dry ice, and an inflatable man with green eyes set the standard for rock pyrotechnics.

ALBUMS: The new heavy-metal band on the block was Deep Purple, a good, not exceptional, collection of British rock veterans led by guitarist Richie Blackmore's occasionally inspired solos. On *Who Do We Think We Are, Made in Japan* and *Machine Head*, you'll find very capable head-banger music and little intelligence.

Much more melodic and considerably more fun were The Doobie Brothers' *The Captain and Me* and *Toulouse Street*. At this time the band was led by guitarist/lead vocalist Tom Johnson with his earthy rock'n'roll aura as reflected by the clean-cut rocker "Long Train Running."

It's a shame that the Edgar Winter group never cultivated the same consistency as the Doobies, because they had enough talent to be America's best rock band. With keyboardist Edgar Winter, guitarist Rick Derringer, and multi-instrumentalist/singer/writer Dan Hartman, they had enough gifted musicians to make excellent music and on *They Only Come Out at Night*, they did. The hit instrumental "Frankenstein" was a creative mesh of rock guitar, percussion, and ARP synthesizer. But Winter couldn't hold the band together and by 1976 Hartman and Derringer had split. Individually neither Winter, Derringer, nor Hartman fulfilled their potential.

Two bands who made major contributions later in the decade made solid impressions in 1973. The Eagles' *Desperado*, an ambitious follow-up to their self-titled debut, was a concept album comparing the life of an old West outlaw with the rock musician's nomad existence. The metaphor was a bit stretched, but the music wasn't. Glen Frey and Don Henley's "Tequila Sunrise" and the title song established a world-weary cynicism and a sharp melodic sense as Eagle trademarks.

Speaking of cynical, Steely Dan debuted with *Can't Buy a Thrill*, pulling off a most difficult double play, impressing musicians and attaining commercial success. Singles' buyers loved "Reelin' in the Years" and "Do It Again" because they sounded great on the radio. Musicians loved the arrangements and changes; critics—basically being "word men"— were fascinated by the sinister insinuations of leader-writers Donald Fagen and Walter Becker. Surprisingly, as Steely Dan's music grew more complex and the lyrics increasingly oblique, sales rose, contradicting record industry truisms.

"The Philly Sound" was now black music's dominant musical production line, replacing Motown and Memphis. Thom Bell's production of the ethereal Stylistics (*Round 2*) and the versatile Spinners ("One of a Kind Love Affair," "Could It Be I'm Falling in Love"), Kenny Gamble and Leon Huff's guidance of The O'Jays ("Back Stabbers," "Love Train"), and Billy Paul ("Me and Mrs. Jones") established some widely imitated production techniques.

Gladys Knight and the Pips emerged as the black singles group of the year with a series of powerful performances ("Neither One of Us," "Midnight Train to Georgia"). During their tenure at Motown, Knight and the Pips were never given the care and consideration their talents deserved, but after shifting to Buddah, they exploded with Knight's intensity, comparing favorably to Aretha Franklin's best work.

SINGLES: There was a tendency in 1973 for pop story songs to do well. Tony Orlando and Dawn's "Tie a Yellow Ribbon," Jim Croce's "Bad, Bad Leroy Brown," Roberta Flack's "Killing Me Softly," Vicki Lawrence's "The Night the Lights Went Out in Georgia," Helen Reddy's "Delta Dawn," Billy Paul's "Me and Mrs. Jones," Cher's "Half Breed," and Paul Simon's "Loves Me Like a Rock" all fit story lines into the verse-chorus-verse pop song format. Far different was Eric Weissberg and Steve Mandell's "Dueling Banjos," a tasty instrumental from the soundtrack of the film *Deliverance*.

It was a good year for novelty records, with Dr. Hook's amusing "Cover of the Rolling Stone" and horrific Bobby (Boris) Pickett's "Monster Mash." "We're an American Band" was a massive AM hit for the maturing Grand Funk Railroad, while Dr. John tasted his only dose of pop success with "Right Place, Wrong Time." Bette Midler also enjoyed some elusive record sales with her remake of The Andrews Sisters' "Boogie Woogie Bugle Boy."

Down South, Charlie Rich's crossover single "Behind Closed Doors" made this the most successful period of the Silver Fox's long and distinguished career. Meanwhile, Johnny Rodriguez became the first Chicano country star with the single "You Always Come Back (Hurting Me)."

The film surprise of the year was George Lucas' *American Graffiti*, steeped in the lore of rock music, fast cars, and California cruising. It grossed $56 million at the box office and sparked a wave of teeny-bopper films heavily laden with rock music. Rock book of the year was Guy Peelaert's *Rock Dreams* with its irreverent and sometimes nasty drawings of rock stars. Nik Cohn's text was appropriately mean-spirited.

Stevie Wonder

Kenneth Gamble

Pink Floyd

Leon Huff

The O'Jays

JANUARY 6, 1973

POP SINGLES

1. ME AND MRS. JONES
   (Billy Paul)
2. YOU'RE SO VAIN
   (Carly Simon)
3. CLAIR
   (Gilbert O'Sullivan)
4. YOU OUGHT TO BE WITH ME
   (Al Green)
5. SUPERSTITION
   (Stevie Wonder)
6. ROCKIN' PNEUMONIA AND BOOGIE
   WOOGIE FLU
   (Johnny Rivers)
7. IT NEVER RAINS IN SOUTHERN
   CALIFORNIA
   (Albert Hammond)
8. I WANNA BE WITH YOU
   (The Raspberries)
9. FUNNY FACE
   (Donna Fargo)
10. YOUR MAMA DON'T DANCE
    (Loggins and Messina)

POP ALBUMS

1. NO SECRETS
   (Carly Simon)
2. SEVENTH SOJOURN
   (The Moody Blues)
3. RHYMES AND REASONS
   (Carole King)
4. LIVING IN THE PAST
   (Jethro Tull)
5. SUMMER BREEZE
   (Seals and Crofts)
6. CATCH BULL AT FOUR
   (Cat Stevens)
7. ONE MAN DOG
   (James Taylor)
8. LOGGINS AND MESSINA
   (Loggins and Messina)
9. I'M STILL IN LOVE WITH YOU
   (Al Green)
10. CARAVANSERAI
    (Santana)

BLACK SINGLES

1. SUPERSTITION
   (Stevie Wonder)
2. KEEPER OF THE CASTLE
   (The Four Tops)
3. WHY CAN'T WE LIVE TOGETHER
   (Timmy Thomas)
4. THE WORLD IS A GHETTO
   (War)
5. LOVE JONES
   (Brighter Side of Darkness)
6. SUPERFLY
   (Curtis Mayfield)
7. ME AND MRS. JONES
   (Billy Paul)
8. TROUBLE IN MY HOME
   (Joe Simon)
9. I GOT A BAG OF MY OWN
   (James Brown)
10. CORNER OF THE SKY
    (The Jackson 5)

JAZZ ALBUMS

1. ON THE CORNER
   (Miles Davis)
2. CHICKEN LICKIN'
   (Funk Inc.)
3. THE ICEMAN'S BAND
   (Jerry Butler)
4. LEAN ON ME
   (Shirley Scott)
5. ENERGY ESSENTIALS
   (Various Artists)
6. ALL THE KING'S HORSES
   (Grover Washington Jr.)
7. PRELUDE
   (Eumir Deodato)
8. LIVE AT FUNKY QUARTERS
   (Cal Tjader)
9. INFINITY
   (John Coltrane)
10. TALK TO THE PEOPLE
    (Les McCann)

COUNTRY SINGLES

1. A PICTURE OF ME (WITHOUT YOU)
   (George Jones)
2. SHE'S GOT TO BE A SAINT
   (Ray Price)
3. LOVIN' ON BACK STREETS
   (Mel Street)
4. SOUL SONG
   (Joe Stampley)
5. PRETEND I NEVER HAPPENED
   (Waylon Jennings)
6. WHITE SILVER SANDS
   (Sonny James)
7. FOOL ME
   (Lynn Anderson)
8. PASS ME BY
   (Johnny Rodriguez)
9. OLD DOGS, CHILDREN AND
   WATERMELON WINE
   (Tom T. Hall)
10. KATY DID
    (Porter Wagoner)

COUNTRY ALBUMS

1. GOT THE ALL OVERS FOR YOU
   (Freddie Hart)
2. HERE I AM AGAIN
   (Loretta Lynn)
3. THE BEST OF THE BEST OF MERLE
   HAGGARD
   (Merle Haggard)
4. MY MAN
   (Tammy Wynette)
5. LYNN ANDERSON'S GREATEST HITS
   (Lynn Anderson)
6. A SUNSHINY DAY
   (Charley Pride)
7. THE HAPPIEST GIRL IN THE WHOLE U.S.A.
   (Donna Fargo)
8. CHARLIE McCOY
   (Charlie McCoy)
9. IT'S NOT LOVE
   (Merle Haggard)
10. WHEEL OF FORTUNE
    (Susan Raye)

JANUARY 13, 1973

POP SINGLES

1. YOU'RE SO VAIN
   (Carly Simon)
2. ME AND MRS. JONES
   (Billy Paul)
3. CLAIR
   (Gilbert O'Sullivan)
4. SUPERSTITION
   (Stevie Wonder)
5. YOUR MAMA DON'T DANCE
   (Loggins and Messina)
6. FUNNY FACE
   (Donna Fargo)
7. I WANNA BE WITH YOU
   (The Raspberries)

8. WHY CAN'T WE LIVE TOGETHER
   (Timmy Thomas)
9. SUPERFLY
   (Curtis Mayfield)
10. KEEPER OF THE CASTLE
    (The Four Tops)

POP ALBUMS

1. NO SECRETS
   (Carly Simon)
2. SEVENTH SOJOURN
   (The Moody Blues)
3. RHYMES AND REASONS
   (Carole King)
4. LIVING IN THE PAST
   (Jethro Tull)
5. SUMMER BREEZE
   (Seals and Crofts)
6. THE WORLD IS A GHETTO
   (War)
7. ONE MAN DOG
   (James Taylor)
8. LOGGINS AND MESSINA
   (Loggins and Messina)
9. CATCH BULL AT FOUR
   (Cat Stevens)
10. TOMMY
    (London Symphony Orchestra and Guest
    Soloists)

BLACK SINGLES

1. SUPERSTITION
   (Stevie Wonder)
2. WHY CAN'T WE LIVE TOGETHER
   (Timmy Thomas)
3. THE WORLD IS A GHETTO
   (War)
4. LOVE JONES
   (Brighter Side of Darkness)
5. TROUBLE MAN
   (Marvin Gaye)
6. KEEPER OF THE CASTLE
   (The Four Tops)
7. SUPERFLY
   (Curtis Mayfield)
8. I'LL BE YOUR SHELTER
   (Luther Ingram)
9. COULD IT BE I'M FALLING IN LOVE
   (Spinners)
10. ME AND MRS. JONES
    (Billy Paul)

JAZZ ALBUMS

1. ENERGY ESSENTIALS
   (Various Artists)
2. CHICKEN LICKIN'
   (Funk Inc.)
3. ALL THE KING'S HORSES
   (Grover Washington Jr.)
4. PRELUDE
   (Eumir Deodato)
5. LEAN ON ME
   (Shirley Scott)
6. ON THE CORNER
   (Miles Davis)
7. CYMANDE
   (Cymande)
8. THE ICEMAN'S BAND
   (Jerry Butler)
9. LIVE AT FUNKY QUARTERS
   (Cal Tjader)
10. TALK TO THE PEOPLE
    (Les McCann)

COUNTRY SINGLES

1. SHE'S GOT TO BE A SAINT
   (Ray Price)

2. LOVIN' ON BACK STREETS
   (Mel Street)
3. SOUL SONG
   (Joe Stampley)
4. A PICTURE OF ME (WITHOUT YOU)
   (George Jones)
5. PASS ME BY
   (Johnny Rodriguez)
6. OLD DOGS, CHILDREN AND
   WATERMELON WINE
   (Tom T. Hall)
7. SHE NEEDS SOMEONE TO HOLD HER
   (Conway Twitty)
8. KATY DID
   (Porter Wagoner)
9. I WONDER IF THEY EVER THINK OF ME
   (Merle Haggard)
10. LOVE'S THE ANSWER/JAMESTOWN FERRY
    (Tanya Tucker)

COUNTRY ALBUMS

1. I GOT THE ALL OVERS FOR YOU
   (Freddie Hart)
2. MY MAN
   (Tammy Wynette)
3. THE BEST OF THE BEST OF MERLE
   HAGGARD
   (Merle Haggard)
4. LYNN ANDERSON'S GREATEST HITS
   (Lynn Anderson)
5. HERE I AM AGAIN
   (Loretta Lynn)
6. IT'A NOT LOVE
   (Merle Haggard)
7. A SUNSHINY DAY
   (Charley Pride)
8. THE HAPPIEST GIRL IN THE WHOLE U.S.A.
   (Donna Fargo)
9. BURNING LOVE
   (Elvis Presley)
10. GLEN TRAVIS CAMPBELL
    (Glen Campbell)

JANUARY 20, 1973

POP SINGLES

1. SUPERSTITION
   (Stevie Wonder)
2. YOU'RE SO VAIN
   (Carly Simon)
3. ME AND MRS. JONES
   (Billy Paul)
4. WHY CAN'T WE LIVE TOGETHER
   (Timmy Thomas)
5. YOUR MAMA DON'T DANCE
   (Loggins and Messina)
6. FUNNY FACE
   (Donna Fargo)
7. SUPERFLY
   (Curtis Mayfield)
8. I WANNA BE WITH YOU
   (The Raspberries)
9. CROCODILE ROCK
   (Elton John)
10. CLAIR
    (Gilbert O'Sullivan)

POP ALBUMS

1. NO SECRETS
   (Carly Simon)
2. THE WORLD IS A GHETTO
   (War)
3. SEVENTH SOJOURN
   (The Moody Blues)
4. RHYMES AND REASONS
   (Carole King)

5. TOMMY
   *(London Symphony Orchestra and Guest
   Soloists)*
6. TALKING BOOK
   (Stevie Wonder)
7. FOR THE ROSES
   (Joni Mitchell)
8. LIVING IN THE PAST
   (Jethro Tull)
9. 360 DEGREES OF BILLY PAUL
   (Billy Paul)
10. ROCKY MOUNTAIN HIGH
    (John Denver)

BLACK SINGLES

1. SUPERSTITION
   (Stevie Wonder)
2. WHY CAN'T WE LIVE TOGETHER
   (Timmy Thomas)
3. LOVE JONES
   (Brighter Side of Darkness)
4. TROUBLE MAN
   (Marvin Gaye)
5. THE WORLD IS A GHETTO
   (War)
6. SUPERFLY
   (Curtis Mayfield)
7. COULD IT BE I'M FALLING IN LOVE
   (Spinners)
8. I'LL BE YOUR SHELTER
   (Luther Ingram)
9. HARRY HIPPIE
   (Bobby Womack and Peace)
10. THE MESSAGE
    (Cymande)

JAZZ ALBUMS

1. PRELUDE
   (Eumir Deodato)
2. CHICKEN LICKIN'
   (Funk Inc.)
3. TALK TO THE PEOPLE
   (Les McCann)
4. SKY DIVE
   (Freddie Hubbard)
5. ON THE CORNER
   (Miles Davis)
6. ALL THE KING'S HORSES
   (Grover Washington Jr.)
7. CYMANDE
   (Cymande)
8. LEAN ON ME
   (Shirley Scott)
9. ENERGY ESSENTIALS
   (Various Artists)
10. NEXT ALBUM
    (Sonny Rollins)

COUNTRY SINGLES

1. LOVIN' ON BACK STREETS
   (Mel Street)
2. SOUL SONG
   (Joe Stampley)
3. SHE'S GOT TO BE A SAINT
   (Ray Price)
4. PASS ME BY
   (Johnny Rodriguez)
5. OLD DOGS, CHILDREN AND
   WATERMELON WINE
   (Tom T. Hall)
6. SHE NEEDS SOMEONE TO HOLD HER
   (Conway Twitty)
7. I WONDER IF THEY EVER THINK OF ME
   (Merle Haggard)
8. KATY DID
   (Porter Wagoner)
9. LOVE'S THE ANSWER/JAMESTOWN FERRY
   (Tanya Tucker)
10. CATFISH JOHN
    (Johnny Russell)

COUNTRY ALBUMS

1. GOT THE ALL OVERS FOR YOU
   (Freddie Hart)
2. MY MAN
   (Tammy Wynette)
3. LYNN ANDERSON'S GREATEST HITS
   (Lynn Anderson)
4. THE BEST OF THE BEST OF MERLE
   HAGGARD
   (Merle Haggard)
5. IT'S NOT LOVE
   (Merle Haggard)
6. HERE I AM AGAIN
   (Loretta Lynn)
7. A SUNSHINY DAY
   (Charley Pride)
8. BURNING LOVE
   (Elvis Presley)
9. GLEN TRAVIS CAMPBELL
   (Glen Campbell)
10. LONELY WOMEN MAKE GOOD LOVERS
    (Bob Luman)

JANUARY 27, 1973

POP SINGLES

1. SUPERSTITION
   (Stevie Wonder)
2. CROCODILE ROCK
   (Elton John)
3. WHY CAN'T WE LIVE TOGETHER
   (Timmy Thomas)
4. YOU'RE SO VAIN
   (Carly Simon)
5. YOUR MAMA DON'T DANCE
   (Loggins and Messina)
6. SUPERFLY
   (Curtis Mayfield)
7. ME AND MRS. JONES
   (Billy Paul)
8. I WANNA BE WITH YOU
   (The Raspberries)
9. OH BABE, WHAT COULD YOU SAY
   (Hurricane Smith)
10. HI HI HI
    (Wings)

POP ALBUMS

1. NO SECRETS
   (Carly Simon)
2. THE WORLD IS A GHETTO
   (War)
3. RHYMES AND REASONS
   (Carole King)
4. TALKING BOOK
   (Stevie Wonder)
5. TOMMY
   *(London Symphony Orchestra and Guest
   Soloists)*
6. SEVENTH SOJOURN
   (The Moody Blues)
7. FOR THE ROSES
   (Joni Mitchell)
8. TROUBLE MAN
   (Marvin Gaye)
9. 360 DEGREES OF BILLY PAUL
   (Billy Paul)
10. ROCKY MOUNTAIN HIGH
    (John Denver)

BLACK SINGLES

1. SUPERSTITION
   (Stevie Wonder)

2. LOVE JONES
   (Brighter Side of Darkness)
3. TROUBLE MAN
   (Marvin Gaye)
4. THE WORLD IS A GHETTO
   (War)
5. SUPERFLY
   (Curtis Mayfield)
6. COULD IT BE I'M FALLING IN LOVE
   (Spinners)
7. WHY CAN'T WE LIVE TOGETHER
   (Timmy Thomas)
8. HARRY HIPPIE
   (Bobby Womack and Peace)
9. THE MESSAGE
   (Cymande)
10. DADDY'S HOME
    (Jermaine Jackson)

BLACK ALBUMS

1. TALKING BOOK
   (Stevie Wonder)
2. THE WORLD IS A GHETTO
   (War)
3. TROUBLE MAN
   (Marvin Gaye)
4. ROUND 2
   (The Stylistics)
5. 360 DEGREES OF BILLY PAUL
   (Billy Paul)
6. SUPERFLY
   (Curtis Mayfield)
7. BACK STABBERS
   (The O'Jays)
8. ALL DIRECTIONS
   (Temptations)
9. 1957–1972
   (Smokey Robinson and the Miracles)
10. I'M STILL IN LOVE WITH YOU
    (Al Green)

JAZZ ALBUMS

1. PRELUDE
   (Eumir Deodato)
2. SKY LOVE
   (Freddie Hubbard)
3. TALK TO THE PEOPLE
   (Les McCann)
4. CHICKEN LICKEN'
   (Funk, Inc.)
5. ALL THE KING'S HORSES
   (Grover Washington Jr.)
6. ON THE CORNER
   (Miles Davis)
7. ELLA LOVES COLE
   (Ella Fitzgerald)
8. THE EVOLUTION OF MANN
   (Herbie Mann)
9. NEXT ALBUM
   (Sonny Rollins)
10. LORD OF LORDS
    (Alice Coltrane)

COUNTRY SINGLES

1. SOUL THING
   (Joe Stampley)
2. OLD DOGS, CHILDREN AND WATER-
   MELON WINE
   (Tom T. Hall)
3. SHE NEEDS SOMEONE TO HOLD HER
   (Conway Twitty)
4. PASS ME BY
   (Johnny Rodriguez)
5. I WONDER IF THEY EVER THINK OF ME
   (Merle Haggard)
6. LOVIN' ON BACK STREETS
   (Mel Street)
7. LOVE'S THE ANSWER/JAMESTOWN FERRY
   (Tanya Tucker)

8. DO YOU KNOW WHAT IT'S LIKE TO BE
   LONESOME
   (Jerry Wallace)
9. RATED X
   (Loretta Lynn)
10. CATFISH JOHN
    (Johnny Russell)

COUNTRY ALBUMS

1. MY MAN
   (Tammy Wynette)
2. GOT THE ALL OVERS FOR YOU
   (Freddie Hart)
3. IT'S NOT LOVE
   (Merle Haggard)
4. THE BEST OF THE BEST OF MERLE
   HAGGARD
   (Merle Haggard)
5. LYNN ANDERSON'S GREATEST HITS
   (Lynn Anderson)
6. THIS MUCH A MAN
   (Marty Robbins)
7. GLEN TRAVIS CAMPBELL
   (Glen Campbell)
8. HERE I AM AGAIN
   (Loretta Lynn)
9. BURNING LOVE
   (Elvis Presley)
10. A SUNSHINY DAY
    (Charley Pride)

FEBRUARY 3, 1973

POP SINGLES

1. CROCODILE ROCK
   (Elton John)
2. WHY CAN'T WE LIVE TOGETHER
   (Timmy Thomas)
3. YOU'RE SO VAIN
   (Carly Simon)
4. SUPERSTITION
   (Stevie Wonder)
5. OH BABE, WHAT COULD YOU SAY
   (Hurricane Smith)
6. YOUR MAMA DON'T DANCE
   (Loggins and Messina)
7. HI HI HI
   (Wings)
8. TROUBLE MAN
   (Marvin Gaye)
9. SUPERFLY
   (Curtis Mayfield)
10. LOVE JONES
    (Brighter Side of Darkness)

POP ALBUMS

1. NO SECRETS
   (Carly Simon)
2. THE WORLD IS A GHETTO
   (War)
3. TALKING BOOK
   (Stevie Wonder)
4. RHYMES ABD REASONS
   (Carole King)
5. TOMMY
   (London Symphony Orchestra and Guest
   Soloists)
6. TROUBLE MAN
   (Marvin Gaye)
7. FOR THE ROSES
   (Joni Mitchell)
8. SEVENTH SOJOURN
   (The Moody Blues)
9. HOMECOMING
   (America)
10. THE DIVINE MISS M
    (Bette Midler)

BLACK SINGLES

1. LOVE TRAIN
   (The O'Jays)
2. LOVE JONES
   (Brighter Side of Darkness)
3. COULD IT BE I'M FALLING IN LOVE
   (Spinners)
4. TROUBLE MAN
   (Marvin Gaye)
5. SUPERSTITION
   (Stevie Wonder)
6. THE WORLD IS A GHETTO
   (War)
7. SUPERFLY
   (Curtis Mayfield)
8. DADDY'S HOME
   (Jermaine Jackson)
9. THE MESSAGE
   (Cymande)
10. HARRY HIPPIE
    (Bobby Womack and Peace)

BLACK ALBUMS

1. TROUBLE MAN
   (Marvin Gaye)
2. TALKING BOOK
   (Stevie Wonder)
3. THE WORLD IS A GHETTO
   (War)
4. LADY SINGS THE BLUES
   (Diana Ross)
5. 360 DEGREES OF BILLY PAUL
   (Billy Paul)
6. BACK STABBERS
   (The O'Jays)
7. ROUND 2
   (The Stylistics)
8. 1957–1972
   (Smokey Robinson and the Miracles)
9. GOOD FOOT
   (James Brown)
10. ALL DIRECTIONS
    (Temptations)

JAZZ ALBUMS

1. PRELUDE
   (Eumir Deodato)
2. SKY DIVE
   (Freddie Hubbard)
3. CHICKEN LICKIN'
   (Funk Inc.)
4. ALL THE KING'S HORSES
   (Grover Washington Jr.)
5. ON THE CORNER
   (Miles Davis)
6. ELLA LOVES COLE
   (Ella Fitzgerald)
7. THE EVOLUTION OF MANN
   (Herbie Mann)
8. TALK TO THE PEOPLE
   (Les McCann)
9. NEXT ALBUM
   (Sonny Rollins)
10. LIVE AT THE EAST
    (Pharaoh Sanders)

COUNTRY SINGLES

1. OLD DOGS, CHILDREN AND
   WATERMELON WINE
   (Tom T. Hall)
2. SHE NEEDS SOMEONE TO HOLD HER
   (Conway Twitty)
3. I WONDER IF THEY EVER THINK OF ME
   (Merle Haggard)
4. PASS ME BY
   (Johnny Rodriguez)
5. DO YOU KNOW WHAT IT'S LIKE TO BE
   LONESOME
   (Jerry Wallace)

6. SOUL SONG
   (*Joe Stampley*)
7. LOVE'S THE ANSWER/JAMESTOWN FERRY
   (*Tanya Tucker*)
8. RATED X
   (*Loretta Lynn*)
9. THE LORD KNOWS I'M DRINKIN'
   (*Cal Smith*)
10. NEON ROSE
   (*Mel Tillis*)

COUNTRY ALBUMS

1. MY MAN
   (*Tammy Wynette*)
2. IT'S NOT LOVE
   (*Merle Haggard*)
3. GOT THE ALL OVERS FOR YOU
   (*Freddie Hart*)
4. THIS MUCH A MAN
   (*Marty Robbins*)
5. THE BEST OF THE BEST OF MERLE HAGGARD
   (*Merle Haggard*)
6. GLEN TRAVIS CAMPBELL
   (*Glen Campbell*)
7. LYNN ANDERSON'S GREATEST HITS
   (*Lynn Anderson*)
8. HERE I AM AGAIN
   (*Loretta Lynn*)
9. A PICTURE OF ME
   (*George Jones*)
10. INCOMPARABLE CHARLEY PRIDE
   (*Charley Pride*)

FEBRUARY 10, 1973

POP SINGLES

1. CROCODILE ROCK
   (*Elton John*)
2. WHY CAN'T WE LIVE TOGETHER
   (*Timmy Thomas*)
3. YOU'RE SO VAIN
   (*Carly Simon*)
4. OH BABE, WHAT COULD YOU SAY
   (*Hurricane Smith*)
5. DUELING BANJOS
   (*Original Soundtrack*)
6. TROUBLE MAN
   (*Marvin Gaye*)
7. HI HI HI
   (*Wings*)
8. LOVE JONES
   (*Brighter Side of Darkness*)
9. THE WORLD IS A GHETTO
   (*War*)
10. COULD IT BE I'M FALLING IN LOVE
   (*Spinners*)

POP ALBUMS

1. NO SECRETS
   (*Carly Simon*)
2. THE WORLD IS A GHETTO
   (*War*)
3. TALKING BOOK
   (*Stevie Wonder*)
4. TROUBLE MAN
   (*Marvin Gaye*)
5. TOMMY
   (*London Symphony Orchestra and Guest Soloists*)
6. THE DIVINE MISS M
   (*Bette Midler*)
7. HOMECOMING
   (*America*)
8. RHYMES AND REASONS
   (*Carole King*)
9. FOR THE ROSES
   (*Joni Mitchell*)

10. HOT AUGUST NIGHT
   (*Neil Diamond*)

BLACK SINGLES

1. LOVE TRAIN
   (*The O'Jays*)
2. COULD IT BE I'M FALLING IN LOVE
   (*Spinners*)
3. LOVE JONES
   (*Brighter Side of Darkness*)
4. DADDY'S HOME
   (*Jermaine Jackson*)
5. TROUBLE MAN
   (*Marvin Gaye*)
6. SUPERSTITION
   (*Stevie Wonder*)
7. THE WORLD IS A GHETTO
   (*War*)
8. GIVE ME YOUR LOVE
   (*Barbara Mason*)
9. I GOT ANTS IN MY PANTS
   (*James Brown*)
10. I WISH I COULD TALK TO YOU
   (*The Sylvers*)

BLACK ALBUMS

1. TROUBLE MAN
   (*Marvin Gaye*)
2. TALKING BOOK
   (*Stevie Wonder*)
3. THE WORLD IS A GHETTO
   (*War*)
4. LADY SINGS THE BLUES
   (*Diana Ross*)
5. BACK STABBERS
   (*The O'Jays*)
6. 360 DEGREES OF BILLY PAUL
   (*Billy Paul*)
7. ROUND 2
   (*The Stylistics*)
8. 1957-1972
   (*Smokey Robinson and the Miracles*)
9. UNDERSTANDING
   (*Bobby Womack*)
10. GOOD FOOT
   (*James Brown*)

JAZZ ALBUMS

1. PRELUDE
   (*Eumir Deodato*)
2. CHICKEN LICKIN'
   (*Funk Inc.*)
3. SKY DIVE
   (*Freddie Hubbard*)
4. THE EVOLUTION OF MANN
   (*Herbie Mann*)
5. ON THE CORNER
   (*Miles Davis*)
6. ALL THE KING'S HORSES
   (*Grover Washington Jr.*)
7. TALK TO THE PEOPLE
   (*Les McCann*)
8. NEXT ALBUM
   (*Sonny Rollins*)
9. LIVE AT THE EAST
   (*Pharoah Sanders*)
10. LIVE AT FUNKY QUARTERS
   (*Cal Tjader*)

COUNTRY SINGLES

1. SHE NEEDS SOMEONE TO HOLD HER
   (*Conway Twitty*)
2. I WONDER IF THEY EVER THINK OF ME
   (*Merle Haggard*)
3. OLD DOGS, CHILDREN AND WATERMELON WINE
   (*Tom T. Hall*)

4. DO YOU KNOW WHAT IT'S LIKE TO BE LONESOME
   (*Jerry Wallace*)
5. THE LORD KNOWS I'M DRINKIN'
   (*Cal Smith*)
6. PASS ME BY
   (*Johnny Rodriquez*)
7. LOVE'S THE ANSWER/JAMESTOWN FERRY
   (*Tanya Tucker*)
8. RATED X
   (*Loretta Lynn*)
9. NEON ROSE
   (*Mel Tillis*)
10. ANY OLD WIND THAT BLOWS
   (*Johnny Cash*)

COUNTRY ALBUMS

1. IT'S NOT LOVE
   (*Merle Haggard*)
2. MY MAN
   (*Tammy Wynette*)
3. THIS MUCH A MAN
   (*Marty Robbins*)
4. GLEN TRAVIS CAMPBELL
   (*Glen Campbell*)
5. GOT THE ALL OVERS FOR YOU
   (*Freddie Hart*)
6. THE BEST OF THE BEST OF MERLE HAGGARD
   (*Merle Haggard*)
7. A PICTURE OF ME
   (*George Jones*)
8. LYNN ANDERSON'S GREATEST HITS
   (*Lynn Anderson*)
9. INCOMPARABLE CHARLEY PRIDE
   (*Charley Pride*)
10. DON'T SHE LOOK GOOD
   (*Bill Anderson*)

FEBRUARY 17, 1973

POP SINGLES

1. DUELING BANJOS
   (*Original Soundtrack*)
2. CROCODILE ROCK
   (*Elton John*)
3. OH BABE, WHAT COULD YOU SAY
   (*Hurricane Smith*)
4. COULD IT BE I'M FALLING IN LOVE
   (*Spinners*)
5. WHY CAN'T WE LIVE TOGETHER
   (*Timmy Thomas*)
6. KILLING ME SOFTLY WITH HIS SONG
   (*Roberta Flack*)
7. DON'T EXPECT ME TO BE YOUR FRIEND
   (*Lobo*)
8. LOVE JONES
   (*Brighter Side of Darkness*)
9. THE WORLD IS A GHETTO
   (*War*)
10. DO IT AGAIN
   (*Steely Dan*)

POP ALBUMS

1. THE WORLD IS A GHETTO
   (*War*)
2. NO SECRETS
   (*Carly Simon*)
3. TALKING BOOK
   (*Stevie Wonder*)
4. TROUBLE MAN
   (*Marvin Gaye*)
5. HOMECOMING
   (*America*)
6. THE DIVINE MISS M
   (*Bette Midler*)

7. TOMMY
   (*London Symphony Orchestra and Guest Soloists*)
8. HOT AUGUST NIGHT
   (*Neil Diamond*)
9. ROCKY MOUNTAIN HIGH
   (*John Denver*)
10. LADY SINGS THE BLUES
    (*Diana Ross*)

BLACK SINGLES

1. LOVE TRAIN
   (*The O'Jays*)
2. COULD IT BE I'M FALLING IN LOVE
   (*Spinners*)
3. DADDY'S HOME
   (*Jermaine Jackson*)
4. LOVE JONES
   (*Brighter Side of Darkness*)
5. GIVE ME YOUR LOVE
   (*Barbara Mason*)
6. I GOT ANTS IN MY PANTS
   (*James Brown*)
7. TROUBLE MAN
   (*Marvin Gaye*)
8. I WISH I COULD TALK TO YOU
   (*The Sylvers*)
9. KILLING ME SOFTLY WITH HIS SONG
   (*Roberta Flack*)
10. THE WORLD IS A GHETTO
    (*War*)

BLACK ALBUMS

1. THE WORLD IS A GHETTO
   (*War*)
2. TROUBLE MAN
   (*Marvin Gaye*)
3. TALKING BOOK
   (*Stevie Wonder*)
4. LADY SINGS THE BLUES
   (*Diana Ross*)
5. BACK STABBERS
   (*The O'Jays*)
6. ROUND 2
   (*The Stylistics*)
7. 360 DEGREES OF BILLY PAUL
   (*Billy Paul*)
8. GREEN IS BLUES
   (*Al Green*)
9. 1957-1972
   (*Smokey Robinson and the Miracles*)
10. UNDERSTANDING
    (*Bobby Womack*)

JAZZ ALBUMS

1. PRELUDE
   (*Eumir Deodato*)
2. THE EVOLUTION OF MANN
   (*Herbie Mann*)
3. CHICKEN LICKIN'
   (*Funk Inc.*)
4. SKY DIVE
   (*Freddie Hubbard*)
5. ON THE CORNER
   (*Miles Davis*)
6. TALK TO THE PEOPLE
   (*Les McCann*)
7. NEXT ALBUM
   (*Sonny Rollins*)
8. LIVE AT THE EAST
   (*Pharaoh Sanders*)
9. LIVE AT FUNKY QUARTERS
   (*Cal Tjader*)
10. LIVE AT THE LIGHTHOUSE
    (*Charles Earland*)

COUNTRY SINGLES

1. I WONDER IF THEY EVER THINK OF ME
   (*Merle Haggard*)

2. THE LORD KNOWS I'M DRINKIN'
   (*Cal Smith*)
3. DO YOU KNOW WHAT IT'S LIKE TO BE LONESOME
   (*Jerry Wallace*)
4. SHE NEEDS SOMEONE TO HOLD HER
   (*Conway Twitty*)
5. RATED X
   (*Loretta Lynn*)
6. NEON ROSE
   (*Mel Tillis*)
7. TIL I GET IT RIGHT
   (*Tammy Wynette*)
8. ANY OLD WIND THAT BLOWS
   (*Johnny Cash*)
9. LOVE'S THE ANSWER/JAMESTOWN FERRY
   (*Tanya Tucker*)
10. YOU LAY SO EASY ON MY MIND
    (*Bobby G. Rice*)

COUNTRY ALBUMS

1. IT'S NOT LOVE
   (*Merle Haggard*)
2. THIS MUCH A MAN
   (*Marty Robbins*)
3. MY MAN
   (*Tammy Wynette*)
4. GLEN TRAVIS CAMPBELL
   (*Glen Campbell*)
5. A PICTURE OF ME
   (*George Jones*)
6. GOT THE ALL OVERS FOR YOU
   (*Freddie Hart*)
7. DON'T SHE LOOK GOOD
   (*Bill Anderson*)
8. INCOMPARABLE CHARLEY PRIDE
   (*Charley Pride*)
9. THE BEST OF THE BEST OF MERLE HAGGARD
   (*Merle Haggard*)
10. LYNN ANDERSON'S GREATEST HITS
    (*Lynn Anderson*)

FEBRUARY 24, 1973

POP SINGLES

1. DUELING BANJOS
   (*Original Soundtrack*)
2. COULD IT BE I'M FALLING IN LOVE
   (*Spinners*)
3. OH BABE, WHAT COULD YOU SAY
   (*Hurricane Smith*)
4. KILLING ME SOFTLY WITH HIS SONG
   (*Roberta Flack*)
5. CROCODILE ROCK
   (*Elton John*)
6. DON'T EXPECT ME TO BE YOUR FRIEND
   (*Lobo*)
7. LOVE TRAIN
   (*The O'Jays*)
8. DO IT AGAIN
   (*Steely Dan*)
9. DADDY'S HOME
   (*Jermaine Jackson*)
10. ROCKY MOUNTAIN HIGH
    (*John Denver*)

POP ALBUMS

1. THE WORLD IS A GHETTO
   (*War*)
2. NO SECRETS
   (*Carly Simon*)
3. TALKING BOOK
   (*Stevie Wonder*)
4. DELIVERANCE
   (*Original Soundtrack*)
5. HOMECOMING
   (*America*)

6. TROUBLE MAN
   (*Marvin Gaye*)
7. HOT AUGUST NIGHT
   (*Neil Diamond*)
8. ROCKY MOUNTAIN HIGH
   (*John Denver*)
9. LADY SINGS THE BLUES
   (*Diana Ross*)
10. DON'T SHOOT ME, I'M ONLY THE PIANO PLAYER
    (*Elton John*)

BLACK SINGLES

1. LOVE TRAIN
   (*The O'Jays*)
2. COULD IT BE I'M FALLING IN LOVE
   (*Spinners*)
3. DADDY'S HOME
   (*Jermaine Jackson*)
4. GIVE ME YOUR LOVE
   (*Barbara Mason*)
5. I GOT ANTS IN MY PANTS
   (*James Brown*)
6. LOVE JONES
   (*Brighter Side of Darkness*)
7. I WISH I COULD TALK TO YOU
   (*The Sylvers*)
8. KILLING ME SOFTLY WITH HIS SONG
   (*Roberta Flack*)
9. NEITHER ONE OF US
   (*Gladys Knight and the Pips*)
10. TROUBLE MAN
    (*Marvin Gaye*)

BLACK ALBUMS

1. THE WORLD IS A GHETTO
   (*War*)
2. TALKING BOOK
   (*Stevie Wonder*)
3. LADY SINGS THE BLUES
   (*Diana Ross*)
4. GREEN IS BLUES
   (*Al Green*)
5. TROUBLE MAN
   (*Marvin Gaye*)
6. BACK STABBERS
   (*The O'Jays*)
7. ROUND 2
   (*The Stylistics*)
8. 360 DEGREES OF BILLY PAUL
   (*Billy Paul*)
9. UNDERSTANDING
   (*Bobby Womack*)
10. 1957-1972
    (*Smokey Robinson and the Miracles*)

JAZZ ALBUMS

1. PRELUDE
   (*Eumir Deodato*)
2. THE EVOLUTION OF MANN
   (*Herbie Mann*)
3. SKY DIVE
   (*Freddie Hubbard*)
4. LIVE AT THE EAST
   (*Pharaoh Sanders*)
5. TALK TO THE PEOPLE
   (*Les McCann*)
6. CHICKEN LICKIN'
   (*Funk Inc.*)
7. NEXT ALBUM
   (*Sonny Rollins*)
8. LIVE AT FUNKY QUARTERS
   (*Cal Tjader*)
9. LIVE AT THE LIGHTHOUSE
   (*Charles Earland*)
10. RAVEN SPEAKS
    (*Woody Herman*)

COUNTRY SINGLES

1. THE LORD KNOWS I'M DRINKIN'
   (*Cal Smith*)

2. DO YOU KNOW WHAT IT'S LIKE TO BE LONESOME
   (Jerry Wallace)
3. TIL I GET IT RIGHT
   (Tammy Wynette)
4. NEON ROSE
   (Mel Tillis)
5. RATED X
   (Loretta Lynn)
6. ANY OLD WIND THAT BLOWS
   (Johnny Cash)
7. TEDDY BEAR SONG
   (Barbara Fairchild)
8. I WONDER IF THEY EVER THINK OF ME
   (Merle Haggard)
9. YOU LAY SO EASY ON MY MIND
   (Bobby G. Rice)
10. SHE NEEDS SOMEONE TO HOLD HER
    (Conway Twitty)

COUNTRY ALBUMS

1. IT'S NOT LOVE
   (Merle Haggard)
2. THIS MUCH A MAN
   (Marty Robbins)
3. A PICTURE OF ME
   (George Jones)
4. MY MAN
   (Tammy Wynette)
5. DON'T SHE LOOK GOOD
   (Bill Anderson)
6. GLEN TRAVIS CAMPBELL
   (Glen Campbell)
7. SONGS OF LOVE BY CHARLEY PRIDE
   (Charley Pride)
8. INCOMPARABLE CHARLEY PRIDE
   (Charley Pride)
9. GOT THE ALL OVERS FOR YOU
   (Freddie Hart)
10. ROY CLARK LIVE
    (Roy Clark)

MARCH 3, 1973

POP SINGLES

1. COULD IT BE I'M FALLING IN LOVE
   (Spinners)
2. KILLING ME SOFTLY WITH HIS SONG
   (Roberta Flack)
3. DUELING BANJOS
   (Original Soundtrack)
4. OH BABE, WHAT COULD YOU SAY
   (Hurricane Smith)
5. LOVE TRAIN
   (The O'Jays)
6. DON'T EXPECT ME TO BE YOUR FRIEND
   (Lobo)
7. LAST SONG
   (Edward Bear)
8. DO IT AGAIN
   (Steely Dan)
9. DADDY'S HOME
   (Jermaine Jackson)
10. ROCKY MOUNTAIN HIGH
    (John Denver)

POP ALBUMS

1. DON'T SHOOT ME, I'M ONLY THE PIANO PLAYER
   (Elton John)
2. HOT AUGUST NIGHT
   (Neil Diamond)
3. DELIVERANCE
   (Original Soundtrack)
4. THE WORLD IS A GHETTO
   (War)

5. NO SECRETS
   (Carly Simon)
6. ROCKY MOUNTAIN HIGH
   (John Denver)
7. LADY SINGS THE BLUES
   (Diana Ross)
8. TALKING BOOK
   (Stevie Wonder)
9. TROUBLE MAN
   (Marvin Gaye)
10. HOMECOMING
    (America)

BLACK SINGLES

1. COULD IT BE I'M FALLING IN LOVE
   (Spinners)
2. LOVE TRAIN
   (The O'Jays)
3. KILLING ME SOFTLY WITH HIS SONG
   (Roberta Flack)
4. GIVE ME YOUR LOVE
   (Barbara Mason)
5. I GOT ANTS IN MY PANTS
   (James Brown)
6. DADDY'S HOME
   (Jermaine Jackson)
7. I WISH I COULD TALK TO YOU
   (The Sylvers)
8. NEITHER ONE OF US
   (Gladys Knight and the Pips)
9. AIN'T NO WOMAN
   (The Four Tops)
10. DON'T LEAVE ME STARVING FOR YOUR LOVE
    (Holland and Dozier)

JAZZ ALBUMS

1. PRELUDE
   (Eumir Deodato)
2. THE EVOLUTION OF MANN
   (Herbie Mann)
3. LIVE AT THE EAST
   (Pharaoh Sanders)
4. LIVE AT THE LIGHTHOUSE
   (Charles Earland)
5. TALK TO THE PEOPLE
   (Les McCann)
6. CHICKEN LICKIN'
   (Funk Inc.)
7. NEXT ALBUM
   (Sonny Rollins)
8. LIVE AT FUNKY QUARTERS
   (Cal Tjader)
9. RAVEN SPEAKS
   (Woody Herman)
10. HIS GREATEST YEARS, VOL. 2
    (John Coltrane)

COUNTRY SINGLES

1. DO YOU KNOW WHAT IT'S LIKE TO BE LONESOME
   (Jerry Wallace)
2. TIL I GET IT RIGHT
   (Tammy Wynette)
3. NEON ROSE
   (Mel Tillis)
4. TEDDY BEAR SONG
   (Barbara Fairchild)
5. THE LORD KNOWS I'M DRINKIN'
   (Cal Smith)
6. ANY OLD WIND THAT BLOWS
   (Johnny Cash)
7. RATED X
   (Loretta Lynn)
8. GOOD THINGS
   (David Houston)
9. YOU LAY SO EASY ON MY MIND
   (Bobby G. Rice)
10. LOVE IS THE LOOK YOU'RE LOOKING FOR
    (Connie Smith)

COUNTRY ALBUMS

1. SONGS OF LOVE BY CHARLEY PRIDE
   (Charley Pride)
2. IT'S NOT LOVE
   (Merle Haggard)
3. A PICTURE OF ME
   (George Jones)
4. THIS MUCH A MAN
   (Marty Robbins)
5. DON'T SHE LOOK GOOD
   (Bill Anderson)
6. MY MAN
   (Tammy Wynette)
7. DELIVERANCE
   (Original Soundtrack)
8. ROY CLARK LIVE
   (Roy Clark)
9. I'VE FOUND SOMEONE OF MY OWN
   (Cal Smith)
10. WHO'S GONNA PLAY THIS OLD PIANO
    (Jerry Lee Lewis)

MARCH 10, 1973

POP SINGLES

1. KILLING ME SOFTLY WITH HIS SONG
   (Roberta Flack)
2. COULD IT BE I'M FALLING IN LOVE
   (Spinners)
3. LAST SONG
   (Edward Bear)
4. LOVE TRAIN
   (The O'Jays)
5. DUELING BANJOS
   (Original Soundtrack)
6. ALSO SPRACH ZARATHUSTRA
   (Eumir Deodato)
7. DADDY'S HOME
   (Jermaine Jackson)
8. ROCKY MOUNTAIN HIGH
   (John Denver)
9. DON'T EXPECT ME TO BE YOUR FRIEND
   (Lobo)
10. COVER OF ROLLING STONE
    (Dr. Hook and the Medicine Show)

POP ALBUMS

1. DON'T SHOOT ME, I'M ONLY THE PIANO PLAYER
   (Elton John)
2. HOT AUGUST NIGHT
   (Neil Diamond)
3. DELIVERANCE
   (Original Soundtrack)
4. THE WORLD IS A GHETTO
   (War)
5. ROCKY MOUNTAIN HIGH
   (John Denver)
6. NO SECRETS
   (Carly Simon)
7. LADY SINGS THE BLUES
   (Diana Ross)
8. PRELUDE
   (Eumir Deodato)
9. TALKING BOOK
   (Stevie Wonder)
10. SHOOT OUT AT THE FANTASY FACTORY
    (Traffic)

BLACK SINGLES

1. KILLING ME SOFTLY WITH HIS SONG
   (Roberta Flack)
2. LOVE TRAIN
   (The O'Jays)
3. COULD IT BE I'M FALLING IN LOVE
   (Spinners)

4. GIVE ME YOUR LOVE
   (Barbara Mason)
5. NEITHER ONE OF US
   (Gladys Knight and the Pips)
6. AIN'T NO WOMAN (LIKE THE ONE I GOT)
   (The Four Tops)
7. I GOT ANTS IN MY PANTS
   (James Brown)
8. DADDY'S HOME
   (Jermaine Jackson)
9. MASTER OF EYES
   (Aretha Franklin)
10. CALL ME
   (Al Green)

JAZZ ALBUMS

1. PRELUDE
   (Eumir Deodato)
2. LIVE AT THE EAST
   (Pharaoh Sanders)
3. LIVE AT THE LIGHTHOUSE
   (Charles Earland)
4. TALK TO THE PEOPLE
   (Les McCann)
5. THE EVOLUTION OF MANN
   (Herbie Mann)
6. CHICKEN LICKIN'
   (Funk Inc.)
7. LIVE AT FUNKY QUARTERS
   (Cal Tjader)
8. NEXT ALBUM
   (Sonny Rollins)
9. RAVEN SPEAKS
   (Woody Herman)
10. SKY DIVE
   (Freddie Hubbard)

COUNTRY SINGLES

1. TIL I GET IT RIGHT
   (Tammy Wynette)
2. TEDDY BEAR SONG
   (Barbara Fairchild)
3. NEON ROSE
   (Mel Tillis)
4. YOU LAY SO EASY ON MY MIND
   (Bobby G. Rice)
5. GOOD THINGS
   (David Houston)
6. THE LORD KNOWS I'M DRINKIN'
   (Cal Smith)
7. DO YOU KNOW WHAT IT'S LIKE TO BE
LONESOME
   (Jerry Wallace)
8. KEEP ME IN MIND
   (Lynn Anderson)
9. LOVE IS THE LOOK YOU'RE LOOKING FOR
   (Connie Smith)
10. SHELTER OF YOUR EYES
   (Don Williams)

COUNTRY ALBUMS

1. SONGS OF LOVE BY CHARLEY PRIDE
   (Charley Pride)
2. IT'S NOT LOVE
   (Merle Haggard)
3. DELIVERANCE
   (Original Soundtrack)
4. I'VE FOUND SOMEONE OF MY OWN
   (Cal Smith)
5. A PICTURE OF ME
   (George Jones)
6. WHO'S GONNA PLAY THIS OLD PIANO
   (Jerry Lee Lewis)
7. ROY CLARK LIVE
   Roy Clark
8. THIS MUCH A MAN
   (Marty Robbins)
9. HOT A'MIGHTY
   (Jerry Reed)
10. ANY OLD WIND THAT BLOWS
   (Johnny Cash)

MARCH 17, 1973

POP SINGLES

1. KILLING ME SOFTLY WITH HIS SONG
   (Roberta Flack)
2. LAST SONG
   (Edward Bear)
3. LOVE TRAIN
   (The O'Jays)
4. COULD IT BE I'M FALLING IN LOVE
   (Spinners)
5. ALSO SPRACH ZARATHUSTRA
   (Eumir Deodato)
6. DADDY'S HOME
   (Jermaine Jackson)
7. ROCKY MOUNTAIN HIGH
   (John Denver)
8. COVER OF ROLLING STONE
   (Dr. Hook and the Medicine Show)
9. DANNY'S SONG
   (Anne Murray)
10. I'M JUST A SINGER IN A ROCK 'N' ROLL
BAND
   (The Moody Blues)

POP ALBUMS

1. DON'T SHOOT ME, I'M ONLY THE PIANO
PLAYER
   (Elton John)
2. DELIVERANCE
   (Original Soundtrack)
3. ROCKY MOUNTAIN HIGH
   (John Denver)
4. THE WORLD IS A GHETTO
   (War)
5. LADY SINGS THE BLUES
   (Diana Ross)
6. PRELUDE
   (Eumir Deodato)
7. NO SECRETS
   (Carly Simon)
8. HOT AUGUST NIGHT
   (Neil Diamond)
9. SHOOT OUT AT THE FANTASY FACTORY
   (Traffic)
10. THE DIVINE MISS M
   (Bette Midler)

BLACK SINGLES

1. KILLING ME SOFTLY WITH HIS SONG
   (Roberta Flack)
2. NEITHER ONE OF US
   (Gladys Knight and the Pips)
3. LOVE TRAIN
   (The O'Jays)
4. GIVE ME YOUR LOVE
   (Barbara Mason)
5. AIN'T NO WOMAN (LIKE THE ONE I GOT)
   (The Four Tops)
6. BREAK UP TO MAKE UP
   (The Stylistics)
7. MASTER OF EYES
   (Aretha Franklin)
8. CALL ME
   (Al Green)
9. DO IT IN THE NAME OF LOVE
   (Candi Staton)
10. WE DID IT
   (Syl Johnson)

BLACK ALBUMS

1. THE WORLD IS A GHETTO
   (War)
2. TALKING BOOK
   (Stevie Wonder)
3. LADY SINGS THE BLUES
   (Diana Ross)

4. ROUND 2
   (The Stylistics)
5. GREEN IS BLUES
   (Al Green)
6. I'M STILL IN LOVE WITH YOU
   (Al Green)
7. TROUBLE MAN
   (Marvin Gaye)
8. WATTSTAX
   (Original Soundtrack)
9. BACK STABBERS
   (The O'Jays)
10. ACROSS 110th STREET
   (Bobby Womack and Peace)

JAZZ ALBUMS

1. PRELUDE
   (Eumir Deodato)
2. LIVE AT THE EAST
   (Pharaoh Sanders)
3. LIVE AT THE LIGHTHOUSE
   (Charles Earland)
4. THE EVOLUTION OF MANN
   (Herbie Mann)
5. TALK TO THE PEOPLE
   (Les McCann)
6. LIVE AT FUNKY QUARTERS
   (Cal Tjader)
7. BIRDS OF FIRE
   (Mahavishnu Orchestra)
8. STRANGE FRUIT
   (Billie Holliday)
9. NEXT ALBUM
   (Sonny Rollins)
10. HUSH 'N' THUNDER
   (Yusef Lateef)

COUNTRY SINGLES

1. TEDDY BEAR SONG
   (Barbara Fairchild)
2. YOU LAY SO EASY ON MY MIND
   (Bobby G. Rice)
3. GOOD THINGS
   (David Houston)
4. TIL I GET IT RIGHT
   (Tammy Wynette)
5. DUELING BANJOS
   (Original Soundtrack)
6. KEEP ME IN MIND
   (Lynn Anderson)
7. NEON ROSE
   (Mel Tillis)
8. SHELTER OF YOUR EYES
   (Don Williams)
9. LOVE IS THE LOOK YOU'RE LOOKING FOR
   (Connie Smith)
10. DANNY'S SONG
   (Anne Murray)

COUNTRY ALBUMS

1. SONGS OF LOVE BY CHARLEY PRIDE
   (Charley Pride)
2. DELIVERANCE
   (Original Soundtrack)
3. I'VE FOUND SOMEONE OF MY OWN
   (Cal Smith)
4. IT'S NOT LOVE
   (Merle Haggard)
5. WHO'S GONNA PLAY THIS OLD PIANO
   (Jerry Lee Lewis)
6. ROY CLARK LIVE
   (Roy Clark)
7. ANY OLD WIND THAT BLOWS
   (Johnny Cash)
8. HOT A'MIGHTY
   (Jerry Reed)
9. A PICTURE OF ME
   (George Jones)
10. THIS MUCH A MAN
   (Marty Robbins)

MARCH 24, 1973

POP SINGLES

1. KILLING ME SOFTLY WITH HIS SONG
   (Roberta Flack)
2. LOVE TRAIN
   (The O'Jays)
3. LAST SONG
   (Edward Bear)
4. ALSO SPRACH ZARATHUSTRA
   (Eumir Deodato)
5. COVER OF ROLLING STONE
   (Dr. Hook and the Medicine Show)
6. DADDY'S HOME
   (Jermaine Jackson)
7. DANNY'S SONG
   (Anne Murray)
8. ROCKY MOUNTAIN HIGH
   (John Denver)
9. NEITHER ONE OF US
   (Gladys Knight and the Pips)
10. I'M JUST A SINGER IN A ROCK 'N' ROLL
    BAND
    (The Moody Blues)

POP ALBUMS

1. DELIVERANCE
   (Original Soundtrack)
2. DON'T SHOOT ME, I'M ONLY THE PIANO
   PLAYER
   (Elton John)
3. ROCKY MOUNTAIN HIGH
   (John Denver)
4. LADY SINGS THE BLUES
   (Diana Ross)
5. THE WORLD IS A GHETTO
   (War)
6. PRELUDE
   (Eumir Deodato)
7. NO SECRETS
   (Carly Simon)
8. SHOOT OUT AT THE FANTASY FACTORY
   (Traffic)
9. THE DIVINE MISS M
   (Bette Midler)
10. CAN'T BUY A THRILL
    (Steely Dan)

BLACK SINGLES

1. NEITHER ONE OF US
   (Gladys Knight and the Pips)
2. KILLING ME SOFTLY WITH HIS SONG
   (Roberta Flack)
3. AIN'T NO WOMAN (LIKE THE ONE I GOT)
   (The Four Tops)
4. BREAK UP TO MAKE UP
   (The Stylistics)
5. MASTER OF EYES
   (Aretha Franklin)
6. LOVE TRAIN
   (The O'Jays)
7. CALL ME
   (Al Green)
8. MASTERPIECE
   (Temptations)
9. DO IT IN THE NAME OF LOVE
   (Candi Staton)
10. WE DID IT
    (Syl Johnson)

BLACK ALBUMS

1. THE WORLD IS A GHETTO
   (War)
2. LADY SINGS THE BLUES
   (Diana Ross)
3. TALKING BOOK
   (Stevie Wonder)

---

4. ROUND 2
   (The Stylistics)
5. WATTSTAX
   (Original Soundtrack)
6. MASTERPIECE
   (Temptations)
7. GREEN IS BLUES
   (Al Green)
8. I'M STILL IN LOVE WITH YOU
   (Al Green)
9. BACK STABBERS
   (The O'Jays)
10. ACROSS 110th STREET
    (Bobby Womack and Peace)

JAZZ ALBUMS

1. PRELUDE
   (Eumir Deodato)
2. BIRDS OF FIRE
   (Mahavishnu Orchestra)
3. LIVE AT THE EAST
   (Pharaoh Sanders)
4. LIVE AT THE LIGHTHOUSE
   (Charles Earland)
5. TALK TO THE PEOPLE
   (Les McCann)
6. STRANGE FRUIT
   (Billie Holliday)
7. LIVE AT FUNKY QUARTERS
   (Cal Tjader)
8. HUSH 'N' THUNDER
   (Yusef Lateef)
9. THE EVOLUTION OF MANN
   (Herbie Mann)
10. HIS GREATEST YEARS, VOL. 2
    (John Coltrane)

COUNTRY SINGLES

1. YOU LAY SO EASY ON MY MIND
   (Bobby G. Rice)
2. GOOD THINGS
   (David Houston)
3. TEDDY BEAR SONG
   (Barbara Fairchild)
4. DUELING BANJOS
   (Original Soundtrack)
5. KEEP ME IN MIND
   (Lynn Anderson)
6. SUPER KIND OF WOMAN
   (Freddie Hart)
7. A SHOULDER TO CRY ON
   (Charley Pride)
8. SHELTER OF YOUR EYES
   (Don Williams)
9. SUPERMAN
   (Donna Fargo)
10. DANNY'S SONG
    (Anne Murray)

COUNTRY ALBUMS

1. DELIVERANCE
   (Original Soundtrack)
2. SONGS OF LOVE BY CHARLEY PRIDE
   (Charley Pride)
3. I'VE FOUND SOMEONE OF MY OWN
   (Cal Smith)
4. WHO'S GONNA PLAY THIS OLD PIANO
   (Jerry Lee Lewis)
5. ROY CLARK LIVE
   (Roy Clark)
6. ANY OLD WIND THAT BLOWS
   (Johnny Cash)
7. IT'S NOT LOVE
   (Merle Haggard)
8. HOT A'MIGHTY
   (Jerry Reed)
9. DO YOU KNOW WHAT IT'S LIKE
   (Jerry Wallace)
10. WILL THE CIRCLE BE UNBROKEN
    (Nitty Gritty Dirt Band)

MARCH 31, 1973

POP SINGLES

1. LOVE TRAIN
   (The O'Jays)
2. KILLING ME SOFTLY WITH HIS SONG
   (Roberta Flack)
3. NEITHER ONE OF US
   (Gladys Knights and the Pips)
4. COVER OF ROLLING STONE
   (Dr. Hook and the Medicine Show)
5. DANNY'S SONG
   (Anne Murray)
6. ALSO SPRACH ZARATHUSTRA
   (Eumir Deodato)
7. AIN'T NO WOMAN (LIKE THE ONE I GOT)
   (The Four Tops)
8. LAST SONG
   (Edward Bear)
9. SING
   (The Carpenters)
10. THE NIGHT THE LIGHTS WENT OUT
    (Vicki Lawrence)

POP ALBUMS

1. LADY SINGS THE BLUES
   (Diana Ross)
2. DELIVERANCE
   (Original Soundtrack)
3. ROCKY MOUNTAIN HIGH
   (John Denver)
4. DON'T SHOOT ME, I'M ONLY THE PIANO
   PLAYER
   (Elton John)
5. THE WORLD IS A GHETTO
   (War)
6. BILLION DOLLAR BABIES
   (Alice Cooper)
7. SHOOT OUT AT THE FANTASY FACTORY
   (Traffic)
8. THE DIVINE MISS M
   (Bette Midler)
9. CAN'T BUY A THRILL
   (Steely Dan)
10. NO SECRETS
    (Carly Simon)

BLACK SINGLES

1. NEITHER ONE OF US
   (Gladys Knight and the Pips)
2. AIN'T NO WOMAN (LIKE THE ONE I GOT)
   (The Four Tops)
3. BREAK UP TO MAKE UP
   (The Stylistics)
4. KILLING ME SOFTLY WITH HIS SONG
   (Roberta Flack)
5. MASTER OF EYES
   (Aretha Franklin)
6. CALL ME
   (Al Green)
7. MASTERPIECE
   (Temptations)
8. LETTER TO MYSELF
   (The Chi-Lites)
9. LOVE TRAIN
   (The O'Jays)
10. STEP BY STEP
    (Joe Simon)

BLACK ALBUMS

1. LADY SINGS THE BLUES
   (Diana Ross)
2. THE WORLD IS A GHETTO
   (War)
3. WATTSTAX
   (Original Soundtrack)

4. MASTERPIECE
   (Temptations)
5. GREEN IS BLUES
   (Al Green)
6. ROUND 2
   (The Stylistics)
7. ACROSS 110TH STREET
   (Bobby Womack and Peace)
8. I'M STILL IN LOVE WITH YOU
   (Al Green)
9. TALKING BOOK
   (Stevie Wonder)
10. KEEPER OF THE CASTLE
    (The Four Tops)

JAZZ ALBUMS

1. PRELUDE
   (Eumir Deodato)
2. BIRDS OF FIRE
   (Mahavishnu Orchestra)
3. LIVE AT THE EAST
   (Pharoah Sanders)
4. STRANGE FRUIT
   (Billie Holliday)
5. HUSH 'N' THUNDER
   (Yusef Lateef)
6. LIVE AT THE LIGHTHOUSE
   (Charles Earland)
7. MORNING STAR
   (Hubert Laws)
8. ON THE CORNER
   (Miles Davis)
9. 'ROUND MIDNIGHT
   (Kenny Burrell)
10. RED BLACK AND GREEN
    (Roy Ayers)

COUNTRY SINGLES

1. GOOD THINGS
   (David Houston)
2. KEEP ME IN MIND
   (Lynn Anderson)
3. SUPER KIND OF WOMAN
   (Freddie Hart)
4. DUELING BANJOS
   (Original Soundtrack)
5. YOU LAY SO EASY ON MY MIND
   (Bobby G. Rice)
6. A SHOULDER TO CRY ON
   (Charley Pride)
7. TEDDY BEAR SONG
   (Barbara Fairchild)
8. SUPERMAN
   (Donna Fargo)
9. NEITHER ONE OF US
   (Bob Luman)
10. I LOVE YOU MORE AND MORE EVERY DAY
    (Sonny James)

COUNTRY ALBUMS

1. DELIVERANCE
   (Original Soundtrack)
2. SONGS OF LOVE BY CHARLEY PRIDE
   (Charley Pride)
3. WHO'S GONNA PLAY THIS OLD PIANO
   (Jerry Lee Lewis)
4. ROY CLARK LIVE
   (Roy Clark)
5. ANY OLD WIND THAT BLOWS
   (Johnny Cash)
6. I'VE FOUND SOMEONE OF MY OWN
   (Cal Smith)
7. DO YOU KNOW WHAT IT'S LIKE
   (Jerry Wallace)
8. WILL THE CIRCLE BE UNBROKEN
   (Nitty Gritty Dirt Band)
9. SONNY JAMES SINGS HITS OF '72
   (Sonny James)
10. IT'S NOT LOVE
    (Merle Haggard)

APRIL 7, 1973

POP SINGLES

1. NEITHER ONE OF US
   (Gladys Knight and the Pips)
2. LOVE TRAIN
   (The O'Jays)
3. AIN'T NO WOMAN (LIKE THE ONE I GOT)
   (The Four Tops)
4. KILLING ME SOFTLY WITH HIS SONG
   (Roberta Flack)
5. DANNY'S SONG
   (Anne Murray)
6. THE NIGHT THE LIGHTS WENT OUT
   (Vicki Lawrence)
7. SING
   (The Carpenters)
8. BREAK UP TO MAKE UP
   (The Stylistics)
9. CALL ME
   (Al Green)
10. TIE A YELLOW RIBBON 'ROUND THE OLD OAK TREE
    (Tony Orlando and Dawn)

POP ALBUMS

1. LADY SINGS THE BLUES
   (Diana Ross)
2. BILLION DOLLAR BABIES
   (Alice Cooper)
3. DELIVERANCE
   (Original Soundtrack)
4. DON'T SHOOT ME, I'M ONLY THE PIANO PLAYER
   (Elton John)
5. ROCKY MOUNTAIN HIGH
   (John Denver)
6. THE WORLD IS A GHETTO
   (War)
7. SHOOT OUT AT THE FANTASY FACTORY
   (Traffic)
8. THE DIVINE MISS M
   (Bette Midler)
9. CAN'T BUY A THRILL
   (Steely Dan)
10. BIRDS OF FIRE
    (Mahavishnu Orchestra)

BLACK SINGLES

1. AIN'T NO WOMAN (LIKE THE ONE I GOT)
   (The Four Tops)
2. BREAK UP TO MAKE UP
   (The Stylistics)
3. NEITHER ONE OF US
   (Gladys Knight and the Pips)
4. CALL ME
   (Al Green)
5. MASTERPIECE
   (Temptations)
6. LETTER TO MYSELF
   (The Chi-Lites)
7. MASTER OF EYES
   (Aretha Franklin)
8. STEP BY STEP
   (Joe Simon)
9. LEAVING ME
   (The Independents)
10. OH LA DE DA
    (The Staple Singers)

BLACK ALBUMS

1. LADY SINGS THE BLUES
   (Diana Ross)
2. WATTSTAX
   (Original Soundtrack)
3. GREEN IS BLUES
   (Al Green)

4. MASTERPIECE
   (Temptations)
5. THE WORLD IS A GHETTO
   (War)
6. ROUND 2
   (The Stylistics)
7. NEITHER ONE OF US
   (Gladys Knight and the Pips)
8. BLACK CAESAR
   (Original Soundtrack)
9. ACROSS 110th STREET
   (Bobby Womack and Peace)
10. I'M STILL IN LOVE WITH YOU
    (Al Green)

JAZZ ALBUMS

1. PRELUDE
   (Eumir Deodato)
2. BIRDS OF FIRE
   (Mahavishnu Orchestra)
3. HUSH 'N' THUNDER
   (Yusef Lateef)
4. STRANGE FRUIT
   (Billie Holliday)
5. LIVE AT THE EAST
   (Pharaoh Sanders)
6. LIVE AT THE LIGHTHOUSE
   (Charles Earland)
7. MORNING STAR
   (Hubert Laws)
8. 'ROUND MIDNIGHT
   (Kenny Burrell)
9. RED BLACK AND GREEN
   (Roy Ayers)
10. ON THE CORNER
    (Miles Davis)

COUNTRY SINGLES

1. KEEP ME IN MIND
   (Lynn Anderson)
2. SUPER KIND OF WOMAN
   (Freddie Hart)
3. A SHOULDER TO CRY ON
   (Charley Pride)
4. SUPERMAN
   (Donna Fargo)
5. GOOD THINGS
   (David Houston)
6. I LOVE YOU MORE AND MORE EVERY DAY
   (Sonny James)
7. BEHIND CLOSED DOORS
   (Charlie Rich)
8. NEITHER ONE OF US
   (Bob Luman)
9. TAKE TIME TO LOVE HER
   (Nat Stuckey)
10. TEDDY BEAR SONG
    (Barbara Fairchild)

COUNTRY ALBUMS

1. DELIVERANCE
   (Original Soundtrack)
2. WHO'S GONNA PLAY THIS OLD PIANO
   (Jerry Lee Lewis)
3. ROY CLARK LIVE
   (Roy Clark)
4. SONGS OF LOVE BY CHARLEY PRIDE
   (Charley Pride)
5. ANY OLD WIND THAT BLOWS
   (Johnny Cash)
6. DO YOU KNOW WHAT IT'S LIKE
   (Jerry Wallace)
7. WILL THE CIRCLE BE UNBROKEN
   (Nitty Gritty Dirt Band)
8. I'VE FOUND SOMEONE OF MY OWN
   (Cal Smith)
9. SONNY JAMES SINGS HITS OF '72
   (Sonny James)
10. ELVIS ALOHA FROM HAWAII (VIA SATELLITE)
    (Elvis Presley)

APRIL 14, 1973

POP SINGLES

1. THE NIGHT THE LIGHTS WENT OUT
   (Vicki Lawrence)
2. AIN'T NO WOMAN (LIKE THE ONE I GOT)
   (The Four Tops)
3. NEITHER ONE OF US
   (Gladys Knight and the Pips)
4. TIE A YELLLOW RIBBON 'ROUND THE OLD
   OAK TREE
   (Tony Orlando and Dawn)
5. SING
   (The Carpenters)
6. BREAK UP TO MAKE UP
   (The Stylistics)
7. CISCO KID
   (War)
8. CALL ME
   (Al Green)
9. KILLING ME SOFTLY WITH HIS SONG
   (Roberta Flack)
10. SPACE ODDITY
    (David Bowie)

POP ALBUMS

1. BILLION DOLLAR BABIES
   (Alice Cooper)
2. LADY SINGS THE BLUES
   (Diana Ross)
3. DARK SIDE OF THE MOON
   (Pink Floyd)
4. DELIVERANCE
   (Original Soundtrack)
5. DON'T SHOOT ME, I'M ONLY THE PIANO
   PLAYER
   (Elton John)
6. ROCKY MOUNTAIN HIGH
   (John Denver)
7. THE WORLD IS A GHETTO
   (War)
8. CAN'T BUY A THRILL
   (Steely Dan)
9. BIRDS OF FIRE
   (Mahavishnu Orchestra)
10. ELVIS ALOHA FROM HAWAII (VIA
    SATELLITE)
    (Elvis Presley)

BLACK SINGLES

1. BREAK UP TO MAKE UP
   (The Stylistics)
2. AIN'T NO WOMAN (LIKE THE ONE I GOT)
   (The Four Tops)
3. MASTERPIECE
   (Temptations)
4. CALL ME
   (Al Green)
5. LEAVING ME
   (The Independents)
6. LETTER TO MYSELF
   (The Chi-Lites)
7. PILLOW TALK
   (Sylvia)
8. STEP BY STEP
   (Joe Simon)
9. OH LA DE DA
   (The Staple Singers)
10. YOU ARE THE SUNSHINE OF MY LIFE
    (Stevie Wonder)

BLACK ALBUMS

1. WATTSTAX
   (Original Soundtrack)
2. LADY SINGS THE BLUES
   (Diana Ross)

3. NEITHER ONE OF US
   (Gladys Knight and the Pips)
4. MASTERPIECE
   (Temptations)
5. GREEN IS BLUES
   (Al Green)
6. BLACK CAESAR
   (Original Soundtrack)
7. THE WORLD IS A GHETTO
   (War)
8. ROUND 2
   (The Stylistics)
9. I'M STILL IN LOVE WITH YOU
   (Al Green)
10. A LETTER TO MYSELF
    (The Chi-Lites)

JAZZ ALBUMS

1. PRELUDE
   (Eumir Deodato)
2. HUSH 'N' THUNDER
   (Yusef Lateef)
3. BIRDS OF FIRE
   (Mahavishnu Orchestra)
4. MORNING STAR
   (Hubert Laws)
5. LIVE AT THE LIGHTHOUSE
   (Charles Earland)
6. LIVE AT THE EAST
   (Pharaoh Sanders)
7. STRANGE FRUIT
   (Billie Holliday)
8. ON THE CORNER
   (Miles Davis)
9. 'ROUND MIDNIGHT
   (Kenny Burrell)
10. RED BLACK AND GREEN
    (Roy Ayers)

COUNTRY SINGLES

1. SUPER KIND OF WOMAN
   (Freddie Hart)
2. A SHOULDER TO CRY ON
   (Charley Pride)
3. SUPERMAN
   (Donna Fargo)
4. BEHIND CLOSED DOORS
   (Charlie Rich)
5. I LOVE YOU MORE AND MORE EVERY DAY
   (Sonny James)
6. KEEP ME IN MIND
   (Lynn Anderson)
7. NEITHER ONE OF US
   (Bob Luman)
8. TAKE TIME TO LOVE HER
   (Nat Stuckey)
9. YOU CAN HAVE HER
   (Waylon Jennings)
10. NOBODY WINS
    (Brenda Lee)

COUNTRY ALBUMS

1. DELIVERANCE
   (Original Soundtrack)
2. ROY CLARK LIVE
   (Roy Clark)
3. WHO'S GONNA PLAY THIS OLD PIANO
   (Jerry Lee Lewis)
4. DO YOU KNOW WHAT IT'S LIKE
   (Jerry Wallace)
5. SONGS OF LOVE BY CHARLEY PRIDE
   (Charley Pride)
6. MY SECOND ALBUM
   (Donna Fargo)
7. ELVIS ALOHA FROM HAWAII (VIA
   SATELLITE)
   (Elvis Presley)
8. WILL THE CIRCLE BE UNBROKEN
   (Nitty Gritty Dirt Band)
9. KEEP ME IN MIND
   (Lynn Anderson)

10. COUNTRY SYMPHONIES IN E MAJOR
    (The Statler Brothers)

APRIL 21, 1973

POP SINGLES

1. THE NIGHT THE LIGHTS WENT OUT
   (Vicki Lawrence)
2. TIE A YELLOW RIBBON 'ROUND THE OLD
   OAK TREE
   (Tony Orlando and Dawn)
3. AIN'T NO WOMAN (LIKE THE ONE I GOT)
   (The Four Tops)
4. SING
   (The Carpenters)
5. CISCO KID
   (War)
6. BREAK UP TO MAKE UP
   (The Stylistics)
7. NEITHER ONE OF US
   (Gladys Knight and the Pips)
8. CALL ME
   (Al Green)
9. LITTLE WILLY
   (Sweet)
10. THE TWELFTH OF NEVER
    (Donny Osmond)

POP ALBUMS

1. DARK SIDE OF THE MOON
   (Pink Floyd)
2. BILLION DOLLAR BABIES
   (Alice Cooper)
3. ELVIS ALOHA FROM HAWAII (VIA
   SATELLITE)
   (Elvis Presley)
4. LADY SINGS THE BLUES
   (Diana Ross)
5. MASTERPIECE
   (Temptations)
6. THE BEST OF BREAD
   (Bread)
7. CAN'T BUY A THRILL
   (Steely Dan)
8. THE WORLD IS A GHETTO
   (War)
9. BIRDS OF FIRE
   (Mahavishnu Orchestra)
10. MOVING WAVES
    (Focus)

BLACK SINGLES

1. MASTERPIECE
   (Temptations)
2. PILLOW TALK
   (Sylvia)
3. AIN'T NO WOMAN (LIKE THE ONE I GOT)
   (The Four Tops)
4. LEAVING ME
   (The Independents)
5. BREAK UP TO MAKE UP
   (The Stylistics)
6. CALL ME
   (Al Green)
7. YOU ARE THE SUNSHINE OF MY LIVE
   (Stevie Wonder)
8. LETTER TO MYSELF
   (The Chi-Lites)
9. OH LA DE DA
   (The Staple Singers)
10. I CAN UNDERSTAND IT
    (New Birth)

BLACK ALBUMS

1. NEITHER ONE OF US
   (Gladys Knight and the Pips)

2. MASTERPIECE
   (Temptations)
3. LADY SINGS THE BLUES
   (Diana Ross)
4. WATTSTAX
   (Original Soundtrack)
5. BLACK CAESAR
   (Original Soundtrack)
6. GREEN IS BLUES
   (Al Green)
7. THE WORLD IS A GHETTO
   (War)
8. A LETTER TO MYSELF
   (The Chi-Lites)
9. ROUND 2
   (The Stylistics)
10. BIRTHDAY
    (New Birth)

JAZZ ALBUMS

1. PRELUDE
   (Eumir Deodato)
2. MORNING STAR
   (Hubert Laws)
3. HUSH 'N' THUNDER
   (Yusef Lateef)
4. LIVE AT THE LIGHTHOUSE
   (Charles Earland)
5. LIVE AT THE EAST
   (Pharaoh Sanders)
6. BIRDS OF FIRE
   (Mahavishnu Orchestra)
7. STRANGE FRUIT
   (Billie Holliday)
8. 'ROUND MIDNIGHT
   (Kenny Burrell)
9. SONG FOR MY LADY
   (McCoy Tyner)
10. ON THE CORNER
    (Miles Davis)

COUNTRY SINGLES

1. A SHOULDER TO CRY ON
   (Charley Pride)
2. BEHIND CLOSED DOORS
   (Charlie Rich)
3. SUPERMAN
   (Donna Fargo)
4. I LOVE YOU MORE AND MORE EVERY DAY
   (Sonny James)
5. TAKE TIME TO LOVE HER
   (Nat Stuckey)
6. SUPER KIND OF WOMAN
   (Freddie Hart)
7. NOBODY WINS
   (Brenda Lee)
8. YOU CAN HAVE HER
   (Wayon Jennings)
9. COME LIVE WITH ME
   (Roy Clark)
10. IF YOU CAN LIVE WITH IT
    (Bill Anderson)

COUNTRY ALBUMS

1. MY SECOND ALBUM
   (Donna Fargo)
2. ELVIS ALOHA FROM HAWAII (VIA SATELLITE)
   (Elvis Presley)
3. DO YOU KNOW WHAT IT'S LIKE
   (Jerry Wallace)
4. DELIVERANCE
   (Original Soundtrack)
5. ROY CLARK LIVE
   (Roy Clark)
6. WHO'S GONNA PLAY THIS OLD PIANO
   (Jerry Lee Lewis)
7. KEEP ME IN MIND
   (Lynn Anderson)
8. SONGS OF LOVE BY CHARLEY PRIDE
   (Charley Pride)

9. SUPER KIND OF WOMAN
   (Freddie Hart)
10. WILL THE CIRCLE BE UNBROKEN
    (Nitty Gritty Dirt Band)

APRIL 28, 1973

POP SINGLES

1. TIE A YELLOW RIBBON 'ROUND THE OLD OAK TREE
   (Tony Orlando and Dawn)
2. THE NIGHT THE LIGHTS WENT OUT
   (Vicki Lawrence)
3. LITTLE WILLY
   (Sweet)
4. CISCO KID
   (War)
5. SING
   (The Carpenters)
6. AIN'T NO WOMAN (LIKE THE ONE I GOT)
   (The Four Tops)
7. THE TWELFTH OF NEVER
   (Donny Osmond)
8. MASTERPIECE
   (Temptations)
9. NEITHER ONE OF US
   (Gladys Knight and the Pips)
10. YOU ARE THE SUNSHINE OF MY LIFE
    (Stevie Wonder)

POP ALBUMS

1. ELVIS ALOHA FROM HAWAII (VIA SATELLITE)
   (Elvis Presley)
2. DARK SIDE OF THE MOON
   (Pink Floyd)
3. BILLION DOLLAR BABIES
   (Alice Cooper)
4. MASTERPIECE
   (Temptations)
5. THE BEST OF BREAD
   (Bread)
6. HOUSES OF THE HOLY
   (Led Zeppelin)
7. CAN'T BUY A THRILL
   (Steely Dan)
8. THEY ONLY COME OUT AT NIGHT
   (Edgar Winter)
9. MOVING WAVES
   (Focus)
10. LADY SINGS THE BLUES
    (Diana Ross)

BLACK SINGLES

1. PILLOW TALK
   (Sylvia)
2. MASTERPIECE
   (Temptations)
3. LEAVING ME
   (The Independents)
4. AIN'T NO WOMAN (LIKE THE ONE I GOT)
   (The Four Tops)
5. YOU ARE THE SUNSHINE OF MY LIFE
   (Stevie Wonder)
6. BREAK UP TO MAKE UP
   (The Stylistics)
7. I CAN UNDERSTAND IT
   (New Birth)
8. CALL ME
   (Al Green)
9. I'M GONNA LOVE YOU JUST A LITTLE MORE BABY
   (Barry White)
10. OH LA DE DA
    (The Staple Singers)

BLACK ALBUMS

1. MASTERPIECE
   (Temptations)
2. NEITHER ONE OF US
   (Gladys Knight and the Pips)
3. BLACK CAESAR
   (Original Soundtrack)
4. LADY SINGS THE BLUES
   (Diana Ross)
5. THE WORLD IS A GHETTO
   (War)
6. A LETTER TO MYSELF
   (The Chi-Lites)
7. GREEN IS BLUES
   (Al Green)
8. BIRTHDAY
   (New Birth)
9. ROUND 2
   (The Stylistics)
10. PLEASURE
    (Ohio Players)

JAZZ ALBUMS

1. PRELUDE
   (Eumir Deodato)
2. HUSH 'N' THUNDER
   (Yusef Lateef)
3. MORNING STAR
   (Hubert Laws)
4. 'ROUND MIDNIGHT
   (Kenny Burrell)
5. SONG FOR MY LADY
   (McCoy Tyner)
6. SECOND CRUSADE
   (Crusaders)
7. GOT MY OWN
   (Gene Ammons)
8. FUNKY SERENITY
   (Ramsey Lewis)
9. ON THE CORNER
   (Miles Davis)
10. STRANGE FRUIT
    (Billie Holliday)

COUNTRY SINGLES

1. BEHIND CLOSED DOORS
   (Charlie Rich)
2. SUPERMAN
   (Donna Fargo)
3. I LOVE YOU MORE AND MORE EVERY DAY
   (Sonny James)
4. NOBODY WINS
   (Brenda Lee)
5. COME LIVE WITH ME
   (Roy Clark)
6. A SHOULDER TO CRY ON
   (Charley Pride)
7. YOU CAN HAVE HER
   (Waylon Jennings)
8. IF YOU CAN LIVE WITH IT
   (Bill Anderson)
9. TAKE TIME TO LOVE HER
   (Nat Stuckey)
10. EMPTIEST ARMS IN THE WORLD
    (Merle Haggard)

COUNTRY ALBUMS

1. MY SECOND ALBUM
   (Donna Fargo)
2. ELVIS ALOHA FROM HAWAII (VIA SATELLITE)
   (Elvis Presley)
3. DO YOU KNOW WHAT IT'S LIKE
   (Jerry Wallace)
4. KEEP ME IN MIND
   (Lynn Anderson)
5. SUPER KIND OF WOMAN
   (Freddie Hart)

6. DELIVERANCE
   (Original Soundtrack)
7. ENTERTAINER OF THE YEAR
   (Loretta Lynn)
8. WHO'S GONNA PLAY THIS OLD PIANO
   (Jerry Lee Lewis)
9. INTRODUCING JOHNNY RODRIGUEZ
   (Johnny Rodriguez)
10. LET'S BUILD A WORLD TOGETHER
    (George Jones and Tammy Wynette)

MAY 5, 1973

POP SINGLES

1. CISCO KID
   (War)
2. TIE A YELLOW RIBBON 'ROUND THE OLD OAK TREE
   (Tony Orlando and Dawn)
3. LITTLE WILLY
   (Sweet)
4. THE NIGHT THE LIGHTS WENT OUT
   (Vicki Lawrence)
5. YOU ARE THE SUNSHINE OF MY LIFE
   (Stevie Wonder)
6. THE TWELFTH OF NEVER
   (Donny Osmond)
7. FRANKENSTEIN
   (Edgar Winter)
8. MASTERPIECE
   (Temptations)
9. DRIFT AWAY
   (Dobie Gray)
10. STUCK IN THE MIDDLE WITH YOU
    (Stealers Wheel)

POP ALBUMS

1. ELVIS ALOHA FROM HAWAII (VIA SATELLITE)
   (Elvis Presley)
2. HOUSES OF THE HOLY
   (Led Zeppelin)
3. THE BEST OF BREAD
   (Bread)
4. MASTERPIECE
   (Temptations)
5. DARK SIDE OF THE MOON
   (Pink Floyd)
6. THEY ONLY COME OUT AT NIGHT
   (Edgar Winter)
7. CAN'T BUY A THRILL
   (Steely Dan)
8. BILLION DOLLAR BABIES
   (Alice Cooper)
9. MOVING WAVES
   (Focus)
10. THE BEATLES/1967-1970
    (The Beatles)

BLACK SINGLES

1. PILLOW TALK
   (Sylvia)
2. LEAVING ME
   (The Independents)
3. MASTERPIECE
   (Temptations)
4. AIN'T NO WOMAN (LIKE THE ONE I GOT)
   (The Four Tops)
5. I CAN UNDERSTAND IT
   (New Birth)
6. YOU ARE THE SUNSHINE OF MY LIFE
   (Stevie Wonder)
7. I'M GONNA LOVE YOU JUST A LITTLE MORE BABY
   (Barry White)
8. BREAK UP TO MAKE UP
   (The Stylistics)

9. FUNKY WORM
   (Ohio Players)
10. ARMED AND EXTREMELY DANGEROUS
    (First Choice)

BLACK ALBUMS

1. MASTERPIECE
   (Temptations)
2. BLACK CAESAR
   (Original Soundtrack)
3. NEITHER ONE OF US
   (Gladys Knight and the Pips)
4. A LETTER TO MYSELF
   (The Chi-Lites)
5. LADY SINGS THE BLUES
   (Diana Ross)
6. THE WORLD IS A GHETTO
   (War)
7. BIRTHDAY
   (New Birth)
8. PLEASURE
   (Ohio Players)
9. GREEN IS BLUES
   (Al Green)
10. ROUND 2
    (The Stylistics)

JAZZ ALBUMS

1. SECOND CRUSADE
   (Crusaders)
2. PRELUDE
   (Eumir Deodato)
3. HUSH 'N' THUNDER
   (Yusef Lateef)
4. 'ROUND MIDNIGHT
   (Kenny Burrell)
5. SONG FOR MY LADY
   (McCoy Tyner)
6. MORNING STAR
   (Hubert Laws)
7. GOT MY OWN
   (Gene Ammons)
8. FUNKY SERENITY
   (Ramsey Lewis)
9. EXTENSIONS
   (McCoy Tyner)
10. SKY DIVE
    (Freddie Hubbard)

COUNTRY SINGLES

1. SUPERMAN
   (Donna Fargo)
2. COME LIVE WITH ME
   (Roy Clark)
3. BEHIND CLOSED DOORS
   (Charlie Rich)
4. NOBODY WINS
   (Brenda Lee)
5. IF YOU CAN LIVE WITH IT
   (Bill Anderson)
6. EMPTIEST ARMS IN THE WORLD
   (Merle Haggard)
7. YOU CAN HAVE HER
   (Waylon Jennings)
8. I LOVE YOU MORE AND MORE EVERY DAY
   (Sonny James)
9. WHAT MY WOMAN CAN'T DO
   (George Jones)
10. WALKIN' PIECE OF HEAVEN
    (Marty Robbins)

COUNTRY ALBUMS

1. ELVIS ALOHA FROM HAWAII (VIA SATELLITE)
   (Elvis Presley)
2. MY SECOND ALBUM
   (Donna Fargo)

3. KEEP ME IN MIND
   (Lynn Anderson)
4. SUPER KIND OF WOMAN
   (Freddie Hart)
5. ENTERTAINER OF THE YEAR
   (Loretta Lynn)
6. INTRODUCING JOHNNY RODRIGUEZ
   (Johnny Rodriguez)
7. DO YOU KNOW WHAT IT'S LIKE
   (Jerry Wallace)
8. DELIVERANCE
   (Original Soundtrack)
9. LET'S BUILD A WORLD TOGETHER
   (George Jones and Tammy Wynette)
10. FIRST SONGS BY THE FIRST LADY
    (Tammy Wynette)

MAY 12, 1973

POP SINGLES

1. YOU ARE THE SUNSHINE OF MY LIFE
   (Stevie Wonder)
2. FRANKENSTEIN
   (Edgar Winter)
3. TIE A YELLOW RIBBON 'ROUND THE OLD OAK TREE
   (Tony Orlando and Dawn)
4. CISCO KID
   (War)
5. LITTLE WILLY
   (Sweet)
6. THE TWELFTH OF NEVER
   (Donny Osmond)
7. STUCK IN THE MIDDLE WITH YOU
   (Stealers Wheel)
8. DRIFT AWAY
   (Dobie Gray)
9. THE NIGHT THE LIGHTS WENT OUT
   (Vicki Lawrence)
10. REELING IN THE YEARS
    (Steely Dan)

POP ALBUMS

1. HOUSES OF THE HOLY
   (Led Zeppelin)
2. THE BEST OF BREAD
   (Bread)
3. ELVIS ALOHA FROM HAWAII (VIA SATELLITE)
   (Elvis Presley)
4. THEY ONLY COME OUT AT NIGHT
   (Edgar Winter)
5. MASTERPIECE
   (Temptations)
6. THE BEATLES/1967-1970
   (The Beatles)
7. THE BEATLES/1962-1966
   (The Beatles)
8. DARK SIDE OF THE MOON
   (Pink Floyd)
9. MOVING WAVES
   (Focus)
10. BILLION DOLLAR BABIES
    (Alice Cooper)

BLACK SINGLES

1. I'M GONNA LOVE YOU JUST A LITTLE MORE BABY
   (Barry White)
2. LEAVING ME
   (The Independents)
3. PILLOW TALK
   (Sylvia)
4. I CAN UNDERSTAND IT
   (New Birth)
5. ARMED AND EXTREMELY DANGEROUS
   (First Choice)

6. MASTERPIECE
   (Temptations)
7. FUNKY WORM
   (Ohio Players)
8. YOU ARE THE SUNSHINE OF MY LIFE
   (Stevie Wonder)
9. WITHOUT YOU IN MY LIFE
   (Tyrone Davis)
10. NATURAL HIGH
    (Bloodstone)

BLACK ALBUMS

1. I'VE GOT SO MUCH TO GIVE
   (Barry White)
2. BIRTHDAY
   (New Birth)
3. A LETTER TO MYSELF
   (The Chi-Lites)
4. MASTERPIECE
   (Temptations)
5. PLEASURE
   (Ohio Players)
6. BLACK CAESAR
   (Original Soundtrack)
7. THE WORLD IS A GHETTO
   (War)
8. NEITHER ONE OF US
   (Gladys Knight and the Pips)
9. SPINNERS
   (Spinners)
10. SECOND CRUSADE
    (Crusaders)

JAZZ ALBUMS

1. SECOND CRUSADE
   (Crusaders)
2. BLACK BYRD
   (Donald Byrd)
3. 'ROUND MIDNIGHT
   (Kenny Burrell)
4. SONG FOR MY LADY
   (McCoy Tyner)
5. PRELUDE
   (Eumir Deodato)
6. GOT MY OWN
   (Gene Ammons)
7. MORNING STAR
   (Hubert Laws)
8. FUNKY SERENITY
   (Ramsey Lewis)
9. EXTENSIONS
   (McCoy Tyner)
10. HUSH 'N' THUNDER
    (Yusef Lateef)

COUNTRY SINGLES

1. COME LIVE WITH ME
   (Roy Clark)
2. IF YOU CAN LIVE WITH IT
   (Bill Anderson)
3. NOBODY WINS
   (Brenda Lee)
4. EMPTIEST ARMS IN THE WORLD
   (Merle Haggard)
5. BEHIND CLOSED DOORS
   (Charlie Rich)
6. SUPERMAN
   (Donna Fargo)
7. WALKIN' PIECE OF HEAVEN
   (Marty Robbins)
8. WHAT MY WOMAN CAN'T DO
   (George Jones)
9. WHAT'S YOUR MAMA'S NAME
   (Tanya Tucker)
10. BABY'S GONE
    (Conway Twitty)

COUNTRY ALBUMS

1. ELVIS ALOHA FROM HAWAII (VIA SATELLITE)
   (Elvis Presley)
2. ENTERTAINER OF THE YEAR
   (Loretta Lynn)
3. KEEP ME IN MIND
   (Lynn Anderson)
4. SUPER KIND OF WOMAN
   (Freddie Hart)
5. INTRODUCING JOHNNY RODRIGUEZ
   (Johnny Rodriguez)
6. MY SECOND ALBUM
   (Donna Fargo)
7. SHE NEEDS SOMEONE TO HOLD HER
   (Conway Twitty)
8. FIRST SONGS BY THE FIRST LADY
   (Tammy Wynette)
9. LET'S BUILD A WORLD TOGETHER
   (George Jones and Tammy Wynette)
10. AMERICA, WHY I LOVE HER
    (John Wayne)

MAY 19, 1973

POP SINGLES

1. FRANKENSTEIN
   (Edgar Winter)
2. YOU ARE THE SUNSHINE OF MY LIFE
   (Stevie Wonder)
3. TIE A YELLOW RIBBON 'ROUND THE OLD OAK TREE
   (Tony Orlando and Dawn)
4. CISCO KID
   (War)
5. DRIFT AWAY
   (Dobie Gray)
6. STUCK IN THE MIDDLE WITH YOU
   (Stealers Wheel)
7. LITTLE WILLY
   (Sweet)
8. REELING IN THE YEARS
   (Steely Dan)
9. DANIEL
   (Elton John)
10. PILLOW TALK
    (Sylvia)

POP ALBUMS

1. HOUSE OF THE HOLY
   (Led Zeppelin)
2. THE BEST OF BREAD
   (Bread)
3. THEY ONLY COME OUT AT NIGHT
   (Edgar Winter)
4. THE BEATLES/1967–1970
   (The Beatles)
5. THE BEATLES/1962–1966
   (The Beatles)
6. MASTERPIECE
   (Temptations)
7. ELVIS ALOHA FROM HAWAII (VIA SATELLITE)
   (Elvis Presley)
8. MOVING WAVES
   (Focus)
9. DARK SIDE OF THE MOON
   (Pink Floyd)
10. BILLION DOLLAR BABIES
    (Alice Cooper)

BLACK SINGLES

1. I'M GONNA LOVE YOU JUST A LITTLE MORE BABY
   (Barry White)
2. I CAN UNDERSTAND IT
   (New Birth)
3. LEAVING ME
   (The Independents)
4. ARMED AND EXTREMELY DANGEROUS
   (First Choice)
5. FUNKY WORM
   (Ohio Players)
6. WITHOUT YOU IN MY LIFE
   (Tyrone Davis)
7. PILLOW TALK
   (Sylvia)
8. NATURAL HIGH
   (Bloodstone)
9. YOU ARE THE SUNSHINE OF MY LIFE
   (Stevie Wonder)
10. CISCO KID
    (War)

BLACK ALBUMS

1. I'VE GOT SO MUCH TO GIVE
   (Barry White)
2. BIRTHDAY
   (New Birth)
3. PLEASURE
   (Ohio Players)
4. A LETTER TO MYSELF
   (The Chi-Lites)
5. SPINNERS
   (Spinners)
6. MASTERPIECE
   (Temptations)
7. BLACK CAESAR
   (Original Soundtrack)
8. SECOND CRUSADE
   (Crusaders)
9. NEITHER ONE OF US
   (Gladys Knight and the Pips)
10. CALL ME
    (Al Green)

COUNTRY SINGLES

1. IF YOU CAN LIVE WITH IT
   (Bill Anderson)
2. EMPTIEST ARMS IN THE WORLD
   (Merle Haggard)
3. NOBODY WINS
   (Brenda Lee)
4. COME LIVE WITH ME
   (Roy Clark)
5. WHAT'S YOUR MAMA'S NAME
   (Tanya Tucker)
6. WHAT MY WOMAN CAN'T DO
   (George Jones)
7. WALKIN' PIECE OF HEAVEN
   (Marty Robbins)
8. BABY'S GONE
   (Conway Twitty)
9. SATIN SHEETS
   (Jeanne Pruett)
10. BEHIND CLOSED DOORS
    (Charlie Rich)

COUNTRY ALBUMS

1. ENTERTAINER OF THE YEAR
   (Loretta Lynn)
2. ELVIS ALOHA FROM HAWAII (VIA SATELLITE)
   (Elvis Presley)
3. INTRODUCING JOHNNY RODRIGUEZ
   (Johnny Rodriquez)
4. SUPER KIND OF WOMAN
   (Freddie Hart)
5. SHE NEEDS SOMEONE TO HOLD HER
   (Conway Twitty)
6. KEEP ME IN MIND
   (Lynn Anderson)
7. LONESOME, ON' RY AND MEAN
   (Waylon Jennings)
8. FIRST SONGS BY THE FIRST LADY
   (Tammy Wynette)

9. RHYMER AND OTHER FIVE AND DIMERS
(*Tom T. Hall*)
10. AMERICA, WHY I LOVE HER
(*John Wayne*)

MAY 26, 1973

POP SINGLES

1. FRANKENSTEIN
(*Edgar Winter*)
2. YOU ARE THE SUNSHINE OF MY LIFE
(*Stevie Wonder*)
3. MY LOVE
(*Paul McCartney and Wings*)
4. DRIFT AWAY
(*Dobie Gray*)
5. DANIEL
(*Elton John*)
6. REELING IN THE YEARS
(*Steely Dan*)
7. TIE A YELLOW RIBBON 'ROUND THE OLD
OAK TREE
(*Tony Orlando and Dawn*)
8. PILLOW TALK
(*Sylvia*)
9. STUCK IN THE MIDDLE WITH YOU
(*Stealers Wheel*)
10. WILDFLOWER
(*Skylark*)

POP ALBUMS

1. THE BEATLES/1967-1970
(*The Beatles*)
2. HOUSES OF THE HOLY
(*Led Zeppelin*)
3. THEY ONLY COME OUT AT NIGHT
(*Edgar Winter*)
4. THE BEATLES/1962-1966
(*The Beatles*)
5. THE BEST OF BREAD
(*Bread*)
6. MOVING WAVES
(*Focus*)
7. MASTERPIECE
(*Temptations*)
8. RED ROSE SPEEDWAY
(*Paul McCartney and Wings*)
9. DARK SIDE OF THE MOON
(*Pink Floyd*)
10. STILL ALIVE AND WELL
(*Johnny Winter*)

BLACK SINGLES

1. I CAN UNDERSTAND IT
(*New Birth*)
2. I'M GONNA LOVE YOU JUST A LITTLE
MORE BABY
(*Barry White*)
3. ARMED AND EXTREMELY DANGEROUS
(*First Choice*)
4. WITHOUT YOU IN MY LIFE
(*Tyrone Davis*)
5. FUNKY WORM
(*Ohio Players*)
6. NATURAL HIGH
(*Bloodstone*)
7. LEAVING ME
(*The Independents*)
8. ONE OF A KIND (LOVE AFFAIR)
(*Spinners*)
9. PILLOW TALK
(*Sylvia*)
10. GIVE YOUR BABY A STANDING OVATION
(*The Dells*)

BLACK ALBUMS

1. I'VE GOT SO MUCH TO GIVE
(*Barry White*)
2. BIRTHDAY
(*New Birth*)
3. SPINNERS
(*Spinners*)
4. PLEASURE
(*Ohio Players*)
5. A LETTER TO MYSELF
(*The Chi-Lites*)
6. CALL ME
(*Al Green*)
7. SECOND CRUSADE
(*Crusaders*)
8. MASTERPIECE
(*Temptations*)
9. BLACK CAESAR
(*Original Soundtrack*)
10. LIVE AT THE SAHARA TAHOE
(*Isaac Hayes*)

JAZZ ALBUMS

1. BLACK BYRD
(*Donald Byrd*)
2. SECOND CRUSADE
(*Crusaders*)
3. GOT MY OWN
(*Gene Ammons*)
4. SONG FOR MY LADY
(*McCoy Tyner*)
5. 'ROUND MIDNIGHT
(*Kenny Burrell*)
6. FUNKY SERENITY
(*Ramsey Lewis*)
7. MORNING STAR
(*Hubert Laws*)
8. SUNFLOWER
(*Milt Jackson*)
9. SKY DIVE
(*Freddie Hubbard*)
10. SNAKE RHYTHM ROCK
(*Ivan Boogaloo Jones*)

COUNTRY SINGLES

1. WHAT'S YOUR MAMA'S NAME
(*Tanya Tucker*)
2. EMPTIEST ARMS IN THE WORLD
(*Merle Haggard*)
3. SATIN SHEETS
(*Jeanne Pruett*)
4. BABY'S GONE
(*Conway Twitty*)
5. YELLOW RIBBON
(*Johnny Carver*)
6. YOU ALWAYS COME BACK
(*Johnny Rodriguez*)
7. COME LIVE WITH ME
(*Roy Clark*)
8. IF YOU CAN LIVE WITH IT
(*Bill Anderson*)
9. KIDS SAY THE DARNDEST THINGS
(*Tammy Wynette*)
10. WALK SOFTLY ON THE BRIDGES
(*Mel Street*)

COUNTRY ALBUMS

1. ENTERTAINER OF THE YEAR
(*Loretta Lynn*)
2. INTRODUCING JOHNNY RODRIGUEZ
(*Johnny Rodriguez*)
3. SUPER KIND OF WOMAN
(*Freddie Hart*)
4. SHE NEEDS SOMEONE TO HOLD HER
(*Conway Twitty*)
5. ELVIS ALOHA FROM HAWAII (VIA
SATELLITE)
(*Elvis Presley*)
6. RHYMER AND OTHER FIVE AND DIMERS
(*Tom T. Hall*)
7. LONESOME, ON'RY AND MEAN
(*Waylon Jennings*)
8. SHE'S GOT TO BE A SAINT
(*Ray Price*)
9. THE SESSION
(*Jerry Lee Lewis*)
10. BEHIND CLOSED DOORS
(*Charlie Rich*)

JUNE 2, 1973

POP SINGLES

1. MY LOVE
(*Paul McCartney and Wings*)
2. FRANKENSTEIN
(*Edgar Winter*)
3. DANIEL
(*Elton John*)
4. DRIFT AWAY
(*Dobie Gray*)
5. PILLOW TALK
(*Sylvia*)
6. REELING IN THE YEARS
(*Steely Dan*)
7. YOU ARE THE SUNSHINE OF MY LIFE
(*Stevie Wonder*)
8. WILDFLOWER
(*Skylark*)
9. HOCUS POCUS
(*Focus*)
10. I'M GONNA LOVE YOU JUST A LITTLE
MORE BABY
(*Barry White*)

POP ALBUMS

1. THE BEATLES/1967-1970
(*The Beatles*)
2. THEY ONLY COME OUT AT NIGHT
(*Edgar Winter*)
3. HOUSES OF THE HOLY
(*Led Zeppelin*)
4. THE BEATLES/1962-1966
(*The Beatles*)
5. RED ROSE SPEEDWAY
(*Paul McCartney and Wings*)
6. MOVING WAVES
(*Focus*)
7. THE BEST OF BREAD
(*Bread*)
8. DIAMOND GIRL
(*Seals and Crofts*)
9. MADE IN JAPAN
(*Deep Purple*)
10. STILL ALIVE AND WELL
(*Johnny Winter*)

BLACK SINGLES

1. ONE OF A KIND (LOVE AFFAIR)
(*Spinners*)
2. I'M GONNA LOVE YOU JUST A LITTLE
MORE BABY
(*Barry White*)
3. ARMED AND EXTREMELY DANGEROUS
(*First Choice*)
4. WITHOUT YOU IN MY LIFE
(*Tyrone Davis*)
5. NATURAL HIGH
(*Bloodstone*)
6. I CAN UNDERSTAND IT
(*New Birth*)
7. GIVE YOUR BABY A STANDING OVATION
(*The Dells*)
8. FUNKY WORM
(*Ohio Players*)
9. WILL IT GO ROUND IN CIRCLES
(*Billy Preston*)

10. BROTHER'S GONNA WORK IT OUT
    (Willie Hutch)

BLACK ALBUMS

1. I'VE GOT SO MUCH TO GIVE
   (Barry White)
2. SPINNERS
   (Spinners)
3. BIRTHDAY
   (New Birth)
4. CALL ME
   (Al Green)
5. PLEASURE
   (Ohio Players)
6. A LETTER TO MYSELF
   (The Chi-Lites)
7. SECOND CRUSADE
   (Crusaders)
8. LIVE AT THE SAHARA TAHOE
   (Isaac Hayes)
9. MASTERPIECE
   (Temptations)
10. LIVE AT CARNEGIE HALL
    (Bill Withers)

JAZZ ALBUMS

1. BLACK BYRD
   (Donald Byrd)
2. SECOND CRUSADE
   (Crusaders)
3. SONG FOR MY LADY
   (McCoy Tyner)
4. GOT MY OWN
   (Gene Ammons)
5. REFLECTIONS ON CREATION AND SPACE
   (Alice Coltrane)
6. 'ROUND MIDNIGHT
   (Kenny Burrell)
7. FUNKY SERENITY
   (Ramsey Lewis)
8. SKY DIVE
   (Freddie Hubbard)
9. LIVE AT THE LIGHTHOUSE
   (Grant Green)
10. SEXTANT
    (Herbie Hancock)

COUNTRY SINGLES

1. SATIN SHEETS
   (Jeanne Pruett)
2. BABY'S GONE
   (Conway Twitty)
3. YELLOW RIBBON
   (Johnny Carver)
4. YOU ALWAYS COME BACK
   (Johnny Rodriguez)
5. WHAT'S YOUR MAMA'S NAME
   (Tanya Tucker)
6. KIDS SAY THE DARNDEST THINGS
   (Tammy Wynette)
7. EMPTIEST ARMS IN THE WORLD
   (Merle Haggard)
8. WALK SOFTLY ON THE BRIDGES
   (Mel Street)
9. BRING IT ON HOME
   (Joe Stampley)
10. GOOD NEWS
    (Jody Miller)

COUNTRY ALBUMS

1. INTRODUCING JOHNNY RODRIGUEZ
   (Johnny Rodriguez)
2. ENTERTAINER OF THE YEAR
   (Loretta Lynn)
3. SHE NEEDS SOMEONE TO HOLD HER
   (Conway Twitty)
4. RHYMER AND OTHER FIVE AND DIMERS
   (Tom T. Hall)

5. SUPER KIND OF WOMAN
   (Freddie Hart)
6. SHE'S GOT TO BE A SAINT
   (Ray Price)
7. THE SESSION
   (Jerry Lee Lewis)
8. BEHIND CLOSED DOORS
   (Charlie Rich)
9. ELVIS ALOHA FROM HAWAII (VIA SATELLITE)
   (Elvis Presley)
10. BRENDA
    (Brenda Lee)

JUNE 9, 1973

POP SINGLES

1. MY LOVE
   (Paul McCartney and Wings)
2. DANIEL
   (Elton John)
3. PILLOW TALK
   (Sylvia)
4. FRANKENSTEIN
   (Edgar Winter)
5. I'M GONNA LOVE YOU JUST A LITTLE MORE BABY
   (Barry White)
6. DRIFT AWAY
   (Dobie Gray)
7. PLAYGROUND IN MY MIND
   (Clint Holmes)
8. WILDFLOWER
   (Skylark)
9. HOCUS POCUS
   (Focus)
10. WILL IT GO ROUND IN CIRCLES
    (Billy Preston)

POP ALBUMS

1. RED ROSE SPEEDWAY
   (Paul McCartney and Wings)
2. THEY ONLY COME OUT AT NIGHT
   (Edgar Winter)
3. THE BEATLES /1967–1970
   (The Beatles)
4. HOUSES OF THE HOLY
   (Led Zeppelin)
5. THE BEATLES/1962–1966
   (The Beatles)
6. DIAMOND GIRL
   (Seals and Crofts)
7. YESSONGS
   (Yes)
8. MADE IN JAPAN
   (Deep Purple)
9. MOVING WAVES
   (Focus)
10. THERE GOES RHYMIN' SIMON
    (Paul Simon)

BLACK SINGLES

1. ONE OF A KIND (LOVE AFFAIR)
   (Spinners)
2. I'M GONNA LOVE YOU JUST A LITTLE MORE BABY
   (Barry White)
3. ARMED AND EXTREMELY DANGEROUS
   (First Choice)
4. GIVE YOUR BABY A STANDING OVATION
   (The Dells)
5. WITHOUT YOU IN MY LIFE
   (Tyrone Davis)
6. WILL IT GO ROUND IN CIRCLES
   (Billy Preston)
7. DADDY COULD SWEAR, I DECLARE
   (Gladys Knight and the Pips)

8. NATURAL HIGH
   (Bloodstone)
9. BROTHER'S GONNA WORK IT OUT
   (Willie Hutch)
10. FINDERS, KEEPERS
    (Chairmen of the Board)

BLACK ALBUMS

1. I'VE GOT SO MUCH TO GIVE
   (Barry White)
2. SPINNERS
   (Spinners)
3. CALL ME
   (Al Green)
4. BIRTHDAY
   (New Birth)
5. PLEASURE
   (Ohio Players)
6. A LETTER TO MYSELF
   (The Chi-Lites)
7. SECOND CRUSADE
   (Crusaders)
8. LIVE AT CARNEGIE HALL
   (Bill Withers)
9. LIVE AT THE SAHARA TAHOE
   (Isaac Hayes)
10. MASTERPIECE
    (Temptations)

JAZZ ALBUMS

1. BLACK BYRD
   (Donald Byrd)
2. REFLECTIONS ON CREATION AND SPACE
   (Alice Coltrane)
3. SONG FOR MY LADY
   (McCoy Tyner)
4. SECOND CRUSADE
   (Crusaders)
5. GOT MY OWN
   (Gene Ammons)
6. SKY DIVE
   (Freddie Hubbard)
7. SEXTANT
   (Herbie Hancock)
8. LIVE AT THE LIGHTHOUSE
   (Grant Green)
9. UNDER FIRE
   (Gato Barbieri)
10. MIZRAB
    (Gabor Szabo)

COUNTRY SINGLES

1. BABY'S GONE
   (Conway Twitty)
2. YELLOW RIBBON
   (Johnny Carver)
3. YOU ALWAYS COME BACK
   (Johnny Rodriguez)
4. KIDS SAY THE DARNDEST THINGS
   (Tammy Wynette)
5. SATIN SHEETS
   (Jeanne Pruett)
6. BRING IT ON HOME
   (Joe Stampley)
7. WHAT'S YOUR MAMA'S NAME
   (Tanya Tucker)
8. WHY ME
   (Kris Kristofferson)
9. WALK SOFTLY ON THE BRIDGES
   (Mel Street)
10. SWEET COUNTRY WOMAN
    (Johnny Duncan)

COUNTRY ALBUMS

1. INTRODUCING JOHNNY RODRIGUEZ
   (Johnny Rodriguez)
2. ENTERTAINER OF THE YEAR
   (Loretta Lynn)

3. RHYMER AND OTHER FIVE AND DIMERS
   (Tom T. Hall)
4. SHE NEEDS SOMEONE TO HOLD HER
   (Conway Twitty)
5. SHE'S GOT TO BE A SAINT
   (Ray Price)
6. THE SESSION
   (Jerry Lee Lewis)
7. BEHIND CLOSED DOORS
   (Charlie Rich)
8. BRENDA
   (Brenda Lee)
9. SUPERPICKER
   (Roy Clark)
10. SUPER KIND OF WOMAN
    (Freddie Hart)

JUNE 16, 1973

POP SINGLES

1. MY LOVE
   (Paul McCartney and Wings)
2. DANIEL
   (Elton John)
3. PILLOW TALK
   (Sylvia)
4. I'M GONNA LOVE YOU JUST A LITTLE
   MORE BABY
   (Barry White)
5. PLAYGROUND IN MY MIND
   (Clint Holmes)
6. WILL IT GO ROUND IN CIRCLES
   (Billy Preston)
7. GIVE ME LOVE (GIVE ME PEACE ON
   EARTH)
   (George Harrison)
8. KODACHROME
   (Paul Simon)
9. HOCUS POCUS
   (Focus)
10. ONE OF A KIND (LOVE AFFAIR)
    (Spinners)

POP ALBUMS

1. RED ROSE SPEEDWAY
   (Paul McCartney and Wings)
2. THEY ONLY COME OUT AT NIGHT
   (Edgar Winter)
3. YESSONGS
   (Yes)
4. THE BEATLES/1967-1970
   (The Beatles)
5. THERE GOES RHYMIN' SIMON
   (Paul Simon)
6. DIAMOND GIRL
   (Seals and Crofts)
7. HOUSES OF THE HOLY
   (Led Zeppelin)
8. MADE IN JAPAN
   (Deep Purple)
9. THE BEATLES/1962-1966
   (The Beatles)
10. BLOODSHOT
    (The J. Geils Band)

BLACK SINGLES

1. GIVE YOUR BABY A STANDING OVATION
   (The Dells)
2. ONE OF A KIND (LOVE AFFAIR)
   (Spinners)
3. I'M GONNA LOVE YOU JUST A LITTLE
   MORE BABY
   (Barry White)
4. WILL IT GO ROUND IN CIRCLES
   (Billy Preston)
5. DADDY COULD SWEAR, I DECLARE
   (Gladys Knight and the Pips)

6. ARMED AND EXTREMELY DANGEROUS
   (First Choice)
7. NATURAL HIGH
   (Bloodstone)
8. FINDERS, KEEPERS
   (Chairmen of the Board)
9. BROTHER'S GONNA WORK IT OUT
   (Willie Hutch)
10. MISDEMEANOR
    (Foster Sylvers)

BLACK ALBUMS

1. CALL ME
   (Al Green)
2. I'VE GOT SO MUCH TO GIVE
   (Barry White)
3. SPINNERS
   (Spinners)
4. BIRTHDAY
   (New Birth)
5. SECOND CRUSADE
   (Crusaders)
6. LIVE AT CARNEGIE HALL
   (Bill Withers)
7. LIVE AT THE SAHARA TAHOE
   (Isaac Hayes)
8. PLEASURE
   (Ohio Players)
9. A LETTER TO MYSELF
   (The Chi-Lites)
10. MASTERPIECE
    (Temptations)

COUNTRY SINGLES

1. YELLOW RIBBON
   (Johnny Carver)
2. YOU ALWAYS COME BACK
   (Johnny Rodriguez)
3. KIDS SAY THE DARNDEST THINGS
   (Tammy Wynette)
4. BABY'S GONE
   (Conway Twitty)
5. SATIN SHEETS
   (Jeanne Pruett)
6. BRING IT ON HOME
   (Joe Stampley)
7. WHY ME
   (Kris Kristofferson)
8. SWEET COUNTRY WOMAN
   (Johnny Duncan)
9. SEND ME NO ROSES
   (Tommy Overstreet)
10. RAVISHING RUBY
    (Tom T. Hall)

COUNTRY ALBUMS

1. INTRODUCING JOHNNY RODRIGUEZ
   (Johnny Rodriguez)
2. RHYMER AND OTHER FIVE AND DIMERS
   (Tom T. Hall)
3. BEHIND CLOSED DOORS
   (Charlie Rich)
4. THE SESSION
   (Jerry Lee Lewis)
5. SHE'S GOT TO BE A SAINT
   (Ray Price)
6. BRENDA
   (Brenda Lee)
7. SUPERPICKER
   (Roy Clark)
8. ENTERTAINER OF THE YEAR
   (Loretta Lynn)
9. DANNY'S SONG
   (Anne Murray)
10. SHE NEEDS SOMEONE TO HOLD HER
    (Conway Twitty)

JUNE 23, 1973

POP SINGLES

1. MY LOVE
   (Paul McCartney and Wings)
2. PLAYGROUND IN MY MIND
   (Clint Holmes)
3. WILL IT GO ROUND IN CIRCLES
   (Billy Preston)
4. I'M GONNA LOVE YOU JUST A LITTLE
   MORE BABY
   (Barry White)
5. KODACHROME
   (Paul Simon)
6. GIVE ME LOVE (GIVE ME PEACE ON
   EARTH)
   (George Harrison)
7. PILLOW TALK
   (Sylvia)
8. DANIEL
   (Elton John)
9. SHAMBALA
   (Three Dog Night)
10. ONE OF A KIND (LOVE AFFAIR)
    (Spinners)

POP ALBUMS

1. LIVING IN THE MATERIAL WORLD
   (George Harrison)
2. THERE GOES RHYMIN' SIMON
   (Paul Simon)
3. YESSONGS
   (Yes)
4. RED ROSE SPEEDWAY
   (Paul McCartney and Wings)
5. THEY ONLY COME OUT AT NIGHT
   (Edgar Winter)
6. THE BEATLES /1967-1970
   (The Beatles)
7. DIAMOND GIRL
   (Seals and Crofts)
8. HOUSES OF THE HOLY
   (Led Zeppelin)
9. BLOODSHOT
   (The J. Geils Band)
10. THE BEATLES/1962-1966
    (The Beatles)

BLACK SINGLES

1. GIVE YOUR BABY A STANDING OVATION
   (The Dells)
2. DADDY COULD SWEAR, I DECLARE
   (Gladys Knight and the Pips)
3. WILL IT GO ROUND IN CIRCLES
   (Billy Preston)
4. ONE OF A KIND (LOVE AFFAIR)
   (Spinners)
5. FINDERS, KEEPERS
   (Chairmen of the Board)
6. MISDEMEANOR
   (Foster Sylvers)
7. NATURAL HIGH
   (Bloodstone)
8. DOIN' IT TO DEATH
   (Fred Wesley and the J.B.'s)
9. I'LL ALWAYS LOVE MY MAMA
   (Intruders)
10. TIME TO GET DOWN
    (The O'Jays)

BLACK ALBUMS

1. CALL ME
   (Al Green)
2. I'VE GOT SO MUCH TO GIVE
   (Barry White)
3. LIVE AT THE SAHARA TAHOE
   (Isaac Hayes)

4. SPINNERS
   (Spinners)
5. BIRTHDAY
   (New Birth)
6. LIVE AT CARNEGIE HALL
   (Bill Withers)
7. SECOND CRUSADE
   (Crusaders)
8. MASTERPIECE
   (Temptations)
9. A LETTER TO MYSELF
   (The Chi-Lites)
10. PILLOW TALK
    (Sylvia)

JAZZ ALBUMS

1. BLACK BYRD
   (Donald Byrd)
2. SWEETNIGHTER
   (Weather Report)
3. SONG FOR MY LADY
   (McCoy Tyner)
4. UNDER FIRE
   (Gato Barbieri)
5. HANGIN' OUT
   (Funk Inc.)
6. SEXTANT
   (Herbie Hancock)
7. SECOND CRUSADE
   (Crusaders)
8. LIVE AT THE EAST
   (Pharaoh Sanders)
9. MILES DAVIS IN CONCERT
   (Miles Davis)
10. REFLECTIONS ON CREATION AND SPACE
    (Alice Coltrane)

COUNTRY SINGLES

1. YOU ALWAYS COME BACK
   (Johnny Rodriguez)
2. KIDS SAY THE DARNDEST THINGS
   (Tammy Wynette)
3. YELLOW RIBBON
   (Johnny Carver)
4. WHY ME
   (Kris Kristofferson)
5. DON'T FIGHT THE FEELINGS
   (Charley Pride)
6. SWEET COUNTRY WOMAN
   (Johnny Duncan)
7. RAVISHING RUBY
   (Tom T. Hall)
8. SEND ME NO ROSES
   (Tommy Overstreet)
9. SATIN SHEETS
   (Jeanne Pruett)
10. RIDE ME DOWN EASY
    (Bobby Bare)

COUNTRY ALBUMS

1. RHYMER AND OTHER FIVE AND DIMERS
   (Tom T. Hall)
2. BEHIND CLOSED DOORS
   (Charlie Rich)
3. INTRODUCING JOHNNY RODRIGUEZ
   (Johnny Rodriguez)
4. THE SESSION
   (Jerry Lee Lewis)
5. KIDS SAY THE DARNDEST THINGS
   (Tammy Wynette)
6. BRENDA
   (Brenda Lee)
7. SUPERPICKER
   (Roy Clark)
8. DANNY'S SONG
   (Anne Murray)
9. GOODTIME CHARLIE
   (Charlie McCoy)
10. SHE'S GOT TO BE A SAINT
    (Ray Price)

JUNE 30, 1973

POP SINGLES

1. MY LOVE
   (Paul McCartney and Wings)
2. PLAYGROUND IN MY MIND
   (Clint Holmes)
3. WILL IT GO ROUND IN CIRCLES
   (Billy Preston)
4. KODACHROME
   (Paul Simon)
5. GIVE ME LOVE (GIVE ME PEACE ON EARTH)
   (George Harrison)
6. I'M GONNA LOVE YOU JUST A LITTLE MORE BABY
   (Barry White)
7. SHAMBALA
   (Three Dog Night)
8. BAD BAD LEROY BROWN
   (Jim Croce)
9. ONE OF A KIND (LOVE AFFAIR)
   (Spinners)
10. RIGHT PLACE WRONG TIME
    (Dr. John)

POP ALBUMS

1. LIVING IN THE MATERIAL WORLD
   (George Harrison)
2. THERE GOES RHYMIN' SIMON
   (Paul Simon)
3. RED ROSE SPEEDWAY
   (Paul McCartney and Wings)
4. YESSONGS
   (Yes)
5. FANTASY
   (Carole King)
6. THE BEATLES/1967–1970
   (The Beatles)
7. DIAMOND GIRL
   (Seals and Crofts)
8. HOUSES OF THE HOLY
   (Led Zeppelin)
9. CALL ME
   (Al Green)
10. NOW AND THEN
    (The Carpenters)

BLACK SINGLES

1. GIVE YOUR BABY A STANDING OVATION
   (The Dells)
2. DADDY COULD SWEAR, I DECLARE
   (Gladys Knight and the Pips)
3. WILL IT GO ROUND IN CIRCLES
   (Billy Preston)
4. MISDEMEANOR
   (Foster Sylvers)
5. FINDERS, KEEPERS
   (Chairmen of the Board)
6. DOIN' IT TO DEATH
   (Fred Wesley and the J.B.'s)
7. I'LL ALWAYS LOVE MY MAMA
   (Intruders)
8. TIME TO GET DOWN
   (The O'Jays)
9. ONE OF A KIND (LOVE AFFAIR)
   (Spinners)
10. NATURAL HIGH
    (Bloodstone)

BLACK ALBUMS

1. LIVE AT THE SAHARA TAHOE
   (Isaac Hayes)
2. CALL ME
   (Al Green)
3. I'VE GOT SO MUCH TO GIVE
   (Barry White)

4. SPINNERS
   (Spinners)
5. LIVE AT CARNEGIE HALL
   (Bill Withers)
6. BIRTHDAY
   (New Birth)
7. SECOND CRUSADE
   (Crusaders)
8. PILLOW TALK
   (Sylvia)
9. MASTERPIECE
   (Temptations)
10. MUSIC IS MY LIFE
    (Billy Preston)

JAZZ ALBUMS

1. SWEETNIGHTER
   (Weather Report)
2. BLACK BYRD
   (Donald Byrd)
3. HANGIN' OUT
   (Funk, Inc.)
4. SONG FOR MY LADY
   (McCoy Tyner)
5. SECOND CRUSADE
   (Crusaders)
6. LIVE AT THE EAST
   (Pharaoh Sanders)
7. UNDER FIRE
   (Gato Barbieri)
8. SEXTANT
   (Herbie Hancock)
9. MILES DAVIS IN CONCERT
   (Miles Davis)
10. WISDOM THROUGH MUSIC
    (Pharaoh Sanders)

COUNTRY SINGLES

1. KIDS SAY THE DARNDEST THINGS
   (Tammy Wynette)
2. DON'T FIGHT THE FEELINGS
   (Charley Pride)
3. RAVISHING RUBY
   (Tom T. Hall)
4. WHY ME
   (Kris Kristofferson)
5. SEND ME NO ROSES
   (Tommy Overstreet)
6. SWEET COUNTRY WOMAN
   (Johnny Duncan)
7. YOU ALWAYS COME BACK
   (Johnny Rodriguez)
8. TOO MUCH MONKEY BUSINESS
   (Freddy Weller)
9. SOUTHERN LOVING
   (Jim Ed Brown)
10. RIDE ME DOWN EASY
    (Bobby Bare)

COUNTRY ALBUMS

1. RHYMER AND OTHER FIVE AND DIMERS
   (Tom T. Hall)
2. BEHIND CLOSED DOORS
   (Charlie Rich)
3. INTRODUCING JOHNNY RODRIGUEZ
   (Johnny Rodriguez)
4. KIDS SAY THE DARNDEST THINGS
   (Tammy Wynette)
5. GOODTIME CHARLIE
   (Charlie McCoy)
6. SUPERPICKER
   (Roy Clark)
7. DANNY'S SONG
   (Anne Murray)
8. THE SESSION
   (Jerry Lee Lewis)
9. BRENDA
   (Brenda Lee)
10. YOU LAY SO EASY ON MY MIND
    (Bobby G. Rice)

JULY 7, 1973

POP SINGLES

1. GIVE ME LOVE (GIVE ME PEACE ON EARTH)
   (George Harrison)
2. PLAYGROUND IN MY MIND
   (Clint Holmes)
3. KODACHROME
   (Paul Simon)
4. MY LOVE
   (Paul McCartney and Wings)
5. BAD BAD LEROY BROWN
   (Jim Croce)
6. SHAMBALA
   (Three Dog Night)
7. WILL IT GO ROUND IN CIRCLES
   (Billy Preston)
8. NATURAL HIGH
   (Bloodstone)
9. LONG TRAIN RUNNING
   (The Doobie Brothers)
10. RIGHT PLACE WRONG TIME
    (Dr. John)

POP ALBUMS

1. LIVING IN THE MATERIAL WORLD
   (George Harrison)
2. THERE GOES RHYMIN' SIMON
   (Paul Simon)
3. FANTASY
   (Carole King)
4. RED ROSE SPEEDWAY
   (Paul McCartney and Wings)
5. NOW AND THEN
   (The Carpenters)
6. DARK SIDE OF THE MOON
   (Pink Floyd)
7. DIAMOND GIRL
   (Seals and Crofts)
8. CALL ME
   (Al Green)
9. YESSONGS
   (Yes)
10. HOUSES OF THE HOLY
    (Led Zeppelin)

BLACK SINGLES

1. DOIN' IT TO DEATH
   (Fred Wesley and the J.B.'s)
2. GIVE YOUR BABY A STANDING OVATION
   (The Dells)
3. TIME TO GET DOWN
   (The O'Jays)
4. MISDEMEANOR
   (Foster Sylvers)
5. DADDY COULD SWEAR, I DECLARE
   (Gladys Knight and the Pips)
6. I'LL ALWAYS LOVE MY MAMA
   (Intruders)
7. WILL IT GO ROUND IN CIRCLES
   (Billy Preston)
8. IT'S FOREVER
   (Ebonys)
9. THERE'S NO ME WITHOUT YOU
   (The Manhattans)
10. YOU'LL NEVER GET TO HEAVEN
    (The Stylistics)

BLACK ALBUMS

1. LIVE AT THE SAHARA TAHOE
   (Isaac Hayes)
2. CALL ME
   (Al Green)
3. I'VE GOT SO MUCH TO GIVE
   (Barry White)

4. SPINNERS
   (Spinners)
5. LIVE AT CARNEGIE HALL
   (Bill Withers)
6. HEAD TO THE SKY
   (Earth, Wind and Fire)
7. MUSIC IS MY LIFE
   (Billy Preston)
8. PILLOW TALK
   (Sylvia)
9. BIRTHDAY
   (New Birth)
10. NATURAL HIGH
    (Bloodstone)

JAZZ ALBUMS

1. SWEETNIGHTER
   (Weather Report)
2. BLACK BYRD
   (Donald Byrd)
3. HANGIN' OUT
   (Funk Inc.)
4. SECOND CRUSADE
   (Crusaders)
5. SEXTANT
   (Herbie Hancock)
6. YOU'VE GOT IT BAD GIRL
   (Quincy Jones)
7. SONG FOR MY LADY
   (McCoy Tyner)
8. MILES DAVIS IN CONCERT
   (Miles Davis)
9. SKY DIVE
   (Freddie Hubbard)
10. LIVE AT MONTREUX
    (Les McCann)

COUNTRY SINGLES

1. DON'T FIGHT THE FEELINGS
   (Charley Pride)
2. RAVISHING RUBY
   (Tom T. Hall)
3. WHY ME
   (Kris Kristofferson)
4. KIDS SAY THE DARNDEST THINGS
   (Tammy Wynette)
5. SEND ME NO ROSES
   (Tommy Overstreet)
6. LOVE IS THE FOUNDATION
   (Loretta Lynn)
7. SOUTHERN LOVING
   (Jim Ed Brown)
8. TOO MUCH MONKEY BUSINESS
   (Freddy Weller)
9. COME EARLY MORNING
   (Don Williams)
10. YOU WERE ALWAYS THERE
    (Donna Fargo)

COUNTRY ALBUMS

1. BEHIND CLOSED DOORS
   (Charlie Rich)
2. RHYMER AND OTHER FIVE AND DIMERS
   (Tom T. Hall)
3. KIDS SAY THE DARNDEST THINGS
   (Tammy Wynette)
4. GOODTIME CHARLIE
   (Charlie McCoy)
5. INTRODUCING JOHNNY RODRIGUEZ
   (Johnny Rodriguez)
6. DANNY'S SONG
   (Anne Murray)
7. SUPERPICKER
   (Roy Clark)
8. YOU LAY SO EASY ON MY MIND
   (Bobby G. Rice)
9. WHAT'S YOUR MAMA'S NAME
   (Tanya Tucker)
10. THE SESSION
    (Jerry Lee Lewis)

JULY 14, 1973

POP SINGLES

1. KODACHROME
   (Paul Simon)
2. GIVE ME LOVE (GIVE ME PEACE ON EARTH)
   (George Harrison)
3. BAD BAD LEROY BROWN
   (Jim Croce)
4. PLAYGROUND IN MY MIND
   (Clint Holmes)
5. SHAMBALA
   (Three Dog Night)
6. YESTERDAY ONCE MORE
   (The Carpenters)
7. NATURAL HIGH
   (Bloodstone)
8. SMOKE ON THE WATER
   (Deep Purple)
9. LONG TRAIN RUNNIN'
   (The Doobie Brothers)
10. WILL IT GO ROUND IN CIRCLES
    (Billy Preston)

POP ALBUMS

1. LIVING IN THE MATERIAL WORLD
   (George Harrison)
2. FANTASY
   (Carole King)
3. THERE GOES RHYMIN' SIMON
   (Paul Simon)
4. NOW AND THEN
   (The Carpenters)
5. DARK SIDE OF THE MOON
   (Pink Floyd)
6. RED ROSE SPEEDWAY
   (Paul McCartney and Wings)
7. DIAMOND GIRL
   (Seals and Crofts)
8. CALL ME
   (Al Green)
9. MACHINE HEAD
   (Deep Purple)
10. MADE IN JAPAN
    (Deep Purple)

BLACK SINGLES

1. TIME TO GET DOWN
   (The O'Jays)
2. DOIN' IT TO DEATH
   (Fred Wesley and the J.B.'s)
3. I BELIEVE IN YOU
   (Johnnie Taylor)
4. THERE'S NO ME WITHOUT YOU
   (The Manhattans)
5. I'LL ALWAYS LOVE MY MAMA
   (Intruders)
6. GIVE YOUR BABY A STANDING OVATION
   (The Dells)
7. IT'S FOREVER
   (Ebonys)
8. WHERE PEACEFUL WATERS FLOW
   (Gladys Knight and the Pips)
9. PLASTIC MAN
   (Temptations)
10. ARE YOU MAN ENOUGH
    (The Four Tops)

BLACK ALBUMS

1. LIVE AT THE SAHARA TAHOE
   (Isaac Hayes)
2. CALL ME
   (Al Green)
3. I'VE GOT SO MUCH TO GIVE
   (Barry White)

4. HEAD TO THE SKY
   (Earth, Wind and Fire)
5. BACK TO THE WORLD
   (Curtis Mayfield)
6. MUSIC IS MY LIFE
   (Billy Preston)
7. PILLOW TALK
   (Sylvia)
8. NATURAL HIGH
   (Bloodstone)
9. BLACK BYRD
   (Donald Byrd)
10. LIVE AT CARNEIGE HALL
    (Bill Withers)

JAZZ ALBUMS

1. SWEETNIGHTER
   (Weather Report)
2. BLACK BYRD
   (Donald Byrd)
3. HANGIN' IN
   (Funk Inc.)
4. SEXTANT
   (Herbie Hancock)
5. YOU'VE GOT IT BAD GIRL
   (Quincy Jones)
6. SONG FOR MY LADY
   (McCoy Tyner)
7. LIVE AT MONTREUX
   (Les McCann)
8. MILES DAVIS IN CONCERT
   (Miles Davis)
9. SECOND CRUSADE
   (Crusaders)
10. SKY DIVE
    (Freddie Hubbard)

COUNTRY SINGLES

1. WHY ME
   (Kris Kristofferson)
2. RAVISHING RUBY
   (Tom T. Hall)
3. LOVE IS THE FOUNDATION
   (Loretta Lynn)
4. DON'T FIGHT THE FEELINGS
   (Charlie Pride)
5. SOUTHERN LOVING
   (Jim Ed Brown)
6. YOU WERE ALWAYS THERE
   (Donna Fargo)
7. COME EARLY MORNING
   (Don Williams)
8. LORD, MR. FORD
   (Jerry Reed)
9. KIDS SAY THE DARNDEST THINGS
   (Tammy Wynette)
10. YOU GIVE ME YOU
    (Bobby G.Rice)

COUNTRY ALBUMS

1. BEHIND CLOSED DOORS
   (Charlie Rich)
2. GOOD TIME CHARLIE
   (Charlie McCoy)
3. KIDS SAY THE DARNDEST THINGS
   (Tammy Wynette)
4. RHYMER AND OTHER FIVE AND DIMERS
   (Tom T. Hall)
5. INTRODUCING JOHNNY RODRIGUEZ
   (Johnny Rodriguez)
6. DANNY'S SONG
   (Anne Murray)
7. YOU LAY SO EASY ON MY MIND
   (Bobby G. Rice)
8. WHAT'S YOUR MAMA'S NAME
   (Tanya Tucker)
9. SUPERPICKER
   (Roy Clark)
10. THE SESSION
    (Jerry Lee Lewis)

JULY 21, 1973

POP SINGLES

1. BAD BAD LEROY BROWN
   (Jim Croce)
2. SHAMBALA
   (Three Dog Night)
3. KODACHROME
   (Paul Simon)
4. YESTERDAY ONCE MORE
   (The Carpenters)
5. GIVE ME LOVE (GIVE ME PEACE ON EARTH)
   (George Harrison)
6. SMOKE ON THE WATER
   (Deep Purple)
7. NATURAL HIGH
   (Bloodstone)
8. BOOGIE WOOGIE BUGLE BOY
   (Bette Midler)
9. PLAYGROUND IN MY MIND
   (Clint Holmes)
10. WILL IT GO ROUND IN CIRCLES
    (Billy Preston)

POP ALBUMS

1. FANTASY
   (Carole King)
2. NOW AND THEN
   (The Carpenters)
3. LIVING IN THE MATERIAL WORLD
   (George Harrison)
4. DARK SIDE OF THE MOON
   (Pink Floyd)
5. THERE GOES RHYMIN' SIMON
   (Paul Simon)
6. RED ROSE SPEEDWAY
   (Paul McCartney and Wings)
7. MACHINE HEAD
   (Deep Purple)
8. MADE IN JAPAN
   (Deep Purple)
9. DIAMOND GIRL
   (Seals and Crofts)
10. FRESH
    (Sly and the Family Stone)

BLACK SINGLES

1. I BELIEVE IN YOU
   (Johnnie Taylor)
2. TIME TO GET DOWN
   (The O'Jays)
3. THERE'S NO ME WITHOUT YOU
   (The Manhattans)
4. DOIN' IT TO DEATH
   (Fred Wesley and the J.B.'s)
5. WHERE PEACEFUL WATERS FLOW
   (Gladys Knight and the Pips)
6. I'LL ALWAYS LOVE MY MAMA
   (Intruders)
7. IT'S FOREVER
   (Ebonys)
8. ARE YOU MAN ENOUGH
   (The Four Tops)
9. PLASTIC MAN
   (Temptations)
10. NOBODY WANTS YOU WHEN YOU'RE DOWN AND OUT
    (Bobby Womack)

BLACK ALBUMS

1. LIVE AT THE SAHARA TAHOE
   (Isaac Hayes)
2. BACK TO THE WORLD
   (Curtis Mayfield)
3. HEAD TO THE SKY
   (Earth, Wind and Fire)

4. I'VE GOT SO MUCH TO GIVE
   (Barry White)
5. MUSIC IS MY LIFE
   (Billy Preston)
6. CALL ME
   (Al Green)
7. NATURAL HIGH
   (Bloodstone)
8. FRESH
   (Sly and the Family Stone)
9. BLACK BYRD
   (Donald Byrd)
10. SPINNERS
    (Spinners)

JAZZ ALBUMS

1. BLACK BYRD
   (Donald Byrd)
2. SWEETNIGHTER
   (Weather Report)
3. YOU'VE GOT IT BAD GIRL
   (Quincy Jones)
4. SEXTANT
   (Herbie Hancock)
5. HANGIN' OUT
   (Funk Inc.)
6. LIVE AT MONTREUX
   (Les McCann)
7. LOVE, DEVOTION, SURRENDER
   (Carlos Santana and Mahavishnu John McLaughlin)
8. MILES DAVIS IN CONCERT
   (Miles Davis)
9. SONG FOR MY LADY
   (McCoy Tyner)
10. SOUL BOX
    (Grover Washington Jr.)

COUNTRY SINGLES

1. RAVISHING RUBY
   (Tom T. Hall)
2. LOVE IS THE FOUNDATION
   (Loretta Lynn)
3. WHY ME
   (Kris Kristofferson)
4. YOU WERE ALWAYS THERE
   (Donna Fargo)
5. SOUTHERN LOVING
   (Jim Ed Brown)
6. LORD, MR. FORD
   (Jerry Reed)
7. COME EARLY MORNING
   (Don Williams)
8. YOU GIVE ME YOU
   (Bobby G. Rice)
9. TRIP TO HEAVEN
   (Freddie Hart)
10. TOP OF THE WORLD
    (Lynn Anderson)

COUNTRY ALBUMS

1. BEHIND CLOSED DOORS
   (Charlie Rich)
2. GOODTIME CHARLIE
   (Charlie McCoy)
3. KIDS SAY THE DARNDEST THINGS
   (Tammy Wynette)
4. RHYMER AND OTHER FIVE AND DIMERS
   (Tom T. Hall)
5. DANNY'S SONG
   (Anne Murray)
6. YOU LAY SO EASY ON MY MIND
   (Bobby G. Rice)
7. WHAT'S YOUR MAMA'S NAME
   (Tanya Tucker)
8. INTRODUCING JOHNNY RODRIGUEZ
   (Johnny Rodriguez)
9. SWEET COUNTRY
   (Charley Pride)
10. SATIN SHEETS
    (Jeanne Pruett)

JULY 28, 1973

POP SINGLES

1. SHAMBALA
   (Three Dog Night)
2. YESTERDAY ONCE MORE
   (The Carpenters)
3. BAD BAD LEROY BROWN
   (Jim Croce)
4. SMOKE ON THE WATER
   (Deep Purple)
5. BOOGIE WOOGIE BUGLE BOY
   (Bette Midler)
6. GET DOWN
   (Gilbert O'Sullivan)
7. NATURAL HIGH
   (Bloodstone)
8. DIAMOND GIRL
   (Seals and Crofts)
9. LIVE AND LET DIE
   (Paul McCartney and Wings)
10. MONSTER MASH
    (Bobby Boris Pickett)

POP ALBUMS

1. NOW AND THEN
   (The Carpenters)
2. FANTASY
   (Carole King)
3. LIVING IN THE MATERIAL WORLD
   (George Harrison)
4. DARK SIDE OF THE MOON
   (Pink Floyd)
5. CHICAGO VI
   (Chicago)
6. MACHINE HEAD
   (Deep Purple)
7. MADE IN JAPAN
   (Deep Purple)
8. FRESH
   (Sly and the Family Stone)
9. THERE GOES RHYMIN' SIMON
   (Paul Simon)
10. RED ROSE SPEEDWAY
    (Paul McCartney and Wings)

BLACK SINGLES

1. I BELIEVE IN YOU
   (Johnnie Taylor)
2. THERE'S NO ME WITHOUT YOU
   (The Manhattans)
3. TIME TO GET DOWN
   (The O'Jays)
4. ARE YOU MAN ENOUGH
   (The Four Tops)
5. WHERE PEACEFUL WATERS FLOW
   (Gladys Knight and the Pips)
6. LET'S GET IT ON
   (Marvin Gaye)
7. SO VERY HARD TO GO
   (Tower of Power)
8. NOBODY WANTS YOU WHEN YOU'RE
   DOWN AND OUT
   (Bobby Womack)
9. ANGEL
   (Aretha Franklin)
10. HERE I AM
    (Al Green)

BLACK ALBUMS

1. BACK TO THE WORLD
   (Curtis Mayfield)
2. HEY NOW HEY
   (Aretha Franklin)
3. HEAD TO THE SKY
   (Earth, Wind and Fire)

4. I'VE GOT SO MUCH TO GIVE
   (Barry White)
5. NATURAL HIGH
   (Bloodstone)
6. FRESH
   (Sly and the Family Stone)
7. LIVE AT THE SAHARA TAHOE
   (Isaac Hayes)
8. TAYLORED IN SILK
   (Johnnie Taylor)
9. CALL ME
   (Al Green)
10. MUSIC IS MY LIFE
    (Billy Preston)

JAZZ ALBUMS

1. YOU'VE GOT IT BAD GIRL
   (Quincy Jones)
2. BLACK BYRD
   (Donald Byrd)
3. SEXTANT
   (Herbie Hancock)
4. SWEETNIGHTER
   (Weather Report)
5. LOVE, DEVOTION, SURRENDER
   (Carlos Santana and Mahavishnu
   John McLaughlin)
6. LIVE AT MONTREUX
   (Les McCann)
7. HANGIN' OUT
   (Funk Inc.)
8. SOUL BOX
   (Grover Washington Jr.)
9. EXCURSIONS
   (Eddie Harris)
10. SECOND CRUSADE
    (Crusaders)

COUNTRY SINGLES

1. LOVE IS THE FOUNDATION
   (Loretta Lynn)
2. YOU WERE ALWAYS THERE
   (Donna Fargo)
3. LORD, MR. FORD
   (Jerry Reed)
4. TRIP TO HEAVEN
   (Freddie Hart)
5. RAVISHING RUBY
   (Tom T. Hall)
6. YOU GIVE ME YOU
   (Bobby G. Rice)
7. TOUCH THE MORNING
   (Don Gibson)
8. TOP OF THE WORLD
   (Lynn Anderson)
9. WHY ME
   (Kris Kristofferson)
10. SOUTHERN LOVING
    (Jim Ed Brown)

COUNTRY ALBUMS

1. GOODTIME CHARLIE
   (Charlie McCoy)
2. BEHIND CLOSED DOORS
   (Charlie Rich)
3. SATIN SHEETS
   (Jeanne Pruett)
4. WHAT'S YOUR MAMA'S NAME
   (Tanya Tucker)
5. DANNY'S SONG
   (Anne Murray)
6. YOU LAY SO EASY ON MY MIND
   (Bobby G. Rice)
7. SWEET COUNTRY
   (Charley Pride)
8. RHYMER AND OTHER FIVE AND DIMERS
   (Tom T. Hall)
9. INTRODUCING JOHNNY RODRIGUEZ
   (Johnny Rodriguez)
10. KIDS SAY THE DARNDEST THINGS
    (Tammy Wynette)

AUGUST 4, 1973

POP SINGLES

1. YESTERDAY ONCE MORE
   (The Carpenters)
2. SMOKE ON THE WATER
   (Deep Purple)
3. SHAMBALA
   (Three Dog Night)
4. GET DOWN
   (Gilbert O'Sullivan)
5. BOOGIE WOOGIE BUGLE BOY
   (Bette Midler)
6. DIAMOND GIRL
   (Seals and Crofts)
7. LIVE AND LET LIVE
   (Paul McCartney and Wings)
8. TOUCH ME IN THE MORNING
   (Diana Ross)
9. MORNING AFTER
   (Maureen McGovern)
10. MONSTER MASH
    (Bobby Boris Pickett)

POP ALBUMS

1. CHICAGO VI
   (Chicago)
2. NOW AND THEN
   (The Carpenters)
3. DARK SIDE OF THE MOON
   (Pink Floyd)
4. FANTASY
   (Carole King)
5. FRESH
   (Sly and the Family Stone)
6. MACHINE HEAD
   (Deep Purple)
7. MADE IN JAPAN
   (Deep Purple)
8. LIVING IN THE MATERIAL WORLD
   (George Harrison)
9. LEON LIVE
   (Leon Russell)
10. LOVE, DEVOTION, SURRENDER
    (Carlos Santana and Mahavishnu
    John McLaughlin)

BLACK SINGLES

1. LET'S GET IT ON
   (Marvin Gaye)
2. I BELIEVE IN YOU
   (Johnnie Taylor)
3. ARE YOU MAN ENOUGH
   (The Four Tops)
4. THERE'S NO ME WITHOUT YOU
   (The Manhattans)
5. NOBODY WANTS YOU WHEN YOU'RE
   DOWN AND OUT
   (Bobby Womack)
6. ANGEL
   (Aretha Franklin)
7. SO VERY HARD TO GO
   (Tower of Power)
8. HERE I AM
   (Al Green)
9. IF YOU WANT ME
   (Sly and the Family Stone)
10. I WAS CHECKIN' OUT, SHE WAS
    CHECKIN' IN
    (Don Covay)

BLACK ALBUMS

1. FRESH
   (Sly and the Family Stone)
2. HEY NOW HEY
   (Aretha Franklin)
3. BACK TO THE WORLD
   (Curtis Mayfield)

4. I'VE GOT SO MUCH TO GIVE
   (Barry White)
5. HEAD TO THE SKY
   (Earth, Wind and Fire)
6. TAYLORED IN SILK
   (Johnnie Taylor)
7. NATURAL HIGH
   (Bloodstone)
8. LIVE AT THE SAHARA TAHOE
   (Isaac Hayes)
9. CALL ME
   (Al Green)
10. TOWER OF POWER
    (Tower of Power)

JAZZ ALBUMS

1. LOVE, DEVOTION, SURRENDER
   (Carlos Santana and Mahavishnu John McLaughlin)
2. YOU'VE GOT IT BAD GIRL
   (Quincy Jones)
3. BLACK BYRD
   (Donald Byrd)
4. SWEETNIGHTER
   (Weather Report)
5. LIVE AT MONTREUX
   (Les McCann)
6. SOUL BOX
   (Grover Washington Jr.)
7. SEXTANT
   (Herbie Hancock)
8. EXCURSIONS
   (Eddie Harris)
9. HANGIN' OUT
   (Funk Inc.)
10. SECOND CRUSADE
    (Crusaders)

COUNTRY SINGLES

1. LORD, MR. FORD
   (Jerry Reed)
2. YOU WERE ALWAYS THERE
   (Donna Fargo)
3. TRIP TO HEAVEN
   (Freddie Hart)
4. LOVE IS THE FOUNDATION
   (Loretta Lynn)
5. TOUCH THE MORNING
   (Don Gibson)
6. TOP OF THE WORLD
   (Lynn Anderson)
7. YOU GIVE ME YOU
   (Bobby Rice)
8. LOUISIANA WOMAN, MISSISSIPPI MAN
   (Loretta Lynn and Conway Twitty)
9. SHE'S ALL WOMAN
   (David Houston)
10. MR. LOVEMAKER
    (Johnny Paycheck)

COUNTRY ALBUMS

1. SATIN SHEETS
   (Jeanne Pruett)
2. GOODTIME CHARLIE
   (Charlie McCoy)
3. WHAT'S YOUR MAMA'S NAME
   (Tanya Tucker)
4. SWEET COUNTRY
   (Charley Pride)
5. BEHIND CLOSED DOORS
   (Charlie Rich)
6. YOU LAY SO EASY ON MY MIND
   (Bobby G. Rice)
7. LORD, MR. FORD
   (Jerry Reed)
8. RHYMER AND OTHER FIVE AND DIMERS
   (Tom T. Hall)
9. INTRODUCING JOHNNY RODRIGUEZ
   (Johnny Rodriguez)
10. I KNEW JESUS (BEFORE HE WAS A STAR)
    (Glen Campbell)

AUGUST 11, 1973

POP SINGLES

1. TOUCH ME IN THE MORNING
   (Diana Ross)
2. MORNING AFTER
   (Maureen McGovern)
3. LIVE AND LET DIE
   (Paul McCartney and Wings)
4. GET DOWN
   (Gilbert O'Sullivan)
5. YESTERDAY ONCE MORE
   (The Carpenters)
6. DIAMOND GIRL
   (Seals and Crofts)
7. SMOKE ON THE WATER
   (Deep Purple)
8. BROTHER LOUIE
   (Stories)
9. LET'S GET IT ON
   (Marvin Gaye)
10. MONEY
    (Pink Floyd)

POP ALBUMS

1. CHICAGO VI
   (Chicago)
2. DARK SIDE OF THE MOON
   (Pink Floyd)
3. NOW AND THEN
   (The Carpenters)
4. FRESH
   (Sly and the Family Stone)
5. FANTASY
   (Carole King)
6. PASSION PLAY
   (Jethro Tull)
7. LEON LIVE
   (Leon Russell)
8. LOVE, DEVOTION, SURRENDER
   (Carlos Santana and Mahavishnu John McLaughlin)
9. MACHINE HEAD
   (Deep Purple)
10. LIVING IN THE MATERIAL WORLD
    (George Harrison)

BLACK SINGLES

1. LET'S GET IT ON
   (Marvin Gaye)
2. I BELIEVE IN YOU
   (Johnnie Taylor)
3. ARE YOU MAN ENOUGH
   (The Four Tops)
4. ANGEL
   (Aretha Franklin)
5. NOBODY WANTS YOU WHEN YOU'RE DOWN AND OUT
   (Bobby Womack)
6. HERE I AM
   (Al Green)
7. IF YOU WANT ME
   (Sly and the Family Stone)
8. I WAS CHECKIN' OUT, SHE WAS CHECKIN' IN
   (Don Covay)
9. TOUCH ME IN THE MORNING
   (Diana Ross)
10. THAT LADY
    (Isley Brothers)

BLACK ALBUMS

1. FRESH
   (Sly and the Family Stone)
2. HEY NOW HEY
   (Aretha Franklin)
3. I'VE GOT SO MUCH TO GIVE
   (Barry White)

4. HEAD TO THE SKY
   (Earth, Wind and Fire)
5. TAYLORED IN SILK
   (Johnnie Taylor)
6. BACK TO THE WORLD
   (Curtis Mayfield)
7. NATURAL HIGH
   (Bloodstone)
8. FACTS OF LIFE
   (Bobby Womack)
9. TOWER OF POWER
   (Tower of Power)
10. TOUCH ME IN THE MORNING
    (Diana Ross)

JAZZ ALBUMS

1. LOVE, DEVOTION, SURRENDER
   (Carlos Santana and Mahavishnu John McLaughlin)
2. BLACK BYRD
   (Donald Byrd)
3. YOU'VE GOT IT BAD GIRL
   (Quincy Jones)
4. SOUL BOX
   (Grover Washington Jr.)
5. LIVE AT MONTREUX
   (Les McCann)
6. SWEETNIGHTER
   (Weather Report)
7. SEXTANT
   (Herbie Hancock)
8. EXCURSIONS
   (Eddie Harris)
9. FIRST LIGHT
   (Freddie Hubbard)
10. SECOND CRUSADE
    (Crusaders)

COUNTRY SINGLES

1. YOU WERE ALWAYS THERE
   (Donna Fargo)
2. TOP OF THE WORLD
   (Lynn Anderson)
3. TRIP TO HEAVEN
   (Freddie Hart)
4. LORD, MR. FORD
   (Jerry Reed)
5. TOUCH THE MORNING
   (Don Gibson)
6. LOUISIANA WOMAN, MISSISSIPPI MAN
   (Loretta Lynn and Conway Twitty)
7. SHE'S ALL WOMAN
   (David Houston)
8. MR. LOVEMAKER
   (Johnny Paycheck)
9. LOVE IS THE FOUNDATION
   (Loretta Lynn)
10. EVERYBODY'S HAD THE BLUES
    (Merle Haggard)

COUNTRY ALBUMS

1. SATIN SHEETS
   (Jeanne Pruett)
2. SWEET COUNTRY
   (Charley Pride)
3. WHAT'S YOUR MAMA'S NAME
   (Tanya Tucker)
4. LORD, MR. FORD
   (Jerry Reed)
5. GOODTIME CHARLIE
   (Charley McCoy)
6. BEHIND CLOSED DOORS
   (Charlie Rich)
7. INTRODUCING JOHNNY RODRIGUEZ
   (Johnny Rodriguez)
8. RHYMER AND OTHER FIVE AND DIMERS
   (Tom T. Hall)
9. YOU LAY SO EASY ON MY MIND
   (Bobby G. Rice)
10. DON WILLIAMS, VOL. 1
    (Don Williams)

AUGUST 18, 1973

POP SINGLES

1. MORNING AFTER
   (Maureen McGovern)
2. LIVE AND LET DIE
   (Paul McCartney and Wings)
3. TOUCH ME IN THE MORNING
   (Diana Ross)
4. BROTHER LOUIE
   (Stories)
5. LET'S GET IT ON
   (Marvin Gaye)
6. GET DOWN
   (Gilbert O'Sullivan)
7. YESTERDAY ONCE MORE
   (The Carpenters)
8. DELTA DAWN
   (Helen Reddy)
9. I BELIEVE IN YOU
   (Johnnie Taylor)
10. SAY, HAS ANYBODY SEEN MY SWEET
    GYPSY ROSE
    (Tony Orlando and Dawn)

POP ALBUMS

1. PASSION PLAY
   (Jethro Tull)
2. DARK SIDE OF THE MOON
   (Pink Floyd)
3. CHICAGO VI
   (Chicago)
4. FRESH
   (Sly and the Family Stone)
5. NOW AND THEN
   (The Carpenters)
6. LEON LIVE
   (Leon Russell)
7. FOREIGNER
   (Cat Stevens)
8. LOVE, DEVOTION, SURRENDER
   *(Carlos Santana and Mahavishnu
   John McLaughlin)*
9. TOUCH ME IN THE MORNING
   (Diana Ross)
10. THE CAPTAIN AND ME
    (The Doobie Brothers)

BLACK SINGLES

1. LET'S GET IT ON
   (Marvin Gaye)
2. ANGEL
   (Aretha Franklin)
3. I BELIEVE IN YOU
   (Johnnie Taylor)
4. HERE I AM
   (Al Green)
5. I WAS CHECKIN' OUT, SHE WAS
   CHECKIN' IN
   (Don Covay)
6. THAT LADY
   (Isley Brothers)
7. IF YOU WANT ME
   (Sly and the Family Stone)
8. TOUCH ME IN THE MORNING
   (Diana Ross)
9. ARE YOU MAN ENOUGH
   (The Four Tops)
10. THERE IT IS
    (Tyrone Davis)

BLACK ALBUMS

1. FRESH
   (Sly and the Family Stone)
2. HEY NOW HEY
   (Aretha Franklin)

3. HEAD TO THE SKY
   (Earth, Wind and Fire)
4. TAYLORED IN SILK
   (Johnnie Taylor)
5. BACK TO THE WORLD
   (Curtis Mayfield)
6. TOUCH ME IN THE MORNING
   (Diana Ross)
7. FACTS OF LIFE
   (Bobby Womack)
8. TOWER OF POWER
   (Tower of Power)
9. I'VE GOT SO MUCH TO GIVE
   (Barry White)
10. EXTENSION OF A MAN
    (Donny Hathaway)

JAZZ ALBUMS

1. LOVE, DEVOTION, SURRENDER
   *(Carlos Santana and Mahavishnu
   John McLaughlin)*
2. BLACK BYRD
   (Donald Byrd)
3. SOUL BOX
   (Grover Washington Jr.)
4. YOU'VE GOT IT BAD GIRL
   (Quincy Jones)
5. SWEETNIGHTER
   (Weather Report)
6. LIVE AT MONTREUX
   (Les McCann)
7. EXCURSIONS
   (Eddie Harris)
8. DEODATO 2
   (Eumir Deodato)
9. FINGERS
   (Airto)
10. SEXTANT
    (Herbie Hancock)

COUNTRY SINGLES

1. LOUISIANA WOMAN, MISSISSIPPI MAN
   (Loretta Lynn and Conway Twitty)
2. TOP OF THE WORLD
   (Lynn Anderson)
3. TRIP TO HEAVEN
   (Freddie Hart)
4. EVERYBODY'S HAD THE BLUES
   (Merle Haggard)
5. MR. LOVEMAKER
   (Johnny Paycheck)
6. SHE'S ALL WOMAN
   (David Houston)
7. YOU WERE ALWAYS THERE
   (Donna Fargo)
8. SLIPPIN' AWAY
   (Jean Shepard)
9. LORD, MR. FORD
   (Jerry Reed)
10. NOTHING EVER HURT ME
    (George Jones)

COUNTRY ALBUMS

1. SATIN SHEETS
   (Jeanne Pruett)
2. SWEET COUNTRY
   (Charley Pride)
3. WHAT'S YOUR MAMA'S NAME
   (Tanya Tucker)
4. LORD, MR. FORD
   (Jerry Reed)
5. BEHIND CLOSED DOORS
   (Charlie Rich)
6. GOODTIME CHARLIE
   (Charlie McCoy)
7. INTRODUCING JOHNNY RODRIGUEZ
   (Johnny Rodriguez)
8. DON WILLIAMS, VOL. 1
   (Don Williams)
9. RHYMER AND OTHER FIVE AND DIMERS
   (Tom T. Hall)

10. AM I THAT EASY TO FORGET
    (Jim Reeves)

AUGUST 25, 1973

POP SINGLES

1. LIVE AND LET DIE
   (Paul McCartney and Wings)
2. LET'S GET IT ON
   (Marvin Gaye)
3. BROTHER LOUIE
   (Stories)
4. MORNING AFTER
   (Maureen McGovern)
5. TOUCH ME IN THE MORNING
   (Diana Ross)
6. DELTA DAWN
   (Helen Reddy)
7. I BELIEVE IN YOU
   (Johnnie Taylor)
8. SAY, HAS ANYBODY SEEN MY SWEET
   GYPSY ROSE
   (Tony Orlando and Dawn)
9. GET DOWN
   (Gilbert O'Sullivan)
10. UNEASY RIDER
    (Charley Daniels)

POP ALBUMS

1. PASSION PLAY
   (Jethro Tull)
2. DARK SIDE OF THE MOON
   (Pink Floyd)
3. CHICAGO VI
   (Chicago)
4. FRESH
   (Sly and the Family Stone)
5. FOREIGNER
   (Cat Stevens)
6. TOUCH ME IN THE MORNING
   (Diana Ross)
7. LEON LIVE
   (Leon Russell)
8. NOW AND THEN
   (The Carpenters)
9. LOVE, DEVOTION, SURRENDER
   *(Carlos Santana and Mahavishnu
   John McLaughlin)*
10. THE CAPTAIN AND ME
    (The Doobie Brothers)

BLACK SINGLES

1. LET'S GET IT ON
   (Marvin Gaye)
2. ANGEL
   (Aretha Franklin)
3. THAT LADY
   (Isley Brothers)
4. HERE I AM
   (Al Green)
5. I WAS CHECKIN' OUT, SHE WAS
   CHECKIN' IN
   (Don Covay)
6. I BELIEVE IN YOU
   (Johnnie Taylor)
7. IF YOU WANT ME
   (Sly and the Family Stone)
8. THERE IT IS
   (Tyrone Davis)
9. BABY I'VE BEEN MISSING YOU
   (The Independents)
10. GYPSY MAN
    (War)

BLACK ALBUMS

1. FRESH
   (Sly and the Family Stone)

2. HEY NOW HEY
   (Aretha Franklin)
3. TOUCH ME IN THE MORNING
   (Diana Ross)
4. TAYLORED IN SILK
   (Johnnie Taylor)
5. HEAD TO THE SKY
   (Earth, Wind and Fire)
6. FACTS OF LIFE
   (Bobby Womack)
7. BACK TO THE WORLD
   (Curtis Mayfield)
8. TOWER OF POWER
   (Tower of Power)
9. EXTENSION OF A MAN
   (Donny Hathaway)
10. INNERVISIONS
   (Stevie Wonder)

JAZZ ALBUMS

1. LOVE, DEVOTION, SURRENDER
   (Carlos Santana and Mahavishnu
   John McLaughlin)
2. DEODATO 2
   (Eumir Deodato)
3. SOUL BOX
   (Grover Washington Jr.)
4. BLACK BYRD
   (Donald Byrd)
5. YOU'VE GOT IT BAD GIRL
   (Quincy Jones)
6. SWEETNIGHTER
   (Weather Report)
7. EXCURSIONS
   (Eddie Harris)
8. LIVE AT MONTREUX
   (Les McCann)
9. FINGERS
   (Airto)
10. JAMAL '73
   (Ahmad Jamal)

COUNTRY SINGLES

1. EVERYBODY'S HAD THE BLUES
   (Merle Haggard)
2. MR. LOVEMAKER
   (Johnny Paycheck)
3. LOUISIANA WOMAN, MISSISSIPPI MAN
   (Loretta Lynn and Conway Twitty)
4. SLIPPIN' AWAY
   (Jean Shepard)
5. TRIP TO HEAVEN
   (Freddie Hart)
6. IF TEARDROPS WERE PENNIES
   (Porter Wagoner and Dolly Parton)
7. THE CORNER OF MY LIFE
   (Bill Anderson)
8. NOTHING EVER HURT ME
   (George Jones)
9. DRIFT AWAY
   (Narvel Felts)
10. YOU'VE NEVER BEEN THIS FAR BEFORE
   (Conway Twitty)

COUNTRY ALBUMS

1. SWEET COUNTRY
   (Charley Pride)
2. SATIN SHEETS
   (Jeanne Pruett)
3. LORD, MR. FORD
   (Jerry Reed)
4. WHAT'S YOUR MAMA'S NAME
   (Tanya Tucker)
5. BEHIND CLOSED DOORS
   (Charlie Rich)
6. GOODTIME CHARLIE
   (Charlie McCoy)
7. DON WILLIAMS, VOL. 1
   (Don Williams)
8. INTRODUCING JOHNNY RODRIGUEZ
   (Johnny Rodriguez)

9. SUPERPICKER
   (Roy Clark)
10. TIE A YELLOW RIBBON
   (Johnny Carver)

SEPTEMBER 1, 1973

POP SINGLES

1. LET'S GET IT ON
   (Marvin Gaye)
2. BROTHER LOUIE
   (Stories)
3. DELTA DAWN
   (Helen Reddy)
4. LIVE AND LET DIE
   (Paul McCartney and Wings)
5. I BELIEVE IN YOU
   (Johnnie Taylor)
6. SAY, HAS ANYBODY SEEN MY SWEET
   GYPSY ROSE
   (Tony Orlando and Dawn)
7. TOUCH ME IN THE MORNING
   (Diana Ross)
8. MORNING AFTER
   (Maureen McGovern)
9. GET DOWN
   (Gilbert O'Sullivan)
10. UNEASY RIDER
   (Charlie Daniels)

POP ALBUMS

1. BROTHERS AND SISTERS
   (Allman Brothers Band)
2. CHICAGO VI
   (Chicago)
3. DARK SIDE OF THE MOON
   (Pink Floyd)
4. TOUCH ME IN THE MORNING
   (Diana Ross)
5. FOREIGNER
   (Cat Stevens)
6. PASSION PLAY
   (Jethro Tull)
7. FRESH
   (Sly and the Family Stone)
8. NOW AND THEN
   (The Carpenters)
9. WE'RE AN AMERICAN BAND
   (Grand Funk Railroad)
10. INNERVISIONS
   (Stevie Wonder)

BLACK SINGLES

1. LET'S GET IT ON
   (Marvin Gaye)
2. THAT LADY
   (Isley Brothers)
3. ANGEL
   (Aretha Franklin)
4. I WAS CHECKIN' OUT, SHE WAS
   CHECKIN' IN
   (Don Covay)
5. HERE I AM
   (Al Green)
6. I BELIEVE IN YOU
   (Johnnie Taylor)
7. THERE IT IS
   (Tyrone Davis)
8. I'VE GOT SO MUCH TO GIVE
   (Barry White)
9. BABY I'VE BEEN MISSING YOU
   (The Independents)
10. GYPSY MAN
   (War)

BLACK ALBUMS

1. FRESH
   (Sly and the Family Stone)

2. TOUCH ME IN THE MORNING
   (Diana Ross)
3. TAYLORED IN SILK
   (Johnnie Taylor)
4. INNERVISIONS
   (Stevie Wonder)
5. HEY NOW HEY
   (Aretha Franklin)
6. EXTENSION OF A MAN
   (Donny Hathaway)
7. TOWER OF POWER
   (Tower of Power)
8. EDDIE KENDRICKS
   (Eddie Kendricks)
9. KILLING ME SOFTLY
   (Roberta Flack)
10. HEAD TO THE SKY
   (Earth, Wind and Fire)

JAZZ ALBUMS

1. LOVE, DEVOTION, SURRENDER
   (Carlos Santana and Mahavishnu
   John McLaughlin)
2. DEODATO 2
   (Eumir Deodato)
3. SOUL BOX
   (Grover Washington Jr.)
4. BLACK BYRD
   (Donald Byrd)
5. LIVE AT MONTREUX
   (Les McCann)
6. JAMAL '73
   (Ahmad Jamal)
7. EXCURSIONS
   (Eddie Harris)
8. SWEETNIGHTER
   (Weather Report)
9. FINGERS
   (Airto)
10. YOU'VE GOT IT BAD GIRL
   (Quincy Jones)

COUNTRY SINGLES

1. SLIPPIN' AWAY
   (Jean Shepard)
2. MR. LOVEMAKER
   (Johnny Paycheck)
3. THE CORNER OF MY LIFE
   (Bill Anderson)
4. IF TEARDROPS WERE PENNIES
   (Porter Wagoner and Dolly Parton)
5. EVERYBODY'S HAD THE BLUES
   (Merle Haggard)
6. YOU'VE NEVER BEEN THIS FAR BEFORE
   (Conway Twitty)
7. DRIFT AWAY
   (Narvel Felts)
8. LOUISIANA WOMAN, MISSISSIPPI MAN
   (Loretta Lynn and Conway Twitty)
9. NOTHING EVER HURT ME
   (George Jones)
10. TRIP TO HEAVEN
   (Freddie Hart)

COUNTRY ALBUMS

1. SATIN SHEETS
   (Jeanne Pruett)
2. LORD, MR. FORD
   (Jerry Reed)
3. SWEET COUNTRY
   (Charley Pride)
4. WHAT'S YOUR MAMA'S NAME
   (Tanya Tucker)
5. BEHIND CLOSED DOORS
   (Charlie Rich)
6. TIE A YELLOW RIBBON
   (Johnny Carver)
7. DON WILLIAMS, VOL. 1
   (Don Williams)
8. SUPERPICKER
   (Roy Clark)

9. GOODTIME CHARLIE
   (Charlie McCoy)
10. COME LIVE WITH ME
   (Roy Clark)

SEPTEMBER 8, 1973

POP SINGLES

1. LET'S GET IT ON
   (Marvin Gaye)
2. DELTA DAWN
   (Helen Reddy)
3. SAY, HAS ANYBODY SEEN MY SWEET
   GYPSY ROSE
   (Tony Orlando and Dawn)
4. BROTHER LOUIE
   (Stories)
5. I BELIEVE IN YOU
   (Johnnie Taylor)
6. LOVES ME LIKE A ROCK
   (Paul Simon)
7. WE'RE AN AMERICAN BAND
   (Grand Funk Railroad)
8. LIVE AND LET DIE
   (Paul McCartney and Wings)
9. MORNING AFTER
   (Maureen McGovern)
10. HERE I AM
   (Al Green)

POP ALBUMS

1. BROTHERS AND SISTERS
   (Allman Brothers Band)
2. CHICAGO VI
   (Chicago)
3. TOUCH ME IN THE MORNING
   (Diana Ross)
4. DARK SIDE OF THE MOON
   (Pink Floyd)
5. WE'RE AN AMERICAN BAND
   (Grand Funk Railroad)
6. FOREIGNER
   (Cat Stevens)
7. INNERVISIONS
   (Stevie Wonder)
8. PASSION PLAY
   (Jethro Tull)
9. FRESH
   (Sly and the Family Stone)
10. KILLING ME SOFTLY
   (Roberta Flack)

BLACK SINGLES

1. LET'S GET IT ON
   (Marvin Gaye)
2. THAT LADY
   (Isley Brothers)
3. I WAS CHECKIN' OUT, SHE WAS
   CHECKIN' IN
   (Don Covay)
4. ANGEL
   (Aretha Franklin)
5. HIGHER GROUND
   (Stevie Wonder)
6. HERE I AM
   (Al Green)
7. I'VE GOT SO MUCH TO GIVE
   (Barry White)
8. THERE IT IS
   (Tyrone Davis)
9. THEME FROM CLEOPATRA JONES
   (Joe Simon)
10. STONED OUT OF MY MIND
   (The Chi-Lites)

BLACK ALBUMS

1. INNERVISIONS
   (Stevie Wonder)
2. TOUCH ME IN THE MORNING
   (Diana Ross)
3. FRESH
   (Sly and the Family Stone)
4. EDDIE KENDRICKS
   (Eddie Kendricks)
5. KILLING ME SOFTLY
   (Roberta Flack)
6. TAYLORED IN SILK
   (Johnnie Taylor)
7. HEY NOW HEY
   (Aretha Franklin)
8. EXTENSION OF A MAN
   (Donny Hathaway)
9. TOWER OF POWER
   (Tower of Power)
10. HEAD TO THE SKY
   (Earth, Wind and Fire)

JAZZ ALBUMS

1. DEODATO 2
   (Eumir Deodato)
2. KILLING ME SOFTLY
   (Roberta Flack)
3. LOVE, DEVOTION, SURRENDER
   *(Carlos Santana and Mahavishnu
   John McLaughlin)*
4. BLACK BYRD
   (Donald Byrd)
5. EXCURSIONS
   (Eddie Harris)
6. JAMAL '73
   (Ahmad Jamal)
7. SWEETNIGHTER
   (Weather Report)
8. LIVE AT MONTREUX
   (Les McCann)
9. FIRST LIGHT
   (Freddie Hubbard)
10. YOU'VE GOT IT BAD GIRL
   (Quincy Jones)

COUNTRY SINGLES

1. THE CORNER OF MY LIFE
   (Bill Anderson)
2. YOU'VE NEVER BEEN THIS FAR BEFORE
   (Conway Twitty)
3. IF TEARDROPS WERE PENNIES
   (Porter Wagoner and Dolly Parton)
4. SLIPPIN' AWAY
   (Jean Shepard)
5. DRIFT AWAY
   (Narvel Felts)
6. EVERYBODY'S HAD THE BLUES
   (Merle Haggard)
7. BLOOD RED AND GOIN' DOWN
   (Tanya Tucker)
8. MR. LOVEMAKER
   (Johnny Paycheck)
9. CAN I SLEEP IN YOUR ARMS
   (Jeannie Seely)
10. I HATE YOU/LET'S FALL APART
   (Ronnie Milsap)

COUNTRY ALBUMS

1. SATIN SHEETS
   (Jeanne Pruett)
2. LORD, MR. FORD
   (Jerry Reed)
3. BEHIND CLOSED DOORS
   (Charlie Rich)
4. SWEET COUNTRY
   (Charley Pride)
5. TIE A YELLOW RIBBON
   (Johnny Carver)

6. WHAT'S YOUR MAMA'S NAME
   (Tanya Tucker)
7. COME LIVE WITH ME
   (Roy Clark)
8. DON WILLIAMS, VOL. 1
   (Don Williams)
9. CLOWER POWER
   (Jerry Clower)
10. TOP OF THE WORLD
   (Lynn Anderson)

SEPTEMBER 15, 1973

POP SINGLES

1. DELTA DAWN
   (Helen Reddy)
2. LET'S GET IT ON
   (Marvin Gaye)
3. SAY, HAS ANYBODY SEEN MY SWEET
   GYPSY ROSE
   (Tony Orlando and Dawn)
4. WE'RE AN AMERICAN BAND
   (Grand Funk Railroad)
5. LOVES ME LIKE A ROCK
   (Paul Simon)
6. BROTHER LOUIE
   (Stories)
7. HALF BREED
   (Cher)
8. SATURDAY NIGHT'S ALRIGHT FOR
   FIGHTING
   (Elton John)
9. HIGHER GROUND
   (Stevie Wonder)
10. HERE I AM
   (Al Green)

POP ALBUMS

1. BROTHERS AND SISTERS
   (Allman Brothers Band)
2. WE'RE AN AMERICAN BAND
   (Grand Funk Railroad)
3. TOUCH ME IN THE MORNING
   (Diana Ross)
4. KILLING ME SOFTLY
   (Roberta Flack)
5. INNERVISIONS
   (Stevie Wonder)
6. DARK SIDE OF THE MOON
   (Pink Floyd)
7. LONG HARD CLIMB
   (Helen Reddy)
8. CHICAGO VI
   (Chicago)
9. FOREIGNER
   (Cat Stevens)
10. PASSION PLAY
   (Jethreo Tull)

BLACK SINGLES

1. LET'S GET IT ON
   (Marvin Gaye)
2. THAT LADY
   (Isley Brothers)
3. I WAS CHECKIN' OUT SHE WAS
   CHECKIN' IN
   (Don Covay)
4. HIGHER GROUND
   (Stevie Wonder)
5. ANGEL
   (Aretha Franklin)
6. THEME FROM CLEOPATRA JONES
   (Joe Simon)
7. I'VE GOT SO MUCH TO GIVE
   (Barry White)
8. STONED OUT OF MY MIND
   (The Chi-Lites)

9. HURTS SO GOOD
   (Millie Jackson)
10. KEEP ON TRUCKIN'
   (Eddie Kendricks)

BLACK ALBUMS

1. KILLING ME SOFTLY
   (Roberta Flack)
2. INNERVISIONS
   (Stevie Wonder)
3. TOUCH ME IN THE MORNING
   (Diana Ross)
4. EDDIE KENDRICKS
   (Eddie Kendricks)
5. FRESH
   (Sly and the Family Stone)
6. TAYLORED IN SILK
   (Johnnie Taylor)
7. EXTENSION OF A MAN
   (Donny Hathaway)
8. HEY NOW HEY
   (Aretha Franklin)
9. TOWER OF POWER
   (Tower of Power)
10. DOIN' IT TO DEATH
   (Fred Wesley and the J.B.'s)

JAZZ ALBUMS

1. KILLING ME SOFTLY
   (Roberta Flack)
2. DEODATO 2
   (Eumir Deodato)
3. LOVE, DEVOTION, SURRENDER
   (Carlos Santana and Mahavishnu
   John McLaughlin)
4. EXCURSION
   (Eddie Harris)
5. BLACK BYRD
   (Donald Byrd)
6. SWEETNIGHTER
   (Weather Report)
7. FIRST LIGHT
   (Freddie Hubbard)
8. JAMAL '73
   (Ahmad Jamal)
9. YOU'VE GOT IT BAD GIRL
   (Quincy Jones)
10. SOUL BOX
   (Grover Washington Jr.)

COUNTRY SINGLES

1. YOU'VE NEVER BEEN THIS FAR BEFORE
   (Conway Twitty)
2. THE CORNER OF MY LIFE
   (Bill Anderson)
3. IF TEARDROPS WERE PENNIES
   (Porter Wagoner and Dolly Parton)
4. DRIFT AWAY
   (Narvel Felts)
5. BLOOD RED AND GOIN' DOWN
   (Tanya Tucker)
6. SLIPPIN' AWAY
   (Jean Shepard)
7. CAN I SLEEP IN YOUR ARMS
   (Jeannie Seely)
8. I HATE YOU/LET'S FALL APART
   (Ronnie Milsap)
9. KID STUFF
   (Barbara Fairchild)
10. YOU'RE THE BEST THING
   (Ray Price)

COUNTRY ALBUMS

1. SATIN SHEETS
   (Jeanne Pruett)
2. LORD, MR. FORD
   (Jerry Reed)

3. BEHIND CLOSED DOORS
   (Charlie Rich)
4. LOUISIANA WOMAN, MISSISSIPPI MAN
   (Loretta Lynn and Conway Twitty)
5. I LOVE DIXIE BLUES
   (Merle Haggard)
6. TOP OF THE WORLD
   (Lynn Anderson)
7. COME LIVE WITH ME
   (Roy Clark)
8. TRIP TO HEAVEN
   (Freddie Hart)
9. CLOWER POWER
   (Jerry Clower)
10. TIE A YELLOW RIBBON
   (Johnny Carver)

SEPTEMBER 22, 1973

POP SINGLES

1. DELTA DAWN
   (Helen Reddy)
2. WE'RE AN AMERICAN BAND
   (Grand Funk Railroad)
3. LET'S GET IT ON
   (Marvin Gaye)
4. LOVES ME LIKE A ROCK
   (Paul Simon)
5. HALF BREED
   (Cher)
6. SAY HAS ANYBODY SEEN MY SWEET
   GYPSY ROSE
   (Tony Orlando and Dawn)
7. HIGHER GROUND
   (Stevie Wonder)
8. SATURDAY NIGHT'S ALRIGHT FOR
   FIGHTING
   (Elton John)
9. MY MARIA
   (B.W. Stevenson)
10. THAT LADY
   (Isley Brothers)

POP ALBUMS

1. BROTHERS AND SISTERS
   (Allman Brothers Band)
2. WE'RE AN AMERICAN BAND
   (Grand Funk Railroad)
3. KILLING ME SOFTLY
   (Roberta Flack)
4. INNERVISIONS
   (Stevie Wonder)
5. TOUCH ME IN THE MORNING
   (Diana Ross)
6. LONG HARD CLIMB
   (Helen Reddy)
7. DARK SIDE OF THE MOON
   (Pink Floyd)
8. CHICAGO VI
   (Chicago)
9. FOREIGNER
   (Cat Stevens)
10. LET'S GET IT ON
   (Marvin Gaye)

BLACK SINGLES

1. LET'S GET IT ON
   (Marvin Gaye)
2. KEEP ON TRUCKIN'
   (Eddie Kendricks)
3. THEME FROM CLEOPATRA JONES
   (Joe Simon)
4. HIGHER GROUND
   (Stevie Wonder)
5. STONED OUT OF MY MIND
   (The Chi-Lites)
6. HURTS SO GOOD
   (Millie Jackson)

7. I'VE GOT SO MUCH TO GIVE
   (Barry White)
8. THAT LADY
   (Isley Brothers)
9. FUNKY STUFF
   (Kool and the Gang)
10. ECSTASY
   (Ohio Players)

BLACK ALBUMS

1. KILLING ME SOFTLY
   (Roberta Flack)
2. INNERVISIONS
   (Stevie Wonder)
3. EDDIE KENDRICKS
   (Eddie Kendricks)
4. TOUCH ME IN THE MORNING
   (Diana Ross)
5. FRESH
   (Sly and the Family Stone)
6. LET'S GET IT ON
   (Marvin Gaye)
7. TAYLORED IN SILK
   (Johnnie Taylor)
8. DELIVER THE WORD
   (War)
9. DOIN' IT TO DEATH
   (Fred Wesley and the J.B.'s)
10. EXTENSION OF A MAN
   (Donny Hathaway)

JAZZ ALBUMS

1. KILLING ME SOFTLY
   (Roberta Flack)
2. DEODATO 2
   (Eumir Deodato)
3. SWEETNIGHTER
   (Weather Report)
4. LOVE, DEVOTION, SURRENDER
   (Carlos Santana and Mahavishnu
   John McLaughlin)
5. FIRST LIGHT
   (Freddie Hubbard)
6. BLACK BYRD
   (Donald Byrd)
7. EXCURSIONS
   (Eddie Harris)
8. JAMAL '73
   (Ahmad Jamal)
9. SOUL BOX
   (Grover Washington Jr.)
10. SUNFLOWER
   (Milt Jackson)

COUNTRY SINGLES

1. BLOOD RED AND GOIN' DOWN
   (Tanya Tucker)
2. YOU'VE NEVER BEEN THIS FAR BEFORE
   (Conway Twitty)
3. THE CORNER OF MY LIFE
   (Bill Anderson)
4. YOU'RE THE BEST THING
   (Ray Price)
5. DRIFT AWAY
   (Narvel Felts)
6. CAN I SLEEP IN YOUR ARMS
   (Jeannie Seely)
7. I HATE YOU/LET'S FALL APART
   (Merle Haggard)
8. KID STUFF
   (Barbara Fairchild)
9. SLIPPIN' AWAY
   (Jean Shepard)
10. RED NECKS, WHITE SOCKS AND BLUE
   RIBBON BEER
   (Johnny Russell)

COUNTRY ALBUMS

1. LOUISIANA WOMAN, MISSISSIPPI MAN
   (Loretta Lynn and Conway Twitty)

2. SATIN SHEETS
   (Jeanne Pruett)
3. I LOVE DIXIE BLUES
   (Merle Haggard)
4. BEHIND CLOSED DOORS
   (Charlie Rich)
5. TOP OF THE WORLD
   (Lynn Anderson)
6. TRIP TO HEAVEN
   (Freddie Hart)
7. JESUS WAS A CAPRICORN
   (Kris Kristofferson)
8. ELVIS
   (Elvis Presley)
9. LORD, MR. FORD
   (Jerry Reed)
10. COME LIVE WITH ME
    (Roy Clark)

SEPTEMBER 29, 1973

POP SINGLES

1. WE'RE AN AMERICAN BAND
   (Grand Funk Railroad)
2. DELTA DAWN
   (Helen Reddy)
3. LOVES ME LIKE A ROCK
   (Paul Simon)
4. HALF BREED
   (Cher)
5. HIGHER GROUND
   (Stevie Wonder)
6. LET'S GET IT ON
   (Marvin Gaye)
7. THAT LADY
   (Isley Brothers)
8. MY MARIA
   (B.W. Stevenson)
9. SAY, HAS ANYBODY SEEN MY SWEET GYPSY ROSE
   (Tony Orlando and Dawn)
10. RAMBLIN' MAN
    (Allman Brothers Band)

POP ALBUMS

1. WE'RE AN AMERICAN BAND
   (Grand Funk Railroad)
2. KILLING ME SOFTLY
   (Roberta Flack)
3. BROTHERS AND SISTERS
   (Allman Brothers Band)
4. INNERVISIONS
   (Stevie Wonder)
5. LET'S GET IT ON
   (Marvin Gaye)
6. LONG HARD CLIMB
   (Helen Reddy)
7. LOS COCHINOS
   (Cheech and Chong)
8. TOUCH ME IN THE MORNING
   (Diana Ross)
9. DARK SIDE OF THE MOON
   (Pink Floyd)
10. DELIVER THE WORD
    (War)

BLACK SINGLES

1. LET'S GET IT ON
   (Marvin Gaye)
2. KEEP ON TRUCKIN'
   (Eddie Kendricks)
3. THEME FROM CLEOPATRA JONES
   (Joe Simon)
4. STONED OUT OF MY MIND
   (The Chi-Lites)
5. HURTS SO GOOD
   (Millie Jackson)

6. HIGHER GROUND
   (Stevie Wonder)
7. ECSTASY
   (Ohio Players)
8. FUNKY STUFF
   (Kool and the Gang)
9. THAT LADY
   (Isley Brothers)
10. MIDNIGHT TRAIN TO GEORGIA
    (Gladys Knight and the Pips)

BLACK ALBUMS

1. KILLING ME SOFTLY
   (Roberta Flack)
2. INNERVISIONS
   (Stevie Wonder)
3. EDDIE KENDRICKS
   (Eddie Kendricks)
4. LET'S GET IT ON
   (Marvin Gaye)
5. DELIVER THE WORD
   (War)
6. FRESH
   (Sly and the Family Stone)
7. TOUCH ME IN THE MORNING
   (Diana Ross)
8. TAYLORED IN SILK
   (Johnnie Taylor)
9. DOIN' IT TO DEATH
   (Fred Wesley and the J.B.'s)
10. POINTER SISTERS
    (The Pointer Sisters)

JAZZ ALBUMS

1. KILLING ME SOFTLY
   (Roberta Flack)
2. DEODATO 2
   (Eumir Deodato)
3. SWEETNIGHTER
   (Weather Report)
4. BLACK BYRD
   (Donald Byrd)
5. SOUL BOX
   (Grover Washington Jr.)
6. LOVE, DEVOTION, SURRENDER
   (Carlos Santana and Mahavishnu John McLaughlin)
7. FIRST LIGHT
   (Freddie Hubbard)
8. JAMAL '73
   (Ahmad Jamal)
9. EXCURSIONS
   (Eddie Harris)
10. SONG OF THE NEW WORLD
    (McCoy Tyner)

COUNTRY SINGLES

1. YOU'RE THE BEST THING
   (Ray Price)
2. YOU'VE NEVER BEEN THIS FAR BEFORE
   (Conway Twitty)
3. BLOOD RED AND GOIN' DOWN
   (Tanya Tucker)
4. CAN I SLEEP IN YOUR ARMS
   (Jeannie Seely)
5. RED NECKS, WHITE SOCKS AND BLUE RIBBON BEER
   (Johnny Russell)
6. KID STUFF
   (Barbara Fairchild)
7. THE CORNER OF MY LIFE
   (Bill Anderson)
8. RIDIN' MY THUMB TO MEXICO
   (Johnny Rodriguez)
9. JUST WHAT I HAD IN MIND
   (Faron Young)
10. YOU REALLY HAVEN'T CHANGED
    (Johnny Carver)

COUNTRY ALBUMS

1. LOUISIANA WOMAN, MISSISSIPPI MAN
   (Loretta Lynn and Conway Twitty)
2. I LOVE DIXIE BLUES
   (Merle Haggard)
3. SATIN SHEETS
   (Jeanne Pruett)
4. BEHIND CLOSED DOORS
   (Charlie Rich)
5. YOU'VE NEVER BEEN THIS FAR BEFORE
   (Conway Twitty)
6. TRIP TO HEAVEN
   (Freddie Hart)
7. JESUS WAS A CAPRICORN
   (Kris Kristofferson)
8. ELVIS
   (Elvis Presley)
9. TOP OF THE WORLD
   (Lynn Anderson)
10. LOVE AND MUSIC
    (Porter Wagoner and Dolly Parton)

OCTOBER 6, 1973

POP SINGLES

1. HALF BREED
   (Cher)
2. WE'RE AN AMERICAN BAND
   (Grand Funk Railroad)
3. LOVES ME LIKE A ROCK
   (Paul Simon)
4. HIGHER GROUND
   (Stevie Wonder)
5. DELTA DAWN
   (Helen Reddy)
6. ANGIE
   (The Rolling Stones)
7. THAT LADY
   (Isley Brothers)
8. RAMBLIN' MAN
   (Allman Brothers Band)
9. MY MARIA
   (B.W. Stevenson)
10. FREE RIDE
    (Edgar Winter)

POP ALBUMS

1. LET'S GET IT ON
   (Marvin Gaye)
2. KILLING ME SOFTLY
   (Roberta Flack)
3. WE'RE AN AMERICAN BAND
   (Grand Funk Railroad)
4. INNERVISIONS
   (Stevie Wonder)
5. LOS COCHINOS
   (Cheech and Chong)
6. BROTHERS AND SISTERS
   (Allman Brothers Band)
7. LONG HARD CLIMB
   (Helen Reddy)
8. GOAT'S HEAD SOUP
   (The Rolling Stones)
9. DELIVER THE WORD
   (War)
10. DARK SIDE OF THE MOON
    (Pink Floyd)

BLACK SINGLES

1. KEEP ON TRUCKIN'
   (Eddie Kendricks)
2. LET'S GET IT ON
   (Marvin Gaye)
3. HURTS SO GOOD
   (Millie Jackson)

4. STONED OUT OF MY MIND
   (The Chi-Lites)
5. THEME FROM CLEOPATRA JONES
   (Joe Simon)
6. MIDNIGHT TRAIN TO GEORGIA
   (Gladys Knight and the Pips)
7. ECSTASY
   (Ohio Players)
8. FUNKY STUFF
   (Kool and the Gang)
9. HIGHER GROUND
   (Stevie Wonder)
10. YES WE CAN CAN
    (The Pointer Sisters)

BLACK ALBUMS

1. LET'S GET IT ON
   (Marvin Gaye)
2. KILLING ME SOFTLY
   (Roberta Flack)
3. INNERVISIONS
   (Stevie Wonder)
4. EDDIE KENDRICKS
   (Eddie Kendricks)
5. DELIVER THE WORD
   (War)
6. 3 PLUS 3
   (Isley Brothers)
7. FRESH
   (Sly and the Family Stone)
8. POINTER SISTERS
   (The Pointer Sisters)
9. TOUCH ME IN THE MORNING
   (Diana Ross)
10. CLEOPATRA JONES
    (Original Soundtrack)

JAZZ ALBUMS

1. KILLING ME SOFTLY
   (Roberta Flack)
2. BLACK BYRD
   (Donald Byrd)
3. SOUL BOX
   (Grover Washington Jr.)
4. SWEETNIGHTER
   (Weather Report)
5. DEODATO 2
   (Eumir Deodato)
6. SONG OF THE NEW WORLD
   (McCoy Tyner)
7. FIRST LIGHT
   (Freddie Hubbard)
8. JAMAL '73
   (Ahmad Jamal)
9. SASSY SOUL STRUT
   (Lou Donaldson)
10. YOU'VE GOT IT BAD GIRL
    (Quincy Jones)

COUNTRY SINGLES

1. RED NECKS, WHITE SOCKS AND BLUE
   RIBBON BEER
   (Johnny Russell)
2. KID STUFF
   (Barbara Fairchild)
3. YOU'RE THE BEST THING
   (Ray Price)
4. CAN I SLEEP IN YOUR ARMS
   (Jeannie Seely)
5. RIDIN' MY THUMB TO MEXICO
   (Johnny Rodriguez)
6. BLOOD RED AND GOIN' DOWN
   (Tanya Tucker)
7. JUST WHAT I HAD IN MIND
   (Faron Young)
8. YOU REALLY HAVEN'T CHANGED
   (Johnny Carver)
9. YOU'VE NEVER BEEN THIS FAR BEFORE
   (Conway Twitty)
10. I NEED SOMEBODY BAD
    (Jack Greene)

COUNTRY ALBUMS

1. I LOVE DIXIE BLUES
   (Merle Haggard)
2. YOU'VE NEVER BEEN THIS FAR BEFORE
   (Conway Twitty)
3. LOUISIANA WOMAN, MISSISSIPPI MAN
   (Loretta Lynn and Conway Twitty)
4. SATIN SHEETS
   (Jeanne Pruett)
5. BEHIND CLOSED DOORS
   (Charlie Rich)
6. LOVE IS THE FOUNDATION
   (Loretta Lynn)
7. TRIP TO HEAVEN
   (Freddie Hart)
8. JESUS WAS A CAPRICORN
   (Kris Kristofferson)
9. ELVIS
   (Elvis Presley)
10. LOVE AND MUSIC
    (Porter Wagoner and Dolly Parton)

OCTOBER 13, 1973

POP SINGLES

1. HIGHER GROUND
   (Stevie Wonder)
2. HALF BREED
   (Cher)
3. ANGIE
   (The Rolling Stones)
4. LOVES ME LIKE A ROCK
   (Paul Simon)
5. RAMBLIN' MAN
   (Allman Brothers Band)
6. WE'RE AN AMERICAN BAND
   (Grand Funk Railroad)
7. THAT LADY
   (Isley Brothers)
8. KEEP ON TRUCKIN'
   (Eddie Kendricks)
9. MIDNIGHT TRAIN TO GEORGIA
   (Gladys Knight and the Pips)
10. FREE RIDE
    (Edgar Winter)

POP ALBUMS

1. LET'S GET IT ON
   (Marvin Gaye)
2. GOAT'S HEAD SOUP
   (The Rolling Stones)
3. LOS COCHINOS
   (Cheech and Chong)
4. INNERVISIONS
   (Stevie Wonder)
5. KILLING ME SOFTLY
   (Roberta Flack)
6. BROTHERS AND SISTERS
   (Allman Brothers Band)
7. WE'RE AN AMERICAN BAND
   (Grand Funk Railroad)
8. DELIVER THE WORD
   (War)
9. LONG HARD CLIMB
   (Helen Reddy)
10. DARK SIDE OF THE MOON
    (Pink Floyd)

BLACK SINGLES

1. MIDNIGHT TRAIN TO GEORGIA
   (Gladys Knight and the Pips)
2. KEEP ON TRUCKIN'
   (Eddie Kendricks)
3. HURTS SO GOOD
   (Millie Jackson)

4. LET'S GET IT ON
   (Marvin Gaye)
5. THEME FROM CLEOPATRA JONES
   (Joe Simon)
6. STONED OUT OF MY MIND
   (The Chi-Lites)
7. ECSTASY
   (Ohio Players)
8. FUNKY STUFF
   (Kool and the Gang)
9. YES WE CAN CAN
   (The Pointer Sisters)
10. HIGHER GROUND
    (Stevie Wonder)

BLACK ALBUMS

1. LET'S GET IT ON
   (Marvin Gaye)
2. INNERVISIONS
   (Stevie Wonder)
3. EDDIE KENDRICKS
   (Eddie Kendricks)
4. KILLING ME SOFTLY
   (Roberta Flack)
5. 3 PLUS 3
   (Isley Brothers)
6. DELIVER THE WORD
   (War)
7. POINTER SISTERS
   (The Pointer Sisters)
8. FRESH
   (Sly and the Family Stone)
9. TOUCH ME IN THE MORNING
   (Diana Ross)
10. CLEOPATRA JONES
    (Original Soundtrack)

JAZZ ALBUMS

1. KILLING ME SOFTLY
   (Roberta Flack)
2. SOUL BOX
   (Grover Washington Jr.)
3. BLACK BYRD
   (Donald Byrd)
4. DEODATO 2
   (Eumir Deodato)
5. SONG OF THE NEW WORLD
   (McCoy Tyner)
6. SWEETNIGHTER
   (Weather Report)
7. SASSY SOUL STRUT
   (Lou Donaldson)
8. JAMAL '73
   (Ahmad Jamal)
9. DON'T MESS WITH MR. T
   (Stanley Turrentine)
10. YOU'VE GOT IT BAD GIRL
    (Quincy Jones)

COUNTRY SINGLES

1. KID STUFF
   (Barbara Fairchild)
2. RED NECKS, WHITE SOCKS AND BLUE
   RIBBON BEER
   (Johnny Russell)
3. RIDIN' MY THUMB TO MEXICO
   (Johnny Rodriguez)
4. YOU'RE THE BEST THING
   (Ray Pride)
5. JUST WHAT I HAD IN MIND
   (Faron Young)
6. THE MIDNIGHT OIL
   (Barbara Mandrell)
7. DON'T GIVE UP ON ME
   (Jerry Wallace)
8. YOU REALLY HAVEN'T CHANGED
   (Johnny Carver)
9. I NEED SOMEBODY BAD
   (Jack Greene)
10. SUNDAY SUNRISE
    (Brenda Lee)

COUNTRY ALBUMS

1. I LOVE DIXIE BLUES
   (Merle Haggard)
2. YOU'VE NEVER BEEN THIS FAR BEFORE
   (Conway Twitty)
3. LOVE IS THE FOUNDATION
   (Loretta Lynn)
4. LOUISIANA WOMAN, MISSISSIPPI MAN
   (Loretta Lynn and Conway Twitty)
5. BEHIND CLOSED DOORS
   (Charlie Rich)
6. SATIN SHEETS
   (Jeanne Pruett)
7. TRIP TO HEAVEN
   (Freddie Hart)
8. JESUS WAS A CAPRICORN
   (Kris Kristofferson)
9. THE BRENDA LEE STORY
   (Brenda Lee)
10. ELVIS
    (Elvis Presley)

OCTOBER 20, 1973

POP SINGLES

1. ANGIE
   (The Rolling Stones)
2. HALF BREED
   (Cher)
3. RAMBLIN' MAN
   (Allman Brothers Band)
4. HIGHER GROUND
   (Stevie Wonder)
5. KEEP ON TRUCKIN'
   (Eddie Kendricks)
6. THAT LADY
   (Isley Brothers)
7. MIDNIGHT TRAIN TO GEORGIA
   (Gladys Knight and the Pips)
8. HEARTBEAT-IT'S A LOVEBEAT
   (DeFranco Family)
9. FREE RIDE
   (Edgar Winter)
10. CHINA GROVE
    (The Doobie Brothers)

POP ALBUMS

1. GOAT'S HEAD SOUP
   (The Rolling Stones)
2. LET'S GET IT ON
   (Marvin Gaye)
3. LOS COCHINOS
   (Cheech and Chong)
4. INNERVISIONS
   (Stevie Wonder)
5. BROTHERS AND SISTERS
   (Allman Brothers Band)
6. ANGEL CLARE
   (Art Garfunkel)
7. WE'RE AN AMERICAN BAND
   (Grand Funk Railroad)
8. LONG HARD CLIMB
   (Helen Reddy)
9. KILLING ME SOFTLY
   (Roberta Flack)
10. DELIVER THE WORD
    (War)

BLACK SINGLES

1. MIDNIGHT TRAIN TO GEORGIA
   (Gladys Knight and the Pips)
2. KEEP ON TRUCKIN'
   (Eddie Kendricks)
3. HURTS SO GOOD
   (Millie Jackson)

4. LET'S GET IT ON
   (Marvin Gaye)
5. THEME FROM CLEOPATRA JONES
   (Joe Simon)
6. ECSTASY
   (Ohio Players)
7. THE LOVE I LOST
   (Harold Melvin and the Blue Notes)
8. CHECK IT OUT
   (Tavares)
9. A SPECIAL PART OF ME
   (Marvin Gaye and Diana Ross)
10. FUNKY STUFF
    (Kool and the Gang)

BLACK ALBUMS

1. LET'S GET IT ON
   (Marvin Gaye)
2. INNERVISIONS
   (Stevie Wonder)
3. 3 PLUS 3
   (Isley Brothers)
4. EDDIE KENDRICKS
   (Eddie Kendricks)
5. DELIVER THE WORD
   (War)
6. KILLING ME SOFTLY
   (Roberta Flack)
7. POINTER SISTERS
   (The Pointer Sisters)
8. FRESH
   (Sly and the Family Stone)
9. TOUCH ME IN THE MORNING
   (Diana Ross)
10. CLEOPATRA JONES
    (Original Soundtrack)

JAZZ ALBUMS

1. KILLING ME SOFTLY
   (Roberta Flack)
2. SOUL BOX
   (Grover Washington Jr.)
3. DEODATO 2
   (Eumir Deodato)
4. SWEETNIGHTER
   (Weather Report)
5. SONG OF THE NEW WORLD
   (McCoy Tyner)
6. BLACK BYRD
   (Donald Byrd)
7. SASSY SOUL STRUT
   (Lou Donaldson)
8. DON'T MESS WITH MR. T
   (Stanley Turrentine)
9. JAMAL '73
   (Ahmad Jamal)
10. TURTLE BAY
    (Herbie Hancock)

COUNTRY SINGLES

1. RIDIN' MY THUMB TO MEXICO
   (Johnny Rodriguez)
2. KID STUFF
   (Barbara Fairchild)
3. THE MIDNIGHT OIL
   (Barbara Mandrell)
4. RED NECKS, WHITE SOCKS AND BLUE
   RIBBON BEER
   (Johnny Russell)
5. JUST WHAT I HAD IN MIND
   (Faron Young)
6. DON'T GIVE UP ON ME
   (Jerry Wallace)
7. SUNDAY SUNRISE
   (Brenda Lee)
8. WE'RE GONNA HOLD ON
   (George Jones and Tammy Wynette)
9. I NEED SOMEONE BAD
   (Jack Greene)
10. SAWMILL
    (Mel Tillis)

COUNTRY ALBUMS

1. YOU'VE NEVER BEEN THIS FAR BEFORE
   (Conway Twitty)
2. LOVE IS THE FOUNDATION
   (Loretta Lynn)
3. I LOVE DIXIE BLUES
   (Merle Haggard)
4. LOUISIANA WOMAN, MISSISSIPPI MAN
   (Loretta Lynn and Conway Twitty)
5. SATIN SHEETS
   (Jeanne Pruett)
6. JESUS WAS A CAPRICORN
   (Kris Kristofferson)
7. BEHIND CLOSED DOORS
   (Charlie Rich)
8. THE BRENDA LEE STORY
   (Brenda Lee)
9. TRIP TO HEAVEN
   (Freddie Hart)
10. ELVIS
    (Elvis Presley)

OCTOBER 27, 1973

POP SINGLES

1. ANGIE
   (The Rolling Stones)
2. RAMBLIN' MAN
   (Allman Brothers Band)
3. KEEP ON TRUCKIN'
   (Eddie Kendricks)
4. HALF BREED
   (Cher)
5. MIDNIGHT TRAIN TO GEORGIA
   (Gladys Knight and the Pips)
6. HEARTBEAT-IT'S A LOVEBEAT
   (DeFranco Family)
7. PAPER ROSES
   (Marie Osmond)
8. THAT LADY
   (Isley Brothers)
9. HIGHER GROUND
   (Stevie Wonder)
10. ALL I KNOW
    (Art Garfunkel)

POP ALBUMS

1. GOAT'S HEAD SOUP
   (The Rolling Stones)
2. LET'S GET IT ON
   (Marvin Gaye)
3. LOS COCHINOS
   (Cheech and Chong)
4. ANGEL CLARE
   (Art Garfunkel)
5. INNERVISIONS
   (Stevie Wonder)
6. BROTHERS AND SISTERS
   (Allman Brothers Band)
7. WE'RE AN AMERICAN BAND
   (Grand Funk Railroad)
8. LONG HARD CLIMB
   (Helen Reddy)
9. 3 PLUS 3
   (Isley Brothers)
10. GOODBYE YELLOW BRICK ROAD
    (Elton John)

BLACK SINGLES

1. MIDNIGHT TRAIN TO GEORGIA
   (Gladys Knight and the Pips)
2. KEEP ON TRUCKIN'
   (Eddie Kendricks)
3. HURTS SO GOOD
   (Millie Jackson)

4. CHECK IT OUT
   (Tavares)
5. THE LOVE I LOST
   (Harold Melvin and the Blue Notes)
6. A SPECIAL PART OF ME
   (Marvin Gaye and Diana Ross)
7. SPACE RACE
   (Billy Preston)
8. LET'S GET IT ON
   (Marvin Gaye)
9. THEME FROM CLEOPATRA JONES
   (Joe Simon)
10. CHEAPER TO KEEP HER
   (Johnnie Taylor)

BLACK ALBUMS

1. LET'S GET IT ON
   (Marvin Gaye)
2. INNERVISIONS
   (Stevie Wonder)
3. 3 PLUS 3
   (Isley Brothers)
4. EDDIE KENDRICKS
   (Eddie Kendricks)
5. DELIVER THE WORD
   (War)
6. KILLING ME SOFTLY
   (Roberta Flack)
7. POINTER SISTERS
   (The Pointer Sisters)
8. FRESH
   (Sly and the Family Stone)
9. ANTHOLOGY
   (Temptations)
10. TOUCH ME IN THE MORNING
   (Diana Ross)

JAZZ ALBUMS

1. KILLING ME SOFTLY
   (Roberta Flack)
2. SOUL BOX
   (Grover Washington Jr.)
3. SWEETNIGHTER
   (Weather Report)
4. SONG OF THE WORLD
   (McCoy Tyner)
5. SASSY SOUL STRUT
   (Lou Donaldson)
6. DON'T MESS WITH MR. T
   (Stanley Turrentine)
7. DEODATO 2
   (Eumir Deodato)
8. TURTLE BAY
   (Herbie Mann)
9. INSIDE STRAIGHT
   (Cannonball Adderley)
10. BODY TALK
   (George Benson)

COUNTRY SINGLES

1. THE MIDNIGHT OIL
   (Barbara Mandrell)
2. RIDIN' MY THUMB TO MEXICO
   (Johnny Rodriguez)
3. DON'T GIVE UP ON ME
   (Jerry Wallace)
4. WE'RE GONNA HOLD ON
   (George Jones and Tammy Wynette)
5. SAWMILL
   (Mel Tillis)
6. SUNDAY SUNRISE
   (Brenda Lee)
7. PAPER ROSES
   (Marie Osmond)
8. RED NECKS, WHITE SOCKS AND BLUE
   RIBBON BEER
   (Johnny Russell)
9. KID STUFF
   (Barbara Fairchild)
10. TOO FAR GONE
   (Joe Stampley)

COUNTRY ALBUMS

1. YOU'VE NEVER BEEN THIS FAR BEFORE
   (Conway Twitty)
2. LOVE IS THE FOUNDATION
   (Loretta Lynn)
3. I LOVE DIXIE BLUES
   (Merle Haggard)
4. JESUS WAS A CAPRICORN
   (Kris Kristofferson)
5. LOUISIANA WOMAN, MISSISSIPPI MAN
   (Conway Twitty and Loretta Lynn)
6. SATIN SHEETS
   (Jeanne Pruett)
7. THE BRENDA LEE STORY
   (Brenda Lee)
8. BEHIND CLOSED DOORS
   (Charlie Rich)
9. ALL I EVER MEANT TO DO WAS SING
   (Johnny Rodriguez)
10. PAPER ROSES
   (Marie Osmond)

NOVEMBER 3, 1973

POP SINGLES

1. MIDNIGHT TRAIN TO GEORGIA
   (Gladys Knight and the Pips)
2. KEEP ON TRUCKIN'
   (Eddie Kendricks)
3. ANGIE
   (The Rolling Stones)
4. HEARTBEAT-IT'S A LOVEBEAT
   (DeFranco Family)
5. PAPER ROSES
   (Marie Osmond)
6. RAMBLIN' MAN
   (Allman Brothers Band)
7. ALL I KNOW
   (Art Garfunkel)
8. TOP OF THE WORLD
   (The Carpenters)
9. PHOTOGRAPH
   (Ringo Starr)
10. HALF BREED
   (Cher)

POP ALBUMS

1. GOAT'S HEAD SOUP
   (The Rolling Stones)
2. GOODBYE YELLOW BRICK ROAD
   (Elton John)
3. LET'S GET IT ON
   (Marvin Gaye)
4. ANGEL CLARE
   (Art Garfunkel)
5. LOS COCHINOS
   (Cheech and Chong)
6. BROTHERS AND SISTERS
   (Allman Brothers Band)
7. 3 PLUS 3
   (Isley Brothers)
8. INNERVISIONS
   (Stevie Wonder)
9. LONG HARD CLIMB
   (Helen Reddy)
10. WE'RE AN AMERICAN BAND
   (Grand Funk Railroad)

BLACK SINGLES

1. MIDNIGHT TRAIN TO GEORGIA
   (Gladys Knight and the Pips)
2. THE LOVE I LOST
   (Harold Melvin and the Blue Notes)
3. CHECK IT OUT
   (Tavares)

4. SPACE RACE
   (Billy Preston)
5. A SPECIAL PART OF ME
   (Marvin Gaye and Diana Ross)
6. KEEP ON TRUCKIN'
   (Eddie Kendricks)
7. HURTS SO GOOD
   (Millie Jackson)
8. CHEAPER TO KEEP HER
   (JohnnieTaylor)
9. LET'S GET IT ON
   (Marvin Gaye)
10. THEME FROM CLEOPATRA JONES
   (Joe Simon)

BLACK ALBUMS

1. 3 PLUS 3
   (Isley Brothers)
2. LET'S GET IT ON
   (Marvin Gaye)
3. EDDIE KENDRICKS
   (Eddie Kendricks)
4. DELIVER THE WORD
   (War)
5. INNERVISIONS
   (Stevie Wonder)
6. ANTHOLOGY
   (Temptations)
7. POINTER SISTERS
   (The Pointer Sisters)
8. FRESH
   (Sly and the Family Stone)
9. KILLING ME SOFTLY
   (Roberta Flack)
10. MAIN STREET PEOPLE
   (The Four Tops)

JAZZ ALBUMS

1. KILLING ME SOFTLY
   (Roberta Flack)
2. SONG OF THE NEW WORLD
   (McCoy Tyner)
3. SASSY SOUL STRUT
   (Lou Donaldson)
4. DON'T MESS WITH MR. T
   (Stanley Turrentine)
5. SWEETNIGHTER
   (Weather Report)
6. DEODATO 2
   (Eumir Deodato)
7. SOUL BOX
   (Grover Washington Jr.)
8. TURTLE BAY
   (Herbie Mann)
9. INSIDE STRAIGHT
   (Cannonball Adderley)
10. BODY TALK
   (George Benson)

COUNTRY SINGLES

1. DON'T GIVE UP ON ME
   (Jerry Wallace)
2. WE'RE GONNA HOLD ON
   (George Jones and Tammy Wynette)
3. PAPER ROSES
   (Marie Osmond)
4. SAWMILL
   (Mel Tillis)
5. RIDIN' MY THUMB TO MEXICO
   (Johnny Rodriguez)
6. SUNDAY SUNRISE
   (Brenda Lee)
7. THE MIDNIGHT OIL
   (Barbara Mandrell)
8. COUNTRY SUNSHINE
   (Dottie West)
9. RED NECKS, WHITE SOCKS AND BLUE
   RIBBON BEER
   (Johnny Russell)
10. TOO FAR GONE
   (Joe Stampley)

COUNTRY ALBUMS

1. LOVE IS THE FOUNDATION
   (Loretta Lynn)
2. YOU'VE NEVER BEEN THIS FAR BEFORE
   (Conway Twitty)
3. JESUS WAS A CAPRICORN
   (Kris Kristofferson)
4. I LOVE DIXIE BLUES
   (Merle Haggard)
5. PAPER ROSES
   (Marie Osmond)
6. ALL I EVER MEANT TO DO WAS SING
   (Johnny Rodriguez)
7. THE BRENDA LEE STORY
   (Brenda Lee)
8. FULL MOON
   (Kris Kristofferson and Rita Coolidge)
9. BEHIND CLOSED DOORS
   (Charlie Rich)
10. SATIN SHEETS
    (Jeanne Pruett)

NOVEMBER 10, 1973

POP SINGLES

1. KEEP ON TRUCKIN'
   (Eddie Kendricks)
2. MIDNIGHT TRAIN TO GEORGIA
   (Gladys Knight and the Pips)
3. HEARTBEAT-IT'S A LOVE BEAT
   (DeFranco Family)
4. PAPER ROSES
   (Marie Osmond)
5. PHOTOGRAPH
   (Ringo Starr)
6. TOP OF THE WORLD
   (The Carpenters)
7. ALL I KNOW
   (Art Garfunkel)
8. ANGIE
   (The Rolling Stones)
9. SPACE RACE
   (Billy Preston)
10. I GOT A NAME
    (Jim Croce)

POP ALBUMS

1. GOODBYE YELLOW BRICK ROAD
   (Elton John)
2. GOAT'S HEAD SOUP
   (The Rolling Stones)
3. LET'S GET IT ON
   (Marvin Gaye)
4. ANGEL CLARE
   (Art Garfunkel)
5. LOS COCHINOS
   (Cheech and Chong)
6. BROTHERS AND SISTERS
   (Allman Brothers Band)
7. 3 PLUS 3
   (Isley Brothers)
8. LIFE AND TIMES
   (Jim Croce)
9. INNERVISIONS
   (Stevie Wonder)
10. YOU DON'T MESS AROUND WITH JIM
    (Jim Croce)

BLACK SINGLES

1. MIDNIGHT TRAIN TO GEORGIA
   (Gladys Knight and the Pips)
2. THE LOVE I LOST
   (Harold Melvin and the Blue Notes)
3. SPACE RACE
   (Billy Preston)

4. CHECK IT OUT
   (Tavares)
5. A SPECIAL PART OF ME
   (Marvin Gaye and Diana Ross)
6. CHEAPER TO KEEP HER
   (Johnnie Taylor)
7. KEEP ON TRUCKIN'
   (Eddie Kendricks)
8. HAVING A PARTY
   (The Ovations)
9. HURTS SO GOOD
   (Millie Jackson)
10. GET IT TOGETHER
    (The Jackson 5)

BLACK ALBUMS

1. LET'S GET IT ON
   (Marvin Gaye)
2. 3 PLUS 3
   (Isley Brothers)
3. EDDIE KENDRICKS
   (Eddie Kendricks)
4. DELIVER THE WORD
   (War)
5. INNERVISIONS
   (Stevie Wonder)
6. ANTHOLOGY
   (Temptations)
7. HEAD TO THE SKY
   (Earth, Wind, and Fire)
8. POINTER SISTERS
   (The Pointer Sisters)
9. FRESH
   (Sly and the Family Stone)
10. MAIN STREET PEOPLE
    (The Four Tops)

JAZZ ALBUMS

1. KILLING ME SOFTLY
   (Roberta Flack)
2. SONG OF THE NEW WORLD
   (McCoy Tyner)
3. SASSY SOUL STRUT
   (Lou Donaldson)
4. DON'T MESS WITH MR. T
   (Stanley Turrentine)
5. DEODATO 2
   (Eumir Deodato)
6. TURTLE BAY
   (Herbie Mann)
7. SWEETNIGHTER
   (Weather Report)
8. SOUL BOX
   (Grover Washington Jr.)
9. INSIDE STRAIGHT
   (Cannonball Adderley)
10. BODY TALK
    (George Benson)

COUNTRY SINGLES

1. PAPER ROSES
   (Marie Osmond)
2. WE'RE GONNA HOLD ON
   (George Jones and Tammy Wynette)
3. COUNTRY SUNSHINE
   (Dottie West)
4. SAWMILL
   (Mel Tillis)
5. DON'T GIVE UP ON ME
   (Jerry Wallace)
6. THE MOST BEAUTIFUL GIRL
   (Charlie Rich)
7. RIDIN' MY THUMB TO MEXICO
   (Johnny Rodriguez)
8. I'M YOUR WOMAN
   (Jeanne Pruett)
9. SUNDAY SUNRISE
   (Brenda Lee)
10. TIL THE WATER STOPS RUNNIN'
    (Billy "Crash" Craddock)

COUNTRY ALBUMS

1. LOVE IS THE FOUNDATION
   (Loretta Lynn)
2. JESUS WAS A CAPRICORN
   (Kris Kristofferson)
3. PAPER ROSES
   (Marie Osmond)
4. YOU'VE NEVER BEEN THIS FAR BEFORE
   (Conway Twitty)
5. ALL I EVER MEANT TO DO WAS SING
   (Johnny Rodriguez)
6. FULL MOON
   (Kris Kristofferson and Rita Coolidge)
7. I LOVE DIXIE BLUES
   (Merle Haggard)
8. THE BRENDA LEE STORY
   (Brenda Lee)
9. BEHIND CLOSED DOORS
   (Charlie Rich)
10. PRIMROSE LANE
    (Jerry Wallace)

NOVEMBER 17, 1973

POP SINGLES

1. HEARTBEAT-IT'S A LOVE BEAT
   (DeFranco Family)
2. PHOTOGRAPH
   (Ringo Starr)
3. KEEP ON TRUCKIN'
   (Eddie Kendricks)
4. PAPER ROSES
   (Marie Osmond)
5. TOP OF THE WORLD
   (The Carpenters)
6. MIDNIGHT TRAIN TO GEORGIA
   (Gladys Knight and the Pips)
7. SPACE RACE
   (Billy Preston)
8. I GOT A NAME
   (Jim Croce)
9. JUST YOU AND ME
   (Chicago)
10. ALL I KNOW
    (Art Garfunkel)

POP ALBUMS

1. GOODBYE YELLOW BRICK ROAD
   (Elton John)
2. GOAT'S HEAD SOUP
   (The Rolling Stones)
3. BROTHERS AND SISTERS
   (Allman Brothers Band)
4. LOS COCHINOS
   (Cheech and Chong)
5. LET'S GET IT ON
   (Marvin Gaye)
6. ANGEL CLARE
   (Art Garfunkel)
7. LIFE AND TIMES
   (Jim Croce)
8. 3 PLUS 3
   (Isley Brothers)
9. YOU DON'T MESS AROUND WITH JIM
   (Jim Croce)
10. THE SMOKER YOU DRINK, THE PLAYER YOU GET
    (Joe Walsh)

BLACK SINGLES

1. THE LOVE I LOST
   (Harold Melvin and the Blue Notes)
2. MIDNIGHT TRAIN TO GEORGIA
   (Gladys Knight and the Pips)
3. SPACE RACE
   (Billy Preston)

4. CHECK IT OUT
(Tavares)
5. CHEAPER TO KEEP HER
(Johnnie Taylor)
6. A SPECIAL PART OF ME
(Marvin Gaye and Diana Ross)
7. KEEP ON TRUCKIN'
(Eddie Kendricks)
8. HAVING A PARTY
(The Ovations)
9. IF YOU'RE READY (COME GO WITH ME)
(The Staple Singers)
10. SOME GUYS HAVE ALL THE LUCK
(The Persuaders)

BLACK ALBUMS

1. LET'S GET IT ON
(Marvin Gaye)
2. DELIVER THE WORD
(War)
3. 3 PLUS 3
(Isley Brothers)
4. EDDIE KENDRICKS
(Eddie Kendricks)
5. ANTHOLOGY
(Temptations)
6. HEAD TO THE SKY
(Earth, Wind and Fire)
7. INNERVISIONS
(Stevie Wonder)
8. POINTER SISTERS
(The Pointer Sisters)
9. MAIN STREET PEOPLE
(The Four Tops)
10. WILD AND PEACEFUL
(Kool and the Gang)

JAZZ ALBUMS

1. KILLING ME SOFTLY
(Roberta Flack)
2. DON'T MESS WITH MR. T
(Stanley Turrentine)
3. SONG OF THE NEW WORLD
(McCoy Tyner)
4. SASSY SOUL STRUT
(Lou Donaldson)
5. DEODATO 2
(Eumir Deodato)
6. TURTLE BAY
(Herbie Mann)
7. SWEETNIGHTER
(Weather Report)
8. INSIDE STRAIGHT
(Cannonball Adderley)
9. SOUL BOX
(Grover Washington Jr.)
10. BODY TALK
(George Benson)

COUNTRY SINGLES

1. COUNTRY SUNSHINE
(Dottie West)
2. THE MOST BEAUTIFUL GIRL
(Charlie Rich)
3. PAPER ROSES
(Marie Osmond)
4. WE'RE GONNA HOLD ON
(George Jones and Tammy Wynette)
5. SAWMILL
(Mel Tillis)
6. I'M YOUR WOMAN
(Jeanne Pruett)
7. TIL THE WATER STOPS RUNNIN'
(Billy "Crash" Craddock)
8. SING ABOUT LOVE
(Lynn Anderson)
9. RIDIN' MY THUMB TO MEXICO
(Johnny Rodriguez)
10. LET ME BE THERE
(Olivia Newton-John)

COUNTRY ALBUMS

1. PAPER ROSES
(Marie Osmond)
2. JESUS WAS A CAPRICORN
(Kris Kristofferson)
3. FULL MOON
(Kris Kristofferson and Rita Coolidge)
4. ALL I EVER MEANT TO DO WAS SING
(Johnny Rodriguez)
5. LOVE IS THE FOUNDATION
(Loretta Lynn)
6. YOU'VE NEVER BEEN THIS FAR BEFORE
(Conway Twitty)
7. PRIMROSE LANE
(Jerry Wallace)
8. I LOVE DIXIE BLUES
(Merle Haggard)
9. BEHIND CLOSED DOORS
(Charlie Rich)
10. SLIPPIN' AWAY
(Jean Shepard)

NOVEMBER 24, 1973

POP SINGLES

1. PHOTOGRAPH
(Ringo Starr)
2. HEARTBEAT-IT'S A LOVE BEAT
(DeFranco Family)
3. TOP OF THE WORLD
(The Carpenters)
4. KEEP ON TRUCKIN'
(Eddie Kendricks)
5. I GOT A NAME
(Jim Croce)
6. SPACE RACE
(Billy Preston)
7. JUST YOU AND ME
(Chicago)
8. GOODBYE YELLOW BRICK ROAD
(Elton John)
9. PAPER ROSES
(Marie Osmond)
10. THE LOVE I LOST
(Harold Melvin and the Blue Notes)

POP ALBUMS

1. RINGO
(Ringo Starr)
2. GOODBYE YELLOW BRICK ROAD
(Elton John)
3. BROTHERS AND SISTERS
(Allman Brothers Band)
4. QUADROPHENIA
(The Who)
5. GOAT'S HEAD SOUP
(The Rolling Stones)
6. LIFE AND TIMES
(Jim Croce)
7. LOS COCHINOS
(Cheech and Chong)
8. YOU DON'T MESS AROUND WITH JIM
(Jim Croce)
9. THE JOKER
(The Steve Miller Band)
10. JONATHAN LIVINGSTON SEAGULL
(Neil Diamond)

BLACK SINGLES

1. THE LOVE I LOST
(Harold Melvin and the Blue Notes)
2. MIDNIGHT TRAIN TO GEORGIA
(Gladys Knight and the Pips)
3. SPACE RACE
(Billy Preston)

4. CHEAPER TO KEEP HER
(Johnnie Taylor)
5. IF YOU'RE READY (COME GO WITH ME)
(The Staple Singers)
6. CHECK IT OUT
(Tavares)
7. A SPECIAL PART OF ME
(Marvin Gaye and Diana Ross)
8. SOME GUYS HAVE ALL THE LUCK
(The Persuaders)
9. ROCKIN' ROLL BABY
(The Stylistics)
10. KEEP ON TRUCKIN'
(Eddie Kendricks)

BLACK ALBUMS

1. LET'S GET IT ON
(Marvin Gaye)
2. DELIVER THE WORD
(War)
3. 3 PLUS 3
(Isley Brothers)
4. EDDIE KENDRICKS
(Eddie Kendricks)
5. HEAD TO THE SKY
(Earth, Wind and Fire)
6. JOY
(Isaac Hayes)
7. IMAGINATION
(Gladys Knight and the Pips)
8. UNDER THE INFLUENCE OF LOVE UNLIMITED
(Love Unlimited)
9. ANTHOLOGY
(Temptations)
10. WILD AND PEACEFUL
(Kool and the Gang)

JAZZ ALBUMS

1. KILLING ME SOFTLY
(Roberta Flack)
2. SPECTRUM
(Billy Cobham)
3. DON'T MESS WITH MR. T
(Stanley Turrentine)
4. TURTLE BAY
(Herbie Mann)
5. SWEETNIGHTER
(Weather Report)
6. DEODATO 2
(Eumir Deodato)
7. SONG OF THE NEW WORLD
(McCoy Tyner)
8. INSIDE STRAIGHT
(Cannonball Adderley)
9. SASSY SOUL STRUT
(Lou Donaldson)
10. CHAPTER ONE: LATIN AMERICA
(Gato Barbieri)

COUNTRY SINGLES

1. THE MOST BEAUTIFUL GIRL
(Charlie Rich)
2. COUNTRY SUNSHINE
(Dottie West)
3. PAPER ROSES
(Marie Osmond)
4. I'M YOUR WOMAN
(Jeanne Pruett)
5. SING ABOUT LOVE
(Lynn Anderson)
6. WE'RE GONNA HOLD ON
(George Jones and Tammy Wynette)
7. TIL THE WATER STOPS RUNNIN'
(Billy "Crash" Craddock)
8. LET ME BE THERE
(Olivia Newton-John)
9. I'LL NEVER BREAK THESE CHAINS
(Tommy Overstreet)
10. LITTLE GIRL GONE
(Donna Fargo)

COUNTRY ALBUMS

1. PAPER ROSES
   (Marie Osmond)
2. FULL MOON
   (Kris Kristofferson and Rita Coolidge)
3. ALL I EVER MEANT TO DO WAS SING
   (Johnny Rodriguez)
4. PRIMROSE LANE
   (Jerry Wallace)
5. JESUS WAS A CAPRICORN
   (Kris Kristofferson)
6. YOU'VE NEVER BEEN THIS FAR BEFORE
   (Conway Twitty)
7. LOVE IS THE FOUNDATION
   (Loretta Lynn)
8. I LOVE DIXIE BLUES
   (Merle Haggard)
9. SATIN SHEETS
   (Jeanne Pruett)
10. SLIPPIN' AWAY
    (Jean Shepard)

DECEMBER 1, 1973

POP SINGLES

1. PHOTOGRAPH
   (Ringo Starr)
2. GOODBYE YELLOW BRICK ROAD
   (Elton John)
3. TOP OF THE WORLD
   (The Carpenters)
4. JUST YOU AND ME
   (Chicago)
5. I GOT A NAME
   (Jim Croce)
6. SPACE RACE
   (Billy Preston)
7. HEARTBEAT-IT'S A LOVE BEAT
   (DeFranco Family)
8. THE LOVE I LOST
   (Harold Melvin and the Blue Notes)
9. THE MOST BEAUTIFUL GIRL
   (Charlie Rich)
10. HELLO, IT'S ME
    (Todd Rundgren)

POP ALBUMS

1. RINGO
   (Ringo Starr)
2. GOODBYE YELLOW BRICK ROAD
   (Elton John)
3. QUADROPHENIA
   (The Who)
4. BROTHERS AND SISTERS
   (Allman Brothers Band)
5. YOU DON'T MESS AROUND WITH JIM
   (Jim Croce)
6. JONATHAN LIVINGSTON SEAGULL
   (Neil Diamond)
7. THE JOKER
   (The Steve Miller Band)
8. LIFE AND TIMES
   (Jim Croce)
9. GOAT'S HEAD SOUP
   (The Rolling Stones)
10. MIND GAMES
    (John Lennon)

BLACK SINGLES

1. THE LOVE I LOST
   (Harold Melvin and the Blue Notes)
2. IF YOU'RE READY (COME GO WITH ME)
   (The Staple Singers)
3. CHEAPER TO KEEP HER
   (Johnnie Taylor)

4. MIDNIGHT TRAIN TO GEORGIA
   (Gladys Knight and the Pips)
5. SPACE RACE
   (Billy Preston)
6. ROCKIN' ROLL BABY
   (The Stylistics)
7. SOME GUYS HAVE ALL THE LUCK
   (The Persuaders)
8. CHECK IT OUT
   (Tavares)
9. NEVER, NEVER GONNA GIVE YA UP
   (Barry White)
10. THIS TIME I'M GONE FOR GOOD
    (Bobby "Blue" Bland)

BLACK ALBUMS

1. JOY
   (Isaac Hayes)
2. LET'S GET IT ON
   (Marvin Gaye)
3. DELIVER THE WORD
   (War)
4. IMAGINATION
   (Gladys Knight and the Pips)
5. 3 PLUS 3
   (Isley Brothers)
6. UNDER THE INFLUENCE OF LOVE
   UNLIMITED
   (Love Unlimited)
7. HEAD TO THE SKY
   (Earth, Wind and Fire)
8. EDDIE KENDRICKS
   (Eddie Kendricks)
9. ANTHOLOGY
   (Temptations)
10. INNERVISIONS
    (Stevie Wonder)

JAZZ ALBUMS

1. SPECTRUM
   (Billy Cobham)
2. DON'T MESS WITH MR. T
   (Stanley Turrentine)
3. KILLING ME SOFTLY
   (Roberta Flack)
4. TURTLE BAY
   (Herbie Mann)
5. SWEETNIGHTER
   (Weather Report)
6. DEODATO 2
   (Eumir Deodato)
7. INSIDE STRAIGHT
   (Cannonball Adderley)
8. CHAPTER ONE: LATIN AMERICA
   (Gato Barbieri)
9. SONG OF THE NEW WORLD
   (McCoy Tyner)
10. BOLIVIA
    (Gato Barbieri)

COUNTRY SINGLES

1. THE MOST BEAUTIFUL GIRL
   (Charlie Rich)
2. AMAZING LOVE
   (Charley Pride)
3. PAPER ROSES
   (Marie Osmond)
4. I'M YOUR WOMAN
   (Jeanne Pruett)
5. SING ABOUT LOVE
   (Lynn Anderson)
6. LITTLE GIRL GONE
   (Donna Fargo)
7. LET ME BE THERE
   (Olivia Newton-John)
8. I'LL NEVER BREAK THESE CHAINS
   (Tommy Overstreet)
9. IF YOU CAN'T FEEL IT
   (Freddie Hart)
10. SOMETIMES A MEMORY AIN'T ENOUGH
    (Jerry Lee Lewis)

COUNTRY ALBUMS

1. PAPER ROSES
   (Marie Osmond)
2. ALL I EVER MEANT TO DO WAS SING
   (Johnny Rodriguez)
3. PRIMROSE LANE
   (Jerry Wallace)
4. FULL MOON
   (Kris Kristofferson and Rita Coolidge)
5. YOU'VE NEVER BEEN THIS FAR BEFORE
   (Conway Twitty)
6. JESUS WAS A CAPRICORN
   (Kris Kristofferson)
7. SATIN SHEETS
   (Jeanne Pruett)
8. LOVE IS THE FOUNDATION
   (Loretta Lynn)
9. I LOVE DIXIE BLUES
   (Merle Haggard)
10. HANK WILSON'S BACK, VOL. 1
    (Hank Wilson)

DECEMBER 8, 1973

POP SINGLES

1. GOODBYE YELLOW BRICK ROAD
   (Elton John)
2. PHOTOGRAPH
   (Ringo Starr)
3. TOP OF THE WORLD
   (The Carpenters)
4. JUST YOU AND ME
   (Chicago)
5. THE MOST BEAUTIFUL GIRL
   (Charlie Rich)
6. HELLO, IT'S ME
   (Todd Rundgren)
7. THE LOVE I LOST
   (Harold Melvin and the Blue Notes)
8. LEAVE ME ALONE (RUBY RED DRESS)
   (Helen Reddy)
9. SPACE RACE
   (Billy Preston)
10. HEARTBEAT-IT'S A LOVE BEAT
    (DeFranco Family)

POP ALBUMS

1. RINGO
   (Ringo Starr)
2. GOODBYE YELLOW BRICK ROAD
   (Elton John)
3. QUADROPHENIA
   (The Who)
4. JONATHAN LIVINGSTON SEAGULL
   (Neil Diamond)
5. YOU DON'T MESS AROUND WITH JIM
   (Jim Croce)
6. THE JOKER
   (The Steve Miller Band)
7. BROTHERS AND SISTERS
   (Allman Brothers Band)
8. MIND GAMES
   (John Lennon)
9. LIFE AND TIMES
   (Jim Croce)
10. GOAT'S HEAD SOUP
    (The Rolling Stones)

BLACK SINGLES

1. IF YOU'RE READY (COME GO WITH ME)
   (The Staple Singers)
2. THE LOVE I LOST
   (Harold Melvin and the Blue Notes)
3. CHEAPER TO KEEP HER
   (Johnnie Taylor)

4. ROCKIN' ROLL BABY
   (The Stylistics)
5. NEVER, NEVER GONNA GIVE YA UP
   (Barry White)
6. SOME GUYS HAVE ALL THE LUCK
   (The Persuaders)
7. THIS TIME I'M GONE FOR GOOD
   (Bobby "Blue" Bland)
8. MIDNIGHT TRAIN TO GEORGIA
   (Gladys Knight and the Pips)
9. SPACE RACE
   (Billy Preston)
10. I WANNA KNOW YOUR NAME
    (Intruders)

BLACK ALBUMS

1. JOY
   (Isaac Hayes)
2. LET'S GET IT ON
   (Marvin Gaye)
3. IMAGINATION
   (Gladys Knight and the Pips)
4. SWEETNIGHTER
   (Weather Report)
5. KILLING ME SOFTLY
   (Roberta Flack)
6. DEODATO 2
   (Eumir Deodato)
7. INSIDE STRAIGHT
   (Cannonball Adderley)
8. HYMN OF THE SEVENTH GALAXY
   (Return to Forever featuring Chick Corea)
9. CHAPTER ONE: LATIN AMERICA
   (Gato Barbieri)
10. UNSUNG HEROES
    (Crusaders)

COUNTRY SINGLES

1. AMAZING LOVE
   (Charley Pride)
2. THE MOST BEAUTIFUL GIRL
   (Charlie Rich)
3. LITTLE GIRL GONE
   (Donna Fargo)
4. YOU ASK ME TO
   (Waylon Jennings)
5. IF WE MAKE IT THROUGH DECEMBER
   (Merle Haggard)
6. SOMETIMES A MEMORY AIN'T ENOUGH
   (Jerry Lee Lewis)
7. IF YOU CAN'T
   (Freddie Hart)
8. I'LL NEVER BREAK THESE CHAINS
   (Tommy Overstreet)
9. SING ABOUT LOVE
   (Lynn Anderson)
10. PAPER ROSES
    (Marie Osmond)

COUNTRY ALBUMS

1. ALL I EVER MEANT TO DO WAS SING
   (Johnny Rodriguez)
2. PAPER ROSES
   (Marie Osmond)
3. PRIMROSE LANE
   (Jerry Wallace)
4. FULL MOON
   (Kris Kristofferson and Rita Coolidge)
5. YOU'VE NEVER BEEN THIS FAR BEFORE
   (Conway Twitty)
6. SATIN SHEETS
   (Jeanne Pruett)
7. BEHIND CLOSED DOORS
   (Charlie Rich)
8. JESUS WAS A CAPRICORN
   (Kris Kristofferson)
9. SAWMILL
   (Mel Tillis)
10. HANK WILSON'S BACK, VOL. 1
    (Hank Wilson)

DECEMBER 15, 1973

POP SINGLES

1. THE MOST BEAUTIFUL GIRL
   (Charlie Rich)
2. JUST YOU AND ME
   (Chicago)
3. GOODBYE YELLOW BRICK ROAD
   (Elton John)
4. HELLO, IT'S ME
   (Todd Rundgren)
5. LEAVE ME ALONE (RUBY RED DRESS)
   (Helen Reddy)
6. THE LOVE I LOST
   (Harold Melvin and the Blue Notes)
7. PHOTOGRAPH
   (Ringo Starr)
8. TIME IN A BOTTLE
   (Jim Croce)
9. THE JOKER
   (The Steve Miller Band)
10. IF YOU'RE READY (COME GO WITH ME)
    (The Staple Singers)

POP ALBUMS

1. GOODBYE YELLOW BRICK ROAD
   (Elton John)
2. RINGO
   (Ringo Starr)
3. THE JOKER
   (The Steve Miller Band)
4. JONATHAN LIVINGSTON SEAGULL
   (Neil Diamond)
5. QUADROPHENIA
   (The Who)
6. YOU DON'T MESS AROUND WITH JIM
   (Jim Croce)
7. MIND GAMES
   (John Lennon)
8. BROTHERS AND SISTERS
   (Allman Brothers Band)
9. LIFE AND TIMES
   (Jim Croce)
10. GOAT'S HEAD SOUP
    (The Rolling Stones)

BLACK SINGLES

1. IF YOU'RE READY (COME GO WITH ME)
   (The Staple Singers)
2. ROCKIN' ROLL BABY
   (The Stylistics)
3. NEVER, NEVER GONNA GIVE YA UP
   (Barry White)
4. THE LOVE I LOST
   (Harold Melvin and the Blue Notes)
5. THIS TIME I'M GONE FOR GOOD
   (Bobby "Blue" Bland)
6. SOME GUYS HAVE ALL THE LUCK
   (The Persuaders)
7. CHEAPER TO KEEP HER
   (Johnnie Taylor)
8. I WANNA KNOW YOUR NAME
   (Intruders)
9. LIVIN' FOR YOU
   (Al Green)
10. COME GET TO THIS
    (Marvin Gaye)

BLACK ALBUMS

1. IMAGINATION
   (Gladys Knight and the Pips)
2. JOY
   (Isaac Hayes)
3. STONE GON'
   (Barry White)
4. UNDER THE INFLUENCE OF LOVE
   UNLIMITED
   (Love Unlimited)

5. LET'S GET IT ON
   (Marvin Gaye)
6. DELIVER THE WORD
   (War)
7. SHIP AHOY
   (The O'Jays)
8. 3 PLUS 3
   (Isley Brothers)
9. DIANA AND MARVIN
   (Diana Ross and Marvin Gaye)
10. BLACK AND BLUE
    (Harold Melvin and the Blue Notes)

JAZZ ALBUMS

1. SPECTRUM
   (Billy Cobham)
2. TURTLE BAY
   (Herbie Mann)
3. SWEETNIGHTER
   (Weather Report)
4. DON'T MESS WITH MR. T
   (Stanley Turrentine)
5. DEODATO 2
   (Eumir Deodato)
6. HYMN OF THE SEVENTH GALAXY
   (Return to Forever featuring Chick Corea)
7. UNSUNG HEROES
   (Crusaders)
8. INSIDE STRAIGHT
   (Cannonball Adderley)
9. CHAPTER ONE: LATIN AMERICA
   (Gato Barbieri)
10. SECOND CRUSADE
    (Crusaders)

COUNTRY SINGLES

1. THE MOST BEAUTIFUL GIRL
   (Charlie Rich)
2. AMAZING LOVE
   (Charley Pride)
3. YOU ASK ME TO
   (Waylon Jennings)
4. IF WE MAKE IT THROUGH DECEMBER
   (Merle Haggard)
5. IF YOU CAN'T FEEL IT
   (Freddie Hart)
6. LITTLE GIRL GONE
   (Donna Fargo)
7. SOMETIMES A MEMORY AIN'T ENOUGH
   (Jerry Lee Lewis)
8. I'LL NEVER BREAK THESE CHAINS
   (Tommy Overstreet)
9. LOVE ME/CRAWLING ON MY KNEES
   (Marty Robbins)
10. THE LAST LOVE SONG
    (Hank Williams Jr.)

COUNTRY ALBUMS

1. ALL I EVER MEANT TO DO WAS SING
   (Johnny Rodriguez)
2. PRIMROSE LANE
   (Jerry Wallace)
3. PAPER ROSES
   (Marie Osmond)
4. BEHIND CLOSED DOORS
   (Charlie Rich)
5. FULL MOON
   (Kris Kristofferson and Rita Coolidge)
6. SATIN SHEETS
   (Jeanne Pruett)
7. SAWMILL
   (Mel Tillis)
8. YOU'VE NEVER BEEN THIS FAR BEFORE
   (Conway Twitty)
9. COME LIVE WITH ME
   (Roy Clark)
10. JESUS WAS A CAPRICORN
    (Kris Kristofferson)

DECEMBER 22, 1973

POP SINGLES

1. THE MOST BEAUTIFUL GIRL
   (Charlie Rich)
2. JUST YOU AND ME
   (Chicago)
3. LEAVE ME ALONE (RUBY RED DRESS)
   (Helen Reddy)
4. HELLO, IT'S ME
   (Todd Rundgren)
5. TIME IN A BOTTLE
   (Jim Croce)
6. THE JOKER
   (The Steve Miller Band)
7. GOODBYE YELLOW BRICK ROAD
   (Elton John)
8. HELEN WHEELS
   (Paul McCartney and Wings)
9. IF YOU'RE READY (COME GO WITH ME)
   (The Staple Singers)
10. MIND GAMES
    (John Lennon)

POP ALBUMS

1. GOODBYE YELLOW BRICK ROAD
   (Elton John)
2. JONATHAN LIVINGSTON SEAGULL
   (Neil Diamond)
3. RINGO
   (Ringo Starr)
4. SINGLES 1969–1973
   (The Carpenters)
5. YOU DON'T MESS AROUND WITH JIM
   (Jim Croce)
6. MIND GAMES
   (John Lennon)
7. BROTHERS AND SISTERS
   (Allman Brothers Band)
8. BETTE MIDLER
   (Bette Midler)
9. QUADROPHENIA
   (The Who)
10. THE JOKER
    (Steve Miller)

BLACK SINGLES

1. NEVER, NEVER GONNA GIVE YA UP
   (Barry White)
2. ROCKIN' ROLL BABY
   (The Stylistics)
3. IF YOU'RE READY (COME GO WITH ME)
   (The Staple Singers)
4. THIS TIME I'M GONE FOR GOOD
   (Bobby "Blue" Bland)
5. I'VE GOT TO USE MY IMAGINATION
   (Gladys Knight and the Pips)
6. LIVIN' FOR YOU
   (Al Green)
7. COME GET TO THIS
   (Marvin Gaye)
8. I WANNA KNOW YOUR NAME
   (Intruders)
9. THE LOVE I LOST
   (Harold Melvin and the Blue Notes)
10. ME AND BABY BROTHER
    (War)

BLACK ALBUMS

1. IMAGINATION
   (Gladys Knight and the Pips)
2. STONE GON'
   (Barry White)
3. JOY
   (Isaac Hayes)
4. UNDER THE INFLUENCE OF LOVE
   UNLIMITED
   (Love Unlimited)
5. SHIP AHOY
   (The O'Jays)

6. LET'S GET IT ON
   (Marvin Gaye)
7. DIANA AND MARVIN
   (Diana Ross and Marvin Gaye)
8. DELIVER THE WORD
   (War)
9. 3 PLUS 3
   (Isley Brothers)
10. BLACK AND BLUE
    (Harold Melvin and the Blue Notes)

COUNTRY SINGLES

1. IF WE MAKE IT THROUGH DECEMBER
   (Merle Haggard)
2. THE MOST BEAUTIFUL GIRL
   (Charlie Rich)
3. YOU ASK ME TO
   (Waylon Jennings)
4. IF YOU CAN'T FEEL IT
   (Freddie Hart)
5. AMAZING LOVE
   (Charley Pride)
6. SOMEWHERE BETWEEN LOVE AND
   TOMORROW
   (Roy Clark)
7. I LOVE
   (Tom T. Hall)
8. THE LAST LOVE SONG
   (Hank Williams Jr.)
9. LOVE ME/CRAWLING ON MY KNEES
   (Marty Robbins)
10. LET ME BE THERE
    (Olivia Newton-John)

COUNTRY ALBUMS

1. PRIMROSE LANE
   (Jerry Wallace)
2. ALL I EVER MEANT TO DO WAS SING
   (Johnny Rodriguez)
3. BEHIND CLOSED DOORS
   (Charlie Rich)
4. PAPER ROSES
   (Marie Osmond)
5. SAWMILL
   (Mel Tillis)
6. COME LIVE WITH ME
   (Roy Clark)
7. DON'T CRY NOW
   (Linda Ronstadt)
8. YOU'VE NEVER BEEN THIS FAR BEFORE
   (Conway Twitty)
9. SATIN SHEETS
   (Jeanne Pruett)
10. FULL MOON
    (Kris Kristofferson and Rita Coolidge)

DECEMBER 29, 1973

POP SINGLES

1. LEAVE ME ALONE (RUBY RED DRESS)
   (Helen Reddy)
2. THE MOST BEAUTIFUL GIRL
   (Charlie Rich)
3. TIME IN A BOTTLE
   (Jim Croce)
4. THE JOKER
   (The Steve Miller Band)
5. HELLO, IT'S ME
   (Todd Rundgren)
6. HELEN WHEELS
   (Paul McCartney and Wings)
7. SHOW AND TELL
   (Al Wilson)
8. IF YOU'RE READY (COME GO WITH ME)
   (The Staple Singers)
9. NEVER, NEVER GONNA GIVE YA UP
   (Barry White)
10. MIND GAMES
    (John Lennon)

POP ALBUMS

1. SINGLES 1969–1973
   (The Carpenters)
2. JONATHAN LIVINGSTON SEAGULL
   (Neil Diamond)
3. GOODBYE YELLOW BRICK ROAD
   (Elton John)
4. THE JOKER
   (The Steve Miller Band)
5. YOU DON'T MESS AROUND WITH JIM
   (Jim Croce)
6. RINGO
   (Ringo Starr)
7. BETTE MIDLER
   (Bette Midler)
8. MIND GAMES
   (John Lennon)
9. BROTHERS AND SISTERS
   (Allman Brothers Band)
10. I GOT A NAME
    (Jim Croce)

BLACK SINGLES

1. NEVER, NEVER GONNA GIVE YA UP
   (Barry White)
2. I'VE GOT TO USE MY IMAGINATION
   (Gladys Knight and the Pips)
3. IF YOU'RE READY (COME GO WITH ME)
   (The Staple Singers)
4. THIS TIME I'M GONE FOR GOOD
   (Bobby "Blue" Bland)
5. LIVIN' FOR YOU
   (Al Green)
6. UNTIL YOU COME BACK TO ME
   (Aretha Franklin)
7. COME GET TO THIS
   (Marvin Gaye)
8. LIVING FOR THE CITY
   (Stevie Wonder)
9. ROCKIN' ROLL BABY
   (The Stylistics)
10. STONE TO THE BONE
    (James Brown)

BLACK ALBUMS

1. IMAGINATION
   (Gladys Knight and the Pips)
2. STONE GON'
   (Barry White)
3. JOY
   (Isaac Hayes)
4. SHIP AHOY
   (The O'Jays)
5. UNDER THE INFLUENCE OF LOVE
   UNLIMITED
   (Love Unlimited)
6. LET'S GET IT ON
   (Marvin Gaye)
7. DIANA AND MARVIN
   (Diana Ross and Marvin Gaye)
8. BLACK AND BLUE
   (Harold Melvin and the Blue Notes)
9. DELIVER THE WORD
   (War)
10. 3 PLUS 3
    (Isley Brothers)

JAZZ ALBUMS

1. SPECTRUM
   (Billy Cobham)
2. TURTLE BAY
   (Herbie Mann)
3. HYMN OF THE SEVENTH GALAXY
   (Return to Forever featuring Chick Corea)
4. HEAD HUNTERS
   (Herbie Hancock)
5. UNSUNG HEROES
   (Crusaders)

6. WELCOME
   (Santana)
7. BETWEEN NOTHINGNESS AND ETERNITY
   (Mahavishnu Orchestra)
8. SWEETNIGHTER
   (Weather Report)
9. DEODATO 2
   (Eumir Deodato)
10. CHAPTER ONE: LATIN AMERICA
    (Gato Barbieri)

COUNTRY SINGLES

1. IF YOU CAN'T FEEL IT
   (Freddie Hart)
2. IF WE MAKE IT THROUGH DECEMBER
   (Merle Haggard)
3. SOMEWHERE BETWEEN LOVE AND
   TOMORROW
   (Roy Clark)
4. I LOVE
   (Tom T. Hall)
5. THE MOST BEAUTIFUL GIRL
   (Charlie Rich)
6. THE LAST LOVE SONG
   (Hank Williams Jr.)
7. AMAZING LOVE
   (Charley Pride)
8. YOU ASK ME TO
   (Waylon Jennings)
9. JOLENE
   (Dolly Parton)
10. LET ME BE THERE
    (Olivia Newton-John)

COUNTRY ALBUMS

1. BEHIND CLOSED DOORS
   (Charlie Rich)
2. ALL I EVER MEANT TO DO WAS SING
   (Johnny Rodriguez)
3. PRIMROSE LANE
   (Jerry Wallace)
4. COME LIVE WITH ME
   (Roy Clark)
5. SAWMILL
   (Mel Tillis)
6. DON'T CRY NOW
   (Linda Ronstadt)
7. SOMETIMES A MEMORY AIN'T ENOUGH
   (Jerry Lee Lewis)
8. YOU'VE NEVER BEEN THIS FAR BEFORE
   (Conway Twitty)
9. PAPER ROSES
   (Marie Osmond)
10. SATIN SHEETS
    (Jeanne Pruett)

1974

Elton John had been building towards superstardom for a couple of years. There were some good albums (*Honky Chateau* the best), some tantalizing singles ("Crocodile Rock," "Rocket Man," "Tiny Dancer," "Levon"), and increasingly flamboyant stage shows—complete with Elton John's garish glittering glasses and equally outrageous costumes. All this showmanship was supported ably by a tight, versatile band composed of drummer Nigel Olson, bassist Dee Anthony, lead guitarist Davey Johnson, and percussionist Ray Cooper.

Finally, with *Goodbye Yellow Brick Road* and *Caribou* in 1974 John put the metal to the pedal and burned rubber, becoming pop music's most ubiquitous presence. His singles were everywhere, charging into homes like a plague of melodic locusts. It was done without malice, but most definitely with aforethought. "Saturday Night's Alright for Fighting," "Goodbye Yellow Brick Road," "Bennie and the Jets," "Don't Let the Sun Go Down on Me," "The Bitch is Back," and an inspired reggae version of The Beatles' "Lucy in the Sky With Diamonds" were creations of a man who thoroughly understood what good pop music was and how to make it. At his peak, John, along with lyricist Bernie Taupin and producer Gus Dudgeon, was a great mass manipulator, in the class of other 1970s pop icons like Richard Pryor, Norman Lear, George Lucas, Steven Spielberg, and Reggie Jackson.

Yes, he finally did burn himself out, but even among the biggest stars that's not unusual. Just ask Paul McCartney. The ability McCartney displayed with The Beatles for writing catchy songs with several layers of meaning had left him by 1974. *Band on the Run* indicated, however, that his ear for melody and an underestimated singing voice were still intact on his most appealing post-Beatles album.

ALBUMS: While there were a number of worthy white pop-rock albums (Bachman-Turner Overdrive's *2*, Joni Mitchell's *Court and Spark*, the late Jim Croce's *I Got a Name* and *You Don't Mess Around With Jim*, and Led Zeppelin's *Houses of the Holy*), it was black music that produced this year's best 33-rpm recordings.

James Brown was in decline. His funk innovations had been adopted and even surpassed by a number of young bands with Kool and the Gang (*Wild and Peaceful*) topping the list. Yet the Godfather wasn't dead. The double album *The Big Payback* showed he could still hit and hit hard. "The Payback" from that album is a deep, evil river of funk with treacherous guitar licks, a hellish bass line, and vicious, blaring horns, surrounding Brown's song-rap about vengeance ("My patience is at an end!") and death. Nasty stuff.

Other top funk albums of 1974 were Herbie Hancock's jazz-funk *Head Hunters*; the street-funk of the Ohio Players' *Skin Tight* and New Birth's *It's Been a Long Time*; Earth, Wind and Fire's sweet-funk *Open Our Eyes* and the Isley Brothers rock-funk *3 Plus 3*, sparked by the addition of brother Ernie on lead guitar and drums.

Gladys Knight and the Pips, with *Imagination* and the soundtrack to *Claudine*, and Marvin Gaye, with the erotic *Let's Get It On*, continued growing. Al Green kept Memphis on the musical map with his fine *Livin' For You*. Richard Pryor's *That Nigger's Crazy* was a major seller and reached audiences his black comic predecessors Moms Mabley and Pigmeat Markum could not because of racism, a reflection of society's changing attitudes and Pryor's special gifts.

Disco was coming into use as a description of music that club dancers enjoyed. At the time, disco just seemed like another genre of black music. Who suspected that Eddie Kendricks's "Boogie Down," the Hues Corporations' "Rock the Boat," George McCrae's "Rock Your Baby," the Jackson 5's "Dancin' Machine," or MFSB's "TSOP" would have such a profound impact? All were long album cuts in the days before 12-inch singles.

Charlie Rich and Olivia Newton-John were the big stories in country. Of the year's best-selling country albums, three were by Rich (*Behind Closed Doors*, *Very Special Love Songs*, *There Won't Be Anymore*) and two by Newton-John (*Let Me Be There*, *If You Love Me Let Me Know*). While both Newton-John's albums were named after hit country singles, this Australian beauty felt no allegiance to that music or audience, and was quickly aiming her white-bread image and emotionless voice at the pop market. Newton-John isn't a no-talent. Just a very little one.

SINGLES: If one has any doubt about Newton-John's vapidity, just compare her voice to that of Barbra Streisand on

"The Way We Were" and Aretha Franklin on "Until You Come Back To Me (That's What I'm Gonna Do)". Both were marvelous marriages of solid songs with exceptional singers that resulted in performances that still linger in memory.

On the flip side, it was a very weak year for male singers. There were some novelty hits (Jim Stafford's "Spiders and Snakes," Ray Stevens's "The Streak"), two mildly interesting one shots (Terry Jacks's "Seasons in the Sun," Al Wilson's "Show and Tell"), and far too many bland voices (David Essex's "Rock On," John Denver's "Annie's Song" and "Sunshine On My Shoulder," Ringo Starr's "You're Sixteen"). For songwriting craftsmanship, Maria Muldaur's "Midnight at the Oasis," Gordon Lightfoot's "Sundown," The Stylistics' "You Make Me Feel Brand New," and the Main Ingredient's "Just Don't Want To Be Lonely" were standouts and, not surprisingly, they have been re-recorded often.

Elton John

James Brown

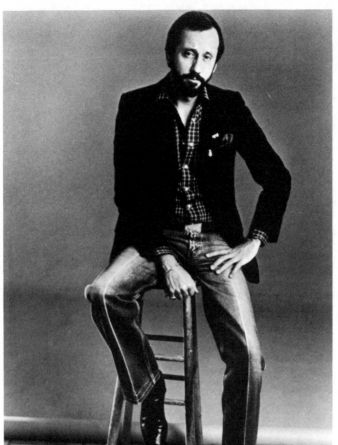

Ray Stevens

Herbie Hancock

JANUARY 5, 1974

POP SINGLES

1. TIME IN A BOTTLE
   (Jim Croce)
2. THE MOST BEAUTIFUL GIRL
   (Charlie Rich)
3. THE JOKER
   (The Steve Miller Band)
4. LEAVE ME ALONE (RUBY RED DRESS)
   (Helen Reddy)
5. HELEN WHEELS
   (Paul McCartney and Wings)
6. SHOW AND TELL
   (Al Wilson)
7. LIVING FOR THE CITY
   (Stevie Wonder)
8. SMOKIN' IN THE BOYS ROOM
   (Brownsville Station)
9. NEVER, NEVER GONNA GIVE YA UP
   (Barry White)
10. I'VE GOT TO USE MY IMAGINATION
    (Gladys Knight and the Pips)

POP ALBUMS

1. SINGLES 1969–1973
   (The Carpenters)
2. YOU DON'T MESS AROUND WITH JIM
   (Jim Croce)
3. GOODBYE YELLOW BRICK ROAD
   (Elton John)
4. I GOT A NAME
   (Jim Croce)
5. JONATHAN LIVINGSTON SEAGULL
   (Neil Diamond)
6. BETTE MIDLER
   (Bette Midler)
7. THE JOKER
   (The Steve Miller Band)
8. RINGO
   (Ringo Starr)
9. MIND GAMES
   (John Lennon)
10. BAND ON THE RUN
    (Paul McCartney and Wings)

BLACK SINGLES

1. I'VE GOT TO USE MY IMAGINATION
   (Gladys Knight and the Pips)
2. UNTIL YOU COME BACK TO ME
   (Aretha Franklin)
3. LIVING FOR THE CITY
   (Stevie Wonder)
4. THIS TIME I'M GONE FOR GOOD
   (Bobby "Blue" Bland)
5. LIVIN' FOR YOU
   (Al Green)
6. NEVER, NEVER GONNA GIVE YA UP
   (Barry White)
7. STONE TO THE BONE
   (James Brown)
8. SHOW AND TELL
   (Al Wilson)
9. IF YOU'RE READY (COME GO WITH ME)
   (The Staple Singers)
10. BABY COME CLOSE
    (Smokey Robinson)

BLACK ALBUMS

1. SHIP AHOY
   (The O'Jays)
2. IMAGINATION
   (Gladys Knight and the Pips)
3. STONE GON'
   (Barry White)
4. JOY
   (Isaac Hayes)

---

5. UNDER THE INFLUENCE OF LOVE UNLIMITED
   (Love Unlimited)
6. INNERVISIONS
   (Stevie Wonder)
7. BLACK AND BLUE
   (Harold Melvin and the Blue Notes)
8. LET'S GET IT ON
   (Marvin Gaye)
9. DELIVER THE WORD
   (War)
10. 3 PLUS 3
    (Isley Brothers)

JAZZ ALBUMS

1. SPECTRUM
   (Billy Cobham)
2. HEAD HUNTERS
   (Herbie Hancock)
3. TURTLE BAY
   (Herbie Mann)
4. WELCOME
   (Santana)
5. BETWEEN NOTHINGNESS AND ETERNITY
   (Mahavishnu Orchestra)
6. HYMN OF THE SEVENTH GALAXY
   (Return to Forever featuring Chick Corea)
7. UNSUNG HEROES
   (Crusaders)
8. DEODATO 2
   (Eumir Deodato)
9. SUPERFUNK
   (Funk Inc.)
10. CHAPTER ONE: LATIN AMERICA
    (Gato Barbieri)

COUNTRY SINGLES

1. SOMEWHERE BETWEEN LOVE AND TOMORROW
   (Roy Clark)
2. I LOVE
   (Tom T. Hall)
3. THE LAST LOVE SONG
   (Hank Williams Jr.)
4. IF WE MAKE IT THROUGH DECEMBER
   (Merle Haggard)
5. IF YOU CAN'T FEEL IT
   (Freddie Hart)
6. JOLENE
   (Dolly Parton)
7. THE MOST BEAUTIFUL GIRL
   (Charlie Rich)
8. HEY LORETTA
   (Loretta Lynn)
9. SONG AND DANCE MAN
   (Johnny Paycheck)
10. AMAZING LOVE
    (Charley Pride)

COUNTRY ALBUMS

1. BEHIND CLOSED DOORS
   (Charlie Rich)
2. ALL I EVER MEANT TO DO WAS SING
   (Johnny Rodriguez)
3. COME LIVE WITH ME
   (Roy Clark)
4. SAWMILL
   (Mel Tillis)
5. DON'T CRY NOW
   (Linda Ronstadt)
6. PRIMROSE LANE
   (Jerry Wallace)
7. YOU'VE NEVER BEEN THIS FAR BEFORE
   (Conway Twitty)
8. SOMETIMES A MEMORY AIN'T ENOUGH
   (Jerry Lee Lewis)
9. PAPER ROSES
   (Marie Osmond)
10. SATIN SHEETS
    (Jeanne Pruett)

JANUARY 12, 1974

POP SINGLES

1. THE JOKER
   (The Steve Miller Band)
2. TIME IN A BOTTLE
   (Jim Croce)
3. SHOW AND TELL
   (Al Wilson)
4. HELEN WHEELS
   (Paul McCartney and Wings)
5. LIVING FOR THE CITY
   (Stevie Wonder)
6. THE MOST BEAUTIFUL GIRL
   (Charlie Rich)
7. SMOKIN' IN THE BOYS ROOM
   (Brownsville Station)
8. I'VE GOT TO USE MY IMAGINATION
   (Gladys Knight and the Pips)
9. NEVER, NEVER GONNA GIVE YA UP
   (Barry White)
10. YOU'RE SIXTEEN
    (Ringo Starr)

POP ALBUMS

1. YOU DON'T MESS AROUND WITH JIM
   (Jim Croce)
2. I GOT A NAME
   (Jim Croce)
3. SINGLES 1969–1973
   (The Carpenters)
4. GOODBYE YELLOW BRICK ROAD
   (Elton John)
5. BETTE MIDLER
   (Bette Midler)
6. THE JOKER
   (The Steve Miller Band)
7. JONATHAN LIVINGSTON SEAGULL
   (Neil Diamond)
8. BAND ON THE RUN
   (Paul McCartney and Wings)
9. BRAIN SALAD SURGERY
   (Emerson, Lake and Palmer)
10. THE MUSCLE OF LOVE
    (Alice Cooper)

BLACK SINGLES

1. UNTIL YOU COME BACK TO ME
   (Aretha Franklin)
2. LIVING FOR THE CITY
   (Stevie Wonder)
3. I'VE GOT TO USE MY IMAGINATION
   (Gladys Knight and the Pips)
4. STONE TO THE BONE
   (James Brown)
5. THIS TIME I'M GONE FOR GOOD
   (Bobby "Blue" Bland)
6. LIVIN' FOR YOU
   (Al Green)
7. BABY COME CLOSE
   (Smokey Robinson)
8. SHOW AND TELL
   (Al Wilson)
9. NEVER, NEVER GONNA GIVE YA UP
   (Barry White)
10. LET YOUR HAIR DOWN
    (Temptations)

BLACK ALBUMS

1. STONE GON'
   (Barry White)
2. IMAGINATION
   (Gladys Knight and the Pips)
3. SHIP AHOY
   (The O'Jays)
4. JOY
   (Isaac Hayes)

5. UNDER THE INFLUENCE OF LOVE
   UNLIMITED
   (Love Unlimited)
6. INNERVISIONS
   (Stevie Wonder)
7. LIVIN' FOR YOU
   (Al Green)
8. BLACK AND BLUE
   (Harold Melvin and the Blue Notes)
9. DELIVER THE WORD
   (War)
10. ROCKIN' ROLL BABY
    (The Stylistics)

JAZZ ALBUMS

1. HEAD HUNTERS
   (Herbie Hancock)
2. SPECTRUM
   (Billy Cobham)
3. WELCOME
   (Santana)
4. BETWEEN NOTHINGNESS AND ETERNITY
   (Mahavishnu Orchestra)
5. TURTLE BAY
   (Herbie Mann)
6. HYMN OF THE SEVENTH GALAXY
   (Return to Forever featuring Chick Corea)
7. DEODATO 2
   (Eumir Deodato)
8. SUPERFUNK
   (Funk Inc.)
9. UNSUNG HEROES
   (Crusaders)
10. CHAPTER ONE: LATIN AMERICA
    (Gato Barbieri)

COUNTRY SINGLES

1. I LOVE
   (Tom T. Hall)
2. THE LAST LOVE SONG
   (Hank Williams Jr.)
3. JOLENE
   (Dolly Parton)
4. SOMEWHERE BETWEEN LOVE AND
   TOMORROW
   (Roy Clark)
5. IF WE MAKE IT THROUGH DECEMBER
   (Merle Haggard)
6. HEY LORETTA
   (Loretta Lynn)
7. SONG AND DANCE MAN
   (Johnny Paycheck)
8. STILL LOVING YOU
   (Bob Luman)
9. IF YOU CAN'T FEEL IT
   (Freddie Hart)
10. AMAZING LOVE
    (Charley Pride)

COUNTRY ALBUMS

1. BEHIND CLOSED DOORS
   (Charlie Rich)
2. COME LIVE WITH ME
   (Roy Clark)
3. SAWMILL
   (Mel Tillis)
4. ALL I EVER MEANT TO DO WAS SING
   (Johnny Rodriguez)
5. DON'T CRY NOW
   (Linda Ronstadt)
6. SOMETIMES A MEMORY AIN'T ENOUGH
   (Jerry Lee Lewis)
7. ROY CLARK'S FAMILY ALBUM
   (Roy Clark)
8. YOU'VE NEVER BEEN THIS FAR BEFORE
   (Conway Twitty)
9. WHERE MY HEART IS
   (Ronnie Milsap)
10. PRIMROSE LANE
    (Jerry Wallace)

JANUARY 19, 1974

POP SINGLES

1. SHOW AND TELL
   (Al Wilson)
2. YOU'RE SIXTEEN
   (Ringo Starr)
3. THE JOKER
   (The Steve Miller Band)
4. HELEN WHEELS
   (Paul McCartney and Wings)
5. LIVING FOR THE CITY
   (Stevie Wonder)
6. SMOKIN' IN THE BOYS ROOM
   (Brownsville Station)
7. I'VE GOT TO USE MY IMAGINATION
   (Gladys Knight and the Pips)
8. LET ME BE THERE
   (Olivia Newton-John)
9. THE WAY WE WERE
   (Barbra Streisand)
10. TIME IN A BOTTLE
    (Jim Croce)

POP ALBUMS

1. I GOT A NAME
   (Jim Croce)
2. YOU DON'T MESS AROUND WITH JIM
   (Jim Croce)
3. SINGLES 1969–1973
   (The Carpenters)
4. BETTE MIDLER
   (Bette Midler)
5. GOODBYE YELLOW BRICK ROAD
   (Elton John)
6. THE JOKER
   (The Steve Miller Band)
7. BAND ON THE RUN
   (Paul McCartney and Wings)
8. BRAIN SALAD SURGERY
   (Emerson, Lake and Palmer)
9. JONATHAN LIVINGSTON SEAGULL
   (Neil Diamond)
10. MUSCLE OF LOVE
    (Alice Cooper)

BLACK SINGLES

1. UNTIL YOU COME BACK TO ME
   (Aretha Franklin)
2. LIVING FOR THE CITY
   (Stevie Wonder)
3. I'VE GOT TO USE MY IMAGINATION
   (Gladys Knight and the Pips)
4. STONE TO THE BONE
   (James Brown)
5. LET YOUR HAIR DOWN
   (Temptations)
6. BABY COME CLOSE
   (Smokey Robinson)
7. WHAT IT COMES DOWN TO
   (Isley Brothers)
8. I MISS YOU
   (The Dells)
9. PUT YOUR HANDS TOGETHER
   (The O'Jays)
10. JUNGLE BOOGIE
    (Kool and the Gang)

BLACK ALBUMS

1. STONE GON'
   (Barry White)
2. IMAGINATION
   (Gladys Knight and the Pips)
3. SHIP AHOY
   (The O'Jays)
4. JOY
   (Isaac Hayes)

5. UNDER THE INFLUENCE OF LOVE
   UNLIMITED
   (Love Unlimited)
6. LIVIN' FOR YOU
   (Al Green)
7. INNERVISIONS
   (Stevie Wonder)
8. 1990
   (Temptations)
9. DELIVER THE WORD
   (War)
10. WILD AND PEACEFUL
    (Kool and the Gang)

JAZZ ALBUMS

1. HEAD HUNTERS
   (Herbie Hancock)
2. SPECTRUM
   (Billy Cobham)
3. BETWEEN NOTHINGNESS AND ETERNITY
   (Mahavishnu Orchestra)
4. WELCOME
   (Santana)
5. TURTLE BAY
   (Herbie Mann)
6. DEODATO 2
   (Eumir Deodato)
7. SWEETNIGHTER
   (Weather Report)
8. HYMN OF THE SEVENTH GALAXY
   (Return to Forever featuring Chick Corea)
9. UNSUNG HEROES
   (Crusaders)
10. SUPERFUNK
    (Funk Inc.)

COUNTRY SINGLES

1. JOLENE
   (Dolly Parton)
2. THE LAST LOVE SONG
   (Hank Williams Jr.)
3. I LOVE
   (Tom T. Hall)
4. HEY LORETTA
   (Loretta Lynn)
5. IF WE MAKE IT THROUGH DECEMBER
   (Merle Haggard)
6. SONG AND DANCE MAN
   (Johnny Paycheck)
7. STILL LOVING YOU
   (Bob Luman)
8. ONCE YOU'VE HAD THE BEST
   (George Jones)
9. SOMEWHERE BETWEEN LOVE AND
   TOMORROW
   (Roy Clark)
10. LOVIN' ON BORROWED TIME
    (Mel Street)

COUNTRY ALBUMS

1. BEHIND CLOSED DOORS
   (Charlie Rich)
2. COME LIVE WITH ME
   (Roy Clark)
3. SAWMILL
   (Mel Tillis)
4. ROY CLARK'S FAMILY ALBUM
   (Roy Clark)
5. SOMETIMES A MEMORY AIN'T ENOUGH
   (Jerry Lee Lewis)
6. WHERE MY HEART IS
   (Ronnie Milsap)
7. ALL I EVER MEANT TO DO WAS SING
   (Johnny Rodriguez)
8. YOU'VE NEVER BEEN THIS FAR BEFORE
   (Conway Twitty)
9. DON'T CRY NOW
   (Linda Ronstadt)
10. AMAZING LOVE
    (Charley Pride)

JANUARY 26, 1974

POP SINGLES

1. YOU'RE SIXTEEN
   (Ringo Starr)
2. SHOW AND TELL
   (Al Wilson)
3. THE WAY WE WERE
   (Barbra Streisand)
4. SMOKIN' IN THE BOYS ROOM
   (Brownsville Station)
5. I'VE GOT TO USE MY IMAGINATION
   (Gladys Knight and the Pips)
6. AMERICANS
   (Byron MacGregor)
7. LET ME BE THERE
   (Olivia Newton-John)
8. LIVING FOR THE CITY
   (Stevie Wonder)
9. LOVE'S THEME
   (Love Unlimited Orchestra)
10. UNTIL YOU COME BACK TO ME
    (Aretha Franklin)

POP ALBUMS

1. I GOT A NAME
   (Jim Croce)
2. YOU DON'T MESS AROUND WITH JIM
   (Jim Croce)
3. SINGLES 1969-1973
   (The Carpenters)
4. BETTE MIDLER
   (Bette Midler)
5. THE JOKER
   (The Steve Miller Band)
6. BAND ON THE RUN
   (Paul McCartney and Wings)
7. BRAIN SALAD SURGERY
   (Emerson, Lake and Palmer)
8. JOHN DENVER'S GREATEST HITS, VOL. 1
   (John Denver)
9. BEHIND CLOSED DOORS
   (Charlie Rich)
10. GOODBYE YELLOW BRICK ROAD
    (Elton John)

BLACK SINGLES

1. PUT YOUR HANDS TOGETHER
   (The O'Jays)
2. UNTIL YOU COME BACK TO ME
   (Aretha Franklin)
3. LET YOUR HAIR DOWN
   (Temptations)
4. LIVING FOR THE CITY
   (Stevie Wonder)
5. WHAT IT COMES DOWN TO
   (Isley Brothers)
6. I'VE GOT TO USE MY IMAGINATION
   (Gladys Knight and the Pips)
7. I MISS YOU
   (The Dells)
8. TRYING TO HOLD ON TO MY WOMAN
   (Lamont Dozier)
9. JUNGLE BOOGIE
   (Kool and the Gang)
10. SEXY MAMA
    (The Moments)

BLACK ALBUMS

1. STONE GON'
   (Barry White)
2. IMAGINATION
   (Gladys Knight and the Pips)
3. SHIP AHOY
   (The O'Jays)
4. LIVIN' FOR YOU
   (Al Green)

5. UNDER THE INFLUENCE OF LOVE UNLIMITED
   (Love Unlimited)
6. JOY
   (Isaac Hayes)
7. INNERVISIONS
   (Stevie Wonder)
8. 1990
   (Temptations)
9. ROCKIN' ROLL BABY
   (The Stylistics)
10. WILD AND PEACEFUL
    (Kool and the Gang)

JAZZ ALBUMS

1. HEAD HUNTERS
   (Herbie Hancock)
2. SPECTRUM
   (Billy Cobham)
3. TURTLE BAY
   (Herbie Mann)
4. DEODATO 2
   (Eumir Deodato)
5. WELCOME
   (Santana)
6. BETWEEN NOTHINGNESS AND ETERNITY
   (Mahavishnu Orchestra)
7. SWEETNIGHTER
   (Weather Report)
8. GIANT BOX
   (Don Sebesky)
9. UNSUNG HEROES
   (Crusaders)
10. HYMNS OF THE SEVENTH GALAXY
    (Return to Forever featuring Chick Corea)

COUNTRY SINGLES

1. I LOVE
   (Tom T. Hall)
2. JOLENE
   (Dolly Parton)
3. HEY LORETTA
   (Loretta Lynn)
4. THE LAST LOVE SONG
   (Hank Williams Jr.)
5. ONCE YOU'VE HAD THE BEST
   (George Jones)
6. SONG AND DANCE MAN
   (Johnny Paycheck)
7. IF WE MAKE IT THROUGH DECEMBER
   (Merle Haggard)
8. GIRL WHO WAITS ON TABLES
   (Ronnie Milsap)
9. SOMEWHERE BETWEEN LOVE AND TOMORROW
   (Roy Clark)
10. LOVIN' ON BORROWED TIME
    (Mel Street)

COUNTRY ALBUMS

1. BEHIND CLOSED DOORS
   (Charlie Rich)
2. ROY CLARK'S FAMILY ALBUM
   (Roy Clark)
3. COME LIVE WITH ME
   (Roy Clark)
4. WHERE MY HEART IS
   (Ronnie Milsap)
5. SAWMILL
   (Mel Tillis)
6. SOMETIMES A MEMORY AIN'T ENOUGH
   (Jerry Lee Lewis)
7. YOU'VE NEVER BEEN THIS FAR BEFORE
   (Conway Twitty)
8. AMAZING LOVE
   (Charley Pride)
9. ALL I EVER MEANT TO DO WAS SING
   (Johnny Rodriguez)
10. ALL ABOUT A FEELING
    (Donna Fargo)

FEBRUARY 2, 1974

POP SINGLES

1. THE WAY WE WERE
   (Barbra Streisand)
2. YOU'RE SIXTEEN
   (Ringo Starr)
3. AMERICANS
   (Byron MacGregor)
4. SMOKIN' IN THE BOYS ROOM
   (Brownsville Station)
5. I'VE GOT TO USE MY IMAGINATION
   (Gladys Knight and the Pips)
6. LOVE'S THEME
   (Love Unlimited Orchestra)
7. LET ME BE THERE
   (Olivia Newton-John)
8. UNTIL YOU COME BACK TO ME
   (Aretha Franklin)
9. SHOW AND TELL
   (Al Wilson)
10. LIVING FOR THE CITY
    (Stevie Wonder)

POP ALBUMS

1. YOU DON'T MESS AROUND WITH JIM
   (Jim Croce)
2. I GOT A NAME
   (Jim Croce)
3. SINGLES 1969-1973
   (The Carpenters)
4. BEHIND CLOSED DOORS
   (Charlie Rich)
5. JOHN DENVER'S GREATEST HITS, VOL. 1
   (John Denver)
6. THE JOKER
   (The Steve Miller Band)
7. BAND ON THE RUN
   (Paul McCartney and Wings)
8. BETTE MIDLER
   (Bette Midler)
9. BRAIN SALAD SURGERY
   (Emerson, Lake and Palmer)
10. GOODBYE YELLOW BRICK ROAD
    (Elton John)

BLACK SINGLES

1. PUT YOUR HANDS TOGETHER
   (The O'Jays)
2. UNTIL YOU COME BACK TO ME
   (Aretha Franklin)
3. LET YOUR HAIR DOWN
   (Temptations)
4. WHAT IT COMES DOWN TO
   (Isley Brothers)
5. JUNGLE BOOGIE
   (Kool and the Gang)
6. TRYING TO HOLD ON TO MY WOMAN
   (Lamont Dozier)
7. I MISS YOU
   (The Dells)
8. SEXY MAMA
   (The Moments)
9. CAN THIS BE REAL
   (The Natural Four)
10. BOOGIE DOWN
    (Eddie Kendricks)

BLACK ALBUMS

1. SHIP AHOY
   (The O'Jays)
2. STONE GON'
   (Barry White)
3. IMAGINATION
   (Gladys Knight and the Pips)
4. LIVIN' FOR YOU
   (Al Green)

5. 1990
   (Temptations)
6. UNDER THE INFLUENCE OF LOVE
   UNLIMITED
   (Love Unlimited)
7. JOY
   (Isaac Hayes)
8. INNERVISIONS
   (Stevie Wonder)
9. WILD AND PEACEFUL
   (Kool and the Gang)
10. THE PAYBACK
    (James Brown)

JAZZ ALBUMS

1. HEAD HUNTERS
   (Herbie Hancock)
2. SPECTRUM
   (Billy Cobham)
3. TURTLE BAY
   (Herbie Mann)
4. DEODATO 2
   (Eumir Deodato)
5. SWEETNIGHTER
   (Weather Report)
6. GIANT BOX
   (Don Sebesky)
7. WELCOME
   (Santana)
8. UNSUNG HEROES
   (Crusaders)
9. BETWEEN NOTHINGNESS AND ETERNITY
   (Mahavishnu Orchestra)
10. SUPERFUNK
    (Funk Inc.)

COUNTRY SINGLES

1. HEY LORETTA
   (Loretta Lynn)
2. I LOVE
   (Tom T. Hall)
3. JOLENE
   (Dolly Parton)
4. ONCE YOU'VE HAD THE BEST
   (George Jones)
5. GIRL WHO WAITS ON TABLES
   (Ronnie Milsap)
6. WORLD OF MAKE BELIEVE
   (Bill Anderson)
7. I'M STILL LOVIN' YOU
   (Joe Stampley)
8. THE LAST LOVE SONG
   (Hank Williams Jr.)
9. BIG GAME HUNTER
   (Buck Owens)
10. LOVE SONG
    (Anne Murray)

COUNTRY ALBUMS

1. ROY CLARK'S FAMILY ALBUM
   (Roy Clark)
2. BEHIND CLOSED DOORS
   (Charlie Rich)
3. WHERE MY HEART IS
   (Ronnie Milsap)
4. COME LIVE WITH ME
   (Roy Clark)
5. AMAZING LOVE
   (Charley Pride)
6. ALL ABOUT A FEELING
   (Donna Fargo)
7. YOU'VE NEVER BEEN THIS FAR BEFORE
   (Conway Twitty)
8. THE FASTEST HARP IN THE SOUTH
   (Charlie McCoy)
9. IF YOU CAN'T FEEL IT
   (Freddie Hart)
10. SAWMILL
    (Mel Tillis)

FEBRUARY 9, 1974

POP SINGLES

1. AMERICANS
   (Byron MacGregor)
2. THE WAY WE WERE
   (Barbra Streisand)
3. LOVE'S THEME
   (Love Unlimited Orchestra)
4. YOU'RE SIXTEEN
   (Ringo Starr)
5. UNTIL YOU COME BACK TO ME
   (Aretha Franklin)
6. LET ME BE THERE
   (Olivia Newton-John)
7. SMOKIN' IN THE BOYS ROOM
   (Brownsville Station)
8. I'VE GOT TO USE MY IMAGINATION
   (Gladys Knight and the Pips)
9. SPIDERS AND SNAKES
   (Jim Stafford)
10. SHOW AND TELL
    (Al Wilson)

POP ALBUMS

1. YOU DON'T MESS AROUND WITH JIM
   (Jim Croce)
2. JOHN DENVER'S GREATEST HITS, VOL. 1
   (John Denver)
3. BEHIND CLOSED DOORS
   (Charlie Rich)
4. I GOT A NAME
   (Jim Croce)
5. SINGLES 1969–1973
   (The Carpenters)
6. BAND ON THE RUN
   (Paul McCartney and Wings)
7. THE JOKER
   (The Steve Miller Band)
8. UNDER THE INFLUENCE OF LOVE
   UNLIMITED
   (Love Unlimited)
9. SHIP AHOY
   (The O'Jays)
10. GOODBYE YELLOW BRICK ROAD
    (Elton John)

BLACK SINGLES

1. PUT YOUR HANDS TOGETHER
   (The O'Jays)
2. JUNGLE BOOGIE
   (Kool and the Gang)
3. BOOGIE DOWN
   (Eddie Kendricks)
4. SEXY MAMA
   (The Moments)
5. CAN THIS BE REAL
   (The Natural Four)
6. TRYING TO HOLD ON TO MY WOMAN
   (Lamont Dozier)
7. WHAT IT COMES DOWN TO
   (Isley Brothers)
8. I LIKE TO LIVE THE LOVE
   (B.B. King)
9. UNTIL YOU COME BACK TO ME
   (Aretha Franklin)
10. LOVE'S THEME
    (Love Unlimited Orchestra)

BLACK ALBUMS

1. SHIP AHOY
   (The O'Jays)
2. STONE GON'
   (Barry White)
3. LIVIN' FOR YOU
   (Al Green)
4. 1990
   (Temptations)

5. UNDER THE INFLUENCE OF LOVE
   UNLIMITED
   (Love Unlimited)
6. IMAGINATION
   (Gladys Knight and the Pips)
7. WILD AND PEACEFUL
   (Kool and the Gang)
8. THE PAYBACK
   (James Brown)
9. INNERVISIONS
   (Stevie Wonder)
10. LAST TIME I SAW HIM
    (Diana Ross)

JAZZ ALBUMS

1. HEAD HUNTERS
   (Herbie Hancock)
2. SPECTRUM
   (Billy Cobham)
3. DEODATO 2
   (Eumir Deodato)
4. TURTLE BAY
   (Herbie Mann)
5. GIANT BOX
   (Don Sebesky)
6. SWEETNIGHTER
   (Weather Report)
7. UNSUNG HEROES
   (Crusaders)
8. LIVE CONCERT IN JAPAN
   (John Coltrane)
9. SUPERFUNK
   (Funk Inc.)
10. BLACK BYRD
    (Donald Byrd)

COUNTRY SINGLES

1. ONCE YOU'VE HAD THE BEST
   (George Jones)
2. WORLD OF MAKE BELIEVE
   (Bill Anderson)
3. I'M STILL LOVIN' YOU
   (Joe Stampley)
4. I LOVE
   (Tom T. Hall)
5. GIRL WHO WAITS ON TABLES
   (Ronnie Milsap)
6. THERE WON'T BE ANYMORE
   (Charlie Rich)
7. THAT'S THE WAY LOVE GOES
   (Johnny Rodriguez)
8. A LOVE SONG
   (Anne Murray)
9. HEY LORETTA
   (Loretta Lynn)
10. THE RIVER'S TOO WIDE
    (Jim Mundy)

COUNTRY ALBUMS

1. ROY CLARK'S FAMILY ALBUM
   (Roy Clark)
2. BEHIND CLOSED DOORS
   (Charlie Rich)
3. WHERE MY HEART IS
   (Ronnie Milsap)
4. AMAZING LOVE
   (Charley Pride)
5. ALL ABOUT A FEELING
   (Donna Fargo)
6. THE FASTEST HARP IN THE SOUTH
   (Charlie McCoy)
7. IF YOU CAN'T FEEL IT
   (Freddie Hart)
8. COME LIVE WITH ME
   (Roy Clark)
9. THE MIDNIGHT OIL
   (Barbara Mandrell)
10. LET ME BE THERE
    (Olivia Newton-John)

FEBRUARY 16, 1974

POP SINGLES

1. LOVE'S THEME
   (Love Unlimited Orchestra)
2. THE WAY WE WERE
   (Barbra Streisand)
3. AMERICANS
   (Byron MacGregor)
4. UNTIL YOU COME BACK TO ME
   (Aretha Franklin)
5. YOU'RE SIXTEEN
   (Ringo Starr)
6. LET ME BE THERE
   (Olivia Newton-John)
7. SPIDERS AND SNAKES
   (Jim Stafford)
8. JUNGLE BOOGIE
   (Kool and the Gang)
9. SEASONS IN THE SUN
   (Terry Jacks)
10. ROCK ON
    (David Essex)

POP ALBUMS

1. YOU DON'T MESS AROUND WITH JIM
   (Jim Croce)
2. JOHN DENVER'S GREATEST HITS, VOL. 1
   (John Denver)
3. BEHIND CLOSED DOORS
   (Charlie Rich)
4. UNDER THE INFLUENCE OF LOVE
   UNLIMITED
   (Love Unlimited)
5. I GOT A NAME
   (Jim Croce)
6. BAND ON THE RUN
   (Paul McCartney and Wings)
7. THE JOKER
   (The Steve Miller Band)
8. SHIP AHOY
   (The O'Jays)
9. SINGLES 1969–1973
   (The Carpenters)
10. GOODBYE YELLOW BRICK ROAD
    (Elton John)

BLACK SINGLES

1. JUNGLE BOOGIE
   (Kool and the Gang)
2. BOOGIE DOWN
   (Eddie Kendricks)
3. SEXY MAMA
   (The Moments)
4. PUT YOUR HANDS TOGETHER
   (The O'Jays)
5. CAN THIS BE REAL
   (The Natural Four)
6. TRYING TO HOLD ON TO MY WOMAN
   (Lamont Dozier)
7. I LIKE TO LIVE THE LOVE
   (B.B. King)
8. I'LL BE THE OTHER WOMAN
   (The Soul Children)
9. LOVE'S THEME
   (Love Unlimited Orchestra)
10. STOP TO START
    (Blue Magic)

BLACK ALBUMS

1. SHIP AHOY
   (The O'Jays)
2. STONE GON'
   (Barry White)
3. LIVIN' FOR YOU
   (Al Green)

---

4. UNDER THE INFLUENCE OF LOVE
   UNLIMITED
   (Love Unlimited)
5. WILD AND PEACEFUL
   (Kool and the Gang)
6. 1990
   (Temptations)
7. LOVE IS THE MESSAGE
   (MFSB)
8. THE PAYBACK
   (James Brown)
9. IMAGINATION
   (Gladys Knight and the Pips)
10. INNERVISIONS
    (Stevie Wonder)

JAZZ ALBUMS

1. HEAD HUNTERS
   (Herbie Hancock)
2. SPECTRUM
   (Billy Cobham)
3. DEODATO 2
   (Eumir Deodato)
4. GIANT BOX
   (Don Sebesky)
5. TURTLE BAY
   (Herbie Mann)
6. SWEETNIGHTER
   (Weather Report)
7. LIVE CONCERT IN JAPAN
   (John Coltrane)
8. UNSUNG HEROES
   (Crusaders)
9. BLACK BYRD
   (Donald Byrd)
10. SUPERFUNK
    (Funk Inc.)

COUNTRY SINGLES

1. WORLD OF MAKE BELIEVE
   (Bill Anderson)
2. THAT'S THE WAY LOVE GOES
   (Johnny Rodriguez)
3. I'M STILL LOVING YOU
   (Joe Stampley)
4. THERE WON'T BE ANYMORE
   (Charlie Rich)
5. DADDY WHAT IF
   (Bobby Bare)
6. ANOTHER LONELY SONG
   (Tammy Wynette)
7. LOVE SONG
   (Anne Murray)
8. ONCE YOU'VE HAD THE BEST
   (George Jones)
9. THE RIVER'S TOO WIDE
   (Jim Mundy)
10. SOMETIME SUNSHINE
    (Jim Ed Brown)

COUNTRY ALBUMS

1. AMAZING LOVE
   (Charley Pride)
2. BEHIND CLOSED DOORS
   (Charlie Rich)
3. THE FASTEST HARP IN THE SOUTH
   (Charlie McCoy)
4. ALL ABOUT A FEELING
   (Donna Fargo)
5. ROY CLARK'S FAMILY ALBUM
   (Roy Clark)
6. LET ME BE THERE
   (Olivia Newton-John)
7. IF YOU CAN'T FEEL IT
   (Freddie Hart)
8. FOR THE PEOPLE IN THE LAST HARD
   TOWN
   (Tom T. Hall)
9. THE MIDNIGHT OIL
   (Barbara Mandrell)
10. WHERE MY HEART IS
    (Ronnie Milsap)

FEBRUARY 23, 1974

POP SINGLES

1. SEASONS IN THE SUN
   (Terry Jacks)
2. THE WAY WE WERE
   (Barbra Streisand)
3. LOVE'S THEME
   (Love Unlimited Orchestra)
4. UNTIL YOU COME BACK TO ME
   (Aretha Franklin)
5. SPIDERS AND SNAKES
   (Jim Stafford)
6. JUNGLE BOOGIE
   (Kool and the Gang)
7. BOOGIE DOWN
   (Eddie Kendricks)
8. ROCK ON
   (David Essex)
9. YOU'RE SIXTEEN
   (Ringo Starr)
10. LAST TIME I SAW HIM
    (Diana Ross)

POP ALBUMS

1. PLANET WAVES
   (Bob Dylan)
2. JOHN DENVER'S GREATEST HITS, VOL. 1
   (John Denver)
3. BEHIND CLOSED DOORS
   (Charlie Rich)
4. UNDER THE INFLUENCE OF LOVE
   UNLIMITED
   (Love Unlimited)
5. YOU DON'T MESS AROUND WITH JIM
   (Jim Croce)
6. COURT AND SPARK
   (Joni Mitchell)
7. BAND ON THE RUN
   (Paul McCartney and Wings)
8. SHIP AHOY
   (The O'Jays)
9. TALES FROM TOPOGRAPHIC OCEANS
   (Yes)
10. HOTCAKES
    (Carly Simon)

BLACK SINGLES

1. BOOGIE DOWN
   (Eddie Kendricks)
2. JUNGLE BOOGIE
   (Kool and the Gang)
3. SEXY MAMA
   (The Moments)
4. I'LL BE THE OTHER WOMAN
   (The Soul Children)
5. TRYING TO HOLD ON TO MY WOMAN
   (Lamont Dozier)
6. I LIKE TO LIVE THE LOVE
   (B.B. King)
7. PUT YOUR HANDS TOGETHER
   (The O'Jays)
8. LOVE'S THEME
   (Love Unlimited Orchestra)
9. STOP TO START
   (Blue Magic)
10. MIGHTY LOVE, PART 1
    (Spinners)

BLACK ALBUMS

1. SHIP AHOY
   (The O'Jays)
2. LOVE IS THE MESSAGE
   (MFSB)
3. WILD AND PEACEFUL
   (Kool and the Gang)

4. STONE GON'
(Barry White)
5. LIVIN' FOR YOU
(Al Green)
6. THE PAYBACK
(James Brown)
7. 1990
(Temptations)
8. UNDER THE INFLUENCE OF LOVE
UNLIMITED
(Love Unlimited)
9. IMAGINATION
(Gladys Knight and the Pips)
10. SHOW AND TELL
(Al Wilson)

JAZZ ALBUMS

1. HEAD HUNTERS
(Herbie Hancock)
2. SPECTRUM
(Billy Cobham)
3. GIANT BOX
(Don Sebesky)
4. DEODATO 2
(Eumir Deodato)
5. SWEETNIGHTER
(Weather Report)
6. TURTLE BAY
(Herbie Mann)
7. UNSUNG HEROES
(Crusaders)
8. BLACK BYRD
(Donald Byrd)
9. LIVE CONCERT IN JAPAN
(John Coltrane)
10. KEEP YOUR SOUL TOGETHER
(Freddie Hubbard)

COUNTRY SINGLES

1. THAT'S THE WAY LOVE GOES
(Johnny Rodriguez)
2. I'M STILL LOVING YOU
(Joe Stampley)
3. THERE WON'T BE ANYMORE
(Charlie Rich)
4. DADDY WHAT IF
(Bobby Bare)
5. ANOTHER LONELY SONG
(Tammy Wynette)
6. LOVE SONG
(Anne Murray)
7. WORLD OF MAKE BELIEVE
(Bill Anderson)
8. SOMETIME SUNSHINE
(Jim Ed Brown)
9. I'VE JUST GOT TO KNOW
(Freddy Weller)
10. THERE'S A HONKY TONK ANGEL
(Conway Twitty)

COUNTRY ALBUMS

1. AMAZING LOVE
(Charley Pride)
2. THE FASTEST HARP IN THE SOUTH
(Charlie McCoy)
3. BEHIND CLOSED DOORS
(Charlie Rich)
4. ALL ABOUT A FEELING
(Donna Fargo)
5. LET ME BE THERE
(Olivia Newton-John)
6. FOR THE PEOPLE IN THE LAST HARD
TOWN
(Tom T. Hall)
7. ROY CLARK'S FAMILY ALBUM
(Roy Clark)
8. SOUTHERN ROOTS
(Jerry Lee Lewis)
9. BOBBY BARE SINGS "LULLABYS, LEGENDS
AND LIES"
(Bobby Bare)

10. WE'RE GONNA HOLD ON
(George Jones and Tammy Wynette)

MARCH 2, 1974

POP SINGLES

1. SEASONS IN THE SUN
(Terry Jacks)
2. THE WAY WE WERE
(Barbra Streisand)
3. BOOGIE DOWN
(Eddie Kendricks)
4. SPIDERS AND SNAKES
(Jim Stafford)
5. JUNGLE BOOGIE
(Kool and the Gang)
6. ROCK ON
(David Essex)
7. LOVE'S THEME
(Love Unlimited Orchestra)
8. DARK LADY
(Cher)
9. LAST TIME I SAW HIM
(Diana Ross)
10. UNTIL YOU COME BACK TO ME
(Aretha Franklin)

POP ALBUMS

1. PLANET WAVES
(Bob Dylan)
2. COURT AND SPARK
(Joni Mitchell)
3. JOHN DENVER'S GREATEST HITS, VOL. 1
(John Denver)
4. BEHIND CLOSED DOORS
(Charlie Rich)
5. HOTCAKES
(Carly Simon)
6. YOU DON'T MESS AROUND WITH JIM
(Jim Croce)
7. TALES FROM TOPOGRAPHIC OCEANS
(Yes)
8. BAND ON THE RUN
(Paul McCartney and Wings)
9. UNDER THE INFLUENCE OF LOVE
UNLIMITED
(Love Unlimited)
10. SHIP AHOY
(The O'Jays)

BLACK SINGLES

1. BOOGIE DOWN
(Eddie Kendricks)
2. I'LL BE THE OTHER WOMAN
(The Soul Children)
3. JUNGLE BOOGIE
(Kool and the Gang)
4. TRYING TO HOLD ON TO MY WOMAN
(Lamont Dozier)
5. MIGHTY LOVE, PART 1
(Spinners)
6. I LIKE TO LIVE THE LOVE
(B.B. King)
7. LOVE'S THEME
(Love Unlimited Orchestra)
8. STOP TO START
(Blue Magic)
9. WE'RE GETTING CARELESS WITH OUR
LOVE
(Johnnie Taylor)
10. SEXY MAMA
(The Moments)

BLACK ALBUMS

1. LOVE IS THE MESSAGE
(MFSB)

2. SHIP AHOY
(The O'Jays)
3. WILD AND PEACEFUL
(Kool and the Gang)
4. RHAPSODY IN WHITE
(Love Unlimited Orchestra)
5. STONE GON'
(Barry White)
6. THE PAYBACK
(James Brown)
7. LIVIN' FOR YOU
(Al Green)
8. UNDER THE INFLUENCE OF LOVE
UNLIMITED
(Love Unlimited)
9. 1990
(Temptations)
10. SHOW AND TELL
(Al Wilson)

JAZZ ALBUMS

1. HEAD HUNTERS
(Herbie Hancock)
2. SPECTRUM
(Billy Cobham)
3. GIANT BOX
(Don Sebesky)
4. DEODATO 2
(Eumir Deodato)
5. SWEETNIGHTER
(Weather Report)
6. UNSUNG HEROES
(Crusaders)
7. KEEP YOUR SOUL TOGETHER
(Freddie Hubbard)
8. BLACK BYRD
(Donald Byrd)
9. TURTLE BAY
(Herbie Mann)
10. WILDFLOWER
(Hank Crawford)

COUNTRY SINGLES

1. THERE WON'T BE ANYMORE
(Charlie Rich)
2. DADDY WHAT IF
(Bobby Bare)
3. ANOTHER LONELY SONG
(Tammy Wynette)
4. THAT'S THE WAY LOVE GOES
(Johnny Rodriguez)
5. I'M STILL LOVING YOU
(Joe Stampley)
6. LOVE SONG
(Anne Murray)
7. THERE'S A HONKY TONK ANGEL
(Conway Twitty)
8. WORLD OF MAKE BELIEVE
(Bill Anderson)
9. SWEET MAGNOLIA BLOSSOM
(Billy "Crash" Craddock)
10. WOULD YOU LAY WITH ME
(Tanya Tucker)

COUNTRY ALBUMS

1. AMAZING LOVE
(Charley Pride)
2. BEHIND CLOSED DOORS
(Charlie Rich)
3. FOR THE PEOPLE IN THE LAST HARD
TOWN
(Tom T. Hall)
4. LET ME BE THERE
(Olivia Newton-John)
5. THE FASTEST HARP IN THE SOUTH
(Charlie McCoy)
6. BOBBY BARE SINGS "LULLABYS, LEGENDS
AND LIES"
(Bobby Bare)
7. SOUTHERN ROOTS
(Jerry Lee Lewis)

8. WE'RE GONNA HOLD ON
   (George Jones and Tammy Wynette)
9. ALL ABOUT A FEELING
   (Donna Fargo)
10. ROY CLARK'S FAMILY ALBUM
    (Roy Clark)

MARCH 9, 1974

POP SINGLES

1. SEASONS IN THE SUN
   (Terry Jacks)
2. BOOGIE DOWN
   (Eddie Kendricks)
3. THE WAY WE WERE
   (Barbra Streisand)
4. ROCK ON
   (David Essex)
5. DARK LADY
   (Cher)
6. SPIDERS AND SNAKES
   (Jim Stafford)
7. SUNSHINE ON MY SHOULDERS
   (John Denver)
8. MOCKINGBIRD
   (Carly Simon and James Taylor)
9. LAST TIME I SAW HIM
   (Diana Ross)
10. JET
    (Paul McCartney and Wings)

POP ALBUMS

1. COURT AND SPARK
   (Joni Mitchell)
2. THE WAY WE WERE
   (Barbra Streisand)
3. PLANET WAVES
   (Bob Dylan)
4. BEHIND CLOSED DOORS
   (Charlie Rich)
5. JOHN DENVER'S GREATEST HITS, VOL. 1
   (John Denver)
6. HOTCAKES
   (Carly Simon)
7. TALES FROM TOPOGRAPHIC OCEANS
   (Yes)
8. YOU DON'T MESS AROUND WITH JIM
   (Jim Croce)
9. BAND ON THE RUN
   (Paul McCartney and Wings)
10. TUBULAR BELLS
    (Mike Oldfield)

BLACK SINGLES

1. MIGHTY LOVE, PART 1
   (Spinners)
2. I'LL BE THE OTHER WOMAN
   (The Soul Children)
3. BOOGIE DOWN
   (Eddie Kendricks)
4. JUNGLE BOOGIE
   (Kool and the Gang)
5. TRYING TO HOLD ON TO MY WOMAN
   (Lamont Dozier)
6. WE'RE GETTING CARELESS WITH OUR LOVE
   (Johnnie Taylor)
7. I LIKE TO LIVE THE LOVE
   (B.B. King)
8. LOVE'S THEME
   (Love Unlimited Orchestra)
9. LOOKIN' FOR A LOVE
   (Bobby Womack)
10. BEST THING THAT EVER HAPPENED TO ME
    (Gladys Knight and the Pips)

BLACK ALBUMS

1. LOVE IS THE MESSAGE
   (MFSB)
2. RHAPSODY IN WHITE
   (Love Unlimited Orchestra)
3. SHIP AHOY
   (The O'Jays)
4. WILD AND PEACEFUL
   (Kool and the Gang)
5. LIVIN' FOR YOU
   (Al Green)
6. 1990
   (Temptations)
7. THE PAYBACK
   (James Brown)
8. STONE GON'
   (Barry White)
9. TO KNOW YOU IS TO LOVE YOU
   (B.B. King)
10. IT'S BEEN A LONG TIME
    (New Birth)

JAZZ ALBUMS

1. HEAD HUNTERS
   (Herbie Hancock)
2. SPECTRUM
   (Billy Cobham)
3. DEODATO 2
   (Eumir Deodato)
4. GIANT BOX
   (Don Sebesky)
5. SWEETNIGHTER
   (Weather Report)
6. KEEP YOUR SOUL TOGETHER
   (Freddie Hubbard)
7. UNSUNG HEROES
   (Crusaders)
8. BLACK BYRD
   (Donald Byrd)
9. WILDFLOWER
   (Hank Crawford)
10. BLACK-EYED BLUES
    (Esther Phillips)

COUNTRY SINGLES

1. DADDY WHAT IF
   (Bobby Bare)
2. ANOTHER LONELY SONG
   (Tammy Wynette)
3. THERE WON'T BE ANYMORE
   (Charlie Rich)
4. THERE'S A HONKY TONK ANGEL
   (Conway Twitty)
5. THAT'S THE WAY LOVE GOES
   (Johnny Rodriguez)
6. SWEET MAGNOLIA BLOSSOM
   (Billy "Crash" Craddock)
7. WOULD YOU LAY WITH ME
   (Tanya Tucker)
8. LOVE SONG
   (Anne Murray)
9. LOVING YOU HAS CHANGED MY LIFE
   (David Rogers)
10. LUCKY LADIES
    (Jeannie Seely)

COUNTRY ALBUMS

1. FOR THE PEOPLE IN THE LAST HARD TOWN
   (Tom T. Hall)
2. BEHIND CLOSED DOORS
   (Charlie Rich)
3. LET ME BE THERE
   (Olivia Newton-John)
4. BOBBY BARE SINGS "LULLABYS, LEGENDS AND LIES"
   (Bobby Bare)
5. AMAZING LOVE
   (Charley Pride)

6. WE'RE GONNA HOLD ON
   (George Jones and Tammy Wynette)
7. SOUTHERN ROOTS
   (Jerry Lee Lewis)
8. THE FASTEST HARP IN THE SOUTH
   (Charlie McCoy)
9. I REMEMBER HANK WILLIAMS
   (Glen Campbell)
10. ROY CLARK'S FAMILY ALBUM
    (Roy Clark)

MARCH 16, 1974

POP SINGLES

1. BOOGIE DOWN
   (Eddie Kendricks)
2. SEASONS IN THE SUN
   (Terry Jacks)
3. ROCK ON
   (David Essex)
4. DARK LADY
   (Cher)
5. SUNSHINE ON MY SHOULDERS
   (John Denver)
6. MOCKINGBIRD
   (Carly Simon and James Taylor)
7. JET
   (Paul McCartney and Wings)
8. THE WAY WE WERE
   (Barbra Streisand)
9. SPIDERS AND SNAKES
   (Jim Stafford)
10. BENNIE AND THE JETS
    (Elton John)

POP ALBUMS

1. THE WAY WE WERE
   (Barbra Streisand)
2. COURT AND SPARK
   (Joni Mitchell)
3. JOHN DENVER'S GREATEST HITS, VOL. 1
   (John Denver)
4. HOTCAKES
   (Carly Simon)
5. BEHIND CLOSED DOORS
   (Charlie Rich)
6. PLANET WAVES
   (Bob Dylan)
7. TALES FROM TOPOGRAPHIC OCEANS
   (Yes)
8. BAND ON THE RUN
   (Paul McCartney and Wings)
9. TUBULAR BELLS
   (Mike Oldfield)
10. YOU DON'T MESS AROUND WITH JIM
    (Jim Croce)

BLACK SINGLES

1. MIGHTY LOVE, PART 1
   (Spinners)
2. I'LL BE THE OTHER WOMAN
   (The Soul Children)
3. LOOKIN' FOR A LOVE
   (Bobby Womack)
4. BOOGIE DOWN
   (Eddie Kendricks)
5. WE'RE GETTING CARELESS WITH OUR LOVE
   (Johnnie Taylor)
6. BEST THING THAT EVER HAPPENED TO ME
   (Gladys Knight and the Pips)
7. HOMELY GIRL
   (The Chi-Lites)
8. JUNGLE BOOGIE
   (Kool and the Gang)
9. I WISH IT WAS ME
   (Tyrone Davis)

10. THAT'S THE SOUND LONELY MAKES
    (Tavares)

BLACK ALBUMS

1. LOVE IS THE MESSAGE
   (MFSB)
2. RHAPSODY IN WHITE
   (Love Unlimited Orchestra)
3. SHIP AHOY
   (The O'Jays)
4. LIVIN' FOR YOU
   (Al Green)
5. 1990
   (Temptations)
6. WILD AND PEACEFUL
   (Kool and the Gang)
7. THE PAYBACK
   (James Brown)
8. STONE GON'
   (Barry White)
9. LOOKIN' FOR A LOVE AGAIN
   (Bobby Womack)
10. UNREAL
    (Bloodstone)

JAZZ ALBUMS

1. HEAD HUNTERS
   (Herbie Hancock)
2. SPECTRUM
   (Billy Cobham)
3. KEEP YOUR SOUL TOGETHER
   (Freddie Hubbard)
4. DEODATO 2
   (Eumir Deodato)
5. GIANT BOX
   (Don Sebesky)
6. WILDFLOWER
   (Hank Crawford)
7. BLACK-EYED BLUES
   (Esther Phillips)
8. LAYERS
   (Les McCann)
9. UNSUNG HEROES
   (Crusaders)
10. BLACK BYRD
    (Donald Byrd)

COUNTRY SINGLES

1. ANOTHER LONELY SONG
   (Tammy Wynette)
2. THERE'S A HONKY TONK ANGEL
   (Conway Twitty)
3. SWEET MAGNOLIA BLOSSOM
   (Billy "Crash" Craddock)
4. WOULD YOU LAY WITH ME
   (Tanya Tucker)
5. THERE WON'T BE ANYMORE
   (Charlie Rich)
6. DADDY WHAT IF
   (Bobby Bare)
7. THAT'S THE WAY LOVE GOES
   (Johnny Rodriguez)
8. LOVING YOU HAS CHANGED MY LIFE
   (David Rogers)
9. WRONG IDEAS
   (Brenda Lee)
10. MIDNIGHT, ME AND THE BLUES
    (Mel Tillis)

COUNTRY ALBUMS

1. FOR THE PEOPLE IN THE LAST HARD
   TOWN
   (Tom T. Hall)
2. LET ME BE THERE
   (Olivia Newton-John)
3. BOBBY BARE SINGS "LULLABYS, LEGENDS
   AND LIES"
   (Bobby Bare)

4. BEHIND CLOSED DOORS
   (Charlie Rich)
5. WE'RE GONNA HOLD ON
   (George Jones and Tammy Wynette)
6. AMAZING LOVE
   (Charley Pride)
7. I REMEMBER HANK WILLIAMS
   (Glen Campbell)
8. SOUTHERN ROOTS
   (Jerry Lee Lewis)
9. THERE WON'T BE ANYMORE
   (Charlie Rich)
10. ROY CLARK'S FAMILY ALBUM
    (Roy Clark)

MARCH 23, 1974

POP SINGLES

1. SUNSHINE ON MY SHOULDERS
   (John Denver)
2. SEASONS IN THE SUN
   (Terry Jacks)
3. DARK LADY
   (Cher)
4. BOOGIE DOWN
   (Eddie Kendricks)
5. MOCKINGBIRD
   (Carly Simon and James Taylor)
6. JET
   (Paul McCartney and Wings)
7. ROCK ON
   (David Essex)
8. BENNIE AND THE JETS
   (Elton John)
9. THE WAY WE WERE
   (Barbra Streisand)
10. ERES TU
    (Mocedades)

POP ALBUMS

1. JOHN DENVER'S GREATEST HITS, VOL. 1
   (John Denver)
2. THE WAY WE WERE
   (Barbra Streisand)
3. COURT AND SPARK
   (Joni Mitchell)
4. BEHIND CLOSED DOORS
   (Charlie Rich)
5. HOTCAKES
   (Carly Simon)
6. TUBULAR BELLS
   (Mike Oldfield)
7. BAND ON THE RUN
   (Paul McCartney and Wings)
8. GOODBYE YELLOW BRICK ROAD
   (Elton John)
9. TALES FROM TOPOGRAPHIC OCEANS
   (Yes)
10. PLANET WAVES
    (Bob Dylan)

BLACK SINGLES

1. LOOKIN' FOR A LOVE
   (Bobby Womack)
2. TSOP
   (MFSB)
3. MIGHTY LOVE, PART 1
   (Spinners)
4. BEST THING THAT EVER HAPPENED TO
   ME
   (Gladys Knight and the Pips)
5. HOMELY GIRL
   (The Chi-Lites)
6. BOOGIE DOWN
   (Eddie Kendricks)
7. I'LL BE THE OTHER WOMAN
   (The Soul Children)

8. JUST DON'T WANT TO BE LONELY
   (Main Ingredient)
9. I WISH IT WAS ME
   (Tyrone Davis)
10. THAT'S THE SOUND LONELY MAKES
    (Tavares)

BLACK ALBUMS

1. LOVE IS THE MESSAGE
   (MFSB)
2. RHAPSODY IN WHITE
   (Love Unlimited Orchestra)
3. SHIP AHOY
   (The O'Jays)
4. 1990
   (Temptations)
5. WILD AND PEACEFUL
   (Kool and the Gang)
6. THE PAYBACK
   (James Brown)
7. LOOKIN' FOR A LOVE AGAIN
   (Bobby Womack)
8. STONE GON'
   (Barry White)
9. HEAD HUNTERS
   (Herbie Hancock)
10. IT'S BEEN A LONG TIME
    (New Birth)

JAZZ ALBUMS

1. HEAD HUNTERS
   (Herbie Hancock)
2. KEEP YOUR SOUL TOGETHER
   (Freddie Hubbard)
3. SPECTRUM
   (Billy Cobham)
4. WILDFLOWER
   (Hank Crawford)
5. LOVE IS THE MESSAGE
   (MFSB)
6. GIANT BOX
   (Don Sebesky)
7. BLACK-EYED BLUES
   (Esther Phillips)
8. LAYERS
   (Les McCann)
9. DEODATO 2
   (Eumir Deodato)
10. UNSUNG HEROES
    (Crusaders)

COUNTRY SINGLES

1. THERE'S A HONKY TONK ANGEL
   (Conway Twitty)
2. SWEET MAGNOLIA BLOSSOM
   (Billy "Crash" Craddock)
3. WOULD YOU LAY WITH ME
   (Tanya Tucker)
4. WRONG IDEAS
   (Brenda Lee)
5. ANOTHER LONELY SONG
   (Tammy Wynette)
6. MIDNIGHT, ME AND THE BLUES
   (Mel Tillis)
7. THERE WON'T BE ANYMORE
   (Charlie Rich)
8. LOVING YOU HAS CHANGED MY LIFE
   (David Rogers)
9. BABY DOLL
   (Barbara Fairchild)
10. I LOVE YOU, I LOVE YOU
    (David Houston and Barbara Mandrell)

COUNTRY ALBUMS

1. LET ME BE THERE
   (Olivia Newton-John)
2. FOR THE PEOPLE IN THE LAST HARD
   TOWN
   (Tom T. Hall)

3. BOBBY BARE SINGS "LULLABYS, LEGENDS AND LIES"
(Bobby Bare)
4. BEHIND CLOSED DOORS
(Charlie Rich)
5. WE'RE GONNA HOLD ON
(George Jones and Tammy Wynette)
6. I REMEMBER HANK WILLIAMS
(Glen Campbell)
7. THERE WON'T BE ANYMORE
(Charlie Rich)
8. ELVIS: A LEGENDARY PERFORMER, VOL. 1
(Elvis Presley)
9. SOUTHERN ROOTS
(Jerry Lee Lewis)
10. AN AMERICAN LEGEND
(Tex Ritter)

MARCH 30, 1974

POP SINGLES

1. BENNIE AND THE JETS
(Elton John)
2. HOOKED ON A FEELING
(Blue Swede)
3. DARK LADY
(Cher)
4. MOCKINGBIRD
(Carly Simon and James Taylor)
5. JET
(Paul McCartney and Wings)
6. SUNSHINE ON MY SHOULDERS
(John Denver)
7. SEASONS IN THE SUN
(Terry Jacks)
8. BOOGIE DOWN
(Eddie Kendricks)
9. ERES TU
(Mocedades)
10. TSOP
(MFSB)

POP ALBUMS

1. JOHN DENVER'S GREATEST HITS, VOL. 1
(John Denver)
2. THE WAY WE WERE
(Barbra Streisand)
3. BEHIND CLOSED DOORS
(Charlie Rich)
4. TUBULAR BELLS
(Mike Oldfield)
5. COURT AND SPARK
(Joni Mitchell)
6. BAND ON THE RUN
(Paul McCartney and Wings)
7. GOODBYE YELLOW BRICK ROAD
(Elton John)
8. HOTCAKES
(Carly Simon)
9. LOVE IS THE MESSAGE
(MFSB)
10. AMERICAN GRAFFITI
(Original Soundtrack)

BLACK SINGLES

1. TSOP
(MFSB)
2. LOOKIN' FOR A LOVE
(Bobby Womack)
3. BEST THING THAT EVER HAPPENED TO ME
(Gladys Knight and the Pips)
4. MIGHTY LOVE, PART 1
(Spinners)
5. HOMELY GIRL
(The Chi-Lites)
6. JUST DON'T WANT TO BE LONELY
(Main Ingredient)

7. OUTSIDE WOMAN
(Bloodstone)
8. KEEP IT IN THE FAMILY
(Leon Haywood)
9. I WISH IT WAS ME
(Tyrone Davis)
10. MY MISTAKE
(Diana Ross and Marvin Gaye)

BLACK ALBUMS

1. LOVE IS THE MESSAGE
(MFSB)
2. RHAPSODY IN WHITE
(Love Unlimited Orchestra)
3. SHIP AHOY
(The O'Jays)
4. LOOKIN' FOR A LOVE AGAIN
(Bobby Womack)
5. THE PAYBACK
(James Brown)
6. EUPHRATES RIVER
(Main Ingredient)
7. 1990
(Temptations)
8. WILD AND PEACEFUL
(Kool and the Gang)
9. HEAD HUNTERS
(Herbie Hancock)
10. LET ME IN YOUR LIFE
(Aretha Franklin)

JAZZ ALBUMS

1. HEAD HUNTERS
(Herbie Hancock)
2. KEEP YOUR SOUL TOGETHER
(Freddie Hubbard)
3. LOVE IS THE MESSAGE
(MFSB)
4. WILDFLOWER
(Hank Crawford)
5. SPECTRUM
(Billy Cobham)
6. GIANT BOX
(Don Sebesky)
7. LAYERS
(Les McCann)
8. BLACK-EYED BLUES
(Esther Phillips)
9. DEODATO 2
(Eumir Deodato)
10. E.H. IN THE U.K.
(Eddie Harris)

COUNTRY SINGLES

1. SWEET MAGNOLIA BLOSSOM
(Billy "Crash" Craddock)
2. WOULD YOU LAY WITH ME
(Tanya Tucker)
3. WRONG IDEAS
(Brenda Lee)
4. MIDNIGHT, ME AND THE BLUES
(Mel Tillis)
5. THERE'S A HONKY TONK ANGEL
(Conway Twitty)
6. BABY DOLL
(Barbara Fairchild)
7. A VERY SPECIAL LOVE SONG
(Charlie Rich)
8. I'M WANTIN' TO/TWENTIETH CENTURY DRIFTER
(Marty Robbins)
9. THERE WON'T BE ANYMORE
(Charlie Rich)
10. I LOVE YOU, I LOVE YOU
(David Houston and Barbara Mandrell)

COUNTRY ALBUMS

1. LET ME BE THERE
(Olivia Newton-John)

2. FOR THE PEOPLE IN THE LAST HARD TOWN
(Tom T. Hall)
3. BEHIND CLOSED DOORS
(Charlie Rich)
4. BOBBY BARE SINGS "LULLABYS, LEGENDS AND LIES"
(Bobby Bare)
5. THERE WON'T BE ANYMORE
(Charlie Rich)
6. ELVIS: A LEGENDARY PERFORMER, VOL. 1
(Elvis Presley)
7. WE'RE GONNA HOLD ON
(George Jones and Tammy Wynette)
8. I'M STILL LOVING YOU
(Joe Stampley)
9. AN AMERICAN LEGEND
(Tex Ritter)
10. I REMEMBER HANK WILLIAMS
(Glen Campbell)

APRIL 6, 1974

POP SINGLES

1. HOOKED ON A FEELING
(Blue Swede)
2. BENNIE AND THE JETS
(Elton John)
3. TSOP
(MFSB)
4. MOCKINGBIRD
(Carly Simon and James Taylor)
5. JET
(Paul McCartney and Wings)
6. SUNSHINE ON MY SHOULDERS
(John Denver)
7. SEASONS IN THE SUN
(Terry Jacks)
8. THE LORD'S PRAYER
(Sister Janet Mead)
9. BEST THING THAT EVER HAPPENED TO ME
(Gladys Knight and the Pips)
10. COME AND GET YOUR LOVE
(Redbone)

POP ALBUMS

1. JOHN DENVER'S GREATEST HITS, VOL. 1
(John Denver)
2. THE WAY WE WERE
(Barbra Streisand)
3. TUBULAR BELLS
(Mike Oldfield)
4. BAND ON THE RUN
(Paul McCartney and Wings)
5. COURT AND SPARK
(Joni Mitchell)
6. BEHIND CLOSED DOORS
(Charlie Rich)
7. GOODBYE YELLOW BRICK ROAD
(Elton John)
8. LOVE IS THE MESSAGE
(MFSB)
9. AMERICAN GRAFFITI
(Original Soundtrack)
10. POEMS, PRAYERS AND PROMISES
(John Denver)

BLACK SINGLES

1. TSOP
(MFSB)
2. BEST THING THAT EVER HAPPENED TO ME
(Gladys Knight and the Pips)
3. LOOKIN' FOR A LOVE
(Bobby Womack)

4. JUST DON'T WANT TO BE LONELY
   (Main Ingredient)
5. MY MISTAKE
   (Diana Ross and Marvin Gaye)
6. OUTSIDE WOMAN
   (Bloodstone)
7. KEEP IT IN THE FAMILY
   (Leon Haywood)
8. MIGHTY LOVE, PART 1
   (Spinners)
9. HOMELY GIRL
   (The Chi-Lites)
10. TOUCH A HAND, MAKE A FRIEND
    (The Staple Singers)

BLACK ALBUMS

1. LOVE IS THE MESSAGE
   (MFSB)
2. RHAPSODY IN WHITE
   (Love Unlimited Orchestra)
3. THE PAYBACK
   (James Brown)
4. LOOKIN' FOR A LOVE AGAIN
   (Bobby Womack)
5. EUPHRATES RIVER
   (Main Ingredient)
6. HEAD HUNTERS
   (Herbie Hancock)
7. LET ME IN YOUR LIFE
   (Aretha Franklin)
8. SHIP AHOY
   (The O'Jays)
9. WILD AND PEACEFUL
   (Kool and the Gang)
10. BOOGIE DOWN
    (Eddie Kendricks)

JAZZ ALBUMS

1. HEAD HUNTERS
   (Herbie Hancock)
2. LOVE IS THE MESSAGE
   (MFSB)
3. KEEP YOUR SOUL TOGETHER
   (Freddie Hubbard)
4. LAYERS
   (Les McCann)
5. SPECTRUM
   (Billy Cobham)
6. WILDFLOWER
   (Hank Crawford)
7. GIANT BOX
   (Don Sebesky)
8. BLACK-EYED BLUES
   (Esther Phillips)
9. E.H. IN THE U.K.
   (Eddie Harris)
10. DEODATO 2
    (Eumir Deodato)

COUNTRY SINGLES

1. WOULD YOU LAY WITH ME
   (Tanya Tucker)
2. A VERY SPECIAL LOVE SONG
   (Charlie Rich)
3. MIDNIGHT, ME AND THE BLUES
   (Mel Tillis)
4. WRONG IDEAS
   (Brenda Lee)
5. BABY DOLL
   (Barbara Fairchild)
6. SWEET MAGNOLIA BLOSSOM
   (Billy "Crash" Craddock)
7. I'M WANTIN' TO
   (Marty Robbins)
8. HANG IN THERE GIRL
   (Freddie Hart)
9. TAKE GOOD CARE OF HER/I'VE GOT A THING ABOUT YOU BABY
   (Elvis Presley)
10. THERE'S A HONKY TONK ANGEL
    (Conway Twitty)

COUNTRY ALBUMS

1. FOR THE PEOPLE IN THE LAST HARD TOWN
   (Tom T. Hall)
2. THERE WON'T BE ANYMORE
   (Charlie Rich)
3. BEHIND CLOSED DOORS
   (Charlie Rich)
4. ELVIS: A LEGENDARY PERFORMER, VOL. 1
   (Elvis Presley)
5. LET ME BE THERE
   (Olivia Newton-John)
6. BOBBY BARE SINGS "LULLABYS, LEGENDS AND LIES"
   (Bobby Bare)
7. I'M STILL LOVING YOU
   (Joe Stampley)
8. AN AMERICAN LEGEND
   (Tex Ritter)
9. WE'RE GONNA HOLD ON
   (George Jones and Tammy Wynette)
10. NEW SUNRISE
    (Brenda Lee)

APRIL 13, 1974

POP SINGLES

1. HOOKED ON A FEELING
   (Blue Swede)
2. TSOP
   (MFSB)
3. BENNIE AND THE JETS
   (Elton John)
4. BEST THING THAT EVER HAPPENED TO ME
   (Gladys Knight and the Pips)
5. THE LORD'S PRAYER
   (Sister Janet Mead)
6. SUNSHINE ON MY SHOULDERS
   (John Denver)
7. OH, MY MY
   (Ringo Starr)
8. COME AND GET YOUR LOVE
   (Redbone)
9. THE LOCO-MOTION
   (Grand Funk Railroad)
10. A VERY SPECIAL LOVE SONG
    (Charlie Rich)

POP ALBUMS

1. BAND ON THE RUN
   (Paul McCartney and Wings)
2. JOHN DENVER'S GREATEST HITS, VOL. 1
   (John Denver)
3. TUBULAR BELLS
   (Mike Oldfield)
4. THE WAY WE WERE
   (Barbra Streisand)
5. COURT AND SPARK
   (Joni Mitchell)
6. BEHIND CLOSED DOORS
   (Charlie Rich)
7. LOVE IS THE MESSAGE
   (MFSB)
8. GOODBYE YELLOW BRICK ROAD
   (Elton John)
9. AMERICAN GRAFFITI
   (Original Soundtrack)
10. POEMS, PRAYERS AND PROMISES
    (John Denver)

BLACK SINGLES

1. BEST THING THAT EVER HAPPENED TO ME
   (Gladys Knight and the Pips)

2. TSOP
   (MFSB)
3. JUST DON'T WANT TO BE LONELY
   (Main Ingredient)
4. LOOKIN' FOR A LOVE
   (Bobby Womack)
5. MY MISTAKE
   (Diana Ross and Marvin Gaye)
6. OUTSIDE WOMAN
   (Bloodstone)
7. TOUCH A HAND, MAKE A FRIEND
   (The Staple Singers)
8. KEEP IT IN THE FAMILY
   (Leon Haywood)
9. THE PAYBACK
   (James Brown)
10. MIGHTY LOVE, PART 1
    (Spinners)

BLACK ALBUMS

1. LOVE IS THE MESSAGE
   (MFSB)
2. LET ME IN YOUR LIFE
   (Aretha Franklin)
3. THE PAYBACK
   (James Brown)
4. EUPHRATES RIVER
   (Main Ingredient)
5. BOOGIE DOWN
   (Eddie Kendricks)
6. RHAPSODY IN WHITE
   (Love Unlimited Orchestra)
7. LOOKIN' FOR A LOVE AGAIN
   (Bobby Womack)
8. HEAD HUNTERS
   (Herbie Hancock)
9. INNERVISIONS
   (Stevie Wonder)
10. OPEN OUR EYES
    (Earth, Wind and Fire)

JAZZ ALBUMS

1. HEAD HUNTERS
   (Herbie Hancock)
2. LOVE IS THE MESSAGE
   (MFSB)
3. LAYERS
   (Les McCann)
4. KEEP YOUR SOUL TOGETHER
   (Freddie Hubbard)
5. SPECTRUM
   (Billy Cobham)
6. E.H. IN THE U.K.
   (Eddie Harris)
7. WILDFLOWER
   (Hank Crawford)
8. DEODATO 2
   (Eumir Deodato)
9. TWO GENERATIONS OF BRUBECK
   (Dave Brubeck)
10. STREET LADY
    (Donald Byrd)

COUNTRY SINGLES

1. A VERY SPECIAL LOVE SONG
   (Charlie Rich)
2. HANG IN THERE GIRL
   (Freddie Hart)
3. WOULD YOU LAY WITH ME
   (Tanya Tucker)
4. HELLO LOVE
   (Hank Snow)
5. BABY DOLL
   (Barbara Fairchild)
6. MIDNIGHT, ME AND THE BLUES
   (Mel Tillis)
7. I'M WANTING TO
   (Marty Robbins)
8. TAKE GOOD CARE OF HER/I'VE GOT A THING ABOUT YOU BABY
   (Elvis Presley)

9. (JEANNE MARIE) YOU WERE A LADY
   (Tommy Overstreet)
10. THINGS AREN'T FUNNY ANYMORE
   (Merle Haggard)

COUNTRY ALBUMS

1. THERE WON'T BE ANYMORE
   (Charlie Rich)
2. ELVIS: A LEGENDARY PERFORMER, VOL. 1
   (Elvis Presley)
3. FOR THE PEOPLE IN THE LAST HARD TOWN
   (Tom T. Hall)
4. BEHIND CLOSED DOORS
   (Charlie Rich)
5. LET ME BE THERE
   (Olivia Newton-John)
6. I'M STILL LOVING YOU
   (Joe Stampley)
7. MY THIRD ALBUM
   (Johnny Rodriguez)
8. IF WE MAKE IT THROUGH DECEMBER
   (Merle Haggard)
9. JOLENE
   (Dolly Parton)
10. VERY SPECIAL LOVE SONGS
   (Charlie Rich)

APRIL 20, 1974

POP SINGLES

1. TSOP
   (MFSB)
2. HOOKED ON A FEELING
   (Blue Swede)
3. BEST THING THAT EVER HAPPENED TO ME
   (Gladys Knight and the Pips)
4. BENNIE AND THE JETS
   (Elton John)
5. THE LORD'S PRAYER
   (Sister Janet Mead)
6. OH, MY MY
   (Ringo Starr)
7. THE LOCO-MOTION
   (Grand Funk Railroad)
8. COME AND GET YOUR LOVE
   (Redbone)
9. LOOKIN' FOR A LOVE
   (Bobby Womack)
10. I'LL HAVE TO SAY I LOVE YOU IN A SONG
   (Jim Croce)

POP ALBUMS

1. JOHN DENVER'S GREATEST HITS, VOL. 1
   (John Denver)
2. BAND ON THE RUN
   (Paul McCartney and Wings)
3. TUBULAR BELLS
   (Mike Oldfield)
4. THE STING
   (Original Soundtrack)
5. CHICAGO VII
   (Chicago)
6. LOVE IS THE MESSAGE
   (MFSB)
7. GOODBYE YELLOW BRICK ROAD
   (Elton John)
8. SHININ' ON
   (Grand Funk Railroad)
9. POEMS, PRAYERS AND PROMISES
   (John Denver)
10. WHAT WERE ONCE VICES ARE NOW HABITS
   (The Doobie Brothers)

BLACK SINGLES

1. THE PAYBACK
   (James Brown)
2. BEST THING THAT EVER HAPPENED TO ME
   (Gladys Knight and the Pips)
3. JUST DON'T WANT TO BE LONELY
   (Main Ingredient)
4. DANCIN' MACHINE
   (The Jackson 5)
5. TSOP
   (MFSB)
6. TOUCH A HAND, MAKE A FRIEND
   (The Staple Singers)
7. LOOKIN' FOR A LOVE
   (Bobby Womack)
8. MIGHTY, MIGHTY
   (Earth, Wind and Fire)
9. KEEP IT IN THE FAMILY
   (Leon Haywood)
10. YOU MAKE ME FEEL BRAND NEW
   (The Stylistics)

BLACK ALBUMS

1. LET ME IN YOUR LIFE
   (Aretha Franklin)
2. LOVE IS THE MESSAGE
   (MFSB)
3. THE PAYBACK
   (James Brown)
4. EUPHRATES RIVER
   (Main Ingredient)
5. BOOGIE DOWN
   (Eddie Kendricks)
6. OPEN OUR EYES
   (Earth, Wind and Fire)
7. INNERVISIONS
   (Stevie Wonder)
8. RHAPSODY IN WHITE
   (Love Unlimited Orchestra)
9. MIGHTY LOVE
   (Spinners)
10. LOOKIN' FOR A LOVE AGAIN
   (Bobby Womack)

JAZZ ALBUMS

1. HEAD HUNTERS
   (Herbie Hancock)
2. LOVE IS THE MESSAGE
   (MFSB)
3. LAYERS
   (Les McCann)
4. E.H. IN THE U.K.
   (Eddie Harris)
5. SPECTRUM
   (Billy Cobham)
6. KEEP YOUR SOUL TOGETHER
   (Freddie Hubbard)
7. TWO GENERATIONS OF BRUBECK
   (Dave Brubeck)
8. WILDFLOWER
   (Hank Crawford)
9. STREET LADY
   (Donald Byrd)
10. LONDON UNDERGROUND
   (Herbie Mann)

COUNTRY SINGLES

1. HANG IN THERE GIRL
   (Freddie Hart)
2. HELLO LOVE
   (Hank Snow)
3. A VERY SPECIAL LOVE SONG
   (Charlie Rich)
4. THINGS AREN'T FUNNY ANYMORE
   (Merle Haggard)
5. COUNTRY BUMPKIN
   (Cal Smith)

6. (JEANNE MARIE) YOU WERE A LADY
   (Tommy Overstreet)
7. I'LL TRY A LITTLE BIT HARDER
   (Donna Fargo)
8. NO CHARGE
   (Melba Montgomery)
9. TAKE GOOD CARE OF HER/I'VE GOT A THING ABOUT YOU BABY
   (Elvis Presley)
10. IS IT WRONG (FOR LOVING YOU)
   (Sonny James)

COUNTRY ALBUMS

1. THERE WON'T BE ANYMORE
   (Charlie Rich)
2. ELVIS: A LEGENDARY PERFORMER, VOL. 1
   (Elvis Presley)
3. BEHIND CLOSED DOORS
   (Charlie Rich)
4. VERY SPECIAL LOVE SONGS
   (Charlie Rich)
5. MY THIRD ALBUM
   (Johnny Rodriguez)
6. IF WE MAKE IT THROUGH DECEMBER
   (Merle Haggard)
7. JOLENE
   (Dolly Parton)
8. WOULD YOU LAY WITH ME
   (Tanya Tucker)
9. FOR THE PEOPLE IN THE LAST HARD TOWN
   (Tom T. Hall)
10. LET ME BE THERE
   (Olivia Newton-John)

APRIL 27, 1974

POP SINGLES

1. TSOP
   (MFSB)
2. BEST THING THAT EVER HAPPENED TO ME
   (Gladys Knight and the Pips)
3. THE LOCO-MOTION
   (Grand Funk Railroad)
4. HOOKED ON A FEELING
   (Blue Swede)
5. OH, MY MY
   (Ringo Starr)
6. DANCIN' MACHINE
   (The Jackson 5)
7. I'LL HAVE TO SAY I LOVE YOU IN A SONG
   (Jim Croce)
8. LOOKIN' FOR A LOVE
   (Bobby Womack)
9. KEEP ON SINGING
   (Helen Reddy)
10. THE SHOW MUST GO ON
   (Three Dog Night)

POP ALBUMS

1. THE STING
   (Original Soundtrack)
2. CHICAGO VII
   (Chicago)
3. JOHN DENVER'S GREATEST HITS, VOL. 1
   (John Denver)
4. BAND ON THE RUN
   (Paul McCartney and Wings)
5. LOVE IS THE MESSAGE
   (MFSB)
6. SHININ' ON
   (Grand Funk Railroad)
7. TUBULAR BELLS
   (Mike Oldfield)
8. GOODBYE YELLOW BRICK ROAD
   (Elton John)

9. WHAT WERE ONCE VICES ARE NOW
   HABITS
   (The Doobie Brothers)
10. POEMS, PRAYERS AND PROMISES
    (John Denver)

BLACK SINGLES

1. DANCIN' MACHINE
   (The Jackson 5)
2. THE PAYBACK
   (James Brown)
3. BEST THING THAT EVER HAPPENED TO
   ME
   (Gladys Knight and the Pips)
4. MIGHTY, MIGHTY
   (Earth, Wind and Fire)
5. JUST DON'T WANT TO BE LONELY
   (Main Ingredient)
6. TOUCH A HAND, MAKE A FRIEND
   (The Staple Singers)
7. TSOP
   (MFSB)
8. YOU MAKE ME FEEL BRAND NEW
   (The Stylistics)
9. HEAVENLY
   (Temptations)
10. HONEY PLEASE, CAN'T YA SEE
    (Barry White)

BLACK ALBUMS

1. OPEN OUR EYES
   (Earth, Wind and Fire)
2. LOVE IS THE MESSAGE
   (MFSB)
3. LET ME IN YOUR LIFE
   (Aretha Franklin)
4. BOOGIE DOWN
   (Eddie Kendricks)
5. EUPHRATES RIVER
   (Main Ingredient)
6. THE PAYBACK
   (James Brown)
7. INNERVISIONS
   (Stevie Wonder)
8. MIGHTY LOVE
   (Spinners)
9. RHAPSODY IN WHITE
   (Love Unlimited Orchestra)
10. HEAD HUNTERS
    (Herbie Hancock)

JAZZ ALBUMS

1. HEAD HUNTERS
   (Herbie Hancock)
2. LOVE IS THE MESSAGE
   (MFSB)
3. LAYERS
   (Les McCann)
4. STREET LADY
   (Donald Byrd)
5. TWO GENERATIONS OF BRUBECK
   (Dave Brubeck)
6. E.H. IN THE U.K.
   (Eddie Harris)
7. LONDON UNDERGROUND
   (Herbie Mann)
8. SPECTRUM
   (Billy Cobham)
9. WILDFLOWERS
   (Hank Crawford)
10. BRIGHT MOMENTS
    (Rahsaan Roland Kirk)

COUNTRY SINGLES

1. HELLO LOVE
   (Hank Snow)
2. COUNTRY BUMPKIN
   (Cal Smith)

3. THINGS AREN'T FUNNY ANYMORE
   (Merle Haggard)
4. NO CHARGE
   (Melba Montgomery)
5. (JEANNE MARIE) YOU WERE A LADY
   (Tommy Overstreet)
6. I'LL TRY A LITTLE BIT HARDER
   (Donna Fargo)
7. IS IT WRONG (FOR LOVING YOU)
   (Sonny James)
8. THE OLDER THE VIOLIN, THE SWEETER
   THE MUSIC
   (Hank Thompson)
9. HANG IN THERE GIRL
   (Freddie Hart)
10. A VERY SPECIAL LOVE SONG
    (Charlie Rich)

COUNTRY ALBUMS

1. THERE WON'T BE ANYMORE
   (Charlie Rich)
2. VERY SPECIAL LOVE SONGS
   (Charlie Rich)
3. BEHIND CLOSED DOORS
   (Charlie Rich)
4. MY THIRD ALBUM
   (Johnny Rodriguez)
5. IF WE MAKE IT THROUGH DECEMBER
   (Merle Haggard)
6. JOLENE
   (Dolly Parton)
7. WOULD YOU LAY WITH ME
   (Tanya Tucker)
8. ELVIS: A LEGENDARY PERFORMER, VOL. 1
   (Elvis Presley)
9. FOR THE PEOPLE IN THE LAST HARD
   TOWN
   (Tom T. Hall)
10. FULLY REALIZED
    (Charlie Rich)

MAY 4, 1974

POP SINGLES

1. THE LOCO-MOTION
   (Grand Funk Railroad)
2. TSOP
   (MFSB)
3. BEST THING THAT EVER HAPPENED TO
   ME
   (Gladys Knight and the Pips)
4. DANCIN' MACHINE
   (The Jackson 5)
5. THE SHOW MUST GO ON
   (Three Dog Night)
6. I'LL HAVE TO SAY I LOVE YOU IN A SONG
   (Jim Croce)
7. TUBULAR BELLS
   (Mike Oldfield)
8. JUST DON'T WANT TO BE LONELY
   (Main Ingredient)
9. KEEP ON SINGING
   (Helen Reddy)
10. THE STREAK
    (Ray Stevens)

POP ALBUMS

1. THE STING
   (Original Soundtrack)
2. CHICAGO VII
   (Chicago)
3. JOHN DENVER'S GREATEST HITS, VOL. 1
   (John Denver)
4. SHININ' ON
   (Grand Funk Railroad)
5. BAND ON THE RUN
   (Paul McCartney and Wings)

6. LOVE IS THE MESSAGE
   (MFSB)
7. TUBULAR BELLS
   (Mike Oldfield)
8. GOODBYE YELLOW BRICK ROAD
   (Elton John)
9. BEHIND CLOSED DOORS
   (Charlie Rich)
10. OPEN OUR EYES
    (Earth, Wind and Fire)

BLACK SINGLES

1. DANCIN' MACHINE
   (The Jackson 5)
2. THE PAYBACK
   (James Brown)
3. BEST THING THAT EVER HAPPENED TO
   ME
   (Gladys Knight and the Pips)
4. MIGHTY, MIGHTY
   (Earth, Wind and Fire)
5. YOU MAKE ME FEEL BRAND NEW
   (The Stylistics)
6. BE THANKFUL FOR WHAT YOU GOT
   (William De Vaughn)
7. LET'S GET MARRIED
   (Al Green)
8. HEAVENLY
   (Temptations)
9. JUST DON'T WANT TO BE LONELY
   (Main Ingredient)
10. TOUCH A HAND, MAKE A FRIEND
    (The Staple Singers)

BLACK ALBUMS

1. OPEN OUR EYES
   (Earth, Wind and Fire)
2. BOOGIE DOWN
   (Eddie Kendricks)
3. LET ME IN YOUR LIFE
   (Aretha Franklin)
4. LOVE IS THE MESSAGE
   (MFSB)
5. THE PAYBACK
   (James Brown)
6. MIGHTY LOVE
   (Spinners)
7. EUPHRATES RIVER
   (Main Ingredient)
8. INNERVISIONS
   (Stevie Wonder)
9. WAR LIVE
   (War)
10. SHIP AHOY
    (The O'Jays)

JAZZ ALBUMS

1. STREET LADY
   (Donald Byrd)
2. HEAD HUNTERS
   (Herbie Hancock)
3. LOVE IS THE MESSAGE
   (MFSB)
4. LAYERS
   (Les McCann)
5. LONDON UNDERGROUND
   (Herbie Mann)
6. SPECTRUM
   (Billy Cobham)
7. JAMAICA
   (Ahmad Jamal)
8. TWO GENERATIONS OF BRUBECK
   (Dave Brubeck)
9. BRIGHT MOMENTS
   (Rahsaan Roland Kirk)
10. E.H. IN THE U.K.
    (Eddie Harris)

COUNTRY SINGLES

1. COUNTRY BUMPKIN
   (Cal Smith)
2. NO CHARGE
   (Melba Montgomery)
3. THINGS AREN'T FUNNY ANYMORE
   (Merle Haggard)
4. HELLO LOVE
   (Hank Snow)
5. IS IT WRONG (FOR LOVING YOU)
   (Sonny James)
6. (JEANNE MARIE) YOU WERE A LADY
   (Tommy Overstreet)
7. I'LL TRY A LITTLE BIT HARDER
   (Donna Fargo)
8. THE OLDER THE VIOLIN, THE SWEETER
   THE MUSIC
   (Hank Thompson)
9. AT THE TIME
   (Jean Shepard)
10. WE SHOULD BE TOGETHER
    (Don Williams)

COUNTRY ALBUMS

1. VERY SPECIAL LOVE SONGS
   (Charlie Rich)
2. THERE WON'T BE ANYMORE
   (Charlie Rich)
3. MY THIRD ALBUM
   (Johnny Rodriguez)
4. WOULD YOU LAY WITH ME
   (Tanya Tucker)
5. IF WE MAKE IT THROUGH DECEMBER
   (Merle Haggard)
6. JOLENE
   (Dolly Parton)
7. BEHIND CLOSED DOORS
   (Charlie Rich)
8. THE ENTERTAINER
   (Roy Clark)
9. FULLY REALIZED
   (Charlie Rich)
10. HELLO LOVE
    (Hank Snow)

MAY 11, 1974

POP SINGLES

1. DANCIN' MACHINE
   (The Jackson 5)
2. THE STREAK
   (Ray Stevens)
3. THE LOCO-MOTION
   (Grand Funk Railroad)
4. THE SHOW MUST GO ON
   (Three Dog Night)
5. TUBULAR BELLS
   (Mike Oldfield)
6. TSOP
   (MFSB)
7. BEST THING THAT EVER HAPPENED
   TO ME
   (Gladys Knight and the Pips)
8. JUST DON'T WANT TO BE LONELY
   (Main Ingredient)
9. (I'VE BEEN) SEARCHIN' SO LONG
   (Chicago)
10. THE ENTERTAINER
    (Marvin Hamlisch)

POP ALBUMS

1. THE STING
   (Original Soundtrack)
2. JOHN DENVER'S GREATEST HITS, VOL. 1
   (John Denver)

3. SHININ' ON
   (Grand Funk Railroad)
4. BUDDHA AND THE CHOCOLATE BOX
   (Cat Stevens)
5. BAND ON THE RUN
   (Paul McCartney and Wings)
6. CHICAGO VII
   (Chicago)
7. LOVE IS THE MESSAGE
   (MFSB)
8. GOODBYE YELLOW BRICK ROAD
   (Elton John)
9. BEHIND CLOSED DOORS
   (Charlie Rich)
10. OPEN OUR EYES
    (Earth, Wind and Fire)

BLACK SINGLES

1. DANCIN' MACHINE
   (The Jackson 5)
2. THE PAYBACK
   (James Brown)
3. YOU MAKE ME FEEL BRAND NEW
   (The Stylistics)
4. BE THANKFUL FOR WHAT YOU GOT
   (William De Vaughn)
5. LET'S GET MARRIED
   (Al Green)
6. MIGHTY, MIGHTY
   (Earth, Wind and Fire)
7. BEST THING THAT EVER HAPPENED
   TO ME
   (Gladys Knight and the Pips)
8. HEAVENLY
   (Temptations)
9. DON'T YOU WORRY 'BOUT A THING
   (Stevie Wonder)
10. HOLLYWOOD SWINGING
    (Kool and the Gang)

BLACK ALBUMS

1. OPEN OUR EYES
   (Earth, Wind and Fire)
2. LET ME IN YOUR LIFE
   (Aretha Franklin)
3. THE PAYBACK
   (James Brown)
4. BOOGIE DOWN
   (Eddie Kendricks)
5. MIGHTY LOVE
   (Spinners)
6. LOVE IS THE MESSAGE
   (MFSB)
7. WAR LIVE
   (War)
8. SHIP AHOY
   (The O'Jays)
9. EUPHRATES RIVER
   (Main Ingredient)
10. INNERVISIONS
    (Stevie Wonder)

JAZZ ALBUMS

1. STREET LADY
   (Donald Byrd)
2. HEAD HUNTERS
   (Herbie Hancock)
3. LOVE IS THE MESSAGE
   (MFSB)
4. SPECTRUM
   (Billy Cobham)
5. LAYERS
   (Les McCann)
6. JAMAICA
   (Ahmad Jamal)
7. LONDON UNDERGROUND
   (Herbie Mann)
8. TWO GENERATIONS OF BRUBECK
   (Dave Brubeck)
9. BRIGHT MOMENTS
   (Rahsaan Roland Kirk)

10. SCRATCH
    (Crusaders)

COUNTRY SINGLES

1. NO CHARGE
   (Melba Montgomery)
2. COUNTRY BUMPKIN
   (Cal Smith)
3. THE STREAK
   (Ray Stevens)
4. IS IT WRONG (FOR LOVING YOU)
   (Sonny James)
5. THINGS AREN'T FUNNY ANYMORE
   (Merle Haggard)
6. HELLO LOVE
   (Hank Snow)
7. WE SHOULD BE TOGETHER
   (Don Williams)
8. HONEYMOON FEELING
   (Roy Clark)
9. AT THE TIME
   (Jean Shepard)
10. I JUST STARTED HATING CHEATING
    SONGS TODAY
    (Moe Bandy)

COUNTRY ALBUMS

1. VERY SPECIAL LOVE SONGS
   (Charlie Rich)
2. THERE WON'T BE ANYMORE
   (Charlie Rich)
3. MY THIRD ALBUM
   (Johnny Rodriguez)
4. WOULD YOU LAY WITH ME
   (Tanya Tucker)
5. THE ENTERTAINER
   (Roy Clark)
6. BEHIND CLOSED DOORS
   (Charlie Rich)
7. HELLO LOVE
   (Hank Snow)
8. IF WE MAKE IT THROUGH DECEMBER
   (Merle Haggard)
9. FULLY REALIZED
   (Charlie Rich)
10. JOLENE
    (Dolly Parton)

MAY 18, 1974

POP SINGLES

1. THE STREAK
   (Ray Stevens)
2. DANCIN' MACHINE
   (The Jackson 5)
3. THE SHOW MUST GO ON
   (Three Dog Night)
4. THE ENTERTAINER
   (Marvin Hamlisch)
5. TUBULAR BELLS
   (Mike Oldfield)
6. (I'VE BEEN) SEARCHIN' SO LONG
   (Chicago)
7. JUST DON'T WANT TO BE LONELY
   (Main Ingredient)
8. THE LOCO-MOTION
   (Grand Funk Railroad)
9. MIDNIGHT AT THE OASIS
   (Maria Muldaur)
10. YOU MAKE ME FEEL BRAND NEW
    (The Stylistics)

POP ALBUMS

1. THE STING
   (Original Soundtrack)

2. BUDDHA AND THE CHOCOLATE BOX
   (Cat Stevens)
3. SHININ' ON
   (Grand Funk Railroad)
4. JOHN DENVER'S GREATEST HITS, VOL. 1
   (John Denver)
5. BAND ON THE RUN
   (Paul McCartney and Wings)
6. CHICAGO VII
   (Chicago)
7. GOODBYE YELLOW BRICK ROAD
   (Elton John)
8. BEHIND CLOSED DOORS
   (Charlie Rich)
9. OPEN OUR EYES
   (Earth, Wind and Fire)
10. INNERVISIONS
    (Stevie Wonder)

BLACK SINGLES

1. BE THANKFUL FOR WHAT YOU GOT
   (William De Vaughn)
2. DANCIN' MACHINE
   (The Jackson 5)
3. YOU MAKE ME FEEL BRAND NEW
   (The Stylistics)
4. THE PAYBACK
   (James Brown)
5. LET'S GET MARRIED
   (Al Green)
6. DON'T YOU WORRY 'BOUT A THING
   (Stevie Wonder)
7. HOLLYWOOD SWINGING
   (Kool and the Gang)
8. I'M IN LOVE
   (Aretha Franklin)
9. BEST THING THAT EVER HAPPENED TO ME
   (Gladys Knight and the Pips)
10. THE SAME LOVE THAT MADE ME LAUGH
    (Bill Withers)

BLACK ALBUMS

1. OPEN OUR EYES
   (Earth, Wind and Fire)
2. THE PAYBACK
   (James Brown)
3. LET ME IN YOUR LIFE
   (Aretha Franklin)
4. MIGHTY LOVE
   (Spinners)
5. BOOGIE DOWN
   (Eddie Kendricks)
6. WAR LIVE
   (War)
7. SHIP AHOY
   (The O'Jays)
8. HEAD HUNTERS
   (Herbie Hancock)
9. STREET LADY
   (Donald Byrd)
10. IMAGINATION
    (Gladys Knight and the Pips)

JAZZ ALBUMS

1. STREET LADY
   (Donald Byrd)
2. HEAD HUNTERS
   (Herbie Hancock)
3. SPECTRUM
   (Billy Cobham)
4. LOVE IS THE MESSAGE
   (MFSB)
5. JAMAICA
   (Ahmad Jamal)
6. LAYERS
   (Les McCann)
7. SCRATCH
   (Crusaders)
8. LONDON UNDERGROUND
   (Herbie Mann)

9. BRIGHT MOMENTS
   (Rahsaan Roland Kirk)
10. STRAIGHT AHEAD
    (Brian Auger's Oblivion Express)

COUNTRY SINGLES

1. THE STREAK
   (Ray Stevens)
2. IS IT WRONG (FOR LOVING YOU)
   (Sonny James)
3. COUNTRY BUMPKIN
   (Cal Smith)
4. NO CHARGE
   (Melba Montgomery)
5. HONEYMOON FEELING
   (Roy Clark)
6. I WILL ALWAYS LOVE YOU
   (Dolly Parton)
7. WE SHOULD BE TOGETHER
   (Don Williams)
8. PURE LOVE
   (Ronnie Milsap)
9. I JUST STARTED HATING CHEATING SONGS TODAY
   (Moe Bandy)
10. SOME KIND OF A WOMAN
    (Faron Young)

COUNTRY ALBUMS

1. VERY SPECIAL LOVE SONGS
   (Charlie Rich)
2. THERE WON'T BE ANYMORE
   (Charlie Rich)
3. THE ENTERTAINER
   (Roy Clark)
4. HELLO LOVE
   (Hank Snow)
5. MY THIRD ALBUM
   (Johnny Rodriguez)
6. BEHIND CLOSED DOORS
   (Charlie Rich)
7. WOULD YOU LAY WITH ME
   (Tanya Tucker)
8. HONKY TONK ANGEL
   (Conway Twitty)
9. ANOTHER LONELY SONG
   (Tammy Wynette)
10. IF WE MAKE IT THROUGH DECEMBER
    (Merle Haggard)

MAY 25, 1974

POP SINGLES

1. THE SHOW MUST GO ON
   (Three Dog Night)
2. THE STREAK
   (Ray Stevens)
3. THE ENTERTAINER
   (Marvin Hamlisch)
4. DANCIN' MACHINE
   (The Jackson 5)
5. (I'VE BEEN) SEARCHIN' SO LONG
   (Chicago)
6. MIDNIGHT AT THE OASIS
   (Maria Muldaur)
7. YOU MAKE ME FEEL BRAND NEW
   (The Stylistics)
8. JUST DON'T WANT TO BE LONELY
   (Main Ingredient)
9. I WON'T LAST A DAY WITHOUT YOU
   (The Carpenters)
10. BAND ON THE RUN
    (Paul McCartney and Wings)

POP ALBUMS

1. THE STING
   (Original Soundtrack)
2. BUDDHA AND THE CHOCOLATE BOX
   (Cat Stevens)
3. SHININ' ON
   (Grand Funk Railroad)
4. BAND ON THE RUN
   (Paul McCartney and Wings)
5. JOHN DENVER'S GREATEST HITS, VOL. 1
   (John Denver)
6. GOODBYE YELLOW BRICK ROAD
   (Elton John)
7. BEHIND CLOSED DOORS
   (Charlie Rich)
8. CHICAGO VII
   (Chicago)
9. BACHMAN-TURNER OVERDRIVE 2
   (Bachman-Turner Overdrive)
10. INNERVISIONS
    (Stevie Wonder)

BLACK SINGLES

1. BE THANKFUL FOR WHAT YOU GOT
   (William De Vaughn)
2. DANCIN' MACHINE
   (The Jackson 5)
3. I'M IN LOVE
   (Aretha Franklin)
4. DON'T WORRY 'BOUT A THING
   (Stevie Wonder)
5. HOLLYWOOD SWINGING
   (Kool and the Gang)
6. YOU MAKE ME FEEL BRAND NEW
   (The Stylistics)
7. LET'S GET MARRIED
   (Al Green)
8. THE SAME LOVE THAT MADE ME LAUGH
   (Bill Withers)
9. CAN YOU HANDLE IT
   (Graham Central Station)
10. THE PAYBACK
    (James Brown)

BLACK ALBUMS

1. OPEN OUR EYES
   (Earth, Wind and Fire)
2. LET ME IN YOUR LIFE
   (Aretha Franklin)
3. MIGHTY LOVE
   (Spinners)
4. SHIP AHOY
   (The O'Jays)
5. THE PAYBACK
   (James Brown)
6. WAR LIVE
   (War)
7. HEAD HUNTERS
   (Herbie Hancock)
8. BOOGIE DOWN
   (Eddie Kendricks)
9. STREET LADY
   (Donald Byrd)
10. IMAGINATION
    (Gladys Knight and the Pips)

JAZZ ALBUMS

1. STREET LADY
   (Donald Byrd)
2. HEAD HUNTERS
   (Herbie Hancock)
3. JAMAICA
   (Ahmad Jamal)
4. SPECTRUM
   (Bill Cobham)
5. LAYERS
   (Les McCann)
6. SCRATCH
   (Crusaders)

7. LOVE IS THE MESSAGE
   (MFSB)
8. STRAIGHT AHEAD
   (Brian Auger's Oblivion Express)
9. LONDON UNDERGROUND
   (Herbie Mann)
10. CROSSWINDS
    (Billy Cobham)

COUNTRY SINGLES

1. THE STREAK
   (Ray Stevens)
2. IS IT WRONG (FOR LOVING YOU)
   (Sonny James)
3. I WILL ALWAYS LOVE YOU
   (Dolly Parton)
4. HONEYMOON FEELING
   (Roy Clark)
5. COUNTRY BUMPKIN
   (Cal Smith)
6. PURE LOVE
   (Ronnie Milsap)
7. SOMETHING
   (Johnny Rodriguez)
8. I JUST STARTED HATING CHEATING
   SONGS TODAY
   (Moe Bandy)
9. SOME KIND OF WOMAN
   (Faron Young)
10. ON THE COVER OF MUSIC CITY NEWS
    (Buck Owens)

COUNTRY ALBUMS

1. THERE WON'T BE ANYMORE
   (Charlie Rich)
2. THE ENTERTAINER
   (Roy Clark)
3. HELLO LOVE
   (Hank Snow)
4. VERY SPECIAL LOVE SONGS
   (Charlie Rich)
5. BEHIND CLOSED DOORS
   (Charlie Rich)
6. HONKY TONK ANGEL
   (Conway Twitty)
7. ANOTHER LONELY SONG
   (Tammy Wynette)
8. MY THIRD ALBUM
   (Johnny Rodriguez)
9. WOULD YOU LAY WITH ME
   (Tanya Tucker)
10. GOOD TIMES
    (Elvis Presley)

JUNE 1, 1974

POP SINGLES

1. THE STREAK
   (Ray Stevens)
2. BAND ON THE RUN
   (Paul McCartney and Wings)
3. THE ENTERTAINER
   (Marvin Hamlisch)
4. YOU MAKE ME FEEL BRAND NEW
   (The Stylistics)
5. MIDNIGHT AT THE OASIS
   (Maria Muldaur)
6. THE SHOW MUST GO ON
   (Three Dog Night)
7. BILLY, DON'T BE A HERO
   (Bo Donaldson and the Heywoods)
8. HELP ME
   (Joni Mitchell)
9. I WON'T LAST A DAY WITHOUT YOU
   (The Carpenters)
10. SUNDOWN
    (Gordon Lightfoot)

POP ALBUMS

1. BAND ON THE RUN
   (Paul McCartney and Wings)
2. THE STING
   (Original Soundtrack)
3. BUDDHA AND THE CHOCOLATE BOX
   (Cat Stevens)
4. SHININ' ON
   (Grand Funk Railroad)
5. JOHN DENVER'S GREATEST HITS, VOL. 1
   (John Denver)
6. GOODBYE YELLOW BRICK ROAD
   (Elton John)
7. BACHMAN-TURNER OVERDRIVE 2
   (Bachman-Turner Overdrive)
8. BEHIND CLOSED DOORS
   (Charlie Rich)
9. CHICAGO VII
   (Chicago)
10. COURT AND SPARK
    (Joni Mitchell)

BLACK SINGLES

1. BE THANKFUL FOR WHAT YOU GOT
   (William De Vaughn)
2. I'M IN LOVE
   (Aretha Franklin)
3. HOLLYWOOD SWINGING
   (Kool and the Gang)
4. DON'T YOU WORRY 'BOUT A THING
   (Stevie Wonder)
5. DANCIN' MACHINE
   (The Jackson 5)
6. FOR THE LOVE OF MONEY
   (The O'Jays)
7. YOU MAKE ME FEEL BRAND NEW
   (The Stylistics)
8. THE SAME LOVE THAT MADE ME LAUGH
   (Bill Withers)
9. CAN YOU HANDLE IT
   (Graham Central Station)
10. LET'S GET MARRIED
    (Al Green)

BLACK ALBUMS

1. MIGHTY LOVE
   (Spinners)
2. OPEN OUR EYES
   (Earth, Wind and Fire)
3. LET ME IN YOUR LIFE
   (Aretha Franklin)
4. SHIP AHOY
   (The O'Jays)
5. THE PAYBACK
   (James Brown)
6. BOOGIE DOWN
   (Eddie Kendricks)
7. HEAD HUNTERS
   (Herbie Hancock)
8. IMAGINATION
   (Gladys Knight and the Pips)
9. STREET LADY
   (Donald Byrd)
10. SKIN TIGHT
    (Ohio Players)

JAZZ ALBUMS

1. STREET LADY
   (Donald Byrd)
2. HEAD HUNTERS
   (Herbie Mann)
3. SPECTRUM
   (Billy Cobham)
4. CROSSWINDS
   (Billy Cobham)
5. LAYERS
   (Les McCann)
6. STRAIGHT AHEAD
   (Brian Auger's Oblivion Express)

7. SCRATCH
   (Crusaders)
8. WHIRLWINDS
   (Eumir Deodato)
9. LOVE IS THE MESSAGE
   (MFSB)
10. JAMAICA
    (Ahmad Jamal)

COUNTRY SINGLES

1. I WILL ALWAYS LOVE YOU
   (Dolly Parton)
2. THE STREAK
   (Ray Stevens)
3. HONEYMOON FEELING
   (Roy Clark)
4. PURE LOVE
   (Ronnie Milsap)
5. IF YOU LOVE ME
   (Olivia Newton-John)
6. SOMETHING
   (Johnny Rodriguez)
7. I JUST STARTED HATING CHEATING
   SONGS TODAY
   (Moe Bandy)
8. ROOM FULL OF ROSES
   (Mickey Gilley)
9. LAST TIME I SAW HIM
   (Dottie West)
10. WE COULD
    (Charley Pride)

COUNTRY ALBUMS

1. THERE WON'T BE ANYMORE
   (Charlie Rich)
2. THE ENTERTAINER
   (Roy Clark)
3. HELLO LOVE
   (Hank Snow)
4. BEHIND CLOSED DOORS
   (Charlie Rich)
5. HONKY TONK ANGEL
   (Conway Twitty)
6. ANOTHER LONELY SONG
   (Tammy Wynette)
7. VERY SPECIAL LOVE SONGS
   (Charlie Rich)
8. GOOD TIMES
   (Elvis Presley)
9. THIS TIME
   (Waylon Jennings)
10. MY THIRD ALBUM
    (Johnny Rodriguez)

JUNE 8, 1974

POP SINGLES

1. BAND ON THE RUN
   (Paul McCartney and Wings)
2. YOU MAKE ME FEEL BRAND NEW
   (The Stylistics)
3. THE STREAK
   (Ray Stevens)
4. BILLY, DON'T BE A HERO
   (Bo Donaldson and the Heywoods)
5. MIDNIGHT AT THE OASIS
   (Maria Muldaur)
6. SUNDOWN
   (Gordon Lightfoot)
7. HELP ME
   (Joni Mitchell)
8. BE THANKFUL FOR WHAT YOU GOT
   (William De Vaughn)
9. FOR THE LOVE OF MONEY
   (The O'Jays)
10. MY GIRL BILL
    (Jim Stafford)

POP ALBUMS

1. BAND ON THE RUN
    (Paul McCartney and Wings)
2. THE STING
    (Original Soundtrack)
3. BUDDHA AND THE CHOCOLATE BOX
    (Cat Stevens)
4. GOODBYE YELLOW BRICK ROAD
    (Elton John)
5. JOHN DENVER'S GREATEST HITS, VOL. 1
    (John Denver)
6. SUNDOWN
    (Gordon Lightfoot)
7. BEHIND CLOSED DOORS
    (Charlie Rich)
8. SHININ' ON
    (Grand Funk Railroad)
9. COURT AND SPARK
    (Joni Mitchell)
10. MARIA MULDAUR
    (Maria Muldaur)

BLACK SINGLES

1. I'M IN LOVE
    (Aretha Franklin)
2. HOLLYWOOD SWINGING
    (Kool and the Gang)
3. BE THANKFUL FOR WHAT YOU GOT
    (William De Vaughn)
4. SIDESHOW
    (Blue Magic)
5. FOR THE LOVE OF MONEY
    (The O'Jays)
6. DANCIN' MACHINE
    (The Jackson 5)
7. YOU MAKE ME FEEL BRAND NEW
    (The Stylistics)
8. DON'T YOU WORRY 'BOUT A THING
    (Stevie Wonder)
9. THE SAME LOVE THAT MADE ME LAUGH
    (Bill Withers)
10. CAN YOU HANDLE IT
    (Graham Central Station)

BLACK ALBUMS

1. MIGHTY LOVE
    (Spinners)
2. OPEN OUR EYES
    (Earth, Wind and Fire)
3. LET ME IN YOUR LIFE
    (Aretha Franklin)
4. HEAD HUNTERS
    (Herbie Hancock)
5. THE PAYBACK
    (James Brown)
6. BOOGIE DOWN
    (Eddie Kendricks)
7. SHIP AHOY
    (The O'Jays)
8. LET'S PUT IT ALL TOGETHER
    (The Stylistics)
9. SKIN TIGHT
    (Ohio Players)
10. CLAUDINE
    (Gladys Knight and the Pips)

JAZZ ALBUMS

1. CROSSWINDS
    (Billy Cobham)
2. STREET LADY
    (Donald Byrd)
3. HEAD HUNTERS
    (Herbie Hancock)
4. SPECTRUM
    (Billy Cobham)
5. STRAIGHT AHEAD
    (Brian Auger's Oblivion Express)
6. WHIRLWINDS
    (Eumir Deodato)

7. SCRATCH
    (Crusaders)
8. LAYERS
    (Les McCann)
9. JAMAICA
    (Ahmad Jamal)
10. LOVE IS THE MESSAGE
    (MFSB)

COUNTRY SINGLES

1. PURE LOVE
    (Ronnie Milsap)
2. I WILL ALWAYS LOVE YOU
    (Dolly Parton)
3. IF YOU LOVE ME
    (Olivia Newton-John)
4. ROOM FULL OF ROSES
    (Mickey Gilley)
5. WE COULD
    (Charley Pride)
6. HONEYMOON FEELING
    (Roy Clark)
7. THE STREAK
    (Ray Stevens)
8. LAST TIME I SAW HIM
    (Dottie West)
9. SOMETHING
    (Johnny Rodriguez)
10. WHEN THE MORNING COMES
    (Hoyt Axton)

COUNTRY ALBUMS

1. THE ENTERTAINER
    (Roy Clark)
2. THERE WON'T BE ANYMORE
    (Charlie Rich)
3. HONKY TONK ANGEL
    (Conway Twitty)
4. ANOTHER LONELY SONG
    (Tammy Wynette)
5. BEHIND CLOSED DOORS
    (Charlie Rich)
6. GOOD TIMES
    (Elvis Presley)
7. THIS TIME
    (Waylon Jennings)
8. HELLO LOVE
    (Hank Snow)
9. VERY SPECIAL LOVE SONGS
    (Charlie Rich)
10. MY THIRD ALBUM
    (Johnny Rodriguez)

JUNE 15, 1974

POP SINGLES

1. YOU MAKE ME FEEL BRAND NEW
    (The Stylistics)
2. BAND ON THE RUN
    (Paul McCartney and Wings)
3. BILLY, DON'T BE A HERO
    (Bo Donaldson and the Heywoods)
4. SUNDOWN
    (Gordon Lightfoot)
5. BE THANKFUL FOR WHAT YOU GOT
    (William De Vaughn)
6. THE STREAK
    (Ray Stevens)
7. HELP ME
    (Joni Mitchell)
8. FOR THE LOVE OF MONEY
    (The O'Jays)
9. MIDNIGHT AT THE OASIS
    (Maria Muldaur)
10. MY GIRL BILL
    (Jim Stafford)

POP ALBUMS

1. SUNDOWN
    (Gordon Lightfoot)
2. BAND ON THE RUN
    (Paul McCartney and Wings)
3. THE STING
    (Original Soundtrack)
4. GOODBYE YELLOW BRICK ROAD
    (Elton John)
5. BUDDHA AND THE CHOCOLATE BOX
    (Cat Stevens)
6. JOHN DENVER'S GREATEST HITS, VOL. 1
    (John Denver)
7. BEHIND CLOSED DOORS
    (Charlie Rich)
8. COURT AND SPARK
    (Joni Mitchell)
9. SHININ' ON
    (Grand Funk Railroad)
10. ON STAGE
    (Loggins and Messina)

BLACK SINGLES

1. HOLLYWOOD SWINGING
    (Kool and the Gang)
2. I'M IN LOVE
    (Aretha Franklin)
3. SIDESHOW
    (Blue Magic)
4. BE THANKFUL FOR WHAT YOU GOT
    (William De Vaughn)
5. FOR THE LOVE OF MONEY
    (The O'Jays)
6. DANCIN' MACHINE
    (The Jackson 5)
7. ONE CHAIN DON'T MAKE NO PRISON
    (The Four Tops)
8. YOU MAKE ME FEEL BRAND NEW
    (The Stylistics)
9. FINALLY GOT MYSELF TOGETHER
    (The Impressions)
10. SON OF SAGITTARIUS
    (Eddie Kendricks)

BLACK ALBUMS

1. MIGHTY LOVE
    (Spinners)
2. OPEN OUR EYES
    (Earth, Wind and Fire)
3. LET ME IN YOUR LIFE
    (Aretha Franklin)
4. SKIN TIGHT
    (Ohio Players)
5. HEAD HUNTERS
    (Herbie Hancock)
6. LET'S PUT IT ALL TOGETHER
    (The Stylistics)
7. SHIP AHOY
    (The O'Jays)
8. THE PAYBACK
    (James Brown)
9. CLAUDINE
    (Gladys Knight and the Pips)
10. BOOGIE DOWN
    (Eddie Kendricks)

JAZZ ALBUMS

1. CROSSWINDS
    (Billy Cobham)
2. STREET LADY
    (Donald Byrd)
3. HEAD HUNTERS
    (Herbie Hancock)
4. WHIRLWINDS
    (Eumir Deodato)
5. SPECTRUM
    (Billy Cobham)
6. STRAIGHT AHEAD
    (Brian Auger's Oblivion Express)

7. SCRATCH
   (Crusaders)
8. BODY HEAT
   (Quincy Jones)
9. LAYERS
   (Les McCann)
10. JAMAICA
    (Ahmad Jamal)

COUNTRY SINGLES

1. IF YOU LOVE ME
   (Olivia Newton-John)
2. ROOM FULL OF ROSES
   (Mickey Gilley)
3. WE COULD
   (Charley Pride)
4. PURE LOVE
   (Ronnie Milsap)
5. I WILL ALWAYS LOVE YOU
   (Dolly Parton)
6. THIS TIME
   (Waylon Jennings)
7. I DON'T SEE ME IN YOUR EYES ANYMORE
   (Charlie Rich)
8. ONE DAY AT A TIME
   (Marilyn Sellars)
9. WHEN THE MORNING COMES
   (Hoyt Axton)
10. LEAN IT ALL ON ME
    (Diana Trask)

COUNTRY ALBUMS

1. HONKY TONK ANGEL
   (Conway Twitty)
2. THE ENTERTAINER
   (Roy Clark)
3. ANOTHER LONELY SONG
   (Tammy Wynette)
4. GOOD TIMES
   (Elvis Presley)
5. BEHIND CLOSED DOORS
   (Charlie Rich)
6. THIS TIME
   (Waylon Jennings)
7. THERE WON'T BE ANYMORE
   (Charlie Rich)
8. VERY SPECIAL LOVE SONGS
   (Charlie Rich)
9. HELLO LOVE
   (Hank Snow)
10. NO CHARGE
    (Melba Montgomery)

JUNE 22, 1974

POP SINGLES

1. BILLY DON'T BE A HERO
   (Bo Donaldson and the Heywoods)
2. SUNDOWN
   (Gordon Lightfoot)
3. YOU MAKE ME FEEL BRAND NEW
   (The Stylistics)
4. BE THANKFUL FOR WHAT YOU GOT
   (William De Vaughn)
5. BAND ON THE RUN
   (Paul McCartney and Wings)
6. THE STREAK
   (Ray Stevens)
7. FOR THE LOVE OF MONEY
   (The O'Jays)
8. IF YOU LOVE ME (LET ME KNOW)
   (Olivia Newton-John)
9. ROCK THE BOAT
   (The Hues Corporation)
10. HAVEN'T GOT TIME FOR THE PAIN
    (Carly Simon)

POP ALBUMS

1. SUNDOWN
   (Gordon Lightfoot)
2. BAND ON THE RUN
   (Paul McCartney and Wings)
3. THE STING
   (Original Soundtrack)
4. GOODBYE YELLOW BRICK ROAD
   (Elton John)
5. COURT AND SPARK
   (Joni Mitchell)
6. JOHN DENVER'S GREATEST HITS, VOL. 1
   (John Denver)
7. BUDDHA AND THE CHOCOLATE BOX
   (Cat Stevens)
8. BEHIND CLOSED DOORS
   (Charlie Rich)
9. ON STAGE
   (Loggins and Messina)
10. BACHMAN-TURNER OVERDRIVE 2
    (Bachman-Turner Overdrive)

BLACK SINGLES

1. SIDESHOW
   (Blue Magic)
2. HOLLYWOOD SWINGING
   (Kool and the Gang)
3. FINALLY GOT MYSELF TOGETHER
   (The Impressions)
4. ONE CHAIN DON'T MAKE NO PRISON
   (The Four Tops)
5. SON OF SAGITTARIUS
   (Eddie Kendricks)
6. ON AND ON
   (Gladys Knight and the Pips)
7. THERE WILL NEVER BE ANY PEACE
   (The Chi-Lites)
8. I'M COMIN' HOME
   (Spinners)
9. ROCK YOUR BABY
   (George McCrae)
10. FISH AIN'T BITIN'
    (Lamont Dozier)

BLACK ALBUMS

1. SKIN TIGHT
   (Ohio Players)
2. MIGHTY LOVE
   (Spinners)
3. OPEN OUR EYES
   (Earth, Wind and Fire)
4. LET'S PUT IT ALL TOGETHER
   (The Stylistics)
5. LET ME IN YOUR LIFE
   (Aretha Franklin)
6. HEAD HUNTERS
   (Herbie Hancock)
7. SHIP AHOY
   (The O'Jays)
8. CLAUDINE
   (Gladys Knight and the Pips)
9. THE PAYBACK
   (James Brown)
10. IMAGINATION
    (Gladys Knight and the Pips)

JAZZ ALBUMS

1. CROSSWINDS
   (Billy Cobham)
2. HEAD HUNTERS
   (Herbie Hancock)
3. BODY HEAT
   (Quincy Jones)
4. STREET LADY
   (Donald Byrd)
5. WHIRLWINDS
   (Eumir Deodato)
6. SPECTRUM
   (Billy Cobham)

7. STRAIGHT AHEAD
   (Brian Auger's Oblivion Express)
8. SCRATCH
   (Crusaders)
9. BIG FUN
   (Miles Davis)
10. LAYERS
    (Les McCann)

COUNTRY SINGLES

1. ROOM FULL OF ROSES
   (Mickey Gilley)
2. WE COULD
   (Charley Pride)
3. THIS TIME
   (Waylon Jennings)
4. I DON'T SEE ME IN YOUR EYES ANYMORE
   (Charlie Rich)
5. IF YOU LOVE ME
   (Olivia Newton-John)
6. MARIE LAVEAU
   (Bobby Bare)
7. ONE DAY AT A TIME
   (Marilyn Sellars)
8. THEY DON'T MAKE 'EM LIKE MY DADDY
   (Loretta Lynn)
9. I'M NOT THROUGH LOVING YOU YET
   (Conway Twitty)
10. HE THINKS I STILL CARE
    (Anne Murray)

COUNTRY ALBUMS

1. HONKY TONK ANGEL
   (Conway Twitty)
2. ANOTHER LONELY SONG
   (Tammy Wynette)
3. GOOD TIMES
   (Elvis Presley)
4. BEHIND CLOSED DOORS
   (Charlie Rich)
5. THIS TIME
   (Waylon Jennings)
6. THERE WON'T BE ANYMORE
   (Charlie Rich)
7. VERY SPECIAL LOVE SONGS
   (Charlie Rich)
8. THE ENTERTAINER
   (Roy Clark)
9. NO CHARGE
   (Melba Montgomery)
10. STOP AND SMELL THE ROSES
    (Mac Davis)

JUNE 29, 1974

POP SINGLES

1. SUNDOWN
   (Gordon Lightfoot)
2. BE THANKFUL FOR WHAT YOU GOT
   (William De Vaughn)
3. BILLY, DON'T BE A HERO
   (Bo Donaldson and the Heywoods)
4. ROCK THE BOAT
   (The Hues Corporation)
5. ROCK YOUR BABY
   (George McCrae)
6. IF YOU LOVE ME (LET ME KNOW)
   (Olivia Newton-John)
7. FOR THE LOVE OF MONEY
   (The O'Jays)
8. THE AIR THAT I BREATHE
   (The Hollies)
9. HOLLYWOOD SWINGING
   (Kool and the Gang)
10. HAVEN'T GOT TIME FOR THE PAIN
    (Carly Simon)

POP ALBUMS

1. BAND ON THE RUN
   (Paul McCartney and Wings)
2. SUNDOWN
   (Gordon Lightfoot)
3. THE STING
   (Original Soundtrack)
4. COURT AND SPARK
   (Joni Mitchell)
5. JOHN DENVER'S GREATEST HITS, VOL. 1
   (John Denver)
6. GOODBYE YELLOW BRICK ROAD
   (Elton John)
7. BUDDHA AND THE CHOCOLATE BOX
   (Cat Stevens)
8. DIAMOND DOGS
   (David Bowie)
9. ON STAGE
   (Loggins and Messina)
10. BACHMAN-TURNER OVERDRIVE 2
    (Bachman-Turner Overdrive)

BLACK SINGLES

1. FINALLY GOT MYSELF TOGETHER
   (The Impressions)
2. ON AND ON
   (Gladys Knight and the Pips)
3. SON OF SAGITTARIUS
   (Eddie Kendricks)
4. ONE CHAIN DON'T MAKE NO PRISON
   (The Four Tops)
5. I'M COMIN' HOME
   (Spinners)
6. ROCK YOUR BABY
   (George McCrae)
7. THERE WILL NEVER BE ANY PEACE
   (The Chi-Lites)
8. FISH AIN'T BITIN'
   (Lamont Dozier)
9. SIDESHOW
   (Blue Magic)
10. ROCK THE BOAT
    (The Hues Corporation)

BLACK ALBUMS

1. SKIN TIGHT
   (Ohio Players)
2. MIGHTY LOVE
   (Spinners)
3. LET'S PUT IT ALL TOGETHER
   (The Stylistics)
4. OPEN OUR EYES
   (Earth, Wind and Fire)
5. SWEET EXORCIST
   (Curtis Mayfield)
6. CLAUDINE
   (Gladys Knight and the Pips)
7. HEAD HUNTERS
   (Herbie Hancock)
8. SHIP AHOY
   (The O'Jays)
9. LET ME IN YOUR LIFE
   (Aretha Franklin)
10. THE PAYBACK
    (James Brown)

JAZZ ALBUMS

1. BODY HEAT
   (Quincy Jones)
2. CROSSWINDS
   (Billy Cobham)
3. HEAD HUNTERS
   (Herbie Hancock)
4. WHIRLWINDS
   (Eumir Deodato)
5. STREET LADY
   (Donald Byrd)
6. SPECTRUM
   (Billy Cobham)

7. BIG FUN
   (Miles Davis)
8. STRAIGHT AHEAD
   (Brian Auger's Oblivion Express)
9. APOCALYPSE
   (Mahavishnu Orchestra)
10. SCRATCH
    (Crusaders)

COUNTRY SINGLES

1. WE COULD
   (Charley Pride)
2. THIS TIME
   (Waylon Jennings)
3. MARIE LAVEAU
   (Bobby Bare)
4. I DON'T SEE ME IN YOUR EYES ANYMORE
   (Charlie Rich)
5. ROOM FULL OF ROSES
   (Mickey Gilley)
6. THEY DON'T MAKE 'EM LIKE MY DADDY
   (Loretta Lynn)
7. ONE DAY AT A TIME
   (Marilyn Sellars)
8. I'M NOT THROUGH LOVING YOU YET
   (Conway Twitty)
9. HE THINKS I STILL CARE
   (Anne Murray)
10. IF YOU LOVE ME
    (Olivia Newton-John)

COUNTRY ALBUMS

1. HONKY TONK ANGEL
   (Conway Twitty)
2. GOOD TIMES
   (Elvis Presley)
3. BEHIND CLOSED DOORS
   (Charlie Rich)
4. THIS TIME
   (Waylon Jennings)
5. THERE WON'T BE ANYMORE
   (Charlie Rich)
6. ANOTHER LONELY SONG
   (Tammy Wynette)
7. VERY SPECIAL LOVE SONGS
   (Charlie Rich)
8. HANG IN THERE GIRL
   (Freddie Hart)
9. THE BEST OF CHARLIE RICH
   (Charlie Rich)
10. STOP AND SMELL THE ROSES
    (Mac Davis)

JULY 6, 1974

POP SINGLES

1. BE THANKFUL FOR WHAT YOU GOT
   (William DeVaughn)
2. ROCK THE BOAT
   (The Hues Corporation)
3. ROCK YOUR BABY
   (George McCrae)
4. SUNDOWN
   (Gordon Lightfoot)
5. IF YOU LOVE ME (LET ME KNOW)
   (Olivia Newton-John)
6. THE AIR THAT I BREATHE
   (The Hollies)
7. HOLLYWOOD SWINGING
   (Kool and the Gang)
8. BILLY, DON'T BE A HERO
   (Bo Donaldson and the Heywoods)
9. ANNIE'S SONG
   (John Denver)
10. FOR THE LOVE OF MONEY
    (The O'Jays)

POP ALBUMS

1. BAND ON THE RUN
   (Paul McCartney and Wings)
2. SUNDOWN
   (Gordon Lightfoot)
3. THE STING
   (Original Soundtrack)
4. COURT AND SPARK
   (Joni Mitchell)
5. JOHN DENVER'S GREATEST HITS, VOL. 1
   (John Denver)
6. DIAMOND DOGS
   (David Bowie)
7. ON STAGE
   (Loggins and Messina)
8. BUDDHA AND THE CHOCOLATE BOX
   (Cat Stevens)
9. GOODBYE YELLOW BRICK ROAD
   (Elton John)
10. BACHMAN-TURNER OVERDRIVE 2
    (Bachman-Turner Overdrive)

BLACK SINGLES

1. ON AND ON
   (Gladys Knight and the Pips)
2. ROCK YOUR BABY
   (George McCrae)
3. SON OF SAGITTARIUS
   (Eddie Kendricks)
4. FISH AIN'T BITIN'
   (Lamont Dozier)
5. I'M COMIN' HOME
   (Spinners)
6. FINALLY GOT MYSELF TOGETHER
   (The Impressions)
7. ROCK THE BOAT
   (The Hues Corporation)
8. ONE CHAIN DON'T MAKE NO PRISON
   (The Four Tops)
9. THERE WILL NEVER BE ANY PEACE
   (The Chi-Lites)
10. SIDESHOW
    (Blue Magic)

BLACK ALBUMS

1. SKIN TIGHT
   (Ohio Players)
2. LET'S PUT IT ALL TOGETHER
   (The Stylistics)
3. SWEET EXORCIST
   (Curtis Mayfield)
4. OPEN OUR EYES
   (Earth, Wind and Fire)
5. CLAUDINE
   (Gladys Knight and the Pips)
6. MIGHTY LOVE
   (Spinners)
7. HEAD HUNTERS
   (Herbie Hancock)
8. SHIP AHOY
   (The O'Jays)
9. INNERVISIONS
   (Stevie Wonder)
10. IMAGINATION
    (Gladys Knight and the Pips)

JAZZ ALBUMS

1. BODY HEAT
   (Quincy Jones)
2. HEAD HUNTERS
   (Herbie Hancock)
3. CROSSWINDS
   (Billy Cobham)
4. STREET LADY
   (Donald Byrd)
5. SPECTRUM
   (Billy Cobham)
6. WHIRLWINDS
   (Eumir Deodato)

7. SCRATCH
   (Crusaders)
8. APOCALYPSE
   (Mahavishnu Orchestra)
9. BIG FUN
   (Miles Davis)
10. STRAIGHT AHEAD
    (Brian Auger's Oblivion Express)

COUNTRY SINGLES

1. THIS TIME
   (Waylon Jennings)
2. MARIE LAVEAU
   (Bobby Bare)
3. THEY DON'T MAKE 'EM LIKE MY DADDY
   (Loretta Lynn)
4. I'M NOT THROUGH LOVING YOU YET
   (Conway Twitty)
5. I DON'T SEE ME IN YOUR EYES ANYMORE
   (Charlie Rich)
6. ONE DAY AT A TIME
   (Marilyn Sellars)
7. WE COULD
   (Charley Pride)
8. HE THINKS I STILL CARE
   (Anne Murray)
9. ONE DAY AT A TIME
   (Don Gibson)
10. ROOM FULL OF ROSES
    (Mickey Gilley)

COUNTRY ALBUMS

1. GOOD TIMES
   (Elvis Presley)
2. BEHIND CLOSED DOORS
   (Charlie Rich)
3. THIS TIME
   (Waylon Jennings)
4. HONKY TONK ANGEL
   (Conway Twitty)
5. THERE WON'T BE ANYMORE
   (Charlie Rich)
6. THE BEST OF CHARLIE RICH
   (Charlie Rich)
7. HANG IN THERE GIRL
   (Freddie Hart)
8. VERY SPECIAL LOVE SONG
   (Charlie Rich)
9. IF YOU LOVE ME
   (Olivia Newton-John)
10. STOP AND SMELL THE ROSES
    (Mac Davis)

JULY 13, 1974

POP SINGLES

1. ROCK THE BOAT
   (The Hues Corporation)
2. ROCK YOUR BABY
   (George McCrae)
3. BE THANKFUL FOR WHAT YOU GOT
   (William DeVaughn)
4. ANNIE'S SONG
   (John Denver)
5. IF YOU LOVE ME (LET ME KNOW)
   (Olivia Newton-John)
6. THE AIR THAT I BREATHE
   (The Hollies)
7. SUNDOWN
   (Gordon Lightfoot)
8. HOLLYWOOD SWINGING
   (Kool and the Gang)
9. ROCK AND ROLL HEAVEN
   (The Righteous Brothers)
10. YOU WON'T SEE ME
    (Anne Murray)

POP ALBUMS

1. CARIBOU
   (Elton John)
2. BAND ON THE RUN
   (Paul McCartney and Wings)
3. BACK HOME AGAIN
   (John Denver)
4. SUNDOWN
   (Gordon Lightfoot)
5. COURT AND SPARK
   (Joni Mitchell)
6. DIAMOND DOGS
   (David Bowie)
7. ON STAGE
   (Loggins and Messina)
8. JOURNEY TO THE CENTER OF THE EARTH
   (Rick Wakeman)
9. THE STING
   (Original Soundtrack)
10. BACHMAN-TURNER OVERDRIVE 2
    (Bachman-Turner Overdrive)

BLACK SINGLES

1. ROCK YOUR BABY
   (George McCrae)
2. ON AND ON
   (Gladys Knight and the Pips)
3. FISH AIN'T BITIN'
   (Lamont Dozier)
4. ROCK THE BOAT
   (The Hues Corporation)
5. MY THANG
   (James Brown)
6. SON OF SAGITTARIUS
   (Eddie Kendricks)
7. I'M COMIN' HOME
   (Spinners)
8. FINALLY GOT MYSELF TOGETHER
   (The Impressions)
9. ONE CHAIN DON'T MAKE NO PRISON
   (The Four Tops)
10. MACHINE GUN
    (Commodores)

BLACK ALBUMS

1. LET'S PUT IT ALL TOGETHER
   (The Stylistics)
2. SWEET EXORCIST
   (Curtis Mayfield)
3. SKIN TIGHT
   (Ohio Players)
4. CLAUDINE
   (Gladys Knight and the Pips)
5. OPEN OUR EYES
   (Earth, Wind and Fire)
6. MIGHTY LOVE
   (Spinners)
7. SHIP AHOY
   (The O'Jays)
8. BODY HEAT
   (Quincy Jones)
9. HEAD HUNTERS
   (Herbie Hancock)
10. LIVE IN LONDON
    (The O'Jays)

JAZZ ALBUMS

1. BODY HEAT
   (Quincy Jones)
2. HEAD HUNTERS
   (Herbie Hancock)
3. CROSSWINDS
   (Billy Cobham)
4. STREET LADY
   (Donald Byrd)
5. WHIRLWINDS
   (Eumir Deodato)
6. SCOTT JOPLIN: THE RED BACK BOOK
   (Gunther Schuller)

7. SPECTRUM
   (Billy Cobham)
8. MYSTERIOUS TRAVELLER
   (Weather Report)
9. SCRATCH
   (Crusaders)
10. APOCALYPSE
    (Mahavishnu Orchestra)

COUNTRY SINGLES

1. MARIE LAVEAU
   (Bobby Bare)
2. I'M NOT THROUGH LOVING YOU YET
   (Conway Twitty)
3. THEY DON'T MAKE 'EM LIKE MY DADDY
   (Loretta Lynn)
4. ONE DAY AT A TIME
   (Marilyn Sellars)
5. ONE DAY AT A TIME
   (Don Gibson)
6. HE THINKS I STILL CARE
   (Anne Murray)
7. THIS TIME
   (Waylon Jennings)
8. STOMP THEM GRAPES
   (Mel Tillis)
9. STATUE OF A FOOL
   (Brian Collins)
10. THAT SONG IS DRIVING ME CRAZY
    (Tom T. Hall)

COUNTRY ALBUMS

1. BEHIND CLOSED DOORS
   (Charlie Rich)
2. GOOD TIMES
   (Elvis Presley)
3. THE BEST OF CHARLIE RICH
   (Charlie Rich)
4. THIS TIME
   (Waylon Jennings)
5. HANG IN THERE GIRL
   (Freddie Hart)
6. IF YOU LOVE ME
   (Olivia Newton-John)
7. THERE WON'T BE ANYMORE
   (Charlie Rich)
8. HONKY TONK ANGEL
   (Conway Twitty)
9. VERY SPECIAL LOVE SONGS
   (Charlie Rich)
10. PURE LOVE
    (Ronnie Milsap)

JULY 20, 1974

POP SINGLES

1. ROCK YOUR BABY
   (George McCrae)
2. ANNIE'S SONG
   (John Denver)
3. ROCK THE BOAT
   (The Hues Corporation)
4. BE THANKFUL FOR WHAT YOU GOT
   (William DeVaughn)
5. THE AIR THAT I BREATHE
   (The Hollies)
6. DON'T LET THE SUN GO DOWN ON ME
   (Elton John)
7. ROCK AND ROLL HEAVEN
   (The Righteous Brothers)
8. ON AND ON
   (Gladys Knight and the Pips)
9. YOU WON'T SEE ME
   (Anne Murray)
10. IF YOU LOVE ME (LET ME KNOW)
    (Olivia Newton-John)

POP ALBUMS

1. BACK HOME AGAIN
   (John Denver)
2. CARIBOU
   (Elton John)
3. BAND ON THE RUN
   (Paul McCartney and Wings)
4. SUNDOWN
   (Gordon Lightfoot)
5. DIAMOND DOGS
   (David Bowie)
6. ON STAGE
   (Loggins and Messina)
7. JOURNEY TO THE CENTER OF THE EARTH
   (Rick Wakeman)
8. JOHN DENVER'S GREATEST HITS, VOL. 1
   (John Denver)
9. THE STING
   (Original Soundtrack)
10. BACHMAN-TURNER OVERDRIVE 2
    (Bachman-Turner Overdrive)

BLACK SINGLES

1. ROCK THE BOAT
   (The Hues Corporation)
2. ROCK YOUR BABY
   (George McCrae)
3. MY THANG
   (James Brown)
4. FISH AIN'T BITIN'
   (Lamont Dozier)
5. ON AND ON
   (Gladys Knight and the Pips)
6. MACHINE GUN
   (Commodores)
7. SON OF SAGITTARIUS
   (Eddie Kendricks)
8. I'M COMING HOME
   (Spinners)
9. YOU'VE GOT MY SOUL ON FIRE
   (Temptations)
10. HOW DO YOU FEEL THE MORNING AFTER
    (Millie Jackson)

BLACK ALBUMS

1. LET'S PUT IT ALL TOGETHER
   (The Stylistics)
2. CLAUDINE
   (Gladys Knight and the Pips)
3. SKIN TIGHT
   (Ohio Players)
4. LIVE IN LONDON
   (The O'Jays)
5. OPEN OUR EYES
   (Earth, Wind and Fire)
6. SWEET EXORCIST
   (Curtis Mayfield)
7. BLUE MAGIC
   (Blue Magic)
8. BODY HEAT
   (Quincy Jones)
9. HEAD HUNTERS
   (Herbie Hancock)
10. FREEDOM FOR THE STALLION
    (The Hues Corporation)

JAZZ ALBUMS

1. BODY HEAT
   (Quincy Jones)
2. HEAD HUNTERS
   (Herbie Hancock)
3. SCOTT JOPLIN: THE RED BACK BOOK
   (Gunther Schuller)
4. MYSTERIOUS TRAVELLER
   (Weather Report)
5. CROSSWINDS
   (Billy Cobham)
6. STREET LADY
   (Donald Byrd)

7. SPECTRUM
   (Billy Cobham)
8. WHIRLWINDS
   (Eumir Deodato)
9. APOCALYPSE
   (Mahavishnu Orchestra)
10. BIG FUN
    (Miles Davis)

COUNTRY SINGLES

1. I'M NOT THROUGH LOVING YOU YET
   (Conway Twitty)
2. THEY DON'T MAKE 'EM LIKE MY DADDY
   (Loretta Lynn)
3. THAT SONG IS DRIVING ME CRAZY
   (Tom T. Hall)
4. STOMP THEM GRAPES
   (Mel Tillis)
5. ONE DAY AT A TIME
   (Don Gibson)
6. MARIE LAVEAU
   (Bobby Bare)
7. RUB IT IN
   (Billy "Crash" Craddock)
8. STATUE OF A FOOL
   (Brian Collins)
9. AS SOON AS I HANG UP THE PHONE
   (Conway Twitty and Loretta Lynn)
10. ONE DAY AT A TIME
    (Marilyn Sellars)

COUNTRY ALBUMS

1. BEST OF CHARLIE RICH
   (Charlie Rich)
2. BEHIND CLOSED DOORS
   (Charlie Rich)
3. IF YOU LOVE ME
   (Olivia Newton-John)
4. HANG IN THERE, GIRL
   (Freddie Hart)
5. GOOD TIMES
   (Elvis Presley)
6. THIS TIME
   (Waylon Jennings)
7. PURE LOVE
   (Ronnie Milsap)
8. COUNTRY FEELING
   (Charley Pride)
9. THERE WON'T BE ANYMORE
   (Charlie Rich)
10. LORETTA LYNN'S GREATEST HITS, VOL. 2
    (Loretta Lynn)

JULY 27, 1974

POP SINGLES

1. ANNIE'S SONG
   (John Denver)
2. ROCK YOUR BABY
   (George McCrae)
3. DON'T LET THE SUN GO DOWN ON ME
   (Elton John)
4. ROCK THE BOAT
   (The Hues Corporation)
5. ROCK AND ROLL HEAVEN
   (The Righteous Brothers)
6. THE AIR THAT I BREATHE
   (The Hollies)
7. ON AND ON
   (Gladys Knight and the Pips)
8. RIKKI, DON'T LOSE THAT NUMBER
   (Steely Dan)
9. SIDESHOW
   (Blue Magic)
10. RADAR LOVE
    (Golden Earring)

POP ALBUMS

1. CARIBOU
   (Elton John)
2. BACK HOME AGAIN
   (John Denver)
3. BAND ON THE RUN
   (Paul McCartney and Wings)
4. SUNDOWN
   (Gordon Lightfoot)
5. BACHMAN-TURNER OVERDRIVE 2
   (Bachman-Turner Overdrive)
6. DIAMOND DOGS
   (David Bowie)
7. JOURNEY TO THE CENTER OF THE EARTH
   (Rick Wakeman)
8. JOHN DENVER'S GREATEST HITS, VOL. 1
   (John Denver)
9. BEFORE THE FLOOD
   (Bob Dylan/The Band)
10. LET'S PUT IT ALL TOGETHER
    (The Stylistics)

BLACK SINGLES

1. MY THANG
   (James Brown)
2. ROCK THE BOAT
   (The Hues Corporation)
3. ROCK YOUR BABY
   (George McCrae)
4. YOU'RE WELCOME, STOP ON BY
   (Bobby Womack)
5. MACHINE GUN
   (Commodores)
6. ON AND ON
   (Gladys Knight and the Pips)
7. FISH AIN'T BITIN'
   (Lamont Dozier)
8. YOU'VE GOT MY SOUL ON FIRE
   (Temptations)
9. MY LOVE
   (Margie Joseph)
10. HOW DO YOU FEEL THE MORNING AFTER
    (Millie Jackson)

BLACK ALBUMS

1. LIVE IN LONDON
   (The O'Jays)
2. LET'S PUT IT ALL TOGETHER
   (The Stylistics)
3. CLAUDINE
   (Gladys Knight and the Pips)
4. SKIN TIGHT
   (Ohio Players)
5. OPEN OUR EYES
   (Earth, Wind and Fire)
6. BLUE MAGIC
   (Blue Magic)
7. BODY HEAT
   (Quincy Jones)
8. SWEET EXORCIST
   (Curtis Mayfield)
9. LIVE
   (Marvin Gaye)
10. THAT NIGGER'S CRAZY
    (Richard Pryor)

COUNTRY SINGLES

1. THEY DON'T MAKE 'EM LIKE MY DADDY
   (Loretta Lynn)
2. THAT SONG IS DRIVING ME CRAZY
   (Tom T. Hall)
3. STOMP THEM GRAPES
   (Mel Tillis)
4. RUB IT IN
   (Billy "Crash" Craddock)
5. YOU CAN'T BE A BEACON
   (Donna Fargo)
6. AS SOON AS I HANG UP THE PHONE
   (Conway Twitty and Loretta Lynn)

7. STATUE OF A FOOL
   (Brian Collins)
8. I'M NOT THROUGH LOVING YOU YET
   (Conway Twitty)
9. MARIE LAVEAU
   (Bobby Bare)
10. THE MAN THAT TURNED MY MAMA ON
    (Tanya Tucker)

COUNTRY ALBUMS

1. IF YOU LOVE ME
   (Olivia Newton-John)
2. THE BEST OF CHARLIE RICH
   (Charlie Rich)
3. BEHIND CLOSED DOORS
   (Charlie Rich)
4. HANG IN THERE GIRL
   (Freddie Hart)
5. PURE LOVE
   (Ronnie Milsap)
6. COUNTRY FEELING
   (Charley Pride)
7. COUNTRY BUMPKIN
   (Cal Smith)
8. LORETTA LYNN'S GREATEST HITS, VOL. 2
   (Loretta Lynn)
9. THERE WON'T BE ANYMORE
   (Charlie Rich)
10. STOP AND SMELL THE ROSES
    (Mac Davis)

AUGUST 3, 1974

POP SINGLES

1. DON'T LET THE SUN GO DOWN ON ME
   (Elton John)
2. ANNIE'S SONG
   (John Denver)
3. ROCK AND ROLL HEAVEN
   (The Righteous Brothers)
4. FEEL LIKE MAKIN' LOVE
   (Roberta Flack)
5. ROCK YOUR BABY
   (George McCrae)
6. RIKKI, DON'T LOSE THAT NUMBER
   (Steely Dan)
7. SIDESHOW
   (Blue Magic)
8. ROCK THE BOAT
   (The Hues Corporation)
9. RADAR LOVE
   (Golden Earring)
10. WATERLOO
    (Abba)

POP ALBUMS

1. CARIBOU
   (Elton John)
2. BACK HOME AGAIN
   (John Denver)
3. BAND ON THE RUN
   (Paul McCartney and Wings)
4. SUNDOWN
   (Gordon Lightfoot)
5. BACHMAN-TURNER OVERDRIVE 2
   (Bachman-Turner Overdrive)
6. JOHN DENVER'S GREATEST HITS, VOL. 1
   (John Denver)
7. BEFORE THE FLOOD
   (Bob Dylan/The Band)
8. JOURNEY TO THE CENTER OF THE EARTH
   (Rick Wakeman)
9. DIAMOND DOGS
   (David Bowie)
10. 461 OCEAN BOULEVARD
    (Eric Clapton)

BLACK SINGLES

1. FEEL LIKE MAKIN' LOVE
   (Roberta Flack)
2. ROCK YOUR BABY
   (George McCrae)
3. YOU'RE WELCOME, STOP ON BY
   (Bobby Womack)
4. MY THANG
   (James Brown)
5. MACHINE GUN
   (Commodores)
6. ROCK THE BOAT
   (The Hues Corporation)
7. MY LOVE
   (Margie Joseph)
8. ON AND ON
   (Gladys Knight and the Pips)
9. TELL ME SOMETHING GOOD
   (Rufus)
10. KUNG FU
    (Curtis Mayfield)

BLACK ALBUMS

1. LIVE IN LONDON
   (The O'Jays)
2. LET'S PUT IT ALL TOGETHER
   (The Stylistics)
3. LIVE
   (Marvin Gaye)
4. SKIN TIGHT
   (Ohio Players)
5. CLAUDINE
   (Gladys Knight and the Pips)
6. BODY HEAT
   (Quincy Jones)
7. FREEDOM FOR THE STALLION
   (The Hues Corporation)
8. THAT NIGGER'S CRAZY
   (Richard Pryor)
9. RAGS TO RUFUS
   (Rufus)
10. OPEN OUR EYES
    (Earth, Wind and Fire)

JAZZ ALBUMS

1. HEAD HUNTERS
   (Herbie Hancock)
2. BODY HEAT
   (Quincy Jones)
3. SCOTT JOPLIN: THE RED BACK BOOK
   (Gunther Schuller)
4. MYSTERIOUS TRAVELLER
   (Weather Report)
5. CROSSWINDS
   (Billy Cobham)
6. STREET LADY
   (Donald Byrd)
7. SPECTRUM
   (Billy Cobham)
8. APOCALYPSE
   (Mahavishnu Orchestra)
9. VISIONS
   (Paul Horn)
10. SCOTT JOPLIN: PIANO RAGS VOLS. 1 AND 2
    (Joshua Rifkin)

COUNTRY SINGLES

1. THAT SONG IS DRIVING ME CRAZY
   (Tom T. Hall)
2. AS SOON AS I HANG UP THE PHONE
   (Conway Twitty and Loretta Lynn)
3. RUB IT IN
   (Billy "Crash" Craddock)
4. YOU CAN'T BE A BEACON
   (Donna Fargo)
5. THE MAN THAT TURNED MY MAMA ON
   (Tanya Tucker)
6. STOMP THEM GRAPES
   (Mel Tillis)

7. STATUE OF A FOOL
   (Brian Collins)
8. THE GRAND TOUR
   (George Jones)
9. MARIE LAVEAU
   (Bobby Bare)
10. HELP ME
    (Elvis Presley)

COUNTRY ALBUMS

1. IF YOU LOVE ME
   (Olivia Newton-John)
2. THE BEST OF CHARLIE RICH
   (Charlie Rich)
3. BEHIND CLOSED DOORS
   (Charlie Rich)
4. COUNTRY FEELING
   (Charley Pride)
5. PURE LOVE
   (Ronnie Milsap)
6. COUNTRY BUMPKIN
   (Cal Smith)
7. LORETTA LYNN'S GREATEST HITS, VOL. 2
   (Loretta Lynn)
8. THERE WON'T BE ANYMORE
   (Charlie Rich)
9. STOP AND SMELL THE ROSES
   (Mac Davis)
10. RUB IT IN
    (Billy "Crash" Craddock)

AUGUST 10, 1974

POP SINGLES

1. FEEL LIKE MAKIN' LOVE
   (Roberta Flack)
2. DON'T LET THE SUN GO DOWN ON ME
   (Elton John)
3. ROCK AND ROLL HEAVEN
   (The Righteous Brothers)
4. THE NIGHT CHICAGO DIED
   (Paper Lace)
5. RIKKI, DON'T LOSE THAT NUMBER
   (Steely Dan)
6. SIDESHOW
   (Blue Magic)
7. ROCK YOUR BABY
   (George McCrae)
8. PLEASE COME TO BOSTON
   (Dave Loggins)
9. ANNIE'S SONG
   (John Denver)
10. WATERLOO
    (Abba)

POP ALBUMS

1. BACK HOME AGAIN
   (John Denver)
2. CARIBOU
   (Elton John)
3. 461 OCEAN BOULEVARD
   (Eric Clapton)
4. BACHMAN-TURNER OVERDRIVE 2
   (Bachman-Turner Overdrive)
5. BEFORE THE FLOOD
   (Bob Dylan/The Band)
6. JOHN DENVER'S GREATEST HITS, VOL. 1
   (John Denver)
7. BAND ON THE RUN
   (Paul McCartney and Wings)
8. SUNDOWN
   (Gordon Lightfoot)
9. JOURNEY TO THE CENTER OF THE EARTH
   (Rick Wakeman)
10. ON STAGE
    (Loggins and Messina)

BLACK SINGLES

1. FEEL LIKE MAKIN' LOVE
   (Roberta Flack)
2. ROCK YOUR BABY
   (George McCrae)
3. YOU'RE WELCOME, STOP ON BY
   (Bobby Womack)
4. TELL ME SOMETHING GOOD
   (Rufus)
5. KUNG FU
   (Curtis Mayfield)
6. MY THANG
   (James Brown)
7. MY LOVE
   (Margie Joseph)
8. TIME FOR LIVIN'
   (Sly and the Family Stone)
9. MACHINE GUN
   (Commodores)
10. HAPPINESS IS JUST AROUND THE BEND
    (Main Ingredient)

BLACK ALBUMS

1. LIVE
   (Marvin Gaye)
2. LIVE IN LONDON
   (The O'Jays)
3. LET'S PUT IT ALL TOGETHER
   (The Stylistics)
4. SKIN TIGHT
   (Ohio Players)
5. FREEDOM FOR THE STALLION
   (The Hues Corporation)
6. BODY HEAT
   (Quincy Jones)
7. THAT NIGGER'S CRAZY
   (Richard Pryor)
8. RAGS TO RUFUS
   (Rufus)
9. CLAUDINE
   (Gladys Knight and the Pips)
10. OPEN OUR EYES
    (Earth, Wind and Fire)

JAZZ ALBUMS

1. HEAD HUNTERS
   (Herbie Hancock)
2. SCOTT JOPLIN: THE RED BACK BOOK
   (Gunther Schuller)
3. BODY HEAT
   (Quincy Jones)
4. CROSSWINDS
   (Billy Cobham)
5. MYSTERIOUS TRAVELLER
   (Weather Report)
6. STREET LADY
   (Donald Byrd)
7. SCOTT JOPLIN: PIANO RAGS VOLS. 1 AND 2
   (Joshua Rifkin)
8. SPECTRUM
   (Billy Cobham)
9. POWER OF SOUL
   (Idris Muhammad)
10. VISIONS
    (Paul Horn)

COUNTRY SINGLES

1. RUB IT IN
   (Billy "Crash" Craddock)
2. AS SOON AS I HANG UP THE PHONE
   (Conway Twitty and Loretta Lynn)
3. YOU CAN'T BE A BEACON
   (Donna Fargo)
4. THE MAN THAT TURNED MY MAMA ON
   (Tanya Tucker)
5. THAT SONG IS DRIVING ME CRAZY
   (Tom T. Hall)
6. THE GRAND TOUR
   (George Jones)
7. OLD MAN FROM THE
   MOUNTAIN/HOLDING THINGS TOGETHER
   (Merle Haggard)
8. HELP ME
   (Elvis Presley)
9. THE WANT TO'S
   (Freddie Hart)
10. DRINKIN' THING
    (Gary Stewart)

COUNTRY ALBUMS

1. IF YOU LOVE ME
   (Olivia Newton-John)
2. BEHIND CLOSED DOORS
   (Charlie Rich)
3. THE BEST OF CHARLIE RICH
   (Charlie Rich)
4. COUNTRY FEELING
   (Charley Pride)
5. COUNTRY BUMPKIN
   (Cal Smith)
6. LORETTA LYNN'S GREATEST HITS, VOL. 2
   (Loretta Lynn)
7. COUNTRY PARTNERS
   (Conway Twitty and Loretta Lynn)
8. RUB IT IN
   (Billy "Crash" Craddock)
9. STOP AND SMELL THE ROSES
   (Mac Davis)
10. BOOGITY BOOGITY
    (Ray Stevens)

AUGUST 17, 1974

POP SINGLES

1. THE NIGHT CHICAGO DIED
   (Paper Lace)
2. FEEL LIKE MAKIN' LOVE
   (Roberta Flack)
3. DON'T LET THE SUN GO DOWN ON ME
   (Elton John)
4. ROCK AND ROLL HEAVEN
   (The Righteous Brothers)
5. SIDESHOW
   (Blue Magic)
6. WILDWOOD WEED
   (Jim Stafford)
7. PLEASE COME TO BOSTON
   (Dave Loggins)
8. (YOU'RE) HAVING MY BABY
   (Paul Anka)
9. WATERLOO
   (Abba)
10. TELL ME SOMETHING GOOD
    (Rufus)

POP ALBUMS

1. 461 OCEAN BOULEVARD
   (Eric Clapton)
2. BACK HOME AGAIN
   (John Denver)
3. CARIBOU
   (Elton John)
4. BACHMAN-TURNER OVERDRIVE 2
   (Bachman-Turner Overdrive)
5. BEFORE THE FLOOD
   (Bob Dylan/The Band)
6. JOHN DENVER'S GREATEST HITS, VOL. 1
   (John Denver)
7. BAND ON THE RUN
   (Paul McCartney and Wings)
8. FULFILLINGNESS' FIRST FINALE
   (Stevie Wonder)
9. JOURNEY TO THE CENTER OF THE EARTH
   (Rick Wakeman)
10. ON STAGE
    (Loggins and Messina)

BLACK SINGLES

1. TELL ME SOMETHING GOOD
   (Rufus)
2. FEEL LIKE MAKIN' LOVE
   (Roberta Flack)
3. ROCK YOUR BABY
   (George McCrae)
4. KUNG FU
   (Curtis Mayfield)
5. HANG ON IN THERE BABY
   (Johnny Bristol)
6. YOU'RE WELCOME, STOP ON BY
   (Bobby Womack)
7. TIME FOR LIVIN'
   (Sly and the Family Stone)
8. MY THANG
   (James Brown)
9. HAPPINESS IS JUST AROUND THE BEND
   (Main Ingredient)
10. CITY IN THE SKY
    (The Staple Singers)

BLACK ALBUMS

1. FULFILLINGNESS' FIRST FINALE
   (Stevie Wonder)
2. LIVE
   (Marvin Gaye)
3. LIVE IN LONDON
   (The O'Jays)
4. SKIN TIGHT
   (Ohio Players)
5. FREEDOM FOR THE STALLION
   (The Hues Corporation)
6. RAGS TO RUFUS
   (Rufus)
7. THAT NIGGER'S CRAZY
   (Richard Pryor)
8. OPEN YOUR EYES
   (Earth, Wind and Fire)
9. BODY HEAT
   (Quincy Jones)
10. LET'S PUT IT ALL TOGETHER
    (The Stylistics)

JAZZ ALBUMS

1. BODY HEAT
   (Quincy Jones)
2. HEAD HUNTERS
   (Herbie Hancock)
3. SCOTT JOPLIN: THE RED BACK BOOK
   (Gunther Schuller)
4. CROSSWINDS
   (Billy Cobham)
5. STREET LADY
   (Donald Byrd)
6. SPECTRUM
   (Billy Cobham)
7. SCOTT JOPLIN: PIANO RAGS VOLS. 1 AND 2
   (Joshua Rifkin)
8. REGGAE
   (Herbie Mann)
9. MYSTERIOUS TRAVELLER
   (Weather Report)
10. APOCALYPSE
    (Mahavishnu Orchestra)

COUNTRY SINGLES

1. AS SOON AS I HANG UP THE PHONE
   (Conway Twitty and Loretta Lynn)
2. YOU CAN'T BE A BEACON
   (Donna Fargo)
3. OLD MAN FROM THE
   MOUNTAIN/HOLDING THINGS TOGETHER
   (Merle Haggard)
4. THE MAN THAT TURNED MY MAMA ON
   (Tanya Tucker)
5. THE GRAND TOUR
   (George Jones)

6. HELP ME
   (Elvis Presley)
7. THE WANT TO'S
   (Freddie Hart)
8. DRINKIN' THING
   (Gary Stewart)
9. RUB IT IN
   (Billy "Crash" Craddock)
10. ANNIE'S SONG
    (John Denver)

COUNTRY ALBUMS

1. IF YOU LOVE ME
   (Olivia Newton-John)
2. BEHIND CLOSED DOORS
   (Charlie Rich)
3. COUNTRY PARTNERS
   (Conway Twitty and Loretta Lynn)
4. THE BEST OF CHARLIE RICH
   (Charlie Rich)
5. RUB IT IN
   (Billy "Crash" Craddock)
6. LORETTA LYNN'S GREATEST HITS, VOL. 2
   (Loretta Lynn)
7. COUNTRY BUMPKIN
   (Cal Smith)
8. COUNTRY FEELING
   (Charley Pride)
9. BOOGITY BOOGITY
   (Ray Stevens)
10. STOP AND SMELL THE ROSES
    (Mac Davis)

AUGUST 24, 1974

POP SINGLES

1. (YOU'RE) HAVING MY BABY
   (Paul Anka)
2. THE NIGHT CHICAGO DIED
   (Paper Lace)
3. FEEL LIKE MAKIN' LOVE
   (Roberta Flack)
4. WILDWOOD WEED
   (Jim Stafford)
5. DON'T LET THE SUN GO DOWN ON ME
   (Elton John)
6. TELL ME SOMETHING GOOD
   (Rufus)
7. PLEASE COME TO BOSTON
   (Dave Loggins)
8. SIDESHOW
   (Blue Magic)
9. I SHOT THE SHERIFF
   (Eric Clapton)
10. I'M LEAVING IT (ALL) UP TO YOU
    (Donny and Marie Osmond)

POP ALBUMS

1. 461 OCEAN BOULEVARD
   (Eric Clapton)
2. BACK HOME AGAIN
   (John Denver)
3. FULFILLINGNESS' FIRST FINALE
   (Stevie Wonder)
4. CARIBOU
   (Elton John)
5. BACHMAN-TURNER OVERDRIVE 2
   (Bachman-Turner Overdrive)
6. BEFORE THE FLOOD
   (Bob Dylan/The Band)
7. JOHN DENVER'S GREATEST HITS, VOL. 1
   (John Denver)
8. BAND ON THE RUN
   (Paul McCartney and Wings)
9. STOP AND SMELL THE ROSES
   (Mac Davis)
10. JOURNEY TO THE CENTER OF THE EARTH
    (Rick Wakeman)

BLACK SINGLES

1. HANG ON IN THERE BABY
   (Johnny Bristol)
2. TELL ME SOMETHING GOOD
   (Rufus)
3. FEEL LIKE MAKIN' LOVE
   (Roberta Flack)
4. KUNG FU
   (Curtis Mayfield)
5. CITY IN THE SKY
   (The Staple Singers)
6. TIME FOR LIVIN'
   (Sly and the Family Stone)
7. KALIMBA STORY
   (Earth, Wind and Fire)
8. HAPPINESS IS JUST AROUND THE BEND
   (Main Ingredient)
9. ROCK YOUR BABY
   (George McRae)
10. NOTHING FROM NOTHING
    (Billy Preston)

BLACK ALBUMS

1. FULFILLINGNESS' FIRST FINALE
   (Stevie Wonder)
2. LIVE
   (Marvin Gaye)
3. LIVE IN LONDON
   (The O'Jays)
4. SKIN TIGHT
   (Ohio Players)
5. RAGS TO RUFUS
   (Rufus)
6. THAT NIGGER'S CRAZY
   (Richard Pryor)
7. OPEN OUR EYES
   (Earth, Wind and Fire)
8. BODY HEAT
   (Quincy Jones)
9. ROCK YOUR BABY
   (George McCrae)
10. HELL
    (James Brown)

JAZZ ALBUMS

1. BODY HEAT
   (Quincy Jones)
2. HEAD HUNTERS
   (Herbie Hancock)
3. CROSSWINDS
   (Billy Cobham)
4. SCOTT JOPLIN: THE RED BACK BOOK
   (Gunther Schuller)
5. REGGAE
   (Herbie Mann)
6. SCOTT JOPLIN: PIANO RAGS VOLS. 1 AND 2
   (Joshua Rifkin)
7. SPECTRUM
   (Billy Cobham)
8. STREET LADY
   (Donald Byrd)
9. MYSTERIOUS TRAVELLER
   (Weather Report)
10. YESTERDAYS
    (Gato Barbieri)

COUNTRY SINGLES

1. YOU CAN'T BE A BEACON
   (Donna Fargo)
2. OLD MAN FROM THE MOUNTAIN/HOLDING THINGS TOGETHER
   (Merle Haggard)
3. AS SOON AS I HANG UP THE PHONE
   (Conway Twitty and Loretta Lynn)
4. THE GRAND TOUR
   (George Jones)
5. HELP ME
   (Elvis Presley)

6. THE WANT TO'S
   (Freddie Hart)
7. ANNIE'S SONG
   (John Denver)
8. DRINKIN' THING
   (Gary Stewart)
9. DANCE WITH ME
   (Johnny Rodriguez)
10. MY WIFE'S HOUSE
    (Jerry Wallace)

COUNTRY ALBUMS

1. COUNTRY PARTNERS
   (Conway Twitty and Loretta Lynn)
2. IF YOU LOVE ME
   (Olivia Newton-John)
3. BEHIND CLOSED DOORS
   (Charlie Rich)
4. RUB IT IN
   (Billy "Crash" Craddock)
5. THE BEST OF CHARLIE RICH
   (Charlie Rich)
6. LORETTA LYNN'S GREATEST HITS, VOL. 2
   (Loretta Lynn)
7. BOOGITY, BOOGITY
   (Ray Stevens)
8. STOP AND SMELL THE ROSES
   (Mac Davis)
9. IN MY LITTLE CORNER OF THE WORLD
   (Marie Osmond)
10. COUNTRY FEELING
    (Charley Pride)

AUGUST 31, 1974

POP SINGLES

1. (YOU'RE) HAVING MY BABY
   (Paul Anka)
2. THE NIGHT CHICAGO DIED
   (Paper Lace)
3. TELL ME SOMETHING GOOD
   (Rufus)
4. WILDWOOD WEED
   (Jim Stafford)
5. I SHOT THE SHERIFF
   (Eric Clapton)
6. FEEL LIKE MAKIN' LOVE
   (Roberta Flack)
7. I'M LEAVING IT (ALL) UP TO YOU
   (Donny and Marie Osmond)
8. ROCK ME GENTLY
   (Andy Kim)
9. PLEASE COME TO BOSTON
   (Dave Loggins)
10. DON'T LET THE SUN GO DOWN ON ME
    (Elton John)

POP ALBUMS

1. FULFILLINGNESS' FIRST FINALE
   (Stevie Wonder)
2. 461 OCEAN BOULEVARD
   (Eric Clapton)
3. BACK HOME AGAIN
   (John Denver)
4. CARIBOU
   (Elton John)
5. BACHMAN-TURNER OVERDRIVE 2
   (Bachman-Turner Overdrive)
6. BAD COMPANY
   (Bad Company)
7. JOHN DENVER'S GREATEST HITS, VOL. 1
   (John Denver)
8. BAND ON THE RUN
   (Paul McCartney and Wings)
9. STOP AND SMELL THE ROSES
   (Mac Davis)

10. THE SOUTHER-HILLMAN-FURAY BAND
    (The Souther-Hillman-Furay Band)

BLACK SINGLES

1. THEN CAME YOU
   (Dionne Warwick and The Spinners)
2. HANG ON IN THERE BABY
   (Johnny Bristol)
3. TELL ME SOMETHING GOOD
   (Rufus)
4. CITY IN THE SKY
   (The Staple Singers)
5. NOTHING FROM NOTHING
   (Billy Preston)
6. KALIMBA STORY
   (Earth, Wind and Fire)
7. CAN'T GET ENOUGH OF YOUR LOVE, BABE
   (Barry White)
8. FEEL LIKE MAKIN' LOVE
   (Roberta Flack)
9. LIVE IT UP (PART 1)
   (Isley Brothers)
10. KUNG FU
    (Curtis Mayfield)

BLACK ALBUMS

1. FULFILLINGNESS' FIRST FINALE
   (Stevie Wonder)
2. LIVE
   (Marvin Gaye)
3. RAGS TO RUFUS
   (Rufus)
4. LIVE IN LONDON
   (The O'Jays)
5. SKIN TIGHT
   (Ohio Players)
6. THAT NIGGER'S CRAZY
   (Richard Pryor)
7. ROCK YOUR BABY
   (George McCrae)
8. HELL
   (James Brown)
9. BODY HEAT
   (Quincy Jones)
10. COMIN' FROM ALL ENDS
    (New Birth)

JAZZ ALBUMS

1. BODY HEAT
   (Quincy Jones)
2. HEAD HUNTERS
   (Herbie Hancock)
3. REGGAE
   (Herbie Mann)
4. CROSSWINDS
   (Billy Cobham)
5. SPECTRUM
   (Billy Cobham)
6. SCOTT JOPLIN: THE RED BACK BOOK
   (Gunther Schuller)
7. YESTERDAYS
   (Gato Barbieri)
8. SCOTT JOPLIN: PIANO RAGS VOLS. 1 AND 2
   (Joshua Rifkin)
9. STREET LADY
   (Donald Byrd)
10. ONE
    (Bob James)

COUNTRY SINGLES

1. OLD MAN FROM THE
   MOUNTAIN/HOLDING THINGS TOGETHER
   (Merle Haggard)
2. THE GRAND TOUR
   (George Jones)
3. YOU CAN'T BE A BEACON
   (Donna Fargo)

4. THE WANT TO'S
   (Freddie Hart)
5. DANCE WITH ME
   (Johnny Rodriguez)
6. PLEASE DON'T TELL ME HOW THE STORY
   ENDS
   (Ronnie Milsap)
7. MY WIFE'S HOUSE
   (Jerry Wallace)
8. I WOULDN'T WANT TO LIVE
   (Don Williams)
9. TALKIN' TO THE WALL
   (Lynn Anderson)

COUNTRY ALBUMS

1. COUNTRY PARTNERS
   (Conway Twitty and Loretta Lynn)
2. IF YOU LOVE ME
   (Olivia Newton-John)
3. BEHIND CLOSED DOORS
   (Charlie Rich)
4. RUB IT IN
   (Billy "Crash" Craddock)
5. BACK HOME AGAIN
   (John Denver)
6. STOP AND SMELL THE ROSES
   (Mac Davis)
7. BOOGITY, BOOGITY
   (Ray Stevens)
8. IN MY LITTLE CORNER OF THE WORLD
   (Marie Osmond)
9. LORETTA LYNN'S GREATEST HITS, VOL. 2
   (Loretta Lynn)
10. ELVIS RECORDED LIVE ON STAGE AT
    MEMPHIS
    (Elvis Presley)

SEPTEMBER 7, 1974

POP SINGLES

1. I SHOT THE SHERIFF
   (Eric Clapton)
2. (YOU'RE) HAVING MY BABY
   (Paul Anka)
3. TELL ME SOMETHING GOOD
   (Rufus)
4. THE NIGHT CHICAGO DIED
   (Paper Lace)
5. I'M LEAVING IT (ALL) UP TO YOU
   (Donny and Marie Osmond)
6. ROCK ME GENTLY
   (Andy Kim)
7. WILDWOOD WEED
   (Jim Stafford)
8. FEEL LIKE MAKIN' LOVE
   (Roberta Flack)
9. CAN'T GET ENOUGH OF YOUR LOVE, BABE
   (Barry White)
10. YOU AND ME AGAINST THE WORLD
    (Helen Reddy)

POP ALBUMS

1. FULFILLINGNESS' FIRST FINALE
   (Stevie Wonder)
2. 461 OCEAN BOULEVARD
   (Eric Clapton)
3. BACK HOME AGAIN
   (John Denver)
4. BAD COMPANY
   (Bad Company)
5. CARIBOU
   (Elton John)
6. BACHMAN-TURNER OVERDRIVE 2
   (Bachman-Turner Overdrive)
7. RAGS TO RUFUS
   (Rufus)
8. STOP AND SMELL THE ROSES
   (Mac Davis)

9. THE SOUTHER-HILLMAN-FURAY BAND
   (The Souther-Hillman-Furay Band)
10. ENDLESS SUMMER
    (The Beach Boys)

BLACK SINGLES

1. CAN'T GET ENOUGH OF YOUR LOVE, BABE
   (Barry White)
2. THEN CAME YOU
   (Dionne Warwick and The Spinners)
3. HANG ON IN THERE BABY
   (Johnny Bristol)
4. NOTHING FROM NOTHING
   (Billy Preston)
5. TELL ME SOMETHING GOOD
   (Rufus)
6. KALIMBA STORY
   (Earth, Wind and Fire)
7. LIVE IT UP (PART 1)
   (Isley Brothers)
8. FEEL LIKE MAKIN' LOVE
   (Roberta Flack)
9. CITY IN THE SKY
   (The Staple Singers)
10. LET'S PUT IT ALL TOGETHER
    (The Stylistics)

BLACK ALBUMS

1. FULFILLINGNESS' FIRST FINALE
   (Stevie Wonder)
2. RAGS TO RUFUS
   (Rufus)
3. LIVE
   (Marvin Gaye)
4. SKIN TIGHT
   (Ohio Players)
5. THAT NIGGER'S CRAZY
   (Richard Pryor)
6. COMIN' FROM ALL ENDS
   (New Birth)
7. LIVE IN LONDON
   (The O'Jays)
8. ROCK YOUR BABY
   (George McCrae)
9. HELL
   (James Brown)
10. BODY HEAT
    (Quincy Jones)

JAZZ ALBUMS

1. BODY HEAT
   (Quincy Jones)
2. REGGAE
   (Herbie Mann)
3. HEAD HUNTERS
   (Herbie Hancock)
4. SPECTRUM
   (Billy Cobham)
5. CROSSWINDS
   (Billy Cobham)
6. SCOTT JOPLIN: THE RED BACK BOOK
   (Gunther Schuller)
7. YESTERDAYS
   (Gato Barbieri)
8. STREET LADY
   (Donald Byrd)
9. ONE
   (Bob James)
10. SCOTT JOPLIN: PIANO RAGS VOLS. 1 AND 2
    (Joshua Rifkin)

COUNTRY SINGLES

1. THE GRAND TOUR
   (George Jones)
2. DANCE WITH ME
   (Johnny Rodriguez)
3. THE WANT TO'S
   (Freddie Hart)

4. PLEASE DON'T TELL ME HOW THE STORY
ENDS
(Ronnie Milsap)
5. OLD MAN FROM THE
MOUNTAIN/HOLDING THINGS TOGETHER
(Merle Haggard)
6. I WOULDN'T WANT TO LIVE
(Don Williams)
7. YOU CAN'T BE A BEACON
(Donna Fargo)
8. MY WIFE'S HOUSE
(Jerry Wallace)
9. TALKIN' TO THE WALL
(Lynn Anderson)
10. I'LL THINK OF SOMETHING
(Hank Williams Jr.)

COUNTRY ALBUMS

1. BACK HOME AGAIN
(John Denver)
2. COUNTRY PARTNERS
(Conway Twitty and Loretta Lynn)
3. IF YOU LOVE ME
(Olivia Newton-John)
4. BEHIND CLOSED DOORS
(Charlie Rich)
5. STOP AND SMELL THE ROSES
(Mac Davis)
6. ELVIS RECORDED LIVE ON STAGE AT
MEMPHIS
(Elvis Presley)
7. IN MY LITTLE CORNER OF THE WORLD
(Marie Osmond)
8. LORETTA LYNN'S GREATEST HITS, VOL. 2
(Loretta Lynn)
9. RUB IT IN
(Billy "Crash" Craddock)
10. VERY SPECIAL LOVE SONGS
(Charlie Rich)

SEPTEMBER 14, 1974

POP SINGLES

1. I SHOT THE SHERIFF
(Eric Clapton)
2. (YOU'RE) HAVING MY BABY
(Paul Anka)
3. CAN'T GET ENOUGH OF YOUR LOVE, BABE
(Barry White)
4. I'M LEAVING IT (ALL) UP TO YOU
(Donny and Marie Osmond)
5. ROCK ME GENTLY
(Andy Kim)
6. TELL ME SOMETHING GOOD
(Rufus)
7. THEN CAME YOU
(Dionne Warwick and The Spinners)
8. NOTHING FROM NOTHING
(Billy Preston)
9. YOU AND ME AGAINST THE WORLD
(Helen Reddy)
10. HANG ON IN THERE BABY
(Johnny Bristol)

POP ALBUMS

1. BACK HOME AGAIN
(John Denver)
2. 461 OCEAN BOULEVARD
(Eric Clapton)
3. FULFILLINGNESS' FIRST FINALE
(Stevie Wonder)
4. BAD COMPANY
(Bad Company)
5. RAGS TO RUFUS
(Rufus)
6. CARIBOU
(Elton John)

7. ENDLESS SUMMER
(The Beach Boys)
8. STOP AND SMELL THE ROSES
(Mac Davis)
9. THE SOUTHER-HILLMAN-FURAY BAND
(The Souther-Hillman-Furay Band)
10. BACHMAN-TURNER OVERDRIVE 2
(Bachman-Turner Overdrive)

BLACK SINGLES

1. CAN'T GET ENOUGH OF YOUR LOVE, BABE
(Barry White)
2. THEN CAME YOU
(Dionne Warwick and The Spinners)
3. HANG ON IN THERE BABY
(Johnny Bristol)
4. NOTHING FROM NOTHING
(Billy Preston)
5. DO IT BABY
(The Miracles)
6. LIVE IT UP (PART 1)
(Isley Brothers)
7. LET'S PUT IT ALL TOGETHER
(The Stylistics)
8. YOU HAVEN'T DONE NOTHIN'
(Stevie Wonder)
9. TELL ME SOMETHING GOOD
(Rufus)
10. SKIN TIGHT
(Ohio Players)

BLACK ALBUMS

1. FULFILLINGNESS' FIRST FINALE
(Stevie Wonder)
2. RAGS TO RUFUS
(Rufus)
3. SKIN TIGHT
(Ohio Players)
4. COMIN' FROM ALL ENDS
(New Birth)
5. LIVE
(Marvin Gaye)
6. THAT NIGGER'S CRAZY
(Richard Pryor)
7. MIGHTY LOVE
(Spinners)
8. STANDING ON THE VERGE
(Funkadelic)
9. ROCK YOUR BABY
(George McCrae)
10. LIVE IN LONDON
(The O'Jays)

JAZZ ALBUMS

1. BODY HEAT
(Quincy Jones)
2. HEAD HUNTERS
(Herbie Hancock)
3. REGGAE
(Herbie Mann)
4. ONE
(Bob James)
5. STREET LADY
(Donald Byrd)
6. SPECTRUM
(Billy Cobham)
7. CROSSWINDS
(Billy Cobham)
8. SCOTT JOPLIN: THE RED BACK BOOK
(Gunther Schuller)
9. SCOTT JOPLIN: PIANO RAGS VOLS. 1 AND 2
(Joshua Rifkin)
10. MAGIC AND MOVEMENT
(John Klemmer)

COUNTRY SINGLES

1. DANCE WITH ME
(Johnny Rodriguez)

2. PLEASE DON'T TELL ME HOW THE STORY
ENDS
(Ronnie Milsap)
3. I WOULDN'T WANT TO LIVE
(Don Williams)
4. THE GRAND TOUR
(George Jones)
5. OLD MAN FROM THE
MOUNTAIN/HOLDING THINGS TOGETHER
(Merle Haggard)
6. THE WANT TO'S
(Freddie Hart)
7. I'LL THINK OF SOMETHING
(Hank Williams Jr.)
8. TALKIN' TO THE WALL
(Lynn Anderson)
9. BIG FOUR-POSTER BED
(Brenda Lee)
10. (IT'S A) MONSTER'S HOLIDAY
(Buck Owens)

COUNTRY ALBUMS

1. BACK HOME AGAIN
(John Denver)
2. COUNTRY PARTNERS
(Conway Twitty and Loretta Lynn)
3. ELVIS RECORDED LIVE ON STAGE AT
MEMPHIS
(Elvis Presley)
4. IF YOU LOVE ME
(Olivia Newton-John)
5. STOP AND SMELL THE ROSES
(Mac Davis)
6. BEHIND CLOSED DOORS
(Charlie Rich)
7. LORETTA LYNN'S GREATEST HITS, VOL. 2
(Loretta Lynn)
8. IN MY LITTLE CORNER OF THE WORLD
(Marie Osmond)
9. GOOD AND COUNTRY
(Marty Robbins)
10. VERY SPECIAL LOVE SONGS
(Charlie Rich)

SEPTEMBER 21, 1974

POP SINGLES

1. CAN'T GET ENOUGH OF YOUR LOVE, BABE
(Barry White)
2. I SHOT THE SHERIFF
(Eric Clapton)
3. I HONESTLY LOVE YOU
(Olivia Newton-John)
4. THEN CAME YOU
(Dionne Warwick and The Spinners)
5. ROCK ME GENTLY
(Andy Kim)
6. NOTHING FROM NOTHING
(Billy Preston)
7. (YOU'RE) HAVING MY BABY
(Paul Anka)
8. I'M LEAVING IT (ALL) UP TO YOU
(Donny and Marie Osmond)
9. YOU HAVEN'T DONE NOTHIN'
(Stevie Wonder)
10. HANG ON IN THERE BABY
(Johnny Bristol)

POP ALBUMS

1. BACK HOME AGAIN
(John Denver)
2. 461 OCEAN BOULEVARD
(Eric Clapton)
3. ENDLESS SUMMER
(The Beach Boys)
4. BAD COMPANY
(Bad Company)

5. RAGS TO RUFUS
   (Rufus)
6. FULFILLINGNESS' FIRST FINALE
   (Stevie Wonder)
7. IF YOU LOVE ME (LET ME KNOW)
   (Olivia Newton-John)
8. CARIBOU
   (Elton John)
9. THE SOUTHER-HILLMAN-FURAY BAND
   (The Souther-Hillman-Furay Band)
10. STOP AND SMELL THE ROSES
    (Mac Davis)

BLACK SINGLES

1. DO IT BABY
   (The Miracles)
2. CAN'T GET ENOUGH OF YOUR LOVE, BABE
   (Barry White)
3. THEN CAME YOU
   (Dionne Warwick and The Spinners)
4. YOU HAVEN'T DONE NOTHIN'
   (Stevie Wonder)
5. SKIN TIGHT
   (Ohio Players)
6. LIVE IT UP (PART 1)
   (Isley Brothers)
7. LET'S PUT IT ALL TOGETHER
   (The Stylistics)
8. MIDNIGHT FLOWER
   (The Four Tops)
9. TELL HER LOVE HAS FELT THE NEED
   (Eddie Kendricks)
10. NOTHING FROM NOTHING
    (Billy Preston)

BLACK ALBUMS

1. RAGS TO RUFUS
   (Rufus)
2. SKIN TIGHT
   (Ohio Players)
3. FULFILLINGNESS' FIRST FINALE
   (Stevie Wonder)
4. BODY HEAT
   (Quincy Jones)
5. COMIN' FROM ALL ENDS
   (New Birth)
6. LIVE
   (Marvin Gaye)
7. MIGHTY LOVE
   (Spinners)
8. STANDING ON THE VERGE
   (Funkadelic)
9. CAN'T GET ENOUGH
   (Barry White)
10. ROCK YOUR BABY
    (George McCrae)

JAZZ ALBUMS

1. BODY HEAT
   (Quincy Jones)
2. ONE
   (Bob James)
3. HEAD HUNTERS
   (Herbie Hancock)
4. REGGAE
   (Herbie Mann)
5. STREET LADY
   (Donald Byrd)
6. CROSSWINDS
   (Billy Cobham)
7. SPECTRUM
   (Billy Cobham)
8. SCOTT JOPLIN: THE RED BACK BOOK
   (Gunther Schuller)
9. WINTER IN AMERICA
   (Gil Scott-Heron)
10. THE BLACKBYRDS
    (Blackbyrds)

COUNTRY SINGLES

1. PLEASE DON'T TELL ME HOW THE STORY
   ENDS
   (Ronnie Milsap)
2. I WOULDN'T WANT TO LIVE
   (Don Williams)
3. BIG FOUR-POSTER BED
   (Brenda Lee)
4. DANCE WITH ME
   (Johnny Rodriguez)
5. (IT'S A) MONSTER'S HOLIDAY
   (Buck Owens)
6. I'M A RAMBLIN' MAN
   (Waylon Jennings)
7. I LOVE MY FRIEND
   (Charlie Rich)
8. I'LL THINK OF SOMETHING
   (Hank Williams Jr.)
9. OLD MAN FROM THE
   MOUNTAIN/HOLDING THINGS TOGETHER
   (Merle Haggard)
10. A MI ESPOSA CON AMOR
    (Sonny James)

COUNTRY ALBUMS

1. BACK HOME AGAIN
   (John Denver)
2. ELVIS RECORDED LIVE ON STAGE AT
   MEMPHIS
   (Elvis Presley)
3. COUNTRY PARTNERS
   (Conway Twitty and Loretta Lynn)
4. STOP AND SMELL THE ROSES
   (Mac Davis)
5. IF YOU LOVE ME
   (Olivia Newton-John)
6. BEHIND CLOSED DOORS
   (Charlie Rich)
7. LORETTA LYNN'S GREATEST HITS, VOL. 2
   (Loretta Lynn)
8. GOOD AND COUNTRY
   (Marty Robbins)
9. VERY SPECIAL LOVE SONGS
   (Charlie Rich)
10. RUB IT IN
    (Billy "Crash" Craddock)

SEPTEMBER 28, 1974

POP SINGLES

1. I HONESTLY LOVE YOU
   (Olivia Newton-John)
2. CAN'T GET ENOUGH OF YOUR LOVE, BABE
   (Barry White)
3. THEN CAME YOU
   (Dionne Warwick and The Spinners)
4. NOTHING FROM NOTHING
   (Billy Preston)
5. ROCK ME GENTLY
   (Andy Kim)
6. I SHOT THE SHERIFF
   (Eric Clapton)
7. YOU HAVEN'T DONE NOTHIN'
   (Stevie Wonder)
8. (YOU'RE) HAVING MY BABY
   (Paul Anka)
9. HANG ON IN THERE BABY
   (Johnny Bristol)
10. EARACHE MY EYE
    (Cheech and Chong)

POP ALBUMS

1. ENDLESS SUMMER
   (The Beach Boys)
2. BACK HOME AGAIN
   (John Denver)

3. BAD COMPANY
   (Bad Company)
4. 461 OCEAN BOULEVARD
   (Eric Clapton)
5. FULFILLINGNESS' FIRST FINALE
   (Stevie Wonder)
6. IF YOU LOVE ME (LET ME KNOW)
   (Olivia Newton-John)
7. RAGS TO RUFUS
   (Rufus)
8. CARIBOU
   (Elton John)
9. WELCOME BACK
   (Emerson, Lake and Palmer)
10. NOT FRAGILE
    (Bachman-Turner Overdrive)

BLACK SINGLES

1. YOU HAVEN'T DONE NOTHIN'
   (Stevie Wonder)
2. DO IT BABY
   (The Miracles)
3. SKIN TIGHT
   (Ohio Players)
4. CAN'T GET ENOUGH OF YOUR LOVE, BABE
   (Barry White)
5. THEN CAME YOU
   (Dionne Warwick and The Spinners)
6. LIVE IT UP (PART 1)
   (Isley Brothers)
7. MIDNIGHT FLOWER
   (The Four Tops)
8. TELL HER LOVE HAS FELT THE NEED
   (Eddie Kendricks)
9. AIN'T NO LOVE IN THE HEART OF THE
   CITY
   (Bobby "Blue" Bland)
10. IN THE BOTTLE
    (Brother to Brother)

BLACK ALBUMS

1. RAGS TO RUFUS
   (Rufus)
2. SKIN TIGHT
   (Ohio Players)
3. CAN'T GET ENOUGH
   (Barry White)
4. BODY HEAT
   (Quincy Jones)
5. COMIN' FROM ALL ENDS
   (New Birth)
6. FULFILLINGNESS' FIRST FINALE
   (Stevie Wonder)
7. MIGHTY LOVE
   (Spinners)
8. STANDING ON THE VERGE
   (Funkadelic)
9. LIVE
   (Marvin Gaye)
10. FRIENDS
    (B.B. King)

JAZZ ALBUMS

1. BODY HEAT
   (Quincy Jones)
2. ONE
   (Bob James)
3. HEAD HUNTERS
   (Herbie Hancock)
4. STREET LADY
   (Donald Byrd)
5. REGGAE
   (Herbie Mann)
6. CROSSWINDS
   (Billy Cobham)
7. WINTER IN AMERICA
   (Gil Scott-Heron)
8. THE BLACKBYRDS
   (Blackbyrds)
9. SPECTRUM
   (Billy Cobham)

10. YESTERDAYS
    (Gato Barbieri)

COUNTRY SINGLES

1. I WOULDN'T WANT TO LIVE
   (Don Williams)
2. BIG FOUR-POSTER BED
   (Brenda Lee)
3. I'M A RAMBLIN' MAN
   (Waylon Jennings)
4. (IT'S A) MONSTER'S HOLIDAY
   (Buck Owens)
5. I LOVE MY FRIEND
   (Charlie Rich)
6. PLEASE DON'T TELL ME HOW THE STORY
   ENDS
   (Ronnie Milsap)
7. A MI ESPOSA CON AMOR
   (Sonny James)
8. BONAPARTE'S RETREAT
   (Glen Campbell)
9. DANCE WITH ME
   (Johnny Rodriguez)
10. IT'LL COME BACK
    (Red Sovine)

COUNTRY ALBUMS

1. BACK HOME AGAIN
   (John Denver)
2. COUNTRY PARTNERS
   (Conway Twitty and Loretta Lynn)
3. ELVIS RECORDED LIVE ON STAGE AT
   MEMPHIS
   (Elvis Presley)
4. STOP AND SMELL THE ROSES
   (Mac Davis)
5. BEHIND CLOSED DOORS
   (Charlie Rich)
6. IF YOU LOVE ME
   (Olivia Newton-John)
7. GOOD AND COUNTRY
   (Marty Robbins)
8. ONE DAY AT A TIME
   (Marilyn Sellars)
9. RUB IT IN
   (Billy "Crash" Craddock)
10. LORETTA LYNN'S GREATEST HITS, VOL. 2
    (Loretta Lynn)

OCTOBER 5, 1974

POP SINGLES

1. I HONESTLY LOVE YOU
   (Olivia Newton-John)
2. THEN CAME YOU
   (Dionne Warwick and The Spinners)
3. NOTHING FROM NOTHING
   (Billy Preston)
4. CAN'T GET ENOUGH OF YOUR LOVE, BABE
   (Barry White)
5. YOU HAVEN'T DONE NOTHIN'
   (Stevie Wonder)
6. ROCK ME GENTLY
   (Andy Kim)
7. JAZZMAN
   (Carole King)
8. NEVER MY LOVE
   (Blue Swede)
9. EARACHE MY EYE
   (Cheech and Chong)
10. SWEET HOME ALABAMA
    (Lynyrd Skynyrd)

POP ALBUMS

1. BAD COMPANY
   (Bad Company)

2. BACK HOME AGAIN
   (John Denver)
3. ENDLESS SUMMER
   (The Beach Boys)
4. IF YOU LOVE ME (LET ME KNOW)
   (Olivia Newton-John)
5. FULFILLINGNESS' FIRST FINALE
   (Stevie Wonder)
6. WELCOME BACK
   (Emerson, Lake and Palmer)
7. NOT FRAGILE
   (Bachman-Turner Overdrive)
8. CARIBOU
   (Elton John)
9. 461 OCEAN BOULEVARD
   (Eric Clapton)
10. CAN'T GET ENOUGH
    (Barry White)

BLACK SINGLES

1. YOU HAVEN'T DONE NOTHIN'
   (Stevie Wonder)
2. SKIN TIGHT
   (Ohio Players)
3. DO IT BABY
   (The Miracles)
4. CAN'T GET ENOUGH OF YOUR LOVE, BABE
   (Barry White)
5. THEN CAME YOU
   (Dionne Warwick and The Spinners)
6. DO IT ('TIL YOU'RE SATISFIED)
   (B.T. Express)
7. IN THE BOTTLE
   (Brother to Brother)
8. PAPA DON'T TAKE NO MESS (PART 1)
   (James Brown)
9. AIN'T NO LOVE IN THE HEART OF THE
   CITY
   (Bobby "Blue" Bland)
10. VIRGIN MAN
    (Smokey Robinson)

BLACK ALBUMS

1. CAN'T GET ENOUGH
   (Barry White)
2. RAGS TO RUFUS
   (Rufus)
3. SKIN TIGHT
   (Ohio Players)
4. BODY HEAT
   (Quincy Jones)
5. MIGHTY LOVE
   (Spinners)
6. COMIN' FROM ALL ENDS
   (New Birth)
7. OPEN OUR EYES
   (Earth, Wind and Fire)
8. FULFILLINGNESS' FIRST FINALE
   (Stevie Wonder)
9. THE KIDS AND ME
   (Billy Preston)
10. DANCING MACHINE
    (The Jackson 5)

JAZZ ALBUMS

1. BODY HEAT
   (Quincy Jones)
2. ONE
   (Bob James)
3. HEAD HUNTERS
   (Herbie Hancock)
4. STREET LADY
   (Donald Byrd)
5. WINTER IN AMERICA
   (Gil Scott-Heron)
6. THE BLACKBYRDS
   (Blackbyrds)
7. HIGH ENERGY
   (Freddie Hubbard)
8. CROSSWINDS
   (Billy Cobham)

9. YESTERDAYS
   (Gato Barbieri)
10. TREASURE ISLAND
    (Keith Jarrett)

COUNTRY SINGLES

1. I'M A RAMBLIN' MAN
   (Waylon Jennings)
2. I LOVE MY FRIEND
   (Charlie Rich)
3. I WOULDN'T WANT TO LIVE
   (Don Williams)
4. BONAPARTE'S RETREAT
   (Glen Campbell)
5. A MI ESPOSA CON AMOR
   (Sonny James)
6. I OVERLOOKED AN ORCHID
   (Mickey Gilley)
7. BIG FOUR-POSTER BED
   (Brenda Lee)
8. PLEASE DON'T TELL ME HOW THE STORY
   ENDS
   (Ronnie Milsap)
9. PLEASE DON'T STOP LOVING ME
   (Porter Wagoner and Dolly Parton)
10. IT'LL COME BACK
    (Red Sovine)

COUNTRY ALBUMS

1. COUNTRY PARTNERS
   (Conway Twitty and Loretta Lynn)
2. BACK HOME AGAIN
   (John Denver)
3. STOP AND SMELL THE ROSES
   (Mac Davis)
4. BEHIND CLOSED DOORS
   (Charlie Rich)
5. IF YOU LOVE ME
   (Olivia Newton-John)
6. ELVIS RECORDED LIVE ON STAGE AT
   MEMPHIS
   (Elvis Presley)
7. ONE DAY AT A TIME
   (Marilyn Sellars)
8. COUNTRY BUMPKIN
   (Cal Smith)
9. ROOM FULL OF ROSES
   (Mickey Gilley)
10. COUNTRY IS
    (Tom T. Hall)

OCTOBER 12, 1974

POP SINGLES

1. THEN CAME YOU
   (Dionne Warwick and The Spinners)
2. NOTHING FROM NOTHING
   (Billy Preston)
3. I HONESTLY LOVE YOU
   (Olivia Newton-John)
4. YOU HAVEN'T DONE NOTHIN'
   (Stevie Wonder)
5. JAZZMAN
   (Carole King)
6. NEVER MY LOVE
   (Blue Swede)
7. CAN'T GET ENOUGH
   (Bad Company)
8. SWEET HOME ALABAMA
   (Lynyrd Skynyrd)
9. STOP AND SMELL THE ROSES
   (Mac Davis)
10. EARACHE MY EYE
    (Cheech and Chong)

POP ALBUMS

1. IF YOU LOVE ME (LET ME KNOW)
   (Olivia Newton-John)

2. BACK HOME AGAIN
   (John Denver)
3. BAD COMPANY
   (Bad Company)
4. NOT FRAGILE
   (Bachman-Turner Overdrive)
5. WELCOME BACK
   (Emerson, Lake and Palmer)
6. FULFILLINGNESS' FIRST FINALE
   (Stevie Wonder)
7. CAN'T GET ENOUGH
   (Barry White)
8. ENDLESS SUMMER
   (The Beach Boys)
9. SO FAR
   (Crosby, Stills, Nash and Young)
10. CARIBOU
    (Elton John)

BLACK SINGLES

1. DO IT ('TIL YOU'RE SATISFIED)
   (B. T. Express)
2. SKIN TIGHT
   (Ohio Players)
3. YOU HAVEN'T DONE NOTHIN'
   (Stevie Wonder)
4. PAPA DON'T TAKE NO MESS (PART 1)
   (James Brown)
5. DO IT BABY
   (The Miracles)
6. IN THE BOTTLE
   (Brother to Brother)
7. THE PLAYER (PART 1)
   (First Choice)
8. VIRGIN MAN
   (Smokey Robinson)
9. HIGHER PLANE
   (Kool and the Gang)
10. AIN'T NOTHING LIKE THE REAL THING
    (Aretha Franklin)

BLACK ALBUMS

1. CAN'T GET ENOUGH
   (Barry White)
2. RAGS TO RUFUS
   (Rufus)
3. SKIN TIGHT
   (Ohio Players)
4. BODY HEAT
   (Quincy Jones)
5. THE KIDS AND ME
   (Billy Preston)
6. COMIN' FROM ALL ENDS
   (New Birth)
7. THRUST
   (Herbie Hancock)
8. FULFILLINGNESS' FIRST FINALE
   (Stevie Wonder)
9. DANCING MACHINE
   (The Jackson 5)
10. LIVE IT UP
    (Isley Brothers)

JAZZ ALBUMS

1. BODY HEAT
   (Quincy Jones)
2. ONE
   (Bob James)
3. HEAD HUNTERS
   (Herbie Hancock)
4. HIGH ENERGY
   (Freddie Hubbard)
5. THE BLACKBYRDS
   (Blackbyrds)
6. STREET LADY
   (Donald Byrd)
7. WINTER IN AMERICA
   (Gil Scott-Heron)
8. CROSSWINDS
   (Billy Cobham)

9. THRUST
   (Herbie Hancock)
10. PERFORMANCE
    (Esther Phillips)

COUNTRY SINGLES

1. BONAPARTE'S RETREAT
   (Glen Campbell)
2. I LOVE MY FRIEND
   (Charlie Rich)
3. I OVERLOOKED AN ORCHID
   (Mickey Gilley)
4. A MI ESPOSA CON AMOR
   (Sonny James)
5. I'M A RAMBLIN' MAN
   (Waylon Jennings)
6. I SEE THE WANT TO IN YOUR EYES
   (Conway Twitty)
7. I HONESTLY LOVE YOU
   (Olivia Newton-John)
8. PLEASE DON'T STOP ME
   (Porter Wagoner and Dolly Parton)
9. I WOULDN'T WANT TO LIVE
   (Don Williams)
10. IF I MISS YOU AGAIN TONIGHT
    (Tommy Overstreet)

COUNTRY ALBUMS

1. BACK HOME AGAIN
   (John Denver)
2. COUNTRY PARTNERS
   (Conway Twitty and Loretta Lynn)
3. STOP AND SMELL THE ROSES
   (Mac Davis)
4. IF YOU LOVE ME
   (Olivia Newton-John)
5. COUNTRY BUMPKIN
   (Cal Smith)
6. BEHIND CLOSED DOORS
   (Charlie Rich)
7. ONE DAY AT A TIME
   (Marilyn Sellars)
8. ROOM FULL OF ROSES
   (Mickey Gilley)
9. COUNTRY IS
   (Tom T. Hall)
10. ANNE MURRAY COUNTRY
    (Anne Murray)

OCTOBER 19, 1974

POP SINGLES

1. NOTHING FROM NOTHING
   (Billy Preston)
2. JAZZMAN
   (Carole King)
3. I HONESTLY LOVE YOU
   (Olivia Newton-John)
4. YOU HAVEN'T DONE NOTHIN'
   (Stevie Wonder)
5. CAN'T GET ENOUGH
   (Bad Company)
6. NEVER MY LOVE
   (Blue Swede)
7. STOP AND SMELL THE ROSES
   (Mac Davis)
8. SWEET HOME ALABAMA
   (Lynyrd Skynyrd)
9. THEN CAME YOU
   (Dionne Warwick and The Spinners)
10. THE BITCH IS BACK
    (Elton John)

POP ALBUMS

1. NOT FRAGILE
   (Bachman-Turner Overdrive)

2. IF YOU LOVE ME (LET ME KNOW)
   (Olivia Newton-John)
3. BACK HOME AGAIN
   (John Denver)
4. CAN'T GET ENOUGH
   (Barry White)
5. WELCOME BACK
   (Emerson, Lake and Palmer)
6. BAD COMPANY
   (Bad Company)
7. CARIBOU
   (Elton John)
8. SO FAR
   (Crosby, Stills, Nash and Young)
9. WRAP AROUND JOY
   (Carole King)
10. FULFILLINGNESS' FIRST FINALE
    (Stevie Wonder)

BLACK SINGLES

1. PAPA DON'T TAKE NO MESS (PART 1)
   (James Brown)
2. SKIN TIGHT
   (Ohio Players)
3. DO IT ('TIL YOU'RE SATISFIED)
   (B.T. Express)
4. HIGHER PLANE
   (Kool and the Gang)
5. YOU HAVEN'T DONE NOTHIN'
   (Stevie Wonder)
6. THE PLAYER (PART 1)
   (First Choice)
7. CAREFUL MAN
   (John Edwards)
8. VIRGIN MAN
   (Smokey Robinson)
9. IN THE BOTTLE
   (Brother to Brother)
10. AIN'T NOTHING LIKE THE REAL THING
    (Aretha Franklin)

BLACK ALBUMS

1. CAN'T GET ENOUGH
   (Barry White)
2. SKIN TIGHT
   (Ohio Players)
3. RAGS TO RUFUS
   (Rufus)
4. THE KIDS AND ME
   (Billy Preston)
5. THRUST
   (Herbie Hancock)
6. BODY HEAT
   (Quincy Jones)
7. LIVE IT UP
   (Isley Brothers)
8. DANCING MACHINE
   (The Jackson 5)
9. FULFILLINGNESS' FIRST FINALE
   (Stevie Wonder)
10. COMIN' FROM ALL ENDS
    (New Birth)

JAZZ ALBUMS

1. BODY HEAT
   (Quincy Jones)
2. THRUST
   (Herbie Hancock)
3. ONE
   (Bob James)
4. HIGH ENERGY
   (Freddie Hubbard)
5. HEAD HUNTERS
   (Herbie Hancock)
6. THE BLACKBYRDS
   (Blackbyrds)
7. WINTER IN AMERICA
   (Gil Scott-Heron)
8. PERFORMANCE
   (Esther Phillips)

9. STREET LADY
   (Donald Byrd)
10. TREASURE ISLAND
   (Keith Jarrett)

COUNTRY SINGLES

1. I OVERLOOKED AN ORCHID
   (Mickey Gilley)
2. I SEE THE WANT TO IN YOUR EYES
   (Conway Twitty)
3. A MI ESPOSA CON AMOR
   (Sonny James)
4. I LOVE MY FRIEND
   (Charlie Rich)
5. I HONESTLY LOVE YOU
   (Olivia Newton-John)
6. PLEASE DON'T STOP LOVING ME
   (Porter Wagoner and Dolly Parton)
7. MISSISSIPPI COTTON PICKIN' DELTA TOWN
   (Charley Pride)
8. WOMAN TO WOMAN
   (Tammy Wynette)
9. IF I MISS YOU AGAIN TONIGHT
   (Tom Overstreet)
10. BETWEEN LUST AND WATCHING TV
   (Cal Smith)

COUNTRY ALBUMS

1. BACK HOME AGAIN
   (John Denver)
2. STOP AND SMELL THE ROSES
   (Mac Davis)
3. COUNTRY PARTNERS
   (Conway Twitty and Loretta Lynn)
4. IF YOU LOVE ME
   (Olivia Newton-John)
5. COUNTRY BUMPKIN
   (Cal Smith)
6. ROOM FULL OF ROSES
   (Mickey Gilley)
7. COUNTRY IS
   (Tom T. Hall)
8. I'M NOT THROUGH LOVING YOU YET
   (Conway Twitty)
9. ANNE MURRAY COUNTRY
   (Anne Murray)
10. PORTER AND DOLLY
   (Porter Wagoner and Dolly Parton)

OCTOBER 26, 1974

POP SINGLES

1. JAZZMAN
   (Carole King)
2. NOTHING FROM NOTHING
   (Billy Preston)
3. YOU HAVEN'T DONE NOTHIN'
   (Stevie Wonder)
4. CAN'T GET ENOUGH
   (Bad Company)
5. STOP AND SMELL THE ROSES
   (Mac Davis)
6. I HONESTLY LOVE YOU
   (Olivia Newton-John)
7. THE BITCH IS BACK
   (Elton John)
8. YOU AIN'T SEEN NOTHING YET
   (Bachman-Turner Overdrive)
9. NEVER MY LOVE
   (Blue Swede)
10. LOVE ME FOR A REASON
   (The Osmonds)

POP ALBUMS

1. CAN'T GET ENOUGH
   (Barry White)

2. NOT FRAGILE
   (Bachman-Turner Overdrive)
3. PHOTOGRAPHS AND MEMORIES
   (Jim Croce)
4. IF YOU LOVE ME (LET ME KNOW)
   (Olivia Newton-John)
5. WELCOME BACK
   (Emerson, Lake and Palmer)
6. CARIBOU
   (Elton John)
7. WRAP AROUND JOY
   (Carole King)
8. WALLS AND BRIDGES
   (John Lennon)
9. BACK HOME AGAIN
   (John Denver)
10. SO FAR
   (Crosby, Stills, Nash and Young)

BLACK SINGLES

1. LET'S STRAIGHTEN IT OUT
   (Latimore)
2. HIGHER PLANE
   (Kool and the Gang)
3. PAPA DON'T TAKE NO MESS (PART 1)
   (James Brown)
4. WOMAN TO WOMAN
   (Shirley Brown)
5. CAREFUL MAN
   (John Edwards)
6. PARTY DOWN (PART 1)
   (Little Beaver)
7. DO IT ('TIL YOU'RE SATISFIED)
   (B.T. Express)
8. SKIN TIGHT
   (Ohio Players)
9. THE PLAYER (PART 1)
   (First Choice)
10. VIRGIN MAN
   (Smokey Robinson)

BLACK ALBUMS

1. CAN'T GET ENOUGH
   (Barry White)
2. THE KIDS AND ME
   (Billy Preston)
3. LIVE IT UP
   (Isley Brothers)
4. THRUST
   (Herbie Hancock)
5. SKIN TIGHT
   (Ohio Players)
6. DANCING MACHINE
   (The Jackson 5)
7. RAGS TO RUFUS
   (Rufus)
8. BODY HEAT
   (Quincy Jones)
9. PERFECT ANGEL
   (Minnie Riperton)
10. MANDRILLAND
   (Mandrill)

JAZZ ALBUMS

1. BODY HEAT
   (Quincy Jones)
2. THRUST
   (Herbie Hancock)
3. HIGH ENERGY
   (Freddie Hubbard)
4. ONE
   (Bob James)
5. HEAD HUNTERS
   (Herbie Hancock)
6. THE BLACKBYRDS
   (Blackbyrds)
7. PERFORMANCE
   (Esther Phillips)
8. WINTER IN AMERICA
   (Gil Scott-Heron)

9. TREASURE ISLAND
   (Keith Jarrett)
10. WHERE HAVE I KNOWN YOU BEFORE
   (Return to Forever featuring Chick Corea)

COUNTRY SINGLES

1. I SEE THE WANT TO IN YOUR EYES
   (Conway Twitty)
2. I HONESTLY LOVE YOU
   (Olivia Newton-John)
3. I OVERLOOKED AN ORCHID
   (Mickey Gilley)
4. MISSISSIPPI COTTON PICKIN' DELTA TOWN
   (Charley Pride)
5. PLEASE DON'T STOP LOVING ME
   (Porter Wagoner and Dolly Parton)
6. WOMAN TO WOMAN
   (Tammy Wynette)
7. LOVE IS LIKE A BUTTERFLY
   (Dolly Parton)
8. TROUBLE IN PARADISE
   (Loretta Lynn)
9. BONEY FINGERS
   (Hoyt Axton)
10. I'M HAVING YOUR BABY
   (Sunday Sharpe)

COUNTRY ALBUMS

1. BACK HOME AGAIN
   (John Denver)
2. STOP AND SMELL THE ROSES
   (Mac Davis)
3. ROOM FULL OF ROSES
   (Mickey Gilley)
4. COUNTRY IS
   (Tom T. Hall)
5. I'M NOT THROUGH LOVING YOU YET
   (Conway Twitty)
6. COUNTRY BUMPKIN
   (Cal Smith)
7. ANNE MURRAY COUNTRY
   (Anne Murray)
8. PORTER AND DOLLY
   (Porter Wagoner and Dolly Parton)
9. GRAND TOUR
   (George Jones)
10. IF YOU LOVE ME
   (Olivia Newton-John)

NOVEMBER 2, 1974

POP SINGLES

1. YOU AIN'T SEEN NOTHING YET
   (Bachman-Turner Overdrive)
2. YOU HAVEN'T DONE NOTHIN'
   (Stevie Wonder)
3. JAZZMAN
   (Carole King)
4. CAN'T GET ENOUGH
   (Bad Company)
5. STOP AND SMELL THE ROSES
   (Mac Davis)
6. THE BITCH IS BACK
   (Elton John)
7. WHATEVER GETS YOU THRU THE NIGHT
   (John Lennon)
8. NOTHING FROM NOTHING
   (Billy Preston)
9. LOVE ME FOR A REASON
   (The Osmonds)
10. TIN MAN
   (America)

POP ALBUMS

1. PHOTOGRAPHS AND MEMORIES
   (Jim Croce)

2. NOT FRAGILE
   (Bachman-Turner Overdrive)
3. WALLS AND BRIDGES
   (John Lennon)
4. CAN'T GET ENOUGH
   (Barry White)
5. WRAP AROUND JOY
   (Carole King)
6. CHEECH AND CHONG'S WEDDING ALBUM
   (Cheech and Chong)
7. IF YOU LOVE ME (LET ME KNOW)
   (Olivia Newton-John)
8. CARIBOU
   (Elton John)
9. SO FAR
   (Crosby, Stills, Nash and Young)
10. WHEN THE EAGLE FLIES
   (Traffic)

BLACK SINGLES

1. HIGHER PLANE
   (Kool and the Gang)
2. WOMAN TO WOMAN
   (Shirley Brown)
3. LET'S STRAIGHTEN IT OUT
   (Latimore)
4. PARTY DOWN (PART 1)
   (Little Beaver)
5. CAREFUL MAN
   (John Edwards)
6. PAPA DON'T TAKE NO MESS (PART 1)
   (James Brown)
7. DO IT ('TIL YOU'RE SATISFIED)
   (B.T. Express)
8. LOVE DON'T LOVE NOBODY (PART 1)
   (Spinners)
9. SKIN TIGHT
   (Ohio Players)
10. SHA-LA-LA (MAKE ME HAPPY)
   (Al Green)

BLACK ALBUMS

1. CAN'T GET ENOUGH
   (Barry White)
2. LIVE IT UP
   (Isley Brothers)
3. THRUST
   (Herbie Hancock)
4. THE KIDS AND ME
   (Billy Preston)
5. DANCING MACHINE
   (The Jackson 5)
6. SKIN TIGHT
   (Ohio Players)
7. PERFECT ANGEL
   (Minnie Riperton)
8. RAGS TO RUFUS
   (Rufus)
9. MANDRILLAND
   (Mandrill)
10. IN HEAT
   (Love Unlimited)

JAZZ ALBUMS

1. BODY HEAT
   (Quincy Jones)
2. THRUST
   (Herbie Hancock)
3. ONE
   (Bob James)
4. HIGH ENERGY
   (Freddie Hubbard)
5. WHERE HAVE I KNOWN YOU BEFORE
   (Return to Forever featuring Chick Corea)
6. THE BLACKBYRDS
   (Blackbyrds)
7. HEAD HUNTERS
   (Herbie Hancock)
8. IS IT IN
   (Eddie Harris)

9. PERFORMANCE
   (Esther Phillips)
10. WINTER IN AMERICA
   (Gil Scott-Heron)

COUNTRY SINGLES

1. I HONESTLY LOVE YOU
   (Olivia Newton-John)
2. I SEE THE WANT TO IN YOUR EYES
   (Conway Twitty)
3. MISSISSIPPI COTTON PICKIN' DELTA TOWN
   (Charley Pride)
4. TROUBLE IN PARADISE
   (Loretta Lynn)
5. LOVE IS LIKE A BUTTERFLY
   (Dolly Parton)
6. WOMAN TO WOMAN
   (Tammy Wynette)
7. I OVERLOOKED AN ORCHID
   (Mickey Gilley)
8. BONEY FINGERS
   (Hoyt Axton)
9. COUNTRY IS
   (Tom T. Hall)
10. PLEASE DON'T STOP LOVING ME
   (Porter Wagoner and Dolly Parton)

COUNTRY ALBUMS

1. BACK HOME AGAIN
   (John Denver)
2. ROOM FULL OF ROSES
   (Mickey Gilley)
3. COUNTRY IS
   (Tom T. Hall)
4. I'M NOT THROUGH LOVING YOU YET
   (Conway Twitty)
5. STOP AND SMELL THE ROSES
   (Mac Davis)
6. PORTER AND DOLLY
   (Porter Wagoner and Dolly Parton)
7. ANNE MURRAY COUNTRY
   (Anne Murray)
8. GRAND TOUR
   (George Jones)
9. LOVE IS LIKE A BUTTERFLY
   (Dolly Parton)
10. I JUST STARTED HATING CHEATING
   SONGS TODAY
   (Moe Bandy)

NOVEMBER 9, 1974

POP SINGLES

1. YOU HAVEN'T DONE NOTHIN'
   (Stevie Wonder)
2. YOU AIN'T SEEN NOTHING YET
   (Bachman-Turner Overdrive)
3. WHATEVER GETS YOU THRU THE NIGHT
   (John Lennon)
4. JAZZMAN
   (Carole King)
5. CAN'T GET ENOUGH
   (Bad Company)
6. THE BITCH IS BACK
   (Elton John)
7. TIN MAN
   (America)
8. LONGFELLOW SERENADE
   (Neil Diamond)
9. DO IT BABY
   (The Miracles)
10. LIFE IS A ROCK (BUT THE RADIO ROLLED
   ME)
   (Reunion)

POP ALBUMS

1. PHOTOGRAPHS AND MEMORIES
   (Jim Croce)
2. WALLS AND BRIDGES
   (John Lennon)
3. CHEECH AND CHONG'S WEDDING ALBUM
   (Cheech and Chong)
4. WRAP AROUND JOY
   (Carole King)
5. NOT FRAGILE
   (Bachman-Turner Overdrive)
6. IF YOU LOVE ME (LET ME KNOW)
   (Olivia Newton-John)
7. CARIBOU
   (Elton John)
8. SO FAR
   (Crosby, Stills, Nash and Young)
9. IT'S ONLY ROCK 'N' ROLL
   (The Rolling Stones)
10. WELCOME BACK
   (Emerson, Lake and Palmer)

BLACK SINGLES

1. WOMAN TO WOMAN
   (Shirley Brown)
2. HIGHER PLANE
   (Kool and the Gang)
3. PARTY DOWN (PART 1)
   (Little Beaver)
4. LOVE DON'T LOVE NOBODY (PART 1)
   (Spinners)
5. LET'S STRAIGHTEN IT OUT
   (Latimore)
6. CAREFUL MAN
   (John Edwards)
7. SHA-LA-LA (MAKE ME HAPPY)
   (Al Green)
8. DO IT ('TIL YOU'RE SATISFIED)
   (B.T. Express)
9. I FEEL A SONG (IN MY HEART)
   (Gladys Knight and the Pips)
10. LET THIS BE A LESSON TO YOU
   (The Independents)

BLACK ALBUMS

1. LIVE IT UP
   (Isley Brothers)
2. CAN'T GET ENOUGH
   (Barry White)
3. THRUST
   (Herbie Hancock)
4. DANCING MACHINE
   (The Jackson 5)
5. THE KIDS AND ME
   (Billy Preston)
6. SKIN TIGHT
   (Ohio Players)
7. PERFECT ANGEL
   (Minnie Riperton)
8. RAGS TO RUFUS
   (Rufus)
9. IN HEAT
   (Love Unlimited)
10. CLIMAX
   (Ohio Players)

JAZZ ALBUMS

1. BODY HEAT
   (Quincy Jones)
2. THRUST
   (Herbie Hancock)
3. ONE
   (Bob James)
4. WHERE HAVE I KNOWN YOU BEFORE
   (Return to Forever featuring Chick Corea)
5. THE BLACKBYRDS
   (The Blackbyrds)
6. HIGH ENERGY
   (Freddie Hubbard)

7. IS IT IN
    (Eddie Harris)
8. PERFORMANCE
    (Esther Phillips)
9. HEAD HUNTERS
    (Herbie Hancock)
10. STREET LADY
    (Donald Byrd)

COUNTRY SINGLES

1. MISSISSIPPI COTTON PICKIN' DELTA TOWN
    (Charley Pride)
2. LOVE IS LIKE A BUTTERFLY
    (Dolly Parton)
3. TROUBLE IN PARADISE
    (Loretta Lynn)
4. I SEE THE WANT TO IN YOUR EYES
    (Conway Twitty)
5. I HONESTLY LOVE YOU
    (Olivia Newton-John)
6. COUNTRY IS
    (Tom T. Hall)
7. BACK HOME AGAIN
    (John Denver)
8. I OVERLOOKED AN ORCHID
    (Mickey Gilley)
9. GET ON MY LOVE TRAIN
    (La Costa)
10. I CAN HELP
    (Billy Swan)

COUNTRY ALBUMS

1. BACK HOME AGAIN
    (John Denver)
2. ROOM FULL OF ROSES
    (Mickey Gilley)
3. COUNTRY IS
    (Tom T. Hall)
4. STOP AND SMELL THE ROSES
    (Mac Davis)
5. PORTER AND DOLLY
    (Porter Wagoner and Dolly Parton)
6. I'M NOT THROUGH LOVING YOU YET
    (Conway Twitty)
7. LOVE IS LIKE A BUTTERFLY
    (Dolly Parton)
8. THE RAMBLIN' MAN
    (Waylon Jennings)
9. THEY DON'T MAKE 'EM LIKE MY DADDY
    (Loretta Lynn)
10. I JUST STARTED HATING CHEATING
    SONGS TODAY
    (Moe Bandy)

NOVEMBER 16, 1974

POP SINGLES

1. WHATEVER GETS YOU THRU THE NIGHT
    (John Lennon)
2. I CAN HELP
    (Billy Swan)
3. YOU HAVEN'T DONE NOTHIN'
    (Stevie Wonder)
4. YOU AIN'T SEEN NOTHING YET
    (Bachman-Turner Overdrive)
5. LONGFELLOW SERENADE
    (Neil Diamond)
6. TIN MAN
    (America)
7. MY MELODY OF LOVE
    (Bobby Vinton)
8. WHEN WILL I SEE YOU AGAIN
    (Three Degrees)
9. LIFE IS A ROCK (BUT THE RADIO ROLLED
    ME)
    (Reunion)
10. BACK HOME AGAIN
    (John Denver)

POP ALBUMS

1. WALLS AND BRIDGES
    (John Lennon)
2. CHEECH AND CHONG'S WEDDING ALBUM
    (Cheech and Chong)
3. WRAP AROUND JOY
    (Carole King)
4. PHOTOGRAPHS AND MEMORIES
    (Jim Croce)
5. NOT FRAGILE
    (Bachman-Turner Overdrive)
6. IT'S ONLY ROCK 'N' ROLL
    (The Rolling Stones)
7. IF YOU LOVE ME (LET ME KNOW)
    (Olivia Newton-John)
8. CARIBOU
    (Elton John)
9. SO FAR
    (Crosby, Stills, Nash and Young)
10. WELCOME BACK
    (Emerson, Lake and Palmer)

BLACK SINGLES

1. WOMAN TO WOMAN
    (Shirley Brown)
2. PARTY DOWN (PART 1)
    (Little Beaver)
3. LOVE DON'T LOVE NOBODY (PART 1)
    (Spinners)
4. HIGHER PLANE
    (Kool and the Gang)
5. SHA-LA-LA (MAKE ME HAPPY)
    (Al Green)
6. I FEEL A SONG (IN MY HEART)
    (Gladys Knight and the Pips)
7. LET'S STRAIGHTEN IT OUT
    (Latimore)
8. CAREFUL MAN
    (John Edwards)
9. DO IT ('TIL YOU'RE SATISFIED)
    (B.T. Express)
10. LET THIS BE A LESSON TO YOU
    (The Independents)

BLACK ALBUMS

1. LIVE IT UP
    (Isley Brothers)
2. THRUST
    (Herbie Hancock)
3. DANCING MACHINE
    (The Jackson 5)
4. CAN'T GET ENOUGH
    (Barry White)
5. CLIMAX
    (Ohio Players)
6. THE KIDS AND ME
    (Billy Preston)
7. PERFECT ANGEL
    (Minnie Riperton)
8. IN HEAT
    (Love Unlimited)
9. SKIN TIGHT
    (Ohio Players)
10. LIGHT OF WORLDS
    (Kool and the Gang)

JAZZ ALBUMS

1. BODY HEAT
    (Quincy Jones)
2. THRUST
    (Herbie Hancock)
3. WHERE HAVE I KNOWN YOU BEFORE
    (Return to Forever featuring Chick Corea)
4. ONE
    (Bob James)
5. IS IT IN
    (Eddie Harris)
6. HIGH ENERGY
    (Freddie Hubbard)

7. THE BLACKBYRDS
    (Blackbyrds)
8. PERFORMANCE
    (Esther Phillips)
9. STREET LADY
    (Donald Byrd)
10. PIECES OF DREAMS
    (Stanley Turrentine)

COUNTRY SINGLES

1. LOVE IS LIKE A BUTTERFLY
    (Dolly Parton)
2. TROUBLE IN PARADISE
    (Loretta Lynn)
3. COUNTRY IS
    (Tom T. Hall)
4. MISSISSIPPI COTTON PICKIN' DELTA TOWN
    (Charley Pride)
5. BACK HOME AGAIN
    (John Denver)
6. I CAN HELP
    (Billy Swan)
7. GET ON MY LOVE TRAIN
    (La Costa)
8. TAKE ME HOME TO SOMEWHERE
    (Joe Stampley)
9. SHE CALLED ME BABY
    (Charlie Rich)
10. I SEE THE WANT TO IN YOUR EYES
    (Conway Twitty)

COUNTRY ALBUMS

1. ROOM FULL OF ROSES
    (Mickey Gilley)
2. BACK HOME AGAIN
    (John Denver)
3. STOP AND SMELL THE ROSES
    (Mac Davis)
4. THE RAMBLIN' MAN
    (Waylon Jennings)
5. LOVE IS LIKE A BUTTERFLY
    (Dolly Parton)
6. THEY DON'T MAKE 'EM LIKE MY DADDY
    (Loretta Lynn)
7. HIS 30th ALBUM
    (Merle Haggard)
8. COUNTRY IS
    (Tom T. Hall)
9. PORTER AND DOLLY
    (Porter Wagoner and Dolly Parton)
10. NASHVILLE HIT MAN
    (Charlie McCoy)

NOVEMBER 23, 1974

POP SINGLES

1. I CAN HELP
    (Billy Swan)
2. WHATEVER GETS YOU THRU THE NIGHT
    (John Lennon)
3. MY MELODY OF LOVE
    (Bobby Vinton)
4. LONGFELLOW SERENADE
    (Neil Diamond)
5. WHEN WILL I SEE YOU AGAIN
    (Three Degrees)
6. YOU AIN'T SEEN NOTHING YET
    (Bachman-Turner Overdrive)
7. CAT'S IN THE CRADLE
    (Harry Chapin)
8. BACK HOME AGAIN
    (John Denver)
9. DO IT ('TIL YOU'RE SATISFIED)
    (B.T. Express)
10. EVERLASTING LOVE
    (Carl Carlton)

POP ALBUMS

1. CHEECH AND CHONG'S WEDDING ALBUM
   (Cheech and Chong)
2. WRAP AROUND JOY
   (Carole King)
3. IT'S ONLY ROCK 'N' ROLL
   (The Rolling Stones)
4. WALLS AND BRIDGES
   (John Lennon)
5. NOT FRAGILE
   (Bachman-Turner Overdrive)
6. WAR CHILD
   (Jethro Tull)
7. IF YOU LOVE ME (LET ME KNOW)
   (Olivia Newton-John)
8. PHOTOGRAPHS AND MEMORIES
   (Jim Croce)
9. CARIBOU
   (Elton John)
10. SERENADE
    (Neil Diamond)

BLACK SINGLES

1. SHA-LA-LA (MAKE ME HAPPY)
   (Al Green)
2. PARTY DOWN (PART 1)
   (Little Beaver)
3. LOVE DON'T LOVE NOBODY (PART 1)
   (Spinners)
4. WOMAN TO WOMAN
   (Shirley Brown)
5. I FEEL A SONG (IN MY HEART)
   (Gladys Knight and the Pips)
6. LET'S STRAIGHTEN IT OUT
   (Latimore)
7. HIGHER PLANE
   (Kool and the Gang)
8. CAREFUL MAN
   (John Edwards)
9. SHE'S GONE
   (Tavares)
10. DO IT ('TIL YOU'RE SATISFIED)
    (B.T. Express)

BLACK ALBUMS

1. LIVE IT UP
   (Isley Brothers)
2. CAUGHT UP
   (Millie Jackson)
3. THRUST
   (Herbie Hancock)
4. CLIMAX
   (Ohio Players)
5. DANCING MACHINE
   (The Jackson 5)
6. PERFECT ANGEL
   (Minnie Riperton)
7. IN HEAT
   (Love Unlimited)
8. LIGHT OF WORLDS
   (Kool and the Gang)
9. THE KIDS AND ME
   (Billy Preston)
10. CAN'T GET ENOUGH
    (Barry White)

JAZZ ALBUMS

1. THRUST
   (Herbie Hancock)
2. BODY HEAT
   (Quincy Jones)
3. WHERE HAVE I KNOWN YOU BEFORE
   (Return to Forever featuring Chick Corea)
4. ONE
   (Bob James)
5. IS IT IN
   (Eddie Harris)
6. PIECES OF DREAMS
   (Stanley Turrentine)

7. HIGH ENERGY
   (Freddie Hubbard)
8. PERFORMANCE
   (Esther Phillips)
9. THE BLACKBYRDS
   (Blackbyrds)
10. HEAD HUNTERS
    (Herbie Hancock)

COUNTRY SINGLES

1. TROUBLE IN PARADISE
   (Loretta Lynn)
2. COUNTRY IS
   (Tom T. Hall)
3. I CAN HELP
   (Billy Swan)
4. BACK HOME AGAIN
   (John Denver)
5. GET ON MY LOVE TRAIN
   (La Costa)
6. SHE CALLED ME BABY
   (Charlie Rich)
7. TAKE ME HOME TO SOMEWHERE
   (Joe Stampley)
8. LOVE IS LIKE A BUTTERFLY
   (Dolly Parton)
9. CREDIT CARD SONG
   (Dick Feller)
10. BRING BACK YOUR LOVE TO ME
    (Don Gibson)

COUNTRY ALBUMS

1. ROOM FULL OF ROSES
   (Mickey Gilley)
2. BACK HOME AGAIN
   (John Denver)
3. THE RAMBLIN' MAN
   (Waylon Jennings)
4. HIS 30th ALBUM
   (Merle Haggard)
5. LOVE IS LIKE A BUTTERFLY
   (Dolly Parton)
6. THEY DON'T MAKE 'EM LIKE MY DADDY
   (Loretta Lynn)
7. STOP AND SMELL THE ROSES
   (Mac Davis)
8. COUNTRY IS
   (Tom T. Hall)
9. NASHVILLE HIT MAN
   (Charlie McCoy)
10. IT'S A MONSTER'S HOLIDAY
    (Buck Owens)

NOVEMBER 30, 1974

POP SINGLES

1. MY MELODY OF LOVE
   (Bobby Vinton)
2. I CAN HELP
   (Billy Swan)
3. WHEN WILL I SEE YOU AGAIN
   (Three Degrees)
4. LONGFELLOW SERENADE
   (Neil Diamond)
5. CAT'S IN THE CRADLE
   (Harry Chapin)
6. KUNG FU FIGHTING
   (Carl Douglas)
7. DO IT ('TIL YOU'RE SATISFIED)
   (B.T. Express)
8. BACK HOME AGAIN
   (John Denver)
9. ANGIE BABY
   (Helen Reddy)
10. SHA-LA-LA (MAKE ME HAPPY)
    (Al Green)

POP ALBUMS

1. WRAP AROUND JOY
   (Carole King)
2. IT'S ONLY ROCK 'N' ROLL
   (The Rolling Stones)
3. CHEECH AND CHONG'S WEDDING ALBUM
   (Cheech and Chong)
4. NOT FRAGILE
   (Bachman-Turner Overdrive)
5. WAR CHILD
   (Jethro Tull)
6. SERENADE
   (Neil Diamond)
7. WALLS AND BRIDGES
   (John Lennon)
8. IF YOU LOVE ME (LET ME KNOW)
   (Olivia Newton-John)
9. CARIBOU
   (Elton John)
10. GREATEST HITS
    (Elton John)

BLACK SINGLES

1. SHA-LA-LA (MAKE ME HAPPY)
   (Al Green)
2. I FEEL A SONG (IN MY HEART)
   (Gladys Knight and the Pips)
3. LOVE DON'T LOVE NOBODY (PART 1)
   (Spinners)
4. WOMAN TO WOMAN
   (Shirley Brown)
5. PARTY DOWN (PART 1)
   (Little Beaver)
6. THREE RING CIRCUS
   (Blue Magic)
7. SHE'S GONE
   (Tavares)
8. WHEN WILL I SEE YOU AGAIN
   (Three Degrees)
9. YOU GOT THE LOVE
   (Rufus)
10. DO IT ('TIL YOU'RE SATISFIED)
    (B.T. Express)

BLACK ALBUMS

1. CAUGHT UP
   (Millie Jackson)
2. LIVE IT UP
   (Isley Brothers)
3. THRUST
   (Herbie Hancock)
4. CLIMAX
   (Ohio Players)
5. LIGHT OF WORLDS
   (Kool and the Gang)
6. IN HEAT
   (Love Unlimited)
7. PERFECT ANGEL
   (Minnie Riperton)
8. DANCING MACHINE
   (The Jackson 5)
9. I FEEL A SONG
   (Gladys Knight and the Pips)
10. FIRE
    (Ohio Players)

JAZZ ALBUMS

1. THRUST
   (Herbie Hancock)
2. BODY HEAT
   (Quincy Jones)
3. WHERE HAVE I KNOWN YOU BEFORE
   (Return to Forever featuring Chick Corea)
4. IS IT IN
   (Eddie Harris)
5. ONE
   (Bob James)
6. PIECES OF DREAMS
   (Stanley Turrentine)

7. HIGH ENERGY
   (Freddie Hubbard)
8. THE BLACKBYRDS
   (Blackbyrds)
9. SOUTHERN COMFORT
   (Crusaders)
10. PERFORMANCE
    (Esther Phillips)

COUNTRY SINGLES

1. COUNTRY IS
   (Tom T. Hall)
2. I CAN HELP
   (Billy Swan)
3. BACK HOME AGAIN
   (John Denver)
4. SHE CALLED ME BABY
   (Charlie Rich)
5. GET ON MY LOVE TRAIN
   (La Costa)
6. TROUBLE IN PARADISE
   (Loretta Lynn)
7. TAKE ME HOME TO SOMEWHERE
   (Joe Stampley)
8. CREDIT CARD SONG
   (Dick Feller)
9. MEMORY MAKER
   (Mel Tillis)
10. BRING BACK YOUR LOVE TO ME
    (Don Gibson)

COUNTRY ALBUMS

1. BACK HOME AGAIN
   (John Denver)
2. HIS 30th ALBUM
   (Merle Haggard)
3. THE RAMBLIN' MAN
   (Waylon Jennings)
4. ROOM FULL OF ROSES
   (Mickey Gilley)
5. THEY DON'T MAKE 'EM LIKE MY DADDY
   (Loretta Lynn)
6. LOVE IS LIKE A BUTTERFLY
   (Dolly Parton)
7. STOP AND SMELL THE ROSES
   (Mac Davis)
8. IT'S A MONSTER'S HOLIDAY
   (Buck Owens)
9. SONGS ABOUT LADIES AND LOVE
   (Johnny Rodriguez)
10. COUNTRY IS
    (Tom T. Hall)

DECEMBER 7, 1974

POP SINGLES

1. WHEN WILL I SEE YOU AGAIN
   (Three Degrees)
2. I CAN HELP
   (Billy Swan)
3. KUNG FU FIGHTING
   (Carl Douglas)
4. CAT'S IN THE CRADLE
   (Harry Chapin)
5. ANGIE BABY
   (Helen Reddy)
6. DO IT ('TIL YOU'RE SATISFIED)
   (B.T. Express)
7. MY MELODY OF LOVE
   (Bobby Vinton)
8. LONGFELLOW SERENADE
   (Neil Diamond)
9. JUNIOR'S FARM
   (Paul McCartney and Wings)
10. SHA-LA-LA (MAKE ME HAPPY)
    (Al Green)

POP ALBUMS

1. IT'S ONLY ROCK 'N' ROLL
   (The Rolling Stones)
2. GREATEST HITS
   (Elton John)
3. SERENADE
   (Neil Diamond)
4. NOT FRAGILE
   (Bachman-Turner Overdrive)
5. WAR CHILD
   (Jethro Tull)
6. WRAP AROUND JOY
   (Carole King)
7. CHEECH AND CHONG'S WEDDING ALBUM
   (Cheech and Chong)
8. BACK HOME AGAIN
   (John Denver)
9. IF YOU LOVE ME (LET ME KNOW)
   (Olivia Newton-John)
10. DAVID LIVE
    (David Bowie)

BLACK SINGLES

1. I FEEL A SONG (IN MY HEART)
   (Gladys Knight and the Pips)
2. SHA-LA-LA (MAKE ME HAPPY)
   (Al Green)
3. SHE'S GONE
   (Tavares)
4. THREE RING CIRCUS
   (Blue Magic)
5. WHEN WILL I SEE YOU AGAIN
   (Three Degrees)
6. WOMAN TO WOMAN
   (Shirley Brown)
7. YOU GOT THE LOVE
   (Rufus)
8. KUNG FU FIGHTING
   (Carl Douglas)
9. COLD BLOODED
   (James Brown)
10. I CAN'T LEAVE YOU ALONE/I GET LIFTED
    (George McCrae)

BLACK ALBUMS

1. CAUGHT UP
   (Millie Jackson)
2. LIVE IT UP
   (Isley Brothers)
3. FIRE
   (Ohio Players)
4. I FEEL A SONG
   (Gladys Knight and the Pips)
5. LIGHT OF WORLDS
   (Kool and the Gang)
6. IN HEAT
   (Love Unlimited)
7. THRUST
   (Herbie Hancock)
8. WHITE GOLD
   (Love Unlimited Orchestra)
9. PERFECT ANGEL
   (Minnie Riperton)
10. DANCING MACHINE
    (The Jackson 5)

JAZZ ALBUMS

1. THRUST
   (Herbie Hancock)
2. IS IT IN
   (Eddie Harris)
3. BODY HEAT
   (Quincy Jones)
4. WHERE HAVE I KNOWN YOU BEFORE
   (Return to Forever featuring Chick Corea)
5. PIECES OF DREAMS
   (Stanley Turrentine)
6. ONE
   (Bob James)

7. SOUTHERN COMFORT
   (Crusaders)
8. CHAPTER THREE: VIVA EMILIANO ZAPATA
   (Gato Barbieri)
9. HIGH ENERGY
   (Freddie Hubbard)
10. THE BLACKBYRDS
    (Blackbyrds)

COUNTRY SINGLES

1. I CAN HELP
   (Billy Swan)
2. BACK HOME AGAIN
   (John Denver)
3. SHE CALLED ME BABY
   (Charlie Rich)
4. MEMORY MAKER
   (Mel Tillis)
5. WE'RE OVER
   (Johnny Rodriguez)
6. GET ON MY LOVE TRAIN
   (La Costa)
7. COUNTRY IS
   (Tom T. Hall)
8. TAKE ME HOME TO SOMEWHERE
   (Joe Stampley)
9. TROUBLE IN PARADISE
   (Loretta Lynn)
10. SON OF A ROTTEN GAMBLER
    (Anne Murray)

COUNTRY ALBUMS

1. HIS 30th ALBUM
   (Merle Haggard)
2. THE RAMBLIN' MAN
   (Waylon Jennings)
3. BACK HOME AGAIN
   (John Denver)
4. ROOM FULL OF ROSES
   (Mickey Gilley)
5. SONGS ABOUT LADIES AND LOVE
   (Johnny Rodriguez)
6. THEY DON'T MAKE 'EM LIKE MY DADDY
   (Loretta Lynn)
7. IT'S A MONSTER'S HOLIDAY
   (Buck Owens)
8. LOVE IS LIKE A BUTTERFLY
   (Dolly Parton)
9. STOP AND SMELL THE ROSES
   (Mac Davis)
10. IF YOU LOVE ME (LET ME KNOW)
    (Olivia Newton-John)

DECEMBER 14, 1974

POP SINGLES

1. KUNG FU FIGHTING
   (Carl Douglas)
2. I CAN HELP
   (Billy Swan)
3. CAT'S IN THE CRADLE
   (Harry Chapin)
4. ANGIE BABY
   (Helen Reddy)
5. WHEN WILL I SEE YOU AGAIN
   (Three Degrees)
6. JUNIOR'S FARM
   (Paul McCartney and Wings)
7. DO IT ('TIL YOU'RE SATISFIED)
   (B.T. Express)
8. MY MELODY OF LOVE
   (Bobby Vinton)
9. YOU'RE THE FIRST, THE LAST, MY EVERYTHING
   (Barry White)
10. SHA-LA-LA (MAKE ME HAPPY)
    (Al Green)

POP ALBUMS

1. GREATEST HITS
   (Elton John)
2. SERENADE
   (Neil Diamond)
3. IT'S ONLY ROCK 'N' ROLL
   (The Rolling Stones)
4. NOT FRAGILE
   (Bachman-Turner Overdrive)
5. WAR CHILD
   (Jethro Tull)
6. BACK HOME AGAIN
   (John Denver)
7. WRAP AROUND JOY
   (Carole King)
8. MOTHER LODE
   (Loggins and Messina)
9. CHEECH AND CHONG'S WEDDING ALBUM
   (Cheech and Chong)
10. DAVID LIVE
    (David Bowie)

BLACK SINGLES

1. SHE'S GONE
   (Tavares)
2. KUNG FU FIGHTING
   (Carl Douglas)
3. YOU GOT THE LOVE
   (Rufus)
4. THREE RING CIRCUS
   (Blue Magic)
5. WHEN WILL I SEE YOU AGAIN
   (Three Degrees)
6. COLD BLOODED
   (James Brown)
7. I FEEL A SONG (IN MY HEART)
   (Gladys Knight and the Pips)
8. SHA-LA-LA (MAKE ME HAPPY)
   (Al Green)
9. YOU'RE THE FIRST, THE LAST, MY EVERYTHING
   (Barry White)
10. WHATEVER YOU GOT, I WANT
    (The Jackson 5)

BLACK ALBUMS

1. FIRE
   (Ohio Players)
2. CAUGHT UP
   (Millie Jackson)
3. I FEEL A SONG
   (Gladys Knight and the Pips)
4. LIVE IT UP
   (Isley Brothers)
5. IN HEAT
   (Love Unlimited)
6. WHITE GOLD
   (Love Unlimited Orchestra)
7. THRUST
   (Herbie Hancock)
8. LIGHT OF WORLDS
   (Kool and the Gang)
9. TOGETHER FOR THE FIRST TIME
   (Bobby "Blue" Bland and B.B. King)
10. PERFECT ANGEL
    (Minnie Riperton)

JAZZ ALBUMS

1. IS IT IN
   (Eddie Harris)
2. THRUST
   (Herbie Hancock)
3. PIECES OF DREAMS
   (Stanley Turrentine)
4. BODY HEAT
   (Quincy Jones)
5. WHERE HAVE I KNOWN YOU BEFORE
   (Return to Forever featuring Chick Corea)
6. SOUTHERN COMFORT
   (Crusaders)
7. ONE
   (Bob James)
8. BAD BENSON
   (George Benson)
9. CHAPTER THREE: VIVA EMILIANO ZAPATA
   (Gato Barbieri)
10. HIGH ENERGY
    (Freddie Hubbard)

COUNTRY SINGLES

1. BACK HOME AGAIN
   (John Denver)
2. SHE CALLED ME BABY
   (Charlie Rich)
3. WE'RE OVER
   (Johnny Rodriguez)
4. MEMORY MAKER
   (Mel Tillis)
5. I CAN HELP
   (Billy Swan)
6. GET ON MY LOVE TRAIN
   (La Costa)
7. SON OF A ROTTEN GAMBLER
   (Anne Murray)
8. EVERY TIME I TURN THE RADIO ON
   (Bill Anderson)
9. HE CAN'T FILL MY SHOES
   (Jerry Lee Lewis)
10. OUT OF HAND
    (Gary Stewart)

COUNTRY ALBUMS

1. HIS 30th ALBUM
   (Merle Haggard)
2. THE RAMBLIN' MAN
   (Waylon Jennings)
3. BACK HOME AGAIN
   (John Denver)
4. SONGS ABOUT LADIES AND LOVE
   (Johnny Rodriguez)
5. ROOM FULL OF ROSES
   (Mickey Gilley)
6. IT'S A MONSTER'S HOLIDAY
   (Buck Owens)
7. THEY DON'T MAKE 'EM LIKE MY DADDY
   (Loretta Lynn)
8. ANNE MURRAY COUNTRY
   (Anne Murray)
9. IF YOU LOVE ME (LET ME KNOW)
   (Olivia Newton-John)
10. LOVE IS LIKE A BUTTERFLY
    (Dolly Parton)

DECEMBER 21, 1974

POP SINGLES

1. CAT'S IN THE CRADLE
   (Harry Chapin)
2. KUNG FU FIGHTING
   (Carl Douglas)
3. ANGIE BABY
   (Helen Reddy)
4. LUCY IN THE SKY WITH DIAMONDS
   (Elton John)
5. JUNIOR'S FARM
   (Paul McCartney and Wings)
6. I CAN HELP
   (Billy Swan)
7. YOU'RE THE FIRST, THE LAST, MY EVERYTHING
   (Barry White)
8. DO IT ('TIL YOU'RE SATISFIED)
   (B.T. Express)
9. WHEN WILL I SEE YOU AGAIN
   (Three Degrees)
10. YOU GOT THE LOVE
    (Rufus)

POP ALBUMS

1. GREATEST HITS
   (Elton John)
2. SERENADE
   (Neil Diamond)
3. NOT FRAGILE
   (Bachman-Turner Overdrive)
4. BACK HOME AGAIN
   (John Denver)
5. MOTHER LODE
   (Loggins and Messina)
6. IT'S ONLY ROCK 'N' ROLL
   (The Rolling Stones)
7. WAR CHILD
   (Jethro Tull)
8. GOODNIGHT VIENNA
   (Ringo Starr)
9. JOHN DENVER'S GREATEST HITS
   (John Denver)
10. VERITIES AND BALDERDASH
    (Harry Chapin)

BLACK SINGLES

1. KUNG FU FIGHTING
   (Carl Douglas)
2. YOU GOT THE LOVE
   (Rufus)
3. SHE'S GONE
   (Tavares)
4. FUNKY PRESIDENT (PEOPLE IT'S BAD)/COLD BLOODED
   (James Brown)
5. WHEN WILL I SEE YOU AGAIN
   (Three Degrees)
6. YOU'RE THE FIRST, THE LAST, MY EVERYTHING
   (Barry White)
7. BOOGIE ON REGGAE WOMAN
   (Stevie Wonder)
8. WHATEVER YOU GOT, I WANT
   (The Jackson 5)
9. HEAVY FALLIN' OUT
   (The Stylistics)
10. I FEEL A SONG (IN MY HEART)
    (Gladys Knight and the Pips)

BLACK ALBUMS

1. FIRE
   (Ohio Players)
2. I FEEL A SONG
   (Gladys Knight and the Pips)
3. CAUGHT UP
   (Millie Jackson)
4. IN HEAT
   (Love Unlimited)
5. WHITE GOLD
   (Love Unlimited Orchestra)
6. LIVE IT UP
   (Isley Brothers)
7. TOGETHER FOR THE FIRST TIME
   (Bobby "Blue" Bland and B.B. King)
8. AL GREEN EXPLORES YOUR MIND
   (Al Green)
9. THRUST
   (Herbie Hancock)
10. LIGHT OF WORLDS
    (Kool and the Gang)

JAZZ ALBUMS

1. PIECES OF DREAMS
   (Stanley Turrentine)
2. SOUTHERN COMFORT
   (Crusaders)
3. IS IT IN
   (Eddie Harris)
4. THRUST
   (Herbie Hancock)
5. BODY HEAT
   (Quincy Jones)

6. BAD BENSON
   (George Benson)
7. WHERE HAVE I KNOWN YOU BEFORE
   (Return to Forever featuring Chick Corea)
8. ONE
   (Bob James)
9. THE BADDEST TURRENTINE
   (Stanley Turrentine)
10. CHAPTER THREE: VIVA EMILIANO ZAPATA
   (Gato Barbieri)

COUNTRY SINGLES

1. SHE CALLED ME BABY
   (Charlie Rich)
2. WE'RE OVER
   (Johnny Rodriguez)
3. BACK HOME AGAIN
   (John Denver)
4. I CAN HELP
   (Billy Swan)
5. OUT OF HAND
   (Gary Stewart)
6. HE CAN'T FILL MY SHOES
   (Jerry Lee Lewis)
7. SON OF A ROTTEN GAMBLER
   (Anne Murray)
8. EVERY TIME I TURN THE RADIO ON
   (Bill Anderson)
9. WHAT A MAN, MY MAN IS
   (Lynn Anderson)
10. IT'S MIDNIGHT/PROMISED LAND
   (Elvis Presley)

COUNTRY ALBUMS

1. HIS 30th ALBUM
   (Merle Haggard)
2. SONGS ABOUT LADIES AND LOVE
   (Johnny Rodriguez)
3. BACK HOME AGAIN
   (John Denver)
4. THE RAMBLIN' MAN
   (Waylon Jennings)
5. ANNE MURRAY COUNTRY
   (Anne Murray)
6. DON WILLIAMS, VOL. III
   (Don Williams)
7. IT'S A MONSTER'S HOLIDAY
   (Buck Owens)
8. MISS DONNA FARGO
   (Donna Fargo)
9. IF YOU LOVE ME (LET ME KNOW)
   (Olivia Newton-John)
10. ROOM FULL OF ROSES
   (Mickey Gilley)

DECEMBER 28, 1974

POP SINGLES

1. ANGIE BABY
   (Helen Reddy)
2. LUCY IN THE SKY WITH DIAMONDS
   (Elton John)
3. KUNG FU FIGHTING
   (Carl Douglas)
4. YOU'RE THE FIRST, THE LAST, MY
   EVERYTHING
   (Barry White)
5. JUNIOR'S FARM
   (Paul McCartney and Wings)
6. CAT'S IN THE CRADLE
   (Harry Chapin)
7. LAUGHTER IN THE RAIN
   (Neil Sedaka)
8. PLEASE MR. POSTMAN
   (The Carpenters)
9. YOU GOT THE LOVE
   (Rufus)

10. ONE MAN WOMAN, ONE WOMAN MAN
   (Paul Anka with Odia Coates)

POP ALBUMS

1. GREATEST HITS
   (Elton John)
2. BACK HOME AGAIN
   (John Denver)
3. NOT FRAGILE
   (Backman-Turner Overdrive)
4. SERENADE
   (Neil Diamond)
5. MOTHER LODE
   (Loggins and Messina)
6. GOODNIGHT VIENNA
   (Ringo Starr)
7. JOHN DENVER'S GREATEST HITS
   (John Denver)
8. BUTTERFLY
   (Barbra Streisand)
9. VERITIES AND BALDERDASH
   (Harry Chapin)
10. FREE AND EASY
   (Helen Reddy)

BLACK SINGLES

1. KUNG FU FIGHTING
   (Carl Douglas)
2. YOU GOT TO LOVE
   (Rufus)
3. FUNKY PRESIDENT (PEOPLE IT'S
   BAD)/COLD BLOODED
   (James Brown)
4. YOU'RE THE FIRST, THE LAST, MY
   EVERYTHING
   (Barry White)
5. BOOGIE ON REGGAE WOMAN
   (Stevie Wonder)
6. WHEN WILL I SEE YOU AGAIN
   (Three Degrees)
7. HEAVY FALLIN' OUT
   (The Stylistics)
8. WHATEVER YOU GOT, I WANT
   (The Jackson 5)
9. SHE'S GONE
   (Tavares)
10. WHERE ARE ALL MY FRIENDS
   (Harold Melvin and The Blue Notes)

BLACK ALBUMS

1. FIRE
   (Ohio Players)
2. I FEEL A SONG
   (Gladys Knight and the Pips)
3. WHITE GOLD
   (Love Unlimited Orchestra)
4. CAUGHT UP
   (Millie Jackson)
5. AL GREEN EXPLORES YOUR MIND
   (Al Green)
6. TOGETHER FOR THE FIRST TIME
   (Bobby "Blue" Bland and B.B. King)
7. IN HEAT
   (Love Unlimited)
8. FULFILLINGNESS' FIRST FINALE
   (Stevie Wonder)
9. DO IT ('TIL YOU'RE SATISFIED)
   (B.T. Express)
10. LIVE IT UP
   (Isley Brothers)

JAZZ ALBUMS

1. PIECES OF DREAMS
   (Stanley Turrentine)
2. SOUTHERN COMFORT
   (Crusaders)
3. IS IT IN
   (Eddie Harris)

4. BAD BENSON
   (George Benson)
5. BODY HEAT
   (Quincy Jones)
6. SATIN DOLL
   (Bobbi Humphrey)
7. THE BADDEST TURRENTINE
   (Stanley Turrentine)
8. LIVE OBLIVION, VOL. 1
   (Brian Auger's Oblivion Express)
9. FLYING START
   (Blackbyrds)
10. ONE
   (Bob James)

COUNTRY SINGLES

1. WE'RE OVER
   (Johnny Rodriguez)
2. OUT OF HAND
   (Gary Stewart)
3. I CAN HELP
   (Billy Swan)
4. WHAT A MAN MY MAN IS
   (Lynn Anderson)
5. HE CAN'T FILL MY SHOES
   (Jerry Lee Lewis)
6. RUBY BABY
   (Billy "Crash" Craddock)
7. KENTUCKY GAMBLER
   (Merle Haggard)
8. LIKE OLD TIMES AGAIN
   (Ray Price)
9. IT'S MIDNIGHT/PROMISED LAND
   (Elvis Presley)
10. U.S. OF A.
   (Donna Fargo)

COUNTRY ALBUMS

1. HIS 30th ALBUM
   (Merle Haggard)
2. SONGS ABOUT LADIES AND LOVE
   (Johnny Rodriguez)
3. BACK HOME AGAIN
   (John Denver)
4. DON WILLIAMS, VOL. III
   (Don Williams)
5. ANNE MURRAY COUNTRY
   (Anne Murray)
6. MISS DONNA FARGO
   (Donna Fargo)
7. PRIDE OF AMERICA
   (Charley Pride)
8. THE RAMBLIN' MAN
   (Waylon Jennings)
9. IT'S A MONSTER'S HOLIDAY
   (Buck Owens)
10. IF YOU LOVE ME (LET ME KNOW)
   (Olivia Newton-John)

1975

A number of bands and performers who'd been building an audience finally broke through in 1975, foremost among them Earth, Wind and Fire. This nine-member band made several albums before *That's the Way of the World* and on each, founder, producer, and spiritual leader Maurice White tinkered with personnel and approaches. With each album, White continued to mold a fresh style out of his primary influences: Sly Stone's driving funk and the cool of the Chicago rhythm and blues scene.

The result was a landmark album, one that enjoyed massive commercial success and established the Earth, Wind and Fire sound as one of pop music's most distinctive. As Joe McEwen wrote: "Cowbells, slight tango rhythm and snatches of James Brown bass lines stand side by side with delicate Latin beats and hard, insistent funk vamps. Voices and strings appear over the choppy, propulsive tracks, swelling and swooping, only to disappear at the snap of a finger, bring the music as close to elegance as funk can come."

This technique not only established Earth, Wind and Fire as black music's premiere band, but pumped life into the career of White's old Chicago employer, pioneering pop-jazzman Ramsey Lewis. The title of Lewis's *Sun Goddess*, produced by Earth, Wind and Fire, was transcendent music with supple, flowing rhythms, and Lewis's gossamer electric piano was as pleasing as awakening to a golden summer sun.

While Earth, Wind and Fire's ascendance was exciting, John Denver's immense popularity was baffling. With a bland voice, mediocre songwriting skills, and a singular lack of charisma, Denver seemed a highly unlikely candidate for superstardom. Yet three of the year's top ten albums (*John Denver's Greatest Hits, Back Home Again, An Evening with John Denver*) were his, a level of acceptance few of his contemporaries could match. Moreover, Denver would parlay his appeal into film roles (*Oh God*), television appearances (he's the Grammy Awards' favorite host), and headline engagements in Las Vegas, a place rock stars fear to tread. It's hard to determine what so many people saw in John Denver and if he knows (probably doubtful), he isn't telling.

Both Phoebe Snow and the Average White Band released self-titled debuts that pleased record buyers and critics, yet neither could manage this marriage again. A major part of their subsequent problems flowed from how they achieved initial acceptance. Snow's LP showcased a singer-songwriter complete with acoustic guitar and sensitive lyrics, an approach fast falling out of favor. In fact, hers would be the last big-selling singer-songwriter album produced in this now anachronistic style. Snow possesses a rich, multi-register voice more reminiscent of Ella Fitzgerald than any pop singer, and this album's simple arrangements beautifully complemented Snow's voice, while her later, more contemporary, recordings confined her expressiveness.

The Average White Band, six white Scots with a passion for rhythm and blues, broke through with music that sounded like James Brown in whiteface. The instrumental "Pick Up the Pieces" was short, sweet, and soulful. Yet that style too was becoming old hat as heavy funk and slick Philly-influenced productions now dominated black pop. As a result, these over-average musicians would flounder directionless through subsequent releases.

ALBUMS: Led Zeppelin's *Physical Graffiti* was a two-record set that displayed the many gifts of the last great heavy-metal band. There was the rumbling, danceable "Trampled Underfoot," featuring John Paul Jones's manic keyboards; the bouncy, happy rock 'n' roll of "Houses of the Holy" (which wasn't on the album of the same name); and "Kashmir," a mesmerizing mesh of rock changes and Eastern musical themes.

On the Border and *One of These Nights* continued The Eagles' progress, producing two great ballads "Best of My Love" and "Nights," plus some memorable rockers like "Already Gone" and "James Dean." Both albums were exceptional.

David Bowie's *Young Americans* was a totally unexpected treat. This arty English rocker always had displayed a remarkable gift for shifting personas from album to album. None were more audacious than his pilgrimage to Philadelphia to cut this strangely captivating approximation of the Philly sound.

Grover Washington Jr.'s gold *Mister Magic* served notice that the fusion of jazz instrumentation and R&B rhythms was now a mature genre. The title song, matching Washington's bluesy tenor sax with an understated funk groove, was the year's best instrumental. His cool, classy sound found favor with the black middle class. Stanley Turrentine's *Pieces of Dreams* and The Crusaders' *Southern Comfort* utilized a similar formula.

SINGLES: This was a great year for totally disposable pop singles. Two of the best were written by comeback performer of the year, Neil Sedaka. He wrote The Captain and Tennille's "Love Will Keep Us Together" and his own "Laughter in the Rain." Grand Funk Railroad recorded the oldie "Some Kind of Wonderful" written by an old Sedaka girl friend, Carole King. "Philadelphia Freedom" kept Elton John's hit streak alive. Freddy Fender emerged from obscurity in Texas to score with "Before the Next Teardrop Falls" and "Wasted Days and Wasted Nights." An atrocious ballad, "My Eyes Adored You," returned ex-Four Seasons lead singer Frankie Valli to the charts, while The Bee Gees had their first success with a disco-influenced song via "Jive Talkin'."

The soon forgotten Carl Douglas tasted short-lived notoriety with the idiotic "Kung Fu Fighting" courtesy of Bruce Lee. Tom Johnson ended his leadership of The Doobie Brothers with "Black Waters." Van McCoy's "The Hustle" laid claim to the hottest dance since "The Twist" and forever marked disco as a musical landscape of anonymous singers and production overkill. Labelle's "Lady Marmalade" was the last blast of pure New Orleans funk to make a national impact. "Mandy" and "Could This Be the Magic" established Barry Manilow as the latest in a long line of nice Jewish stars from Brooklyn. Major Harris's "Love Won't Let Me Wait" was a campy, erotic masterpiece and America's "Sister Golden Hair" wonderfully captured The Beach Boys' California spirit.

Still, one can't remember 1975 without mentioning Morris Albert's "Feelings," a song so icky doctors feared it would turn earlobes into bubble gum. No surprise then that it was the world's most recorded song for the next two years. Ugh!

Bruce Springsteen's *Born to Run* was the year's most critically praised and hyped album, though both rock radio and buyers were more cautious in their accepting this high-spirited New Jersey rocker. Columbia Records' publicists pulled off a major coup when *Time* and *Newsweek* ran cover stories on "the Boss" the same week. Columbia was elated. Editors at *Time* and *Newsweek* were not amused.

One of the best books written about rock, Griel Marcus's *Mystery Train*, was published. Marcus, a founding father of rock criticism, merged images from American literature (Moby-Dick, for one) and a personal view of American history into an evaluation of rock's key figures, including a lengthy essay on Elvis Presley. This was deservedly the first book about rock to be nominated for the National Book Award.

David Bowie

**John Denver
and the Muppets**

The Grateful Dead

Earth, Wind and Fire

JANUARY 4, 1975

POP SINGLES

1. LUCY IN THE SKY WITH DIAMONDS
   (Elton John)
2. KUNG FU FIGHTING
   (Carl Douglas)
3. YOU'RE THE FIRST, THE LAST, MY EVERYTHING
   (Barry White)
4. PLEASE MR. POSTMAN
   (The Carpenters)
5. JUNIOR'S FARM
   (Paul McCartney and Wings)
6. LAUGHTER IN THE RAIN
   (Neil Sedaka)
7. ANGIE BABY
   (Helen Reddy)
8. MANDY
   (Barry Manilow)
9. ONE MAN WOMAN, ONE WOMAN MAN
   (Paul Anka with Odia Coates)
10. BUNGLE IN THE JUNGLE
    (Jethro Tull)

POP ALBUMS

1. GREATEST HITS
   (Elton John)
2. BACK HOME AGAIN
   (John Denver)
3. NOT FRAGILE
   (Bachman-Turner Overdrive)
4. JOHN DENVER'S GREATEST HITS
   (John Denver)
5. GOODNIGHT VIENNA
   (Ringo Starr)
6. FIRE
   (Ohio Players)
7. SERENADE
   (Neil Diamond)
8. BUTTERFLY
   (Barbra Streisand)
9. THIS IS THE MOODY BLUES
   (The Moody Blues)
10. FREE AND EASY
    (Helen Reddy)

BLACK SINGLES

1. KUNG FU FIGHTING
   (Carl Douglas)
2. BOOGIE ON REGGAE WOMAN
   (Stevie Wonder)
3. YOU'RE THE FIRST, THE LAST, MY EVERYTHING
   (Barry White)
4. FUNKY PRESIDENT (PEOPLE IT'S BAD)
   (James Brown)
5. YOU GOT THE LOVE
   (Rufus featuring Chaka Khan)
6. WHEN WILL I SEE YOU AGAIN
   (The Three Degrees)
7. HEAVY FALLIN' OUT
   (The Stylistics)
8. DON'T TAKE YOUR LOVE FROM ME
   (The Manhattans)
9. FIRE
   (Ohio Players)
10. FROM HIS WOMAN TO YOU
    (Barbara Mason)

BLACK ALBUMS

1. FIRE
   (Ohio Players)
2. I FEEL A SONG
   (Gladys Knight and the Pips)
3. WHITE GOLD
   (Love Unlimited Orchestra)

---

4. AL GREEN EXPLORES YOUR MIND
   (Al Green)
5. FULFILLINGNESS' FIRST FINALE
   (Stevie Wonder)
6. TOGETHER FOR THE FIRST TIME
   (Bobby "Blue" Bland and B.B. King)
7. DO IT 'TIL YOU'RE SATISFIED
   (B.T. Express)
8. CAUGHT UP
   (Millie Jackson)
9. NEW AND IMPROVED
   (Spinners)
10. SOUTHERN COMFORT
    (Crusaders)

JAZZ ALBUMS

1. SOUTHERN COMFORT
   (Crusaders)
2. PIECES OF DREAMS
   (Stanley Turrentine)
3. BAD BENSON
   (George Benson)
4. SATIN DOLL
   (Bobbi Humphrey)
5. LIVE OBLIVION, VOL. I
   (Brian Auger's Oblivion Express)
6. FLYING START
   (Blackbyrds)
7. IS IT IN
   (Eddie Harris)
8. BODY HEAT
   (Quincy Jones)
9. ONE
   (Bob James)
10. TOTAL ECLIPSE
    (Billy Cobham)

COUNTRY SINGLES

1. OUT OF HAND
   (Gary Stewart)
2. WHAT A MAN, MY MAN IS
   (Lynn Anderson)
3. RUBY BABY
   (Billy "Crash" Craddock)
4. KENTUCKY GAMBLER
   (Merle Haggard)
5. LIKE OLD TIMES AGAIN
   (Ray Price)
6. WE'RE OVER
   (Johnny Rodriguez)
7. THE DOOR
   (George Jones)
8. IT'S MIDNIGHT/PROMISED LAND
   (Elvis Presley)
9. (I'D BE) A LEGEND IN MY TIME
   (Ronnie Milsap)
10. MY WOMAN'S MAN
    (Freddie Hart)

COUNTRY ALBUMS

1. HIS 30th ALBUM
   (Merle Haggard)
2. DON WILLIAMS, VOL. III
   (Don Williams)
3. PRIDE OF AMERICA
   (Charley Pride)
4. BACK HOME AGAIN
   (John Denver)
5. MISS DONNA FARGO
   (Donna Fargo)
6. SONGS ABOUT LADIES AND LOVE
   (Johnny Rodriguez)
7. ANNE MURRAY COUNTRY
   (Anne Murray)
8. THE RAMBLIN' MAN
   (Waylon Jennings)
9. IF YOU LOVE ME (LET ME KNOW)
   (Olivia Newton-John)
10. ROOM FULL OF ROSES
    (Mickey Gilley)

JANUARY 11, 1975

POP SINGLES

1. LUCY IN THE SKY WITH DIAMONDS
   (Elton John)
2. YOU'RE THE FIRST, THE LAST, MY EVERYTHING
   (Barry White)
3. PLEASE MR. POSTMAN
   (The Carpenters)
4. LAUGHTER IN THE RAIN
   (Neil Sedaka)
5. MANDY
   (Barry Manilow)
6. JUNIOR'S FARM
   (Paul McCartney and Wings)
7. BOOGIE ON REGGAE WOMAN
   (Stevie Wonder)
8. ONE MAN WOMAN, ONE WOMAN MAN
   (Paul Anka with Odia Coates)
9. KUNG FU FIGHTING
   (Carl Douglas)
10. ONLY YOU
    (Ringo Starr)

POP ALBUMS

1. GREATEST HITS
   (Elton John)
2. BACK HOME AGAIN
   (John Denver)
3. FIRE
   (Ohio Players)
4. JOHN DENVER'S GREATEST HITS
   (John Denver)
5. GOODNIGHT VIENNA
   (Ringo Starr)
6. NOT FRAGILE
   (Bachman-Turner Overdrive)
7. MILES OF AISLES
   (Joni Mitchell)
8. BUTTERFLY
   (Barbra Streisand)
9. THIS IS THE MOODY BLUES
   (The Moody Blues)
10. SERENADE
    (Neil Diamond)

BLACK SINGLES

1. BOOGIE ON REGGAE WOMAN
   (Stevie Wonder)
2. KUNG FU FIGHTING
   (Carl Douglas)
3. YOU'RE THE FIRST, THE LAST, MY EVERYTHING
   (Barry White)
4. FIRE
   (Ohio Players)
5. FUNKY PRESIDENT (PEOPLE IT'S BAD)
   (James Brown)
6. DON'T TAKE YOUR LOVE FROM ME
   (The Manhattans)
7. YOU GOT THE LOVE
   (Rufus featuring Chaka Khan)
8. FROM HIS WOMAN TO YOU
   (Barbara Mason)
9. AS LONG AS HE TAKES CARE OF HOME
   (Candi Staton)
10. WHEN WILL I SEE YOU AGAIN
    (The Three Degrees)

BLACK ALBUMS

1. FIRE
   (Ohio Players)
2. AL GREEN EXPLORES YOUR MIND
   (Al Green)
3. FULFILLINGNESS' FIRST FINALE
   (Stevie Wonder)

4. WHITE GOLD
 (Love Unlimited Orchestra)
5. TOGETHER FOR THE FIRST TIME
 (Bobby "Blue" Bland and B.B. King)
6. DO IT 'TIL YOU'RE SATISFIED
 (B.T. Express)
7. NEW AND IMPROVED
 (Spinners)
8. I FEEL A SONG
 (Gladys Knight and the Pips)
9. CAN'T GET ENOUGH
 (Barry White)
10. KUNG FU FIGHTING
 (Carl Douglas)

JAZZ ALBUMS

1. SOUTHERN COMFORT
 (Crusaders)
2. PIECES OF DREAMS
 (Stanley Turrentine)
3. BAD BENSON
 (George Benson)
4. SATIN DOLL
 (Bobbi Humphrey)
5. LIVE OBLIVION, VOL. I
 (Brian Auger's Oblivion Express)
6. FLYING START
 (Blackbyrds)
7. TOTAL ECLIPSE
 (Billy Cobham)
8. BODY HEAT
 (Quincy Jones)
9. ONE
 (Bob James)
10. FEEL
 (George Duke)

COUNTRY SINGLES

1. RUBY BABY
 (Billy "Crash" Craddock)
2. WHAT A MAN, MY MAN IS
 (Lynn Anderson)
3. KENTUCKY GAMBLER
 (Merle Haggard)
4. (I'D BE) A LEGEND IN MY TIME
 (Ronnie Milsap)
5. LIKE OLD TIMES AGAIN
 (Ray Price)
6. OUT OF HAND
 (Gary Stewart)
7. THE DOOR
 (George Jones)
8. IT'S MIDNIGHT/PROMISED LAND
 (Elvis Presley)
9. MY WOMAN'S MAN
 (Freddie Hart)
10. FOR A MINUTE THERE
 (Johnny Paycheck)

COUNTRY ALBUMS

1. PRIDE OF AMERICA
 (Charley Pride)
2. DON WILLIAMS, VOL. III
 (Don Williams)
3. BACK HOME AGAIN
 (John Denver)
4. HIS 30th ALBUM
 (Merle Haggard)
5. MISS DONNA FARGO
 (Donna Fargo)
6. SONGS ABOUT LADIES AND LOVE
 (Johnny Rodriguez)
7. THE RAMBLIN' MAN
 (Waylon Jennings)
8. IF YOU LOVE ME (LET ME KNOW)
 (Olivia Newton-John)
9. ANNE MURRAY COUNTRY
 (Anne Murray)
10. COUNTRY PARTNERS
 (Conway Twitty and Loretta Lynn)

JANUARY 18, 1975

POP SINGLES

1. MANDY
 (Barry Manilow)
2. PLEASE MR. POSTMAN
 (The Carpenters)
3. YOU'RE THE FIRST, THE LAST, MY EVERYTHING
 (Barry White)
4. LAUGHTER IN THE RAIN
 (Neil Sedaka)
5. LUCY IN THE SKY WITH DIAMONDS
 (Elton John)
6. BOOGIE ON REGGAE WOMAN
 (Stevie Wonder)
7. JUNIOR'S FARM
 (Paul McCartney and Wings)
8. ONE MAN WOMAN, ONE WOMAN MAN
 (Paul Anka with Odia Coates)
9. ONLY YOU
 (Ringo Starr)
10. FIRE
 (Ohio Players)

POP ALBUMS

1. GREATEST HITS
 (Elton John)
2. BACK HOME AGAIN
 (John Denver)
3. FIRE
 (Ohio Players)
4. JOHN DENVER'S GREATEST HITS
 (John Denver)
5. MILES OF AISLES
 (Joni Mitchell)
6. NOT FRAGILE
 (Bachman-Turner Overdrive)
7. RELAYER
 (Yes)
8. DARK HORSE
 (George Harrison)
9. GOODNIGHT VIENNA
 (Ringo Starr)
10. HEART LIKE A WHEEL
 (Linda Ronstadt)

BLACK SINGLES

1. FIRE
 (Ohio Players)
2. BOOGIE ON REGGAE WOMAN
 (Stevie Wonder)
3. KUNG FU FIGHTING
 (Carl Douglas)
4. DON'T TAKE YOUR LOVE FROM ME
 (The Manhattans)
5. YOU'RE THE FIRST, THE LAST, MY EVERYTHING
 (Barry White)
6. FROM HIS WOMAN TO YOU
 (Barbara Mason)
7. FUNKY PRESIDENT (PEOPLE IT'S BAD)
 (James Brown)
8. AS LONG AS HE TAKES CARE OF HOME
 (Candi Staton)
9. I BELONG TO YOU
 (Love Unlimited)
10. YOU GOT THE LOVE
 (Rufus featuring Chaka Khan)

BLACK ALBUMS

1. FIRE
 (Ohio Players)
2. AL GREEN EXPLORES YOUR MIND
 (Al Green)
3. FULFILLINGNESS' FIRST FINALE
 (Stevie Wonder)

4. DO IT 'TIL YOU'RE SATISFIED
 (B.T. Express)
5. TOGETHER FOR THE FIRST TIME
 (Bobby "Blue" Bland and B.B. King)
6. NEW AND IMPROVED
 (Spinners)
7. KUNG FU FIGHTING
 (Carl Douglas)
8. WHITE GOLD
 (Love Unlimited Orchestra)
9. CAN'T GET ENOUGH
 (Barry White)
10. RUFUSIZED
 (Rufus featuring Chaka Khan)

JAZZ ALBUMS

1. PIECES OF DREAMS
 (Stanley Turrentine)
2. SOUTHERN COMFORT
 (Crusaders)
3. SATIN DOLL
 (Bobbi Humphrey)
4. BAD BENSON
 (George Benson)
5. LIVE OBLIVION, VOL. I
 (Brian Auger's Oblivion Express)
6. FLYING START
 (Blackbyrds)
7. TOTAL ECLIPSE
 (Billy Cobham)
8. FEEL
 (George Duke)
9. SUN GODDESS
 (Ramsey Lewis)
10. ANOTHER BEGINNING
 (Les McCann)

COUNTRY SINGLES

1. KENTUCKY GAMBLER
 (Merle Haggard)
2. (I'D BE) A LEGEND IN MY TIME
 (Ronnie Milsap)
3. RUBY BABY
 (Billy "Crash" Craddock)
4. MY WOMAN'S MAN
 (Freddie Hart)
5. LIKE OLD TIMES AGAIN
 (Ray Price)
6. FOR A MINUTE THERE
 (Johnny Paycheck)
7. OUT OF HAND
 (Gary Stewart)
8. CITY LIGHTS
 (Mickey Gilley)
9. ROCK ON BABY
 (Brenda Lee)
10. THE DOOR
 (George Jones)

COUNTRY ALBUMS

1. PRIDE IN AMERICA
 (Charley Pride)
2. BACK HOME AGAIN
 (John Denver)
3. HIS 30th ALBUM
 (Merle Haggard)
4. DON WILLIAMS, VOL. III
 (Don Williams)
5. MISS DONNA FARGO
 (Donna Fargo)
6. GET ON MY LOVE TRAIN
 (La Costa)
7. THE SILVER FOX
 (Charlie Rich)
8. THE RAMBLIN' MAN
 (Waylon Jennings)
9. I CAN HELP
 (Billy Swan)
10. CITY LIGHTS
 (Mickey Gilley)

JANUARY 25, 1975

POP SINGLES

1. PLEASE MR. POSTMAN
   (The Carpenters)
2. MANDY
   (Barry Manilow)
3. LAUGHTER IN THE RAIN
   (Neil Sedaka)
4. YOU'RE THE FIRST, THE LAST, MY EVERYTHING
   (Barry White)
5. BOOGIE ON REGGAE WOMAN
   (Stevie Wonder)
6. FIRE
   (Ohio Players)
7. JUNIOR'S FARM
   (Paul McCartney and Wings)
8. YOU'RE NO GOOD
   (Linda Ronstadt)
9. BEST OF MY LOVE
   (The Eagles)
10. NEVER CAN SAY GOODBYE
    (Gloria Gaynor)

POP ALBUMS

1. GREATEST HITS
   (Elton John)
2. FIRE
   (Ohio Players)
3. JOHN DENVER'S GREATEST HITS
   (John Denver)
4. MILES OF AISLES
   (Joni Mitchell)
5. RELAYER
   (Yes)
6. DARK HORSE
   (George Harrison)
7. BACK HOME AGAIN
   (John Denver)
8. HEART LIKE A WHEEL
   (Linda Ronstadt)
9. AVERAGE WHITE BAND
   (Average White Band)
10. NOT FRAGILE
    (Bachman-Turner Overdrive)

BLACK SINGLES

1. FIRE
   (Ohio Players)
2. BOOGIE ON REGGAE WOMAN
   (Stevie Wonder)
3. DON'T TAKE YOUR LOVE FROM ME
   (The Manhattans)
4. KUNG FU FIGHTING
   (Carl Douglas)
5. FROM HIS WOMAN TO YOU
   (Barbara Mason)
6. I BELONG TO YOU
   (Love Unlimited)
7. AS LONG AS HE TAKES CARE OF HOME
   (Candi Staton)
8. YOU'RE THE FIRST, THE LAST, MY EVERYTHING
   (Barry White)
9. FUNKY PRESIDENT (PEOPLE IT'S BAD)
   (James Brown)
10. PICK UP THE PIECES
    (Average White Band)

BLACK ALBUMS

1. FIRE
   (Ohio Players)
2. AL GREEN EXPLORES YOUR MIND
   (Al Green)
3. FULFILLINGNESS' FIRST FINALE
   (Stevie Wonder)

4. DO IT 'TIL YOU'RE SATISFIED
   (B.T. Express)
5. NEW AND IMPROVED
   (Spinners)
6. RUFUSIZED
   (Rufus featuring Chaka Khan)
7. KUNG FU FIGHTING
   (Carl Douglas)
8. WHITE GOLD
   (Love Unlimited Orchestra)
9. AVERAGE WHITE BAND
   (Average White Band)
10. CAN'T GET ENOUGH
    (Barry White)

JAZZ ALBUMS

1. PIECES OF DREAMS
   (Stanley Turrentine)
2. SATIN DOLL
   (Bobbi Humphrey)
3. SOUTHERN COMFORT
   (Crusaders)
4. BAD BENSON
   (George Benson)
5. FEEL
   (George Duke)
6. TOTAL ECLIPSE
   (Billy Cobham)
7. SUN GODDESS
   (Ramsey Lewis)
8. LIVE OBLIVION, VOL. I
   (Brian Auger's Oblivion Express)
9. ANOTHER BEGINNING
   (Les McCann)
10. FLYING START
    (Blackbyrds)

COUNTRY SINGLES

1. (I'D BE) A LEGEND IN MY TIME
   (Ronnie Milsap)
2. KENTUCKY GAMBLER
   (Merle Haggard)
3. CITY LIGHTS
   (Mickey Gilley)
4. MY WOMAN'S MAN
   (Freddie Hart)
5. FOR A MINUTE THERE
   (Johnny Paycheck)
6. RUBY BABY
   (Billy "Crash" Craddock)
7. THEN WHO AM I
   (Charley Pride)
8. IT'S TIME TO PAY THE FIDDLER
   (Cal Smith)
9. OUT OF HAND
   (Gary Stewart)
10. WRONG ROAD AGAIN
    (Crystal Gayle)

COUNTRY ALBUMS

1. THE SILVER FOX
   (Charlie Rich)
2. BACK HOME AGAIN
   (John Denver)
3. I CAN HELP
   (Billy Swan)
4. CITY LIGHTS
   (Mickey Gilley)
5. GET ON MY LOVE TRAIN
   (La Costa)
6. PRIDE OF AMERICA
   (Charley Pride)
7. HIS 30th ALBUM
   (Merle Haggard)
8. SONGS OF FOX HOLLOW
   (Tom T. Hall)
9. DON WILLIAMS, VOL. III
   (Don Williams)
10. MISS DONNA FARGO
    (Donna Fargo)

FEBRUARY 1, 1975

POP SINGLES

1. LAUGHTER IN THE RAIN
   (Neil Sedaka)
2. BOOGIE ON REGGAE WOMAN
   (Stevie Wonder)
3. MANDY
   (Barry Manilow)
4. FIRE
   (Ohio Players)
5. PLEASE MR. POSTMAN
   (The Carpenters)
6. YOU'RE NO GOOD
   (Linda Ronstadt)
7. BEST OF MY LOVE
   (The Eagles)
8. PICK UP THE PIECES
   (Average White Band)
9. NEVER CAN SAY GOODBYE
   (Gloria Gaynor)
10. SOME KIND OF WONDERFUL
    (Grand Funk Railroad)

POP ALBUMS

1. FIRE
   (Ohio Players)
2. GREATEST HITS
   (Elton John)
3. MILES OF AISLES
   (Joni Mitchell)
4. DARK HORSE
   (George Harrison)
5. RELAYER
   (Yes)
6. HEART LIKE A WHEEL
   (Linda Ronstadt)
7. AVERAGE WHITE BAND
   (Average White Band)
8. JOHN DENVER'S GREATEST HITS
   (John Denver)
9. BACK HOME AGAIN
   (John Denver)
10. WAR CHILD
    (Jethro Tull)

BLACK SINGLES

1. FIRE
   (Ohio Players)
2. BOOGIE ON REGGAE WOMAN
   (Stevie Wonder)
3. DON'T TAKE YOUR LOVE FROM ME
   (The Manhattans)
4. I BELONG TO YOU
   (Love Unlimited)
5. FROM HIS WOMAN TO YOU
   (Barbara Mason)
6. KUNG FU FIGHTING
   (Carl Douglas)
7. AS LONG AS HE TAKES CARE OF HOME
   (Candi Staton)
8. PICK UP THE PIECES
   (Average White Band)
9. YOU'RE THE FIRST, THE LAST, MY EVERYTHING
   (Barry White)
10. STRUTTIN'/YOU'RE SO BEAUTIFUL
    (Billy Preston)

BLACK ALBUMS

1. FIRE
   (Ohio Players)
2. AL GREEN EXPLORES YOUR MIND
   (Al Green)
3. FULFILLINGNESS' FIRST FINALE
   (Stevie Wonder)

4. NEW AND IMPROVED
   (Spinners)
5. DO IT 'TIL YOU'RE SATISFIED
   (B.T. Express)
6. RUFUSIZED
   (Rufus featuring Chaka Khan)
7. AVERAGE WHITE BAND
   (Average White Band)
8. NIGHTBIRDS
   (Labelle)
9. WITH EVERYTHING I FEEL IN ME
   (Aretha Franklin)
10. FLYING START
    (Blackbyrds)

JAZZ ALBUMS

1. SATIN DOLL
   (Bobbi Humphrey)
2. SOUTHERN COMFORT
   (Crusaders)
3. PIECES OF DREAMS
   (Stanley Turrentine)
4. FEEL
   (George Duke)
5. SUN GODDESS
   (Ramsey Lewis)
6. TOTAL ECLIPSE
   (Billy Cobham)
7. BAD BENSON
   (George Benson)
8. FLYING START
   (Blackbyrds)
9. LIVE OBLIVION, VOL. I
   (Brian Auger's Oblivion Express)
10. ANOTHER BEGINNING
    (Les McCann)

COUNTRY SINGLES

1. CITY LIGHTS
   (Mickey Gilley)
2. (I'D BE) A LEGEND IN MY TIME
   (Ronnie Milsap)
3. THEN WHO AM I
   (Charley Pride)
4. IT'S TIME TO PAY THE FIDDLER
   (Cal Smith)
5. KENTUCKY GAMBLER
   (Merle Haggard)
6. I CARE/SNEAKY SNAKE
   (Tom T. Hall)
7. THE TIES THAT BIND
   (Don Williams)
8. DEVIL IN THE BOTTLE
   (T.G. Sheppard)
9. WRONG ROAD AGAIN
   (Crystal Gayle)
10. THERE'S A SONG ON THE JUKEBOX
    (David Wills)

COUNTRY ALBUMS

1. CITY LIGHTS
   (Mickey Gilley)
2. I CAN HELP
   (Billy Swan)
3. THE SILVER FOX
   (Charlie Rich)
4. BACK HOME AGAIN
   (John Denver)
5. GET ON MY LOVE TRAIN
   (La Costa)
6. SONGS OF FOX HOLLOW
   (Tom T. Hall)
7. PRIDE OF AMERICA
   (Charley Pride)
8. HEART LIKE A WHEEL
   (Linda Ronstadt)
9. HIS 30th ALBUM
   (Merle Haggard)
10. DON WILLIAMS, VOL. III
    (Don Williams)

FEBRUARY 8, 1975

POP SINGLES

1. BOOGIE ON REGGAE WOMAN
   (Stevie Wonder)
2. FIRE
   (Ohio Players)
3. YOU'RE NO GOOD
   (Linda Ronstadt)
4. LAUGHTER IN THE RAIN
   (Neil Sedaka)
5. PICK UP THE PIECES
   (Average White Band)
6. BEST OF MY LOVE
   (The Eagles)
7. MANDY
   (Barry Manilow)
8. SOME KIND OF WONDERFUL
   (Grand Funk Railroad)
9. PLEASE MR. POSTMAN
   (The Carpenters)
10. MORNING SIDE OF THE MOUNTAIN
    (Donny and Marie Osmond)

POP ALBUMS

1. GREATEST HITS
   (Elton John)
2. FIRE
   (Ohio Players)
3. MILES OF AISLES
   (Joni Mitchell)
4. DARK HORSE
   (George Harrison)
5. HEART LIKE A WHEEL
   (Linda Ronstadt)
6. AVERAGE WHITE BAND
   (Average White Band)
7. RELAYER
   (Yes)
8. JOHN DENVER'S GREATEST HITS
   (John Denver)
9. WAR CHILD
   (Jethro Tull)
10. RUFUSIZED
    (Rufus featuring Chaka Khan)

BLACK SINGLES

1. FIRE
   (Ohio Players)
2. I BELONG TO YOU
   (Love Unlimited)
3. BOOGIE ON REGGAE WOMAN
   (Stevie Wonder)
4. PICK UP THE PIECES
   (Average White Band)
5. DON'T TAKE YOUR LOVE FROM ME
   (The Manhattans)
6. FROM HIS WOMAN TO YOU
   (Barbara Mason)
7. STRUTTIN'/YOU ARE SO BEAUTIFUL
   (Billy Preston)
8. KUNG FU FIGHTING
   (Carl Douglas)
9. HAPPY PEOPLE
   (Temptations)
10. I AM, I AM
    (Smokey Robinson)

BLACK ALBUMS

1. FIRE
   (Ohio Players)
2. FULFILLINGNESS' FIRST FINALE
   (Stevie Wonder)
3. NEW AND IMPROVED
   (Spinners)
4. AVERAGE WHITE BAND
   (Average White Band)

5. DO IT 'TIL YOU'RE SATISFIED
   (B.T. Express)
6. AL GREEN EXPLORES YOUR MIND
   (Al Green)
7. RUFUSIZED
   (Rufus featuring Chaka Khan)
8. NIGHTBIRDS
   (Labelle)
9. SUN GODDESS
   (Ramsey Lewis)
10. WITH EVERYTHING I FEEL IN ME
    (Aretha Franklin)

JAZZ ALBUMS

1. SUN GODDESS
   (Ramsey Lewis)
2. SATIN DOLL
   (Bobbi Humphrey)
3. SOUTHERN COMFORT
   (Crusaders)
4. FEEL
   (George Duke)
5. TOTAL ECLIPSE
   (Billy Cobham)
6. PIECES OF DREAMS
   (Stanley Turrentine)
7. FLYING START
   (Blackbyrds)
8. BAD BENSON
   (George Benson)
9. LIVE OBLIVION, VOL. I
   (Brian Auger's Oblivion Express)
10. TIM WEISBERG 4
    (Tim Weisberg)

COUNTRY SINGLES

1. THEN WHO AM I
   (Charley Pride)
2. IT'S TIME TO PAY THE FIDDLER
   (Cal Smith)
3. CITY LIGHTS
   (Mickey Gilley)
4. I CARE/SNEAKY SNAKE
   (Tom T. Hall)
5. THE TIES THAT BIND
   (Don Williams)
6. DEVIL IN THE BOTTLE
   (T.G. Sheppard)
7. (I'D BE) A LEGEND IN MY TIME
   (Ronnie Milsap)
8. IT WAS ALWAYS SO EASY
   (Moe Bandy)
9. WRONG ROAD AGAIN
   (Crystal Gayle)
10. THERE'S A SONG ON THE JUKEBOX
    (David Wills)

COUNTRY ALBUMS

1. CITY LIGHTS
   (Mickey Gilley)
2. I CAN HELP
   (Billy Swan)
3. THE SILVER FOX
   (Charlie Rich)
4. SONGS OF FOX HOLLOW
   (Tom T. Hall)
5. BACK HOME AGAIN
   (John Denver)
6. HEART LIKE A WHEEL
   (Linda Ronstadt)
7. PRIDE OF AMERICA
   (Charley Pride)
8. GET ON MY LOVE TRAIN
   (La Costa)
9. HIS 30th ALBUM
   (Merle Haggard)
10. THE RAMBLIN' MAN
    (Waylon Jennings)

FEBRUARY 15, 1975

POP SINGLES

1. FIRE
   (Ohio Players)
2. YOU'RE NO GOOD
   (Linda Ronstadt)
3. PICK UP THE PIECES
   (Average White Band)
4. BLACK WATER
   (The Doobie Brothers)
5. BEST OF MY LOVE
   (The Eagles)
6. SOME KIND OF WONDERFUL
   (Grand Funk Railroad)
7. BOOGIE ON REGGAE WOMAN
   (Stevie Wonder)
8. MANDY
   (Barry Manilow)
9. MY EYES ADORED YOU
   (Frankie Valli)
10. MORNING SIDE OF THE MOUNTAIN
    (Donny and Marie Osmond)

POP ALBUMS

1. HEART LIKE A WHEEL
   (Linda Ronstadt)
2. BLOOD ON THE TRACKS
   (Bob Dylan)
3. FIRE
   (Ohio Players)
4. GREATEST HITS
   (Elton John)
5. AVERAGE WHITE BAND
   (Average White Band)
6. MILES OF AISLES
   (Joni Mitchell)
7. DARK HORSE
   (George Harrison)
8. WAR CHILD
   (Jethro Tull)
9. RUFUSIZED
   (Rufus featuring Chaka Khan)
10. BARRY MANILOW II
    (Barry Manilow)

BLACK SINGLES

1. FIRE
   (Ohio Players)
2. I BELONG TO YOU
   (Love Unlimited)
3. PICK UP THE PIECES
   (Average White Band)
4. BOOGIE ON REGGAE WOMAN
   (Stevie Wonder)
5. DON'T TAKE YOUR LOVE FROM ME
   (The Manhattans)
6. HAPPY PEOPLE
   (Temptations)
7. STRUTTIN'/YOU ARE SO BEAUTIFUL
   (Billy Preston)
8. RHYME TYME PEOPLE
   (Kool and the Gang)
9. MIDNIGHT SKY, PART 1
   (Isley Brothers)
10. I AM, I AM
    (Smokey Robinson)

BLACK ALBUMS

1. FIRE
   (Ohio Players)
2. AVERAGE WHITE BAND
   (Average White Band)
3. NEW AND IMPROVED
   (Spinners)
4. FULFILLINGNESS' FIRST FINALE
   (Stevie Wonder)

---

5. DO IT 'TIL YOU'RE SATISFIED
   (B.T. Express)
6. RUFUSIZED
   (Rufus featuring Chaka Khan)
7. NIGHTBIRDS
   (Labelle)
8. SUN GODDESS
   (Ramsey Lewis)
9. URBAN RENEWAL
   (Tower of Power)
10. REALITY
    (James Brown)

JAZZ ALBUMS

1. SUN GODDESS
   (Ramsey Lewis)
2. FLYING START
   (Blackbyrds)
3. SATIN DOLL
   (Bobbi Humphrey)
4. SOUTHERN COMFORT
   (Crusaders)
5. FEEL
   (George Duke)
6. TOTAL ECLIPSE
   (Billy Cobham)
7. BAD BENSON
   (George Benson)
8. PIECES OF DREAMS
   (Stanley Turrentine)
9. TIM WEISBERG 4
   (Tim Weisberg)
10. STANLEY CLARKE
    (Stanley Clarke)

COUNTRY SINGLES

1. IT'S TIME TO PAY THE FIDDLER
   (Cal Smith)
2. I CARE/SNEAKY SNAKE
   (Tom T. Hall)
3. THE TIES THAT BIND
   (Don Williams)
4. DEVIL IN THE BOTTLE
   (T.G. Sheppard)
5. RAINY DAY WOMAN
   (Waylon Jennings)
6. I CAN'T HELP IT
   (Linda Ronstadt)
7. WRONG ROAD AGAIN
   (Crystal Gayle)
8. IT WAS ALWAYS SO EASY
   (Moe Bandy)
9. LINDA ON MY MIND
   (Conway Twitty)
10. THEN WHO AM I
    (Charley Pride)

COUNTRY ALBUMS

1. I CAN HELP
   (Billy Swan)
2. SONGS OF FOX HOLLOW
   (Tom T. Hall)
3. CITY LIGHTS
   (Mickey Gilley)
4. HEART LIKE A WHEEL
   (Linda Ronstadt)
5. THE SILVER FOX
   (Charlie Rich)
6. BACK HOME AGAIN
   (John Denver)
7. LIKE OLD TIMES AGAIN
   (Ray Price)
8. HIS 30th ALBUM
   (Merle Haggard)
9. THE RAMBLIN' MAN
   (Waylon Jennings)
10. HIGHLY PRIZED POSSESSION
    (Anne Murray)

FEBRUARY 22, 1975

POP SINGLES

1. YOU'RE NO GOOD
   (Linda Ronstadt)
2. PICK UP THE PIECES
   (Average White Band)
3. BLACK WATER
   (The Doobie Brothers)
4. BEST OF MY LOVE
   (The Eagles)
5. SOME KIND OF WONDERFUL
   (Grand Funk Railroad)
6. FIRE
   (Ohio Players)
7. MY EYES ADORED YOU
   (Frankie Valli)
8. LADY
   (Styx)
9. HAVE YOU NEVER BEEN MELLOW
   (Olivia Newton-John)
10. LONELY PEOPLE
    (America)

POP ALBUMS

1. BLOOD ON THE TRACKS
   (Bob Dylan)
2. HEART LIKE A WHEEL
   (Linda Ronstadt)
3. AVERAGE WHITE BAND
   (Average White Band)
4. GREATEST HITS
   (Elton John)
5. FIRE
   (Ohio Players)
6. RUFUSIZED
   (Rufus featuring Chaka Khan)
7. MILES OF AISLES
   (Joni Mitchell)
8. BARRY MANILOW II
   (Barry Manilow)
9. SO WHAT
   (Joe Walsh)
10. WAR CHILD
    (Jethro Tull)

BLACK SINGLES

1. I BELONG TO YOU
   (Love Unlimited)
2. PICK UP THE PIECES
   (Average White Band)
3. FIRE
   (Ohio Players)
4. HAPPY PEOPLE
   (Temptations)
5. LADY MARMALADE
   (Labelle)
6. RHYME TYME PEOPLE
   (Kool and the Gang)
7. MIDNIGHT SKY, PART 1
   (Isley Brothers)
8. DON'T CHA LOVE IT
   (The Miracles)
9. I GET LIFTED
   (George McCrae)
10. SUPER DUPER LOVE, PART 1
    (Sugar Billy)

BLACK ALBUMS

1. FIRE
   (Ohio Players)
2. AVERAGE WHITE BAND
   (Average White Band)
3. NEW AND IMPROVED
   (Spinners)
4. NIGHTBIRDS
   (Labelle)

5. URBAN RENEWAL
   (Tower of Power)
6. SUN GODDESS
   (Ramsey Lewis)
7. RUFUSIZED
   (Rufus featuring Chaka Khan)
8. DO IT 'TIL YOU'RE SATISFIED
   (B.T. Express)
9. REALITY
   (James Brown)
10. FULFILLINGNESS' FIRST FINALE
    (Stevie Wonder)

JAZZ ALBUMS

1. SUN GODDESS
   (Ramsey Lewis)
2. FLYING START
   (Blackbyrds)
3. SOUTHERN COMFORT
   (Crusaders)
4. SATIN DOLL
   (Bobbi Humphrey)
5. FEEL
   (George Duke)
6. BAD BENSON
   (George Benson)
7. FIRST MINUTE OF A NEW DAY
   (Gil Scott-Heron and Brian Jackson)
8. STANLEY CLARKE
   (Stanley Clarke)
9. PIECES OF DREAMS
   (Stanley Turrentine)
10. URBAN RENEWAL
    (Tower of Power)

COUNTRY SINGLES

1. I CARE/SNEAKY SNAKE
   (Tom T. Hall)
2. DEVIL IN THE BOTTLE
   (T.G. Sheppard)
3. THE TIES THAT BIND
   (Don Williams)
4. RAINY DAY WOMAN
   (Waylon Jennings)
5. LINDA ON MY MIND
   (Conway Twitty)
6. I CAN'T HELP IT
   (Linda Ronstadt)
7. WRONG ROAD AGAIN
   (Crystal Gayle)
8. IT'S TIME TO PAY THE FIDDLER
   (Cal Smith)
9. BEFORE THE NEXT TEARDROP FALLS
   (Freddy Fender)
10. WOLF CREEK PASS
    (C.W. McCall)

COUNTRY ALBUMS

1. SONGS OF FOX HOLLOW
   (Tom T. Hall)
2. HEART LIKE A WHEEL
   (Linda Ronstadt)
3. I CAN HELP
   (Billy Swan)
4. CITY LIGHTS
   (Mickey Gilley)
5. LIKE OLD TIMES AGAIN
   (Ray Price)
6. THE SILVER FOX
   (Charlie Rich)
7. BACK HOME AGAIN
   (John Denver)
8. HIGHLY PRIZED POSSESSION
   (Anne Murray)
9. HIS 30th ALBUM
   (Merle Haggard)
10. THE RAMBLIN' MAN
    (Waylon Jennings)

MARCH 1, 1975

POP SINGLES

1. PICK UP THE PIECES
   (Average White Band)
2. BLACK WATER
   (The Doobie Brothers)
3. BEST OF MY LOVE
   (The Eagles)
4. YOU'RE NO GOOD
   (Linda Ronstadt)
5. MY EYES ADORED YOU
   (Frankie Valli)
6. HAVE YOU NEVER BEEN MELLOW
   (Olivia Newton-John)
7. LADY
   (Styx)
8. LADY MARMALADE
   (Labelle)
9. LONELY PEOPLE
   (America)
10. FIRE
    (Ohio Players)

POP ALBUMS

1. BLOOD ON THE TRACKS
   (Bob Dylan)
2. HEART LIKE A WHEEL
   (Linda Ronstadt)
3. AVERAGE WHITE BAND
   (Average White Band)
4. GREATEST HITS
   (Elton John)
5. FIRE
   (Ohio Players)
6. RUFUSIZED
   (Rufus featuring Chaka Khan)
7. EMPTY SKY
   (Elton John)
8. WHAT WERE ONCE VICES ARE NOW
   HABITS
   (The Doobie Brothers)
9. SO WHAT
   (Joe Walsh)
10. NOT FRAGILE
    (Bachman-Turner Overdrive)

BLACK SINGLES

1. PICK UP THE PIECES
   (Average White Band)
2. I BELONG TO YOU
   (Love Unlimited)
3. LADY MARMALADE
   (Labelle)
4. HAPPY PEOPLE
   (Temptations)
5. SUPERNATURAL THING, PART 1
   (Ben E. King)
6. RHYME TYME PEOPLE
   (Kool and the Gang)
7. DON'T CHA LOVE IT
   (The Miracles)
8. SUPER DUPER LOVE, PART 1
   (Sugar Billy)
9. I GET LIFTED
   (George McCrae)
10. SHAME, SHAME, SHAME
    (Shirley and Company)

BLACK ALBUMS

1. AVERAGE WHITE BAND
   (Average White Band)
2. FIRE
   (Ohio Players)
3. NIGHTBIRDS
   (Labelle)
4. SUN GODDESS
   (Ramsey Lewis)

5. URBAN RENEWAL
   (Tower of Power)
6. NEW AND IMPROVED
   (Spinners)
7. DO IT 'TIL YOU'RE SATISFIED
   (B.T. Express)
8. RUFUSIZED
   (Rufus featuring Chaka Khan)
9. A SONG FOR YOU
   (Temptations)
10. PERFECT ANGEL
    (Minnie Riperton)

JAZZ ALBUMS

1. SUN GODDESS
   (Ramsey Lewis)
2. FLYING START
   (Blackbyrds)
3. SATIN DOLL
   (Bobbi Humphrey)
4. BAD BENSON
   (George Benson)
5. FEEL
   (George Duke)
6. FIRST MINUTE OF A NEW DAY
   (Gil Scott-Heron and Brian Jackson)
7. STANLEY CLARKE
   (Stanley Clarke)
8. SOUTHERN COMFORT
   (Crusaders)
9. URBAN RENEWAL
   (Tower of Power)
10. IN CONCERT, VOL. 2
    (Various Artists)

COUNTRY SINGLES

1. DEVIL IN THE BOTTLE
   (T.G. Sheppard)
2. THE TIES THAT BIND
   (Don Williams)
3. LINDA ON MY MIND
   (Conway Twitty)
4. RAINY DAY WOMAN
   (Waylon Jennings)
5. BEFORE THE NEXT TEARDROP FALLS
   (Freddy Fender)
6. I CARE/SNEAKY SNAKE
   (Tom T. Hall)
7. I CAN'T HELP IT
   (Linda Ronstadt)
8. WRONG ROAD AGAIN
   (Crystal Gayle)
9. IT'S TIME TO PAY THE FIDDLER
   (Cal Smith)
10. WOLF CREEK PASS
    (C.W. McCall)

COUNTRY ALBUMS

1. SONGS OF FOX HOLLOW
   (Tom T. Hall)
2. HEART LIKE A WHEEL
   (Linda Ronstadt)
3. LINDA ON MY MIND
   (Conway Twitty)
4. LIKE OLD TIMES AGAIN
   (Ray Price)
5. CITY LIGHTS
   (Mickey Gilley)
6. THE SILVER FOX
   (Charlie Rich)
7. BACK HOME AGAIN
   (John Denver)
8. HIGHLY PRIZED POSSESSION
   (Anne Murray)
9. PROMISED LAND
   (Elvis Presley)
10. A LEGEND IN MY TIME
    (Ronnie Milsap)

MARCH 8, 1975

POP SINGLES

1. BLACK WATER
   (The Doobie Brothers)
2. HAVE YOU NEVER BEEN MELLOW
   (Olivia Newton-John)
3. MY EYES ADORED YOU
   (Frankie Valli)
4. PICK UP THE PIECES
   (Average White Band)
5. LADY MARMALADE
   (Labelle)
6. BEST OF MY LOVE
   (The Eagles)
7. LADY
   (Styx)
8. LOVIN' YOU
   (Minnie Riperton)
9. YOU'RE NO GOOD
   (Linda Ronstadt)
10. POETRY MAN
    (Phoebe Snow)

POP ALBUMS

1. BLOOD ON THE TRACKS
   (Bob Dylan)
2. AVERAGE WHITE BAND
   (Average White Band)
3. GREATEST HITS
   (Elton John)
4. FIRE
   (Ohio Players)
5. HEART LIKE A WHEEL
   (Linda Ronstadt)
6. WHAT WERE ONCE VICES ARE NOW
   HABITS
   (The Doobie Brothers)
7. EMPTY SKY
   (Elton John)
8. HAVE YOU NEVER BEEN MELLOW
   (Olivia Newton-John)
9. RUFUSIZED
   (Rufus)
10. NOT FRAGILE
    (Bachman-Turner Overdrive)

BLACK SINGLES

1. LADY MARMALADE
   (Labelle)
2. PICK UP THE PIECES
   (Average White Band)
3. SUPERNATURAL THING, PART 1
   (Ben E. King)
4. I BELONG TO YOU
   (Love Unlimited)
5. SHAME, SHAME, SHAME
   (Shirley and Company)
6. SUPER DUPER LOVE, PART 1
   (Sugar Billy)
7. HAPPY PEOPLE
   (Temptations)
8. I AM LOVE
   (The Jackson 5)
9. EXPRESS
   (B.T. Express)
10. LOVIN' YOU
    (Minnie Riperton)

BLACK ALBUMS

1. AVERAGE WHITE BAND
   (Average White Band)
2. NIGHTBIRDS
   (Labelle)
3. SUN GODDESS
   (Ramsey Lewis)
4. FIRE
   (Ohio Players)

5. URBAN RENEWAL
   (Tower of Power)
6. DO IT 'TIL YOU'RE SATISFIED
   (B.T. Express)
7. A SONG FOR YOU
   (Temptations)
8. PERFECT ANGEL
   (Minnie Riperton)
9. FLYING START
   (Blackbyrds)
10. NEW AND IMPROVED
    (Spinners)

JAZZ ALBUMS

1. SUN GODDESS
   (Ramsey Lewis)
2. FLYING START
   (Blackbyrds)
3. BAD BENSON
   (George Benson)
4. FEEL
   (George Duke)
5. FIRST MINUTE OF A NEW DAY
   (Gil Scott-Heron and Brian Jackson)
6. STANLEY CLARKE
   (Stanley Clarke)
7. SATIN DOLL
   (Bobbi Humphrey)
8. SOUTHERN COMFORT
   (Crusaders)
9. IN CONCERT, VOL. 2
   (Various Artists)
10. URBAN RENEWAL
    (Tower of Power)

COUNTRY SINGLES

1. LINDA ON MY MIND
   (Conway Twitty)
2. BEFORE THE NEXT TEARDROP FALLS
   (Freddy Fender)
3. RAINY DAY WOMAN
   (Waylon Jennings)
4. DEVIL IN THE BOTTLE
   (T.G. Sheppard)
5. THE TIES THAT BIND
   (Don Williams)
6. I CAN'T HELP IT
   (Linda Ronstadt)
7. THE BARGAIN STORE
   (Dolly Parton)
8. SWEET SURRENDER
   (John Denver)
9. LOVIN' YOU WILL NEVER GROW OLD
   (Lois Johnson)
10. I'M A BELIEVER
    (Tommy Overstreet)

COUNTRY ALBUMS

1. LINDA ON MY MIND
   (Conway Twitty)
2. HEART LIKE A WHEEL
   (Linda Ronstadt)
3. PROMISED LAND
   (Elvis Presley)
4. SONGS OF FOX HOLLOW
   (Tom T. Hall)
5. A LEGEND IN MY TIME
   (Ronnie Milsap)
6. LIKE OLD TIMES AGAIN
   (Ray Price)
7. THE SILVER FOX
   (Charlie Rich)
8. BACK HOME AGAIN
   (John Denver)
9. IT'S TIME TO PAY THE FIDDLER
   (Cal Smith)
10. CITY LIGHTS
    (Mickey Gilley)

MARCH 15, 1975

POP SINGLES

1. HAVE YOU NEVER BEEN MELLOW
   (Olivia Newton-John)
2. MY EYES ADORED YOU
   (Frankie Valli)
3. BLACK WATER
   (The Doobie Brothers)
4. LADY MARMALADE
   (Labelle)
5. LOVIN' YOU
   (Minnie Riperton)
6. PICK UP THE PIECES
   (Average White Band)
7. LADY
   (Styx)
8. POETRY MAN
   (Phoebe Snow)
9. NO NO SONG
   (Ringo Starr)
10. EXPRESS
    (B.T. Express)

POP ALBUMS

1. HAVE YOU NEVER BEEN MELLOW
   (Olivia Newton-John)
2. BLOOD ON THE TRACKS
   (Bob Dylan)
3. AVERAGE WHITE BAND
   (Average White Band)
4. GREATEST HITS
   (Elton John)
5. PHYSICAL GRAFFITI
   (Led Zeppelin)
6. WHAT WERE ONCE VICES ARE NOW
   HABITS
   (The Doobie Brothers)
7. FIRE
   (Ohio Players)
8. EMPTY SKY
   (Elton John)
9. HEART LIKE A WHEEL
   (Linda Ronstadt)
10. NIGHTBIRDS
    (Labelle)

BLACK SINGLES

1. SUPERNATURAL THING, PART 1
   (Ben E. King)
2. SHAME, SHAME, SHAME
   (Shirley and Company)
3. LADY MARMALADE
   (Labelle)
4. EXPRESS
   (B.T. Express)
5. SUPER DUPER LOVE, PART 1
   (Sugar Billy)
6. I AM LOVE
   (The Jackson 5)
7. LOVIN' YOU
   (Minnie Riperton)
8. SHINING STAR
   (Earth, Wind and Fire)
9. PICK UP THE PIECES
   (Average White Band)
10. HAPPY PEOPLE
    (Temptations)

BLACK ALBUMS

1. AVERAGE WHITE BAND
   (Average White Band)
2. NIGHTBIRDS
   (Labelle)
3. SUN GODDESS
   (Ramsey Lewis)
4. FIRE
   (Ohio Players)

MARCH 22, 1975

5. DO IT 'TIL YOU'RE SATISFIED
   (B.T. Express)
6. A SONG FOR YOU
   (Temptations)
7. PERFECT ANGEL
   (Minnie Riperton)
8. NEVER CAN SAY GOODBYE
   (Gloria Gaynor)
9. FLYING START
   (Blackbyrds)
10. URBAN RENEWAL
    (Tower of Power)

JAZZ ALBUMS

1. SUN GODDESS
   (Ramsey Lewis)
2. FLYING START
   (Blackbyrds)
3. BAD BENSON
   (George Benson)
4. FEEL
   (George Duke)
5. FIRST MINUTE OF A NEW DAY
   (Gil Scott-Heron and Brian Jackson)
6. SATIN DOLL
   (Bobbi Humphrey)
7. STANLEY CLARKE
   (Stanley Clarke)
8. IN CONCERT, VOL. 2
   (Various Artists)
9. URBAN RENEWAL
   (Tower of Power)
10. SOUTHERN COMFORT
    (Crusaders)

COUNTRY SINGLES

1. BEFORE THE NEXT TEARDROP FALLS
   (Freddy Fender)
2. LINDA ON MY MIND
   (Conway Twitty)
3. THE BARGAIN STORE
   (Dolly Parton)
4. I CAN'T HELP IT
   (Linda Ronstadt)
5. RAINY DAY WOMAN
   (Waylon Jennings)
6. LOVIN' YOU WILL NEVER GROW OLD
   (Lois Johnson)
7. MY ELUSIVE DREAMS
   (Charlie Rich)
8. SWEET SURRENDER
   (John Denver)
9. HAVE YOU NEVER BEEN MELLOW
   (Olivia Newton-John)
10. PENNY
    (Joe Stampley)

COUNTRY ALBUMS

1. LINDA ON MY MIND
   (Conway Twitty)
2. PROMISED LAND
   (Elvis Presley)
3. A LEGEND IN MY TIME
   (Ronnie Milsap)
4. HEART LIKE A WHEEL
   (Linda Ronstadt)
5. SONGS OF FOX HOLLOW
   (Tom T. Hall)
6. LIKE OLD TIMES AGAIN
   (Ray Price)
7. IT'S TIME TO PAY THE FIDDLER
   (Cal Smith)
8. ALL THE LOVE IN THE WORLD
   (Mac Davis)
9. BACK HOME AGAIN
   (John Denver)
10. THE SILVER FOX
    (Charlie Rich)

POP SINGLES

1. MY EYES ADORED YOU
   (Frankie Valli)
2. HAVE YOU NEVER BEEN MELLOW
   (Olivia Newton-John)
3. LADY MARMALADE
   (Labelle)
4. LOVIN' YOU
   (Minnie Riperton)
5. BLACK WATER
   (The Doobie Brothers)
6. NO NO SONG
   (Ringo Starr)
7. POETRY MAN
   (Phoebe Snow)
8. EXPRESS
   (B.T. Express)
9. YOU ARE SO BEAUTIFUL
   (Joe Cocker)
10. DON'T CALL US, WE'LL CALL YOU
    (Sugarloaf/Jerry Corbetta)

POP ALBUMS

1. PHYSICAL GRAFFITI
   (Led Zeppelin)
2. HAVE YOU NEVER BEEN MELLOW
   (Olivia Newton-John)
3. BLOOD ON THE TRACKS
   (Bob Dylan)
4. AVERAGE WHITE BAND
   (Average White Band)
5. GREATEST HITS
   (Elton John)
6. WHAT WERE ONCE VICES ARE NOW HABITS
   (The Doobie Brothers)
7. FIRE
   (Ohio Players)
8. AN EVENING WITH JOHN DENVER
   (John Denver)
9. NIGHTBIRDS
   (Labelle)
10. PHOEBE SNOW
    (Phoebe Snow)

BLACK SINGLES

1. SHAME, SHAME, SHAME
   (Shirley and Company)
2. EXPRESS
   (B.T. Express)
3. SUPERNATURAL THING, PART 1
   (Ben E. King)
4. LOVIN' YOU
   (Minnie Riperton)
5. SHINING STAR
   (Earth, Wind and Fire)
6. I AM LOVE
   (The Jackson 5)
7. SHOESHINE BOY
   (Eddie Kendricks)
8. SUPER DUPER LOVE, PART 1
   (Sugar Billy)
9. LADY MARMALADE
   (Labelle)
10. SATIN SOUL
    (Love Unlimited Orchestra)

BLACK ALBUMS

1. AVERAGE WHITE BAND
   (Average White Band)
2. NIGHTBIRDS
   (Labelle)
3. SUN GODDESS
   (Ramsey Lewis)

4. DO IT 'TIL YOU'RE SATISFIED
   (B.T. Express)
5. A SONG FOR YOU
   (Temptations)
6. PERFECT ANGEL
   (Minnie Riperton)
7. FIRE
   (Ohio Players)
8. NEVER CAN SAY GOODBYE
   (Gloria Gaynor)
9. FLYING START
   (Blackbyrds)
10. URBAN RENEWAL
    (Tower of Power)

JAZZ ALBUMS

1. SUN GODDESS
   (Ramsey Lewis)
2. FLYING START
   (Blackbyrds)
3. BAD BENSON
   (George Benson)
4. FEEL
   (George Duke)
5. STANLEY CLARKE
   (Stanley Clarke)
6. FIRST MINUTE OF A NEW DAY
   (Gil Scott-Heron and Brian Jackson)
7. SATIN DOLL
   (Bobbi Humphrey)
8. URBAN RENEWAL
   (Tower of Power)
9. IN CONCERT, VOL. 2
   (Various Artists)
10. MISTER MAGIC
    (Grover Washington Jr.)

COUNTRY SINGLES

1. THE BARGAIN STORE
   (Dolly Parton)
2. BEFORE THE NEXT TEARDROP FALLS
   (Freddy Fender)
3. LINDA ON MY MIND
   (Conway Twitty)
4. MY ELUSIVE DREAMS
   (Charlie Rich)
5. LOVIN' YOU WILL NEVER GROW OLD
   (Lois Johnson)
6. A LITTLE BIT SOUTH OF SASKATOON
   (Sonny James)
7. HAVE YOU NEVER BEEN MELLOW
   (Olivia Newton-John)
8. I JUST CAN'T GET HER OUT OF MY MIND
   (Johnny Rodriguez)
9. PENNY
   (Joe Stampley)
10. WRITE ME A LETTER
    (Bobby G. Rice)

COUNTRY ALBUMS

1. LINDA ON MY MIND
   (Conway Twitty)
2. PROMISED LAND
   (Elvis Presley)
3. A LEGEND IN MY TIME
   (Ronnie Milsap)
4. HAVE YOU NEVER BEEN MELLOW
   (Olivia Newton-John)
5. IT'S TIME TO PAY THE FIDDLER
   (Cal Smith)
6. ALL THE LOVE IN THE WORLD
   (Mac Davis)
7. BACK IN THE COUNTRY
   (Loretta Lynn)
8. SONGS OF FOX HOLLOW
   (Tom T. Hall)
9. HEART LIKE A WHEEL
   (Linda Ronstadt)
10. LIKE OLD TIMES
    (Ray Price)

MARCH 29, 1975

POP SINGLES

1. LADY MARMALADE
   (Labelle)
2. LOVIN' YOU
   (Minnie Riperton)
3. MY EYES ADORED YOU
   (Frankie Valli)
4. NO NO SONG
   (Ringo Starr)
5. HAVE YOU NEVER BEEN MELLOW
   (Olivia Newton-John)
6. POETRY MAN
   (Phoebe Snow)
7. PHILADELPHIA FREEDOM
   (Elton John Band)
8. EXPRESS
   (B.T. Express)
9. YOU ARE SO BEAUTIFUL
   (Joe Cocker)
10. SUPERNATURAL THING, PART 1
    (Ben E. King)

POP ALBUMS

1. PHYSICAL GRAFFITI
   (Led Zeppelin)
2. HAVE YOU NEVER BEEN MELLOW
   (Olivia Newton-John)
3. AN EVENING WITH JOHN DENVER
   (John Denver)
4. BLOOD ON THE TRACKS
   (Bob Dylan)
5. AVERAGE WHITE BAND
   (Average White Band)
6. WHAT WERE ONCE VICES ARE NOW
   HABITS
   (The Doobie Brothers)
7. GREATEST HITS
   (Elton John)
8. ROCK 'N' ROLL
   (John Lennon)
9. FOR EARTH BELOW
   (Robin Trower)
10. NIGHTBIRDS
    (Labelle)

BLACK SINGLES

1. EXPRESS
   (B.T. Express)
2. LOVIN' YOU
   (Minnie Riperton)
3. SHINING STAR
   (Earth, Wind and Fire)
4. SHAME, SHAME, SHAME
   (Shirley and Company)
5. SHOESHINE BOY
   (Eddie Kendricks)
6. SUPERNATURAL THING, PART 1
   (Ben E. King)
7. I AM LOVE
   (The Jackson 5)
8. SATIN SOUL
   (Love Unlimited Orchestra)
9. SUPER DUPER LOVE, PART 1
   (Sugar Billy)
10. LOVE FINDS ITS OWN WAY
    (Gladys Knight and the Pips)

BLACK ALBUMS

1. NIGHTBIRDS
   (Labelle)
2. AVERAGE WHITE BAND
   (Average White Band)
3. SUN GODDESS
   (Ramsey Lewis)

---

4. DO IT 'TIL YOU'RE SATISFIED
   (B.T. Express)
5. PERFECT ANGEL
   (Minnie Riperton)
6. FIRE
   (Ohio Players)
7. THAT'S THE WAY OF THE WORLD
   (Earth, Wind and Fire)
8. A SONG FOR YOU
   (Temptations)
9. FLYING START
   (Blackbyrds)
10. NEVER CAN SAY GOODBYE
    (Gloria Gaynor)

JAZZ ALBUMS

1. SUN GODDESS
   (Ramsey Lewis)
2. FLYING START
   (Blackbyrds)
3. FEEL
   (George Duke)
4. BAD BENSON
   (George Benson)
5. MISTER MAGIC
   (Grover Washington Jr.)
6. FIRST MINUTE OF A NEW DAY
   (Gil Scott-Heron and Brian Jackson)
7. URBAN RENEWAL
   (Tower of Power)
8. STANLEY CLARKE
   (Stanley Clarke)
9. HOT CITY
   (Gene Page)
10. NO MYSTERY
    (Return to Forever featuring Chick Corea)

COUNTRY SINGLES

1. MY ELUSIVE DREAMS
   (Charlie Rich)
2. BEFORE THE NEXT TEARDROP FALLS
   (Freddy Fender)
3. THE BARGAIN STORE
   (Dolly Parton)
4. A LITTLE BIT SOUTH OF SASKATOON
   (Sonny James)
5. I JUST CAN'T GET HER OUT OF MY MIND
   (Johnny Rodriguez)
6. HAVE YOU NEVER BEEN MELLOW
   (Olivia Newton-John)
7. ALWAYS WANTING YOU
   (Merle Haggard)
8. ROSES AND LOVE SONGS
   (Ray Price)
9. THE PILL
   (Loretta Lynn)
10. LINDA ON MY MIND
    (Conway Twitty)

COUNTRY ALBUMS

1. HAVE YOU NEVER BEEN MELLOW
   (Olivia Newton-John)
2. LINDA ON MY MIND
   (Conway Twitty)
3. A LEGEND IN MY TIME
   (Ronnie Milsap)
4. BACK IN THE COUNTRY
   (Loretta Lynn)
5. IT'S TIME TO PAY THE FIDDLER
   (Cal Smith)
6. ALL THE LOVE IN THE WORLD
   (Mac Davis)
7. PROMISED LAND
   (Elvis Presley)
8. AN EVENING WITH JOHN DENVER
   (John Denver)
9. HEART LIKE A WHEEL
   (Linda Ronstadt)
10. SONGS OF FOX HOLLOW
    (Tom T. Hall)

APRIL 5, 1975

POP SINGLES

1. LOVIN' YOU
   (Minnie Riperton)
2. LADY MARMALADE
   (Labelle)
3. NO NO SONG
   (Ringo Starr)
4. PHILADELPHIA FREEDOM
   (Elton John Band)
5. POETRY MAN
   (Phoebe Snow)
6. MY EYES ADORED YOU
   (Frankie Valli)
7. HAVE YOU NEVER BEEN MELLOW
   (Olivia Newton-John)
8. SUPERNATURAL THING, PART 1
   (Ben E. King)
9. EMMA
   (Hot Chocolate)
10. (HEY WON'T YOU PLAY) ANOTHER
    SOMEBODY DONE SOMEBODY WRONG
    SONG
    (B.J. Thomas)

POP ALBUMS

1. PHYSICAL GRAFFITI
   (Led Zeppelin)
2. AN EVENING WITH JOHN DENVER
   (John Denver)
3. HAVE YOU NEVER BEEN MELLOW
   (Olivia Newton-John)
4. ROCK 'N' ROLL
   (John Lennon)
5. BLOOD ON THE TRACKS
   (Bob Dylan)
6. FOR EARTH BELOW
   (Robin Trower)
7. YOUNG AMERICANS
   (David Bowie)
8. AVERAGE WHITE BAND
   (Average White Band)
9. WHAT WERE ONCE VICES ARE NOW
   HABITS
   (The Doobie Brothers)
10. PERFECT ANGEL
    (Minnie Riperton)

BLACK SINGLES

1. LOVIN' YOU
   (Minnie Riperton)
2. SHINING STAR
   (Earth, Wind and Fire)
3. SHOESHINE BOY
   (Eddie Kendricks)
4. EXPRESS
   (B.T. Express)
5. LOVE FINDS ITS OWN WAY
   (Gladys Knight and the Pips)
6. L-O-V-E (LOVE)
   (Al Green)
7. ONCE YOU GET STARTED
   (Rufus)
8. SATIN SOUL
   (Love Unlimited Orchestra)
9. WALKING IN RHYTHM
   (Blackbyrds)
10. SHAME, SHAME, SHAME
    (Shirley and Company)

BLACK ALBUMS

1. NIGHTBIRDS
   (Labelle)
2. SUN GODDESS
   (Ramsey Lewis)

3. PERFECT ANGEL
   (Minnie Riperton)
4. DO IT 'TIL YOU'RE SATISFIED
   (B.T. Express)
5. AVERAGE WHITE BAND
   (Average White Band)
6. THAT'S THE WAY OF THE WORLD
   (Earth, Wind and Fire)
7. FIRE
   (Ohio Players)
8. A SONG FOR YOU
   (Temptations)
9. FLYING START
   (Blackbyrds)
10. THE DRAMATIC JACKPOT
    (Ron Banks and the Dramatics)

JAZZ ALBUMS

1. SUN GODDESS
   (Ramsey Lewis)
2. FLYING START
   (Blackbyrds)
3. MISTER MAGIC
   (Grover Washington Jr.)
4. NO MYSTERY
   (Return to Forever featuring Chick Corea)
5. FIRST MINUTE OF A NEW DAY
   (Gil Scott-Heron and Brian Jackson)
6. BAD BENSON
   (George Benson)
7. STEPPING INTO TOMORROW
   (Donald Byrd)
8. FEEL
   (George Duke)
9. VISIONS OF THE EMERALD BEYOND
   (Mahavishnu Orchestra)
10. STANLEY CLARKE
    (Stanley Clarke)

COUNTRY SINGLES

1. I JUST CAN'T GET HER OUT OF MY MIND
   (Johnny Rodriguez)
2. ALWAYS WANTING YOU
   (Merle Haggard)
3. MY ELUSIVE DREAMS
   (Charlie Rich)
4. A LITTLE BIT SOUTH OF SASKATOON
   (Sonny James)
5. HAVE YOU NEVER BEEN MELLOW
   (Olivia Newton-John)
6. ROSES AND LOVE SONGS
   (Ray Price)
7. THE PILL
   (Loretta Lynn)
8. BLANKET ON THE GROUND
   (Billie Jo Spears)
9. BEFORE THE NEXT TEARDROP FALLS
   (Freddy Fender)
10. STILL THINKING ABOUT YOU
    (Billy "Crash" Craddock)

COUNTRY ALBUMS

1. HAVE YOU NEVER BEEN MELLOW
   (Olivia Newton-John)
2. BACK IN THE COUNTRY
   (Loretta Lynn)
3. LINDA ON MY MIND
   (Conway Twitty)
4. A LEGEND IN MY TIME
   (Ronnie Milsap)
5. AN EVENING WITH JOHN DENVER
   (John Denver)
6. IT'S TIME TO PAY THE FIDDLER
   (Cal Smith)
7. PROMISED LAND
   (Elvis Presley)
8. ALL THE LOVE IN THE WORLD
   (Mac Davis)
9. SONGS OF FOX HOLLOW
   (Tom T. Hall)
10. HEART LIKE A WHEEL
    (Linda Ronstadt)

APRIL 12, 1975

POP SINGLES

1. PHILADELPHIA FREEDOM
   (Elton John Band)
2. LOVIN' YOU
   (Minnie Riperton)
3. LADY MARMALADE
   (Labelle)
4. NO NO SONG
   (Ringo Starr)
5. POETRY MAN
   (Phoebe Snow)
6. SUPERNATURAL THING, PART 1
   (Ben E. King)
7. EMMA
   (Hot Chocolate)
8. (HEY WON'T YOU PLAY) ANOTHER
   SOMEBODY DONE SOMEBODY WRONG
   SONG
   (B.J. Thomas)
9. CHEVY VAN
   (Sammy Johns)
10. MY EYES ADORED YOU
    (Frankie Valli)

POP ALBUMS

1. PHYSICAL GRAFFITI
   (Led Zeppelin)
2. AN EVENING WITH JOHN DENVER
   (John Denver)
3. HAVE YOU NEVER BEEN MELLOW
   (Olivia Newton-John)
4. ROCK 'N' ROLL
   (John Lennon)
5. FOR EARTH BELOW
   (Robin Trower)
6. YOUNG AMERICANS
   (David Bowie)
7. BLOOD ON THE TRACKS
   (Bob Dylan)
8. AVERAGE WHITE BAND
   (Average White Band)
9. PERFECT ANGEL
   (Minnie Riperton)
10. A SONG FOR YOU
    (Temptations)

BLACK SINGLES

1. SHINING STAR
   (Earth, Wind and Fire)
2. SHOESHINE BOY
   (Eddie Kendricks)
3. L-O-V-E (LOVE)
   (Al Green)
4. ONCE YOU GET STARTED
   (Rufus)
5. LOVE FINDS ITS OWN WAY
   (Gladys Knight and the Pips)
6. LOVIN' YOU
   (Minnie Riperton)
7. WALKING IN RHYTHM
   (Blackbyrds)
8. WHAT AM I GONNA DO WITH YOU
   (Barry White)
9. EXPRESS
   (B.T. Express)
10. ONE BEAUTIFUL DAY
    (Ecstasy, Passion and Pain)

BLACK ALBUMS

1. SUN GODDESS
   (Ramsey Lewis)
2. NIGHTBIRDS
   (Labelle)
3. PERFECT ANGEL
   (Minnie Riperton)

4. THAT'S THE WAY OF THE WORLD
   (Earth, Wind and Fire)
5. DO IT 'TIL YOU'RE SATISFIED
   (B.T. Express)
6. AVERAGE WHITE BAND
   (Average White Band)
7. A SONG FOR YOU
   (Temptations)
8. THE DRAMATIC JACKPOT
   (Ron Banks and the Dramatics)
9. MISTER MAGIC
   (Grover Washington Jr.)
10. GREATEST HITS
    (Kool and the Gang)

JAZZ ALBUMS

1. SUN GODDESS
   (Ramsey Lewis)
2. FLYING START
   (Blackbyrds)
3. MISTER MAGIC
   (Grover Washington Jr.)
4. STEPPING INTO TOMORROW
   (Donald Byrd)
5. NO MYSTERY
   (Return to Forever featuring Chick Corea)
6. FIRST MINUTE OF A NEW DAY
   (Gil Scott-Heron and Brian Jackson)
7. BAD BENSON
   (George Benson)
8. FEEL
   (George Duke)
9. VISIONS OF THE EMERALD BEYOND
   (Mahavishnu Orchestra)
10. STANLEY CLARKE
    (Stanley Clarke)

COUNTRY SINGLES

1. ALWAYS WANTING YOU
   (Merle Haggard)
2. I JUST CAN'T GET HER OUT OF MY MIND
   (Johnny Rodriguez)
3. BLANKET ON THE GROUND
   (Billie Jo Spears)
4. STILL THINKING ABOUT YOU
   (Billy "Crash" Craddock)
5. HAVE YOU NEVER BEEN MELLOW
   (Olivia Newton-John)
6. ROSES AND LOVE SONGS
   (Ray Price)
7. THE PILL
   (Loretta Lynn)
8. BEST WAY I KNOW HOW
   (Mel Tillis)
9. IT DO FEEL GOOD
   (Donna Fargo)
10. (HEY WON'T YOU PLAY) ANOTHER
    SOMEBODY DONE SOMEBODY WRONG
    SONG
    (B.J. Thomas)

COUNTRY ALBUMS

1. BACK IN THE COUNTRY
   (Loretta Lynn)
2. AN EVENING WITH JOHN DENVER
   (John Denver)
3. HAVE YOU NEVER BEEN MELLOW
   (Olivia Newton-John)
4. A LEGEND IN MY TIME
   (Ronnie Milsap)
5. LINDA ON MY MIND
   (Conway Twitty)
6. PROMISED LAND
   (Elvis Presley)
7. OUT OF HAND
   (Gary Stewart)
8. A PAIR OF FIVES (BANJOS THAT IT)
   (Roy Clark and Buck Trent)
9. SONGS OF FOX HOLLOW
   (Tom T. Hall)
10. BARROOMS AND BEDROOMS
    (David Wills)

APRIL 19, 1975

POP SINGLES

1. PHILADELPHIA FREEDOM
   (Elton John Band)
2. LOVIN' YOU
   (Minnie Riperton)
3. (HEY WON'T YOU PLAY) ANOTHER SOMEBODY DONE SOMEBODY WRONG SONG
   (B.J. Thomas)
4. EMMA
   (Hot Chocolate)
5. SUPERNATURAL THING, PART 1
   (Ben E. King)
6. LADY MARMALADE
   (Labelle)
7. CHEVY VAN
   (Sammy Johns)
8. LONG TALL GLASSES (I CAN DANCE)
   (Leo Sayer)
9. SHINING STAR
   (Earth, Wind and Fire)
10. ONCE YOU GET STARTED
    (Rufus featuring Chaka Khan)

POP ALBUMS

1. HAVE YOU NEVER BEEN MELLOW
   (Olivia Newton-John)
2. PHYSICAL GRAFFITI
   (Led Zeppelin)
3. AN EVENING WITH JOHN DENVER
   (John Denver)
4. YOUNG AMERICANS
   (David Bowie)
5. FOR EARTH BELOW
   (Robin Trower)
6. ROCK 'N' ROLL
   (John Lennon)
7. CHICAGO VIII
   (Chicago)
8. A SONG FOR YOU
   (Temptations)
9. THAT'S THE WAY OF THE WORLD
   (Earth, Wind and Fire)
10. AUTOBAHN
    (Kraftwerk)

BLACK SINGLES

1. SHOESHINE BOY
   (Eddie Kendricks)
2. L-O-V-E (LOVE)
   (Al Green)
3. ONCE YOU GET STARTED
   (Rufus featuring Chaka Khan)
4. SHINING STAR
   (Earth, Wind and Fire)
5. WHAT AM I GONNA DO WITH YOU
   (Barry White)
6. SHAKY GROUND
   (Temptations)
7. WALKING IN RHYTHM
   (Blackbyrds)
8. ONE BEAUTIFUL DAY
   (Ecstasy, Passion and Pain)
9. LIVING A LITTLE, LAUGHING A LITTLE
   (Spinners)
10. MY LITTLE LADY
    (Bloodstone)

BLACK ALBUMS

1. THAT'S THE WAY OF THE WORLD
   (Earth, Wind and Fire)
2. PERFECT ANGEL
   (Minnie Riperton)
3. SUN GODDESS
   (Ramsey Lewis)

---

4. A SONG FOR YOU
   (Temptations)
5. FEEL LIKE MAKIN' LOVE
   (Roberta Flack)
6. NIGHTBIRDS
   (Labelle)
7. THE DRAMATIC JACKPOT
   (Ron Banks and the Dramatics)
8. MISTER MAGIC
   (Grover Washington Jr.)
9. GREATEST HITS
   (Kool and the Gang)
10. DO IT 'TIL YOU'RE SATISFIED
    (B.T. Express)

JAZZ ALBUMS

1. FLYING START
   (Blackbyrds)
2. STEPPING INTO TOMORROW
   (Donald Byrd)
3. MISTER MAGIC
   (Grover Washington Jr.)
4. SUN GODDESS
   (Ramsey Lewis)
5. NO MYSTERY
   (Return to Forever featuring Chick Corea)
6. VISIONS OF THE EMERALD BEYOND
   (Mahavishnu Orchestra)
7. FIRST MINUTE OF A NEW DAY
   (Gil Scott-Heron and Brian Jackson)
8. BAD BENSON
   (George Benson)
9. FEEL
   (George Duke)
10. SUGARMAN
    (Stanley Turrentine)

COUNTRY SINGLES

1. BLANKET ON THE GROUND
   (Billie Jo Spears)
2. ALWAYS WANTING YOU
   (Merle Haggard)
3. STILL THINKING ABOUT YOU
   (Billy "Crash" Craddock)
4. (HEY WON'T YOU PLAY) ANOTHER SOMEBODY DONE SOMEBODY WRONG SONG
   (B.J. Thomas)
5. I'M NOT LISA
   (Jessi Colter)
6. ROLL ON BIG MAMA
   (Joe Stampley)
7. HAVE YOU NEVER BEEN MELLOW
   (Olivia Newton-John)
8. BEST WAY I KNOW HOW
   (Mel Tillis)
9. IT DO FEEL GOOD
   (Donna Fargo)
10. SHE'S ACTIN' SINGLE (I'M DRINKIN' DOUBLES)
    (Gary Stewart)

COUNTRY ALBUMS

1. AN EVENING WITH JOHN DENVER
   (John Denver)
2. BACK IN THE COUNTRY
   (Loretta Lynn)
3. HAVE YOU NEVER BEEN MELLOW
   (Olivia Newton-John)
4. OUT OF HAND
   (Gary Stewart)
5. A LEGEND IN MY TIME
   (Ronnie Milsap)
6. A PAIR OF FIVES (BANJOS THAT IS)
   (Roy Clark and Buck Trent)
7. LINDA ON MY MIND
   (Conway Twitty)
8. BARGAIN STORE
   (Dolly Parton)
9. BARROOMS AND BEDROOMS
   (David Wills)

---

10. I'M JESSI COLTER
    (Jessi Colter)

APRIL 26, 1975

POP SINGLES

1. PHILADELPHIA FREEDOM
   (Elton John Band)
2. (HEY WON'T YOU PLAY) ANOTHER SOMEBODY DONE SOMEBODY WRONG SONG
   (B.J. Thomas)
3. LOVIN' YOU
   (Minnie Riperton)
4. EMMA
   (Hot Chocolate)
5. SHINING STAR
   (Earth, Wind and Fire)
6. HE DON'T LOVE YOU (LIKE I LOVE YOU)
   (Tony Orlando and Dawn)
7. CHEVY VAN
   (Sammy Johns)
8. LONG TALL GLASSES (I CAN DANCE)
   (Leo Sayer)
9. SUPERNATURAL THING, PART 1
   (Ben E. King)
10. JACKIE BLUE
    (Ozark Mountain Daredevils)

POP ALBUMS

1. CHICAGO VIII
   (Chicago)
2. HAVE YOU NEVER BEEN MELLOW
   (Olivia Newton-John)
3. PHYSICAL GRAFFITI
   (Led Zeppelin)
4. YOUNG AMERICANS
   (David Bowie)
5. AN EVENING WITH JOHN DENVER
   (John Denver)
6. THAT'S THE WAY OF THE WORLD
   (Earth, Wind and Fire)
7. A SONG FOR YOU
   (Temptations)
8. BLUEJAYS
   (Justin Hayward and John Lodge)
9. FUNNY LADY
   (Original Soundtrack)
10. AUTOBAHN
    (Kraftwerk)

BLACK SINGLES

1. L-O-V-E (LOVE)
   (Al Green)
2. ONCE YOU GET STARTED
   (Rufus)
3. SHAKY GROUND
   (Temptations)
4. WHAT AM I GONNA DO WITH YOU
   (Barry White)
5. SHOESHINE BOY
   (Eddie Kendricks)
6. SHINING STAR
   (Earth, Wind and Fire)
7. BAD LUCK (PART 1)
   (Harold Melvin and the Blue Notes)
8. ONE BEAUTIFUL DAY
   (Ecstasy, Passion and Pain)
9. LIVING A LITTLE, LAUGHING A LITTLE
   (Spinners)
10. MY LITTLE LADY
    (Bloodstone)

BLACK ALBUMS

1. THAT'S THE WAY OF THE WORLD
   (Earth, Wind and Fire)

2. A SONG FOR YOU
   (Temptations)
3. PERFECT ANGEL
   (Minnie Riperton)
4. SUN GODDESS
   (Ramsey Lewis)
5. FEEL LIKE MAKIN' LOVE
   (Roberta Flack)
6. THE DRAMATIC JACKPOT
   (Ron Banks and the Dramatics)
7. MISTER MAGIC
   (Grover Washington Jr.)
8. JUST ANOTHER WAY TO SAY I LOVE YOU
   (Barry White)
9. GREATEST HITS
   (Kool and the Gang)
10. GREATEST HITS
    (Al Green)

JAZZ ALBUMS

1. STEPPING INTO TOMORROW
   (Donald Byrd)
2. MISTER MAGIC
   (Grover Washington Jr.)
3. SUN GODDESS
   (Ramsey Lewis)
4. NO MYSTERY
   (Return to Forever featuring Chick Corea)
5. FLYING START
   (Blackbyrds)
6. VISIONS OF THE EMERALD BEYOND
   (Mahavishnu Orchestra)
7. SUGARMAN
   (Stanley Turrentine)
8. EXPANSIONS
   (Lonnie Liston Smith)
9. FIRST MINUTE OF A NEW DAY
   (Gil Scott-Heron and Brian Jackson)
10. ALTERNATE TAKES
    (John Coltrane)

COUNTRY SINGLES

1. STILL THINKING ABOUT YOU
   (Billy "Crash" Craddock)
2. (HEY WON'T YOU PLAY) ANOTHER SOMEBODY DONE SOMEBODY WRONG SONG
   (B.J. Thomas)
3. ALWAYS WANTING YOU
   (Merle Haggard)
4. I'M NOT LISA
   (Jessi Colter)
5. ROLL ON BIG MAMA
   (Joe Stampley)
6. BLANKET ON THE GROUND
   (Billie Jo Spears)
7. SHE'S ACTIN' SINGLE (I'M DRINKIN' DOUBLES)
   (Gary Stewart)
8. (YOU MAKE ME WANT TO BE) A MOTHER
   (Tammy Wynette)
9. BEST WAY I KNOW HOW
   (Mel Tillis)
10. TOO LATE TO WORRY, TOO BLUE TO CRY
    (Ronnie Milsap)

COUNTRY ALBUMS

1. AN EVENING WITH JOHN DENVER
   (John Denver)
2. HAVE YOU NEVER BEEN MELLOW
   (Olivia Newton-John)
3. OUT OF HAND
   (Gary Stewart)
4. BACK IN THE COUNTRY
   (Loretta Lynn)
5. A PAIR OF FIVES (BANJOS THAT IS)
   (Roy Clark and Buck Trent)
6. I'M JESSI COLTER
   (Jessi Colter)
7. BARGAIN STORE
   (Dolly Parton)

8. BARROOMS AND BEDROOMS
   (David Wills)
9. LINDA ON MY MIND
   (Conway Twitty)
10. WOLF CREEK PASS
    (C.W. McCall)

MAY 3, 1975

POP SINGLES

1. (HEY WON'T YOU PLAY) ANOTHER SOMEBODY DONE SOMEBODY WRONG SONG
   (B.J. Thomas)
2. HE DON'T LOVE YOU (LIKE I LOVE YOU)
   (Tony Orlando and Dawn)
3. PHILADELPHIA FREEDOM
   (Elton John Band)
4. SHINING STAR
   (Earth, Wind and Fire)
5. LOVIN' YOU
   (Minnie Riperton)
6. JACKIE BLUE
   (Ozark Mountain Daredevils)
7. HOW LONG
   (Ace)
8. LONG TALL GLASSES (I CAN DANCE)
   (Leo Sayer)
9. ONLY YESTERDAY
   (The Carpenters)
10. IT'S A MIRACLE
    (Barry Manilow)

POP ALBUMS

1. CHICAGO VIII
   (Chicago)
2. THAT'S THE WAY OF THE WORLD
   (Earth, Wind and Fire)
3. HAVE YOU NEVER BEEN MELLOW
   (Olivia Newton-John)
4. PHYSICAL GRAFFITI
   (Led Zeppelin)
5. AN EVENING WITH JOHN DENVER
   (John Denver)
6. BLUEJAYS
   (Justin Hayward and John Lodge)
7. A SONG FOR YOU
   (Temptations)
8. FUNNY LADY
   (Original Soundtrack)
9. STRAIGHT SHOOTER
   (Bad Company)
10. TOMMY
    (Original Soundtrack)

BLACK SINGLES

1. SHAKY GROUND
   (Temptations)
2. ONCE YOU GET STARTED
   (Rufus)
3. L-O-V-E (LOVE)
   (Al Green)
4. WHAT AM I GONNA DO WITH YOU
   (Barry White)
5. BAD LUCK (PART 1)
   (Harold Melvin and the Blue Notes)
6. SHOESHINE BOY
   (Eddie Kendricks)
7. SHINING STAR
   (Earth, Wind and Fire)
8. GET DOWN, GET DOWN (GET ON THE FLOOR)
   (Joe Simon)
9. BABY THAT'S BACKATCHA
   (Smokey Robinson)
10. WE'RE ALMOST THERE
    (Michael Jackson)

BLACK ALBUMS

1. THAT'S THE WAY OF THE WORLD
   (Earth, Wind and Fire)
2. A SONG FOR YOU
   (Temptations)
3. THE DRAMATIC JACKPOT
   (Ron Banks and the Dramatics)
4. JUST ANOTHER WAY TO SAY I LOVE YOU
   (Barry White)
5. MISTER MAGIC
   (Grover Washington Jr.)
6. FEEL LIKE MAKIN' LOVE
   (Roberta Flack)
7. PERFECT ANGEL
   (Minnie Riperton)
8. SUN GODDESS
   (Ramsey Lewis)
9. GREATEST HITS
   (Kool and the Gang)
10. TO BE TRUE
    (Harold Melvin and the Blue Notes)

JAZZ ALBUMS

1. STEPPING INTO TOMORROW
   (Donald Byrd)
2. MISTER MAGIC
   (Grover Washington Jr.)
3. SUN GODDESS
   (Ramsey Lewis)
4. FLYING START
   (Blackbyrds)
5. EXPANSIONS
   (Lonnie Liston Smith)
6. SUGARMAN
   (Stanley Turrentine)
7. ASTRAL SIGN
   (Gene Harris)
8. CUTTING EDGE
   (Sonny Rollins)
9. ALTERNATE TAKES
   (John Coltrane)
10. VISIONS OF THE EMERALD BEYOND
    (Mahavishnu Orchestra)

COUNTRY SINGLES

1. (HEY WON'T YOU PLAY) ANOTHER SOMEBODY DONE SOMEBODY WRONG SONG
   (B.J. Thomas)
2. I'M NOT LISA
   (Jessi Colter)
3. SHE'S ACTIN' SINGLE (I'M DRINKIN' DOUBLES)
   (Gary Stewart)
4. ROLL ON BIG MAMA
   (Joe Stampley)
5. STILL THINKING ABOUT YOU
   (Billy "Crash" Craddock)
6. WINDOW UP ABOVE
   (Mickey Gilley)
7. TOO LATE TO WORRY, TOO BLUE TO CRY
   (Ronnie Milsap)
8. (YOU MAKE ME WANT TO BE) A MOTHER
   (Tammy Wynette)
9. I'D LIKE TO SLEEP 'TIL I GET OVER YOU
   (Freddie Hart)
10. THANK GOD, I'M A COUNTRY BOY
    (John Denver)

COUNTRY ALBUMS

1. AN EVENING WITH JOHN DENVER
   (John Denver)
2. OUT OF HAND
   (Gary Stewart)
3. HAVE YOU NEVER BEEN MELLOW
   (Olivia Newton-John)
4. I'M JESSI COLTER
   (Jessi Colter)

5. A PAIR OF FIVES (BANJOS THAT IS)
    (Roy Clark and Buck Trent)
6. BARGAIN STORE
    (Dolly Parton)
7. WOLF CREEK PASS
    (C.W. McCall)
8. BARROOMS AND BEDROOMS
    (David Wills)
9. BACK IN THE COUNTRY
    (Loretta Lynn)
10. SONGS OF FOX HOLLOW
    (Tom T. Hall)

MAY 10, 1975

POP SINGLES

1. HE DON'T LOVE YOU (LIKE I LOVE YOU)
    (Tony Orlando and Dawn)
2. (HEY WON'T YOU PLAY) ANOTHER SOMEBODY DONE SOMEBODY WRONG SONG
    (B.J. Thomas)
3. JACKIE BLUE
    (Ozark Mountain Daredevils)
4. SHINING STAR
    (Earth, Wind and Fire)
5. HOW LONG
    (Ace)
6. PHILADELPHIA FREEDOM
    (Elton John Band)
7. ONLY YESTERDAY
    (The Carpenters)
8. LONG TALL GLASSES (I CAN DANCE)
    (Leo Sayer)
9. WALKING IN RHYTHM
    (Blackbyrds)
10. BEFORE THE NEXT TEARDROP FALLS
    (Freddy Fender)

POP ALBUMS

1. THAT'S THE WAY OF THE WORLD
    (Earth, Wind and Fire)
2. HAVE YOU NEVER BEEN MELLOW
    (Olivia Newton-John)
3. CHICAGO VIII
    (Chicago)
4. PHYSICAL GRAFFITI
    (Led Zeppelin)
5. TOMMY
    (Original Soundtrack)
6. BLUEJAYS
    (Justin Hayward and John Lodge)
7. STRAIGHT SHOOTER
    (Bad Company)
8. A SONG FOR YOU
    (Temptations)
9. FUNNY LADY
    (Original Soundtrack)
10. AN EVENING WITH JOHN DENVER
    (John Denver)

BLACK SINGLES

1. GET DOWN, GET DOWN (GET ON THE FLOOR)
    (Joe Simon)
2. SHAKY GROUND
    (Temptations)
3. WHAT AM I GONNA DO WITH YOU
    (Barry White)
4. BAD LUCK (PART 1)
    (Harold Melvin and the Blue Notes)
5. ROCKIN' CHAIR
    (Gwen McCrae)
6. L-O-V-E (LOVE)
    (Al Green)
7. SHOESHINE BOY
    (Eddie Kendricks)
8. BABY THAT'S BACKATCHA
    (Smokey Robinson)
9. SHINING STAR
    (Earth, Wind and Fire)
10. SPIRIT OF THE BOOGIE/SUMMER MADNESS
    (Kool and the Gang)

BLACK ALBUMS

1. THAT'S THE WAY OF THE WORLD
    (Earth, Wind and Fire)
2. THE DRAMATIC JACKPOT
    (Ron Banks and the Dramatics)
3. MISTER MAGIC
    (Grover Washington Jr.)
4. JUST ANOTHER WAY TO SAY I LOVE YOU
    (Barry White)
5. A SONG FOR YOU
    (Temptations)
6. TO BE TRUE
    (Harold Melvin and the Blue Notes)
7. FEEL LIKE MAKIN' LOVE
    (Roberta Flack)
8. SUN GODDESS
    (Ramsey Lewis)
9. DISCOTHEQUE
    (Herbie Mann)
10. GREATEST HITS
    (Al Green)

JAZZ ALBUMS

1. MISTER MAGIC
    (Grover Washington Jr.)
2. STEPPING INTO TOMORROW
    (Donald Byrd)
3. SUN GODDESS
    (Ramsey Lewis)
4. EXPANSIONS
    (Lonnie Liston Smith)
5. FLYING START
    (Blackbyrds)
6. TWO
    (Bob James)
7. ALTERNATE TAKES
    (John Coltrane)
8. CUTTING EDGE
    (Sonny Rollins)
9. DISCOTHEQUE
    (Herbie Mann)
10. TOM CAT
    (Tom Scott and the L.A. Express)

COUNTRY SINGLES

1. I'M NOT LISA
    (Jessi Colter)
2. SHE'S ACTIN' SINGLE (I'M DRINKIN' DOUBLES)
    (Gary Stewart)
3. THANK GOD, I'M A COUNTRY BOY
    (John Denver)
4. ROLL ON BIG MAMA
    (Joe Stampley)
5. WINDOW UP ABOVE
    (Mickey Gilley)
6. TOO LATE TO WORRY, TOO BLUE TO CRY
    (Ronnie Milsap)
7. (HEY WON'T YOU PLAY) ANOTHER SOMEBODY DONE SOMEBODY WRONG SONG
    (B.J. Thomas)
8. MISTY
    (Ray Stevens)
9. I'D LIKE TO SLEEP 'TIL I GET OVER YOU
    (Freddie Hart)
10. SMOKEY MOUNTAIN MEMORIES
    (Mel Street)

COUNTRY ALBUMS

1. OUT OF HAND
    (Gary Stewart)
2. AN EVENING WITH JOHN DENVER
    (John Denver)
3. I'M JESSI COLTER
    (Jessi Colter)
4. HAVE YOU NEVER BEEN MELLOW
    (Olivia Newton-John)
5. WOLF CREEK PASS
    (C.W. McCall)
6. BARGAIN STORE
    (Dolly Parton)
7. A PAIR OF FIVES (BANJOS THAT IS)
    (Roy Clark and Buck Trent)
8. REUNION
    (B.J. Thomas)
9. SONGS OF FOX HOLLOW
    (Tom T. Hall)
10. FREDDIE HART'S GREATEST HITS
    (Freddie Hart)

MAY 17, 1975

POP SINGLES

1. JACKIE BLUE
    (Ozark Mountain Daredevils)
2. HE DON'T LOVE YOU (LIKE I LOVE YOU)
    (Tony Orlando and Dawn)
3. HOW LONG
    (Ace)
4. SHINING STAR
    (Earth, Wind and Fire)
5. (HEY WON'T YOU PLAY) ANOTHER SOMEBODY DONE SOMEBODY WRONG SONG
    (B.J. Thomas)
6. ONLY YESTERDAY
    (The Carpenters)
7. THANK GOD, I'M A COUNTRY BOY
    (John Denver)
8. WALKING IN RHYTHM
    (Blackbyrds)
9. BEFORE THE NEXT TEARDROP FALLS
    (Freddy Fender)
10. I DON'T LIKE TO SLEEP ALONE
    (Paul Anka)

POP ALBUMS

1. THAT'S THE WAY OF THE WORLD
    (Earth, Wind and Fire)
2. CHICAGO VIII
    (Chicago)
3. HAVE YOU NEVER BEEN MELLOW
    (Olivia Newton-John)
4. TOMMY
    (Original Soundtrack)
5. STRAIGHT SHOOTER
    (Bad Company)
6. PHYSICAL GRAFFITI
    (Led Zeppelin)
7. A SONG FOR YOU
    (Temptations)
8. NUTHIN' FANCY
    (Lynyrd Skynyrd)
9. HEARTS
    (America)
10. KATY LIED
    (Steely Dan)

BLACK SINGLES

1. GET DOWN, GET DOWN (GET ON THE FLOOR)
    (Joe Simon)
2. SHAKY GROUND
    (Temptations)

3. BAD LUCK (PART 1)
   (Harold Melvin and the Blue Notes)
4. ROCKIN' CHAIR
   (Gwen McCrae)
5. WHAT AM I GONNA DO WITH YOU
   (Barry White)
6. L-O-V-E (LOVE)
   (Al Green)
7. BABY THAT'S BACKATCHA
   (Smokey Robinson)
8. SPIRIT OF THE BOOGIE/SUMMER MADNESS
   (Kool and the Gang)
9. LOVE WON'T LET ME WAIT
   (Major Harris)
10. SHOESHINE BOY
    (Eddie Kendricks)

BLACK ALBUMS

1. THAT'S THE WAY OF THE WORLD
   (Earth, Wind and Fire)
2. THE DRAMATIC JACKPOT
   (Ron Banks and the Dramatics)
3. MISTER MAGIC
   (Grover Washington Jr.)
4. TO BE TRUE
   (Harold Melvin and the Blue Notes)
5. JUST ANOTHER WAY TO SAY I LOVE YOU
   (Barry White)
6. DISCOTHEQUE
   (Herbie Mann)
7. SUN GODDESS
   (Ramsey Lewis)
8. GREATEST HITS
   (Al Green)
9. A SONG FOR YOU
   (Temptations)
10. SURVIVAL
    (The O'Jays)

JAZZ ALBUMS

1. MISTER MAGIC
   (Grover Washington Jr.)
2. SUN GODDESS
   (Ramsey Lewis)
3. STEPPING INTO TOMORROW
   (Donald Byrd)
4. EXPANSIONS
   (Lonnie Liston Smith)
5. TWO
   (Ron James)
6. DISCOTHEQUE
   (Herbie Mann)
7. FLYING START
   (Blackbyrds)
8. ALTERNATE TAKES
   (John Coltrane)
9. TOM CAT
   (Tom Scott and the L.A. Express)
10. RESTFUL MIND
    (Larry Coryell)

COUNTRY SINGLES

1. SHE'S ACTIN' SINGLE (I'M DRINKING DOUBLES)
   (Gary Stewart)
2. THANK GOD, I'M A COUNTRY BOY
   (John Denver)
3. I'M NOT LISA
   (Jessi Colter)
4. WINDOW UP ABOVE
   (Mickey Gilley)
5. TOO LATE TO WORRY, TOO BLUE TO CRY
   (Ronnie Milsap)
6. MISTY
   (Ray Stevens)
7. ROLL ON BIG MAMA
   (Joe Stampley)
8. I'D LIKE TO SLEEP 'TIL I GET OVER YOU
   (Freddie Hart)

9. I AIN'T ALL BAD
   (Charley Pride)
10. SMOKEY MOUNTAIN MEMORIES
    (Mel Street)

COUNTRY ALBUMS

1. OUT OF HAND
   (Gary Stewart)
2. I'M JESSI COLTER
   (Jessi Colter)
3. AN EVENING WITH JOHN DENVER
   (John Denver)
4. WOLF CREEK PASS
   (C.W. McCall)
5. REUNION
   (B.J. Thomas)
6. BEFORE THE NEXT TEARDROP FALLS
   (Freddy Fender)
7. HAVE YOU NEVER BEEN MELLOW
   (Olivia Newton-John)
8. BLANKET ON THE GROUND
   (Billie Jo Spears)
9. SONGS OF FOX HOLLOW
   (Tom T. Hall)
10. FREDDIE HART'S GREATEST HITS
    (Freddie Hart)

MAY 24, 1975

POP SINGLES

1. SHINING STAR
   (Earth, Wind and Fire)
2. BEFORE THE NEXT TEARDROP FALLS
   (Freddy Fender)
3. HOW LONG
   (Ace)
4. THANK GOD, I'M A COUNTRY BOY
   (John Denver)
5. JACKIE BLUE
   (Ozark Mountain Daredevils)
6. ONLY YESTERDAY
   (The Carpenters)
7. SISTER GOLDEN HAIR
   (America)
8. HE DON'T LOVE YOU (LIKE I LOVE YOU)
   (Tony Orlando and Dawn)
9. I DON'T LIKE TO SLEEP ALONE
   (Paul Anka)
10. BAD TIME
    (Grand Funk Railroad)

POP ALBUMS

1. THAT'S THE WAY OF THE WORLD
   (Earth, Wind and Fire)
2. CHICAGO VIII
   (Chicago)
3. TOMMY
   (Original Soundtrack)
4. STRAIGHT SHOOTER
   (Bad Company)
5. HAVE YOU NEVER BEEN MELLOW
   (Olivia Newton-John)
6. NUTHIN' FANCY
   (Lynyrd Skynyrd)
7. PHYSICAL GRAFFITI
   (Led Zeppelin)
8. A SONG FOR YOU
   (Temptations)
9. HEARTS
   (America)
10. WELCOME TO MY NIGHTMARE
    (Alice Cooper)

BLACK SINGLES

1. GET DOWN, GET DOWN (GET ON THE FLOOR)
   (Joe Simon)
2. ROCKIN' CHAIR
   (Gwen McCrae)
3. BAD LUCK (PART 1)
   (Harold Melvin and the Blue Notes)
4. SPIRIT OF THE BOOGIE/SUMMER MADNESS
   (Kool and the Gang)
5. SHAKY GROUND
   (Temptations)
6. BABY THAT'S BACKATCHA
   (Smokey Robinson)
7. LOVE WON'T LET ME WAIT
   (Major Harris)
8. WHAT AM I GONNA DO WITH YOU
   (Barry White)
9. CUT THE CAKE/PERSON TO PERSON
   (Average White Band)
10. L-O-V-E (LOVE)
    (Al Green)

BLACK ALBUMS

1. THAT'S THE WAY OF THE WORLD
   (Earth, Wind and Fire)
2. MISTER MAGIC
   (Grover Washington Jr.)
3. THE DRAMATIC JACKPOT
   (Ron Banks and the Dramatics)
4. TO BE TRUE
   (Harold Melvin and the Blue Notes)
5. SURVIVAL
   (The O'Jays)
6. DISCOTHEQUE
   (Herbie Mann)
7. A SONG FOR YOU
   (Temptations)
8. JUST ANOTHER WAY TO SAY I LOVE YOU
   (Barry White)
9. A QUIET STORM
   (Smokey Robinson)
10. MY WAY
    (Major Harris)

JAZZ ALBUMS

1. MISTER MAGIC
   (Grover Washington Jr.)
2. SUN GODDESS
   (Ramsey Lewis)
3. EXPANSIONS
   (Lonnie Liston Smith)
4. DISCOTHEQUE
   (Herbie Mann)
5. TWO
   (Bob James)
6. STEPPING INTO TOMORROW
   (Donald Byrd)
7. TOM CAT
   (Tom Scott and the L.A. Express)
8. RESTFUL MIND
   (Larry Coryell)
9. IN THE POCKET
   (Stanley Turrentine)
10. FEEL
    (George Duke)

COUNTRY SINGLES

1. THANK GOD, I'M A COUNTRY BOY
   (John Denver)
2. MISTY
   (Ray Stevens)
3. WINDOW UP ABOVE
   (Mickey Gilley)
4. I'M NOT LISA
   (Jessi Colter)
5. TOO LATE TO WORRY, TOO BLUE TO CRY
   (Ronnie Milsap)

6. SHE'S ACTIN' SINGLE (I'M DRINKIN' DOUBLES)
   (Gary Stewart)
7. I AIN'T ALL BAD
   (Charley Pride)
8. YOU'RE MY BEST FRIEND
   (Don Williams)
9. RECONSIDER ME
   (Narvel Felts)
10. HURT
   (Connie Cato)

COUNTRY ALBUMS

1. I'M JESSI COLTER
   (Jessi Colter)
2. REUNION
   (B.J. Thomas)
3. BEFORE THE NEXT TEARDROP FALLS
   (Freddy Fender)
4. WOLF CREEK PASS
   (C.W. McCall)
5. BLANKET ON THE GROUND
   (Billie Jo Spears)
6. OUT OF HAND
   (Gary Stewart)
7. AN EVENING WITH JOHN DENVER
   (John Denver)
8. PHONE CALL FROM GOD
   (Jerry Jordan)
9. HAVE YOU NEVER BEEN MELLOW
   (Olivia Newton-John)
10. SONGS OF FOX HOLLOW
   (Tom T. Hall)

MAY 31, 1975

POP SINGLES

1. BEFORE THE NEXT TEARDROP FALLS
   (Freddy Fender)
2. SHINING STAR
   (Earth, Wind and Fire)
3. THANK GOD, I'M A COUNTRY BOY
   (John Denver)
4. HOW LONG
   (Ace)
5. SISTER GOLDEN HAIR
   (America)
6. ONLY YESTERDAY
   (The Carpenters)
7. JACKIE BLUE
   (Ozark Mountain Daredevils)
8. BAD TIME
   (Grand Funk Railroad)
9. OLD DAYS
   (Chicago)
10. TAKE ME IN YOUR ARMS (ROCK ME)
   (The Doobie Brothers)

POP ALBUMS

1. THAT'S THE WAY OF THE WORLD
   (Earth, Wind and Fire)
2. CHICAGO VIII
   (Chicago)
3. TOMMY
   (Original Soundtrack)
4. STRAIGHT SHOOTER
   (Bad Company)
5. NUTHIN' FANCY
   (Lynyrd Skynyrd)
6. WELCOME TO MY NIGHTMARE
   (Alice Cooper)
7. STAMPEDE
   (The Doobie Brothers)
8. A SONG FOR YOU
   (Temptations)
9. PLAYING POSSUM
   (Carly Simon)

10. BLOW BY BLOW
   (Jeff Beck)

BLACK SINGLES

1. ROCKIN' CHAIR
   (Gwen McCrae)
2. GET DOWN, GET DOWN (GET ON THE FLOOR)
   (Joe Simon)
3. SPIRIT OF THE BOOGIE/SUMMER MADNESS
   (Kool and the Gang)
4. LOVE WON'T LET ME WAIT
   (Major Harris)
5. BABY THAT'S BACKATCHA
   (Smokey Robinson)
6. BAD LUCK (PART 1)
   (Harold Melvin and the Blue Notes)
7. CUT THE CAKE/PERSON TO PERSON
   (Average White Band)
8. SHAKY GROUND
   (Temptations)
9. GIVE THE PEOPLE WHAT THEY WANT
   (The O'Jays)
10. L-O-V-E (LOVE)
   (Al Green)

BLACK ALBUMS

1. THAT'S THE WAY OF THE WORLD
   (Earth, Wind and Fire)
2. MISTER MAGIC
   (Grover Washington Jr.)
3. SURVIVAL
   (The O'Jays)
4. TO BE TRUE
   (Harold Melvin and the Blue Notes)
5. DISCOTHEQUE
   (Herbie Mann)
6. THE DRAMATIC JACKPOT
   (Ron Banks and the Dramatics)
7. A SONG FOR YOU
   (Temptations)
8. MY WAY
   (Major Harris)
9. A QUIET STORM
   (Smokey Robinson)
10. CHOCOLATE CITY
   (Parliament)

JAZZ ALBUMS

1. MISTER MAGIC
   (Grover Washington Jr.)
2. EXPANSIONS
   (Lonnie Liston Smith)
3. DISCOTHEQUE
   (Herbie Mann)
4. IN THE POCKET
   (Stanley Turrentine)
5. TWO
   (Bob James)
6. TOM CAT
   (Tom Scott and the L.A. Express)
7. SUN GODDESS
   (Ramsey Lewis)
8. RESTFUL MIND
   (Larry Coryell)
9. I NEED SOME MONEY
   (Eddie Harris)
10. CHASE THE CLOUDS AWAY
   (Chuck Mangione)

COUNTRY SINGLES

1. MISTY
   (Ray Stevens)
2. WINDOW UP ABOVE
   (Mickey Gilley)
3. THANK GOD, I'M A COUNTRY BOY
   (John Denver)

4. I'M NOT LISA
   (Jessi Colter)
5. I AIN'T ALL BAD
   (Charley Pride)
6. YOU'RE MY BEST FRIEND
   (Don Williams)
7. RECONSIDER ME
   (Narvel Felts)
8. WHEN WILL I BE LOVED
   (Linda Ronstadt)
9. FROM BARROOMS TO BEDROOMS
   (David Wills)
10. HURT
   (Connie Cato)

COUNTRY ALBUMS

1. BEFORE THE NEXT TEARDROP FALLS
   (Freddy Fender)
2. REUNION
   (B.J. Thomas)
3. I'M JESSI COLTER
   (Jessi Colter)
4. BLANKET ON THE GROUND
   (Billie Jo Spears)
5. WOLF CREEK PASS
   (C.W. McCall)
6. PHONE CALL FROM GOD
   (Jerry Jordan)
7. MICKEY'S MOVIN' ON
   (Mickey Gilley)
8. AN EVENING WITH JOHN DENVER
   (John Denver)
9. HAVE YOU NEVER BEEN MELLOW
   (Olivia Newton-John)
10. OUT OF HAND
   (Gary Stewart)

JUNE 7, 1975

POP SINGLES

1. THANK GOD, I'M A COUNTRY BOY
   (John Denver)
2. SISTER GOLDEN HAIR
   (America)
3. BEFORE THE NEXT TEARDROP FALLS
   (Freddy Fender)
4. SHINING STAR
   (Earth, Wind and Fire)
5. WILDFIRE
   (Michael Murphey)
6. TAKE ME IN YOUR ARMS (ROCK ME)
   (The Doobie Brothers)
7. BAD TIME
   (Grand Funk Railroad)
8. OLD DAYS
   (Chicago)
9. HOW LONG
   (Ace)
10. GET DOWN, GET DOWN (GET ON THE FLOOR)
   (Joe Simon)

POP ALBUMS

1. CAPTAIN FANTASTIC AND THE BROWN DIRT COWBOY
   (Elton John)
2. STAMPEDE
   (The Doobie Brothers)
3. THAT'S THE WAY OF THE WORLD
   (Earth, Wind and Fire)
4. CHICAGO VIII
   (Chicago)
5. TOMMY
   (Original Soundtrack)
6. WELCOME TO MY NIGHTMARE
   (Alice Cooper)
7. PLAYING POSSUM
   (Carly Simon)

8. FANDANGO
   (ZZ Top)
9. BLOW BY BLOW
   (Jeff Beck)
10. SPIRIT OF AMERICA
    (The Beach Boys)

BLACK SINGLES

1. ROCKIN' CHAIR
   (Gwen McCrae)
2. LOVE WON'T LET ME WAIT
   (Major Harris)
3. SPIRIT OF THE BOOGIE/SUMMER MADNESS
   (Kool and the Gang)
4. GET DOWN, GET DOWN (GET ON THE FLOOR)
   (Joe Simon)
5. CUT THE CAKE/PERSON TO PERSON
   (Average White Band)
6. GIVE THE PEOPLE WHAT THEY WANT
   (The O'Jays)
7. BABY THAT'S BACKATCHA
   (Smokey Robinson)
8. LOOK AT ME (I'M IN LOVE)
   (The Moments)
9. THE WAY WE WERE/TRY TO REMEMBER
   (Gladys Knight and the Pips)
10. SLIPPERY WHEN WET
    (Commodores)

BLACK ALBUMS

1. THAT'S THE WAY OF THE WORLD
   (Earth, Wind and Fire)
2. SURVIVAL
   (The O'Jays)
3. MISTER MAGIC
   (Grover Washington Jr.)
4. TO BE TRUE
   (Harold Melvin and the Blue Notes)
5. DISCOTHEQUE
   (Herbie Mann)
6. A SONG FOR YOU
   (Temptations)
7. MY WAY
   (Major Harris)
8. A QUIET STORM
   (Smokey Robinson)
9. CHOCOLATE CITY
   (Parliament)
10. THE DRAMATIC JACKPOT
    (Ron Banks and the Dramatics)

JAZZ ALBUMS

1. MISTER MAGIC
   (Grover Washington Jr.)
2. DISCOTHEQUE
   (Herbie Mann)
3. EXPANSIONS
   (Lonnie Liston Smith)
4. IN THE POCKET
   (Stanley Turrentine)
5. TWO
   (Bob James)
6. TOM CAT
   (Tom Scott and the L.A. Express)
7. CHASE THE CLOUDS AWAY
   (Chuck Mangione)
8. I NEED SOME MONEY
   (Eddie Harris)
9. POLAR AC
   (Freddie Hubbard)
10. SUN GODDESS
    (Ramsey Lewis)

COUNTRY SINGLES

1. WINDOW UP ABOVE
   (Mickey Gilley)
2. MISTY
   (Ray Stevens)
3. I AIN'T ALL BAD
   (Charley Pride)
4. YOU'RE MY BEST FRIEND
   (Don Williams)
5. RECONSIDER ME
   (Narvel Felts)
6. WHEN WILL I BE LOVED
   (Linda Ronstadt)
7. TRYIN' TO BEAT THE MORNING HOME
   (T.G. Sheppard)
8. THANK GOD, I'M A COUNTRY BOY
   (John Denver)
9. FROM BARROOMS TO BEDROOMS
   (David Wills)
10. BRASS BUCKLES
    (Barbi Benton)

COUNTRY ALBUMS

1. BEFORE THE NEXT TEARDROP FALLS
   (Freddy Fender)
2. PHONE CALL FROM GOD
   (Jerry Jordan)
3. BLANKET ON THE GROUND
   (Billie Jo Spears)
4. WOLF CREEK PASS
   (C.W. McCall)
5. MICKEY'S MOVIN' ON
   (Mickey Gilley)
6. I'M JESSI COLTER
   (Jessi Colter)
7. REUNION
   (B.J. Thomas)
8. IN CONCERT, VOL. 2
   (Various Artists)
9. AN EVENING WITH JOHN DENVER
   (John Denver)
10. KEEP MOVIN' ON
    (Merle Haggard)

JUNE 14, 1975

POP SINGLES

1. SISTER GOLDEN HAIR
   (America)
2. THANK GOD, I'M A COUNTRY BOY
   (John Denver)
3. LOVE WILL KEEP US TOGETHER
   (The Captain and Tennille)
4. WILDFIRE
   (Michael Murphey)
5. TAKE ME IN YOUR ARMS (ROCK ME)
   (The Doobie Brothers)
6. LOVE WON'T LET ME WAIT
   (Major Harris)
7. BAD TIME
   (Grand Funk Railroad)
8. WHEN WILL I BE LOVED
   (Linda Ronstadt)
9. GET DOWN, GET DOWN (GET ON THE FLOOR)
   (Joe Simon)
10. ONLY WOMEN
    (Alice Cooper)

POP ALBUMS

1. CAPTAIN FANTASTIC AND THE BROWN DIRT COWBOY
   (Elton John)
2. STAMPEDE
   (The Doobie Brothers)
3. THAT'S THE WAY OF THE WORLD
   (Earth, Wind and Fire)
4. FOUR-WHEEL DRIVE
   (Bachman-Turner Overdrive)
5. PLAYING POSSUM
   (Carly Simon)
6. FANDANGO
   (ZZ Top)
7. WELCOME TO MY NIGHTMARE
   (Alice Cooper)
8. BLOW BY BLOW
   (Jeff Beck)
9. SURVIVAL
   (The O'Jays)
10. HEARTS
    (America)

BLACK SINGLES

1. ROCKIN' CHAIR
   (Gwen McCrae)
2. LOVE WON'T LET ME WAIT
   (Major Harris)
3. GIVE THE PEOPLE WHAT THEY WANT
   (The O'Jays)
4. LOOK AT ME (I'M IN LOVE)
   (The Moments)
5. CUT THE CAKE/PERSON TO PERSON
   (Average White Band)
6. SPIRIT OF THE BOOGIE/SUMMER MADNESS
   (Kool and the Gang)
7. THE WAY WE WERE/TRY TO REMEMBER
   (Gladys Knight and the Pips)
8. SLIPPERY WHEN WET
   (Commodores)
9. THE HUSTLE
   (Van McCoy and the Soul City Symphony)
10. SHACKIN' UP
    (Barbara Mason)

BLACK ALBUMS

1. THAT'S THE WAY OF THE WORLD
   (Earth, Wind and Fire)
2. MISTER MAGIC
   (Grover Washington Jr.)
3. TO BE TRUE
   (Harold Melvin and the Blue Notes)
4. SURVIVAL
   (The O'Jays)
5. A SONG FOR YOU
   (Temptations)
6. DISCO BABY
   (Van McCoy and the Soul City Symphony)
7. CHOCOLATE CITY
   (Parliament)
8. MY WAY
   (Major Harris)
9. DISCOTHEQUE
   (Herbie Mann)
10. THE DRAMATIC JACKPOT
    (Ron Banks and the Dramatics)

JAZZ ALBUMS

1. MISTER MAGIC
   (Grover Washington Jr.)
2. DISCOTHEQUE
   (Herbie Mann)
3. IN THE POCKET
   (Stanley Turrentine)
4. EXPANSIONS
   (Lonnie Liston Smith)
5. TWO
   (Bob James)
6. CHASE THE CLOUDS AWAY
   (Chuck Mangione)
7. TOM CAT
   (Tom Scott and the L.A. Express)
8. I NEED SOME MONEY
   (Eddie Harris)
9. THE AURA WILL PREVAIL
   (George Duke)
10. TALE SPINNIN'
    (Weather Report)

COUNTRY SINGLES

1. I AIN'T ALL BAD
   (Charley Pride)
2. YOU'RE MY BEST FRIEND
   (Don Williams)
3. WHEN WILL I BE LOVED
   (Linda Ronstadt)
4. TRYIN' TO BEAT THE MORNING HOME
   (T.G. Sheppard)
5. RECONSIDER ME
   (Narvel Felts)
6. LIZZIE AND THE RAINMAN
   (Tanya Tucker)
7. WINDOW UP ABOVE
   (Mickey Gilley)
8. MISTY
   (Ray Stevens)
9. THERE I SAID IT
   (Margo Smith)
10. LITTLE BAND OF GOLD
    (Sonny James)

COUNTRY ALBUMS

1. PHONE CALL FROM GOD
   (Jerry Jordan)
2. BEFORE THE NEXT TEARDROP FALLS
   (Freddy Fender)
3. MICKEY'S MOVIN' ON
   (Mickey Gilley)
4. KEEP MOVIN' ON
   (Merle Haggard)
5. WOLF CREEK PASS
   (C.W. McCall)
6. BLANKET ON THE GROUND
   (Billy Jo Spears)
7. IN CONCERT, VOL. 2
   (Various Artists)
8. I'M JESSI COLTER
   (Jessi Colter)
9. REUNION
   (B.J. Thomas)
10. AN EVENING WITH JOHN DENVER
    (John Denver)

JUNE 21, 1975

POP SINGLES

1. LOVE WILL KEEP US TOGETHER
   (The Captain and Tennille)
2. SISTER GOLDEN HAIR
   (America)
3. WILDFIRE
   (Michael Murphey)
4. LOVE WON'T LET ME WAIT
   (Major Harris)
5. TAKE ME IN YOUR ARMS (ROCK ME)
   (The Doobie Brothers)
6. WHEN WILL I BE LOVED
   (Linda Ronstadt)
7. THANK GOD, I'M A COUNTRY BOY
   (John Denver)
8. I'M NOT LISA
   (Jessi Colter)
9. ONLY WOMEN
   (Alice Cooper)
10. GET DOWN, GET DOWN (GET ON THE FLOOR)
    (Joe Simon)

POP ALBUMS

1. CAPTAIN FANTASTIC AND THE BROWN DIRT COWBOY
   (Elton John)
2. FOUR-WHEEL DRIVE
   (Bachman-Turner Overdrive)

3. STAMPEDE
   (The Doobie Brothers)
4. VENUS AND MARS
   (Paul McCartney and Wings)
5. PLAYING POSSUM
   (Carly Simon)
6. FANDANGO
   (ZZ Top)
7. THAT'S THE WAY OF THE WORLD
   (Earth, Wind and Fire)
8. HEARTS
   (America)
9. SURVIVAL
   (The O'Jays)
10. WELCOME TO MY NIGHTMARE
    (Alice Cooper)

BLACK SINGLES

1. LOVE WON'T LET ME WAIT
   (Major Harris)
2. ROCKIN' CHAIR
   (Gwen McCrae)
3. GIVE THE PEOPLE WHAT THEY WANT
   (The O'Jays)
4. LOOK AT ME (I'M IN LOVE)
   (The Moments)
5. THE HUSTLE
   (Van McCoy and the Soul City Symphony)
6. SLIPPERY WHEN WET
   (Commodores)
7. THE WAY WE WERE/TRY TO REMEMBER
   (Gladys Knight and the Pips)
8. CUT THE CAKE/PERSON TO PERSON
   (Average White Band)
9. SPIRIT OF THE BOOGIE/SUMMER MADNESS
   (Kool and the Gang)
10. SHACKIN' UP
    (Barbara Mason)

BLACK ALBUMS

1. THAT'S THE WAY OF THE WORLD
   (Earth, Wind and Fire)
2. MISTER MAGIC
   (Grover Washington Jr.)
3. SURVIVAL
   (The O'Jays)
4. TO BE TRUE
   (Harold Melvin and the Blue Notes)
5. A SONG FOR YOU
   (Temptations)
6. DISCO BABY
   (Van McCoy and the Soul City Symphony)
7. CHOCOLATE CITY
   (Parliament)
8. ADVENTURES IN PARADISE
   (Minnie Riperton)
9. MY WAY
   (Major Harris)
10. THE DRAMATIC JACKPOT
    (Ron Banks and the Dramatics)

JAZZ ALBUMS

1. MISTER MAGIC
   (Grover Washington Jr.)
2. DISCOTHEQUE
   (Herbie Mann)
3. IN THE POCKET
   (Stanley Turrentine)
4. TALE SPINNIN'
   (Weather Report)
5. CHASE THE CLOUDS AWAY
   (Chuck Mangione)
6. THE AURA WILL PREVAIL
   (George Duke)
7. TWO
   (Bob James)
8. TOM CAT
   (Tom Scott and the L.A. Express)
9. EXPANSIONS
   (Lonnie Liston Smith)

10. I NEED SOME MONEY
    (Eddie Harris)

COUNTRY SINGLES

1. YOU'RE MY BEST FRIEND
   (Don Williams)
2. WHEN WILL I BE LOVED
   (Linda Ronstadt)
3. TRYIN' TO BEAT THE MORNING HOME
   (T.G. Sheppard)
4. RECONSIDER ME
   (Narvel Felts)
5. LIZZIE AND THE RAINMAN
   (Tanya Tucker)
6. THERE I SAID IT
   (Margo Smith)
7. I AIN'T ALL BAD
   (Charley Pride)
8. LITTLE BAND OF GOLD
   (Sonny James)
9. MISTY
   (Ray Stevens)
10. FORGIVE AND FORGET
    (Eddie Rabbitt)

COUNTRY ALBUMS

1. PHONE CALL FROM GOD
   (Jerry Jordan)
2. KEEP MOVIN' ON
   (Merle Haggard)
3. MICKEY'S MOVIN' ON
   (Mickey Gilley)
4. BEFORE THE NEXT TEARDROP FALLS
   (Freddy Fender)
5. WOLF CREEK PASS
   (C.W. McCall)
6. YOU'RE MY BEST FRIEND
   (Don Williams)
7. TANYA TUCKER
   (Tanya Tucker)
8. IN CONCERT, VOL. 2
   (Various Artists)
9. I'M JESSI COLTER
   (Jessi Colter)
10. REUNION
    (B.J. Thomas)

JUNE 28, 1975

POP SINGLES

1. LOVE WILL KEEP US TOGETHER
   (The Captain and Tennille)
2. WILDFIRE
   (Michael Murphey)
3. LOVE WON'T LET ME WAIT
   (Major Harris)
4. WHEN WILL I BE LOVED
   (Linda Ronstadt)
5. SISTER GOLDEN HAIR
   (America)
6. I'M NOT LISA
   (Jessi Colter)
7. THE HUSTLE
   (Van McCoy and the Soul City Symphony)
8. MAGIC
   (Pilot)
9. ONLY WOMEN
   (Alice Cooper)
10. LISTEN TO WHAT THE MAN SAID
    (Paul McCartney and Wings)

POP ALBUMS

1. CAPTAIN FANTASTIC AND THE BROWN DIRT COWBOY
   (Elton John)

2. FOUR-WHEEL DRIVE
   (Bachman-Turner Overdrive)
3. VENUS AND MARS
   (Paul McCartney and Wings)
4. STAMPEDE
   (The Doobie Brothers)
5. HEARTS
   (America)
6. THAT'S THE WAY OF THE WORLD
   (Earth, Wind and Fire)
7. SURVIVAL
   (The O'Jays)
8. LOVE WILL KEEP US TOGETHER
   (The Captain and Tennille)
9. WELCOME TO MY NIGHTMARE
   (Alice Cooper)
10. MISTER MAGIC
    (Grover Washington Jr.)

BLACK SINGLES

1. LOVE WON'T LET ME WAIT
   (Major Harris)
2. ROCKIN' CHAIR
   (Gwen McCrae)
3. THE HUSTLE
   (Van McCoy and the Soul City Symphony)
4. LOOK AT ME (I'M IN LOVE)
   (The Moments)
5. SLIPPERY WHEN WET
   (Commodores)
6. GIVE THE PEOPLE WHAT THEY WANT
   (The O'Jays)
7. THE WAY WE WERE/TRY TO REMEMBER
   (Gladys Knight and the Pips)
8. CUT THE CAKE/PERSON TO PERSON
   (Average White Band)
9. SPIRIT OF THE BOOGIE/SUMMER MADNESS
   (Kool and the Gang)
10. SHACKIN' UP
    (Barbara Mason)

BLACK ALBUMS

1. THAT'S THE WAY OF THE WORLD
   (Earth, Wind and Fire)
2. THE HEAT IS ON
   (Isley Brothers)
3. MISTER MAGIC
   (Grover Washington Jr.)
4. SURVIVAL
   (The O'Jays)
5. TO BE TRUE
   (Harold Melvin and the Blue Notes)
6. DISCO BABY
   (Van McCoy and the Soul City Symphony)
7. A SONG FOR YOU
   (Temptations)
8. ADVENTURES IN PARADISE
   (Adventures in Paradise)
9. BLIND BABY
   (New Birth)
10. THE DRAMATIC JACKPOT
    (Ron Banks and the Dramatics)

JAZZ ALBUMS

1. MISTER MAGIC
   (Grover Washington Jr.)
2. DISCOTHEQUE
   (Herbie Mann)
3. TALE SPINNIN'
   (Weather Report)
4. IN THE POCKET
   (Stanley Turrentine)
5. THE AURA WILL PREVAIL
   (George Duke)
6. NATIVE DANCER
   (Wayne Shorter)
7. CHASE THE CLOUDS AWAY
   (Chuck Mangione)
8. TWO
   (Bob James)

9. EXPANSIONS
   (Lonnie Liston Smith)
10. SUN GODDESS
    (Ramsey Lewis)

COUNTRY SINGLES

1. WHEN WILL I BE LOVED
   (Linda Ronstadt)
2. RECONSIDER ME
   (Narvel Felts)
3. TRYIN' TO BEAT THE MORNING HOME
   (T.G. Sheppard)
4. LIZZIE AND THE RAINMAN
   (Tanya Tucker)
5. THERE I SAID IT
   (Margo Smith)
6. LITTLE BAND OF GOLD
   (Sonny James)
7. YOU'RE MY BEST FRIEND
   (Don Williams)
8. TOUCH THE HAND
   (Conway Twitty)
9. HE'S MY ROCK
   (Brenda Lee)
10. WORD GAMES
    (Billy Walker)

COUNTRY ALBUMS

1. KEEP MOVIN' ON
   (Merle Haggard)
2. PHONE CALL FROM GOD
   (Jerry Jordan)
3. BEFORE THE NEXT TEARDROP FALLS
   (Freddy Fender)
4. MICKEY'S MOVIN' ON
   (Mickey Gilley)
5. YOU'RE MY BEST FRIEND
   (Don Williams)
6. TANYA TUCKER
   (Tanya Tucker)
7. WOLF CREEK PASS
   (C.W. McCall)
8. I'M JESSI COLTER
   (Jessi Colter)
9. LAST FAREWELL
   (Roger Whittaker)
10. AN EVENING WITH JOHN DENVER
    (John Denver)

JULY 5, 1975

POP SINGLES

1. LOVE WILL KEEP US TOGETHER
   (The Captain and Tennille)
2. WILDFIRE
   (Michael Murphey)
3. LOVE WON'T LET ME WAIT
   (Major Harris)
4. WHEN WILL I BE LOVED
   (Linda Ronstadt)
5. THE HUSTLE
   (Van McCoy and the Soul City Symphony)
6. I'M NOT LISA
   (Jessi Colter)
7. MAGIC
   (Pilot)
8. LISTEN TO WHAT THE MAN SAID
   (Paul McCartney and Wings)
9. SISTER GOLDEN HAIR
   (America)
10. SWEARIN' TO GOD
    (Frankie Valli)

POP ALBUMS

1. CAPTAIN FANTASTIC AND THE BROWN DIRT COWBOY
   (Elton John)
2. VENUS AND MARS
   (Paul McCartney and Wings)
3. STAMPEDE
   (The Doobie Brothers)
4. FOUR-WHEEL DRIVE
   (Bachman-Turner Overdrive)
5. HEARTS
   (America)
6. LOVE WILL KEEP US TOGETHER
   (The Captain and Tennille)
7. SURVIVAL
   (The O'Jays)
8. THE HEAT IS ON
   (Isley Brothers)
9. ONE OF THESE NIGHTS
   (The Eagles)
10. MISTER MAGIC
    (Grover Washington Jr.)

BLACK SINGLES

1. THE HUSTLE
   (Van McCoy and the Soul City Symphony)
2. LOVE WON'T LET ME WAIT
   (Major Harris)
3. ROCKIN' CHAIR
   (Gwen McCrae)
4. SLIPPERY WHEN WET
   (Commodores)
5. LOOK AT ME (I'M IN LOVE)
   (The Moments)
6. JUST A LITTLE BIT OF YOU
   (Michael Jackson)
7. GIVE THE PEOPLE WHAT THEY WANT
   (The O'Jays)
8. THE WAY WE WERE/TRY TO REMEMBER
   (Gladys Knight and the Pips)
9. CUT THE CAKE/PERSON TO PERSON
   (Average White Band)
10. SOONER OR LATER
    (The Impressions)

BLACK ALBUMS

1. THE HEAT IS ON
   (Isley Brothers)
2. THAT'S THE WAY OF THE WORLD
   (Earth, Wind and Fire)
3. SURVIVAL
   (The O'Jays)
4. MISTER MAGIC
   (Grover Washington Jr.)
5. TO BE TRUE
   (Harold Melvin and the Blue Notes)
6. DISCO BABY
   (Van McCoy and the Soul City Symphony)
7. BLIND BABY
   (New Birth)
8. A SONG FOR YOU
   (Temptations)
9. CHOCOLATE CHIP
   (Isaac Hayes)
10. MOVING VIOLATION
    (The Jackson 5)

JAZZ ALBUMS

1. MISTER MAGIC
   (Grover Washington Jr.)
2. TALE SPINNIN'
   (Weather Report)
3. DISCOTHEQUE
   (Herbie Mann)
4. THE AURA WILL PREVAIL
   (George Duke)
5. IN THE POCKET
   (Stanley Turrentine)

6. SUN GODDESS
   (Ramsey Lewis)
7. EXPANSIONS
   (Lonnie Liston Smith)
8. CHASE THE CLOUDS AWAY
   (Chuck Mangione)
9. NATIVE DANCER
   (Wayne Shorter)
10. TWO
    (Bob James)

COUNTRY SINGLES

1. RECONSIDER ME
   (Narvel Felts)
2. MOVIN' ON
   (Merle Haggard)
3. TOUCH THE HAND
   (Conway Twitty)
4. LIZZIE AND THE RAINMAN
   (Tanya Tucker)
5. THERE I SAID IT
   (Margo Smith)
6. LITTLE BAND OF GOLD
   (Sonny James)
7. TRYIN' TO BEAT THE MORNING HOME
   (T.G. Sheppard)
8. WHEN WILL I BE LOVED
   (Linda Ronstadt)
9. JUST GET UP AND CLOSE THE DOOR
   (Johnny Rodriguez)
10. THAT'S WHEN MY WOMAN BEGINS
    (Tommy Overstreet)

COUNTRY ALBUMS

1. KEEP MOVIN' ON
   (Merle Haggard)
2. PHONE CALL FROM GOD
   (Jerry Jordan)
3. BEFORE THE NEXT TEARDROP FALLS
   (Freddy Fender)
4. YOU'RE MY BEST FRIEND
   (Don Williams)
5. TANYA TUCKER
   (Tanya Tucker)
6. MICKEY'S MOVIN' ON
   (Mickey Gilley)
7. I'M JESSI COLTER
   (Jessi Colter)
8. JUST GET UP AND CLOSE THE DOOR
   (Johnny Rodriguez)
9. LAST FAREWELL
   (Roger Whittaker)
10. STILL THINKIN' ABOUT YOU
    (Billy "Crash" Craddock)

JULY 12, 1975

POP SINGLES

1. THE HUSTLE
   (Van McCoy and the Soul City Symphony)
2. LOVE WILL KEEP US TOGETHER
   (The Captain and Tennille)
3. WILDFIRE
   (Michael Murphey)
4. LISTEN TO WHAT THE MAN SAID
   (Paul McCartney and Wings)
5. MAGIC
   (Pilot)
6. LOVE WON'T LET ME WAIT
   (Major Harris)
7. SWEARIN' TO GOD
   (Frankie Valli)
8. I'M NOT IN LOVE
   (10 C.C.)
9. ONE OF THESE NIGHTS
   (The Eagles)
10. ROCKIN' CHAIR
    (Gwen McCrae)

POP ALBUMS

1. VENUS AND MARS
   (Paul McCartney and Wings)
2. CAPTAIN FANTASTIC AND THE BROWN
   DIRT COWBOY
   (Elton John)
3. ONE OF THESE NIGHTS
   (The Eagles)
4. THE HEAT IS ON
   (Isley Brothers)
5. LOVE WILL KEEP US TOGETHER
   (The Captain and Tennille)
6. STAMPEDE
   (The Doobie Brothers)
7. FOUR-WHEEL DRIVE
   (Bachman-Turner Overdrive)
8. HEARTS
   (America)
9. SURVIVAL
   (The O'Jays)
10. THAT'S THE WAY OF THE WORLD
    (Earth, Wind and Fire)

BLACK SINGLES

1. THE HUSTLE
   (Van McCoy and the Soul City Symphony)
2. LOVE WON'T LET ME WAIT
   (Major Harris)
3. ROCKIN' CHAIR
   (Gwen McCrae)
4. FIGHT THE POWER, PART 1
   (Isley Brothers)
5. JUST A LITTLE BIT OF YOU
   (Michael Jackson)
6. SOONER OR LATER
   (The Impressions)
7. SLIPPERY WHEN WET
   (Commodores)
8. LOOK AT ME (I'M IN LOVE)
   (The Moments)
9. THE WAY WE WERE/TRY TO REMEMBER
   (Gladys Knight and the Pips)
10. SEXY
    (MFSB)

BLACK ALBUMS

1. THE HEAT IS ON
   (Isley Brothers)
2. THAT'S THE WAY OF THE WORLD
   (Earth, Wind and Fire)
3. SURVIVAL
   (The O'Jays)
4. MISTER MAGIC
   (Grover Washington, Jr.)
5. DISCO BABY
   (Van McCoy and the Soul City Symphony)
6. CHOCOLATE CHIP
   (Isaac Hayes)
7. A SONG FOR YOU
   (Temptations)
8. TO BE TRUE
   (Harold Melvin and the Blue Notes)
9. CUT THE CAKE
   (Average White Band)
10. UNIVERSAL LOVE
    (MFSB)

JAZZ ALBUMS

1. MISTER MAGIC
   (Grover Washington Jr.)
2. TALE SPINNIN'
   (Weather Report)
3. DISCOTHEQUE
   (Herbie Mann)
4. SUN GODDESS
   (Ramsey Lewis)
5. IN THE POCKET
   (Stanley Turrentine)

6. EXPANSIONS
   (Lonnie Liston Smith)
7. THE AURA WILL PREVAIL
   (George Duke)
8. CHICAGO THEME
   (Hubert Laws)
9. BRECKER BROTHERS
   (Brecker Brothers)
10. NO MYSTERY
    (Return to Forever featuring Chick Corea)

COUNTRY SINGLES

1. MOVIN' ON
   (Merle Haggard)
2. TOUCH THE HAND
   (Conway Twitty)
3. LIZZIE AND THE RAINMAN
   (Tanya Tucker)
4. JUST GET UP AND CLOSE THE DOOR
   (Johnny Rodriguez)
5. RECONSIDER ME
   (Narvel Felts)
6. EVERYTIME YOU TOUCH ME (I GET HIGH)
   (Charlie Rich)
7. THERE I SAID IT
   (Margo Smith)
8. LITTLE BAND OF GOLD
   (Sonny James)
9. THAT'S WHEN MY WOMAN BEGINS
   (Tommy Overstreet)
10. CLASSIFIED
    (C.W. McCall)

COUNTRY ALBUMS

1. KEEP MOVIN' ON
   (Merle Haggard)
2. BEFORE THE NEXT TEARDROP FALLS
   (Freddy Fender)
3. YOU'RE MY BEST FRIEND
   (Don Williams)
4. TANYA TUCKER
   (Tanya Tucker)
5. PHONE CALL FROM GOD
   (Jerry Jordan)
6. JUST GET UP AND CLOSE THE DOOR
   (Johnny Rodriguez)
7. I'M JESSI COLTER
   (Jessi Colter)
8. MICKEY'S MOVIN' ON
   (Mickey Gilley)
9. STILL THINKIN' ABOUT YOU
   (Billy "Crash" Craddock)
10. EVERYTIME YOU TOUCH ME (I GET HIGH)
    (Charlie Rich)

JULY 19, 1975

POP SINGLES

1. LISTEN TO WHAT THE MAN SAID
   (Paul McCartney and Wings)
2. LOVE WILL KEEP US TOGETHER
   (The Captain and Tennille)
3. THE HUSTLE
   (Van McCoy and the Soul City Symphony)
4. ONE OF THESE NIGHTS
   (The Eagles)
5. MAGIC
   (Pilot)
6. SWEARIN' TO GOD
   (Frankie Valli)
7. I'M NOT IN LOVE
   (10 C.C.)
8. MIDNIGHT BLUE
   (Melissa Manchester)
9. PLEASE MR. PLEASE
   (Olivia Newton-John)
10. ROCKIN' CHAIR
    (Gwen McCrae)

POP ALBUMS

1. ONE OF THESE NIGHTS
   (The Eagles)
2. THE HEAT IS ON
   (Isley Brothers)
3. CAPTAIN FANTASTIC AND THE BROWN DIRT COWBOY
   (Elton John)
4. VENUS AND MARS
   (Paul McCartney and Wings)
5. LOVE WILL KEEP US TOGETHER
   (The Captain and Tennille)
6. STAMPEDE
   (The Doobie Brothers)
7. FOUR-WHEEL DRIVE
   (Bachman-Turner Overdrive)
8. HEARTS
   (America)
9. THAT'S THE WAY OF THE WORLD
   (Earth, Wind and Fire)
10. MADE IN THE SHADE
    (The Rolling Stones)

BLACK SINGLES

1. THE HUSTLE
   (Van McCoy and the Soul City Symphony)
2. FIGHT THE POWER, PART 1
   (Isley Brothers)
3. ROCKIN' CHAIR
   (Gwen McCrae)
4. SOONER OR LATER
   (The Impressions)
5. LOVE WON'T LET ME WAIT
   (Major Harris)
6. JUST A LITTLE BIT OF YOU
   (Michael Jackson)
7. SLIPPERY WHEN WET
   (Commodores)
8. FREE MAN
   (South Shore Commission)
9. SEXY
   (MFSB)
10. GET DOWN TONIGHT
    (KC and the Sunshine Band)

BLACK ALBUMS

1. THE HEAT IS ON
   (Isley Brothers)
2. SURVIVAL
   (The O'Jays)
3. THAT'S THE WAY OF THE WORLD
   (Earth, Wind and Fire)
4. MISTER MAGIC
   (Grover Washington Jr.)
5. CHOCOLATE CHIP
   (Isaac Hayes)
6. A SONG FOR YOU
   (Temptations)
7. DISCO BABY
   (Van McCoy and the Soul City Symphony)
8. CUT THE CAKE
   (Average White Band)
9. TO BE TRUE
   (Harold Melvin and the Blue Notes)
10. THE HIT MAN
    (Eddie Kendricks)

JAZZ ALBUMS

1. MISTER MAGIC
   (Grover Washington Jr.)
2. TALE SPINNIN'
   (Weather Report)
3. DISCOTHEQUE
   (Herbie Mann)
4. SUN GODDESS
   (Ramsey Lewis)
5. CHICAGO THEME
   (Hubert Laws)
6. EXPANSIONS
   (Lonnie Liston Smith)

7. BRECKER BROTHERS
   (Brecker Brothers)
8. IN THE POCKET
   (Stanley Turrentine)
9. THE AURA WILL PREVAIL
   (George Duke)
10. SHABAZZ
    (Billy Cobham)

COUNTRY SINGLES

1. TOUCH THE HAND
   (Conway Twitty)
2. MOVIN' ON
   (Merle Haggard)
3. JUST GET UP AND CLOSE THE DOOR
   (Johnny Rodriguez)
4. EVERYTIME YOU TOUCH ME (I GET HIGH)
   (Charlie Rich)
5. THAT'S WHEN MY WOMAN BEGINS
   (Tommy Overstreet)
6. RECONSIDER ME
   (Narvel Felts)
7. WASTED DAYS AND WASTED NIGHTS
   (Freddy Fender)
8. LIZZIE AND THE RAINMAN
   (Tanya Tucker)
9. LOVE IN THE HOT AFTERNOON
   (Gene Watson)
10. CLASSIFIED
    (C.W. McCall)

COUNTRY ALBUMS

1. BEFORE THE NEXT TEARDROP FALLS
   (Freddy Fender)
2. KEEP MOVIN' ON
   (Merle Haggard)
3. YOU'RE MY BEST FRIEND
   (Don Williams)
4. TANYA TUCKER
   (Tanya Tucker)
5. JUST GET UP AND CLOSE THE DOOR
   (Johnny Rodriguez)
6. PHONE CALL FROM GOD
   (Jerry Jordan)
7. EVERYTIME YOU TOUCH ME (I GET HIGH)
   (Charlie Rich)
8. MICKEY'S MOVIN' ON
   (Mickey Gilley)
9. STILL THINKIN' ABOUT YOU
   (Billy "Crash" Craddock)
10. I'M JESSI COLTER
    (Jessi Colter)

JULY 26, 1975

POP SINGLES

1. LISTEN TO WHAT THE MAN SAID
   (Paul McCartney and Wings)
2. LOVE WILL KEEP US TOGETHER
   (The Captain and Tennille)
3. ONE OF THESE NIGHTS
   (The Eagles)
4. I'M NOT IN LOVE
   (10 C.C.)
5. MIDNIGHT BLUE
   (Melissa Manchester)
6. SWEARIN' TO GOD
   (Frankie Valli)
7. PLEASE MR. PLEASE
   (Olivia Newton-John)
8. THE HUSTLE
   (Van McCoy and the Soul City Symphony)
9. WHY CAN'T WE BE FRIENDS
   (War)
10. JIVE TALKIN'
    (The Bee Gees)

POP ALBUMS

1. ONE OF THESE NIGHTS
   (The Eagles)
2. THE HEAT IS ON
   (Isley Brothers)
3. CAPTAIN FANTASTIC AND THE BROWN DIRT COWBOY
   (Elton John)
4. VENUS AND MARS
   (Paul McCartney and Wings)
5. LOVE WILL KEEP US TOGETHER
   (The Captain and Tennille)
6. CUT THE CAKE
   (Average White Band)
7. THAT'S THE WAY OF THE WORLD
   (Earth, Wind and Fire)
8. WHY CAN'T WE BE FRIENDS
   (War)
9. MADE IN THE SHADE
   (The Rolling Stones)
10. METAMORPHOSIS
    (The Rolling Stones)

BLACK SINGLES

1. FIGHT THE POWER, PART 1
   (Isley Brothers)
2. THE HUSTLE
   (Van McCoy and the Soul City Symphony)
3. ROCKIN' CHAIR
   (Gwen McCrae)
4. SOONER OR LATER
   (The Impressions)
5. GET DOWN TONIGHT
   (KC and the Sunshine Band)
6. FREE MAN
   (South Shore Commission)
7. HOPE THAT WE CAN BE TOGETHER SOON
   (Sharon Paige and Harold Melvin and the Blue Notes)
8. LOVE WON'T LET ME WAIT
   (Major Harris)
9. SEXY
   (MFSB)
10. JUST A LITTLE BIT OF YOU
    (Michael Jackson)

BLACK ALBUMS

1. THE HEAT IS ON
   (Isley Brothers)
2. SURVIVAL
   (The O'Jays)
3. THAT'S THE WAY OF THE WORLD
   (Earth, Wind and Fire)
4. MISTER MAGIC
   (Grover Washington Jr.)
5. CHOCOLATE CHIP
   (Isaac Hayes)
6. A SONG FOR YOU
   (Temptations)
7. CUT THE CAKE
   (Average White Band)
8. TO BE TRUE
   (Harold Melvin and the Blue Notes)
9. DISCO BABY
   (Van McCoy and the Soul City Symphony)
10. THE HIT MAN
    (Eddie Kendricks)

JAZZ ALBUMS

1. MISTER MAGIC
   (Grover Washington Jr.)
2. CHICAGO THEME
   (Hubert Laws)
3. SUN GODDESS
   (Ramsey Lewis)
4. TALE SPINNIN'
   (Weather Report)
5. EXPANSIONS
   (Lonnie Liston Smith)

6. DISCOTHEQUE
   (Herbie Mann)
7. BRECKER BROTHERS
   (Brecker Brothers)
8. SHABAZZ
   (Billy Cobham)
9. TWO
   (Bob James)
10. IN THE POCKET
    (Stanley Turrentine)

COUNTRY SINGLES

1. JUST GET UP AND CLOSE THE DOOR
   (Johnny Rodriguez)
2. EVERYTIME YOU TOUCH ME (I GET HIGH)
   (Charlie Rich)
3. TOUCH THE HAND
   (Conway Twitty)
4. THAT'S WHEN MY WOMAN BEGINS
   (Tommy Overstreet)
5. WASTED DAYS AND WASTED NIGHTS
   (Freddy Fender)
6. LOVE IN THE HOT AFTERNOON
   (Gene Watson)
7. MOVIN' ON
   (Merle Haggard)
8. FEELINS'
   (Conway Twitty and Loretta Lynn)
9. PLEASE MR. PLEASE
   (Olivia Newton-John)
10. I WANT TO HOLD YOU IN MY DREAMS
    TONIGHT
    (Stella Parton)

COUNTRY ALBUMS

1. BEFORE THE NEXT TEARDROP FALLS
   (Freddy Fender)
2. KEEP MOVIN' ON
   (Merle Haggard)
3. JUST GET UP AND CLOSE THE DOOR
   (Johnny Rodriguez)
4. EVERYTIME YOU TOUCH ME (I GET HIGH)
   (Charlie Rich)
5. YOU'RE MY BEST FRIEND
   (Don Williams)
6. PHONE CALL FROM GOD
   (Jerry Jordan)
7. TANYA TUCKER
   (Tanya Tucker)
8. NARVEL FELTS
   (Narvel Felts)
9. FEELINS'
   (Conway Twitty and Loretta Lynn)
10. REDHEADED STRANGER
    (Willie Nelson)

AUGUST 2, 1975

POP SINGLES

1. ONE OF THESE NIGHTS
   (The Eagles)
2. LISTEN TO WHAT THE MAN SAID
   (Paul McCartney and Wings)
3. I'M NOT IN LOVE
   (10 C.C.)
4. JIVE TALKIN'
   (The Bee Gees)
5. MIDNIGHT BLUE
   (Melissa Manchester)
6. PLEASE MR. PLEASE
   (Olivia Newton-John)
7. WHY CAN'T WE BE FRIENDS
   (War)
8. LOVE WILL KEEP US TOGETHER
   (The Captain and Tennille)
9. SOMEONE SAVED MY LIFE TONIGHT
   (Elton John)
10. THE WAY WE WERE/TRY TO REMEMBER
    (Gladys Knight and the Pips)

POP ALBUMS

1. THE HEAT IS ON
   (Isley Brothers)
2. ONE OF THESE NIGHTS
   (The Eagles)
3. CAPTAIN FANTASTIC AND THE BROWN
   DIRT COWBOY
   (Elton John)
4. CUT THE CAKE
   (Average White Band)
5. LOVE WILL KEEP US TOGETHER
   (The Captain and Tennille)
6. WHY CAN'T WE BE FRIENDS
   (War)
7. VENUS AND MARS
   (Paul McCartney and Wings)
8. THAT'S THE WAY OF THE WORLD
   (Earth, Wind and Fire)
9. MADE IN THE SHADE
   (The Rolling Stones)
10. RED OCTOPUS
    (The Jefferson Starship)

BLACK SINGLES

1. FIGHT THE POWER, PART 1
   (Isley Brothers)
2. GET DOWN TONIGHT
   (KC and the Sunshine Band)
3. HOPE THAT WE CAN BE TOGETHER SOON
   *(Sharon Paige and Harold Melvin and the
   Blue Notes)*
4. SOONER OR LATER
   (The Impressions)
5. THE HUSTLE
   (Van McCoy and the Soul City Symphony)
6. FREE MAN
   (South Shore Commission)
7. ROCKIN' CHAIR
   (Gwen McCrae)
8. LOVE WON'T LET ME WAIT
   (Major Harris)
9. SEXY
   (MFSB)
10. THREE STEPS FROM TRUE LOVE
    (The Reflections)

BLACK ALBUMS

1. THE HEAT IS ON
   (Isley Brothers)
2. SURVIVAL
   (The O'Jays)
3. THAT'S THE WAY OF THE WORLD
   (Earth, Wind and Fire)
4. CHOCOLATE CHIP
   (Isaac Hayes)
5. TO BE TRUE
   (Harold Melvin and the Blue Notes)
6. MISTER MAGIC
   (Grover Washington Jr.)
7. CUT THE CAKE
   (Average White Band)
8. WHY CAN'T WE BE FRIENDS
   (War)
9. DISCO BABY
   (Van McCoy and the Soul City Symphony)
10. A SONG FOR YOU
    (Temptations)

JAZZ ALBUMS

1. MISTER MAGIC
   (Grover Washington Jr.)
2. EXPANSIONS
   (Lonnie Liston Smith)
3. CHICAGO THEME
   (Hubert Laws)
4. SUN GODDESS
   (Ramsey Lewis)
5. TALE SPINNIN'
   (Weather Report)

6. DISCOTHEQUE
   (Herbie Mann)
7. SHABAZZ
   (Billy Cobham)
8. TWO
   (Bob James)
9. BRECKER BROTHERS
   (Brecker Brothers)
10. NO MYSTERY
    (Return to Forever featuring Chick Corea)

COUNTRY SINGLES

1. EVERYTIME YOU TOUCH ME (I GET HIGH)
   (Charlie Rich)
2. WASTED DAYS AND WASTED NIGHTS
   (Freddy Fender)
3. FEELINS'
   (Conway Twitty and Loretta Lynn)
4. THAT'S WHEN MY WOMAN BEGINS
   (Tommy Overstreet)
5. LOVE IN THE HOT AFTERNOON
   (Gene Watson)
6. PLEASE MR. PLEASE
   (Olivia Newton-John)
7. THE SEEKER
   (Dolly Parton)
8. RHINESTONE COWBOY
   (Glen Campbell)
9. I WANT TO HOLD YOU IN MY DREAMS
   TONIGHT
   (Stella Parton)
10. DEAL
    (Tom T. Hall)

COUNTRY ALBUMS

1. BEFORE THE NEXT TEARDROP FALLS
   (Freddy Fender)
2. EVERYTIME YOU TOUCH ME (I GET HIGH)
   (Charlie Rich)
3. JUST GET UP AND CLOSE THE DOOR
   (Johnny Rodriguez)
4. KEEP MOVIN' ON
   (Merle Haggard)
5. FEELINS'
   (Conway Twitty and Loretta Lynn)
6. NARVEL FELTS
   (Narvel Felts)
7. MISTY
   (Ray Stevens)
8. REDHEADED STRANGER
   (Willie Nelson)
9. TODAY
   (Elvis Presley)
10. PHONE CALL FROM GOD
    (Jerry Jordan)

AUGUST 9, 1975

POP SINGLES

1. JIVE TALKIN'
   (The Bee Gees)
2. LISTEN TO WHAT THE MAN SAID
   (Paul McCartney and Wings)
3. I'M NOT IN LOVE
   (10 C.C.)
4. ONE OF THESE NIGHTS
   (The Eagles)
5. PLEASE MR. PLEASE
   (Olivia Newton-John)
6. WHY CAN'T WE BE FRIENDS
   (War)
7. SOMEONE SAVED MY LIFE TONIGHT
   (Elton John)
8. MIDNIGHT BLUE
   (Melissa Manchester)
9. THE WAY WE WERE/TRY TO REMEMBER
   (Gladys Knight and the Pips)

10. DYNOMITE
    (Tony Camillo's Bazuka)

POP ALBUMS

1. THE HEAT IS ON
   (Isley Brothers)
2. ONE OF THESE NIGHTS
   (The Eagles)
3. CAPTAIN FANTASTIC AND THE BROWN
   DIRT COWBOY
   (Elton John)
4. CUT THE CAKE
   (Average White Band)
5. LOVE WILL KEEP US TOGETHER
   (The Captain and Tennille)
6. WHY CAN'T WE BE FRIENDS
   (War)
7. RED OCTOPUS
   (The Jefferson Starship)
8. THAT'S THE WAY OF THE WORLD
   (Earth, Wind and Fire)
9. VENUS AND MARS
   (Paul McCartney and Wings)
10. CAT STEVENS' GREATEST HITS
    (Cat Stevens)

BLACK SINGLES

1. FIGHT THE POWER, PART 1
   (Isley Brothers)
2. GET DOWN TONIGHT
   (KC and the Sunshine Band)
3. HOPE THAT WE CAN BE TOGETHER
   (Sharon Paige and Harold Melvin and the
   Blue Notes)
4. SOONER OR LATER
   (The Impressions)
5. THE HUSTLE
   (Van McCoy and the Soul City Symphony)
6. FREE MAN
   (South Shore Commission)
7. ROCKIN' CHAIR
   (Gwen McCrae)
8. THREE STEPS FROM TRUE LOVE
   (The Reflections)
9. 7-6-5-4-3-2-1 (BLOW YOUR WHISTLE)
   (Gary Toms Empire)
10. YOUR LOVE
    (Graham Central Station)

BLACK ALBUMS

1. THE HEAT IS ON
   (Isley Brothers)
2. SURVIVAL
   (The O'Jays)
3. THAT'S THE WAY OF THE WORLD
   (Earth, Wind and Fire)
4. CHOCOLATE CHIP
   (Isaac Hayes)
5. TO BE TRUE
   (Harold Melvin and the Blue Notes)
6. MISTER MAGIC
   (Grover Washington Jr.)
7. WHY CAN'T WE BE FRIENDS
   (War)
8. DISCO BABY
   (Van McCoy and the Soul City Symphony)
9. CUT THE CAKE
   (Average White Band)
10. GET DOWN
    (Joe Simon)

JAZZ ALBUMS

1. MISTER MAGIC
   (Grover Washington Jr.)
2. EXPANSIONS
   (Lonnie Liston Smith)

3. CHICAGO THEME
   (Hubert Laws)
4. TALE SPINNIN'
   (Weather Report)
5. SHABAZZ
   (Billy Cobham)
6. DISCOTHEQUE
   (Herbie Mann)
7. SUN GODDESS
   (Ramsey Lewis)
8. TWO
   (Bob James)
9. LIQUID LOVE
   (Freddie Hubbard)
10. NO MYSTERY
    (Return to Forever featuring Chick Corea)

COUNTRY SINGLES

1. WASTED DAYS AND WASTED NIGHTS
   (Freddy Fender)
2. FEELINS'
   (Conway Twitty and Loretta Lynn)
3. RHINESTONE COWBOY
   (Glen Campbell)
4. PLEASE MR. PLEASE
   (Olivia Newton-John)
5. LOVE IN THE HOT AFTERNOON
   (Gene Watson)
6. THE SEEKER
   (Dolly Parton)
7. EVERYTIME YOU TOUCH ME (I GET HIGH)
   (Charlie Rich)
8. I WANT TO HOLD YOU IN MY DREAMS
   TONIGHT
   (Stella Parton)
9. DEAL
   (Tom T. Hall)
10. THAT'S WHEN MY WOMAN BEGINS
    (Tommy Overstreet)

COUNTRY ALBUMS

1. BEFORE THE NEXT TEARDROP FALLS
   (Freddy Fender)
2. EVERYTIME YOU TOUCH ME (I GET HIGH)
   (Charlie Rich)
3. FEELINS'
   (Conway Twitty and Loretta Lynn)
4. NARVEL FELTS
   (Narvel Felts)
5. KEEP MOVIN' ON
   (Merle Haggard)
6. MISTY
   (Ray Stevens)
7. REDHEADED STRANGER
   (Willie Nelson)
8. TODAY
   (Elvis Presley)
9. JUST GET UP AND CLOSE THE DOOR
   (Johnny Rodriguez)
10. DREAMING MY DREAMS
    (Waylon Jennings)

AUGUST 16, 1975

POP SINGLES

1. JIVE TALKIN'
   (The Bee Gees)
2. SOMEONE SAVED MY LIFE TONIGHT
   (Elton John)
3. LISTEN TO WHAT THE MAN SAID
   (Paul McCartney and Wings)
4. I'M NOT IN LOVE
   (10 C.C.)
5. WHY CAN'T WE BE FRIENDS
   (War)
6. GET DOWN TONIGHT
   (KC and the Sunshine Band)

7. PLEASE MR. PLEASE
   (Olivia Newton-John)
8. FALLIN' IN LOVE
   (Hamilton, Joe Frank and Reynolds)
9. HOW SWEET IT IS
   (James Taylor)
10. RHINESTONE COWBOY
    (Glen Campbell)

POP ALBUMS

1. ONE OF THESE NIGHTS
   (The Eagles)
2. THE HEAT IS ON
   (Isley Brothers)
3. CAPTAIN FANTASTIC AND THE BROWN
   DIRT COWBOY
   (Elton John)
4. RED OCTOPUS
   (The Jefferson Starship)
5. CUT THE CAKE
   (Average White Band)
6. WHY CAN'T WE BE FRIENDS
   (War)
7. CAT STEVENS' GREATEST HITS
   (Cat Stevens)
8. THAT'S THE WAY OF THE WORLD
   (Earth, Wind and Fire)
9. LOVE WILL KEEP US TOGETHER
   (The Captain and Tennille)
10. VENUS AND MARS
    (Paul McCartney and Wings)

BLACK SINGLES

1. GET DOWN TONIGHT
   (KC and the Sunshine Band)
2. FIGHT THE POWER, PART 1
   (Isley Brothers)
3. HOPE THAT WE CAN BE TOGETHER SOON
   (Sharon Paige and Harold Melvin and the
   Blue Notes)
4. YOUR LOVE
   (Graham Central Station)
5. SOONER OR LATER
   (The Impressions)
6. THE HUSTLE
   (Van McCoy and the Soul City Symphony)
7. ROCKIN' CHAIR
   (Gwen McCrae)
8. DREAM MERCHANT
   (New Birth)
9. DREAMING A DREAM
   (Crown Heights Affair)
10. FREE MAN
    (South Shore Commission)

BLACK ALBUMS

1. THE HEAT IS ON
   (Isley Brothers)
2. THAT'S THE WAY OF THE WORLD
   (Earth, Wind and Fire)
3. SURVIVAL
   (The O'Jays)
4. CHOCOLATE CHIP
   (Isaac Hayes)
5. TO BE TRUE
   (Harold Melvin and the Blue Notes)
6. WHY CAN'T WE BE FRIENDS
   (War)
7. NON-STOP
   (B.T. Express)
8. AIN'T NO 'BOUT-A-DOUBT IT
   (Graham Central Station)
9. DISCO BABY
   (Van McCoy and the Soul City Symphony)
10. GET DOWN
    (Joe Simon)

JAZZ ALBUMS

1. MISTER MAGIC
   (Grover Washington Jr.)
2. EXPANSIONS
   (Lonnie Liston Smith)
3. CHICAGO THEME
   (Hubert Laws)
4. TALE SPINNIN'
   (Weather Report)
5. SUN GODDESS
   (Ramsey Lewis)
6. LIQUID LOVE
   (Freddie Hubbard)
7. SHABAZZ
   (Billy Cobham)
8. DISCOTHEQUE
   (Herbie Mann)
9. LEVEL ONE
   (Eleventh House featuring Larry Coryell)
10. BECK
    (Joe Beck)

COUNTRY SINGLES

1. FEELINS'
   (Conway Twitty and Loretta Lynn)
2. RHINESTONE COWBOY
   (Glen Campbell)
3. WASTED DAYS AND WASTED NIGHTS
   (Freddy Fender)
4. PLEASE MR. PLEASE
   (Olivia Newton-John)
5. THE SEEKER
   (Dolly Parton)
6. LOVE IN THE HOT AFTERNOON
   (Gene Watson)
7. I WANT TO HOLD YOU IN MY DREAMS
   TONIGHT
   (Stella Parton)
8. SPRING
   (Tanya Tucker)
9. DEAL
   (Tom T. Hall)
10. I LOVE THE BLUES AND THE BOOGIE
    WOOGIE
    (Billy "Crash" Craddock)

COUNTRY ALBUMS

1. EVERYTIME YOU TOUCH ME (I GET HIGH)
   (Charlie Rich)
2. FEELINS'
   (Conway Twitty and Loretta Lynn)
3. NARVEL FELTS
   (Narvel Felts)
4. BEFORE THE NEXT TEARDROP FALLS
   (Freddy Fender)
5. REDHEADED STRANGER
   (Willie Nelson)
6. MISTY
   (Ray Stevens)
7. TODAY
   (Elvis Presley)
8. DREAMING MY DREAMS
   (Waylon Jennings)
9. KEEP MOVIN' ON
   (Merle Haggard)
10. CHARLEY
    (Charley Pride)

AUGUST 23, 1975

POP SINGLES

1. SOMEONE SAVED MY LIFE TONIGHT
   (Elton John)
2. JIVE TALKIN'
   (The Bee Gees)

3. GET DOWN TONIGHT
   (KC and the Sunshine Band)
4. FALLIN' IN LOVE
   (Hamilton, Joe Frank and Reynolds)
5. LISTEN TO WHAT THE MAN SAID
   (Paul McCartney and Wings)
6. AT SEVENTEEN
   (Janis Ian)
7. HOW SWEET IT IS
   (James Taylor)
8. I'M NOT IN LOVE
   (10 C.C.)
9. WHY CAN'T WE BE FRIENDS
   (War)
10. RHINESTONE COWBOY
    (Glen Campbell)

POP ALBUMS

1. THE HEAT IS ON
   (Isley Brothers)
2. ONE OF THESE NIGHTS
   (The Eagles)
3. RED OCTOPUS
   (The Jefferson Starship)
4. CAPTAIN FANTASTIC AND THE BROWN
   DIRT COWBOY
   (Elton John)
5. CUT THE CAKE
   (Average White Band)
6. WHY CAN'T WE BE FRIENDS
   (War)
7. CAT STEVENS' GREATEST HITS
   (Cat Stevens)
8. THAT'S THE WAY OF THE WORLD
   (Earth, Wind and Fire)
9. LOVE WILL KEEP US TOGETHER
   (The Captain and Tennille)
10. VENUS AND MARS
    (Paul McCartney and Wings)

BLACK SINGLES

1. GET DOWN TONIGHT
   (KC and the Sunshine Band)
2. FIGHT THE POWER, PART 1
   (Isley Brothers)
3. YOUR LOVE
   (Graham Central Station)
4. HOPE THAT WE CAN BE TOGETHER SOON
   (Sharon Paige and Harold Melvin and the
   Blue Notes)
5. DREAM MERCHANT
   (New Birth)
6. THE HUSTLE
   (Van McCoy and the Soul City Symphony)
7. DREAMING A DREAM
   (Crown Heights Affair)
8. ROCKIN' CHAIR
   (Gwen McCrae)
9. GET THE CREAM OFF THE TOP
   (Eddie Kendricks)
10. THAT'S THE WAY OF THE WORLD
    (Earth, Wind and Fire)

BLACK ALBUMS

1. THE HEAT IS ON
   (Isley Brothers)
2. THAT'S THE WAY OF THE WORLD
   (Earth, Wind and Fire)
3. CHOCOLATE CHIP
   (Isaac Hayes)
4. NON-STOP
   (B.T. Express)
5. WHY CAN'T WE BE FRIENDS
   (War)
6. AIN'T NO 'BOUT-A-DOUBT IT
   (Graham Central Station)
7. PICK OF THE LITTER
   (Spinners)
8. SURVIVAL
   (The O'Jays)

9. DISCO BABY
   (Van McCoy and the Soul City Symphony)
10. TO BE TRUE
    (Harold Melvin and the Blue Notes)

JAZZ ALBUMS

1. MISTER MAGIC
   (Grover Washington Jr.)
2. EXPANSIONS
   (Lonnie Liston Smith)
3. CHICAGO THEME
   (Hubert Laws)
4. TALE SPINNIN'
   (Weather Report)
5. LIQUID LOVE
   (Freddie Hubbard)
6. SUN GODDESS
   (Ramsey Lewis)
7. LEVEL ONE
   (The Eleventh House featuring Larry Coryell)
8. DISCOTHEQUE
   (Herbie Mann)
9. BECK
   (Joe Beck)
10. SHABAZZ
    (Billy Cobham)

COUNTRY SINGLES

1. RHINESTONE COWBOY
   (Glen Campbell)
2. FEELINS'
   (Conway Twitty and Loretta Lynn)
3. PLEASE MR. PLEASE
   (Olivia Newton-John)
4. WASTED DAYS AND WASTED NIGHTS
   (Freddy Fender)
5. THE SEEKER
   (Dolly Parton)
6. LOVE IN THE HOT AFTERNOON
   (Gene Watson)
7. THE FIRST TIME
   (Freddie Hart)
8. SPRING
   (Tanya Tucker)
9. I LOVE THE BLUES AND THE BOOGIE
   WOOGIE
   (Billy "Crash" Craddock)
10. WOMAN IN THE BACK OF MY MIND
    (Mel Tillis)

COUNTRY ALBUMS

1. FEELINS'
   (Conway Twitty and Loretta Lynn)
2. EVERYTIME YOU TOUCH ME (I GET HIGH)
   (Charlie Rich)
3. NARVEL FELTS
   (Narvel Felts)
4. REDHEADED STRANGER
   (Willie Nelson)
5. BEFORE THE NEXT TEARDROP FALLS
   (Freddy Fender)
6. MISTY
   (Ray Stevens)
7. TODAY
   (Elvis Presley)
8. DREAMING MY DREAMS
   (Waylon Jennings)
9. CHARLEY
   (Charley Pride)
10. KEEP MOVIN' ON
    (Merle Haggard)

AUGUST 30, 1975

POP SINGLES

1. FALLIN' IN LOVE
   (Hamilton, Joe Frank and Reynolds)

2. GET DOWN TONIGHT
   (KC and the Sunshine Band)
3. JIVE TALKIN'
   (The Bee Gees)
4. AT SEVENTEEN
   (Janis Ian)
5. SOMEONE SAVED MY LIFE TONIGHT
   (Elton John)
6. HOW SWEET IT IS
   (James Taylor)
7. FIGHT THE POWER, PART 1
   (Isley Brothers)
8. FAME
   (David Bowie)
9. COULD IT BE MAGIC
   (Barry Manilow)
10. RHINESTONE COWBOY
    (Glen Campbell)

POP ALBUMS

1. ONE OF THESE NIGHTS
   (The Eagles)
2. THE HEAT IS ON
   (Isley Brothers)
3. RED OCTOPUS
   (The Jefferson Starship)
4. CAPTAIN FANTASTIC AND THE BROWN DIRT COWBOY
   (Elton John)
5. THAT'S THE WAY OF THE WORLD
   (Earth, Wind and Fire)
6. LOVE WILL KEEP US TOGETHER
   (The Captain and Tennille)
7. CAT STEVENS' GREATEST HITS
   (Cat Stevens)
8. WHY CAN'T WE BE FRIENDS
   (War)
9. HONEY
   (Ohio Players)
10. FANDANGO
    (ZZ Top)

BLACK SINGLES

1. GET DOWN TONIGHT
   (KC and the Sunshine Band)
2. FIGHT THE POWER, PART 1
   (Isley Brothers)
3. YOUR LOVE
   (Graham Central Station)
4. DREAM MERCHANT
   (New Birth)
5. HOPE THAT WE CAN BE TOGETHER SOON
   (Sharon Paige and Harold Melvin and the Blue Notes)
6. MAKE ME FEEL LIKE A WOMAN
   (Jackie Moore)
7. DREAMING A DREAM
   (Crown Heights Affair)
8. DO IT ANY WAY YOU WANNA
   (People's Choice)
9. GET THE CREAM OFF THE TOP
   (Eddie Kendricks)
10. THAT'S THE WAY OF THE WORLD
    (Earth, Wind and Fire)

BLACK ALBUMS

1. THE HEAT IS ON
   (Isley Brothers)
2. THAT'S THE WAY OF THE WORLD
   (Earth, Wind and Fire)
3. PICK OF THE LITTER
   (Spinners)
4. NON-STOP
   (B.T. Express)
5. WHY CAN'T WE BE FRIENDS
   (War)
6. AIN'T NO 'BOUT-A-DOUBT IT
   (Graham Central Station)
7. CHOCOLATE CHIP
   (Isaac Hayes)

8. SURVIVAL
   (The O'Jays)
9. HONEY
   (Ohio Players)
10. IS IT SOMETHING I SAID
    (Richard Pryor)

JAZZ ALBUMS

1. MISTER MAGIC
   (Grover Washington Jr.)
2. CHICAGO THEME
   (Hubert Laws)
3. EXPANSIONS
   (Lonnie Liston Smith)
4. LIQUID LOVE
   (Freddie Hubbard)
5. TALE SPINNIN'
   (Weather Report)
6. DISCOTHEQUE
   (Herbie Mann)
7. SUN GODDESS
   (Ramsey Lewis)
8. BECK
   (Joe Beck)
9. LEVEL ONE
   (Eleventh House featuring Larry Coryell)
10. SHABAZZ
    (Billy Cobham)

COUNTRY SINGLES

1. RHINESTONE COWBOY
   (Glen Campbell)
2. FEELINS'
   (Conway Twitty and Loretta Lynn)
3. WASTED DAYS AND WASTED NIGHTS
   (Freddy Fender)
4. I'LL GO TO MY GRAVE LOVING YOU
   (The Statler Brothers)
5. PLEASE MR. PLEASE
   (Olivia Newton-John)
6. THE FIRST TIME
   (Freddie Hart)
7. LOVE IN THE HOT AFTERNOON
   (Gene Watson)
8. WOMAN IN THE BACK OF MY MIND
   (Mel Tillis)
9. I LOVE THE BLUES AND THE BOOGIE WOOGIE
   (Billy "Crash" Craddock)
10. THIRD RATE ROMANCE
    (Amazing Rhythm Aces)

COUNTRY ALBUMS

1. FEELINS'
   (Conway Twitty and Loretta Lynn)
2. EVERYTIME YOU TOUCH ME (I GET HIGH)
   (Charlie Rich)
3. REDHEADED STRANGER
   (Willie Nelson)
4. NARVEL FELTS
   (Narvel Felts)
5. BEFORE THE NEXT TEARDROP FALLS
   (Freddy Fender)
6. MISTY
   (Ray Stevens)
7. DREAMING MY DREAMS
   (Waylon Jennings)
8. CHARLEY
   (Charley Pride)
9. LIVE IN PICAYUNE
   (Jerry Clower)
10. THE HIGH PRIEST OF COUNTRY MUSIC
    (Conway Twitty)

SEPTEMBER 6, 1975

POP SINGLES

1. GET DOWN TONIGHT
   (KC and the Sunshine Band)

2. FALLIN' IN LOVE
   (Hamilton, Joe Frank and Reynolds)
3. FAME
   (David Bowie)
4. AT SEVENTEEN
   (Janis Ian)
5. FIGHT THE POWER, PART I
   (Isley Brothers)
6. HOW SWEET IT IS
   (James Taylor)
7. RHINESTONE COWBOY
   (Glen Campbell)
8. COULD IT BE MAGIC
   (Barry Manilow)
9. JIVE TALKIN'
   (The Bee Gees)
10. THAT'S THE WAY OF THE WORLD
    (Earth, Wind and Fire)

POP ALBUMS

1. CAPTAIN FANTASTIC AND THE BROWN DIRT COWBOY
   (Elton John)
2. ONE OF THESE NIGHTS
   (The Eagles)
3. RED OCTOPUS
   (The Jefferson Starship)
4. THE HEAT IS ON
   (Isley Brothers)
5. THAT'S THE WAY OF THE WORLD
   (Earth, Wind and Fire)
6. LOVE WILL KEEP US TOGETHER
   (The Captain and Tennille)
7. HONEY
   (Ohio Players)
8. AIN'T NO 'BOUT-A-DOUBT IT
   (Graham Central Station)
9. FANDANGO
   (ZZ Top)
10. BETWEEN THE LINES
    (Janis Ian)

BLACK SINGLES

1. GET DOWN TONIGHT
   (KC and the Sunshine Band)
2. YOUR LOVE
   (Graham Central Station)
3. DO IT ANY WAY YOU WANNA
   (People's Choice)
4. DREAM MERCHANT
   (New Birth)
5. MAKE ME FEEL LIKE A WOMAN
   (Jackie Moore)
6. FIGHT THE POWER, PART I
   (Isley Brothers)
7. HOW LONG (BETCHA GOT A CHICK ON THE SIDE)
   (The Pointer Sisters)
8. HOPE THAT WE CAN BE TOGETHER SOON
   (Sharon Paige and Harold Melvin and the Blue Notes)
9. DREAMING A DREAM
   (Crown Heights Affair)
10. THIS WILL BE
    (Natalie Cole)

BLACK ALBUMS

1. THE HEAT IS ON
   (Isley Brothers)
2. PICK OF THE LITTER
   (Spinners)
3. HONEY
   (Ohio Players)
4. IS IT SOMETHING I SAID
   (Richard Pryor)
5. AIN'T NO 'BOUT-A-DOUBT IT
   (Graham Central Station)
6. NON-STOP
   (B.T. Express)
7. THAT'S THE WAY OF THE WORLD
   (Earth, Wind and Fire)

8. WHY CAN'T WE BE FRIENDS
   (War)
9. CHOCOLATE CHIP
   (Isaac Hayes)
10. MELLOW MADNESS
    (Quincy Jones)

JAZZ ALBUMS

1. MISTER MAGIC
   (Grover Washington Jr.)
2. CHICAGO THEME
   (Hubert Laws)
3. EXPANSIONS
   (Lonnie Liston Smith)
4. TALE SPINNIN'
   (Weather Report)
5. LIQUID LOVE
   (Freddie Hubbard)
6. SUN GODDESS
   (Ramsey Lewis)
7. DISCOTHEQUE
   (Herbie Mann)
8. WHAT A DIFFERENCE A DAY MADE
   (Esther Phillips with Joe Beck)
9. STEPPING INTO TOMORROW
   (Donald Byrd)
10. MELLOW MADNESS
    (Quincy Jones)

COUNTRY SINGLES

1. I'LL GO TO MY GRAVE LOVING YOU
   (The Statler Brothers)
2. RHINESTONE COWBOY
   (Glen Campbell)
3. IF I COULD ONLY WIN YOUR LOVE
   (Emmylou Harris)
4. BLUE EYES CRYING IN THE RAIN
   (Willie Nelson)
5. THE FIRST TIME
   (Freddie Hart)
6. DAYDREAMS ABOUT NIGHT THINGS
   (Ronnie Mislap)
7. THIRD RATE ROMANCE
   (Amazing Rhythm Aces)
8. WOMAN IN THE BACK OF MY MIND
   (Mel Tillis)
9. WASTED DAYS AND WASTED NIGHTS
   (Freddy Fender)
10. BANDY THE RODEO CLOWN
    (Moe Bandy)

COUNTRY ALBUMS

1. REDHEADED STRANGER
   (Willie Nelson)
2. FEELINS'
   (Conway Twitty and Loretta Lynn)
3. EVERYTIME YOU TOUCH ME (I GET HIGH)
   (Charlie Rich)
4. DREAMING MY DREAMS
   (Waylon Jennings)
5. MISTY
   (Ray Stevens)
6. THE HIGH PRIEST OF COUNTRY MUSIC
   (Conway Twitty)
7. CHARLEY
   (Charley Pride)
8. LIVE IN PICAYUNE
   (Jerry Clower)
9. RHINESTONE COWBOY
   (Glen Campbell)
10. BEFORE THE NEXT TEARDROP FALLS
    (Freddy Fender)

SEPTEMBER 13, 1975

POP SINGLES

1. GET DOWN TONIGHT
   (KC and the Sunshine Band)

2. FAME
   (David Bowie)
3. FALLIN' IN LOVE
   (Hamilton, Joe Frank and Reynolds)
4. RHINESTONE COWBOY
   (Glen Campbell)
5. FIGHT THE POWER, PART I
   (Isley Brothers)
6. AT SEVENTEEN
   (Janis Ian)
7. THAT'S THE WAY OF THE WORLD
   (Earth, Wind and Fire)
8. COULD IT BE MAGIC
   (Barry Manilow)
9. RUN JOEY RUN
   (David Geddes)
10. WASTED DAYS AND WASTED NIGHTS
    (Freddy Fender)

POP ALBUMS

1. RED OCTOPUS
   (The Jefferson Starship)
2. CAPTAIN FANTASTIC AND THE BROWN
   DIRT COWBOY
   (Elton John)
3. ONE OF THESE NIGHTS
   (The Eagles)
4. THE HEAT IS ON
   (Isley Brothers)
5. THAT'S THE WAY OF THE WORLD
   (Earth, Wind and Fire)
6. HONEY
   (Ohio Players)
7. IS IT SOMETHING I SAID
   (Richard Pryor)
8. AIN'T NO 'BOUT-A-DOUBT IT
   (Graham Central Station)
9. PICK OF THE LITTER
   (Spinners)
10. BORN TO RUN
    (Bruce Springsteen)

BLACK SINGLES

1. DO IT ANY WAY YOU WANNA
   (People's Choice)
2. GET DOWN TONIGHT
   (KC and the Sunshine Band)
3. YOUR LOVE
   (Graham Central Station)
4. HOW LONG (BETCHA GOT A CHICK ON
   THE SIDE)
   (The Pointer Sisters)
5. MAKE ME FEEL LIKE A WOMAN
   (Jackie Moore)
6. DREAM MERCHANT
   (New Birth)
7. THIS WILL BE
   (Natalie Cole)
8. FIGHT THE POWER, PART I
   (Isley Brothers)
9. IT ONLY TAKES A MINUTE
   (Tavares)
10. GLASS HOUSE
    (Temptations)

BLACK ALBUMS

1. THE HEAT IS ON
   (Isley Brothers)
2. PICK OF THE LITTER
   (Spinners)
3. HONEY
   (Ohio Players)
4. IS IT SOMETHING I SAID
   (Richard Pryor)
5. AIN'T NO 'BOUT-A-DOUBT IT
   (Graham Central Station)
6. NON-STOP
   (B.T. Express)
7. THAT'S THE WAY OF THE WORLD
   (Earth, Wind and Fire)
8. MELLOW MADNESS
   (Quincy Jones)

9. WHY CAN'T WE BE FRIENDS
   (War)
10. SPIRIT OF THE BOOGIE
    (Kool and the Gang)

JAZZ ALBUMS

1. MISTER MAGIC
   (Grover Washington Jr.)
2. CHICAGO THEME
   (Hubert Laws)
3. EXPANSIONS
   (Lonnie Liston Smith)
4. TALE SPINNIN'
   (Weather Report)
5. SUN GODDESS
   (Ramsey Lewis)
6. MELLOW MADNESS
   (Quincy Jones)
7. WHAT A DIFFERENCE A DAY MADE
   (Esther Phillips with Joe Beck)
8. STEPPING INTO TOMORROW
   (Donald Byrd)
9. DISCOTHEQUE
   (Herbie Mann)
10. LIQUID LOVE
    (Freddie Hubbard)

COUNTRY SINGLES

1. IF I COULD ONLY WIN YOUR LOVE
   (Emmylou Harris)
2. BLUE EYES CRYING IN THE RAIN
   (Willie Nelson)
3. DAYDREAMS ABOUT NIGHT THINGS
   (Ronnie Milsap)
4. THE FIRST TIME
   (Freddie Hart)
5. THIRD RATE ROMANCE
   (Amazing Rhythm Aces)
6. I'LL GO TO MY GRAVE LOVING YOU
   (The Statler Brothers)
7. BANDY THE RODEO CLOWN
   (Moe Bandy)
8. RHINESTONE COWBOY
   (Glen Campbell)
9. YOU NEVER EVEN CALLED ME BY MY
   NAME
   (David Allen Coe)
10. DON'T CRY JONI
    (Conway Twitty)

COUNTRY ALBUMS

1. REDHEADED STRANGER
   (Willie Nelson)
2. FEELINS'
   (Conway Twitty and Loretta Lynn)
3. DREAMING MY DREAMS
   (Waylon Jennings)
4. THE HIGH PRIEST OF COUNTRY MUSIC
   (Conway Twitty)
5. MISTY
   (Ray Stevens)
6. RHINESTONE COWBOY
   (Glen Campbell)
7. CHARLEY
   (Charley Pride)
8. LIVE IN PICAYUNE
   (Jerry Clower)
9. THE BEST OF THE STATLER BROTHERS
   (The Statler Brothers)
10. EVERYTIME YOU TOUCH ME (I GET HIGH)
    (Charlie Rich)

SEPTEMBER 20, 1975

POP SINGLES

1. RHINESTONE COWBOY
   (Glen Campbell)

2. FAME
   (David Bowie)
3. GET DOWN TONIGHT
   (KC and the Sunshine Band)
4. WASTED DAYS AND WASTED NIGHTS
   (Freddy Fender)
5. RUN JOEY RUN
   (David Geddes)
6. THAT'S THE WAY OF THE WORLD
   (Earth, Wind and Fire)
7. I'M SORRY/CALYPSO
   (John Denver)
8. DANCE WITH ME
   (Orleans)
9. HOW LONG (BETCHA GOT A CHICK ON THE SIDE)
   (The Pointer Sisters)
10. ROCKY
    (Austin Roberts)

POP ALBUMS

1. CAPTAIN FANTASTIC AND THE BROWN DIRT COWBOY
   (Elton John)
2. ONE OF THESE NIGHTS
   (The Eagles)
3. BORN TO RUN
   (Bruce Springsteen)
4. RED OCTOPUS
   (The Jefferson Starship)
5. THE HEAT IS ON
   (Isley Brothers)
6. HONEY
   (Ohio Players)
7. IS IT SOMETHING I SAID
   (Richard Pryor)
8. PICK OF THE LITTER
   (Spinners)
9. THAT'S THE WAY OF THE WORLD
   (Earth, Wind and Fire)
10. BETWEEN THE LINES
    (Janis Ian)

BLACK SINGLES

1. DO IT ANYWAY YOU WANNA
   (People's Choice)
2. HOW LONG (BETCHA GOT A CHICK ON THE SIDE)
   (The Pointer Sisters)
3. GET DOWN TONIGHT
   (KC and the Sunshine Band)
4. THIS WILL BE
   (Natalie Cole)
5. YOUR LOVE
   (Graham Central Station)
6. IT ONLY TAKES A MINUTE
   (Tavares)
7. MAKE ME FEEL LIKE A WOMAN
   (Jackie Moore)
8. THEY JUST CAN'T STOP IT (THE GAMES PEOPLE PLAY)
   (Spinners)
9. DREAM MERCHANT
   (New Birth)
10. FIGHT THE POWER, PART I
    (Isley Brothers)

BLACK ALBUMS

1. THE HEAT IS ON
   (Isley Brothers)
2. PICK OF THE LITTER
   (Spinners)
3. HONEY
   (Ohio Players)
4. IS IT SOMETHING I SAID
   (Richard Pryor)
5. AIN'T NO 'BOUT-A-DOUBT IT
   (Graham Central Station)
6. NON-STOP
   (B.T. Express)

7. THAT'S THE WAY OF THE WORLD
   (Earth, Wind and Fire)
8. MELLOW MADNESS
   (Quincy Jones)
9. SPIRIT OF THE BOOGIE
   (Kool and the Gang)
10. KC AND THE SUNSHINE BAND
    (KC and the Sunshine Band)

JAZZ ALBUMS

1. MELLOW MADNESS
   (Quincy Jones)
2. CHAIN REACTION
   (Crusaders)
3. MISTER MAGIC
   (Grover Washington Jr.)
4. CHICAGO THEME
   (Hubert Laws)
5. WHAT A DIFFERENCE A DAY MADE
   (Esther Phillips with Joe Beck)
6. TALE SPINNIN'
   (Weather Report)
7. EXPANSIONS
   (Lonnie Liston Smith)
8. STEPPING INTO TOMORROW
   (Donald Byrd)
9. SUN GODDESS
   (Ramsey Lewis)
10. FIRST CUCKOO
    (Deodato)

COUNTRY SINGLES

1. BLUE EYES CRYING IN THE RAIN
   (Willie Nelson)
2. DAYDREAMS ABOUT NIGHT THINGS
   (Ronnie Milsap)
3. IF I COULD ONLY WIN YOUR LOVE
   (Emmylou Harris)
4. THE FIRST TIME
   (Freddie Hart)
5. THIRD RATE ROMANCE
   (Amazing Rhythm Aces)
6. BANDY THE RODEO CLOWN
   (Moe Bandy)
7. DON'T CRY JONI
   (Conway Twitty)
8. YOU NEVER EVEN CALLED ME BY MY NAME
   (David Allen Coe)
9. RHINESTONE COWBOY
   (Glen Campbell)
10. SAY FOREVER YOU'LL BE MINE
    (Porter Wagoner and Dolly Parton)

COUNTRY ALBUMS

1. RHINESTONE COWBOY
   (Glen Campbell)
2. DREAMING MY DREAMS
   (Waylon Jennings)
3. REDHEADED STRANGER
   (Willie Nelson)
4. THE HIGH PRIEST OF COUNTRY MUSIC
   (Conway Twitty)
5. FEELINS'
   (Conway Twitty and Loretta Lynn)
6. THE BEST OF THE STATLER BROTHERS
   (The Statler Brothers)
7. MISTY
   (Ray Stevens)
8. CHARLEY
   (Charley Pride)
9. THE BEST OF DOLLY PARTON
   (Dolly Parton)
10. ANNIVERSARY SPECIAL
    (Earl Scruggs Revue)

SEPTEMBER 27, 1975

POP SINGLES

1. FAME
   (David Bowie)
2. RHINESTONE COWBOY
   (Glen Campbell)
3. WASTED DAYS AND WASTED NIGHTS
   (Freddy Fender)
4. RUN JOEY RUN
   (David Geddes)
5. I'M SORRY/CALYPSO
   (John Denver)
6. DANCE WITH ME
   (Orleans)
7. HOW LONG (BETCHA GOT A CHICK ON THE SIDE)
   (The Pointer Sisters)
8. ROCKY
   (Austin Roberts)
9. GET DOWN TONIGHT
   (KC and the Sunshine Band)
10. MR. JAWS
    (Dickie Goodman)

POP ALBUMS

1. BORN TO RUN
   (Bruce Springsteen)
2. CAPTAIN FANTASTIC AND THE BROWN DIRT COWBOY
   (Elton John)
3. ONE OF THESE NIGHTS
   (The Eagles)
4. RED OCTOPUS
   (The Jefferson Starship)
5. THE HEAT IS ON
   (Isley Brothers)
6. HONEY
   (Ohio Players)
7. BLUES FOR ALLAH
   (Grateful Dead)
8. ATLANTIC CROSSING
   (Rod Stewart)
9. KC AND THE SUNSHINE BAND
   (KC and the Sunshine Band)
10. IS IT SOMETHING I SAID
    (Richard Pryor)

BLACK SINGLES

1. DO IT ANY WAY YOU WANNA
   (People's Choice)
2. HOW LONG (BETCHA GOT A CHICK ON THE SIDE)
   (The Pointer Sisters)
3. THIS WILL BE
   (Natalie Cole)
4. IT ONLY TAKES A MINUTE
   (Tavares)
5. THEY JUST CAN'T STOP IT (THE GAMES PEOPLE PLAY)
   (Spinners)
6. GET DOWN
   (KC and the Sunshine Band)
7. YOUR LOVE
   (Graham Central Station)
8. MAKE ME FEEL LIKE A WOMAN
   (Jackie Moore)
9. TO EACH HIS OWN
   (Faith, Hope and Charity)
10. BRAZIL
    (The Ritchie Family)

BLACK ALBUMS

1. IS IT SOMETHING I SAID
   (Richard Pryor)
2. THE HEAT IS ON
   (Isley Brothers)

3. KC AND THE SUNSHINE BAND
   (KC and the Sunshine Band)
4. AIN'T NO 'BOUT-A-DOUBT IT
   (Graham Central Station)
5. PICK OF THE LITTER
   (Spinners)
6. HONEY
   (Ohio Players)
7. NON-STOP
   (B.T. Express)
8. MELLOW MADNESS
   (Quincy Jones)
9. BOOGIE DOWN U.S.A.
   (People's Choice)
10. SPIRIT OF THE BOOGIE
    (Kool and the Gang)

JAZZ ALBUMS

1. MELLOW MADNESS
   (Quincy Jones)
2. CHAIN REACTION
   (Crusaders)
3. MISTER MAGIC
   (Grover Washington Jr.)
4. WHAT A DIFFERENCE A DAY MADE
   (Esther Phillips with Joe Beck)
5. CHICAGO THEME
   (Hubert Laws)
6. FIRST CUCKOO
   (Deodato)
7. PRESSURE SENSITIVE
   (Ronnie Laws)
8. TALE SPINNIN'
   (Weather Report)
9. EXPANSIONS
   (Lonnie Liston Smith)
10. LIQUID LOVE
    (Freddie Hubbard)

COUNTRY SINGLES

1. DAYDREAMS ABOUT NIGHT THINGS
   (Ronnie Milsap)
2. BLUE EYES CRYING IN THE RAIN
   (Willie Nelson)
3. IF I COULD ONLY WIN YOUR LOVE
   (Emmylou Harris)
4. DON'T CRY JONI
   (Conway Twitty)
5. I HOPE YOU'RE FEELING ME
   (Charley Pride)
6. BANDY THE RODEO CLOWN
   (Moe Bandy)
7. THE FIRST TIME
   (Freddie Hart)
8. YOU NEVER EVEN CALLED ME BY MY
   NAME
   (David Allen Coe)
9. SAY FOREVER YOU'LL BE MINE
   (Porter Wagoner and Dolly Parton)
10. (TURN OUT THE LIGHTS) AND LOVE ME
    TONIGHT
    (Don Williams)

COUNTRY ALBUMS

1. RHINESTONE COWBOY
   (Glen Campbell)
2. DREAMING MY DREAMS
   (Waylon Jennings)
3. THE HIGH PRIEST OF COUNTRY MUSIC
   (Conway Twitty)
4. REDHEADED STRANGER
   (Willie Nelson)
5. THE BEST OF THE STATLER BROTHERS
   (The Statler Brothers)
6. THE BEST OF DOLLY PARTON
   (Dolly Parton)
7. FEELINS'
   (Conway Twitty and Loretta Lynn)
8. CHARLEY
   (Charley Pride)
9. MISTY
   (Ray Stevens)

10. ONCE UPON A RHYME
    (David Allen Coe)

OCTOBER 4, 1975

POP SINGLES

1. FAME
   (David Bowie)
2. I'M SORRY/CALYPSO
   (John Denver)
3. MR. JAWS
   (Dickie Goodman)
4. RUN JOEY RUN
   (David Geddes)
5. DANCE WITH ME
   (Orleans)
6. ROCKY
   (Austin Roberts)
7. HOW LONG (BETCHA GOT A CHICK ON
   THE SIDE)
   (The Pointer Sisters)
8. RHINESTONE COWBOY
   (Glen Campbell)
9. AIN'T NO WAY TO TREAT A LADY
   (Helen Reddy)
10. WASTED DAYS AND WASTED NIGHTS
    (Freddy Fender)

POP ALBUMS

1. WISH YOU WERE HERE
   (Pink Floyd)
2. BORN TO RUN
   (Bruce Springsteen)
3. ONE OF THESE NIGHTS
   (The Eagles)
4. CAPTAIN FANTASTIC AND THE BROWN
   DIRT COWBOY
   (Elton John)
5. RED OCTOPUS
   (The Jefferson Starship)
6. BLUES FOR ALLAH
   (Grateful Dead)
7. ATLANTIC CROSSING
   (Rod Stewart)
8. WIN, LOSE OR DRAW
   (Allman Brothers Band)
9. KC AND THE SUNSHINE BAND
   (KC and the Sunshine Band)
10. THE HEAT IS ON
    (Isley Brothers)

BLACK SINGLES

1. THEY JUST CAN'T STOP IT (THE GAMES
   PEOPLE PLAY)
   (Spinners)
2. DO IT ANY WAY YOU WANNA
   (People's Choice)
3. THIS WILL BE
   (Natalie Cole)
4. IT ONLY TAKES A MINUTE
   (Tavares)
5. HOW LONG (BETCHA GOT A CHICK ON
   THE SIDE)
   (The Pointer Sisters)
6. TO EACH HIS OWN
   (Faith, Hope and Charity)
7. GET DOWN TONIGHT
   (KC and the Sunshine Band)
8. BRAZIL
   (The Ritchie Family)
9. PEACE PIPE/GIVE IT WHAT YOU GOT
   (B.T. Express)
10. MONEY
    (Gladys Knight and the Pips)

BLACK ALBUMS

1. IS IT SOMETHING I SAID
   (Richard Pryor)
2. PICK OF THE LITTER
   (Spinners)
3. KC AND THE SUNSHINE BAND
   (KC and the Sunshine Band)
4. HONEY
   (Ohio Players)
5. AIN'T NO 'BOUT-A-DOUBT IT
   (Graham Central Station)
6. THE HEAT IS ON
   (Isley Brothers)
7. WHY CAN'T WE BE FRIENDS
   (War)
8. BOOGIE DOWN U.S.A.
   (People's Choice)
9. AL GREEN IS LOVE
   (Al Green)
10. PHOENIX
    (Labelle)

JAZZ ALBUMS

1. MELLOW MADNESS
   (Quincy Jones)
2. CHAIN REACTION
   (Crusaders)
3. MISTER MAGIC
   (Grover Washington Jr.)
4. WHAT A DIFFERENCE A DAY MADE
   (Esther Phillips with Joe Beck)
5. CHICAGO THEME
   (Hubert Laws)
6. FIRST CUCKOO
   (Deodato)
7. PRESSURE SENSITIVE
   (Ronnie Laws)
8. TALE SPINNIN'
   (Weather Report)
9. LIQUID LOVE
   (Freddie Hubbard)
10. SATURDAY NIGHT SPECIAL
    (Norman Connors)

COUNTRY SINGLES

1. DON'T CRY JONI
   (Conway Twitty)
2. BLUE EYES CRYING IN THE RAIN
   (Willie Nelson)
3. DAYDREAMS ABOUT NIGHT THINGS
   (Ronnie Milsap)
4. I HOPE YOU'RE FEELING ME
   (Charley Pride)
5. IF I COULD ONLY WIN YOUR LOVE
   (Emmylou Harris)
6. (TURN OUT THE LIGHTS) AND LOVE ME
   TONIGHT
   (Don Williams)
7. SAN ANTONIO STROLL
   (Tanya Tucker)
8. HOME
   (Loretta Lynn)
9. SAY FOREVER YOU'LL BE MINE
   (Porter Wagoner and Dolly Parton)
10. I'M SORRY
    (John Denver)

COUNTRY ALBUMS

1. RHINESTONE COWBOY
   (Glen Campbell)
2. THE HIGH PRIEST OF COUNTRY MUSIC
   (Conway Twitty)
3. THE BEST OF THE STATLER BROTHERS
   (The Statler Brothers)
4. REDHEADED STRANGER
   (Willie Nelson)
5. THE BEST OF DOLLY PARTON
   (Dolly Parton)

6. DREAMING MY DREAMS
(*Waylon Jennings*)
7. ONCE UPON A RHYME
(*David Allen Coe*)
8. FEELINS'
(*Conway Twitty and Loretta Lynn*)
9. CHARLEY
(*Charley Pride*)
10. BURNIN' THING
(*Mac Davis*)

OCTOBER 11, 1975

POP SINGLES

1. I'M SORRY/CALYPSO
(*John Denver*)
2. MR. JAWS
(*Dickie Goodman*)
3. FAME
(*David Bowie*)
4. DANCE WITH ME
(*Orleans*)
5. RUN JOEY RUN
(*David Geddes*)
6. ROCKY
(*Austin Roberts*)
7. AIN'T NO WAY TO TREAT A LADY
(*Helen Reddy*)
8. THEY JUST CAN'T STOP IT (THE GAMES PEOPLE PLAY)
(*Spinners*)
9. BAD BLOOD
(*Neil Sedaka*)
10. IT ONLY TAKES A MINUTE
(*Tavares*)

POP ALBUMS

1. WINDSONG
(*John Denver*)
2. WISH YOU WERE HERE
(*Pink Floyd*)
3. BORN TO RUN
(*Bruce Springsteen*)
4. RED OCTOPUS
(*The Jefferson Starship*)
5. WIN, LOSE OR DRAW
(*Allman Brothers Band*)
6. ONE OF THESE NIGHTS
(*The Eagles*)
7. CAPTAIN FANTASTIC AND THE BROWN DIRT COWBOY
(*Elton John*)
8. BLUES FOR ALLAH
(*Grateful Dead*)
9. PRISONER IN DISGUISE
(*Linda Ronstadt*)
10. KC AND THE SUNSHINE BAND
(*KC and the Sunshine Band*)

BLACK SINGLES

1. THEY JUST CAN'T STOP IT (THE GAMES PEOPLE PLAY)
(*Spinners*)
2. DO IT ANY WAY YOU WANNA
(*People's Choice*)
3. TO EACH HIS OWN
(*Faith, Hope and Charity*)
4. IT ONLY TAKES A MINUTE
(*Tavares*)
5. THIS WILL BE
(*Natalie Cole*)
6. HOW LONG (BETCHA GOT A CHICK ON THE SIDE)
(*The Pointer Sisters*)
7. GET DOWN TONIGHT
(*KC and the Sunshine Band*)
8. BRAZIL
(*The Ritchie Family*)

9. PEACE PIPE/GIVE IT WHAT YOU GOT
(*B.T. Express*)
10. WHAT A DIFFERENCE A DAY MADE
(*Esther Phillips*)

BLACK ALBUMS

1. IS IT SOMETHING I SAID
(*Richard Pryor*)
2. HONEY
(*Ohio Players*)
3. PICK OF THE LITTER
(*Spinners*)
4. KC AND THE SUNSHINE BAND
(*KC and the Sunshine Band*)
5. AIN'T NO 'BOUT-A-DOUBT IT
(*Graham Central Station*)
6. WHY CAN'T WE BE FRIENDS
(*War*)
7. AL GREEN IS LOVE
(*Al Green*)
8. THE HEAT IS ON
(*Isley Brothers*)
9. PHOENIX
(*Labelle*)
10. BOOGIE DOWN U.S.A.
(*People's Choice*)

JAZZ ALBUMS

1. CHAIN REACTION
(*Crusaders*)
2. MELLOW MADNESS
(*Quincy Jones*)
3. WHAT A DIFFERENCE A DAY MADE
(*Esther Phillips with Joe Beck*)
4. PRESSURE SENSITIVE
(*Ronnie Laws*)
5. FIRST CUCKOO
(*Deodato*)
6. CHICAGO THEME
(*Hubert Laws*)
7. MISTER MAGIC
(*Grover Washington Jr.*)
8. SATURDAY NIGHT SPECIAL
(*Norman Connors*)
9. LIQUID LOVE
(*Freddie Hubbard*)
10. DON'T IT FEEL GOOD
(*Ramsey Lewis*)

COUNTRY SINGLES

1. I HOPE YOU'RE FEELING ME
(*Charley Pride*)
2. BLUE EYES CRYING IN THE RAIN
(*Willie Nelson*)
3. DAYDREAMS ABOUT NIGHT THINGS
(*Ronnie Milsap*)
4. (TURN OUT THE LIGHTS) AND LOVE ME TONIGHT
(*Don Williams*)
5. SAN ANTONIO STROLL
(*Tanya Tucker*)
6. I'M SORRY
(*John Denver*)
7. HOME
(*Loretta Lynn*)
8. SAY FOREVER YOU'LL BE MINE
(*Porter Wagoner and Dolly Parton*)
9. ROCKY
(*Dickey Lee*)
10. DON'T CRY JONI
(*Conway Twitty*)

COUNTRY ALBUMS

1. THE HIGH PRIEST OF COUNTRY MUSIC
(*Conway Twitty*)
2. THE BEST OF THE STATLER BROTHERS
(*The Statler Brothers*)

3. RHINESTONE COWBOY
(*Glen Campbell*)
4. REDHEADED STRANGER
(*Willie Nelson*)
5. THE BEST OF DOLLY PARTON
(*Dolly Parton*)
6. ONCE UPON A RHYME
(*David Allen Coe*)
7. DREAMING MY DREAMS
(*Waylon Jennings*)
8. CHARLEY
(*Charley Pride*)
9. HOME
(*Loretta Lynn*)
10. BURNIN' THING
(*Mac Davis*)

OCTOBER 18, 1975

POP SINGLES

1. MR. JAWS
(*Dickie Goodman*)
2. BAD BLOOD
(*Neil Sedaka*)
3. THEY JUST CAN'T STOP IT (THE GAMES PEOPLE PLAY)
(*Spinners*)
4. DANCE WITH ME
(*Orleans*)
5. I'M SORRY/CALYPSO
(*John Denver*)
6. LYIN' EYES
(*The Eagles*)
7. AIN'T NO WAY TO TREAT A LADY
(*Helen Reddy*)
8. IT ONLY TAKES A MINUTE
(*Tavares*)
9. FEELINGS
(*Morris Albert*)
10. FAME
(*David Bowie*)

POP ALBUMS

1. WINDSONG
(*John Denver*)
2. WISH YOU WERE HERE
(*Pink Floyd*)
3. RED OCTOPUS
(*The Jefferson Starship*)
4. BORN TO RUN
(*Bruce Springsteen*)
5. WIN, LOSE OR DRAW
(*Allman Brothers Band*)
6. ONE OF THESE NIGHTS
(*The Eagles*)
7. PRISONER IN DISGUISE
(*Linda Ronstadt*)
8. CAPTAIN FANTASTIC AND THE BROWN DIRT COWBOY
(*Elton John*)
9. MINSTREL IN THE GALLERY
(*Jethro Tull*)
10. BLUES FOR ALLAH
(*Grateful Dead*)

BLACK SINGLES

1. THEY JUST CAN'T STOP IT (THE GAMES PEOPLE PLAY)
(*Spinners*)
2. TO EACH HIS OWN
(*Faith, Hope and Charity*)
3. DO IT ANY WAY YOU WANNA
(*People's Choice*)
4. THIS WILL BE
(*Natalie Cole*)
5. IT ONLY TAKES A MINUTE
(*Tavares*)

6. LOW RIDER
   (War)
7. WHAT A DIFFERENCE A DAY MADE
   (Esther Phillips)
8. HOW LONG (BETCHA GOT A CHICK ON
   THE SIDE)
   (The Pointer Sisters)
9. PEACE PIPE/GIVE IT WHAT YOU GOT
   (B.T. Express)
10. BRAZIL
    (The Ritchie Family)

BLACK ALBUMS

1. IS IT SOMETHING I SAID
   (Richard Pryor)
2. HONEY
   (Ohio Players)
3. PICK OF THE LITTER
   (Spinners)
4. KC AND THE SUNSHINE BAND
   (KC and the Sunshine Band)
5. AIN'T NO 'BOUT-A-DOUBT IT
   (Graham Central Station)
6. WHY CAN'T WE BE FRIENDS
   (War)
7. AL GREEN IS LOVE
   (Al Green)
8. THE HEAT IS ON
   (Isley Brothers)
9. SAVE ME
   (Silver Convention)
10. PHOENIX
    (Labelle)

JAZZ ALBUMS

1. DON'T IT FEEL GOOD
   (Ramsey Lewis)
2. MELLOW MADNESS
   (Quincy Jones)
3. PRESSURE SENSITIVE
   (Ronnie Laws)
4. CHAIN REACTION
   (Crusaders)
5. FIRST CUCKOO
   (Deodato)
6. CHICAGO THEME
   (Hubert Laws)
7. MISTER MAGIC
   (Grover Washington Jr.)
8. SATURDAY NIGHT SPECIAL
   (Norman Connors)
9. WATERBED
   (Herbie Mann)
10. LIQUID LOVE
    (Freddie Hubbard)

COUNTRY SINGLES

1. (TURN OUT THE LIGHTS) AND LOVE ME
   TONIGHT
   (Don Williams)
2. SAN ANTONIO STROLL
   (Tanya Tucker)
3. I'M SORRY
   (John Denver)
4. BLUE EYES CRYING IN THE RAIN
   (Willie Nelson)
5. DAYDREAMS ABOUT NIGHT THINGS
   (Ronnie Milsap)
6. ROCKY
   (Dickey Lee)
7. I HOPE YOU'RE FEELING ME
   (Charley Pride)
8. WHAT'S HAPPENED TO BLUE EYES
   (Jessi Colter)
9. ARE YOU SURE HANK DONE IT THIS
   WAY?/BOB WILLS IS STILL THE KING
   (Waylon Jennings)
10. WHAT IN THE WORLD'S COME OVER YOU
    (Sonny James)

COUNTRY ALBUMS

1. THE BEST OF THE STATLER BROTHERS
   (The Statler Brothers)
2. THE HIGH PRIEST OF COUNTRY MUSIC
   (Conway Twitty)
3. REDHEADED STRANGER
   (Willie Nelson)
4. RHINESTONE COWBOY
   (Glen Campbell)
5. ONCE UPON A RHYME
   (David Allen Coe)
6. THE BEST OF DOLLY PARTON
   (Dolly Parton)
7. DREAMING MY DREAMS
   (Waylon Jennings)
8. HOME
   (Loretta Lynn)
9. CHARLEY
   (Charley Pride)
10. LOVE IN THE HOT AFTERNOON
    (Gene Watson)

OCTOBER 25, 1975

POP SINGLES

1. BAD BLOOD
   (Neil Sedaka)
2. THEY JUST CAN'T STOP IT (THE GAMES
   PEOPLE PLAY)
   (Spinners)
3. MR. JAWS
   (Dickie Goodman)
4. LYIN' EYES
   (The Eagles)
5. I'M SORRY/CALYPSO
   (John Denver)
6. MIRACLES
   (The Jefferson Starship)
7. FEELINGS
   (Morris Albert)
8. IT ONLY TAKES A MINUTE
   (Tavares)
9. DANCE WITH ME
   (Orleans)
10. WHO LOVES YOU
    (The Four Seasons)

POP ALBUMS

1. WINDSONG
   (John Denver)
2. WISH YOU WERE HERE
   (Pink Floyd)
3. RED OCTOPUS
   (The Jefferson Starship)
4. ONE OF THESE NIGHTS
   (The Eagles)
5. PRISONER IN DISGUISE
   (Linda Ronstadt)
6. WIN, LOSE OR DRAW
   (Allman Brothers Band)
7. BORN TO RUN
   (Bruce Springsteen)
8. MINSTREL IN THE GALLERY
   (Jethro Tull)
9. CAPTAIN FANTASTIC AND THE BROWN
   DIRT COWBOY
   (Elton John)
10. EXTRA TEXTURE
    (George Harrison)

BLACK SINGLES

1. THEY JUST CAN'T STOP IT (THE GAMES
   PEOPLE PLAY)
   (Spinners)
2. TO EACH HIS OWN
   (Faith, Hope and Charity)

3. THIS WILL BE
   (Natalie Cole)
4. LOW RIDER
   (War)
5. DO IT ANYWAY YOU WANNA
   (People's Choice)
6. FLY, ROBIN, FLY
   (Silver Convention)
7. WHAT A DIFFERENCE A DAY MADE
   (Esther Phillips)
8. I GET HIGH ON YOU
   (Sly Stone)
9. PEACE PIPE/GIVE IT WHAT YOU GOT
   (B.T. Express)
10. SO IN LOVE
    (Curtis Mayfield)

BLACK ALBUMS

1. IS IT SOMETHING I SAID
   (Richard Pryor)
2. HONEY
   (Ohio Players)
3. KC AND THE SUNSHINE BAND
   (KC and the Sunshine Band)
4. PICK OF THE LITTER
   (Spinners)
5. WHY CAN'T WE BE FRIENDS
   (War)
6. AIN'T NO 'BOUT-A-DOUBT IT
   (Graham Central Station)
7. INSEPARABLE
   (Natalie Cole)
8. THE HEAT IS ON
   (Isley Brothers)
9. SAVE ME
   (Silver Convention)
10. THIRTEEN BLUE MAGIC LANE
    (Blue Magic)

JAZZ ALBUMS

1. DON'T IT FEEL GOOD
   (Ramsey Lewis)
2. MELLOW MADNESS
   (Quincy Jones)
3. PRESSURE SENSITIVE
   (Ronnie Laws)
4. FIRST CUCKOO
   (Deodato)
5. CHAIN REACTION
   (Crusaders)
6. WATERBED
   (Herbie Mann)
7. MISTER MAGIC
   (Grover Washington Jr.)
8. CHICAGO THEME
   (Hubert Laws)
9. SATURDAY NIGHT SPECIAL
   (Norman Connors)
10. SONG FOR MY LADY
    (Jon Lucien)

COUNTRY SINGLES

1. SAN ANTONIO STROLL
   (Tanya Tucker)
2. I'M SORRY
   (John Denver)
3. (TURN OUT THE LIGHTS) AND LOVE ME
   TONIGHT
   (Don Williams)
4. ROCKY
   (Dickey Lee)
5. WHAT'S HAPPENED TO BLUE EYES
   (Jessi Colter)
6. ARE YOU SURE HANK DONE IT THIS
   WAY?/BOB WILLS IS STILL THE KING
   (Waylon Jennings)
7. BLUE EYES CRYING IN THE RAIN
   (Willie Nelson)
8. I LIKE BEER
   (Tom T. Hall)
9. FUNNY HOW TIME SLIPS AWAY
   (Narvel Felts)

10. WHAT IN THE WORLD'S COME OVER YOU
    (Sonny James)

COUNTRY ALBUMS

1. THE BEST OF THE STATLER BROTHERS
   (The Statler Brothers)
2. REDHEADED STRANGER
   (Willie Nelson)
3. THE HIGH PRIEST OF COUNTRY MUSIC
   (Conway Twitty)
4. RHINESTONE COWBOY
   (Glen Campbell)
5. WINDSONG
   (John Denver)
6. THE BEST OF DOLLY PARTON
   (Dolly Parton)
7. ONCE UPON A RHYME
   (David Allen Coe)
8. LOVE IN THE HOT AFTERNOON
   (Gene Watson)
9. SAY FOREVER YOU'LL BE MINE
   (Porter Wagoner and Dolly Parton)
10. HOME
    (Loretta Lynn)

NOVEMBER 1, 1975

POP SINGLES

1. THEY JUST CAN'T STOP IT (THE GAMES
   PEOPLE PLAY)
   (Spinners)
2. BAD BLOOD
   (Neil Sedaka)
3. LYIN' EYES
   (The Eagles)
4. MIRACLES
   (The Jefferson Starship)
5. I'M SORRY/CALYPSO
   (John Denver)
6. FEELINGS
   (Morris Albert)
7. WHO LOVES YOU
   (The Four Seasons)
8. IT ONLY TAKES A MINUTE
   (Tavares)
9. ISLAND GIRL
   (Elton John)
10. HEAT WAVE/LOVE IS A ROSE
    (Linda Ronstadt)

POP ALBUMS

1. WINDSONG
   (John Denver)
2. RED OCTOPUS
   (The Jefferson Starship)
3. ONE OF THESE NIGHTS
   (The Eagles)
4. WISH YOU WERE HERE
   (Pink Floyd)
5. PRISONER IN DISGUISE
   (Linda Ronstadt)
6. CAPTAIN FANTASTIC AND THE BROWN
   DIRT COWBOY
   (Elton John)
7. BORN TO RUN
   (Bruce Springsteen)
8. MINSTREL IN THE GALLERY
   (Jethro Tull)
9. EXTRA TEXTURE
   (George Harrison)
10. CLEARLY LOVE
    (Olivia Newton-John)

BLACK SINGLES

1. THEY JUST CAN'T STOP IT (THE GAMES
   PEOPLE PLAY)
   (Spinners)

2. LOW RIDER
   (War)
3. FLY, ROBIN, FLY
   (Silver Convention)
4. TO EACH HIS OWN
   (Faith, Hope and Charity)
5. THIS WILL BE
   (Natalie Cole)
6. DO IT ANY WAY YOU WANNA
   (People's Choice)
7. I WANTA DO SOMETHING FREAKY TO YOU
   (Leon Haywood)
8. I GET HIGH ON YOU
   (Sly Stone)
9. SO IN LOVE
   (Curtis Mayfield)
10. THE AGONY AND THE ECSTASY
    (Smokey Robinson)

BLACK ALBUMS

1. HONEY
   (Ohio Players)
2. KC AND THE SUNSHINE BAND
   (KC and the Sunshine Band)
3. INSEPARABLE
   (Natalie Cole)
4. IS IT SOMETHING I SAID
   (Richard Pryor)
5. PICK OF THE LITTER
   (Spinners)
6. SAVE ME
   (Silver Convention)
7. WHY CAN'T WE BE FRIENDS
   (War)
8. THIRTEEN BLUE MAGIC LANE
   (Blue Magic)
9. DON'T IT FEEL GOOD
   (Ramsey Lewis)
10. AIN'T NO 'BOUT-A-DOUBT-IT
    (Graham Central Station)

JAZZ ALBUMS

1. MELLOW MADNESS
   (Quincy Jones)
2. PRESSURE SENSITIVE
   (Ronnie Laws)
3. DON'T IT FEEL GOOD
   (Ramsey Lewis)
4. MAN-CHILD
   (Herbie Hancock)
5. CHAIN REACTION
   (Crusaders)
6. FIRST CUCKOO
   (Deodato)
7. VISIONS OF A NEW WORLD
   (Lonnie Liston Smith and The Cosmic
   Echoes)
8. WATERBED
   (Herbie Mann)
9. CHICAGO THEME
   (Hubert Laws)
10. SONG FOR MY LADY
    (Jon Lucien)

COUNTRY SINGLES

1. I'M SORRY
   (John Denver)
2. ROCKY
   (Dickey Lee)
3. ARE YOU SURE HANK DONE IT THIS
   WAY?/BOB WILLS IS STILL THE KING
   (Waylon Jennings)
4. WHAT'S HAPPENED TO BLUE EYES
   (Jessie Colter)
5. SAN ANTONIO STROLL
   (Tanya Tucker)
6. I LIKE BEER
   (Tom T. Hall)
7. ALL OVER ME
   (Charlie Rich)
8. FUNNY HOW TIME SLIPS AWAY
   (Narvel Felts)

9. LOVE IS A ROSE
   (Linda Ronstadt)
10. ANOTHER WOMAN
    (T.G. Sheppard)

COUNTRY ALBUMS

1. WINDSONG
   (John Denver)
2. REDHEADED STRANGER
   (Willie Nelson)
3. THE BEST OF THE STATLER BROTHERS
   (The Statler Brothers)
4. RHINESTONE COWBOY
   (Glen Campbell)
5. THE HIGH PRIEST OF COUNTRY MUSIC
   (Conway Twitty)
6. LOVE IN THE HOT AFTERNOON
   (Gene Watson)
7. SAY FOREVER YOU'LL BE MINE
   (Porter Wagoner and Dolly Parton)
8. THE BEST OF DOLLY PARTON
   (Dolly Parton)
9. ONCE UPON A RHYME
   (David Allen Coe)
10. HOME
    (Loretta Lynn)

NOVEMBER 8, 1975

POP SINGLES

1. ISLAND GIRL
   (Elton John)
2. LYIN' EYES
   (The Eagles)
3. MIRACLES
   (The Jefferson Starship)
4. THEY JUST CAN'T STOP IT (THE GAMES
   PEOPLE PLAY)
   (Spinners)
5. FEELINGS
   (Morris Albert)
6. WHO LOVES YOU
   (The Four Seasons)
7. BAD BLOOD
   (Neil Sedaka)
8. HEAT WAVE/LOVE IS A ROSE
   (Linda Ronstadt)
9. THE WAY I WANT TO TOUCH YOU
   (The Captain and Tennille)
10. LADY BLUE
    (Leon Russell)

POP ALBUMS

1. WINDSONG
   (John Denver)
2. RED OCTOPUS
   (The Jefferson Starship)
3. ONE OF THESE NIGHTS
   (The Eagles)
4. WISH YOU WERE HERE
   (Pink Floyd)
5. ROCK OF THE WESTIES
   (Elton John)
6. CAPTAIN FANTASTIC AND THE BROWN
   DIRT COWBOY
   (Elton John)
7. STILL CRAZY AFTER ALL THESE YEARS
   (Paul Simon)
8. PRISONER IN DISGUISE
   (Linda Ronstadt)
9. CLEARLY LOVE
   (Olivia Newton-John)
10. BORN TO RUN
    (Bruce Springsteen)

BLACK SINGLES

1. LOW RIDER
   (War)
2. FLY, ROBIN, FLY
   (Silver Convention)
3. THEY JUST CAN'T STOP IT (THE GAMES PEOPLE PLAY)
   (Spinners)
4. LET'S DO IT AGAIN
   (The Staple Singers)
5. TO EACH HIS OWN
   (Faith, Hope and Charity)
6. THIS WILL BE
   (Natalie Cole)
7. I WANT'A DO SOMETHING FREAKY TO YOU
   (Leon Haywood)
8. DO IT ANY WAY YOU WANNA
   (People's Choice)
9. SAME THING IT TOOK
   (The Impressions)
10. LOVE POWER
   (Willie Hutch)

BLACK ALBUMS

1. KC AND THE SUNSHINE BAND
   (KC and the Sunshine Band)
2. HONEY
   (Ohio Players)
3. SAVE ME
   (Silver Convention)
4. INSEPARABLE
   (Natalie Cole)
5. PICK OF THE LITTER
   (Spinners)
6. IS IT SOMETHING I SAID
   (Richard Pryor)
7. DON'T IT FEEL GOOD
   (Ramsey Lewis)
8. SECOND ANNIVERSARY
   (Gladys Knight and the Pips)
9. THIRTEEN BLUE MAGIC LANE
   (Blue Magic)
10. WHY CAN'T WE BE FRIENDS
   (War)

JAZZ ALBUMS

1. MAN-CHILD
   (Herbie Hancock)
2. PRESSURE SENSITIVE
   (Ronnie Laws)
3. DON'T IT FEEL GOOD
   (Ramsey Lewis)
4. MELLOW MADNESS
   (Quincy Jones)
5. CHAIN REACTION
   (Crusaders)
6. VISIONS OF A NEW WORLD
   (Lonnie Liston Smith and The Cosmic Echoes)
7. FIRST CUCKOO
   (Deodato)
8. WATERBED
   (Herbie Mann)
9. SATURDAY NIGHT SPECIAL
   (Norman Connors)
10. CHICAGO THEME
   (Hubert Laws)

COUNTRY SINGLES

1. ROCKY
   (Dickey Lee)
2. ARE YOU SURE HANK DONE IT THIS WAY?/BOB WILLS IS STILL THE KING
   (Waylon Jennings)
3. I'M SORRY
   (John Denver)
4. WHAT'S HAPPENED TO BLUE EYES
   (Jessi Colter)
5. I LIKE BEER
   (Tom T. Hall)
6. ALL OVER ME
   (Charlie Rich)
7. LOVE IS A ROSE
   (Linda Ronstadt)
8. SAN ANTONIO STROLL
   (Tanya Tucker)
9. IT'S ALL IN THE MOVIES/LIVIN' WITH THE SHADES PULLED DOWN
   (Merle Haggard)
10. I SHOULD HAVE MARRIED YOU
   (Eddie Rabbitt)

COUNTRY ALBUMS

1. WINDSONG
   (John Denver)
2. REDHEADED STRANGER
   (Willie Nelson)
3. RHINESTONE COWBOY
   (Glen Campbell)
4. THE BEST OF THE STATLER BROTHERS
   (The Statler Brothers)
5. LOVE IN THE HOT AFTERNOON
   (Gene Watson)
6. SAY FOREVER YOU'LL BE MINE
   (Porter Wagoner and Dolly Parton)
7. THE HIGH PRIEST OF COUNTRY MUSIC
   (Conway Twitty)
8. TEXAS GOLD
   (Asleep at the Wheel)
9. THE BEST OF DOLLY PARTON
   (Dolly Parton)
10. HOME
   (Loretta Lynn)

NOVEMBER 15, 1975

POP SINGLES

1. ISLAND GIRL
   (Elton John)
2. MIRACLES
   (The Jefferson Starship)
3. LYIN' EYES
   (The Eagles)
4. FEELINGS
   (Morris Albert)
5. WHO LOVES YOU
   (The Four Seasons)
6. HEAT WAVE/LOVE IS A ROSE
   (Linda Ronstadt)
7. THE WAY I WANT TO TOUCH YOU
   (The Captain and Tennille)
8. LOW RIDER
   (War)
9. THIS WILL BE
   (Natalie Cole)
10. S O S
   (Abba)

POP ALBUMS

1. ROCK OF THE WESTIES
   (Elton John)
2. WINDSONG
   (John Denver)
3. RED OCTOPUS
   (The Jefferson Starship)
4. ONE OF THESE NIGHTS
   (The Eagles)
5. STILL CRAZY AFTER ALL THESE YEARS
   (Paul Simon)
6. CAPTAIN FANTASTIC AND THE BROWN DIRT COWBOY
   (Elton John)
7. WISH YOU WERE HERE
   (Pink Floyd)
8. PRISONER IN DISGUISE
   (Linda Ronstadt)

9. CLEARLY LOVE
   (Olivia Newton-John)
10. WIND ON THE WATER
   (David Crosby and Graham Nash)

BLACK SINGLES

1. FLY, ROBIN, FLY
   (Silver Convention)
2. LET'S DO IT AGAIN
   (The Staple Singers)
3. LOW RIDER
   (War)
4. THEY JUST CAN'T STOP IT (THE GAMES PEOPLE PLAY)
   (Spinners)
5. TO EACH HIS OWN
   (Faith, Hope and Charity)
6. I LOVE MUSIC (PART 1)
   (The O'Jays)
7. THIS WILL BE
   (Natalie Cole)
8. THAT'S THE WAY (I LIKE IT)
   (KC and the Sunshine Band)
9. SAME THING IT TOOK
   (The Impressions)
10. I WANT'A DO SOMETHING FREAKY TO YOU
   (Leon Haywood)

BLACK ALBUMS

1. KC AND THE SUNSHINE BAND
   (KC and the Sunshine Band)
2. HONEY
   (Ohio Players)
3. SAVE ME
   (Silver Convention)
4. INSEPARABLE
   (Natalie Cole)
5. SECOND ANNIVERSARY
   (Gladys Knight and the Pips)
6. PICK OF THE LITTER
   (Spinners)
7. LET'S DO IT AGAIN
   (Original Soundtrack)
8. LOVE TO LOVE YOU BABY
   (Donna Summer)
9. THIRTEEN BLUE MAGIC LANE
   (Blue Magic)
10. FEELS SO GOOD
   (Grover Washington Jr.)

JAZZ ALBUMS

1. MAN-CHILD
   (Herbie Hancock)
2. PRESSURE SENSITIVE
   (Ronnie Laws)
3. MELLOW MADNESS
   (Quincy Jones)
4. VISIONS OF A NEW WORLD
   (Lonnie Liston Smith and The Cosmic Echoes)
5. DON'T IT FEEL GOOD
   (Ramsey Lewis)
6. CHAIN REACTION
   (Crusaders)
7. JOURNEY TO LOVE
   (Stanley Clarke)
8. FIRST CUCKOO
   (Deodato)
9. SATURDAY NIGHT SPECIAL
   (Norman Connors)
10. WATERBED
   (Herbie Mann)

COUNTRY SINGLES

1. ARE YOU SURE HANK DONE IT THIS WAY?/BOB WILLS IS STILL THE KING
   (Waylon Jennings)

2. I LIKE BEER
   (Tom T. Hall)
3. ROCKY
   (Dickey Lee)
4. ALL OVER ME
   (Charlie Rich)
5. IT'S ALL IN THE MOVIES/LIVIN' WITH THE SHADES PULLED DOWN
   (Merle Haggard)
6. LOVE IS A ROSE
   (Linda Ronstadt)
7. WHAT'S HAPPENED TO BLUE EYES
   (Jessi Colter)
8. I'M SORRY
   (John Denver)
9. SECRET LOVE
   (Freddy Fender)
10. I SHOULD HAVE MARRIED YOU
    (Eddie Rabbitt)

COUNTRY ALBUMS

1. WINDSONG
   (John Denver)
2. REDHEADED STRANGER
   (Willie Nelson)
3. LOVE IN THE HOT AFTERNOON
   (Gene Watson)
4. RHINESTONE COWBOY
   (Glen Campbell)
5. THE BEST OF THE STATLER BROTHERS
   (The Statler Brothers)
6. SAY FOREVER YOU'LL BE MINE
   (Porter Wagoner and Dolly Parton)
7. THE HIGH PRIEST OF COUNTRY MUSIC
   (Conway Twitty)
8. TEXAS GOLD
   (Asleep at the Wheel)
9. CLEARLY LOVE
   (Olivia Newton-John)
10. TOM T. HALL'S GREATEST HITS
    (Tom T. Hall)

NOVEMBER 22, 1975

POP SINGLES

1. ISLAND GIRL
   (Elton John)
2. THAT'S THE WAY (I LIKE IT)
   (KC and the Sunshine Band)
3. FLY, ROBIN, FLY
   (Silver Convention)
4. THE WAY I WANT TO TOUCH YOU
   (The Captain and Tennille)
5. FEELINGS
   (Morris Albert)
6. HEAT WAVE/LOVE IS A ROSE
   (Linda Ronstadt)
7. LOW RIDER
   (War)
8. THIS WILL BE
   (Natalie Cole)
9. MIRACLES
   (The Jefferson Starship)
10. S O S
    (Abba)

POP ALBUMS

1. ROCK OF THE WESTIES
   (Elton John)
2. WINDSONG
   (John Denver)
3. RED OCTOPUS
   (The Jefferson Starship)
4. ONE OF THESE NIGHTS
   (The Eagles)
5. STILL CRAZY AFTER ALL THESE YEARS
   (Paul Simon)

6. CAPTAIN FANTASTIC AND THE BROWN DIRT COWBOY
   (Elton John)
7. PRISONER IN DISGUISE
   (Linda Ronstadt)
8. WISH YOU WERE HERE
   (Pink Floyd)
9. WIND ON THE WATER
   (David Crosby and Graham Nash)
10. CLEARLY LOVE
    (Olivia Newton-John)

BLACK SINGLES

1. LET'S DO IT AGAIN
   (The Staple Singers)
2. FLY, ROBIN, FLY
   (Silver Convention)
3. LOW RIDER
   (War)
4. THAT'S THE WAY (I LIKE IT)
   (KC and the Sunshine Band)
5. I LOVE MUSIC (PART 1)
   (The O'Jays)
6. THEY JUST CAN'T STOP IT (THE GAMES PEOPLE PLAY)
   (Spinners)
7. THIS WILL BE
   (Natalie Cole)
8. SAME THING IT TOOK
   (The Impressions)
9. TO EACH HIS OWN
   (Faith, Hope and Charity)
10. I WANT'A DO SOMETHING FREAKY TO YOU
    (Leon Haywood)

BLACK ALBUMS

1. HONEY
   (Ohio Players)
2. KC AND THE SUNSHINE BAND
   (KC and the Sunshine Band)
3. LET'S DO IT AGAIN
   (Original Soundtrack)
4. SAVE ME
   (Silver Convention)
5. INSEPARABLE
   (Natalie Cole)
6. PICK OF THE LITTER
   (Spinners)
7. LOVE TO LOVE YOU BABY
   (Donna Summer)
8. FEELS SO GOOD
   (Grover Washington Jr.)
9. YOU
   (Aretha Franklin)
10. SECOND ANNIVERSARY
    (Gladys Knight and the Pips)

JAZZ ALBUMS

1. FEELS SO GOOD
   (Grover Washington Jr.)
2. JOURNEY TO LOVE
   (Stanley Clarke)
3. MAN-CHILD
   (Herbie Hancock)
4. VISIONS OF A NEW WORLD
   (Lonnie Liston Smith and The Cosmic Echoes)
5. MELLOW MADNESS
   (Quincy Jones)
6. DON'T IT FEEL GOOD
   (Ramsey Lewis)
7. PRESSURE SENSITIVE
   (Ronnie Laws)
8. CHAIN REACTION
   (Crusaders)
9. FIRST CUCKOO
   (Deodato)
10. SATURDAY NIGHT SPECIAL
    (Norman Connors)

COUNTRY SINGLES

1. I LIKE BEER
   (Tom T. Hall)
2. IT'S ALL IN THE MOVIES/LIVIN' WITH THE SHADES PULLED DOWN
   (Merle Haggard)
3. ARE YOU SURE HANK DONE IT THIS WAY?/BOB WILLS IS STILL THE KING
   (Waylon Jennings)
4. ALL OVER ME
   (Charlie Rich)
5. SECRET LOVE
   (Freddy Fender)
6. LOVE IS A ROSE
   (Linda Ronstadt)
7. ROCKY
   (Dickey Lee)
8. LOVE PUT A SONG IN MY HEART
   (Johnny Rodriguez)
9. I'M SORRY
   (John Denver)
10. SHE EVEN WOKE ME UP TODAY TO SAY GOODBYE
    (Ronnie Milsap)

COUNTRY ALBUMS

1. REDHEADED STRANGER
   (Willie Nelson)
2. LOVE IN THE HOT AFTERNOON
   (Gene Watson)
3. WINDSONG
   (John Denver)
4. RHINESTONE COWBOY
   (Glen Campbell)
5. ARE YOU READY FOR FREDDY
   (Freddy Fender)
6. TEXAS GOLD
   (Asleep at the Wheel)
7. SAY FOREVER YOU'LL BE MINE
   (Porter Wagoner and Dolly Parton)
8. THE BEST OF THE STATLER BROTHERS
   (The Statler Brothers)
9. CLEARLY LOVE
   (Olivia Newton-John)
10. TOM T. HALL'S GREATEST HITS
    (Tom T. Hall)

NOVEMBER 29, 1975

POP SINGLES

1. THAT'S THE WAY (I LIKE IT)
   (KC and the Sunshine Band)
2. FLY, ROBIN, FLY
   (Silver Convention)
3. ISLAND GIRL
   (Elton John)
4. THE WAY I WANT TO TOUCH YOU
   (The Captain and Tennille)
5. LET'S DO IT AGAIN
   (The Staple Singers)
6. FEELINGS
   (Morris Albert)
7. THIS WILL BE
   (Natalie Cole)
8. SATURDAY NIGHT
   (Bay City Rollers)
9. NIGHTS ON BROADWAY
   (The Bee Gees)
10. SKY HIGH
    (Jigsaw)

POP ALBUMS

1. ROCK OF THE WESTIES
   (Elton John)
2. WINDSONG
   (John Denver)

3. RED OCTOPUS
    (The Jefferson Starship)
4. ONE OF THESE NIGHTS
    (The Eagles)
5. STILL CRAZY AFTER ALL THESE YEARS
    (Paul Simon)
6. SEALS AND CROFTS GREATEST HITS
    (Seals and Crofts)
7. HISTORY: AMERICA'S GREATEST HITS
    (America)
8. CAPTAIN FANTASTIC AND THE BROWN
    DIRT COWBOY
    (Elton John)
9. PRISONER IN DISGUISE
    (Linda Ronstadt)
10. BREAKAWAY
    (Art Garfunkel)

BLACK SINGLES

1. LET'S DO IT AGAIN
    (The Staple Singers)
2. THAT'S THE WAY (I LIKE IT)
    (KC and the Sunshine Band)
3. FLY, ROBIN, FLY
    (Silver Convention)
4. I LOVE MUSIC (PART 1)
    (The O'Jays)
5. LOW RIDER
    (War)
6. THEY JUST CAN'T STOP IT (THE GAMES
    PEOPLE PLAY)
    (Spinners)
7. THIS WILL BE
    (Natalie Cole)
8. PART TIME LOVE
    (Gladys Knight and the Pips)
9. SAME THING IT TOOK
    (The Impressions)
10. TO EACH HIS OWN
    (Faith, Hope and Charity)

BLACK ALBUMS

1. HONEY
    (Ohio Players)
2. LET'S DO IT AGAIN
    (Original Soundtrack)
3. KC AND THE SUNSHINE BAND
    (KC and the Sunshine Band)
4. SAVE ME
    (Silver Convention)
5. LOVE TO LOVE YOU BABY
    (Donna Summer)
6. PICK OF THE LITTER
    (Spinners)
7. FEELS SO GOOD
    (Grover Washington Jr.)
8. MOVIN' ON
    (Commodores)
9. YOU
    (Aretha Franklin)
10. SECOND ANNIVERSARY
    (Gladys Knight and the Pips)

JAZZ ALBUMS

1. FEELS SO GOOD
    (Grover Washington Jr.)
2. JOURNEY TO LOVE
    (Stanley Clarke)
3. MAN-CHILD
    (Herbie Hancock)
4. VISIONS OF A NEW WORLD
    (Lonnie Liston Smith and The Cosmic
    Echoes)
5. DON'T IT FEEL GOOD
    (Ramsey Lewis)
6. MELLOW MADNESS
    (Quincy Jones)
7. PLACES AND SPACES
    (Donald Byrd)
8. PRESSURE SENSITIVE
    (Ronnie Laws)

9. FUNKY THIDE OF SINGS
    (Billy Cobham)
10. FIRST CUCKOO
    (Deodato)

COUNTRY SINGLES

1. IT'S ALL IN THE MOVIES/LIVIN' WITH THE
    SHADES PULLED DOWN
    (Merle Haggard)
2. SECRET LOVE
    (Freddy Fender)
3. LOVE PUT A SONG IN MY HEART
    (Johnny Rodriguez)
4. I LIKE BEER
    (Tom T. Hall)
5. ALL OVER ME
    (Charlie Rich)
6. ARE YOU SURE HANK DONE IT THIS
    WAY?/BOB WILLS IS STILL THE KING
    (Waylon Jennings)
7. LOVE IS A ROSE
    (Linda Ronstadt)
8. WE USED TO
    (Dolly Parton)
9. ROCKY
    (Dickey Lee)
10. TODAY I STARTED LOVING YOU AGAIN
    (Sammi Stewart)

COUNTRY ALBUMS

1. REDHEADED STRANGER
    (Willie Nelson)
2. LOVE IN THE HOT AFTERNOON
    (Gene Watson)
3. ARE YOU READY FOR FREDDY
    (Freddy Fender)
4. WINDSONG
    (John Denver)
5. RHINESTONE COWBOY
    (Glen Campbell)
6. TEXAS GOLD
    (Asleep at the Wheel)
7. PRISONER IN DISGUISE
    (Linda Ronstadt)
8. CLEARLY LOVE
    (Olivia Newton-John)
9. SAY FOREVER YOU'LL BE MINE
    (Porter Wagoner and Dolly Parton)
10. THE BEST OF THE STATLER BROTHERS
    (The Statler Brothers)

DECEMBER 6, 1975

POP SINGLES

1. FLY, ROBIN, FLY
    (Silver Convention)
2. THAT'S THE WAY (I LIKE IT)
    (KC and the Sunshine Band)
3. ISLAND GIRL
    (Elton John)
4. LET'S DO IT AGAIN
    (The Staple Singers)
5. SATURDAY NIGHT
    (Bay City Rollers)
6. THE WAY I WANT TO TOUCH YOU
    (The Captain and Tennille)
7. NIGHTS ON BROADWAY
    (The Bee Gees)
8. SKY HIGH
    (Jigsaw)
9. FEELINGS
    (Morris Albert)
10. THIS WILL BE
    (Natalie Cole)

POP ALBUMS

1. CHICAGO IX-GREATEST HITS
    (Chicago)
2. RED OCTOPUS
    (The Jefferson Starship)
3. ROCK OF THE WESTIES
    (Elton John)
4. WINDSONG
    (John Denver)
5. HISTORY: AMERICA'S GREATEST HITS
    (America)
6. SEALS AND CROFTS GREATEST HITS
    (Seals and Crofts)
7. STILL CRAZY AFTER ALL THESE YEARS
    (Paul Simon)
8. ONE OF THESE NIGHTS
    (The Eagles)
9. CAPTAIN FANTASTIC AND THE BROWN
    DIRT COWBOY
    (Elton John)
10. BREAKAWAY
    (Art Garfunkel)

BLACK SINGLES

1. THAT'S THE WAY (I LIKE IT)
    (KC and the Sunshine Band)
2. LET'S DO IT AGAIN
    (The Staple Singers)
3. I LOVE MUSIC (PART 1)
    (The O'Jays)
4. FLY, ROBIN, FLY
    (Silver Convention)
5. PART TIME LOVE
    (Gladys Knight and the Pips)
6. LOW RIDER
    (War)
7. THEY JUST CAN'T STOP IT (THE GAMES
    PEOPLE PLAY)
    (Spinners)
8. THIS WILL BE
    (Natalie Cole)
9. FULL OF FIRE
    (Al Green)
10. I'M ON FIRE
    (Jim Gilstrap)

BLACK ALBUMS

1. LET'S DO IT AGAIN
    (Original Soundtrack)
2. KC AND THE SUNSHINE BAND
    (KC and the Sunshine Band)
3. LOVE TO LOVE YOU BABY
    (Donna Summer)
4. HONEY
    (Ohio Players)
5. FEELS SO GOOD
    (Grover Washington Jr.)
6. MOVIN' ON
    (Commodores)
7. PICK OF THE LITTER
    (Spinners)
8. WHO I AM
    (David Ruffin)
9. SAVE ME
    (Silver Convention)
10. FAMILY REUNION
    (The O'Jays)

JAZZ ALBUMS

1. FEELS SO GOOD
    (Grover Washington Jr.)
2. MAN-CHILD
    (Herbie Hancock)
3. JOURNEY TO LOVE
    (Stanley Clarke)
4. DON'T IT FEEL GOOD
    (Ramsey Lewis)
5. VISIONS OF A NEW WORLD
    (Lonnie Liston Smith and The Cosmic
    Echoes)

6. PLACES AND SPACES
   (Donald Byrd)
7. MELLOW MADNESS
   (Quincy Jones)
8. FUNKY THIDE OF SINGS
   (Billy Cobham)
9. HAVE YOU EVER SEEN THE RAIN
   (Stanley Turrentine)
10. PRESSURE SENSITIVE
   (Ronnie Laws)

COUNTRY SINGLES

1. SECRET LOVE
   (Freddy Fender)
2. LOVE PUT A SONG IN MY HEART
   (Johnny Rodriguez)
3. IT'S ALL IN THE MOVIES/LIVIN' WITH THE
   SHADES PULLED DOWN
   (Merle Haggard)
4. EASY AS PIE
   (Billy "Crash" Craddock)
5. WE USED TO
   (Dolly Parton)
6. WHERE LOVE BEGINS
   (Gene Watson)
7. ALL OVER ME
   (Charlie Rich)
8. LYIN' EYES
   (The Eagles)
9. SINCE I MET YOU BABY
   (Freddy Fender)
10. THE BLIND MAN IN THE BLEACHERS
   (Kenny Starr)

COUNTRY ALBUMS

1. ARE YOU READY FOR FREDDY
   (Freddy Fender)
2. REDHEADED STRANGER
   (Willie Nelson)
3. LOVE IN THE HOT AFTERNOON
   (Gene Watson)
4. PRISONER IN DISGUISE
   (Linda Ronstadt)
5. WINDSONG
   (John Denver)
6. RHINESTONE COWBOY
   (Glen Campbell)
7. CLEARLY LOVE
   (Olivia Newton-John)
8. GREATEST HITS
   (Don Williams)
9. BLACK BEAR ROAD
   (C.W. McCall)
10. THE BEST OF THE STATLER BROTHERS
   (The Statler Brothers)

DECEMBER 13, 1975

POP SINGLES

1. THAT'S THE WAY (I LIKE IT)
   (KC and the Sunshine Band)
2. FLY, ROBIN, FLY
   (Silver Convention)
3. LET'S DO IT AGAIN
   (The Staple Singers)
4. SATURDAY NIGHT
   (Bay City Rollers)
5. ISLAND GIRL
   (Elton John)
6. SKY HIGH
   (Jigsaw)
7. NIGHTS ON BROADWAY
   (The Bee Gees)
8. LOVE ROLLERCOASTER
   (Ohio Players)
9. I WRITE THE SONGS
   (Barry Manilow)

10. THEME FROM MAHOGANY (DO YOU KNOW
   WHERE YOU'RE GOING TO)
   (Diana Ross)

POP ALBUMS

1. CHICAGO IX-GREATEST HITS
   (Chicago)
2. HISTORY: AMERICA'S GREATEST HITS
   (America)
3. ROCK OF THE WESTIES
   (Elton John)
4. WINDSONG
   (John Denver)
5. THE HISSING OF SUMMER LAWNS
   (Joni Mitchell)
6. RED OCTOPUS
   (The Jefferson Starship)
7. SEALS AND CROFTS GREATEST HITS
   (Seals and Crofts)
8. STILL CRAZY AFTER ALL THESE YEARS
   (Paul Simon)
9. GRATITUDE
   (Earth, Wind and Fire)
10. KC AND THE SUNSHINE BAND
   (KC and the Sunshine Band)

BLACK SINGLES

1. THAT'S THE WAY (I LIKE IT)
   (KC and the Sunshine Band)
2. LET'S DO IT AGAIN
   (The Staple Singers)
3. I LOVE MUSIC (PART 1)
   (The O'Jays)
4. PART TIME LOVE
   (Gladys Knight and the Pips)
5. FLY, ROBIN, FLY
   (Silver Convention)
6. FULL OF FIRE
   (Al Green)
7. LOW RIDER
   (War)
8. LOVE ROLLERCOASTER
   (Ohio Players)
9. CARIBBEAN FESTIVAL
   (Kool and the Gang)
10. THEY JUST CAN'T STOP IT (THE GAMES
   PEOPLE PLAY)
   (Spinners)

BLACK ALBUMS

1. LET'S DO IT AGAIN
   (Original Soundtrack)
2. FAMILY REUNION
   (The O'Jays)
3. LOVE TO LOVE YOU BABY
   (Donna Summer)
4. KC AND THE SUNSHINE BAND
   (KC and the Sunshine Band)
5. FEELS SO GOOD
   (Grover Washington Jr.)
6. HONEY
   (Ohio Players)
7. MOVIN' ON
   (Commodores)
8. WHO I AM
   (David Ruffin)
9. SAVE ME
   (Silver Convention)
10. MAKING MUSIC
   (Bill Withers)

JAZZ ALBUMS

1. FEELS SO GOOD
   (Grover Washington Jr.)
2. MAN-CHILD
   (Herbie Hancock)
3. DON'T IT FEEL GOOD
   (Ramsey Lewis)

4. JOURNEY TO LOVE
   (Stanley Clarke)
5. VISIONS OF A NEW WORLD
   (Lonnie Liston Smith and The Cosmic
   Echoes)
6. HAVE YOU EVER SEEN THE RAIN
   (Stanley Turrentine)
7. PLACES AND SPACES
   (Donald Byrd)
8. MELLOW MADNESS
   (Quincy Jones)
9. FUNKY THIDE OF SINGS
   (Billy Cobham)
10. PRESSURE SENSITIVE
   (Ronnie Laws)

COUNTRY SINGLES

1. LOVE PUT A SONG IN MY HEART
   (Johnny Rodriguez)
2. SECRET LOVE
   (Freddy Fender)
3. EASY AS PIE
   (Billy "Crash" Craddock)
4. WHERE LOVE BEGINS
   (Gene Watson)
5. WE USED TO
   (Dolly Parton)
6. THE BLIND MAN IN THE BLEACHERS
   (Kenny Starr)
7. WARM SIDE OF YOU
   (Freddie Hart)
8. LYIN' EYES
   (The Eagles)
9. SINCE I MET YOU BABY
   (Freddy Fender)
10. JUST IN CASE
   (Ronnie Milsap)

COUNTRY ALBUMS

1. ARE YOU READY FOR FREDDY
   (Freddy Fender)
2. PRISONER IN DISGUISE
   (Linda Ronstadt)
3. LOVE IN THE HOT AFTERNOON
   (Gene Watson)
4. REDHEADED STRANGER
   (Willie Nelson)
5. WINDSONG
   (John Denver)
6. GREATEST HITS
   (Don Williams)
7. BLACK BEAR ROAD
   (C.W. McCall)
8. SINCE I MET YOU BABY
   (Freddy Fender)
9. CLEARLY LOVE
   (Olivia Newton-John)
10. NIGHT THINGS
   (Ronnie Milsap)

DECEMBER 20, 1975

POP SINGLES

1. THAT'S THE WAY (I LIKE IT)
   (KC and the Sunshine Band)
2. SATURDAY NIGHT
   (Bay City Rollers)
3. LET'S DO IT AGAIN
   (The Staple Singers)
4. LOVE ROLLERCOASTER
   (Ohio Players)
5. SKY HIGH
   (Jigsaw)
6. I WRITE THE SONGS
   (Barry Manilow)
7. THEME FROM MAHOGANY (DO YOU KNOW
   WHERE YOU'RE GOING TO)
   (Diana Ross)

8. FLY, ROBIN, FLY
   (Silver Convention)
9. ISLAND GIRL
   (Elton John)
10. I LOVE MUSIC (PART 1)
    (The O'Jays)

POP ALBUMS

1. CHICAGO IX-GREATEST HITS
   (Chicago)
2. HISTORY: AMERICA'S GREATEST HITS
   (America)
3. THE HISSING OF SUMMER LAWNS
   (Joni Mitchell)
4. WINDSONG
   (John Denver)
5. ROCK OF THE WESTIES
   (Elton John)
6. RED OCTOPUS
   (The Jefferson Starship)
7. GRATITUDE
   (Earth, Wind and Fire)
8. KC AND THE SUNSHINE BAND
   (KC and the Sunshine Band)
9. SEALS AND CROFTS GREATEST HITS
   (Seals and Crofts)
10. STILL CRAZY AFTER ALL THESE YEARS
    (Paul Simon)

BLACK SINGLES

1. THAT'S THE WAY (I LIKE IT)
   (KC and the Sunshine Band)
2. I LOVE MUSIC (PART 1)
   (The O'Jays)
3. LET'S DO IT AGAIN
   (The Staple Singers)
4. LOVE ROLLERCOASTER
   (Ohio Players)
5. FLY, ROBIN, FLY
   (Silver Convention)
6. FULL OF FIRE
   (Al Green)
7. PART TIME LOVE
   (Gladys Knight and the Pips)
8. LOW RIDER
   (War)
9. CARIBBEAN FESTIVAL
   (Kool and the Gang)
10. LOVE MACHINE, PART 1
    (The Miracles)

BLACK ALBUMS

1. FAMILY REUNION
   (The O'Jays)
2. GRATITUDE
   (Earth, Wind and Fire)
3. LET'S DO IT AGAIN
   (Original Soundtrack)
4. LOVE TO LOVE YOU BABY
   (Donna Summer)
5. FEELS SO GOOD
   (Grover Washington Jr.)
6. HONEY
   (Ohio Players)
7. KC AND THE SUNSHINE BAND
   (KC and the Sunshine Band)
8. RUFUS . . . FEATURING CHAKA KHAN
   (Rufus featuring Chaka Khan)
9. MAKING MUSIC
   (Bill Withers)
10. MOVIN' ON
    (Commodores)

JAZZ ALBUMS

1. FEELS SO GOOD
   (Grover Washington Jr.)
2. MAN-CHILD
   (Herbie Hancock)

3. JOURNEY TO LOVE
   (Stanley Clarke)
4. DON'T IT FEEL GOOD
   (Ramsey Lewis)
5. HAVE YOU EVER SEEN THE RAIN
   (Stanley Turrentine)
6. VISIONS OF A NEW WORLD
   (Lonnie Liston Smith and The Cosmic Echoes)
7. PLACES AND SPACES
   (Donald Byrd)
8. MELLOW MADNESS
   (Quincy Jones)
9. PRESSURE SENSITIVE
   (Ronnie Laws)
10. FUNKY THIDE OF SINGS
    (Billy Cobham)

COUNTRY SINGLES

1. EASY AS PIE
   (Billy "Crash" Craddock)
2. WHERE LOVE BEGINS
   (Gene Watson)
3. LOVE PUT A SONG IN MY HEART
   (Johnny Rodriguez)
4. THE BLIND MAN IN THE BLEACHERS
   (Kenny Starr)
5. WARM SIDE OF YOU
   (Freddie Hart)
6. SECRET LOVE
   (Freddy Fender)
7. JUST IN CASE
   (Ronnie Milsap)
8. COUNTRY BOY
   (Glen Campbell)
9. CONVOY
   (C.W. McCall)
10. LYIN' EYES
    (The Eagles)

COUNTRY ALBUMS

1. ARE YOU READY FOR FREDDY
   (Freddy Fender)
2. PRISONER IN DISGUISE
   (Linda Ronstadt)
3. REDHEADED STRANGER
   (Willie Nelson)
4. BLACK BEAR ROAD
   (C.W. McCall)
5. GREATEST HITS
   (Don Williams)
6. LOVE IN THE HOT AFTERNOON
   (Gene Watson)
7. WINDSONG
   (John Denver)
8. SINCE I MET YOU BABY
   (Freddy Fender)
9. NIGHT THINGS
   (Ronnie Milsap)
10. CLEARLY LOVE
    (Olivia Newton-John)

DECEMBER 27, 1975

POP SINGLES

1. SATURDAY NIGHT
   (Bay City Rollers)
2. THAT'S THE WAY (I LIKE IT)
   (KC and the Sunshine Band)
3. THEME FROM MAHOGANY (DO YOU KNOW WHERE YOU'RE GOING TO)
   (Diana Ross)
4. LOVE ROLLERCOASTER
   (Ohio Players)
5. I WRITE THE SONGS
   (Barry Manilow)
6. LET'S DO IT AGAIN
   (The Staple Singers)

7. SKY HIGH
   (Jigsaw)
8. I LOVE MUSIC (PART 1)
   (The O'Jays)
9. FOX ON THE RUN
   (Sweet)
10. CONVOY
    (C.W. McCall)

POP ALBUMS

1. CHICAGO IX-GREATEST HITS
   (Chicago)
2. HISTORY: AMERICA'S GREATEST HITS
   (America)
3. THE HISSING OF SUMMER LAWNS
   (Joni Mitchell)
4. WINDSONG
   (John Denver)
5. GRATITUDE
   (Earth, Wind and Fire)
6. ROCK OF THE WESTIES
   (Elton John)
7. RED OCTOPUS
   (The Jefferson Starship)
8. KC AND THE SUNSHINE BAND
   (KC and the Sunshine Band)
9. ROCKY MOUNTAIN CHRISTMAS
   (John Denver)
10. SEALS AND CROFTS GREATEST HITS
    (Seals and Crofts)

BLACK SINGLES

1. I LOVE MUSIC (PART 1)
   (The O'Jays)
2. LOVE ROLLERCOASTER
   (Ohio Players)
3. THAT'S THE WAY (I LIKE IT)
   (KC and the Sunshine Band)
4. LET'S DO IT AGAIN
   (The Staple Singers)
5. FULL OF FIRE
   (Al Green)
6. FLY, ROBIN, FLY
   (Silver Convention)
7. LOVE MACHINE (PART 1)
   (The Miracles)
8. WALK AWAY FROM LOVE
   (David Ruffin)
9. SING A SONG
   (Earth, Wind and Fire)
10. PART TIME LOVE
    (Gladys Knight and the Pips)

BLACK ALBUMS

1. FAMILY REUNION
   (The O'Jays)
2. GRATITUDE
   (Earth, Wind and Fire)
3. LOVE TO LOVE YOU BABY
   (Donna Summer)
4. LET'S DO IT AGAIN
   (Original Soundtrack)
5. FEELS SO GOOD
   (Grover Washington Jr.)
6. HONEY
   (Ohio Players)
7. KC AND THE SUNSHINE BAND
   (KC and the Sunshine Band)
8. RUFUS . . . FEATURING CHAKA KHAN
   (Rufus featuring Chaka Khan)
9. MAKING MUSIC
   (Bill Withers)
10. WAKE UP EVERYBODY
    (Harold Melvin and the Blue Notes)

JAZZ ALBUMS

1. FEELS SO GOOD
   (Grover Washington Jr.)

2. MAN-CHILD
   (Herbie Hancock)
3. HAVE YOU EVER SEEN THE RAIN
   (Stanley Turrentine)
4. JOURNEY TO LOVE
   (Stanley Clarke)
5. DON'T IT FEEL GOOD
   (Ramsey Lewis)
6. VISIONS OF A NEW WORLD
   *(Lonnie Liston Smith and The Cosmic
   Echoes)*
7. PLACES AND SPACES
   (Donald Byrd)
8. MELLOW MADNESS
   (Quincy Jones)
9. PRESSURE SENSITIVE
   (Ronnie Laws)
10. CITY LIFE
    (Blackbyrds)

COUNTRY SINGLES

1. WHERE LOVE BEGINS
   (Gene Watson)
2. THE BLIND MAN IN THE BLEACHERS
   (Kenny Starr)
3. CONVOY
   (C.W. McCall)
4. JUST IN CASE
   (Ronnie Milsap)
5. WARM SIDE OF YOU
   (Freddie Hart)
6. EASY AS PIE
   (Billy "Crash" Craddock)
7. COUNTRY BOY
   (Glen Campbell)
8. WHEN THE TINGLE BECOMES A CHILL
   (Loretta Lynn)
9. SECRET LOVE
   (Freddy Fender)
10. JASON'S FARM
    (Cal Smith)

COUNTRY ALBUMS

1. ARE YOU READY FOR FREDDY
   (Freddy Fender)
2. BLACK BEAR ROAD
   (C.W. McCall)
3. REDHEADED STRANGER
   (Willie Nelson)
4. GREATEST HITS
   (Don Williams)
5. NIGHT THINGS
   (Ronnie Milsap)
6. PRISONER IN DISGUISE
   (Linda Ronstadt)
7. LOVE IN THE HOT AFTERNOON
   (Gene Wilson)
8. WINDSONG
   (John Denver)
9. WHAT CAN YOU DO TO ME NOW
   (Willie Nelson)
10. ROCKY
    (Dickey Lee)

1976

Platinum singles for sales of two million copies were awarded for the first time in history. Three of the four singles, Johnnie Taylor's "Disco Lady," Wild Cherry's "Play That Funky Music White Boy," and Rick Dees and His Cast of Idiots' "Disco Duck" were disco songs (the last really a stupid parody of the form), while The Manhattans' "Kiss and Say Goodbye" was an old-fashioned love song. As the entries by Wild Cherry and Rick Dees suggested, 1976 was not a big year for quality singles. In fact, the year's most significant single didn't crack *Billboard's* top one hundred.

The Sex Pistols' "Anarchy in the UK," a mean, vicious expression of punk passion, articulated the disdain of many young Englishmen for social and economic conditions there. Sex Pistol leader Johnny Rotten didn't want to construct any brave new world. His contribution was to spit on what existed and laugh bitterly at everyone in sight. At least that is what the group's music and concerts suggested. The indulgences of rock stardom truly disgusted Rotten, so with a real sense of punk commitment Rotten quit, effectively destroying the Sex Pistols before the band was totally co-opted by the money and idolatry.

The two most successful album artists of the year, Peter Frampton and Fleetwood Mac (both English expatriates), were the kind of musicians Rotten called "old farts." Both had been around since the mid-1960s, shifting from the blues to heavy metal to streamlined pop-rock with more professionalism than commitment.

Frampton's music was a vacuous mix of spritely melodies and guileless vocals and his image was that of a cute rock version of John Denver. His *Frampton Comes Alive* was the biggest seller in A&M Records' history and the largest-selling live album to date. But for Frampton, his burst of fame and fortune proved brief. He followed *Alive* with the so-so *I'm In You*, the lead role in a terrible movie, *Sgt. Pepper*, an auto accident, and a break-up with his long-time manager. This succession of misfortunes sent his career in perhaps an irreversible tailspin.

The music on Fleetwood Mac's self-titled album was as pop as Frampton's, but within that framework they injected an amazing amount of emotion and personal drama. With original members drummer John McVie and bassist Mick Fleetwood as the solid bottom, singer-writers Christine McVie, Stevie Nicks, and Lindsay Buckingham fashioned durable, ingratiating songs whose lyrical and melodic textures grew denser and more intense with repeated listenings. If possible, *Rumours* was even better, with captivating songwriting and glowing performances again the norm. No other band was able to come up with successive albums so strong as these in the 1970s.

ALBUMS: Queen's *A Night at the Opera* was this British quartet's first major American seller, largely due to the classical rock puzzle of "Bohemian Rhapsody." Most of the album was heavy metal, establishing a Queen tradition of great singles and disposable 33-rpms.

Brass Construction's self-titled debut was heaven for disco goers. Each of this large Brooklyn band's songs contained a funky vamp, a chant vocal and some gritty horn charts—monotonous in spots but highly functional.

Still Crazy After All These Years is Paul Simon's most musically varied LP. Always an incisive and thoughtful lyricist, here Simon utilizes a variety of melodic and rhythmic ideas to give backbone to his melancholy tales. The title song is a classic of pre-middle-aged yearning, while the rest of the album is stuffed with wry meditations on "adult" relationships.

Red Octopus briefly revived The Jefferson Starship as Grace Slick and Marty Balin ceased hostilities long enough to weave their voices through several fine songs. Balin's "Miracles," and Slick's "Play on Love" and "Fast Buck Freddy" re-established the band in the marketplace, though sadly little of the band's Airplane-era street energy was to be found.

Aerosmith's *Toys in the Attic* and Foghat's *Fool for the City* made each group a truckload of money, and allowed each to fill huge concert halls and curse on stage as often as they wished. If a good song struck them, they played it. Good songs just didn't often pass their way.

George Benson is black and Boz Scaggs is white, but they both used polished, self-consciously sophisticated vocal styles to charm the ladies on *Breezin'*. Benson's jazz guitar took second billing to his voice on "This Masquerade," projecting a suave, debonair image he'd continue to refine. Scaggs's *Silk Degrees* had a similar feel, though he managed to touch a funk nerve with "Lowdown," an eminently tasteful dance track.

With The Brothers Johnson's *Look Out for #1*, producer Quincy Jones showed a surprising facility for contemporary pop. Everyone knew he could do soundtracks and that his pop-jazz albums were pleasant enough.

But here Jones's sumptuous arrangements and hi-tech gross were unveiled for the first time to a young audience. His ability to make bassist Louis and guitarist George Johnson, two gifted instrumentalists and weak vocalists, across-the-board hit makers, foreshadowed Jones's future triumphs.

Wheeler-dealer president Neil Bogart fashioned Casablanca Records in his own flamboyant image and his two biggest acts of 1976 could upstage any costume party. Kiss and Parliament were loud and wild, wore theatrical make-up, and were raunchy in the extreme. Kiss made do with decidedly limited musical gifts, so they specialized in straight-ahead arena rock with a minimum of taste and a maximum of wham-bang-thank-you groupies. Check Kiss's *Alive* for the gory details.

Parliament's scam was considerably more conceptual. This huge aggregation (composed of members of Funkadelic and several offshoot bands) was a tribe with George Clinton as chieftain, Bootsy Collins as witch doctor, and Fred Wesley, Maceo Parker, Junie Morrison, and Bernie Worrell as spear carriers. *Mothership Connection* introduced Clinton to white audiences, though for years his P-Funk army had been favorites of hip black folks. Funk was their forte and with "Tear the Roof Off the Sucker," they made the deepest, darkest funk you ever heard.

Steve Miller had none of Elton John's flamboyance, but on *Fly Like an Eagle*, he showed an ear for writing songs that were suspiciously like previous hits by others that rivaled Elton John's. His next album, *Book of Dreams*, was recorded at the same time as *Eagle* and has the same "doesn't that sound familiar" quality. Just for the record, "Rock 'n' Me" was based on Free's "Alright Now" and "Jet Airliner" on Cream's version of Robert Johnson's "Crossroads."

Marvin Gaye's *I Want You* is soothing and sexy and really has no songs. There are smooth silky grooves like "After the Dance" and the title cut with pieces of lyrics that Gaye's pliant voice delivers with sensual conviction. Mood music for an evening at home.

This was the year of the outlaws in country music. Willie Nelson's *The Sound in Your Mind*, Waylon Jennings's *Are You Ready for the Country*, and the definitive statement, *Wanted: The Outlaws*, featuring Nelson, Jennings, Jessi Colter, and Tompall Glaser, who thumbed their collective nose at the stiff, embalmed sound of Nashville. Drawing from diverse musical traditions (rock, R&B, Tin Pan Alley standards) Nelson and Jennings went their own way. By refusing to be stereotyped, they expanded the scope and audience for country, aiding its growth immensely. Nelson's eccentric ways and vocal and songwriting brilliance made him the symbol of outlaw country and landed him several film roles, including his own vehicle *Honeysuckle Rose*.

Paul Simon

George Benson

The Manhattans

Supertramp

Willie Nelson

The Jefferson Starship

Courtesy Grunt Records

Johnnie Taylor

The Brothers Johnson

Courtesy A & M Records

Funkadelic

Photograph by Diem Jones

JANUARY 3, 1976

POP SINGLES

1. CONVOY
   (C.W. McCall)
2. THEME FROM MAHOGANY (DO YOU KNOW WHERE YOU'RE GOING TO)
   (Diana Ross)
3. SATURDAY NIGHT
   (Bay City Rollers)
4. I WRITE THE SONGS
   (Barry Manilow)
5. LOVE ROLLERCOASTER
   (Ohio Players)
6. FOX ON THE RUN
   (Sweet)
7. I LOVE MUSIC (PART 1)
   (The O'Jays)
8. THAT'S THE WAY (I LIKE IT)
   (KC and the Sunshine Band)
9. LET'S DO IT AGAIN
   (The Staple Singers)
10. YOU SEXY THING
    (Hot Chocolate)

POP ALBUMS

1. CHICAGO IX- GREATEST HITS
   (Chicago)
2. HISTORY: AMERICA'S GREATEST HITS
   (America)
3. GRATITUDE
   (Earth, Wind and Fire)
4. WINDSONG
   (John Denver)
5. THE HISSING OF SUMMER LAWNS
   (Joni Mitchell)
6. ROCK OF THE WESTIES
   (Elton John)
7. ROCKY MOUNTAIN CHRISTMAS
   (John Denver)
8. RED OCTOPUS
   (The Jefferson Starship)
9. SEALS AND CROFTS GREATEST HITS
   (Seals and Crofts)
10. ALIVE
    (Kiss)

BLACK SINGLES

1. I LOVE MUSIC (PART 1)
   (The O'Jays)
2. LOVE ROLLERCOASTER
   (Ohio Players)
3. WALK AWAY FROM LOVE
   (David Ruffin)
4. LOVE MACHINE (PART 1)
   (The Miracles)
5. SING A SONG
   (Earth, Wind and Fire)
6. THAT'S THE WAY (I LIKE IT)
   (KC and the Sunshine Band)
7. LET'S DO IT AGAIN
   (The Staple Singers)
8. LOVE TO LOVE YOU BABY
   (Donna Summer)
9. THEME FROM MAHOGANY (DO YOU KNOW WHERE YOU'RE GOING TO)
   (Diana Ross)
10. WAKE UP EVERYBODY (PART 1)
    (Harold Melvin and the Blue Notes)

BLACK ALBUMS

1. FAMILY REUNION
   (The O'Jays)
2. GRATITUDE
   (Earth, Wind and Fire)
3. LOVE TO LOVE YOU BABY
   (Donna Summer)

---

4. FEELS SO GOOD
   (Grover Washington Jr.)
5. LET'S DO IT AGAIN
   (Original Soundtrack)
6. KC AND THE SUNSHINE BAND
   (KC and the Sunshine Band)
7. HONEY
   (Ohio Players)
8. WAKE UP EVERYBODY
   (Harold Melvin and the Blue Notes)
9. RUFUS . . . FEATURING CHAKA KHAN
   (Rufus featuring Chaka Khan)
10. MAKING MUSIC
    (Bill Withers)

JAZZ ALBUMS

1. FEELS SO GOOD
   (Grover Washington Jr.)
2. MAN-CHILD
   (Herbie Hancock)
3. JOURNEY TO LOVE
   (Stanley Clarke)
4. HAVE YOU EVER SEEN THE RAIN
   (Stanley Turrentine)
5. CITY LIFE
   (Blackbyrds)
6. VISIONS OF A NEW WORLD
   (Lonnie Liston Smith and The Cosmic Echoes)
7. PLACES AND SPACES
   (Donald Byrd)
8. DON'T IT FEEL GOOD
   (Ramsey Lewis)
9. TOUCH
   (John Klemmer)
10. MELLOW MADNESS
    (Quincy Jones)

COUNTRY SINGLES

1. THE BLIND MAN IN THE BLEACHERS
   (Kenny Starr)
2. CONVOY
   (C.W. McCall)
3. JUST IN CASE
   (Ronnie Milsap)
4. COUNTRY BOY
   (Glen Campbell)
5. WHEN THE TINGLE BECOMES A CHILL
   (Loretta Lynn)
6. WHERE LOVE BEGINS
   (Gene Watson)
7. EASY AS PIE
   (Billy "Crash" Craddock)
8. THIS TIME I'VE HURT HER MORE THAN SHE LOVES ME
   (Conway Twitty)
9. OVERNIGHT SENSATION
   (Mickey Gilley)
10. JASON'S FARM
    (Cal Smith)

COUNTRY ALBUMS

1. BLACK BEAR ROAD
   (C.W. McCall)
2. ARE YOU READY FOR FREDDY
   (Freddy Fender)
3. NIGHT THINGS
   (Ronnie Milsap)
4. GREATEST HITS
   (Don Williams)
5. REDHEADED STRANGER
   (Willie Nelson)
6. PRISONER IN DISGUISE
   (Linda Ronstadt)
7. WHAT CAN YOU DO TO ME NOW
   (Willie Nelson)
8. LOVE IN THE HOT AFTERNOON
   (Gene Watson)
9. ROCKY
   (Dickey Lee)
10. WINDSONG
    (John Denver)

JANUARY 10, 1976

POP SINGLES

1. THEME FROM MAHOGANY (DO YOU KNOW WHERE YOU'RE GOING TO)
   (Diana Ross)
2. CONVOY
   (C.W. McCall)
3. I WRITE THE SONGS
   (Barry Manilow)
4. SATURDAY NIGHT
   (Bay City Rollers)
5. FOX ON THE RUN
   (Sweet)
6. LOVE ROLLERCOASTER
   (Ohio Players)
7. I LOVE MUSIC (PART 1)
   (The O'Jays)
8. YOU SEXY THING
   (Hot Chocolate)
9. THAT'S THE WAY (I LIKE IT)
   (KC and the Sunshine Band)
10. SING A SONG
    (Earth, Wind and Fire)

POP ALBUMS

1. CHICAGO IX-GREATEST HITS
   (Chicago)
2. HISTORY: AMERICA'S GREATEST HITS
   (America)
3. GRATITUDE
   (Earth, Wind and Fire)
4. WINDSONG
   (John Denver)
5. THE HISSING OF SUMMER LAWNS
   (Joni Mitchell)
6. ROCK OF THE WESTIES
   (Elton John)
7. ROCKY MOUNTAIN CHRISTMAS
   (John Denver)
8. STILL CRAZY AFTER ALL THESE YEARS
   (Paul Simon)
9. HELEN REDDY'S GREATEST HITS
   (Helen Reddy)
10. ALIVE
    (Kiss)

BLACK SINGLES

1. I LOVE MUSIC (PART 1)
   (The O'Jays)
2. WALK AWAY FROM LOVE
   (David Ruffin)
3. LOVE MACHINE (PART 1)
   (The Miracles)
4. SING A SONG
   (Earth, Wind and Fire)
5. LOVE TO LOVE YOU BABY
   (Donna Summer)
6. THEME FROM MAHOGANY (DO YOU KNOW WHERE YOU'RE GOING TO)
   (Diana Ross)
7. LOVE ROLLERCOASTER
   (Ohio Players)
8. TURNING POINT
   (Tyrone Davis)
9. WAKE UP EVERYBODY (PART 1)
   (Harold Melvin and the Blue Notes)
10. THAT'S THE WAY (I LIKE IT)
    (KC and the Sunshine Band)

BLACK ALBUMS

1. FAMILY REUNION
   (The O'Jays)
2. GRATITUDE
   (Earth, Wind and Fire)
3. FEELS SO GOOD
   (Grover Washington Jr.)

4. LOVE TO LOVE YOU BABY
   (Donna Summer)
5. WAKE UP EVERYBODY
   (Harold Melvin and the Blue Notes)
6. KC AND THE SUNSHINE BAND
   (KC and the Sunshine Band)
7. LET'S DO IT AGAIN
   (Original Soundtrack)
8. HONEY
   (Ohio Players)
9. RUFUS . . . FEATURING CHAKA KHAN
   (Rufus featuring Chaka Khan)
10. WHO I AM
    (David Ruffin)

JAZZ ALBUMS

1. FEELS SO GOOD
   (Grover Washington Jr.)
2. MAN-CHILD
   (Herbie Hancock)
3. JOURNEY TO LOVE
   (Stanley Clarke)
4. CITY LIFE
   (Blackbyrds)
5. HAVE YOU EVER SEEN THE RAIN
   (Stanley Turrentine)
6. PLACES AND SPACES
   (Donald Byrd)
7. TOUCH
   (John Klemmer)
8. DON'T IT FEEL GOOD
   (Ramsey Lewis)
9. VISIONS OF A NEW WORLD
   (Lonnie Liston Smith and The Cosmic Echoes)
10. MELLOW MADNESS
    (Quincy Jones)

COUNTRY SINGLES

1. CONVOY
   (C.W. McCall)
2. THE BLIND MAN IN THE BLEACHERS
   (Kenny Starr)
3. JUST IN CASE
   (Ronnie Milsap)
4. WHEN THE TINGLE BECOMES A CHILL
   (Loretta Lynn)
5. COUNTRY BOY
   (Glen Campbell)
6. THIS TIME I'VE HURT HER MORE THAN
   SHE LOVES ME
   (Conway Twitty)
7. EASY AS PIE
   (Billy "Crash" Craddock)
8. OVERNIGHT SENSATION
   (Mickey Gilley)
9. SOMETIMES
   (Bill Anderson and Mary Lou Turner)
10. SOMETIMES I TALK IN MY SLEEP
    (Randy Cornor)

COUNTRY ALBUMS

1. BLACK BEAR ROAD
   (C.W. McCall)
2. ARE YOU READY FOR FREDDY
   (Freddy Fender)
3. NIGHT THINGS
   (Ronnie Milsap)
4. REDHEADED STRANGER
   (Willie Nelson)
5. GREATEST HITS
   (Don Williams)
6. WHAT CAN YOU DO TO ME NOW
   (Willie Nelson)
7. ROCKY
   (Dickey Lee)
8. THE HAPPINESS OF HAVING YOU
   (Charley Pride)
9. PRISONER IN DISGUISE
   (Linda Ronstadt)
10. LOVE IN THE HOT AFTERNOON
    (Gene Watson)

JANUARY 17, 1976

POP SINGLES

1. I WRITE THE SONGS
   (Barry Manilow)
2. CONVOY
   (C.W. McCall)
3. THEME FROM MAHOGANY (DO YOU KNOW
   WHERE YOU'RE GOING TO)
   (Diana Ross)
4. FOX ON THE RUN
   (Sweet)
5. LOVE ROLLERCOASTER
   (Ohio Players)
6. YOU SEXY THING
   (Hot Chocolate)
7. I LOVE MUSIC (PART 1)
   (The O'Jays)
8. SING A SONG
   (Earth, Wind and Fire)
9. LOVE TO LOVE YOU BABY
   (Donna Summer)
10. WALK AWAY FROM LOVE
    (David Ruffin)

POP ALBUMS

1. CHICAGO IX-GREATEST HITS
   (Chicago)
2. GRATITUDE
   (Earth, Wind and Fire)
3. HISTORY: AMERICA'S GREATEST HITS
   (America)
4. WINDSONG
   (John Denver)
5. ROCK OF THE WESTIES
   (Elton John)
6. STILL CRAZY AFTER ALL THESE YEARS
   (Paul Simon)
7. HELEN REDDY'S GREATEST HITS
   (Helen Reddy)
8. THE HISSING OF SUMMER LAWNS
   (Joni Mitchell)
9. ALIVE
   (Kiss)
10. BLACK BEAR ROAD
    (C.W. McCall)

BLACK SINGLES

1. WALK AWAY FROM LOVE
   (David Ruffin)
2. SING A SONG
   (Earth, Wind and Fire)
3. LOVE MACHINE (PART I)
   (The Miracles)
4. LOVE TO LOVE YOU BABY
   (Donna Summer)
5. THEME FROM MAHOGANY (DO YOU KNOW
   WHERE YOU'RE GOING TO)
   (Diana Ross)
6. I LOVE MUSIC (PART 1)
   (The O'Jays)
7. TURNING POINT
   (Tyrone Davis)
8. LOVE ROLLERCOASTER
   (Ohio Players)
9. WAKE UP EVERYBODY (PART 1)
   (Harold Melvin and the Blue Notes)
10. THAT'S THE WAY (I LIKE IT)
    (KC and the Sunshine Band)

BLACK ALBUMS

1. GRATITUDE
   (Earth, Wind and Fire)
2. FAMILY REUNION
   (The O'Jays)
3. WAKE UP EVERYBODY
   (Harold Melvin and the Blue Notes)

4. FEELS SO GOOD
   (Grover Washington Jr.)
5. LOVE TO LOVE YOU BABY
   (Donna Summer)
6. KC AND THE SUNSHINE BAND
   (KC and the Sunshine Band)
7. RUFUS . . . FEATURING CHAKA KHAN
   (Rufus featuring Chaka Khan)
8. SPINNERS LIVE
   (Spinners)
9. WHO I AM
   (David Ruffin)
10. HONEY
    (Ohio Players)

JAZZ ALBUMS

1. FEELS SO GOOD
   (Grover Washington Jr.)
2. MAN-CHILD
   (Herbie Hancock)
3. JOURNEY TO LOVE
   (Stanley Clarke)
4. CITY LIFE
   (Blackbyrds)
5. HAVE YOU EVER SEEN THE RAIN
   (Stanley Turrentine)
6. PLACES AND SPACES
   (Donald Byrd)
7. DON'T IT FEEL GOOD
   (Ramsey Lewis)
8. VISIONS OF A NEW WORLD
   (Lonnie Liston Smith and The Cosmic Echoes)
9. TOUCH
   (John Klemmer)
10. NEW YORK CONNECTION
    (Tom Scott)

COUNTRY SINGLES

1. CONVOY
   (C.W. McCall)
2. WHEN THE TINGLE BECOMES A CHILL
   (Loretta Lynn)
3. THE BLIND MAN IN THE BLEACHERS
   (Kenny Starr)
4. THIS TIME I'VE HURT HER MORE THAN
   SHE LOVES ME
   (Conway Twitty)
5. SOMETIMES
   (Bill Anderson and Mary Lou Turner)
6. JUST IN CASE
   (Ronnie Milsap)
7. OVERNIGHT SENSATION
   (Mickey Gilley)
8. SOMETIMES I TALK IN MY SLEEP
   (Randy Cornor)
9. LET IT SHINE
   (Olivia Newton-John)
10. THE WHITE KNIGHT
    (Cledus Maggard)

COUNTRY ALBUMS

1. BLACK BEAR ROAD
   (C.W. McCall)
2. NIGHT THINGS
   (Ronnie Milsap)
3. ARE YOU READY FOR FREDDY
   (Freddy Fender)
4. THE HAPPINESS OF HAVING YOU
   (Charley Pride)
5. ROCKY
   (Dickey Lee)
6. WHAT CAN YOU DO TO ME NOW
   (Willie Nelson)
7. REDHEADED STRANGER
   (Willie Nelson)
8. GREATEST HITS
   (Don Williams)
9. PRISONER IN DISGUISE
   (Linda Ronstadt)
10. LOVE IN THE HOT AFTERNOON
    (Gene Watson)

JANUARY 24, 1976

POP SINGLES

1. CONVOY
   (C.W. McCall)
2. I WRITE THE SONGS
   (Barry Manilow)
3. LOVE ROLLERCOASTER
   (Ohio Players)
4. FOX ON THE RUN
   (Sweet)
5. SING A SONG
   (Earth, Wind and Fire)
6. YOU SEXY THING
   (Hot Chocolate)
7. LOVE TO LOVE YOU BABY
   (Donna Summer)
8. 50 WAYS TO LEAVE YOUR LOVER
   (Paul Simon)
9. WALK AWAY FROM LOVE
   (David Ruffin)
10. EVIL WOMAN
    (Electric Light Orchestra)

POP ALBUMS

1. CHICAGO IX-GREATEST HITS
   (Chicago)
2. GRATITUDE
   (Earth, Wind and Fire)
3. WINDSONG
   (John Denver)
4. STILL CRAZY AFTER ALL THESE YEARS
   (Paul Simon)
5. HISTORY: AMERICA'S GREATEST HITS
   (America)
6. ROCK OF THE WESTIES
   (Elton John)
7. HELEN REDDY'S GREATEST HITS
   (Helen Reddy)
8. BLACK BEAR ROAD
   (C.W. McCall)
9. ALIVE
   (Kiss)
10. SEALS AND CROFTS GREATEST HITS
    (Seals and Crofts)

BLACK SINGLES

1. SING A SONG
   (Earth, Wind and Fire)
2. LOVE TO LOVE YOU BABY
   (Donna Summer)
3. WALK AWAY FROM LOVE
   (David Ruffin)
4. THEME FROM MAHOGANY (DO YOU KNOW
   WHERE YOU'RE GOING TO)
   (Diana Ross)
5. TURNING POINT
   (Tyrone Davis)
6. LOVE MACHINE (PART 1)
   (The Miracles)
7. I LOVE MUSIC (PART 1)
   (The O'Jays)
8. LOVE ROLLERCOASTER
   (Ohio Players)
9. THEME FROM S.W.A.T.
   (Rhythm Heritage)
10. ONCE YOU HIT THE ROAD
    (Dionne Warwick)

BLACK ALBUMS

1. GRATITUDE
   (Earth, Wind and Fire)
2. FAMILY REUNION
   (The O'Jays)
3. RUFUS . . . FEATURING CHAKA KHAN
   (Rufus featuring Chaka Khan)

---

4. WAKE UP EVERYBODY
   (Harold Melvin and the Blue Notes)
5. SPINNERS LIVE
   (Spinners)
6. KC AND THE SUNSHINE BAND
   (KC and the Sunshine Band)
7. FEELS SO GOOD
   (Grover Washington Jr.)
8. WHO I AM
   (David Ruffin)
9. LOVE TO LOVE YOU BABY
   (Donna Summer)
10. HONEY
    (Ohio Players)

JAZZ ALBUMS

1. FEELS SO GOOD
   (Grover Washington Jr.)
2. MAN-CHILD
   (Herbie Hancock)
3. CITY LIFE
   (Blackbyrds)
4. HAVE YOU EVER SEEN THE RAIN
   (Stanley Turrentine)
5. PLACES AND SPACES
   (Donald Byrd)
6. DON'T IT FEEL GOOD
   (Ramsey Lewis)
7. JOURNEY TO LOVE
   (Stanley Clarke)
8. PRESSURE SENSITIVE
   (Ronnie Laws)
9. NEW YORK CONNECTION
   (Tom Scott)
10. TOUCH
    (John Klemmer)

COUNTRY SINGLES

1. WHEN THE TINGLE BECOMES A CHILL
   (Loretta Lynn)
2. CONVOY
   (C.W. McCall)
3. THIS TIME I'VE HURT HER MORE THAN
   SHE LOVES ME
   (Conway Twitty)
4. SOMETIMES
   (Bill Anderson and Mary Lou Turner)
5. THE BLIND MAN IN THE BLEACHERS
   (Kenny Starr)
6. THE WHITE KNIGHT
   (Cledus Maggard)
7. OVERNIGHT SENSATION
   (Mickey Gilley)
8. SOMETIMES I TALK IN MY SLEEP
   (Randy Cornor)
9. LET IT SHINE
   (Olivia Newton-John)
10. AMAZING GRACE (USED TO BE HER
    FAVORITE SONG)
    (Amazing Rhythm Aces)

COUNTRY ALBUMS

1. BLACK BEAR ROAD
   (C.W. McCall)
2. NIGHT THINGS
   (Ronnie Milsap)
3. THE HAPPINESS OF HAVING YOU
   (Charley Pride)
4. ARE YOU READY FOR FREDDY
   (Freddy Fender)
5. ROCKY
   (Dickey Lee)
6. REDHEADED STRANGER
   (Willie Nelson)
7. WHAT CAN YOU DO TO ME NOW
   (Willie Nelson)
8. PRISONER IN DISGUISE
   (Linda Ronstadt)
9. COUNTRY WILLIE
   (Willie Nelson)
10. GREATEST HITS
    (Don Williams)

JANUARY 31, 1976

POP SINGLES

1. CONVOY
   (C.W. McCall)
2. I WRITE THE SONGS
   (Barry Manilow)
3. LOVE ROLLERCOASTER
   (Ohio Players)
4. LOVE TO LOVE YOU BABY
   (Donna Summer)
5. SING A SONG
   (Earth, Wind and Fire)
6. YOU SEXY THING
   (Hot Chocolate)
7. 50 WAYS TO LEAVE YOUR LOVER
   (Paul Simon)
8. WALK AWAY FROM LOVE
   (David Ruffin)
9. EVIL WOMAN
   (Electric Light Orchestra)
10. LOVE MACHINE (PART 1)
    (The Miracles)

POP ALBUMS

1. GRATITUDE
   (Earth, Wind and Fire)
2. CHICAGO IX-GREATEST HITS
   (Chicago)
3. STILL CRAZY AFTER ALL THESE YEARS
   (Paul Simon)
4. DESIRE
   (Bob Dylan)
5. HISTORY: AMERICA'S GREATEST HITS
   (America)
6. WINDSONG
   (John Denver)
7. HELEN REDDY'S GREATEST HITS
   (Helen Reddy)
8. BLACK BEAR ROAD
   (C.W. McCall)
9. TRYIN' TO GET THE FEELING
   (Barry Manilow)
10. ALIVE
    (Kiss)

BLACK SINGLES

1. LOVE TO LOVE YOU BABY
   (Donna Summer)
2. SING A SONG
   (Earth, Wind and Fire)
3. THEME FROM MAHOGANY (DO YOU KNOW
   WHERE YOU'RE GOING TO)
   (Diana Ross)
4. TURNING POINT
   (Tyrone Davis)
5. WALK AWAY FROM LOVE
   (David Ruffin)
6. THEME FROM S.W.A.T.
   (Rhythm Heritage)
7. LOVE MACHINE (PART 1)
   (The Miracles)
8. ONCE YOU HIT THE ROAD
   (Dionne Warwick)
9. I LOVE MUSIC (PART 1)
   (The Miracles)
10. SWEET LOVE
    (Commodores)

BLACK ALBUMS

1. GRATITUDE
   (Earth, Wind and Fire)
2. FAMILY REUNION
   (The O'Jays)
3. RUFUS . . . FEATURING CHAKA KHAN
   (Rufus featuring Chaka Khan)
4. WAKE UP EVERYBODY
   (Harold Melvin and the Blue Notes)

5. SPINNERS LIVE
   (Spinners)
6. RATTLESNAKE
   (Ohio Players)
7. FEELS SO GOOD
   (Grover Washington Jr.)
8. WHO I AM
   (David Ruffin)
9. LOVE TO LOVE YOU BABY
   (Donna Summer)
10. HONEY
    (Ohio Players)

JAZZ ALBUMS

1. FEELS SO GOOD
   (Grover Washington Jr.)
2. CITY LIFE
   (Blackbyrds)
3. HAVE YOU EVER SEEN THE RAIN
   (Stanley Turrentine)
4. PLACES AND SPACES
   (Donald Byrd)
5. MAN-CHILD
   (Herbie Hancock)
6. NEW YORK CONNECTION
   (Tom Scott)
7. JOURNEY TO LOVE
   (Stanley Clarke)
8. DON'T IT FEEL GOOD
   (Ramsey Lewis)
9. TOUCH
   (John Klemmer)
10. MELLOW MADNESS
    (Quincy Jones)

COUNTRY SINGLES

1. THIS TIME I'VE HURT HER MORE THAN
   SHE LOVES ME
   (Conway Twitty)
2. CONVOY
   (C.W. McCall)
3. SOMETIMES
   (Bill Anderson and Mary Lou Turner)
4. THE WHITE KNIGHT
   (Cledus Maggard)
5. THE BLIND MAN IN THE BLEACHERS
   (Kenny Starr)
6. WHEN THE TINGLE BECOMES A CHILL
   (Loretta Lynn)
7. SOMEBODY LOVES YOU
   (Crystal Gayle)
8. DON'T BELIEVE MY HEART CAN STAND
   ANOTHER YOU
   (Tanya Tucker)
9. AMAZING GRACE (USED TO BE HER
   FAVORITE SONG)
   (Amazing Rhythm Aces)
10. THE HAPPINESS OF HAVING YOU
    (Charley Pride)

COUNTRY ALBUMS

1. BLACK BEAR ROAD
   (C.W. McCall)
2. NIGHT THINGS
   (Ronnie Milsap)
3. THE HAPPINESS OF HAVING YOU
   (Charley Pride)
4. REDHEADED STRANGER
   (Willie Nelson)
5. ARE YOU READY FOR FREDDY
   (Freddy Fender)
6. ROCKY
   (Dickey Lee)
7. OVERNIGHT SENSATION
   (Mickey Gilley)
8. COUNTRY WILLIE
   (Willie Nelson)
9. PRISONER IN DISGUISE
   (Linda Ronstadt)
10. WHAT CAN YOU DO TO ME NOW
    (Willie Nelson)

FEBRUARY 7, 1976

POP SINGLES

1. 50 WAYS TO LEAVE YOUR LOVER
   (Paul Simon)
2. CONVOY
   (C.W. McCall)
3. LOVE TO LOVE YOU BABY
   (Donna Summer)
4. I WRITE THE SONGS
   (Barry Manilow)
5. LOVE ROLLERCOASTER
   (Ohio Players)
6. YOU SEXY THING
   (Hot Chocolate)
7. SING A SONG
   (Earth, Wind and Fire)
8. LOVE MACHINE (PART 1)
   (The Miracles)
9. EVIL WOMAN
   (Electric Light Orchestra)
10. THEME FROM S.W.A.T.
    (Rhythm Heritage)

POP ALBUMS

1. DESIRE
   (Bob Dylan)
2. GRATITUDE
   (Earth, Wind and Fire)
3. CHICAGO IX-GREATEST HITS
   (Chicago)
4. STILL CRAZY AFTER ALL THESE YEARS
   (Paul Simon)
5. HISTORY: AMERICA'S GREATEST HITS
   (America)
6. HELEN REDDY'S GREATEST HITS
   (Helen Reddy)
7. WINDSONG
   (John Denver)
8. TRYIN' TO GET THE FEELING
   (Barry Manilow)
9. ALIVE
   (Kiss)
10. BLACK BEAR ROAD
    (C.W. McCall)

BLACK SINGLES

1. THEME FROM S.W.A.T.
   (Rhythm Heritage)
2. LOVE TO LOVE YOU BABY
   (Donna Summer)
3. THEME FROM MAHOGANY (DO YOU KNOW
   WHERE YOU'RE GOING TO)
   (Diana Ross)
4. TURNING POINT
   (Tyrone Davis)
5. SING A SONG
   (Earth, Wind and Fire)
6. WALK AWAY FROM LOVE
   (David Ruffin)
7. SWEET LOVE
   (Commodores)
8. ONCE YOU HIT THE ROAD
   (Dionne Warwick)
9. LOVE MACHINE (PART 1)
   (The Miracles)
10. YOU SEXY THING
    (Hot Chocolate)

BLACK ALBUMS

1. GRATITUDE
   (Earth, Wind and Fire)
2. RUFUS . . . FEATURING CHAKA KHAN
   (Rufus featuring Chaka Khan)
3. FAMILY REUNION
   (The O'Jays)
4. WAKE UP EVERYBODY
   (Harold Melvin and the Blue Notes)

5. SPINNERS LIVE
   (Spinners)
6. FEELS SO GOOD
   (Grover Washington Jr.)
7. RATTLESNAKE
   (Ohio Players)
8. WHO I AM
   (David Ruffin)
9. LOVE TO LOVE YOU BABY
   (Donna Summer)
10. MOVIN' ON
    (Commodores)

JAZZ ALBUMS

1. FEELS SO GOOD
   (Grover Washington Jr.)
2. CITY LIFE
   (Blackbyrds)
3. PLACES AND SPACES
   (Donald Byrd)
4. HAVE YOU EVER SEEN THE RAIN
   (Stanley Turrentine)
5. NEW YORK CONNECTION
   (Tom Scott)
6. MAN-CHILD
   (Herbie Hancock)
7. JOURNEY TO LOVE
   (Stanley Clarke)
8. TOUCH
   (John Klemmer)
9. MELLOW MADNESS
   (Quincy Jones)
10. DON'T IT FEEL GOOD
    (Ramsey Lewis)

COUNTRY SINGLES

1. SOMETIMES
   (Bill Anderson and Mary Lou Turner)
2. THE WHITE KNIGHT
   (Cledus Maggard)
3. CONVOY
   (C.W. McCall)
4. THIS TIME I'VE HURT HER MORE THAN
   SHE LOVES ME
   (Conway Twitty)
5. DON'T BELIEVE MY HEART CAN STAND
   ANOTHER YOU
   (Tanya Tucker)
6. GOODHEARTED WOMAN
   (Waylon Jennings and Willie Nelson)
7. SOMEBODY LOVES YOU
   (Crystal Gayle)
8. AMAZING GRACE (USED TO BE HER
   FAVORITE SONG)
   (Amazing Rhythm Aces)
9. THE HAPPINESS OF HAVING YOU
   (Charley Pride)
10. SOMEBODY HOLD ME (UNTIL SHE PASSES
    BY)
    (Narvel Felts)

COUNTRY ALBUMS

1. BLACK BEAR ROAD
   (C.W. McCall)
2. THE HAPPINESS OF HAVING YOU
   (Charley Pride)
3. NIGHT THINGS
   (Ronnie Milsap)
4. OVERNIGHT SENSATION
   (Mickey Gilley)
5. REDHEADED STRANGER
   (Willie Nelson)
6. ARE YOU READY FOR FREDDY
   (Freddy Fender)
7. ROCKY
   (Dickey Lee)
8. COUNTRY WILLIE
   (Willie Nelson)
9. PRISONER IN DISGUISE
   (Linda Ronstadt)
10. LOVE PUT A SONG IN MY HEART
    (Johnny Rodriguez)

FEBRUARY 14, 1976

POP SINGLES

1. LOVE TO LOVE YOU BABY
   (Donna Summer)
2. 50 WAYS TO LEAVE YOUR LOVER
   (Paul Simon)
3. CONVOY
   (C.W. McCall)
4. THEME FROM S.W.A.T.
   (Rhythm Heritage)
5. LOVE MACHINE (PART 1)
   (The Miracles)
6. I WRITE THE SONGS
   (Barry Manilow)
7. YOU SEXY THING
   (Hot Chocolate)
8. LOVE ROLLERCOASTER
   (Ohio Players)
9. SING A SONG
   (Earth, Wind and Fire)
10. BREAKING UP IS HARD TO DO
    (Neil Sedaka)

POP ALBUMS

1. DESIRE
   (Bob Dylan)
2. CHICAGO IX-GREATEST HITS
   (Chicago)
3. GRATITUDE
   (Earth, Wind and Fire)
4. STILL CRAZY AFTER ALL THESE YEARS
   (Paul Simon)
5. HISTORY: AMERICA'S GREATEST HITS
   (America)
6. HELEN REDDY'S GREATEST HITS
   (Helen Reddy)
7. WINDSONG
   (John Denver)
8. TRYIN' TO GET THE FEELING
   (Barry Manilow)
9. FLEETWOOD MAC
   (Fleetwood Mac)
10. ALIVE
    (Kiss)

BLACK SINGLES

1. TURNING POINT
   (Tyrone Davis)
2. THEME FROM S.W.A.T.
   (Rhythm Heritage)
3. LOVE TO LOVE YOU BABY
   (Donna Summer)
4. SWEET THING
   (Rufus featuring Chaka Khan)
5. SWEET LOVE
   (Commodores)
6. THEME FROM MAHOGANY (DO YOU KNOW WHERE YOU'RE GOING TO)
   (Diana Ross)
7. SING A SONG
   (Earth, Wind and Fire)
8. WALK AWAY FROM LOVE
   (David Ruffin)
9. YOU SEXY THING
   (Hot Chocolate)
10. INSEPARABLE
    (Natalie Cole)

BLACK ALBUMS

1. RUFUS . . . FEATURING CHAKA KHAN
   (Rufus featuring Chaka Khan)
2. GRATITUDE
   (Earth, Wind and Fire)
3. FAMILY REUNION
   (The O'Jays)

4. WAKE UP EVERYBODY
   (Harold Melvin and the Blue Notes)
5. SPINNERS LIVE
   (Spinners)
6. FEELS SO GOOD
   (Grover Washington Jr.)
7. WHO I AM
   (David Ruffin)
8. RATTLESNAKE
   (Ohio Players)
9. MOVIN' ON
   (Commodores)
10. DANCE YOUR TROUBLES AWAY
    (Archie Bell and the Drells)

JAZZ ALBUMS

1. CITY LIFE
   (Blackbyrds)
2. FEELS SO GOOD
   (Grover Washington Jr.)
3. PLACES AND SPACES
   (Donald Byrd)
4. NEW YORK CONNECTION
   (Tom Scott)
5. HAVE YOU EVER SEEN THE RAIN
   (Stanley Turrentine)
6. JOURNEY TO LOVE
   (Stanley Clarke)
7. MAN-CHILD
   (Herbie Hancock)
8. TOUCH
   (John Klemmer)
9. I LOVE THE BLUES/SHE HEARD MY CRY
   (George Duke)
10. MELLOW MADNESS
    (Quincy Jones)

COUNTRY SINGLES

1. THE WHITE KNIGHT
   (Cledus Maggard)
2. SOMETIMES
   (Bill Anderson and Mary Lou Turner)
3. GOODHEARTED WOMAN
   (Waylon Jennings and Willie Nelson)
4. DON'T BELIEVE MY HEART CAN STAND ANOTHER YOU
   (Tanya Tucker)
5. THIS TIME I'VE HURT HER MORE THAN SHE LOVES ME
   (Conway Twitty)
6. CONVOY
   (C.W. McCall)
7. HANK WILLIAMS, YOU WROTE MY LIFE
   (Moe Bandy)
8. SOMEBODY HOLD ME (UNTIL SHE PASSES BY)
   (Narvel Felts)
9. THE HAPPINESS OF HAVING YOU
   (Charley Pride)
10. REMEMBER ME
    (Willie Nelson)

COUNTRY ALBUMS

1. BLACK BEAR ROAD
   (C.W. McCall)
2. THE HAPPINESS OF HAVING YOU
   (Charley Pride)
3. OVERNIGHT SENSATION
   (Mickey Gilley)
4. NIGHT THINGS
   (Ronnie Milsap)
5. LOVE PUT A SONG IN MY HEART
   (Johnny Rodriguez)
6. ARE YOU READY FOR FREDDY
   (Freddy Fender)
7. TWITTY
   (Conway Twitty)
8. PRISONER IN DISGUISE
   (Linda Ronstadt)
9. COUNTRY WILLIE
   (Willie Nelson)

10. SOMEBODY LOVES YOU
    (Crystal Gayle)

FEBRUARY 21, 1976

POP SINGLES

1. THEME FROM S.W.A.T.
   (Rhythm Heritage)
2. 50 WAYS TO LEAVE YOUR LOVER
   (Paul Simon)
3. LOVE TO LOVE YOU BABY
   (Donna Summer)
4. LOVE MACHINE (PART 1)
   (The Miracles)
5. CONVOY
   (C.W. McCall)
6. I WRITE THE SONGS
   (Barry Manilow)
7. YOU SEXY THING
   (Hot Chocolate)
8. ALL BY MYSELF
   (Eric Carmen)
9. TAKE IT TO THE LIMIT
   (The Eagles)
10. LOVE HURTS
    (Nazareth)

POP ALBUMS

1. DESIRE
   (Bob Dylan)
2. STILL CRAZY AFTER ALL THESE YEARS
   (Paul Simon)
3. GRATITUDE
   (Earth, Wind and Fire)
4. CHICAGO IX-GREATEST HITS
   (Chicago)
5. HISTORY: AMERICA'S GREATEST HITS
   (America)
6. FRAMPTON COMES ALIVE
   (Peter Frampton)
7. STATION TO STATION
   (David Bowie)
8. FLEETWOOD MAC
   (Fleetwood Mac)
9. RUN WITH THE PACK
   (Bad Company)
10. TRYIN' TO GET THE FEELING
    (Barry Manilow)

BLACK SINGLES

1. TURNING POINT
   (Tyrone Davis)
2. SWEET THING
   (Rufus featuring Chaka Khan)
3. THEME FROM S.W.A.T.
   (Rhythm Heritage)
4. SWEET LOVE
   (Commodores)
5. LOVE TO LOVE YOU BABY
   (Donna Summer)
6. THEME FROM MAHOGANY (DO YOU KNOW WHERE YOU'RE GOING TO)
   (Diana Ross)
7. SING A SONG
   (Earth, Wind and Fire)
8. INSEPARABLE
   (Natalie Cole)
9. YOU SEXY THING
   (Hot Chocolate)
10. WALK AWAY FROM LOVE
    (David Ruffin)

BLACK ALBUMS

1. RUFUS . . . FEATURING CHAKA KHAN
   (Rufus featuring Chaka Khan)

2. GRATITUDE
    (Earth, Wind and Fire)
3. WAKE UP EVERYBODY
    (Harold Melvin and the Blue Notes)
4. FAMILY REUNION
    (The O'Jays)
5. BRASS CONSTRUCTION
    (Brass Construction)
6. WHO I AM
    (David Ruffin)
7. SPINNERS LIVE
    (Spinners)
8. MOVIN' ON
    (Commodores)
9. FEELS SO GOOD
    (Grover Washington Jr.)
10. DANCE YOUR TROUBLES AWAY
    (Archie Bell and the Drells)

JAZZ ALBUMS

1. CITY LIFE
    (Blackbyrds)
2. FEELS SO GOOD
    (Grover Washington Jr.)
3. PLACES AND SPACES
    (Donald Byrd)
4. NEW YORK CONNECTION
    (Tom Scott)
5. JOURNEY TO LOVE
    (Stanley Clarke)
6. HAVE YOU EVER SEEN THE RAIN
    (Stanley Turrentine)
7. TOUCH
    (John Klemmer)
8. VISIONS OF A NEW WORLD
    (Lonnie Liston Smith and The Cosmic Echoes)
9. MAN-CHILD
    (Herbie Hancock)
10. I LOVE THE BLUES/SHE HEARD MY CRY
    (George Duke)

COUNTRY SINGLES

1. GOODHEARTED WOMAN
    (Waylon Jennings and Willie Nelson)
2. THE WHITE KNIGHT
    (Cledus Maggard)
3. SOMETIMES
    (Bill Anderson and Mary Lou Turner)
4. DON'T BELIEVE MY HEART CAN STAND ANOTHER YOU
    (Tanya Tucker)
5. REMEMBER ME
    (Willie Nelson)
6. HANK WILLIAMS, YOU WROTE MY LIFE
    (Moe Bandy)
7. SOMEBODY HOLD ME (UNTIL SHE PASSES BY)
    (Narvel Felts)
8. STANDING ROOM ONLY
    (Barbara Mandrell)
9. THE ROOTS OF MY RAISING
    (Merle Haggard)
10. SOMEBODY LOVES YOU
    (Crystal Gayle)

COUNTRY ALBUMS

1. THE HAPPINESS OF HAVING YOU
    (Charley Pride)
2. OVERNIGHT SENSATION
    (Mickey Gilley)
3. BLACK BEAR ROAD
    (C.W. McCall)
4. LOVE PUT A SONG IN MY HEART
    (Johnny Rodriguez)
5. TWITTY
    (Conway Twitty)
6. NIGHT THINGS
    (Ronnie Milsap)
7. ARE YOU READY FOR FREDDY
    (Freddy Fender)

8. PRISONER IN DISGUISE
    (Linda Ronstadt)
9. LOVIN' AND LEARNIN'
    (Tanya Tucker)
10. SOMEBODY LOVES YOU
    (Crystal Gayle)

FEBRUARY 28, 1976

POP SINGLES

1. THEME FROM S.W.A.T.
    (Rhythm Heritage)
2. 50 WAYS TO LEAVE YOUR LOVER
    (Paul Simon)
3. LOVE MACHINE (PART 1)
    (The Miracles)
4. ALL BY MYSELF
    (Eric Carmen)
5. LOVE TO LOVE YOU BABY
    (Donna Summer)
6. TAKE IT TO THE LIMIT
    (The Eagles)
7. CONVOY
    (C.W. McCall)
8. DREAM WEAVER
    (Gary Wright)
9. LOVE HURTS
    (Nazareth)
10. DECEMBER, 1963 (OH WHAT A NIGHT)
    (The Four Seasons)

POP ALBUMS

1. DESIRE
    (Bob Dylan)
2. STILL CRAZY AFTER ALL THESE YEARS
    (Paul Simon)
3. RUN WITH THE PACK
    (Bad Company)
4. FRAMPTON COMES ALIVE
    (Peter Frampton)
5. CHICAGO IX-GREATEST HITS
    (Chicago)
6. STATION TO STATION
    (David Bowie)
7. HISTORY: AMERICA'S GREATEST HITS
    (America)
8. GRATITUDE
    (Earth, Wind and Fire)
9. FLEETWOOD MAC
    (Fleetwood Mac)
10. RUFUS . . . FEATURING CHAKA KHAN
    (Rufus featuring Chaka Khan)

BLACK SINGLES

1. SWEET THING
    (Rufus featuring Chaka Khan)
2. TURNING POINT
    (Tyrone Davis)
3. THEME FROM S.W.A.T.
    (Rhythm Heritage)
4. SWEET LOVE
    (Commodores)
5. DISCO LADY
    (Johnnie Taylor)
6. LOVE TO LOVE YOU BABY
    (Donna Summer)
7. INSEPARABLE
    (Natalie Cole)
8. BOOGIE FEVER
    (The Sylvers)
9. THEME FROM MAHOGANY (DO YOU KNOW WHERE YOU'RE GOING TO)
    (Diana Ross)
10. I NEED YOU, YOU NEED ME
    (Joe Simon)

BLACK ALBUMS

1. RUFUS . . . FEATURING CHAKA KHAN
    (Rufus featuring Chaka Khan)
2. GRATITUDE
    (Earth, Wind and Fire)
3. WAKE UP EVERYBODY
    (Harold Melvin and the Blue Notes)
4. BRASS CONSTRUCTION
    (Brass Construction)
5. FAMILY REUNION
    (The O'Jays)
6. WHO I AM
    (David Ruffin)
7. HE'S A FRIEND
    (Eddie Kendricks)
8. MOVIN' ON
    (Commodores)
9. THE SALSOUL ORCHESTRA
    (Salsoul)
10. DANCE YOUR TROUBLES AWAY
    (Archie Bell and the Drells)

JAZZ ALBUMS

1. CITY LIFE
    (Blackbyrds)
2. FEELS SO GOOD
    (Grover Washington Jr.)
3. PLACES AND SPACES
    (Donald Byrd)
4. NEW YORK CONNECTION
    (Tom Scott)
5. TOUCH
    (John Klemmer)
6. JOURNEY TO LOVE
    (Stanley Clarke)
7. VISIONS OF A NEW WORLD
    (Lonnie Liston Smith and The Cosmic Echoes)
8. HAVE YOU EVER SEEN THE RAIN
    (Stanley Turrentine)
9. MAN-CHILD
    (Herbie Hancock)
10. BRASS CONSTRUCTION
    (Brass Construction)

COUNTRY SINGLES

1. REMEMBER ME
    (Willie Nelson)
2. GOODHEARTED WOMAN
    (Waylon Jennings and Willie Nelson)
3. HANK WILLIAMS, YOU WROTE MY LIFE
    (Moe Bandy)
4. THE ROOTS OF MY RAISING
    (Merle Haggard)
5. FASTER HORSES
    (Tom T. Hall)
6. DON'T BELIEVE MY HEART CAN STAND ANOTHER YOU
    (Tanya Tucker)
7. STANDING ROOM ONLY
    (Barbara Mandrell)
8. SOMEBODY HOLD ME (UNTIL SHE PASSES BY)
    (Narvel Felts)
9. MOTELS AND MEMORIES
    (T.G. Sheppard)
10. SOMEBODY LOVES YOU
    (Crystal Gayle)

COUNTRY ALBUMS

1. OVERNIGHT SENSATION
    (Mickey Gilley)
2. TWITTY
    (Conway Twitty)
3. LOVE PUT A SONG IN MY HEART
    (Johnny Rodriguez)
4. THE HAPPINESS OF HAVING YOU
    (Charley Pride)

5. THE OUTLAWS
   (Waylon, Willie, Jessi and Tompall)
6. BLACK BEAR ROAD
   (C.W. McCall)
7. LOVIN' AND LEARNIN'
   (Tanya Tucker)
8. ELITE HOTEL
   (Emmylou Harris)
9. NIGHT THINGS
   (Ronnie Milsap)
10. BLIND MAN IN THE BLEACHERS
    (Kenny Starr)

MARCH 6, 1976

POP SINGLES

1. LOVE MACHINE (PART 1)
   (The Miracles)
2. THEME FROM S.W.A.T.
   (Rhythm Heritage)
3. ALL BY MYSELF
   (Eric Carmen)
4. DECEMBER, 1963 (OH WHAT A NIGHT)
   (The Four Seasons)
5. DREAM WEAVER
   (Gary Wright)
6. TAKE IT TO THE LIMIT
   (The Eagles)
7. 50 WAYS TO LEAVE YOUR LOVER
   (Paul Simon)
8. LOVE HURTS
   (Nazareth)
9. LONELY NIGHT (ANGEL FACE)
   (The Captain and Tennille)
10. FANNY (BE TENDER WITH MY LOVE)
    (The Bee Gees)

POP ALBUMS

1. FRAMPTON COMES ALIVE
   (Peter Frampton)
2. DESIRE
   (Bob Dylan)
3. RUN WITH THE PACK
   (Bad Company)
4. STILL CRAZY AFTER ALL THESE YEARS
   (Paul Simon)
5. CHICAGO IX-GREATEST HITS
   (Chicago)
6. STATION TO STATION
   (David Bowie)
7. HISTORY: AMERICA'S GREATEST HITS
   (America)
8. FLEETWOOD MAC
   (Fleetwood Mac)
9. ONE OF THESE NIGHTS
   (The Eagles)
10. RUFUS . . . FEATURING CHAKA KHAN
    (Rufus featuring Chaka Khan)

BLACK SINGLES

1. DISCO LADY
   (Johnnie Taylor)
2. SWEET THING
   (Rufus featuring Chaka Khan)
3. THEME FROM S.W.A.T.
   (Rhythm Heritage)
4. TURNING POINT
   (Tyrone Davis)
5. SWEET LOVE
   (Commodores)
6. BOOGIE FEVER
   (The Sylvers)
7. INSEPARABLE
   (Natalie Cole)
8. LOVE TO LOVE YOU BABY
   (Donna Summer)

9. I NEED YOU, YOU NEED ME
   (Joe Simon)
10. THEME FROM MAHOGANY (DO YOU KNOW WHERE YOU'RE GOING TO)
    (Diana Ross)

BLACK ALBUMS

1. RUFUS . . . FEATURING CHAKA KHAN
   (Rufus featuring Chaka Khan)
2. BRASS CONSTRUCTION
   (Brass Construction)
3. GRATITUDE
   (Earth, Wind and Fire)
4. WAKE UP EVERYBODY
   (Harold Melvin and the Blue Notes)
5. FAMILY REUNION
   (The O'Jays)
6. HE'S A FRIEND
   (Eddie Kendricks)
7. DANCE YOUR TROUBLES AWAY
   (Archie Bell and the Drells)
8. MOVIN' ON
   (Commodores)
9. THE SALSOUL ORCHESTRA
   (Salsoul)
10. MOTHERSHIP CONNECTION
    (Parliament)

JAZZ ALBUMS

1. CITY LIFE
   (Blackbyrds)
2. FEELS SO GOOD
   (Grover Washington Jr.)
3. PLACES AND SPACES
   (Donald Byrd)
4. NEW YORK CONNECTION
   (Tom Scott)
5. TOUCH
   (John Klemmer)
6. VISIONS OF A NEW WORLD
   (Lonnie Liston Smith and The Cosmic Echoes)
7. JOURNEY TO LOVE
   (Stanley Clarke)
8. MAN-CHILD
   (Herbie Hancock)
9. BRASS CONSTRUCTION
   (Brass Construction)
10. MYSTIC VOYAGE
    (Roy Ayers Ubiquity)

COUNTRY SINGLES

1. THE ROOTS OF MY RAISING
   (Merle Haggard)
2. FASTER HORSES
   (Tom T. Hall)
3. HANK WILLIAMS, YOU WROTE MY LIFE
   (Moe Bandy)
4. REMEMBER ME
   (Willie Nelson)
5. GOODHEARTED WOMAN
   (Waylon Jennings and Willie Nelson)
6. STANDING ROOM ONLY
   (Barbara Mandrell)
7. MOTELS AND MEMORIES
   (T.G. Sheppard)
8. BROKEN LADY
   (Larry Gatlin)
9. DON'T BELIEVE MY HEART CAN STAND ANOTHER YOU
   (Tanya Tucker)
10. TILL THE RIVERS ALL RUN DRY
    (Don Williams)

COUNTRY ALBUMS

1. THE OUTLAWS
   (Waylon, Willie, Jessi and Tompall)

2. TWITTY
   (Conway Twitty)
3. LOVE PUT A SONG IN MY HEART
   (Johnny Rodriguez)
4. OVERNIGHT SENSATION
   (Mickey Gilley)
5. ELITE HOTEL
   (Emmylou Harris)
6. LOVIN' AND LEARNIN'
   (Tanya Tucker)
7. JESSI
   (Jessi Colter)
8. BLACK BEAR ROAD
   (C.W. McCall)
9. BLIND MAN IN THE BLEACHERS
   (Kenny Starr)
10. THE HAPPINESS OF HAVING YOU
    (Charley Pride)

MARCH 13, 1976

POP SINGLES

1. ALL BY MYSELF
   (Eric Carmen)
2. DECEMBER, 1963 (OH WHAT A NIGHT)
   (The Four Seasons)
3. DREAM WEAVER
   (Gary Wright)
4. LOVE MACHINE (PART 1)
   (The Miracles)
5. THEME FROM S.W.A.T.
   (Rhythm Heritage)
6. LONELY NIGHT (ANGEL FACE)
   (The Captain and Tennille)
7. TAKE IT TO THE LIMIT
   (The Eagles)
8. LOVE HURTS
   (Nazareth)
9. SWEET THING
   (Rufus featuring Chaka Khan)
10. DREAM ON
    (Aerosmith)

POP ALBUMS

1. THEIR GREATEST HITS
   (The Eagles)
2. FRAMPTON COMES ALIVE
   (Peter Frampton)
3. DESIRE
   (Bob Dylan)
4. RUN WITH THE PACK
   (Bad Company)
5. STILL CRAZY AFTER ALL THESE YEARS
   (Paul Simon)
6. CHICAGO IX-GREATEST HITS
   (Chicago)
7. FLEETWOOD MAC
   (Fleetwood Mac)
8. ONE OF THESE NIGHTS
   (The Eagles)
9. STATION TO STATION
   (David Bowie)
10. HISTORY: AMERICA'S GREATEST HITS
    (America)

BLACK SINGLES

1. DISCO LADY
   (Johnnie Taylor)
2. BOOGIE FEVER
   (The Sylvers)
3. SWEET THING
   (Rufus featuring Chaka Khan)
4. THEME FROM S.W.A.T.
   (Rhythm Heritage)
5. TURNING POINT
   (Tyrone Davis)
6. MISTY BLUE
   (Dorothy Moore)

7. SWEET LOVE
   (Commodores)
8. LOVE TO LOVE YOU BABY
   (Donna Summer)
9. INSEPARABLE
   (Natalie Cole)
10. I NEED YOU, YOU NEED ME
    (Joe Simon)

BLACK ALBUMS

1. RUFUS . . . FEATURING CHAKA KHAN
   (Rufus featuring Chaka Khan)
2. BRASS CONSTRUCTION
   (Brass Construction)
3. GRATITUDE
   (Earth, Wind and Fire)
4. WAKE UP EVERYBODY
   (Harold Melvin and the Blue Notes)
5. HE'S A FRIEND
   (Eddie Kendricks)
6. FAMILY REUNION
   (The O'Jays)
7. MOTHERSHIP CONNECTION
   (Parliament)
8. DANCE YOUR TROUBLES AWAY
   (Archie Bell and the Drells)
9. THE SALSOUL ORCHESTRA
   (Salsoul)
10. LET THE MUSIC PLAY
    (Barry White)

JAZZ ALBUMS

1. CITY LIFE
   (Blackbyrds)
2. PLACES AND SPACES
   (Donald Byrd)
3. FEELS SO GOOD
   (Grover Washington Jr.)
4. NEW YORK CONNECTION
   (Tom Scott)
5. THE LEPRECHAUN
   (Chick Corea)
6. TOUCH
   (John Klemmer)
7. VISIONS OF A NEW WORLD
   (Lonnie Liston Smith and The Cosmic Echoes)
8. MAN-CHILD
   (Herbie Hancock)
9. BRASS CONSTRUCTION
   (Brass Construction)
10. HAVE YOU EVER SEEN THE RAIN
    (Stanley Turrentine)

COUNTRY SINGLES

1. FASTER HORSES
   (Tom T. Hall)
2. THE ROOTS OF MY RAISING
   (Merle Haggard)
3. REMEMBER ME
   (Willie Nelson)
4. GOODHEARTED WOMAN
   (Waylon Jennings and Willie Nelson)
5. BROKEN LADY
   (Larry Gatlin)
6. STANDING ROOM ONLY
   (Barbara Mandrell)
7. TILL THE RIVERS ALL RUN DRY
   (Don Williams)
8. MOTELS AND MEMORIES
   (T.G. Sheppard)
9. IF I HAD IT TO DO ALL OVER AGAIN
   (Roy Clark)
10. YOU'LL LOSE A GOOD THING
    (Freddy Fender)

COUNTRY ALBUMS

1. THE OUTLAWS
   (Waylon, Willie, Jessi and Tompall)

2. ELITE HOTEL
   (Emmylou Harris)
3. TWITTY
   (Conway Twitty)
4. LOVIN' AND LEARNIN'
   (Tanya Tucker)
5. JESSI
   (Jessi Colter)
6. LOVE PUT A SONG IN MY HEART
   (Johnny Rodriguez)
7. OVERNIGHT SENSATION
   (Mickey Gilley)
8. BLIND MAN IN THE BLEACHERS
   (Kenny Starr)
9. BLACK BEAR ROAD
   (C.W. McCall)
10. 200 YEARS OF COUNTRY MUSIC
    (Sonny James)

MARCH 20, 1976

POP SINGLES

1. DECEMBER, 1963 (OH WHAT A NIGHT)
   (The Four Seasons)
2. DREAM WEAVER
   (Gary Wright)
3. ALL BY MYSELF
   (Eric Carmen)
4. LONELY NIGHT (ANGEL FACE)
   (The Captain and Tennille)
5. DISCO LADY
   (Johnnie Taylor)
6. SWEET THING
   (Rufus featuring Chaka Khan)
7. LOVE MACHINE (PART 1)
   (The Miracles)
8. DREAM ON
   (Aerosmith)
9. THEME FROM S.W.A.T.
   (Rhythm Heritage)
10. TAKE IT TO THE LIMIT
    (The Eagles)

POP ALBUMS

1. THEIR GREATEST HITS
   (The Eagles)
2. FRAMPTON COMES ALIVE
   (Peter Frampton)
3. DESIRE
   (Bob Dylan)
4. RUN WITH THE PACK
   (Bad Company)
5. STILL CRAZY AFTER ALL THESE YEARS
   (Paul Simon)
6. CHICAGO IX-GREATEST HITS
   (Chicago)
7. ONE OF THESE NIGHTS
   (The Eagles)
8. FLEETWOOD MAC
   (Fleetwood Mac)
9. HISTORY: AMERICA'S GREATEST HITS
   (America)
10. STATION TO STATION
    (David Bowie)

BLACK SINGLES

1. DISCO LADY
   (Johnnie Taylor)
2. BOOGIE FEVER
   (The Sylvers)
3. MISTY BLUE
   (Dorothy Moore)
4. SWEET THING
   (Rufus featuring Chaka Khan)
5. THEME FROM S.W.A.T.
   (Rhythm Heritage)
6. TURNING POINT
   (Tyrone Davis)

7. SWEET LOVE
   (Commodores)
8. (CALL ME) THE TRAVELING MAN
   (Masqueraders)
9. HE'S A FRIEND
   (Eddie Kendricks)
10. FROM US TO YOU
    (The Stairsteps)

BLACK ALBUMS

1. RUFUS . . . FEATURING CHAKA KHAN
   (Rufus featuring Chaka Khan)
2. BRASS CONSTRUCTION
   (Brass Construction)
3. GRATITUDE
   (Earth, Wind and Fire)
4. HE'S A FRIEND
   (Eddie Kendricks)
5. WAKE UP EVERYBODY
   (Harold Melvin and the Blue Notes)
6. FAMILY REUNION
   (The O'Jays)
7. MOTHERSHIP CONNECTION
   (Parliament)
8. DANCE YOUR TROUBLES AWAY
   (Archie Bell and the Drells)
9. EARGASM
   (Johnnie Taylor)
10. TURNING POINT
    (Tyrone Davis)

JAZZ ALBUMS

1. PLACES AND SPACES
   (Donald Byrd)
2. CITY LIFE
   (Blackbyrds)
3. THE LEPRECHAUN
   (Chick Corea)
4. NEW YORK CONNECTION
   (Tom Scott)
5. FEELS SO GOOD
   (Grover Washington Jr.)
6. TOUCH
   (John Klemmer)
7. VISIONS OF A NEW WORLD
   (Lonnie Liston Smith and The Cosmic Echoes)
8. HAVE YOU EVER SEEN THE RAIN
   (Stanley Turrentine)
9. BRASS CONSTRUCTION
   (Brass Construction)
10. MAN-CHILD
    (Herbie Hancock)

COUNTRY SINGLES

1. TILL THE RIVERS ALL RUN DRY
   (Don Williams)
2. FASTER HORSES
   (Tom T. Hall)
3. REMEMBER ME
   (Willie Nelson)
4. BROKEN LADY
   (Larry Gatlin)
5. IF I HAD IT TO DO ALL OVER AGAIN
   (Roy Clark)
6. THE ROOTS OF MY RAISING
   (Merle Haggard)
7. YOU'LL LOSE A GOOD THING
   (Freddy Fender)
8. GOODHEARTED WOMAN
   (Waylon Jennings and Willie Nelson)
9. STANDING ROOM ONLY
   (Barbara Mandrell)
10. MOTELS AND MEMORIES
    (T.G. Sheppard)

COUNTRY ALBUMS

1. THE OUTLAWS
   (Waylon, Willie, Jessi and Tompall)

2. ELITE HOTEL
   (Emmylou Harris)
3. LOVIN' AND LEARNIN'
   (Tanya Tucker)
4. JESSI
   (Jessi Colter)
5. TWITTY
   (Conway Twitty)
6. ROCK 'N' COUNTRY
   (Freddy Fender)
7. 200 YEARS OF COUNTRY MUSIC
   (Sonny James)
8. BLIND MAN IN THE BLEACHERS
   (Kenny Starr)
9. OVERNIGHT SENSATION
   (Mickey Gilley)
10. WHEN THE TINGLE BECOMES A CHILL
    (Loretta Lynn)

MARCH 27, 1976

POP SINGLES

1. DREAM WEAVER
   (Gary Wright)
2. DECEMBER, 1963 (OH WHAT A NIGHT)
   (The Four Seasons)
3. LONELY NIGHT (ANGEL FACE)
   (The Captain and Tennille)
4. DISCO LADY
   (Johnnie Taylor)
5. ALL BY MYSELF
   (Eric Carmen)
6. SWEET THING
   (Rufus featuring Chaka Khan)
7. DREAM ON
   (Aerosmith)
8. LOVE MACHINE (PART 1)
   (The Miracles)
9. SWEET LOVE
   (Commodores)
10. MONEY HONEY
    (Bay City Rollers)

POP ALBUMS

1. THEIR GREATEST HITS
   (The Eagles)
2. FRAMPTON COMES ALIVE
   (Peter Frampton)
3. DESIRE
   (Bob Dylan)
4. STILL CRAZY AFTER ALL THESE YEARS
   (Paul Simon)
5. RUN WITH THE PACK
   (Bad Company)
6. ONE OF THESE NIGHTS
   (The Eagles)
7. CHICAGO IX-GREATEST HITS
   (Chicago)
8. FLEETWOOD MAC
   (Fleetwood Mac)
9. HISTORY: AMERICA'S GREATEST HITS
   (America)
10. RUFUS . . . FEATURING CHAKA KHAN
    (Rufus featuring Chaka Khan)

BLACK SINGLES

1. DISCO LADY
   (Johnnie Taylor)
2. MISTY BLUE
   (Dorothy Moore)
3. BOOGIE FEVER
   (The Sylvers)
4. HE'S A FRIEND
   (Eddie Kendricks)
5. LET'S GROOVE
   (Archie Bell and the Drells)
6. SWEET THING
   (Rufus featuring Chaka Khan)

7. THEME FROM S.W.A.T.
   (Rhythm Heritage)
8. (CALL ME) THE TRAVELING MAN
   (Masqueraders)
9. NEW ORLEANS
   (The Staple Singers)
10. SWEET LOVE
    (Commodores)

BLACK ALBUMS

1. RUFUS . . . FEATURING CHAKA KHAN
   (Rufus featuring Chaka Khan)
2. BRASS CONSTRUCTION
   (Brass Construction)
3. HE'S A FRIEND
   (Eddie Kendricks)
4. WAKE UP EVERYBODY
   (Harold Melvin and the Blue Notes)
5. MOTHERSHIP CONNECTION
   (Parliament)
6. EARGASM
   (Johnnie Taylor)
7. FAMILY REUNION
   (The O'Jays)
8. GRATITUDE
   (Earth, Wind and Fire)
9. TURNING POINT
   (Tyrone Davis)
10. DANCE YOUR TROUBLES AWAY
    (Archie Bell and the Drells)

JAZZ ALBUMS

1. CITY LIFE
   (Blackbyrds)
2. PLACES AND SPACES
   (Donald Byrd)
3. THE LEPRECHAUN
   (Chick Corea)
4. NEW YORK CONNECTION
   (Tom Scott)
5. FEELS SO GOOD
   (Grover Washington Jr.)
6. BRASS CONSTRUCTION
   (Brass Construction)
7. TOUCH
   (John Klemmer)
8. HAVE YOU EVER SEEN THE RAIN
   (Stanley Turrentine)
9. VISIONS OF A NEW WORLD
   (Lonnie Liston Smith and The Cosmic Echoes)
10. BACK TO BACK
    (Brecker Brothers)

COUNTRY SINGLES

1. BROKEN LADY
   (Larry Gatlin)
2. TILL THE RIVERS ALL RUN DRY
   (Don Williams)
3. IF I HAD IT TO DO ALL OVER AGAIN
   (Roy Clark)
4. YOU'LL LOSE A GOOD THING
   (Freddy Fender)
5. FASTER HORSES
   (Tom T. Hall)
6. REMEMBER ME
   (Willie Nelson)
7. THE ROOTS OF MY RAISING
   (Merle Haggard)
8. DRINKIN' MY BABY (OFF MY MIND)
   (Eddie Rabbitt)
9. IF I LET HER COME IN
   (Ray Griff)
10. YOU ARE THE SONG
    (Freddie Hart)

COUNTRY ALBUMS

1. THE OUTLAWS
   (Waylon, Willie, Jessi and Tompall)

2. ELITE HOTEL
   (Emmylou Harris)
3. LOVIN' AND LEARNIN'
   (Tanya Tucker)
4. ROCK 'N' COUNTRY
   (Freddy Fender)
5. JESSI
   (Jessi Colter)
6. 200 YEARS OF COUNTRY MUSIC
   (Sonny James)
7. WHEN THE TINGLE BECOMES A CHILL
   (Loretta Lynn)
8. TWITTY
   (Conway Twitty)
9. SOMETIMES
   (Bill Anderson and Mary Lou Turner)
10. OVERNIGHT SENSATION
    (Mickey Gilley)

APRIL 3, 1976

POP SINGLES

1. LONELY NIGHT (ANGEL FACE)
   (The Captain and Tennille)
2. DISCO LADY
   (Johnnie Taylor)
3. DECEMBER, 1963 (OH WHAT A NIGHT)
   (The Four Seasons)
4. DREAM WEAVER
   (Gary Wright)
5. SWEET THING
   (Rufus featuring Chaka Khan)
6. DREAM ON
   (Aerosmith)
7. SWEET LOVE
   (Commodores)
8. ALL BY MYSELF
   (Eric Carmen)
9. RIGHT BACK WHERE WE STARTED FROM
   (Maxine Nightingale)
10. BOHEMIAN RHAPSODY
    (Queen)

POP ALBUMS

1. THEIR GREATEST HITS
   (The Eagles)
2. FRAMPTON COMES ALIVE
   (Peter Frampton)
3. STILL CRAZY AFTER ALL THESE YEARS
   (Paul Simon)
4. ONE OF THESE NIGHTS
   (The Eagles)
5. DESIRE
   (Bob Dylan)
6. FLEETWOOD MAC
   (Fleetwood Mac)
7. RUN WITH THE PACK
   (Bad Company)
8. CHICAGO IX-GREATEST HITS
   (Chicago)
9. HISTORY: AMERICA'S GREATEST HITS
   (America)
10. LOVE WILL KEEP US TOGETHER
    (The Captain and Tennille)

BLACK SINGLES

1. DISCO LADY
   (Johnnie Taylor)
2. MISTY BLUE
   (Dorothy Moore)
3. HE'S A FRIEND
   (Eddie Kendricks)
4. LET'S GROOVE
   (Archie Bell and the Drells)
5. BOOGIE FEVER
   (The Sylvers)
6. SWEET THING
   (Rufus featuring Chaka Khan)

7. FOPP
   (Ohio Players)
8. HAPPY MUSIC
   (Blackbyrds)
9. NEW ORLEANS
   (The Staple Singers)
10. I'VE GOT A FEELING (WE'LL BE SEEING
    EACH OTHER AGAIN)
    (Al Wilson)

BLACK ALBUMS

1. EARGASM
   (Johnnie Taylor)
2. RUFUS . . . FEATURING CHAKA KHAN
   (Rufus featuring Chaka Khan)
3. BRASS CONSTRUCTION
   (Brass Construction)
4. HE'S A FRIEND
   (Eddie Kendricks)
5. MOTHERSHIP CONNECTION
   (Parliament)
6. WAKE UP EVERYBODY
   (Harold Melvin and the Blue Notes)
7. FAMILY REUNION
   (The O'Jays)
8. GRATITUDE
   (Earth, Wind and Fire)
9. TURNING POINT
   (Tyrone Davis)
10. DANCE YOUR TROUBLES AWAY
    (Archie Bell and the Drells)

JAZZ ALBUMS

1. CITY LIFE
   (Blackbyrds)
2. THE LEPRECHAUN
   (Chick Corea)
3. PLACES AND SPACES
   (Donald Byrd)
4. BRASS CONSTRUCTION
   (Brass Construction)
5. NEW YORK CONNECTION
   (Tom Scott)
6. FEELS SO GOOD
   (Grover Washington Jr.)
7. TROPEA
   (John Tropea)
8. TOUCH
   (John Klemmer)
9. BACK TO BACK
   (Brecker Brothers)
10. MYSTIC VOYAGE
    (Roy Ayers Ubiquity)

COUNTRY SINGLES

1. IF I HAD IT TO DO ALL OVER AGAIN
   (Roy Clark)
2. YOU'LL LOSE A GOOD THING
   (Freddy Fender)
3. TILL THE RIVERS ALL RUN DRY
   (Don Williams)
4. BROKEN LADY
   (Larry Gatlin)
5. DRINKIN' MY BABY (OFF MY MIND)
   (Eddie Rabbitt)
6. FASTER HORSES
   (Tom T. Hall)
7. 'TIL I CAN MAKE IT ON MY OWN
   (Tammy Wynette)
8. IF I LET HER COME IN
   (Ray Griff)
9. ANGELS, ROSES AND RAIN
   (Dickey Lee)
10. THE PRISONER'S SONG/BACK IN THE
    SADDLE AGAIN
    (Sonny James)

COUNTRY ALBUMS

1. ELITE HOTEL
   (Emmylou Harris)

2. ROCK 'N' COUNTRY
   (Freddy Fender)
3. THE OUTLAWS
   (Waylon, Willie, Jessi and Tompall)
4. WHEN THE TINGLE BECOMES A CHILL
   (Loretta Lynn)
5. LOVIN' AND LEARNIN'
   (Tanya Tucker)
6. 200 YEARS OF COUNTRY MUSIC
   (Sonny James)
7. SOMETIMES
   (Bill Anderson and Mary Lou Turner)
8. THE WHITE KNIGHT
   (Cledus Maggard and The Citizens Band)
9. IT'S ALL IN THE MOVIES
   (Merle Haggard)
10. EASY AS PIE
    (Billy "Crash" Craddock)

APRIL 10, 1976

POP SINGLES

1. DISCO LADY
   (Johnnie Taylor)
2. LONELY NIGHT (ANGEL FACE)
   (The Captain and Tennille)
3. DECEMBER, 1963 (OH WHAT A NIGHT)
   (The Four Seasons)
4. RIGHT BACK WHERE WE STARTED FROM
   (Maxine Nightingale)
5. DREAM WEAVER
   (Gary Wright)
6. SWEET LOVE
   (Commodores)
7. DREAM ON
   (Aerosmith)
8. BOHEMIAN RHAPSODY
   (Queen)
9. BOOGIE FEVER
   (The Sylvers)
10. LET YOUR LOVE FLOW
    (The Bellamy Brothers)

POP ALBUMS

1. THEIR GREATEST HITS
   (The Eagles)
2. FRAMPTON COMES ALIVE
   (Peter Frampton)
3. FLEETWOOD MAC
   (Fleetwood Mac)
4. ONE OF THESE NIGHTS
   (The Eagles)
5. STILL CRAZY AFTER ALL THESE YEARS
   (Paul Simon)
6. DESIRE
   (Bob Dylan)
7. SONG OF JOY
   (The Captain and Tennille)
8. COME ON OVER
   (Olivia Newton-John)
9. RUN WITH THE PACK
   (Bad Company)
10. EARGASM
    (Johnnie Taylor)

BLACK SINGLES

1. DISCO LADY
   (Johnnie Taylor)
2. MISTY BLUE
   (Dorothy Moore)
3. HAPPY MUSIC
   (Blackbyrds)
4. LET'S GROOVE
   (Archie Bell and the Drells)
5. FOPP
   (Ohio Players)
6. HE'S A FRIEND
   (Eddie Kendricks)

7. I'VE GOT A FEELING (WE'LL BE SEEING
   EACH OTHER AGAIN)
   (Al Wilson)
8. BOOGIE FEVER
   (The Sylvers)
9. SWEET THING
   (Rufus featuring Chaka Khan)
10. NEW ORLEANS
    (Bobby Womack)

BLACK ALBUMS

1. EARGASM
   (Johnnie Taylor)
2. RUFUS . . . FEATURING CHAKA KHAN
   (Rufus featuring Chaka Khan)
3. BRASS CONSTRUCTION
   (Brass Construction)
4. HE'S A FRIEND
   (Eddie Kendricks)
5. FAMILY REUNION
   (The O'Jays)
6. MOTHERSHIP CONNECTION
   (Parliament)
7. WAKE UP EVERYBODY
   (Harold Melvin and the Blue Notes)
8. TURNING POINT
   (Tyrone Davis)
9. CITY LIFE
   (Blackbyrds)
10. INSEPARABLE
    (Natalie Cole)

JAZZ ALBUMS

1. CITY LIFE
   (Blackbyrds)
2. THE LEPRECHAUN
   (Chick Corea)
3. PLACES AND SPACES
   (Donald Byrd)
4. BRASS CONSTRUCTION
   (Brass Construction)
5. TROPEA
   (John Tropea)
6. NEW YORK CONNECTION
   (Tom Scott)
7. MYSTIC VOYAGE
   (Roy Ayers Ubiquity)
8. BACK TO BACK
   (Brecker Brothers)
9. FEELS SO GOOD
   (Grover Washington Jr.)
10. TOUCH
    (John Klemmer)

COUNTRY SINGLES

1. YOU'LL LOSE A GOOD THING
   (Freddy Fender)
2. DRINKIN' MY BABY (OFF MY MIND)
   (Eddie Rabbitt)
3. TILL THE RIVERS ALL RUN DRY
   (Don Williams)
4. IF I HAD IT TO DO ALL OVER AGAIN
   (Roy Clark)
5. 'TIL I CAN MAKE IT ON MY OWN
   (Tammy Wynette)
6. ANGELS, ROSES AND RAIN
   (Dickey Lee)
7. IF I LET HER COME IN
   (Ray Griff)
8. TOGETHER AGAIN
   (Emmylou Harris)
9. YOU COULD KNOW AS MUCH ABOUT A
   STRANGER
   (Gene Watson)
10. DON'T THE GIRLS ALL GET PRETTIER AT
    CLOSING TIME
    (Mickey Gilley)

COUNTRY ALBUMS

1. ELITE HOTEL
   (Emmylou Harris)
2. ROCK 'N' COUNTRY
   (Freddy Fender)
3. THE OUTLAWS
   (Waylon, Willie, Jessi and Tompall)
4. WHEN THE TINGLE BECOMES A CHILL
   (Loretta Lynn)
5. THE WHITE KNIGHT
   (Cledus Maggard and The Citizens Band)
6. SOMETIMES
   (Bill Anderson and Mary Lou Turner)
7. IT'S ALL IN THE MOVIES
   (Merle Haggard)
8. NARVEL THE MARVEL
   (Narvel Felts)
9. EASY AS PIE
   (Billy "Crash" Craddock)
10. LOVIN' AND LEARNIN'
    (Tanya Tucker)

APRIL 17, 1976

POP SINGLES

1. DISCO LADY
   (Johnnie Taylor)
2. DECEMBER, 1963 (OH WHAT A NIGHT)
   (The Four Seasons)
3. RIGHT BACK WHERE WE STARTED FROM
   (Maxine Nightingale)
4. LONELY NIGHT (ANGEL FACE)
   (The Captain and Tennille)
5. BOHEMIAN RHAPSODY
   (Queen)
6. BOOGIE FEVER
   (The Sylvers)
7. LET YOUR LOVE FLOW
   (The Bellamy Brothers)
8. SWEET LOVE
   (Commodores)
9. DREAM WEAVER
   (Gary Wright)
10. ONLY 16
    (Dr. Hook)

POP ALBUMS

1. THEIR GREATEST HITS
   (The Eagles)
2. FRAMPTON COMES ALIVE
   (Peter Frampton)
3. FLEETWOOD MAC
   (Fleetwood Mac)
4. DESTROYER
   (Kiss)
5. SONG OF JOY
   (The Captain and Tennille)
6. WINGS AT THE SPEED OF SOUND
   (Paul McCartney and Wings)
7. COME ON OVER
   (Olivia Newton-John)
8. EARGASM
   (Johnnie Taylor)
9. A NIGHT AT THE OPERA
   (Queen)
10. ONE OF THESE NIGHTS
    (The Eagles)

BLACK SINGLES

1. DISCO LADY
   (Johnnie Taylor)
2. MISTY BLUE
   (Dorothy Moore)
3. HAPPY MUSIC
   (Blackbyrds)

4. I'VE GOT A FEELING (WE'LL BE SEEING EACH OTHER AGAIN)
   (Al Wilson)
5. FOPP
   (Ohio Players)
6. HE'S A FRIEND
   (Eddie Kendricks)
7. LET'S GROOVE
   (Archie Bell and the Drells)
8. BOOGIE FEVER
   (The Sylvers)
9. LOVE HANGOVER
   (Diana Ross)
10. HEAVY LOVE
    (David Ruffin)

BLACK ALBUMS

1. EARGASM
   (Johnnie Taylor)
2. I WANT YOU
   (Marvin Gaye)
3. BRASS CONSTRUCTION
   (Brass Construction)
4. MOTHERSHIP CONNECTION
   (Parliament)
5. RUFUS . . . FEATURING CHAKA KHAN
   (Rufus featuring Chaka Khan)
6. FAMILY REUNION
   (The O'Jays)
7. HE'S A FRIEND
   (Eddie Kendricks)
8. WAKE UP EVERYBODY
   (Harold Melvin and the Blue Notes)
9. CITY LIFE
   (Blackbyrds)
10. DIANA ROSS
    (Diana Ross)

JAZZ ALBUMS

1. CITY LIFE
   (Blackbyrds)
2. THE LEPRECHAUN
   (Chick Corea)
3. BRASS CONSTRUCTION
   (Brass Construction)
4. PLACES AND SPACES
   (Donald Byrd)
5. TROPEA
   (John Tropea)
6. BACK TO BACK
   (Brecker Brothers)
7. MYSTIC VOYAGE
   (Roy Ayers Ubiquity)
8. NEW YORK CONNECTION
   (Tom Scott)
9. TOUCH
   (John Klemmer)
10. LOOK OUT FOR #1
    (The Brothers Johnson)

COUNTRY SINGLES

1. DRINKIN' MY BABY (OFF MY MIND)
   (Eddie Rabbitt)
2. 'TIL I CAN MAKE IT ON MY OWN
   (Tammy Wynette)
3. YOU'LL LOSE A GOOD THING
   (Freddy Fender)
4. TILL THE RIVERS ALL RUN DRY
   (Don Williams)
5. DON'T THE GIRLS ALL GET PRETTIER AT CLOSING TIME
   (Mickey Gilley)
6. ANGELS, ROSES AND RAIN
   (Dickey Lee)
7. TOGETHER AGAIN
   (Emmylou Harris)
8. YOU COULD KNOW AS MUCH ABOUT A STRANGER
   (Gene Watson)
9. I COULDN'T BE ME WITHOUT YOU
   (Johnny Rodriguez)

10. IF I HAD IT TO DO ALL OVER AGAIN
    (Roy Clark)

COUNTRY ALBUMS

1. ELITE HOTEL
   (Emmylou Harris)
2. IT'S ALL IN THE MOVIES
   (Merle Haggard)
3. THE WHITE KNIGHT
   (Cledus Maggard and The Citizens Band)
4. THE OUTLAWS
   (Waylon, Willie, Jessi and Tompall)
5. SOMETIMES
   (Bill Anderson and Mary Lou Turner)
6. ROCK 'N' COUNTRY
   (Freddy Fender)
7. THE SOUND IN YOUR MIND
   (Willie Nelson)
8. NARVEL THE MARVEL
   (Narvel Felts)
9. EASY AS PIE
   (Billy "Crash" Craddock)
10. WHEN THE TINGLE BECOMES A CHILL
    (Loretta Lynn)

APRIL 24, 1976

POP SINGLES

1. DISCO LADY
   (Johnnie Taylor)
2. RIGHT BACK WHERE WE STARTED FROM
   (Maxine Nightingale)
3. BOOGIE FEVER
   (The Sylvers)
4. BOHEMIAN RHAPSODY
   (Queen)
5. LET YOUR LOVE FLOW
   (The Bellamy Brothers)
6. DECEMBER, 1963 (OH WHAT A NIGHT)
   (The Four Seasons)
7. LONELY NIGHT (ANGEL FACE)
   (The Captain and Tennille)
8. SHOW ME THE WAY
   (Peter Frampton)
9. WELCOME BACK
   (John Sebastian)
10. ONLY 16
    (Dr. Hook)

POP ALBUMS

1. PRESENCE
   (Led Zeppelin)
2. THEIR GREATEST HITS
   (The Eagles)
3. WINGS AT THE SPEED OF SOUND
   (Paul McCartney and Wings)
4. DESTROYER
   (Kiss)
5. FRAMPTON COMES ALIVE
   (Peter Frampton)
6. SONG OF JOY
   (The Captain and Tennille)
7. COME ON OVER
   (Olivia Newton-John)
8. EARGASM
   (Johnnie Taylor)
9. A NIGHT AT THE OPERA
   (Queen)
10. FLEETWOOD MAC
    (Fleetwood Mac)

BLACK SINGLES

1. DISCO LADY
   (Johnnie Taylor)

2. MISTY BLUE
   (Dorothy Moore)
3. HAPPY MUSIC
   (Blackbyrds)
4. I'VE GOT A FEELING (WE'LL BE SEEING EACH OTHER AGAIN)
   (Al Wilson)
5. LOVE HANGOVER
   (Diana Ross)
6. HE'S A FRIEND
   (Eddie Kendricks)
7. MOVIN'
   (Brass Construction)
8. IT'S COOL
   (The Tymes)
9. HEAVY LOVE
   (David Ruffin)
10. FOPP
    (Ohio Players)

BLACK ALBUMS

1. EARGASM
   (Johnnie Taylor)
2. I WANT YOU
   (Marvin Gaye)
3. BRASS CONSTRUCTION
   (Brass Construction)
4. MOTHERSHIP CONNECTION
   (Parliament)
5. RUFUS . . . FEATURING CHAKA KHAN
   (Rufus featuring Chaka Khan)
6. FAMILY REUNION
   (The O'Jays)
7. DIANA ROSS
   (Diana Ross)
8. CITY LIFE
   (Blackbyrds)
9. LOOK OUT FOR #1
   (The Brothers Johnson)
10. LOVE AND UNDERSTANDING
    (Kool and the Gang)

JAZZ ALBUMS

1. THE LEPRECHAUN
   (Chick Corea)
2. CITY LIFE
   (Blackbyrds)
3. BRASS CONSTRUCTION
   (Brass Construction)
4. ROMANTIC WARRIOR, WITH RETURN TO FOREVER
   (Chick Corea with Return to Forever)
5. PLACES AND SPACES
   (Donald Byrd)
6. BACK TO BACK
   (Brecker Brothers)
7. MYSTIC VOYAGE
   (Roy Ayers Ubiquity)
8. TOUCH
   (John Klemmer)
9. TROPEA
   (John Tropea)
10. LOOK OUT FOR #1
    (The Brothers Johnson)

COUNTRY SINGLES

1. 'TIL I CAN MAKE IT ON MY OWN
   (Tammy Wynette)
2. DRINKIN' MY BABY (OFF MY MIND)
   (Eddie Rabbitt)
3. TOGETHER AGAIN
   (Emmylou Harris)
4. DON'T THE GIRLS ALL GET PRETTIER AT CLOSING TIME
   (Mickey Gilley)
5. YOU'LL LOSE A GOOD THING
   (Freddy Fender)
6. I COULDN'T BE ME WITHOUT YOU
   (Johnny Rodriguez)
7. TILL THE RIVERS ALL RUN DRY
   (Don Williams)

8. YOU COULD KNOW AS MUCH ABOUT A STRANGER
   (Gene Watson)
9. WHAT I'VE GOT IN MIND
   (Billie Jo Spears)
10. COME ON OVER
    (Olivia Newton-John)

COUNTRY ALBUMS

1. IT'S ALL IN THE MOVIES
   (Merle Haggard)
2. THE WHITE KNIGHT
   (Cledus Maggard and The Citizens Band)
3. ELITE HOTEL
   (Emmylou Harris)
4. THE SOUND IN YOUR MIND
   (Willie Nelson)
5. SOMETIMES
   (Bill Anderson and Mary Lou Turner)
6. THE OUTLAWS
   (Waylon, Willie, Jessi and Tompall)
7. COME ON OVER
   (Olivia Newton-John)
8. EASY AS PIE
   (Billy "Crash" Craddock)
9. ROCK 'N' COUNTRY
   (Freddy Fender)
10. NARVEL THE MARVEL
    (Narvel Felts)

MAY 1, 1976

POP SINGLES

1. RIGHT BACK WHERE WE STARTED FROM
   (Maxine Nightingale)
2. WELCOME BACK
   (John Sebastian)
3. BOOGIE FEVER
   (The Sylvers)
4. BOHEMIAN RHAPSODY
   (Queen)
5. LET YOUR LOVE FLOW
   (The Bellamy Brothers)
6. DISCO LADY
   (Johnnie Taylor)
7. SHOW ME THE WAY
   (Peter Frampton)
8. DECEMBER, 1963 (OH WHAT A NIGHT)
   (The Four Seasons)
9. FOOLED AROUND AND FELL IN LOVE
   (Elvin Bishop)
10. LONELY NIGHT (ANGEL FACE)
    (The Captain and Tennille)

POP ALBUMS

1. PRESENCE
   (Led Zeppelin)
2. THEIR GREATEST HITS
   (The Eagles)
3. WINGS AT THE SPEED OF SOUND
   (Paul McCartney and Wings)
4. FRAMPTON COMES ALIVE
   (Peter Frampton)
5. DESTROYER
   (Kiss)
6. FLEETWOOD MAC
   (Fleetwood Mac)
7. EARGASM
   (Johnnie Taylor)
8. COME ON OVER
   (Olivia Newton-John)
9. A NIGHT AT THE OPERA
   (Queen)
10. I WANT YOU
    (Marvin Gaye)

BLACK SINGLES

1. MISTY BLUE
   (Dorothy Moore)
2. DISCO LADY
   (Johnnie Taylor)
3. LOVE HANGOVER
   (Diana Ross)
4. MOVIN'
   (Brass Construction)
5. HAPPY MUSIC
   (Blackbyrds)
6. IT'S COOL
   (The Tymes)
7. I'VE GOT A FEELING (WE'LL BE SEEING EACH OTHER AGAIN)
   (Al Wilson)
8. HE'S A FRIEND
   (Eddie Kendricks)
9. GET UP AND BOOGIE
   (Silver Convention)
10. LIVIN' FOR THE WEEKEND
    (The O'Jays)

BLACK ALBUMS

1. EARGASM
   (Johnnie Taylor)
2. I WANT YOU
   (Marvin Gaye)
3. MOTHERSHIP CONNECTION
   (Parliament)
4. BRASS CONSTRUCTION
   (Brass Construction)
5. RUFUS . . . FEATURING CHAKA KHAN
   (Rufus featuring Chaka Khan)
6. LOOK OUT FOR #1
   (The Brothers Johnson)
7. DIANA ROSS
   (Diana Ross)
8. CITY LIFE
   (Blackbyrds)
9. FAMILY REUNION
   (The O'Jays)
10. WINGS OF LOVE
    (Temptations)

JAZZ ALBUMS

1. BREEZIN'
   (George Benson)
2. THE LEPRECHAUN
   (Chick Corea)
3. CITY LIFE
   (Blackbyrds)
4. ROMANTIC WARRIOR, WITH RETURN TO FOREVER
   (Chick Corea with Return to Forever)
5. BRASS CONSTRUCTION
   (Brass Construction)
6. MYSTIC VOYAGE
   (Roy Ayers Ubiquity)
7. TOUCH
   (John Klemmer)
8. REFLECTIONS OF A GOLDEN DREAM
   (Lonnie Liston Smith and The Cosmic Echoes)
9. LOOK OUT FOR #1
   (The Brothers Johnson)
10. PLACES AND SPACES
    (Donald Byrd)

COUNTRY SINGLES

1. TOGETHER AGAIN
   (Emmylou Harris)
2. DON'T THE GIRLS ALL GET PRETTIER AT CLOSING TIME
   (Mickey Gilley)
3. 'TIL I CAN MAKE IT ON MY OWN
   (Tammy Wynette)
4. I COULDN'T BE ME WITHOUT YOU
   (Johnny Rodriguez)

5. WHAT I'VE GOT IN MIND
   (Billie Jo Spears)
6. MY EYES CAN ONLY SEE AS FAR AS YOU
   (Charley Pride)
7. YOU COULD KNOW AS MUCH ABOUT A STRANGER
   (Gene Watson)
8. WHAT GOES ON WHEN THE SUN GOES DOWN
   (Ronnie Milsap)
9. COME ON OVER
   (Olivia Newton-John)
10. LONE STAR BEER AND BOB WILLS MUSIC
    (Red Steagall)

COUNTRY ALBUMS

1. THE SOUND IN YOUR MIND
   (Willie Nelson)
2. IT'S ALL IN THE MOVIES
   (Merle Haggard)
3. THE WHITE KNIGHT
   (Cledus Maggard and The Citizens Band)
4. COME ON OVER
   (Olivia Newton-John)
5. THE OUTLAWS
   (Waylon, Willie, Jessi and Tompall)
6. ELITE HOTEL
   (Emmylou Harris)
7. 'TIL I CAN MAKE IT ON MY OWN
   (Tammy Wynette)
8. SOMETIMES
   (Bill Anderson and Mary Lou Turner)
9. EASY AS PIE
   (Billy "Crash" Craddock)
10. LONGHAIRED REDNECK
    (David Allen Coe)

MAY 8, 1976

POP SINGLES

1. WELCOME BACK
   (John Sebastian)
2. BOOGIE FEVER
   (The Sylvers)
3. RIGHT BACK WHERE WE STARTED FROM
   (Maxine Nightingale)
4. LET YOUR LOVE FLOW
   (The Bellamy Brothers)
5. FOOLED AROUND AND FELL IN LOVE
   (Elvin Bishop)
6. SHOW ME THE WAY
   (Peter Frampton)
7. DISCO LADY
   (Johnnie Taylor)
8. BOHEMIAN RHAPSODY
   (Queen)
9. LOVE HANGOVER
   (Diana Ross)
10. SILLY LOVE SONGS
    (Paul McCartney and Wings)

POP ALBUMS

1. PRESENCE
   (Led Zeppelin)
2. THEIR GREATEST HITS
   (The Eagles)
3. FRAMPTON COMES ALIVE
   (Peter Frampton)
4. WINGS AT THE SPEED OF SOUND
   (Paul McCartney and Wings)
5. FLEETWOOD MAC
   (Fleetwood Mac)
6. DESTROYER
   (Kiss)
7. I WANT YOU
   (Marvin Gaye)
8. A NIGHT AT THE OPERA
   (Queen)

9. BLACK AND BLUE
   (The Rolling Stones)
10. TAKIN' IT TO THE STREETS
    (The Doobie Brothers)

BLACK SINGLES

1. MISTY BLUE
   (Dorothy Moore)
2. LOVE HANGOVER
   (Diana Ross)
3. MOVIN'
   (Brass Construction)
4. DISCO LADY
   (Johnnie Taylor)
5. GET UP AND BOOGIE
   (Silver Convention)
6. IT'S COOL
   (The Tymes)
7. KISS AND SAY GOODBYE
   (The Manhattans)
8. I'VE GOT A FEELING (WE'LL BE SEEING EACH OTHER AGAIN)
   (Al Wilson)
9. LIVIN' FOR THE WEEKEND
   (The O'Jays)
10. YOUNG HEARTS RUN FREE
    (Candi Staton)

BLACK ALBUMS

1. I WANT YOU
   (Marvin Gaye)
2. EARGASM
   (Johnnie Taylor)
3. LOOK OUT FOR #1
   (The Brothers Johnson)
4. MOTHERSHIP CONNECTION
   (Parliament)
5. BRASS CONSTRUCTION
   (Brass Construction)
6. DIANA ROSS
   (Diana Ross)
7. RUFUS . . . FEATURING CHAKA KHAN
   (Rufus featuring Chaka Khan)
8. CITY LIFE
   (Blackbyrds)
9. BREEZIN'
   (George Benson)
10. AMIGOS
    (Santana)

JAZZ ALBUMS

1. BREEZIN'
   (George Benson)
2. THE LEPRECHAUN
   (Chick Corea)
3. ROMANTIC WARRIOR, WITH RETURN TO FOREVER
   (Chick Corea with Return to Forever)
4. CITY LIFE
   (Blackbyrds)
5. BLACK MARKET
   (Weather Report)
6. MYSTIC VOYAGE
   (Roy Ayers Ubiquity)
7. REFLECTIONS OF A GOLDEN DREAM
   (Lonnie Liston Smith and The Cosmic Echoes)
8. TOUCH
   (John Klemmer)
9. LOOK OUT FOR #1
   (The Brothers Johnson)
10. BRASS CONSTRUCTION
    (Brass Construction)

COUNTRY SINGLES

1. DON'T THE GIRLS ALL GET PRETTIER AT CLOSING TIME
   (Mickey Gilley)

2. I COULDN'T BE ME WITHOUT YOU
   (Johnny Rodriguez)
3. MY EYES CAN ONLY SEE AS FAR AS YOU
   (Charley Pride)
4. WHAT I'VE GOT IN MIND
   (Billie Jo Spears)
5. TOGETHER AGAIN
   (Emmylou Harris)
6. WHAT GOES ON WHEN THE SUN GOES DOWN
   (Ronnie Milsap)
7. COME ON OVER
   (Olivia Newton-John)
8. AFTER ALL THE GOOD IS GONE
   (Conway Twitty)
9. 'TIL I CAN MAKE IT ON MY OWN
   (Tammy Wynette)
10. LONE STAR BEER AND BOB WILLS MUSIC
    (Red Steagall)

COUNTRY ALBUMS

1. THE SOUND IN YOUR MIND
   (Willie Nelson)
2. IT'S ALL IN THE MOVIES
   (Merle Haggard)
3. COME ON OVER
   (Olivia Newton-John)
4. THE WHITE KNIGHT
   (Cledus Maggard and The Citizens Band)
5. THE OUTLAWS
   (Waylon, Willie, Jessi and Tompall)
6. 'TIL I CAN MAKE IT ON MY OWN
   (Tammy Wynette)
7. ELITE HOTEL
   (Emmylou Harris)
8. GREATEST HITS OF JOHNNY RODRIGUEZ
   (Johnny Rodriguez)
9. FASTER HORSES
   (Tom T. Hall)
10. LONGHAIRED REDNECK
    (David Allen Coe)

MAY 15, 1976

POP SINGLES

1. WELCOME BACK
   (John Sebastian)
2. BOOGIE FEVER
   (The Sylvers)
3. FOOLED AROUND AND FELL IN LOVE
   (Elvin Bishop)
4. RIGHT BACK WHERE WE STARTED FROM
   (Maxine Nightingale)
5. LOVE HANGOVER
   (Diana Ross)
6. SILLY LOVE SONGS
   (Paul McCartney and Wings)
7. LET YOUR LOVE FLOW
   (The Bellamy Brothers)
8. DISCO LADY
   (Johnnie Taylor)
9. SHOW ME THE WAY
   (Peter Frampton)
10. SHANNON
    (Henry Gross)

POP ALBUMS

1. PRESENCE
   (Led Zeppelin)
2. FRAMPTON COMES ALIVE
   (Peter Frampton)
3. BLACK AND BLUE
   (The Rolling Stones)
4. THEIR GREATEST HITS
   (The Eagles)
5. WINGS AT THE SPEED OF SOUND
   (Paul McCartney and Wings)

6. I WANT YOU
   (Marvin Gaye)
7. FLEETWOOD MAC
   (Fleetwood Mac)
8. A NIGHT AT THE OPERA
   (Queen)
9. TAKIN' IT TO THE STREETS
   (The Doobie Brothers)
10. DESTROYER
    (Kiss)

BLACK SINGLES

1. LOVE HANGOVER
   (Diana Ross)
2. MISTY BLUE
   (Dorothy Moore)
3. MOVIN'
   (Brass Construction)
4. GET UP AND BOOGIE
   (Silver Convention)
5. KISS AND SAY GOODBYE
   (The Manhattans)
6. DISCO LADY
   (Johnnie Taylor)
7. YOUNG HEARTS RUN FREE
   (Candi Staton)
8. IT'S COOL
   (The Tymes)
9. I'VE GOT A FEELING (WE'LL BE SEEING
   EACH OTHER AGAIN)
   (Al Wilson)
10. LIVIN' FOR THE WEEKEND
    (The O'Jays)

BLACK ALBUMS

1. I WANT YOU
   (Marvin Gaye)
2. EARGASM
   (Johnnie Taylor)
3. LOOK OUT FOR #1
   (The Brothers Johnson)
4. MOTHERSHIP CONNECTION
   (Parliament)
5. DIANA ROSS
   (Diana Ross)
6. BREEZIN'
   (George Benson)
7. BRASS CONSTRUCTION
   (Brass Construction)
8. RUFUS . . . FEATURING CHAKA KHAN
   (Rufus featuring Chaka Khan)
9. AMIGOS
   (Santana)
10. THE MANHATTANS
    (The Manhattans)

JAZZ ALBUMS

1. BREEZIN'
   (George Benson)
2. THE LEPRECHAUN
   (Chick Corea)
3. ROMANTIC WARRIOR, WITH RETURN TO
   FOREVER
   (Chick Corea with Return to Forever)
4. BLACK MARKET
   (Weather Report)
5. CITY LIFE
   (Blackbyrds)
6. REFLECTIONS OF A GOLDEN DREAM
   *(Lonnie Liston Smith and The Cosmic
   Echoes)*
7. MYSTIC VOYAGE
   (Roy Ayers Ubiquity)
8. TOUCH
   (John Klemmer)
9. BACK TO BACK
   (Brecker Brothers)
10. LOOK OUT FOR #1
    (The Brothers Johnson)

COUNTRY SINGLES

1. I COULDN'T BE ME WITHOUT YOU
   (Johnny Rodriguez)
2. MY EYES CAN ONLY SEE AS FAR AS YOU
   (Charley Pride)
3. WHAT GOES ON WHEN THE SUN GOES
   DOWN
   (Ronnie Milsap)
4. WHAT I'VE GOT IN MIND
   (Billie Jo Spears)
5. AFTER ALL THE GOOD IS GONE
   (Conway Twitty)
6. COME ON OVER
   (Olivia Newton-John)
7. I'LL GET OVER YOU
   (Crystal Gayle)
8. ONE PIECE AT A TIME
   (Johnny Cash)
9. LONE STAR BEER AND BOB WILLS MUSIC
   (Red Steagall)
10. THAT'S WHAT MADE ME LOVE YOU
    (Bill Anderson and Mary Lou Turner)

COUNTRY ALBUMS

1. THE SOUND IN YOUR MIND
   (Willie Nelson)
2. COME ON OVER
   (Olivia Newton-John)
3. GREATEST HITS OF JOHNNY RODRIGUEZ
   (Johnny Rodriguez)
4. 'TIL I CAN MAKE IT ON MY OWN
   (Tammy Wynette)
5. IT'S ALL IN THE MOVIES
   (Merle Haggard)
6. FASTER HORSES
   (Tom T. Hall)
7. THE OUTLAWS
   (Waylon, Willie, Jessi and Tompall)
8. ELITE HOTEL
   (Emmylou Harris)
9. SUN SESSIONS
   (Elvis Presley)
10. GILLEY'S GREATEST HITS, VOL. 1
    (Mickey Gilley)

MAY 22, 1976

POP SINGLES

1. BOOGIE FEVER
   (The Sylvers)
2. WELCOME BACK
   (John Sebastian)
3. FOOLED AROUND AND FELL IN LOVE
   (Elvin Bishop)
4. LOVE HANGOVER
   (Diana Ross)
5. SILLY LOVE SONGS
   (Paul McCartney and Wings)
6. RIGHT BACK WHERE WE STARTED FROM
   (Maxine Nightingale)
7. GET UP AND BOOGIE
   (Silver Convention)
8. SHANNON
   (Henry Gross)
9. HAPPY DAYS
   (Pratt and McLain)
10. MISTY BLUE
    (Dorothy Moore)

POP ALBUMS

1. PRESENCE
   (Led Zeppelin)
2. BLACK AND BLUE
   (The Rolling Stones)
3. FRAMPTON COMES ALIVE
   (Peter Frampton)

4. THEIR GREATEST HITS
   (The Eagles)
5. WINGS AT THE SPEED OF SOUND
   (Paul McCartney and Wings)
6. I WANT YOU
   (Marvin Gaye)
7. FLEETWOOD MAC
   (Fleetwood Mac)
8. A NIGHT AT THE OPERA
   (Queen)
9. DESTROYER
   (Kiss)
10. TAKIN' IT TO THE STREETS
    (The Doobie Brothers)

BLACK SINGLES

1. LOVE HANGOVER
   (Diana Ross)
2. KISS AND SAY GOODBYE
   (The Manhattans)
3. GET UP AND BOOGIE
   (Silver Convention)
4. YOUNG HEARTS RUN FREE
   (Candi Staton)
5. MISTY BLUE
   (Dorothy Moore)
6. MOVIN'
   (Brass Construction)
7. DISCO LADY
   (Johnnie Taylor)
8. DANCE WIT ME
   (Rufus featuring Chaka Khan)
9. IT'S COOL
   (The Tymes)
10. I WANT YOU
    (Marvin Gaye)

BLACK ALBUMS

1. I WANT YOU
   (Marvin Gaye)
2. MOTHERSHIP CONNECTION
   (Parliament)
3. LOOK OUT FOR #1
   (The Brothers Johnson)
4. DIANA ROSS
   (Diana Ross)
5. EARGASM
   (Johnnie Taylor)
6. BREEZIN'
   (George Benson)
7. THE MANHATTANS
   (The Manhattans)
8. BRASS CONSTRUCTION
   (Brass Construction)
9. AMIGOS
   (Santana)
10. STRETCHIN' OUT IN BOOTSY'S RUBBER
    BAND
    (Bootsy's Rubber Band)

JAZZ ALBUMS

1. BREEZIN'
   (George Benson)
2. ROMANTIC WARRIOR, WITH RETURN TO
   FOREVER
   (Chick Corea with Return to Forever)
3. THE LEPRECHAUN
   (Chick Corea)
4. BLACK MARKET
   (Weather Report)
5. REFLECTIONS OF A GOLDEN DREAM
   *(Lonnie Liston Smith and The Cosmic
   Echoes)*
6. CITY LIFE
   (Blackbyrds)
7. MYSTIC VOYAGE
   (Roy Ayers Ubiquity)
8. TOUCH
   (John Klemmer)
9. LOOK OUT FOR #1
   (The Brothers Johnson)

10. LAND OF THE MIDNIGHT SUN
     (Al DiMeola)

COUNTRY SINGLES

1. WHAT I'VE GOT IN MIND
    (Billie Jo Spears)
2. MY EYES CAN ONLY SEE AS FAR AS YOU
    (Charley Pride)
3. WHAT GOES ON WHEN THE SUN GOES DOWN
    (Ronnie Milsap)
4. AFTER ALL THE GOOD IS GONE
    (Conway Twitty)
5. ONE PIECE AT A TIME
    (Johnny Cash)
6. I'LL GET OVER YOU
    (Crystal Gayle)
7. COME ON OVER
    (Olivia Newton-John)
8. HURT/FOR THE HEART
    (Elvis Presley)
9. THAT'S WHAT MADE ME LOVE YOU
    (Bill Anderson and Mary Lou Turner)
10. I COULDN'T BE ME WITHOUT YOU
    (Johnny Rodriguez)

COUNTRY ALBUMS

1. THE SOUND IN YOUR MIND
    (Willie Nelson)
2. GREATEST HITS OF JOHNNY RODRIGUEZ
    (Johnny Rodriguez)
3. COME ON OVER
    (Olivia Newton-John)
4. 'TIL I CAN MAKE IT ON MY OWN
    (Tammy Wynette)
5. IT'S ALL IN THE MOVIES
    (Merle Haggard)
6. FASTER HORSES
    (Tom T. Hall)
7. GILLEY'S GREATEST HITS, VOL. 1
    (Mickey Gilley)
8. SUN SESSIONS
    (Elvis Presley)
9. ELITE HOTEL
    (Emmylou Harris)
10. BLOODLINE
    (Glen Campbell)

MAY 29, 1976

POP SINGLES

1. SILLY LOVE SONGS
    (Paul McCartney and Wings)
2. BOOGIE FEVER
    (The Sylvers)
3. LOVE HANGOVER
    (Diana Ross)
4. WELCOME BACK
    (John Sebastian)
5. GET UP AND BOOGIE
    (Silver Convention)
6. SHANNON
    (Henry Cross)
7. HAPPY DAYS
    (Pratt and McLain)
8. FOOLED AROUND AND FELL IN LOVE
    (Elvin Bishop)
9. MISTY BLUE
    (Dorothy Moore)
10. TRYIN' TO GET THE FEELING AGAIN
    (Barry Manilow)

POP ALBUMS

1. BLACK AND BLUE
    (The Rolling Stones)

2. FRAMPTON COMES ALIVE
    (Peter Frampton)
3. PRESENCE
    (Led Zeppelin)
4. THEIR GREATEST HITS
    (The Eagles)
5. WINGS AT THE SPEED OF SOUND
    (Paul McCartney and Wings)
6. FLEETWOOD MAC
    (Fleetwood Mac)
7. HERE AND THERE
    (Elton John)
8. I WANT YOU
    (Marvin Gaye)
9. A NIGHT AT THE OPERA
    (Queen)
10. TAKIN' IT TO THE STREETS
    (The Doobie Brothers)

BLACK SINGLES

1. KISS AND SAY GOODBYE
    (The Manhattans)
2. LOVE HANGOVER
    (Diana Ross)
3. GET UP AND BOOGIE
    (Silver Convention)
4. YOUNG HEARTS RUN FREE
    (Candi Staton)
5. MISTY BLUE
    (Dorothy Moore)
6. MOVIN'
    (Brass Construction)
7. DANCE WIT ME
    (Rufus featuring Chaka Khan)
8. I WANT YOU
    (Marvin Gaye)
9. TEAR THE ROOF OFF THE SUCKER (GIVE UP THE FUNK)
    (Parliament)
10. I'LL BE GOOD TO YOU
    (The Brothers Johnson)

BLACK ALBUMS

1. I WANT YOU
    (Marvin Gaye)
2. LOOK OUT FOR #1
    (The Brothers Johnson)
3. MOTHERSHIP CONNECTION
    (Parliament)
4. DIANA ROSS
    (Diana Ross)
5. BREEZIN'
    (George Benson)
6. THE MANHATTANS
    (The Manhattans)
7. EARGASM
    (Johnnie Taylor)
8. STRETCHIN' OUT IN BOOTSY'S RUBBER BAND
    (Bootsy's Rubber Band)
9. BRASS CONSTRUCTION
    (Brass Construction)
10. AMIGOS
    (Santana)

JAZZ ALBUMS

1. BREEZIN'
    (George Benson)
2. ROMANTIC WARRIOR, WITH RETURN TO FOREVER
    (Chick Corea with Return to Forever)
3. THE LEPRECHAUN
    (Chick Corea)
4. BLACK MARKET
    (Weather Report)
5. CITY LIFE
    (Blackbyrds)
6. REFLECTIONS OF A GOLDEN DREAM
    (Lonnie Liston Smith and The Cosmic Echoes)
7. TOUCH
    (John Klemmer)

8. LOOK OUT FOR #1
    (The Brothers Johnson)
9. MYSTIC VOYAGE
    (Roy Ayers Ubiquity)
10. LAND OF THE MIDNIGHT SUN
    (Al DiMeola)

COUNTRY SINGLES

1. MY EYES CAN ONLY SEE AS FAR AS YOU
    (Charley Pride)
2. WHAT GOES ON WHEN THE SUN GOES DOWN
    (Ronnie Milsap)
3. ONE PIECE AT A TIME
    (Johnny Cash)
4. AFTER ALL THE GOOD IS GONE
    (Conway Twitty)
5. I'LL GET OVER YOU
    (Crystal Gayle)
6. WHAT I'VE GOT IN MIND
    (Billie Jo Spears)
7. HURT/FOR THE HEART
    (Elvis Presley)
8. DON'T PULL YOUR LOVE/THEN YOU CAN TELL ME GOODBYE
    (Glen Campbell)
9. THAT'S WHAT MADE ME LOVE YOU
    (Bill Anderson and Mary Lou Turner)
10. WALK SOFTLY
    (Billy "Crash" Craddock)

COUNTRY ALBUMS

1. GREATEST HITS OF JOHNNY RODRIGUEZ
    (Johnny Rodriguez)
2. THE SOUND IN YOUR MIND
    (Willie Nelson)
3. COME ON OVER
    (Olivia Newton-John)
4. 'TIL I CAN MAKE IT ON MY OWN
    (Tammy Wynette)
5. SUN SESSIONS
    (Elvis Presley)
6. FASTER HORSES
    (Tom T. Hall)
7. GILLEY'S GREATEST HITS, VOL. 1
    (Mickey Gilley)
8. BLOODLINE
    (Glen Campbell)
9. WILDERNESS
    (C.W. McCall)
10. HARMONY
    (Don Williams)

JUNE 5, 1976

POP SINGLES

1. SILLY LOVE SONGS
    (Paul McCartney and Wings)
2. LOVE HANGOVER
    (Diana Ross)
3. GET UP AND BOOGIE
    (Silver Convention)
4. BOOGIE FEVER
    (The Sylvers)
5. SHANNON
    (Henry Gross)
6. HAPPY DAYS
    (Pratt and McLain)
7. WELCOME BACK
    (John Sebastian)
8. MISTY BLUE
    (Dorothy Moore)
9. FOOLED AROUND AND FELL IN LOVE
    (Elvin Bishop)
10. RHIANNON (WILL YOU EVER)
    (Fleetwood Mac)

POP ALBUMS

1. FRAMPTON COMES ALIVE
   (Peter Frampton)
2. WINGS AT THE SPEED OF SOUND
   (Paul McCartney and Wings)
3. BLACK AND BLUE
   (The Rolling Stones)
4. PRESENCE
   (Led Zeppelin)
5. HERE AND THERE
   (Elton John)
6. FLEETWOOD MAC
   (Fleetwood Mac)
7. THEIR GREATEST HITS
   (The Eagles)
8. ROCKS
   (Aerosmith)
9. A NIGHT AT THE OPERA
   (Queen)
10. TAKIN' IT TO THE STREETS
    (The Doobie Brothers)

BLACK SINGLES

1. KISS AND SAY GOODBYE
   (The Manhattans)
2. LOVE HANGOVER
   (Diana Ross)
3. GET UP AND BOOGIE
   (Silver Convention)
4. YOUNG HEARTS RUN FREE
   (Candi Staton)
5. TEAR THE ROOF OFF THE SUCKER (GIVE
   UP THE FUNK)
   (Parliament)
6. DANCE WIT ME
   (Rufus featuring Chaka Khan)
7. I WANT YOU
   (Marvin Gaye)
8. MISTY BLUE
   (Dorothy Moore)
9. OPEN
   (Smokey Robinson)
10. I'LL BE GOOD TO YOU
    (The Brothers Johnson)

BLACK ALBUMS

1. I WANT YOU
   (Marvin Gaye)
2. BREEZIN'
   (George Benson)
3. LOOK OUT FOR #1
   (The Brothers Johnson)
4. MOTHERSHIP CONNECTION
   (Parliament)
5. DIANA ROSS
   (Diana Ross)
6. THE MANHATTANS
   (The Manhattans)
7. STRETCHIN' OUT IN BOOTSY'S RUBBER
   BAND
   (Bootsy's Rubber Band)
8. EARGASM
   (Johnnie Taylor)
9. WHERE THE HAPPY PEOPLE GO
   (Trammps)
10. RASTAMAN VIBRATION
    (Bob Marley and the Wailers)

JAZZ ALBUMS

1. BREEZIN'
   (George Benson)
2. ROMANTIC WARRIOR, WITH RETURN TO
   FOREVER
   (Chick Corea with Return to Forever)
3. BLACK MARKET
   (Weather Report)
4. THE LEPRECHAUN
   (Chick Corea)

5. CITY LIFE
   (Blackbyrds)
6. LOOK OUT FOR #1
   (The Brothers Johnson)
7. TOUCH
   (John Klemmer)
8. REFLECTIONS OF A GOLDEN DREAM
   (Lonnie Liston Smith and The Cosmic
   Echoes)
9. LAND OF THE MIDNIGHT SUN
   (Al DiMeola)
10. ODYSSEY
    (Charles Earland)

COUNTRY SINGLES

1. WHAT GOES ON WHEN THE SUN GOES
   DOWN
   (Ronnie Milsap)
2. ONE PIECE AT A TIME
   (Johnny Cash)
3. I'LL GET OVER YOU
   (Crystal Gayle)
4. AFTER ALL THE GOOD IS GONE
   (Conway Twitty)
5. DON'T PULL YOUR LOVE/THEN YOU CAN
   TELL ME GOODBYE
   (Glen Campbell)
6. HURT/FOR THE HEART
   (Elvis Presley)
7. WALK SOFTLY
   (Billy "Crash" Craddock)
8. YOU'VE GOT ME TO HOLD ON TO
   (Tanya Tucker)
9. EL PASO CITY
   (Marty Robbins)
10. LONELY TEARDROPS
    (Narvel Felts)

COUNTRY ALBUMS

1. GREATEST HITS OF JOHNNY RODRIGUEZ
   (Johnny Rodriguez)
2. THE SOUND IN YOUR MIND
   (Willie Nelson)
3. SUN SESSIONS
   (Elvis Presley)
4. 'TIL I CAN MAKE IT ON MY OWN
   (Tammy Wynette)
5. FASTER HORSES
   (Tom T. Hall)
6. BLOODLINE
   (Glen Campbell)
7. GILLEY'S GREATEST HITS, VOL. 1
   (Mickey Gilley)
8. HARMONY
   (Don Williams)
9. WILDERNESS
   (C.W. McCall)
10. COME ON OVER
    (Olivia Newton-John)

JUNE 12, 1976

POP SINGLES

1. LOVE HANGOVER
   (Diana Ross)
2. SILLY LOVE SONGS
   (Paul McCartney and Wings)
3. GET UP AND BOOGIE
   (Silver Convention)
4. BOOGIE FEVER
   (The Sylvers)
5. SHANNON
   (Henry Gross)
6. MISTY BLUE
   (Dorothy Moore)
7. HAPPY DAYS
   (Pratt and McLain)

8. MORE, MORE, MORE
   (Andrea True Connection)
9. WELCOME BACK
   (John Sebastian)
10. SARA SMILE
    (Daryl Hall and John Oates)

POP ALBUMS

1. FRAMPTON COMES ALIVE
   (Peter Frampton)
2. WINGS AT THE SPEED OF SOUND
   (Paul McCartney and Wings)
3. FLEETWOOD MAC
   (Fleetwood Mac)
4. ROCKS
   (Aerosmith)
5. HERE AND THERE
   (Elton John)
6. PRESENCE
   (Led Zeppelin)
7. THEIR GREATEST HITS
   (The Eagles)
8. BLACK AND BLUE
   (The Rolling Stones)
9. TAKIN' IT TO THE STREETS
   (The Doobie Brothers)
10. A NIGHT AT THE OPERA
    (Queen)

BLACK SINGLES

1. TEAR THE ROOF OFF THE SUCKER (GIVE
   UP THE FUNK)
   (Parliament)
2. KISS AND SAY GOODBYE
   (The Manhattans)
3. YOUNG HEARTS RUN FREE
   (Candi Staton)
4. LOVE HANGOVER
   (Diana Ross)
5. SOPHISTICATED LADY
   (Natalie Cole)
6. I WANT YOU
   (Marvin Gaye)
7. BARETTA'S THEME: KEEP YOUR EYE ON
   THE SPARROW
   (Rhythm Heritage)
8. OPEN
   (Smokey Robinson)
9. GET UP AND BOOGIE
   (Silver Convention)
10. THAT'S WHERE THE HAPPY PEOPLE GO
    (Trammps)

BLACK ALBUMS

1. BREEZIN'
   (George Benson)
2. I WANT YOU
   (Marvin Gaye)
3. LOOK OUT FOR #1
   (The Brothers Johnson)
4. MOTHERSHIP CONNECTION
   (Parliament)
5. THE MANHATTANS
   (The Manhattans)
6. DIANA ROSS
   (Diana Ross)
7. STRETCHIN' OUT IN BOOTSY'S RUBBER
   BAND
   (Bootsy's Rubber Band)
8. WHERE THE HAPPY PEOPLE GO
   (Trammps)
9. NATALIE
   (Natalie Cole)
10. HARVEST FOR THE WORLD
    (Isley Brothers)

JAZZ ALBUMS

1. BREEZIN'
   (George Benson)

2. ROMANTIC WARRIOR, WITH RETURN TO FOREVER
   (Chick Corea with Return to Forever)
3. BLACK MARKET
   (Weather Report)
4. LOOK OUT FOR #1
   (The Brothers Johnson)
5. THOSE SOUTHERN KNIGHTS
   (Crusaders)
6. THE LEPRECHAUN
   (Chick Corea)
7. SALONGO
   (Ramsey Lewis)
8. REFLECTIONS OF A GOLDEN DREAM
   (Lonnie Liston Smith and The Cosmic Echoes)
9. TOUCH
   (John Klemmer)
10. CITY LIFE
    (Blackbyrds)

COUNTRY SINGLES

1. ONE PIECE AT A TIME
   (Johnny Cash)
2. I'LL GET OVER YOU
   (Crystal Gayle)
3. EL PASO CITY
   (Marty Robbins)
4. AFTER ALL THE GOOD IS GONE
   (Conway Twitty)
5. HURT/FOR THE HEART
   (Elvis Presley)
6. WALK SOFTLY
   (Billy "Crash" Craddock)
7. YOU'VE GOT ME TO HOLD ON TO
   (Tanya Tucker)
8. LONELY TEARDROPS
   (Narvel Felts)
9. THE DOOR IS ALWAYS OPEN
   (Dave and Sugar)
10. STRANGER
    (Johnny Duncan)

COUNTRY ALBUMS

1. SUN SESSIONS
   (Elvis Presley)
2. GREATEST HITS OF JOHNNY RODRIGUEZ
   (Johnny Rodriguez)
3. THE SOUND IN YOUR MIND
   (Willie Nelson)
4. BLOODLINE
   (Glen Campbell)
5. HARMONY
   (Don Williams)
6. GILLEY'S GREATEST HITS, VOL. 1
   (Mickey Gilley)
7. FASTER HORSES
   (Tom T. Hall)
8. 'TIL I CAN MAKE IT ON MY OWN
   (Tammy Wynette)
9. WILLIE NELSON LIVE
   (Willie Nelson)
10. HAROLD, LEW, PHIL AND DON
    (The Statler Brothers)

JUNE 19, 1976

POP SINGLES

1. SILLY LOVE SONGS
   (Paul McCartney and Wings)
2. GET UP AND BOOGIE
   (Silver Convention)
3. LOVE HANGOVER
   (Diana Ross)
4. SHANNON
   (Henry Gross)
5. MORE, MORE, MORE
   (Andrea True Connection)

6. MISTY BLUE
   (Dorothy Moore)
7. BOOGIE FEVER
   (The Sylvers)
8. WELCOME BACK
   (John Sebastian)
9. SHOP AROUND
   (The Captain and Tennille)
10. NEVER GONNA FALL IN LOVE AGAIN
    (Eric Carmen)

POP ALBUMS

1. WINGS AT THE SPEED OF SOUND
   (Paul McCartney and Wings)
2. FRAMPTON COMES ALIVE
   (Peter Frampton)
3. FLEETWOOD MAC
   (Fleetwood Mac)
4. ROCKS
   (Aerosmith)
5. HERE AND THERE
   (Elton John)
6. THEIR GREATEST HITS
   (The Eagles)
7. PRESENCE
   (Led Zeppelin)
8. BLACK AND BLUE
   (The Rolling Stones)
9. TAKIN' IT TO THE STREETS
   (The Doobie Brothers)
10. THE DREAM WEAVER
    (Gary Wright)

BLACK SINGLES

1. KISS AND SAY GOODBYE
   (The Manhattans)
2. YOUNG HEARTS RUN FREE
   (Candi Staton)
3. SOPHISTICATED LADY
   (Natalie Cole)
4. TEAR THE ROOF OFF THE SUCKER (GIVE UP THE FUNK)
   (Parliament)
5. BARETTA'S THEME: KEEP YOUR EYE ON THE SPARROW
   (Rhythm Heritage)
6. I WANT YOU
   (Marvin Gaye)
7. LOVE HANGOVER
   (Diana Ross)
8. OPEN
   (Smokey Robinson)
9. THAT'S WHERE THE HAPPY PEOPLE GO
   (Trammps)
10. THE LONELY ONE
    (Special Delivery)

BLACK ALBUMS

1. LOOK OUT FOR #1
   (The Brothers Johnson)
2. BREEZIN'
   (George Benson)
3. I WANT YOU
   (Marvin Gaye)
4. NATALIE
   (Natalie Cole)
5. MOTHERSHIP CONNECTION
   (Parliament)
6. THE MANHATTANS
   (The Manhattans)
7. HARVEST FOR THE WORLD
   (Isley Brothers)
8. DIANA ROSS
   (Diana Ross)
9. STRETCHIN' OUT IN BOOTSY'S RUBBER BAND
   (Bootsy's Rubber Band)
10. WHERE THE HAPPY PEOPLE GO
    (Trammps)

JAZZ ALBUMS

1. BREEZIN'
   (George Benson)
2. THOSE SOUTHERN KNIGHTS
   (Crusaders)
3. LOOK OUT FOR #1
   (The Brothers Johnson)
4. SALONGO
   (Ramsey Lewis)
5. BLACK MARKET
   (Weather Report)
6. ROMANTIC WARRIOR, WITH RETURN TO FOREVER
   (Chick Corea with Return to Forever)
7. THE LEPRECHAUN
   (Chick Corea)
8. REFLECTIONS OF A GOLDEN DREAM
   (Lonnie Liston Smith and The Cosmic Echoes)
9. TOUCH
   (John Klemmer)
10. CITY LIFE
    (Blackbyrds)

COUNTRY SINGLES

1. I'LL GET OVER YOU
   (Crystal Gayle)
2. EL PASO CITY
   (Marty Robbins)
3. ONE PIECE AT A TIME
   (Johnny Cash)
4. ALL THESE THINGS
   (Joe Stampley)
5. STRANGER
   (Johnny Duncan)
6. WALK SOFTLY
   (Billy "Crash" Craddock)
7. THE DOOR IS ALWAYS OPEN
   (Dave and Sugar)
8. LONELY TEARDROPS
   (Narvel Felts)
9. YOU'VE GOT ME TO HOLD ON TO
   (Tanya Tucker)
10. SHE'LL THROW STONES AT YOU
    (Freddie Hart)

COUNTRY ALBUMS

1. SUN SESSIONS
   (Elvis Presley)
2. BLOODLINE
   (Glen Campbell)
3. HARMONY
   (Don Williams)
4. THE SOUND IN YOUR MIND
   (Willie Nelson)
5. GREATEST HITS OF JOHNNY RODRIGUEZ
   (Johnny Rodriguez)
6. WILLIE NELSON LIVE
   (Willie Nelson)
7. FASTER HORSES
   (Tom T. Hall)
8. GILLEY'S GREATEST HITS, VOL. 1
   (Mickey Gilley)
9. HAROLD, LEW, PHIL AND DON
   (The Statler Brothers)
10. SUNDAY MORNING WITH CHARLEY PRIDE
    (Charley Pride)

JUNE 26, 1976

POP SINGLES

1. GET UP AND BOOGIE
   (Silver Convention)
2. SILLY LOVE SONGS
   (Paul McCartney and Wings)

3. LOVE HANGOVER
   (Diana Ross)
4. MORE, MORE, MORE
   (Andrea True Connection)
5. KISS AND SAY GOODBYE
   (The Manhattans)
6. MISTY BLUE
   (Dorothy Moore)
7. SHOP AROUND
   (The Captain and Tennille)
8. SHANNON
   (Henry Gross)
9. NEVER GONNA FALL IN LOVE AGAIN
   (Eric Carmen)
10. AFTERNOON DELIGHT
    (Starland Vocal Band)

POP ALBUMS

1. WINGS AT THE SPEED OF SOUND
   (Paul McCartney and Wings)
2. FLEETWOOD MAC
   (Fleetwood Mac)
3. FRAMPTON COMES ALIVE
   (Peter Frampton)
4. ROCKS
   (Aerosmith)
5. THEIR GREATEST HITS
   (The Eagles)
6. HERE AND THERE
   (Elton John)
7. PRESENCE
   (Led Zeppelin)
8. BLACK AND BLUE
   (The Rolling Stones)
9. THE DREAM WEAVER
   (Gary Wright)
10. TAKIN' IT TO THE STREETS
    (The Doobie Brothers)

BLACK SINGLES

1. KISS AND SAY GOODBYE
   (The Manhattans)
2. YOUNG HEARTS RUN FREE
   (Candi Staton)
3. SOPHISTICATED LADY
   (Natalie Cole)
4. SOMETHING HE CAN FEEL
   (Aretha Franklin)
5. BARETTA'S THEME: KEEP YOUR EYE ON
   THE SPARROW
   (Rhythm Heritage)
6. YOU'LL NEVER FIND ANOTHER LOVE LIKE
   MINE
   (Lou Rawls)
7. TEAR THE ROOF OFF THE SUCKER (GIVE
   UP THE FUNK)
   (Parliament)
8. THAT'S WHERE THE HAPPY PEOPLE GO
   (Trammps)
9. THE LONELY ONE
   (Special Delivery)
10. I WANT YOU
    (Marvin Gaye)

BLACK ALBUMS

1. BREEZIN'
   (George Benson)
2. LOOK OUT FOR #1
   (The Brothers Johnson)
3. NATALIE
   (Natalie Cole)
4. I WANT YOU
   (Marvin Gaye)
5. HARVEST FOR THE WORLD
   (Isley Brothers)
6. THE MANHATTANS
   (The Manhattans)
7. MOTHERSHIP CONNECTION
   (Parliament)
8. DIANA ROSS
   (Diana Ross)

9. STRETCHIN' OUT IN BOOTSY'S RUBBER
   BAND
   (Bootsy's Rubber Band)
10. THOSE SOUTHERN KNIGHTS
    (Crusaders)

JAZZ ALBUMS

1. BREEZIN'
   (George Benson)
2. THOSE SOUTHERN KNIGHTS
   (Crusaders)
3. SALONGO
   (Ramsey Lewis)
4. LOOK OUT FOR #1
   (The Brothers Johnson)
5. BLACK MARKET
   (Weather Report)
6. ROMANTIC WARRIOR, WITH RETURN TO
   FOREVER
   (Chick Corea with Return to Forever)
7. FEVER
   (Ronnie Laws)
8. FLY WITH THE WIND
   (McCoy Tyner)
9. TOUCH
   (John Klemmer)
10. CITY LIFE
    (Blackbyrds)

COUNTRY SINGLES

1. EL PASO CITY
   (Marty Robbins)
2. ALL THESE THINGS
   (Joe Stampley)
3. STRANGER
   (Johnny Duncan)
4. THE DOOR IS ALWAYS OPEN
   (Dave and Sugar)
5. I'LL GET OVER YOU
   (Crystal Gaye)
6. SUSPICIOUS MINDS
   (Waylon Jennings and Jessi Colter)
7. ONE PIECE AT A TIME
   (Johnny Cash)
8. HERE COMES THE FREEDOM TRAIN
   (Merle Haggard)
9. LONELY TEARDROPS
   (Narvel Felts)
10. SHE'LL THROW STONES AT YOU
    (Freddie Hart)

COUNTRY ALBUMS

1. HARMONY
   (Don Williams)
2. BLOODLINE
   (Glen Campbell)
3. SUN SESSIONS
   (Elvis Presley)
4. THE SOUND IN YOUR MIND
   (Willie Nelson)
5. WILLIE NELSON LIVE
   (Willie Nelson)
6. GREATEST HITS OF JOHNNY RODRIGUEZ
   (Johnny Rodriguez)
7. GILLEY'S GREATEST HITS, VOL. 1
   (Mickey Gilley)
8. FASTER HORSES
   (Tom T. Hall)
9. SUNDAY MORNING WITH CHARLEY PRIDE
   (Charley Pride)
10. ONE PIECE AT A TIME
    (Johnny Cash)

JULY 3, 1976

POP SINGLES

1. SILLY LOVE SONGS
   (Paul McCartney and Wings)

2. GET UP AND BOOGIE
   (Silver Convention)
3. MORE, MORE, MORE
   (Andrea True Connection)
4. KISS AND SAY GOODBYE
   (The Manhattans)
5. AFTERNOON DELIGHT
   (Starland Vocal Band)
6. SHOP AROUND
   (The Captain and Tennille)
7. LOVE HANGOVER
   (Diana Ross)
8. MISTY BLUE
   (Dorothy Moore)
9. LOVE IS ALIVE
   (Gary Wright)
10. MOONLIGHT FEELS RIGHT
    (Starbuck)

POP ALBUMS

1. WINGS AT THE SPEED OF SOUND
   (Paul McCartney and Wings)
2. FRAMPTON COMES ALIVE
   (Peter Frampton)
3. FLEETWOOD MAC
   (Fleetwood Mac)
4. ROCKS
   (Aerosmith)
5. THEIR GREATEST HITS
   (The Eagles)
6. HERE AND THERE
   (Elton John)
7. THE DREAM WEAVER
   (Gary Wright)
8. BLACK AND BLUE
   (The Rolling Stones)
9. BREEZIN'
   (George Benson)
10. HARVEST FOR THE WORLD
    (Isley Brothers)

BLACK SINGLES

1. SOMETHING HE CAN FEEL
   (Aretha Franklin)
2. YOU'LL NEVER FIND ANOTHER LOVE LIKE
   MINE
   (Lou Rawls)
3. KISS AND SAY GOODBYE
   (The Manhattans)
4. SOPHISTICATED LADY
   (Natalie Cole)
5. YOUNG HEARTS RUN FREE
   (Candi Staton)
6. THIS MASQUERADE
   (George Benson)
7. TEAR THE ROOF OFF THE SUCKER (GIVE
   UP THE FUNK)
   (Parliament)
8. THAT'S WHERE THE HAPPY PEOPLE GO
   (Trammps)
9. THE LONELY ONE
   (Special Delivery)
10. SOMEBODY'S GETTIN' IT
    (Johnnie Taylor)

BLACK ALBUMS

1. BREEZIN'
   (George Benson)
2. LOOK OUT FOR #1
   (The Brothers Johnson)
3. NATALIE
   (Natalie Cole)
4. HARVEST FOR THE WORLD
   (Isley Brothers)
5. I WANT YOU
   (Marvin Gaye)
6. CONTRADICTION
   (Ohio Players)
7. SPARKLE
   (Aretha Franklin)

8. THE MANHATTANS
(The Manhattans)
9. THOSE SOUTHERN KNIGHTS
(Crusaders)
10. DIANA ROSS
(Diana Ross)

JAZZ ALBUMS

1. BREEZIN'
(George Benson)
2. THOSE SOUTHERN KNIGHTS
(Crusaders)
3. LOOK OUT FOR #1
(The Brothers Johnson)
4. FEVER
(Ronnie Laws)
5. FLY WITH THE WIND
(McCoy Tyner)
6. SALONGO
(Ramsey Lewis)
7. BLACK MARKET
(Weather Report)
8. ROMANTIC WARRIOR, WITH RETURN TO
FOREVER
(Chick Corea with Return to Forever)
9. EVERYBODY COME ON OUT
(Stanley Turrentine)
10. CITY LIFE
(Blackbyrds)

COUNTRY SINGLES

1. ALL THESE THINGS
(Joe Stampley)
2. STRANGER
(Johnny Duncan)
3. THE DOOR IS ALWAYS OPEN
(Dave and Sugar)
4. EL PASO CITY
(Marty Robbins)
5. SUSPICIOUS MINDS
(Waylon Jennings and Jessi Colter)
6. I'LL GET OVER YOU
(Crystal Gayle)
7. HERE COMES THE FREEDOM TRAIN
(Merle Haggard)
8. ONE PIECE AT A TIME
(Johnny Cash)
9. I'D HAVE TO BE CRAZY
(Willie Nelson)
10. VAYA CON DIOS
(Freddy Fender)

COUNTRY ALBUMS

1. HARMONY
(Don Williams)
2. BLOODLINE
(Glen Campbell)
3. SUN SESSIONS
(Elvis Presley)
4. ONE PIECE AT A TIME
(Johnny Cash)
5. WILLIE NELSON LIVE
(Willie Nelson)
6. THE SOUND IN YOUR MIND
(Willie Nelson)
7. GREATEST HITS OF JOHNNY RODRIGUEZ
(Johnny Rodriguez)
8. 20-20 VISION
(Ronnie Milsap)
9. NOW AND THEN
(Conway Twitty)
10. FROM ELVIS PRESLEY BOULEVARD,
MEMPHIS, TENNESSEE
(Elvis Presley)

JULY 10, 1976

POP SINGLES

1. KISS AND SAY GOODBYE
(The Manhattans)
2. AFTERNOON DELIGHT
(Starland Vocal Band)
3. MORE, MORE, MORE
(Andrea True Connection)
4. SILLY LOVE SONGS
(Paul McCartney and Wings)
5. SHOP AROUND
(The Captain and Tennille)
6. GET UP AND BOOGIE
(Silver Convention)
7. LOVE IS ALIVE
(Gary Wright)
8. MOONLIGHT FEELS RIGHT
(Starbuck)
9. LOVE HANGOVER
(Diana Ross)
10. MISTY BLUE
(Dorothy Moore)

POP ALBUMS

1. FLEETWOOD MAC
(Fleetwood Mac)
2. FRAMPTON COMES ALIVE
(Peter Frampton)
3. WINGS AT THE SPEED OF SOUND
(Paul McCartney and Wings)
4. THEIR GREATEST HITS
(The Eagles)
5. THE DREAM WEAVER
(Gary Wright)
6. ROCKS
(Aerosmith)
7. BREEZIN'
(George Benson)
8. ROCK 'N' ROLL MUSIC
(The Beatles)
9. BLACK AND BLUE
(The Rolling Stones)
10. HARVEST FOR THE WORLD
(Isley Brothers)

BLACK SINGLES

1. SOMETHING HE CAN FEEL
(Aretha Franklin)
2. YOU'LL NEVER FIND ANOTHER LOVE LIKE
MINE
(Lou Rawls)
3. THIS MASQUERADE
(George Benson)
4. SOPHISTICATED LADY
(Natalie Cole)
5. YOUNG HEARTS RUN FREE
(Candi Staton)
6. KISS AND SAY GOODBYE
(The Manhattans)
7. TEAR THE ROOF OFF THE SUCKER (GIVE
UP THE FUNK)
(Parliament)
8. THAT'S WHERE THE HAPPY PEOPLE GO
(Trammps)
9. SOMEBODY'S GETTIN' IT
(Johnnie Taylor)
10. THE LONELY ONE
(Special Delivery)

BLACK ALBUMS

1. BREEZIN'
(George Benson)
2. NATALIE
(Natalie Cole)
3. LOOK OUT FOR #1
(The Brothers Johnson)

4. SPARKLE
(Aretha Franklin)
5. CONTRADICTION
(Ohio Players)
6. HARVEST FOR THE WORLD
(Isley Brothers)
7. I WANT YOU
(Marvin Gaye)
8. THOSE SOUTHERN KNIGHTS
(Crusaders)
9. THE MANHATTANS
(The Manhattans)
10. ALL THINGS IN TIME
(Lou Rawls)

JAZZ ALBUMS

1. BREEZIN'
(George Benson)
2. THOSE SOUTHERN KNIGHTS
(Crusaders)
3. LOOK OUT FOR #1
(The Brothers Johnson)
4. FEVER
(Ronnie Laws)
5. FLY WITH THE WIND
(McCoy Tyner)
6. THREE
(Bob James)
7. SALONGO
(Ramsey Lewis)
8. EVERYBODY COME ON OUT
(Stanley Turrentine)
9. ROMANTIC WARRIOR, WITH RETURN TO
FOREVER
(Chick Corea with Return to Forever)
10. GOOD KING BAD
(George Benson)

COUNTRY SINGLES

1. STRANGER
(Johnny Duncan)
2. THE DOOR IS ALWAYS OPEN
(Dave and Sugar)
3. ALL THESE THINGS
(Joe Stampley)
4. EL PASO CITY
(Marty Robbins)
5. SUSPICIOUS MINDS
(Waylon Jennings and Jessi Colter)
6. TEDDY BEAR
(Red Sovine)
7. HERE COMES THE FREEDOM TRAIN
(Merle Haggard)
8. VAYA CON DIOS
(Freddy Fender)
9. IS FOREVER LONGER THAN ALWAYS
(Porter Wagoner and Dolly Parton)
10. GOLDEN RING
(George Jones and Tammy Wynette)

COUNTRY ALBUMS

1. HARMONY
(Don Williams)
2. ONE PIECE AT A TIME
(Johnny Cash)
3. FROM ELVIS PRESLEY BOULEVARD,
MEMPHIS, TENNESSEE
(Elvis Presley)
4. BLOODLINE
(Glen Campbell)
5. WILLIE NELSON LIVE
(Willie Nelson)
6. 20-20 VISION
(Ronnie Milsap)
7. NOW AND THEN
(Conway Twitty)
8. THE SOUND IN YOUR MIND
(Willie Nelson)
9. SADDLE TRAMP
(Charlie Daniels Band)

10. SUN SESSIONS
    (Elvis Presley)

JULY 17, 1976

POP SINGLES

1. AFTERNOON DELIGHT
   (Starland Vocal Band)
2. MORE, MORE, MORE
   (Andrea True Connection)
3. KISS AND SAY GOODBYE
   (The Manhattans)
4. SHOP AROUND
   (The Captain and Tennille)
5. LOVE IS ALIVE
   (Gary Wright)
6. MOONLIGHT FEELS RIGHT
   (Starbuck)
7. SILLY LOVE SONGS
   (Paul McCartney and Wings)
8. GET UP AND BOOGIE
   (Silver Convention)
9. I'LL BE GOOD TO YOU
   (The Brothers Johnson)
10. GET CLOSER
    (Seals and Crofts)

POP ALBUMS

1. FRAMPTON COMES ALIVE
   (Peter Frampton)
2. FLEETWOOD MAC
   (Fleetwood Mac)
3. WINGS AT THE SPEED OF SOUND
   (Paul McCartney and Wings)
4. THEIR GREATEST HITS
   (The Eagles)
5. THE DREAM WEAVER
   (Gary Wright)
6. ROCK 'N' ROLL MUSIC
   (The Beatles)
7. BREEZIN'
   (George Benson)
8. BEAUTIFUL NOISE
   (Neil Diamond)
9. CHICAGO X
   (Chicago)
10. ROCKS
    (Aerosmith)

BLACK SINGLES

1. SOMETHING HE CAN FEEL
   (Aretha Franklin)
2. YOU'LL NEVER FIND ANOTHER LOVE LIKE MINE
   (Lou Rawls)
3. THIS MASQUERADE
   (George Benson)
4. SOPHISTICATED LADY
   (Natalie Cole)
5. YOUNG HEARTS RUN FREE
   (Candi Staton)
6. KISS AND SAY GOODBYE
   (The Manhattans)
7. TEAR THE ROOF OFF THE SUCKER (GIVE UP THE FUNK)
   (Parliament)
8. HEAVEN MUST BE MISSING AN ANGEL
   (Tavares)
9. SOMEBODY'S GETTIN' IT
   (Johnnie Taylor)
10. GET UP OFFA THAT THING
    (James Brown)

BLACK ALBUMS

1. BREEZIN'
   (George Benson)

2. SPARKLE
   (Aretha Franklin)
3. NATALIE
   (Natalie Cole)
4. LOOK OUT FOR #1
   (The Brothers Johnson)
5. HARVEST FOR THE WORLD
   (Isley Brothers)
6. I WANT YOU
   (Marvin Gaye)
7. CONTRADICTION
   (Ohio Players)
8. ALL THINGS IN TIME
   (Lou Rawls)
9. THOSE SOUTHERN KNIGHTS
   (Crusaders)
10. STRETCHIN' OUT IN BOOTSY'S RUBBER BAND
    (Bootsy's Rubber Band)

JAZZ ALBUMS

1. BREEZIN'
   (George Benson)
2. THOSE SOUTHERN KNIGHTS
   (Crusaders)
3. FEVER
   (Ronnie Laws)
4. THREE
   (Bob James)
5. LOOK OUT FOR #1
   (The Brothers Johnson)
6. EVERYBODY COME ON OUT
   (Stanley Turrentine)
7. FLY WITH THE WIND
   (McCoy Tyner)
8. GOOD KING BAD
   (George Benson)
9. SALONGO
   (Ramsey Lewis)
10. TOUCH
    (John Klemmer)

COUNTRY SINGLES

1. THE DOOR IS ALWAYS OPEN
   (Dave and Sugar)
2. TEDDY BEAR
   (Red Sovine)
3. ALL THESE THINGS
   (Joe Stampley)
4. STRANGER
   (Johnny Duncan)
5. SUSPICIOUS MINDS
   (Waylon Jennings and Jessi Colter)
6. VAYA CON DIOS
   (Freddy Fender)
7. IS FOREVER LONGER THAN ALWAYS
   (Porter Wagoner and Dolly Parton)
8. HERE COMES THE FREEDOM TRAIN
   (Merle Haggard)
9. GOLDEN RING
   (George Jones and Tammy Wynette)
10. WHEN SOMETHING'S WRONG WITH MY BABY
    (Sonny James)

COUNTRY ALBUMS

1. FROM ELVIS PRESLEY BOULEVARD, MEMPHIS, TENNESSEE
   (Elvis Presley)
2. ONE PIECE AT A TIME
   (Johnny Cash)
3. HARMONY
   (Don Williams)
4. 20-20 VISION
   (Ronnie Milsap)
5. NOW AND THEN
   (Conway Twitty)
6. BLOODLINE
   (Glen Campbell)
7. WILLIE NELSON LIVE
   (Willie Nelson)

8. SADDLE TRAMP
   (Charlie Daniels Band)
9. THE SOUND IN YOUR MIND
   (Willie Nelson)
10. SOMEBODY LOVES YOU
    (Crystal Gayle)

JULY 24, 1976

POP SINGLES

1. MORE, MORE, MORE
   (Andrea True Connection)
2. KISS AND SAY GOODBYE
   (The Manhattans)
3. AFTERNOON DELIGHT
   (Starland Vocal Band)
4. LOVE IS ALIVE
   (Gary Wright)
5. MOONLIGHT FEELS RIGHT
   (Starbuck)
6. SHOP AROUND
   (The Captain and Tennille)
7. GET CLOSER
   (Seals and Crofts)
8. I'LL BE GOOD TO YOU
   (The Brothers Johnson)
9. TEAR THE ROOF OFF THE SUCKER (GIVE UP THE FUNK)
   (Parliament)
10. DON'T GO BREAKING MY HEART
    (Elton John and Kiki Dee)

POP ALBUMS

1. FRAMPTON COMES ALIVE
   (Peter Frampton)
2. FLEETWOOD MAC
   (Fleetwood Mac)
3. ROCK 'N' ROLL MUSIC
   (The Beatles)
4. SPITFIRE
   (The Jefferson Starship)
5. WINGS AT THE SPEED OF SOUND
   (Paul McCartney and Wings)
6. BEAUTIFUL NOISE
   (Neil Diamond)
7. THEIR GREATEST HITS
   (The Eagles)
8. CHICAGO X
   (Chicago)
9. THE DREAM WEAVER
   (Gary Wright)
10. BREEZIN'
    (George Benson)

BLACK SINGLES

1. SOMETHING HE CAN FEEL
   (Aretha Franklin)
2. YOU'LL NEVER FIND ANOTHER LOVE LIKE MINE
   (Lou Rawls)
3. THIS MASQUERADE
   (George Benson)
4. SOPHISTICATED LADY
   (Natalie Cole)
5. HEAVEN MUST BE MISSING AN ANGEL
   (Tavares)
6. GET UP OFFA THAT THING
   (James Brown)
7. KISS AND SAY GOODBYE
   (The Manhattans)
8. YOUNG HEARTS RUN FREE
   (Candi Staton)
9. TEAR THE ROOF OFF THE SUCKER (GIVE UP THE FUNK)
   (Parliament)
10. WHO'D SHE COO?
    (Ohio Players)

BLACK ALBUMS

1. BREEZIN'
   (George Benson)
2. SPARKLE
   (Aretha Franklin)
3. NATALIE
   (Natalie Cole)
4. HARVEST FOR THE WORLD
   (Isley Brothers)
5. LOOK OUT FOR #1
   (The Brothers Johnson)
6. I WANT YOU
   (Marvin Gaye)
7. HOT ON THE TRACKS
   (Commodores)
8. CONTRADICTIONS
   (Ohio Players)
9. ALL THINGS IN TIME
   (Lou Rawls)
10. THOSE SOUTHERN KNIGHTS
    (Crusaders)

JAZZ ALBUMS

1. BREEZIN'
   (George Benson)
2. THOSE SOUTHERN KNIGHTS
   (Crusaders)
3. THREE
   (Bob James)
4. FEVER
   (Ronnie Laws)
5. LOOK OUT FOR #1
   (The Brothers Johnson)
6. GOOD KING BAD
   (George Benson)
7. EVERYBODY COME ON OUT
   (Stanley Turrentine)
8. FLY WITH THE WIND
   (McCoy Tyner)
9. SALONGO
   (Ramsey Lewis)
10. HARD WORK
    (John Handy)

COUNTRY SINGLES

1. TEDDY BEAR
   (Red Sovine)
2. THE DOOR IS ALWAYS OPEN
   (Dave and Sugar)
3. GOLDEN RING
   (George Jones and Tammy Wynette)
4. ALL THESE THINGS
   (Joe Stampley)
5. THE LETTER
   (Conway Twitty and Loretta Lynn)
6. VAYA CON DIOS
   (Freddy Fender)
7. IS FOREVER LONGER THAN ALWAYS
   (Porter Wagoner and Dolly Parton)
8. SAY IT AGAIN
   (Don Williams)
9. WHEN SOMETHING'S WRONG WITH MY BABY
   (Sonny James)
10. STRANGER
    (Johnny Duncan)

COUNTRY ALBUMS

1. FROM ELVIS PRESLEY BOULEVARD, MEMPHIS, TENNESSEE
   (Elvis Presley)
2. ONE PIECE AT A TIME
   (Johnny Cash)
3. 20-20 VISION
   (Ronnie Milsap)
4. NOW AND THEN
   (Conway Twitty)
5. HARMONY
   (Don Williams)

6. UNITED TALENT
   (Loretta Lynn and Conway Twitty)
7. BLOODLINE
   (Glen Campbell)
8. SADDLE TRAMP
   (Charlie Daniels Band)
9. WILLIE NELSON LIVE
   (Willie Nelson)
10. SOMEBODY LOVES YOU
    (Crystal Gayle)

JULY 31, 1976

POP SINGLES

1. AFTERNOON DELIGHT
   (Starland Vocal Band)
2. KISS AND SAY GOODBYE
   (The Manhattans)
3. MORE, MORE, MORE
   (Andrea True Connection)
4. MOONLIGHT FEELS RIGHT
   (Starbuck)
5. GET CLOSER
   (Seals and Crofts)
6. DON'T GO BREAKING MY HEART
   (Elton John and Kiki Dee)
7. LOVE IS ALIVE
   (Gary Wright)
8. TEAR THE ROOF OFF THE SUCKER (GIVE UP THE FUNK)
   (Parliament)
9. GOT TO GET YOU INTO MY LIFE
   (The Beatles)
10. ROCK AND ROLL MUSIC
    (The Beach Boys)

POP ALBUMS

1. FRAMPTON COMES ALIVE
   (Peter Frampton)
2. ROCK 'N' ROLL MUSIC
   (The Beatles)
3. SPITFIRE
   (The Jefferson Starship)
4. FLEETWOOD MAC
   (Fleetwood Mac)
5. BEAUTIFUL NOISE
   (Neil Diamond)
6. THEIR GREATEST HITS
   (The Eagles)
7. CHICAGO X
   (Chicago)
8. WINGS AT THE SPEED OF SOUND
   (Paul McCartney and Wings)
9. BREEZIN'
   (George Benson)
10. ROCKS
    (Aerosmith)

BLACK SINGLES

1. YOU'LL NEVER FIND ANOTHER LOVE LIKE MINE
   (Lou Rawls)
2. SOMETHING HE CAN FEEL
   (Aretha Franklin)
3. HEAVEN MUST BE MISSING AN ANGEL
   (Tavares)
4. GET UP OFFA THAT THING
   (James Brown)
5. GETAWAY
   (Earth, Wind and Fire)
6. THIS MASQUERADE
   (George Benson)
7. WHO'D SHE COO?
   (Ohio Players)
8. (SHAKE, SHAKE, SHAKE) SHAKE YOUR BOOTY
   (KC and the Sunshine Band)

9. KISS AND SAY GOODBYE
   (The Manhattans)
10. SOPHISTICATED LADY
    (Natalie Cole)

BLACK ALBUMS

1. SPARKLE
   (Aretha Franklin)
2. BREEZIN'
   (George Benson)
3. HARVEST FOR THE WORLD
   (Isley Brothers)
4. HOT ON THE TRACKS
   (Commodores)
5. CONTRADICTION
   (Ohio Players)
6. NATALIE
   (Natalie Cole)
7. ALL THINGS IN TIME
   (Lou Rawls)
8. LOOK OUT FOR #1
   (The Brothers Johnson)
9. I WANT YOU
   (Marvin Gaye)
10. MOTHERSHIP CONNECTION
    (Parliament)

JAZZ ALBUMS

1. BREEZIN'
   (George Benson)
2. THOSE SOUTHERN KNIGHTS
   (Crusaders)
3. THREE
   (Bob James)
4. GOOD KING BAD
   (George Benson)
5. EVERYBODY COME ON OUT
   (Stanley Turrentine)
6. FEVER
   (Ronnie Laws)
7. LOOK OUT FOR #1
   (The Brothers Johnson)
8. FLY WITH THE WIND
   (McCoy Tyner)
9. HARD WORK
   (John Handy)
10. MYSTERIES
    (Keith Jarrett)

COUNTRY SINGLES

1. TEDDY BEAR
   (Red Sovine)
2. GOLDEN RING
   (George Jones and Tammy Wynette)
3. THE LETTER
   (Conway Twitty and Loretta Lynn)
4. THE DOOR IS ALWAYS OPEN
   (Dave and Sugar)
5. SAY IT AGAIN
   (Don Williams)
6. ONE OF THESE DAYS
   (Emmylou Harris)
7. VAYA CON DIOS
   (Freddy Fender)
8. IS FOREVER LONGER THAN ALWAYS
   (Porter Wagoner and Dolly Parton)
9. ROCKY MOUNTAIN MUSIC/DO YOU RIGHT TONIGHT
   (Eddie Rabbitt)
10. SAVE YOUR KISSES FOR ME
    (Margo Smith)

COUNTRY ALBUMS

1. ONE PIECE AT A TIME
   (Johnny Cash)
2. 20-20 VISION
   (Ronnie Milsap)

3. NOW AND THEN
   (Conway Twitty)
4. UNITED TALENT
   (Loretta Lynn and Conway Twitty)
5. FROM ELVIS PRESLEY BOULEVARD,
   MEMPHIS, TENNESSEE
   (Elvis Presley)
6. HARMONY
   (Don Williams)
7. ARE YOU READY FOR THE COUNTRY
   (Waylon Jennings)
8. BLOODLINE
   (Glen Campbell)
9. WHAT I'VE GOT IN MIND
   (Billie Jo Spears)
10. SADDLE TRAMP
    (Charlie Daniels Band)

AUGUST 7, 1976

POP SINGLES

1. DON'T GO BREAKING MY HEART
   (Elton John and Kiki Dee)
2. AFTERNOON DELIGHT
   (Starland Vocal Band)
3. KISS AND SAY GOODBYE
   (The Manhattans)
4. GET CLOSER
   (Seals and Crofts)
5. MOONLIGHT FEELS RIGHT
   (Starbuck)
6. LET 'EM IN
   (Paul McCartney and Wings)
7. YOU'LL NEVER FIND ANOTHER LOVE LIKE
   MINE
   (Lou Rawls)
8. ROCK AND ROLL MUSIC
   (The Beach Boys)
9. GOT TO GET YOU INTO MY LIFE
   (The Beatles)
10. PLAY THAT FUNKY MUSIC
    (Wild Cherry)

POP ALBUMS

1. FRAMPTON COMES ALIVE
   (Peter Frampton)
2. ROCK 'N' ROLL MUSIC
   (The Beatles)
3. SPITFIRE
   (The Jefferson Starship)
4. BEAUTIFUL NOISE
   (Neil Diamond)
5. FLEETWOOD MAC
   (Fleetwood Mac)
6. THEIR GREATEST HITS
   (The Eagles)
7. CHICAGO X
   (Chicago)
8. WINGS AT THE SPEED OF SOUND
   (Paul McCartney and Wings)
9. BREEZIN'
   (George Benson)
10. 15 BIG ONES
    (The Beach Boys)

BLACK SINGLES

1. YOU'LL NEVER FIND ANOTHER LOVE LIKE
   MINE
   (Lou Rawls)
2. GETAWAY
   (Earth, Wind and Fire)
3. HEAVEN MUST BE MISSING AN ANGEL
   (Tavares)
4. GET UP OFFA THAT THING
   (James Brown)
5. (SHAKE, SHAKE, SHAKE) SHAKE YOUR
   BOOTY
   (KC and the Sunshine Band)

6. WHO'D SHE COO?
   (Ohio Players)
7. SOMETHING HE CAN FEEL
   (Aretha Franklin)
8. THIS MASQUERADE
   (George Benson)
9. PLAY THAT FUNKY MUSIC
   (Wild Cherry)
10. KISS AND SAY GOODBYE
    (The Manhattans)

BLACK ALBUMS

1. SPARKLE
   (Aretha Franklin)
2. BREEZIN'
   (George Benson)
3. HOT ON THE TRACKS
   (Commodores)
4. HARVEST FOR THE WORLD
   (Isley Brothers)
5. CONTRADICTION
   (Ohio Players)
6. ALL THINGS IN TIME
   (Lou Rawls)
7. NATALIE
   (Natalie Cole)
8. LOOK OUT FOR #1
   (The Brothers Johnson)
9. MIRROR
   (Graham Central Station)
10. MOTHERSHIP CONNECTION
    (Parliament)

JAZZ ALBUMS

1. BREEZIN'
   (George Benson)
2. THOSE SOUTHERN KNIGHTS
   (Crusaders)
3. THREE
   (Bob James)
4. LOOK OUT FOR #1
   (The Brothers Johnson)
5. GOOD KING BAD
   (George Benson)
6. EVERYBODY COME ON OUT
   (Stanley Turrentine)
7. FEVER
   (Ronnie Laws)
8. FLY WITH THE WIND
   (McCoy Tyner)
9. HARD WORK
   (John Handy)
10. MYSTERIES
    (Keith Jarrett)

COUNTRY SINGLES

1. GOLDEN RING
   (George Jones and Tammy Wynette)
2. THE LETTER
   (Conway Twitty and Loretta Lynn)
3. TEDDY BEAR
   (Red Sovine)
4. SAY IT AGAIN
   (Don Williams)
5. ONE OF THESE DAYS
   (Emmylou Harris)
6. ROCKY MOUNTAIN MUSIC/DO YOU RIGHT
   TONIGHT
   (Eddie Rabbitt)
7. BRING IT ON HOME TO ME
   (Mickey Gilley)
8. THE DOOR IS ALWAYS OPEN
   (Dave and Sugar)
9. SAVE YOUR KISSES FOR ME
   (Margo Smith)
10. IS FOREVER LONGER THAN ALWAYS
    (Porter Wagoner and Dolly Parton)

COUNTRY ALBUMS

1. 20-20 VISION
   (Ronnie Milsap)
2. ONE PIECE AT A TIME
   (Johnny Cash)
3. UNITED TALENT
   (Loretta Lynn and Conway Twitty)
4. NOW AND THEN
   (Conway Twitty)
5. ARE YOU READY FOR THE COUNTRY
   (Waylon Jennings)
6. FROM ELVIS PRESLEY BOULEVARD,
   MEMPHIS, TENNESSEE
   (Elvis Presley)
7. HARMONY
   (Don Williams)
8. WHAT I'VE GOT IN MIND
   (Billie Jo Spears)
9. TEDDY BEAR
   (Red Sovine)
10. THE BEST OF JOHNNY DUNCAN
    (Johnny Duncan)

AUGUST 14, 1976

POP SINGLES

1. DON'T GO BREAKING MY HEART
   (Elton John and Kiki Dee)
2. AFTERNOON DELIGHT
   (Starland Vocal Band)
3. YOU'LL NEVER FIND ANOTHER LOVE LIKE
   MINE
   (Lou Rawls)
4. KISS AND SAY GOODBYE
   (The Manhattans)
5. LET 'EM IN
   (Paul McCartney and Wings)
6. PLAY THAT FUNKY MUSIC
   (Wild Cherry)
7. ROCK AND ROLL MUSIC
   (The Beach Boys)
8. GET CLOSER
   (Seals and Crofts)
9. YOU SHOULD BE DANCING
   (The Bee Gees)
10. THIS MASQUERADE
    (George Benson)

POP ALBUMS

1. FRAMPTON COMES ALIVE
   (Peter Frampton)
2. SPITFIRE
   (The Jefferson Starship)
3. BEAUTIFUL NOISE
   (Neil Diamond)
4. FLEETWOOD MAC
   (Fleetwood Mac)
5. THEIR GREATEST HITS
   (The Eagles)
6. ROCK 'N' ROLL MUSIC
   (The Beatles)
7. WINGS AT THE SPEED OF SOUND
   (Paul McCartney and Wings)
8. BREEZIN'
   (George Benson)
9. 15 BIG ONES
   (The Beach Boys)
10. CHICAGO X
    (Chicago)

BLACK SINGLES

1. YOU'LL NEVER FIND ANOTHER LOVE LIKE
   MINE
   (Lou Rawls)
2. GETAWAY
   (Earth, Wind and Fire)

3. (SHAKE, SHAKE, SHAKE) SHAKE YOUR
   BOOTY
   (KC and the Sunshine Band)
4. HEAVEN MUST BE MISSING AN ANGEL
   (Tavares)
5. WHO'D SHE COO?
   (Ohio Players)
6. PLAY THAT FUNKY MUSIC
   (Wild Cherry)
7. GET UP OFFA THAT THING
   (James Brown)
8. SOMETHING HE CAN FEEL
   (Aretha Franklin)
9. THIS MASQUERADE
   (George Benson)
10. ONE FOR THE MONEY
    (Whispers)

BLACK ALBUMS

1. SPARKLE
   (Aretha Franklin)
2. BREEZIN'
   (George Benson)
3. HOT ON THE TRACKS
   (Commodores)
4. ALL THINGS IN TIME
   (Lou Rawls)
5. CONTRADICTION
   (Ohio Players)
6. HARVEST FOR THE WORLD
   (Isley Brothers)
7. LOOK OUT FOR #1
   (The Brothers Johnson)
8. MIRROR
   (Graham Central Station)
9. NATALIE
   (Natalie Cole)
10. SOUL SEARCHING
    (Average White Band)

JAZZ ALBUMS

1. BREEZIN'
   (George Benson)
2. THOSE SOUTHERN KNIGHTS
   (Crusaders)
3. THREE
   (Bob James)
4. LOOK OUT FOR #1
   (The Brothers Johnson)
5. EVERYBODY COME ON OUT
   (Stanley Turrentine)
6. GOOD KING BAD
   (George Benson)
7. FEVER
   (Ronnie Laws)
8. FLY WITH THE WIND
   (McCoy Tyner)
9. HARD WORK
   (John Handy)
10. YOU ARE MY STARSHIP
    (Norman Connors)

COUNTRY SINGLES

1. THE LETTER
   (Conway Twitty and Loretta Lynn)
2. GOLDEN RING
   (George Jones and Tammy Wynette)
3. SAY IT AGAIN
   (Don Williams)
4. ONE OF THESE DAYS
   (Emmylou Harris)
5. ROCKY MOUNTAIN MUSIC/DO YOU RIGHT
   TONIGHT
   (Eddie Rabbitt)
6. BRING IT ON HOME TO ME
   (Mickey Gilley)
7. (I'M A) STAND BY MY WOMAN MAN
   (Ronnie Milsap)
8. TEDDY BEAR
   (Red Sovine)
9. SAVE YOUR KISSES FOR ME
   (Margo Smith)

10. MISTY BLUE
    (Billie Jo Spears)

COUNTRY ALBUMS

1. UNITED TALENT
   (Loretta Lynn and Conway Twitty)
2. 20-20 VISION
   (Ronnie Milsap)
3. ARE YOU READY FOR THE COUNTRY
   (Waylon Jennings)
4. ONE PIECE AT A TIME
   (Johnny Cash)
5. TEDDY BEAR
   (Red Sovine)
6. FROM ELVIS PRESLEY BOULEVARD,
   MEMPHIS, TENNESSEE
   (Elvis Presley)
7. NOW AND THEN
   (Conway Twitty)
8. GREATEST HITS, VOL. 1
   (Charlie Rich)
9. THE BEST OF JOHNNY DUNCAN
   (Johnny Duncan)
10. WHAT I'VE GOT IN MIND
    (Billie Jo Spears)

AUGUST 21, 1976

POP SINGLES

1. DON'T GO BREAKING MY HEART
   (Elton John and Kiki Dee)
2. YOU'LL NEVER FIND ANOTHER LOVE LIKE
   MINE
   (Lou Rawls)
3. AFTERNOON DELIGHT
   (Starland Vocal Band)
4. LET 'EM IN
   (Paul McCartney and Wings)
5. PLAY THAT FUNKY MUSIC
   (Wild Cherry)
6. YOU SHOULD BE DANCING
   (The Bee Gees)
7. KISS AND SAY GOODBYE
   (The Manhattans)
8. THIS MASQUERADE
   (George Benson)
9. I'D REALLY LOVE TO SEE YOU TONIGHT
   (England Dan and John Ford Coley)
10. (SHAKE, SHAKE, SHAKE) SHAKE YOUR
    BOOTY
    (KC and the Sunshine Band)

POP ALBUMS

1. FRAMPTON COMES ALIVE
   (Peter Frampton)
2. SPITFIRE
   (The Jefferson Starship)
3. FLEETWOOD MAC
   (Fleetwood Mac)
4. BEAUTIFUL NOISE
   (Neil Diamond)
5. THEIR GREATEST HITS
   (The Eagles)
6. WINGS AT THE SPEED OF SOUND
   (Paul McCartney and Wings)
7. BREEZIN'
   (George Benson)
8. ROCK 'N' ROLL MUSIC
   (The Beatles)
9. CHICAGO X
   (Chicago)
10. 15 BIG ONES
    (The Beach Boys)

BLACK SINGLES

1. YOU'LL NEVER FIND ANOTHER LOVE LIKE
   MINE
   (Lou Rawls)

2. GETAWAY
   (Earth, Wind and Fire)
3. (SHAKE, SHAKE, SHAKE) SHAKE YOUR
   BOOTY
   (KC and the Sunshine Band)
4. PLAY THAT FUNKY MUSIC
   (Wild Cherry)
5. WHO'D SHE COO?
   (Ohio Players)
6. HEAVEN MUST BE MISSING AN ANGEL
   (Tavares)
7. GET UP OFFA THAT THING
   (James Brown)
8. SOMETHING HE CAN FEEL
   (Aretha Franklin)
9. ONE FOR THE MONEY
   (Whispers)
10. THIS MASQUERADE
    (George Benson)

BLACK ALBUMS

1. HOT ON THE TRACKS
   (Commodores)
2. SPARKLE
   (Aretha Franklin)
3. BREEZIN'
   (George Benson)
4. ALL THINGS IN TIME
   (Lou Rawls)
5. CONTRADICTION
   (Ohio Players)
6. MIRROR
   (Graham Central Station)
7. LOOK OUT FOR #1
   (The Brothers Johnson)
8. WILD CHERRY
   (Wild Cherry)
9. SOUL SEARCHING
   (Average White Band)
10. HARVEST FOR THE WORLD
    (Isley Brothers)

JAZZ ALBUMS

1. BREEZIN'
   (George Benson)
2. THREE
   (Bob James)
3. THOSE SOUTHERN KNIGHTS
   (Crusaders)
4. LOOK OUT FOR #1
   (The Brothers Johnson)
5. GOOD KING BAD
   (George Benson)
6. EVERYBODY COME ON OUT
   (Stanley Turrentine)
7. FEVER
   (Ronnie Laws)
8. YOU ARE MY STARSHIP
   (Norman Connors)
9. HARD WORK
   (John Handy)
10. FLY WITH THE WIND
    (McCoy Tyner)

COUNTRY SINGLES

1. SAY IT AGAIN
   (Don Williams)
2. ONE OF THESE DAYS
   (Emmylou Harris)
3. BRING IT ON HOME TO ME
   (Mickey Gilley)
4. (I'M A) STAND BY MY WOMAN MAN
   (Ronnie Milsap)
5. ROCKY MOUNTAIN MUSIC/DO YOU RIGHT
   TONIGHT
   (Eddie Rabbitt)
6. MISTY BLUE
   (Billie Jo Spears)
7. GOLDEN RING
   (George Jones and Tammy Wynette)

8. THE LETTER
   (Conway Twitty and Loretta Lynn)
9. YOU RUBBED IT IN ALL WRONG
   (Billy "Crash" Craddock)
10. I WONDER IF I EVER SAID GOODBYE
    (Johnny Rodriguez)

COUNTRY ALBUMS

1. ARE YOU READY FOR THE COUNTRY
   (Waylon Jennings)
2. UNITED TALENT
   (Loretta Lynn and Conway Twitty)
3. TEDDY BEAR
   (Red Sovine)
4. 20-20 VISION
   (Ronnie Milsap)
5. ONE PIECE AT A TIME
   (Johnny Cash)
6. GREATEST HITS, VOL. 1
   (Charlie Rich)
7. FROM ELVIS PRESLEY BOULEVARD,
   MEMPHIS, TENNESSEE
   (Elvis Presley)
8. THE BEST OF JOHNNY DUNCAN
   (Johnny Duncan)
9. WHAT I'VE GOT IN MIND
   (Billie Jo Spears)
10. HARMONY
    (Don Williams)

AUGUST 28, 1976

POP SINGLES

1. DON'T GO BREAKING MY HEART
   (Elton John and Kiki Dee)
2. YOU'LL NEVER FIND ANOTHER LOVE LIKE
   MINE
   (Lou Rawls)
3. PLAY THAT FUNKY MUSIC
   (Wild Cherry)
4. LET 'EM IN
   (Paul McCartney and Wings)
5. YOU SHOULD BE DANCING
   (The Bee Gees)
6. (SHAKE, SHAKE, SHAKE) SHAKE YOUR
   BOOTY
   (KC and the Sunshine Band)
7. I'D REALLY LOVE TO SEE YOU TONIGHT
   (England Dan and John Ford Coley)
8. THIS MASQUERADE
   (George Benson)
9. AFTERNOON DELIGHT
   (Starland Vocal Band)
10. A FIFTH OF BEETHOVEN
    (Walter Murphy and The Big Apple Band)

POP ALBUMS

1. FRAMPTON COMES ALIVE
   (Peter Frampton)
2. FLEETWOOD MAC
   (Fleetwood Mac)
3. SPITFIRE
   (The Jefferson Starship)
4. THEIR GREATEST HITS
   (The Eagles)
5. WINGS AT THE SPEED OF SOUND
   (Paul McCartney and Wings)
6. BREEZIN'
   (George Benson)
7. BEAUTIFUL NOISE
   (Neil Diamond)
8. CHICAGO X
   (Chicago)
9. 15 BIG ONES
   (The Beach Boys)
10. WILD CHERRY
    (Wild Cherry)

BLACK SINGLES

1. PLAY THAT FUNKY MUSIC
   (Wild Cherry)
2. GETAWAY
   (Earth, Wind and Fire)
3. WHO'D SHE COO?
   (Ohio Players)
4. YOU'LL NEVER FIND ANOTHER LOVE LIKE
   MINE
   (Lou Rawls)
5. (SHAKE, SHAKE, SHAKE) SHAKE YOUR
   BOOTY
   (KC and the Sunshine Band)
6. GET UP OFFA THAT THING
   (James Brown)
7. ONE FOR THE MONEY
   (Whispers)
8. THIS MASQUERADE
   (George Benson)
9. SOMETHING HE CAN FEEL
   (Aretha Franklin)
10. HEAVEN MUST BE MISSING AN ANGEL
    (Tavares)

BLACK ALBUMS

1. HOT ON THE TRACKS
   (Commodores)
2. SPARKLE
   (Aretha Franklin)
3. ALL THINGS IN TIME
   (Lou Rawls)
4. BREEZIN'
   (George Benson)
5. CONTRADICTION
   (Ohio Players)
6. MIRROR
   (Graham Central Station)
7. WILD CHERRY
   (Wild Cherry)
8. SOUL SEARCHING
   (Average White Band)
9. YOU ARE MY STARSHIP
   (Norman Connors)
10. HAPPINESS IS BEING WITH THE SPINNERS
    (Spinners)

JAZZ ALBUMS

1. BREEZIN'
   (George Benson)
2. THREE
   (Bob James)
3. THOSE SOUTHERN KNIGHTS
   (Crusaders)
4. LOOK OUT FOR #1
   (The Brothers Johnson)
5. EVERYBODY COME ON OUT
   (Stanley Turrentine)
6. YOU ARE MY STARSHIP
   (Norman Connors)
7. EVERYBODY LOVES THE SUNSHINE
   (Roy Ayers Ubiquity)
8. GOOD KING BAD
   (George Benson)
9. FEVER
   (Ronnie Laws)
10. FLY WITH THE WIND
    (McCoy Tyner)

COUNTRY SINGLES

1. ONE OF THESE DAYS
   (Emmylou Harris)
2. BRING IT ON HOME TO ME
   (Mickey Gilley)
3. (I'M A) STAND BY MY WOMAN MAN
   (Ronnie Milsap)
4. MISTY BLUE
   (Billie Jo Spears)
5. SAY IT AGAIN
   (Don Williams)

6. ROCKY MOUNTAIN MUSIC/DO YOU RIGHT
   TONIGHT
   (Eddie Rabbitt)
7. I WONDER IF I EVER SAID GOODBYE
   (Johnny Rodriguez)
8. YOU RUBBED IT IN ALL WRONG
   (Billy "Crash" Craddock)
9. I DON'T WANT TO HAVE TO MARRY YOU
   (Jim Ed Brown and Helen Cornelius)
10. GOLDEN RING
    (George Jones and Tammy Wynette)

COUNTRY ALBUMS

1. ARE YOU READY FOR THE COUNTRY
   (Waylon Jennings)
2. TEDDY BEAR
   (Red Sovine)
3. UNITED TALENT
   (Loretta Lynn and Conway Twitty)
4. 20-20 VISION
   (Ronnie Milsap)
5. THE BEST OF JOHNNY DUNCAN
   (Johnny Duncan)
6. GREATEST HITS, VOL. 1
   (Charlie Rich)
7. FROM ELVIS PRESLEY BOULEVARD,
   MEMPHIS, TENNESSEE
   (Elvis Presley)
8. ALL THESE THINGS
   (Joe Stampley)
9. MY LOVE AFFAIR WITH TRAINS
   (Merle Haggard)
10. WHAT I'VE GOT IN MIND
    (Billie Jo Spears)

SEPTEMBER 4, 1976

POP SINGLES

1. DON'T GO BREAKING MY HEART
   (Elton John and Kiki Dee)
2. PLAY THAT FUNKY MUSIC
   (Wild Cherry)
3. (SHAKE, SHAKE, SHAKE) SHAKE YOUR
   BOOTY
   (KC and the Sunshine Band)
4. YOU SHOULD BE DANCING
   (The Bee Gees)
5. YOU'LL NEVER FIND ANOTHER LOVE LIKE
   MINE
   (Lou Rawls)
6. I'D REALLY LOVE TO SEE YOU TONIGHT
   (England Dan and John Ford Coley)
7. LET 'EM IN
   (Paul McCartney and Wings)
8. A FIFTH OF BEETHOVEN
   (Walter Murphy and The Big Apple Band)
9. THIS MASQUERADE
   (George Benson)
10. AFTERNOON DELIGHT
    (Starland Vocal Band)

POP ALBUMS

1. FRAMPTON COMES ALIVE
   (Peter Frampton)
2. FLEETWOOD MAC
   (Fleetwood Mac)
3. SPITFIRE
   (The Jefferson Starship)
4. THEIR GREATEST HITS
   (The Eagles)
5. BREEZIN'
   (George Benson)
6. WINGS AT THE SPEED OF SOUND
   (Paul McCartney and Wings)
7. CHICAGO X
   (Chicago)
8. WILD CHERRY
   (Wild Cherry)

9. 15 BIG ONES
  (The Beach Boys)
10. BEAUTIFUL NOISE
  (Neil Diamond)

BLACK SINGLES

1. PLAY THAT FUNKY MUSIC
  (Wild Cherry)
2. GETAWAY
  (Earth, Wind and Fire)
3. WHO'D SHE COO?
  (Ohio Players)
4. (SHAKE, SHAKE, SHAKE) SHAKE YOUR BOOTY
  (KC and the Sunshine Band)
5. YOU'LL NEVER FIND ANOTHER LOVE LIKE MINE
  (Lou Rawls)
6. GET UP OFFA THAT THING
  (James Brown)
7. THIS MASQUERADE
  (George Benson)
8. SOMETHING HE CAN FEEL
  (Aretha Franklin)
9. ONE FOR THE MONEY
  (Whispers)
10. SUMMER
  (War)

BLACK ALBUMS

1. HOT ON THE TRACKS
  (Commodores)
2. WILD CHERRY
  (Wild Cherry)
3. ALL THINGS IN TIME
  (Lou Rawls)
4. CONTRADICTION
  (Ohio Players)
5. SPARKLE
  (Aretha Franklin)
6. SOUL SEARCHING
  (Average White Band)
7. YOU ARE MY STARSHIP
  (Norman Connors)
8. BREEZIN'
  (George Benson)
9. MIRROR
  (Graham Central Station)
10. HAPPINESS IS BEING WITH THE SPINNERS
  (Spinners)

JAZZ ALBUMS

1. BREEZIN'
  (George Benson)
2. THREE
  (Bob James)
3. LOOK OUT FOR #1
  (The Brothers Johnson)
4. YOU ARE MY STARSHIP
  (Norman Connors)
5. EVERYBODY LOVES THE SUNSHINE
  (Roy Ayers Ubiquity)
6. THOSE SOUTHERN KNIGHTS
  (Crusaders)
7. GOOD KING BAD
  (George Benson)
8. EVERYBODY COME ON OUT
  (Stanley Turrentine)
9. FEVER
  (Ronnie Laws)
10. HARD WORK
  (John Handy)

COUNTRY SINGLES

1. BRING IT ON HOME TO ME
  (Mickey Gilley)
2. (I'M A) STAND BY MY WOMAN MAN
  (Ronnie Milsap)

3. MISTY BLUE
  (Billie Jo Spears)
4. I WONDER IF I EVER SAID GOODBYE
  (Johnny Rodriguez)
5. ONE OF THESE DAYS
  (Emmylou Harris)
6. YOU RUBBED IT IN ALL WRONG
  (Billy "Crash" Craddock)
7. I DON'T WANT TO HAVE TO MARRY YOU
  (Jim Ed Brown and Helen Cornelius)
8. IF YOU'VE GOT THE MONEY, I'VE GOT THE TIME
  (Willie Nelson)
9. SAY IT AGAIN
  (Don Williams)
10. COWBOY
  (Eddy Arnold)

COUNTRY ALBUMS

1. TEDDY BEAR
  (Red Sovine)
2. ARE YOU READY FOR THE COUNTRY
  (Waylon Jennings)
3. UNITED TALENT
  (Loretta Lynn and Conway Twitty)
4. THE BEST OF JOHNNY DUNCAN
  (Johnny Duncan)
5. 20-20 VISION
  (Ronnie Milsap)
6. GREATEST HITS, VOL. 1
  (Charlie Rich)
7. MY LOVE AFFAIR WITH TRAINS
  (Merle Haggard)
8. ALL THESE THINGS
  (Joe Stampley)
9. FROM ELVIS PRESLEY BOULEVARD, MEMPHIS, TENNESSEE
  (Elvis Presley)
10. DIAMOND IN THE ROUGH
  (Jessi Colter)

SEPTEMBER 11, 1976

POP SINGLES

1. PLAY THAT FUNKY MUSIC
  (Wild Cherry)
2. DON'T GO BREAKING MY HEART
  (Elton John and Kiki Dee)
3. (SHAKE, SHAKE, SHAKE) SHAKE YOUR BOOTY
  (KC and the Sunshine Band)
4. YOU SHOULD BE DANCING
  (The Bee Gees)
5. I'D REALLY LOVE TO SEE YOU TONIGHT
  (England Dan and John Ford Coley)
6. A FIFTH OF BEETHOVEN
  (Walter Murphy and The Big Apple Band)
7. YOU'LL NEVER FIND ANOTHER LOVE LIKE MINE
  (Lou Rawls)
8. LET 'EM IN
  (Paul McCartney and Wings)
9. LOWDOWN
  (Boz Scaggs)
10. DEVIL WOMAN
  (Cliff Richard)

POP ALBUMS

1. FRAMPTON COMES ALIVE
  (Peter Frampton)
2. FLEETWOOD MAC
  (Fleetwood Mac)
3. SPIRIT
  (John Denver)
4. SPITFIRE
  (The Jefferson Starship)
5. HASTEN DOWN THE WIND
  (Linda Ronstadt)

6. BREEZIN'
  (George Benson)
7. WILD CHERRY
  (Wild Cherry)
8. CHICAGO X
  (Chicago)
9. THEIR GREATEST HITS
  (The Eagles)
10. WINGS AT THE SPEED OF SOUND
  (Paul McCartney and Wings)

BLACK SINGLES

1. PLAY THAT FUNKY MUSIC
  (Wild Cherry)
2. (SHAKE, SHAKE, SHAKE) SHAKE YOUR BOOTY
  (KC and the Sunshine Band)
3. WHO'D SHE COO?
  (Ohio Players)
4. GETAWAY
  (Earth, Wind and Fire)
5. YOU'LL NEVER FIND ANOTHER LOVE LIKE MINE
  (Lou Rawls)
6. YOU SHOULD BE DANCING
  (The Bee Gees)
7. THIS MASQUERADE
  (George Benson)
8. SOMETHING HE CAN FEEL
  (Aretha Franklin)
9. GET UP OFFA THAT THING
  (James Brown)
10. SUMMER
  (War)

BLACK ALBUMS

1. HOT ON THE TRACKS
  (Commodores)
2. WILD CHERRY
  (Wild Cherry)
3. SOUL SEARCHING
  (Average White Band)
4. ALL THINGS IN TIME
  (Lou Rawls)
5. YOU ARE MY STARSHIP
  (Norman Connors)
6. SPARKLE
  (Aretha Franklin)
7. CONTRADICTION
  (Ohio Players)
8. HAPPINESS IS BEING WITH THE SPINNERS
  (Spinners)
9. BREEZIN'
  (George Benson)
10. MIRROR
  (Graham Central Station)

JAZZ ALBUMS

1. BREEZIN'
  (George Benson)
2. YOU ARE MY STARSHIP
  (Norman Connors)
3. THREE
  (Bob James)
4. EVERYBODY LOVES THE SUNSHINE
  (Roy Ayers Ubiquity)
5. LOOK OUT FOR #1
  (The Brothers Johnson)
6. THOSE SOUTHERN KNIGHTS
  (Crusaders)
7. GOOD KING BAD
  (George Benson)
8. FEVER
  (Ronnie Laws)
9. EVERYBODY COME ON OUT
  (Stanley Turrentine)
10. HARD WORK
  (John Handy)

COUNTRY SINGLES

1. (I'M A) STAND BY MY WOMAN MAN
   (Ronnie Milsap)
2. I WONDER IF I EVER SAID GOODBYE
   (Johnny Rodriguez)
3. I DON'T WANT TO HAVE TO MARRY YOU
   (Jim Ed Brown and Helen Cornelius)
4. MISTY BLUE
   (Billie Jo Spears)
5. IF YOU'VE GOT THE MONEY, I'VE GOT THE TIME
   (Willie Nelson)
6. YOU RUBBED IT IN ALL WRONG
   (Billy "Crash" Craddock)
7. ONE OF THESE DAYS
   (Emmylou Harris)
8. AFTERNOON DELIGHT
   (Johnny Carver)
9. CAN'T YOU SEE/I'LL GO BACK TO HER
   (Waylon Jennings)
10. ALL I CAN DO
    (Dolly Parton)

COUNTRY ALBUMS

1. TEDDY BEAR
   (Red Sovine)
2. ARE YOU READY FOR THE COUNTRY
   (Waylon Jennings)
3. UNITED TALENT
   (Loretta Lynn and Conway Twitty)
4. THE BEST OF JOHNNY DUNCAN
   (Johnny Duncan)
5. MY LOVE AFFAIR WITH TRAINS
   (Merle Haggard)
6. ALL THESE THINGS
   (Joe Stampley)
7. DIAMOND IN THE ROUGH
   (Jessi Colter)
8. GREATEST HITS, VOL. 1
   (Charlie Rich)
9. 20-20 VISION
   (Ronnie Milsap)
10. FROM ELVIS PRESLEY BOULEVARD, MEMPHIS, TENNESSEE
    (Elvis Presley)

SEPTEMBER 18, 1976

POP SINGLES

1. (SHAKE, SHAKE, SHAKE) SHAKE YOUR BOOTY
   (KC and the Sunshine Band)
2. PLAY THAT FUNKY MUSIC
   (Wild Cherry)
3. DON'T GO BREAKING MY HEART
   (Elton John and Kiki Dee)
4. A FIFTH OF BEETHOVEN
   (Walter Murphy and The Big Apple Band)
5. I'D REALLY LOVE TO SEE YOU TONIGHT
   (England Dan and John Ford Coley)
6. LOWDOWN
   (Boz Scaggs)
7. DEVIL WOMAN
   (Cliff Richard)
8. YOU SHOULD BE DANCING
   (The Bee Gees)
9. YOU'LL NEVER FIND ANOTHER LOVE LIKE MINE
   (Lou Rawls)
10. IF YOU LEAVE ME NOW
    (Chicago)

POP ALBUMS

1. FRAMPTON COMES ALIVE
   (Peter Frampton)

2. SPIRIT
   (John Denver)
3. FLEETWOOD MAC
   (Fleetwood Mac)
4. HASTEN DOWN THE WIND
   (Linda Ronstadt)
5. SPITFIRE
   (The Jefferson Starship)
6. BREEZIN'
   (George Benson)
7. WILD CHERRY
   (Wild Cherry)
8. CHICAGO X
   (Chicago)
9. SILK DEGREES
   (Boz Scaggs)
10. WAR'S GREATEST HITS
    (War)

BLACK SINGLES

1. PLAY THAT FUNKY MUSIC
   (Wild Cherry)
2. (SHAKE, SHAKE, SHAKE) SHAKE YOUR BOOTY
   (KC and the Sunshine Band)
3. GETAWAY
   (Earth, Wind and Fire)
4. WHO'D SHE COO?
   (Ohio Players)
5. YOU'LL NEVER FIND ANOTHER LOVE LIKE MINE
   (Lou Rawls)
6. YOU SHOULD BE DANCING
   (The Bee Gees)
7. LOWDOWN
   (Boz Scaggs)
8. THIS MASQUERADE
   (George Benson)
9. SOMETHING HE CAN FEEL
   (Aretha Franklin)
10. GET THE FUNK OUT MA FACE
    (The Brothers Johnson)

BLACK ALBUMS

1. HOT ON THE TRACKS
   (Commodores)
2. WILD CHERRY
   (Wild Cherry)
3. SOUL SEARCHING
   (Average White Band)
4. YOU ARE MY STARSHIP
   (Norman Connors)
5. ALL THINGS IN TIME
   (Lou Rawls)
6. HAPPINESS IS BEING WITH THE SPINNERS
   (Spinners)
7. SPARKLE
   (Aretha Franklin)
8. CONTRADICTION
   (Ohio Players)
9. BREEZIN'
   (George Benson)
10. MIRROR
    (Graham Central Station)

JAZZ ALBUMS

1. BREEZIN'
   (George Benson)
2. EVERYBODY LOVES THE SUNSHINE
   (Roy Ayers Ubiquity)
3. YOU ARE MY STARSHIP
   (Norman Connors)
4. THREE
   (Bob James)
5. LOOK OUT FOR #1
   (The Brothers Johnson)
6. FEVER
   (Ronnie Laws)
7. THOSE SOUTHERN KNIGHTS
   (Crusaders)

8. GOOD KING BAD
   (George Benson)
9. EVERYBODY COME ON OUT
   (Stanley Turrentine)
10. GLOW
    (Al Jarreau)

COUNTRY SINGLES

1. I WONDER IF I EVER SAID GOODBYE
   (Johnny Rodriguez)
2. I DON'T WANT TO HAVE TO MARRY YOU
   (Jim Ed Brown and Helen Cornelius)
3. IF YOU'VE GOT THE MONEY, I'VE GOT THE TIME
   (Willie Nelson)
4. (I'M A) STAND BY MY WOMAN MAN
   (Ronnie Milsap)
5. CAN'T YOU SEE/I'LL GO BACK TO HER
   (Waylon Jennings)
6. ALL I CAN DO
   (Dolly Parton)
7. AFTERNOON DELIGHT
   (Johnny Carver)
8. HERE'S SOME LOVE
   (Tanya Tucker)
9. MISTY BLUE
   (Billie Jo Spears)
10. LET'S PUT IT BACK TOGETHER AGAIN
    (Jerry Lee Lewis)

COUNTRY ALBUMS

1. ARE YOU READY FOR THE COUNTRY
   (Waylon Jennings)
2. TEDDY BEAR
   (Red Sovine)
3. MY LOVE AFFAIR WITH TRAINS
   (Merle Haggard)
4. DIAMOND IN THE ROUGH
   (Jessi Colter)
5. UNITED TALENT
   (Loretta Lynn and Conway Twitty)
6. ALL THESE THINGS
   (Joe Stampley)
7. GOLDEN RING
   (George Jones and Tammy Wynette)
8. THE BEST OF JOHNNY DUNCAN
   (Johnny Duncan)
9. 20-20 VISION
   (Ronnie Milsap)
10. GREATEST HITS, VOL. 1
    (Charlie Rich)

SEPTEMBER 25, 1976

POP SINGLES

1. A FIFTH OF BEETHOVEN
   (Walter Murphy and The Big Apple Band)
2. PLAY THAT FUNKY MUSIC
   (Wild Cherry)
3. (SHAKE, SHAKE, SHAKE) SHAKE YOUR BOOTY
   (KC and the Sunshine Band)
4. DON'T GO BREAKING MY HEART
   (Elton John and Kiki Dee)
5. LOWDOWN
   (Boz Scaggs)
6. DEVIL WOMAN
   (Cliff Richard)
7. I'D REALLY LOVE TO SEE YOU TONIGHT
   (England Dan and John Ford Coley)
8. IF YOU LEAVE ME NOW
   (Chicago)
9. DISCO DUCK (PART 1)
   (Rick Dees and His Cast Of Idiots)
10. YOU SHOULD BE DANCING
    (The Bee Gees)

POP ALBUMS

1. FRAMPTON COMES ALIVE
   (Peter Frampton)
2. SPIRIT
   (John Denver)
3. HASTEN DOWN THE WIND
   (Linda Ronstadt)
4. FLEETWOOD MAC
   (Fleetwood Mac)
5. CHICAGO X
   (Chicago)
6. WILD CHERRY
   (Wild Cherry)
7. SILK DEGREES
   (Boz Scaggs)
8. WAR'S GREATEST HITS
   (War)
9. BREEZIN'
   (George Benson)
10. SPITFIRE
    (The Jefferson Starship)

BLACK SINGLES

1. (SHAKE, SHAKE, SHAKE) SHAKE YOUR BOOTY
   (KC and the Sunshine Band)
2. PLAY THAT FUNKY MUSIC
   (Wild Cherry)
3. GETAWAY
   (Earth, Wind and Fire)
4. LOWDOWN
   (Boz Scaggs)
5. WHO'D SHE COO?
   (Ohio Players)
6. YOU SHOULD BE DANCING
   (The Bee Gees)
7. GET THE FUNK OUT MA FACE
   (The Brothers Johnson)
8. YOU'LL NEVER FIND ANOTHER LOVE LIKE MINE
   (Lou Rawls)
9. GIVE IT UP (TURN IT LOOSE)
   (Tyrone Davis)
10. JUST TO BE CLOSE TO YOU
    (Commodores)

BLACK ALBUMS

1. HOT ON THE TRACKS
   (Commodores)
2. WILD CHERRY
   (Wild Cherry)
3. SOUL SEARCHING
   (Average White Band)
4. YOU ARE MY STARSHIP
   (Norman Connors)
5. HAPPINESS IS BEING WITH THE SPINNERS
   (Spinners)
6. ALL THINGS IN TIME
   (Lou Rawls)
7. SPARKLE
   (Aretha Franklin)
8. CONTRADICTION
   (Ohio Players)
9. MIRROR
   (Graham Central Station)
10. BREEZIN'
    (George Benson)

JAZZ ALBUMS

1. BREEZIN'
   (George Benson)
2. EVERYBODY LOVES THE SUNSHINE
   (Roy Ayers Ubiquity)
3. YOU ARE MY STARSHIP
   (Norman Connors)
4. THREE
   (Bob James)
5. LOOK OUT FOR #1
   (The Brothers Johnson)
6. WINDJAMMER
   (Freddie Hubbard)
7. BAREFOOT BALLET
   (John Klemmer)
8. SECRETS
   (Herbie Hancock)
9. GLOW
   (Al Jarreau)
10. FEVER
    (Ronnie Laws)

COUNTRY SINGLES

1. I DON'T WANT TO HAVE TO MARRY YOU
   (Jim Ed Brown and Helen Cornelius)
2. IF YOU'VE GOT THE MONEY, I'VE GOT THE TIME
   (Willie Nelson)
3. HERE'S SOME LOVE
   (Tanya Tucker)
4. ALL I CAN DO
   (Dolly Parton)
5. CAN'T YOU SEE/I'LL GO BACK TO HER
   (Waylon Jennings)
6. I WONDER IF I EVER SAID GOODBYE
   (Johnny Rodriguez)
7. LET'S PUT IT BACK TOGETHER AGAIN
   (Jerry Lee Lewis)
8. THE GAMES THAT DADDIES PLAY
   (Conway Twitty)
9. AFTER THE STORM
   (Wynn Stewart)
10. (I'M A) STAND BY MY WOMAN MAN
    (Ronnie Milsap)

COUNTRY ALBUMS

1. ARE YOU READY FOR THE COUNTRY
   (Waylon Jennings)
2. MY LOVE AFFAIR WITH TRAINS
   (Merle Haggard)
3. TEDDY BEAR
   (Red Sovine)
4. DIAMOND IN THE ROUGH
   (Jessi Colter)
5. GOLDEN RING
   (George Jones and Tammy Wynette)
6. HASTEN DOWN THE WIND
   (Linda Ronstadt)
7. UNITED TALENT
   (Loretta Lynn and Conway Twitty)
8. ALL THESE THINGS
   (Joe Stampley)
9. EL PASO CITY
   (Marty Robbins)
10. 20-20 VISION
    (Ronnie Milsap)

OCTOBER 2, 1976

POP SINGLES

1. PLAY THAT FUNKY MUSIC
   (Wild Cherry)
2. A FIFTH OF BEETHOVEN
   (Walter Murphy and The Big Apple Band)
3. DISCO DUCK (PART 1)
   (Rick Dees and His Cast of Idiots)
4. LOWDOWN
   (Boz Scaggs)
5. DEVIL WOMAN
   (Cliff Richard)
6. IF YOU LEAVE ME NOW
   (Chicago)
7. (SHAKE, SHAKE, SHAKE) SHAKE YOUR BOOTY
   (KC and the Sunshine Band)
8. DON'T GO BREAKING MY HEART
   (Elton John and Kiki Dee)
9. I'D REALLY LOE TO SEE YOU TONIGHT
   (England Dan and John Ford Coley)
10. STILL THE ONE
    (Orleans)

POP ALBUMS

1. FRAMPTON COMES ALIVE
   (Peter Frampton)
2. HASTEN DOWN THE WIND
   (Linda Ronstadt)
3. FLEETWOOD MAC
   (Fleetwood Mac)
4. CHICAGO X
   (Chicago)
5. SILK DEGREES
   (Boz Scaggs)
6. SPIRIT
   (John Denver)
7. WAR'S GREATEST HITS
   (War)
8. WILD CHERRY
   (Wild Cherry)
9. SPITFIRE
   (The Jefferson Starship)
10. BREEZIN'
    (George Benson)

BLACK SINGLES

1. JUST TO BE CLOSE TO YOU
   (Commodores)
2. (SHAKE, SHAKE, SHAKE) SHAKE YOUR BOOTY
   (KC and the Sunshine Band)
3. LOWDOWN
   (Boz Scaggs)
4. PLAY THAT FUNKY MUSIC
   (Wild Cherry)
5. GIVE IT UP (TURN IT LOOSE)
   (Tyrone Davis)
6. A FIFTH OF BEETHOVEN
   (Walter Murphy and The Big Apple Band)
7. GET THE FUNK OUT MA FACE
   (The Brothers Johnson)
8. GETAWAY
   (Earth, Wind and Fire)
9. MESSAGE IN OUR MUSIC
   (The O'Jays)
10. WHO'D SHE COO?
    (Ohio Players)

BLACK ALBUMS

1. HOT ON THE TRACKS
   (Commodores)
2. WILD CHERRY
   (Wild Cherry)
3. YOU ARE MY STARSHIP
   (Norman Connors)
4. HAPPINESS IS BEING WITH THE SPINNERS
   (Spinners)
5. SOUL SEARCHING
   (Average White Band)
6. SPARKLE
   (Aretha Franklin)
7. ALL THINGS IN TIME
   (Lou Rawls)
8. EVERYBODY LOVES THE SUNSHINE
   (Roy Ayers Ubiquity)
9. MIRROR
   (Graham Central Station)
10. AIN'T THAT A BITCH
    (Johnny Guitar Watson)

JAZZ ALBUMS

1. BREEZIN'
   (George Benson)
2. EVERYBODY LOVES THE SUNSHINE
   (Roy Ayers Ubiquity)
3. YOU ARE MY STARSHIP
   (Norman Connors)

4. WINDJAMMER
   (Freddie Hubbard)
5. BAREFOOT BALLET
   (John Klemmer)
6. SECRETS
   (Herbie Hancock)
7. THREE
   (Bob James)
8. SCHOOL DAYS
   (Stanley Clarke)
9. LOOK OUT FOR #1
   (The Brothers Johnson)
10. GLOW
    (Al Jarreau)

COUNTRY SINGLES

1. IF YOU'VE GOT THE MONEY, I'VE GOT THE
   TIME
   (Willie Nelson)
2. HERE'S SOME LOVE
   (Tanya Tucker)
3. THE GAMES THAT DADDIES PLAY
   (Conway Twitty)
4. ALL I CAN DO
   (Dolly Parton)
5. CAN'T YOU SEE/I'LL GO BACK TO HER
   (Waylon Jennings)
6. LET'S PUT IT BACK TOGETHER AGAIN
   (Jerry Lee Lewis)
7. YOU AND ME
   (Tammy Wynette)
8. I DON'T WANT TO HAVE TO MARRY YOU
   (Jim Ed Brown and Helen Cornelius)
9. AFTER THE STORM
   (Wynn Stewart)
10. I WONDER IF I EVER SAID GOODBYE
    (Johnny Rodriguez)

COUNTRY ALBUMS

1. GOLDEN RING
   (George Jones and Tammy Wynette)
2. HASTEN DOWN THE WIND
   (Linda Ronstadt)
3. ARE YOU READY FOR THE COUNTRY
   (Waylon Jennings)
4. MY LOVE AFFAIR WITH TRAINS
   (Merle Haggard)
5. DIAMOND IN THE ROUGH
   (Jessi Colter)
6. TEDDY BEAR
   (Red Sovine)
7. EL PASO CITY
   (Marty Robbins)
8. SPIRIT
   (John Denver)
9. ALL I CAN DO
   (Dolly Parton)
10. 20-20 VISION
    (Ronnie Milsap)

OCTOBER 9, 1976

POP SINGLES

1. DISCO DUCK (PART 1)
   (Rick Dees and His Cast of Idiots)
2. PLAY THAT FUNKY MUSIC
   (Wild Cherry)
3. IF YOU LEAVE ME NOW
   (Chicago)
4. LOWDOWN
   (Boz Scaggs)
5. A FIFTH OF BEETHOVEN
   (Walter Murphy and The Big Apple Band)
6. DEVIL WOMAN
   (Cliff Richard)
7. (SHAKE, SHAKE, SHAKE) SHAKE YOUR
   BOOTY
   (KC and the Sunshine Band)

8. DON'T GO BREAKING MY HEART
   (Elton John and Kiki Dee)
9. STILL THE ONE
   (Orleans)
10. MAGIC MAN
    (Heart)

POP ALBUMS

1. FRAMPTON COMES ALIVE
   (Peter Frampton)
2. FLEETWOOD MAC
   (Fleetwood Mac)
3. SILK DEGREES
   (Boz Scaggs)
4. CHICAGO X
   (Chicago)
5. HASTEN DOWN THE WIND
   (Linda Ronstadt)
6. SPIRIT
   (John Denver)
7. FLY LIKE AN EAGLE
   (The Steve Miller Band)
8. WAR'S GREATEST HITS
   (War)
9. SPITFIRE
   (The Jefferson Starship)
10. DREAMBOAT ANNIE
    (Heart)

BLACK SINGLES

1. JUST TO BE CLOSE TO YOU
   (Commodores)
2. GIVE IT UP (TURN IT LOOSE)
   (Tyrone Davis)
3. A FIFTH OF BEETHOVEN
   (Walter Murphy and The Big Apple Band)
4. (SHAKE, SHAKE, SHAKE) SHAKE YOUR
   BOOTY
   (KC and the Sunshine Band)
5. LOWDOWN
   (Boz Scaggs)
6. MESSAGE IN OUR MUSIC
   (The O'Jays)
7. PLAY THAT FUNKY MUSIC
   (Wild Cherry)
8. GET THE FUNK OUT MA FACE
   (The Brothers Johnson)
9. GETAWAY
   (Earth, Wind and Fire)
10. YOU ARE MY STARSHIP
    (Norman Connors)

BLACK ALBUMS

1. HOT ON THE TRACKS
   (Commodores)
2. YOU ARE MY STARSHIP
   (Norman Connors)
3. HAPPINESS IS BEING WITH THE SPINNERS
   (Spinners)
4. WILD CHERRY
   (Wild Cherry)
5. EVERYBODY LOVES THE SUNSHINE
   (Roy Ayers Ubiquity)
6. SPARKLE
   (Aretha Franklin)
7. SOUL SEARCHING
   (Average White Band)
8. ALL THINGS IN TIME
   (Lou Rawls)
9. AIN'T THAT A BITCH
   (Johnny Guitar Watson)
10. LOVE TO THE WORLD
    (L.T.D.)

JAZZ ALBUMS

1. BREEZIN'
   (George Benson)
2. YOU ARE MY STARSHIP
   (Norman Connors)

3. EVERYBODY LOVES THE SUNSHINE
   (Roy Ayers Ubiquity)
4. BAREFOOT BALLET
   (John Klemmer)
5. SECRETS
   (Herbie Hancock)
6. SCHOOL DAYS
   (Stanley Clarke)
7. WINDJAMMER
   (Freddie Hubbard)
8. THREE
   (Bob James)
9. LOOK OUT FOR #1
   (The Brothers Johnson)
10. I HEARD THAT!!
    (Quincy Jones)

COUNTRY SINGLES

1. HERE'S SOME LOVE
   (Tanya Tucker)
2. THE GAMES THAT DADDIES PLAY
   (Conway Twitty)
3. YOU AND ME
   (Tammy Wynette)
4. ALL I CAN DO
   (Dolly Parton)
5. LET'S PUT IT BACK TOGETHER AGAIN
   (Jerry Lee Lewis)
6. CAN'T YOU SEE/I'LL GO BACK TO HER
   (Waylon Jennings)
7. IF YOU'VE GOT THE MONEY, I'VE GOT THE
   TIME
   (Willie Nelson)
8. AFTER THE STORM
   (Wynn Stewart)
9. A WHOLE LOTTA THINGS TO SING ABOUT
   (Charley Pride)
10. I DON'T WANT TO HAVE TO MARRY YOU
    (Jim Ed Brown and Helen Cornelius)

COUNTRY ALBUMS

1. GOLDEN RING
   (George Jones and Tammy Wynette)
2. HASTEN DOWN THE WIND
   (Linda Ronstadt)
3. SPIRIT
   (John Denver)
4. EL PASO CITY
   (Marty Robbins)
5. ALL I CAN DO
   (Dolly Parton)
6. ARE YOU READY FOR THE COUNTRY
   (Waylon Jennings)
7. CRYSTAL
   (Crystal Gayle)
8. TEDDY BEAR
   (Red Sovine)
9. MY LOVE AFFAIR WITH TRAINS
   (Merle Haggard)
10. DIAMOND IN THE ROUGH
    (Jessi Colter)

OCTOBER 16, 1976

POP SINGLES

1. DISCO DUCK (PART 1)
   (Rick Dees and His Cast of Idiots)
2. IF YOU LEAVE ME NOW
   (Chicago)
3. PLAY THAT FUNKY MUSIC
   (Wild Cherry)
4. LOWDOWN
   (Boz Scaggs)
5. A FIFTH OF BEETHOVEN
   (Walter Murphy and The Big Apple Band)
6. DEVIL WOMAN
   (Cliff Richard)
7. MAGIC MAN
   (Heart)

8. STILL THE ONE
   (Orleans)
9. (SHAKE, SHAKE, SHAKE) SHAKE YOUR BOOTY
   (KC and the Sunshine Band)
10. ROCK 'N' ME
    (The Steve Miller Band)

POP ALBUMS

1. FRAMPTON COMES ALIVE
   (Peter Frampton)
2. SONGS IN THE KEY OF LIFE
   (Stevie Wonder)
3. SILK DEGREES
   (Boz Scaggs)
4. FLEETWOOD MAC
   (Fleetwood Mac)
5. CHICAGO X
   (Chicago)
6. FLY LIKE AN EAGLE
   (The Steve Miller Band)
7. DREAMBOAT ANNIE
   (Heart)
8. HARD RAIN
   (Bob Dylan)
9. HASTEN DOWN THE WIND
   (Linda Ronstadt)
10. SPIRIT
    (Earth, Wind and Fire)

BLACK SINGLES

1. JUST TO BE CLOSE TO YOU
   (Commodores)
2. GIVE IT UP (TURN IT LOOSE)
   (Tyrone Davis)
3. A FIFTH OF BEETHOVEN
   (Walter Murphy and The Big Apple Band)
4. YOU ARE MY STARSHIP
   (Norman Connors)
5. MESSAGE IN OUR MUSIC
   (The O'Jays)
6. (SHAKE, SHAKE, SHAKE) SHAKE YOUR BOOTY
   (KC and the Sunshine Band)
7. LOWDOWN
   (Boz Scaggs)
8. PLAY THAT FUNKY MUSIC
   (Wild Cherry)
9. GET THE FUNK OUT MA FACE
   (The Brothers Johnson)
10. GETAWAY
    (Earth, Wind and Fire)

BLACK ALBUMS

1. SONGS IN THE KEY OF LIFE
   (Stevie Wonder)
2. HOT ON THE TRACKS
   (Commodores)
3. YOU ARE MY STARSHIP
   (The Jefferson Starship)
4. SPIRIT
   (Earth, Wind and Fire)
5. HAPPINESS IS BEING WITH THE SPINNERS
   (Spinners)
6. EVERYBODY LOVES THE SUNSHINE
   (Roy Ayers Ubiquity)
7. AIN'T THAT A BITCH
   (Johnny Guitar Watson)
8. SOUL SEARCHING
   (Average White Band)
9. LOVE TO THE WORLD
   (L.T.D.)
10. MESSAGE IN OUR MUSIC
    (The O'Jays)

JAZZ ALBUMS

1. BREEZIN'
   (George Benson)

2. YOU ARE MY STARSHIP
   (Norman Connors)
3. EVERYBODY LOVES THE SUNSHINE
   (Roy Ayers Ubiquity)
4. BAREFOOT BALLET
   (John Klemmer)
5. SECRETS
   (Herbie Hancock)
6. SCHOOL DAYS
   (Stanley Clarke)
7. I HEARD THAT!!
   (Quincy Jones)
8. WINDJAMMER
   (Freddie Hubbard)
9. THREE
   (Bob James)
10. LOOK OUT FOR #1
    (The Brothers Johnson)

COUNTRY SINGLES

1. THE GAMES THAT DADDIES PLAY
   (Conway Twitty)
2. YOU AND ME
   (Tammy Wynette)
3. HERE'S SOME LOVE
   (Tanya Tucker)
4. A WHOLE LOTTA THINGS TO SING ABOUT
   (Charley Pride)
5. LET'S PUT IT BACK TOGETHER AGAIN
   (Jerry Lee Lewis)
6. AMONG MY SOUVENIRS
   (Marty Robbins)
7. CHEROKEE MAIDEN/WHAT HAVE YOU GOT PLANNED TONIGHT DIANA
   (Merle Haggard)
8. ALL I CAN DO
   (Dolly Parton)
9. PEANUTS AND DIAMONDS
   (Bill Anderson)
10. HER NAME IS
    (George Jones)

COUNTRY ALBUMS

1. HASTEN DOWN THE WIND
   (Linda Ronstadt)
2. SPIRIT
   (John Denver)
3. EL PASO CITY
   (Marty Robbins)
4. ALL I CAN DO
   (Dolly Parton)
5. GOLDEN RING
   (George Jones and Tammy Wynette)
6. CRYSTAL
   (Crystal Gayle)
7. ARE YOU READY FOR THE COUNTRY
   (Waylon Jennings)
8. HERE'S SOME LOVE
   (Tanya Tucker)
9. TEDDY BEAR
   (Red Sovine)
10. DAVE AND SUGAR
    (Dave and Sugar)

OCTOBER 23, 1976

POP SINGLES

1. IF YOU LEAVE ME NOW
   (Chicago)
2. DISCO DUCK (PART 1)
   (Rick Dees and His Cast Of Idiots)
3. PLAY THAT FUNKY MUSIC
   (Wild Cherry)
4. ROCK 'N' ME
   (The Steve Miller Band)
5. A FIFTH OF BEETHOVEN
   (Walter Murphy and The Big Apple Band)

6. MAGIC MAN
   (Heart)
7. STILL THE ONE
   (Orleans)
8. LOWDOWN
   (Boz Scaggs)
9. THE WRECK OF THE EDMUND FITZGERALD
   (Gordon Lightfoot)
10. I ONLY WANT TO BE WITH YOU
    (Bay City Rollers)

POP ALBUMS

1. SONGS IN THE KEY OF LIFE
   (Stevie Wonder)
2. FRAMPTON COMES ALIVE
   (Peter Frampton)
3. SPIRIT
   (Earth, Wind and Fire)
4. DREAMBOAT ANNIE
   (Heart)
5. SILK DEGREES
   (Boz Scaggs)
6. FLY LIKE AN EAGLE
   (The Steve Miller Band)
7. HARD RAIN
   (Bob Dylan)
8. FLEETWOOD MAC
   (Fleetwood Mac)
9. ONE MORE FROM THE ROAD
   (Lynyrd Skynyrd)
10. CHICAGO X
    (Chicago)

BLACK SINGLES

1. JUST TO BE CLOSE TO YOU
   (Commodores)
2. GIVE IT UP (TURN IT LOOSE)
   (Tyrone Davis)
3. YOU ARE MY STARSHIP
   (Norman Connors)
4. A FIFTH OF BEETHOVEN
   (Walter Murphy and The Big Apple Band)
5. MESSAGE IN OUR MUSIC
   (The O'Jays)
6. (SHAKE, SHAKE, SHAKE) SHAKE YOUR BOOTY
   (KC and the Sunshine Band)
7. LOVE BALLAD
   (L.T.D.)
8. THE RUBBERBAND MAN
   (Spinners)
9. LOWDOWN
   (Boz Scaggs)
10. PLAY THAT FUNKY MUSIC
    (Wild Cherry)

BLACK ALBUMS

1. SONGS IN THE KEY OF LIFE
   (Stevie Wonder)
2. SPIRIT
   (Earth, Wind and Fire)
3. HOT ON THE TRACKS
   (Commodores)
4. YOU ARE MY STARSHIP
   (Norman Connors)
5. HAPPINESS IS BEING WITH THE SPINNERS
   (Spinners)
6. AIN'T THAT A BITCH
   (Johnny Guitar Watson)
7. MESSAGE IN OUR MUSIC
   (The O'Jays)
8. LOVE TO THE WORLD
   (L.T.D.)
9. EVERYBODY LOVES THE SUNSHINE
   (Roy Ayers Ubiquity)
10. DO THE TEMPTATIONS
    (Temptations)

JAZZ ALBUMS

1. BREEZIN'
   (George Benson)
2. YOU ARE MY STARSHIP
   (Norman Connors)
3. BAREFOOT BALLET
   (John Klemmer)
4. SECRETS
   (Herbie Hancock)
5. I HEARD THAT!!
   (Quincy Jones)
6. EVERYBODY LOVES THE SUNSHINE
   (Roy Ayers Ubiquity)
7. SCHOOL DAYS
   (Stanley Clarke)
8. WINDJAMMER
   (Freddie Hubbard)
9. THREE
   (Bob James)
10. GLOW
    (Al Jarreau)

COUNTRY SINGLES

1. YOU AND ME
   (Tammy Wynette)
2. A WHOLE LOTTA THINGS TO SING ABOUT
   (Charley Pride)
3. AMONG MY SOUVENIRS
   (Marty Robbins)
4. CHEROKEE MAIDEN/WHAT HAVE YOU GOT PLANNED TONIGHT DIANA
   (Merle Haggard)
5. THE GAMES THAT DADDIES PLAY
   (Conway Twitty)
6. LET'S PUT IT BACK TOGETHER AGAIN
   (Jerry Lee Lewis)
7. HER NAME IS
   (George Jones)
8. PEANUTS AND DIAMONDS
   (Bill Anderson)
9. SOMEBODY SOMEWHERE
   (Loretta Lynn)
10. COME ON IN
    (Sonny James)

COUNTRY ALBUMS

1. HASTEN DOWN THE WIND
   (Linda Ronstadt)
2. SPIRIT
   (John Denver)
3. EL PASO CITY
   (Marty Robbins)
4. ALL I CAN DO
   (Dolly Parton)
5. HERE'S SOME LOVE
   (Tanya Tucker)
6. CRYSTAL
   (Crystal Gayle)
7. DAVE AND SUGAR
   (Dave and Sugar)
8. GOLDEN RING
   (George Jones and Tammy Wynette)
9. ARE YOU READY FOR THE COUNTRY
   (Waylon Jennings)
10. TEDDY BEAR
    (Red Sovine)

OCTOBER 30, 1976

POP SINGLES

1. IF YOU LEAVE ME NOW
   (Chicago)
2. DISCO DUCK (PART 1)
   (Rick Dees and His Cast Of Idiots)
3. ROCK 'N' ME
   (The Steve Miller Band)
4. PLAY THAT FUNKY MUSIC
   (Wild Cherry)
5. MAGIC MAN
   (Heart)
6. A FIFTH OF BEETHOVEN
   (Walter Murphy and The Big Apple Band)
7. THE WRECK OF THE EDMUND FITZGERALD
   (Gordon Lightfoot)
8. STILL THE ONE
   (Orleans)
9. MUSKRAT LOVE
   (The Captain and Tennille)
10. SHE'S GONE
    (Daryl Hall and John Oates)

POP ALBUMS

1. SONGS IN THE KEY OF LIFE
   (Stevie Wonder)
2. FRAMPTON COMES ALIVE
   (Peter Frampton)
3. SPIRIT
   (Earth, Wind and Fire)
4. DREAMBOAT ANNIE
   (Heart)
5. FLY LIKE AN EAGLE
   (The Steve Miller Band)
6. SILK DEGREES
   (Boz Scaggs)
7. ONE MORE FROM THE ROAD
   (Lynyrd Skynyrd)
8. BOSTON
   (Boston)
9. CHICAGO X
   (Chicago)
10. CHILDREN OF THE WORLD
    (The Bee Gees)

BLACK SINGLES

1. JUST TO BE CLOSE TO YOU
   (Commodores)
2. GIVE IT UP (TURN IT LOOSE)
   (Tyrone Davis)
3. YOU ARE MY STARSHIP
   (Norman Connors)
4. LOVE BALLAD
   (L.T.D.)
5. THE RUBBERBAND MAN
   (Spinners)
6. A FIFTH OF BEETHOVEN
   (Walter Murphy and The Big Apple Band)
7. MESSAGE IN OUR MUSIC
   (The O'Jays)
8. (SHAKE, SHAKE, SHAKE) SHAKE YOUR BOOTY
   (KC and the Sunshine Band)
9. YOU DON'T HAVE TO BE A STAR (TO BE IN MY SHOW)
   (Marilyn McCoo and Billy Davis Jr.)
10. LOWDOWN
    (Boz Scaggs)

BLACK ALBUMS

1. SONGS IN THE KEY OF LIFE
   (Stevie Wonder)
2. SPIRIT
   (Earth, Wind and Fire)
3. HOT ON THE TRACKS
   (Commodores)
4. HAPPINESS IS BEING WITH THE SPINNERS
   (Spinners)
5. MESSAGE IN OUR MUSIC
   (The O'Jays)
6. YOU ARE MY STARSHIP
   (Norman Connors)
7. AIN'T THAT A BITCH
   (Johnny Guitar Watson)
8. LOVE TO THE WORLD
   (L.T.D.)
9. DO THE TEMPTATIONS
   (Temptations)
10. EVERYBODY LOVES THE SUNSHINE
    (Roy Ayers Ubiquity)

JAZZ ALBUMS

1. BREEZIN'
   (George Benson)
2. YOU ARE MY STARSHIP
   (Norman Connors)
3. BAREFOOT BALLET
   (John Klemmer)
4. I HEARD THAT!!
   (Quincy Jones)
5. SECRETS
   (Herbie Hancock)
6. EVERYBODY LOVES THE SUNSHINE
   (Roy Ayers Ubiquity)
7. SCHOOL DAYS
   (Stanley Clarke)
8. WINDJAMMER
   (Freddie Hubbard)
9. GLOW
   (Al Jarreau)
10. THREE
    (Bob James)

COUNTRY SINGLES

1. A WHOLE LOTTA THINGS TO SING ABOUT
   (Charley Pride)
2. AMONG MY SOUVENIRS
   (Marty Robbins)
3. CHEROKEE MAIDEN/WHAT HAVE YOU GOT PLANNED TONIGHT DIANA
   (Merle Haggard)
4. YOU AND ME
   (Tammy Wynette)
5. SOMEBODY SOMEWHERE
   (Loretta Lynn)
6. HER NAME IS
   (George Jones)
7. COME ON IN
   (Sonny James)
8. PEANUTS AND DIAMONDS
   (Bill Anderson)
9. I'M GONNA LOVE YOU
   (Dave and Sugar)
10. LIVING IT DOWN
    (Freddy Fender)

COUNTRY ALBUMS

1. HASTEN DOWN THE WIND
   (Linda Ronstadt)
2. EL PASO CITY
   (Marty Robbins)
3. HERE'S SOME LOVE
   (Tanya Tucker)
4. SPIRIT
   (John Denver)
5. ALL I CAN DO
   (Dolly Parton)
6. DAVE AND SUGAR
   (Dave and Sugar)
7. CRYSTAL
   (Crystal Gayle)
8. GOLDEN RING
   (George Jones and Tammy Wynette)
9. ARE YOU READY FOR THE COUNTRY
   (Waylon Jennings)
10. 20-20 VISION
    (Ronnie Milsap)

NOVEMBER 6, 1976

POP SINGLES

1. DISCO DUCK (PART 1)
   (Rick Dees and His Cast Of Idiots)

2. ROCK 'N' ME
(The Steve Miller Band)
3. IF YOU LEAVE ME NOW
(Chicago)
4. PLAY THAT FUNKY MUSIC
(Wild Cherry)
5. MUSKRAT LOVE
(The Captain and Tennille)
6. THE WRECK OF THE EDMUND FITZGERALD
(Gordon Lightfoot)
7. MAGIC MAN
(Heart)
8. A FIFTH OF BEETHOVEN
(Walter Murphy and The Big Apple Band)
9. THE RUBBERBAND MAN
(Spinners)
10. SHE'S GONE
(Daryl Hall and John Oates)

POP ALBUMS

1. SONGS IN THE KEY OF LIFE
(Stevie Wonder)
2. FRAMPTON COMES ALIVE
(Peter Frampton)
3. SPIRIT
(Earth, Wind and Fire)
4. DREAMBOAT ANNIE
(Heart)
5. FLY LIKE AN EAGLE
(The Steve Miller Band)
6. ONE MORE FROM THE ROAD
(Lynyrd Skynyrd)
7. THE SONG REMAINS THE SAME
(Led Zeppelin)
8. BOSTON
(Boston)
9. CHICAGO X
(Chicago)
10. CHILDREN OF THE WORLD
(The Bee Gees)

BLACK SINGLES

1. JUST TO BE CLOSE TO YOU
(Commodores)
2. LOVE BALLAD
(L.T.D.)
3. THE RUBBERBAND MAN
(Spinners)
4. GIVE IT UP (TURN IT LOOSE)
(Tyrone Davis)
5. YOU ARE MY STARSHIP
(Norman Connors)
6. YOU DON'T HAVE TO BE A STAR (TO BE IN MY SHOW)
(Marilyn McCoo and Billy Davis Jr.)
7. A FIFTH OF BEETHOVEN
(Walter Murphy and The Big Apple Band)
8. MESSAGE IN OUR MUSIC
(The O'Jays)
9. (SHAKE, SHAKE, SHAKE) SHAKE YOUR BOOTY
(KC and the Sunshine Band)
10. PLAY THAT FUNKY MUSIC
(Wild Cherry)

BLACK ALBUMS

1. SONGS IN THE KEY OF LIFE
(Stevie Wonder)
2. SPIRIT
(Earth, Wind and Fire)
3. HOT ON THE TRACKS
(Commodores)
4. MESSAGE IN OUR MUSIC
(The O'Jays)
5. HAPPINESS IS BEING WITH THE SPINNERS
(Spinners)
6. YOU ARE MY STARSHIP
(Norman Connors)
7. FEELING GOOD
(Walter Jackson)

8. LOVE TO THE WORLD
(L.T.D.)
9. AIN'T THAT A BITCH
(Johnny Guitar Watson)
10. THE CLONES OF DR. FUNKENSTEIN
(Parliament)

JAZZ ALBUMS

1. BREEZIN'
(George Benson)
2. I HEARD THAT!!
(Quincy Jones)
3. BAREFOOT BALLET
(John Klemmer)
4. YOU ARE MY STARSHIP
(Norman Connors)
5. SECRETS
(Herbie Hancock)
6. SCHOOL DAYS
(Stanley Clarke)
7. EVERYBODY LOVES THE SUNSHINE
(Roy Ayers Ubiquity)
8. VERY TOGETHER
(Deodato)
9. WINDJAMMER
(Freddie Hubbard)
10. GLOW
(Al Jarreau)

COUNTRY SINGLES

1. AMONG MY SOUVENIRS
(Marty Robbins)
2. CHEROKEE MAIDEN/WHAT HAVE YOU GOT PLANNED TONIGHT DIANA
(Merle Haggard)
3. SOMEBODY SOMEWHERE
(Loretta Lynn)
4. YOU AND ME
(Tammy Wynette)
5. I'M GONNA LOVE YOU
(Dave and Sugar)
6. HER NAME IS
(George Jones)
7. COME ON IN
(Sonny James)
8. 9,999,999 TEARS
(Dickey Lee)
9. LIVING IT DOWN
(Freddy Fender)
10. A WHOLE LOTTA THINGS TO SING ABOUT
(Charley Pride)

COUNTRY ALBUMS

1. HASTEN DOWN THE WIND
(Linda Ronstadt)
2. EL PASO CITY
(Marty Robbins)
3. HERE'S SOME LOVE
(Tanya Tucker)
4. DAVE AND SUGAR
(Dave and Sugar)
5. ALL I CAN DO
(Dolly Parton)
6. SPIRIT
(John Denver)
7. YOU AND ME
(Tammy Wynette)
8. THE TROUBLEMAKER
(Willie Nelson)
9. GOLDEN RING
(George Jones and Tammy Wynette)
10. ARE YOU READY FOR THE COUNTRY
(Waylon Jennings)

NOVEMBER 13, 1976

POP SINGLES

1. ROCK 'N' ME
(The Steve Miller Band)
2. MUSKRAT LOVE
(The Captain and Tennille)
3. IF YOU LEAVE ME NOW
(Chicago)
4. DISCO DUCK (PART 1)
(Rick Dees and His Cast Of Idiots)
5. THE WRECK OF THE EDMUND FITZGERALD
(Gordon Lightfoot)
6. PLAY THAT FUNKY MUSIC
(Wild Cherry)
7. THE RUBBERBAND MAN
(Spinners)
8. MAGIC MAN
(Heart)
9. TONIGHT'S THE NIGHT (GONNA BE ALRIGHT)
(Rod Stewart)
10. BETH
(Kiss)

POP ALBUMS

1. SONGS IN THE KEY OF LIFE
(Stevie Wonder)
2. SPIRIT
(Earth, Wind and Fire)
3. THE SONG REMAINS THE SAME
(Led Zeppelin)
4. FRAMPTON COMES ALIVE
(Peter Frampton)
5. FLY LIKE AN EAGLE
(The Steve Miller Band)
6. BOSTON
(Boston)
7. BLUE MOVES
(Elton John)
8. DREAMBOAT ANNIE
(Heart)
9. ONE MORE FROM THE ROAD
(Lynyrd Skynyrd)
10. CHICAGO X
(Chicago)

BLACK SINGLES

1. LOVE BALLAD
(L.T.D.)
2. THE RUBBERBAND MAN
(Spinners)
3. JUST TO BE CLOSE TO YOU
(Commodores)
4. YOU DON'T HAVE TO BE A STAR (TO BE IN MY SHOW)
(Marilyn McCoo and Billy Davis Jr.)
5. GIVE IT UP (TURN IT LOOSE)
(Tyrone Davis)
6. YOU ARE MY STARSHIP
(Norman Connors)
7. MESSAGE IN OUR MUSIC
(The O'Jays)
8. A FIFTH OF BEETHOVEN
(Walter Murphy and The Big Apple Band)
9. (SHAKE, SHAKE, SHAKE) SHAKE YOUR BOOTY
(KC and the Sunshine Band)
10. CAR WASH
(Rose Royce)

BLACK ALBUMS

1. SONGS IN THE KEY OF LIFE
(Stevie Wonder)
2. SPIRIT
(Earth, Wind and Fire)

3. MESSAGE IN OUR MUSIC
   (The O'Jays)
4. HOT ON THE TRACKS
   (Commodores)
5. THE CLONES OF DR. FUNKENSTEIN
   (Parliament)
6. HAPPINESS IS BEING WITH THE SPINNERS
   (Spinners)
7. FEELING GOOD
   (Walter Jackson)
8. LOVE TO THE WORLD
   (L.T.D.)
9. YOU ARE MY STARSHIP
   (Norman Connors)
10. AIN'T THAT A BITCH
    (Johnny Guitar Watson)

JAZZ ALBUMS

1. BREEZIN'
   (George Benson)
2. I HEARD THAT!!
   (Quincy Jones)
3. BAREFOOT BALLET
   (John Klemmer)
4. SECRETS
   (Herbie Hancock)
5. YOU ARE MY STARSHIP
   (Norman Connors)
6. SCHOOL DAYS
   (Stanley Clarke)
7. VERY TOGETHER
   (Deodato)
8. EVERYBODY LOVES THE SUNSHINE
   (Roy Ayers Ubiquity)
9. LIVE ON TOUR IN EUROPE
   (Cobham/Duke Band)
10. WINDJAMMER
    (Freddie Hubbard)

COUNTRY SINGLES

1. CHEROKEE MAIDEN/WHAT HAVE YOU GOT PLANNED TONIGHT DIANA
   (Merle Haggard)
2. SOMEBODY SOMEWHERE
   (Loretta Lynn)
3. I'M GONNA LOVE YOU
   (Dave and Sugar)
4. AMONG MY SOUVENIRS
   (Marty Robbins)
5. HER NAME IS
   (George Jones)
6. 9,999,999 TEARS
   (Dickey Lee)
7. LIVING IT DOWN
   (Freddy Fender)
8. SHOW ME A MAN
   (T.G. Sheppard)
9. THANK GOD I'VE GOT YOU
   (The Statler Brothers)
10. THINKIN' OF A RENDEZVOUS
    (Johnny Duncan)

COUNTRY ALBUMS

1. HERE'S SOME LOVE
   (Tanya Tucker)
2. EL PASO CITY
   (Marty Robbins)
3. DAVE AND SUGAR
   (Dave and Sugar)
4. THE TROUBLEMAKER
   (Willie Nelson)
5. YOU AND ME
   (Tammy Wynette)
6. HASTEN DOWN THE WIND
   (Linda Ronstadt)
7. ALL I CAN DO
   (Dolly Parton)
8. GOLDEN RING
   (George Jones and Tammy Wynette)
9. ARE YOU READY FOR THE COUNTRY
   (Waylon Jennings)

10. IF YOU'RE EVER IN TEXAS
    (Freddy Fender)

NOVEMBER 20, 1976

POP SINGLES

1. TONIGHT'S THE NIGHT (GONNA BE ALRIGHT)
   (Rod Stewart)
2. MUSKRAT LOVE
   (The Captain and Tennille)
3. ROCK 'N' ME
   (The Steve Miller Band)
4. DISCO DUCK (PART 1)
   (Rick Dees and His Cast Of Idiots)
5. THE RUBBERBAND MAN
   (Spinners)
6. THE WRECK OF THE EDMUND FITZGERALD
   (Gordon Lightfoot)
7. IF YOU LEAVE ME NOW
   (Chicago)
8. PLAY THAT FUNKY MUSIC
   (Wild Cherry)
9. BETH
   (Kiss)
10. JUST TO BE CLOSE TO YOU
    (Commodores)

POP ALBUMS

1. SONGS IN THE KEY OF LIFE
   (Stevie Wonder)
2. THE SONG REMAINS THE SAME
   (Led Zeppelin)
3. SPIRIT
   (Earth, Wind and Fire)
4. FRAMPTON COMES ALIVE
   (Peter Frampton)
5. BLUE MOVES
   (Elton John)
6. BOSTON
   (Boston)
7. FLY LIKE AN EAGLE
   (The Steve Miller Band)
8. A NIGHT ON THE TOWN
   (Rod Stewart)
9. DREAMBOAT ANNIE
   (Heart)
10. CHICAGO X
    (Chicago)

BLACK SINGLES

1. LOVE BALLAD
   (L.T.D.)
2. THE RUBBERBAND MAN
   (Spinners)
3. YOU DON'T HAVE TO BE A STAR (TO BE IN MY SHOW)
   (Marilyn McCoo and Billy Davis Jr.)
4. JUST TO BE CLOSE TO YOU
   (Commodores)
5. CAR WASH
   (Rose Royce)
6. GIVE IT UP (TURN IT LOOSE)
   (Tyrone Davis)
7. MESSAGE IN OUR MUSIC
   (The O'Jays)
8. YOU ARE MY STARSHIP
   (Norman Connors)
9. A FIFTH OF BEETHOVEN
   (Walter Murphy and The Big Apple Band)
10. (SHAKE, SHAKE, SHAKE) SHAKE YOUR BOOTY
    (KC and the Sunshine Band)

BLACK ALBUMS

1. SONGS IN THE KEY OF LIFE
   (Stevie Wonder)
2. SPIRIT
   (Earth, Wind and Fire)
3. MESSAGE IN OUR MUSIC
   (The O'Jays)
4. THE CLONES OF DR. FUNKENSTEIN
   (Parliament)
5. HOT ON THE TRACKS
   (Commodores)
6. HAPPINESS IS BEING WITH THE SPINNERS
   (Spinners)
7. FEELING GOOD
   (Walter Jackson)
8. LOVE TO THE WORLD
   (L.T.D.)
9. FLOWERS
   (Emotions)
10. BICENTENNIAL NIGGER
    (Richard Pryor)

JAZZ ALBUMS

1. BREEZIN'
   (George Benson)
2. I HEARD THAT!!
   (Quincy Jones)
3. BAREFOOT BALLET
   (John Klemmer)
4. SCHOOL DAYS
   (Stanley Clarke)
5. SECRETS
   (Herbie Hancock)
6. YOU ARE MY STARSHIP
   (Norman Connors)
7. VERY TOGETHER
   (Deodato)
8. LIVE ON TOUR IN EUROPE
   (Cobham/Duke Band)
9. EVERYBODY LOVES THE SUNSHINE
   (Roy Ayers Ubiquity)
10. THREE
    (Bob James)

COUNTRY SINGLES

1. SOMEBODY SOMEWHERE
   (Loretta Lynn)
2. I'M GONNA LOVE YOU
   (Dave and Sugar)
3. 9,999,999 TEARS
   (Dickey Lee)
4. HER NAME IS
   (George Jones)
5. LIVING IT DOWN
   (Freddy Fender)
6. CHEROKEE MAIDEN/WHAT HAVE YOU GOT PLANNED TONIGHT DIANA
   (Merle Haggard)
7. THANK GOD I'VE GOT YOU
   (The Statler Brothers)
8. SHOW ME A MAN
   (T.G. Sheppard)
9. THINKIN' OF A RENDEZVOUS
   (Johnny Duncan)
10. GOOD WOMAN BLUES
    (Mel Tillis)

COUNTRY ALBUMS

1. EL PASO CITY
   (Marty Robbins)
2. HERE'S SOME LOVE
   (Tanya Tucker)
3. DAVE AND SUGAR
   (Dave and Sugar)
4. THE TROUBLEMAKER
   (Willie Nelson)
5. YOU AND ME
   (Tammy Wynette)

6. IF YOU'RE EVER IN TEXAS
   (Freddy Fender)
7. SOMEBODY SOMEWHERE
   (Loretta Lynn)
8. GOLDEN RING
   (George Jones and Tammy Wynette)
9. ALL I CAN DO
   (Dolly Parton)
10. REFLECTING
    (Johnny Rodriguez)

NOVEMBER 27, 1976

POP SINGLES

1. TONIGHT'S THE NIGHT (GONNA BE ALRIGHT)
   (Rod Stewart)
2. MUSKRAT LOVE
   (The Captain and Tennille)
3. THE RUBBERBAND MAN
   (Spinners)
4. ROCK 'N' ME
   (The Steve Miller Band)
5. DISCO DUCK (PART 1)
   (Rick Dees and His Cast Of Idiots)
6. THE WRECK OF THE EDMUND FITZGERALD
   (Gordon Lightfoot)
7. MORE THAN A FEELING
   (Boston)
8. BETH
   (Kiss)
9. YOU DON'T HAVE TO BE A STAR (TO BE IN MY SHOW)
   (Marilyn McCoo and Billy Davis Jr.)
10. NADIA'S THEME (THE YOUNG AND THE RESTLESS)
    (Barry DeVorzon and Perry Botkin Jr.)

POP ALBUMS

1. SONGS IN THE KEY OF LIFE
   (Stevie Wonder)
2. THE SONG REMAINS THE SAME
   (Led Zeppelin)
3. BLUE MOVES
   (Elton John)
4. BOSTON
   (Boston)
5. FRAMPTON COMES ALIVE
   (Peter Frampton)
6. A NIGHT ON THE TOWN
   (Rod Stewart)
7. SPIRIT
   (Earth, Wind and Fire)
8. FLY LIKE AN EAGLE
   (Steve Miller Band)
9. DREAMBOAT ANNIE
   (Heart)
10. CHICAGO X
    (Chicago)

BLACK SINGLES

1. YOU DON'T HAVE TO BE A STAR (TO BE IN MY SHOW)
   (Marilyn McCoo and Billy Davis Jr.)
2. CAR WASH
   (Rose Royce)
3. DAZZ
   (Brick)
4. LOVE BALLAD
   (L.T.D.)
5. THE RUBBERBAND MAN
   (Spinners)
6. JUST TO BE CLOSE TO YOU
   (Commodores)
7. GIVE IT UP (TURN IT LOOSE)
   (Tyrone Davis)

8. YOU ARE MY STARSHIP
   (Norman Connors)
9. MESSAGE IN OUR MUSIC
   (The O'Jays)
10. SHAKE YOUR RUMP TO THE FUNK
    (Bar-Kays)

BLACK ALBUMS

1. SONGS IN THE KEY OF LIFE
   (Stevie Wonder)
2. SPIRIT
   (Earth, Wind and Fire)
3. THE CLONES OF DR. FUNKENSTEIN
   (Parliament)
4. MESSAGE IN OUR MUSIC
   (The O'Jays)
5. HOT ON THE TRACKS
   (Commodores)
6. FLOWERS
   (Emotions)
7. HAPPINESS IS BEING WITH THE SPINNERS
   (Spinners)
8. FEELING GOOD
   (Walter Jackson)
9. LOVE TO THE WORLD
   (L.T.D.)
10. PART 3
    (KC and the Sunshine Band)

JAZZ ALBUMS

1. BREEZIN'
   (George Benson)
2. I HEARD THAT!!
   (Quincy Jones)
3. SCHOOL DAYS
   (Stanley Clarke)
4. BAREFOOT BALLET
   (John Klemmer)
5. SECRETS
   (Herbie Hancock)
6. LIVE ON TOUR IN EUROPE
   (Cobham/Duke Band)
7. VERY TOGETHER
   (Deodato)
8. YOU ARE MY STARSHIP
   (Norman Connors)
9. BENSON AND FARRELL
   (George Benson and Joe Farrell)
10. CALIENTE
    (Gato Barbieri)

COUNTRY SINGLES

1. I'M GONNA LOVE YOU
   (Dave and Sugar)
2. 9,999,999 TEARS
   (Dickey Lee)
3. LIVING IT DOWN
   (Freddy Fender)
4. SOMEBODY SOMEWHERE
   (Loretta Lynn)
5. THINKIN' OF A RENDEZVOUS
   (Johnny Duncan)
6. GOOD WOMAN BLUES
   (Mel Tillis)
7. THANK GOD I'VE GOT YOU
   (The Statler Brothers)
8. HER NAME IS
   (George Jones)
9. HILLBILLY HEART
   (Johnny Rodriguez)
10. TAKE MY BREATH AWAY
    (Margo Smith)

COUNTRY ALBUMS

1. THE TROUBLEMAKER
   (Willie Nelson)
2. DAVE AND SUGAR
   (Dave and Sugar)

3. EL PASO CITY
   (Marty Robbins)
4. SOMEBODY SOMEWHERE
   (Loretta Lynn)
5. YOU AND ME
   (Tammy Wynette)
6. IF YOU'RE EVER IN TEXAS
   (Freddy Fender)
7. HERE'S SOME LOVE
   (Tanya Tucker)
8. GOLDEN RING
   (George Jones and Tammy Wynette)
9. REFLECTING
   (Johnny Rodriguez)
10. ALONE AGAIN
    (George Jones)

DECEMBER 4, 1976

POP SINGLES

1. TONIGHT'S THE NIGHT (GONNA BE ALRIGHT)
   (Rod Stewart)
2. THE RUBBERBAND MAN
   (Spinners)
3. MUSKRAT LOVE
   (The Captain and Tennille)
4. ROCK 'N' ME
   (The Steve Miller Band)
5. MORE THAN A FEELING
   (Boston)
6. YOU DON'T HAVE TO BE A STAR (TO BE IN MY SHOW)
   (Marilyn McCoo and Billy Davis Jr.)
7. BETH
   (Kiss)
8. NADIA'S THEME (THE YOUNG AND THE RESTLESS)
   (Barry DeVorzon and Perry Botkin Jr.)
9. DISCO DUCK (PART 1)
   (Rick Dees and His Cast Of Idiots)
10. NIGHTS ARE FOREVER WITHOUT YOU
    (England Dan and John Ford Coley)

POP ALBUMS

1. SONGS IN THE KEY OF LIFE
   (Stevie Wonder)
2. BOSTON
   (Boston)
3. BLUE MOVES
   (Elton John)
4. THE SONG REMAINS THE SAME
   (Led Zeppelin)
5. A NIGHT ON THE TOWN
   (Rod Stewart)
6. FRAMPTON COMES ALIVE
   (Peter Frampton)
7. SPIRIT
   (Earth, Wind and Fire)
8. FLY LIKE AN EAGLE
   (The Steve Miller Band)
9. A NEW WORLD RECORD
   (Electric Light Orchestra)
10. CHICAGO X
    (Chicago)

BLACK SINGLES

1. DAZZ
   (Brick)
2. CAR WASH
   (Rose Royce)
3. YOU DON'T HAVE TO BE A STAR (TO BE IN MY SHOW)
   (Marilyn McCoo and Billy Davis Jr.)
4. LOVE BALLAD
   (L.T.D.)
5. THE RUBBERBAND MAN
   (Spinners)

6. ENJOY YOURSELF
   (The Jacksons)
7. JUST TO BE CLOSE TO YOU
   (Commodores)
8. GIVE IT UP (TURN IT LOOSE)
   (Tyrone Davis)
9. SHAKE YOUR RUMP TO THE FUNK
   (Bar-Kays)
10. CATFISH
    (The Four Tops)

BLACK ALBUMS

1. SONGS IN THE KEY OF LIFE
   (Stevie Wonder)
2. SPIRIT
   (Earth, Wind and Fire)
3. CAR WASH
   (Original Soundtrack)
4. THE CLONES OF DR. FUNKENSTEIN
   (Parliament)
5. HOT ON THE TRACKS
   (Commodores)
6. FLOWERS
   (Emotions)
7. MESSAGE IN OUR MUSIC
   (The O'Jays)
8. FEELING GOOD
   (Walter Jackson)
9. THIS IS NIECY
   (Deniece Williams)
10. PART 3
    (KC and the Sunshine Band)

JAZZ ALBUMS

1. BREEZIN'
   (George Benson)
2. I HEARD THAT!!
   (Quincy Jones)
3. SCHOOL DAYS
   (Stanley Clarke)
4. BAREFOOT BALLET
   (John Klemmer)
5. LIVE ON TOUR IN EUROPE
   (Cobham/Duke Band)
6. SECRETS
   (Herbie Hancock)
7. VERY TOGETHER
   (Deodato)
8. CALIENTE
   (Gato Barbieri)
9. MAIN SQUEEZE
   (Chuck Mangione)
10. BENSON AND FARRELL
    (George Benson and Joe Farrell)

COUNTRY SINGLES

1. 9,999,999 TEARS
   (Dickey Lee)
2. THINKIN' OF A RENDEZVOUS
   (Johnny Duncan)
3. LIVING IT DOWN
   (Freddy Fender)
4. GOOD WOMAN BLUES
   (Mel Tillis)
5. I'M GONNA LOVE YOU
   (Dave and Sugar)
6. HILLBILLY HEART
   (Johnny Rodriquez)
7. TAKE MY BREATH AWAY
   (Margo Smith)
8. LAWDY MISS CLAWDY
   (Mickey Gilley)
9. BABY BOY
   (Mary Kay Place)
10. SHE NEVER KNEW ME
    (Don Williams)

COUNTRY ALBUMS

1. THE TROUBLEMAKER
   (Willie Nelson)

2. DAVE AND SUGAR
   (Dave and Sugar)
3. SOMEBODY SOMEWHERE
   (Loretta Lynn)
4. EL PASO CITY
   (Marty Robbins)
5. YOU AND ME
   (Tammy Wynette)
6. IF YOU'RE EVER IN TEXAS
   (Freddy Fender)
7. HERE'S SOME LOVE
   (Tanya Tucker)
8. REFLECTING
   (Johnny Rodriguez)
9. ALONE AGAIN
   (George Jones)
10. MARY KAY PLACE
    (Mary Kay Place)

DECEMBER 11, 1976

POP SINGLES

1. TONIGHT'S THE NIGHT (GONNA BE
   ALRIGHT)
   (Rod Stewart)
2. THE RUBBERBAND MAN
   (Spinners)
3. YOU DON'T HAVE TO BE A STAR (TO BE IN
   MY SHOW)
   (Marilyn McCoo and Billy Davis Jr.)
4. MORE THAN A FEELING
   (Boston)
5. MUSKRAT LOVE
   (The Captain and Tennille)
6. ROCK 'N' ME
   (The Steve Miller Band)
7. NADIA'S THEME (THE YOUNG AND THE
   RESTLESS)
   (Barry DeVorzon and Perry Botkin Jr.)
8. YOU MAKE ME FEEL LIKE DANCING
   (Leo Sayer)
9. NIGHTS ARE FOREVER WITHOUT YOU
   (England Dan and John Ford Coley)
10. LOVE SO RIGHT
    (The Bee Gees)

POP ALBUMS

1. SONGS IN THE KEY OF LIFE
   (Stevie Wonder)
2. BOSTON
   (Boston)
3. A NIGHT ON THE TOWN
   (Rod Stewart)
4. BLUE MOVES
   (Elton John)
5. FRAMPTON COMES ALIVE
   (Peter Frampton)
6. THE SONG REMAINS THE SAME
   (Led Zeppelin)
7. BEST OF THE DOOBIES
   (The Doobie Brothers)
8. A NEW WORLD RECORD
   (Electric Light Orchestra)
9. THE PRETENDER
   (Jackson Browne)
10. ROCK AND ROLL OVER
    (Kiss)

BLACK SINGLES

1. CAR WASH
   (Rose Royce)
2. DAZZ
   (Brick)
3. YOU DON'T HAVE TO BE A STAR (TO BE IN
   MY SHOW)
   (Marilyn McCoo and Billy Davis Jr.)
4. ENJOY YOURSELF
   (The Jacksons)

5. LOVE BALLAD
   (L.T.D.)
6. THE RUBBERBAND MAN
   (Spinners)
7. HOT LINE
   (The Sylvers)
8. JUST TO BE CLOSE TO YOU
   (Commodores)
9. SHAKE YOUR RUMP TO THE FUNK
   (Bar-Kays)
10. DO IT TO MY MIND
    (Johnny Bristol)

BLACK ALBUMS

1. SONGS IN THE KEY OF LIFE
   (Stevie Wonder)
2. CAR WASH
   (Original Soundtrack)
3. SPIRIT
   (Earth, Wind and Fire)
4. THE CLONES OF DR. FUNKENSTEIN
   (Parliament)
5. FLOWERS
   (Emotions)
6. THIS IS NIECY
   (Deniece Williams)
7. HOT ON THE TRACKS
   (Commodores)
8. FEELING GOOD
   (Walter Jackson)
9. PART 3
   (KC and the Sunshine Band)
10. GOOD HIGH
    (Brick)

JAZZ ALBUMS

1. BREEZIN'
   (George Benson)
2. I HEARD THAT!!
   (Quincy Jones)
3. SCHOOL DAYS
   (Stanley Clarke)
4. BAREFOOT BALLET
   (John Klemmer)
5. MAIN SQUEEZE
   (Chuck Mangione)
6. VERY TOGETHER
   (Deodato)
7. CALIENTE
   (Gato Barbieri)
8. SECRETS
   (Herbie Hancock)
9. LIVE ON TOUR IN EUROPE
   (Cobham/Duke Band)
10. ROMEO AND JULIET
    (Hubert Laws)

COUNTRY SINGLES

1. THINKIN' OF A RENDEZVOUS
   (Johnny Duncan)
2. GOOD WOMAN BLUES
   (Mel Tillis)
3. 9,999,999 TEARS
   (Dickey Lee)
4. SHE NEVER KNEW ME
   (Don Williams)
5. TAKE MY BREATH AWAY
   (Margo Smith)
6. HILLBILLY HEART
   (Johnny Rodriquez)
7. BABY BOY
   (Mary Kay Place)
8. LAWDY MISS CLAWDY
   (Mickey Gilley)
9. SWEET DREAMS
   (Emmylou Harris)
10. BROKEN DOWN IN TINY PIECES
    (Billy "Crash" Craddock)

COUNTRY ALBUMS

1. SOMEBODY SOMEWHERE
   (Loretta Lynn)
2. THE TROUBLEMAKER
   (Willie Nelson)
3. DAVE AND SUGAR
   (Dave and Sugar)
4. EL PASO CITY
   (Marty Robbins)
5. IF YOU'RE EVER IN TEXAS
   (Freddy Fender)
6. BEST OF CHARLEY PRIDE, VOL. III
   (Charley Pride)
7. DON'T STOP BELIEVIN'
   (Olivia Newton-John)
8. MARY KAY PLACE
   (Mary Kay Place)
9. HERE'S SOME LOVE
   (Tanya Tucker)
10. YOU AND ME
    (Tammy Wynette)

DECEMBER 18, 1976

POP SINGLES

1. TONIGHT'S THE NIGHT (GONNA BE ALRIGHT)
   (Rod Stewart)
2. THE RUBBERBAND MAN
   (Spinners)
3. YOU DON'T HAVE TO BE A STAR (TO BE IN MY SHOW)
   (Marilyn McCoo and Billy Davis Jr.)
4. MORE THAN A FEELING
   (Boston)
5. YOU MAKE ME FEEL LIKE DANCING
   (Leo Sayer)
6. MUSKRAT LOVE
   (The Captain and Tennille)
7. NADIA'S THEME (THE YOUNG AND THE RESTLESS)
   (Barry DeVorzon and Perry Botkin Jr.)
8. HOT LINE
   (The Sylvers)
9. I NEVER CRY
   (Alice Cooper)
10. YOU ARE THE WOMAN
    (Firefall)

POP ALBUMS

1. SONGS IN THE KEY OF LIFE
   (Stevie Wonder)
2. BOSTON
   (Boston)
3. A NIGHT ON THE TOWN
   (Rod Stewart)
4. FRAMPTON COMES ALIVE
   (Peter Frampton)
5. BEST OF THE DOOBIES
   (The Doobie Brothers)
6. BLUE MOVES
   (Elton John)
7. THE PRETENDER
   (Jackson Browne)
8. ROCK AND ROLL OVER
   (Kiss)
9. A NEW WORLD RECORD
   (Electric Light Orchestra)
10. THE SONG REMAINS THE SAME
    (Led Zeppelin)

BLACK SINGLES

1. DAZZ
   (Brick)
2. CAR WASH
   (Rose Royce)

3. ENJOY YOURSELF
   (The Jacksons)
4. YOU DON'T HAVE TO BE A STAR (TO BE IN MY SHOW)
   (Marilyn McCoo and Billy Davis Jr.)
5. HOT LINE
   (The Sylvers)
6. DO IT TO MY MIND
   (Johnny Bristol)
7. LOVE BALLAD
   (L.T.D.)
8. THE RUBBERBAND MAN
   (Spinners)
9. SHAKE YOUR RUMP TO THE FUNK
   (Bar-Kays)
10. JUST TO BE CLOSE TO YOU
    (Commodores)

BLACK ALBUMS

1. SONGS IN THE KEY OF LIFE
   (Stevie Wonder)
2. CAR WASH
   (Original Soundtrack)
3. SPIRIT
   (Earth, Wind and Fire)
4. GOOD HIGH
   (Brick)
5. FLOWERS
   (Emotions)
6. THE CLONES OF DR. FUNKENSTEIN
   (Parliament)
7. THIS IS NIECY
   (Deniece Williams)
8. II
   (Brass Construction)
9. HOT ON THE TRACKS
   (Commodores)
10. PART 3
    (KC and the Sunshine Band)

JAZZ ALBUMS

1. BREEZIN'
   (George Benson)
2. I HEARD THAT!!
   (Quincy Jones)
3. BAREFOOT BALLET
   (John Klemmer)
4. MAIN SQUEEZE
   (Chuck Mangione)
5. MAN WITH THE SAD FACE
   (Stanley Turrentine)
6. VERY TOGETHER
   (Deodato)
7. UNFINISHED BUSINESS
   (Blackbyrds)
8. SCHOOL DAYS
   (Stanley Clarke)
9. CALIENTE
   (Gato Barbieri)
10. BENSON AND FARRELL
    (George Benson and Joe Farrell)

COUNTRY SINGLES

1. GOOD WOMAN BLUES
   (Mel Tillis)
2. SHE NEVER KNEW ME
   (Don Williams)
3. THINKIN' OF A RENDEZVOUS
   (Johnny Duncan)
4. TAKE MY BREATH AWAY
   (Margo Smith)
5. SWEET DREAMS
   (Emmylou Harris)
6. BABY BOY
   (Mary Kay Place)
7. HILLBILLY HEART
   (Johnny Rodriguez)
8. BROKEN DOWN IN TINY PIECES
   (Billy "Crash" Craddock)
9. LAWDY MISS CLAWDY
   (Mickey Gilley)

10. STATUES WITHOUT HEARTS
    (Larry Gatlin)

COUNTRY ALBUMS

1. SOMEBODY SOMEWHERE
   (Loretta Lynn)
2. THE TROUBLEMAKER
   (Willie Nelson)
3. DON'T STOP BELIEVIN'
   (Olivia Newton-John)
4. BEST OF CHARLEY PRIDE, VOL. III
   (Charley Pride)
5. IF YOU'RE EVER IN TEXAS
   (Freddy Fender)
6. GREATEST HITS, VOL. II
   (Conway Twitty)
7. MARY KAY PLACE
   (Mary Kay Place)
8. ARE YOU READY FOR THE COUNTRY
   (Waylon Jennings)
9. EL PASO CITY
   (Marty Robbins)
10. DAVE AND SUGAR
    (Dave and Sugar)

DECEMBER 25, 1976

POP SINGLES

1. TONIGHT'S THE NIGHT (GONNA BE ALRIGHT)
   (Rod Stewart)
2. YOU DON'T HAVE TO BE A STAR (TO BE IN MY SHOW)
   (Marilyn McCoo and Billy Davis Jr.)
3. YOU MAKE ME FEEL LIKE DANCING
   (Leo Sayer)
4. THE RUBBERBAND MAN
   (Spinners)
5. HOT LINE
   (The Sylvers)
6. MUSKRAT LOVE
   (The Captain and Tennille)
7. CAR WASH
   (Rose Royce)
8. I NEVER CRY
   (Alice Cooper)
9. STAND TALL
   (Burton Cummings)
10. SORRY SEEMS TO BE THE HARDEST WORD
    (Elton John)

POP ALBUMS

1. SONGS IN THE KEY OF LIFE
   (Stevie Wonder)
2. BOSTON
   (Boston)
3. FRAMPTON COMES ALIVE
   (Peter Frampton)
4. A NIGHT ON THE TOWN
   (Rod Stewart)
5. BEST OF THE DOOBIES
   (The Doobie Brothers)
6. THE PRETENDER
   (Jackson Browne)
7. ROCK AND ROLL OVER
   (Kiss)
8. HOTEL CALIFORNIA
   (The Eagles)
9. A NEW WORLD RECORD
   (Electric Light Orchestra)
10. THEIR GREATEST HITS
    (The Eagles)

BLACK SINGLES

1. DAZZ
   (Brick)

2. CAR WASH
    (Rose Royce)
3. ENJOY YOURSELF
    (The Jacksons)
4. YOU DON'T HAVE TO BE A STAR (TO BE IN MY SHOW)
    (Marilyn McCoo and Billy Davis Jr.)
5. HOT LINE
    (The Sylvers)
6. DO IT TO MY MIND
    (Johnny Bristol)
7. I WISH
    (Stevie Wonder)
8. LOVE BALLAD
    (L.T.D.)
9. THE RUBBERBAND MAN
    (Spinners)
10. SHAKE YOUR RUMP TO THE FUNK
    (Bar-Kays)

BLACK ALBUMS

1. SONGS IN THE KEY OF LIFE
    (Stevie Wonder)
2. CAR WASH
    (Original Soundtrack)
3. SPIRIT
    (Earth, Wind and Fire)
4. GOOD HIGH
    (Brick)
5. II
    (Brass Construction)
6. THE CLONES OF DR. FUNKENSTEIN
    (Parliament)
7. THIS IS NIECY
    (Deniece Williams)
8. FLOWERS
    (Emotions)
9. PART 3
    (KC and the Sunshine Band)
10. OPEN SESAME
    (Kool and the Gang)

JAZZ ALBUMS

1. MAIN SQUEEZE
    (Chuck Mangione)
2. BREEZIN'
    (George Benson)
3. I HEARD THAT!!
    (Quincy Jones)
4. MAN WITH THE SAD FACE
    (Stanley Turrentine)
5. UNFINISHED BUSINESS
    (Blackbyrds)
6. SCHOOL DAYS
    (Stanley Clarke)
7. CALIENTE
    (Gato Barbieri)
8. BAREFOOT BALLET
    (John Klemmer)
9. VERY TOGETHER
    (Deodato)
10. BENSON AND FARRELL
    (George Benson and Joe Farrell)

COUNTRY SINGLES

1. SHE NEVER KNEW ME
    (Don Williams)
2. SWEET DREAMS
    (Emmylou Harris)
3. GOOD WOMAN BLUES
    (Mel Tillis)
4. BROKEN DOWN IN TINY PIECES
    (Billy "Crash" Craddock)
5. BABY BOY
    (Mary Kay Place)
6. THINKIN' OF A RENDEZVOUS
    (Johnny Duncan)
7. STATUES WITHOUT HEARTS
    (Larry Gatlin)

8. YOU NEVER MISS A REAL GOOD THING (TILL HE SAYS GOODBYE)
    (Crystal Gayle)
9. DON'T BE ANGRY
    (Donna Fargo)
10. TWO DOLLARS IN THE JUKEBOX
    (Eddie Rabbitt)

COUNTRY ALBUMS

1. DON'T STOP BELIEVIN'
    (Olivia Newton-John)
2. BEST OF CHARLEY PRIDE, VOL. III
    (Charley Pride)
3. THE TROUBLEMAKER
    (Willie Nelson)
4. SOMEBODY SOMEWHERE
    (Loretta Lynn)
5. GREATEST HITS, VOL. II
    (Conway Twitty)
6. ARE YOU READY FOR THE COUNTRY
    (Waylon Jennings)
7. TONIGHT! AT THE CAPRI LOUNGE
    (Mary Kay Place)
8. GILLEY'S SMOKING
    (Mickey Gilley)
9. RONNIE MILSAP LIVE
    (Ronnie Milsap)
10. THE BEST OF GLEN CAMPBELL
    (Glen Campbell)

1977

The Eagles' *Hotel California* was 1977's masterpiece. It crystalized all the images of love, lust, and greed in the Eagles' best work since *Desperado*. Just as The Beach Boys defined a certain vision of life in America's most glamorous state in the 1960s, so The Eagles portrayed California in the 1970s. The golden-haired women still were living there. So were the fast cars and the promise of high living. But it wasn't all fun, fun, fun to The Eagles. The women had turned sinister as in "Hotel California" or two-faced as in "New Kid in Town." The good life crumbled in cocaine flakes for the Hollywood couple described in "Life in the Fast Lane" and cruel sex for the naive girl in "Victim of Love." The Eagles had a love-hate relationship with Southern California apparent in the lyrics of the title song and "The Last Resort."

This imagery was supported by The Eagles' finest music. Henley's voice was mean, nasty, and sarcastic, even on love songs. For other bands this might have been limiting, but with The Eagles' material, written primarily by Henley and guitarist Glenn Frey, his bitterness was just right. Guitarist Joe Walsh joined The Eagles on this album, making a fine band a great one. His sinuous, driving play on "Hotel California" and "Life in the Fast Lane" enhanced their bleak mood and made for the most mesmerizing music of 1977.

Stevie Wonder's *Songs in the Key of Life* is a near masterpiece. Unlike *Hotel California*, where images and music link into one central vision, Wonder's music bubbles all over the place, almost giving the listeners too much of everything. What should have been Wonder's greatest single album turned out to be an overblown double album plus a seven-inch single with four songs. Much of it ("I Wish," "Sir Duke," "Love's In Need of Love Today") was brilliant and would have been presented better in a smaller package.

ALBUMS: Bob Seger's *Night Moves* introduced this rocking singer-songwriter to most of the country. In his native Michigan, Seger was a legend, headlining over many national attractions when they invaded his turf. It wasn't until this album with its nostalgic title track that his name spread outside the Midwest. Folks who listened to the entire LP found that Seger was more than melancholy. No, he was a rocker who wrote good, lean songs and possessed a soulful singing voice.

Foreigner and Boston's self-titled debut albums both went platinum, the music of each setting standards for an upcoming wave of pop-rock bands. Foreigner was a collection of well-respected American and English rockers. Their music suggested heavy metal, but in essence it was pop with a calculation that, like their first single, was as "Cold as Ice."

Boston was more benign, but just as shrewd at hit-making. The difference was that Boston's mastermind Tom Scholz somehow concocted a mix of rock hooks and mellow middle of the road (MOR) sensibility that worked. Foreigner and Boston's approach would influence the early 1980s hits of Journey, R.E.O. Speedwagon, Loverboy, and Styx.

Linda Ronstadt's *Greatest Hits* culled music from her previous albums—*Heart Like A Wheel*, *Prisoner in Disguise*, *Hasten Down the Wind*, and *Simple Dreams*—the music that made her the mid-1970s' most salable female vocalist. Her steely multi-octave voice, backed by producer Peter Asher's super-clean state-of-the-art production, yielded numerous hit singles ("You're No Good," "Blue Bayou," "When Will I Be Loved"). In the process, she became one of America's favorite sex symbols, right along with Farah Fawcett and the rest of "Charlie's Angels." The Ronstadt-Asher team would reach its creative nadir with her next release, *Living in the U.S.A.* Subsequently, she'd vacation from recording, savor her success, and appear on Broadway in the musical *Pirates of Penzance*.

Is Jackson Browne a poet? Only his high school English teacher knows for sure. He does, however, have a gift for words. Browne's problem until *The Pretender* was finding music that matched his pretentions. On this, his fourth album, it all came together. "Here Come Those Tears Again," "The Pretender," and "The Fuse" were all beautiful, heartfelt songs with solid melodies and even better music, the latter provided by a crew of crack Los Angeles session players.

Dr. Buzzard's Original Savannah Band was the most ambitious and audacious disco recording up to that time. Incorporating equal parts of 1940s backlot musical, statement of mulatto independence, and musical hybrid (big-band horns, disco pulse, Philly sound strings), songs like "Cherchez La Femme," "I'll Play the Fool," and "Bitter Honey" possessed the sophistication and élan that all disco aspired to, with a wit none could match.

This was a great year for new acts in black music. Teddy Pendergrass began his solo career auspiciously after breaking with Harold Melvin and the Blue Notes. The soprano of Deniece Williams led Maurice White to produce *This Is Niecy*, while George Clinton supervised the introduction of William "Bootsy" Collins's cartoon vocals and innovative funk rhythms on *Ahh . . . The Name Is Bootsy, Baby*. For the boogie children, the latest hot new funk band was Slave, an energetic aggregation from Dayton; while for the mature, mellow crowd, Maze, featuring Frankie Beverly, was now standard background music.

The "outlaws" continued their reign over country with Waylon Jennings leading the way with *Ol' Waylon* and his duet with Willie Nelson on "Luckenbach, Texas." However, a new force was on the country horizon. The name was Kenny Rogers and with the hardcore "Lucille," he built a country base that would serve him well in the coming years.

Weather Report was one of the few acts that at this late date was still upholding the adventurous jazz-rock tradition of Miles Davis's *Bitches Brew*. Co-founders saxophonist Wayne Shorter and keyboardist Joe Zawinal never compromised their work to be commercial, instead winning sales on the music's considerable merits. On *Heavy Weather* they created fusion's anthem—"Birdland"—a song that managed simultaneously to be melodic and daring.

SINGLES: The biggest-selling singles of this year have few classics among them. "Tonight's the Night" and "Love Theme from *A Star is Born*" are hardly the best work that Rod Stewart and Barbra Streisand have done. Andy Gibb's "I Just Want To Be Your Everything" and the Emotions' "Best of My Love" were effervescent, but in the long run forgettable. Leo Sayer's "You Make Me Feel Like Dancing" incredibly won the Grammy as "Best R&B Song of the Year" over the Commodores' "Easy," one of Lionel Richie's best songs.

Jimmy Buffett's "Margaritaville" was a whimsical, amusing little gem that added a much needed touch of personality to the chart. Manfred Mann's reworking of Bruce Springsteen's "Blinded by the Light" was clever and revived this veteran British group. Marvin Gaye's "Got to Give It Up (Part I)" was a shortened version of an 11:48-minute dance epic, one of the rare disco efforts by a longstanding black star that didn't condescend to the trend. In America, disco was at its commercial peak with the film *Saturday Night Fever* on its way to grossing $74 million, the most for a pop music flick since the dawn of rock 'n' roll. The soundtrack and the Bee Gee juggernaut were just making waves at the end of the year.

The Nitty Gritty Dirt Band became the first American pop group to go to Russia. In England, The Sex Pistols made news. Soon after signing with EMI Records, the quartet was dropped after an intentionally obscene appearance on the BBC. The Sex Pistols also were dropped soon after signing with A&M Records in Britain, following protest from company personnel about their subversive music. The band, quite happily, kept the advances.

Elvis Presley died of a drug overdose in August. The genuine emotion displayed by fans over this pioneering rock 'n' roller's passing was quite touching, a tribute to the man's charisma and broad impact. Unfortunately, the sleazy exploitation of his memory by his "friends" mirrored the dark side of Presley's life.

Elvis Presley

William "Bootsy" Collins

The Eagles

The Beach Boys

Weather Report

Waylon Jennings

Foreigner

JANUARY 1, 1977

POP SINGLES

1. YOU DON'T HAVE TO BE A STAR (TO BE IN MY SHOW)
   (Marilyn McCoo and Billy Davis Jr.)
2. YOU MAKE ME FEEL LIKE DANCING
   (Leo Sayer)
3. TONIGHT'S THE NIGHT (GONNA BE ALRIGHT)
   (Rod Stewart)
4. HOT LINE
   (The Sylvers)
5. CAR WASH
   (Rose Royce)
6. THE RUBBERBAND MAN
   (Spinners)
7. DAZZ
   (Brick)
8. SORRY SEEMS TO BE THE HARDEST WORD
   (Elton John)
9. STAND TALL
   (Burton Cummings)
10. LIVIN' THING
    (Electric Light Orchestra)

POP ALBUMS

1. SONGS IN THE KEY OF LIFE
   (Stevie Wonder)
2. HOTEL CALIFORNIA
   (The Eagles)
3. FRAMPTON COMES ALIVE
   (Peter Frampton)
4. BOSTON
   (Boston)
5. WINGS OVER AMERICA
   (Paul McCartney and Wings)
6. A NIGHT ON THE TOWN
   (Rod Stewart)
7. BEST OF THE DOOBIES
   (The Doobie Brothers)
8. THE PRETENDER
   (Jackson Browne)
9. ROCK AND ROLL OVER
   (Kiss)
10. THEIR GREATEST HITS
    (The Eagles)

BLACK SINGLES

1. DAZZ
   (Brick)
2. CAR WASH
   (Rose Royce)
3. I WISH
   (Stevie Wonder)
4. HOT LINE
   (The Sylvers)
5. ENJOY YOURSELF
   (The Jacksons)
6. YOU DON'T HAVE TO BE A STAR (TO BE IN MY SHOW)
   (Marilyn McCoo and Billy Davis Jr.)
7. DO IT TO MY MIND
   (Johnny Bristol)
8. LOVE BALLAD
   (L.T.D.)
9. FREE
   (Deniece Williams)
10. I KINDA MISS YOU
    (The Manhattans)

BLACK ALBUMS

1. SONGS IN THE KEY OF LIFE
   (Stevie Wonder)
2. CAR WASH
   (Original Soundtrack)
3. GOOD HIGH
   (Brick)

4. SPIRIT
   (Earth, Wind and Fire)
5. II
   (Brass Construction)
6. THIS IS NIECY
   (Deniece Williams)
7. THE CLONES OF DR. FUNKENSTEIN
   (Parliament)
8. OPEN SESAME
   (Kool and the Gang)
9. FLOWERS
   (Emotions)
10. TOO HOT TO STOP
    (Bar-Kays)

JAZZ ALBUMS

1. BREEZIN'
   (George Benson)
2. MAIN SQUEEZE
   (Chuck Mangione)
3. I HEARD THAT!!
   (Quincy Jones)
4. MAN WITH THE SAD FACE
   (Stanley Turrentine)
5. UNFINISHED BUSINESS
   (Blackbyrds)
6. SCHOOL DAYS
   (Stanley Clarke)
7. BAREFOOT BALLET
   (John Klemmer)
8. CALIENTE
   (Gato Barbieri)
9. RENAISSANCE
   (Lonnie Liston Smith)
10. VERY TOGETHER
    (Deodato)

COUNTRY SINGLES

1. SWEET DREAMS
   (Emmylou Harris)
2. BROKEN DOWN IN TINY PIECES
   (Billy "Crash" Craddock)
3. STATUES WITHOUT HEARTS
   (Larry Gatlin)
4. BABY BOY
   (Mary Kay Place)
5. SHE NEVER KNEW ME
   (Don Williams)
6. YOU NEVER MISS A REAL GOOD THING (TILL HE SAYS GOODBYE)
   (Crystal Gayle)
7. DON'T BE ANGRY
   (Donna Fargo)
8. I CAN'T BELIEVE (SHE GIVES IT ALL TO ME)
   (Conway Twitty)
9. TWO DOLLARS IN THE JUKEBOX
   (Eddie Rabbitt)
10. GOOD WOMAN BLUES
    (Mel Tillis)

COUNTRY ALBUMS

1. ARE YOU READY FOR THE COUNTRY
   (Waylon Jennings)
2. BEST OF CHARLEY PRIDE, VOL. III
   (Charley Pride)
3. DON'T STOP BELIEVIN'
   (Olivia Newton-John)
4. CONWAY TWITTY'S GREATEST HITS, VOL. II
   (Conway Twitty)
5. THE TROUBLEMAKER
   (Willie Nelson)
6. RONNIE MISLAP LIVE
   (Ronnie Mislap)
7. GILLEY'S SMOKIN'
   (Mickey Gilley)
8. TONIGHT! AT THE CAPRI LOUNGE
   (Mary Kay Place)
9. THE BEST OF GLEN CAMPBELL
   (Glen Campbell)

10. SOMEBODY SOMEWHERE
    (Loretta Lynn)

JANUARY 8, 1977

POP SINGLES

1. YOU MAKE ME FEEL LIKE DANCING
   (Leo Sayer)
2. YOU DON'T HAVE TO BE A STAR (TO BE IN MY SHOW)
   (Marilyn McCoo and Billy Davis Jr.)
3. HOT LINE
   (The Sylvers)
4. CAR WASH
   (Rose Royce)
5. TONIGHT'S THE NIGHT (GONNA BE ALRIGHT)
   (Rod Stewart)
6. DAZZ
   (Brick)
7. THE RUBBERBAND MAN
   (Spinners)
8. SORRY SEEMS TO BE THE HARDEST WORD
   (Elton John)
9. I WISH
   (Stevie Wonder)
10. LIVIN' THING
    (Electric Light Orchestra)

POP ALBUMS

1. HOTEL CALIFORNIA
   (The Eagles)
2. SONGS IN THE KEY OF LIFE
   (Stevie Wonder)
3. FRAMPTON COMES ALIVE
   (Peter Frampton)
4. WINGS OVER AMERICA
   (Paul McCartney and Wings)
5. BOSTON
   (Boston)
6. A NIGHT ON THE TOWN
   (Rod Stewart)
7. BEST OF THE DOOBIES
   (The Doobie Brothers)
8. ROCK AND ROLL OVER
   (Kiss)
9. GREATEST HITS
   (Linda Ronstadt)
10. THEIR GREATEST HITS
    (The Eagles)

BLACK SINGLES

1. CAR WASH
   (Rose Royce)
2. I WISH
   (Stevie Wonder)
3. DAZZ
   (Brick)
4. HOT LINE
   (The Sylvers)
5. ENJOY YOURSELF
   (The Jacksons)
6. FREE
   (Deniece Williams)
7. DO IT TO MY MIND
   (Johnny Bristol)
8. YOU DON'T HAVE TO BE A STAR (TO BE IN MY SHOW)
   (Marilyn McCoo and Billy Davis Jr.)
9. I LIKE TO DO IT
   (KC and the Sunshine Band)
10. I KINDA MISS YOU
    (The Manhattans)

BLACK ALBUMS

1. SONGS IN THE KEY OF LIFE
   (Stevie Wonder)
2. CAR WASH
   (Original Soundtrack)
3. GOOD HIGH
   (Brick)
4. SPIRIT
   (Earth, Wind and Fire)
5. THIS IS NIECY
   (Deniece Williams)
6. II
   (Brass Construction)
7. THE CLONES OF DR. FUNKENSTEIN
   (Parliament)
8. OPEN SESAME
   (Kool and the Gang)
9. TOO HOT TO STOP
   (Bar-Kays)
10. FLOWERS
   (Emotions)

JAZZ ALBUMS

1. BREEZIN'
   (George Benson)
2. MAIN SQUEEZE
   (Chuck Mangione)
3. I HEARD THAT!!
   (Quincy Jones)
4. MAN WITH THE SAD FACE
   (Stanley Turrentine)
5. UNFINISHED BUSINESS
   (Blackbyrds)
6. SCHOOL DAYS
   (Stanley Clarke)
7. BAREFOOT BALLET
   (John Klemmer)
8. RENAISSANCE
   (Lonnie Liston Smith)
9. CALIENTE
   (Gato Barbieri)
10. VERY TOGETHER
   (Deodato)

COUNTRY SINGLES

1. BROKEN DOWN IN TINY PIECES
   (Billy "Crash" Craddock)
2. STATUES WITHOUT HEARTS
   (Larry Gatlin)
3. SWEET DREAMS
   (Emmylou Harris)
4. YOU NEVER MISS A REAL GOOD THING
   (TILL HE SAYS GOODBYE)
   (Crystal Gayle)
5. I CAN'T BELIEVE (SHE GIVES IT ALL TO
   ME)
   (Conway Twitty)
6. DON'T BE ANGRY
   (Donna Fargo)
7. SHE NEVER KNEW ME
   (Don Williams)
8. TWO DOLLARS IN THE JUKEBOX
   (Eddie Rabbitt)
9. BABY BOY
   (Mary Kay Place)
10. ARE YOU READY FOR THE COUNTRY/SO
   GOOD WOMAN
   (Waylon Jennings)

COUNTRY ALBUMS

1. ARE YOU READY FOR THE COUNTRY
   (Waylon Jennings)
2. CONWAY TWITTY'S GREATEST HITS, VOL.
   II
   (Conway Twitty)
3. BEST OF CHARLEY PRIDE, VOL. III
   (Charley Pride)
4. RONNIE MILSAP LIVE
   (Ronnie Milsap)

5. DON'T STOP BELIEVIN'
   (Olivia Newton-John)
6. THE TROUBLEMAKER
   (Willie Nelson)
7. GILLEY'S SMOKIN'
   (Mickey Gilley)
8. THE BEST OF GLEN CAMPBELL
   (Glen Campbell)
9. WAYLON LIVE
   (Waylon Jennings)
10. I DON'T WANNA HAVE TO MARRY YOU
   (Jim Ed Brown and Helen Cornelius)

JANUARY 15, 1977

POP SINGLES

1. CAR WASH
   (Rose Royce)
2. HOT LINE
   (The Sylvers)
3. YOU MAKE ME FEEL LIKE DANCING
   (Leo Sayer)
4. DAZZ
   (Brick)
5. YOU DON'T HAVE TO BE A STAR (TO BE IN
   MY SHOW)
   (Marilyn McCoo and Billy Davis Jr.)
6. I WISH
   (Stevie Wonder)
7. TONIGHT'S THE NIGHT (GONNA BE
   ALRIGHT)
   (Rod Stewart)
8. THE RUBBERBAND MAN
   (Spinners)
9. WALK THIS WAY
   (Aerosmith)
10. BLINDED BY THE LIGHT
   (Manfred Mann's Earth Band)

POP ALBUMS

1. HOTEL CALIFORNIA
   (The Eagles)
2. SONGS IN THE KEY OF LIFE
   (Stevie Wonder)
3. WINGS OVER AMERICA
   (Paul McCartney and Wings)
4. FRAMPTON COMES ALIVE
   (Peter Frampton)
5. BOSTON
   (Boston)
6. GREATEST HITS
   (Linda Ronstadt)
7. BEST OF THE DOOBIES
   (The Doobie Brothers)
8. ROCK AND ROLL OVER
   (Kiss)
9. THEIR GREATEST HITS
   (The Eagles)
10. A NIGHT ON THE TOWN
   (Rod Stewart)

BLACK SINGLES

1. CAR WASH
   (Rose Royce)
2. I WISH
   (Stevie Wonder)
3. DAZZ
   (Brick)
4. HOT LINE
   (The Sylvers)
5. FREE
   (Deniece Williams)
6. ENJOY YOURSELF
   (The Jacksons)
7. I LIKE TO DO IT
   (KC and the Sunshine Band)
8. DO IT TO MY MIND
   (Johnny Bristol)

9. YOU DON'T HAVE TO BE A STAR (TO BE IN
   MY SHOW)
   (Marilyn McCoo and Billy Davis Jr.)
10. I KINDA MISS YOU
   (The Manhattans)

BLACK ALBUMS

1. SONGS IN THE KEY OF LIFE
   (Stevie Wonder)
2. CAR WASH
   (Original Soundtrack)
3. GOOD HIGH
   (Brick)
4. SPIRIT
   (Earth, Wind and Fire)
5. THIS IS NIECY
   (Deniece Williams)
6. II
   (Brass Construction)
7. OPEN SESAME
   (Kool and the Gang)
8. UNFINISHED BUSINESS
   (Blackbyrds)
9. TOO HOT TO STOP
   (Bar-Kays)
10. THE CLONES OF DR. FUNKENSTEIN
   (Parliament)

JAZZ ALBUMS

1. BREEZIN'
   (George Benson)
2. MAIN SQUEEZE
   (Chuck Mangione)
3. A SECRET PLACE
   (Grover Washington Jr.)
4. I HEARD THAT!!
   (Quincy Jones)
5. UNFINISHED BUSINESS
   (Blackbyrds)
6. SCHOOL DAYS
   (Stanley Clarke)
7. MAN WITH THE SAD FACE
   (Stanley Turrentine)
8. RENAISSANCE
   (Lonnie Liston Smith)
9. BAREFOOT BALLET
   (John Klemmer)
10. CALIENTE
   (Gato Barbieri)

COUNTRY SINGLES

1. STATUES WITHOUT HEARTS
   (Larry Gatlin)
2. YOU NEVER MISS A REAL GOOD THING
   (TILL HE SAYS GOODBYE)
   (Crystal Gayle)
3. I CAN'T BELIEVE (SHE GIVES IT ALL TO
   ME)
   (Conway Twitty)
4. BROKEN DOWN IN TINY PIECES
   (Billy "Crash" Craddock)
5. TWO DOLLARS IN THE JUKEBOX
   (Eddie Rabbitt)
6. DON'T BE ANGRY
   (Donna Fargo)
7. LET MY LOVE BE YOUR PILLOW
   (Ronnie Milsap)
8. ARE YOU READY FOR THE COUNTRY/SO
   GOOD WOMAN
   (Waylon Jennings)
9. SWEET DREAMS
   (Emmylou Harris)
10. SAYING HELLO, SAYING I LOVE YOU,
   SAYING GOODBYE
   (Jim Ed Brown and Helen Cornelius)

COUNTRY ALBUMS

1. CONWAY TWITTY'S GREATEST HITS, VOL.
   II
   (Conway Twitty)

2. ARE YOU READY FOR THE COUNTRY
   (*Waylon Jennings*)
3. RONNIE MILSAP LIVE
   (*Ronnie Milsap*)
4. WAYLON LIVE
   (*Waylon Jennings*)
5. BEST OF CHARLEY PRIDE, VOL. III
   (*Charley Pride*)
6. THE TROUBLEMAKER
   (*Willie Nelson*)
7. GILLEY'S SMOKIN'
   (*Mickey Gilley*)
8. THE BEST OF GLEN CAMPBELL
   (*Glen Campbell*)
9. I DON'T WANNA HAVE TO MARRY YOU
   (*Jim Ed Brown and Helen Cornelius*)
10. THE ROOTS OF MY RAISING
   (*Merle Haggard*)

JANUARY 22, 1977

POP SINGLES

1. I WISH
   (*Stevie Wonder*)
2. HOT LINE
   (*The Sylvers*)
3. CAR WASH
   (*Rose Royce*)
4. DAZZ
   (*Brick*)
5. YOU MAKE ME FEEL LIKE DANCING
   (*Leo Sayer*)
6. BLINDED BY THE LIGHT
   (*Manfred Mann's Earth Band*)
7. WALK THIS WAY
   (*Aerosmith*)
8. YOU DON'T HAVE TO BE A STAR (TO BE IN MY SHOW)
   (*Marilyn McCoo and Billy Davis Jr.*)
9. NEW KID IN TOWN
   (*The Eagles*)
10. TORN BETWEEN TWO LOVERS
   (*Mary MacGregor*)

POP ALBUMS

1. HOTEL CALIFORNIA
   (*The Eagles*)
2. SONGS IN THE KEY OF LIFE
   (*Stevie Wonder*)
3. WINGS OVER AMERICA
   (*Paul McCartney and Wings*)
4. BOSTON
   (*Boston*)
5. FRAMPTON COMES ALIVE
   (*Peter Frampton*)
6. GREATEST HITS
   (*Linda Ronstadt*)
7. A STAR IS BORN
   (*Original Soundtrack*)
8. BEST OF THE DOOBIES
   (*The Doobie Brothers*)
9. THEIR GREATEST HITS
   (*The Eagles*)
10. FLY LIKE AN EAGLE
   (*The Steve Miller Band*)

BLACK SINGLES

1. CAR WASH
   (*Rose Royce*)
2. I WISH
   (*Stevie Wonder*)
3. DAZZ
   (*Brick*)
4. FREE
   (*Deniece Williams*)
5. HOT LINE
   (*The Sylvers*)
6. ENJOY YOURSELF
   (*The Jacksons*)

7. I LIKE TO DO IT
   (*KC and the Sunshine Band*)
8. DO IT TO MY MIND
   (*Johnny Bristol*)
9. I KINDA MISS YOU
   (*The Manhattans*)
10. DARLIN' DARLIN' BABY (SWEET TENDER LOVE)
   (*The O'Jays*)

BLACK ALBUMS

1. SONGS IN THE KEY OF LIFE
   (*Stevie Wonder*)
2. CAR WASH
   (*Original Soundtrack*)
3. GOOD HIGH
   (*Brick*)
4. SPIRIT
   (*Earth, Wind and Fire*)
5. THIS IS NIECY
   (*Deniece Williams*)
6. II
   (*Brass Construction*)
7. UNFINISHED BUSINESS
   (*Blackbyrds*)
8. OPEN SESAME
   (*Kool and the Gang*)
9. TOO HOT TO STOP
   (*Bar-Kays*)
10. I HOPE WE GET TO LOVE IN TIME
   (*Marilyn McCoo and Billy Davis Jr.*)

JAZZ ALBUMS

1. A SECRET PLACE
   (*Grover Washington Jr.*)
2. UNFINISHED BUSINESS
   (*Blackbyrds*)
3. MAIN SQUEEZE
   (*Chuck Mangione*)
4. BREEZIN'
   (*George Benson*)
5. I HEARD THAT!!
   (*Quincy Jones*)
6. SCHOOL DAYS
   (*Stanley Clarke*)
7. MAN WITH THE SAD FACE
   (*Stanley Turrentine*)
8. MY SPANISH HEART
   (*Chick Corea*)
9. BAREFOOT BALLET
   (*John Klemmer*)
10. CALIENTE
   (*Gato Barbieri*)

COUNTRY SINGLES

1. YOU NEVER MISS A REAL GOOD THING (TILL HE SAYS GOODBYE)
   (*Crystal Gayle*)
2. I CAN'T BELIEVE (SHE GIVES IT ALL TO ME)
   (*Conway Twitty*)
3. TWO DOLLARS IN THE JUKEBOX
   (*Eddie Rabbitt*)
4. LET MY LOVE BE YOUR PILLOW
   (*Ronnie Milsap*)
5. DON'T BE ANGRY
   (*Donna Fargo*)
6. STATUES WITHOUT HEARTS
   (*Larry Gatlin*)
7. ARE YOU READY FOR THE COUNTRY/SO GOOD WOMAN
   (*Waylon Jennings*)
8. SAYING HELLO, SAYING I LOVE YOU, SAYING GOODBYE
   (*Jim Ed Brown and Helen Cornelius*)
9. BROKEN DOWN IN TINY PIECES
   (*Billy "Crash" Craddock*)
10. C.B. SAVAGE
   (*Rod Hart*)

COUNTRY ALBUMS

1. WAYLON LIVE
   (*Waylon Jennings*)
2. ARE YOU READY FOR THE COUNTRY
   (*Waylon Jennings*)
3. RONNIE MILSAP LIVE
   (*Ronnie Milsap*)
4. THE TROUBLEMAKER
   (*Willie Nelson*)
5. CONWAY TWITTY'S GREATEST HITS, VOL. II
   (*Conway Twitty*)
6. BEST OF CHARLEY PRIDE, VOL. III
   (*Charley Pride*)
7. THE BEST OF GLEN CAMPBELL
   (*Glen Campbell*)
8. THE ROOTS OF MY RAISING
   (*Merle Haggard*)
9. GILLEY'S SMOKIN'
   (*Mickey Gilley*)
10. GREATEST HITS
   (*Linda Ronstadt*)

JANUARY 29, 1977

POP SINGLES

1. CAR WASH
   (*Rose Royce*)
2. I WISH
   (*Stevie Wonder*)
3. DAZZ
   (*Brick*)
4. BLINDED BY THE LIGHT
   (*Manfred Mann's Earth Band*)
5. WALK THIS WAY
   (*Aerosmith*)
6. HOT LINE
   (*The Sylvers*)
7. NEW KID IN TOWN
   (*The Eagles*)
8. TORN BETWEEN TWO LOVERS
   (*Mary MacGregor*)
9. YOU MAKE ME FEEL LIKE DANCING
   (*Leo Sayer*)
10. AFTER THE LOVIN'
   (*Englebert Humperdinck*)

POP ALBUMS

1. HOTEL CALIFORNIA
   (*The Eagles*)
2. SONGS IN THE KEY OF LIFE
   (*Stevie Wonder*)
3. A STAR IS BORN
   (*Original Soundtrack*)
4. WINGS OVER AMERICA
   (*Paul McCartney and Wings*)
5. BOSTON
   (*Boston*)
6. FRAMPTON COMES ALIVE
   (*Peter Frampton*)
7. GREATEST HITS
   (*Linda Ronstadt*)
8. FLY LIKE AN EAGLE
   (*The Steve Miller Band*)
9. THEIR GREATEST HITS
   (*The Eagles*)
10. BEST OF THE DOOBIES
   (*The Doobie Brothers*)

BLACK SINGLES

1. I WISH
   (*Stevie Wonder*)
2. CAR WASH
   (*Rose Royce*)
3. DAZZ
   (*Brick*)

4. FREE
   (Deniece Williams)
5. ENJOY YOURSELF
   (The Jacksons)
6. I LIKE TO DO IT
   (KC and the Sunshine Band)
7. HOT LINE
   (The Sylvers)
8. FANCY DANCER
   (Commodores)
9. DARLIN' DARLIN' BABY (SWEET TENDER LOVE)
   (The O'Jays)
10. I KINDA MISS YOU
   (The Manhattans)

BLACK ALBUMS

1. SONGS IN THE KEY OF LIFE
   (Stevie Wonder)
2. CAR WASH
   (Original Soundtrack)
3. GOOD HIGH
   (Brick)
4. THIS IS NIECY
   (Deniece Williams)
5. SPIRIT
   (Earth, Wind and Fire)
6. II
   (Brass Construction)
7. UNFINISHED BUSINESS
   (Blackbyrds)
8. OPEN SESAME
   (Kool and the Gang)
9. TOO HOT TO STOP
   (Bar-Kays)
10. FEELING GOOD
   (Walter Jackson)

JAZZ ALBUMS

1. A SECRET PLACE
   (Grover Washington Jr.)
2. UNFINISHED BUSINESS
   (Blackbyrds)
3. BREEZIN'
   (George Benson)
4. MAIN SQUEEZE
   (Chuck Mangione)
5. VIBRATIONS
   (Roy Ayers Ubiquity)
6. I HEARD THAT!!
   (Quincy Jones)
7. SCHOOL DAYS
   (Stanley Clarke)
8. MY SPANISH HEART
   (Chick Corea)
9. CALIENTE
   (Gato Barbieri)
10. IMAGINARY VOYAGE
   (Jean Luc Ponty)

COUNTRY SINGLES

1. I CAN'T BELIEVE (SHE GIVES IT ALL TO ME)
   (Conway Twitty)
2. LET MY LOVE BE YOUR PILLOW
   (Ronnie Milsap)
3. TWO DOLLARS IN THE JUKEBOX
   (Eddie Rabbitt)
4. YOU NEVER MISS A REAL GOOD THING (TILL HE SAYS GOODBYE)
   (Crystal Gayle)
5. DON'T BE ANGRY
   (Donna Fargo)
6. SAYING HELLO, SAYING I LOVE YOU, SAYING GOODBYE
   (Jim Ed Brown and Helen Cornelius)
7. ARE YOU READY FOR THE COUNTRY/SO GOOD WOMAN
   (Waylon Jennings)
8. NEAR YOU
   (George Jones and Tammy Wynette)

9. STATUES WITHOUT HEARTS
   (Larry Gatlin)
10. LIARS ONE, BELIEVERS ZERO
   (Bill Anderson)

COUNTRY ALBUMS

1. WAYLON LIVE
   (Waylon Jennings)
2. ARE YOU READY FOR THE COUNTRY
   (Waylon Jennings)
3. RONNIE MILSAP LIVE
   (Ronnie Milsap)
4. THE TROUBLEMAKER
   (Willie Nelson)
5. GREATEST HITS
   (Linda Ronstadt)
6. CONWAY TWITTY'S GREATEST HITS, VOL. II
   (Conway Twitty)
7. THE ROOTS OF MY RAISING
   (Merle Haggard)
8. THE BEST OF GLEN CAMPBELL
   (Glen Campbell)
9. BEST OF CHARLEY PRIDE, VOL. III
   (Charley Pride)
10. TONIGHT! AT THE CAPRI LOUNGE
   (Mary Kay Place)

FEBRUARY 5, 1977

POP SINGLES

1. TORN BETWEEN TWO LOVERS
   (Mary MacGregor)
2. CAR WASH
   (Rose Royce)
3. BLINDED BY THE LIGHT
   (Manfred Mann's Earth Band)
4. I WISH
   (Stevie Wonder)
5. WALK THIS WAY
   (Aerosmith)
6. NEW KID IN TOWN
   (The Eagles)
7. YOU MAKE ME FEEL LIKE DANCING
   (Leo Sayer)
8. HOT LINE
   (The Sylvers)
9. DAZZ
   (Brick)
10. ENJOY YOURSELF
   (The Jacksons)

POP ALBUMS

1. A STAR IS BORN
   (Original Soundtrack)
2. HOTEL CALIFORNIA
   (The Eagles)
3. SONGS IN THE KEY OF LIFE
   (Stevie Wonder)
4. WINGS OVER AMERICA
   (Paul McCartney and Wings)
5. BOSTON
   (Boston)
6. FRAMPTON COMES ALIVE
   (Peter Frampton)
7. FLY LIKE AN EAGLE
   (The Steve Miller Band)
8. GREATEST HITS
   (Linda Ronstadt)
9. A DAY AT THE RACES
   (Queen)
10. BEST OF THE DOOBIES
   (The Doobie Brothers)

BLACK SINGLES

1. I WISH
   (Stevie Wonder)

2. CAR WASH
   (Rose Royce)
3. FREE
   (Deniece Williams)
4. DAZZ
   (Brick)
5. I LIKE TO DO IT
   (KC and the Sunshine Band)
6. ENJOY YOURSELF
   (The Jacksons)
7. FANCY DANCER
   (Commodores)
8. DARLIN' DARLIN' BABY (SWEET TENDER LOVE)
   (The O'Jays)
9. HOT LINE
   (The Sylvers)
10. WHEN LOVE IS NEW
   (Arthur Prysock)

BLACK ALBUMS

1. SONGS IN THE KEY OF LIFE
   (Stevie Wonder)
2. GOOD HIGH
   (Brick)
3. CAR WASH
   (Original Soundtrack)
4. THIS IS NIECY
   (Deniece Williams)
5. BRASS CONSTRUCTION
   (Brass Construction)
6. UNFINISHED BUSINESS
   (Blackbyrds)
7. SPIRIT
   (Earth, Wind and Fire)
8. II
   (Brass Construction)
9. TOO HOT TO STOP
   (Bar-Kays)
10. THE JACKSONS
   (The Jacksons)

JAZZ ALBUMS

1. A SECRET PLACE
   (Grover Washington Jr.)
2. UNFINISHED BUSINESS
   (Blackbyrds)
3. BREEZIN'
   (George Benson)
4. MAIN SQUEEZE
   (Chuck Mangione)
5. VIBRATIONS
   (Roy Ayers Ubiquity)
6. SCHOOL DAYS
   (Stanley Clarke)
7. MY SPANISH HEART
   (Chick Corea)
8. IMAGINARY VOYAGE
   (Jean Luc Ponty)
9. CALIENTE
   (Gato Barbieri)
10. RENAISSANCE
   (Lonnie Liston Smith)

COUNTRY SINGLES

1. LET MY LOVE BE YOUR PILLOW
   (Ronnie Milsap)
2. I CAN'T BELIEVE (SHE GIVES IT ALL TO ME)
   (Conway Twitty)
3. SAYING HELLO, SAYING I LOVE YOU, SAYING GOODBYE
   (Jim Ed Brown and Helen Cornelius)
4. NEAR YOU
   (George Jones and Tammy Wynette)
5. DON'T BE ANGRY
   (Donna Fargo)
6. TWO DOLLARS IN THE JUKEBOX
   (Eddie Rabbitt)
7. LIARS ONE, BELIEVERS ZERO
   (Bill Anderson)

8. SAY YOU'LL STAY UNTIL TOMORROW
   (Tom Jones)
9. UNCLOUDY DAY
   (Willie Nelson)
10. MOODY BLUE
    (Elvis Presley)

COUNTRY ALBUMS

1. WAYLON LIVE
   (Waylon Jennings)
2. RONNIE MILSAP LIVE
   (Ronnie Milsap)
3. GREATEST HITS
   (Linda Ronstadt)
4. THE TROUBLEMAKER
   (Willie Nelson)
5. CONWAY TWITTY'S GREATEST HITS, VOL. II
   (Conway Twitty)
6. ARE YOU READY FOR THE COUNTRY
   (Waylon Jennings)
7. THE ROOTS OF MY RAISING
   (Merle Haggard)
8. BEST OF CHARLEY PRIDE, VOL. III
   (Charley Pride)
9. THE BEST OF GLEN CAMPBELL
   (Glen Campbell)
10. TONIGHT! AT THE CAPRI LOUNGE
    (Mary Kay Place)

FEBRUARY 12, 1977

POP SINGLES

1. TORN BETWEEN TWO LOVERS
   (Mary MacGregor)
2. BLINDED BY THE LIGHT
   (Manfred Mann's Earth Band)
3. CAR WASH
   (Rose Royce)
4. NEW KID IN TOWN
   (The Eagles)
5. I WISH
   (Stevie Wonder)
6. YOU MAKE ME FEEL LIKE DANCING
   (Leo Sayer)
7. WEEKEND IN NEW ENGLAND
   (Barry Manilow)
8. YEAR OF THE CAT
   (Al Stewart)
9. ENJOY YOURSELF
   (The Jacksons)
10. LOST WITHOUT YOUR LOVE
    (Bread)

POP ALBUMS

1. A STAR IS BORN
   (Original Soundtrack)
2. HOTEL CALIFORNIA
   (The Eagles)
3. SONGS IN THE KEY OF LIFE
   (Stevie Wonder)
4. BOSTON
   (Boston)
5. FLY LIKE AN EAGLE
   (The Steve Miller Band)
6. WINGS OVER AMERICA
   (Paul McCartney and Wings)
7. GREATEST HITS
   (Linda Ronstadt)
8. FRAMPTON COMES ALIVE
   (Peter Frampton)
9. A DAY AT THE RACES
   (Queen)
10. TEJAS
    (ZZ Top)

BLACK SINGLES

1. I WISH
   (Stevie Wonder)

2. FREE
   (Deniece Williams)
3. CAR WASH
   (Rose Royce)
4. DAZZ
   (Brick)
5. DON'T LEAVE ME THIS WAY
   (Thelma Houston)
6. FANCY DANCER
   (Commodores)
7. I LIKE TO DO IT
   (KC and the Sunshine Band)
8. DARLIN' DARLIN' BABY (SWEET TENDER LOVE)
   (The O'Jays)
9. ENJOY YOURSELF
   (The Jacksons)
10. WHEN LOVE IS NEW
    (Arthur Prysock)

BLACK ALBUMS

1. SONGS IN THE KEY OF LIFE
   (Stevie Wonder)
2. CAR WASH
   (Original Soundtrack)
3. THIS IS NIECY
   (Deniece Williams)
4. II
   (Brass Construction)
5. GOOD HIGH
   (Brick)
6. UNFINISHED BUSINESS
   (Blackbyrds)
7. THE JACKSONS
   (The Jacksons)
8. TOO HOT TO STOP
   (Bar-Kays)
9. ASK RUFUS
   (Rufus)
10. SPIRIT
    (Earth, Wind and Fire)

JAZZ ALBUMS

1. A SECRET PLACE
   (Grover Washington Jr.)
2. UNFINISHED BUSINESS
   (Blackbyrds)
3. MAIN SQUEEZE
   (Chuck Mangione)
4. VIBRATIONS
   (Roy Ayers Ubiquity)
5. BREEZIN'
   (George Benson)
6. MY SPANISH HEART
   (Chick Corea)
7. IMAGINARY VOYAGE
   (Jean Luc Ponty)
8. CALIENTE
   (Gato Barbieri)
9. RENAISSANCE
   (Lonnie Liston Smith)
10. SCHOOL DAYS
    (Stanley Clarke)

COUNTRY SINGLES

1. NEAR YOU
   (George Jones and Tammy Wynette)
2. LET MY LOVE BE YOUR PILLOW
   (Ronnie Milsap)
3. SAYING HELLO, SAYING I LOVE YOU, SAYING GOODBYE
   (Jim Ed Brown and Helen Cornelius)
4. I CAN'T BELIEVE (SHE GIVES IT ALL TO ME)
   (Conway Twitty)
5. LIARS ONE, BELIEVERS ZERO
   (Bill Anderson)
6. SAY YOU'LL STAY UNTIL TOMORROW
   (Tom Jones)
7. MOODY BLUE
   (Elvis Presley)

8. UNCLOUDY DAY
   (Willie Nelson)
9. CRAZY
   (Linda Ronstadt)
10. WHY LOVERS TURN TO STRANGERS
    (Freddie Hart)

COUNTRY ALBUMS

1. WAYLON LIVE
   (Waylon Jennings)
2. RONNIE MILSAP LIVE
   (Ronnie Milsap)
3. GREATEST HITS
   (Linda Ronstadt)
4. THE TROUBLEMAKER
   (Willie Nelson)
5. ARE YOU READY FOR THE COUNTRY
   (Waylon Jennings)
6. THE ROOTS OF MY RAISING
   (Merle Haggard)
7. CONWAY TWITTY'S GREATEST HITS, VOL. II
   (Conway Twitty)
8. BEST OF CHARLEY PRIDE, VOL. III
   (Charley Pride)
9. LUXURY LINER
   (Emmylou Harris)
10. THE BEST OF GLEN CAMPBELL
    (Glen Campbell)

FEBRUARY 19, 1977

POP SINGLES

1. BLINDED BY THE LIGHT
   (Manfred Mann's Earth Band)
2. TORN BETWEEN TWO LOVERS
   (Mary MacGregor)
3. NEW KID IN TOWN
   (The Eagles)
4. CAR WASH
   (Rose Royce)
5. YEAR OF THE CAT
   (Al Stewart)
6. WEEKEND IN NEW ENGLAND
   (Barry Manilow)
7. FLY LIKE AN EAGLE
   (The Steve Miller Band)
8. ENJOY YOURSELF
   (The Jacksons)
9. LOVE THEME FROM "A STAR IS BORN" (EVERGREEN)
   (Barbra Streisand)
10. LOST WITHOUT YOUR LOVE
    (Bread)

POP ALBUMS

1. A STAR IS BORN
   (Original Soundtrack)
2. HOTEL CALIFORNIA
   (The Eagles)
3. SONGS IN THE KEY OF LIFE
   (Stevie Wonder)
4. BOSTON
   (Boston)
5. FLY LIKE AN EAGLE
   (The Steve Miller Band)
6. GREATEST HITS
   (Linda Ronstadt)
7. WINGS OVER AMERICA
   (Paul McCartney and Wings)
8. FRAMPTON COMES ALIVE
   (Peter Frampton)
9. TEJAS
   (ZZ Top)
10. YEAR OF THE CAT
    (Al Stewart)

BLACK SINGLES

1. I WISH
   (Stevie Wonder)
2. DON'T LEAVE ME THIS WAY
   (Thelma Houston)
3. FREE
   (Deniece Williams)
4. CAR WASH
   (Rose Royce)
5. DAZZ
   (Brick)
6. GLORIA
   (Enchantment)
7. I'VE GOT LOVE ON MY MIND
   (Natalie Cole)
8. BE MY GIRL
   (The Dramatics)
9. SOMETHING 'BOUT 'CHA
   (Latimore)
10. FANCY DANCER
    (Commodores)

BLACK ALBUMS

1. SONGS IN THE KEY OF LIFE
   (Stevie Wonder)
2. ASK RUFUS
   (Rufus)
3. CAR WASH
   (Original Soundtrack)
4. THIS IS NIECY
   (Deniece Williams)
5. UNFINISHED BUSINESS
   (Blackbyrds)
6. II
   (Brass Construction)
7. THE JACKSONS
   (The Jacksons)
8. GOOD HIGH
   (Brick)
9. ANY WAY YOU LIKE IT
   (Thelma Houston)
10. TOO HOT TO STOP
    (Bar-Kays)

JAZZ ALBUMS

1. IN FLIGHT
   (George Benson)
2. A SECRET PLACE
   (Grover Washington Jr.)
3. UNFINISHED BUSINESS
   (Blackbyrds)
4. VIBRATIONS
   (Roy Ayers Ubiquity)
5. IMAGINARY VOYAGE
   (Jean Luc Ponty)
6. MY SPANISH HEART
   (Chick Corea)
7. BREEZIN'
   (George Benson)
8. CALIENTE
   (Gato Barbieri)
9. MAIN SQUEEZE
   (Chuck Mangione)
10. RENAISSANCE
    (Lonnie Liston Smith)

COUNTRY SINGLES

1. SAY YOU'LL STAY UNTIL TOMORROW
   (Tom Jones)
2. NEAR YOU
   (George Jones and Tammy Wynette)
3. MOODY BLUE
   (Elvis Presley)
4. CRAZY
   (Linda Ronstadt)
5. LIARS ONE, BELIEVERS ZERO
   (Bill Anderson)
6. UNCLOUDY DAY
   (Willie Nelson)

7. SAYING HELLO, SAYING I LOVE YOU, SAYING GOODBYE
   (Jim Ed Brown and Helen Cornelius)
8. LET MY LOVE BE YOUR PILLOW
   (Ronnie Milsap)
9. I CAN'T BELIEVE (SHE GIVES IT ALL TO ME)
   (Conway Twitty)
10. WHY LOVERS TURN TO STRANGERS
    (Freddie Hart)

COUNTRY ALBUMS

1. WAYLON LIVE
   (Waylon Jennings)
2. LUXURY LINER
   (Emmylou Harris)
3. GREATEST HITS
   (Linda Ronstadt)
4. RONNIE MILSAP LIVE
   (Ronnie Milsap)
5. ARE YOU READY FOR THE COUNTRY
   (Waylon Jennings)
6. THE ROOTS OF MY RAISING
   (Merle Haggard)
7. THE TROUBLEMAKER
   (Willie Nelson)
8. BEST OF CHARLEY PRIDE, VOL. III
   (Charley Pride)
9. CONWAY TWITTY'S GREATEST HITS, VOL. II
   (Conway Twitty)
10. DON'T STOP BELIEVIN'
    (Olivia Newton-John)

FEBRUARY 26, 1977

POP SINGLES

1. TORN BETWEEN TWO LOVERS
   (Mary MacGregor)
2. BLINDED BY THE LIGHT
   (Manfred Mann's Earth Band)
3. LOVE THEME FROM "A STAR IS BORN" (EVERGREEN)
   (Barbra Streisand)
4. YEAR OF THE CAT
   (Al Stewart)
5. NEW KID IN TOWN
   (The Eagles)
6. FLY LIKE AN EAGLE
   (The Steve Miller Band)
7. ENJOY YOURSELF
   (The Jacksons)
8. WEEKEND IN NEW ENGLAND
   (Barry Manilow)
9. NIGHT MOVES
   (Bob Seger and the Silver Bullet Band)
10. I LIKE DREAMIN'
    (Kenny Nolan)

POP ALBUMS

1. A STAR IS BORN
   (Original Soundtrack)
2. HOTEL CALIFORNIA
   (The Eagles)
3. SONGS IN THE KEY OF LIFE
   (Stevie Wonder)
4. BOSTON
   (Boston)
5. FLY LIKE AN EAGLE
   (The Steve Miller Band)
6. GREATEST HITS
   (Linda Ronstadt)
7. FRAMPTON COMES ALIVE
   (Peter Frampton)
8. WINGS OVER AMERICA
   (Paul McCartney and Wings)
9. ANIMALS
   (Pink Floyd)

10. YEAR OF THE CAT
    (Al Stewart)

BLACK SINGLES

1. I'VE GOT LOVE ON MY MIND
   (Natalie Cole)
2. DON'T LEAVE ME THIS WAY
   (Thelma Houston)
3. GLORIA
   (Enchantment)
4. SOMETIMES
   (The Facts of Life)
5. I WISH
   (Stevie Wonder)
6. FREE
   (Deniece Williams)
7. SOMETHING 'BOUT 'CHA
   (Latimore)
8. BE MY GIRL
   (The Dramatics)
9. CAR WASH
   (Rose Royce)
10. DAZZ
    (Brick)

BLACK ALBUMS

1. SONGS IN THE KEY OF LIFE
   (Stevie Wonder)
2. ASK RUFUS
   (Rufus)
3. CAR WASH
   (Original Soundtrack)
4. UNFINISHED BUSINESS
   (Blackbyrds)
5. THIS IS NIECY
   (Deniece Williams)
6. AHH . . . THE NAME IS BOOTSY, BABY!
   (Bootsy's Rubber Band)
7. ANY WAY YOU LIKE IT
   (Thelma Houston)
8. THE JACKSONS
   (The Jacksons)
9. PERSON TO PERSON
   (Average White Band)
10. A SECRET PLACE
    (Grover Washington Jr.)

JAZZ ALBUMS

1. IN FLIGHT
   (George Benson)
2. A SECRET PLACE
   (Grover Washington Jr.)
3. UNFINISHED BUSINESS
   (Blackbyrds)
4. VIBRATIONS
   (Roy Ayers Ubiquity)
5. IMAGINARY VOYAGE
   (Jean Luc Ponty)
6. MY SPANISH HEART
   (Chick Corea)
7. BREEZIN'
   (George Benson)
8. CALIENTE
   (Gato Barbieri)
9. GEORGE BENSON IN CONCERT— CARNEGIE HALL
   (George Benson)
10. RENAISSANCE
    (Lonnie Liston Smith)

COUNTRY SINGLES

1. MOODY BLUE
   (Elvis Presley)
2. SAY YOU'LL STAY UNTIL TOMORROW
   (Tom Jones)
3. NEAR YOU
   (George Jones and Tammy Wynette)
4. CRAZY
   (Linda Ronstadt)

5. UNCLOUDY DAY
   (Willie Nelson)
6. TORN BETWEEN TWO LOVERS
   (Mary MacGregor)
7. LIARS ONE, BELIEVERS ZERO
   (Bill Anderson)
8. HEART HEALER
   (Mel Tillis)
9. SAYING HELLO, SAYING I LOVE YOU,
   SAYING GOODBYE
   (Jim Ed Brown and Helen Cornelius)
10. TWO LESS LONELY PEOPLE
    (Rex Allen Jr.)

COUNTRY ALBUMS

1. LUXURY LINER
   (Emmylou Harris)
2. WAYLON LIVE
   (Waylon Jennings)
3. GREATEST HITS
   (Linda Ronstadt)
4. ARE YOU READY FOR THE COUNTRY
   (Waylon Jennings)
5. RONNIE MILSAP LIVE
   (Ronnie Milsap)
6. THE ROOTS OF MY RAISING
   (Merle Haggard)
7. THE TROUBLEMAKER
   (Willie Nelson)
8. BEST OF CHARLEY PRIDE, VOL. III
   (Charley Pride)
9. CONWAY TWITTY'S GREATEST HITS, VOL.
   II
   (Conway Twitty)
10. DON'T STOP BELIEVIN'
    (Olivia Newton-John)

MARCH 5, 1977

POP SINGLES

1. TORN BETWEEN TWO LOVERS
   (Mary MacGregor)
2. LOVE THEME FROM "A STAR IS BORN"
   (EVERGREEN)
   (Barbra Streisand)
3. BLINDED BY THE LIGHT
   (Manfred Mann's Earth Band)
4. YEAR OF THE CAT
   (Al Stewart)
5. FLY LIKE AN EAGLE
   (The Steve Miller Band)
6. NIGHT MOVES
   (Bob Seger and the Silver Bullet Band)
7. DANCING QUEEN
   (Abba)
8. I LIKE DREAMIN'
   (Kenny Nolan)
9. NEW KID IN TOWN
   (The Eagles)
10. ENJOY YOURSELF
    (The Jacksons)

POP ALBUMS

1. A STAR IS BORN
   (Original Soundtrack)
2. HOTEL CALIFORNIA
   (The Eagles)
3. SONGS IN THE KEY OF LIFE
   (Stevie Wonder)
4. BOSTON
   (Boston)
5. FLY LIKE AN EAGLE
   (The Steve Miller Band)
6. GREATEST HITS
   (Linda Ronstadt)
7. ANIMALS
   (Pink Floyd)

8. FRAMPTON COMES ALIVE
   (Peter Frampton)
9. RUMOURS
   (Fleetwood Mac)
10. WINGS OVER AMERICA
    (Paul McCartney and Wings)

BLACK SINGLES

1. I'VE GOT LOVE ON MY MIND
   (Natalie Cole)
2. SOMETIMES
   (The Facts of Life)
3. GLORIA
   (Enchantment)
4. DON'T LEAVE ME THIS WAY
   (Thelma Houston)
5. I WISH
   (Stevie Wonder)
6. SOMETHING 'BOUT 'CHA
   (Latimore)
7. BE MY GIRL
   (The Dramatics)
8. FREE
   (Deniece Williams)
9. CAR WASH
   (Rose Royce)
10. TRYING TO LOVE TWO
    (William Bell)

BLACK ALBUMS

1. SONGS IN THE KEY OF LIFE
   (Stevie Wonder)
2. ASK RUFUS
   (Rufus)
3. AHH . . . THE NAME IS BOOTSY, BABY!
   (Bootsy's Rubber Band)
4. UNFINISHED BUSINESS
   (Blackbyrds)
5. CAR WASH
   (Original Soundtrack)
6. THIS IS NIECY
   (Deniece Williams)
7. ANY WAY YOU LIKE IT
   (Thelma Houston)
8. PERSON TO PERSON
   (Average White Band)
9. IN FLIGHT
   (George Benson)
10. THE JACKSONS
    (The Jacksons)

JAZZ ALBUMS

1. IN FLIGHT
   (George Benson)
2. A SECRET PLACE
   (Grover Washington Jr.)
3. UNFINISHED BUSINESS
   (Blackbyrds)
4. ROOTS
   (Quincy Jones)
5. IMAGINARY VOYAGE
   (Jean Luc Ponty)
6. VIBRATIONS
   (Roy Ayers Ubiquity)
7. CALIENTE
   (Gato Barbieri)
8. MY SPANISH HEART
   (Chick Corea)
9. GEORGE BENSON IN CONCERT—
   CARNEGIE HALL
   (George Benson)
10. RENAISSANCE
    (Lonnie Liston Smith)

COUNTRY SINGLES

1. TORN BETWEEN TWO LOVERS
   (Mary MacGregor)

2. SAY YOU'LL STAY UNTIL TOMORROW
   (Tom Jones)
3. MOODY BLUE
   (Elvis Presley)
4. HEART HEALER
   (Mel Tillis)
5. CRAZY
   (Linda Ronstadt)
6. THERE SHE GOES AGAIN
   (Joe Stampley)
7. UNCLOUDY DAY
   (Willie Nelson)
8. DESPERADO
   (Johnny Rodriguez)
9. IF LOVE WAS A BOTTLE OF WINE
   (Tommy Overstreet)
10. SHE'S JUST AN OLD LOVE TURNED
    MEMORY
    (Charley Pride)

COUNTRY ALBUMS

1. LUXURY LINER
   (Emmylou Harris)
2. WAYLON LIVE
   (Waylon Jennings)
3. GREATEST HITS
   (Linda Ronstadt)
4. VISIONS
   (Don Williams)
5. RONNIE MILSAP LIVE
   (Ronnie Milsap)
6. THE TROUBLEMAKER
   (Willie Nelson)
7. THE COUNTRY AMERICA LOVES
   (The Statler Brothers)
8. TORN BETWEEN TWO LOVERS
   (Mary MacGregor)
9. CONWAY TWITTY'S GREATEST HITS, VOL.
   II
   (Conway Twitty)
10. RUBBER DUCK
    (C.W. McCall)

MARCH 12, 1977

POP SINGLES

1. LOVE THEME FROM "A STAR IS BORN"
   (EVERGREEN)
   (Barbra Streisand)
2. TORN BETWEEN TWO LOVERS
   (Mary MacGregor)
3. BLINDED BY THE LIGHT
   (Manfred Mann's Earth Band)
4. DANCING QUEEN
   (Abba)
5. NIGHT MOVES
   (Bob Seger and the Silver Bullet Band)
6. YEAR OF THE CAT
   (Al Stewart)
7. FLY LIKE AN EAGLE
   (The Steve Miller Band)
8. I LIKE DREAMIN'
   (Kenny Nolan)
9. CARRY ON WAYWARD SON
   (Kansas)
10. GO YOUR OWN WAY
    (Fleetwood Mac)

POP ALBUMS

1. A STAR IS BORN
   (Original Soundtrack)
2. HOTEL CALIFORNIA
   (The Eagles)
3. RUMOURS
   (Fleetwood Mac)
4. SONGS IN THE KEY OF LIFE
   (Stevie Wonder)
5. BOSTON
   (Boston)

6. ANIMALS
   (Pink Floyd)
7. FLY LIKE AN EAGLE
   (The Steve Miller Band)
8. GREATEST HITS
   (Linda Ronstadt)
9. FRAMPTON COMES ALIVE
   (Peter Frampton)
10. BEST OF THE DOOBIES
    (The Doobie Brothers)

BLACK SINGLES

1. I'VE GOT LOVE ON MY MIND
   (Natalie Cole)
2. SOMETIMES
   (The Facts of Life)
3. GLORIA
   (Enchantment)
4. DON'T LEAVE ME THIS WAY
   (Thelma Houston)
5. TRYING TO LOVE TWO
   (William Bell)
6. SOMETHING 'BOUT 'CHA
   (Latimore)
7. BE MY GIRL
   (The Dramatics)
8. I WISH
   (Stevie Wonder)
9. FREE
   (Deniece Williams)
10. AT MIDNIGHT (MY LOVE WILL LIFT YOU
    UP)
    (Rufus featuring Chaka Khan)

BLACK ALBUMS

1. ASK RUFUS
   (Rufus)
2. SONGS IN THE KEY OF LIFE
   (Stevie Wonder)
3. UNPREDICTABLE
   (Natalie Cole)
4. AHH . . . THE NAME IS BOOTSY, BABY!
   (Bootsy's Rubber Band)
5. UNFINISHED BUSINESS
   (Blackbyrds)
6. ANY WAY YOU LIKE IT
   (Thelma Houston)
7. ROOTS
   (Quincy Jones)
8. IN FLIGHT
   (George Benson)
9. PERSON TO PERSON
   (Average White Band)
10. CAR WASH
    (Original Soundtrack)

JAZZ ALBUMS

1. IN FLIGHT
   (George Benson)
2. ROOTS
   (Quincy Jones)
3. A SECRET PLACE
   (Grover Washington Jr.)
4. UNFINISHED BUSINESS
   (Blackbyrds)
5. IMAGINARY VOYAGE
   (Jean Luc Ponty)
6. CARICATURES
   (Donald Byrd)
7. VIBRATIONS
   (Roy Ayers Ubiquity)
8. CALIENTE
   (Gato Barbieri)
9. BREEZIN'
   (George Benson)
10. GEORGE BENSON IN CONCERT—
    CARNEGIE HALL
    (George Benson)

COUNTRY SINGLES

1. HEART HEALER
   (Mel Tillis)
2. SAY YOU'LL STAY UNTIL TOMORROW
   (Tom Jones)
3. TORN BETWEEN TWO LOVERS
   (Mary MacGregor)
4. MOODY BLUE
   (Elvis Presley)
5. SHE'S JUST AN OLD LOVE TURNED
   MEMORY
   (Charley Pride)
6. THERE SHE GOES AGAIN
   (Joe Stampley)
7. DESPERADO
   (Johnny Rodriguez)
8. SOUTHERN NIGHTS
   (Glen Campbell)
9. IF LOVE WAS A BOTTLE OF WINE
   (Tommy Overstreet)
10. LUCILLE
    (Kenny Rogers)

COUNTRY ALBUMS

1. LUXURY LINER
   (Emmylou Harris)
2. WAYLON LIVE
   (Waylon Jennings)
3. VISIONS
   (Don Williams)
4. RONNIE MILSAP LIVE
   (Ronnie Milsap)
5. GREATEST HITS
   (Linda Ronstadt)
6. THE TROUBLEMAKER
   (Willie Nelson)
7. THE COUNTRY AMERICA LOVES
   (The Statler Brothers)
8. TORN BETWEEN TWO LOVERS
   (Mary MacGregor)
9. CONWAY TWITTY'S GREATEST HITS, VOL.
   II
   (Conway Twitty)
10. RUBBER DUCK
    (C.W. McCall)

MARCH 19, 1977

POP SINGLES

1. LOVE THEME FROM "A STAR IS BORN"
   (EVERGREEN)
   (Barbra Streisand)
2. TORN BETWEEN TWO LOVERS
   (Mary MacGregor)
3. DANCING QUEEN
   (Abba)
4. RICH GIRL
   (Daryl Hall and John Oates)
5. BLINDED BY THE LIGHT
   (Manfred Mann's Earth Band)
6. NIGHT MOVES
   (Bob Seger and the Silver Bullet Band)
7. I LIKE DREAMIN'
   (Kenny Nolan)
8. CARRY ON WAYWARD SON
   (Kansas)
9. DON'T LEAVE ME THIS WAY
   (Thelma Houston)
10. THE THINGS WE DO FOR LOVE
    (10 C.C.)

POP ALBUMS

1. A STAR IS BORN
   (Original Soundtrack)
2. RUMOURS
   (Fleetwood Mac)

3. HOTEL CALIFORNIA
   (The Eagles)
4. BOSTON
   (Boston)
5. SONGS IN THE KEY OF LIFE
   (Stevie Wonder)
6. ANIMALS
   (Pink Floyd)
7. FLY LIKE AN EAGLE
   (The Steve Miller Band)
8. GREATEST HITS
   (Linda Ronstadt)
9. LOVE AT THE GREEK
   (Neil Diamond)
10. NIGHT MOVES
    (Bob Seger and the Silver Bullet Band)

BLACK SINGLES

1. I'VE GOT LOVE ON MY MIND
   (Natalie Cole)
2. SOMETIMES
   (The Facts of Life)
3. TRYING TO LOVE TWO
   (William Bell)
4. GLORIA
   (Enchantment)
5. DON'T LEAVE ME THIS WAY
   (Thelma Houston)
6. AT MIDNIGHT (MY LOVE WILL LIFT YOU
   UP)
   (Rufus featuring Chaka Khan)
7. SOMETHING 'BOUT 'CHA
   (Latimore)
8. BE MY GIRL
   (The Dramatics)
9. I WISH
   (Stevie Wonder)
10. FREE
    (Deniece Williams)

BLACK ALBUMS

1. ASK RUFUS
   (Rufus)
2. UNPREDICTABLE
   (Natalie Cole)
3. SONGS IN THE KEY OF LIFE
   (Stevie Wonder)
4. AHH . . . THE NAME IS BOOTSY, BABY!
   (Bootsy's Rubber Band)
5. IN FLIGHT
   (George Benson)
6. ANY WAY YOU LIKE IT
   (Thelma Houston)
7. ROOTS
   (Quincy Jones)
8. UNFINISHED BUSINESS
   (Blackbyrds)
9. PERSON TO PERSON
   (Average White Band)
10. IT FEELS SO GOOD
    (The Manhattans)

JAZZ ALBUMS

1. IN FLIGHT
   (George Benson)
2. ROOTS
   (Quincy Jones)
3. A SECRET PLACE
   (Grover Washington Jr.)
4. IMAGINARY VOYAGE
   (Jean Luc Ponty)
5. CARICATURES
   (Donald Byrd)
6. UNFINISHED BUSINESS
   (Blackbyrds)
7. VIBRATIONS
   (Roy Ayers Ubiquity)
8. BREEZIN'
   (George Benson)
9. CALIENTE
   (Gato Barbieri)

10. MY SPANISH HEART
    (Chick Corea)

COUNTRY SINGLES

1. SHE'S JUST AN OLD LOVE TURNED
   MEMORY
   (Charley Pride)
2. SOUTHERN NIGHTS
   (Glen Campbell)
3. TORN BETWEEN TWO LOVERS
   (Mary MacGregor)
4. SAY YOU'LL STAY UNTIL TOMORROW
   (Tom Jones)
5. DESPERADO
   (Johnny Rodriguez)
6. LUCILLE
   (Kenny Rogers)
7. HEART HEALER
   (Mel Tillis)
8. IT COULDN'T HAVE BEEN ANY BETTER
   (Johnny Duncan)
9. YOU'RE FREE TO GO
   (Sonny James)
10. ADIOS AMIGO
    (Marty Robbins)

COUNTRY ALBUMS

1. WAYLON LIVE
   (Waylon Jennings)
2. LUXURY LINER
   (Emmylou Harris)
3. VISIONS
   (Don Williams)
4. RONNIE MILSAP LIVE
   (Ronnie Milsap)
5. THE COUNTRY AMERICA LOVES
   (The Statler Brothers)
6. TORN BETWEEN TWO LOVERS
   (Mary MacGregor)
7. GREATEST HITS
   (Linda Ronstadt)
8. THE TROUBLEMAKER
   (Willie Nelson)
9. SAY YOU'LL STAY UNTIL TOMORROW
   (Tom Jones)
10. BEST OF CHARLEY PRIDE, VOL. III
    (Charley Pride)

MARCH 26, 1977

POP SINGLES

1. DANCING QUEEN
   (Abba)
2. RICH GIRL
   (Daryl Hall and John Oates)
3. LOVE THEME FROM "A STAR IS BORN"
   (EVERGREEN)
   (Barbra Streisand)
4. TORN BETWEEN TWO LOVERS
   (Mary MacGregor)
5. DON'T LEAVE ME THIS WAY
   (Thelma Houston)
6. BLINDED BY THE LIGHT
   (Manfred Mann's Earth Band)
7. THE THINGS WE DO FOR LOVE
   (10 C.C.)
8. DON'T GIVE UP ON US
   (David Soul)
9. CARRY ON WAYWARD SON
   (Kansas)
10. I LIKE DREAMIN'
    (Kenny Nolan)

POP ALBUMS

1. RUMOURS
   (Fleetwood Mac)

---

2. A STAR IS BORN
   (Original Soundtrack)
3. HOTEL CALIFORNIA
   (The Eagles)
4. BOSTON
   (Boston)
5. THIS ONE'S FOR YOU
   (Barry Manilow)
6. LOVE AT THE GREEK
   (Neil Diamond)
7. SONGS IN THE KEY OF LIFE
   (Stevie Wonder)
8. ANIMALS
   (Pink Floyd)
9. FLY LIKE AN EAGLE
   (The Steve Miller Band)
10. NIGHT MOVES
    (Bob Seger and the Silver Bullet Band)

BLACK SINGLES

1. I'VE GOT LOVE ON MY MIND
   (Natalie Cole)
2. SOMETIMES
   (The Facts of Life)
3. TRYING TO LOVE TWO
   (William Bell)
4. AT MIDNIGHT (MY LOVE WILL LIFT YOU
   UP)
   (Rufus featuring Chaka Khan)
5. GLORIA
   (Enchantment)
6. DON'T LEAVE ME THIS WAY
   (Thelma Houston)
7. LOVE IS BETTER IN THE A.M.
   (Johnnie Taylor)
8. SOMETHING 'BOUT 'CHA
   (Latimore)
9. BE MY GIRL
   (The Dramatics)
10. FREE
    (Deniece Williams)

BLACK ALBUMS

1. ASK RUFUS
   (Rufus)
2. UNPREDICTABLE
   (Natalie Cole)
3. SONGS IN THE KEY OF LIFE
   (Stevie Wonder)
4. AHH . . . THE NAME IS BOOTSY, BABY!
   (Bootsy's Rubber Band)
5. IN FLIGHT
   (George Benson)
6. ROOTS
   (Quincy Jones)
7. ANY WAY YOU LIKE IT
   (Thelma Houston)
8. UNFINISHED BUSINESS
   (Blackbyrds)
9. TEDDY PENDERGRASS
   (Teddy Pendergrass)
10. IT FEELS SO GOOD
    (The Manhattans)

JAZZ ALBUMS

1. IN FLIGHT
   (George Benson)
2. ROOTS
   (Quincy Jones)
3. A SECRET PLACE
   (Grover Washington Jr.)
4. IMAGINARY VOYAGE
   (Jean Luc Ponty)
5. BREEZIN'
   (George Benson)
6. CARICATURES
   (Donald Byrd)
7. VIBRATIONS
   (Roy Ayers Ubiquity)
8. UNFINISHED BUSINESS
   (Blackbyrds)

---

9. CALIENTE
   (Gato Barbieri)
10. MY SPANISH HEART
    (Chick Corea)

COUNTRY SINGLES

1. SOUTHERN NIGHTS
   (Glen Campbell)
2. SHE'S JUST AN OLD LOVE TURNED
   MEMORY
   (Charley Pride)
3. LUCILLE
   (Kenny Rogers)
4. TORN BETWEEN TWO LOVERS
   (Mary MacGregor)
5. DESPERADO
   (Johnny Rodriguez)
6. IT COULDN'T HAVE BEEN ANY BETTER
   (Johnny Duncan)
7. ADIOS AMIGO
   (Marty Robbins)
8. PAPER ROSIE
   (Gene Watson)
9. YOU'RE FREE TO GO
   (Sonny James)
10. DON'T THROW IT ALL AWAY
    (Dave and Sugar)

COUNTRY ALBUMS

1. LUXURY LINER
   (Emmylou Harris)
2. VISIONS
   (Don Williams)
3. WAYLON LIVE
   (Waylon Jennings)
4. RONNIE MILSAP LIVE
   (Ronnie Milsap)
5. THE COUNTRY AMERICA LOVES
   (The Statler Brothers)
6. TORN BETWEEN TWO LOVERS
   (Mary MacGregor)
7. SAY YOU'LL STAY UNTIL TOMORROW
   (Tom Jones)
8. GREATEST HITS
   (Linda Ronstadt)
9. NEW HARVEST . . . FIRST GATHERING
   (Dolly Parton)
10. BEST OF CHARLEY PRIDE, VOL. III
    (Charley Pride)

APRIL 2, 1977

POP SINGLES

1. RICH GIRL
   (Daryl Hall and John Oates)
2. DANCING QUEEN
   (Abba)
3. LOVE THEME FROM "A STAR IS BORN"
   (EVERGREEN)
   (Barbra Streisand)
4. DON'T LEAVE ME THIS WAY
   (Thelma Houston)
5. THE THINGS WE DO FOR LOVE
   (10 C.C.)
6. DON'T GIVE UP ON US
   (David Soul)
7. TORN BETWEEN TWO LOVERS
   (Mary MacGregor)
8. HOTEL CALIFORNIA
   (The Eagles)
9. I'VE GOT LOVE ON MY MIND
   (Natalie Cole)
10. CARRY ON WAYWARD SON
    (Kansas)

POP ALBUMS

1. RUMOURS
   (Fleetwood Mac)

2. HOTEL CALIFORNIA
   (The Eagles)
3. A STAR IS BORN
   (Original Soundtrack)
4. BOSTON
   (Boston)
5. THIS ONE'S FOR YOU
   (Barry Manilow)
6. LOVE AT THE GREEK
   (Neil Diamond)
7. SONGS IN THE KEY OF LIFE
   (Stevie Wonder)
8. FLY LIKE AN EAGLE
   (The Steve Miller Band)
9. NIGHT MOVES
   (Bob Seger and the Silver Bullet Band)
10. LEFTOVERTURE
    (Kansas)

BLACK SINGLES

1. I'VE GOT LOVE ON MY MIND
   (Natalie Cole)
2. TRYING TO LOVE TWO
   (William Bell)
3. SOMETIMES
   (The Facts of Life)
4. AT MIDNIGHT (MY LOVE WILL LIFT YOU UP)
   (Rufus featuring Chaka Khan)
5. LOVE IS BETTER IN THE A.M.
   (Johnnie Taylor)
6. GLORIA
   (Enchantment)
7. DON'T LEAVE ME THIS WAY
   (Thelma Houston)
8. I WANNA GET NEXT TO YOU
   (Rose Royce)
9. THERE WILL COME A DAY (I'M GONNA HAPPEN TO YOU)
   (Smokey Robinson)
10. SOMETHING 'BOUT 'CHA
    (Latimore)

BLACK ALBUMS

1. ASK RUFUS
   (Rufus)
2. UNPREDICTABLE
   (Natalie Cole)
3. AHH . . . THE NAME IS BOOTSY, BABY!
   (Bootsy's Rubber Band)
4. SONGS IN THE KEY OF LIFE
   (Stevie Wonder)
5. IN FLIGHT
   (George Benson)
6. TEDDY PENDERGRASS
   (Teddy Pendergrass)
7. ROOTS
   (Quincy Jones)
8. ANY WAY YOU LIKE IT
   (Thelma Houston)
9. UNFINISHED BUSINESS
   (Blackbyrds)
10. SWEET BEGINNINGS
    (Marlena Shaw)

JAZZ ALBUMS

1. IN FLIGHT
   (George Benson)
2. ROOTS
   (Quincy Jones)
3. BREEZIN'
   (George Benson)
4. A SECRET PLACE
   (Grover Washington Jr.)
5. IMAGINARY VOYAGE
   (Jean Luc Ponty)
6. SWEET BEGINNINGS
   (Marlena Shaw)
7. VIBRATIONS
   (Roy Ayers Ubiquity)
8. HEAVY WEATHER
   (Weather Report)

9. UNFINISHED BUSINESS
   (Blackbyrds)
10. CARICATURES
    (Donald Byrd)

COUNTRY SINGLES

1. LUCILLE
   (Kenny Rogers)
2. SOUTHERN NIGHTS
   (Glen Campbell)
3. IT COULDN'T HAVE BEEN ANY BETTER
   (Johnny Duncan)
4. SHE'S JUST AN OLD LOVE TURNED MEMORY
   (Charley Pride)
5. ADIOS AMIGO
   (Marty Robbins)
6. PAPER ROSIE
   (Gene Watson)
7. DON'T THROW IT ALL AWAY
   (Dave and Sugar)
8. TORN BETWEEN TWO LOVERS
   (Mary MacGregor)
9. SHE'S GOT YOU
   (Loretta Lynn)
10. SLIDE OFF OF YOUR SATIN SHEETS
    (Johnny Paycheck)

COUNTRY ALBUMS

1. LUXURY LINER
   (Emmylou Harris)
2. VISIONS
   (Don Williams)
3. WAYLON LIVE
   (Waylon Jennings)
4. NEW HARVEST . . . FIRST GATHERING
   (Dolly Parton)
5. SAY YOU'LL STAY UNTIL TOMORROW
   (Tom Jones)
6. TORN BETWEEN TWO LOVERS
   (Mary MacGregor)
7. HEART HEALER
   (Mel Tillis)
8. GREATEST HITS
   (Linda Ronstadt)
9. BEST OF DONNA FARGO
   (Donna Fargo)
10. RIDIN' RAINBOWS
    (Tanya Tucker)

APRIL 9, 1977

POP SINGLES

1. RICH GIRL
   (Daryl Hall and John Oates)
2. DON'T GIVE UP ON US
   (David Soul)
3. THE THINGS WE DO FOR LOVE
   (10 C.C.)
4. DON'T LEAVE ME THIS WAY
   (Thelma Houston)
5. LOVE THEME FROM "A STAR IS BORN" EVERGREEN
   (Barbra Streisand)
6. HOTEL CALIFORNIA
   (The Eagles)
7. I'VE GOT LOVE ON MY MIND
   (Natalie Cole)
8. DANCING QUEEN
   (Abba)
9. SOUTHERN NIGHTS
   (Glen Campbell)
10. TRYING TO LOVE TWO
    (William Bell)

POP ALBUMS

1. HOTEL CALIFORNIA
   (The Eagles)

2. A STAR IS BORN
   (Original Soundtrack)
3. RUMOURS
   (Fleetwood Mac)
4. BOSTON
   (Boston)
5. THIS ONE'S FOR YOU
   (Barry Manilow)
6. SONGS IN THE KEY OF LIFE
   (Stevie Wonder)
7. LOVE AT THE GREEK
   (Neil Diamond)
8. NIGHT MOVES
   (Bob Seger and the Silver Bullet Band)
9. LEFTOVERTURE
   (Kansas)
10. UNPREDICTABLE
    (Natalie Cole)

BLACK SINGLES

1. TRYING TO LOVE TWO
   (William Bell)
2. I'VE GOT LOVE ON MY MIND
   (Natalie Cole)
3. AT MIDNIGHT (MY LOVE WILL LIFT YOU UP)
   (Rufus featuring Chaka Khan)
4. SOMETIMES
   (The Facts of Life)
5. LOVE IS BETTER IN THE A.M.
   (Johnnie Taylor)
6. I WANNA GET NEXT TO YOU
   (Rose Royce)
7. I'M YOUR BOOGIE MAN
   (KC and the Sunshine Band)
8. GLORIA
   (Enchantment)
9. THERE WILL COME A DAY (I'M GONNA HAPPEN TO YOU)
   (Smokey Robinson)
10. AIN'T GONNA BUMP (WITH NO BIG FAT WOMAN)
    (Joe Tex)

BLACK ALBUMS

1. UNPREDICTABLE
   (Natalie Cole)
2. ASK RUFUS
   (Rufus)
3. SONGS IN THE KEY OF LIFE
   (Stevie Wonder)
4. IN FLIGHT
   (George Benson)
5. AHH . . . THE NAME IS BOOTSY, BABY!
   (Bootsy's Rubber Band)
6. TEDDY PENDERGRASS
   (Teddy Pendergrass)
7. ROOTS
   (Quincy Jones)
8. SWEET BEGINNINGS
   (Marlena Shaw)
9. DISCO INFERNO
   (Trammps)
10. ANY WAY YOU LIKE IT
    (Thelma Houston)

JAZZ ALBUMS

1. IN FLIGHT
   (George Benson)
2. ROOTS
   (Quincy Jones)
3. HEAVY WEATHER
   (Weather Report)
4. BREEZIN'
   (George Benson)
5. A SECRET PLACE
   (Grover Washington Jr.)
6. SWEET BEGINNINGS
   (Marlena Shaw)
7. IMAGINARY VOYAGE
   (Jean Luc Ponty)

8. VIBRATIONS
   (Roy Ayers Ubiquity)
9. UNFINISHED BUSINESS
   (Blackbyrds)
10. CARICATURES
    (Donald Byrd)

COUNTRY SINGLES

1. IT COULDN'T HAVE BEEN ANY BETTER
   (Johnny Duncan)
2. LUCILLE
   (Kenny Rogers)
3. SOUTHERN NIGHTS
   (Glen Campbell)
4. PAPER ROSIE
   (Gene Watson)
5. ADIOS AMIGO
   (Marty Robbins)
6. DON'T THROW IT ALL AWAY
   (Dave and Sugar)
7. SHE'S GOT YOU
   (Loretta Lynn)
8. SLIDE OFF OF YOUR SATIN SHEETS
   (Johnny Paycheck)
9. SHE'S JUST AN OLD LOVE TURNED
   MEMORY
   (Charley Pride)
10. SHE'S PULLING ME BACK AGAIN
    (Mickey Gilley)

COUNTRY ALBUMS

1. NEW HARVEST . . . FIRST GATHERING
   (Dolly Parton)
2. LUXURY LINER
   (Emmylou Harris)
3. SAY YOU'LL STAY UNTIL TOMORROW
   (Tom Jones)
4. VISIONS
   (Don Williams)
5. SOUTHERN NIGHTS
   (Glen Campbell)
6. WAYLON LIVE
   (Waylon Jennings)
7. HEART HEALER
   (Mel Tillis)
8. BEST OF DONNA FARGO
   (Donna Fargo)
9. RIDIN' RAINBOWS
   (Tanya Tucker)
10. GREATEST HITS
    (Linda Ronstadt)

APRIL 16, 1977

POP SINGLES

1. DON'T GIVE UP ON US
   (David Soul)
2. RICH GIRL
   (Daryl Hall and John Oates)
3. THE THINGS WE DO FOR LOVE
   (10 C.C.)
4. HOTEL CALIFORNIA
   (The Eagles)
5. SOUTHERN NIGHTS
   (Glen Campbell)
6. I'VE GOT LOVE ON MY MIND
   (Natalie Cole)
7. DON'T LEAVE ME THIS WAY
   (Thelma Houston)
8. TRYING TO LOVE TWO
   (William Bell)
9. SO IN TO YOU
   (Atlanta Rhythm Section)
10. WHEN I NEED YOU
    (Leo Sayer)

POP ALBUMS

1. HOTEL CALIFORNIA
   (The Eagles)
2. RUMOURS
   (Fleetwood Mac)
3. A STAR IS BORN
   (Original Soundtrack)
4. BOSTON
   (Boston)
5. THIS ONE'S FOR YOU
   (Barry Manilow)
6. SONGS IN THE KEY OF LIFE
   (Stevie Wonder)
7. NIGHT MOVES
   (Bob Seger and the Silver Bullet Band)
8. LEFTOVERTURE
   (Kansas)
9. UNPREDICTABLE
   (Natalie Cole)
10. FLY LIKE AN EAGLE
    (The Steve Miller Band)

BLACK SINGLES

1. TRYING TO LOVE TWO
   (William Bell)
2. I WANNA GET NEXT TO YOU
   (Rose Royce)
3. AT MIDNIGHT (MY LOVE WILL LIFT YOU
   UP)
   (Rufus featuring Chaka Khan)
4. I'M YOUR BOOGIE MAN
   (KC and the Sunshine Band)
5. I'VE GOT LOVE ON MY MIND
   (Natalie Cole)
6. AIN'T GONNA BUMP (WITH NO BIG FAT
   WOMAN)
   (Joe Tex)
7. DISCO INFERNO
   (Trammps)
8. SOMETIMES
   (The Facts of Life)
9. THERE WILL COME A DAY (I'M GONNA
   HAPPEN TO YOU)
   (Smokey Robinson)
10. LOVE IS BETTER IN THE A.M.
    (Johnnie Taylor)

BLACK ALBUMS

1. MARVIN GAYE LIVE AT THE LONDON
   PALLADIUM
   (Marvin Gaye)
2. UNPREDICTABLE
   (Natalie Cole)
3. SONGS IN THE KEY OF LIFE
   (Stevie Wonder)
4. ASK RUFUS
   (Rufus)
5. COMMODORES
   (Commodores)
6. GO FOR YOUR GUNS
   (Isley Brothers)
7. AHH . . . THE NAME IS BOOTSY, BABY!
   (Bootsy's Rubber Band)
8. TEDDY PENDERGRASS
   (Teddy Pendergrass)
9. IN FLIGHT
   (George Benson)
10. ANY WAY YOU LIKE IT
    (Thelma Houston)

JAZZ ALBUMS

1. IN FLIGHT
   (George Benson)
2. ROOTS
   (Quincy Jones)
3. HEAVY WEATHER
   (Weather Report)
4. BREEZIN'
   (George Benson)

5. A SECRET PLACE
   (Grover Washington Jr.)
6. SWEET BEGINNINGS
   (Marlena Shaw)
7. MUSICMAGIC
   (Return to Forever)
8. IMAGINARY VOYAGE
   (Jean Luc Ponty)
9. VIBRATIONS
   (Roy Ayers Ubiquity)
10. BIRD IN A SILVER CAGE
    (Herbie Mann)

COUNTRY SINGLES

1. PAPER ROSIE
   (Gene Watson)
2. LUCILLE
   (Kenny Rogers)
3. IT COULDN'T HAVE BEEN ANY BETTER
   (Johnny Duncan)
4. SHE'S GOT YOU
   (Loretta Lynn)
5. SHE'S PULLING ME BACK AGAIN
   (Mickey Gilley)
6. DON'T THROW IT ALL AWAY
   (Dave and Sugar)
7. SLIDE OFF OF YOUR SATIN SHEETS
   (Johnny Paycheck)
8. (YOU NEVER CAN TELL) C'EST LA VIE
   (Emmylou Harris)
9. SOUTHERN NIGHTS
   (Glen Campbell)
10. PLAY GUITAR PLAY
    (Conway Twitty)

COUNTRY ALBUMS

1. NEW HARVEST . . . FIRST GATHERING
   (Dolly Parton)
2. LUXURY LINER
   (Emmylou Harris)
3. SAY YOU'LL STAY UNTIL TOMORROW
   (Tom Jones)
4. SOUTHERN NIGHTS
   (Glen Campbell)
5. VISIONS
   (Don Williams)
6. WAYLON LIVE
   (Waylon Jennings)
7. BEST OF DONNA FARGO
   (Donna Fargo)
8. GREATEST HITS, VOL. 2
   (John Denver)
9. HEART HEALER
   (Mel Tillis)
10. GREATEST HITS
    (Linda Ronstadt)

APRIL 23, 1977

POP SINGLES

1. HOTEL CALIFORNIA
   (The Eagles)
2. DON'T GIVE UP ON US
   (David Soul)
3. SOUTHERN NIGHTS
   (Glen Campbell)
4. RICH GIRL
   (Daryl Hall and John Oates)
5. I'VE GOT LOVE ON MY MIND
   (Natalie Cole)
6. WHEN I NEED YOU
   (Leo Sayer)
7. TRYING TO LOVE TWO
   (William Bell)
8. SO IN TO YOU
   (Atlanta Rhythm Section)
9. THE THINGS WE DO FOR LOVE
   (10 C.C.)
10. I WANNA GET NEXT TO YOU
    (Rose Royce)

POP ALBUMS

1. HOTEL CALIFORNIA
   (The Eagles)
2. A STAR IS BORN
   (Original Soundtrack)
3. RUMOURS
   (Fleetwood Mac)
4. BOSTON
   (Boston)
5. SONGS IN THE KEY OF LIFE
   (Stevie Wonder)
6. LEFTOVERTURE
   (Kansas)
7. COMMODORES
   (Commodores)
8. MARVIN GAYE LIVE AT THE LONDON
   PALLADIUM
   (Marvin Gaye)
9. THIS ONE'S FOR YOU
   (Barry Manilow)
10. GO FOR YOUR GUNS
   (Isley Brothers)

BLACK SINGLES

1. TRYING TO LOVE TWO
   (William Bell)
2. I WANNA GET NEXT TO YOU
   (Rose Royce)
3. GOT TO GIVE IT UP
   (Marvin Gaye)
4. I'M YOUR BOOGIE MAN
   (KC and the Sunshine Band)
5. AIN'T GONNA BUMP (WITH NO BIG FAT
   WOMAN)
   (Joe Tex)
6. DISCO INFERNO
   (Trammps)
7. AT MIDNIGHT (MY LOVE WILL LIFT YOU
   UP)
   (Rufus featuring Chaka Khan)
8. I'VE GOT LOVE ON MY MIND
   (Natalie Cole)
9. THE PRIDE
   (Isley Brothers)
10. I WANNA DO IT TO YOU
   (Jerry Butler)

BLACK ALBUMS

1. MARVIN GAYE LIVE AT THE LONDON
   PALLADIUM
   (Marvin Gaye)
2. COMMODORES
   (Commodores)
3. UNPREDICTABLE
   (Natalie Cole)
4. GO FOR YOUR GUNS
   (Isley Brothers)
5. SONGS IN THE KEY OF LIFE
   (Stevie Wonder)
6. ASK RUFUS
   (Rufus)
7. TEDDY PENDERGRASS
   (Teddy Pendergrass)
8. AH ... THE NAME IS BOOTSY, BABY!
   (Bootsy's Rubber Band)
9. IN FLIGHT
   (George Benson)
10. SWEET BEGINNINGS
   (Marlena Shaw)

JAZZ ALBUMS

1. IN FLIGHT
   (George Benson)
2. HEAVY WEATHER
   (Weather Report)
3. BOOTS
   (Quincy Jones)
4. MUSICMAGIC
   (Return to Forever)

5. CONQUISTADOR
   (Maynard Ferguson)
6. BREEZIN'
   (George Benson)
7. BOB JAMES FOUR
   (Bob James)
8. A SECRET PLACE
   (Grover Washington Jr.)
9. IMAGINARY VOYAGE
   (Jean Luc Ponty)
10. BIRD IN A SILVER CAGE
   (Herbie Mann)

COUNTRY SINGLES

1. SHE'S GOT YOU
   (Loretta Lynn)
2. PAPER ROSIE
   (Gene Watson)
3. LUCILLE
   (Kenny Rogers)
4. SHE'S PULLING ME BACK AGAIN
   (Mickey Gilley)
5. PLAY GUITAR PLAY
   (Conway Twitty)
6. (YOU NEVER CAN TELL) C'EST LA VIE
   (Emmylou Harris)
7. SLIDE OFF OF YOUR SATIN SHEETS
   (Johnny Paycheck)
8. SOME BROKEN HEARTS NEVER MEND
   (Don Williams)
9. IT COULDN'T HAVE BEEN ANY BETTER
   (Johnny Duncan)
10. SOUTHERN NIGHTS
   (Glen Campbell)

COUNTRY ALBUMS

1. SOUTHERN NIGHTS
   (Glen Campbell)
2. NEW HARVEST ... FIRST GATHERING
   (Dolly Parton)
3. SAY YOU'LL STAY UNTIL TOMORROW
   (Tom Jones)
4. LUXURY LINER
   (Emmylou Harris)
5. WAYLON LIVE
   (Waylon Jennings)
6. BEST OF DONNA FARGO
   (Donna Fargo)
7. GREATEST HITS, VOL. 2
   (John Denver)
8. PLAY GUITAR PLAY
   (Conway Twitty)
9. HEART HEALER
   (Mel Tillis)
10. VISIONS
   (Don Williams)

APRIL 30, 1977

POP SINGLES

1. SOUTHERN NIGHTS
   (Glen Campbell)
2. WHEN I NEED YOU
   (Leo Sayer)
3. HOTEL CALIFORNIA
   (The Eagles)
4. RICH GIRL
   (Daryl Hall and John Oates)
5. I'VE GOT LOVE ON MY MIND
   (Natalie Cole)
6. DON'T GIVE UP ON US
   (David Soul)
7. TRYING TO LOVE TWO
   (William Bell)
8. SO IN TO YOU
   (Atlanta Rhythm Section)
9. I WANNA GET NEXT TO YOU
   (Rose Royce)

10. THE THINGS WE DO FOR LOVE
   (10 C.C.)

POP ALBUMS

1. HOTEL CALIFORNIA
   (The Eagles)
2. RUMOURS
   (Fleetwood Mac)
3. A STAR IS BORN
   (Original Soundtrack)
4. BOSTON
   (Boston)
5. COMMODORES
   (Commodores)
6. LEFTOVERTURE
   (Kansas)
7. MARVIN GAYE LIVE AT THE LONDON
   PALLADIUM
   (Marvin Gaye)
8. GO FOR YOUR GUNS
   (Isley Brothers)
9. SONGS IN THE KEY OF LIFE
   (Stevie Wonder)
10. THIS ONE'S FOR YOU
   (Barry Manilow)

BLACK SINGLES

1. GOT TO GIVE IT UP
   (Marvin Gaye)
2. TRYING TO LOVE TWO
   (William Bell)
3. I'M YOUR BOOGIE MAN
   (KC and the Sunshine Band)
4. AIN'T GONNA BUMP (WITH NO BIG FAT
   WOMAN)
   (Joe Tex)
5. I WANNA GET NEXT TO YOU
   (Rose Royce)
6. DISCO INFERNO
   (Trammps)
7. I'VE GOT LOVE ON MY MIND
   (Natalie Cole)
8. THE PRIDE
   (Isley Brothers)
9. I WANNA DO IT TO YOU
   (Jerry Butler)
10. YOU'RE THROWING A GOOD LOVE AWAY
   (Spinners)

BLACK ALBUMS

1. MARVIN GAYE LIVE AT THE LONDON
   PALLADIUM
   (Marvin Gaye)
2. COMMODORES
   (Commodores)
3. GO FOR YOUR GUNS
   (Isley Brothers)
4. SONGS IN THE KEY OF LIFE
   (Stevie Wonder)
5. ASK RUFUS
   (Rufus)
6. TEDDY PENDERGRASS
   (Teddy Pendergrass)
7. UNPREDICTABLE
   (Natalie Cole)
8. AHH ... THE NAME IS BOOTSY, BABY!
   (Bootsy's Rubber Band)
9. SLAVE
   (Slave)
10. ANGEL
   (Ohio Players)

JAZZ ALBUMS

1. IN FLIGHT
   (George Benson)
2. HEAVY WEATHER
   (Weather Report)

3. MUSICMAGIC
   (Return to Forever)
4. CONQUISTADOR
   (Maynard Ferguson)
5. BOB JAMES FOUR
   (Bob James)
6. ROOTS
   (Quincy Jones)
7. BREEZIN'
   (George Benson)
8. ELEGANT GYPSY
   (Al DiMeola)
9. GINSENG WOMAN
   (Eric Gale)
10. FROM ME TO YOU
   (George Duke)

COUNTRY SINGLES

1. SHE'S PULLING ME BACK AGAIN
   (Mickey Gilley)
2. PLAY GUITAR PLAY
   (Conway Twitty)
3. SHE'S GOT YOU
   (Loretta Lynn)
4. SOME BROKEN HEARTS NEVER MEND
   (Don Williams)
5. PAPER ROSIE
   (Gene Watson)
6. (YOU NEVER CAN TELL) C'EST LA VIE
   (Emmylou Harris)
7. LUCILLE
   (Kenny Rogers)
8. SLIDE OFF OF YOUR SATIN SHEETS
   (Johnny Paycheck)
9. YESTERDAY'S GONE
   (Vern Gosdin)
10. I'D DO IT ALL OVER AGAIN
   (Crystal Gayle)

COUNTRY ALBUMS

1. SOUTHERN NIGHTS
   (Glen Campbell)
2. NEW HARVEST . . . FIRST GATHERING
   (Dolly Parton)
3. LUXURY LINER
   (Emmylou Harris)
4. PLAY GUITAR PLAY
   (Conway Twitty)
5. WAYLON LIVE
   (Waylon Jennings)
6. SAY YOU'LL STAY UNTIL TOMORROW
   (Tom Jones)
7. GREATEST HITS, VOL. 2
   (John Denver)
8. HEART HEALER
   (Mel Tillis)
9. BEST OF DONNA FARGO
   (Donna Fargo)
10. VISIONS
   (Don Williams)

MAY 7, 1977

POP SINGLES

1. WHEN I NEED YOU
   (Leo Sayer)
2. SOUTHERN NIGHTS
   (Glen Campbell)
3. HOTEL CALIFORNIA
   (The Eagles)
4. RICH GIRL
   (Daryl Hall and John Oates)
5. DON'T GIVE UP ON US
   (David Soul)
6. I'VE GOT LOVE ON MY MIND
   (Natalie Cole)
7. SIR DUKE
   (Stevie Wonder)

8. I WANNA GET NEXT TO YOU
   (Rose Royce)
9. I'M YOUR BOOGIE MAN
   (KC and the Sunshine Band)
10. RIGHT TIME OF THE NIGHT
   (Jennifer Warnes)

POP ALBUMS

1. HOTEL CALIFORNIA
   (The Eagles)
2. RUMOURS
   (Fleetwood Mac)
3. A STAR IS BORN
   (Original Soundtrack)
4. BOSTON
   (Boston)
5. COMMODORES
   (Commodores)
6. MARVIN GAYE LIVE AT THE LONDON PALLADIUM
   (Marvin Gaye)
7. GO FOR YOUR GUNS
   (Isley Brothers)
8. SONGS IN THE KEY OF LIFE
   (Stevie Wonder)
9. LEFTOVERTURE
   (Kansas)
10. THIS ONE'S FOR YOU
   (Barry Manilow)

BLACK SINGLES

1. GOT TO GIVE IT UP
   (Marvin Gaye)
2. I'M YOUR BOOGIE MAN
   (KC and the Sunshine Band)
3. AIN'T GONNA BUMP (WITH NO BIG FAT WOMAN)
   (Joe Tex)
4. TRYING TO LOVE TWO
   (William Bell)
5. DISCO INFERNO
   (Trammps)
6. I WANNA GET NEXT TO YOU
   (Rose Royce)
7. THE PRIDE
   (Isley Brothers)
8. I'VE GOT LOVE ON MY MIND
   (Natalie Cole)
9. YOU'RE THROWING A GOOD LOVE AWAY
   (Spinners)
10. I WANNA DO IT TO YOU
   (Jerry Butler)

BLACK ALBUMS

1. MARVIN GAYE LIVE AT THE LONDON PALLADIUM
   (Marvin Gaye)
2. GO FOR YOUR GUNS
   (Isley Brothers)
3. COMMODORES
   (Commodores)
4. SONGS IN THE KEY OF LIFE
   (Stevie Wonder)
5. TEDDY PENDERGRASS
   (Teddy Pendergrass)
6. ASK RUFUS
   (Rufus)
7. UNPREDICTABLE
   (Natalie Cole)
8. SLAVE
   (Slave)
9. ANGEL
   (Ohio Players)
10. AHH . . . THE NAME IS BOOTSY, BABY!
   (Bootsy's Rubber Band)

JAZZ ALBUMS

1. IN FLIGHT
   (George Benson)

2. HEAVY WEATHER
   (Weather Report)
3. MUSICMAGIC
   (Return to Forever)
4. CONQUISTADOR
   (Maynard Ferguson)
5. BOB JAMES FOUR
   (Bob James)
6. BREEZIN'
   (George Benson)
7. ELEGANT GYPSY
   (Al DiMeola)
8. GINSENG WOMAN
   (Eric Gale)
9. BIRD IN A SILVER CAGE
   (Herbie Mann)
10. FROM ME TO YOU
   (George Duke)

COUNTRY SINGLES

1. PLAY GUITAR PLAY
   (Conway Twitty)
2. SOME BROKEN HEARTS NEVER MEND
   (Don Williams)
3. SHE'S PULLING ME BACK AGAIN
   (Mickey Gilley)
4. SHE'S GOT YOU
   (Loretta Lynn)
5. I'D DO IT ALL OVER AGAIN
   (Crystal Gayle)
6. PAPER ROSIE
   (Gene Watson)
7. IF WE'RE NOT BACK IN LOVE BY MONDAY
   (Merle Haggard)
8. YESTERDAY'S GONE
   (Vern Gosdin)
9. THE RAINS CAME/SUGAR-COATED LOVE
   (Freddy Fender)
10. LUCKENBACH, TEXAS
   (Waylon Jennings)

COUNTRY ALBUMS

1. NEW HARVEST . . . FIRST GATHERING
   (Dolly Parton)
2. SOUTHERN NIGHTS
   (Glen Campbell)
3. LUXURY LINER
   (Emmylou Harris)
4. PLAY GUITAR PLAY
   (Conway Twitty)
5. SHE'S JUST AN OLD LOVE TURNED MEMORY
   (Charley Pride)
6. SAY YOU'LL STAY UNTIL TOMORROW
   (Tom Jones)
7. GREATEST HITS, VOL. 2
   (John Denver)
8. WAYLON LIVE
   (Waylon Jennings)
9. VISIONS
   (Don Williams)
10. THE OUTLAWS
   (Waylon, Willie, Jessi and Tompall)

MAY 14, 1977

POP SINGLES

1. WHEN I NEED YOU
   (Leo Sayer)
2. SOUTHERN NIGHTS
   (Glen Campbell)
3. SIR DUKE
   (Stevie Wonder)
4. HOTEL CALIFORNIA
   (The Eagles)
5. RICH GIRL
   (Daryl Hall and John Oates)
6. I'M YOUR BOOGIE MAN
   (KC and the Sunshine Band)

7. DON'T GIVE UP ON US
   (David Soul)
8. I'VE GOT LOVE ON MY MIND
   (Natalie Cole)
9. I WANNA GET NEXT TO YOU
   (Rose Royce)
10. RIGHT TIME OF THE NIGHT
    (Jennifer Warnes)

POP ALBUMS

1. HOTEL CALIFORNIA
   (The Eagles)
2. RUMOURS
   (Fleetwood Mac)
3. BOSTON
   (Boston)
4. MARVIN GAYE LIVE AT THE LONDON
   PALLADIUM
   (Marvin Gaye)
5. A STAR IS BORN
   (Original Soundtrack)
6. GO FOR YOUR GUNS
   (Isley Brothers)
7. SONGS IN THE KEY OF LIFE
   (Stevie Wonder)
8. COMMODORES
   (Commodores)
9. THIS ONE'S FOR YOU
   (Barry Manilow)
10. ROCKY
    (Original Soundtrack)

BLACK SINGLES

1. GOT TO GIVE IT UP
   (Marvin Gaye)
2. I'M YOUR BOOGIE MAN
   (KC and the Sunshine Band)
3. AIN'T GONNA BUMP (WITH NO BIG FAT
   WOMAN)
   (Joe Tex)
4. TRYING TO LOVE TWO
   (William Bell)
5. SIR DUKE
   (Stevie Wonder)
6. DISCO INFERNO
   (Trammps)
7. THE PRIDE
   (Isley Brothers)
8. I WANNA GET NEXT TO YOU
   (Rose Royce)
9. I'VE GOT LOVE ON MY MIND
   (Natalie Cole)
10. YOUR LOVE——
    (Marilyn McCoo and Billy Davis Jr.)

BLACK ALBUMS

1. MARVIN GAYE LIVE AT THE LONDON
   PALLADIUM
   (Marvin Gaye)
2. GO FOR YOUR GUNS
   (Isley Brothers)
3. COMMODORES
   (Commodores)
4. SONGS IN THE KEY OF LIFE
   (Stevie Wonder)
5. ASK RUFUS
   (Rufus)
6. TEDDY PENDERGRASS
   (Teddy Pendergrass)
7. SLAVE
   (Slave)
8. ANGEL
   (Ohio Players)
9. A REAL MOTHER FOR YA
   (Johnny Guitar Watson)
10. UNPREDICTABLE
    (Natalie Cole)

JAZZ ALBUMS

1. IN FLIGHT
   (George Benson)
2. HEAVY WEATHER
   (Weather Report)
3. MUSICMAGIC
   (Return to Forever)
4. CONQUISTADOR
   (Maynard Ferguson)
5. BOB JAMES FOUR
   (Bob James)
6. BREEZIN'
   (George Benson)
7. ELEGANT GYPSY
   (Al DiMeola)
8. GINSENG WOMAN
   (Eric Gale)
9. FROM ME TO YOU
   (George Duke)
10. V.S.O.P.
    (Herbie Hancock)

COUNTRY SINGLES

1. SOME BROKEN HEARTS NEVER MEND
   (Don Williams)
2. PLAY GUITAR PLAY
   (Conway Twitty)
3. I'D DO IT ALL OVER AGAIN
   (Crystal Gayle)
4. LUCKENBACH, TEXAS
   (Waylon Jennings)
5. IF WE'RE NOT BACK IN LOVE BY MONDAY
   (Merle Haggard)
6. SHE'S PULLING ME BACK AGAIN
   (Mickey Gilley)
7. THE RAINS CAME/SUGAR-COATED LOVE
   (Freddy Fender)
8. YESTERDAY'S GONE
   (Vern Gosdin)
9. I CAN'T HELP MYSELF
   (Eddie Rabbitt)
10. LET'S GET TOGETHER (ONE LAST TIME)
    (Tammy Wynette)

COUNTRY ALBUMS

1. NEW HARVEST . . . FIRST GATHERING
   (Dolly Parton)
2. SOUTHERN NIGHTS
   (Glen Campbell)
3. LUXURY LINER
   (Emmylou Harris)
4. SHE'S JUST AN OLD LOVE TURNED
   MEMORY
   (Charley Pride)
5. PLAY GUITAR PLAY
   (Conway Twitty)
6. I REMEMBER PATSY
   (Loretta Lynn)
7. KENNY ROGERS
   (Kenny Rogers)
8. WELCOME TO MY WORLD
   (Elvis Presley)
9. VISIONS
   (Don Williams)
10. THE OUTLAWS
    (Waylon, Willie, Jessi and Tompall)

MAY 21, 1977

POP SINGLES

1. WHEN I NEED YOU
   (Leo Sayer)
2. SIR DUKE
   (Stevie Wonder)
3. SOUTHERN NIGHTS
   (Glen Campbell)

4. I'M YOUR BOOGIE MAN
   (KC and the Sunshine Band)
5. HOTEL CALIFORNIA
   (The Eagles)
6. RICH GIRL
   (Daryl Hall and John Oates)
7. GOT TO GIVE IT UP
   (Marvin Gaye)
8. DREAMS
   (Fleetwood Mac)
9. DON'T GIVE UP ON US
   (David Soul)
10. COULDN'T GET IT RIGHT
    (Climax Blues Band)

POP ALBUMS

1. HOTEL CALIFORNIA
   (The Eagles)
2. RUMOURS
   (Fleetwood Mac)
3. MARVIN GAYE LIVE AT THE LONDON
   PALLADIUM
   (Marvin Gaye)
4. BOSTON
   (Boston)
5. GO FOR YOUR GUNS
   (Isley Brothers)
6. COMMODORES
   (Commodores)
7. SONGS IN THE KEY OF LIFE
   (Stevie Wonder)
8. A STAR IS BORN
   (Original Soundtrack)
9. ROCKY
   (Original Soundtrack)
10. THIS ONE'S FOR YOU
    (Barry Manilow)

BLACK SINGLES

1. GOT TO GIVE IT UP
   (Marvin Gaye)
2. I'M YOUR BOOGIE MAN
   (KC and the Sunshine Band)
3. SIR DUKE
   (Stevie Wonder)
4. AIN'T GONNA BUMP (WITH NO BIG FAT
   WOMAN)
   (Joe Tex)
5. TRYING TO LOVE TWO
   (William Bell)
6. THE PRIDE
   (Isley Brothers)
7. DISCO INFERNO
   (Trammps)
8. YOUR LOVE
   (Marilyn McCoo and Billy Davis Jr.)
9. SHOW YOU THE WAY TO GO
   (The Jacksons)
10. I WANNA GET NEXT TO YOU
    (Rose Royce)

BLACK ALBUMS

1. MARVIN GAYE LIVE AT THE LONDON
   PALLADIUM
   (Marvin Gaye)
2. GO FOR YOUR GUNS
   (Isley Brothers)
3. COMMODORES
   (Commodores)
4. SONGS IN THE KEY OF LIFE
   (Stevie Wonder)
5. A REAL MOTHER FOR YA
   (Johnny Guitar Watson)
6. TEDDY PENDERGRASS
   (Teddy Pendergrass)
7. SLAVE
   (Slave)
8. ASK RUFUS
   (Rufus)
9. NOW DO-U-WANTA DANCE
   (Graham Central Station)

10. UNPREDICTABLE
    (Natalie Cole)

JAZZ ALBUMS

1. HEAVY WEATHER
   (Weather Report)
2. IN FLIGHT
   (George Benson)
3. CONQUISTADOR
   (Maynard Ferguson)
4. MUSICMAGIC
   (Return to Forever)
5. ELEGANT GYPSY
   (Al DiMeola)
6. BOB JAMES FOUR
   (Bob James)
7. FRIENDS AND STRANGERS
   (Ronnie Laws)
8. GINSENG WOMAN
   (Eric Gale)
9. BREEZIN'
   (George Benson)
10. FROM ME TO YOU
    (George Duke)

COUNTRY SINGLES

1. LUCKENBACH, TEXAS
   (Waylon Jennings)
2. SOME BROKEN HEARTS NEVER MEND
   (Don Williams)
3. I'D DO IT ALL OVER AGAIN
   (Crystal Gayle)
4. IF WE'RE NOT BACK IN LOVE BY MONDAY
   (Merle Haggard)
5. PLAY GUITAR PLAY
   (Conway Twitty)
6. THE RAINS CAME/SUGAR-COATED LOVE
   (Freddy Fender)
7. I CAN'T HELP MYSELF
   (Eddie Rabbitt)
8. SHE'S PULLING ME BACK AGAIN
   (Mickey Gilley)
9. LET'S GET TOGETHER (ONE LAST TIME)
   (Tammy Wynette)
10. BLUEST HEARTACHE OF THE YEAR
    (Kenny Dale)

COUNTRY ALBUMS

1. OL' WAYLON
   (Waylon Jennings)
2. KENNY ROGERS
   (Kenny Rogers)
3. NEW HARVEST . . . FIRST GATHERING
   (Dolly Parton)
4. SHE'S JUST AN OLD LOVE TURNED MEMORY
   (Charley Pride)
5. PLAY GUITAR PLAY
   (Conway Twitty)
6. I REMEMBER PATSY
   (Loretta Lynn)
7. WELCOME TO MY WORLD
   (Elvis Presley)
8. SOUTHERN NIGHTS
   (Glen Campbell)
9. LUXURY LINER
   (Emmylou Harris)
10. YOUR PLACE OR MINE
    (Gary Stewart)

MAY 28, 1977

POP SINGLES

1. SIR DUKE
   (Stevie Wonder)
2. WHEN I NEED YOU
   (Leo Sayer)
3. I'M YOUR BOOGIE MAN
   (KC and the Sunshine Band)
4. GOT TO GIVE IT UP
   (Marvin Gaye)
5. DREAMS
   (Fleetwood Mac)
6. HOTEL CALIFORNIA
   (The Eagles)
7. GONNA FLY NOW (THEME FROM "ROCKY")
   (Bill Conti)
8. LUCILLE
   (Kenny Rogers)
9. COULDN'T GET IT RIGHT
   (Climax Blues Band)
10. LONELY BOY
    (Andrew Gold)

POP ALBUMS

1. RUMOURS
   (Fleetwood Mac)
2. HOTEL CALIFORNIA
   (The Eagles)
3. MARVIN GAYE LIVE AT THE LONDON PALLADIUM
   (Marvin Gaye)
4. BOSTON
   (Boston)
5. GO FOR YOUR GUNS
   (Isley Brothers)
6. COMMODORES
   (Commodores)
7. SONGS IN THE KEY OF LIFE
   (Stevie Wonder)
8. ROCKY
   (Original Soundtrack)
9. THE BEATLES LIVE AT THE HOLLYWOOD BOWL
   (The Beatles)
10. A STAR IS BORN
    (Original Soundtrack)

BLACK SINGLES

1. GOT TO GIVE IT UP
   (Marvin Gaye)
2. SIR DUKE
   (Stevie Wonder)
3. I'M YOUR BOOGIE MAN
   (KC and the Sunshine Band)
4. AIN'T GONNA BUMP (WITH NO BIG FAT WOMAN)
   (Joe Tex)
5. THE PRIDE
   (Isley Brothers)
6. WHODUNIT
   (Tavares)
7. TRYING TO LOVE TWO
   (William Bell)
8. HOLLYWOOD
   (Rufus featuring Chaka Khan)
9. I DON'T LOVE YOU ANYMORE
   (Teddy Pendergrass)
10. HIGH SCHOOL DANCE
    (The Sylvers)

BLACK ALBUMS

1. MARVIN GAYE LIVE AT THE LONDON PALLADIUM
   (Marvin Gaye)
2. GO FOR YOUR GUNS
   (Isley Brothers)
3. COMMODORES
   (Commodores)
4. SONGS IN THE KEY OF LIFE
   (Stevie Wonder)
5. RIGHT ON TIME
   (The Brothers Johnson)
6. TEDDY PENDERGRASS
   (Teddy Pendergrass)
7. A REAL MOTHER FOR YA
   (Johnny Guitar Watson)
8. SLAVE
   (Slave)
9. NOW DO-U-WANTA DANCE
   (Graham Central Station)
10. ASK RUFUS
    (Rufus)

JAZZ ALBUMS

1. HEAVY WEATHER
   (Weather Report)
2. IN FLIGHT
   (George Benson)
3. CONQUISTADOR
   (Maynard Ferguson)
4. MUSICMAGIC
   (Return to Forever)
5. ELEGANT GYPSY
   (Al DiMeola)
6. FRIENDS AND STRANGERS
   (Ronnie Laws)
7. BOB JAMES FOUR
   (Bob James)
8. LOVE NOTES
   (Ramsey Lewis)
9. BREEZIN'
   (George Benson)
10. GINSENG WOMAN
    (Eric Gale)

COUNTRY SINGLES

1. LUCKENBACH, TEXAS
   (Waylon Jennings)
2. SOME BROKEN HEARTS NEVER MEND
   (Don Williams)
3. I'D DO IT ALL OVER AGAIN
   (Crystal Gayle)
4. IF WE'RE NOT BACK IN LOVE BY MONDAY
   (Merle Haggard)
5. I CAN'T HELP MYSELF
   (Eddie Rabbitt)
6. THE RAINS CAME/SUGAR-COATED LOVE
   (Freddy Fender)
7. MARRIED BUT NOT TO EACH OTHER
   (Barbara Mandrell)
8. YOUR MAN LOVES YOU HONEY
   (Tom T. Hall)
9. PLAY GUITAR PLAY
   (Conway Twitty)
10. BLUEST HEARTACHE OF THE YEAR
    (Kenny Dale)

COUNTRY ALBUMS

1. OL' WAYLON
   (Waylon Jennings)
2. KENNY ROGERS
   (Kenny Rogers)
3. NEW HARVEST . . . FIRST GATHERING
   (Dolly Parton)
4. I REMEMBER PATSY
   (Loretta Lynn)
5. SHE'S JUST AN OLD LOVE TURNED MEMORY
   (Charley Pride)
6. PLAY GUITAR PLAY
   (Conway Twitty)
7. BEFORE HIS TIME
   (Willie Nelson)
8. YOUR PLACE OR MINE
   (Gary Stewart)
9. LUXURY LINER
   (Emmylou Harris)
10. WELCOME TO MY WORLD
    (Elvis Presley)

JUNE 4, 1977

POP SINGLES

1. SIR DUKE
   (Stevie Wonder)
2. GOT TO GIVE IT UP
   (Marvin Gaye)
3. I'M YOUR BOOGIE MAN
   (KC and the Sunshine Band)
4. DREAMS
   (Fleetwood Mac)
5. WHEN I NEED YOU
   (Leo Sayer)
6. GONNA FLY NOW (THEME FROM "ROCKY")
   (Bill Conti)
7. LUCILLE
   (Kenny Rogers)
8. LONELY BOY
   (Andrew Gold)
9. UNDERCOVER ANGEL
   (Alan O'Day)
10. AIN'T GONNA BUMP (WITH NO BIG FAT WOMAN)
    (Joe Tex)

POP ALBUMS

1. RUMOURS
   (Fleetwood Mac)
2. HOTEL CALIFORNIA
   (The Eagles)
3. MARVIN GAYE LIVE AT THE LONDON PALLADIUM
   (Marvin Gaye)
4. GO FOR YOUR GUNS
   (Isley Brothers)
5. COMMODORES
   (Commodores)
6. BOSTON
   (Boston)
7. THE BEATLES LIVE AT THE HOLLYWOOD BOWL
   (The Beatles)
8. ROCKY
   (Original Soundtrack)
9. SONGS IN THE KEY OF LIFE
   (Stevie Wonder)
10. A STAR IS BORN
    (Original Soundtrack)

BLACK SINGLES

1. GOT TO GIVE IT UP
   (Marvin Gaye)
2. SIR DUKE
   (Stevie Wonder)
3. I'M YOUR BOOGIE MAN
   (KC and the Sunshine Band)
4. HOLLYWOOD
   (Rufus featuring Chaka Khan)
5. AIN'T GONNA BUMP (WITH NO BIG FAT WOMAN)
   (Joe Tex)
6. WHODUNIT
   (Tavares)
7. I DON'T LOVE YOU ANYMORE
   (Teddy Pendergrass)
8. THE PRIDE
   (Isley Brothers)
9. HIGH SCHOOL DANCE
   (The Sylvers)
10. TRYING TO LOVE TWO
    (William Bell)

BLACK ALBUMS

1. MARVIN GAYE LIVE AT THE LONDON PALLADIUM
   (Marvin Gaye)
2. GO FOR YOUR GUNS
   (Isley Brothers)

3. COMMODORES
   (Commodores)
4. RIGHT ON TIME
   (The Brothers Johnson)
5. SONGS IN THE KEY OF LIFE
   (Stevie Wonder)
6. TEDDY PENDERGRASS
   (Teddy Pendergrass)
7. A REAL MOTHER FOR YA
   (Johnny Guitar Watson)
8. PARLIAMENT LIVE
   (Parliament)
9. SLAVE
   (Slave)
10. NOW DO-U-WANTA DANCE
    (Graham Central Station)

JAZZ ALBUMS

1. HEAVY WEATHER
   (Weather Report)
2. CONQUISTADOR
   (Maynard Ferguson)
3. IN FLIGHT
   (George Benson)
4. ELEGANT GYPSY
   (Al DiMeola)
5. FRIENDS AND STRANGERS
   (Ronnie Laws)
6. MUSICMAGIC
   (Return to Forever)
7. BREEZIN'
   (George Benson)
8. LOVE NOTES
   (Ramsey Lewis)
9. BOB JAMES FOUR
   (Bob James)
10. DON'T STOP THE MUSIC
    (Brecker Brothers)

COUNTRY SINGLES

1. LUCKENBACH, TEXAS
   (Waylon Jennings)
2. IF WE'RE NOT BACK IN LOVE BY MONDAY
   (Merle Haggard)
3. I'D DO IT ALL OVER AGAIN
   (Crystal Gayle)
4. I CAN'T HELP MYSELF
   (Eddie Rabbitt)
5. MARRIED BUT NOT TO EACH OTHER
   (Barbara Mandrell)
6. YOUR MAN LOVES YOU HONEY
   (Tom T. Hall)
7. SOME BROKEN HEARTS NEVER MEND
   (Don Williams)
8. IT'S A COWBOY LOVIN' NIGHT
   (Tanya Tucker)
9. THAT WAS YESTERDAY
   (Donna Fargo)
10. I'M GETTING GOOD AT MISSING YOU (SOLITAIRE)
    (Rex Allen Jr.)

COUNTRY ALBUMS

1. OL' WAYLON
   (Waylon Jennings)
2. KENNY ROGERS
   (Kenny Rogers)
3. I REMEMBER PATSY
   (Loretta Lynn)
4. NEW HARVEST . . . FIRST GATHERING
   (Dolly Parton)
5. BEFORE HIS TIME
   (Willie Nelson)
6. SHE'S JUST AN OLD LOVE TURNED MEMORY
   (Charley Pride)
7. PLAY GUITAR PLAY
   (Conway Twitty)
8. YOUR PLACE OR MINE
   (Gary Stewart)

9. CHANGES IN LATITUDES, CHANGES IN ATTITUDES
   (Jimmy Buffett)
10. WELCOME TO MY WORLD
    (Elvis Presley)

JUNE 11, 1977

POP SINGLES

1. I'M YOUR BOOGIE MAN
   (KC and the Sunshine Band)
2. GOT TO GIVE IT UP
   (Marvin Gaye)
3. DREAMS
   (Fleetwood Mac)
4. SIR DUKE
   (Stevie Wonder)
5. GONNA FLY NOW (THEME FROM "ROCKY")
   (Bill Conti)
6. LONELY BOY
   (Andrew Gold)
7. UNDERCOVER ANGEL
   (Alan O'Day)
8. LUCILLE
   (Kenny Rogers)
9. WHEN I NEED YOU
   (Leo Sayer)
10. FEELS LIKE THE FIRST TIME
    (Foreigner)

POP ALBUMS

1. RUMOURS
   (Fleetwood Mac)
2. HOTEL CALIFORNIA
   (The Eagles)
3. MARVIN GAYE LIVE AT THE LONDON PALLADIUM
   (Marvin Gaye)
4. ROCKY
   (Original Soundtrack)
5. COMMODORES
   (Commodores)
6. BOOK OF DREAMS
   (The Steve Miller Band)
7. THE BEATLES LIVE AT THE HOLLYWOOD BOWL
   (The Beatles)
8. BARRY MANILOW LIVE
   (Barry Manilow)
9. GO FOR YOUR GUNS
   (Isley Brothers)
10. SONGS IN THE KEY OF LIFE
    (Stevie Wonder)

BLACK SINGLES

1. GOT TO GIVE IT UP
   (Marvin Gaye)
2. HOLLYWOOD
   (Rufus featuring Chaka Khan)
3. SIR DUKE
   (Stevie Wonder)
4. I'M YOUR BOOGIE MAN
   (KC and the Sunshine Band)
5. WHODUNIT
   (Tavares)
6. I DON'T LOVE YOU ANYMORE
   (Teddy Pendergrass)
7. AIN'T GONNA BUMP (WITH NO BIG FAT WOMAN)
   (Joe Tex)
8. HIGH SCHOOL DANCE
   (The Sylvers)
9. THE PRIDE
   (Isley Brothers)
10. TRYING TO LOVE TWO
    (William Bell)

BLACK ALBUMS

1. MARVIN GAYE LIVE AT THE LONDON PALLADIUM
   (Marvin Gaye)
2. COMMODORES
   (Commodores)
3. GO FOR YOUR GUNS
   (Isley Brothers)
4. RIGHT ON TIME
   (The Brothers Johnson)
5. SONGS IN THE KEY OF LIFE
   (Stevie Wonder)
6. A REAL MOTHER FOR YA
   (Johnny Guitar Watson)
7. TEDDY PENDERGRASS
   (Teddy Pendergrass)
8. PARLIAMENT LIVE
   (Parliament)
9. TRAVELIN' AT THE SPEED OF THOUGHT
   (The O'Jays)
10. SLAVE
    (Slave)

JAZZ ALBUMS

1. HEAVY WEATHER
   (Weather Report)
2. CONQUISTADOR
   (Maynard Ferguson)
3. FRIENDS AND STRANGERS
   (Ronnie Laws)
4. ELEGANT GYPSY
   (Al DiMeola)
5. IN FLIGHT
   (George Benson)
6. MUSICMAGIC
   (Return to Forever)
7. BREEZIN'
   (George Benson)
8. LOVE NOTES
   (Ramsey Lewis)
9. BOB JAMES FOUR
   (Bob James)
10. DON'T STOP THE MUSIC
    (Brecker Brothers)

COUNTRY SINGLES

1. LUCKENBACH, TEXAS
   (Waylon Jennings)
2. IF WE'RE NOT BACK IN LOVE BY MONDAY
   (Merle Haggard)
3. I CAN'T HELP MYSELF
   (Eddie Rabbitt)
4. MARRIED BUT NOT TO EACH OTHER
   (Barbara Mandrell)
5. YOUR MAN LOVES YOU HONEY
   (Tom T. Hall)
6. IT'S A COWBOY LOVIN' NIGHT
   (Tanya Tucker)
7. THAT WAS YESTERDAY
   (Donna Fargo)
8. I'D DO IT ALL OVER AGAIN
   (Crystal Gayle)
9. BURNING MEMORIES
   (Mel Tillis)
10. I'M GETTING GOOD AT MISSING YOU (SOLITAIRE)
    (Rex Allen Jr.)

COUNTRY ALBUMS

1. OL' WAYLON
   (Waylon Jennings)
2. KENNY ROGERS
   (Kenny Rogers)
3. I REMEMBER PATSY
   (Loretta Lynn)
4. BEFORE HIS TIME
   (Willie Nelson)
5. NEW HARVEST . . . FIRST GATHERING
   (Dolly Parton)

6. CHANGES IN LATITUDES, CHANGES IN ATTITUDES
   (Jimmy Buffett)
7. BEST OF FREDDY FENDER
   (Freddy Fender)
8. SHE'S JUST AN OLD LOVE TURNED MEMORY
   (Charley Pride)
9. SONGS I'LL ALWAYS SING
   (Merle Haggard)
10. YOUR PLACE OR MINE
    (Gary Stewart)

JUNE 18, 1977

POP SINGLES

1. GOT TO GIVE IT UP
   (Marvin Gaye)
2. DREAMS
   (Fleetwood Mac)
3. I'M YOUR BOOGIE MAN
   (KC and the Sunshine Band)
4. GONNA FLY NOW (THEME FROM "ROCKY")
   (Bill Conti)
5. UNDERCOVER ANGEL
   (Alan O'Day)
6. LONELY BOY
   (Andrew Gold)
7. SIR DUKE
   (Stevie Wonder)
8. WHEN I NEED YOU
   (Leo Sayer)
9. FEELS LIKE THE FIRST TIME
   (Foreigner)
10. DA DOO RON RON
    (Shaun Cassidy)

POP ALBUMS

1. RUMOURS
   (Fleetwood Mac)
2. HOTEL CALIFORNIA
   (The Eagles)
3. BOOK OF DREAMS
   (The Steve Miller Band)
4. ROCKY
   (Original Soundtrack)
5. MARVIN GAYE LIVE AT THE LONDON PALLADIUM
   (Marvin Gaye)
6. BARRY MANILOW LIVE
   (Barry Manilow)
7. COMMODORES
   (Commodores)
8. GO FOR YOUR GUNS
   (Isley Brothers)
9. SONGS IN THE KEY OF LIFE
   (Stevie Wonder)
10. BOSTON
    (Boston)

BLACK SINGLES

1. GOT TO GIVE IT UP
   (Marvin Gaye)
2. HOLLYWOOD
   (Rufus featuring Chaka Khan)
3. EASY
   (Commodores)
4. SIR DUKE
   (Stevie Wonder)
5. I DON'T LOVE YOU ANYMORE
   (Teddy Pendergrass)
6. I'M YOUR BOOGIE MAN
   (KC and the Sunshine Band)
7. HIGH SCHOOL DANCE
   (The Sylvers)
8. SEE YOU WHEN I GET THERE
   (Lou Rawls)
9. WHODUNIT
   (Tavares)

10. GOOD THING MAN
    (Frank Lucas)

BLACK ALBUMS

1. COMMODORES
   (Commodores)
2. MARVIN GAYE LIVE AT THE LONDON PALLADIUM
   (Marvin Gaye)
3. GO FOR YOUR GUNS
   (Isley Brothers)
4. RIGHT ON TIME
   (The Brothers Johnson)
5. SONGS IN THE KEY OF LIFE
   (Stevie Wonder)
6. TRAVELIN' AT THE SPEED OF THOUGHT
   (The O'Jays)
7. A REAL MOTHER FOR YA
   (Johnny Guitar Watson)
8. TEDDY PENDERGRASS
   (Teddy Pendergrass)
9. PARLIAMENT LIVE
   (Parliament)
10. SLAVE
    (Slave)

JAZZ ALBUMS

1. HEAVY WEATHER
   (Weather Report)
2. CONQUISTADOR
   (Maynard Ferguson)
3. FRIENDS AND STRANGERS
   (Ronnie Laws)
4. FREE AS THE WIND
   (Crusaders)
5. LOVE NOTES
   (Ramsey Lewis)
6. IN FLIGHT
   (George Benson)
7. ELEGANT GYPSY
   (Al DiMeola)
8. MUSICMAGIC
   (Return to Forever)
9. TURN THIS MUTHA OUT
   (Idris Muhammad)
10. SEAWIND
    (Seawind)

COUNTRY SINGLES

1. LUCKENBACH, TEXAS
   (Waylon Jennings)
2. MARRIED BUT NOT TO EACH OTHER
   (Barbara Mandrell)
3. I CAN'T HELP MYSELF
   (Eddie Rabbitt)
4. YOUR MAN LOVES YOU HONEY
   (Tom T. Hall)
5. THAT WAS YESTERDAY
   (Donna Fargo)
6. IT'S A COWBOY LOVIN' NIGHT
   (Tanya Tucker)
7. IF WE'RE NOT BACK IN LOVE BY MONDAY
   (Merle Haggard)
8. BURNING MEMORIES
   (Mel Tillis)
9. I'D DO IT ALL OVER AGAIN
   (Crystal Gayle)
10. LIGHT OF A CLEAR BLUE MORNING
    (Dolly Parton)

COUNTRY ALBUMS

1. OL' WAYLON
   (Waylon Jennings)
2. KENNY ROGERS
   (Kenny Rogers)
3. BEFORE HIS TIME
   (Willie Nelson)

4. CHANGES IN LATITUDES, CHANGES IN
   ATTITUDES
   (Jimmy Buffett)
5. NEW HARVEST . . . FIRST GATHERING
   (Dolly Parton)
6. BEST OF FREDDY FENDER
   (Freddy Fender)
7. I REMEMBER PATSY
   (Loretta Lynn)
8. SONGS I'LL ALWAYS SING
   (Merle Haggard)
9. SHE'S JUST AN OLD LOVE TURNED
   MEMORY
   (Charley Pride)
10. SONGS OF KRISTOFFERSON
    (Kris Kristofferson)

JUNE 25, 1977

POP SINGLES

1. DREAMS
   (Fleetwood Mac)
2. GOT TO GIVE IT UP
   (Marvin Gaye)
3. UNDERCOVER ANGEL
   (Alan O'Day)
4. GONNA FLY NOW (THEME FROM "ROCKY")
   (Bill Conti)
5. DA DOO RON RON
   (Shaun Cassidy)
6. I'M YOUR BOOGIE MAN
   (KC and the Sunshine Band)
7. LONELY BOY
   (Andrew Gold)
8. SIR DUKE
   (Stevie Wonder)
9. FEELS LIKE THE FIRST TIME
   (Foreigner)
10. JET AIRLINER
    (The Steve Miller Band)

POP ALBUMS

1. RUMOURS
   (Fleetwood Mac)
2. BOOK OF DREAMS
   (The Steve Miller Band)
3. BARRY MANILOW LIVE
   (Barry Manilow)
4. ROCKY
   (Original Soundtrack)
5. MARVIN GAYE LIVE AT THE LONDON
   PALLADIUM
   (Marvin Gaye)
6. HOTEL CALIFORNIA
   (The Eagles)
7. COMMODORES
   (Commodores)
8. SONGS IN THE KEY OF LIFE
   (Stevie Wonder)
9. BOSTON
   (Boston)
10. LITTLE QUEEN
    (Heart)

BLACK SINGLES

1. EASY
   (Commodores)
2. GOT TO GIVE IT UP
   (Marvin Gaye)
3. BEST OF MY LOVE
   (Emotions)
4. I DON'T LOVE YOU ANYMORE
   (Teddy Pendergrass)
5. SIR DUKE
   (Stevie Wonder)
6. SEE YOU WHEN I GET THERE
   (Lou Rawls)

7. HOLLYWOOD
   (Rufus featuring Chaka Khan)
8. I'M YOUR BOOGIE MAN
   (KC and the Sunshine Band)
9. SLIDE
   (Slave)
10. HIGH SCHOOL DANCE
    (The Sylvers)

BLACK ALBUMS

1. COMMODORES
   (Commodores)
2. GO FOR YOUR GUNS
   (Isley Brothers)
3. MARVIN GAYE LIVE AT THE LONDON
   PALLADIUM
   (Marvin Gaye)
4. RIGHT ON TIME
   (The Brothers Johnson)
5. SONGS IN THE KEY OF LIFE
   (Stevie Wonder)
6. TRAVELIN' AT THE SPEED OF THOUGHT
   (The O'Jays)
7. A REAL MOTHER FOR YA
   (Johnny Guitar Watson)
8. TEDDY PENDERGRASS
   (Teddy Pendergrass)
9. SLAVE
   (Slave)
10. UNMISTAKABLY LOU
    (Lou Rawls)

JAZZ ALBUMS

1. FREE AS THE WIND
   (Crusaders)
2. HEAVY WEATHER
   (Weather Report)
3. FRIENDS AND STRANGERS
   (Ronnie Laws)
4. CONQUISTADOR
   (Maynard Ferguson)
5. IN FLIGHT
   (George Benson)
6. LIFESTYLE
   (John Klemmer)
7. LOVE NOTES
   (Ramsey Lewis)
8. SEAWIND
   (Seawind)
9. TURN THIS MUTHA OUT
   (Idris Muhammad)
10. ELEGANT GYPSY
    (Al DiMeola)

COUNTRY SINGLES

1. LUCKENBACH, TEXAS
   (Waylon Jennings)
2. MARRIED BUT NOT TO EACH OTHER
   (Barbara Mandrell)
3. THAT WAS YESTERDAY
   (Donna Fargo)
4. YOUR MAN LOVES YOU HONEY
   (Tom T. Hall)
5. I CAN'T HELP MYSELF
   (Eddie Rabbitt)
6. IT'S A COWBOY LOVIN' NIGHT
   (Tanya Tucker)
7. I WAS THERE
   (The Statler Brothers)
8. BURNING MEMORIES
   (Mel Tillis)
9. HEAD TO TOE
   (Bill Anderson)
10. DON'T GO CITY GIRL ON ME
    (Tommy Overstreet)

COUNTRY ALBUMS

1. OL' WAYLON
   (Waylon Jennings)

2. KENNY ROGERS
   (Kenny Rogers)
3. BEFORE HIS TIME
   (Willie Nelson)
4. CHANGES IN LATITUDES, CHANGES IN
   ATTITUDES
   (Jimmy Buffett)
5. NEW HARVEST . . . FIRST GATHERING
   (Dolly Parton)
6. BEST OF FREDDY FENDER
   (Freddy Fender)
7. I REMEMBER PATSY
   (Loretta Lynn)
8. RAMBLIN' FEVER
   (Merle Haggard)
9. SONGS OF KRISTOFFERSON
   (Kris Kristofferson)
10. SONGS I'LL ALWAYS SING
    (Merle Haggard)

JULY 2, 1977

POP SINGLES

1. UNDERCOVER ANGEL
   (Alan O'Day)
2. DA DOO RON RON
   (Shaun Cassidy)
3. DREAMS
   (Fleetwood Mac)
4. GONNA FLY NOW (THEME FROM "ROCKY")
   (Bill Conti)
5. GOT TO GIVE IT UP
   (Marvin Gaye)
6. I'M YOUR BOOGIE MAN
   (KC and the Sunshine Band)
7. LOOKS LIKE WE MADE IT
   (Barry Manilow)
8. JET AIRLINER
   (The Steve Miller Band)
9. LONELY BOY
   (Andrew Gold)
10. I'M IN YOU
    (Peter Frampton)

POP ALBUMS

1. BARRY MANILOW LIVE
   (Barry Manilow)
2. RUMOURS
   (Fleetwood Mac)
3. I'M IN YOU
   (Peter Frampton)
4. BOOK OF DREAMS
   (The Steve Miller Band)
5. ROCKY
   (Original Soundtrack)
6. MARVIN GAYE LIVE AT THE LONDON
   PALLADIUM
   (Marvin Gaye)
7. COMMODORES
   (Commodores)
8. LITTLE QUEEN
   (Heart)
9. BOSTON
   (Boston)
10. FOREIGNER
    (Foreigner)

BLACK SINGLES

1. EASY
   (Commodores)
2. BEST OF MY LOVE
   (Emotions)
3. GOT TO GIVE IT UP
   (Marvin Gaye)
4. SEE YOU WHEN I GET THERE
   (Lou Rawls)
5. SLIDE
   (Slave)

6. I DON'T LOVE YOU ANYMORE
   (Teddy Pendergrass)
7. SIR DUKE
   (Stevie Wonder)
8. THIS I SWEAR
   (Tyrone Davis)
9. I'M YOUR BOOGIE MAN
   (KC and the Sunshine Band)
10. HOLLYWOOD
    (Rufus featuring Chaka Khan)

BLACK ALBUMS

1. COMMODORES
   (Commodores)
2. GO FOR YOUR GUNS
   (Isley Brothers)
3. MARVIN GAYE LIVE AT THE LONDON PALLADIUM
   (Marvin Gaye)
4. RIGHT ON TIME
   (The Brothers Johnson)
5. TRAVELIN' AT THE SPEED OF THOUGHT
   (The O'Jays)
6. SONGS IN THE KEY OF LIFE
   (Stevie Wonder)
7. A REAL MOTHER FOR YA
   (Johnny Guitar Watson)
8. TEDDY PENDERGRASS
   (Teddy Pendergrass)
9. SLAVE
   (Slave)
10. REJOICE
    (Emotions)

JAZZ ALBUMS

1. FREE AS THE WIND
   (Crusaders)
2. FRIENDS AND STRANGERS
   (Ronnie Laws)
3. HEAVY WEATHER
   (Weather Report)
4. CONQUISTADOR
   (Maynard Ferguson)
5. LIFESTYLE
   (John Klemmer)
6. IN FLIGHT
   (George Benson)
7. LOVE NOTES
   (Ramsey Lewis)
8. SEAWIND
   (Seawind)
9. TURN THIS MUTHA OUT
   (Idris Muhammad)
10. RIGHT ON TIME
    (The Brothers Johnson)

COUNTRY SINGLES

1. THAT WAS YESTERDAY
   (Donna Fargo)
2. LUCKENBACH, TEXAS
   (Waylon Jennings)
3. MARRIED BUT NOT TO EACH OTHER
   (Barbara Mandrell)
4. YOUR MAN LOVES YOU HONEY
   (Tom T. Hall)
5. DON'T GO CITY GIRL ON ME
   (Tommy Overstreet)
6. I WAS THERE
   (The Statler Brothers)
7. IF PRACTICE MAKES PERFECT
   (Johnny Rodriguez)
8. HEAD TO TOE
   (Bill Anderson)
9. I'LL BE LEAVING ALONE
   (Charley Pride)
10. IT WAS ALMOST LIKE A SONG
    (Ronnie Milsap)

COUNTRY ALBUMS

1. OL' WAYLON
   (Waylon Jennings)

2. KENNY ROGERS
   (Kenny Rogers)
3. BEFORE HIS TIME
   (Willie Nelson)
4. CHANGES IN LATITUDES, CHANGES IN ATTITUDES
   (Jimmy Buffett)
5. NEW HARVEST . . . FIRST GATHERING
   (Dolly Parton)
6. RAMBLIN' FEVER
   (Merle Haggard)
7. BEST OF FREDDY FENDER
   (Freddy Fender)
8. I REMEMBER PATSY
   (Loretta Lynn)
9. A MAN MUST CARRY ON
   (Jerry Jeff Walker)
10. SONGS OF KRISTOFFERSON
    (Kris Kristofferson)

JULY 9, 1977

POP SINGLES

1. DA DOO RON RON
   (Shaun Cassidy)
2. UNDERCOVER ANGEL
   (Alan O'Day)
3. DREAMS
   (Fleetwood Mac)
4. GONNA FLY NOW (THEME FROM "ROCKY")
   (Bill Conti)
5. LOOKS LIKE WE MADE IT
   (Barry Manilow)
6. I'M IN YOU
   (Peter Frampton)
7. JET AIRLINER
   (The Steve Miller Band)
8. GOT TO GIVE IT UP
   (Marvin Gaye)
9. I'M YOUR BOOGIE MAN
   (KC and the Sunshine Band)
10. LONELY BOY
    (Andrew Gold)

POP ALBUMS

1. RUMOURS
   (Fleetwood Mac)
2. I'M IN YOU
   (Peter Frampton)
3. BARRY MANILOW LIVE
   (Barry Manilow)
4. BOOK OF DREAMS
   (The Steve Miller Band)
5. COMMODORES
   (Commodores)
6. MARVIN GAYE LIVE AT THE LONDON PALLADIUM
   (Marvin Gaye)
7. LITTLE QUEEN
   (Heart)
8. BOSTON
   (Boston)
9. FOREIGNER
   (Foreigner)
10. ROCKY
    (Original Soundtrack)

BLACK SINGLES

1. BEST OF MY LOVE
   (Emotions)
2. EASY
   (Commodores)
3. SLIDE
   (Slave)
4. SEE YOU WHEN I GET THERE
   (Lou Rawls)
5. GOT TO GIVE IT UP
   (Marvin Gaye)

6. I DON'T LOVE YOU ANYMORE
   (Teddy Pendergrass)
7. THIS I SWEAR
   (Tyrone Davis)
8. SIR DUKE
   (Stevie Wonder)
9. I'M YOUR BOOGIE MAN
   (KC and the Sunshine Band)
10. HOLLYWOOD
    (Rufus featuring Chaka Khan)

BLACK ALBUMS

1. COMMODORES
   (Commodores)
2. GO FOR YOUR GUNS
   (Isley Brothers)
3. MARVIN GAYE LIVE AT THE LONDON PALLADIUM
   (Marvin Gaye)
4. RIGHT ON TIME
   (The Brothers Johnson)
5. REJOICE
   (Emotions)
6. SONGS IN THE KEY OF LIFE
   (Stevie Wonder)
7. A REAL MOTHER FOR YA
   (Johnny Guitar Watson)
8. TRAVELIN' AT THE SPEED OF THOUGHT
   (The O'Jays)
9. FLOAT ON
   (The Floaters)
10. SLAVE
    (Slave)

JAZZ ALBUMS

1. FREE AS THE WIND
   (Crusaders)
2. HEAVY WEATHER
   (Weather Report)
3. FRIENDS AND STRANGERS
   (Ronnie Laws)
4. LIFESTYLE
   (John Klemmer)
5. CONQUISTADOR
   (Maynard Ferguson)
6. IN FLIGHT
   (George Benson)
7. RIGHT ON TIME
   (The Brothers Johnson)
8. LOVE NOTES
   (Ramsey Lewis)
9. SEAWIND
   (Seawind)
10. TURN THIS MUTHA OUT
    (Idris Muhammad)

COUNTRY SINGLES

1. THAT WAS YESTERDAY
   (Donna Fargo)
2. I'LL BE LEAVING ALONE
   (Charley Pride)
3. LUCKENBACH, TEXAS
   (Waylon Jennings)
4. DON'T GO CITY GIRL ON ME
   (Tommy Overstreet)
5. IF PRACTICE MAKES PERFECT
   (Johnny Rodriguez)
6. IT WAS ALMOST LIKE A SONG
   (Ronnie Milsap)
7. HEAD TO TOE
   (Bill Anderson)
8. CHEAP PERFUME AND CANDLELIGHT
   (Bobby Borchers)
9. IF YOU WANT ME
   (Billie Jo Spears)
10. MARGARITAVILLE
    (Jimmy Buffett)

COUNTRY ALBUMS

1. OL' WAYLON
   (Waylon Jennings)

2. KENNY ROGERS
   (Kenny Rogers)
3. CHANGES IN LATITUDES, CHANGES IN
   ATTITUDES
   (Jimmy Buffett)
4. NEW HARVEST . . . FIRST GATHERING
   (Dolly Parton)
5. RAMBLIN' FEVER
   (Merle Haggard)
6. BEST OF FREDDY FENDER
   (Freddy Fender)
7. A MAN MUST CARRY ON
   (Jerry Jeff Walker)
8. I REMEMBER PATSY
   (Loretta Lynn)
9. BEFORE HIS TIME
   (Willie Nelson)
10. CRYSTAL
    (Crystal Gayle)

JULY 16, 1977

POP SINGLES

1. UNDERCOVER ANGEL
   (Alan O'Day)
2. DA DOO RON RON
   (Shaun Cassidy)
3. LOOKS LIKE WE MADE IT
   (Barry Manilow)
4. I'M IN YOU
   (Peter Frampton)
5. DREAMS
   (Fleetwood Mac)
6. GONNA FLY NOW (THEME FROM "ROCKY")
   (Bill Conti)
7. JET AIRLINER
   (The Steve Miller Band)
8. DO YOU WANNA MAKE LOVE
   (Peter McCann)
9. MARGARITAVILLE
   (Jimmy Buffett)
10. I JUST WANT TO BE YOUR EVERYTHING
    (Andy Gibb)

POP ALBUMS

1. RUMOURS
   (Fleetwood Mac)
2. I'M IN YOU
   (Peter Frampton)
3. BARRY MANILOW LIVE
   (Barry Manilow)
4. BOOK OF DREAMS
   (The Steve Miller Band)
5. COMMODORES
   (Commodores)
6. LOVE GUN
   (Kiss)
7. LITTLE QUEEN
   (Heart)
8. MARVIN GAYE LIVE AT THE LONDON
   PALLADIUM
   (Marvin Gaye)
9. STREISAND SUPERMAN
   (Barbra Streisand)
10. CSN
    (Crosby, Stills and Nash)

BLACK SINGLES

1. BEST OF MY LOVE
   (Emotions)
2. EASY
   (Commodores)
3. SLIDE
   (Slave)
4. LIVIN' IN THE LIFE
   (Isley Brothers)
5. SEE YOU WHEN I GET THERE
   (Lou Rawls)

6. THIS I SWEAR
   (Tyrone Davis)
7. GOT TO GIVE IT UP
   (Marvin Gaye)
8. I DON'T LOVE YOU ANYMORE
   (Teddy Pendergrass)
9. A REAL MOTHER FOR YA
   (Johnny Guitar Watson)
10. STRAWBERRY LETTER 23
    (The Brothers Johnson)

BLACK ALBUMS

1. COMMODORES
   (Commodores)
2. GO FOR YOUR GUNS
   (Isley Brothers)
3. RIGHT ON TIME
   (The Brothers Johnson)
4. REJOICE
   (Emotions)
5. MARVIN GAYE LIVE AT THE LONDON
   PALLADIUM
   (Marvin Gaye)
6. A REAL MOTHER FOR YA
   (Johnny Guitar Watson)
7. FLOAT ON
   (The Floaters)
8. SONGS IN THE KEY OF LIFE
   (Stevie Wonder)
9. TRAVELIN' AT THE SPEED OF THOUGHT
   (The O'Jays)
10. SLAVE
    (Slave)

JAZZ ALBUMS

1. FREE AS THE WIND
   (Crusaders)
2. FRIENDS AND STRANGERS
   (Ronnie Laws)
3. HEAVY WEATHER
   (Weather Report)
4. LIFESTYLE
   (John Klemmer)
5. CONQUISTADOR
   (Maynard Ferguson)
6. RIGHT ON TIME
   (The Brothers Johnson)
7. IN FLIGHT
   (George Benson)
8. LOVE NOTES
   (Ramsey Lewis)
9. TURN THIS MUTHA OUT
   (Idris Muhammad)
10. LIFELINE
    (Roy Ayers Ubiquity)

COUNTRY SINGLES

1. I'LL BE LEAVING ALONE
   (Charley Pride)
2. IT WAS ALMOST LIKE A SONG
   (Ronnie Milsap)
3. THAT WAS YESTERDAY
   (Donna Fargo)
4. DON'T GO CITY GIRL ON ME
   (Tommy Overstreet)
5. IF PRACTICE MAKES PERFECT
   (Johnny Rodriguez)
6. I CAN'T LOVE YOU ENOUGH
   (Loretta Lynn and Conway Twitty)
7. CHEAP PERFUME AND CANDLELIGHT
   (Bobby Borchers)
8. IF YOU WANT ME
   (Billie Jo Spears)
9. MARGARITAVILLE
   (Jimmy Buffett)
10. I DON'T WANNA CRY
    (Larry Gatlin)

COUNTRY ALBUMS

1. OL' WAYLON
   (Waylon Jennings)

2. CHANGES IN LATITUDES, CHANGES IN
   ATTITUDES
   (Jimmy Buffett)
3. KENNY ROGERS
   (Kenny Rogers)
4. NEW HARVEST . . . FIRST GATHERING
   (Dolly Parton)
5. RAMBLIN' FEVER
   (Merle Haggard)
6. BEST OF FREDDY FENDER
   (Freddy Fender)
7. A MAN MUST CARRY ON
   (Jerry Jeff Walker)
8. DYNAMIC DUO
   (Conway Twitty and Loretta Lynn)
9. BEFORE HIS TIME
   (Willie Nelson)
10. CRYSTAL
    (Crystal Gayle)

JULY 23, 1977

POP SINGLES

1. UNDERCOVER ANGEL
   (Alan O'Day)
2. DA DOO RON RON
   (Shaun Cassidy)
3. LOOKS LIKE WE MADE IT
   (Barry Manilow)
4. I'M IN YOU
   (Peter Frampton)
5. I JUST WANT TO BE YOUR EVERYTHING
   (Andy Gibb)
6. DREAMS
   (Fleetwood Mac)
7. DO YOU WANNA MAKE LOVE
   (Peter McCann)
8. (YOUR LOVE HAS LIFTED ME) HIGHER
   AND HIGHER
   (Rita Coolidge)
9. MARGARITAVILLE
   (Jimmy Buffett)
10. WHATCHA GONNA DO?
    (Pablo Cruise)

POP ALBUMS

1. RUMOURS
   (Fleetwood Mac)
2. I'M IN YOU
   (Peter Frampton)
3. BARRY MANILOW LIVE
   (Barry Manilow)
4. LOVE GUN
   (Kiss)
5. BOOK OF DREAMS
   (Steve Miller Band)
6. CSN
   (Crosby, Stills and Nash)
7. STREISAND SUPERMAN
   (Barbra Streisand)
8. LITTLE QUEEN
   (Heart)
9. COMMODORES
   (Commodores)
10. BOSTON
    (Boston)

BLACK SINGLES

1. BEST OF MY LOVE
   (Emotions)
2. EASY
   (Commodores)
3. SLIDE
   (Slave)
4. LIVIN' IN THE LIFE
   (Isley Brothers)
5. FLOAT ON
   (The Floaters)

6. STRAWBERRY LETTER 23
   (The Brothers Johnson)
7. THIS I SWEAR
   (Tyrone Davis)
8. A REAL MOTHER FOR YA
   (Johnny Guitar Watson)
9. SEE YOU WHEN I GET THERE
   (Lou Rawls)
10. SUNSHINE
    (Enchantment)

BLACK ALBUMS

1. COMMODORES
   (Commodores)
2. RIGHT ON TIME
   (The Brothers Johnson)
3. REJOICE
   (Emotions)
4. GO FOR YOUR GUNS
   (Isley Brothers)
5. FLOAT ON
   (The Floaters)
6. SLAVE
   (Slave)
7. A REAL MOTHER FOR YA
   (Johnny Guitar Watson)
8. MARVIN GAYE LIVE AT THE LONDON
   PALLADIUM
   (Marvin Gaye)
9. TRAVELIN' AT THE SPEED OF THOUGHT
   (The O'Jays)
10. SONGS IN THE KEY OF LIFE
    (Stevie Wonder)

JAZZ ALBUMS

1. LIFESTYLE
   (John Klemmer)
2. FRIENDS AND STRANGERS
   (Ronnie Laws)
3. FREE AS THE WIND
   (Crusaders)
4. LIFELINE
   (Roy Ayers Ubiquity)
5. RIGHT ON TIME
   (The Brothers Johnson)
6. HEAVY WEATHER
   (Weather Report)
7. CONQUISTADOR
   (Maynard Ferguson)
8. TURN THIS MUTHA OUT
   (Idris Muhammad)
9. LOOK TO THE RAINBOW
   (Al Jarreau)
10. LOVE NOTES
    (Ramsey Lewis)

COUNTRY SINGLES

1. IT WAS ALMOST LIKE A SONG
   (Ronnie Milsap)
2. I'LL BE LEAVING ALONE
   (Charley Pride)
3. I CAN'T LOVE YOU ENOUGH
   (Loretta Lynn and Conway Twitty)
4. THAT WAS YESTERDAY
   (Donna Fargo)
5. ROLLIN' WITH THE FLOW
   (Charlie Rich)
6. I DON'T WANNA CRY
   (Larry Gatlin)
7. CHEAP PERFUME AND CANDLELIGHT
   (Bobby Borchers)
8. MAKIN' BELIEVE
   (Emmylou Harris)
9. IF PRACTICE MAKES PERFECT
   (Johnny Rodriguez)
10. DON'T GO CITY GIRL ON ME
    (Tommy Overstreet)

COUNTRY ALBUMS

1. OL' WAYLON
   (Waylon Jennings)

2. CHANGES IN LATITUDES, CHANGES IN
   ATTITUDES
   (Jimmy Buffett)
3. KENNY ROGERS
   (Kenny Rogers)
4. RAMBLIN' FEVER
   (Merle Haggard)
5. NEW HARVEST . . . FIRST GATHERING
   (Dolly Parton)
6. TO LEFTY FROM WILLIE
   (Willie Nelson)
7. A MAN MUST CARRY ON
   (Jerry Jeff Walker)
8. DYNAMIC DUO
   (Conway Twitty and Loretta Lynn)
9. BEFORE HIS TIME
   (Willie Nelson)
10. RABBITT
    (Eddie Rabbitt)

JULY 30, 1977

POP SINGLES

1. UNDERCOVER ANGEL
   (Alan O'Day)
2. I JUST WANT TO BE YOUR EVERYTHING
   (Andy Gibb)
3. I'M IN YOU
   (Peter Frampton)
4. DA DOO RON RON
   (Shaun Cassidy)
5. BEST OF MY LOVE
   (Emotions)
6. (YOUR LOVE HAS LIFTED ME) HIGHER
   AND HIGHER
   (Rita Coolidge)
7. LOOKS LIKE WE MADE IT
   (Barry Manilow)
8. WATCHA GONNA DO?
   (Pablo Cruise)
9. YOU MADE ME BELIEVE IN MAGIC
   (Bay City Rollers)
10. EASY
    (Commodores)

POP ALBUMS

1. RUMOURS
   (Fleetwood Mac)
2. I'M IN YOU
   (Peter Frampton)
3. BARRY MANILOW LIVE
   (Barry Manilow)
4. LOVE GUN
   (Kiss)
5. CSN
   (Crosby, Stills and Nash)
6. STREISAND SUPERMAN
   (Barbra Streisand)
7. BOOK OF DREAMS
   (The Steve Miller Band)
8. LITTLE QUEEN
   (Heart)
9. JT
   (James Taylor)
10. COMMODORES
    (Commodores)

BLACK SINGLES

1. BEST OF MY LOVE
   (Emotions)
2. FLOAT ON
   (The Floaters)
3. EASY
   (Commodores)
4. SLIDE
   (Slave)
5. STRAWBERRY LETTER 23
   (The Brothers Johnson)

6. LIVIN' IN THE LIFE
   (Isley Brothers)
7. A REAL MOTHER FOR YA
   (Johnny Guitar Watson)
8. THIS I SWEAR
   (Tyrone Davis)
9. SUNSHINE
   (Enchantment)
10. SEE YOU WHEN I GET THERE
    (Lou Rawls)

BLACK ALBUMS

1. REJOICE
   (Emotions)
2. COMMODORES
   (Commodores)
3. RIGHT ON TIME
   (The Brothers Johnson)
4. FLOAT ON
   (The Floaters)
5. GO FOR YOUR GUNS
   (Isley Brothers)
6. SLAVE
   (Slave)
7. A REAL MOTHER FOR YA
   (Johnny Guitar Watson)
8. TRAVELIN' AT THE SPEED OF THOUGHT
   (The O'Jays)
9. MARVIN GAYE LIVE AT THE LONDON
   PALLADIUM
   (Marvin Gaye)
10. SONGS IN THE KEY OF LIFE
    (Stevie Wonder)

JAZZ ALBUMS

1. FREE AS THE WIND
   (Crusaders)
2. LIFELINE
   (Roy Ayers Ubiquity)
3. LIFESTYLE
   (John Klemmer)
4. FRIENDS AND STRANGERS
   (Ronnie Laws)
5. RIGHT ON TIME
   (The Brothers Johnson)
6. TURN THIS MUTHA OUT
   (Idris Muhammad)
7. LOOK TO THE RAINBOW
   (Al Jarreau)
8. HEAVY WEATHER
   (Weather Report)
9. IN FLIGHT
   (George Benson)
10. LIVE
    (Lonnie Liston Smith)

COUNTRY SINGLES

1. IT WAS ALMOST LIKE A SONG
   (Ronnie Milsap)
2. ROLLIN' WITH THE FLOW
   (Charlie Rich)
3. I CAN'T LOVE YOU ENOUGH
   (Loretta Lynn and Conway Twitty)
4. I DON'T WANNA CRY
   (Larry Gatlin)
5. I'LL BE LEAVING ALONE
   (Charley Pride)
6. MAKIN' BELIEVE
   (Emmylou Harris)
7. A SONG IN THE NIGHT
   (Johnny Duncan)
8. WAY DOWN/PLEDGING MY LOVE
   (Elvis Presley)
9. HONKY TONK MEMORIES
   (Mickey Gilley)
10. A TEAR FELL
    (Billy "Crash" Craddock)

COUNTRY ALBUMS

1. OL' WAYLON
   (Waylon Jennings)

2. KENNY ROGERS
   (Kenny Rogers)
3. TO LEFTY FROM WILLIE
   (Willie Nelson)
4. RAMBLIN' FEVER
   (Merle Haggard)
5. CHANGES IN LATITUDES, CHANGES IN
   ATTITUDES
   (Jimmy Buffett)
6. DYNAMIC DUO
   (Conway Twitty and Loretta Lynn)
7. A MAN MUST CARRY ON
   (Jerry Jeff Walker)
8. NEW HARVEST . . . FIRST GATHERING
   (Dolly Parton)
9. RABBITT
   (Eddie Rabbitt)
10. MOODY BLUE
    (Elvis Presley)

AUGUST 6, 1977

POP SINGLES

1. I JUST WANT TO BE YOUR EVERYTHING
   (Andy Gibb)
2. UNDERCOVER ANGEL
   (Alan O'Day)
3. BEST OF MY LOVE
   (Emotions)
4. I'M IN YOU
   (Peter Frampton)
5. (YOUR LOVE HAS LIFTED ME) HIGHER
   AND HIGHER
   (Rita Coolidge)
6. WHATCHA GONNA DO?
   (Pablo Cruise)
7. DA DOO RON RON
   (Shaun Cassidy)
8. EASY
   (Commodores)
9. YOU MADE ME BELIEVE IN MAGIC
   (Bay City Rollers)
10. HANDY MAN
    (James Taylor)

POP ALBUMS

1. RUMOURS
   (Fleetwood Mac)
2. CSN
   (Crosby, Stills and Nash)
3. I'M IN YOU
   (Peter Frampton)
4. BARRY MANILOW LIVE
   (Barry Manilow)
5. STREISAND SUPERMAN
   (Barbra Streisand)
6. LOVE GUN
   (Kiss)
7. JT
   (James Taylor)
8. LITTLE QUEEN
   (Heart)
9. BOOK OF DREAMS
   (The Steve Miller Band)
10. COMMODORES
    (Commodores)

BLACK SINGLES

1. FLOAT ON
   (The Floaters)
2. BEST OF MY LOVE
   (Emotions)
3. EASY
   (Commodores)
4. STRAWBERRY LETTER 23
   (The Brothers Johnson)
5. SLIDE
   (Slave)
6. A REAL MOTHER FOR YA
   (Johnny Guitar Watson)

7. LIVIN' IN THE LIFE
   (Isley Brothers)
8. SUNSHINE
   (Enchantment)
9. I BELIEVE YOU
   (Dorothy Moore)
10. THIS I SWEAR
    (Tyrone Davis)

BLACK ALBUMS

1. REJOICE
   (Emotions)
2. COMMODORES
   (Commodores)
3. FLOAT ON
   (The Floaters)
4. RIGHT ON TIME
   (The Brothers Johnson)
5. GO FOR YOUR GUNS
   (Isley Brothers)
6. SLAVE
   (Slave)
7. TRAVELIN' AT THE SPEED OF THOUGHT
   (The O'Jays)
8. A REAL MOTHER FOR YA
   (Johnny Guitar Watson)
9. PLATINUM JAZZ
   (War)
10. MARVIN GAYE LIVE AT THE LONDON
    PALLADIUM
    (Marvin Gaye)

JAZZ ALBUMS

1. FREE AS THE WIND
   (Crusaders)
2. LIFELINE
   (Roy Ayers Ubiquity)
3. LIFESTYLE
   (John Klemmer)
4. RIGHT ON TIME
   (The Brothers Johnson)
5. FRIENDS AND STRANGERS
   (Ronnie Laws)
6. LOOK TO THE RAINBOW
   (Al Jarreau)
7. HEAVY WEATHER
   (Weather Report)
8. LIVE
   (Lonnie Liston Smith)
9. TURN THIS MUTHA OUT
   (Idris Muhammad)
10. IN FLIGHT
    (George Benson)

COUNTRY SINGLES

1. ROLLIN' WITH THE FLOW
   (Charlie Rich)
2. IT WAS ALMOST LIKE A SONG
   (Ronnie Milsap)
3. I DON'T WANNA CRY
   (Larry Gatlin)
4. I CAN'T LOVE YOU ENOUGH
   (Loretta Lynn and Conway Twitty)
5. A SONG IN THE NIGHT
   (Johnny Duncan)
6. MAKIN' BELIEVE
   (Emmylou Harris)
7. WAY DOWN/PLEDGING MY LOVE
   (Elvis Presley)
8. HONKY TONK MEMORIES
   (Mickey Gilley)
9. A TEAR FELL
   (Billy "Crash" Craddock)
10. RAMBLIN' FEVER
    (Merle Haggard)

COUNTRY ALBUMS

1. OL' WAYLON
   (Waylon Jennings)

2. KENNY ROGERS
   (Kenny Rogers)
3. TO LEFTY FROM WILLIE
   (Willie Nelson)
4. MOODY BLUE
   (Elvis Presley)
5. CHANGES IN LATITUDES, CHANGES IN
   ATTITUDES
   (Jimmy Buffett)
6. DYNAMIC DUO
   (Conway Twitty and Loretta Lynn)
7. RAMBLIN' FEVER
   (Merle Haggard)
8. RABBITT
   (Eddie Rabbitt)
9. WE MUST BELIEVE IN MAGIC
   (Crystal Gayle)
10. NEW HARVEST . . . FIRST GATHERING
    (Dolly Parton)

AUGUST 13, 1977

POP SINGLES

1. I JUST WANT TO BE YOUR EVERYTHING
   (Andy Gibb)
2. BEST OF MY LOVE
   (Emotions)
3. UNDERCOVER ANGEL
   (Alan O'Day)
4. (YOUR LOVE HAS LIFTED ME) HIGHER
   AND HIGHER
   (Rita Coolidge)
5. WHATCHA GONNA DO?
   (Pablo Cruise)
6. EASY
   (Commodores)
7. I'M IN YOU
   (Peter Frampton)
8. HANDY MAN
   (James Taylor)
9. YOU MADE ME BELIEVE IN MAGIC
   (Bay City Rollers)
10. DA DOO RON RON
    (Shaun Cassidy)

POP ALBUMS

1. RUMOURS
   (Fleetwood Mac)
2. CSN
   (Crosby, Stills and Nash)
3. I'M IN YOU
   (Peter Frampton)
4. STREISAND SUPERMAN
   (Barbra Streisand)
5. JT
   (James Taylor)
6. BARRY MANILOW LIVE
   (Barry Manilow)
7. LOVE GUN
   (Kiss)
8. LITTLE QUEEN
   (Heart)
9. STAR WARS
   (Original Soundtrack)
10. BOOK OF DREAMS
    (The Steve Miller Band)

BLACK SINGLES

1. FLOAT ON
   (The Floaters)
2. BEST OF MY LOVE
   (Emotions)
3. STRAWBERRY LETTER 23
   (The Brothers Johnson)
4. EASY
   (Commodores)
5. SLIDE
   (Slave)

6. A REAL MOTHER FOR YA
   (Johnny Guitar Watson)
7. I BELIEVE YOU
   (Dorothy Moore)
8. SUNSHINE
   (Enchantment)
9. LIVIN' IN THE LIFE
   (Isley Brothers)
10. THE GREATEST LOVE OF ALL
    (George Benson)

BLACK ALBUMS

1. REJOICE
   (Emotions)
2. FLOAT ON
   (The Floaters)
3. RIGHT ON TIME
   (The Brothers Johnson)
4. COMMODORES
   (Commodores)
5. SLAVE
   (Slave)
6. PLATINUM JAZZ
   (War)
7. TRAVELIN' AT THE SPEED OF THOUGHT
   (The O'Jays)
8. GO FOR YOUR GUNS
   (Isley Brothers)
9. A REAL MOTHER FOR YA
   (Johnny Guitar Watson)
10. SONGS IN THE KEY OF LIFE
    (Stevie Wonder)

JAZZ ALBUMS

1. FREE AS THE WIND
   (Crusaders)
2. LIFESTYLE
   (John Klemmer)
3. LIFELINE
   (Roy Ayers Ubiquity)
4. RIGHT ON TIME
   (The Brothers Johnson)
5. FRIENDS AND STRANGERS
   (Ronnie Laws)
6. LOOK TO THE RAINBOW
   (Al Jarreau)
7. LIVE
   (Lonnie Liston Smith)
8. HEAVY WEATHER
   (Weather Report)
9. TURN THIS MUTHA OUT
   (Idris Muhammad)
10. FINGER PAINTING
    (Earl Klugh)

COUNTRY SINGLES

1. ROLLIN' WITH THE FLOW
   (Charlie Rich)
2. IT WAS ALMOST LIKE A SONG
   (Ronnie Milsap)
3. I DON'T WANNA CRY
   (Larry Gatlin)
4. A SONG IN THE NIGHT
   (Johnny Duncan)
5. WAY DOWN/PLEDGING MY LOVE
   (Elvis Presley)
6. I CAN'T LOVE YOU ENOUGH
   (Loretta Lynn and Conway Twitty)
7. RAMBLIN' FEVER
   (Merle Haggard)
8. HONKY TONK MEMORIES
   (Mickey Gilley)
9. A TEAR FELL
   (Billy "Crash" Craddock)
10. TILL THE END
    (Vern Gosdin)

COUNTRY ALBUMS

1. OL' WAYLON
   (Waylon Jennings)

2. TO LEFTY FROM WILLIE
   (Willie Nelson)
3. KENNY ROGERS
   (Kenny Rogers)
4. MOODY BLUE
   (Elvis Presley)
5. CHANGES IN LATITUDES, CHANGES IN
   ATTITUDES
   (Jimmy Buffett)
6. WE MUST BELIEVE IN MAGIC
   (Crystal Gayle)
7. DYNAMIC DUO
   (Conway Twitty and Loretta Lynn)
8. RABBITT
   (Eddie Rabbitt)
9. RAMBLIN' FEVER
   (Merle Haggard)
10. NEW HARVEST . . . FIRST GATHERING
    (Dolly Parton)

AUGUST 20, 1977

POP SINGLES

1. I JUST WANT TO BE YOUR EVERYTHING
   (Andy Gibb)
2. BEST OF MY LOVE
   (Emotions)
3. UNDERCOVER ANGEL
   (Alan O'Day)
4. (YOUR LOVE HAS LIFTED ME) HIGHER
   AND HIGHER
   (Rita Coolidge)
5. EASY
   (Commodores)
6. HANDY MAN
   (James Taylor)
7. WHATCHA GONNA DO?
   (Pablo Cruise)
8. I'M IN YOU
   (Peter Frampton)
9. FLOAT ON
   (The Floaters)
10. DON'T STOP
    (Fleetwood Mac)

POP ALBUMS

1. RUMOURS
   (Fleetwood Mac)
2. STREISAND SUPERMAN
   (Barbra Streisand)
3. I'M IN YOU
   (Peter Frampton)
4. JT
   (James Taylor)
5. CSN
   (Crosby, Stills and Nash)
6. STAR WARS
   (Original Soundtrack)
7. BARRY MANILOW LIVE
   (Barry Manilow)
8. REJOICE
   (Emotions)
9. LOVE GUN
   (Kiss)
10. LITTLE QUEEN
    (Heart)

BLACK SINGLES

1. FLOAT ON
   (The Floaters)
2. BEST OF MY LOVE
   (Emotions)
3. STRAWBERRY LETTER 23
   (The Brothers Johnson)
4. EASY
   (Commodores)
5. THE GREATEST LOVE OF ALL
   (George Benson)

6. I BELIEVE YOU
   (Dorothy Moore)
7. SLIDE
   (Slave)
8. A REAL MOTHER FOR YA
   (Johnny Guitar Watson)
9. SUNSHINE
   (Enchantment)
10. L.A. SUNSHINE
    (War)

BLACK ALBUMS

1. FLOAT ON
   (The Floaters)
2. REJOICE
   (Emotions)
3. COMMODORES
   (Commodores)
4. RIGHT ON TIME
   (The Brothers Johnson)
5. SLAVE
   (Slave)
6. GO FOR YOUR GUNS
   (Isley Brothers)
7. PLATINUM JAZZ
   (War)
8. TRAVELIN' AT THE SPEED OF THOUGHT
   (The O'Jays)
9. A REAL MOTHER FOR YA
   (Johnny Guitar Watson)
10. SOMETHING TO LOVE
    (L.T.D.)

JAZZ ALBUMS

1. FREE AS THE WIND
   (Crusaders)
2. LIFELINE
   (Roy Ayers Ubiquity)
3. LIFESTYLE
   (John Klemmer)
4. RIGHT ON TIME
   (The Brothers Johnson)
5. FRIENDS AND STRANGERS
   (Ronnie Laws)
6. LOOK TO THE RAINBOW
   (Al Jarreau)
7. MORE STUFF
   (Stuff)
8. LIVE
   (Lonnie Liston Smith)
9. HEAVY WEATHER
   (Weather Report)
10. FINGER PAINTING
    (Earl Klugh)

COUNTRY SINGLES

1. ROLLIN' WITH THE FLOW
   (Charlie Rich)
2. WAY DOWN/PLEDGING MY LOVE
   (Elvis Presley)
3. I DON'T WANNA CRY
   (Larry Gatlin)
4. A SONG IN THE NIGHT
   (Johnny Duncan)
5. RAMBLIN' FEVER
   (Merle Haggard)
6. DON'T IT MAKE MY BROWN EYES BLUE
   (Crystal Gayle)
7. SUNFLOWER
   (Glen Campbell)
8. TILL THE END
   (Vern Gosdin)
9. HONKY TONK MEMORIES
   (Mickey Gilley)
10. I'M THE ONLY HELL (MAMA EVER RAISED)
    (Johnny Paycheck)

COUNTRY ALBUMS

1. OL' WAYLON
   (Waylon Jennings)

2. TO LEFTY FROM WILLIE
   (Willie Nelson)
3. MOODY BLUE
   (Elvis Presley)
4. WE MUST BELIEVE IN MAGIC
   (Crystal Gayle)
5. KENNY ROGERS
   (Kenny Rogers)
6. CHANGES IN LATITUDES, CHANGES IN ATTITUDES
   (Jimmy Buffett)
7. DYNAMIC DUO
   (Conway Twitty and Loretta Lynn)
8. RABBITT
   (Eddie Rabbitt)
9. RAMBLIN' FEVER
   (Merle Haggard)
10. A MAN MUST CARRY ON
    (Jerry Jeff Walker)

AUGUST 27, 1977

POP SINGLES

1. BEST OF MY LOVE
   (Emotions)
2. I JUST WANT TO BE YOUR EVERYTHING
   (Andy Gibb)
3. (YOUR LOVE HAS LIFTED ME) HIGHER AND HIGHER
   (Rita Coolidge)
4. HANDY MAN
   (James Taylor)
5. EASY
   (Commodores)
6. FLOAT ON
   (The Floaters)
7. UNDERCOVER ANGEL
   (Alan O'Day)
8. DON'T STOP
   (Fleetwood Mac)
9. STRAWBERRY LETTER 23
   (The Brothers Johnson)
10. WHATCHA GONNA DO?
    (Pablo Cruise)

POP ALBUMS

1. RUMOURS
   (Fleetwood Mac)
2. STREISAND SUPERMAN
   (Barbra Streisand)
3. JT
   (James Taylor)
4. STAR WARS
   (Original Soundtrack)
5. CSN
   (Crosby, Stills and Nash)
6. I'M IN YOU
   (Peter Frampton)
7. BARRY MANILOW LIVE
   (Barry Manilow)
8. REJOICE
   (Emotions)
9. LITTLE QUEEN
   (Heart)
10. GOING FOR THE ONE
    (Yes)

BLACK SINGLES

1. FLOAT ON
   (The Floaters)
2. STRAWBERRY LETTER 23
   (The Brothers Johnson)
3. BEST OF MY LOVE
   (Emotions)
4. THE GREATEST LOVE OF ALL
   (George Benson)
5. EASY
   (Commodores)

6. I BELIEVE YOU
   (Dorothy Moore)
7. SLIDE
   (Slave)
8. SUNSHINE
   (Enchantment)
9. L.A. SUNSHINE
   (War)
10. WORK ON ME
    (The O'Jays)

BLACK ALBUMS

1. FLOAT ON
   (The Floaters)
2. COMMODORES
   (Commodores)
3. REJOICE
   (Emotions)
4. RIGHT ON TIME
   (The Brothers Johnson)
5. PLATINUM JAZZ
   (War)
6. GO FOR YOUR GUNS
   (Isley Brothers)
7. SLAVE
   (Slave)
8. TRAVELIN' AT THE SPEED OF THOUGHT
   (The O'Jays)
9. SOMETHING TO LOVE
   (L.T.D.)
10. A REAL MOTHER FOR YA
    (Johnny Guitar Watson)

JAZZ ALBUMS

1. FREE AS THE WIND
   (Crusaders)
2. LIFELINE
   (Roy Ayers Ubiquity)
3. LOOK TO THE RAINBOW
   (Al Jarreau)
4. MORE STUFF
   (Stuff)
5. LIFESTYLE
   (John Klemmer)
6. RIGHT ON TIME
   (The Brothers Johnson)
7. FRIENDS AND STRANGERS
   (Ronnie Laws)
8. LIVE
   (Lonnie Liston Smith)
9. FINGER PAINTING
   (Earl Klugh)
10. HEAVY WEATHER
    (Weather Report)

COUNTRY SINGLES

1. WAY DOWN/PLEDGING MY LOVE
   (Elvis Presley)
2. ROLLIN' WITH THE FLOW
   (Charlie Rich)
3. DON'T IT MAKE MY BROWN EYES BLUE
   (Crystal Gayle)
4. RAMBLIN' FEVER
   (Merle Haggard)
5. SUNFLOWER
   (Glen Campbell)
6. A SONG IN THE NIGHT
   (Johnny Duncan)
7. TILL THE END
   (Vern Gosdin)
8. I DON'T WANNA CRY
   (Larry Gatlin)
9. SOUTHERN CALIFORNIA
   (George Jones and Tammy Wynette)
10. I'VE ALREADY LOVED YOU IN MY MIND
    (Conway Twitty)

COUNTRY ALBUMS

1. OL' WAYLON
   (Waylon Jennings)

2. TO LEFTY FROM WILLIE
   (Willie Nelson)
3. MOODY BLUE
   (Elvis Presley)
4. WE MUST BELIEVE IN MAGIC
   (Crystal Gayle)
5. KENNY ROGERS
   (Kenny Rogers)
6. CHANGES IN LATITUDES, CHANGES IN ATTITUDES
   (Jimmy Buffett)
7. RABBITT
   (Eddie Rabbitt)
8. DYNAMIC DUO
   (Conway Twitty and Loretta Lynn)
9. RAMBLIN' FEVER
   (Merle Haggard)
10. A MAN MUST CARRY ON
    (Jerry Jeff Walker)

SEPTEMBER 3, 1977

POP SINGLES

1. I JUST WANT TO BE YOUR EVERYTHING
   (Andy Gibb)
2. BEST OF MY LOVE
   (Emotions)
3. (YOUR LOVE HAS LIFTED ME) HIGHER AND HIGHER
   (Rita Coolidge)
4. HANDY MAN
   (James Taylor)
5. FLOAT ON
   (The Floaters)
6. DON'T STOP
   (Fleetwood Mac)
7. EASY
   (Commodores)
8. STRAWBERRY LETTER 23
   (The Brothers Johnson)
9. UNDERCOVER ANGEL
   (Alan O'Day)
10. TELEPHONE LINE
    (Electric Light Orchestra)

POP ALBUMS

1. RUMOURS
   (Fleetwood Mac)
2. STAR WARS
   (Original Soundtrack)
3. STREISAND SUPERMAN
   (Barbra Streisand)
4. JT
   (James Taylor)
5. CSN
   (Crosby, Stills and Nash)
6. MOODY BLUE
   (Elvis Presley)
7. REJOICE
   (Emotions)
8. LITTLE QUEEN
   (Heart)
9. GOING FOR THE ONE
   (Yes)
10. I'M IN YOU
    (Peter Frampton)

BLACK SINGLES

1. FLOAT ON
   (The Floaters)
2. STRAWBERRY LETTER 23
   (The Brothers Johnson)
3. BEST OF MY LOVE
   (Emotions)
4. THE GREATEST LOVE OF ALL
   (George Benson)
5. EASY
   (Commodores)

6. I BELIEVE YOU
   (Dorothy Moore)
7. SUNSHINE
   (Enchantment)
8. WORK ON ME
   (The O'Jays)
9. L.A. SUNSHINE
   (War)
10. LET'S CLEAN UP THE GHETTO
    (Philadelphia International All Stars)

BLACK ALBUMS

1. FLOAT ON
   (The Floaters)
2. COMMODORES
   (Commodores)
3. REJOICE
   (Emotions)
4. RIGHT ON TIME
   (The Brothers Johnson)
5. GO FOR YOUR GUNS
   (Isley Brothers)
6. PLATINUM JAZZ
   (War)
7. TRAVELIN' AT THE SPEED OF THOUGHT
   (The O'Jays)
8. SOMETHING TO LOVE
   (L.T.D.)
9. SLAVE
   (Slave)
10. TOO HOT TO HANDLE
    (Heatwave)

JAZZ ALBUMS

1. FREE AS THE WIND
   (Crusaders)
2. LIFELINE
   (Roy Ayers Ubiquity)
3. LOOK TO THE RAINBOW
   (Al Jarreau)
4. LIFESTYLE
   (John Klemmer)
5. MORE STUFF
   (Stuff)
6. RIGHT ON TIME
   (The Brothers Johnson)
7. LIVE
   (Lonnie Liston Smith)
8. FRIENDS AND STRANGERS
   (Ronnie Laws)
9. HEAVY WEATHER
   (Weather Report)
10. FINGER PAINTING
    (Earl Klugh)

COUNTRY SINGLES

1. DON'T IT MAKE MY BROWN EYES BLUE
   (Crystal Gayle)
2. WAY DOWN/PLEDGING MY LOVE
   (Elvis Presley)
3. SUNFLOWER
   (Glen Campbell)
4. RAMBLIN' FEVER
   (Merle Haggard)
5. ROLLIN' WITH THE FLOW
   (Charlie Rich)
6. TILL THE END
   (Vern Gosdin)
7. I'VE ALREADY LOVED YOU IN MY MIND
   (Conway Twitty)
8. SOUTHERN CALIFORNIA
   (George Jones and Tammy Wynette)
9. DAYTIME FRIENDS
   (Kenny Rogers)
10. THAT'S THE WAY LOVE SHOULD BE
    (Dave and Sugar)

COUNTRY ALBUMS

1. MOODY BLUE
   (Elvis Presley)

2. OL' WAYLON
   (Waylon Jennings)
3. TO LEFTY FROM WILLIE
   (Willie Nelson)
4. WE MUST BELIEVE IN MAGIC
   (Crystal Gayle)
5. RABBITT
   (Eddie Rabbitt)
6. KENNY ROGERS
   (Kenny Rogers)
7. CHANGES IN LATITUDES, CHANGES IN ATTITUDES
   (Jimmy Buffett)
8. DAYTIME FRIENDS
   (Kenny Rogers)
9. RAMBLIN' FEVER
   (Merle Haggard)
10. A MAN MUST CARRY ON
    (Jerry Jeff Walker)

SEPTEMBER 10, 1977

POP SINGLES

1. I JUST WANT TO BE YOUR EVERYTHING
   (Andy Gibb)
2. BEST OF MY LOVE
   (Emotions)
3. (YOUR LOVE HAS LIFTED ME) HIGHER AND HIGHER
   (Rita Coolidge)
4. FLOAT ON
   (The Floaters)
5. DON'T STOP
   (Fleetwood Mac)
6. HANDY MAN
   (James Taylor)
7. STRAWBERRY LETTER 23
   (The Brothers Johnson)
8. TELEPHONE LINE
   (Electric Light Orchestra)
9. EASY
   (Commodores)
10. UNDERCOVER ANGEL
    (Alan O'Day)

POP ALBUMS

1. RUMOURS
   (Fleetwood Mac)
2. STAR WARS
   (Original Soundtrack)
3. CSN
   (Crosby, Stills and Nash)
4. JT
   (James Taylor)
5. MOODY BLUE
   (Elvis Presley)
6. STREISAND SUPERMAN
   (Barbra Streisand)
7. LITTLE QUEEN
   (Heart)
8. COMMODORES
   (Commodores)
9. SHAUN CASSIDY
   (Shaun Cassidy)
10. FOREIGNER
    (Foreigner)

BLACK SINGLES

1. FLOAT ON
   (The Floaters)
2. STRAWBERRY LETTER 23
   (The Brothers Johnson)
3. BEST OF MY LOVE
   (Emotions)
4. THE GREATEST LOVE OF ALL
   (George Benson)
5. IT'S ECSTASY WHEN YOU LAY DOWN NEXT TO ME
   (Barry White)

6. KEEP IT COMIN' LOVE
   (KC and the Sunshine Band)
7. SUNSHINE
   (Enchantment)
8. WORK ON ME
   (The O'Jays)
9. EASY
   (Commodores)
10. LET'S CLEAN UP THE GHETTO
    (Philadelphia International All Stars)

BLACK ALBUMS

1. COMMODORES
   (Commodores)
2. FLOAT ON
   (The Floaters)
3. REJOICE
   (Emotions)
4. RIGHT ON TIME
   (The Brothers Johnson)
5. TOO HOT TO HANDLE
   (Heatwave)
6. IN FULL BLOOM
   (Rose Royce)
7. PLATINUM JAZZ
   (War)
8. SOMETHING TO LOVE
   (L.T.D.)
9. GO FOR YOUR GUNS
   (Isley Brothers)
10. TRAVELIN' AT THE SPEED OF THOUGHT
    (The O'Jays)

JAZZ ALBUMS

1. LIFELINE
   (Roy Ayers Ubiquity)
2. FREE AS THE WIND
   (Crusaders)
3. LIFESTYLE
   (John Klemmer)
4. MORE STUFF
   (Stuff)
5. LOOK TO THE RAINBOW
   (Al Jarreau)
6. LIVE
   (Lonnie Liston Smith)
7. RIGHT ON TIME
   (The Brothers Johnson)
8. FRIENDS AND STRANGERS
   (Ronnie Laws)
9. FINGER PAINTING
   (Earl Klugh)
10. HEAVY WEATHER
    (Weather Report)

COUNTRY SINGLES

1. DON'T IT MAKE MY BROWN EYES BLUE
   (Crystal Gayle)
2. WAY DOWN/PLEDGING MY LOVE
   (Elvis Presley)
3. SUNFLOWER
   (Glen Campbell)
4. I'VE ALREADY LOVED YOU IN MY MIND
   (Conway Twitty)
5. RAMBLIN' FEVER
   (Merle Haggard)
6. DAYTIME FRIENDS
   (Kenny Rogers)
7. SOUTHERN CALIFORNIA
   (George Jones and Tammy Wynette)
8. TILL THE END
   (Vern Gosdin)
9. THAT'S THE WAY LOVE SHOULD BE
   (Dave and Sugar)
10. ROLLIN' WITH THE FLOW
    (Charlie Rich)

COUNTRY ALBUMS

1. MOODY BLUE
   (Elvis Presley)

2. OL' WAYLON
   (Waylon Jennings)
3. WELCOME TO MY WORLD
   (Elvis Presley)
4. TO LEFTY FROM WILLIE
   (Willie Nelson)
5. RABBITT
   (Eddie Rabbitt)
6. DAYTIME FRIENDS
   (Kenny Rogers)
7. CHANGES IN LATITUDES, CHANGES IN ATTITUDES
   (Jimmy Buffett)
8. WE MUST BELIEVE IN MAGIC
   (Crystal Gayle)
9. WORLD WIDE FIFTY GOLD AWARD HITS, VOL. 1
   (Elvis Presley)
10. MAKING A GOOD THING BETTER
    (Olivia Newton-John)

SEPTEMBER 17, 1977

POP SINGLES

1. BEST OF MY LOVE
   (Emotions)
2. I JUST WANT TO BE YOUR EVERYTHING
   (Andy Gibb)
3. DON'T STOP
   (Fleetwood Mac)
4. FLOAT ON
   (The Floaters)
5. (YOUR LOVE HAS LIFTED ME) HIGHER AND HIGHER
   (Rita Coolidge)
6. THAT'S ROCK 'N' ROLL
   (Shaun Cassidy)
7. TELEPHONE LINE
   (Electric Light Orchestra)
8. HANDY MAN
   (James Taylor)
9. "STAR WARS" THEME/CANTINA BAND
   (Meco)
10. ON AND ON
    (Stephen Bishop)

POP ALBUMS

1. RUMOURS
   (Fleetwood Mac)
2. STAR WARS
   (Original Soundtrack)
3. CSN
   (Crosby, Stills and Nash)
4. JT
   (James Taylor)
5. LITTLE QUEEN
   (Heart)
6. COMMODORES
   (Commodores)
7. SHAUN CASSIDY
   (Shaun Cassidy)
8. STREISAND SUPERMAN
   (Barbra Streisand)
9. FOREIGNER
   (Foreigner)
10. MOODY BLUE
    (Elvis Presley)

BLACK SINGLES

1. FLOAT ON
   (The Floaters)
2. STRAWBERRY LETTER 23
   (The Brothers Johnson)
3. IT'S ECSTASY WHEN YOU LAY DOWN NEXT TO ME
   (Barry White)
4. BEST OF MY LOVE
   (Emotions)

5. KEEP IT COMIN' LOVE
   (KC and the Sunshine Band)
6. BOOGIE NIGHTS
   (Heatwave)
7. THE GREATEST LOVE OF ALL
   (George Benson)
8. WORK ON ME
   (The O'Jays)
9. SUNSHINE
   (Enchantment)
10. EASY
    (Commodores)

BLACK ALBUMS

1. COMMODORES
   (Commodores)
2. FLOAT ON
   (The Floaters)
3. REJOICE
   (Emotions)
4. TOO HOT TO HANDLE
   (Heatwave)
5. IN FULL BLOOM
   (Rose Royce)
6. RIGHT ON TIME
   (The Brothers Johnson)
7. BRICK
   (Brick)
8. SOMETHING TO LOVE
   (L.T.D.)
9. GO FOR YOUR GUNS
   (Isley Brothers)
10. PLATINUM JAZZ
    (War)

JAZZ ALBUMS

1. LIFELINE
   (Roy Ayers Ubiquity)
2. FREE AS THE WIND
   (Crusaders)
3. LIFESTYLE
   (John Klemmer)
4. LOOK TO THE RAINBOW
   (Al Jarreau)
5. NIGHTWINGS
   (Stanley Turrentine)
6. LIVE
   (Lonnie Liston Smith)
7. MORE STUFF
   (Stuff)
8. FRIENDS AND STRANGERS
   (Ronnie Laws)
9. RIGHT ON TIME
   (The Brothers Johnson)
10. TURN THIS MUTHA OUT
    (Idris Muhammad)

COUNTRY SINGLES

1. DON'T IT MAKE MY BROWN EYES BLUE
   (Crystal Gayle)
2. WAY DOWN/PLEDGING MY LOVE
   (Elvis Presley)
3. I'VE ALREADY LOVED YOU IN MY MIND
   (Conway Twitty)
4. DAYTIME FRIENDS
   (Kenny Rogers)
5. SUNFLOWER
   (Glen Campbell)
6. SOUTHERN CALIFORNIA
   (George Jones and Tammy Wynette)
7. RAMBLIN' FEVER
   (Merle Haggard)
8. Y'ALL COME BACK SALOON
   (The Oak Ridge Boys)
9. THAT'S THE WAY LOVE SHOULD BE
   (Dave and Sugar)
10. I LOVE YOU A THOUSAND WAYS
    (Willie Nelson)

COUNTRY ALBUMS

1. MOODY BLUE
   (Elvis Presley)

2. ELVIS: A LEGENDARY PERFORMER, VOL. 1
   (Elvis Presley)
3. WELCOME TO MY WORLD
   (Elvis Presley)
4. OL' WAYLON
   (Waylon Jennings)
5. DAYTIME FRIENDS
   (Kenny Rogers)
6. CHANGES IN LATITUDES, CHANGES IN ATTITUDES
   (Jimmy Buffett)
7. WE MUST BELIEVE IN MAGIC
   (Crystal Gayle)
8. TO LEFTY FROM WILLIE
   (Willie Nelson)
9. WORLD WIDE FIFTY GOLD AWARD HITS, VOL. 1
   (Elvis Presley)
10. MAKING A GOOD THING BETTER
    (Olivia Newton-John)

SEPTEMBER 24, 1977

POP SINGLES

1. BEST OF MY LOVE
   (Emotions)
2. I JUST WANT TO BE YOUR EVERYTHING
   (Andy Gibb)
3. DON'T STOP
   (Fleetwood Mac)
4. "STAR WARS" THEME/CANTINA BAND
   (Meco)
5. THAT'S ROCK 'N' ROLL
   (Shaun Cassidy)
6. KEEP IT COMIN' LOVE
   (KC and the Sunshine Band)
7. TELEPHONE LINE
   (Electric Light Orchestra)
8. FLOAT ON
   (The Floaters)
9. COLD AS ICE
   (Foreigner)
10. ON AND ON
    (Stephen Bishop)

POP ALBUMS

1. RUMOURS
   (Fleetwood Mac)
2. STAR WARS
   (Original Soundtrack)
3. JT
   (James Taylor)
4. LITTLE QUEEN
   (Heart)
5. CSN
   (Crosby, Stills and Nash)
6. COMMODORES
   (Commodores)
7. SHAUN CASSIDY
   (Shaun Cassidy)
8. FOREIGNER
   (Foreigner)
9. MOODY BLUE
   (Elvis Presley)
10. FLOAT ON
    (The Floaters)

BLACK SINGLES

1. IT'S ECSTASY WHEN YOU LAY DOWN NEXT TO ME
   (Barry White)
2. FLOAT ON
   (The Floaters)
3. STRAWBERRY LETTER 23
   (The Brothers Johnson)
4. BOOGIE NIGHTS
   (Heatwave)

5. KEEP IT COMIN' LOVE
   (KC and the Sunshine Band)
6. BEST OF MY LOVE
   (Emotions)
7. THE GREATEST LOVE OF ALL
   (George Benson)
8. WORK ON ME
   (The O'Jays)
9. EASY
   (Commodores)
10. WE NEVER DANCED TO A LOVE SONG
    (The Manhattans)

BLACK ALBUMS

1. COMMODORES
   (Commodores)
2. REJOICE
   (Emotions)
3. FLOAT ON
   (The Floaters)
4. TOO HOT TO HANDLE
   (Heatwave)
5. IN FULL BLOOM
   (Rose Royce)
6. BRICK
   (Brick)
7. RIGHT ON TIME
   (The Brothers Johnson)
8. SOMETHING TO LOVE
   (L.T.D.)
9. STAR WARS AND OTHER GALACTIC FUNK
   (Meco)
10. BARRY WHITE SINGS FOR SOMEONE YOU
    LOVE
    (Barry White)

JAZZ ALBUMS

1. LIFELINE
   (Roy Ayers Ubiquity)
2. NIGHTWINGS
   (Stanley Turrentine)
3. FREE AS THE WIND
   (Crusaders)
4. LIFESTYLE
   (John Klemmer)
5. LOOK TO THE RAINBOW
   (Al Jarreau)
6. BLOW IT OUT
   (Tom Scott)
7. TURN THIS MUTHA OUT
   (Idris Muhammad)
8. FRIENDS AND STRANGERS
   (Ronnie Laws)
9. MORE STUFF
   (Stuff)
10. LIVE
    (Lonnie Liston Smith)

COUNTRY SINGLES

1. DON'T IT MAKE MY BROWN EYES BLUE
   (Crystal Gayle)
2. I'VE ALREADY LOVED YOU IN MY MIND
   (Conway Twitty)
3. DAYTIME FRIENDS
   (Kenny Rogers)
4. WAY DOWN/PLEDGING MY LOVE
   (Elvis Presley)
5. Y'ALL COME BACK SALOON
   (The Oak Ridge Boys)
6. SOUTHERN CALIFORNIA
   (George Jones and Tammy Wynette)
7. HEAVEN'S JUST A SIN AWAY
   (The Kendalls)
8. WHY CAN'T HE BE YOU
   (Loretta Lynn)
9. EAST BOUND AND DOWN
   (Jerry Reed)
10. I LOVE YOU A THOUSAND WAYS
    (Willie Nelson)

COUNTRY ALBUMS

1. MOODY BLUE
   (Elvis Presley)

2. ELVIS: A LEGENDARY PERFORMER, VOL. 1
   (Elvis Presley)
3. WELCOME TO MY WORLD
   (Elvis Presley)
4. OL' WAYLON
   (Waylon Jennings)
5. DAYTIME FRIENDS
   (Kenny Rogers)
6. SIMPLE DREAM
   (Linda Ronstadt)
7. TO LEFTY FROM WILLIE
   (Willie Nelson)
8. WE MUST BELIEVE IN MAGIC
   (Crystal Gayle)
9. IT WAS ALMOST LIKE A SONG
   (Ronnie Milsap)
10. PURE GOLD
    (Elvis Presley)

OCTOBER 1, 1977

POP SINGLES

1. "STAR WARS" THEME/CANTINA BAND
   (Meco)
2. BEST OF MY LOVE
   (Emotions)
3. THAT'S ROCK 'N' ROLL
   (Shaun Cassidy)
4. KEEP IT COMIN' LOVE
   (KC and the Sunshine Band)
5. I JUST WANT TO BE YOUR EVERYTHING
   (Andy Gibb)
6. DON'T STOP
   (Fleetwood Mac)
7. NOBODY DOES IT BETTER
   (Carly Simon)
8. YOU LIGHT UP MY LIFE
   (Debby Boone)
9. COLD AS ICE
   (Foreigner)
10. BOOGIE NIGHTS
    (Heatwave)

POP ALBUMS

1. RUMOURS
   (Fleetwood Mac)
2. STAR WARS
   (Original Soundtrack)
3. LITTLE QUEEN
   (Heart)
4. SHAUN CASSIDY
   (Shaun Cassidy)
5. COMMODORES
   (Commodores)
6. CSN
   (Crosby, Stills and Nash)
7. JT
   (James Taylor)
8. FOREIGNER
   (Foreigner)
9. MOODY BLUE
   (Elvis Presley)
10. SIMPLE DREAMS
    (Linda Ronstadt)

BLACK SINGLES

1. IT'S ECSTASY WHEN YOU LAY DOWN NEXT
   TO ME
   (Barry White)
2. BOOGIE NIGHTS
   (Heatwave)
3. FLOAT ON
   (The Floaters)
4. KEEP IT COMIN' LOVE
   (KC and the Sunshine Band)
5. STRAWBERRY LETTER 23
   (The Brothers Johnson)
6. BEST OF MY LOVE
   (Emotions)

7. WORK ON ME
   (The O'Jays)
8. WE NEVER DANCED TO A LOVE SONG
   (The Manhattans)
9. THE GREATEST LOVE OF ALL
   (George Benson)
10. BRICK
    (Brick)

BLACK ALBUMS

1. COMMODORES
   (Commodores)
2. IN FULL BLOOM
   (Rose Royce)
3. REJOICE
   (Emotions)
4. TOO HOT TO HANDLE
   (Heatwave)
5. BRICK
   (Brick)
6. FLOAT ON
   (The Floaters)
7. BARRY WHITE SINGS FOR SOMEONE YOU
   LOVE
   (Barry White)
8. STAR WARS AND OTHER GALACTIC FUNK
   (Meco)
9. SOMETHING TO LOVE
   (L.T.D.)
10. RIGHT ON TIME
    (The Brothers Johnson)

JAZZ ALBUMS

1. LIFELINE
   (Roy Ayers Ubiquity)
2. NIGHTWINGS
   (Stanley Turrentine)
3. FREE AS THE WIND
   (Crusaders)
4. BLOW IT OUT
   (Tom Scott)
5. LOOK TO THE RAINBOW
   (Al Jarreau)
6. LIFESTYLE
   (John Klemmer)
7. TURN THIS MUTHA OUT
   (Idris Muhammad)
8. FRIENDS AND STRANGERS
   (Ronnie Laws)
9. MORE STUFF
   (Stuff)
10. LIVE
    (Lonnie Liston Smith)

COUNTRY SINGLES

1. I'VE ALREADY LOVED YOU IN MY MIND
   (Conway Twitty)
2. DAYTME FRIENDS
   (Kenny Rogers)
3. DON'T IT MAKE MY BROWN EYES BLUE
   (Crystal Gayle)
4. HEAVEN'S JUST A SIN AWAY
   (The Kendalls)
5. Y'ALL COME BACK SALOON
   (The Oak Ridge Boys)
6. EAST BOUND AND DOWN
   (Jerry Reed)
7. I GOT THE HOSS
   (Mel Tillis)
8. WHY CAN'T HE BE YOU
   (Loretta Lynn)
9. SOUTHERN CALIFORNIA
   (George Jones and Tammy Wynette)
10. IT'S ALL IN THE GAME
    (Tom T. Hall)

COUNTRY ALBUMS

1. MOODY BLUE
   (Elvis Presley)

2. ELVIS' GOLDEN RECORDS, VOL. 4
   (*Elvis Presley*)
3. ELVIS' GOLDEN RECORDS, VOL. 2
   (*Elvis Presley*)
4. OL' WAYLON
   (*Waylon Jennings*)
5. DAYTIME FRIENDS
   (*Kenny Rogers*)
6. SIMPLE DREAMS
   (*Linda Ronstadt*)
7. WE MUST BELIEVE IN MAGIC
   (*Crystal Gayle*)
8. ELVIS' GOLDEN RECORDS, VOL. 1
   (*Elvis Presley*)
9. IT WAS ALMOST LIKE A SONG
   (*Ronnie Milsap*)
10. PURE GOLD
    (*Elvis Presley*)

OCTOBER 8, 1977

POP SINGLES

1. "STAR WARS" THEME/CANTINA BAND
   (*Meco*)
2. KEEP IT COMIN' LOVE
   (*KC and the Sunshine Band*)
3. THAT'S ROCK 'N' ROLL
   (*Shaun Cassidy*)
4. YOU LIGHT UP MY LIFE
   (*Debby Boone*)
5. NOBODY DOES IT BETTER
   (*Carly Simon*)
6. BEST OF MY LOVE
   (*Emotions*)
7. BOOGIE NIGHTS
   (*Heatwave*)
8. COLD AS ICE
   (*Foreigner*)
9. I JUST WANT TO BE YOUR EVERYTHING
   (*Andy Gibb*)
10. WAY DOWN
    (*Elvis Presley*)

POP ALBUMS

1. RUMOURS
   (*Fleetwood Mac*)
2. STAR WARS
   (*Original Soundtrack*)
3. SIMPLE DREAMS
   (*Linda Ronstadt*)
4. SHAUN CASSIDY
   (*Shaun Cassidy*)
5. LITTLE QUEEN
   (*Heart*)
6. FOREIGNER
   (*Foreigner*)
7. CSN
   (*Crosby, Stills and Nash*)
8. MOODY BLUE
   (*Elvis Presley*)
9. COMMODORES
   (*Commodores*)
10. JT
    (*James Taylor*)

BLACK SINGLES

1. IT'S ECSTASY WHEN YOU LAY DOWN NEXT
   TO ME
   (*Barry White*)
2. BOOGIE NIGHTS
   (*Heatwave*)
3. KEEP IT COMIN' LOVE
   (*KC and the Sunshine Band*)
4. BRICK HOUSE
   (*Commodores*)
5. DUSIC
   (*Brick*)
6. DO YOUR DANCE (PART 1)
   (*Rose Royce*)

7. FLOAT ON
   (*The Floaters*)
8. WE NEVER DANCED TO A LOVE SONG
   (*The Manhattans*)
9. WORK ON ME
   (*The O'Jays*)
10. STRAWBERRY LETTER 23
    (*The Brothers Johnson*)

BLACK ALBUMS

1. COMMODORES
   (*Commodores*)
2. IN FULL BLOOM
   (*Rose Royce*)
3. BARRY WHITE SINGS FOR SOMEONE YOU
   LOVE
   (*Barry White*)
4. TOO HOT TO HANDLE
   (*Heatwave*)
5. BRICK
   (*Brick*)
6. REJOICE
   (*Emotions*)
7. FLOAT ON
   (*The Floaters*)
8. STAR WARS AND OTHER GALACTIC FUNK
   (*Meco*)
9. SOMETHING TO LOVE
   (*L.T.D.*)
10. SHAKE IT WELL
    (*The Dramatics*)

JAZZ ALBUMS

1. NIGHTWINGS
   (*Stanley Turrentine*)
2. LIFELINE
   (*Roy Ayers Ubiquity*)
3. FREE AS THE WIND
   (*Crusaders*)
4. ENIGMATIC OCEAN
   (*Jean Luc Ponty*)
5. BLOW IT OUT
   (*Tom Scott*)
6. LOOK TO THE RAINBOW
   (*Al Jarreau*)
7. LIFESTYLE
   (*John Klemmer*)
8. FRIENDS AND STRANGERS
   (*Ronnie Laws*)
9. TURN THIS MUTHA OUT
   (*Idris Muhammad*)
10. MORE STUFF
    (*Stuff*)

COUNTRY SINGLES

1. HEAVEN'S JUST A SIN AWAY
   (*The Kendalls*)
2. DAYTIME FRIENDS
   (*Kenny Rogers*)
3. Y'ALL COME BACK SALOON
   (*The Oak Ridge Boys*)
4. I'VE ALREADY LOVED YOU IN MY MIND
   (*Conway Twitty*)
5. EAST BOUND AND DOWN
   (*Jerry Reed*)
6. I GOT THE HOSS
   (*Mel Tillis*)
7. I'M JUST A COUNTRY BOY
   (*Don Williams*)
8. WE CAN'T GO ON LIVING LIKE THIS
   (*Eddie Rabbitt*)
9. WHY CAN'T HE BE YOU
   (*Loretta Lynn*)
10. IT'S ALL IN THE GAME
    (*Tom T. Hall*)

COUNTRY ALBUMS

1. MOODY BLUE
   (*Elvis Presley*)

2. ELVIS' GOLDEN RECORDS, VOL. 4
   (*Elvis Presley*)
3. ELVIS' GOLDEN RECORDS, VOL. 2
   (*Elvis Presley*)
4. WE MUST BELIEVE IN MAGIC
   (*Crystal Gayle*)
5. OL' WAYLON
   (*Waylon Jennings*)
6. DAYTIME FRIENDS
   (*Kenny Rogers*)
7. SIMPLE DREAMS
   (*Linda Ronstadt*)
8. ELVIS' GOLDEN RECORDS, VOL. 1
   (*Elvis Presley*)
9. TO LEFTY FROM WILLIE
   (*Willie Nelson*)
10. IT WAS ALMOST LIKE A SONG
    (*Ronnie Milsap*)

OCTOBER 15, 1977

POP SINGLES

1. YOU LIGHT UP MY LIFE
   (*Debby Boone*)
2. KEEP IT COMIN' LOVE
   (*KC and the Sunshine Band*)
3. "STAR WARS" THEME/CANTINA BAND
   (*Meco*)
4. NOBODY DOES IT BETTER
   (*Carly Simon*)
5. THAT'S ROCK 'N' ROLL
   (*Shaun Cassidy*)
6. BOOGIE NIGHTS
   (*Heatwave*)
7. BEST OF MY LOVE
   (*Emotions*)
8. COLD AS ICE
   (*Foreigner*)
9. I JUST WANT TO BE YOUR EVERYTHING
   (*Andy Gibb*)
10. I FEEL LOVE
    (*Donna Summer*)

POP ALBUMS

1. RUMOURS
   (*Fleetwood Mac*)
2. STAR WARS
   (*Original Soundtrack*)
3. SIMPLE DREAMS
   (*Linda Ronstadt*)
4. SHAUN CASSIDY
   (*Shaun Cassidy*)
5. FOREIGNER
   (*Foreigner*)
6. MOODY BLUE
   (*Elvis Presley*)
7. CSN
   (*Crosby, Stills and Nash*)
8. COMMODORES
   (*Commodores*)
9. CHICAGO X
   (*Chicago*)
10. LITTLE QUEEN
    (*Heart*)

BLACK SINGLES

1. IT'S ECSTASY WHEN YOU LAY DOWN NEXT
   TO ME
   (*Barry White*)
2. DO YOUR DANCE (PART 1)
   (*Rose Royce*)
3. BOOGIE NIGHTS
   (*Heatwave*)
4. BRICK HOUSE
   (*Commodores*)
5. DUSIC
   (*Brick*)

6. KEEP IT COMIN' LOVE
   (*KC and the Sunshine Band*)
7. (EVERY TIME I TURN AROUND) BACK IN LOVE AGAIN
   (*L.T.D.*)
8. WE NEVER DANCED TO A LOVE SONG
   (*The Manhattans*)
9. FLOAT ON
   (*The Floaters*)
10. DO YOU WANNA GET FUNKY WITH ME
    (*Peter Brown*)

BLACK ALBUMS

1. COMMODORES
   (*Commodores*)
2. IN FULL BLOOM
   (*Rose Royce*)
3. BARRY WHITE SINGS FOR SOMEONE YOU LOVE
   (*Barry White*)
4. TOO HOT TO HANDLE
   (*Heatwave*)
5. REJOICE
   (*Emotions*)
6. BRICK
   (*Brick*)
7. FLOAT ON
   (*The Floaters*)
8. SOMETHING TO LOVE
   (*L.T.D.*)
9. STAR WARS AND OTHER GALACTIC FUNK
   (*Meco*)
10. SHAKE IT WELL
    (*The Dramatics*)

JAZZ ALBUMS

1. NIGHTWINGS
   (*Stanley Turrentine*)
2. ENIGMATIC OCEAN
   (*Jean Luc Ponty*)
3. LIFELINE
   (*Roy Ayers Ubiquity*)
4. FREE AS THE WIND
   (*Crusaders*)
5. BLOW IT OUT
   (*Tom Scott*)
6. LOOK TO THE RAINBOW
   (*Al Jarreau*)
7. LIFESTYLE
   (*John Klemmer*)
8. ACTION
   (*Blackbyrds*)
9. FRIENDS AND STRANGERS
   (*Ronnie Laws*)
10. MORE STUFF
    (*Stuff*)

COUNTRY SINGLES

1. HEAVEN'S JUST A SIN AWAY
   (*The Kendalls*)
2. EASTBOUND AND DOWN
   (*Jerry Reed*)
3. Y'ALL COME BACK SALOON
   (*The Oak Ridge Boys*)
4. I GOT THE HOSS
   (*Mel Tillis*)
5. I'M JUST A COUNTRY BOY
   (*Don Williams*)
6. WE CAN'T GO ON LIVING LIKE THIS
   (*Eddie Rabbitt*)
7. DAYTIME FRIENDS
   (*Kenny Rogers*)
8. I'VE ALREADY LOVED YOU IN MY MIND
   (*Conway Twitty*)
9. WHY CAN'T HE BE YOU
   (*Loretta Lynn*)
10. THE KING IS GONE
    (*Ronnie McDowell*)

COUNTRY ALBUMS

1. MOODY BLUE
   (*Elvis Presley*)
2. SIMPLE DREAMS
   (*Linda Ronstadt*)
3. DAYTIME FRIENDS
   (*Kenny Rogers*)
4. WE MUST BELIEVE IN MAGIC
   (*Crystal Gayle*)
5. OL' WAYLON
   (*Waylon Jennings*)
6. IT WAS ALMOST LIKE A SONG
   (*Ronnie Milsap*)
7. TO LEFTY FROM WILLIE
   (*Willie Nelson*)
8. I'VE ALREADY LOVED YOU IN MY MIND
   (*Conway Twitty*)
9. WELCOME TO MY WORLD
   (*Elvis Presley*)
10. CHANGES IN LATITUDES, CHANGES IN ATTITUDES
    (*Jimmy Buffett*)

OCTOBER 22, 1977

POP SINGLES

1. YOU LIGHT UP MY LIFE
   (*Debby Boone*)
2. KEEP IT COMIN' LOVE
   (*KC and the Sunshine Band*)
3. NOBODY DOES IT BETTER
   (*Carly Simon*)
4. "STAR WARS" THEME/CANTINA BAND
   (*Meco*)
5. BOOGIE NIGHTS
   (*Heatwave*)
6. THAT'S ROCK 'N' ROLL
   (*Shaun Cassidy*)
7. COLD AS ICE
   (*Foreigner*)
8. I FEEL LOVE
   (*Donna Summer*)
9. I JUST WANT TO BE YOUR EVERYTHING
   (*Andy Gibb*)
10. BRICK HOUSE
    (*Commodores*)

POP ALBUMS

1. RUMOURS
   (*Fleetwood Mac*)
2. SHAUN CASSIDY
   (*Shaun Cassidy*)
3. SIMPLE DREAMS
   (*Linda Ronstadt*)
4. STAR WARS
   (*Original Soundtrack*)
5. FOREIGNER
   (*Foreigner*)
6. MOODY BLUE
   (*Elvis Presley*)
7. CHICAGO X
   (*Chicago*)
8. AJA
   (*Steely Dan*)
9. ANYTIME . . . ANYWHERE
   (*Rita Coolidge*)
10. COMMODORES
    (*Commodores*)

BLACK SINGLES

1. IT'S ECSTASY WHEN YOU LAY DOWN NEXT TO ME
   (*Barry White*)
2. DO YOUR DANCE (PART 1)
   (*Rose Royce*)

3. (EVERY TIME I TURN AROUND) BACK IN LOVE AGAIN
   (*L.T.D.*)
4. DUSIC
   (*Brick*)
5. BRICK HOUSE
   (*Commodores*)
6. BOOGIE NIGHTS
   (*Heatwave*)
7. KEEP IT COMIN' LOVE
   (*KC and the Sunshine Band*)
8. WE NEVER DANCED TO A LOVE SONG
   (*The Manhattans*)
9. DO YOU WANNA GET FUNKY WITH ME
   (*Peter Brown*)
10. FLOAT ON
    (*The Floaters*)

BLACK ALBUMS

1. BARRY WHITE SINGS FOR SOMEONE YOU LOVE
   (*Barry White*)
2. IN FULL BLOOM
   (*Rose Royce*)
3. COMMODORES
   (*Commodores*)
4. TOO HOT TO HANDLE
   (*Heatwave*)
5. SOMETHING TO LOVE
   (*L.T.D.*)
6. REJOICE
   (*Emotions*)
7. BRICK
   (*Brick*)
8. FLOAT ON
   (*The Floaters*)
9. SHAKE IT WELL
   (*Dramatics*)
10. STAR WARS AND OTHER GALACTIC FUNK
    (*Meco*)

JAZZ ALBUMS

1. ENIGMATIC OCEAN
   (*Jean Luc Ponty*)
2. LIFELINE
   (*Roy Ayers Ubiquity*)
3. NIGHTWINGS
   (*Stanley Turrentine*)
4. FREE AS THE WIND
   (*Crusaders*)
5. BLOW IT OUT
   (*Tom Scott*)
6. ACTION
   (*Blackbyrds*)
7. LOOK TO THE RAINBOW
   (*Al Jarreau*)
8. LIFESTYLE
   (*John Klemmer*)
9. FRIENDS AND STRANGERS
   (*Ronnie Laws*)
10. MORE STUFF
    (*Stuff*)

COUNTRY SINGLES

1. HEAVEN'S JUST A SIN AWAY
   (*The Kendalls*)
2. EASTBOUND AND DOWN
   (*Jerry Reed*)
3. I GOT THE HOSS
   (*Mel Tillis*)
4. I'M JUST A COUNTRY BOY
   (*Don Williams*)
5. WE CAN'T GO ON LIVING LIKE THIS
   (*Eddie Rabbitt*)
6. Y'ALL COME BACK SALOON
   (*The Oak Ridge Boys*)
7. DAYTIME FRIENDS
   (*Kenny Rogers*)
8. ROSES FOR MAMA
   (*C.W. McCall*)

9. ONCE IN A LIFETIME THING
   (John Wesley Ryles)
10. THE KING IS GONE
    (Ronnie McDowell)

COUNTRY ALBUMS

1. MOODY BLUE
   (Elvis Presley)
2. SIMPLE DREAMS
   (Linda Ronstadt)
3. DAYTIME FRIENDS
   (Kenny Rogers)
4. WE MUST BELIEVE IN MAGIC
   (Crystal Gayle)
5. IT WAS ALMOST LIKE A SONG
   (Ronnie Milsap)
6. OL' WAYLON
   (Waylon Jennings)
7. TO LEFTY FROM WILLIE
   (Willie Nelson)
8. I'VE ALREADY LOVED YOU IN MY MIND
   (Conway Twitty)
9. WELCOME TO MY WORLD
   (Elvis Presley)
10. CHANGES IN LATITUDES, CHANGES IN ATTITUDES
    (Jimmy Buffett)

OCTOBER 29, 1977

POP SINGLES

1. YOU LIGHT UP MY LIFE
   (Debby Boone)
2. NOBODY DOES IT BETTER
   (Carly Simon)
3. BOOGIE NIGHTS
   (Heatwave)
4. KEEP IT COMIN' LOVE
   (KC and the Sunshine Band)
5. "STAR WARS" THEME/CANTINA BAND
   (Meco)
6. I FEEL LOVE
   (Donna Summer)
7. THAT'S ROCK 'N' ROLL
   (Shaun Cassidy)
8. IT'S ECSTASY WHEN YOU LAY DOWN NEXT TO ME
   (Barry White)
9. BRICK HOUSE
   (Commodores)
10. COLD AS ICE
    (Foreigner)

POP ALBUMS

1. RUMOURS
   (Fleetwood Mac)
2. SHAUN CASSIDY
   (Shaun Cassidy)
3. SIMPLE DREAMS
   (Linda Ronstadt)
4. FOREIGNER
   (Foreigner)
5. AJA
   (Steely Dan)
6. MOODY BLUE
   (Elvis Presley)
7. CHICAGO X
   (Chicago)
8. STAR WARS
   (Original Soundtrack)
9. ANYTIME . . . ANYWHERE
   (Rita Coolidge)
10. ELVIS IN CONCERT
    (Elvis Presley)

BLACK SINGLES

1. IT'S ECSTASY WHEN YOU LAY DOWN NEXT TO ME
   (Barry White)
2. (EVERY TIME I TURN AROUND) BACK IN LOVE AGAIN
   (L.T.D.)
3. DO YOUR DANCE (PART 1)
   (Rose Royce)
4. DUSIC
   (Brick)
5. BRICK HOUSE
   (Commodores)
6. KEEP IT COMIN' LOVE
   (KC and the Sunshine Band)
7. BOOGIE NIGHTS
   (Heatwave)
8. DO YOU WANNA GET FUNKY WITH ME
   (Peter Brown)
9. YOU CAN'T TURN ME OFF (IN THE MIDDLE OF TURNING ME ON)
   (High Inergy)
10. WE NEVER DANCED TO A LOVE SONG
    (The Manhattans)

BLACK ALBUMS

1. BARRY WHITE SINGS FOR SOMEONE YOU LOVE
   (Barry White)
2. IN FULL BLOOM
   (Rose Royce)
3. COMMODORES
   (Commodores)
4. TOO HOT TO HANDLE
   (Heatwave)
5. SOMETHING TO LOVE
   (L.T.D.)
6. BRICK
   (Brick)
7. REJOICE
   (Emotions)
8. SHAKE IT WELL
   (The Dramatics)
9. FLOAT ON
   (The Floaters)
10. STAR WARS AND OTHER GALACTIC FUNK
    (Meco)

JAZZ ALBUMS

1. ENIGMATIC OCEAN
   (Jean Luc Ponty)
2. LIFELINE
   (Roy Ayers Ubiquity)
3. NIGHTWINGS
   (Stanley Turrentine)
4. ACTION
   (Blackbyrds)
5. BLOW IT OUT
   (Tom Scott)
6. FREE AS THE WIND
   (Crusaders)
7. LIFESTYLE
   (John Klemmer)
8. LOOK TO THE RAINBOW
   (Al Jarreau)
9. FRIENDS AND STRANGERS
   (Ronnie Laws)
10. BRIDGES
    (Gil Scott-Heron and Brian Jackson)

COUNTRY SINGLES

1. EASTBOUND AND DOWN
   (Jerry Reed)
2. HEAVEN'S JUST A SIN AWAY
   (The Kendalls)
3. I GOT THE HOSS
   (Mel Tillis)
4. I'M JUST A COUNTRY BOY
   (Don Williams)

5. WE CAN'T GO ON LIVING LIKE THIS
   (Eddie Rabbitt)
6. ROSES FOR MAMA
   (C.W. McCall)
7. ONCE IN A LIFETIME THING
   (John Wesley Ryles)
8. LOVE IS JUST A GAME
   (Larry Gatlin)
9. BLUE BAYOU
   (Linda Ronstadt)
10. MORE TO ME
    (Charley Pride)

COUNTRY ALBUMS

1. MOODY BLUE
   (Elvis Presley)
2. ELVIS IN CONCERT
   (Elvis)
3. SIMPLE DREAMS
   (Linda Ronstadt)
4. IT WAS ALMOST LIKE A SONG
   (Ronnie Milsap)
5. WE MUST BELIEVE IN MAGIC
   (Crystal Gayle)
6. DAYTIME FRIENDS
   (Kenny Rogers)
7. OL' WAYLON
   (Waylon Jennings)
8. HOW GREAT THOU ART
   (Elvis Presley)
9. PURE GOLD
   (Elvis Presley)
10. SMOKEY AND THE BANDIT
    (Original Soundtrack)

NOVEMBER 5, 1977

POP SINGLES

1. YOU LIGHT UP MY LIFE
   (Debby Boone)
2. BOOGIE NIGHTS
   (Heatwave)
3. NOBODY DOES IT BETTER
   (Carly Simon)
4. I FEEL LOVE
   (Donna Summer)
5. KEEP IT COMIN' LOVE
   (KC and the Sunshine Band)
6. IT'S ECSTASY WHEN YOU LAY DOWN NEXT TO ME
   (Barry White)
7. "STAR WARS" THEME/CANTINA BAND
   (Meco)
8. DON'T IT MAKE MY BROWN EYES BLUE
   (Crystal Gayle)
9. BRICK HOUSE
   (Commodores)
10. WE'RE ALL ALONE
    (Rita Coolidge)

POP ALBUMS

1. RUMOURS
   (Fleetwood Mac)
2. SIMPLE DREAMS
   (Linda Ronstadt)
3. SHAUN CASSIDY
   (Shaun Cassidy)
4. AJA
   (Steely Dan)
5. ELVIS IN CONCERT
   (Elvis Presley)
6. FOREIGNER
   (Foreigner)
7. MOODY BLUE
   (Elvis Presley)
8. CHICAGO X
   (Chicago)

9. STAR WARS
   (Original Soundtrack)
10. FOGHAT LIVE
   (Foghat)

BLACK SINGLES

1. (EVERY TIME I TURN AROUND) BACK IN LOVE AGAIN
   (L.T.D.)
2. IT'S ECSTASY WHEN YOU LAY DOWN NEXT TO ME
   (Barry White)
3. DUSIC
   (Brick)
4. DO YOUR DANCE (PART 1)
   (Rose Royce)
5. KEEP IT COMIN' LOVE
   (KC and the Sunshine Band)
6. YOU CAN'T TURN ME OFF (IN THE MIDDLE OF TURNING ME ON)
   (High Inergy)
7. DO YOU WANNA GET FUNKY WITH ME
   (Peter Brown)
8. IF YOU'RE NOT BACK IN LOVE BY MONDAY
   (Millie Jackson)
9. BRICK HOUSE
   (Commodores)
10. SERPENTINE FIRE
   (Earth, Wind and Fire)

BLACK ALBUMS

1. IN FULL BLOOM
   (Rose Royce)
2. BARRY WHITE SINGS FOR SOMEONE YOU LOVE
   (Barry White)
3. SOMETHING TO LOVE
   (L.T.D.)
4. COMMODORES
   (Commodores)
5. TOO HOT TO HANDLE
   (Heatwave)
6. REJOICE
   (Emotions)
7. BRICK
   (Brick)
8. SHAKE IT WELL
   (The Dramatics)
9. STAR WARS AND OTHER GALACTIC FUNK
   (Meco)
10. FEELIN' BITCHY
   (Millie Jackson)

JAZZ ALBUMS

1. ENIGMATIC OCEAN
   (Jean Luc Ponty)
2. LIFETIME
   (Roy Ayers Ubiquity)
3. ACTION
   (Blackbyrds)
4. NIGHTWINGS
   (Stanley Turrentine)
5. FEELS SO GOOD
   (Chuck Mangione)
6. BLOW IT OUT
   (Tom Scott)
7. FREE AS THE WIND
   (Crusaders)
8. LIFESTYLE
   (John Klemmer)
9. LOOK TO THE RAINBOW
   (Al Jarreau)
10. BRIDGES
   (Gil Scott-Heron and Brian Jackson)

COUNTRY SINGLES

1. I'M JUST A COUNTRY BOY
   (Don Williams)

2. HEAVEN'S JUST A SIN AWAY
   (The Kendalls)
3. ROSES FOR MAMA
   (C.W. McCall)
4. BLUE BAYOU
   (Linda Ronstadt)
5. MORE TO ME
   (Charley Pride)
6. ONCE IN A LIFETIME THING
   (John Wesley Ryles)
7. LOVE IS JUST A GAME
   (Larry Gatlin)
8. EASTBOUND AND DOWN
   (Jerry Reed)
9. WURLITZER PRIZE/LOOKIN' FOR A FEELING
   (Waylon Jennings)
10. LET ME DOWN EASY
   (Cristy Lane)

COUNTRY ALBUMS

1. ELVIS IN CONCERT
   (Elvis Presley)
2. MOODY BLUE
   (Elvis Presley)
3. SIMPLE DREAMS
   (Linda Ronstadt)
4. IT WAS ALMOST LIKE A SONG
   (Ronnie Milsap)
5. WELCOME TO MY WORLD
   (Elvis Presley)
6. ELVIS' GOLDEN RECORDS, VOL. 3
   (Elvis Presley)
7. PURE GOLD
   (Elvis Presley)
8. HOW GREAT THOU ART
   (Elvis Presley)
9. DAYTIME FRIENDS
   (Kenny Rogers)
10. SMOKEY AND THE BANDIT
   (Original Soundtrack)

NOVEMBER 12, 1977

POP SINGLES

1. YOU LIGHT UP MY LIFE
   (Debby Boone)
2. BOOGIE NIGHTS
   (Heatwave)
3. NOBODY DOES IT BETTER
   (Carly Simon)
4. I FEEL LOVE
   (Donna Summer)
5. IT'S ECSTASY WHEN YOU LAY DOWN NEXT TO ME
   (Barry White)
6. DON'T IT MAKE MY BROWN EYES BLUE
   (Crystal Gayle)
7. WE'RE ALL ALONE
   (Rita Coolidge)
8. KEEP IT COMIN' LOVE
   (KC and the Sunshine Band)
9. BABY, WHAT A BIG SURPRISE
   (Chicago)
10. "STAR WARS" THEME/CANTINA BAND
   (Meco)

POP SINGLES

1. RUMOURS
   (Fleetwood Mac)
2. SIMPLE DREAMS
   (Linda Ronstadt)
3. ELVIS IN CONCERT
   (Elvis Presley)
4. AJA
   (Steely Dan)
5. FOREIGNER
   (Foreigner)

6. MOODY BLUE
   (Elvis Presley)
7. SHAUN CASSIDY
   (Shaun Cassidy)
8. CHICAGO X
   (Chicago)
9. STAR WARS
   (Original Soundtrack)
10. STREET SURVIVORS
   (Lynyrd Skynyrd)

BLACK SINGLES

1. (EVERY TIME I TURN AROUND) BACK IN LOVE AGAIN
   (L.T.D.)
2. IT'S ECSTASY WHEN YOU LAY DOWN NEXT TO ME
   (Barry White)
3. DUSIC
   (Brick)
4. YOU CAN'T TURN ME OFF (IN THE MIDDLE OF TURNING ME ON)
   (High Inergy)
5. IF YOU'RE NOT BACK IN LOVE BY MONDAY
   (Millie Jackson)
6. DO YOUR DANCE (PART 1)
   (Rose Royce)
7. SERPENTINE FIRE
   (Earth, Wind and Fire)
8. KEEP IT COMIN' LOVE
   (KC and the Sunshine Band)
9. DO YOU WANNA GET FUNKY WITH ME
   (Peter Brown)
10. BRICK HOUSE
   (Commodores)

BLACK ALBUMS

1. IN FULL BLOOM
   (Rose Royce)
2. BARRY WHITE SINGS FOR SOMEONE YOU LOVE
   (Barry White)
3. SOMETHING TO LOVE
   (L.T.D.)
4. TOO HOT TO HANDLE
   (Heatwave)
5. COMMODORES
   (Commodores)
6. BRICK
   (Brick)
7. FEELIN' BITCHY
   (Millie Jackson)
8. REJOICE
   (Emotions)
9. STAR WARS AND OTHER GALACTIC FUNK
   (Meco)
10. SHAKE IT WELL
   (The Dramatics)

JAZZ ALBUMS

1. REACH FOR IT
   (George Duke)
2. FEELS SO GOOD
   (Chuck Mangione)
3. ENIGMATIC OCEAN
   (Jean Luc Ponty)
4. LIFELINE
   (Roy Ayers Ubiquity)
5. ACTION
   (Blackbyrds)
6. NIGHTWINGS
   (Stanley Turrentine)
7. BLOW IT OUT
   (Tom Scott)
8. LIFESTYLE
   (John Klemmer)
9. FREE AS THE WIND
   (Crusaders)
10. BRIDGES
   (Gil Scott-Heron and Brian Jackson)

COUNTRY SINGLES

1. ROSES FOR MAMA
   (C.W. McCall)
2. I'M JUST A COUNTRY BOY
   (Don Williams)
3. BLUE BAYOU
   (Linda Ronstadt)
4. MORE TO ME
   (Charley Pride)
5. LOVE IS JUST A GAME
   (Charley Pride)
6. WURLITZER PRIZE/LOOKIN' FOR A
   FEELING
   (Waylon Jennings)
7. ONCE IN A LIFETIME THING
   (John Wesley Ryles)
8. FROM GRACELAND TO THE PROMISED
   LAND
   (Merle Haggard)
9. SHAME ON ME
   (Donna Fargo)
10. LET ME DOWN EASY
    (Cristy Lane)

COUNTRY ALBUMS

1. ELVIS IN CONCERT
   (Elvis Presley)
2. MOODY BLUE
   (Elvis Presley)
3. SIMPLE DREAMS
   (Linda Ronstadt)
4. IT WAS ALMOST LIKE A SONG
   (Ronnie Milsap)
5. WELCOME TO MY WORLD
   (Elvis Presley)
6. ELVIS' GOLDEN RECORDS, VOL. 3
   (Elvis Presley)
7. PURE GOLD
   (Elvis Presley)
8. WE MUST BELIEVE IN MAGIC
   (Crystal Gayle)
9. OL' WAYLON
   (Waylon Jennings)
10. DAYTIME FRIENDS
    (Kenny Rogers)

NOVEMBER 19, 1977

POP SINGLES

1. YOU LIGHT UP MY LIFE
   (Debby Boone)
2. BOOGIE NIGHTS
   (Heatwave)
3. NOBODY DOES IT BETTER
   (Carly Simon)
4. DON'T IT MAKE MY BROWN EYES BLUE
   (Crystal Gayle)
5. WE'RE ALL ALONE
   (Rita Coolidge)
6. IT'S ECSTASY WHEN YOU LAY DOWN NEXT
   TO ME
   (Barry White)
7. I FEEL LOVE
   (Donna Summer)
8. BABY, WHAT A BIG SURPRISE
   (Chicago)
9. BLUE BAYOU
   (Linda Ronstadt)
10. HOW DEEP IS YOUR LOVE
    (The Bee Gees)

POP ALBUMS

1. RUMOURS
   (Fleetwood Mac)
2. SIMPLE DREAMS
   (Linda Ronstadt)

3. ELVIS IN CONCERT
   (Elvis Presley)
4. AJA
   (Steely Dan)
5. MOODY BLUE
   (Elvis Presley)
6. FOREIGNER
   (Foreigner)
7. SHAUN CASSIDY
   (Shaun Cassidy)
8. STREET SURVIVORS
   (Lynyrd Skynyrd)
9. STAR WARS
   (Original Soundtrack)
10. YOU LIGHT UP MY LIFE
    (Original Soundtrack)

BLACK SINGLES

1. (EVERY TIME I TURN AROUND) BACK IN
   LOVE AGAIN
   (L.T.D.)
2. IT'S ECSTASY WHEN YOU LAY DOWN NEXT
   TO ME
   (Barry White)
3. YOU CAN'T TURN ME OFF (IN THE
   MIDDLE OF TURNING ME ON)
   (High Inergy)
4. IF YOU'RE NOT BACK IN LOVE BY MONDAY
   (Millie Jackson)
5. SERPENTINE FIRE
   (Earth, Wind and Fire)
6. DUSIC
   (Brick)
7. DO YOUR DANCE (PART 1)
   (Rose Royce)
8. KEEP IT COMIN' LOVE
   (KC and the Sunshine Band)
9. GOIN' PLACES
   (The Jacksons)
10. DO YOU WANNA GET FUNKY WITH ME
    (Peter Brown)

BLACK ALBUMS

1. IN FULL BLOOM
   (Rose Royce)
2. BARRY WHITE SINGS FOR SOMEONE YOU
   LOVE
   (Barry White)
3. SOMETHING TO LOVE
   (L.T.D.)
4. TOO HOT TO HANDLE
   (Heatwave)
5. FEELIN' BITCHY
   (Millie Jackson)
6. COMMODORES
   (Commodores)
7. BRICK
   (Brick)
8. REJOICE
   (Emotions)
9. STAR WARS AND OTHER GALACTIC FUNK
   (Meco)
10. PATTI LABELLE
    (Patti Labelle)

JAZZ ALBUMS

1. REACH FOR IT
   (George Duke)
2. FEELS SO GOOD
   (Chuck Mangione)
3. ENIGMATIC OCEAN
   (Jean Luc Ponty)
4. LIFELINE
   (Roy Ayers Ubiquity)
5. ACTION
   (Blackbyrds)
6. BLOW IT OUT
   (Tom Scott)
7. RUBY, RUBY
   (Gato Barbieri)

8. NIGHTWINGS
   (Stanley Turrentine)
9. BRIDGES
   (Gil Scott-Heron and Brian Jackson)
10. LIFESTYLE
    (John Klemmer)

COUNTRY SINGLES

1. BLUE BAYOU
   (Linda Ronstadt)
2. WURLITZER PRIZE/LOOKIN' FOR A
   FEELING
   (Waylon Jennings)
3. MORE TO ME
   (Charley Pride)
4. ROSES FOR MAMA
   (C.W. McCall)
5. LOVE IS JUST A GAME
   (Larry Gatlin)
6. FROM GRACELAND TO THE PROMISED
   LAND
   (Merle Haggard)
7. HERE YOU COME AGAIN
   (Dolly Parton)
8. SHAME ON ME
   (Donna Fargo)
9. FOOLS FALL IN LOVE
   (Jacky Ward)
10. I'M JUST A COUNTRY BOY
    (Don Williams)

COUNTRY ALBUMS

1. ELVIS IN CONCERT
   (Elvis Presley)
2. WE MUST BELIEVE IN MAGIC
   (Crystal Gayle)
3. MOODY BLUE
   (Elvis Presley)
4. SIMPLE DREAMS
   (Linda Ronstadt)
5. IT WAS ALMOST LIKE A SONG
   (Ronnie Milsap)
6. HERE YOU COME AGAIN
   (Dolly Parton)
7. DAYTIME FRIENDS
   (Kenny Rogers)
8. OLIVIA NEWTON-JOHN'S GREATEST HITS
   (Olivia Newton-John)
9. OL' WAYLON
   (Waylon Jennings)
10. COUNTRY BOY
    (Don Williams)

NOVEMBER 26, 1977

POP SINGLES

1. YOU LIGHT UP MY LIFE
   (Debby Boone)
2. BOOGIE NIGHTS
   (Heatwave)
3. DON'T IT MAKE MY BROWN EYES BLUE
   (Crystal Gayle)
4. WE'RE ALL ALONE
   (Rita Coolidge)
5. NOBODY DOES IT BETTER
   (Carly Simon)
6. BLUE BAYOU
   (Linda Ronstadt)
7. HOW DEEP IS YOUR LOVE
   (The Bee Gees)
8. BABY, WHAT A BIG SURPRISE
   (Chicago)
9. IT'S ECSTASY WHEN YOU LAY DOWN NEXT
   TO ME
   (Barry White)
10. YOU MAKE LOVING FUN
    (Fleetwood Mac)

POP ALBUMS

1. RUMOURS
   (Fleetwood Mac)
2. SIMPLE DREAMS
   (Linda Ronstadt)
3. ELVIS IN CONCERT
   (Elvis Presley)
4. AJA
   (Steely Dan)
5. MOODY BLUE
   (Elvis Presley)
6. STREET SURVIVORS
   (Lynyrd Skynyrd)
7. SHAUN CASSIDY
   (Shaun Cassidy)
8. YOU LIGHT UP MY LIFE
   (Original Soundtrack)
9. YOU LIGHT UP MY LIFE
   (Debby Boone)
10. STAR WARS
    (Original Soundtrack)

BLACK SINGLES

1. (EVERY TIME I TURN AROUND) BACK IN
   LOVE AGAIN
   (L.T.D.)
2. YOU CAN'T TURN ME OFF (IN THE
   MIDDLE OF TURNING ME ON)
   (High Inergy)
3. IF YOU'RE NOT BACK IN LOVE BY MONDAY
   (Millie Jackson)
4. SERPENTINE FIRE
   (Earth, Wind and Fire)
5. IT'S ECSTASY WHEN YOU LAY DOWN NEXT
   TO ME
   (Barry White)
6. DUSIC
   (Brick)
7. DO YOUR DANCE (PART 1)
   (Rose Royce)
8. GOIN' PLACES
   (The Jacksons)
9. KEEP IT COMIN' LOVE
   (KC and the Sunshine Boys)
10. DON'T ASK MY NEIGHBORS
    (Emotions)

BLACK ALBUMS

1. IN FULL BLOOM
   (Rose Royce)
2. BARRY WHITE SINGS FOR SOMEONE YOU
   LOVE
   (Barry White)
3. SOMETHING TO LOVE
   (L.T.D.)
4. TOO HOT TO HANDLE
   (Heatwave)
5. COMMODORES LIVE
   (Commodores)
6. FEELIN' GOOD
   (Millie Jackson)
7. BRICK
   (Brick)
8. REJOICE
   (Emotions)
9. COMMODORES
   (Commodores)
10. BABY IT'S ME
    (Diana Ross)

JAZZ ALBUMS

1. REACH FOR IT
   (George Duke)
2. FEELS SO GOOD
   (Chuck Mangione)
3. ENIGMATIC OCEAN
   (Jean Luc Ponty)
4. ACTION
   (Blackbyrds)

5. LIFELINE
   (Roy Ayers Ubiquity)
6. RUBY, RUBY
   (Gato Barbieri)
7. BLOW IT OUT
   (Tom Scott)
8. BRIDGES
   (Gil Scott-Heron and Brian Jackson)
9. HEADS
   (Bob James)
10. NIGHTWINGS
    (Stanley Turrentine)

COUNTRY SINGLES

1. WURLITZER PRIZE/LOOKIN' FOR A
   FEELING
   (Waylon Jennings)
2. BLUE BAYOU
   (Linda Ronstadt)
3. MORE TO ME
   (Charley Pride)
4. FROM GRACELAND TO THE PROMISED
   LAND
   (Merle Haggard)
5. HERE YOU COME AGAIN
   (Dolly Parton)
6. ROSES FOR MAMA
   (C.W. McCall)
7. FOOLS FALL IN LOVE
   (Jacky Ward)
8. SHAME ON ME
   (Donna Fargo)
9. YOU LIGHT UP MY LIFE
   (Debby Boone)
10. ONE OF A KIND
    (Tammy Wynette)

COUNTRY ALBUMS

1. ELVIS IN CONCERT
   (Elvis Presley)
2. WE MUST BELIEVE IN MAGIC
   (Crystal Gayle)
3. MOODY BLUE
   (Elvis Presley)
4. SIMPLE DREAMS
   (Linda Ronstadt)
5. IT WAS ALMOST LIKE A SONG
   (Ronnie Milsap)
6. HERE YOU COME AGAIN
   (Dolly Parton)
7. DAYTIME FRIENDS
   (Kenny Rogers)
8. OLIVIA NEWTON-JOHN'S GREATEST HITS
   (Olivia Newton-John)
9. OL' WAYLON
   (Waylon Jennings)
10. COUNTRY BOY
    (Don Williams)

DECEMBER 3, 1977

POP SINGLES

1. YOU LIGHT UP MY LIFE
   (Debby Boone)
2. BOOGIE NIGHTS
   (Heatwave)
3. DON'T IT MAKE MY BROWN EYES BLUE
   (Crystal Gayle)
4. WE'RE ALL ALONE
   (Rita Coolidge)
5. BLUE BAYOU
   (Linda Ronstadt)
6. HOW DEEP IS YOUR LOVE
   (The Bee Gees)
7. NOBODY DOES IT BETTER
   (Carly Simon)
8. (EVERY TIME I TURN AROUND) BACK IN
   LOVE AGAIN
   (L.T.D.)

9. YOU MAKE LOVING FUN
   (Fleetwood Mac)
10. HEAVEN ON THE SEVENTH FLOOR
    (Paul Nicholas)

POP ALBUMS

1. RUMOURS
   (Fleetwood Mac)
2. SIMPLE DREAMS
   (Linda Ronstadt)
3. ELVIS IN CONCERT
   (Elvis Presley)
4. STREET SURVIVORS
   (Lynyrd Skynyrd)
5. AJA
   (Steely Dan)
6. MOODY BLUE
   (Elvis Presley)
7. SHAUN CASSIDY
   (Shaun Cassidy)
8. YOU LIGHT UP MY LIFE
   (Original Soundtrack)
9. YOU LIGHT UP MY LIFE
   (Debby Boone)
10. STAR WARS
    (Original Soundtrack)

BLACK SINGLES

1. (EVERY TIME I TURN AROUND) BACK IN
   LOVE AGAIN
   (L.T.D.)
2. YOU CAN'T TURN ME OFF (IN THE
   MIDDLE OF TURNING ME ON)
   (High Inergy)
3. SERPENTINE FIRE
   (Earth, Wind and Fire)
4. IF YOU'RE NOT BACK IN LOVE BY MONDAY
   (Millie Jackson)
5. IT'S ECSTASY WHEN YOU LAY DOWN NEXT
   TO ME
   (Barry White)
6. REACH FOR IT
   (George Duke)
7. NATIVE NEW YORKER
   (Odyssey)
8. GOIN' PLACES
   (The Jacksons)
9. DUSIC
   (Brick)
10. DON'T ASK MY NEIGHBORS
    (Emotions)

BLACK ALBUMS

1. IN FULL BLOOM
   (Rose Royce)
2. COMMODORES LIVE
   (Commodores)
3. SOMETHING TO LOVE
   (L.T.D.)
4. BARRY WHITE SINGS FOR SOMEONE YOU
   LOVE
   (Barry White)
5. TOO HOT TO HANDLE
   (Heatwave)
6. FEELIN' BITCHY
   (Millie Jackson)
7. BRICK
   (Brick)
8. REACH FOR IT
   (George Duke)
9. REJOICE
   (Emotions)
10. TURNIN' ON
    (High Inergy)

JAZZ ALBUMS

1. REACH FOR IT
   (George Duke)

2. FEELS SO GOOD
   (Chuck Mangione)
3. HEADS
   (Bob James)
4. ENIGMATIC OCEAN
   (Jean Luc Ponty)
5. ACTION
   (Blackbyrds)
6. RUBY, RUBY
   (Gato Barbieri)
7. BLOW IT OUT
   (Tom Scott)
8. LIFELINE
   (Roy Ayers Ubiquity)
9. MAGIC
   (Billy Cobham)
10. NIGHTWINGS
    (Stanley Turrentine)

COUNTRY SINGLES

1. HERE YOU COME AGAIN
   (Dolly Parton)
2. BLUE BAYOU
   (Linda Ronstadt)
3. WURLITZER PRIZE/LOOKIN' FOR A
   FEELING
   (Waylon Jennings)
4. FROM GRACELAND TO THE PROMISED
   LAND
   (Merle Haggard)
5. YOU LIGHT UP MY LIFE
   (Debby Boone)
6. ROSES FOR MAMA
   (C.W. McCall)
7. FOOLS FALL IN LOVE
   (Jacky Ward)
8. MORE TO ME
   (Charley Pride)
9. ONE OF A KIND
   (Tammy Wynette)
10. I'M KNEE DEEP IN LOVING YOU
    (Dave and Sugar)

COUNTRY ALBUMS

1. ELVIS IN CONCERT
   (Elvis Presley)
2. MOODY BLUE
   (Elvis Presley)
3. WE MUST BELIEVE IN MAGIC
   (Crystal Gayle)
4. SIMPLE DREAMS
   (Linda Ronstadt)
5. IT WAS ALMOST LIKE A SONG
   (Ronnie Milsap)
6. HERE YOU COME AGAIN
   (Dolly Parton)
7. DAYTIME FRIENDS
   (Kenny Rogers)
8. OLIVIA NEWTON-JOHN'S GREATEST HITS
   (Olivia Newton-John)
9. HEAVEN'S JUST A SIN AWAY
   (The Kendalls)
10. MY FAREWELL TO ELVIS
    (Merle Haggard)

DECEMBER 10, 1977

POP SINGLES

1. YOU LIGHT UP MY LIFE
   (Debby Boone)
2. DON'T IT MAKE MY BROWN EYES BLUE
   (Crystal Gayle)
3. BLUE BAYOU
   (Linda Ronstadt)
4. WE'RE ALL ALONE
   (Rita Coolidge)
5. HOW DEEP IS YOUR LOVE
   (The Bee Gees)

6. BOOGIE NIGHTS
   (Heatwave)
7. (EVERY TIME I TURN AROUND) BACK IN
   LOVE AGAIN
   (L.T.D.)
8. YOU MAKE LOVING FUN
   (Fleetwood Mac)
9. HEAVEN ON THE SEVENTH FLOOR
   (Paul Nicholas)
10. NOBODY DOES IT BETTER
    (Carly Simon)

POP ALBUMS

1. RUMOURS
   (Fleetwood Mac)
2. SIMPLE DREAMS
   (Linda Ronstadt)
3. ALIVE 2
   (Kiss)
4. STREET SURVIVORS
   (Lynyrd Skynyrd)
5. SHAUN CASSIDY
   (Shaun Cassidy)
6. COMMODORES
   (Commodores)
7. ELVIS IN CONCERT
   (Elvis Presley)
8. YOU LIGHT UP MY LIFE
   (Debby Boone)
9. YOU LIGHT UP MY LIFE
   (Original Soundtrack)
10. AJA
    (Steely Dan)

BLACK SINGLES

1. YOU CAN'T TURN ME OFF (IN THE
   MIDDLE OF TURNING ME ON)
   (High Inergy)
2. SERPENTINE FIRE
   (Earth, Wind and Fire)
3. (EVERY TIME I TURN AROUND) BACK IN
   LOVE AGAIN
   (L.T.D.)
4. REACH FOR IT
   (George Duke)
5. IF YOU'RE NOT BACK IN LOVE BY MONDAY
   (Millie Jackson)
6. NATIVE NEW YORKER
   (Odyssey)
7. IT'S ECSTASY WHEN YOU LAY DOWN NEXT
   TO ME
   (Barry White)
8. GOIN' PLACES
   (The Jacksons)
9. SOMEBODY'S GOTTA WIN, SOMEBODY'S
   GOTTA LOSE
   (The Controllers)
10. DUSIC
    (Brick)

BLACK ALBUMS

1. ALL 'N ALL
   (Earth, Wind and Fire)
2. COMMODORES LIVE
   (Commodores)
3. IN FULL BLOOM
   (Rose Royce)
4. SOMETHING TO LOVE
   (L.T.D.)
5. TOO HOT TO HANDLE
   (Heatwave)
6. FEELIN' BITCHY
   (Millie Jackson)
7. BARRY WHITE SINGS FOR SOMEONE YOU
   LOVE
   (Barry White)
8. REACH OUT
   (George Duke)
9. BRICK
   (Brick)

10. TURNIN' ON
    (High Inergy)

JAZZ ALBUMS

1. REACH FOR IT
   (George Duke)
2. HEADS
   (Bob James)
3. FEELS SO GOOD
   (Chuck Mangione)
4. ENIGMATIC OCEAN
   (Jean Luc Ponty)
5. ACTION
   (Blackbyrds)
6. RUBY, RUBY
   (Gato Barbieri)
7. MAGIC
   (Billy Cobham)
8. BLOW IT OUT
   (Tom Scott)
9. NEW VINTAGE
   (Maynard Ferguson)
10. LIFELINE
    (Roy Ayers Ubiquity)

COUNTRY SINGLES

1. HERE YOU COME AGAIN
   (Dolly Parton)
2. YOU LIGHT UP MY LIFE
   (Debby Boone)
3. BLUE BAYOU
   (Linda Ronstadt)
4. WURLITZER PRIZE/LOOKIN' FOR A
   FEELING
   (Waylon Jennings)
5. I'M KNEE DEEP IN LOVING YOU
   (Dave and Sugar)
6. FROM GRACELAND TO THE PROMISED
   LAND
   (Merle Haggard)
7. TAKE THIS JOB AND SHOVE IT
   (Johnny Paycheck)
8. ONE OF A KIND
   (Tammy Wynette)
9. DON'T LET ME TOUCH YOU
   (Marty Robbins)
10. GEORGIA KEEPS PULLING ON MY RING
    (Conway Twitty)

COUNTRY ALBUMS

1. ELVIS IN CONCERT
   (Elvis Presley)
2. MOODY BLUE
   (Elvis Presley)
3. WE MUST BELIEVE IN MAGIC
   (Crystal Gayle)
4. SIMPLE DREAMS
   (Linda Ronstadt)
5. HERE YOU COME AGAIN
   (Dolly Parton)
6. IT WAS ALMOST LIKE A SONG
   (Ronnie Milsap)
7. OLIVIA NEWTON-JOHN'S GREATEST HITS
   (Olivia Newton-John)
8. YOU LIGHT UP MY LIFE
   (Debby Boone)
9. HEAVEN'S JUST A SIN AWAY
   (The Kendalls)
10. MY FAREWELL TO ELVIS
    (Merle Haggard)

DECEMBER 17, 1977

POP SINGLES

1. YOU LIGHT UP MY LIFE
   (Debby Boone)

2. DON'T IT MAKE MY BROWN EYES BLUE
   (Crystal Gayle)
3. BLUE BAYOU
   (Linda Ronstadt)
4. HOW DEEP IS YOUR LOVE
   (The Bee Gees)
5. WE'RE ALL ALONE
   (Rita Coolidge)
6. (EVERY TIME I TURN AROUND) BACK IN LOVE AGAIN
   (L.T.D.)
7. BOOGIE NIGHTS
   (Heatwave)
8. HEAVEN ON THE SEVENTH FLOOR
   (Paul Nicholas)
9. SENTIMENTAL LADY
   (Bob Welch)
10. BABY COME BACK
    (Player)

POP ALBUMS

1. RUMOURS
   (Fleetwood Mac)
2. SIMPLE DREAMS
   (Linda Ronstadt)
3. ALIVE 2
   (Kiss)
4. SHAUN CASSIDY
   (Shaun Cassidy)
5. COMMODORES LIVE
   (Commodores)
6. ALL 'N ALL
   (Earth, Wind and Fire)
7. ELVIS IN CONCERT
   (Elvis Presley)
8. STREET SURVIVORS
   (Lynyrd Skynyrd)
9. FOOT LOOSE AND FANCY FREE
   (Rod Stewart)
10. OUT OF THE BLUE
    (Electric Light Orchestra)

BLACK SINGLES

1. SERPENTINE FIRE
   (Earth, Wind and Fire)
2. YOU CAN'T TURN ME OFF (IN THE MIDDLE OF TURNING ME ON)
   (High Inergy)
3. REACH FOR IT
   (George Duke)
4. (EVERY TIME I TURN AROUND) BACK IN LOVE AGAIN
   (L.T.D.)
5. NATIVE NEW YORKER
   (Odyssey)
6. IF YOU'RE NOT BACK IN LOVE BY MONDAY
   (Millie Jackson)
7. SOMEBODY'S GOTTA WIN, SOMEBODY'S GOTTA LOSE
   (The Controllers)
8. IT'S ECSTASY WHEN YOU LAY DOWN NEXT TO ME
   (Barry White)
9. DANCE, DANCE, DANCE (YOWSAH, YOWSAH, YOWSAH)
   (Chic)
10. DUSIC
    (Brick)

BLACK ALBUMS

1. ALL 'N ALL
   (Earth, Wind and Fire)
2. COMMODORES LIVE
   (Commodores)
3. IN FULL BLOOM
   (Rose Royce)
4. REACH FOR IT
   (George Duke)
5. FEELIN' BITCHY
   (Millie Jackson)

6. TOO HOT TO HANDLE
   (Heatwave)
7. SOMETHING TO LOVE
   (L.T.D.)
8. BARRY WHITE SINGS TO SOMEONE YOU LOVE
   (Barry White)
9. TURNIN' ON
   (High Inergy)
10. SECRETS
    (Con Funk Shun)

JAZZ ALBUMS

1. REACH FOR IT
   (George Duke)
2. HEADS
   (Bob James)
3. FEELS SO GOOD
   (Chuck Mangione)
4. ENIGMATIC OCEAN
   (Jean Luc Ponty)
5. ACTION
   (Blackbyrds)
6. MAGIC
   (Billy Cobham)
7. RUBY, RUBY
   (Gato Barbieri)
8. NEW VINTAGE
   (Maynard Ferguson)
9. BLOW IT OUT
   (Tom Scott)
10. LIFETIME
    (Roy Ayers Ubiquity)

COUNTRY SINGLES

1. HERE YOU COME AGAIN
   (Dolly Parton)
2. YOU LIGHT UP MY LIFE
   (Debby Boone)
3. BLUE BAYOU
   (Linda Ronstadt)
4. I'M KNEE DEEP IN LOVING YOU
   (Dave and Sugar)
5. TAKE THIS JOB AND SHOVE IT
   (Johnny Paycheck)
6. WURLITZER PRIZE/LOOKIN' FOR A FEELING
   (Waylon Jennings)
7. GEORGIA KEEPS PULLING ON MY RING
   (Conway Twitty)
8. COME A LITTLE BIT CLOSER
   (Johnny Duncan with Janie Fricke)
9. DON'T LET ME TOUCH YOU
   (Marty Robbins)
10. MY WAY
    (Elvis Presley)

COUNTRY ALBUMS

1. ELVIS IN CONCERT
   (Elvis Presley)
2. MOODY BLUE
   (Elvis Presley)
3. HERE YOU COME AGAIN
   (Dolly Parton)
4. WE MUST BELIEVE IN MAGIC
   (Crystal Gayle)
5. SIMPLE DREAMS
   (Linda Ronstadt)
6. IT WAS ALMOST LIKE A SONG
   (Ronnie Milsap)
7. DAYTIME FRIENDS
   (Kenny Rogers)
8. YOU LIGHT UP MY LIFE
   (Debby Boone)
9. MY FAREWELL TO ELVIS
   (Merle Haggard)
10. OL' WAYLON
    (Waylon Jennings)

DECEMBER 24, 1977

POP SINGLES

1. YOU LIGHT UP MY LIFE
   (Debby Boone)
2. HOW DEEP IS YOUR LOVE
   (The Bee Gees)
3. DON'T IT MAKE MY BROWN EYES BLUE
   (Crystal Gayle)
4. BLUE BAYOU
   (Linda Ronstadt)
5. BABY COME BACK
   (Player)
6. (EVERY TIME I TURN AROUND) BACK IN LOVE AGAIN
   (L.T.D.)
7. WE'RE ALL ALONE
   (Rita Coolidge)
8. SENTIMENTAL LADY
   (Bob Welch)
9. HEAVEN ON THE SEVENTH FLOOR
   (Paul Nicholas)
10. YOU'RE IN MY HEART (THE FINAL ACCLAIM)
    (Rod Stewart)

POP ALBUMS

1. RUMOURS
   (Fleetwood Mac)
2. SIMPLE DREAMS
   (Linda Ronstadt)
3. ALIVE 2
   (Kiss)
4. SHAUN CASSIDY
   (Shaun Cassidy)
5. ALL 'N ALL
   (Earth, Wind and Fire)
6. FOOT LOOSE AND FANCY FREE
   (Rod Stewart)
7. COMMODORES LIVE
   (Commodores)
8. OUT OF THE BLUE
   (Electric Light Orchestra)
9. BORN LATE
   (Shaun Cassidy)
10. ELVIS IN CONCERT
    (Elvis Presley)

BLACK SINGLES

1. SERPENTINE FIRE
   (Earth, Wind and Fire)
2. REACH FOR IT
   (George Duke)
3. YOU CAN'T TURN ME OFF (IN THE MIDDLE OF TURNING ME ON)
   (High Inergy)
4. NATIVE NEW YORKER
   (Odyssey)
5. (EVERY TIME I TURN AROUND) BACK IN LOVE AGAIN
   (L.T.D.)
6. SOMEBODY'S GOTTA WIN, SOMEBODY'S GOTTA LOSE
   (Controllers)
7. DANCE, DANCE, DANCE (YOWSAH, YOWSAH, YOWSAH)
   (Chic)
8. IF YOU'RE NOT BACK IN LOVE BY MONDAY
   (Millie Jackson)
9. LOVELY DAY
   (Bill Withers)
10. FFUN
    (Con Funk Shun)

BLACK ALBUMS

1. ALL 'N ALL
   (Earth, Wind and Fire)

2. COMMODORES LIVE
   (Commodores)
3. IN FULL BLOOM
   (Rose Royce)
4. REACH FOR IT
   (George Duke)
5. FEELIN' BITCHY
   (Millie Jackson)
6. TOO HOT TO HANDLE
   (Heatwave)
7. THANKFUL
   (Natalie Cole)
8. TURNIN' ON
   (High Inergy)
9. SOMETHING TO LOVE
   (L.T.D.)
10. FLYING HIGH ON YOUR LOVE
    (Bar-Kays)

JAZZ ALBUMS

1. REACH FOR IT
   (George Duke)
2. HEADS
   (Bob James)
3. FEELS SO GOOD
   (Chuck Mangione)
4. ENIGMATIC OCEAN
   (Jean Luc Ponty)
5. ACTION
   (Blackbyrds)
6. LIVE AT THE BIJOU
   (Grover Washington Jr.)
7. RUBY, RUBY
   (Gato Barbieri)
8. MAGIC
   (Billy Cobham)
9. TEQUILA MOCKINGBIRD
   (Ramsey Lewis)
10. NEW VINTAGE
    (Maynard Ferguson)

COUNTRY SINGLES

1. HERE YOU COME AGAIN
   (Dolly Parton)
2. I'M KNEE DEEP IN LOVING YOU
   (Dave and Sugar)
3. TAKE THIS JOB AND SHOVE IT
   (Johnny Paycheck)
4. YOU LIGHT UP MY LIFE
   (Debby Boone)
5. GEORGIA KEEPS PULLING ON MY RING
   (Conway Twitty)
6. COME A LITTLE BIT CLOSER
   (Johnny Duncan with Janie Fricke)
7. MY WAY
   (Elvis Presley)
8. DON'T LET ME TOUCH YOU
   (Marty Robbins)
9. MIDDLE AGE CRAZY
   (Jerry Lee Lewis)
10. SWEET MUSIC MAN
    (Kenny Rogers)

COUNTRY ALBUMS

1. ELVIS IN CONCERT
   (Elvis Presley)
2. SIMPLE DREAMS
   (Linda Ronstadt)
3. HERE YOU COME AGAIN
   (Dolly Parton)
4. MOODY BLUE
   (Elvis Presley)
5. OLIVIA NEWTON-JOHN'S GREATEST HITS
   (Olivia Newton-John)
6. WE MUST BELIEVE IN MAGIC
   (Crystal Gayle)
7. DAYTIME FRIENDS
   (Kenny Rogers)
8. I WANT TO LIVE
   (John Denver)
9. IT WAS ALMOST LIKE A SONG
   (Ronnie Milsap)
10. OL' WAYLON
    (Waylon Jennings)

DECEMBER 31, 1977

POP SINGLES

1. YOU LIGHT UP MY LIFE
   (Debby Boone)
2. HOW DEEP IS YOUR LOVE
   (The Bee Gees)
3. BABY COME BACK
   (Player)
4. DON'T IT MAKE MY BROWN EYES BLUE
   (Crystal Gayle)
5. BLUE BAYOU
   (Linda Ronstadt)
6. YOU'RE IN MY HEART (THE FINAL ACCLAIM)
   (Rod Stewart)
7. SENTIMENTAL LADY
   (Bob Welch)
8. (EVERY TIME I TURN AROUND) BACK IN LOVE AGAIN
   (L.T.D.)
9. WE'RE ALL ALONE
   (Rita Coolidge)
10. HEAVEN ON THE SEVENTH FLOOR
    (Paul Nicholas)

POP ALBUMS

1. RUMOURS
   (Fleetwood Mac)
2. SIMPLE DREAMS
   (Linda Ronstadt)
3. SHAUN CASSIDY
   (Shaun Cassidy)
4. ALIVE 2
   (Kiss)
5. ALL 'N ALL
   (Earth, Wind and Fire)
6. FOOT LOOSE AND FANCY FREE
   (Rod Stewart)
7. OUT OF THE BLUE
   (Electric Light Orchestra)
8. BORN LATE
   (Shaun Cassidy)
9. COMMODORES LIVE
   (Commodores)
10. NEWS OF THE WORLD
    (Queen)

BLACK SINGLES

1. SERPENTINE FIRE
   (Earth, Wind and Fire)
2. REACH FOR IT
   (George Duke)
3. YOU CAN'T TURN ME OFF (IN THE MIDDLE OF TURNING ME ON)
   (High Inergy)
4. DANCE, DANCE, DANCE (YOWSAH, YOWSAH, YOWSAH)
   (Chic)
5. NATIVE NEW YORKER
   (Odyssey)
6. LOVELY DAY
   (Bill Withers)
7. FFUN
   (Con Funk Shun)
8. OUR LOVE
   (Natalie Cole)
9. (EVERY TIME I TURN AROUND) BACK IN LOVE AGAIN
   (L.T.D.)
10. OOH BOY
    (Rose Royce)

BLACK ALBUMS

1. ALL 'N ALL
   (Earth, Wind and Fire)
2. COMMODORES LIVE
   (Commodores)
3. IN FULL BLOOM
   (Rose Royce)

4. REACH FOR IT
   (George Duke)
5. THANKFUL
   (Natalie Cole)
6. FUNKENTELECHY VS. THE PLACEBO SYNDROME
   (Parliament)
7. FEELIN' BITCHY
   (Millie Jackson)
8. GALAXY
   (War)
9. FLYING HIGH ON YOUR LOVE
   (Bar-Kays)
10. TOO HOT TO HANDLE
    (Heatwave)

JAZZ ALBUMS

1. REACH FOR IT
   (George Duke)
2. LIVE AT THE BIJOU
   (Grover Washington Jr.)
3. HEADS
   (Bob James)
4. FEELS SO GOOD
   (Chuck Mangione)
5. ENIGMATIC OCEAN
   (Jean Luc Ponty)
6. TEQUILA MOCKINGBIRD
   (Ramsey Lewis)
7. ACTION
   (Blackbyrds)
8. MAGIC
   (Billy Cobham)
9. NEW VINTAGE
   (Maynard Ferguson)
10. MULTIPLICATION
    (Eric Gale)

COUNTRY SINGLES

1. I'M KNEE DEEP IN LOVING YOU
   (Dave and Sugar)
2. TAKE THIS JOB AND SHOVE IT
   (Johnny Paycheck)
3. HERE YOU COME AGAIN
   (Dolly Parton)
4. MY WAY
   (Elvis Presley)
5. GEORGIA KEEPS PULLING ON MY RING
   (Conway Twitty)
6. COME A LITTLE BIT CLOSER
   (Johnny Duncan with Janie Fricke)
7. MIDDLE AGE CRAZY
   (Jerry Lee Lewis)
8. WHAT A DIFFERENCE YOU'VE MADE IN MY LIFE
   (Ronnie Milsap)
9. CHAINS OF LOVE
   (Mickey Gilley)
10. SWEET MUSIC MAN
    (Kenny Rogers)

COUNTRY ALBUMS

1. ELVIS IN CONCERT
   (Elvis Presley)
2. SIMPLE DREAMS
   (Linda Ronstadt)
3. HERE YOU COME AGAIN
   (Dolly Parton)
4. OLIVIA NEWTON-JOHN'S GREATEST HITS
   (Olivia Newton-John)
5. WE MUST BELIEVE IN MAGIC
   (Crystal Gayle)
6. MOODY BLUE
   (Elvis Presley)
7. I WANT TO LIVE
   (John Denver)
8. IT WAS ALMOST LIKE A SONG
   (Ronnie Milsap)
9. YOU LIGHT UP MY LIFE
   (Debby Boone)
10. DAYTIME FRIENDS
    (Kenny Rogers)

1978

This was the record industry's last full year of optimism, skyrocketing sales, and excess. Double and triple platinum albums were so plentiful that artists who merely went gold felt inferior in the presence of The Bee Gees, Fleetwood Mac, Billy Joel, Steely Dan, Meat Loaf, or any of their other platinum-plated contemporaries. Yet the recession was about to strike this "recession-proof" business, helped in large part by its executives. The classic example was the late Neil Bogart of Casablanca. Believing his own hype, Bogart released solo albums by the four members of Kiss at the same time, attempting to squeeze more cash from their young fans. He literally shipped almost a million albums and they were returned by the hundred thousands. By glutting the Kiss market, he destroyed it, at the same time forcing Casablanca to eat all those unsold LPs. The company never recovered and within three years was gobbled up by the multi-national PolyGram Records operation. Bogart, his promotional gifts intact, was able to get financing to begin Boardwalk Records and start the hype machine all over again.

RSO Records, owned by Australian media mogul Robert Stigwood, also would be disabled by the end of 1981, despite having three of 1978's top 10 recordings: "Saturday Night Fever," "Grease," and Eric Clapton's "Slowhand." Overshipping, mammoth returns, bootleg versions of RSO's music and the failure of the expensive *Sgt. Pepper's* film and soundtrack brought this mighty company to its knees.

Until *Sgt. Pepper*, Stigwood had proved himself a shrewd businessman. His wedding of The Bee Gee's newly discotized music and John Travolta's swaggering presence was simply brilliant. Tom Smucker described the impact this way: "Before *Saturday Night Fever* was released, there had been little way for most people to explore the burgeoning new (disco) scene. Outside of New York, Philadelphia, and Miami there were few discos to visit. Music that was specifically disco was still boycotted by many pop stations. And because the genre did not feature recognizable stars, there was no handle for an outsider to use to sort through the disco section in the record store.

"*Saturday Night Fever*—the movie and the soundtrack music—changed all that. First, there was the setting: a straight, white working-class disco. Shot at a real club—2001 Odyssey in Bay Ridge, Brooklyn—the movie accurately conveyed the unintimidating and non-elitist aspects of disco culture, while conveniently sidestepping its gay elements. There was John Travolta's wonderful average-Joe performance—a fleshing out of the dumb, arrogant, but lovable Brooklynite Barbarino he was playing on T.V.'s popular "Welcome Back, Kotter." There were the old and familiar Bee Gees on the soundtrack with a black-influenced sound that approached disco without straying too far from established pop conventions. And there was the pleasing assortment of disco classics (by The Trammps, Kool and the Gang, KC and the Sunshine Band, etc.)."

The other big story of 1978 was made by a guy who could have passed for a scruffy John Travolta, not in *Saturday Night Fever*, but as his leather-jacket character in *Grease*. Billy Joel was his name and with *The Stranger* he usurped Elton John's throne as pop's leading piano man. His "Just the Way You Are," a soft, sugar-coated ballad, established him as an across-the-board star. The album revealed Joel as a snappy pop rocker with a limited, but expressive, voice and an ear for pleasing hooks. Many critics detested him and in interviews Joel replied in kind, reflecting an combative nature that often appeared in his music.

Some Girls was The Rolling Stones' best work since *Exile on Main Street* and contained "Miss You"—a disco-ish, very New York record—their best single since "Brown Sugar." On "When the Whip Comes Down" and "Shattered" Mick Jagger, Keith Richard, and comrades displayed the ragged power that has, quite literally, made them legends in their own time.

The mountainous Meat Loaf was the year's surprise. His *Bat Out of Hell*—equal parts Springsteen, Steppenwolf, and Phil Spector—was the perfect vehicle for Mr. Loaf's operatic shouts. Be it the rocking "All Dressed Up with No Place to Go," the cold-hearted "Two Out of Three Ain't Bad," or the hilarious parody of teen lust "Paradise By the Dashboard Light," the album held together as an menagerie of ridiculous rock 'n' roll.

Though it upset her loyal country fans, Dolly Parton seduced the pop world with "Here You Come Again," cooing pop that her little-bird voice pushed onto top-40 radio. Moreover, Parton, with her impressive physique and winning personality, quickly moved on to "The Tonight Show" and films. Though musically gifted, Parton clearly wasn't afraid of using her most obvious assets to get ahead.

Waylon Jennings and Willie Nelson were so ubiquitous in the country market that they released an LP simply titled, *Waylon and Willie*. Their duet on "Mammas, Don't Let Your Babies Grow Up To Be Cowboys" made the song an instant classic. On *Stardust*, Nelson essayed a collection of Tin Pan Alley standards, stretching out vocally and in the process taking on the aura of a white Ray Charles.

The most striking country single of the year was Johnny Paycheck's "Take This Job and Shove It," a working-class anthem that reflected Waylon and Willie's influence over country.

The trend in black music was toward large self-contained bands: Earth, Wind and Fire's *All 'n All*, the Commodores' *Natural High*, Parliament's *Funkentelechy vs. the Placebo Syndrome*, Rose Royce's *In Full Bloom*, the Isley Brothers' *Showdown*. Yet there was one young act so traditional he seemed to have just stepped out of 1965. Peabo Bryson is a smooth, soulful, singer-songwriter whose catalogue overflows with love ballads. There was more than a touch of Sam Cooke and Donny Hathaway in his voice and his songwriting. *Reaching for the Sky* set a level of quality that Bryson has managed to maintain throughout the years. It yielded his most powerful love song, "Feel the Fire," a wedding of carnal and religious fervor that made it one of the 1970s' greatest ballads.

SINGLES: The top two jazz albums also contained two major pop singles. The title song from Chuck Mangione's *Feels So Good*, a bright, melodic instrumental, and George Benson's up tempo remake of "On Broadway," from his live *Weekend in L.A.*, showed that the term "jazz," at least in reference to the major sellers on the jazz chart, now meant almost nothing. What these men were doing was as mass oriented as anything by The Bee Gees.

And, man, did The Bee Gees turn out singles. Brothers Maurice, Robin, and Barry either wrote, sang on, or produced in 1979: their own "Night Fever," "How Deep is Your Love," and "Staying Alive"; kid brother Andy's "Shadow Dancing," "An Everlasting Love," and "Love is Thicker Than Water"; Samantha Sang's "Emotion"; and Yvonne Elliman's great "If I Can't Have You." Chic made its presence known outside disco with the campy "Dance, Dance, Dance (Yowsah, Yowsah, Yowsah.)" Lionel Richie attacked the pop audience in earnest with the banal "Three Times a Lady" for The Commodores. Kansas, once a boring art rock band, found redemption in the world of pop with the philosophical and depressing "Dust in the Wind" and the title song of *Point of Know Return*.

Arnold Shaw's *Honkers and Shouters* was the first book to study in depth rhythm and blues, the dominant form of black pop music before soul. "Thank God It's Friday" tried to match the success of "Saturday Night Fever" but instead was a waste of film stock. The soundtrack did contain two fine songs, Donna Summer's "Last Dance," her first real attempt at pop, and The Commodore's last great dance record "Too Hot Ta Trot."

The rock film event of the year was Martin Scorsese's documentary about The Band's 1976 farewell concert. Called *The Last Waltz*, it in fact had the timeless quality the title suggested. This was due in large part to The Band's lead guitarist-lyricist Robbie Robertson, who cut a romantic figure on screen, and Scorsese's abilities as a director. An all-star cast, including Eric Clapton, Muddy Waters, Bob Dylan, Joni Mitchell, Van Morrison, and many others, added to the film's historic significance. Perhaps the most memorable sequence is a studio scene in which The Band and The Staple Singers perform "The Weight." Stunning.

Tom Petty and the Heartbreakers

Courtesy MCA Records

Courtesy EPA Records

Isley Brothers

Courtesy Partee Records

Richard Pryor

The Bee Gees

The Staple Singers

The Clash

Bob Marley and the Commodores

JANUARY 14, 1978

POP SINGLES

1. WE ARE THE CHAMPIONS/WE WILL ROCK YOU
   (Queen)
2. BABY COME BACK
   (Player)
3. YOU LIGHT UP MY LIFE
   (Debby Boone)
4. YOU'RE IN MY HEART (THE FINAL ACCLAIM)
   (Rod Stewart)
5. HOW DEEP IS YOUR LOVE
   (The Bee Gees)
6. JUST THE WAY YOU ARE
   (Billy Joel)
7. HERE YOU COME AGAIN
   (Dolly Parton)
8. SHORT PEOPLE
   (Randy Newman)
9. COME SAIL AWAY
   (Styx)
10. BLUE BAYOU
    (Linda Ronstadt)

POP ALBUMS

1. RUMOURS
   (Fleetwood Mac)
2. SIMPLE DREAMS
   (Linda Ronstadt)
3. SHAUN CASSIDY
   (Shaun Cassidy)
4. ALIVE 2
   (Kiss)
5. SATURDAY NIGHT FEVER
   (Original Soundtrack)
6. FOOT LOOSE AND FANCY FREE
   (Rod Stewart)
7. ALL 'N ALL
   (Earth, Wind and Fire)
8. NEWS OF THE WORLD
   (Queen)
9. DRAW THE LINE
   (Aerosmith)
10. RUNNING ON EMPTY
    (Jackson Browne)

BLACK SINGLES

1. REACH FOR IT
   (George Duke)
2. SERPENTINE FIRE
   (Earth, Wind and Fire)
3. LOVELY DAY
   (Bill Withers)
4. DANCE DANCE, DANCE (YOWSAH, YOWSAH, YOWSAH)
   (Chic)
5. FFUN
   (Con Funk Shun)
6. OUR LOVE
   (Natalie Cole)
7. YOU CAN'T TURN ME OFF (IN THE MIDDLE OF TURNING ME ON)
   (High Inergy)
8. OOH BOY
   (Rose Royce)
9. NATIVE NEW YORKER
   (Odyssey)
10. (EVERY TIME I TURN AROUND) BACK IN LOVE AGAIN
    (L.T.D.)

BLACK ALBUMS

1. ALL 'N ALL
   (Earth, Wind and Fire)

2. FUNKENTELECHY VS. THE PLACEBO SYNDROME
   (Parliament)
3. IN FULL BLOOM
   (Rose Royce)
4. COMMODORES LIVE
   (Commodores)
5. REACH FOR IT
   (George Duke)
6. THANKFUL
   (Natalie Cole)
7. GALAXY
   (War)
8. TOO HOT TO HANDLE
   (Heatwave)
9. FEELIN' BITCHY
   (Millie Jackson)
10. SECRETS
    (Con Funk Shun)

JAZZ ALBUMS

1. REACH FOR IT
   (George Duke)
2. LIVE AT THE BIJOU
   (Grover Washington Jr.)
3. HEADS
   (Bob James)
4. FEELS SO GOOD
   (Chuck Mangione)
5. TEQUILA MOCKINGBIRD
   (Ramsey Lewis)
6. ACTION
   (Blackbyrds)
7. ENIGMATIC OCEAN
   (Jean Luc Ponty)
8. RUBY, RUBY
   (Gato Barbieri)
9. MULTIPLICATION
   (Eric Gale)
10. TRUE TO LIFE
    (Ray Charles)

COUNTRY SINGLES

1. TAKE THIS JOB AND SHOVE IT
   (Johnny Paycheck)
2. MY WAY
   (Elvis Presley)
3. WHAT A DIFFERENCE YOU'VE MADE IN MY LIFE
   (Ronnie Milsap)
4. MIDDLE AGE CRAZY
   (Jerry Lee Lewis)
5. I'M KNEE DEEP IN LOVING YOU
   (Dave and Sugar)
6. HERE YOU COME AGAIN
   (Dolly Parton)
7. COME A LITTLE BIT CLOSER
   (Johnny Duncan With Janie Fricke)
8. LONELY STREET
   (Rex Allen Jr.)
9. OUT OF MY HEAD AND BACK IN MY BED
   (Loretta Lynn)
10. CHAINS OF LOVE
    (Mickey Gilley)

COUNTRY ALBUMS

1. SIMPLE DREAMS
   (Linda Ronstadt)
2. ELVIS IN CONCERT
   (Elvis Presley)
3. HERE YOU COME AGAIN
   (Dolly Parton)
4. WE MUST BELIEVE IN MAGIC
   (Crystal Gayle)
5. OLIVIA NEWTON-JOHN'S GREATEST HITS
   (Olivia Newton-John)
6. MOODY BLUE
   (Elvis Presley)
7. YOU LIGHT UP MY LIFE
   (Debby Boone)
8. IT WAS ALMOST LIKE A SONG
   (Ronnie Milsap)

9. MY FAREWELL TO ELVIS
   (Merle Haggard)
10. DAYTIME FRIENDS
    (Kenny Rogers)

JANUARY 21, 1978

POP SINGLES

1. WE ARE THE CHAMPIONS/WE WILL ROCK YOU
   (Queen)
2. BABY COME BACK
   (Player)
3. SHORT PEOPLE
   (Randy Newman)
4. YOU'RE IN MY HEART (THE FINAL ACCLAIM)
   (Rod Stewart)
5. JUST THE WAY YOU ARE
   (Billy Joel)
6. HERE YOU COME AGAIN
   (Dolly Parton)
7. STAYIN' ALIVE
   (The Bee Gees)
8. YOU LIGHT UP MY LIFE
   (Debby Boone)
9. COME SAIL AWAY
   (Styx)
10. TURN TO STONE
    (Electric Light Orchestra)

POP ALBUMS

1. SATURDAY NIGHT FEVER
   (Original Soundtrack)
2. RUMOURS
   (Fleetwood Mac)
3. SIMPLE DREAMS
   (Linda Ronstadt)
4. SHAUN CASSIDY
   (Shaun Cassidy)
5. FOOT LOOSE AND FANCY FREE
   (Rod Stewart)
6. ALIVE 2
   (Kiss)
7. NEWS OF THE WORLD
   (Queen)
8. DRAW THE LINE
   (Aerosmith)
9. RUNNING ON EMPTY
   (Jackson Browne)
10. ALL 'N ALL
    (Earth, Wind and Fire)

BLACK SINGLES

1. FFUN
   (Con Funk Shun)
2. LOVELY DAY
   (Bill Withers)
3. DANCE, DANCE, DANCE (YOWSAH, YOWSAH, YOWSAH)
   (Chic)
4. OUR LOVE
   (Natalie Cole)
5. SERPENTINE FIRE
   (Earth, Wind and Fire)
6. REACH FOR IT
   (George Duke)
7. YOU CAN'T TURN ME OFF (IN THE MIDDLE OF TURNING ME ON)
   (High Inergy)
8. OOH BOY
   (Rose Royce)
9. GALAXY
   (War)
10. JACK AND JILL
    (Raydio)

BLACK ALBUMS

1. ALL 'N ALL
   (Earth, Wind and Fire)
2. FUNKENTELECHY VS. THE PLACEBO
   SYNDROME
   (Parliament)
3. COMMODORES LIVE
   (Commodores)
4. THANKFUL
   (Natalie Cole)
5. GALAXY
   (War)
6. IN FULL BLOOM
   (Rose Royce)
7. TOO HOT TO HANDLE
   (Heatwave)
8. MENAGERIE
   (Bill Withers)
9. SECRETS
   (Con Funk Shun)
10. SATURDAY NIGHT FEVER
    (Original Soundtrack)

JAZZ ALBUMS

1. LIVE AT THE BIJOU
   (Grover Washington Jr.)
2. REACH FOR IT
   (George Duke)
3. HEADS
   (Bob James)
4. FEELS SO GOOD
   (Chuck Mangione)
5. TEQUILA MOCKINGBIRD
   (Ramsey Lewis)
6. ENIGMATIC OCEAN
   (Jean Luc Ponty)
7. ACTION
   (Blackbyrds)
8. RUBY, RUBY
   (Gato Barbieri)
9. HAVANA CANDY
   (Patti Austin)
10. INNER VOICES
    (McCoy Tyner)

COUNTRY SINGLES

1. SIMPLE DREAMS
   (Linda Ronstadt)
2. HERE YOU COME AGAIN
   (Dolly Parton)
3. WE MUST BELIEVE IN MAGIC
   (Crystal Gayle)
4. ELVIS IN CONCERT
   (Elvis Presley)
5. DAYTIME FRIENDS
   (Kenny Rogers)
6. I WANT TO LIVE
   (John Denver)
7. OL' WAYLON
   (Waylon Jennings)
8. IT WAS ALMOST LIKE A SONG
   (Ronnie Milsap)
9. OLIVIA NEWTON-JOHN'S GREATEST HITS
   (Olivia Newton-John)
10. MY FAREWELL TO ELVIS
    (Merle Haggard)

COUNTRY ALBUMS

1. TAKE THIS JOB AND SHOVE IT
   (Johnny Paycheck)
2. WHAT A DIFFERENCE YOU'VE MADE IN
   MY LIFE
   (Ronnie Milsap)
3. MY WAY
   (Elvis Presley)
4. MIDDLE AGE CRAZY
   (Jerry Lee Lewis)
5. OUT OF MY HEAD AND BACK IN MY BED
   (Loretta Lynn)

6. I'M KNEE DEEP IN LOVING YOU
   (Dave and Sugar)
7. HERE YOU COME AGAIN
   (Dolly Parton)
8. LONELY STREET
   (Rex Allen Jr.)
9. TO DADDY
   (Emmylou Harris)
10. THE FIRST TIME
    (Billy "Crash" Craddock)

JANUARY 28, 1978

POP SINGLES

1. WE ARE THE CHAMPIONS/WE WILL ROCK
   YOU
   (Queen)
2. BABY COME BACK
   (Player)
3. SHORT PEOPLE
   (Randy Newman)
4. YOU'RE IN MY HEART (THE FINAL
   ACCLAIM)
   (Rod Stewart)
5. JUST THE WAY YOU ARE
   (Billy Joel)
6. STAYIN' ALIVE
   (The Bee Gees)
7. HERE YOU COME AGAIN
   (Dolly Parton)
8. SOMETIMES WHEN WE TOUCH
   (Dan Hill)
9. TURN TO STONE
   (Electric Light Orchestra)
10. SERPENTINE FIRE
    (Earth, Wind and Fire)

POP ALBUMS

1. SATURDAY NIGHT FEVER
   (Original Soundtrack)
2. RUMOURS
   (Fleetwood Mac)
3. NEWS OF THE WORLD
   (Queen)
4. FOOT LOOSE AND FANCY FREE
   (Rod Stewart)
5. ALL 'N ALL
   (Earth, Wind and Fire)
6. SIMPLE DREAMS
   (Linda Ronstadt)
7. RUNNING ON EMPTY
   (Jackson Browne)
8. DRAW THE LINE
   (Aerosmith)
9. ALIVE 2
   (Kiss)
10. BORN LATE
    (Shaun Cassidy)

BLACK SINGLES

1. FFUN
   (Con Funk Shun)
2. OUR LOVE
   (Natalie Cole)
3. DANCE, DANCE, DANCE (YOWSAH,
   YOWSAH, YOWSAH)
   (Chic)
4. LOVELY DAY
   (Bill Withers)
5. SERPENTINE FIRE
   (Earth, Wind and Fire)
6. REACH FOR IT
   (George Duke)
7. GALAXY
   (War)
8. JACK AND JILL
   (Raydio)

9. TOO HOT TA TROT
   (Commodores)
10. WHICH WAY IS UP
    (Stargard)

BLACK ALBUMS

1. ALL 'N ALL
   (Earth, Wind and Fire)
2. FUNKENTELECHY VS. THE PLACEBO
   SYNDROME
   (Parliament)
3. COMMODORES LIVE
   (Commodores)
4. GALAXY
   (War)
5. THANKFUL
   (Natalie Cole)
6. SATURDAY NIGHT FEVER
   (Original Soundtrack)
7. TOO HOT TO HANDLE
   (Heatwave)
8. IN FULL BLOOM
   (Rose Royce)
9. SECRETS
   (Con Funk Shun)
10. MENAGERIE
    (Bill Withers)

JAZZ ALBUMS

1. LIVE AT THE BIJOU
   (Grover Washington Jr.)
2. REACH FOR IT
   (George Duke)
3. HEADS
   (Bob James)
4. FEELS SO GOOD
   (Chuck Mangione)
5. TEQUILA MOCKINGBIRD
   (Ramsey Lewis)
6. ENIGMATIC OCEAN
   (Jean Luc Ponty)
7. HAVANA CANDY
   (Patti Austin)
8. ACTION
   (Blackbyrds)
9. RUBY, RUBY
   (Gato Barbieri)
10. MULTIPLICATION
    (Eric Gale)

COUNTRY SINGLES

1. WHAT A DIFFERENCE YOU'VE MADE IN
   MY LIFE
   (Ronnie Milsap)
2. TAKE THIS JOB AND SHOVE IT
   (Johnny Paycheck)
3. OUT OF MY HEAD AND BACK IN MY BED
   (Loretta Lynn)
4. MIDDLE AGE CRAZY
   (Jerry Lee Lewis)
5. MY WAY
   (Elvis Presley)
6. TO DADDY
   (Emmylou Harris)
7. YOU'RE THE ONE
   (The Oak Ridge Boys)
8. LONELY STREET
   (Rex Allen Jr.)
9. I JUST WISH YOU WERE SOMEONE I LOVE
   (Larry Gatlin)
10. THE FIRST TIME
    (Billy "Crash" Craddock)

COUNTRY ALBUMS

1. HERE YOU COME AGAIN
   (Dolly Parton)
2. SIMPLE DREAMS
   (Linda Ronstadt)

3. WE MUST BELIEVE IN MAGIC
   (Crystal Gayle)
4. TAKE THIS JOB AND SHOVE IT
   (Johnny Paycheck)
5. DAYTIME FRIENDS
   (Kenny Rogers)
6. I WANT TO LIVE
   (John Denver)
7. OL' WAYLON
   (Waylon Jennings)
8. OLIVIA NEWTON-JOHN'S GREATEST HITS
   (Olivia Newton-John)
9. YOU LIGHT UP MY LIFE
   (Debby Boone)
10. IT WAS ALMOST LIKE A SONG
    (Ronnie Milsap)

FEBRUARY 4, 1978

POP SINGLES

1. STAYIN' ALIVE
   (The Bee Gees)
2. WE ARE THE CHAMPIONS/WE WILL ROCK YOU
   (Queen)
3. BABY COME BACK
   (Player)
4. JUST THE WAY YOU ARE
   (Billy Joel)
5. SHORT PEOPLE
   (Randy Newman)
6. SOMETIMES WHEN WE TOUCH
   (Dan Hill)
7. YOU'RE IN MY HEART (THE FINAL ACCLAIM)
   (Rod Stewart)
8. HERE YOU COME AGAIN
   (Dolly Parton)
9. DANCE, DANCE, DANCE (YOWSAH, YOWSAH, YOWSAH)
   (Chic)
10. SERPENTINE FIRE
    (Earth, Wind and Fire)

POP ALBUMS

1. SATURDAY NIGHT FEVER
   (Original Soundtrack)
2. RUMOURS
   (Fleetwood Mac)
3. NEWS OF THE WORLD
   (Queen)
4. FOOT LOOSE AND FANCY FREE
   (Rod Stewart)
5. ALL 'N ALL
   (Earth, Wind and Fire)
6. RUNNING ON EMPTY
   (Jackson Browne)
7. SIMPLE DREAMS
   (Linda Ronstadt)
8. ALIVE 2
   (Kiss)
9. BORN LATE
   (Shaun Cassidy)
10. I'M GLAD YOU'RE HERE WITH ME TONIGHT
    (Neil Diamond)

BLACK SINGLES

1. FFUN
   (Con Funk Shun)
2. OUR LOVE
   (Natalie Cole)
3. DANCE, DANCE, DANCE (YOWSAH, YOWSAH, YOWSAH)
   (Chic)
4. WHICH WAY IS UP
   (Stargard)

5. JACK AND JILL
   (Raydio)
6. TOO HOT TA TROT
   (Commodores)
7. GALAXY
   (War)
8. LOVELY DAY
   (Bill Withers)
9. ALWAYS AND FOREVER
   (Heatwave)
10. SERPENTINE FIRE
    (Earth, Wind and Fire)

BLACK ALBUMS

1. ALL 'N ALL
   (Earth, Wind and Fire)
2. SATURDAY NIGHT FEVER
   (Original Soundtrack)
3. FUNKENTELECHY VS. THE PLACEBO SYNDROME
   (Parliament)
4. THANKFUL
   (Natalie Cole)
5. GALAXY
   (War)
6. COMMODORES LIVE
   (Commodores)
7. SECRETS
   (Con Funk Shun)
8. IN FULL BLOOM
   (Rose Royce)
9. FLYING HIGH ON YOUR LOVE
   (Bar-Kays)
10. MENAGERIE
    (Bill Withers)

JAZZ ALBUMS

1. LIVE AT THE BIJOU
   (Grover Washington Jr.)
2. HEADS
   (Bob James)
3. FEELS SO GOOD
   (Chuck Mangione)
4. REACH FOR IT
   (George Duke)
5. TEQUILA MOCKINGBIRD
   (Ramsey Lewis)
6. HAVANA CANDY
   (Patti Austin)
7. ENIGMATIC OCEAN
   (Jean Luc Ponty)
8. ACTION
   (Blackbyrds)
9. RUBY, RUBY
   (Gato Barbieri)
10. MULTIPLICATION
    (Eric Gale)

COUNTRY SINGLES

1. OUT OF MY HEAD AND BACK IN MY BED
   (Loretta Lynn)
2. TAKE THIS JOB AND SHOVE IT
   (Johnny Paycheck)
3. WHAT A DIFFERENCE YOU'VE MADE IN MY LIFE
   (Ronnie Milsap)
4. TO DADDY
   (Emmylou Harris)
5. YOU'RE THE ONE
   (The Oak Ridge Boys)
6. I JUST WISH YOU WERE SOMEONE I LOVE
   (Larry Gatlin)
7. MIDDLE AGE CRAZY
   (Jerry Lee Lewis)
8. DON'T BREAK THE HEART THAT LOVES YOU
   (Margo Smith)
9. WHAT DID I PROMISE HER LAST NIGHT
   (Mel Tillis)
10. SOMETHING TO BRAG ABOUT
    (Mary Kay Place)

COUNTRY ALBUMS

1. HERE YOU COME AGAIN
   (Dolly Parton)
2. SIMPLE DREAMS
   (Linda Ronstadt)
3. WE MUST BELIEVE IN MAGIC
   (Crystal Gayle)
4. TAKE THIS JOB AND SHOVE IT
   (Johnny Paycheck)
5. OLIVIA NEWTON-JOHN'S GREATEST HITS
   (Olivia Newton-John)
6. IT WAS ALMOST LIKE A SONG
   (Ronnie Milsap)
7. DAYTIME FRIENDS
   (Kenny Rogers)
8. YOU LIGHT UP MY LIFE
   (Debby Boone)
9. OL' WAYLON
   (Waylon Jennings)
10. TEN YEARS OF GOLD
    (Kenny Rogers)

FEBRUARY 11, 1978

POP SINGLES

1. STAYIN' ALIVE
   (The Bee Gees)
2. WE ARE THE CHAMPIONS/WE WILL ROCK YOU
   (Queen)
3. JUST THE WAY YOU ARE
   (Billy Joel)
4. BABY COME BACK
   (Player)
5. SOMETIMES WHEN WE TOUCH
   (Dan Hill)
6. SHORT PEOPLE
   (Randy Newman)
7. (LOVE IS) THICKER THAN WATER
   (Andy Gibb)
8. DANCE, DANCE, DANCE (YOWSAH, YOWSAH, YOWSAH)
   (Chic)
9. YOU'RE IN MY HEART (THE FINAL ACCLAIM)
   (Rod Stewart)
10. EMOTION
    (Samantha Sang)

POP ALBUMS

1. SATURDAY NIGHT FEVER
   (Original Soundtrack)
2. NEWS OF THE WORLD
   (Queen)
3. RUMOURS
   (Fleetwood Mac)
4. FOOT LOOSE AND FANCY FREE
   (Rod Stewart)
5. ALL 'N ALL
   (Earth, Wind and Fire)
6. RUNNING ON EMPTY
   (Jackson Browne)
7. SIMPLE DREAMS
   (Linda Ronstadt)
8. THE STRANGER
   (Billy Joel)
9. ALIVE 2
   (Kiss)
10. BORN LATE
    (Shaun Cassidy)

BLACK SINGLES

1. OUR LOVE
   (Natalie Cole)
2. WHICH WAY IS UP
   (Stargard)

3. DANCE, DANCE, DANCE (YOWSAH, YOWSAH, YOWSAH)
   (Chic)
4. TOO HOT TA TROT
   (Commodores)
5. JACK AND JILL
   (Raydio)
6. FFUN
   (Con Funk Shun)
7. ALWAYS AND FOREVER
   (Heatwave)
8. GALAXY
   (War)
9. LOVELY DAY
   (Bill Withers)
10. LOVE ME RIGHT
    (Denise LaSalle)

BLACK ALBUMS

1. SATURDAY NIGHT FEVER
   (Original Soundtrack)
2. ALL 'N ALL
   (Earth, Wind and Fire)
3. FUNKENTELECHY VS. THE PLACEBO SYNDROME
   (Parliament)
4. THANKFUL
   (Natalie Cole)
5. COMMODORES LIVE
   (Commodores)
6. SECRETS
   (Con Funk Shun)
7. GALAXY
   (War)
8. FLYING HIGH ON YOUR LOVE
   (Bar-Kays)
9. BLUE LIGHTS IN THE BASEMENT
   (Roberta Flack)
10. WHEN YOU HEAR LOU, YOU'VE HEARD IT ALL
    (Lou Rawls)

JAZZ ALBUMS

1. LIVE AT THE BIJOU
   (Grover Washington Jr.)
2. WEEKEND IN L.A.
   (George Benson)
3. HEADS
   (Bob James)
4. FEELS SO GOOD
   (Chuck Mangione)
5. REACH FOR IT
   (George Duke)
6. TEQUILA MOCKINGBIRD
   (Ramsey Lewis)
7. HAVANA CANDY
   (Patti Austin)
8. ENIGMATIC OCEAN
   (Jean Luc Ponty)
9. RUBY, RUBY
   (Gato Barbieri)
10. INNER VOICES
    (McCoy Tyner)

COUNTRY SINGLES

1. OUT OF MY HEAD AND BACK IN MY BED
   (Loretta Lynn)
2. TO DADDY
   (Emmylou Harris)
3. YOU'RE THE ONE
   (The Oak Ridge Boys)
4. I JUST WISH YOU WERE SOMEONE I LOVE
   (Larry Gatlin)
5. WHAT A DIFFERENCE YOU'VE MADE IN MY LIFE
   (Ronnie Milsap)
6. DON'T BREAK THE HEART THAT LOVES YOU
   (Margo Smith)
7. WHAT DID I PROMISE HER LAST NIGHT
   (Mel Tillis)

8. WOMAN TO WOMAN
   (Barbara Mandrell)
9. SOMETHING TO BRAG ABOUT
   (Mary Kay Place)
10. DO I LOVE YOU (YES IN EVERY WAY)
    (Donna Fargo)

COUNTRY ALBUMS

1. WAYLON AND WILLIE
   (Waylon Jennings and Willie Nelson)
2. HERE YOU COME AGAIN
   (Dolly Parton)
3. SIMPLE DREAMS
   (Linda Ronstadt)
4. TEN YEARS OF GOLD
   (Kenny Rogers)
5. OLIVIA NEWTON-JOHN'S GREATEST HITS
   (Olivia Newton-John)
6. IT WAS ALMOST LIKE A SONG
   (Ronnie Milsap)
7. TAKE THIS JOB AND SHOVE IT
   (Johnny Paycheck)
8. WE MUST BELIEVE IN MAGIC
   (Crystal Gayle)
9. QUARTER MOON IN A TEN CENT TOWN
   (Emmylou Harris)
10. DAYTIME FRIENDS
    (Kenny Rogers)

FEBRUARY 18, 1978

POP SINGLES

1. STAYIN' ALIVE
   (The Bee Gees)
2. WE ARE THE CHAMPIONS/WE WILL ROCK YOU
   (Queen)
3. JUST THE WAY YOU ARE
   (Billy Joel)
4. SOMETIMES WHEN WE TOUCH
   (Dan Hill)
5. (LOVE IS) THICKER THAN WATER
   (Andy Gibb)
6. BABY COME BACK
   (Player)
7. EMOTION
   (Samantha Sang)
8. DANCE, DANCE, DANCE (YOWSAH, YOWSAH, YOWSAH)
   (Chic)
9. SHORT PEOPLE
   (Randy Newman)
10. YOU'RE IN MY HEART (THE FINAL ACCLAIM)
    (Rod Stewart)

POP ALBUMS

1. SATURDAY NIGHT FEVER
   (Original Soundtrack)
2. NEWS OF THE WORLD
   (Queen)
3. RUMOURS
   (Fleetwood Mac)
4. FOOT LOOSE AND FANCY FREE
   (Rod Stewart)
5. ALL 'N ALL
   (Earth, Wind and Fire)
6. RUNNING ON EMPTY
   (Jackson Browne)
7. SIMPLE DREAMS
   (Linda Ronstadt)
8. THE STRANGER
   (Billy Joel)
9. BORN LATE
   (Shaun Cassidy)
10. I'M GLAD YOU'RE HERE WITH ME TONIGHT
    (Neil Diamond)

BLACK SINGLES

1. OUR LOVE
   (Natalie Cole)
2. WHICH WAY IS UP
   (Stargard)
3. TOO HOT TA TROT
   (Commodores)
4. ALWAYS AND FOREVER
   (Heatwave)
5. JACK AND JILL
   (Raydio)
6. DANCE, DANCE, DANCE (YOWSAH, YOWSAH, YOWSAH)
   (Chic)
7. FFUN
   (Con Funk Shun)
8. LOVE ME RIGHT
   (Denise LaSalle)
9. LOVELY DAY
   (Bill Withers)
10. IT'S YOU THAT I NEED
    (Enchantment)

BLACK ALBUMS

1. SATURDAY NIGHT FEVER
   (Original Soundtrack)
2. ALL 'N ALL
   (Earth, Wind and Fire)
3. THANKFUL
   (Natalie Cole)
4. FUNKENTELECHY VS. THE PLACEBO SYNDROME
   (Parliament)
5. COMMODORES LIVE
   (Commodores)
6. BLUE LIGHTS IN THE BASEMENT
   (Roberta Flack)
7. GOLDEN TIME OF DAY
   (Maze featuring Frankie Beverly)
8. WEEKEND IN L.A.
   (George Benson)
9. FLYING HIGH ON YOUR LOVE
   (Bar-Kays)
10. STREET PLAYER
    (Rufus/Chaka Khan)

JAZZ ALBUMS

1. WEEKEND IN L.A.
   (George Benson)
2. LIVE AT THE BIJOU
   (Grover Washington Jr.)
3. HEADS
   (Bob James)
4. FEELS SO GOOD
   (Chuck Mangione)
5. REACH FOR IT
   (George Duke)
6. TEQUILA MOCKINGBIRD
   (Ramsey Lewis)
7. HAVANA CANDY
   (Patti Austin)
8. ENIGMATIC OCEAN
   (Jean Luc Ponty)
9. INNER VOICES
   (McCoy Tyner)
10. WINDOW OF A CHILD
    (Seawind)

COUNTRY SINGLES

1. DON'T BREAK THE HEART THAT LOVES YOU
   (Margo Smith)
2. TO DADDY
   (Emmylou Harris)
3. YOU'RE THE ONE
   (The Oak Ridge Boys)
4. I JUST WISH YOU WERE SOMEONE I LOVE
   (Larry Gatlin)

5. OUT OF MY HEAD AND BACK IN MY BED
   (Loretta Lynn)
6. WHAT DID I PROMISE HER LAST NIGHT
   (Mel Tillis)
7. WOMAN TO WOMAN
   (Barbara Mandrell)
8. DO I LOVE YOU (YES IN EVERY WAY)
   (Donna Fargo)
9. MAMMAS, DON'T LET YOUR BABIES GROW UP TO BE COWBOYS
   (Waylon Jennings and Willie Nelson)
10. I DON'T NEED A THING AT ALL
    (Gene Watson)

COUNTRY ALBUMS

1. WAYLON AND WILLIE
   (Waylon Jennings and Willie Nelson)
2. TEN YEARS OF GOLD
   (Kenny Rogers)
3. QUARTER MOON IN A TEN CENT TOWN
   (Emmylou Harris)
4. HERE YOU COME AGAIN
   (Dolly Parton)
5. SIMPLE DREAMS
   (Linda Ronstadt)
6. WE MUST BELIEVE IN MAGIC
   (Crystal Gayle)
7. TAKE THIS JOB AND SHOVE IT
   (Johnny Paycheck)
8. OLIVIA NEWTON-JOHN'S GREATEST HITS
   (Olivia Newton-John)
9. IT WAS ALMOST LIKE A SONG
   (Ronnie Milsap)
10. GEORGIA KEEPS PULLING ON MY RING
    (Conway Twitty)

FEBRUARY 25, 1978

POP SINGLES

1. STAYIN' ALIVE
   (The Bee Gees)
2. (LOVE IS) THICKER THAN WATER
   (Andy Gibb)
3. SOMETIMES WHEN WE TOUCH
   (Dan Hill)
4. WE ARE THE CHAMPIONS/WE WILL ROCK YOU
   (Queen)
5. JUST THE WAY YOU ARE
   (Billy Joel)
6. EMOTION
   (Samantha Sang)
7. BABY COME BACK
   (Player)
8. DANCE, DANCE, DANCE (YOWSAH, YOWSAH, YOWSAH)
   (Chic)
9. SHORT PEOPLE
   (Randy Newman)
10. YOU'RE IN MY HEART (THE FINAL ACCLAIM)
    (Rod Stewart)

POP ALBUMS

1. SATURDAY NIGHT FEVER
   (Original Soundtrack)
2. NEWS OF THE WORLD
   (Queen)
3. RUMOURS
   (Fleetwood Mac)
4. RUNNING ON EMPTY
   (Jackson Browne)
5. THE STRANGER
   (Billy Joel)
6. ALL 'N ALL
   (Earth, Wind and Fire)
7. FOOT LOOSE AND FANCY FREE
   (Rod Stewart)

8. SIMPLE DREAMS
   (Linda Ronstadt)
9. BORN LATE
   (Shaun Cassidy)
10. I'M GLAD YOU'RE HERE WITH ME TONIGHT
    (Neil Diamond)

BLACK SINGLES

1. WHICH WAY IS UP
   (Stargard)
2. OUR LOVE
   (Natalie Cole)
3. ALWAYS AND FOREVER
   (Heatwave)
4. TOO HOT TA TROT
   (Commodores)
5. FLASH LIGHT
   (Parliament)
6. JACK AND JILL
   (Raydio)
7. IT'S YOU THAT I NEED
   (Enchantment)
8. LOVE ME RIGHT
   (Denise LaSalle)
9. DANCE, DANCE, DANCE (YOWSAH, YOWSAH, YOWSAH)
   (Chic)
10. BABY COME BACK
    (Player)

BLACK ALBUMS

1. SATURDAY NIGHT FEVER
   (Original Soundtrack)
2. ALL 'N ALL
   (Earth, Wind and Fire)
3. FUNKENTELECHY VS. THE PLACEBO SYNDROME
   (Parliament)
4. THANKFUL
   (Natalie Cole)
5. BLUE LIGHTS IN THE BASEMENT
   (Roberta Flack)
6. GOLDEN TIME OF DAY
   (Maze featuring Frankie Beverly)
7. WEEKEND IN L.A.
   (George Benson)
8. STREET PLAYER
   (Rufus/Chaka Khan)
9. COMMODORES LIVE
   (Commodores)
10. FLYING HIGH ON YOUR LOVE
    (Bar-Kays)

JAZZ ALBUMS

1. WEEKEND IN L.A.
   (George Benson)
2. LIVE AT THE BIJOU
   (Grover Washington Jr.)
3. HEADS
   (Bob James)
4. FEELS SO GOOD
   (Chuck Mangione)
5. REACH FOR IT
   (George Duke)
6. TEQUILA MOCKINGBIRD
   (Ramsey Lewis)
7. HAVANA CANDY
   (Patti Austin)
8. WINDOW OF A CHILD
   (Seawind)
9. HERB ALPERT-HUGH MASEKELA
   (Herb Alpert and Hugh Masekela)
10. HOLD ON
    (Noel Pointer)

COUNTRY SINGLES

1. DON'T BREAK THE HEART THAT LOVES YOU
   (Margo Smith)

2. MAMMAS, DON'T LET YOUR BABIES GROW UP TO BE COWBOYS
   (Waylon Jennings and Willie Nelson)
3. DO I LOVE YOU (YES IN EVERY WAY)
   (Donna Fargo)
4. WHAT DID I PROMISE HER LAST NIGHT
   (Mel Tillis)
5. WOMAN TO WOMAN
   (Barbara Mandrell)
6. I JUST WISH YOU WERE SOMEONE I LOVE
   (Larry Gatlin)
7. YOU'RE THE ONE
   (The Oak Ridge Boys)
8. I LOVE YOU, I LOVE YOU, I LOVE YOU
   (Ronnie McDowell)
9. TO DADDY
   (Emmylou Harris)
10. I DON'T NEED A THING AT ALL
    (Gene Watson)

COUNTRY ALBUMS

1. WAYLON AND WILLIE
   (Waylon Jennings and Willie Nelson)
2. TEN YEARS OF GOLD
   (Kenny Rogers)
3. QUARTER MOON IN A TEN CENT TOWN
   (Emmylou Harris)
4. HERE YOU COME AGAIN
   (Dolly Parton)
5. TAKE THIS JOB AND SHOVE IT
   (Johnny Paycheck)
6. WE MUST BELIEVE IN MAGIC
   (Crystal Gayle)
7. SIMPLE DREAMS
   (Linda Ronstadt)
8. OLIVIA NEWTON-JOHN'S GREATEST HITS
   (Olivia Newton-John)
9. IT WAS ALMOST LIKE A SONG
   (Ronnie Milsap)
10. GEORGIA KEEPS PULLING ON MY RING
    (Conway Twitty)

MARCH 4, 1978

POP SINGLES

1. (LOVE IS) THICKER THAN WATER
   (Andy Gibb)
2. STAYIN' ALIVE
   (The Bee Gees)
3. SOMETIMES WHEN WE TOUCH
   (Dan Hill)
4. WE ARE THE CHAMPIONS/WE WILL ROCK YOU
   (Queen)
5. EMOTION
   (Samantha Sang)
6. JUST THE WAY YOU ARE
   (Billy Joel)
7. NIGHT FEVER
   (The Bee Gees)
8. BABY COME BACK
   (Player)
9. SHORT PEOPLE
   (Randy Newman)
10. THEME FROM "CLOSE ENCOUNTERS OF THE THIRD KIND"
    (John Williams)

POP ALBUMS

1. SATURDAY NIGHT FEVER
   (Original Soundtrack)
2. NEWS OF THE WORLD
   (Queen)
3. THE STRANGER
   (Billy Joel)
4. RUNNING ON EMPTY
   (Jackson Browne)

5. RUMOURS
    (Fleetwood Mac)
6. ALL 'N ALL
    (Earth, Wind and Fire)
7. FOOT LOOSE AND FANCY FREE
    (Rod Stewart)
8. SIMPLE DREAMS
    (Linda Ronstadt)
9. THE GRAND ILLUSION
    (Styx)
10. BORN LATE
    (Shaun Cassidy)

BLACK SINGLES

1. FLASH LIGHT
    (Parliament)
2. OUR LOVE
    (Natalie Cole)
3. WHICH WAY IS UP
    (Stargard)
4. ALWAYS AND FOREVER
    (Heatwave)
5. IT'S YOU THAT I NEED
    (Enchantment)
6. TOO HOT TA TROT
    (Commodores)
7. JACK AND JILL
    (Raydio)
8. LOVE ME RIGHT
    (Denise LaSalle)
9. STAYIN' ALIVE
    (The Bee Gees)
10. BOOTZILLA
    (Bootsy's Rubber Band)

BLACK ALBUMS

1. SATURDAY NIGHT FEVER
    (Original Soundtrack)
2. ALL 'N ALL
    (Earth, Wind and Fire)
3. FUNKENTELECHY VS. THE PLACEBO
    SYNDROME
    (Parliament)
4. THANKFUL
    (Natalie Cole)
5. BLUE LIGHTS IN THE BASEMENT
    (Roberta Flack)
6. GOLDEN TIME OF DAY
    (Maze featuring Frankie Beverly)
7. WEEKEND IN L.A.
    (George Benson)
8. STREET PLAYER
    (Rufus/Chaka Khan)
9. BOOTSY: PLAYER OF THE YEAR
    (Bootsy's Rubber Band)
10. LIVE AT THE BIJOU
    (Grover Washington Jr.)

JAZZ ALBUMS

1. WEEKEND IN L.A.
    (George Benson)
2. LIVE AT THE BIJOU
    (Grover Washington Jr.)
3. HEADS
    (Bob James)
4. FEELS SO GOOD
    (Chuck Mangione)
5. TEQUILA MOCKINGBIRD
    (Ramsey Lewis)
6. HERB ALPERT-HUGH MASEKELA
    (Herb Alpert and Hugh Masekela)
7. HOLD ON
    (Noel Pointer)
8. HAVANA CANDY
    (Patti Austin)
9. WINDOW OF A CHILD
    (Seawind)
10. RAINBOW SEEKER
    (Joe Sample)

COUNTRY SINGLES

1. DON'T BREAK THE HEART THAT LOVES
    YOU
    (Margo Smith)
2. MAMMAS, DON'T LET YOUR BABIES GROW
    UP TO BE COWBOYS
    (Waylon Jennings and Willie Nelson)
3. DO I LOVE YOU (YES IN EVERY WAY)
    (Donna Fargo)
4. WHAT DID I PROMISE HER LAST NIGHT
    (Mel Tillis)
5. WOMAN TO WOMAN
    (Barbara Mandrell)
6. I LOVE YOU, I LOVE YOU, I LOVE YOU
    (Ronnie McDowell)
7. BARTENDER'S BLUES
    (George Jones)
8. I JUST WISH YOU WERE SOMEONE I LOVE
    (Larry Gatlin)
9. GOD MADE LOVE
    (Mel McDaniel)
10. TWO DOORS DOWN
    (Zella Lehr)

COUNTRY ALBUMS

1. WAYLON AND WILLIE
    (Waylon Jennings and Willie Nelson)
2. TEN YEARS OF GOLD
    (Kenny Rogers)
3. QUARTER MOON IN A TEN CENT TOWN
    (Emmylou Harris)
4. HERE YOU COME AGAIN
    (Dolly Parton)
5. TAKE THIS JOB AND SHOVE IT
    (Johnny Paycheck)
6. SIMPLE DREAMS
    (Linda Ronstadt)
7. WE MUST BELIEVE IN MAGIC
    (Crystal Gayle)
8. IT WAS ALMOST LIKE A SONG
    (Ronnie Milsap)
9. OLIVIA NEWTON-JOHN'S GREATEST HITS
    (Olivia Newton-John)
10. GEORGIA KEEPS PULLING ON MY RING
    (Conway Twitty)

MARCH 11, 1978

POP SINGLES

1. STAYIN' ALIVE
    (The Bee Gees)
2. (LOVE IS) THICKER THAN WATER
    (Andy Gibb)
3. EMOTION
    (Samantha Sang)
4. SOMETIMES WHEN WE TOUCH
    (Dan Hill)
5. NIGHT FEVER
    (The Bee Gees)
6. WE ARE THE CHAMPIONS/WE WILL ROCK
    YOU
    (Queen)
7. JUST THE WAY YOU ARE
    (Billy Joel)
8. BABY COME BACK
    (Player)
9. OUR LOVE
    (Natalie Cole)
10. JACK AND JILL
    (Raydio)

POP ALBUMS

1. SATURDAY NIGHT FEVER
    (Original Soundtrack)
2. THE STRANGER
    (Billy Joel)

3. NEWS OF THE WORLD
    (Queen)
4. EVEN NOW
    (Barry Manilow)
5. RUNNING ON EMPTY
    (Jackson Browne)
6. ALL 'N ALL
    (Earth, Wind and Fire)
7. RUMOURS
    (Fleetwood Mac)
8. FOOT LOOSE AND FANCY FREE
    (Rod Stewart)
9. THE GRAND ILLUSION
    (Styx)
10. SLOWHAND
    (Eric Clapton)

BLACK SINGLES

1. FLASH LIGHT
    (Parliament)
2. OUR LOVE
    (Natalie Cole)
3. IT'S YOU THAT I NEED
    (Enchantment)
4. WHICH WAY IS UP
    (Stargard)
5. STAYIN' ALIVE
    (The Bee Gees)
6. ALWAYS AND FOREVER
    (Heatwave)
7. BOOTZILLA
    (Bootsy's Rubber Band)
8. JACK AND JILL
    (Raydio)
9. THE CLOSER I GET TO YOU
    (Roberta Flack with Donny Hathaway)
10. LOVE ME RIGHT
    (Denise LaSalle)

BLACK ALBUMS

1. SATURDAY NIGHT FEVER
    (Original Soundtrack)
2. FUNKENTELECHY VS. THE PLACEBO
    SYNDROME
    (Parliament)
3. ALL 'N ALL
    (Earth, Wind and Fire)
4. WEEKEND IN L.A.
    (George Benson)
5. BLUE LIGHTS IN THE BASEMENT
    (Roberta Flack)
6. THANKFUL
    (Natalie Cole)
7. GOLDEN TIME OF DAY
    (Maze featuring Frankie Beverly)
8. BOOTSY: PLAYER OF THE YEAR
    (Bootsy's Rubber Band)
9. STREET PLAYER
    (Rufus/Chaka Khan)
10. ONCE UPON A DREAM
    (Enchantment)

JAZZ ALBUMS

1. WEEKEND IN L.A.
    (George Benson)
2. LIVE AT THE BIJOU
    (Grover Washington Jr.)
3. FEELS SO GOOD
    (Chuck Mangione)
4. HOLD ON
    (Noel Pointer)
5. HEADS
    (Bob James)
6. HERB ALPERT-HUGH MASEKELA
    (Herb Alpert and Hugh Masekela)
7. RAINBOW SEEKER
    (Joe Sample)
8. TEQUILA MOCKINGBIRD
    (Ramsey Lewis)
9. WINDOW OF A CHILD
    (Seawind)

10. FUNK IN A MASON JAR
    (Harvey Mason)

COUNTRY SINGLES

1. MAMMAS, DON'T LET YOUR BABIES GROW
   UP TO BE COWBOYS
   (Waylon Jennings and Willie Nelson)
2. DO I LOVE YOU (YES IN EVERY WAY)
   (Donna Fargo)
3. DON'T BREAK THE HEART THAT LOVES
   YOU
   (Margo Smith)
4. I LOVE YOU, I LOVE YOU, I LOVE YOU
   (Ronnie McDowell)
5. WHAT DID I PROMISE HER LAST NIGHT
   (Mel Tillis)
6. BARTENDER'S BLUES
   (George Jones)
7. TWO DOORS DOWN
   (Zella Lehr)
8. WALK RIGHT BACK
   (Anne Murray)
9. GOD MADE LOVE
   (Mel McDaniel)
10. RETURN TO ME
    (Marty Robbins)

COUNTRY ALBUMS

1. WAYLON AND WILLIE
   (Waylon Jennings and Willie Nelson)
2. HERE YOU COME AGAIN
   (Dolly Parton)
3. TEN YEARS OF GOLD
   (Kenny Rogers)
4. QUARTER MOON IN A TEN CENT TOWN
   (Emmylou Harris)
5. SIMPLE DREAMS
   (Linda Ronstadt)
6. WE MUST BELIEVE IN MAGIC
   (Crystal Gayle)
7. TAKE THIS JOB AND SHOVE IT
   (Johnny Paycheck)
8. GEORGIA KEEPS PULLING ON MY RING
   (Conway Twitty)
9. OL' WAYLON
   (Waylon Jennings)
10. IT WAS ALMOST LIKE A SONG
    (Ronnie Milsap)

MARCH 18, 1978

POP SINGLES

1. STAYIN' ALIVE
   (The Bee Gees)
2. NIGHT FEVER
   (The Bee Gees)
3. EMOTION
   (Samantha Sang)
4. (LOVE IS) THICKER THAN WATER
   (Andy Gibb)
5. SOMETIMES WHEN WE TOUCH
   (Dan Hill)
6. WE ARE THE CHAMPIONS/WE WILL ROCK
   YOU
   (Queen)
7. CAN'T SMILE WITHOUT YOU
   (Barry Manilow)
8. OUR LOVE
   (Natalie Cole)
9. JACK AND JILL
   (Raydio)
10. LAY DOWN SALLY
    (Eric Clapton)

POP ALBUMS

1. SATURDAY NIGHT FEVER
   (Original Soundtrack)
2. EVEN NOW
   (Barry Manilow)
3. THE STRANGER
   (Billy Joel)
4. RUNNING ON EMPTY
   (Jackson Browne)
5. NEWS OF THE WORLD
   (Queen)
6. ALL 'N ALL
   (Earth, Wind and Fire)
7. RUMOURS
   (Fleetwood Mac)
8. SLOWHAND
   (Eric Clapton)
9. FOOT LOOSE AND FANCY FREE
   (Rod Stewart)
10. POINT OF KNOW RETURN
    (Kansas)

BLACK SINGLES

1. FLASH LIGHT
   (Parliament)
2. OUR LOVE
   (Natalie Cole)
3. IT'S YOU THAT I NEED
   (Enchantment)
4. STAYIN' ALIVE
   (The Bee Gees)
5. THE CLOSER I GET TO YOU
   (Roberta Flack with Donny Hathaway)
6. BOOTZILLA
   (Bootsy's Rubber Band)
7. WHICH WAY IS UP
   (Stargard)
8. ALWAYS AND FOREVER
   (Heatwave)
9. JACK AND JILL
   (Raydio)
10. REACHING FOR THE SKY
    (Peabo Bryson)

BLACK ALBUMS

1. SATURDAY NIGHT FEVER
   (Original Soundtrack)
2. FUNKENTELECHY VS. THE PLACEBO
   SYNDROME
   (Parliament)
3. ALL 'N ALL
   (Earth, Wind and Fire)
4. WEEKEND IN L.A.
   (George Benson)
5. BLUE LIGHTS IN THE BASEMENT
   (Roberta Flack)
6. THANKFUL
   (Natalie Cole)
7. GOLDEN TIME OF DAY
   (Maze featuring Frankie Beverly)
8. BOOTSY: PLAYER OF THE YEAR
   (Bootsy's Rubber Band)
9. STREET PLAYER
   (Rufus/Chaka Khan)
10. STARGARD
    (Stargard)

JAZZ ALBUMS

1. WEEKEND IN L.A.
   (George Benson)
2. LIVE AT THE BIJOU
   (Grover Washington Jr.)
3. FEELS SO GOOD
   (Chuck Mangione)
4. HOLD ON
   (Noel Pointer)
5. RAINBOW SEEKER
   (Joe Sample)

6. HERB ALPERT-HUGH MASEKELA
   (Herb Alpert and Hugh Masekela)
7. HEADS
   (Bob James)
8. TEQUILA MOCKINGBIRD
   (Ramsey Lewis)
9. FUNK IN A MASON JAR
   (Harvey Mason)
10. LET'S DO IT
    (Roy Ayers)

COUNTRY SINGLES

1. MAMMAS, DON'T LET YOUR BABIES GROW
   UP TO BE COWBOYS
   (Waylon Jennings and Willie Nelson)
2. DO I LOVE YOU (YES IN EVERY WAY)
   (Donna Fargo)
3. I LOVE YOU, I LOVE YOU, I LOVE YOU
   (Ronnie McDowell)
4. DON'T BREAK THE HEART THAT LOVES
   YOU
   (Margo Smith)
5. TWO DOORS DOWN
   (Zella Lehr)
6. WALK RIGHT BACK
   (Anne Murray)
7. READY FOR THE TIMES TO GET BETTER
   (Crystal Gayle)
8. RETURN TO ME
   (Marty Robbins)
9. SOMEONE LOVES YOU HONEY
   (Charley Pride)
10. IF I HAD A CHEATING HEART
    (Mel Street)

COUNTRY ALBUMS

1. WAYLON AND WILLIE
   (Waylon Jennings and Willie Nelson)
2. HERE YOU COME AGAIN
   (Dolly Parton)
3. TEN YEARS OF GOLD
   (Kenny Rogers)
4. QUARTER MOON IN A TEN CENT TOWN
   (Emmylou Harris)
5. SIMPLE DREAMS
   (Linda Ronstadt)
6. TAKE THIS JOB AND SHOVE IT
   (Johnny Paycheck)
7. WE MUST BELIEVE IN MAGIC
   (Crystal Gayle)
8. GEORGIA KEEPS PULLING ON MY RING
   (Conway Twitty)
9. OL' WAYLON
   (Waylon Jennings)
10. IT WAS ALMOST LIKE A SONG
    (Ronnie Milsap)

MARCH 25, 1978

POP SINGLES

1. NIGHT FEVER
   (The Bee Gees)
2. STAYIN' ALIVE
   (The Bee Gees)
3. EMOTION
   (Samantha Sang)
4. (LOVE IS) THICKER THAN WATER
   (Andy Gibb)
5. CAN'T SMILE WITHOUT YOU
   (Barry Manilow)
6. SOMETIMES WHEN WE TOUCH
   (Dan Hill)
7. OUR LOVE
   (Natalie Cole)
8. JACK AND JILL
   (Raydio)

9. LAY DOWN SALLY
(Eric Clapton)
10. WE ARE THE CHAMPIONS/WE WILL ROCK YOU
(Queen)

POP ALBUMS

1. SATURDAY NIGHT FEVER
(Original Soundtrack)
2. EVEN NOW
(Barry Manilow)
3. THE STRANGER
(Billy Joel)
4. RUNNING ON EMPTY
(Jackson Browne)
5. NEWS OF THE WORLD
(Queen)
6. SLOWHAND
(Eric Clapton)
7. ALL 'N ALL
(Earth, Wind and Fire)
8. RUMOURS
(Fleetwood Mac)
9. POINT OF KNOW RETURN
(Kansas)
10. AJA
(Steely Dan)

BLACK SINGLES

1. FLASH LIGHT
(Parliament)
2. THE CLOSER I GET TO YOU
(Roberta Flack with Donny Hathaway)
3. STAYIN' ALIVE
(The Bee Gees)
4. BOOTZILLA
(Bootsy's Rubber Band)
5. OUR LOVE
(Natalie Cole)
6. IT'S YOU THAT I NEED
(Enchantment)
7. WHICH WAY IS UP
(Stargard)
8. TOO MUCH, TOO LITTLE, TOO LATE
(Johnny Mathis and Deniece Williams)
9. JACK AND JILL
(Raydio)
10. REACHING FOR THE SKY
(Peabo Bryson)

BLACK ALBUMS

1. SATURDAY NIGHT FEVER
(Original Soundtrack)
2. FUNKENTELECHY VS. THE PLACEBO SYNDROME
(Parliament)
3. WEEKEND IN L.A.
(George Benson)
4. ALL 'N ALL
(Earth, Wind and Fire)
5. BLUE LIGHTS IN THE BASEMENT
(Roberta Flack)
6. BOOTSY: PLAYER OF THE YEAR
(Bootsy's Rubber Band)
7. THANKFUL
(Natalie Cole)
8. GOLDEN TIME OF DAY
(Maze featuring Frankie Beverly)
9. STREET PLAYER
(Rufus/Chaka Khan)
10. STARGARD
(Stargard)

JAZZ ALBUMS

1. WEEKEND IN L.A.
(George Benson)
2. LIVE AT THE BIJOU
(Grover Washington Jr.)

3. FEELS SO GOOD
(Chuck Mangione)
4. HOLD ON
(Noel Pointer)
5. RAINBOW SEEKER
(Joe Sample)
6. HERB ALPERT-HUGH MASEKELA
(Herb Alpert and Hugh Masekela)
7. LET'S DO IT
(Roy Ayers)
8. THE PATH
(Ralph MacDonald)
9. FUNK IN A MASON JAR
(Harvey Mason)
10. WEST SIDE HIGHWAY
(Stanley Turrentine)

COUNTRY SINGLES

1. MAMMAS, DON'T LET YOUR BABIES GROW UP TO BE COWBOYS
(Waylon Jennings and Willie Nelson)
2. READY FOR THE TIMES TO GET BETTER
(Crystal Gayle)
3. SOMEONE LOVES YOU HONEY
(Charley Pride)
4. WALK RIGHT BACK
(Anne Murray)
5. TWO DOORS DOWN
(Zella Lehr)
6. DO I LOVE YOU (YES IN EVERY WAY)
(Donna Fargo)
7. RETURN TO ME
(Marty Robbins)
8. A LOVER'S QUESTION
(Jacky Ward)
9. I LOVE YOU, I LOVE YOU, I LOVE YOU
(Ronnie McDowell)
10. IT DON'T FEEL LIKE SINNIN' TO ME
(The Kendalls)

COUNTRY ALBUMS

1. WAYLON AND WILLIE
(Waylon Jennings and Willie Nelson)
2. TEN YEARS OF GOLD
(Kenny Rogers)
3. QUARTER MOON IN A TEN CENT TOWN
(Emmylou Harris)
4. HERE YOU COME AGAIN
(Dolly Parton)
5. SIMPLE DREAMS
(Linda Ronstadt)
6. TAKE THIS JOB AND SHOVE IT
(Johnny Paycheck)
7. WE MUST BELIEVE IN MAGIC
(Crystal Gayle)
8. IT WAS ALMOST LIKE A SONG
(Ronnie Milsap)
9. Y'ALL COME BACK SALOON
(The Oak Ridge Boys)
10. THE BEST OF THE STATLER BROTHERS
(The Statler Brothers)

APRIL 1, 1978

POP SINGLES

1. NIGHT FEVER
(The Bee Gees)
2. STAYIN' ALIVE
(The Bee Gees)
3. CAN'T SMILE WITHOUT YOU
(Barry Manilow)
4. EMOTION
(Samantha Sang)
5. (LOVE IS) THICKER THAN WATER
(Andy Gibb)
6. OUR LOVE
(Natalie Cole)

7. JACK AND JILL
(Raydio)
8. LAY DOWN SALLY
(Eric Clapton)
9. SOMETIMES WHEN WE TOUCH
(Dan Hill)
10. DUST IN THE WIND
(Kansas)

POP ALBUMS

1. SATURDAY NIGHT FEVER
(Original Soundtrack)
2. EVEN NOW
(Barry Manilow)
3. RUNNING ON EMPTY
(Jackson Browne)
4. THE STRANGER
(Billy Joel)
5. SLOWHAND
(Eric Clapton)
6. POINT OF KNOW RETURN
(Kansas)
7. NEWS OF THE WORLD
(Queen)
8. AJA
(Steely Dan)
9. RUMOURS
(Fleetwood Mac)
10. ALL 'N ALL
(Earth, Wind and Fire)

BLACK SINGLES

1. THE CLOSER I GET TO YOU
(Roberta Flack with Donny Hathaway)
2. FLASH LIGHT
(Parliament)
3. BOOTZILLA
(Bootsy's Rubber Band)
4. STAYIN' ALIVE
(The Bee Gees)
5. TOO MUCH, TOO LITTLE, TOO LATE
(Johnny Mathis and Deniece Williams)
6. OUR LOVE
(Natalie Cole)
7. IT'S YOU THAT I NEED
(Enchantment)
8. WHICH WAY IS UP
(Stargard)
9. DANCE WITH ME
(Peter Brown)
10. REACHING FOR THE SKY
(Peabo Bryson)

BLACK ALBUMS

1. SATURDAY NIGHT FEVER
(Original Soundtrack)
2. WEEKEND IN L.A.
(George Benson)
3. FUNKENTELECHY VS. THE PLACEBO SYNDROME
(Parliament)
4. BLUE LIGHTS IN THE BASEMENT
(Roberta Flack)
5. BOOTSY: PLAYER OF THE YEAR
(Bootsy's Rubber Band)
6. ALL 'N ALL
(Earth, Wind and Fire)
7. THANKFUL
(Natalie Cole)
8. STREET PLAYER
(Rufus/Chaka Khan)
9. GOLDEN TIME OF DAY
(Maze featuring Frankie Beverly)
10. STARGARD
(Stargard)

JAZZ ALBUMS

1. WEEKEND IN L.A.
(George Benson)

2. LIVE AT THE BIJOU
   (Grover Washington Jr.)
3. FEELS SO GOOD
   (Chuck Mangione)
4. HOLD ON
   (Noel Pointer)
5. RAINBOW SEEKER
   (Joe Sample)
6. LET'S DO IT
   (Roy Ayers)
7. HERB ALPERT-HUGH MASEKELA
   (Herb Alpert and Hugh Masekela)
8. THE PATH
   (Ralph MacDonald)
9. WEST SIDE HIGHWAY
   (Stanley Turrentine)
10. FUNK IN A MASON JAR
    (Harvey Mason)

COUNTRY SINGLES

1. READY FOR THE TIMES TO GET BETTER
   (Crystal Gayle)
2. SOMEONE LOVES YOU HONEY
   (Charley Pride)
3. WALK RIGHT BACK
   (Anne Murray)
4. MAMMAS, DON'T LET YOUR BABIES GROW
   UP TO BE COWBOYS
   (Waylon Jennings and Willie Nelson)
5. A LOVER'S QUESTION
   (Jacky Ward)
6. IT DON'T FEEL LIKE SINNIN' TO ME
   (The Kendalls)
7. TWO DOORS DOWN
   (Zella Lehr)
8. I CHEATED ON A GOOD WOMAN'S LOVE
   (Billy "Crash" Craddock)
9. I'VE GOT A WINNER IN YOU
   (Don Williams)
10. HEARTS ON FIRE
    (Eddie Rabbitt)

COUNTRY ALBUMS

1. WAYLON AND WILLIE
   (Waylon Jennings and Willie Nelson)
2. TEN YEARS OF GOLD
   (Kenny Rogers)
3. QUARTER MOON IN A TEN CENT TOWN
   (Emmylou Harris)
4. HERE YOU COME AGAIN
   (Dolly Parton)
5. SIMPLE DREAMS
   (Linda Ronstadt)
6. TAKE THIS JOB AND SHOVE IT
   (Johnny Paycheck)
7. SOMEONE LOVES YOU HONEY
   (Charley Pride)
8. IT WAS ALMOST LIKE A SONG
   (Ronnie Milsap)
9. Y'ALL COME BACK SALOON
   (The Oak Ridge Boys)
10. THE BEST OF THE STATLER BROTHERS
    (The Statler Brothers)

APRIL 8, 1978

POP SINGLES

1. NIGHT FEVER
   (The Bee Gees)
2. CAN'T SMILE WITHOUT YOU
   (Barry Manilow)
3. STAYIN' ALIVE
   (The Bee Gees)
4. EMOTION
   (Samantha Sang)
5. IF I CAN'T HAVE YOU
   (Yvonne Elliman)

6. DUST IN THE WIND
   (Kansas)
7. JACK AND JILL
   (Raydio)
8. LAY DOWN SALLY
   (Eric Clapton)
9. OUR LOVE
   (Natalie Cole)
10. (LOVE IS) THICKER THAN WATER
    (Andy Gibb)

POP ALBUMS

1. SATURDAY NIGHT FEVER
   (Original Soundtrack)
2. EVEN NOW
   (Barry Manilow)
3. RUNNING ON EMPTY
   (Jackson Browne)
4. SLOWHAND
   (Eric Clapton)
5. POINT OF KNOW RETURN
   (Kansas)
6. THE STRANGER
   (Billy Joel)
7. AJA
   (Steely Dan)
8. NEWS OF THE WORLD
   (Queen)
9. RUMOURS
   (Fleetwood Mac)
10. WEEKEND IN L.A.
    (George Benson)

BLACK SINGLES

1. THE CLOSER I GET TO YOU
   (Roberta Flack with Donny Hathaway)
2. TOO MUCH, TOO LITTLE, TOO LATE
   (Johnny Mathis and Deniece Williams)
3. BOOTZILLA
   (Bootsy's Rubber Band)
4. FLASH LIGHT
   (Parliament)
5. STAYIN' ALIVE
   (The Bee Gees)
6. DANCE WITH ME
   (Peter Brown)
7. OUR LOVE
   (Natalie Cole)
8. IT'S YOU THAT I NEED
   (Enchantment)
9. WHICH WAY IS UP
   (Stargard)
10. ON BROADWAY
    (George Benson)

BLACK ALBUMS

1. SATURDAY NIGHT FEVER
   (Original Soundtrack)
2. WEEKEND IN L.A.
   (George Benson)
3. BLUE LIGHTS IN THE BASEMENT
   (Roberta Flack)
4. BOOTSY: PLAYER OF THE YEAR
   (Bootsy's Rubber Band)
5. FUNKENTELECHY VS. THE PLACEBO
   SYNDROME
   (Parliament)
6. STREET PLAYER
   (Rufus/Chaka Khan)
7. THANKFUL
   (Natalie Cole)
8. ALL 'N ALL
   (Earth, Wind and Fire)
9. GOLDEN TIME OF DAY
   (Maze featuring Frankie Beverly)
10. STARGARD
    (Stargard)

JAZZ ALBUMS

1. WEEKEND IN L.A.
   (George Benson)

2. LIVE AT THE BIJOU
   (Grover Washington Jr.)
3. RAINBOW SEEKER
   (Joe Sample)
4. FEELS SO GOOD
   (Chuck Mangione)
5. LET'S DO IT
   (Roy Ayers)
6. HOLD ON
   (Noel Pointer)
7. THE PATH
   (Ralph MacDonald)
8. THE MAD HATTER
   (Chick Corea)
9. SAY IT WITH SILENCE
   (Hubert Laws)
10. WEST SIDE HIGHWAY
    (Stanley Turrentine)

COUNTRY SINGLES

1. SOMEONE LOVES YOU HONEY
   (Charley Pride)
2. READY FOR THE TIMES TO GET BETTER
   (Crystal Gayle)
3. WALK RIGHT BACK
   (Anne Murray)
4. IT DON'T FEEL LIKE SINNIN' TO ME
   (The Kendalls)
5. A LOVER'S QUESTION
   (Jacky Ward)
6. I CHEATED ON A GOOD WOMAN'S LOVE
   (Billy "Crash" Craddock)
7. I'VE GOT A WINNER IN YOU
   (Don Williams)
8. HEARTS ON FIRE
   (Eddie Rabbitt)
9. EVERY TIME TWO FOOLS COLLIDE
   (Kenny Rogers and Dottie West)
10. SWEET SWEET SMILE
    (The Carpenters)

COUNTRY ALBUMS

1. WAYLON AND WILLIE
   (Waylon Jennings and Willie Nelson)
2. TEN YEARS OF GOLD
   (Kenny Rogers)
3. HERE YOU COME AGAIN
   (Dolly Parton)
4. TAKE THIS JOB AND SHOVE IT
   (Johnny Paycheck)
5. QUARTER MOON IN A TEN CENT TOWN
   (Emmylou Harris)
6. SIMPLE DREAMS
   (Linda Ronstadt)
7. SOMEONE LOVES YOU HONEY
   (Charley Pride)
8. WE MUST BELIEVE IN MAGIC
   (Crystal Gayle)
9. Y'ALL COME BACK SALOON
   (The Oak Ridge Boys)
10. THE BEST OF THE STATLER BROTHERS
    (The Statler Brothers)

APRIL 15, 1978

POP SINGLES

1. NIGHT FEVER
   (The Bee Gees)
2. CAN'T SMILE WITHOUT YOU
   (Barry Manilow)
3. STAYIN' ALIVE
   (The Bee Gees)
4. IF I CAN'T HAVE YOU
   (Yvonne Elliman)
5. DUST IN THE WIND
   (Kansas)
6. EMOTION
   (Samantha Sang)

7. THE CLOSER I GET TO YOU
   (Roberta Flack with Donny Hathaway)
8. LAY DOWN SALLY
   (Eric Clapton)
9. JACK AND JILL
   (Raydio)
10. EBONY EYES
   (Bob Welch)

POP ALBUMS

1. SATURDAY NIGHT FEVER
   (Original Soundtrack)
2. EVEN NOW
   (Barry Manilow)
3. RUNNING ON EMPTY
   (Jackson Browne)
4. SLOWHAND
   (Eric Clapton)
5. POINT OF KNOW RETURN
   (Kansas)
6. THE STRANGER
   (Billy Joel)
7. NEWS OF THE WORLD
   (Queen)
8. AJA
   (Steely Dan)
9. EARTH
   (Jefferson Starship)
10. WEEKEND IN L.A.
   (George Benson)

BLACK SINGLES

1. TOO MUCH, TOO LITTLE, TOO LATE
   (Johnny Mathis and Deniece Williams)
2. THE CLOSER I GET TO YOU
   (Roberta Flack with Donny Hathaway)
3. BOOTZILLA
   (Bootsy's Rubber Band)
4. FLASH LIGHT
   (Parliament)
5. DANCE WITH ME
   (Peter Brown)
6. ON BROADWAY
   (George Benson)
7. STAYIN' ALIVE
   (The Bee Gees)
8. OUR LOVE
   (Natalie Cole)
9. IT'S YOU THAT I NEED
   (Enchantment)
10. WHICH WAY IS UP
   (Stargard)

BLACK ALBUMS

1. SATURDAY NIGHT FEVER
   (Original Soundtrack)
2. WEEKEND IN L.A.
   (George Benson)
3. BLUE LIGHTS IN THE BASEMENT
   (Roberta Flack)
4. FUNKENTELECHY VS. THE PLACEBO SYNDROME
   (Parliament)
5. BOOTSY: PLAYER OF THE YEAR
   (Bootsy's Rubber Band)
6. STREET PLAYER
   (Rufus/Chaka Khan)
7. THANKFUL
   (Natalie Cole)
8. ALL 'N ALL
   (Earth, Wind and Fire)
9. RAYDIO
   (Raydio)
10. WARMER COMMUNICATIONS
   (Average White Band)

JAZZ ALBUMS

1. WEEKEND IN L.A.
   (George Benson)

2. LIVE AT THE BIJOU
   (Grover Washington Jr.)
3. RAINBOW SEEKER
   (Joe Sample)
4. FEELS SO GOOD
   (Chuck Mangione)
5. LET'S DO IT
   (Roy Ayers)
6. HOLD ON
   (Noel Pointer)
7. SAY IT WITH SILENCE
   (Hubert Laws)
8. THE MAD HATTER
   (Chick Corea)
9. THE PATH
   (Ralph MacDonald)
10. WEST SIDE HIGHWAY
   (Stanley Turrentine)

COUNTRY SINGLES

1. SOMEONE LOVES YOU HONEY
   (Charley Pride)
2. IT DON'T FEEL LIKE SINNIN' TO ME
   (The Kendalls)
3. I CHEATED ON A GOOD WOMAN'S LOVE
   (Billy "Crash" Craddock)
4. HEARTS ON FIRE
   (Eddie Rabbitt)
5. EVERY TIME TWO FOOLS COLLIDE
   (Kenny Rogers and Dottie West)
6. I'VE GOT A WINNER IN YOU
   (Don Williams)
7. A LOVER'S QUESTION
   (Jacky Ward)
8. SWEET SWEET SMILE
   (The Carpenters)
9. IT'S ALL WRONG, BUT IT'S ALL RIGHT
   (Dolly Parton)
10. WE BELIEVE IN HAPPY ENDINGS
   (Johnny Rodriguez)

COUNTRY ALBUMS

1. WAYLON AND WILLIE
   (Waylon Jennings and Willie Nelson)
2. TEN YEARS OF GOLD
   (Kenny Rogers)
3. HERE YOU COME AGAIN
   (Dolly Parton)
4. TAKE THIS JOB AND SHOVE IT
   (Johnny Paycheck)
5. SIMPLE DREAMS
   (Linda Ronstadt)
6. QUARTER MOON IN A TEN CENT TOWN
   (Emmylou Harris)
7. THE BEST OF THE STATLER BROTHERS
   (The Statler Brothers)
8. WE MUST BELIEVE IN MAGIC
   (Crystal Gayle)
9. SOMEONE LOVES YOU HONEY
   (Charley Pride)
10. IT WAS ALMOST LIKE A SONG
   (Ronnie Milsap)

APRIL 22, 1978

POP SINGLES

1. NIGHT FEVER
   (The Bee Gees)
2. CAN'T SMILE WITHOUT YOU
   (Barry Manilow)
3. IF I CAN'T HAVE YOU
   (Yvonne Elliman)
4. STAYIN' ALIVE
   (The Bee Gees)
5. THE CLOSER I GET TO YOU
   (Roberta Flack with Donny Hathaway)
6. DUST IN THE WIND
   (Kansas)

7. EMOTION
   (Samantha Sang)
8. JACK AND JILL
   (Raydio)
9. LAY DOWN SALLY
   (Eric Clapton)
10. EBONY EYES
   (Bob Welch)

POP ALBUMS

1. SATURDAY NIGHT FEVER
   (Original Soundtrack)
2. EVEN NOW
   (Barry Manilow)
3. LONDON TOWN
   (Paul McCartney and Wings)
4. RUNNING ON EMPTY
   (Jackson Browne)
5. POINT OF KNOW RETURN
   (Kansas)
6. THE STRANGER
   (Billy Joel)
7. SLOWHAND
   (Eric Clapton)
8. EARTH
   (The Jefferson Starship)
9. AJA
   (Steely Dan)
10. WEEKEND IN L.A.
   (George Benson)

BLACK SINGLES

1. TOO MUCH, TOO LITTLE, TOO LATE
   (Johnny Mathis and Deniece Williams)
2. THE CLOSER I GET TO YOU
   (Roberta Flack with Donny Hathaway)
3. BOOTZILLA
   (Bootsy's Rubber Band)
4. ON BROADWAY
   (George Benson)
5. DANCE WITH ME
   (Peter Brown)
6. FLASH LIGHT
   (Parliament)
7. STAYIN' ALIVE
   (The Bee Gees)
8. OUR LOVE
   (Natalie Cole)
9. NIGHT FEVER
   (The Bee Gees)
10. IT'S YOU THAT I NEED
   (Enchantment)

BLACK ALBUMS

1. SATURDAY NIGHT FEVER
   (Original Soundtrack)
2. WEEKEND IN L.A.
   (George Benson)
3. BLUE LIGHTS IN THE BASEMENT
   (Roberta Flack)
4. STREET PLAYER
   (Rufus/Chaka Khan)
5. BOOTSY: PLAYER OF THE YEAR
   (Bootsy's Rubber Band)
6. FUNKENTELECHY VS. THE PLACEBO SYNDROME
   (Parliament)
7. SHOWDOWN
   (Isley Brothers)
8. THANKFUL
   (Natalie Cole)
9. RAYDIO
   (Raydio)
10. WARMER COMMUNICATIONS
   (Average White Band)

JAZZ ALBUMS

1. WEEKEND IN L.A.
   (George Benson)

2. RAINBOW SEEKER
   (Joe Sample)
3. LIVE AT THE BIJOU
   (Grover Washington Jr.)
4. FEELS SO GOOD
   (Chuck Mangione)
5. LET'S DO IT
   (Roy Ayers)
6. SAY IT WITH SILENCE
   (Hubert Laws)
7. HOLD ON
   (Noel Pointer)
8. THE MAD HATTER
   (Chick Corea)
9. THE PATH
   (Ralph MacDonald)
10. WEST SIDE HIGHWAY
    (Stanley Turrentine)

COUNTRY SINGLES

1. EVERY TIME TWO FOOLS COLLIDE
   (Kenny Rogers and Dottie West)
2. IT DON'T FEEL LIKE SINNIN' TO ME
   (The Kendalls)
3. I CHEATED ON A GOOD WOMAN'S LOVE
   (Billy "Crash" Craddock)
4. HEARTS ON FIRE
   (Eddie Rabbitt)
5. SOMEONE LOVES YOU HONEY
   (Charley Pride)
6. I'VE GOT A WINNER IN YOU
   (Don Williams)
7. IT'S ALL WRONG, BUT IT'S ALL RIGHT
   (Dolly Parton)
8. SWEET SWEET SMILE
   (The Carpenters)
9. WE BELIEVE IN HAPPY ENDINGS
   (Johnny Rodriguez)
10. SHE CAN PUT HER SHOES UNDER MY BED
    (ANYTIME)
    (Johnny Duncan)

COUNTRY ALBUMS

1. WAYLON AND WILLIE
   (Waylon Jennings and Willie Nelson)
2. TEN YEARS OF GOLD
   (Kenny Rogers)
3. HERE YOU COME AGAIN
   (Dolly Parton)
4. SIMPLE DREAMS
   (Linda Ronstadt)
5. QUARTER MOON IN A TEN CENT TOWN
   (Emmylou Harris)
6. THE BEST OF THE STATLER BROTHERS
   (The Statler Brothers)
7. WE MUST BELIEVE IN MAGIC
   (Crystal Gayle)
8. HE WALKS BESIDE ME
   (Elvis Presley)
9. SON OF A SON OF A SAILOR
   (Jimmy Buffett)
10. TAKE THIS JOB AND SHOVE IT
    (Johnny Paycheck)

APRIL 29, 1978

POP SINGLES

1. NIGHT FEVER
   (The Bee Gees)
2. CAN'T SMILE WITHOUT YOU
   (Barry Manilow)
3. IF I CAN'T HAVE YOU
   (Yvonne Elliman)
4. THE CLOSER I GET TO YOU
   (Roberta Flack with Donny Hathaway)
5. STAYIN' ALIVE
   (The Bee Gees)

6. DUST IN THE WIND
   (Kansas)
7. JACK AND JILL
   (Raydio)
8. EMOTION
   (Samantha Sang)
9. WITH A LITTLE LUCK
   (Paul McCartney and Wings)
10. LAY DOWN SALLY
    (Eric Clapton)

POP ALBUMS

1. SATURDAY NIGHT FEVER
   (Original Soundtrack)
2. LONDON TOWN
   (Paul McCartney and Wings)
3. EVEN NOW
   (Barry Manilow)
4. RUNNING ON EMPTY
   (Jackson Browne)
5. POINT OF KNOW RETURN
   (Kansas)
6. SLOWHAND
   (Eric Clapton)
7. THE STRANGER
   (Billy Joel)
8. EARTH
   (The Jefferson Starship)
9. WEEKEND IN L.A.
   (George Benson)
10. AJA
    (Steely Dan)

BLACK SINGLES

1. TOO MUCH, TOO LITTLE, TOO LATE
   (Johnny Mathis and Deniece Williams)
2. THE CLOSER I GET TO YOU
   (Roberta Flack with Donny Hathaway)
3. ON BROADWAY
   (George Benson)
4. DANCE WITH ME
   (Peter Brown)
5. BOOTZILLA
   (Bootsy's Rubber Band)
6. TAKE ME TO THE NEXT PHASE (PART 1)
   (Isley Brothers)
7. FLASH LIGHT
   (Parliament)
8. STAY
   (Rufus/Chaka Khan)
9. NIGHT FEVER
   (The Bee Gees)
10. USE TA BE MY GIRL
    (The O'Jays)

BLACK ALBUMS

1. SATURDAY NIGHT FEVER
   (Original Soundtrack)
2. SHOWDOWN
   (Isley Brothers)
3. CENTRAL HEATING
   (Heatwave)
4. WEEKEND IN L.A.
   (George Benson)
5. STREET PLAYER
   (Rufus/Chaka Khan)
6. BLUE LIGHTS IN THE BASEMENT
   (Roberta Flack)
7. BOOTSY: PLAYER OF THE YEAR
   (Bootsy's Rubber Band)
8. SO FULL OF LOVE
   (The O'Jays)
9. FUNKENTELECHY VS. THE PLACEBO
   SYNDROME
   (Parliament)
10. WARMER COMMUNICATIONS
    (Average White Band)

JAZZ ALBUMS

1. WEEKEND IN L.A.
   (George Benson)
2. RAINBOW SEEKER
   (Joe Sample)
3. LIVE AT THE BIJOU
   (Grover Washington Jr.)
4. FEELS SO GOOD
   (Chuck Mangione)
5. SAY IT WITH SILENCE
   (Hubert Laws)
6. HOLD ON
   (Noel Pointer)
7. THE PATH
   (Ralph MacDonald)
8. LET'S DO IT
   (Roy Ayers)
9. WEST SIDE HIGHWAY
   (Stanley Turrentine)
10. MODERN MAN
    (Stanley Clarke)

COUNTRY SINGLES

1. HEARTS ON FIRE
   (Eddie Rabbitt)
2. EVERY TIME TWO FOOLS COLLIDE
   (Kenny Rogers and Dottie West)
3. IT'S ALL WRONG, BUT IT'S ALL RIGHT
   (Dolly Parton)
4. I CHEATED ON A GOOD WOMAN'S LOVE
   (Billy "Crash" Craddock)
5. IT DON'T FEEL LIKE SINNIN' TO ME
   (The Kendalls)
6. SHE CAN PUT HER SHOES UNDER MY BED
   (ANYTIME)
   (Johnny Duncan)
7. SWEET SWEET SMILE
   (The Carpenters)
8. WE BELIEVE IN HAPPY ENDINGS
   (Johnny Rodriguez)
9. I'M ALWAYS ON A MOUNTAIN WHEN I
   FALL
   (Merle Haggard)
10. MAYBE BABY
    (Susie Allanson)

COUNTRY ALBUMS

1. WAYLON AND WILLIE
   (Waylon Jennings and Willie Nelson)
2. TEN YEARS OF GOLD
   (Kenny Rogers)
3. HERE YOU COME AGAIN
   (Dolly Parton)
4. SON OF A SON OF A SAILOR
   (Jimmy Buffett)
5. QUARTER MOON IN A TEN CENT TOWN
   (Emmylou Harris)
6. SIMPLE DREAMS
   (Linda Ronstadt)
7. EVERY TIME TWO FOOLS COLLIDE
   (Kenny Rogers and Dottie West)
8. HE WALKS BESIDE ME
   (Elvis Presley)
9. THE BEST OF THE STATLER BROTHERS
   (The Statler Brothers)
10. TAKE THIS JOB AND SHOVE IT
    (Johnny Paycheck)

MAY 6, 1978

POP SINGLES

1. NIGHT FEVER
   (The Bee Gees)
2. IF I CAN'T HAVE YOU
   (Yvonne Elliman)

3. THE CLOSER I GET TO YOU
   (Roberta Flack and Donny Hathaway)
4. CAN'T SMILE WITHOUT YOU
   (Barry Manilow)
5. STAYIN' ALIVE
   (The Bee Gees)
6. WITH A LITTLE LUCK
   (Paul McCartney and Wings)
7. JACK AND JILL
   (Raydio)
8. TOO MUCH, TOO LITTLE, TOO LATE
   (Johnny Mathis and Deniece Williams)
9. DUST IN THE WIND
   (Kansas)
10. COUNT ON ME
    (The Jefferson Starship)

POP ALBUMS

1. SATURDAY NIGHT FEVER
   (Original Soundtrack)
2. LONDON TOWN
   (Paul McCartney and Wings)
3. EVEN NOW
   (Barry Manilow)
4. RUNNING ON EMPTY
   (Jackson Browne)
5. POINT OF KNOW RETURN
   (Kansas)
6. SLOWHAND
   (Eric Clapton)
7. THE STRANGER
   (Billy Joel)
8. SHOWDOWN
   (Isley Brothers)
9. EARTH
   (The Jefferson Starship)
10. WEEKEND IN L.A.
    (George Benson)

BLACK SINGLES

1. TOO MUCH, TOO LITTLE, TOO LATE
   (Johnny Mathis and Deniece Williams)
2. THE CLOSER I GET TO YOU
   (Roberta Flack with Donny Hathaway)
3. ON BROADWAY
   (George Benson)
4. DANCE WITH ME
   (Peter Brown)
5. TAKE ME TO THE NEXT PHASE (PART 1)
   (Isley Brothers)
6. USE TA BE MY GIRL
   (The O'Jays)
7. STAY
   (Rufus/Chaka Khan)
8. FLASH LIGHT
   (Parliament)
9. BOOTZILLA
   (Bootsy's Rubber Band)
10. THE GROOVE LINE
    (Heatwave)

BLACK ALBUMS

1. SHOWDOWN
   (Isley Brothers)
2. SATURDAY NIGHT FEVER
   (Original Soundtrack)
3. CENTRAL HEATING
   (Heatwave)
4. SO FULL OF LOVE
   (The O'Jays)
5. WEEKEND IN L.A.
   (George Benson)
6. STREET PLAYER
   (Rufus/Chaka Khan)
7. BOOTSY: PLAYER OF THE YEAR
   (Bootsy's Rubber Band)
8. YOU LIGHT UP MY LIFE
   (Johnny Mathis)
9. BLUE LIGHTS IN THE BASEMENT
   (Roberta Flack)

10. FUNKENTELECHY VS. THE PLACEBO
    SYNDROME
    (Parliament)

JAZZ ALBUMS

1. WEEKEND IN L.A.
   (George Benson)
2. RAINBOW SEEKER
   (Joe Sample)
3. FEELS SO GOOD
   (Chuck Mangione)
4. LIVE AT THE BIJOU
   (Grover Washington Jr.)
5. SAY IT WITH SILENCE
   (Hubert Laws)
6. MODERN MAN
   (Stanley Clarke)
7. HOLD ON
   (Noel Pointer)
8. WEST SIDE HIGHWAY
   (Stanley Turrentine)
9. THE PATH
   (Ralph MacDonald)
10. LOVE ISLAND
    (Deodato)

COUNTRY SINGLES

1. IT'S ALL WRONG, BUT IT'S ALL RIGHT
   (Dolly Parton)
2. EVERY TIME TWO FOOLS COLLIDE
   (Kenny Rogers and Dottie West)
3. HEARTS ON FIRE
   (Eddie Rabbitt)
4. SHE CAN PUT HER SHOES UNDER MY BED
   (ANYTIME)
   (Johnny Duncan)
5. I'M ALWAYS ON A MOUNTAIN WHEN I
   FALL
   (Merle Haggard)
6. IT DON'T FEEL LIKE SINNIN' TO ME
   (The Kendalls)
7. SOFTLY, AS I LEAVE YOU/UNCHAINED
   MELODY
   (Elvis Presley)
8. MAYBE BABY
   (Susie Allanson)
9. DO YOU KNOW YOU ARE MY SUNSHINE
   (The Statler Brothers)
10. I'LL NEVER BE FREE
    (Jim Ed Brown and Helen Cornelius)

COUNTRY ALBUMS

1. WAYLON AND WILLIE
   (Waylon Jennings and Willie Nelson)
2. TEN YEARS OF GOLD
   (Kenny Rogers)
3. HERE YOU COME AGAIN
   (Dolly Parton)
4. SON OF A SON OF A SAILOR
   (Jimmy Buffett)
5. QUARTER MOON IN A TEN CENT TOWN
   (Emmylou Harris)
6. EVERY TIME TWO FOOLS COLLIDE
   (Kenny Rogers and Dottie West)
7. SIMPLE DREAMS
   (Linda Ronstadt)
8. THE BEST OF THE STATLER BROTHERS
   (The Statler Brothers)
9. HE WALKS BESIDE ME
   (Elvis Presley)
10. TAKE THIS JOB AND SHOVE IT
    (Johnny Paycheck)

MAY 13, 1978

POP SINGLES

1. NIGHT FEVER
   (The Bee Gees)

2. IF I CAN'T HAVE YOU
   (Yvonne Elliman)
3. THE CLOSER I GET TO YOU
   (Roberta Flack with Donny Hathaway)
4. TOO MUCH, TOO LITTLE, TOO LATE
   (Johnny Mathis and Deniece Williams)
5. WITH A LITTLE LUCK
   (Paul McCartney and Wings)
6. YOU'RE THE ONE THAT I WANT
   (John Travolta and Olivia Newton-John)
7. CAN'T SMILE WITHOUT YOU
   (Barry Manilow)
8. ON BROADWAY
   (George Benson)
9. SHADOW DANCING
   (Andy Gibb)
10. COUNT ON ME
    (Jefferson Starship)

POP ALBUMS

1. SATURDAY NIGHT FEVER
   (Original Soundtrack)
2. LONDON TOWN
   (Paul McCartney and Wings)
3. SHOWDOWN
   (Isley Brothers)
4. EVEN NOW
   (Barry Manilow)
5. RUNNING ON EMPTY
   (Jackson Browne)
6. POINT OF KNOW RETURN
   (Kansas)
7. SLOWHAND
   (Eric Clapton)
8. THE STRANGER
   (Billy Joel)
9. EARTH
   (The Jefferson Starship)
10. SON OF A SON OF A SAILOR
    (Jimmy Buffett)

BLACK SINGLES

1. TOO MUCH, TOO LITTLE, TOO LATE
   (Johnny Mathis and Deniece Williams)
2. USE TA BE MY GIRL
   (The O'Jays)
3. TAKE ME TO THE NEXT PHASE (PART 1)
   (Isley Brothers)
4. ON BROADWAY
   (George Benson)
5. THE CLOSER I GET TO YOU
   (Roberta Flack with Donny Hathaway)
6. DANCE WITH ME
   (Peter Brown)
7. STAY
   (Rufus/Chaka Khan)
8. THE GROOVE LINE
   (Heatwave)
9. FLASH LIGHT
   (Parliament)
10. BOOTZILLA
    (Bootsy's Rubber Band)

BLACK ALBUMS

1. SHOWDOWN
   (Isley Brothers)
2. SATURDAY NIGHT FEVER
   (Original Soundtrack)
3. CENTRAL HEATING
   (Heatwave)
4. SO FULL OF LOVE
   (The O'Jays)
5. WEEKEND IN L.A.
   (George Benson)
6. BOOTSY: PLAYER OF THE YEAR
   (Bootsy's Rubber Band)
7. STREET PLAYER
   (Rufus/Chaka Khan)
8. YOU LIGHT UP MY LIFE
   (Johnny Mathis)
9. RAYDIO
   (Raydio)

10. FUNKENTELECHY VS. THE PLACEBO
SYNDROME
(Parliament)

JAZZ ALBUMS

1. WEEKEND IN L.A.
(George Benson)
2. FEELS SO GOOD
(Chuck Mangione)
3. RAINBOW SEEKER
(Joe Sample)
4. MODERN MAN
(Stanley Clarke)
5. SAY IT WITH SILENCE
(Hubert Laws)
6. LIVE AT THE BIJOU
(Grover Washington Jr.)
7. LOVE ISLAND
(Deodato)
8. CASINO
(Al DiMeola)
9. LOVELAND
(Lonnie Liston Smith)
10. WEST SIDE HIGHWAY
(Stanley Turrentine)

COUNTRY SINGLES

1. IT'S ALL WRONG, BUT IT'S ALL RIGHT
(Dolly Parton)
2. SHE CAN PUT HER SHOES UNDER MY BED
(ANYTIME)
(Johnny Duncan)
3. I'M ALWAYS ON A MOUNTAIN WHEN I
FALL
(Merle Haggard)
4. EVERY TIME TWO FOOLS COLLIDE
(Kenny Rogers and Dottie West)
5. DO YOU KNOW YOU ARE MY SUNSHINE
(The Statler Brothers)
6. SOFTLY, AS I LEAVE YOU/UNCHAINED
MELODY
(Elvis Presley)
7. GEORGIA ON MY MIND
(Willie Nelson)
8. MAYBE BABY
(Susie Allanson)
9. I'LL NEVER BE FREE
(Jim Ed Brown and Helen Cornelius)
10. IF YOU CAN TOUCH HER AT ALL
(Willie Nelson)

COUNTRY ALBUMS

1. WAYLON AND WILLIE
(Waylon Jennings and Willie Nelson)
2. TEN YEARS OF GOLD
(Kenny Rogers)
3. EVERY TIME TWO FOOLS COLLIDE
(Kenny Rogers and Dottie West)
4. SON OF A SON OF A SAILOR
(Jimmy Buffett)
5. HERE YOU COME AGAIN
(Dolly Parton)
6. SIMPLE DREAMS
(Linda Ronstadt)
7. THE BEST OF THE STATLER BROTHERS
(The Statler Brothers)
8. ENTERTAINERS . . . ON AND OFF THE
RECORD
(The Statler Brothers)
9. TAKE THIS JOB AND SHOVE IT
(Johnny Paycheck)
10. QUARTER MOON IN A TEN CENT TOWN
(Emmylou Harris)

MAY 20, 1978

POP SINGLES

1. TOO MUCH, TOO LITTLE, TOO LATE
(Johnny Mathis and Deniece Williams)
2. WITH A LITTLE LUCK
(Paul McCartney and Wings)
3. THE CLOSER I GET TO YOU
(Roberta Flack with Donny Hathaway)
4. YOU'RE THE ONE THAT I WANT
(John Travolta and Olivia Newton-John)
5. NIGHT FEVER
(The Bee Gees)
6. SHADOW DANCING
(Andy Gibb)
7. ON BROADWAY
(George Benson)
8. IF I CAN'T HAVE YOU
(Yvonne Elliman)
9. FEELS SO GOOD
(Chuck Mangione)
10. IMAGINARY LOVER
(Atlanta Rhythm Section)

POP ALBUMS

1. SATURDAY NIGHT FEVER
(Original Soundtrack)
2. LONDON TOWN
(Paul McCartney and Wings)
3. SHOWDOWN
(Isley Brothers)
4. RUNNING ON EMPTY
(Jackson Browne)
5. EVEN NOW
(Barry Manilow)
6. POINT OF KNOW RETURN
(Kansas)
7. SLOWHAND
(Eric Clapton)
8. EARTH
(The Jefferson Starship)
9. THE STRANGER
(Billy Joel)
10. FEELS SO GOOD
(Chuck Mangione)

BLACK SINGLES

1. USE TA BE MY GIRL
(The O'Jays)
2. TOO MUCH, TOO LITTLE, TOO LATE
(Johnny Mathis and Deniece Williams)
3. TAKE ME TO THE NEXT PHASE (PART 1)
(Isley Brothers)
4. ON BROADWAY
(George Benson)
5. THE GROOVE LINE
(Heatwave)
6. THE CLOSER I GET TO YOU
(Roberta Flack with Donny Hathaway)
7. STAY
(Rufus/Chaka Khan)
8. DANCE WITH ME
(Peter Brown)
9. FLASH LIGHT
(Parliament)
10. OH WHAT A NIGHT FOR DANCING
(Barry White)

BLACK ALBUMS

1. SHOWDOWN
(Isley Brothers)
2. SATURDAY NIGHT FEVER
(Original Soundtrack)
3. SO FULL OF LOVE
(The O'Jays)
4. CENTRAL HEATING
(Heatwave)

5. WEEKEND IN L.A.
(George Benson)
6. STREET PLAYER
(Rufus/Chaka Khan)
7. YOU LIGHT UP MY LIFE
(Johnny Mathis)
8. BOOTSY: PLAYER OF THE YEAR
(Bootsy's Rubber Band)
9. RAYDIO
(Raydio)
10. THANKFUL
(Natalie Cole)

JAZZ ALBUMS

1. WEEKEND IN L.A.
(George Benson)
2. FEELS SO GOOD
(Chuck Mangione)
3. RAINBOW SEEKER
(Joe Sample)
4. MODERN MAN
(Stanley Clarke)
5. SAY IT WITH SILENCE
(Hubert Laws)
6. LIVE AT THE BIJOU
(Grover Washington Jr.)
7. CASINO
(Al DiMeola)
8. LOVE ISLAND
(Deodato)
9. LOVELAND
(Lonnie Liston Smith)
10. WEST SIDE HIGHWAY
(Stanley Turrentine)

COUNTRY SINGLES

1. SHE CAN PUT HER SHOES UNDER MY BED
(ANYTIME)
(Johnny Duncan)
2. IT'S ALL WRONG, BUT IT'S ALL RIGHT
(Dolly Parton)
3. I'M ALWAYS ON A MOUNTAIN WHEN I
FALL
(Merle Haggard)
4. DO YOU KNOW YOU ARE MY SUNSHINE
(The Statler Brothers)
5. GEORGIA ON MY MIND
(Willie Nelson)
6. SOFTLY, AS I LEAVE YOU/UNCHAINED
MELODY
(Elvis Presley)
7. RED WINE AND BLUE MEMORIES
(Joe Stampley)
8. IF YOU CAN TOUCH HER AT ALL
(Willie Nelson)
9. NO, NO, NO (I'D RATHER BE FREE)
(Rex Allen Jr.)
10. PUTTIN' IN OVERTIME AT HOME
(Charlie Rich)

COUNTRY ALBUMS

1. WAYLON AND WILLIE
(Waylon Jennings and Willie Nelson)
2. HERE YOU COME AGAIN
(Dolly Parton)
3. EVERY TIME TWO FOOLS COLLIDE
(Kenny Rogers and Dottie West)
4. SON OF A SON OF A SAILOR
(Jimmy Buffett)
5. TEN YEARS OF GOLD
(Kenny Rogers)
6. SIMPLE DREAMS
(Linda Ronstadt)
7. STARDUST
(Willie Nelson)
8. ENTERTAINERS . . . ON AND OFF THE
RECORD
(The Statler Brothers)
9. VARIATIONS
(Eddie Rabbitt)
10. QUARTER MOON IN A TEN CENT TOWN
(Emmylou Harris)

MAY 27, 1978

POP SINGLES

1. WITH A LITTLE LUCK
   (Paul McCartney and Wings)
2. TOO MUCH, TOO LITTLE, TOO LATE
   (Johnny Mathis and Deniece Williams)
3. YOU'RE THE ONE THAT I WANT
   (John Travolta and Olivia Newton-John)
4. SHADOW DANCING
   (Andy Gibb)
5. THE CLOSER I GET TO YOU
   (Roberta Flack with Donny Hathaway)
6. ON BROADWAY
   (George Benson)
7. NIGHT FEVER
   (The Bees Gees)
8. FEELS SO GOOD
   (Chuck Mangione)
9. IMAGINARY LOVER
   (Atlanta Rhythm Section)
10. IT'S A HEARTACHE
    (Bonnie Tyler)

POP ALBUMS

1. SATURDAY NIGHT FEVER
   (Original Soundtrack)
2. LONDON TOWN
   (Paul McCartney and Wings)
3. SHOWDOWN
   (Isley Brothers)
4. FEELS SO GOOD
   (Chuck Mangione)
5. POINT OF KNOW RETURN
   (Kansas)
6. RUNNING ON EMPTY
   (Jackson Browne)
7. EVEN NOW
   (Barry Manilow)
8. THE STRANGER
   (Billy Joel)
9. SLOWHAND
   (Eric Clapton)
10. EARTH
    (The Jefferson Starship)

BLACK SINGLES

1. USE TA BE MY GIRL
   (The O'Jays)
2. TOO MUCH, TOO LITTLE, TOO LATE
   (Johnny Mathis and Deniece Williams)
3. TAKE ME TO THE NEXT PHASE (PART 1)
   (Isley Brothers)
4. THE GROOVE LINE
   (Heatwave)
5. ON BROADWAY
   (George Benson)
6. THE CLOSER I GET TO YOU
   (Roberta Flack with Donny Hathaway)
7. STAY
   (Rufus/Chaka Khan)
8. DANCE WITH ME
   (Peter Brown)
9. FLASH LIGHT
   (Parliament)
10. OH WHAT A NIGHT FOR DANCING
    (Barry White)

BLACK ALBUMS

1. SHOWDOWN
   (Isley Brothers)
2. SO FULL OF LOVE
   (The O'Jays)
3. CENTRAL HEATING
   (Heatwave)
4. SATURDAY NIGHT FEVER
   (Original Soundtrack)

5. WEEKEND IN L.A.
   (George Benson)
6. YOU LIGHT UP MY LIFE
   (Johnny Mathis)
7. NATURAL HIGH
   (Commodores)
8. STREET PLAYER
   (Rufus/Chaka Khan)
9. BOOTSY: PLAYER OF THE YEAR
   (Bootsy's Rubber Band)
10. THANKFUL
    (Natalie Cole)

JAZZ ALBUMS

1. WEEKEND IN L.A.
   (George Benson)
2. FEELS SO GOOD
   (Chuck Mangione)
3. RAINBOW SEEKER
   (Joe Sample)
4. MODERN MAN
   (Stanley Clarke)
5. SAY IT WITH SILENCE
   (Hubert Laws)
6. CASINO
   (Al DiMeola)
7. LIVE AT THE BIJOU
   (Grover Washington Jr.)
8. LOVELAND
   (Lonnie Liston Smith)
9. LOVE ISLAND
   (Deodato)
10. SPINOZZA
    (David Spinozza)

COUNTRY SINGLES

1. DO YOU KNOW YOU ARE MY SUNSHINE
   (The Statler Brothers)
2. GEORGIA ON MY MIND
   (Willie Nelson)
3. I'M ALWAYS ON A MOUNTAIN WHEN I FALL
   (Merle Haggard)
4. SHE CAN PUT HER SHOES UNDER MY BED (ANYTIME)
   (Johnny Duncan)
5. RED WINE AND BLUE MEMORIES
   (Joe Stampley)
6. IF YOU CAN TOUCH HER AT ALL
   (Willie Nelson)
7. PUTTIN' IN OVERTIME AT HOME
   (Charlie Rich)
8. NO, NO, NO (I'D RATHER BE FREE)
   (Rex Allen Jr.)
9. NIGHT TIME MAGIC
   (Larry Gatlin)
10. GOTTA QUIT LOOKIN' AT YOU BABY
    (Dave and Sugar)

COUNTRY ALBUMS

1. WAYLON AND WILLIE
   (Waylon Jennings and Willie Nelson)
2. HERE YOU COME AGAIN
   (Dolly Parton)
3. STARDUST
   (Willie Nelson)
4. TEN YEARS OF GOLD
   (Kenny Rogers)
5. EVERY TIME TWO FOOLS COLLIDE
   (Kenny Rogers and Dottie West)
6. ENTERTAINERS . . . ON AND OFF THE RECORD
   (The Statler Brothers)
7. SIMPLE DREAMS
   (Linda Ronstadt)
8. SON OF A SON OF A SAILOR
   (Jimmy Buffett)
9. VARIATIONS
   (Eddie Rabbitt)
10. Y'ALL COME BACK SALOON
    (The Oak Ridge Boys)

JUNE 3, 1978

POP SINGLES

1. SHADOW DANCING
   (Andy Gibb)
2. YOU'RE THE ONE THAT I WANT
   (John Travolta and Olivia Newton-John)
3. WITH A LITTLE LUCK
   (Paul McCartney and Wings)
4. TOO MUCH, TOO LITTLE, TOO LATE
   (Johnny Mathis and Deniece Williams)
5. ON BROADWAY
   (George Benson)
6. THE CLOSER I GET TO YOU
   (Roberta Flack with Donny Hathaway)
7. FEELS SO GOOD
   (Chuck Mangione)
8. IT'S A HEARTACHE
   (Bonnie Tyler)
9. IMAGINARY LOVER
   (Atlanta Rhythm Section)
10. USE TA BE MY GIRL
    (The O'Jays)

POP ALBUMS

1. SATURDAY NIGHT FEVER
   (Original Soundtrack)
2. FEELS SO GOOD
   (Chuck Mangione)
3. LONDON TOWN
   (Paul McCartney and Wings)
4. SHOWDOWN
   (Isley Brothers)
5. RUNNING ON EMPTY
   (Jackson Browne)
6. POINT OF KNOW RETURN
   (Kansas)
7. EVEN NOW
   (Barry Manilow)
8. THE STRANGER
   (Billy Joel)
9. SO FULL OF LOVE
   (The O'Jays)
10. SLOWHAND
    (Eric Clapton)

BLACK SINGLES

1. USE TA BE MY GIRL
   (The O'Jays)
2. THE GROOVE LINE
   (Heatwave)
3. TAKE ME TO THE NEXT PHASE (PART 1)
   (Isley Brothers)
4. TOO MUCH, TOO LITTLE, TOO LATE
   (Johnny Mathis and Deniece Williams)
5. ON BROADWAY
   (George Benson)
6. DUKEY STICK (PART 1)
   (George Duke)
7. STAY
   (Rufus/Chaka Khan)
8. THE CLOSER I GET TO YOU
   (Roberta Flack with Donny Hathaway)
9. OH WHAT A NIGHT FOR DANCING
   (Barry White)
10. MS
    (David Oliver)

BLACK ALBUMS

1. SHOWDOWN
   (Isley Brothers)
2. SO FULL OF LOVE
   (The O'Jays)
3. CENTRAL HEATING
   (Heatwave)
4. NATURAL HIGH
   (Commodores)

5. SATURDAY NIGHT FEVER
   (Original Soundtrack)
6. WEEKEND IN L.A.
   (George Benson)
7. YOU LIGHT UP MY LIFE
   (Johnny Mathis)
8. STREET PLAYER
   (Rufus/Chaka Khan)
9. THANK GOD IT'S FRIDAY
   (Original Soundtrack)
10. BOOTSY: PLAYER OF THE YEAR
    (Bootsy's Rubber Band)

JAZZ ALBUMS

1. FEELS SO GOOD
   (Chuck Mangione)
2. WEEKEND IN L.A.
   (George Benson)
3. MODERN MAN
   (Stanley Clarke)
4. RAINBOW SEEKER
   (Joe Sample)
5. SAY IT WITH SILENCE
   (Hubert Laws)
6. CASINO
   (Al DiMeola)
7. DON'T LET GO
   (George Duke)
8. LOVELAND
   (Lonnie Liston Smith)
9. LOVE ISLAND
   (Deodato)
10. LIVE AT THE BIJOU
    (Grover Washington Jr.)

COUNTRY SINGLES

1. GEORGIA ON MY MIND
   (Willie Nelson)
2. DO YOU KNOW YOU ARE MY SUNSHINE
   (The Statler Brothers)
3. NIGHT TIME MAGIC
   (Larry Gatlin)
4. RED WINE AND BLUE MEMORIES
   (Joe Stampley)
5. IF YOU CAN TOUCH HER AT ALL
   (Willie Nelson)
6. PUTTIN' IN OVERTIME AT HOME
   (Charlie Rich)
7. NO, NO, NO (I'D RATHER BE FREE)
   (Rex Allen Jr.)
8. GOTTA QUIT LOOKIN' AT YOU BABY
   (Dave and Sugar)
9. TWO MORE BOTTLES OF WINE
   (Emmylou Harris)
10. I'LL BE TRUE TO YOU
    (The Oak Ridge Boys)

COUNTRY ALBUMS

1. WAYLON AND WILLIE
   (Waylon Jennings and Willie Nelson)
2. STARDUST
   (Willie Nelson)
3. HERE YOU COME AGAIN
   (Dolly Parton)
4. TEN YEARS OF GOLD
   (Kenny Rogers)
5. ENTERTAINERS . . . ON AND OFF THE
   RECORD
   (The Statler Brothers)
6. EVERY TIME TWO FOOLS COLLIDE
   (Kenny Rogers and Dottie West)
7. THE BEST OF THE STATLER BROTHERS
   (The Statler Brothers)
8. SIMPLE DREAMS
   (Linda Ronstadt)
9. SON OF A SON OF A SAILOR
   (Jimmy Buffett)
10. VARIATIONS
    (Eddie Rabbitt)

JUNE 10, 1978

POP SINGLES

1. SHADOW DANCING
   (Andy Gibb)
2. YOU'RE THE ONE THAT I WANT
   (John Travolta and Olivia Newton-John)
3. WITH A LITTLE LUCK
   (Paul McCartney and Wings)
4. TOO MUCH, TOO LITTLE, TOO LATE
   (Johnny Mathis and Deniece Williams)
5. IT'S A HEARTACHE
   (Bonnie Tyler)
6. FEELS SO GOOD
   (Chuck Mangione)
7. USE TA BE MY GIRL
   (The O'Jays)
8. BAKER STREET
   (Gerry Rafferty)
9. ON BROADWAY
   (George Benson)
10. YOU BELONG TO ME
    (Carly Simon)

POP ALBUMS

1. SATURDAY NIGHT FEVER
   (Original Soundtrack)
2. FEELS SO GOOD
   (Chuck Mangione)
3. LONDON TOWN
   (Paul McCartney and Wings)
4. SO FULL OF LOVE
   (The O'Jays)
5. RUNNING ON EMPTY
   (Jackson Browne)
6. NATURAL HIGH
   (Commodores)
7. THE STRANGER
   (Billy Joel)
8. SHOWDOWN
   (Isley Brothers)
9. FM
   (Original Soundtrack)
10. EVEN NOW
    (Barry Manilow)

BLACK SINGLES

1. USE TA BE MY GIRL
   (The O'Jays)
2. THE GROOVE LINE
   (Heatwave)
3. TAKE ME TO THE NEXT PHASE (PART 1)
   (Isley Brothers)
4. DUKEY STICK (PART 1)
   (George Duke)
5. TOO MUCH, TOO LITTLE, TOO LATE
   (Johnny Mathis and Deniece Williams)
6. ON BROADWAY
   (George Benson)
7. RUNAWAY LOVE
   (Linda Clifford)
8. STAY
   (Rufus/Chaka Khan)
9. DANCE ACROSS THE FLOOR
   (Jimmy "Bo" Horne)
10. OH WHAT A NIGHT FOR DANCING
    (Barry White)

BLACK ALBUMS

1. SO FULL OF LOVE
   (The O'Jays)
2. NATURAL HIGH
   (Commodores)
3. SHOWDOWN
   (Isley Brothers)
4. CENTRAL HEATING
   (Heatwave)

5. SATURDAY NIGHT FEVER
   (Original Soundtrack)
6. WEEKEND IN L.A.
   (George Benson)
7. THANK GOD IT'S FRIDAY
   (Original Soundtrack)
8. YOU LIGHT UP MY LIFE
   (Johnny Mathis)
9. STREET PLAYER
   (Rufus/Chaka Khan)
10. DO WHAT YOU WANNA DO
    (The Dramatics)

JAZZ ALBUMS

1. FEELS SO GOOD
   (Chuck Mangione)
2. WEEKEND IN L.A.
   (George Benson)
3. MODERN MAN
   (Stanley Clarke)
4. DON'T LET GO
   (George Duke)
5. RAINBOW SEEKER
   (Joe Sample)
6. CASINO
   (Al DiMeola)
7. SAY IT WITH SILENCE
   (Hubert Laws)
8. LOVE ISLAND
   (Deodato)
9. LIVE AT THE BIJOU
   (Grover Washington Jr.)
10. LOVELAND
    (Lonnie Liston Smith)

COUNTRY SINGLES

1. GEORGIA ON MY MIND
   (Willie Nelson)
2. NIGHT TIME MAGIC
   (Larry Gatlin)
3. DO YOU KNOW YOU ARE MY SUNSHINE
   (The Statler Brothers)
4. TWO MORE BOTTLES OF WINE
   (Emmylou Harris)
5. PUTTIN' IN OVERTIME AT HOME
   (Charlie Rich)
6. GOTTA QUIT LOOKIN' AT YOU BABY
   (Dave and Sugar)
7. NO, NO, NO (I'D RATHER BE FREE)
   (Rex Allen Jr.)
8. I'LL BE TRUE TO YOU
   (The Oak Ridge Boys)
9. RED WINE AND BLUE MEMORIES
   (Joe Stampley)
10. COWBOYS DON'T GET LUCKY ALL THE
    TIME
    (Gene Watson)

COUNTRY ALBUMS

1. WAYLON AND WILLIE
   (Waylon Jennings and Willie Nelson)
2. STARDUST
   (Willie Nelson)
3. HERE YOU COME AGAIN
   (Dolly Parton)
4. EVERY TIME TWO FOOLS COLLIDE
   (Kenny Rogers and Dottie West)
5. ENTERTAINERS . . . ON AND OFF THE
   RECORD
   (The Statler Brothers)
6. TEN YEARS OF GOLD
   (Kenny Rogers)
7. THE BEST OF THE STATLER BROTHERS
   (The Statler Brothers)
8. HE WALKS BESIDE ME
   (Elvis Presley)
9. SON OF A SON OF A SAILOR
   (Jimmy Buffett)
10. TAKE THIS JOB AND SHOVE IT
    (Johnny Paycheck)

JUNE 17, 1978

POP SINGLES

1. SHADOW DANCING
   (Andy Gibb)
2. YOU'RE THE ONE THAT I WANT
   (John Travolta and Olivia Newton-John)
3. IT'S A HEARTACHE
   (Bonnie Tyler)
4. BAKER STREET
   (Gerry Rafferty)
5. USE TA BE MY GIRL
   (The O'Jays)
6. WITH A LITTLE LUCK
   (Paul McCartney and Wings)
7. FEELS SO GOOD
   (Chuck Mangione)
8. TOO MUCH, TOO LITTLE, TOO LATE
   (Johnny Mathis and Deniece Williams)
9. YOU BELONG TO ME
   (Carly Simon)
10. THE GROOVE LINE
    (Heatwave)

POP ALBUMS

1. SATURDAY NIGHT FEVER
   (Original Soundtrack)
2. FEELS SO GOOD
   (Chuck Mangione)
3. NATURAL HIGH
   (Commodores)
4. SO FULL OF LOVE
   (The O'Jays)
5. STRANGER IN TOWN
   (Bob Seger and The Silver Bullet Band)
6. THE STRANGER
   (Billy Joel)
7. FM
   (Original Soundtrack)
8. RUNNING ON EMPTY
   (Jackson Browne)
9. LONDON TOWN
   (Paul McCartney and Wings)
10. SHOWDOWN
    (Isley Brothers)

BLACK SINGLES

1. USE TA BE MY GIRL
   (The O'Jays)
2. THE GROOVE LINE
   (Heatwave)
3. TAKE ME TO THE NEXT PHASE (PART 1)
   (Isley Brothers)
4. RUNAWAY LOVE
   (Linda Clifford)
5. DUKEY STICK (PART 1)
   (George Duke)
6. SHAME
   (Evelyn "Champagne" King)
7. TOO MUCH, TOO LITTLE, TOO LATE
   (Johnny Mathis and Deniece Williams)
8. ON BROADWAY
   (George Benson)
9. DANCE ACROSS THE FLOOR
   (Jimmy "Bo" Horne)
10. STUFF LIKE THAT
    (Quincy Jones)

BLACK ALBUMS

1. SO FULL OF LOVE
   (The O'Jays)
2. NATURAL HIGH
   (Commodores)
3. SHOWDOWN
   (Isley Brothers)
4. CENTRAL HEATING
   (Heatwave)

5. SATURDAY NIGHT FEVER
   (Original Soundtrack)
6. THANK GOD IT'S FRIDAY
   (Original Soundtrack)
7. STREET PLAYER
   (Rufus/Chaka Khan)
8. YOU LIGHT UP MY LIFE
   (Johnny Mathis)
9. WEEKEND IN L.A.
   (George Benson)
10. DO WHAT YOU WANNA DO
    (The Dramatics)

JAZZ ALBUMS

1. FEELS SO GOOD
   (Chuck Mangione)
2. WEEKEND IN L.A.
   (George Benson)
3. MODERN MAN
   (Stanley Clarke)
4. DON'T LET GO
   (George Duke)
5. RAINBOW SEEKER
   (Joe Sample)
6. CASINO
   (Al DiMeola)
7. SAY IT WITH SILENCE
   (Hubert Laws)
8. LOVELAND
   (Lonnie Liston Smith)
9. LOVE ISLAND
   (Deodato)
10. ELECTRIC GUITARIST
    (John McLaughlin)

COUNTRY SINGLES

1. NIGHT TIME MAGIC
   (Larry Gatlin)
2. TWO MORE BOTTLES OF WINE
   (Emmylou Harris)
3. GEORGIA ON MY MIND
   (Willie Nelson)
4. I'LL BE TRUE TO YOU
   (The Oak Ridge Boys)
5. IT ONLY HURTS FOR A LITTLE WHILE
   (Margo Smith)
6. GOTTA QUIT LOOKIN' AT YOU BABY
   (Dave and Sugar)
7. I CAN'T WAIT ANY LONGER
   (Bill Anderson)
8. DO YOU KNOW YOU ARE MY SUNSHINE
   (The Statler Brothers)
9. COWBOYS DON'T GET LUCKY ALL THE TIME
   (Gene Watson)
10. I BELIEVE IN YOU
    (Mel Tillis)

COUNTRY ALBUMS

1. STARDUST
   (Willie Nelson)
2. WAYLON AND WILLIE
   (Waylon Jennings and Willie Nelson)
3. TEN YEARS OF GOLD
   (Kenny Rogers)
4. EVERY TIME TWO FOOLS COLLIDE
   (Kenny Rogers and Dottie West)
5. HERE YOU COME AGAIN
   (Dolly Parton)
6. ENTERTAINERS . . . ON AND OFF THE RECORD
   (The Statler Brothers)
7. THE BEST OF THE STATLER BROTHERS
   (The Statler Brothers)
8. HE WALKS BESIDE ME
   (Elvis Presley)
9. SON OF A SON OF A SAILOR
   (Jimmy Buffett)
10. TAKE THIS JOB AND SHOVE IT
    (Johnny Paycheck)

JUNE 24, 1978

POP SINGLES

1. SHADOW DANCING
   (Andy Gibb)
2. BAKER STREET
   (Gerry Rafferty)
3. IT'S A HEARTACHE
   (Bonnie Tyler)
4. USE TA BE MY GIRL
   (The O'Jays)
5. YOU'RE THE ONE THAT I WANT
   (John Travolta and Olivia Newton-John)
6. WITH A LITTLE LUCK
   (Paul McCartney and Wings)
7. THE GROOVE LINE
   (Heatwave)
8. YOU BELONG TO ME
   (Carly Simon)
9. STILL THE SAME
   (Bob Seger and The Silver Bullet Band)
10. TWO OUT OF THREE AIN'T BAD
    (Meat Loaf)

POP ALBUMS

1. SATURDAY NIGHT FEVER
   (Original Soundtrack)
2. NATURAL HIGH
   (Commodores)
3. FEELS SO GOOD
   (Chuck Mangione)
4. STRANGER IN TOWN
   (Bob Seger and The Silver Bullet Band)
5. SO FULL OF LOVE
   (The O'Jays)
6. CITY TO CITY
   (Gerry Rafferty)
7. FM
   (Original Soundtrack)
8. THE STRANGER
   (Billy Joel)
9. SHADOW DANCING
   (Andy Gibb)
10. DARKNESS ON THE EDGE OF TOWN
    (Bruce Springsteen)

BLACK SINGLES

1. USE TA BE MY GIRL
   (The O'Jays)
2. THE GROOVE LINE
   (Heatwave)
3. RUNAWAY LOVE
   (Linda Clifford)
4. SHAME
   (Evelyn "Champagne" King)
5. DUKEY STICK (PART 1)
   (George Duke)
6. TAKE ME TO THE NEXT PHASE (PART 1)
   (Isley Brothers)
7. STUFF LIKE THAT
   (Quincy Jones)
8. CLOSE THE DOOR
   (Teddy Pendergrass)
9. DANCE ACROSS THE FLOOR
   (Jimmy "Bo" Horne)
10. ANNIE MAE
    (Natalie Cole)

BLACK ALBUMS

1. NATURAL HIGH
   (Commodores)
2. SO FULL OF LOVE
   (The O'Jays)
3. SHOWDOWN
   (Isley Brothers)
4. CENTRAL HEATING
   (Heatwave)

5. LIFE IS A SONG WORTH SINGING
   (*Teddy Pendergrass*)
6. THANK GOD IT'S FRIDAY
   (*Original Soundtrack*)
7. IF MY FRIENDS COULD SEE ME NOW
   (*Linda Clifford*)
8. SATURDAY NIGHT FEVER
   (*Original Soundtrack*)
9. COME GET IT
   (*Rick James Stone City Band*)
10. DON'T LET GO
    (*George Duke*)

JAZZ ALBUMS

1. FEELS SO GOOD
   (*Chuck Mangione*)
2. WEEKEND IN L.A.
   (*George Benson*)
3. MODERN MAN
   (*Stanley Clarke*)
4. DON'T LET GO
   (*George Duke*)
5. ARABESQUE
   (*John Klemmer*)
6. CASINO
   (*Al DiMeola*)
7. RAINBOW SEEKER
   (*Joe Sample*)
8. SAY IT WITH SILENCE
   (*Hubert Laws*)
9. ELECTRIC GUITARIST
   (*John McLaughlin*)
10. LOVELAND
    (*Lonnie Liston Smith*)

COUNTRY SINGLES

1. TWO MORE BOTTLES OF WINE
   (*Emmylou Harris*)
2. I'LL BE TRUE TO YOU
   (*The Oak Ridge Boys*)
3. IT ONLY HURTS FOR A LITTLE WHILE
   (*Margo Smith*)
4. NIGHT TIME MAGIC
   (*Larry Gatlin*)
5. I CAN'T WAIT ANY LONGER
   (*Bill Anderson*)
6. GEORGIA ON MY MIND
   (*Willie Nelson*)
7. I BELIEVE IN YOU
   (*Mel Tillis*)
8. GOTTA QUIT LOOKIN' AT YOU BABY
   (*Dave and Sugar*)
9. IT'S A HEARTACHE
   (*Bonnie Tyler*)
10. SLOW AND EASY
    (*Randy Barlow*)

COUNTRY ALBUMS

1. STARDUST
   (*Willie Nelson*)
2. WAYLON AND WILLIE
   (*Waylon Jennings and Willie Nelson*)
3. TEN YEARS OF GOLD
   (*Kenny Rogers*)
4. THE BEST OF THE STATLER BROTHERS
   (*The Statler Brothers*)
5. HERE YOU COME AGAIN
   (*Dolly Parton*)
6. ENTERTAINERS . . . ON AND OFF THE
   RECORD
   (*The Statler Brothers*)
7. OH! BROTHER
   (*Larry Gatlin*)
8. SON OF A SON OF A SAILOR
   (*Jimmy Buffett*)
9. EVERY TIME TWO FOOLS COLLIDE
   (*Kenny Rogers and Dottie West*)
10. QUARTER MOON IN A TEN CENT TOWN
    (*Emmylou Harris*)

JULY 1, 1978

POP SINGLES

1. SHADOW DANCING
   (*Andy Gibb*)
2. BAKER STREET
   (*Gerry Rafferty*)
3. USE TA BE MY GIRL
   (*The O'Jays*)
4. IT'S A HEARTACHE
   (*Bonnie Tyler*)
5. YOU'RE THE ONE THAT I WANT
   (*John Travolta and Olivia Newton-John*)
6. STILL THE SAME
   (*Bob Seger and The Silver Bullet Band*)
7. THE GROOVE LINE
   (*Heatwave*)
8. YOU BELONG TO ME
   (*Carly Simon*)
9. TWO OUT OF THREE AIN'T BAD
   (*Meat Loaf*)
10. TAKE A CHANCE ON ME
    (*Abba*)

POP ALBUMS

1. SATURDAY NIGHT FEVER
   (*Original Soundtrack*)
2. NATURAL HIGH
   (*Commodores*)
3. SHADOW DANCING
   (*Andy Gibb*)
4. STRANGER IN TOWN
   (*Bob Seger and The Silver Bullet Band*)
5. SOME GIRLS
   (*The Rolling Stones*)
6. CITY TO CITY
   (*Gerry Rafferty*)
7. FEELS SO GOOD
   (*Chuck Mangione*)
8. DARKNESS ON THE EDGE OF TOWN
   (*Bruce Springsteen*)
9. SO FULL OF LOVE
   (*The O'Jays*)
10. THE STRANGER
    (*Billy Joel*)

BLACK SINGLES

1. USE TA BE MY GIRL
   (*The O'Jays*)
2. CLOSE THE DOOR
   (*Teddy Pendergrass*)
3. RUNAWAY LOVE
   (*Linda Clifford*)
4. SHAME
   (*Evelyn "Champagne" King*)
5. STUFF LIKE THAT
   (*Quincy Jones*)
6. THE GROOVE LINE
   (*Heatwave*)
7. DUKEY STICK (PART 1)
   (*George Duke*)
8. ANNIE MAE
   (*Natalie Cole*)
9. YOU AND I
   (*Rick James Stone City Band*)
10. TAKE ME TO THE NEXT PHASE (PART 1)
    (*Isley Brothers*)

BLACK ALBUMS

1. NATURAL HIGH
   (*Commodores*)
2. SO FULL OF LOVE
   (*The O'Jays*)
3. SHOWDOWN
   (*Isley Brothers*)
4. LIFE IS A SONG WORTH SINGING
   (*Teddy Pendergrass*)

5. CENTRAL HEATING
   (*Heatwave*)
6. THANK GOD IT'S FRIDAY
   (*Original Soundtrack*)
7. IF MY FRIENDS COULD SEE ME NOW
   (*Linda Clifford*)
8. SOUNDS . . . AND STUFF LIKE THAT!!
   (*Quincy Jones*)
9. COME GET IT
   (*Rick James Stone City Band*)
10. TOGETHERNESS
    (*L.T.D.*)

JAZZ ALBUMS

1. FEELS SO GOOD
   (*Chuck Mangione*)
2. MODERN MAN
   (*Stanley Clarke*)
3. DON'T LET GO
   (*George Duke*)
4. WEEKEND IN L.A.
   (*George Benson*)
5. ARABESQUE
   (*John Klemmer*)
6. SOUNDS . . . AND STUFF LIKE THAT!!
   (*Quincy Jones*)
7. CASINO
   (*Al DiMeola*)
8. MAGIC IN YOUR EYES
   (*Earl Klugh*)
9. ELECTRIC GUITARIST
   (*John McLaughlin*)
10. FREESTYLE
    (*Bobbi Humphrey*)

COUNTRY SINGLES

1. I'LL BE TRUE TO YOU
   (*The Oak Ridge Boys*)
2. IT ONLY HURTS FOR A LITTLE WHILE
   (*Margo Smith*)
3. I BELIEVE IN YOU
   (*Mel Tillis*)
4. I CAN'T WAIT ANY LONGER
   (*Bill Anderson*)
5. TWO MORE BOTTLES OF WINE
   (*Emmylou Harris*)
6. THERE AIN'T NO GOOD CHAIN GANGS
   (*Johnny Cash and Waylon Jennings*)
7. ONLY ONE LOVE IN MY LIFE
   (*Ronnie Milsap*)
8. I NEVER WILL MARRY
   (*Linda Ronstadt*)
9. IT'S A HEARTACHE
   (*Bonnie Tyler*)
10. SLOW AND EASY
    (*Randy Barlow*)

COUNTRY ALBUMS

1. STARDUST
   (*Willie Nelson*)
2. WAYLON AND WILLIE
   (*Waylon Jennings and Willie Nelson*)
3. OH! BROTHER
   (*Larry Gatlin*)
4. THE BEST OF THE STATLER BROTHERS
   (*The Statler Brothers*)
5. TEN YEARS OF GOLD
   (*Kenny Rogers*)
6. ROOM SERVICE
   (*The Oak Ridge Boys*)
7. HERE YOU COME AGAIN
   (*Dolly Parton*)
8. ONLY ONE LOVE IN MY LIFE
   (*Ronnie Milsap*)
9. EVERY TIME TWO FOOLS COLLIDE
   (*Kenny Rogers and Dottie West*)
10. IT'S A HEARTACHE
    (*Bonnie Tyler*)

JULY 8, 1978

POP SINGLES

1. SHADOW DANCING
   (Andy Gibb)
2. BAKER STREET
   (Gerry Rafferty)
3. USE TA BE MY GIRL
   (The O'Jays)
4. YOU'RE THE ONE THAT I WANT
   (John Travolta and Olivia Newton-John)
5. IT'S A HEARTACHE
   (Bonnie Tyler)
6. STILL THE SAME
   (Bob Seger and The Silver Bullet Band)
7. THE GROOVE LINE
   (Heatwave)
8. TWO OUT OF THREE AIN'T BAD
   (Meat Loaf)
9. TAKE A CHANCE ON ME
   (Abba)
10. MISS YOU
    (The Rolling Stones)

POP ALBUMS

1. SATURDAY NIGHT FEVER
   (Original Soundtrack)
2. SHADOW DANCING
   (Andy Gibb)
3. SOME GIRLS
   (The Rolling Stones)
4. NATURAL HIGH
   (Commodores)
5. CITY TO CITY
   (Gerry Rafferty)
6. STRANGER IN TOWN
   (Bob Seger and The Silver Bullet Band)
7. FEELS SO GOOD
   (Chuck Mangione)
8. DARKNESS ON THE EDGE OF TOWN
   (Bruce Springsteen)
9. THE STRANGER
   (Billy Joel)
10. SO FULL OF LOVE
    (The O'Jays)

BLACK SINGLES

1. USE TA BE MY GIRL
   (The O'Jays)
2. CLOSE THE DOOR
   (Teddy Pendergrass)
3. RUNAWAY LOVE
   (Linda Clifford)
4. SHAME
   (Evelyn "Champagne" King)
5. STUFF LIKE THAT
   (Quincy Jones)
6. YOU AND I
   (Rick James Stone City Band)
7. ANNIE MAE
   (Natalie Cole)
8. BOOGIE, OOGIE OOGIE
   (A Taste of Honey)
9. THE GROOVE LINE
   (Heatwave)
10. LAST DANCE
    (Donna Summer)

BLACK ALBUMS

1. NATURAL HIGH
   (Commodores)
2. SO FULL OF LOVE
   (The O'Jays)
3. LIFE IS A SONG WORTH SINGING
   (Teddy Pendergrass)
4. SHOWDOWN
   (Isley Brothers)

5. THANK GOD IT'S FRIDAY
   (Original Soundtrack)
6. CENTRAL HEATING
   (Heatwave)
7. SOUNDS . . . AND STUFF LIKE THAT!!
   (Quincy Jones)
8. IF MY FRIENDS COULD SEE ME NOW
   (Linda Clifford)
9. COME GET IT
   (Rick James Stone City Band)
10. TOGETHERNESS
    (L.T.D.)

JAZZ ALBUMS

1. FEELS SO GOOD
   (Chuck Mangione)
2. MODERN MAN
   (Stanley Clarke)
3. SOUNDS . . . AND STUFF LIKE THAT!!
   (Quincy Jones)
4. DON'T LET GO
   (George Duke)
5. ARABESQUE
   (John Klemmer)
6. WEEKEND IN L.A.
   (George Benson)
7. FREESTYLE
   (Bobbi Humphrey)
8. SAY IT WITH SILENCE
   (Hubert Laws)
9. ELECTRIC GUITARIST
   (John McLaughlin)
10. MAGIC IN YOUR EYES
    (Earl Klugh)

COUNTRY SINGLES

1. IT ONLY HURTS FOR A LITTLE WHILE
   (Margo Smith)
2. I BELIEVE IN YOU
   (Mel Tillis)
3. THERE AIN'T NO GOOD CHAIN GANGS
   (Johnny Cash and Waylon Jennings)
4. I CAN'T WAIT ANY LONGER
   (Bill Anderson)
5. ONLY ONE LOVE IN MY LIFE
   (Ronnie Milsap)
6. LOVE OR SOMETHING LIKE IT
   (Kenny Rogers)
7. TONIGHT
   (Barbara Mandrell)
8. I NEVER WILL MARRY
   (Linda Ronstadt)
9. I'LL BE TRUE TO YOU
   (The Oak Ridge Boys)
10. NEVER MY LOVE
    (Vern Gosdin)

COUNTRY ALBUMS

1. STARDUST
   (Willie Nelson)
2. WAYLON AND WILLIE
   (Waylon Jennings and Willie Nelson)
3. OH! BROTHER
   (Larry Gatlin)
4. ONLY ONE LOVE IN MY LIFE
   (Ronnie Milsap)
5. WHEN I DREAM
   (Crystal Gayle)
6. ROOM SERVICE
   (The Oak Ridge Boys)
7. HERE YOU COME AGAIN
   (Dolly Parton)
8. IT'S A HEARTACHE
   (Bonnie Tyler)
9. THE BEST OF THE STATLER BROTHERS
   (The Statler Brothers)
10. ENTERTAINERS . . . ON AND OFF THE RECORD
    (The Statler Brothers)

JULY 15, 1978

POP SINGLES

1. SHADOW DANCING
   (Andy Gibb)
2. BAKER STREET
   (Gerry Rafferty)
3. USE TA BE MY GIRL
   (The O'Jays)
4. YOU'RE THE ONE THAT I WANT
   (John Travolta and Olivia Newton-John)
5. STILL THE SAME
   (Bob Seger and The Silver Bullet Band)
6. MISS YOU
   (The Rolling Stones)
7. TWO OUT OF THREE AIN'T BAD
   (Meat Loaf)
8. LAST DANCE
   (Donna Summer)
9. TAKE A CHANCE ON ME
   (Abba)
10. THE GROOVE LINE
    (Heatwave)

POP ALBUMS

1. SOME GIRLS
   (The Rolling Stones)
2. SHADOW DANCING
   (Andy Gibb)
3. GREASE
   (Original Soundtrack)
4. NATURAL HIGH
   (Commodores)
5. CITY TO CITY
   (Gerry Rafferty)
6. SATURDAY NIGHT FEVER
   (Original Soundtrack)
7. STRANGER IN TOWN
   (Bob Seger and The Silver Bullet Band)
8. FEELS SO GOOD
   (Chuck Mangione)
9. DARKNESS ON THE EDGE OF TOWN
   (Bruce Springsteen)
10. DOUBLE VISION
    (Foreigner)

BLACK SINGLES

1. CLOSE THE DOOR
   (Teddy Pendergrass)
2. USE TA BE MY GIRL
   (The O'Jays)
3. SHAME
   (Evelyn "Champagne" King)
4. STUFF LIKE THAT
   (Quincy Jones)
5. YOU AND I
   (Rick James Stone City Band)
6. BOOGIE, OOGIE OOGIE
   (A Taste of Honey)
7. THREE TIMES A LADY
   (Commodores)
8. LAST DANCE
   (Donna Summer)
9. RUNAWAY LOVE
   (Linda Clifford)
10. ANNIE MAE
    (Natalie Cole)

BLACK ALBUMS

1. NATURAL HIGH
   (Commodores)
2. LIFE IS A SONG WORTH SINGING
   (Teddy Pendergrass)
3. SO FULL OF LOVE
   (The O'Jays)
4. SOUNDS . . . AND STUFF LIKE THAT!!
   (Quincy Jones)

5. COME GET IT
   (*Rick James Stone City Band*)
6. TOGETHERNESS
   (*L.T.D.*)
7. CENTRAL HEATING
   (*Heatwave*)
8. THANK GOD IT'S FRIDAY
   (*Original Soundtrack*)
9. SMOOTH TALK
   (*Evelyn "Champagne" King*)
10. A TASTE OF HONEY
   (*A Taste of Honey*)

JAZZ ALBUMS

1. SOUNDS . . . AND STUFF LIKE THAT!!
   (*Quincy Jones*)
2. FEELS SO GOOD
   (*Chuck Mangione*)
3. ARABESQUE
   (*John Klemmer*)
4. DON'T LET GO
   (*George Duke*)
5. WEEKEND IN L.A.
   (*George Benson*)
6. MODERN MAN
   (*Stanley Clarke*)
7. SUNLIGHT
   (*Herbie Hancock*)
8. FREESTYLE
   (*Bobbi Humphrey*)
9. ELECTRIC GUITARIST
   (*John McLaughlin*)
10. CASINO
   (*Al DiMeola*)

COUNTRY SINGLES

1. I BELIEVE IN YOU
   (*Mel Tillis*)
2. ONLY ONE LOVE IN MY LIFE
   (*Ronnie Milsap*)
3. THERE AIN'T NO GOOD CHAIN GANGS
   (*Johnny Cash and Waylon Jennings*)
4. LOVE OR SOMETHING LIKE IT
   (*Kenny Rogers*)
5. IT ONLY HURTS FOR A LITTLE WHILE
   (*Margo Smith*)
6. TONIGHT
   (*Barbara Mandrell*)
7. WHEN CAN WE DO THIS AGAIN
   (*T.G. Sheppard*)
8. NEVER MY LOVE
   (*Vern Gosdin*)
9. PITTSBURGH STEALERS
   (*The Kendalls*)
10. YOU DON'T LOVE ME ANYMORE
   (*Eddie Rabbitt*)

COUNTRY ALBUMS

1. STARDUST
   (*Willie Nelson*)
2. WHEN I DREAM
   (*Crystal Gayle*)
3. WAYLON AND WILLIE
   (*Waylon Jennings and Willie Nelson*)
4. ONLY ONE LOVE IN MY LIFE
   (*Ronnie Milsap*)
5. ROOM SERVICE
   (*The Oak Ridge Boys*)
6. OH! BROTHER
   (*Larry Gatlin*)
7. IT'S A HEARTACHE
   (*Bonnie Tyler*)
8. THE BEST OF THE STATLER BROTHERS
   (*The Statler Brothers*)
9. HERE YOU COME AGAIN
   (*Dolly Parton*)
10. VARIATIONS
   (*Eddie Rabbitt*)

JULY 22, 1978

POP SINGLES

1. SHADOW DANCING
   (*Andy Gibb*)
2. YOU'RE THE ONE THAT I WANT
   (*John Travolta and Olivia Newton-John*)
3. BAKER STREET
   (*Gerry Rafferty*)
4. MISS YOU
   (*The Rolling Stones*)
5. STILL THE SAME
   (*Bob Seger and The Silver Bullet Band*)
6. LAST DANCE
   (*Donna Summer*)
7. USE TA BE MY GIRL
   (*The O'Jays*)
8. TWO OUT OF THREE AIN'T BAD
   (*Meat Loaf*)
9. THREE TIMES A LADY
   (*Commodores*)
10. GREASE
   (*Frankie Valli*)

POP ALBUMS

1. GREASE
   (*Original Soundtrack*)
2. SOME GIRLS
   (*The Rolling Stones*)
3. NATURAL HIGH
   (*Commodores*)
4. SHADOW DANCING
   (*Andy Gibb*)
5. SATURDAY NIGHT FEVER
   (*Original Soundtrack*)
6. DOUBLE VISION
   (*Foreigner*)
7. CITY TO CITY
   (*Gerry Rafferty*)
8. STRANGER IN TOWN
   (*Bob Seger and The Silver Bullet Band*)
9. DARKNESS ON THE EDGE OF TOWN
   (*Bruce Springsteen*)
10. FEELS SO GOOD
   (*Chuck Mangione*)

BLACK SINGLES

1. CLOSE THE DOOR
   (*Teddy Pendergrass*)
2. STUFF LIKE THAT
   (*Quincy Jones*)
3. SHAME
   (*Evelyn "Champagne" King*)
4. YOU AND I
   (*Rick James Stone City Band*)
5. BOOGIE, OOGIE OOGIE
   (*A Taste of Honey*)
6. THREE TIMES A LADY
   (*Commodores*)
7. LAST DANCE
   (*Donna Summer*)
8. USE TA BE MY GIRL
   (*The O'Jays*)
9. RUNAWAY LOVE
   (*Linda Clifford*)
10. ANNIE MAE
   (*Natalie Cole*)

BLACK ALBUMS

1. NATURAL HIGH
   (*Commodores*)
2. LIFE IS A SONG WORTH SINGING
   (*Teddy Pendergrass*)
3. SO FULL OF LOVE
   (*The O'Jays*)
4. SOUNDS . . . AND STUFF LIKE THAT!!
   (*Quincy Jones*)

5. COME GET IT
   (*Rick James Stone City Band*)
6. TOGETHERNESS
   (*L.T.D.*)
7. A TASTE OF HONEY
   (*A Taste of Honey*)
8. SMOOTH TALK
   (*Evelyn "Champagne" King*)
9. THANK GOD IT'S FRIDAY
   (*Original Soundtrack*)
10. NATALIE . . . LIVE!
   (*Natalie Cole*)

JAZZ ALBUMS

1. SOUNDS . . . AND STUFF LIKE THAT!!
   (*Quincy Jones*)
2. FEELS SO GOOD
   (*Chuck Mangione*)
3. ARABESQUE
   (*John Klemmer*)
4. DON'T LET GO
   (*George Duke*)
5. WEEKEND IN L.A.
   (*George Benson*)
6. SUNLIGHT
   (*Herbie Hancock*)
7. FREESTYLE
   (*Bobbi Humphrey*)
8. IMAGES
   (*The Crusaders*)
9. MODERN MAN
   (*Stanley Clarke*)
10. CASINO
   (*Al DiMeola*)

COUNTRY SINGLES

1. ONLY ONE LOVE IN MY LIFE
   (*Ronnie Milsap*)
2. LOVE OR SOMETHING LIKE IT
   (*Kenny Rogers*)
3. THERE AIN'T NO GOOD CHAIN GANGS
   (*Johnny Cash and Waylon Jennings*)
4. I BELIEVE IN YOU
   (*Mel Tillis*)
5. YOU DON'T LOVE ME ANYMORE
   (*Eddie Rabbitt*)
6. PITTSBURGH STEALERS
   (*The Kendalls*)
7. WHEN CAN WE DO THIS AGAIN
   (*T.G. Sheppard*)
8. NEVER MY LOVE
   (*Vern Gosdin*)
9. SPRING FEVER
   (*Loretta Lynn*)
10. YOU NEEDED ME
   (*Anne Murray*)

COUNTRY ALBUMS

1. STARDUST
   (*Willie Nelson*)
2. WHEN I DREAM
   (*Crystal Gayle*)
3. WAYLON AND WILLIE
   (*Waylon Jennings and Willie Nelson*)
4. ONLY ONE LOVE IN MY LIFE
   (*Ronnie Milsap*)
5. ROOM SERVICE
   (*The Oak Ridge Boys*)
6. OH! BROTHER
   (*Larry Gatlin*)
7. IT'S A HEARTACHE
   (*Bonnie Tyler*)
8. TEN YEARS OF GOLD
   (*Kenny Rogers*)
9. EVERY TIME TWO FOOLS COLLIDE
   (*Kenny Rogers and Dottie West*)
10. VARIATIONS
   (*Eddie Rabbitt*)

JULY 29, 1978

POP SINGLES

1. YOU'RE THE ONE THAT I WANT
   (John Travolta and Olivia Newton-John)
2. SHADOW DANCING
   (Andy Gibb)
3. MISS YOU
   (The Rolling Stones)
4. GREASE
   (Frankie Valli)
5. LAST DANCE
   (Donna Summer)
6. THREE TIMES A LADY
   (Commodores)
7. BAKER STREET
   (Gerry Rafferty)
8. TWO OUT OF THREE AIN'T BAD
   (Meat Loaf)
9. COPACABANA (AT THE COPA)
   (Barry Manilow)
10. STILL THE SAME
    (Bob Seger and The Silver Bullet Band)

POP ALBUMS

1. GREASE
   (Original Soundtrack)
2. SOME GIRLS
   (The Rolling Stones)
3. NATURAL HIGH
   (Commodores)
4. SHADOW DANCING
   (Andy Gibb)
5. DOUBLE VISION
   (Foreigner)
6. SATURDAY NIGHT FEVER
   (Original Soundtrack)
7. CITY TO CITY
   (Gerry Rafferty)
8. STRANGER IN TOWN
   (Bob Seger and The Silver Bullet Band)
9. DARKNESS ON THE EDGE OF TOWN
   (Bruce Springsteen)
10. BUT SERIOUSLY, FOLKS . . .
    (Joe Walsh)

BLACK SINGLES

1. CLOSE THE DOOR
   (Teddy Pendergrass)
2. STUFF LIKE THAT
   (Quincy Jones)
3. YOU AND I
   (Rick James Stone City Band)
4. BOOGIE, OOGIE OOGIE
   (A Taste of Honey)
5. THREE TIMES A LADY
   (Commodores)
6. SHAME
   (Evelyn "Champagne" King)
7. LAST DANCE
   (Donna Summer)
8. USE TA BE MY GIRL
   (The O'Jays)
9. RUNAWAY LOVE
   (Linda Clifford)
10. ANNIE MAE
    (Natalie Cole)

BLACK ALBUMS

1. NATURAL HIGH
   (Commodores)
2. LIFE IS A SONG WORTH SINGING
   (Teddy Pendergrass)
3. COME GET IT
   (Rick James Stone City Band)
4. SOUNDS . . . AND STUFF LIKE THAT!!
   (Quincy Jones)

---

5. TOGETHERNESS
   (L.T.D.)
6. SO FULL OF LOVE
   (The O'Jays)
7. A TASTE OF HONEY
   (A Taste of Honey)
8. SMOOTH TALK
   (Evelyn "Champagne" King)
9. NATALIE . . . LIVE!
   (Natalie Cole)
10. LOVESHINE
    (Con Funk Shun)

JAZZ ALBUMS

1. SOUNDS . . . AND STUFF LIKE THAT!!
   (Quincy Jones)
2. FEELS SO GOOD
   (Chuck Mangione)
3. IMAGES
   (Crusaders)
4. SUNLIGHT
   (Herbie Hancock)
5. ARABESQUE
   (John Klemmer)
6. WEEKEND IN L.A.
   (George Benson)
7. FREESTYLE
   (Bobbi Humphrey)
8. DON'T LET GO
   (George Duke)
9. MODERN MAN
   (Stanley Clarke)
10. CASINO
    (Al DiMeola)

COUNTRY SINGLES

1. LOVE OR SOMETHING LIKE IT
   (Kenny Rogers)
2. ONLY ONE LOVE IN MY LIFE
   (Ronnie Milsap)
3. YOU DON'T LOVE ME ANYMORE
   (Eddie Rabbitt)
4. THERE AIN'T NO GOOD CHAIN GANGS
   (Johnny Cash and Waylon Jennings)
5. PITTSBURGH STEALERS
   (The Kendalls)
6. WHEN CAN WE DO THIS AGAIN
   (T.G. Sheppard)
7. TALKING IN YOUR SLEEP
   (Crystal Gayle)
8. YOU NEEDED ME
   (Anne Murray)
9. SPRING FEVER
   (Loretta Lynn)
10. WE BELONG TOGETHER
    (Susie Allanson)

COUNTRY ALBUMS

1. STARDUST
   (Willie Nelson)
2. WHEN I DREAM
   (Crystal Gayle)
3. WAYLON AND WILLIE
   (Waylon Jennings and Willie Nelson)
4. ONLY ONE LOVE IN MY LIFE
   (Ronnie Milsap)
5. ROOM SERVICE
   (The Oak Ridge Boys)
6. OH! BROTHER
   (Larry Gatlin)
7. IT'S A HEARTACHE
   (Bonnie Tyler)
8. TEN YEARS OF GOLD
   (Kenny Rogers)
9. EVERY TIME TWO FOOLS COLLIDE
   (Kenny Rogers and Dotty West)
10. LOVE OR SOMETHING LIKE IT
    (Kenny Rogers)

AUGUST 5, 1978

POP SINGLES

1. THREE TIMES A LADY
   (Commodores)
2. GREASE
   (Frankie Valli)
3. MISS YOU
   (The Rolling Stones)
4. LAST DANCE
   (Donna Summer)
5. YOU'RE THE ONE THAT I WANT
   (John Travolta and Olivia Newton-John)
6. SHADOW DANCING
   (Andy Gibb)
7. COPACABANA (AT THE COPA)
   (Barry Manilow)
8. TWO OUT OF THREE AIN'T BAD
   (Meat Loaf)
9. BAKER STREET
   (Gerry Rafferty)
10. LOVE WILL FIND A WAY
    (Pablo Cruise)

POP ALBUMS

1. GREASE
   (Original Soundtrack)
2. SOME GIRLS
   (The Rolling Stones)
3. NATURAL HIGH
   (Commodores)
4. DOUBLE VISION
   (Foreigner)
5. SHADOW DANCING
   (Andy Gibb)
6. SATURDAY NIGHT FEVER
   (Original Soundtrack)
7. STRANGER IN TOWN
   (Bob Seger and The Silver Bullet Band)
8. CITY TO CITY
   (Gerry Rafferty)
9. BUT SERIOUSLY, FOLKS . . .
   (Joe Walsh)
10. WORLDS AWAY
    (Pablo Cruise)

BLACK SINGLES

1. BOOGIE, OOGIE OOGIE
   (A Taste of Honey)
2. YOU AND I
   (Rick James Stone City Band)
3. CLOSE THE DOOR
   (Teddy Pendergrass)
4. THREE TIMES A LADY
   (Commodores)
5. STUFF LIKE THAT
   (Quincy Jones)
6. SHAME
   (Evelyn "Champagne" King)
7. LAST DANCE
   (Donna Summer)
8. GET OFF
   (Foxy)
9. USE TA BE MY GIRL
   (The O'Jays)
10. ANNIE MAE
    (Natalie Cole)

BLACK ALBUMS

1. NATURAL HIGH
   (Commodores)
2. LIFE IS A SONG WORTH SINGING
   (Teddy Pendergrass)
3. COME GET IT
   (Rick James Stone City Band)
4. TOGETHERNESS
   (L.T.D.)

5. SOUNDS . . . AND STUFF LIKE THAT!!
   (Quincy Jones)
6. A TASTE OF HONEY
   (A Taste of Honey)
7. SMOOTH TALK
   (Evelyn "Champagne" King)
8. NATALIE . . . LIVE!
   (Natalie Cole)
9. SO FULL OF LOVE
   (The O'Jays)
10. GET IT OUTCHA SYSTEM
    (Millie Jackson)

JAZZ ALBUMS

1. SOUNDS . . . AND STUFF LIKE THAT!!
   (Quincy Jones)
2. IMAGES
   (Crusaders)
3. FEELS SO GOOD
   (Chuck Mangione)
4. SUNLIGHT
   (Herbie Hancock)
5. ARABESQUE
   (John Klemmer)
6. WEEKEND IN L.A.
   (George Benson)
7. FREESTYLE
   (Bobbi Humphrey)
8. DON'T LET GO
   (George Duke)
9. TROPICO
   (Gato Barbieri)
10. MODERN MAN
    (Stanley Clarke)

COUNTRY SINGLES

1. LOVE OR SOMETHING LIKE IT
   (Kenny Rogers)
2. YOU DON'T LOVE ME ANYMORE
   (Eddie Rabbitt)
3. ONLY ONE LOVE IN MY LIFE
   (Ronnie Milsap)
4. TALKING IN YOUR SLEEP
   (Crystal Gayle)
5. PITTSBURGH STEALERS
   (The Kendalls)
6. YOU NEEDED ME
   (Anne Murray)
7. WE BELONG TOGETHER
   (Susie Allanson)
8. FROM SEVEN TILL TEN
   (Loretta Lynn and Conway Twitty)
9. WHEN I STOP LEAVING (I'LL BE GONE)
   (Charley Pride)
10. ROSE COLORED GLASSES
    (John Conlee)

COUNTRY ALBUMS

1. STARDUST
   (Willie Nelson)
2. WHEN I DREAM
   (Crystal Gayle)
3. WAYLON AND WILLIE
   (Waylon Jennings and Willie Nelson)
4. ONLY ONE LOVE IN MY LIFE
   (Ronnie Milsap)
5. LOVE OR SOMETHING LIKE IT
   (Kenny Rogers)
6. OH! BROTHER
   (Larry Gatlin)
7. ROOM SERVICE
   (The Oak Ridge Boys)
8. VARIATIONS
   (Eddie Rabbitt)
9. IT'S A HEARTACHE
   (Bonnie Tyler)
10. HERE YOU COME AGAIN
    (Dolly Parton)

AUGUST 12, 1978

POP SINGLES

1. GREASE
   (Frankie Valli)
2. THREE TIMES A LADY
   (Commodores)
3. MISS YOU
   (The Rolling Stones)
4. LAST DANCE
   (Donna Summer)
5. YOU'RE THE ONE THAT I WANT
   (John Travolta and Olivia Newton-John)
6. COPACABANA (AT THE COPA)
   (Barry Manilow)
7. SHADOW DANCING
   (Andy Gibb)
8. LOVE WILL FIND A WAY
   (Pablo Cruise)
9. BOOGIE, OOGIE OOGIE
   (A Taste of Honey)
10. HOT BLOODED
    (Foreigner)

POP ALBUMS

1. GREASE
   (Original Soundtrack)
2. SOME GIRLS
   (The Rolling Stones)
3. NATURAL HIGH
   (Commodores)
4. DOUBLE VISION
   (Foreigner)
5. SGT. PEPPER'S LONELY HEARTS CLUB BAND
   (Original Soundtrack)
6. SATURDAY NIGHT FEVER
   (Original Soundtrack)
7. SHADOW DANCING
   (Andy Gibb)
8. STRANGER IN TOWN
   (Bob Seger and The Silver Bullet Band)
9. WORLDS AWAY
   (Pablo Cruise)
10. BUT SERIOUSLY, FOLKS . . .
    (Joe Walsh)

BLACK SINGLES

1. BOOGIE, OOGIE OOGIE
   (A Taste of Honey)
2. YOU AND I
   (Rick James Stone City Band)
3. THREE TIMES A LADY
   (Commodores)
4. CLOSE THE DOOR
   (Teddy Pendergrass)
5. GET OFF
   (Foxy)
6. SHAME
   (Evelyn "Champagne" King)
7. LAST DANCE
   (Donna Summer)
8. SHAKE AND DANCE WITH ME
   (Con Funk Shun)
9. STUFF LIKE THAT
   (Quincy Jones)
10. HOLDING ON (WHEN LOVE IS GONE)
    (L.T.D.)

BLACK ALBUMS

1. NATURAL HIGH
   (Commodores)
2. LIFE IS A SONG WORTH SINGING
   (Teddy Pendergrass)
3. COME GET IT
   (Rick James Stone City Band)
4. TOGETHERNESS
   (L.T.D.)

5. A TASTE OF HONEY
   (A Taste of Honey)
6. SOUNDS . . . AND STUFF LIKE THAT!!
   (Quincy Jones)
7. SMOOTH TALK
   (Evelyn "Champagne" King)
8. BLAM!!
   (The Brothers Johnson)
9. NATALIE . . . LIVE!
   (Natalie Cole)
10. IN THE NIGHT-TIME
    (Michael Henderson)

JAZZ ALBUMS

1. SOUNDS . . . AND STUFF LIKE THAT!!
   (Quincy Jones)
2. IMAGES
   (Crusaders)
3. FEELS SO GOOD
   (Chuck Mangione)
4. SUNLIGHT
   (Herbie Hancock)
5. TROPICO
   (Gato Barbieri)
6. ARABESQUE
   (John Klemmer)
7. WEEKEND IN L.A.
   (George Benson)
8. FREESTYLE
   (Bobbi Humphrey)
9. DON'T LET GO
   (George Duke)
10. MODERN MAN
    (Stanley Clarke)

COUNTRY SINGLES

1. YOU DON'T LOVE ME ANYMORE
   (Eddie Rabbitt)
2. TALKING IN YOUR SLEEP
   (Crystal Gayle)
3. LOVE OR SOMETHING LIKE IT
   (Kenny Rogers)
4. YOU NEEDED ME
   (Anne Murray)
5. WHEN I STOP LEAVING (I'LL BE GONE)
   (Charley Pride)
6. WE BELONG TOGETHER
   (Susie Allanson)
7. FROM SEVEN TILL TEN
   (Loretta Lynn and Conway Twitty)
8. RAKE AND RAMBLIN' MAN
   (Don Williams)
9. ROSE COLORED GLASSES
   (John Conlee)
10. (I LOVE YOU) WHAT CAN I SAY
    (Jerry Reed)

COUNTRY ALBUMS

1. STARDUST
   (Willie Nelson)
2. WHEN I DREAM
   (Crystal Gayle)
3. LOVE OR SOMETHING LIKE IT
   (Kenny Rogers)
4. WAYLON AND WILLIE
   (Waylon Jennings and Willie Nelson)
5. ONLY ONE LOVE IN MY LIFE
   (Ronnie Milsap)
6. OH! BROTHER
   (Larry Gatlin)
7. ROOM SERVICE
   (The Oak Ridge Boys)
8. VARIATIONS
   (Eddie Rabbitt)
9. IT'S A HEARTACHE
   (Bonnie Tyler)
10. HERE YOU COME AGAIN
    (Dolly Parton)

AUGUST 19, 1978

POP SINGLES

1. GREASE
   (Frankie Valli)
2. THREE TIMES A LADY
   (Commodores)
3. MISS YOU
   (The Rolling Stones)
4. BOOGIE, OOGIE OOGIE
   (A Taste of Honey)
5. LAST DANCE
   (Donna Summer)
6. LOVE WILL FIND A WAY
   (Pablo Cruise)
7. HOT BLOODED
   (Foreigner)
8. COPACABANA (AT THE COPA)
   (Barry Manilow)
9. YOU'RE THE ONE THAT I WANT
   (John Travolta and Olivia Newton-John)
10. LIFE'S BEEN GOOD
    (Joe Walsh)

POP ALBUMS

1. GREASE
   (Original Soundtrack)
2. SOME GIRLS
   (The Rolling Stones)
3. NATURAL HIGH
   (Commodores)
4. DOUBLE VISION
   (Foreigner)
5. SGT. PEPPER'S LONELY HEARTS CLUB BAND
   (Original Soundtrack)
6. SATURDAY NIGHT FEVER
   (Original Soundtrack)
7. SHADOW DANCING
   (Andy Gibb)
8. WORLDS AWAY
   (Pablo Cruise)
9. STRANGER IN TOWN
   (Bob Seger and The Silver Bullet Band)
10. BUT SERIOUSLY, FOLKS . . .
    (Joe Walsh)

BLACK SINGLES

1. BOOGIE, OOGIE OOGIE
   (A Taste of Honey)
2. THREE TIMES A LADY
   (Commodores)
3. YOU AND I
   (Rick James Stone City Band)
4. GET OFF
   (Foxy)
5. CLOSE THE DOOR
   (Teddy Pendergrass)
6. SHAKE AND DANCE WITH ME
   (Con Funk Shun)
7. SHAME
   (Evelyn "Champagne" King)
8. HOLDING ON (WHEN LOVE IS GONE)
   (L.T.D.)
9. GOT TO GET YOU INTO MY LIFE
   (Earth, Wind and Fire)
10. STUFF LIKE THAT
    (Quincy Jones)

BLACK ALBUMS

1. NATURAL HIGH
   (Commodores)
2. LIFE IS A SONG WORTH SINGING
   (Teddy Pendergrass)
3. COME GET IT
   (Rick James Stone City Band)

4. TOGETHERNESS
   (L.T.D.)
5. A TASTE OF HONEY
   (A Taste of Honey)
6. SOUNDS . . . AND STUFF LIKE THAT!!
   (Quincy Jones)
7. BLAM!!
   (The Brothers Johnson)
8. SMOOTH TALK
   (Evelyn "Champagne" King)
9. LOVESHINE
   (Con Funk Shun)
10. IN THE NIGHT-TIME
    (Michael Henderson)

JAZZ ALBUMS

1. IMAGES
   (Crusaders)
2. SOUNDS . . . AND STUFF LIKE THAT!!
   (Quincy Jones)
3. FEELS SO GOOD
   (Chuck Mangione)
4. SUNLIGHT
   (Herbie Hancock)
5. TROPICO
   (Gato Barbieri)
6. WEEKEND IN L.A.
   (George Benson)
7. ARABESQUE
   (John Klemmer)
8. FREESTYLE
   (Bobbi Humphrey)
9. MODERN MAN
   (Stanley Clarke)
10. THIS IS YOUR LIFE
    (Norman Connors)

COUNTRY SINGLES

1. TALKING IN YOUR SLEEP
   (Crystal Gayle)
2. YOU DON'T LOVE ME ANYMORE
   (Eddie Rabbitt)
3. WHEN I STOP LEAVING (I'LL BE GONE)
   (Charley Pride)
4. YOU NEEDED ME
   (Anne Murray)
5. WE BELONG TOGETHER
   (Susie Allanson)
6. RAKE AND RAMBLIN' MAN
   (Don Williams)
7. FROM SEVEN TILL TEN
   (Loretta Lynn and Conway Twitty)
8. I'LL FIND IT WHERE I CAN
   (Jerry Lee Lewis)
9. ROSE COLORED GLASSES
   (John Conlee)
10. LOVE ME WITH ALL YOUR HEART
    (CUANDO CALIENTE EL SOL)
    (Johnny Rodriguez)

COUNTRY ALBUMS

1. STARDUST
   (Willie Nelson)
2. WHEN I DREAM
   (Crystal Gayle)
3. LOVE OR SOMETHING LIKE IT
   (Kenny Rogers)
4. HEARTBREAKER
   (Dolly Parton)
5. WAYLON AND WILLIE
   (Waylon Jennings and Willie Nelson)
6. ONLY ONE LOVE IN MY LIFE
   (Ronnie Milsap)
7. OH! BROTHER
   (Larry Gatlin)
8. ROOM SERVICE
   (The Oak Ridge Boys)
9. VARIATIONS
   (Eddie Rabbitt)
10. IT'S A HEARTACHE
    (Bonnie Tyler)

AUGUST 26, 1978

POP SINGLES

1. THREE TIMES A LADY
   (Commodores)
2. GREASE
   (Frankie Valli)
3. BOOGIE OOGIE OOGIE
   (A Taste of Honey)
4. MISS YOU
   (The Rolling Stones)
5. HOT BLOODED
   (Foreigner)
6. LOVE WILL FIND A WAY
   (Pablo Cruise)
7. LAST DANCE
   (Donna Summer)
8. HOPELESSLY DEVOTED TO YOU
   (Olivia Newton-John)
9. LIFE'S BEEN GOOD
   (Joe Walsh)
10. COPACABANA (AT THE COPA)
    (Barry Manilow)

POP ALBUMS

1. GREASE
   (Original Soundtrack)
2. NATURAL HIGH
   (Commodores)
3. DOUBLE VISION
   (Foreigner)
4. SOME GIRLS
   (The Rolling Stones)
5. SGT. PEPPER'S LONELY HEARTS CLUB BAND
   (Original Soundtrack)
6. WORLDS AWAY
   (Pablo Cruise)
7. SATURDAY NIGHT FEVER
   (Original Soundtrack)
8. SHADOW DANCING
   (Andy Gibb)
9. STRANGER IN TOWN
   (Bob Seger and The Silver Bullet Band)
10. LIFE IS A SONG WORTH SINGING
    (Teddy Pendergrass)

BLACK SINGLES

1. THREE TIMES A LADY
   (Commodores)
2. BOOGIE OOGIE OOGIE
   (A Taste of Honey)
3. GET OFF
   (Foxy)
4. YOU AND I
   (Rick James Stone City Band)
5. SHAKE AND DANCE WITH ME
   (Con Funk Shun)
6. HOLDING ON (WHEN LOVE IS GONE)
   (L.T.D.)
7. GOT TO GET YOU INTO MY LIFE
   (Earth, Wind and Fire)
8. CLOSE THE DOOR
   (Teddy Pendergrass)
9. SHAME
   (Evelyn "Champagne" King)
10. TAKE ME I'M YOURS
    (Michael Henderson)

BLACK ALBUMS

1. NATURAL HIGH
   (Commodores)
2. LIFE IS A SONG WORTH SINGING
   (Teddy Pendergrass)
3. COME GET IT
   (Rick James Stone City Band)

4. TOGETHERNESS
   (L.T.D.)
5. A TASTE OF HONEY
   (A Taste of Honey)
6. BLAM!!
   (The Brothers Johnson)
7. SOUNDS . . . AND STUFF LIKE THAT!!
   (Quincy Jones)
8. SMOOTH TALK
   (Evelyn "Champagne" King)
9. GET OFF
   (Foxy)
10. IN THE NIGHT-TIME
    (Michael Henderson)

JAZZ ALBUMS

1. IMAGES
   (Crusaders)
2. SOUNDS . . . AND STUFF LIKE THAT!!
   (Quincy Jones)
3. FEELS SO GOOD
   (Chuck Mangione)
4. SUNLIGHT
   (Herbie Hancock)
5. TROPICO
   (Gato Barbieri)
6. WEEKEND IN L.A.
   (George Benson)
7. YOU SEND ME
   (Roy Ayers)
8. FRIENDS
   (Chick Corea)
9. RAINBOW SEEKER
   (Joe Sample)
10. FREESTYLE
    (Bobbi Humphrey)

COUNTRY SINGLES

1. TALKING IN YOUR SLEEP
   (Crystal Gayle)
2. WHEN I STOP LEAVING (I'LL BE GONE)
   (Charley Pride)
3. RAKE AND RAMBLIN' MAN
   (Don Williams)
4. WE BELONG TOGETHER
   (Susie Allanson)
5. YOU DON'T LOVE ME ANYMORE
   (Eddie Rabbitt)
6. BOOGIE GRASS BAND
   (Conway Twitty)
7. I'LL FIND IT WHERE I CAN
   (Jerry Lee Lewis)
8. LOVE ME WITH ALL YOUR HEART
   (CUANDO CALIENTE EL SOL)
   (Johnny Rodriguez)
9. BLUE SKIES
   (Willie Nelson)
10. BEAUTIFUL WOMAN
    (Charlie Rich)

COUNTRY ALBUMS

1. LOVE OR SOMETHING LIKE IT
   (Kenny Rogers)
2. HEARTBREAKER
   (Dolly Parton)
3. STARDUST
   (Willie Nelson)
4. WHEN I DREAM
   (Crystal Gayle)
5. WAYLON AND WILLIE
   (Waylon Jennings and Willie Nelson)
6. OH! BROTHER
   (Larry Gatlin)
7. ONLY ONE LOVE IN MY LIFE
   (Ronnie Milsap)
8. VARIATIONS
   (Eddie Rabbitt)
9. ROOM SERVICE
   (The Oak Ridge Boys)
10. THE BEST OF THE STATLER BROTHERS
    (The Statler Brothers)

SEPTEMBER 2, 1978

POP SINGLES

1. THREE TIMES A LADY
   (Commodores)
2. GREASE
   (Frankie Valli)
3. BOOGIE, OOGIE OOGIE
   (A Taste of Honey)
4. HOT BLOODED
   (Foreigner)
5. MISS YOU
   (The Rolling Stones)
6. HOPELESSLY DEVOTED TO YOU
   (Olivia Newton-John)
7. LOVE WILL FIND A WAY
   (Pablo Cruise)
8. LAST DANCE
   (Donna Summer)
9. LIFE'S BEEN GOOD
   (Joe Walsh)
10. SHAME
    (Evelyn "Champagne" King)

POP ALBUMS

1. GREASE
   (Original Soundtrack)
2. NATURAL HIGH
   (Commodores)
3. DOUBLE VISION
   (Foreigner)
4. SOME GIRLS
   (The Rolling Stones)
5. SGT. PEPPER'S LONELY HEARTS CLUB
   BAND
   (Original Soundtrack)
6. WORLDS AWAY
   (Pablo Cruise)
7. DON'T LOOK BACK
   (Boston)
8. SATURDAY NIGHT FEVER
   (Original Soundtrack)
9. SHADOW DANCING
   (Andy Gibb)
10. LIFE IS A SONG WORTH SINGING
    (Teddy Pendergrass)

BLACK SINGLES

1. GET OFF
   (Foxy)
2. BOOGIE, OOGIE OOGIE
   (A Taste of Honey)
3. THREE TIMES A LADY
   (Commodores)
4. YOU AND I
   (Rick James Stone City Band)
5. SHAKE AND DANCE WITH ME
   (Con Funk Shun)
6. HOLDING ON (WHEN LOVE IS GONE)
   (L.T.D.)
7. GOT TO GET YOU INTO MY LIFE
   (Earth, Wind and Fire)
8. CLOSE THE DOOR
   (Teddy Pendergrass)
9. TAKE ME I'M YOURS
   (Michael Henderson)
10. YOU
    (The McCrarys)

BLACK ALBUMS

1. LIFE IS A SONG WORTH SINGING
   (Teddy Pendergrass)
2. NATURAL HIGH
   (Commodores)
3. COME GET IT
   (Rick James Stone City Band)

4. BLAM!!
   (The Brothers Johnson)
5. TOGETHERNESS
   (L.T.D.)
6. A TASTE OF HONEY
   (A Taste of Honey)
7. SUNBEAM
   (Emotions)
8. GET OFF
   (Foxy)
9. IN THE NIGHT-TIME
   (Michael Henderson)
10. SMOOTH TALK
    (Evelyn "Champagne" King)

JAZZ ALBUMS

1. IMAGES
   (Crusaders)
2. SOUNDS . . . AND STUFF LIKE THAT!!
   (Quincy Jones)
3. YOU SEND ME
   (Roy Ayers)
4. SUNLIGHT
   (Herbie Hancock)
5. TROPICO
   (Gato Barbieri)
6. FEELS SO GOOD
   (Chuck Mangione)
7. FRIENDS
   (Chick Corea)
8. WEEKEND IN L.A.
   (George Benson)
9. RAINBOW SEEKER
   (Joe Sample)
10. FREESTYLE
    (Bobbi Humphrey)

COUNTRY SINGLES

1. RAKE AND RAMBLIN' MAN
   (Don Williams)
2. WHEN I STOP LEAVING (I'LL BE GONE)
   (Charley Pride)
3. TALKING IN YOUR SLEEP
   (Crystal Gayle)
4. BLUE SKIES
   (Willie Nelson)
5. BOOGIE GRASS BAND
   (Conway Twitty)
6. LOVE ME WITH ALL YOUR HEART
   (CUANDO CALIENTE EL SOL)
   (Johnny Rodriguez)
7. WE BELONG TOGETHER
   (Susie Allanson)
8. I'VE ALWAYS BEEN CRAZY
   (Waylon Jennings)
9. BEAUTIFUL WOMAN
   (Charlie Rich)
10. WOMANHOOD
    (Tammy Wynette)

COUNTRY ALBUMS

1. LOVE OR SOMETHING LIKE IT
   (Kenny Rogers)
2. HEARTBREAKER
   (Dolly Parton)
3. WHEN I DREAM
   (Crystal Gayle)
4. STARDUST
   (Willie Nelson)
5. WAYLON AND WILLIE
   (Waylon Jennings and Willie Nelson)
6. OH! BROTHER
   (Larry Gatlin)
7. ONLY ONE LOVE IN MY LIFE
   (Ronnie Milsap)
8. VARIATIONS
   (Eddie Rabbitt)
9. ROOM SERVICE
   (The Oak Ridge Boys)
10. THE BEST OF STATLER BROTHERS
    (The Statler Brothers)

SEPTEMBER 9, 1978

POP SINGLES

1. THREE TIMES A LADY
   (Commodores)
2. BOOGIE OOGIE OOGIE
   (A Taste of Honey)
3. GREASE
   (Frankie Valli)
4. HOT BLOODED
   (Foreigner)
5. HOPELESSLY DEVOTED TO YOU
   (Olivia Newton-John)
6. MISS YOU
   (The Rolling Stones)
7. KISS YOU ALL OVER
   (Exile)
8. LOVE WILL FIND A WAY
   (Pablo Cruise)
9. SHAME
   (Evelyn "Champagne" King)
10. AN EVERLASTING LOVE
    (Andy Gibb)

POP ALBUMS

1. GREASE
   (Original Soundtrack)
2. DON'T LOOK BACK
   (Boston)
3. DOUBLE VISION
   (Foreigner)
4. SOME GIRLS
   (The Rolling Stones)
5. SGT. PEPPER'S LONELY HEARTS CLUB
   BAND
   (Original Soundtrack)
6. NATURAL HIGH
   (Commodores)
7. WORLDS AWAY
   (Pablo Cruise)
8. SATURDAY NIGHT FEVER
   (Original Soundtrack)
9. SHADOW DANCING
   (Andy Gibb)
10. STRANGER IN TOWN
    (Bob Seger and The Silver Bullet Band)

BLACK SINGLES

1. GET OFF
   (Foxy)
2. BOOGIE OOGIE OOGIE
   (A Taste of Honey)
3. GOT TO GET YOU INTO MY LIFE
   (Earth, Wind and Fire)
4. SHAKE AND DANCE WITH ME
   (Con Funk Shun)
5. HOLDING ON (WHEN LOVE IS GONE)
   (L.T.D.)
6. THREE TIMES A LADY
   (Commodores)
7. YOU AND I
   (Rick James Stone City Band)
8. TAKE ME I'M YOURS
   (Michael Henderson)
9. YOU
   (The McCrarys)
10. CLOSE THE DOOR
    (Teddy Pendergrass)

BLACK ALBUMS

1. LIFE IS A SONG WORTH SINGING
   (Teddy Pendergrass)
2. NATURAL HIGH
   (Commodores)
3. BLAM!!
   (The Brothers Johnson)
4. COME GET IT
   (Rick James Stone City Band)

---

5. TOGETHERNESS
   (L.T.D.)
6. A TASTE OF HONEY
   (A Taste of Honey)
7. SUNBEAM
   (Emotions)
8. GET OFF
   (Foxy)
9. IN THE NIGHT-TIME
   (Michael Henderson)
10. SMOOTH TALK
    (Evelyn "Champagne" King)

JAZZ ALBUMS

1. IMAGES
   (Crusaders)
2. YOU SEND ME
   (Roy Ayers)
3. SOUNDS . . . AND STUFF LIKE THAT!!
   (Quincy Jones)
4. SUNLIGHT
   (Herbie Hancock)
5. TROPICO
   (Gato Barbieri)
6. FRIENDS
   (Chick Corea)
7. FEELS SO GOOD
   (Chuck Mangione)
8. COSMIC MESSENGER
   (Jean Luc Ponty)
9. WEEKEND IN L.A.
   (George Benson)
10. FREESTYLE
    (Bobbi Humphrey)

COUNTRY SINGLES

1. BLUE SKIES
   (Willie Nelson)
2. I'VE ALWAYS BEEN CRAZY
   (Waylon Jennings)
3. BOOGIE GRASS BAND
   (Conway Twitty)
4. RAKE AND RAMBLIN' MAN
   (Don Williams)
5. LOVE ME WITH ALL YOUR HEART
   (CUANDO CALIENTE EL SOL)
   (Johnny Rodriguez)
6. WHEN I STOP LEAVING (I'LL BE GONE)
   (Charley Pride)
7. WOMANHOOD
   (Tammy Wynette)
8. HELLO MEXICO (AND ADIOS BABY TO
   YOU)
   (Johnny Duncan)
9. IF YOU'VE GOT TEN MINUTES (LET'S FALL
   IN LOVE)
   (Joe Stampley)
10. LET'S SHAKE HANDS AND COME OUT
    LOVIN'
    (Kenny O'Dell)

COUNTRY ALBUMS

1. LOVE OR SOMETHING LIKE IT
   (Kenny Rogers)
2. HEARTBREAKER
   (Dolly Parton)
3. STARDUST
   (Willie Nelson)
4. WHEN I DREAM
   (Crystal Gayle)
5. WAYLON AND WILLIE
   (Waylon Jennings and Willie Nelson)
6. OH! BROTHER
   (Larry Gatlin)
7. LET'S KEEP IT THAT WAY
   (Anne Murray)
8. WOMANHOOD
   (Tammy Wynette)
9. ONLY ONE LOVE IN MY LIFE
   (Ronnie Milsap)
10. ROOM SERVICE
    (The Oak Ridge Boys)

SEPTEMBER 16, 1978

POP SINGLES

1. THREE TIMES A LADY
   (Commodores)
2. BOOGIE OOGIE OOGIE
   (A Taste of Honey)
3. GREASE
   (Frankie Valli)
4. HOPELESSLY DEVOTED TO YOU
   (Olivia Newton-John)
5. KISS YOU ALL OVER
   (Exile)
6. HOT BLOODED
   (Foreigner)
7. MISS YOU
   (The Rolling Stones)
8. SUMMER NIGHTS
   (John Travolta and Olivia Newton-John)
9. AN EVERLASTING LOVE
   (Andy Gibb)
10. SHAME
    (Evelyn "Champagne" King)

POP ALBUMS

1. GREASE
   (Original Soundtrack)
2. DON'T LOOK BACK
   (Boston)
3. DOUBLE VISION
   (Foreigner)
4. SOME GIRLS
   (The Rolling Stones)
5. SGT. PEPPER'S LONELY HEARTS CLUB
   BAND
   (Original Soundtrack)
6. NATURAL HIGH
   (Commodores)
7. WORLDS AWAY
   (Pablo Cruise)
8. WHO ARE YOU
   (The Who)
9. SATURDAY NIGHT FEVER
   (Original Soundtrack)
10. STRANGER IN TOWN
    (Bob Seger and The Silver Bullet Band)

BLACK SINGLES

1. GET OFF
   (Foxy)
2. HOLDING ON (WHEN LOVE IS GONE)
   (L.T.D.)
3. GOT TO GET YOU INTO MY LIFE
   (Earth, Wind and Fire)
4. SHAKE AND DANCE WITH ME
   (Con Funk Shun)
5. BOOGIE OOGIE OOGIE
   (A Taste of Honey)
6. THREE TIMES A LADY
   (Commodores)
7. TAKE ME I'M YOURS
   (Michael Henderson)
8. YOU
   (The McCrarys)
9. YOU AND I
   (Rick James Stone City Band)
10. SMILE
    (Emotions)

BLACK ALBUMS

1. LIFE IS A SONG WORTH SINGING
   (Teddy Pendergrass)
2. BLAM!!
   (The Brothers Johnson)
3. TOGETHERNESS
   (L.T.D.)
4. COME GET IT
   (Rick James Stone City Band)

SEPTEMBER 23, 1978

5. A TASTE OF HONEY
   (A Taste of Honey)
6. NATURAL HIGH
   (Commodores)
7. SUNBEAM
   (Emotions)
8. GET OFF
   (Foxy)
9. IN THE NIGHT-TIME
   (Michael Henderson)
10. THE CONCEPT
    (Slave)

JAZZ ALBUMS

1. IMAGES
   (Crusaders)
2. YOU SEND ME
   (Roy Ayers)
3. SOUNDS . . . AND STUFF LIKE THAT!!
   (Quincy Jones)
4. COSMIC MESSENGER
   (Jean Luc Ponty)
5. TROPICO
   (Gato Barbieri)
6. SUNLIGHT
   (Herbie Hancock)
7. FRIENDS
   (Chick Corea)
8. FEELS SO GOOD
   (Chuck Mangione)
9. WEEKEND IN L.A.
   (George Benson)
10. FREESTYLE
    (Bobbi Humphrey)

COUNTRY SINGLES

1. I'VE ALWAYS BEEN CRAZY
   (Waylon Jennings)
2. BLUE SKIES
   (Willie Nelson)
3. BOOGIE GRASS BAND
   (Conway Twitty)
4. WOMANHOOD
   (Tammy Wynette)
5. HELLO MEXICO (AND ADIOS BABY TO YOU)
   (Johnny Duncan)
6. IF YOU'VE GOT TEN MINUTES (LET'S FALL IN LOVE)
   (Joe Stampley)
7. WHO AM I TO SAY
   (The Statler Brothers)
8. WITH LOVE
   (Rex Allen Jr.)
9. IT'S BEEN A GREAT AFTERNOON
   (Merle Haggard)
10. LET'S SHAKE HANDS AND COME OUT LOVIN'
    (Kenny O'Dell)

COUNTRY ALBUMS

1. STARDUST
   (Willie Nelson)
2. LOVE OR SOMETHING LIKE IT
   (Kenny Rogers)
3. HEARTBREAKER
   (Dolly Parton)
4. WHEN I DREAM
   (Crystal Gayle)
5. WAYLON AND WILLIE
   (Waylon Jennings and Willie Nelson)
6. OH! BROTHER
   (Larry Gatlin)
7. LET'S KEEP IT THAT WAY
   (Anne Murray)
8. WOMANHOOD
   (Tammy Wynette)
9. ONLY ONE LOVE IN MY LIFE
   (Ronnie Milsap)
10. THE BEST OF THE STATLER BROTHERS
    (The Statler Brothers)

POP SINGLES

1. BOOGIE OOGIE OOGIE
   (A Taste of Honey)
2. THREE TIMES A LADY
   (Commodores)
3. KISS YOU ALL OVER
   (Exile)
4. HOPELESSLY DEVOTED TO YOU
   (Olivia Newton-John)
5. SUMMER NIGHTS
   (John Travolta and Olivia Newton-John)
6. HOT BLOODED
   (Foreigner)
7. GREASE
   (Frankie Valli)
8. MISS YOU
   (The Rolling Stones)
9. HOT CHILD IN THE CITY
   (Nick Gilder)
10. AN EVERLASTING LOVE
    (Andy Gibb)

POP ALBUMS

1. GREASE
   (Original Soundtrack)
2. DON'T LOOK BACK
   (Boston)
3. DOUBLE VISION
   (Foreigner)
4. WHO ARE YOU
   (The Who)
5. SOME GIRLS
   (The Rolling Stones)
6. WORLDS AWAY
   (Pablo Cruise)
7. NATURAL HIGH
   (Commodores)
8. SGT. PEPPER'S LONELY HEARTS CLUB BAND
   (Original Soundtrack)
9. STRANGER IN TOWN
   (Bob Seger and The Silver Bullet Band)
10. SATURDAY NIGHT FEVER
    (Original Soundtrack)

BLACK SINGLES

1. GET OFF
   (Foxy)
2. HOLDING ON (WHEN LOVE IS GONE)
   (L.T.D.)
3. GOT TO GET YOU INTO MY LIFE
   (Earth, Wind and Fire)
4. SHAKE AND DANCE WITH ME
   (Con Funk Shun)
5. BOOGIE OOGIE OOGIE
   (A Taste of Honey)
6. ONE NATION UNDER A GROOVE
   (Funkadelic)
7. TAKE ME I'M YOURS
   (Michael Henderson)
8. YOU
   (The McCrarys)
9. SMILE
   (Emotions)
10. THREE TIMES A LADY
    (Commodores)

BLACK ALBUMS

1. BLAM!!
   (The Brothers Johnson)
2. LIFE IS A SONG WORTH SINGING
   (Teddy Pendergrass)
3. TOGETHERNESS
   (L.T.D.)

4. A TASTE OF HONEY
   (A Taste of Honey)
5. COME GET IT
   (Rick James Stone City Band)
6. NATURAL HIGH
   (Commodores)
7. SUNBEAM
   (Emotions)
8. IN THE NIGHT-TIME
   (Michael Henderson)
9. IS IT STILL GOOD TO YA
   (Ashford and Simpson)
10. GET OFF
    (Foxy)

JAZZ ALBUMS

1. IMAGES
   (Crusaders)
2. YOU SEND ME
   (Roy Ayers)
3. COSMIC MESSENGER
   (Jean Luc Ponty)
4. SOUNDS . . . AND STUFF LIKE THAT!!
   (Quincy Jones)
5. SUNLIGHT
   (Herbie Hancock)
6. FRIENDS
   (Chick Corea)
7. TROPICO
   (Gato Barbieri)
8. FEELS SO GOOD
   (Chuck Mangione)
9. IN THE NIGHT-TIME
   (Michael Henderson)
10. CHILDREN OF SANCHEZ
    (Chuck Mangione)

COUNTRY SINGLES

1. I'VE ALWAYS BEEN CRAZY
   (Waylon Jennings)
2. HELLO MEXICO (AND ADIOS BABY TO YOU)
   (Johnny Duncan)
3. WOMANHOOD
   (Tammy Wynette)
4. WHO AM I TO SAY
   (The Statler Brothers)
5. IF YOU'VE GOT TEN MINUTES (LET'S FALL IN LOVE)
   (Joe Stampley)
6. IT'S BEEN A GREAT AFTERNOON
   (Merle Haggard)
7. HEARTBREAKER
   (Dolly Parton)
8. WITH LOVE
   (Rex Allen Jr.)
9. PENNY ARCADE
   (Cristy Lane)
10. BOOGIE GRASS BAND
    (Conway Twitty)

COUNTRY ALBUMS

1. STARDUST
   (Willie Nelson)
2. LOVE OR SOMETHING LIKE IT
   (Kenny Rogers)
3. HEARTBREAKER
   (Dolly Parton)
4. WHEN I DREAM
   (Crystal Gayle)
5. LET'S KEEP IT THAT WAY
   (Anne Murray)
6. OH! BROTHER
   (Larry Gatlin)
7. WAYLON AND WILLIE
   (Waylon Jennings and Willie Nelson)
8. TEN YEARS OF GOLD
   (Kenny Rogers)
9. WOMANHOOD
   (Tammy Wynette)

10. TEAR TIME
    (Dave and Sugar)

SEPTEMBER 30, 1978

POP SINGLES

1. KISS YOU ALL OVER
   (Exile)
2. BOOGIE OOGIE OOGIE
   (A Taste of Honey)
3. THREE TIMES A LADY
   (Commodores)
4. SUMMER NIGHTS
   (John Travolta and Olivia Newton-John)
5. HOPELESSLY DEVOTED TO YOU
   (Olivia Newton-John)
6. HOT CHILD IN THE CITY
   (Nick Gilder)
7. HOT BLOODED
   (Foreigner)
8. GREASE
   (Frankie Valli)
9. DON'T LOOK BACK
   (Boston)
10. YOU NEEDED ME
    (Anne Murray)

POP ALBUMS

1. GREASE
   (Original Soundtrack)
2. DON'T LOOK BACK
   (Boston)
3. DOUBLE VISION
   (Foreigner)
4. WHO ARE YOU
   (The Who)
5. SOME GIRLS
   (The Rolling Stones)
6. WORLDS AWAY
   (Pablo Cruise)
7. SGT. PEPPER'S LONELY HEARTS CLUB BAND
   (Original Soundtrack)
8. NATURAL HIGH
   (Commodores)
9. TWIN SONS OF DIFFERENT MOTHERS
   (Dan Fogelberg and Tim Weisberg)
10. STRANGER IN TOWN
    (Bob Seger and The Silver Bullet Band)

BLACK SINGLES

1. GET OFF
   (Foxy)
2. HOLDING ON (WHEN LOVE IS GONE)
   (L.T.D.)
3. ONE NATION UNDER A GROOVE
   (Funkadelic)
4. GOT TO GET YOU INTO MY LIFE
   (Earth, Wind and Fire)
5. SHAKE AND DANCE WITH ME
   (Con Funk Shun)
6. BOOGIE OOGIE OOGIE
   (A Taste of Honey)
7. TAKE ME I'M YOURS
   (Michael Henderson)
8. YOU
   (The McCrarys)
9. SMILE
   (Emotions)
10. THREE TIMES A LADY
    (Commodores)

BLACK ALBUMS

1. BLAM!!
   (The Brothers Johnson)

2. TOGETHERNESS
   (L.T.D.)
3. LIFE IS A SONG WORTH SINGING
   (Teddy Pendergrass)
4. A TASTE OF HONEY
   (A Taste of Honey)
5. COME GET IT
   (Rick James Stone City Band)
6. IS IT STILL GOOD TO YA
   (Ashford and Simpson)
7. STRIKES AGAIN
   (Rose Royce)
8. SUNBEAM
   (Emotions)
9. IN THE NIGHT-TIME
   (Michael Henderson)
10. LIVE AND MORE
    (Donna Summer)

JAZZ ALBUMS

1. IMAGES
   (Crusaders)
2. YOU SEND ME
   (Roy Ayers)
3. COSMIC MESSENGER
   (Jean Luc Ponty)
4. CHILDREN OF SANCHEZ
   (Chuck Mangione)
5. SOUNDS . . . AND STUFF LIKE THAT!!
   (Quincy Jones)
6. FRIENDS
   (Chick Corea)
7. SUNLIGHT
   (Herbie Hancock)
8. FEELS SO GOOD
   (Chuck Mangione)
9. SECRETS
   (Gil Scott-Heron and Brian Jackson)
10. TROPICO
    (Gato Barbieri)

COUNTRY SINGLES

1. WHO AM I TO SAY
   (The Statler Brothers)
2. HELLO MEXICO (AND ADIOS BABY TO YOU)
   (Johnny Duncan)
3. HEARTBREAKER
   (Dolly Parton)
4. IT'S BEEN A GREAT AFTERNOON
   (Merle Haggard)
5. I'VE ALWAYS BEEN CRAZY
   (Waylon Jennings)
6. TEAR TIME
   (Dave and Sugar)
7. IF THE WORLD RAN OUT OF LOVE TONIGHT
   (Jim Ed Brown and Helen Cornelius)
8. WITH LOVE
   (Rex Allen Jr.)
9. PENNY ARCADE
   (Cristy Lane)
10. HERE COMES THE HURT AGAIN
    (Mickey Gilley)

COUNTRY ALBUMS

1. HEARTBREAKER
   (Dolly Parton)
2. STARDUST
   (Willie Nelson)
3. WHEN I DREAM
   (Crystal Gayle)
4. LOVE OR SOMETHING LIKE IT
   (Kenny Rogers)
5. LET'S KEEP IT THAT WAY
   (Anne Murray)
6. OH! BROTHER
   (Larry Gatlin)
7. WAYLON AND WILLIE
   (Waylon Jennings and Willie Nelson)
8. TEN YEARS OF GOLD
   (Kenny Rogers)

9. WOMANHOOD
   (Tammy Wynette)
10. TEAR TIME
    (Dave and Sugar)

OCTOBER 7, 1978

POP SINGLES

1. KISS YOU ALL OVER
   (Exile)
2. BOOGIE OOGIE OOGIE
   (A Taste of Honey)
3. HOT CHILD IN THE CITY
   (Nick Gilder)
4. THREE TIMES A LADY
   (Commodores)
5. SUMMER NIGHTS
   (John Travolta and Olivia Newton-John)
6. YOU NEEDED ME
   (Anne Murray)
7. HOPELESSLY DEVOTED TO YOU
   (Olivia Newton-John)
8. DON'T LOOK BACK
   (Boston)
9. REMINISCING
   (Little River Band)
10. WHENEVER I CALL YOU "FRIEND"
    (Kenny Loggins)

POP ALBUMS

1. GREASE
   (Original Soundtrack)
2. DON'T LOOK BACK
   (Boston)
3. DOUBLE VISION
   (Foreigner)
4. WHO ARE YOU
   (The Who)
5. SOME GIRLS
   (The Rolling Stones)
6. NATURAL HIGH
   (Commodores)
7. TWIN SONS OF DIFFERENT MOTHERS
   (Dan Fogelberg and Tim Weisberg)
8. NIGHTWATCH
   (Kenny Loggins)
9. WORLDS AWAY
   (Pablo Cruise)
10. SGT. PEPPER'S LONELY HEARTS CLUB BAND
    (Original Soundtrack)

BLACK SINGLES

1. ONE NATION UNDER A GROOVE
   (Funkadelic)
2. GET OFF
   (Foxy)
3. HOLDING ON (WHEN LOVE IS GONE)
   (L.T.D.)
4. IT SEEMS TO HANG ON
   (Ashford and Simpson)
5. DANCE (DISCO HEAT)
   (Sylvester)
6. BOOGIE OOGIE OOGIE
   (A Taste of Honey)
7. I'M IN LOVE (AND I LOVE THE FEELING)
   (Rose Royce)
8. SHAKE AND DANCE WITH ME
   (Con Funk Shun)
9. TAKE ME I'M YOURS
   (Michael Henderson)
10. THERE'LL NEVER BE
    (Switch)

BLACK ALBUMS

1. ONE NATION UNDER A GROOVE
   (Funkadelic)

2. BLAM!!
   (The Brothers Johnson)
3. TOGETHERNESS
   (L.T.D.)
4. STRIKES AGAIN
   (Rose Royce)
5. IS IT STILL GOOD TO YA
   (Ashford and Simpson)
6. LIVE AND MORE
   (Donna Summer)
7. LIFE IS A SONG WORTH SINGING
   (Teddy Pendergrass)
8. A TASTE OF HONEY
   (A Taste of Honey)
9. STEP TWO
   (Sylvester)
10. COME GET IT
    (Rick James Stone City Band)

JAZZ ALBUMS

1. IMAGES
   (Crusaders)
2. COSMIC MESSENGERS
   (Jean Luc Ponty)
3. YOU SEND ME
   (Roy Ayers)
4. CHILDREN OF SANCHEZ
   (Chuck Mangione)
5. SOUNDS . . . AND STUFF LIKE THAT!!
   (Quincy Jones)
6. FRIENDS
   (Chick Corea)
7. SECRETS
   (Gil Scott-Heron and Brian Jackson)
8. WHAT ABOUT YOU?
   (Stanley Turrentine)
9. PAT METHENY GROUP
   (Pat Metheny)
10. FEELS SO GOOD
    (Chuck Mangione)

COUNTRY SINGLES

1. HEARTBREAKER
   (Dolly Parton)
2. IT'S BEEN A GREAT AFTERNOON
   (Merle Haggard)
3. WHO AM I TO SAY
   (The Statler Brothers)
4. TEAR TIME
   (Dave and Sugar)
5. IF THE WORLD RAN OUT OF LOVE
   TONIGHT
   (Jim Ed Brown and Helen Cornelius)
6. LET'S TAKE THE LONG WAY AROUND THE
   WORLD
   (Ronnie Milsap)
7. I'VE ALWAYS BEEN CRAZY
   (Waylon Jennings)
8. HELLO MEXICO (AND ADIOS BABY TO
   YOU)
   (Johnny Duncan)
9. HERE COMES THE HURT AGAIN
   (Mickey Gilley)
10. CRYIN' AGAIN
    (The Oak Ridge Boys)

COUNTRY ALBUMS

1. HEARTBREAKER
   (Dolly Parton)
2. STARDUST
   (Willie Nelson)
3. WHEN I DREAM
   (Crystal Gayle)
4. LET'S KEEP IT THAT WAY
   (Anne Murray)
5. LOVE OR SOMETHING LIKE IT
   (Kenny Rogers)
6. WAYLON AND WILLIE
   (Waylon Jennings and Willie Nelson)
7. ELVIS SINGS FOR CHILDREN AND
   GROWNUPS TOO
   (Elvis Presley)

8. OH! BROTHER
   (Larry Gatlin)
9. TEAR TIME
   (Dave and Sugar)
10. TEN YEARS OF GOLD
    (Kenny Rogers)

OCTOBER 14, 1978

POP SINGLES

1. KISS YOU ALL OVER
   (Exile)
2. BOOGIE OOGIE OOGIE
   (A Taste of Honey)
3. HOT CHILD IN THE CITY
   (Nick Gilder)
4. YOU NEEDED ME
   (Anne Murray)
5. SUMMER NIGHTS
   (John Travolta and Olivia Newton-John)
6. THREE TIMES A LADY
   (Commodores)
7. REMINISCING
   (Little River Band)
8. DON'T LOOK BACK
   (Boston)
9. WHENEVER I CALL YOU "FRIEND"
   (Kenny Loggins)
10. RIGHT DOWN THE LINE
    (Gerry Rafferty)

POP ALBUMS

1. GREASE
   (Original Soundtrack)
2. DON'T LOOK BACK
   (Boston)
3. DOUBLE VISION
   (Foreigner)
4. WHO ARE YOU
   (The Who)
5. SOME GIRLS
   (The Rolling Stones)
6. NATURAL HIGH
   (Commodores)
7. TWIN SONS OF DIFFERENT MOTHERS
   (Dan Fogelberg and Tim Weisberg)
8. NIGHTWATCH
   (Kenny Loggins)
9. LIVING IN THE U.S.A.
   (Linda Ronstadt)
10. PIECES OF EIGHT
    (Styx)

BLACK SINGLES

1. ONE NATION UNDER A GROOVE
   (Funkadelic)
2. IT SEEMS TO HANG ON
   (Ashford and Simpson)
3. GET OFF
   (Foxy)
4. DANCE (DISCO HEAT)
   (Sylvester)
5. HOLDING ON (WHEN LOVE IS GONE)
   (L.T.D.)
6. I'M IN LOVE (AND I LOVE THE FEELING)
   (Rose Royce)
7. BOOGIE OOGIE OOGIE
   (A Taste of Honey)
8. BLAME IT ON THE BOOGIE
   (The Jacksons)
9. THERE'LL NEVER BE
   (Switch)
10. TAKE ME I'M YOURS
    (Michael Henderson)

BLACK ALBUMS

1. ONE NATION UNDER A GROOVE
   (Funkadelic)
2. BLAM!!
   (The Brothers Johnson)
3. STRIKES AGAIN
   (Rose Royce)
4. LIVE AND MORE
   (Donna Summer)
5. IS IT STILL GOOD TO YA
   (Ashford and Simpson)
6. TOGETHERNESS
   (L.T.D.)
7. LIFE IS A SONG WORTH SINGING
   (Teddy Pendergrass)
8. A TASTE OF HONEY
   (A Taste of Honey)
9. STEP TWO
   (Sylvester)
10. COME GET IT
    (Rick James Stone City Band)

JAZZ ALBUMS

1. CHILDREN OF SANCHEZ
   (Chuck Mangione)
2. COSMIC MESSENGER
   (Jean Luc Ponty)
3. IMAGES
   (Crusaders)
4. YOU SEND ME
   (Roy Ayers)
5. SECRETS
   (Gil Scott-Heron and Brian Jackson)
6. FRIENDS
   (Chick Corea)
7. WHAT ABOUT YOU?
   (Stanley Turrentine)
8. PAT METHENY GROUP
   (Pat Metheny)
9. SOUNDS . . . AND STUFF LIKE THAT!!
   (Quincy Jones)
10. REED SEED
    (Grover Washington Jr.)

COUNTRY SINGLES

1. HEARTBREAKER
   (Dolly Parton)
2. IT'S BEEN A GREAT AFTERNOON
   (Merle Haggard)
3. TEAR TIME
   (Dave and Sugar)
4. LET'S TAKE THE LONG WAY AROUND THE
   WORLD
   (Ronnie Milsap)
5. IF THE WORLD RAN OUT OF LOVE
   TONIGHT
   (Jim Ed Brown and Helen Cornelius)
6. WHO AM I TO SAY
   (The Statler Brothers)
7. CRYIN' AGAIN
   (The Oak Ridge Boys)
8. ANYONE WHO ISN'T ME TONIGHT
   (Kenny Rogers and Dottie West)
9. AIN'T NO CALIFORNIA
   (Mel Tillis)
10. SLEEPING SINGLE IN A DOUBLE BED
    (Barbara Mandrell)

COUNTRY ALBUMS

1. STARDUST
   (Willie Nelson)
2. HEARTBREAKER
   (Dolly Parton)
3. I'VE ALWAYS BEEN CRAZY
   (Waylon Jennings)
4. LET'S KEEP IT THAT WAY
   (Anne Murray)
5. WHEN I DREAM
   (Crystal Gayle)

6. LIVING IN THE U.S.A.
  (Linda Ronstadt)
7. ELVIS SINGS FOR CHILDREN AND
  GROWNUPS TOO
  (Elvis Presley)
8. THE BEST OF THE STATLER BROTHERS
  (The Statler Brothers)
9. LOVE OR SOMETHING LIKE IT
  (Kenny Rogers)
10. EXPRESSIONS
  (Don Williams)

OCTOBER 21, 1978

POP SINGLES

1. HOT CHILD IN THE CITY
  (Nick Gilder)
2. KISS YOU ALL OVER
  (Exile)
3. YOU NEEDED ME
  (Anne Murray)
4. BOOGIE OOGIE OOGIE
  (A Taste of Honey)
5. REMINISCING
  (Little River Band)
6. WHENEVER I CALL YOU "FRIEND"
  (Kenny Loggins)
7. MacARTHUR PARK
  (Donna Summer)
8. GET OFF
  (Foxy)
9. RIGHT DOWN THE LINE
  (Gerry Rafferty)
10. WHO ARE YOU
  (The Who)

POP ALBUMS

1. GREASE
  (Original Soundtrack)
2. DON'T LOOK BACK
  (Boston)
3. LIVING IN THE U.S.A.
  (Linda Ronstadt)
4. DOUBLE VISION
  (Foreigner)
5. WHO ARE YOU
  (The Who)
6. SOME GIRLS
  (The Rolling Stones)
7. PIECES OF EIGHT
  (Styx)
8. TWIN SONS OF DIFFERENT MOTHERS
  (Dan Fogelberg and Tim Weisberg)
9. LIVE AND MORE
  (Donna Summer)
10. NIGHTWATCH
  (Kenny Loggins)

BLACK SINGLES

1. ONE NATION UNDER A GROOVE
  (Funkadelic)
2. IT SEEMS TO HANG ON
  (Ashford and Simpson)
3. DANCE (DISCO HEAT)
  (Sylvester)
4. GET OFF
  (Foxy)
5. I'M IN LOVE (AND I LOVE THE FEELING)
  (Rose Royce)
6. HOLDING ON (WHEN LOVE IS GONE)
  (L.T.D.)
7. BLAME IT ON THE BOOGIE
  (The Jacksons)
8. THERE'LL NEVER BE
  (Switch)
9. BOOGIE OOGIE OOGIE
  (A Taste of Honey)

10. TONIGHT IS THE NIGHT (PART 2)
  (Betty Wright)

BLACK ALBUMS

1. ONE NATION UNDER A GROOVE
  (Funkadelic)
2. LIVE AND MORE
  (Donna Summer)
3. STRIKES AGAIN
  (Rose Royce)
4. IS IT STILL GOOD TO YA
  (Ashford and Simpson)
5. BLAM!!
  (The Brothers Johnson)
6. TOGETHERNESS
  (L.T.D.)
7. LIFE IS A SONG WORTH SINGING
  (Teddy Pendergrass)
8. THE MAN
  (Barry White)
9. STEP TWO
  (Sylvester)
10. IN THE NIGHT-TIME
  (Michael Henderson)

JAZZ ALBUMS

1. CHILDREN OF SANCHEZ
  (Chuck Mangione)
2. REED SEED
  (Grover Washington Jr.)
3. COSMIC MESSENGER
  (Jean Luc Ponty)
4. MR. GONE
  (Weather Report)
5. SECRETS
  (Gil Scott-Heron and Brian Jackson)
6. IMAGES
  (Crusaders)
7. YOU SEND ME
  (Roy Ayers)
8. CARNIVAL
  (Maynard Ferguson)
9. WHAT ABOUT YOU?
  (Stanley Turrentine)
10. PAT METHENY GROUP
  (Pat Metheny)

COUNTRY SINGLES

1. IT'S BEEN A GREAT AFTERNOON
  (Merle Haggard)
2. TEAR TIME
  (Dave and Sugar)
3. LET'S TAKE THE LONG WAY AROUND THE
  WORLD
  (Ronnie Milsap)
4. HEARTBREAKER
  (Dolly Parton)
5. CRYIN' AGAIN
  (The Oak Ridge Boys)
6. ANYONE WHO ISN'T ME TONIGHT
  (Kenny Rogers and Dottie West)
7. AIN'T NO CALIFORNIA
  (Mel Tillis)
8. SLEEPING SINGLE IN A DOUBLE BED
  (Barbara Mandrell)
9. IF THE WORLD RAN OUT OF LOVE
  TONIGHT
  (Jim Ed Brown and Helen Cornelius)
10. LITTLE THINGS MEAN A LOT
  (Margo Smith)

COUNTRY ALBUMS

1. I'VE ALWAYS BEEN CRAZY
  (Waylon Jennings)
2. STARDUST
  (Willie Nelson)
3. HEARTBREAKER
  (Dolly Parton)

4. LET'S KEEP IT THAT WAY
  (Anne Murray)
5. WHEN I DREAM
  (Crystal Gayle)
6. LIVING IN THE U.S.A.
  (Linda Ronstadt)
7. THE BEST OF THE STATLER BROTHERS
  (The Statler Brothers)
8. LOVE OR SOMETHING LIKE IT
  (Kenny Rogers)
9. ONLY ONE LOVE IN MY LIFE
  (Ronnie Milsap)
10. EXPRESSIONS
  (Don Williams)

OCTOBER 28, 1978

POP SINGLES

1. HOT CHILD IN THE CITY
  (Nick Gilder)
2. KISS YOU ALL OVER
  (Exile)
3. YOU NEEDED ME
  (Anne Murray)
4. MacARTHUR PARK
  (Donna Summer)
5. REMINISCING
  (Little River Band)
6. WHENEVER I CALL YOU "FRIEND"
  (Kenny Loggins)
7. BOOGIE OOGIE OOGIE
  (A Taste of Honey)
8. GET OFF
  (Foxy)
9. WHO ARE YOU
  (The Who)
10. ONE NATION UNDER A GROOVE
  (Funkadelic)

POP ALBUMS

1. GREASE
  (Original Soundtrack)
2. DON'T LOOK BACK
  (Boston)
3. LIVING IN THE U.S.A.
  (Linda Ronstadt)
4. DOUBLE VISION
  (Foreigner)
5. SOME GIRLS
  (The Rolling Stones)
6. PIECES OF EIGHT
  (Styx)
7. WHO ARE YOU
  (The Who)
8. LIVE AND MORE
  (Donna Summer)
9. TWIN SONS OF DIFFERENT MOTHERS
  (Dan Fogelberg and Tim Weisberg)
10. ONE NATION UNDER A GROOVE
  (Funkadelic)

BLACK SINGLES

1. ONE NATION UNDER A GROOVE
  (Funkadelic)
2. IT SEEMS TO HANG ON
  (Ashford and Simpson)
3. DANCE (DISCO HEAT)
  (Sylvester)
4. THERE'LL NEVER BE
  (Switch)
5. I'M IN LOVE (AND I LOVE THE FEELING)
  (Rose Royce)
6. BLAME IT ON THE BOOGIE
  (The Jacksons)
7. GET OFF
  (Foxy)
8. TONIGHT IS THE NIGHT (PART 2)
  (Betty Wright)

9. YOUR SWEETNESS IS MY WEAKNESS
   (Barry White)
10. MacARTHUR PARK
    (Donna Summer)

BLACK ALBUMS

1. ONE NATION UNDER A GROOVE
   (Funkadelic)
2. LIVE AND MORE
   (Donna Summer)
3. IS IT STILL GOOD TO YA
   (Ashford and Simpson)
4. STRIKES AGAIN
   (Rose Royce)
5. THE MAN
   (Barry White)
6. BLAM!!
   (The Brothers Johnson)
7. SWITCH
   (Switch)
8. LIFE IS A SONG WORTH SINGING
   (Teddy Pendergrass)
9. IN THE NIGHT-TIME
   (Michael Henderson)
10. CRUISIN'
    (Village People)

JAZZ ALBUMS

1. CHILDREN OF SANCHEZ
   (Chuck Mangione)
2. REED SEED
   (Grover Washington Jr.)
3. MR. GONE
   (Weather Report)
4. COSMIC MESSENGER
   (Jean Luc Ponty)
5. SECRETS
   (Gil Scott-Heron and Brian Jackson)
6. ALL FLY HOME
   (Al Jarreau)
7. CARNIVAL
   (Maynard Ferguson)
8. LEGACY
   (Ramsey Lewis)
9. PAT METHENY GROUP
   (Pat Metheny)
10. IMAGES
    (Crusaders)

COUNTRY SINGLES

1. TEAR TIME
   (Dave and Sugar)
2. LET'S TAKE THE LONG WAY AROUND THE WORLD
   (Ronnie Milsap)
3. CRYIN' AGAIN
   (The Oak Ridge Boys)
4. ANYONE WHO ISN'T ME TONIGHT
   (Kenny Rogers and Dottie West)
5. AIN'T NO CALIFORNIA
   (Mel Tillis)
6. SLEEPING SINGLE IN A DOUBLE BED
   (Barbara Mandrell)
7. IT'S BEEN A GREAT AFTERNOON
   (Merle Haggard)
8. LITTLE THINGS MEAN A LOT
   (Margo Smith)
9. ONE-SIDED CONVERSATION
   (Gene Watson)
10. ANOTHER GOODBYE
    (Donna Fargo)

COUNTRY ALBUMS

1. I'VE ALWAYS BEEN CRAZY
   (Waylon Jennings)
2. LET'S KEEP IT THAT WAY
   (Anne Murray)

3. STARDUST
   (Willie Nelson)
4. HEARTBREAKER
   (Dolly Parton)
5. WHEN I DREAM
   (Crystal Gayle)
6. LIVING IN THE U.S.A.
   (Linda Ronstadt)
7. TEAR TIME
   (Dave and Sugar)
8. ONLY ONE LOVE IN MY LIFE
   (Ronnie Milsap)
9. EXPRESSIONS
   (Don Williams)
10. ROOM SERVICE
    (The Oak Ridge Boys)

NOVEMBER 4, 1978

POP SINGLES

1. HOT CHILD IN THE CITY
   (Nick Gilder)
2. YOU NEEDED ME
   (Anne Murray)
3. MacARTHUR PARK
   (Donna Summer)
4. KISS YOU ALL OVER
   (Exile)
5. REMINISCING
   (Little River Band)
6. WHENEVER I CALL YOU "FRIEND"
   (Kenny Loggins)
7. BOOGIE OOGIE OOGIE
   (A Taste of Honey)
8. READY TO TAKE A CHANCE AGAIN
   (Barry Manilow)
9. ONE NATION UNDER A GROOVE
   (Funkadelic)
10. YOU NEVER DONE IT LIKE THAT
    (The Captain and Tennille)

POP ALBUMS

1. GREASE
   (Original Soundtrack)
2. LIVING IN THE U.S.A.
   (Linda Ronstadt)
3. DON'T LOOK BACK
   (Boston)
4. DOUBLE VISION
   (Foreigner)
5. SOME GIRLS
   (The Rolling Stones)
6. PIECES OF EIGHT
   (Styx)
7. LIVE AND MORE
   (Donna Summer)
8. WHO ARE YOU
   (The Who)
9. ONE NATION UNDER A GROOVE
   (Funkadelic)
10. 52nd STREET
    (Billy Joel)

BLACK SINGLES

1. ONE NATION UNDER A GROOVE
   (Funkadelic)
2. THERE'LL NEVER BE
   (Switch)
3. DANCE (DISCO HEAT)
   (Sylvester)
4. IT SEEMS TO HANG ON
   (Ashford and Simpson)
5. YOUR SWEETNESS IS MY WEAKNESS
   (Barry White)
6. BLAME IT ON THE BOOGIE
   (The Jacksons)
7. TONIGHT IS THE NIGHT (PART 2)
   (Betty Wright)

8. MacARTHUR PARK
   (Donna Summer)
9. I'M EVERY WOMAN
   (Chaka Khan)
10. MARY JANE
    (Rick James)

BLACK ALBUMS

1. ONE NATION UNDER A GROOVE
   (Funkadelic)
2. LIVE AND MORE
   (Donna Summer)
3. IS IT STILL GOOD TO YA
   (Ashford and Simpson)
4. THE MAN
   (Barry White)
5. STRIKES AGAIN
   (Rose Royce)
6. SWITCH
   (Switch)
7. CRUISIN'
   (The Village People)
8. REED SEED
   (Grover Washington Jr.)
9. LIFE IS A SONG WORTH SINGING
   (Teddy Pendergrass)
10. BLAM!!
    (The Brothers Johnson)

JAZZ ALBUMS

1. REED SEED
   (Grover Washington Jr.)
2. CHILDREN OF SANCHEZ
   (Chuck Mangione)
3. MR. GONE
   (Weather Report)
4. COSMIC MESSENGER
   (Jean Luc Ponty)
5. SECRETS
   (Gil Scott-Heron and Brian Jackson)
6. ALL FLY HOME
   (Al Jarreau)
7. LEGACY
   (Ramsey Lewis)
8. FLAME
   (Ronnie Laws)
9. CARNIVAL
   (Maynard Ferguson)
10. WHAT ABOUT YOU?
    (Stanley Turrentine)

COUNTRY SINGLES

1. LET'S TAKE THE LONG WAY AROUND THE WORLD
   (Ronnie Milsap)
2. ANYONE WHO ISN'T ME TONIGHT
   (Kenny Rogers and Dottie West)
3. CRYIN' AGAIN
   (The Oak Ridge Boys)
4. SLEEPING SINGLE IN A DOUBLE BED
   (Barbara Mandrell)
5. AIN'T NO CALIFORNIA
   (Mel Tillis)
6. LITTLE THINGS MEAN A LOT
   (Margo Smith)
7. SWEET DESIRE
   (The Kendalls)
8. ONE-SIDED CONVERSATION
   (Gene Watson)
9. ANOTHER GOODBYE
   (Donna Fargo)
10. I JUST WANT TO LOVE YOU
    (Eddie Rabbitt)

COUNTRY ALBUMS

1. LET'S KEEP IT THAT WAY
   (Anne Murray)

2. I'VE ALWAYS BEEN CRAZY
   (Waylon Jennings)
3. STARDUST
   (Willie Nelson)
4. HEARTBREAKER
   (Dolly Parton)
5. LIVING IN THE U.S.A.
   (Linda Ronstadt)
6. WHEN I DREAM
   (Crystal Gayle)
7. TEAR TIME
   (Dave and Sugar)
8. ROOM SERVICE
   (The Oak Ridge Boys)
9. ONLY ONE LOVE IN MY LIFE
   (Ronnie Milsap)
10. LOVE OR SOMETHING LIKE IT
    (Kenny Rogers)

NOVEMBER 11, 1978

POP SINGLES

1. HOT CHILD IN THE CITY
   (Nick Gilder)
2. YOU NEEDED ME
   (Anne Murray)
3. MacARTHUR PARK
   (Donna Summer)
4. KISS YOU ALL OVER
   (Exile)
5. READY TO TAKE A CHANCE AGAIN
   (Barry Manilow)
6. YOU NEVER DONE IT LIKE THAT
   (The Captain and Tennille)
7. WHENEVER I CALL YOU "FRIEND"
   (Kenny Loggins)
8. ONE NATION UNDER A GROOVE
   (Funkadelic)
9. HOW MUCH I FEEL
   (Ambrosia)
10. DOUBLE VISION
    (Foreigner)

POP ALBUMS

1. 52nd STREET
   (Billy Joel)
2. LIVING IN THE U.S.A.
   (Linda Ronstadt)
3. GREASE
   (Original Soundtrack)
4. DOUBLE VISION
   (Foreigner)
5. DON'T LOOK BACK
   (Boston)
6. LIVE AND MORE
   (Donna Summer)
7. SOME GIRLS
   (The Rolling Stones)
8. PIECES OF EIGHT
   (Styx)
9. ONE NATION UNDER A GROOVE
   (Funkadelic)
10. A WILD AND CRAZY GUY
    (Steve Martin)

BLACK SINGLES

1. ONE NATION UNDER A GROOVE
   (Funkadelic)
2. THERE'LL NEVER BE
   (Switch)
3. YOUR SWEETNESS IS MY WEAKNESS
   (Barry White)
4. I'M EVERY WOMAN
   (Chaka Khan)
5. MacARTHUR PARK
   (Donna Summer)
6. IT SEEMS TO HANG ON
   (Ashford and Simpson)

7. TONIGHT IS THE NIGHT (PART 2)
   (Betty Wright)
8. BLAME IT ON THE BOOGIE
   (The Jacksons)
9. MARY JANE
   (Rick James)
10. DANCE (DISCO HEAT)
    (Sylvester)

BLACK ALBUMS

1. ONE NATION UNDER A GROOVE
   (Funkadelic)
2. LIVE AND MORE
   (Donna Summer)
3. IS IT STILL GOOD TO YA
   (Ashford and Simpson)
4. THE MAN
   (Barry White)
5. CHAKA
   (Chaka Khan)
6. STRIKES AGAIN
   (Rose Royce)
7. SWITCH
   (Switch)
8. CRUISIN'
   (The Village People)
9. REED SEED
   (Grover Washington Jr.)
10. BLAM!!
    (The Brothers Johnson)

JAZZ ALBUMS

1. REED SEED
   (Grover Washington Jr.)
2. CHILDREN OF SANCHEZ
   (Chuck Mangione)
3. MR. GONE
   (Weather Report)
4. FLAME
   (Ronnie Laws)
5. SECRETS
   (Gil Scott-Heron and Brian Jackson)
6. ALL FLY HOME
   (Al Jarreau)
7. COSMIC MESSENGER
   (Jean Luc Ponty)
8. LEGACY
   (Ramsey Lewis)
9. SOFT SPACE
   (The Jeff Lorber Fusion)
10. CARNIVAL
    (Maynard Ferguson)

COUNTRY SINGLES

1. SLEEPING SINGLE IN A DOUBLE BED
   (Barbara Mandrell)
2. ANYONE WHO ISN'T ME TONIGHT
   (Kenny Rogers and Dottie West)
3. LITTLE THINGS MEAN A LOT
   (Margo Smith)
4. AIN'T NO CALIFORNIA
   (Mel Tillis)
5. SWEET DESIRE
   (The Kendalls)
6. LET'S TAKE THE LONG WAY AROUND THE
   WORLD
   (Ronnie Milsap)
7. I JUST WANT TO LOVE YOU
   (Eddie Rabbitt)
8. DAYLIGHT
   (T.G. Sheppard)
9. CRYIN' AGAIN
   (The Oak Ridge Boys)
10. TWO LONELY PEOPLE
    (Moe Bandy)

COUNTRY ALBUMS

1. LET'S KEEP IT THAT WAY
   (Anne Murray)

2. I'VE ALWAYS BEEN CRAZY
   (Waylon Jennings)
3. STARDUST
   (Willie Nelson)
4. HEARTBREAKER
   (Dolly Parton)
5. WHEN I DREAM
   (Crystal Gayle)
6. LIVING IN THE U.S.A.
   (Linda Ronstadt)
7. LOVE OR SOMETHING LIKE IT
   (Kenny Rogers)
8. ROOM SERVICE
   (The Oak Ridge Boys)
9. TEAR TIME
   (Dave and Sugar)
10. WAYLON AND WILLIE
    (Waylon Jennings and Willie Nelson)

NOVEMBER 18, 1978

POP SINGLES

1. MacARTHUR PARK
   (Donna Summer)
2. YOU NEEDED ME
   (Anne Murray)
3. HOT CHILD IN THE CITY
   (Nick Gilder)
4. YOU DON'T BRING ME FLOWERS
   (Barbra Streisand and Neil Diamond)
5. READY TO TAKE A CHANCE AGAIN
   (Barry Manilow)
6. YOU NEVER DONE IT LIKE THAT
   (The Captain and Tennille)
7. ONE NATION UNDER A GROOVE
   (Funkadelic)
8. DOUBLE VISION
   (Foreigner)
9. HOW MUCH I FEEL
   (Ambrosia)
10. KISS YOU ALL OVER
    (Exile)

POP ALBUMS

1. 52nd STREET
   (Billy Joel)
2. LIVE AND MORE
   (Donna Summer)
3. LIVING IN THE U.S.A.
   (Linda Ronstadt)
4. GREASE
   (Original Soundtrack)
5. A WILD AND CRAZY GUY
   (Steve Martin)
6. DOUBLE VISION
   (Foreigner)
7. SOME GIRLS
   (The Rolling Stones)
8. DON'T LOOK BACK
   (Boston)
9. ONE NATION UNDER A GROOVE
   (Funkadelic)
10. PIECES OF EIGHT
    (Styx)

BLACK SINGLES

1. I'M EVERY WOMAN
   (Chaka Khan)
2. YOUR SWEETNESS IS MY WEAKNESS
   (Barry White)
3. ONE NATION UNDER A GROOVE
   (Funkadelic)
4. MacARTHUR PARK
   (Donna Summer)
5. THERE'LL NEVER BE
   (Switch)
6. LE FREAK
   (Chic)

7. IT SEEMS TO HANG ON
   (Ashford and Simpson)
8. MARY JANE
   (Rick James)
9. TONIGHT IS THE NIGHT (PART 2)
   (Betty Wright)
10. GOT TO BE REAL
    (Cheryl Lynn)

BLACK ALBUMS

1. LIVE AND MORE
   (Donna Summer)
2. ONE NATION UNDER A GROOVE
   (Funkadelic)
3. THE MAN
   (Barry White)
4. CHAKA
   (Chaka Khan)
5. IS IT STILL GOOD TO YA
   (Ashford and Simpson)
6. STRIKES AGAIN
   (Rose Royce)
7. SWITCH
   (Switch)
8. CRUISIN'
   (The Village People)
9. REED SEED
   (Grover Washington Jr.)
10. FUNK OR WALK
    (The Brides of Funkenstein)

JAZZ ALBUMS

1. REED SEED
   (Grover Washington Jr.)
2. MR. GONE
   (Weather Report)
3. FLAME
   (Ronnie Laws)
4. CHILDREN OF SANCHEZ
   (Chuck Mangione)
5. SECRETS
   (Gil Scott-Heron and Brian Jackson)
6. ALL FLY HOME
   (Al Jarreau)
7. COSMIC MESSENGER
   (Jean Luc Ponty)
8. SOFT SPACE
   (The Jeff Lorber Fusion)
9. LEGACY
   (Ramsey Lewis)
10. THANK YOU . . . FOR F.U.M.L. (FUNKING UP
    MY LIFE)
    (Donald Byrd)

COUNTRY SINGLES

1. SLEEPING SINGLE IN A DOUBLE BED
   (Barbara Mandrell)
2. SWEET DESIRE
   (The Kendalls)
3. LITTLE THINGS MEAN A LOT
   (Margo Smith)
4. I JUST WANT TO LOVE YOU
   (Eddie Rabbitt)
5. ANYONE WHO ISN'T ME TONIGHT
   (Kenny Rogers and Dottie West)
6. ON MY KNEES
   (Charlie Rich and Janie Fricke)
7. DAYLIGHT
   (T.G. Sheppard)
8. TWO LONELY PEOPLE
   (Moe Bandy)
9. FADIN' IN, FADIN' OUT
   (Tommy Overstreet)
10. WHAT HAVE YOU GOT TO LOSE
    (Tom T. Hall)

COUNTRY ALBUMS

1. I'VE ALWAYS BEEN CRAZY
   (Waylon Jennings)

2. LET'S KEEP IT THAT WAY
   (Anne Murray)
3. STARDUST
   (Willie Nelson)
4. WHEN I DREAM
   (Crystal Gayle)
5. HEARTBREAKER
   (Dolly Parton)
6. LIVING IN THE U.S.A.
   (Linda Ronstadt)
7. LOVE OR SOMETHING LIKE IT
   (Kenny Rogers)
8. MOODS
   (Barbara Mandrell)
9. EXPRESSIONS
   (Don Williams)
10. TEAR TIME
    (Dave and Sugar)

NOVEMBER 25, 1978

POP SINGLES

1. MacARTHUR PARK
   (Donna Summer)
2. YOU DON'T BRING ME FLOWERS
   (Barbra Streisand and Neil Diamond)
3. YOU NEEDED ME
   (Anne Murray)
4. HOT CHILD IN THE CITY
   (Nick Gilder)
5. READY TO TAKE A CHANCE AGAIN
   (Barry Manilow)
6. HOW MUCH I FEEL
   (Ambrosia)
7. ONE NATION UNDER A GROOVE
   (Funkadelic)
8. DOUBLE VISION
   (Foreigner)
9. I JUST WANNA STOP
   (Gino Vannelli)
10. SHARING THE NIGHT TOGETHER
    (Dr. Hook)

POP ALBUMS

1. 52nd STREET
   (Billy Joel)
2. LIVE AND MORE
   (Donna Summer)
3. A WILD AND CRAZY GUY
   (Steve Martin)
4. LIVING IN THE U.S.A.
   (Linda Ronstadt)
5. GREASE
   (Original Soundtrack)
6. DOUBLE VISION
   (Foreigner)
7. SOME GIRLS
   (The Rolling Stones)
8. PIECES OF EIGHT
   (Styx)
9. DON'T LOOK BACK
   (Boston)
10. HOT STREETS
    (Chicago)

BLACK SINGLES

1. I'M EVERY WOMAN
   (Chaka Khan)
2. YOUR SWEETNESS IS MY WEAKNESS
   (Barry White)
3. LE FREAK
   (Chic)
4. MacARTHUR PARK
   (Donna Summer)
5. ONE NATION UNDER A GROOVE
   (Funkadelic)
6. THERE'LL NEVER BE
   (Switch)

7. MARY JANE
   (Rick James)
8. GOT TO BE REAL
   (Cheryl Lynn)
9. TONIGHT IS THE NIGHT (PART 2)
   (Betty Wright)
10. LOVE DON'T LIVE HERE ANYMORE
    (Rose Royce)

BLACK ALBUMS

1. LIVE AND MORE
   (Donna Summer)
2. THE MAN
   (Barry White)
3. CHAKA
   (Chaka Khan)
4. ONE NATION UNDER A GROOVE
   (Funkadelic)
5. IS IT STILL GOOD TO YA
   (Ashford and Simpson)
6. STRIKES AGAIN
   (Rose Royce)
7. CRUISIN'
   (The Village People)
8. SWITCH
   (Switch)
9. REED SEED
   (Grover Washington Jr.)
10. FUNK OR WALK
    (The Brides of Funkenstein)

JAZZ ALBUMS

1. REED SEED
   (Grover Washington Jr.)
2. MR. GONE
   (Weather Report)
3. FLAME
   (Ronnie Laws)
4. CHILDREN OF SANCHEZ
   (Chuck Mangione)
5. SECRETS
   (Gil Scott-Heron and Brian Jackson)
6. ALL FLY HOME
   (Al Jarreau)
7. COSMIC MESSENGER
   (Jean Luc Ponty)
8. SOFT SPACE
   (The Jeff Lorber Fusion)
9. LEGACY
   (Ramsey Lewis)
10. THANK YOU . . . FOR F.U.M.L. (FUNKING UP
    MY LIFE)
    (Donald Byrd)

COUNTRY SINGLES

1. SWEET DESIRE
   (The Kendalls)
2. I JUST WANT TO LOVE YOU
   (Eddie Rabbitt)
3. SLEEPING SINGLE IN A DOUBLE BED
   (Barbara Mandrell)
4. ON MY KNEES
   (Charlie Rich and Janie Fricke)
5. LITTLE THINGS MEAN A LOT
   (Margo Smith)
6. FADIN' IN, FADIN' OUT
   (Tommy Overstreet)
7. TWO LONELY PEOPLE
   (Moe Bandy)
8. THAT'S WHAT YOU DO TO ME
   (Charly McClain)
9. YOU'VE STILL GOT A PLACE IN MY HEART
   (Con Hunley)
10. BREAK MY MIND
    (Vern Gosdin)

COUNTRY ALBUMS

1. I'VE ALWAYS BEEN CRAZY
   (Waylon Jennings)

2. LET'S KEEP IT THAT WAY
   (Anne Murray)
3. STARDUST
   (Willie Nelson)
4. HEARTBREAKER
   (Dolly Parton)
5. LIVING IN THE U.S.A.
   (Linda Ronstadt)
6. WHEN I DREAM
   (Crystal Gayle)
7. LOVE OR SOMETHING LIKE IT
   (Kenny Rogers)
8. MOODS
   (Barbara Mandrell)
9. EXPRESSIONS
   (Don Williams)
10. LARRY GATLIN'S GREATEST HITS
    (Larry Gatlin)

DECEMBER 2, 1978

POP SINGLES

1. YOU DON'T BRING ME FLOWERS
   (Barbra Streisand and Neil Diamond)
2. MacARTHUR PARK
   (Donna Summer)
3. LE FREAK
   (Chic)
4. YOU NEEDED ME
   (Anne Murray)
5. HOT CHILD IN THE CITY
   (Nick Gilder)
6. HOW MUCH I FEEL
   (Ambrosia)
7. ONE NATION UNDER A GROOVE
   (Funkadelic)
8. I JUST WANNA STOP
   (Gino Vannelli)
9. SHARING THE NIGHT TOGETHER
   (Dr. Hook)
10. I LOVE THE NIGHT LIFE (DISCO ROUND)
    (Alicia Bridges)

POP ALBUMS

1. 52nd STREET
   (Billy Joel)
2. LIVE AND MORE
   (Donna Summer)
3. A WILD AND CRAZY GUY
   (Steve Martin)
4. LIVING IN THE U.S.A.
   (Linda Ronstadt)
5. DOUBLE VISION
   (Foreigner)
6. PIECES OF EIGHT
   (Styx)
7. LIVE BOOTLEG
   (Aerosmith)
8. SOME GIRLS
   (The Rolling Stones)
9. GREASE
   (Original Soundtrack)
10. HOT STREETS
    (Chicago)

BLACK SINGLES

1. LE FREAK
   (Chic)
2. I'M EVERY WOMAN
   (Chaka Khan)
3. YOUR SWEETNESS IS MY WEAKNESS
   (Barry White)
4. GOT TO BE REAL
   (Cheryl Lynn)
5. ONE NATION UNDER A GROOVE
   (Funkadelic)
6. MARY JANE
   (Rick James)

7. MacARTHUR PARK
   (Donna Summer)
8. LOVE DON'T LIVE HERE ANYMORE
   (Rose Royce)
9. THERE'LL NEVER BE
   (Switch)
10. TONIGHT IS THE NIGHT (PART 2)
    (Betty Wright)

BLACK ALBUMS

1. THE MAN
   (Barry White)
2. LIVE AND MORE
   (Donna Summer)
3. CHAKA
   (Chaka Khan)
4. ONE NATION UNDER A GROOVE
   (Funkadelic)
5. IS IT STILL GOOD TO YA
   (Ashford and Simpson)
6. STRIKES AGAIN
   (Rose Royce)
7. SWITCH
   (Switch)
8. CRUISIN'
   (The Village People)
9. FOR THE SAKE OF LOVE
   (Isaac Hayes)
10. CHERYL LYNN
    (Cheryl Lynn)

JAZZ ALBUMS

1. MR. GONE
   (Weather Report)
2. REED SEED
   (Grover Washington Jr.)
3. FLAME
   (Ronnie Laws)
4. CHILDREN OF SANCHEZ
   (Chuck Mangione)
5. SECRETS
   (Gil Scott-Heron and Brian Jackson)
6. ALL FLY HOME
   (Al Jarreau)
7. COSMIC MESSENGER
   (Jean Luc Ponty)
8. CRY
   (John Klemmer)
9. INTIMATE STRANGERS
   (Tom Scott)
10. THANK YOU . . . FOR F.U.M.L. (FUNKING UP
    MY LIFE)
    (Donald Byrd)

COUNTRY SINGLES

1. I JUST WANT TO LOVE YOU
   (Eddie Rabbitt)
2. ON MY KNEES
   (Charlie Rich and Janie Fricke)
3. SWEET DESIRE
   (The Kendalls)
4. BURGERS AND FRIES
   (Charley Pride)
5. THE GAMBLER
   (Kenny Rogers)
6. FADIN' IN, FADIN' OUT
   (Tommy Overstreet)
7. YOU'VE STILL GOT A PLACE IN MY HEART
   (Con Hunley)
8. THAT'S WHAT YOU DO TO ME
   (Charly McClain)
9. SLEEP TIGHT, GOOD NIGHT MAN
   (Bobby Bare)
10. BREAK MY MIND
    (Vern Gosdin)

COUNTRY ALBUMS

1. I'VE ALWAYS BEEN CRAZY
   (Waylon Jennings)

2. LET'S KEEP IT THAT WAY
   (Anne Murray)
3. STARDUST
   (Willie Nelson)
4. WILLIE AND FAMILY LIVE
   (Willie Nelson)
5. HEARTBREAKER
   (Dolly Parton)
6. WHEN I DREAM
   (Crystal Gayle)
7. LOVE OR SOMETHING LIKE IT
   (Kenny Rogers)
8. MOODS
   (Barbara Mandrell)
9. LARRY GATLIN'S GREATEST HITS
   (Larry Gatlin)
10. TNT
    (Tanya Tucker)

DECEMBER 9, 1978

POP SINGLES

1. YOU DON'T BRING ME FLOWERS
   (Barbra Streisand and Neil Diamond)
2. LE FREAK
   (Chic)
3. MacARTHUR PARK
   (Donna Summer)
4. SHARING THE NIGHT TOGETHER
   (Dr. Hook)
5. YOU NEEDED ME
   (Anne Murray)
6. HOW MUCH I FEEL
   (Ambrosia)
7. I LOVE THE NIGHT LIFE (DISCO ROUND)
   (Alicia Bridges)
8. I JUST WANNA STOP
   (Gino Vannelli)
9. MY LIFE
   (Billy Joel)
10. TOO MUCH HEAVEN
    (The Bee Gees)

POP ALBUMS

1. 52nd STREET
   (Billy Joel)
2. LIVE AND MORE
   (Donna Summer)
3. A WILD AND CRAZY GUY
   (Steve Martin)
4. BARBRA STREISAND'S GREATEST HITS,
   VOL. 2
   (Barbra Streisand)
5. DOUBLE VISION
   (Foreigner)
6. PIECES OF EIGHT
   (Styx)
7. LIVE BOOTLEG
   (Aerosmith)
8. LIVING IN THE U.S.A.
   (Linda Ronstadt)
9. GREASE
   (Original Soundtrack)
10. SOME GIRLS
    (The Rolling Stones)

BLACK SINGLES

1. LE FREAK
   (Chic)
2. I'M EVERY WOMAN
   (Chaka Khan)
3. GOT TO BE REAL
   (Cheryl Lynn)
4. YOUR SWEETNESS IS MY WEAKNESS
   (Barry White)
5. LOVE DON'T LIVE HERE ANYMORE
   (Rose Royce)

6. MARY JANE
   (Rick James)
7. ONE NATION UNDER A GROOVE
   (Funkadelic)
8. MacARTHUR PARK
   (Donna Summer)
9. THERE'LL NEVER BE
   (Switch)
10. LONG STROKE
    (ADC Band)

BLACK ALBUMS

1. THE MAN
   (Barry White)
2. C'EST CHIC
   (Chic)
3. CHAKA
   (Chaka Khan)
4. THE BEST OF EARTH, WIND AND FIRE,
   VOL. 1
   (Earth, Wind and Fire)
5. LIVE AND MORE
   (Donna Summer)
6. ONE NATION UNDER A GROOVE
   (Funkadelic)
7. IS IT STILL GOOD TO YA
   (Ashford and Simpson)
8. STRIKES AGAIN
   (Rose Royce)
9. FOR THE SAKE OF LOVE
   (Isaac Hayes)
10. CHERYL LYNN
    (Cheryl Lynn)

JAZZ ALBUMS

1. REED SEED
   (Grover Washington Jr.)
2. MR. GONE
   (Weather Report)
3. FLAME
   (Ronnie Laws)
4. CHILDREN OF SANCHEZ
   (Chuck Mangione)
5. INTIMATE STRANGERS
   (Tom Scott)
6. SECRETS
   (Gil Scott-Heron and Brian Jackson)
7. COSMIC MESSENGER
   (Jean Luc Ponty)
8. CRY
   (John Klemmer)
9. THANK YOU . . . FOR F.U.M.L. (FUNKING UP
   MY LIFE)
   (Donald Byrd)
10. ALL FLY HOME
    (Al Jarreau)

COUNTRY SINGLES

1. ON MY KNEES
   (Charlie Rich and Janie Fricke)
2. BURGERS AND FRIES
   (Charley Pride)
3. THE GAMBLER
   (Kenny Rogers)
4. I JUST WANT TO LOVE YOU
   (Eddie Rabbitt)
5. ALL OF ME
   (Willie Nelson)
6. DON'T YOU THINK THIS OUTLAW BIT'S
   DONE GOT OUT OF HAND
   (Waylon Jennings)
7. YOU'VE STILL GOT A PLACE IN MY HEART
   (Con Hunley)
8. FRIEND, LOVER, WIFE
   (Johnny Paycheck)
9. SLEEP TIGHT, GOOD NIGHT MAN
   (Bobby Bare)
10. TULSA TIME
    (Don Williams)

COUNTRY ALBUMS

1. I'VE ALWAYS BEEN CRAZY
   (Waylon Jennings)
2. LET'S KEEP IT THAT WAY
   (Anne Murray)
3. STARDUST
   (Willie Nelson)
4. WILLIE AND FAMILY LIVE
   (Willie Nelson)
5. WHEN I DREAM
   (Crystal Gayle)
6. PROFILES/BEST OF EMMYLOU HARRIS
   (Emmylou Harris)
7. HEARTBREAKER
   (Dolly Parton)
8. TNT
   (Tanya Tucker)
9. ARMED AND CRAZY
   (Johnny Paycheck)
10. LOVE OR SOMETHING LIKE IT
    (Kenny Rogers)

DECEMBER 16, 1978

POP SINGLES

1. LE FREAK
   (Chic)
2. YOU DON'T BRING ME FLOWERS
   (Barbra Streisand and Neil Diamond)
3. TOO MUCH HEAVEN
   (The Bee Gees)
4. SHARING THE NIGHT TOGETHER
   (Dr. Hook)
5. MY LIFE
   (Billy Joel)
6. YMCA
   (The Village People)
7. I LOVE THE NIGHT LIFE (DISCO ROUND)
   (Alicia Bridges)
8. MacARTHUR PARK
   (Donna Summer)
9. I JUST WANNA STOP
   (Gino Vannelli)
10. OUR LOVE (DON'T THROW IT ALL AWAY)
    (Andy Gibb)

POP ALBUMS

1. 52nd STREET
   (Billy Joel)
2. A WILD AND CRAZY GUY
   (Steve Martin)
3. BARBRA STREISAND'S GREATEST HITS,
   VOL. 2
   (Barbra Streisand)
4. LIVE AND MORE
   (Donna Summer)
5. DOUBLE VISION
   (Foreigner)
6. GREASE
   (Original Soundtrack)
7. LIVE BOOTLEG
   (Aerosmith)
8. PIECES OF EIGHT
   (Styx)
9. LIVING IN THE U.S.A.
   (Linda Ronstadt)
10. SOME GIRLS
    (The Rolling Stones)

BLACK SINGLES

1. LE FREAK
   (Chic)
2. I'M EVERY WOMAN
   (Chaka Khan)
3. GOT TO BE REAL
   (Cheryl Lynn)

4. LOVE DON'T LIVE HERE ANYMORE
   (Rose Royce)
5. YOUR SWEETNESS IS MY WEAKNESS
   (Barry White)
6. SEPTEMBER
   (Earth, Wind and Fire)
7. ONE NATION UNDER A GROOVE
   (Funkadelic)
8. LONG STROKE
   (ADC Band)
9. GET DOWN
   (Gene Chandler)
10. DON'T HOLD BACK
    (Chanson)

BLACK ALBUMS

1. THE MAN
   (Barry White)
2. C'EST CHIC
   (Chic)
3. CHAKA
   (Chaka Khan)
4. MOTOR BOOTY AFFAIR
   (Parliament)
5. THE BEST OF EARTH, WIND AND FIRE
   VOL. 1
   (Earth, Wind and Fire)
6. LIVE AND MORE
   (Donna Summer)
7. IS IT STILL GOOD TO YA
   (Ashford and Simpson)
8. STRIKES AGAIN
   (Rose Royce)
9. ONE NATION UNDER A GROOVE
   (Funkadelic)
10. CHERYL LYNN
    (Cheryl Lynn)

JAZZ ALBUMS

1. REED SEED
   (Grover Washington Jr.)
2. MR. GONE
   (Weather Report)
3. FLAME
   (Ronnie Laws)
4. TOUCH DOWN
   (Bob James)
5. CHILDREN OF SANCHEZ
   (Chuck Mangione)
6. SECRETS
   (Gil Scott-Heron and Brian Jackson)
7. INTIMATE STRANGERS
   (Tom Scott)
8. COSMIC MESSENGER
   (Jean Luc Ponty)
9. ALL FLY HOME
   (Al Jarreau)
10. CRY
    (John Klemmer)

COUNTRY SINGLES

1. BURGERS AND FRIES
   (Charley Pride)
2. THE GAMBLER
   (Kenny Rogers)
3. ON MY KNEES
   (Charlie Rich and Janie Fricke)
4. ALL OF ME
   (Willie Nelson)
5. DON'T YOU THINK THIS OUTLAW BIT'S
   DONE GOT OUT OF HAND
   (Waylon Jennings)
6. TULSA TIME
   (Don Williams)
7. FRIEND, LOVER, WIFE
   (Johnny Paycheck)
8. I JUST WANT TO LOVE YOU
   (Eddie Rabbitt)
9. LADY LAY DOWN
   (John Conlee)
10. THE BULL AND THE BEAVER
    (Merle Haggard and Leona Williams)

COUNTRY ALBUMS

1. WILLIE AND FAMILY LIVE
   (Willie Nelson)
2. LET'S KEEP IT THAT WAY
   (Anne Murray)
3. I'VE ALWAYS BEEN CRAZY
   (Waylon Jennings)
4. PROFILES/BEST OF EMMYLOU HARRIS
   (Emmylou Harris)
5. WHEN I DREAM
   (Crystal Gayle)
6. ELVIS: A LEGENDARY PERFORMER, VOL. 3
   (Elvis Presley)
7. THE GAMBLER
   (Kenny Rogers)
8. TNT
   (Tanya Tucker)
9. ARMED AND CRAZY
   (Johnny Paycheck)
10. STARDUST
    (Willie Nelson)

DECEMBER 23, 1978

POP SINGLES

1. LE FREAK
   (Chic)
2. TOO MUCH HEAVEN
   (The Bee Gees)
3. YOU DON'T BRING ME FLOWERS
   (Barbra Streisand and Neil Diamond)
4. MY LIFE
   (Billy Joel)
5. YMCA
   (The Village People)
6. SHARING THE NIGHT TOGETHER
   (Dr. Hook)
7. I LOVE THE NIGHT LIFE (DISCO ROUND)
   (Alicia Bridges)
8. MacARTHUR PARK
   (Donna Summer)
9. OUR LOVE (DON'T THROW IT ALL AWAY)
   (Andy Gibb)
10. SEPTEMBER
    (Earth, Wind and Fire)

POP ALBUMS

1. BARBRA STREISAND'S GREATEST HITS, VOL. 2
   (Barbra Streisand)
2. A WILD AND CRAZY GUY
   (Steve Martin)
3. 52nd STREET
   (Billy Joel)
4. LIVE AND MORE
   (Donna Summer)
5. GREASE
   (Original Soundtrack)
6. DOUBLE VISION
   (Foreigner)
7. GREATEST HITS
   (Barry Manilow)
8. C'EST CHIC
   (Chic)
9. THE BEST OF EARTH, WIND AND FIRE, VOL. 1
   (Earth, Wind and Fire)
10. SOME GIRLS
    (The Rolling Stones)

BLACK SINGLES

1. LE FREAK
   (Chic)
2. GOT TO BE REAL
   (Cheryl Lynn)
3. I'M EVERY WOMAN
   (Chaka Khan)
4. LOVE DON'T LIVE HERE ANYMORE
   (Rose Royce)
5. SEPTEMBER
   (Earth, Wind and Fire)
6. YOUR SWEETNESS IS MY WEAKNESS
   (Barry White)
7. LONG STROKE
   (ADC Band)
8. GET DOWN
   (Gene Chandler)
9. WHAT YOU WON'T DO FOR LOVE
   (Bobby Caldwell)
10. DON'T HOLD BACK
    (Chanson)

BLACK ALBUMS

1. C'EST CHIC
   (Chic)
2. THE BEST OF EARTH, WIND AND FIRE, VOL. 1
   (Earth, Wind and Fire)
3. MOTOR BOOTY AFFAIR
   (Parliament)
4. THE MAN
   (Barry White)
5. CHAKA
   (Chaka Khan)
6. LIVE AND MORE
   (Donna Summer)
7. CHERYL LYNN
   (Cheryl Lynn)
8. CROSSWINDS
   (Peabo Bryson)
9. FOR THE SAKE OF LOVE
   (Isaac Hayes)
10. IS IT STILL GOOD TO YA
    (Ashford and Simpson)

JAZZ ALBUMS

1. REED SEED
   (Grover Washington Jr.)
2. TOUCH DOWN
   (Bob James)
3. FLAME
   (Ronnie Laws)
4. MR. GONE
   (Weather Report)
5. CHILDREN OF SANCHEZ
   (Chuck Mangione)
6. SECRETS
   (Gil Scott-Heron and Brian Jackson)
7. INTIMATE STRANGERS
   (Tom Scott)
8. COSMIC MESSENGER
   (Jean Luc Ponty)
9. ALL FLY HOME
   (Al Jarreau)
10. THANK YOU . . . FOR F.U.M.L. (FUNKING UP MY LIFE)
    (Donald Byrd)

COUNTRY SINGLES

1. THE GAMBLER
   (Kenny Rogers)
2. BURGERS AND FRIES
   (Charley Pride)
3. TULSA TIME
   (Don Williams)
4. ALL OF ME
   (Willie Nelson)
5. DON'T YOU THINK THIS OUTLAW BIT'S DONE GOT OUT OF HAND
   (Waylon Jennings)
6. LADY LAY DOWN
   (John Conlee)
7. DO YOU EVER FOOL AROUND
   (Joe Stampley)
8. RHYTHM OF THE RAIN
   (Jacky Ward)

9. THE BULL AND THE BEAVER
   (Merle Haggard and Leona Williams)
10. WE'VE COME A LONG WAY BABY
    (Loretta Lynn)

COUNTRY ALBUMS

1. WILLIE AND FAMILY LIVE
   (Willie Nelson)
2. THE GAMBLER
   (Kenny Rogers)
3. LET'S KEEP IT THAT WAY
   (Anne Murray)
4. PROFILES/BEST OF EMMYLOU HARRIS
   (Emmylou Harris)
5. I'VE ALWAYS BEEN CRAZY
   (Waylon Jennings)
6. ELVIS: A LEGENDARY PERFORMER, VOL. 3
   (Elvis Presley)
7. WHEN I DREAM
   (Crystal Gayle)
8. LARRY GATLIN'S GREATEST HITS
   (Larry Gatlin)
9. STARDUST
   (Willie Nelson)
10. HEARTBREAKER
    (Dolly Parton)

DECEMBER 30, 1978

POP SINGLES

1. LE FREAK
   (Chic)
2. TOO MUCH HEAVEN
   (The Bee Gees)
3. MY LIFE
   (Billy Joel)
4. YOU DON'T BRING ME FLOWERS
   (Barbra Streisand and Neil Diamond)
5. YMCA
   (The Village People)
6. SHARING THE NIGHT TOGETHER
   (Dr. Hook)
7. SEPTEMBER
   (Earth, Wind and Fire)
8. HOLD THE LINE
   (Toto)
9. OUR LOVE (DON'T THROW IT ALL AWAY)
   (Andy Gibb)
10. I LOVE THE NIGHT LIFE (DISCO ROUND)
    (Alicia Bridges)

POP ALBUMS

1. BARBRA STREISAND'S GREATEST HITS, VOL. 2
   (Barbra Streisand)
2. 52nd STREET
   (Billy Joel)
3. A WILD AND CRAZY GUY
   (Steve Martin)
4. GREASE
   (Original Soundtrack)
5. DOUBLE VISION
   (Foreigner)
6. GREATEST HITS
   (Barry Manilow)
7. C'EST CHIC
   (Chic)
8. YOU DON'T BRING ME FLOWERS
   (Neil Diamond)
9. THE BEST OF EARTH, WIND AND FIRE, VOL. 1
   (Earth, Wind and Fire)
10. LIVE AND MORE
    (Donna Summer)

BLACK SINGLES

1. LE FREAK
   (Chic)
2. GOT TO BE REAL
   (Cheryl Lynn)
3. SEPTEMBER
   (Earth, Wind and Fire)
4. I'M EVERY WOMAN
   (Chaka Khan)
5. GET DOWN
   (Gene Chandler)
6. LOVE DON'T LIVE HERE ANYMORE
   (Rose Royce)
7. LONG STROKE
   (ADC Band)
8. WHAT YOU WON'T DO FOR LOVE
   (Bobby Caldwell)
9. YOUR SWEETNESS IS MY WEAKNESS
   (Barry White)
10. I DON'T KNOW IF IT'S RIGHT
    (Evelyn "Champagne" King)

BLACK ALBUMS

1. C'EST CHIC
   (Chic)
2. THE BEST OF EARTH, WIND AND FIRE, VOL. 1
   (Earth, Wind and Fire)
3. MOTOR BOOTY AFFAIR
   (Parliament)
4. THE MAN
   (Barry White)
5. CHAKA
   (Chaka Khan)
6. LIVE AND MORE
   (Donna Summer)
7. CHERYL LYNN
   (Cheryl Lynn)
8. CROSSWINDS
   (Peabo Bryson)
9. FOR THE SAKE OF LOVE
   (Isaac Hayes)
10. IS IT STILL GOOD TO YA
    (Ashford and Simpson)

JAZZ ALBUMS

1. REED SEED
   (Grover Washington Jr.)
2. TOUCH DOWN
   (Bob James)
3. FLAME
   (Ronnie Laws)
4. CHILDREN OF SANCHEZ
   (Chuck Mangione)
5. MR. GONE
   (Weather Report)
6. INTIMATE STRANGERS
   (Tom Scott)
7. SECRETS
   (Gil Scott-Heron and Brian Jackson)
8. ALL FLY HOME
   (Al Jarreau)
9. COSMIC MESSENGER
   (Jean Luc Ponty)
10. SECRET AGENT
    (Chick Corea)

COUNTRY SINGLES

1. TULSA TIME
   (Don Williams)
2. THE GAMBLER
   (Kenny Rogers)
3. BURGERS AND FRIES
   (Charley Pride)
4. LADY LAY DOWN
   (John Conlee)
5. ALL OF ME
   (Willie Nelson)

6. DO YOU EVER FOOL AROUND
   (Joe Stampley)
7. RHYTHM OF THE RAIN
   (Jacky Ward)
8. YOUR LOVE HAD TAKEN ME THAT HIGH
   (Conway Twitty)
9. I'VE DONE ENOUGH DYIN' TODAY
   (Larry Gatlin)
10. WE'VE COME A LONG WAY BABY
    (Loretta Lynn)

COUNTRY ALBUMS

1. WILLIE AND FAMILY LIVE
   (Willie Nelson)
2. THE GAMBLER
   (Kenny Rogers)
3. LET'S KEEP IT THAT WAY
   (Anne Murray)
4. I'VE ALWAYS BEEN CRAZY
   (Waylon Jennings)
5. PROFILES/BEST OF EMMYLOU HARRIS
   (Emmylou Harris)
6. LARRY GATLIN'S GREATEST HITS
   (Larry Gatlin)
7. MOODS
   (Barbara Mandrell)
8. STARDUST
   (Willie Nelson)
9. ELVIS: A LEGENDARY PERFORMER, VOL. 3
   (Elvis Presley)
10. TNT
    (Tanya Tucker)

1979

A female singer with a carefully cultivated image and a band with no image at all were the major stories of an active year in pop music, one that also introduced an eclectic collection of young rock bands.

Starting with her first orgasmic hit single in 1977, "Love to Love You Baby," Donna Summer played the sex siren on records, in concert, and on screen in *Thank God It's Friday*. The difference between *Bad Girls* and her previous albums was producer Giorgio Moroder's decision to give several songs a tough, rock edge aimed at convincing the skeptical that Summer was a genuine pop star, not just another disco diva. His strategy worked magnificently as "Bad Girls" and the explosive "Hot Stuff" broke Summer completely into the pop and rock markets. In 1979, she overshadowed every other female performer, including Barbra Streisand, with whom Summer recorded the redundant "Enough Is Enough."

It's doubtful most of the folks who purchased the Supertramp's album *Breakfast in America* could name the group members or tell how many there were. All fans could attest to truly was that Supertramp's music, as the title suggested, had a slight, precious tone and exquisitely hummable melodies. The chief example was the big single, "The Logical Song," which indulged in prep-school wordplay, ("watch what you say or they'll be calling you a liberal/intellectual/cynical"), over a charming melody. Supertramp's chief virtue was its cleverness, and considering disco's influence on pop wordplay, this was definitely an admirable quality.

Van Halen, The Cars, The Knack, Dire Straits, Toto, and The Police all achieved radio acceptance with debut albums, sold loads of records, and suggested the range of music squeezed, often uncomfortably, under the banner of rock.

Van Halen was discovered playing bars and getting drunk around the San Fernando Valley. As with most bar bands, Van Halen was better at sounding like other people than projecting any originality. Lead screamer David Lee Roth imitates Robert Plant by way of Eric Burdon; and guitarist Eddie Van Halen emulated guitar "heroes" Jimi Hendrix and Jimmy Page. Appropriately, Van Halen's rock radio hit was a faithful, though extended, version of The Kinks' heavy metal classic "You Really Got Me." Still, this quartet's third-generation heavy-metal sound had a certain élan, especially after you've had seven beers, the minimum for Van Halen fans.

The Cars came on the scene like a Maserati: cool, sleek, short, and metallic. Behind sun glasses and monotone vocals, Cars leader Rick Ocasek guided his four comrades around the course, producing hooky rock ("Best Friend's Girl," "Just What I Needed") with splashes of synthesizer, crisp guitar breaks, and lyrics never quite so simple as they sounded. Their self-titled debut album received huge sales and tremendous reviews, and deserved both.

But did The Knack deserve the attention they received? "My Sharona" was the most infectious single of that summer, and Doug Fiegler's lyrics and lecherous vocals on *Get the Knack* were no dirtier than, say, the Stones. But there was definitely something sleazy about The Knack and their new-Beatles hype. Certainly the music didn't merit it. But in the long run it didn't matter, since two years later the band self-destructed, due to pressure generated by its own hype.

Dire Straits received no hype. They were a quartet from London whose first single, "Sultans of Swing," was exposed on a local radio show, and subsequently purchased by a major record label. "Sultans" was the surprise single of the year and led by guitarist-singer-writer Mark Knopfler, the album *Dire Straits* was as stirring as the single. Knopfler's Dylanesque imagery and sinuous guitar lines gave Dire Straits' music a captivating cinematic quality.

Toto's music was professional. Too professional. These five Los Angeles session cats play and write pop-rock so polished they sound like training records for aspiring players. Toto's debut single "Hold the Line" not only went top 10, but also was the first commercially available picture disk.

Reggae was the "in" music throughout England and most of the young bands tried to imitate Jamaican reggae originators as closely as possible. The Police—assist-singer Sting, drummer Stewart Copeland, and guitarist Andy Summers—developed their own way of playing reggae, so that it still has an idiomatic pulse, but didn't slavishly follow their

Jamaican models. "Roxanne" set the style, one that would quickly grow more sophisticated.

ALBUMS: Billy Joel's *52nd Street* and The Bee Gees' *Spirits Having Flown* sold well, primarily because they followed up the artistically more interesting *Stranger* and *Saturday Night Fever* albums. Across-the-board acceptance of Kenny Rogers album and single "The Gambler" made him the king of both country and the burgeoning adult-contemporary market—radio's new name for MOR recordings. The jazz phrasing and poetic ramblings of Rickie Lee Jones found an audience, as did the revivalist rock 'n' roll of George Thorogood and the Destroyers. English rock war-horses Led Zeppelin (*In Through the Out Door*), Foreigner (*Double Vision*), Eric Clapton (*Backless*), and Bad Company (*Desolation Angels*) offered their wares to anxious anglophiles. Meanwhile, two young American bands, Heart (*Dog and Butterfly*), and Cheap Trick (*Live at Budokan*) made their mark.

SINGLES: Dance music (some of it disco, some not) dominated the singles chart. There was rock disco (Rod Stewart's "Da Ya Think I'm Sexy?" Kiss's "I Was Made for Loving You," Blondie's "Hearts of Glass"); sophisticated funk (Chic's "Le Freak" and "Good Times," Sister Sledge's "He's the Greatest Dancer" and "We Are Family"); soap-opera disco (Gloria Gaynor's "I Will Survive"); shake disco (The Jacksons' "Shake Your Body," Peaches and Herb's "Shake Your Groove Thing"); novelty disco (The Village Peoples' "YMCA" and "In the Navy"); and disco disco (Anita Ward's "Ring My Bell," Amii Stewart's "Knock on Wood," Summer's "MacArthur Park"). Even Van Halen had a single called "Dance the Night Away."

Despite disco's impact, hard-core funk (Chuck Brown and the Soul Searchers' "Bustin' Loose," Instant Funk's "I Got My Mind Made Up," Parliament's "Aqua Boogie," Funkadelic's "One Nation Under a Groove"), schmaltzy ballads (Peaches and Herb's "Reunited"), Philly music (McFadden

and Whitehead's "Ain't No Stoppin'" and Teddy Pendergrass's "Turn Out the Lights"), and great voices (Michael Jackson's "Don't Stop 'Til You Get Enough," Chaka Khan's "I'm Every Woman") still persevered on the black charts. The collaboration of Randy Crawford with the Crusaders produced a slick, exciting single, "Street Life," one of the rare examples of intelligent pop-jazz.

Country contributed some very likable singles. The Bellamy Brothers posed the musical question, "If I Said You Had a Beautiful Body, Would You Hold It Against Me?" Barbara Mandrell's ("Sleeping Single in a Double Bed," "If Loving You Is Wrong, I Don't Want to Be Right") and Eddie Rabbitt's ("Every Which Way But Loose," "Suspicions") stock rose considerably, boosting sales and leading to lucrative television and commercial work.

Lots of news in 1979. Paul Simon jumped from Columbia Records to Warner Brothers for $14 million. Paul McCartney skipped from Capital to Columbia for reportedly much cash and a piece of CBS's vast April/Blackwood publishing catalogue. Bette Midler garnered an Oscar nomination for her role as a Janis Joplin–like singer in *The Rose*. Jeff Stein directed an excellent documentary history of The Who, entitled *The Kids Are Alright*. Worst rock film of the year was *Rust Never Sleeps*, starring Neil Young and directed by him under a pseudonym.

For rock literature this was an epochal year. Books about various aspects of pop music and culture had been appearing with regularity since the mid-1960s. However, it wasn't until Dave Marsh's *Born to Run*, a biography of Bruce Springsteen, made *The New York Times* best-seller list that the publishing industry realized there was a large audience for rock books. Next year Jerry Hopkins and David Sugarman's *No One Gets Out Alive*, a biography of The Doors' Jim Morrison, repeated that feat and a deluge of rock books was underway.

Randy Crawford

Donna Summer

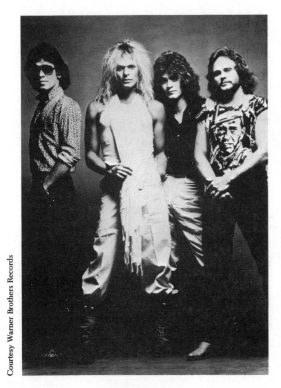

Van Halen

The Police

Chic

Rick Ocasek (The Cars)

Teddy Pendergrass

Mark Knolfer (Dire Straits)

Bad Company

JANUARY 6, 1979

POP SINGLES

1. LE FREAK
   (Chic)
2. TOO MUCH HEAVEN
   (The Bee Gees)
3. MY LIFE
   (Billy Joel)
4. YOU DON'T BRING ME FLOWERS
   (Barbra Streisand and Neil Diamond)
5. YMCA
   (The Village People)
6. SHARING THE NIGHT TOGETHER
   (Dr. Hook)
7. SEPTEMBER
   (Earth, Wind and Fire)
8. HOLD THE LINE
   (Toto)
9. OUR LOVE (DON'T THROW IT ALL AWAY)
   (Andy Gibb)
10. I LOVE THE NIGHT LIFE (DISCO ROUND)
    (Alicia Bridges)

POP ALBUMS

1. BARBRA STREISAND'S GREATEST HITS,
   VOL. 2
   (Barbra Streisand)
2. 52nd STREET
   (Billy Joel)
3. A WILD AND CRAZY GUY
   (Steve Martin)
4. GREASE
   (Original Soundtrack)
5. DOUBLE VISION
   (Foreigner)
6. GREATEST HITS
   (Barry Manilow)
7. C'EST CHIC
   (Chic)
8. YOU DON'T BRING ME FLOWERS
   (Neil Diamond)
9. THE BEST OF EARTH, WIND AND FIRE,
   VOL. 1
   (Earth, Wind and Fire)
10. BRIEFCASE FULL OF BLUES
    (The Blues Brothers)

BLACK SINGLES

1. LE FREAK
   (Chic)
2. GOT TO BE REAL
   (Cheryl Lynn)
3. SEPTEMBER
   (Earth, Wind and Fire)
4. I'M EVERY WOMAN
   (Chaka Khan)
5. GET DOWN
   (Gene Chandler)
6. LOVE DON'T LIVE HERE ANYMORE
   (Rose Royce)
7. LONG STROKE
   (ADC Band)
8. WHAT YOU WON'T DO FOR LOVE
   (Bobby Caldwell)
9. YOUR SWEETNESS IS MY WEAKNESS
   (Barry White)
10. I DON'T KNOW IF IT'S RIGHT
    (Evelyn "Champagne" King)

BLACK ALBUMS

1. C'EST CHIC
   (Chic)
2. THE BEST OF EARTH, WIND AND FIRE,
   VOL. 1
   (Earth, Wind and Fire)

3. MOTOR BOOTY AFFAIR
   (Parliament)
4. THE MAN
   (Barry White)
5. CHAKA
   (Chaka Khan)
6. LIVE AND MORE
   (Donna Summer)
7. CHERYL LYNN
   (Cheryl Lynn)
8. CROSSWINDS
   (Peabo Bryson)
9. IS IT STILL GOOD TO YA
   (Ashford and Simpson)
10. GET DOWN
    (Gene Chandler)

JAZZ ALBUMS

1. TOUCH DOWN
   (Bob James)
2. REED SEED
   (Grover Washington Jr.)
3. CHILDREN OF SANCHEZ
   (Chuck Mangione)
4. FLAME
   (Ronnie Laws)
5. SECRET AGENT
   (Chick Corea)
6. ALL FLY HOME
   (Al Jarreau)
7. MR. GONE
   (Weather Report)
8. INTIMATE STRANGERS
   (Tom Scott)
9. PATRICE
   (Patrice Rushen)
10. COSMIC MESSENGER
    (Jean Luc Ponty)

COUNTRY SINGLES

1. TULSA TIME
   (Don Williams)
2. LADY LAY DOWN
   (John Conlee)
3. THE GAMBLER
   (Kenny Rogers)
4. YOUR LOVE HAD TAKEN ME THAT HIGH
   (Conway Twitty)
5. BURGERS AND FRIES
   (Charley Pride)
6. BABY, I'M BURNIN'/I REALLY GOT THE
   FEELING
   (Dolly Parton)
7. I'VE DONE ENOUGH DYIN' TODAY
   (Larry Gatlin)
8. WHY HAVE YOU LEFT THE ONE YOU LEFT
   ME FOR
   (Crystal Gayle)
9. THE OFFICIAL HISTORIAN ON SHIRLEY
   JEAN BERRELL
   (The Statler Brothers)
10. GIMME BACK MY BLUES
    (Jerry Reed)

COUNTRY ALBUMS

1. WILLIE AND FAMILY LIVE
   (Willie Nelson)
2. THE GAMBLER
   (Kenny Rogers)
3. I'VE ALWAYS BEEN CRAZY
   (Waylon Jennings)
4. LET'S KEEP IT THAT WAY
   (Anne Murray)
5. TNT
   (Tanya Tucker)
6. LARRY GATLIN'S GREATEST HITS
   (Larry Gatlin)
7. MOODS
   (Barbara Mandrell)
8. PROFILES/BEST OF EMMYLOU HARRIS
   (Emmylou Harris)

9. STARDUST
   (Willie Nelson)
10. WHEN I DREAM
    (Crystal Gayle)

JANUARY 13, 1979

POP SINGLES

1. LE FREAK
   (Chic)
2. GOT TO BE REAL
   (Cheryl Lynn)
3. SEPTEMBER
   (Earth, Wind and Fire)
4. GET DOWN
   (Gene Chandler)
5. LOVE DON'T LIVE HERE ANYMORE
   (Rose Royce)
6. WHAT YOU WON'T DO FOR LOVE
   (Bobby Caldwell)
7. I'M EVERY WOMAN
   (Chaka Khan)
8. I DON'T KNOW IF IT'S RIGHT
   (Evelyn "Champagne" King)
9. I'M SO INTO YOU
   (Peabo Bryson)
10. AQUA BOOGIE
    (Parliament)

POP ALBUMS

1. 52nd STREET
   (Billy Joel)
2. BARBRA STREISAND'S GREATEST HITS,
   VOL. 2
   (Barbra Streisand)
3. A WILD AND CRAZY GUY
   (Steve Martin)
4. GREASE
   (Original Soundtrack)
5. GREATEST HITS
   (Barry Manilow)
6. BRIEFCASE FULL OF BLUES
   (The Blues Brothers)
7. C'EST CHIC
   (Chic)
8. DOUBLE VISION
   (Foreigner)
9. YOU DON'T BRING ME FLOWERS
   (Neil Diamond)
10. THE BEST OF EARTH, WIND AND FIRE,
    VOL. 1
    (Earth, Wind and Fire)

BLACK SINGLES

1. LE FREAK
   (Chic)
2. GOT TO BE REAL
   (Cheryl Lynn)
3. SEPTEMBER
   (Earth, Wind and Fire)
4. GET DOWN
   (Gene Chandler)
5. LOVE DON'T LIVE HERE ANYMORE
   (Rose Royce)
6. WHAT YOU WON'T DO FOR LOVE
   (Bobby Caldwell)
7. I'M EVERY WOMAN
   (Chaka Khan)
8. I DON'T KNOW IF IT'S RIGHT
   (Evelyn "Champagne" King)
9. I'M SO INTO YOU
   (Peabo Bryson)
10. AQUA BOOGIE
    (Parliament)

BLACK ALBUMS

1. C'EST CHIC
   (Chic)
2. THE BEST OF EARTH, WIND AND FIRE,
   VOL. 1
   (Earth, Wind and Fire)
3. MOTOR BOOTY AFFAIR
   (Parliament)
4. THE MAN
   (Barry White)
5. CHAKA
   (Chaka Khan)
6. CROSSWINDS
   (Peabo Bryson)
7. CHERYL LYNN
   (Cheryl Lynn)
8. HERE, MY DEAR
   (Marvin Gaye)
9. GET DOWN
   (Gene Chandler)
10. LIVE AND MORE
    (Donna Summer)

JAZZ ALBUMS

1. TOUCH DOWN
   (Bob James)
2. REED SEED
   (Grover Washington Jr.)
3. CHILDREN OF SANCHEZ
   (Chuck Mangione)
4. FLAME
   (Ronnie Laws)
5. SECRET AGENT
   (Chick Corea)
6. ALL FLY HOME
   (Al Jarreau)
7. MR. GONE
   (Weather Report)
8. INTIMATE STRANGERS
   (Tom Scott)
9. PATRICE
   (Patrice Rushen)
10. COSMIC MESSENGER
    (Jean Luc Ponty)

COUNTRY SINGLES

1. LADY LAY DOWN
   (John Conlee)
2. TULSA TIME
   (Don Williams)
3. YOUR LOVE HAD TAKEN ME THAT HIGH
   (Conway Twitty)
4. BABY, I'M BURNIN'/I REALLY GOT THE
   FEELING
   (Dolly Parton)
5. WHY HAVE YOU LEFT THE ONE YOU LEFT
   ME FOR
   (Crystal Gayle)
6. I'VE DONE ENOUGH DYIN' TODAY
   (Larry Gatlin)
7. THE OFFICIAL HISTORIAN ON SHIRLEY
   JEAN BERRELL
   (The Statler Brothers)
8. TEXAS (WHEN I DIE)
   (Tanya Tucker)
9. GIMME BACK MY BLUES
   (Jerry Reed)
10. AS LONG AS I CAN WAKE UP IN YOUR ARMS
    (Kenny O'Dell)

COUNTRY ALBUMS

1. THE GAMBLER
   (Kenny Rogers)
2. WILLIE AND FAMILY LIVE
   (Willie Nelson)
3. I'VE ALWAYS BEEN CRAZY
   (Waylon Jennings)
4. TNT
   (Tanya Tucker)

5. LARRY GATLIN'S GREATEST HITS
   (Larry Gatlin)
6. LET'S KEEP IT THAT WAY
   (Anne Murray)
7. EVERY WHICH WAY BUT LOOSE
   (Original Soundtrack)
8. STARDUST
   (Willie Nelson)
9. PROFILES/BEST OF EMMYLOU HARRIS
   (Emmylou Harris)
10. WHEN I DREAM
    (Crystal Gayle)

JANUARY 20, 1979

POP SINGLES

1. LE FREAK
   (Chic)
2. YMCA
   (The Village People)
3. TOO MUCH HEAVEN
   (The Bee Gees)
4. MY LIFE
   (Billy Joel)
5. HOLD THE LINE
   (Toto)
6. SEPTEMBER
   (Earth, Wind and Fire)
7. SHARING THE NIGHT TOGETHER
   (Dr. Hook)
8. EVERY 1's A WINNER
   (Hot Chocolate)
9. OUR LOVE (DON'T THROW IT ALL AWAY)
   (Andy Gibb)
10. GOT TO BE REAL
    (Cheryl Lynn)

POP ALBUMS

1. 52nd STREET
   (Billy Joel)
2. BARBRA STREISAND'S GREATEST HITS,
   VOL. 2
   (Barbra Streisand)
3. BRIEFCASE FULL OF BLUES
   (The Blues Brothers)
4. A WIND AND CRAZY GUY
   (Steve Martin)
5. GREATEST HITS
   (Barry Manilow)
6. BLONDES HAVE MORE FUN
   (Rod Stewart)
7. C'EST CHIC
   (Chic)
8. GREASE
   (Original Soundtrack)
9. DOUBLE VISION
   (Foreigner)
10. THE BEST OF EARTH, WIND AND FIRE,
    VOL. 1
    (Earth, Wind and Fire)

BLACK SINGLES

1. GOT TO BE REAL
   (Cheryl Lynn)
2. SEPTEMBER
   (Earth, Wind and Fire)
3. LE FREAK
   (Chic)
4. GET DOWN
   (Gene Chandler)
5. WHAT YOU WON'T DO FOR LOVE
   (Bobby Caldwell)
6. I'M SO INTO YOU
   (Peabo Bryson)
7. I DON'T KNOW IF IT'S RIGHT
   (Evelyn "Champagne" King)
8. LOVE DON'T LIVE HERE ANYMORE
   (Rose Royce)

9. AQUA BOOGIE
   (Parliament)
10. I'M EVERY WOMAN
    (Chaka Khan)

BLACK ALBUMS

1. C'EST CHIC
   (Chic)
2. THE BEST OF EARTH, WIND AND FIRE,
   VOL. 1
   (Earth, Wind and Fire)
3. MOTOR BOOTY AFFAIR
   (Parliament)
4. THE MAN
   (Barry White)
5. CROSSWINDS
   (Peabo Bryson)
6. HERE, MY DEAR
   (Marvin Gaye)
7. CHERYL LYNN
   (Cheryl Lynn)
8. CHAKA
   (Chaka Khan)
9. GET DOWN
   (Gene Chandler)
10. LIGHT OF LIFE
    (Bar-Kays)

JAZZ ALBUMS

1. TOUCH DOWN
   (Bob James)
2. REED SEED
   (Grover Washington Jr.)
3. FLAME
   (Ronnie Laws)
4. CHILDREN OF SANCHEZ
   (Chuck Mangione)
5. ALL FLY HOME
   (Al Jarreau)
6. SECRET AGENT
   (Chick Corea)
7. INTIMATE STRANGERS
   (Tom Scott)
8. PATRICE
   (Patrice Rushen)
9. WE ALL HAVE A STAR
   (Wilton Felder)
10. STEP INTO OUR LIFE
    (Roy Ayers and Wayne Henderson)

COUNTRY SINGLES

1. BABY, I'M BURNIN'/I REALLY GOT THE
   FEELING
   (Dolly Parton)
2. LADY LAY DOWN
   (John Conlee)
3. YOUR LOVE HAD TAKEN ME THAT HIGH
   (Conway Twitty)
4. WHY HAVE YOU LEFT THE ONE YOU LEFT
   ME FOR
   (Crystal Gayle)
5. THE OFFICIAL HISTORIAN ON SHIRLEY
   JEAN BERRELL
   (The Statler Brothers)
6. TEXAS (WHEN I DIE)
   (Tanya Tucker)
7. COME ON IN
   (The Oak Ridge Boys)
8. EVERY WHICH WAY BUT LOOSE
   (Eddie Rabbitt)
9. BACK ON MY MIND AGAIN
   (Ronnie Milsap)
10. AS LONG AS I CAN WAKE UP IN YOUR ARMS
    (Kenny O'Dell)

COUNTRY ALBUMS

1. WILLIE AND FAMILY LIVE
   (Willie Nelson)

2. THE GAMBLER
   (Kenny Rogers)
3. TNT
   (Tanya Tucker)
4. STARDUST
   (Willie Nelson)
5. LARRY GATLIN'S GREATEST HITS
   (Larry Gatlin)
6. I'VE ALWAYS BEEN CRAZY
   (Waylon Jennings)
7. EVERY WHICH WAY BUT LOOSE
   (Original Soundtrack)
8. LET'S KEEP IT THAT WAY
   (Anne Murray)
9. PROFILES/BEST OF EMMYLOU HARRIS
   (Emmylou Harris)
10. WHEN I DREAM
    (Crystal Gayle)

JANUARY 27, 1979

POP SINGLES

1. LE FREAK
   (Chic)
2. YMCA
   (The Village People)
3. TOO MUCH HEAVEN
   (The Bee Gees)
4. MY LIFE
   (Billy Joel)
5. SEPTEMBER
   (Earth, Wind and Fire)
6. FIRE
   (The Pointer Sisters)
7. A LITTLE MORE LOVE
   (Olivia Newton-John)
8. EVERY 1's A WINNER
   (Hot Chocolate)
9. GOT TO BE REAL
   (Cheryl Lynn)
10. LOTTA LOVE
    (Nicolette Larson)

POP ALBUMS

1. BARBRA STREISAND'S GREATEST HITS,
   VOL. 2
   (Barbra Streisand)
2. BLONDES HAVE MORE FUN
   (Rod Stewart)
3. BRIEFCASE FULL OF BLUES
   (The Blues Brothers)
4. 52nd STREET
   (Billy Joel)
5. A WILD AND CRAZY GUY
   (Steve Martin)
6. GREATEST HITS
   (Barry Manilow)
7. THE BEST OF EARTH, WIND AND FIRE,
   VOL. 1
   (Earth, Wind and Fire)
8. C'EST CHIC
   (Chic)
9. DOUBLE VISION
   (Foreigner)
10. TOTALLY HOT
    (Olivia Newton-John)

BLACK SINGLES

1. LE FREAK
   (Chic)
2. SEPTEMBER
   (Earth, Wind and Fire)
3. GET DOWN
   (Gene Chandler)
4. GOT TO BE REAL
   (Cheryl Lynn)

5. WHAT YOU WON'T DO FOR LOVE
   (Bobby Caldwell)
6. I'M SO INTO YOU
   (Peabo Bryson)
7. I DON'T KNOW IF IT'S RIGHT
   (Evelyn "Champagne" King)
8. AQUA BOOGIE
   (Parliament)
9. SHAKE YOUR GROOVE THING
   (Peaches and Herb)
10. EVERY 1's A WINNER
    (Hot Chocolate)

BLACK ALBUMS

1. C'EST CHIC
   (Chic)
2. THE BEST OF EARTH, WIND AND FIRE,
   VOL. 1
   (Earth, Wind and Fire)
3. MOTOR BOOTY AFFAIR
   (Parliament)
4. CROSSWINDS
   (Peabo Bryson)
5. HERE, MY DEAR
   (Marvin Gaye)
6. THE MAN
   (Barry White)
7. GET DOWN
   (Gene Chandler)
8. "WANTED" RICHARD PRYOR LIVE IN
   CONCERT
   (Richard Pryor)
9. CHERYL LYNN
   (Cheryl Lynn)
10. CHAKA
    (Chaka Khan)

JAZZ ALBUMS

1. TOUCH DOWN
   (Bob James)
2. REED SEED
   (Grover Washington Jr.)
3. FLAME
   (Ronnie Laws)
4. CHILDREN OF SANCHEZ
   (Chuck Mangione)
5. ALL FLY HOME
   (Al Jarreau)
6. PATRICE
   (Patrice Rushen)
7. WE ALL HAVE A STAR
   (Wilton Felder)
8. SECRET AGENT
   (Chick Corea)
9. INTIMATE STRANGERS
   (Tom Scott)
10. STEP INTO OUR LIFE
    (Roy Ayers and Wayne Henderson)

COUNTRY SINGLES

1. WHY HAVE YOU LEFT THE ONE YOU LEFT
   ME FOR
   (Crystal Gayle)
2. BABY, I'M BURNIN'/I REALLY GOT THE
   FEELING
   (Dolly Parton)
3. COME ON IN
   (The Oak Ridge Boys)
4. EVERY WHICH WAY BUT LOOSE
   (Eddie Rabbitt)
5. THE OFFICIAL HISTORIAN ON SHIRLEY
   JEAN BERRELL
   (The Statler Brothers)
6. TEXAS (WHEN I DIE)
   (Tanya Tucker)
7. BACK ON MY MIND AGAIN
   (Ronnie Milsap)
8. YOUR LOVE HAD TAKEN ME THAT HIGH
   (Conway Twitty)
9. LADY LAY DOWN
   (John Conlee)

10. IT'S TIME WE TALK THINGS OVER
    (Rex Allen Jr.)

COUNTRY ALBUMS

1. WILLIE AND FAMILY LIVE
   (Willie Nelson)
2. THE GAMBLER
   (Kenny Rogers)
3. TNT
   (Tanya Tucker)
4. STARDUST
   (Willie Nelson)
5. I'VE ALWAYS BEEN CRAZY
   (Waylon Jennings)
6. LARRY GATLIN'S GREATEST HITS
   (Larry Gatlin)
7. LET'S KEEP IT THAT WAY
   (Anne Murray)
8. EVERY WHICH WAY BUT LOOSE
   (Original Soundtrack)
9. WHEN I DREAM
   (Crystal Gayle)
10. HEARTBREAKER
    (Dolly Parton)

FEBRUARY 3, 1979

POP SINGLES

1. LE FREAK
   (Chic)
2. DA YA THINK I'M SEXY?
   (Rod Stewart)
3. YMCA
   (The Village People)
4. SEPTEMBER
   (Earth, Wind and Fire)
5. FIRE
   (The Pointer Sisters)
6. A LITTLE MORE LOVE
   (Olivia Newton-John)
7. EVERY 1's A WINNER
   (Hot Chocolate)
8. LOTTA LOVE
   (Nicolette Larson)
9. GOT TO BE REAL
   (Cheryl Lynn)
10. TOO MUCH HEAVEN
    (The Bee Gees)

POP ALBUMS

1. BLONDES HAVE MORE FUN
   (Rod Stewart)
2. BRIEFCASE FULL OF BLUES
   (The Blues Brothers)
3. 52nd STREET
   (Billy Joel)
4. BARBRA STREISAND'S GREATEST HITS,
   VOL. 2
   (Barbra Streisand)
5. THE BEST OF EARTH, WIND AND FIRE,
   VOL. 1
   (Earth, Wind and Fire)
6. TOTALLY HOT
   (Olivia Newton-John)
7. GREATEST HITS
   (Barry Manilow)
8. C'EST CHIC
   (Chic)
9. TOTO
   (Toto)
10. CRUISIN'
    (The Village People)

BLACK SINGLES

1. I'M SO INTO YOU
   (Peabo Bryson)
2. LE FREAK
   (Chic)
3. GET DOWN
   (Gene Chandler)
4. SHAKE YOUR GROOVE THING
   (Peaches and Herb)
5. AQUA BOOGIE
   (Parliament)
6. WHAT YOU WON'T DO FOR LOVE
   (Bobby Caldwell)
7. I DON'T KNOW IF IT'S RIGHT
   (Evelyn "Champagne" King)
8. SEPTEMBER
   (Earth, Wind and Fire)
9. GOT TO BE REAL
   (Cheryl Lynn)
10. EVERY 1's A WINNER
    (Hot Chocolate)

BLACK ALBUMS

1. C'EST CHIC
   (Chic)
2. MOTOR BOOTY AFFAIR
   (Parliament)
3. THE BEST OF EARTH, WIND AND FIRE, VOL. 1
   (Earth, Wind and Fire)
4. CROSSWINDS
   (Peabo Bryson)
5. HERE, MY DEAR
   (Marvin Gaye)
6. "WANTED" RICHARD PRYOR LIVE IN CONCERT
   (Richard Pryor)
7. GET DOWN
   (Gene Chandler)
8. THE MAN
   (Barry White)
9. CHERYL LYNN
   (Cheryl Lynn)
10. 2 HOT!
    (Peaches and Herb)

JAZZ ALBUMS

1. TOUCH DOWN
   (Bob James)
2. REED SEED
   (Grover Washington Jr.)
3. FLAME
   (Ronnie Laws)
4. CHILDREN OF SANCHEZ
   (Chuck Mangione)
5. ALL FLY HOME
   (Al Jarreau)
6. PATRICE
   (Patrice Rushen)
7. WE ALL HAVE A STAR
   (Wilton Felder)
8. SECRET AGENT
   (Chick Corea)
9. INTIMATE STRANGERS
   (Tom Scott)
10. MR. GONE
    (Weather Report)

COUNTRY SINGLES

1. WHY HAVE YOU LEFT THE ONE YOU LEFT ME FOR
   (Crystal Gayle)
2. EVERY WHICH WAY BUT LOOSE
   (Eddie Rabbitt)
3. COME ON IN
   (The Oak Ridge Boys)
4. BACK ON MY MIND AGAIN
   (Ronnie Milsap)

5. THE OFFICIAL HISTORIAN ON SHIRLEY JEAN BERRELL
   (The Statler Brothers)
6. TEXAS (WHEN I DIE)
   (Tanya Tucker)
7. BABY, I'M BURNIN'/I REALLY GOT THE FEELING
   (Dolly Parton)
8. MABELLENE
   (George Jones and Johnny Paycheck)
9. I JUST CAN'T STAY MARRIED TO YOU
   (Cristy Lane)
10. YOU DON'T BRING ME FLOWERS
    (Jim Ed Brown and Helen Cornelius)

COUNTRY ALBUMS

1. THE GAMBLER
   (Kenny Rogers)
2. WILLIE AND FAMILY LIVE
   (Willie Nelson)
3. TNT
   (Tanya Tucker)
4. JOHN DENVER
   (John Denver)
5. LET'S KEEP IT THAT WAY
   (Anne Murray)
6. I'VE ALWAYS BEEN CRAZY
   (Waylon Jennings)
7. LARRY GATLIN'S GREATEST HITS
   (Larry Gatlin)
8. WHEN I DREAM
   (Crystal Gayle)
9. EVERY WHICH WAY BUT LOOSE
   (Original Soundtrack)
10. HEARTBREAKER
    (Dolly Parton)

FEBRUARY 10, 1979

POP SINGLES

1. DA YA THINK I'M SEXY?
   (Rod Stewart)
2. LE FREAK
   (Chic)
3. FIRE
   (The Pointer Sisters)
4. SEPTEMBER
   (Earth, Wind and Fire)
5. A LITTLE MORE LOVE
   (Olivia Newton-John)
6. YMCA
   (The Village People)
7. EVERY 1's A WINNER
   (Hot Chocolate)
8. LOTTA LOVE
   (Nicolette Larson)
9. I WILL SURVIVE
   (Gloria Gaynor)
10. TOO MUCH HEAVEN
    (The Bee Gees)

POP ALBUMS

1. BLONDES HAVE MORE FUN
   (Rod Stewart)
2. BRIEFCASE FULL OF BLUES
   (The Blues Brothers)
3. BARBRA STREISAND'S GREATEST HITS, VOL. 2
   (Barbra Streisand)
4. 52nd STREET
   (Billy Joel)
5. THE BEST OF EARTH, WIND AND FIRE, VOL. 1
   (Earth, Wind and Fire)
6. TOTALLY HOT
   (Olivia Newton-John)
7. GREATEST HITS
   (Barry Manilow)

8. C'EST CHIC
   (Chic)
9. TOTO
   (Toto)
10. CRUISIN'
    (The Village People)

BLACK SINGLES

1. I'M SO INTO YOU
   (Peabo Bryson)
2. SHAKE YOUR GROOVE THING
   (Peaches and Herb)
3. LE FREAK
   (Chic)
4. AQUA BOOGIE
   (Parliament)
5. GET DOWN
   (Gene Chandler)
6. BUSTIN' LOOSE
   (Chuck Brown and the Soul Searchers)
7. I DON'T KNOW IF IT'S RIGHT
   (Evelyn "Champagne" King)
8. WHAT YOU WON'T DO FOR LOVE
   (Bobby Caldwell)
9. NEVER HAD A LOVE LIKE THIS BEFORE
   (Tavares)
10. EVERY 1's A WINNER
    (Hot Chocolate)

BLACK ALBUMS

1. C'EST CHIC
   (Chic)
2. THE BEST OF EARTH, WIND AND FIRE, VOL. 1
   (Earth, Wind and Fire)
3. MOTOR BOOTY AFFAIR
   (Parliament)
4. CROSSWINDS
   (Peabo Bryson)
5. HERE, MY DEAR
   (Marvin Gaye)
6. "WANTED" RICHARD PRYOR LIVE IN CONCERT
   (Richard Pryor)
7. 2 HOT!
   (Peaches and Herb)
8. THE MAN
   (Barry White)
9. CHERYL LYNN
   (Cheryl Lynn)
10. GET DOWN
    (Gene Chandler)

JAZZ ALBUMS

1. TOUCH DOWN
   (Bob James)
2. REED SEED
   (Grover Washington Jr.)
3. FLAME
   (Ronnie Laws)
4. CHILDREN OF SANCHEZ
   (Chuck Mangione)
5. PATRICE
   (Patrice Rushen)
6. WE ALL HAVE A STAR
   (Wilton Felder)
7. ALL FLY HOME
   (Al Jarreau)
8. SECRET AGENT
   (Chick Corea)
9. INTIMATE STRANGERS
   (Tom Scott)
10. MR. GONE
    (Weather Report)

COUNTRY SINGLES

1. EVERY WHICH WAY BUT LOOSE
   (Eddie Rabbitt)

2. BACK ON MY MIND AGAIN
    (Ronnie Milsap)
3. COME ON IN
    (The Oak Ridge Boys)
4. WHY HAVE YOU LEFT THE ONE YOU LEFT ME FOR
    (Crystal Gayle)
5. TEXAS (WHEN I DIE)
    (Tanya Tucker)
6. MABELLENE
    (George Jones and Johnny Paycheck)
7. I JUST CAN'T STAY MARRIED TO YOU
    (Cristy Lane)
8. HAPPY TOGETHER
    (T.G. Sheppard)
9. TONIGHT SHE'S GONNA LOVE ME
    (Razzy Bailey)
10. THE OFFICIAL HISTORIAN ON SHIRLEY JEAN BERRELL
    (The Statler Brothers)

COUNTRY ALBUMS

1. THE GAMBLER
    (Kenny Rogers)
2. WILLIE AND FAMILY LIVE
    (Willie Nelson)
3. TNT
    (Tanya Tucker)
4. JOHN DENVER
    (John Denver)
5. LET'S KEEP IT THAT WAY
    (Anne Murray)
6. WHEN I DREAM
    (Crystal Gayle)
7. I'VE ALWAYS BEEN CRAZY
    (Waylon Jennings)
8. EVERY WHICH WAY BUT LOOSE
    (Original Soundtrack)
9. LARRY GATLIN'S GREATEST HITS
    (Larry Gatlin)
10. STARDUST
    (Willie Nelson)

FEBRUARY 17, 1979

POP SINGLES

1. DA YA THINK I'M SEXY?
    (Rod Stewart)
2. FIRE
    (The Pointer Sisters)
3. LE FREAK
    (Chic)
4. A LITTLE MORE LOVE
    (Olivia Newton-John)
5. I WILL SURVIVE
    (Gloria Gaynor)
6. YMCA
    (The Village People)
7. TOO MUCH HEAVEN
    (The Bee Gees)
8. LOTTA LOVE
    (Nicolette Larson)
9. SEPTEMBER
    (Earth, Wind and Fire)
10. SHAKE IT
    (Ian Matthews)

POP ALBUMS

1. BLONDES HAVE MORE FUN
    (Rod Stewart)
2. BRIEFCASE FULL OF BLUES
    (The Blues Brothers)
3. SPIRITS HAVING FLOWN
    (The Bee Gees)
4. 52nd STREET
    (Billy Joel)
5. BARBRA STREISAND'S GREATEST HITS, VOL. 2
    (Barbra Streisand)

6. TOTALLY HOT
    (Olivia Newton-John)
7. THE BEST OF EARTH, WIND AND FIRE, VOL. 1
    (Earth, Wind and Fire)
8. GREATEST HITS
    (Barry Manilow)
9. C'EST CHIC
    (Chic)
10. MINUTE BY MINUTE
    (The Doobie Brothers)

BLACK SINGLES

1. SHAKE YOUR GROOVE THING
    (Peaches and Herb)
2. I'M SO INTO YOU
    (Peabo Bryson)
3. BUSTIN' LOOSE
    (Chuck Brown and the Soul Searchers)
4. AQUA BOOGIE
    (Parliament)
5. LE FREAK
    (Chic)
6. NEVER HAD A LOVE LIKE THIS BEFORE
    (Tavares)
7. GET DOWN
    (Gene Chandler)
8. I DON'T KNOW IF IT'S RIGHT
    (Evelyn "Champagne" King)
9. IT'S ALL THE WAY LIVE
    (Lakeside)
10. DA YA THINK I'M SEXY?
    (Rod Stewart)

BLACK ALBUMS

1. C'EST CHIC
    (Chic)
2. THE BEST OF EARTH, WIND AND FIRE, VOL. 1
    (Earth, Wind and Fire)
3. MOTOR BOOTY AFFAIR
    (Parliament)
4. HERE, MY DEAR
    (Marvin Gaye)
5. 2 HOT!
    (Peaches and Herb)
6. CROSSWINDS
    (Peabo Bryson)
7. "WANTED" RICHARD PRYOR LIVE IN CONCERT
    (Richard Pryor)
8. BUSTIN' OUT OF L SEVEN
    (Rick James)
9. LOVE TRACKS
    (Gloria Gaynor)
10. THE MAN
    (Barry White)

JAZZ ALBUMS

1. TOUCH DOWN
    (Bob James)
2. REED SEED
    (Grover Washington Jr.)
3. FLAME
    (Ronnie Laws)
4. CHILDREN OF SANCHEZ
    (Chuck Mangione)
5. PATRICE
    (Patrice Rushen)
6. WE ALL HAVE A STAR
    (Wilton Felder)
7. ALL FLY HOME
    (Al Jarreau)
8. CARMEL
    (Joe Sample)
9. ANGIE
    (Angela Bofill)
10. MILESTONE JAZZ STARS IN CONCERT
    (Milestone)

COUNTRY SINGLES

1. EVERY WHICH WAY BUT LOOSE
    (Eddie Rabbitt)
2. BACK ON MY MIND AGAIN
    (Ronnie Milsap)
3. COME ON IN
    (The Oak Ridge Boys)
4. I JUST CAN'T STAY MARRIED TO YOU
    (Cristy Lane)
5. HAPPY TOGETHER
    (T.G. Sheppard)
6. MABELLENE
    (George Jones and Johnny Paycheck)
7. TONIGHT SHE'S GONNA LOVE ME
    (Razzy Bailey)
8. I'LL WAKE YOU UP WHEN I GET HOME
    (Charlie Rich)
9. IF I COULD WRITE A SONG AS BEAUTIFUL AS YOU
    (Billy "Crash" Craddock)
10. SEND ME DOWN TO TUCSON/CHARLIE'S ANGELS
    (Mel Tillis)

COUNTRY ALBUMS

1. THE GAMBLER
    (Kenny Rogers)
2. WILLIE AND FAMILY LIVE
    (Willie Nelson)
3. TNT
    (Tanya Tucker)
4. STARDUST
    (Willie Nelson)
5. EVERY WHICH WAY BUT LOOSE
    (Original Soundtrack)
6. WHEN I DREAM
    (Crystal Gayle)
7. JOHN DENVER
    (John Denver)
8. LET'S KEEP IT THAT WAY
    (Anne Murray)
9. LARRY GATLIN'S GREATEST HITS
    (Larry Gatlin)
10. NEW KIND OF FEELING
    (Anne Murray)

FEBRUARY 24, 1979

POP SINGLES

1. DA YA THINK I'M SEXY?
    (Rod Stewart)
2. FIRE
    (The Pointer Sisters)
3. I WILL SURVIVE
    (Gloria Gaynor)
4. A LITTLE MORE LOVE
    (Olivia Newton-John)
5. YMCA
    (The Village People)
6. LE FREAK
    (Chic)
7. TOO MUCH HEAVEN
    (The Bee Gees)
8. HEAVEN KNOWS
    (Donna Summer with Brooklyn Dreams)
9. SEPTEMBER
    (Earth, Wind and Fire)
10. SHAKE IT
    (Ian Matthews)

POP ALBUMS

1. SPIRITS HAVING FLOWN
    (The Bee Gees)
2. BLONDES HAVE MORE FUN
    (Rod Stewart)

3. BRIEFCASE FULL OF BLUES
   (The Blues Brothers)
4. 52nd STREET
   (Billy Joel)
5. CRUISIN'
   (The Village People)
6. TOTALLY HOT
   (Olivia Newton-John)
7. MINUTE BY MINUTE
   (The Doobie Brothers)
8. C'EST CHIC
   (Chic)
9. BARBRA STREISAND'S GREATEST HITS, VOL. 2
   (Barbra Streisand)
10. DIRE STRAITS
    (Dire Straits)

BLACK SINGLES

1. BUSTIN' LOOSE
   (Chuck Brown and the Soul Searchers)
2. SHAKE YOUR GROOVE THING
   (Peaches and Herb)
3. I'M SO INTO YOU
   (Peabo Bryson)
4. NEVER HAD A LOVE LIKE THIS BEFORE
   (Tavares)
5. DA YA THINK I'M SEXY?
   (Rod Stewart)
6. IT'S ALL THE WAY LIVE
   (Lakeside)
7. LE FREAK
   (Chic)
8. AQUA BOOGIE
   (Parliament)
9. I GOT MY MIND MADE UP (YOU CAN GET IT GIRL)
   (Instant Funk)
10. LIVIN' IT UP (FRIDAY NIGHT)
    (Bell and James)

BLACK ALBUMS

1. 2 HOT!
   (Peaches and Herb)
2. C'EST CHIC
   (Chic)
3. THE BEST OF EARTH, WIND AND FIRE, VOL. 1
   (Earth, Wind and Fire)
4. BUSTIN' OUT OF L SEVEN
   (Rick James)
5. MOTOR BOOTY AFFAIR
   (Parliament)
6. CROSSWINDS
   (Peabo Bryson)
7. LOVE TRACKS
   (Gloria Gaynor)
8. HERE, MY DEAR
   (Marvin Gaye)
9. SHOT OF LOVE
   (Lakeside)
10. "WANTED" RICHARD PRYOR LIVE IN CONCERT
    (Richard Pryor)

JAZZ ALBUMS

1. TOUCH DOWN
   (Bob James)
2. CARMEL
   (Joe Sample)
3. REED SEED
   (Grover Washington Jr.)
4. FLAME
   (Ronnie Laws)
5. PATRICE
   (Patrice Rushen)
6. CHILDREN OF SANCHEZ
   (Chuck Mangione)
7. ANGIE
   (Angela Bofill)

8. WE ALL HAVE A STAR
   (Wilton Felder)
9. EXOTIC MYSTERIES
   (Lonnie Liston Smith)
10. MILESTONE JAZZ STARS IN CONCERT
    (Milestone)

COUNTRY SINGLES

1. BACK ON MY MIND AGAIN
   (Ronnie Milsap)
2. EVERY WHICH WAY BUT LOOSE
   (Eddie Rabbitt)
3. I'LL WAKE YOU UP WHEN I GET HOME
   (Charlie Rich)
4. I JUST CAN'T STAY MARRIED TO YOU
   (Cristy Lane)
5. HAPPY TOGETHER
   (T.G. Sheppard)
6. TONIGHT SHE'S GONNA LOVE ME
   (Razzy Bailey)
7. IF I COULD WRITE A SONG AS BEAUTIFUL AS YOU
   (Billy "Crash" Craddock)
8. SEND ME DOWN TO TUCSON/CHARLIE'S ANGELS
   (Mel Tillis)
9. GOLDEN TEARS
   (Dave and Sugar)
10. I HAD A LOVELY TIME
    (The Kendalls)

COUNTRY ALBUMS

1. THE GAMBLER
   (Kenny Rogers)
2. WILLIE AND FAMILY LIVE
   (Willie Nelson)
3. NEW KIND OF FEELING
   (Anne Murray)
4. STARDUST
   (Willie Nelson)
5. EVERY WHICH WAY BUT LOOSE
   (Original Soundtrack)
6. JOHN DENVER
   (John Denver)
7. TNT
   (Tanya Tucker)
8. WHEN I DREAM
   (Crystal Gayle)
9. LARRY GATLIN'S GREATEST HITS
   (Larry Gatlin)
10. I'VE ALWAYS BEEN CRAZY
    (Waylon Jennings)

MARCH 3, 1979

POP SINGLES

1. DA YA THINK I'M SEXY?
   (Rod Stewart)
2. I WILL SURVIVE
   (Gloria Gaynor)
3. YMCA
   (The Village People)
4. FIRE
   (The Pointer Sisters)
5. TRAGEDY
   (The Bee Gees)
6. HEAVEN KNOWS
   (Donna Summer with Brooklyn Dreams)
7. LE FREAK
   (Chic)
8. A LITTLE MORE LOVE
   (Olivia Newton-John)
9. SHAKE YOUR GROOVE THING
   (Peaches and Herb)
10. TOO MUCH HEAVEN
    (The Bee Gees)

POP ALBUMS

1. SPIRITS HAVING FLOWN
   (The Bee Gees)
2. BLONDES HAVE MORE FUN
   (Rod Stewart)
3. BRIEFCASE FULL OF BLUES
   (The Blues Brothers)
4. CRUISIN'
   (The Village People)
5. 52nd STREET
   (Billy Joel)
6. TOTALLY HOT
   (Olivia Newton-John)
7. MINUTE BY MINUTE
   (The Doobie Brothers)
8. DIRE STRAITS
   (Dire Straits)
9. BARBRA STREISAND'S GREATEST HITS, VOL. 2
   (Barbra Streisand)
10. C'EST CHIC
    (Chic)

BLACK SINGLES

1. DA YA THINK I'M SEXY?
   (Rod Stewart)
2. BUSTIN' LOOSE
   (Chuck Brown and the Soul Searchers)
3. SHAKE YOUR GROOVE THING
   (Peaches and Herb)
4. NEVER HAD A LOVE LIKE THIS BEFORE
   (Tavares)
5. I GOT MY MIND MADE UP (YOU CAN GET IT GIRL)
   (Instant Funk)
6. IT'S ALL THE WAY LIVE
   (Lakeside)
7. I WILL SURVIVE
   (Gloria Gaynor)
8. I'M SO INTO YOU
   (Peabo Bryson)
9. LIVIN' IT UP (FRIDAY NIGHT)
   (Bell and James)
10. LE FREAK
    (Chic)

BLACK ALBUMS

1. 2 HOT!
   (Peaches and Herb)
2. BUSTIN' OUT OF L SEVEN
   (Rick James)
3. C'EST CHIC
   (Chic)
4. LOVE TRACKS
   (Gloria Gaynor)
5. MOTOR BOOTY AFFAIR
   (Parliament)
6. THE BEST OF EARTH, WIND AND FIRE, VOL. 1
   (Earth, Wind and Fire)
7. HERE, MY DEAR
   (Marvin Gaye)
8. CROSSWINDS
   (Peabo Bryson)
9. DESTINY
   (The Jacksons)
10. SPIRITS HAVING FLOWN
    (The Bee Gees)

JAZZ ALBUMS

1. TOUCH DOWN
   (Bob James)
2. CARMEL
   (Joe Sample)
3. REED SEED
   (Grover Washington Jr.)
4. FLAME
   (Ronnie Laws)

5. PATRICE
   (Patrice Rushen)
6. ANGIE
   (Angela Bofill)
7. CHILDREN OF SANCHEZ
   (Chuck Mangione)
8. EXOTIC MYSTERIES
   (Lonnie Liston Smith)
9. MILESTONE JAZZ STARS IN CONCERT
   (Milestone)
10. PAT METHENY GROUP
    (Pat Metheny)

COUNTRY SINGLES

1. BACK ON MY MIND AGAIN
   (Ronnie Milsap)
2. I'LL WAKE YOU UP WHEN I GET HOME
   (Charlie Rich)
3. EVERY WHICH WAY BUT LOOSE
   (Eddie Rabbitt)
4. IF I COULD WRITE A SONG AS BEAUTIFUL
   AS YOU
   (Billy "Crash" Craddock)
5. SEND ME DOWN TO TUCSON/CHARLIE'S
   ANGELS
   (Mel Tillis)
6. TONIGHT SHE'S GONNA LOVE ME
   (Razzy Bailey)
7. GOLDEN TEARS
   (Dave and Sugar)
8. I HAD A LOVELY TIME
   (The Kendalls)
9. I JUST CAN'T STAY MARRIED TO YOU
   (Cristy Lane)
10. I JUST FALL IN LOVE AGAIN
    (Anne Murray)

COUNTRY ALBUMS

1. THE GAMBLER
   (Kenny Rogers)
2. NEW KIND OF FEELING
   (Anne Murray)
3. WILLIE AND FAMILY LIVE
   (Willie Nelson)
4. JOHN DENVER
   (John Denver)
5. SWEET MEMORIES
   (Willie Nelson)
6. TNT
   (Tanya Tucker)
7. WHEN I DREAM
   (Crystal Gayle)
8. EVERY WHICH WAY BUT LOOSE
   (Original Soundtrack)
9. I'VE ALWAYS BEEN CRAZY
   (Waylon Jennings)
10. STARDUST
    (Willie Nelson)

MARCH 10, 1979

POP SINGLES

1. I WILL SURVIVE
   (Gloria Gaynor)
2. DA YA THINK I'M SEXY?
   (Rod Stewart)
3. YMCA
   (The Village People)
4. TRAGEDY
   (The Bee Gees)
5. FIRE
   (The Pointer Sisters)
6. HEAVEN KNOWS
   (Donna Summer with Brooklyn Dreams)
7. LE FREAK
   (Chic)
8. SHAKE YOUR GROOVE THING
   (Peaches and Herb)

9. A LITTLE MORE LOVE
   (Olivia Newton-John)
10. WHAT A FOOL BELIEVES
    (The Doobie Brothers)

POP ALBUMS

1. SPIRITS HAVING FLOWN
   (The Bee Gees)
2. BLONDES HAVE MORE FUN
   (Rod Stewart)
3. BRIEFCASE FULL OF BLUES
   (The Blues Brothers)
4. MINUTE BY MINUTE
   (The Doobie Brothers)
5. 52nd STREET
   (Billy Joel)
6. DIRE STRAITS
   (Dire Straits)
7. TOTALLY HOT
   (Olivia Newton-John)
8. CRUISIN'
   (The Village People)
9. C'EST CHIC
   (Chic)
10. LOVE TRACKS
    (Gloria Gaynor)

BLACK SINGLES

1. DA YA THINK I'M SEXY?
   (Rod Stewart)
2. BUSTIN' LOOSE
   (Chuck Brown and the Soul Searchers)
3. SHAKE YOUR GROOVE THING
   (Peaches and Herb)
4. I GOT MY MIND MADE UP (YOU CAN GET
   IT GIRL)
   (Instant Funk)
5. I WILL SURVIVE
   (Gloria Gaynor)
6. NEVER HAD A LOVE LIKE THIS BEFORE
   (Tavares)
7. IT'S ALL THE WAY LIVE
   (Lakeside)
8. LIVIN' IT UP (FRIDAY NIGHT)
   (Bell and James)
9. I'M SO INTO YOU
   (Peabo Bryson)
10. OH HONEY
    (The Delegation)

BLACK ALBUMS

1. 2 HOT!
   (Peaches and Herb)
2. BUSTIN' OUT OF L SEVEN
   (Rick James)
3. C'EST CHIC
   (Chic)
4. LOVE TRACKS
   (Gloria Gaynor)
5. DESTINY
   (The Jacksons)
6. HERE, MY DEAR
   (Marvin Gaye)
7. MOTOR BOOTY AFFAIR
   (Parliament)
8. INSTANT FUNK
   (Instant Funk)
9. BUSTIN' LOOSE
   (Chuck Brown and the Soul Searchers)
10. SPIRITS HAVING FLOWN
    (The Bee Gees)

JAZZ ALBUMS

1. CARMEL
   (Joe Sample)
2. TOUCH DOWN
   (Bob James)
3. REED SEED
   (Grover Washington Jr.)

4. PATRICE
   (Patrice Rushen)
5. ANGIE
   (Angela Bofill)
6. FLAME
   (Ronnie Laws)
7. EXOTIC MYSTERIES
   (Lonnie Liston Smith)
8. MILESTONE JAZZ STARS IN CONCERT
   (Milestone)
9. CHILDREN OF SANCHEZ
   (Chuck Mangione)
10. PAT METHENY GROUP
    (Pat Metheny)

COUNTRY SINGLES

1. I'LL WAKE YOU UP WHEN I GET HOME
   (Charlie Rich)
2. GOLDEN TEARS
   (Dave and Sugar)
3. IF I COULD WRITE A SONG AS BEAUTIFUL
   AS YOU
   (Billy "Crash" Craddock)
4. SEND ME DOWN TO TUCSON/CHARLIE'S
   ANGELS
   (Mel Tillis)
5. I JUST FALL IN LOVE AGAIN
   (Anne Murray)
6. I HAD A LOVELY TIME
   (The Kendalls)
7. BACK ON MY MIND AGAIN
   (Ronnie Milsap)
8. EVERY WHICH WAY BUT LOOSE
   (Eddie Rabbitt)
9. SOMEBODY SPECIAL
   (Donna Fargo)
10. STILL A WOMAN
    (Margo Smith)

COUNTRY ALBUMS

1. THE GAMBLER
   (Kenny Rogers)
2. NEW KIND OF FEELING
   (Anne Murray)
3. WILLIE AND FAMILY LIVE
   (Willie Nelson)
4. JOHN DENVER
   (John Denver)
5. SWEET MEMORIES
   (Willie Nelson)
6. TNT
   (Tanya Tucker)
7. WHEN I DREAM
   (Crystal Gayle)
8. EVERY WHICH WAY BUT LOOSE
   (Original Soundtrack)
9. STARDUST
   (Willie Nelson)
10. HEARTBREAKER
    (Dolly Parton)

MARCH 17, 1979

POP SINGLES

1. TRAGEDY
   (The Bee Gees)
2. DA YA THINK I'M SEXY?
   (Rod Stewart)
3. I WILL SURVIVE
   (Gloria Gaynor)
4. YMCA
   (The Village People)
5. FIRE
   (The Pointer Sisters)
6. HEAVEN KNOWS
   (Donna Summer with Brooklyn Dreams)
7. SHAKE YOUR GROOVE THING
   (Peaches and Herb)

8. WHAT A FOOL BELIEVES
   (The Doobie Brothers)
9. LE FREAK
   (Chic)
10. A LITTLE MORE LOVE
    (Olivia Newton-John)

POP ALBUMS

1. SPIRITS HAVING FLOWN
   (The Bee Gees)
2. BLONDES HAVE MORE FUN
   (Rod Stewart)
3. BRIEFCASE FULL OF BLUES
   (The Blues Brothers)
4. MINUTE BY MINUTE
   (The Doobie Brothers)
5. DIRE STRAITS
   (Dire Straits)
6. 52nd STREET
   (Billy Joel)
7. TOTALLY HOT
   (Olivia Newton-John)
8. CRUISIN'
   (The Village People)
9. LOVE TRACKS
   (Gloria Gaynor)
10. 2 HOT!
    (Peaches and Herb)

BLACK SINGLES

1. I GOT MY MIND MADE UP (YOU CAN GET IT GIRL)
   (Instant Funk)
2. DA YA THINK I'M SEXY?
   (Rod Stewart)
3. I WILL SURVIVE
   (Gloria Gaynor)
4. BUSTIN' LOOSE
   (Chuck Brown and the Soul Searchers)
5. SHAKE YOUR GROOVE THING
   (Peaches and Herb)
6. HE'S THE GREATEST DANCER
   (Sister Sledge)
7. OH HONEY
   (The Delegation)
8. SHAKE YOUR BODY (DOWN TO THE GROUND)
   (The Jacksons)
9. LIVIN' IT UP (FRIDAY NIGHT)
   (Bell and James)
10. HEAVEN KNOWS
    (Donna Summer with Brooklyn Dreams)

BLACK ALBUMS

1. 2 HOT!
   (Peaches and Herb)
2. BUSTIN' OUT OF L SEVEN
   (Rick James)
3. LOVE TRACKS
   (Gloria Gaynor)
4. C'EST CHIC
   (Chic)
5. DESTINY
   (The Jacksons)
6. HERE, MY DEAR
   (Marvin Gaye)
7. INSTANT FUNK
   (Instant Funk)
8. BUSTIN' LOOSE
   (Chuck Brown and the Soul Searchers)
9. SPIRITS HAVING FLOWN
   (The Bee Gees)
10. MOTOR BOOTY AFFAIR
    (Parliament)

JAZZ ALBUMS

1. CARMEL
   (Joe Sample)

2. TOUCH DOWN
   (Bob James)
3. PATRICE
   (Patrice Rushen)
4. ANGIE
   (Angela Bofill)
5. REED SEED
   (Grover Washington Jr.)
6. EXOTIC MYSTERIES
   (Lonnie Liston Smith)
7. MILESTONE JAZZ STARS IN CONCERT
   (Milestone)
8. FLAME
   (Ronnie Laws)
9. CHILDREN OF SANCHEZ
   (Chuck Mangione)
10. PAT METHENY GROUP
    (Pat Metheny)

COUNTRY SINGLES

1. SEND ME DOWN TO TUCSON/CHARLIE'S ANGELS
   (Mel Tillis)
2. GOLDEN TEARS
   (Dave and Sugar)
3. IF I COULD WRITE A SONG AS BEAUTIFUL AS YOU
   (Billy "Crash" Craddock)
4. I JUST FALL IN LOVE AGAIN
   (Anne Murray)
5. I HAD A LOVELY TIME
   (The Kendalls)
6. STILL A WOMAN
   (Margo Smith)
7. SOMEBODY SPECIAL
   (Donna Fargo)
8. I'LL WAKE YOU UP WHEN I GET HOME
   (Charlie Rich)
9. IT'S A CHEATING SITUATION
   (Moe Bandy)
10. MY HEART HAS A MIND OF ITS OWN
    (Debby Boone)

COUNTRY ALBUMS

1. THE GAMBLER
   (Kenny Rogers)
2. NEW KIND OF FEELING
   (Anne Murray)
3. WILLIE AND FAMILY LIVE
   (Willie Nelson)
4. TNT
   (Tanya Tucker)
5. WHEN I DREAM
   (Crystal Gayle)
6. EVERY WHICH WAY BUT LOOSE
   (Original Soundtrack)
7. STARDUST
   (Willie Nelson)
8. SWEET MEMORIES
   (Willie Nelson)
9. JOHN DENVER
   (John Denver)
10. HEARTBREAKER
    (Dolly Parton)

MARCH 24, 1979

POP SINGLES

1. DA YA THINK I'M SEXY?
   (Rod Stewart)
2. TRAGEDY
   (The Bee Gees)
3. I WILL SURVIVE
   (Gloria Gaynor)
4. YMCA
   (The Village People)
5. HEAVEN KNOWS
   (Donna Summer with Brooklyn Dreams)

6. WHAT A FOOL BELIEVES
   (The Doobie Brothers)
7. SHAKE YOUR GROOVE THING
   (Peaches and Herb)
8. FIRE
   (The Pointer Sisters)
9. LADY
   (Little River Band)
10. MUSIC BOX DANCER
    (Frank Mills)

POP ALBUMS

1. SPIRITS HAVING FLOWN
   (The Bee Gees)
2. BLONDES HAVE MORE FUN
   (Rod Stewart)
3. MINUTE BY MINUTE
   (The Doobie Brothers)
4. DIRE STRAITS
   (Dire Straits)
5. CRUISIN'
   (The Village People)
6. BRIEFCASE FULL OF BLUES
   (The Blues Brothers)
7. 52nd STREET
   (Billy Joel)
8. 2 HOT!
   (Peaches and Herb)
9. LOVE TRACKS
   (Gloria Gaynor)
10. TOTALLY HOT
    (Olivia Newton-John)

BLACK SINGLES

1. I GOT MY MIND MADE UP (YOU CAN GET IT GIRL)
   (Instant Funk)
2. DA YA THINK I'M SEXY?
   (Rod Stewart)
3. I WILL SURVIVE
   (Gloria Gaynor)
4. BUSTIN' LOOSE
   (Chuck Brown and The Soul Searchers)
5. SHAKE YOUR BODY (DOWN TO THE GROUND)
   (The Jacksons)
6. HE'S THE GREATEST DANCER
   (Sister Sledge)
7. OH HONEY
   (The Delegation)
8. SHAKE YOUR GROOVE THING
   (Peaches and Herb)
9. DISCO NIGHTS (ROCK FREAK)
   (G.Q.)
10. HEAVEN KNOWS
    (Donna Summer with Brooklyn Dreams)

BLACK ALBUMS

1. 2 HOT!
   (Peaches and Herb)
2. BUSTIN' OUT OF L SEVEN
   (Rick James)
3. DESTINY
   (The Jacksons)
4. LOVE TRACKS
   (Gloria Gaynor)
5. INSTANT FUNK
   (Instant Funk)
6. C'EST CHIC
   (Chic)
7. LIVIN' INSIDE YOUR LOVE
   (George Benson)
8. BUSTIN' LOOSE
   (Chuck Brown and the Soul Searchers)
9. HERE, MY DEAR
   (Marvin Gaye)
10. SPIRITS HAVING FLOWN
    (The Bee Gees)

JAZZ ALBUMS

1. CARMEL
   (Joe Sample)
2. TOUCH DOWN
   (Bob James)
3. ANGIE
   (Angela Bofill)
4. PATRICE
   (Patrice Rushen)
5. LIVIN' INSIDE YOUR LOVE
   (George Benson)
6. REED SEED
   (Grover Washington Jr.)
7. EXOTIC MYSTERIES
   (Lonnie Liston Smith)
8. MILESTONE JAZZ STARS IN CONCERT
   (Milestone)
9. FOLLOW THE RAINBOW
   (George Duke)
10. SUPER MANN
    (Herbie Mann)

COUNTRY SINGLES

1. I JUST FALL IN LOVE AGAIN
   (Anne Murray)
2. SEND ME DOWN TO TUCSON/CHARLIE'S ANGELS
   (Mel Tillis)
3. GOLDEN TEARS
   (Dave and Sugar)
4. SOMEBODY SPECIAL
   (Donna Fargo)
5. I HAD A LOVELY TIME
   (The Kendalls)
6. STILL A WOMAN
   (Margo Smith)
7. IT'S A CHEATING SITUATION
   (Moe Bandy)
8. (IF LOVING YOU IS WRONG) I DON'T WANT TO BE RIGHT
   (Barbara Mandrell)
9. TRYIN' TO SATISFY YOU
   (Dottsy)
10. I'VE BEEN WAITING FOR YOU ALL OF MY LIFE
    (Con Hunley)

COUNTRY ALBUMS

1. THE GAMBLER
   (Kenny Rogers)
2. WILLIE AND FAMILY LIVE
   (Willie Nelson)
3. NEW KIND OF FEELING
   (Anne Murray)
4. TNT
   (Tanya Tucker)
5. WHEN I DREAM
   (Crystal Gayle)
6. EVERY WHICH WAY BUT LOOSE
   (Original Soundtrack)
7. STARDUST
   (Willie Nelson)
8. SWEET MEMORIES
   (Willie Nelson)
9. I'VE ALWAYS BEEN CRAZY
   (Waylon Jennings)
10. HEARTBREAKER
    (Dolly Parton)

MARCH 31, 1979

POP SINGLES

1. TRAGEDY
   (The Bee Gees)

---

2. DA YA THINK I'M SEXY?
   (Rod Stewart)
3. I WILL SURVIVE
   (Gloria Gaynor)
4. WHAT A FOOL BELIEVES
   (The Doobie Brothers)
5. YMCA
   (The Village People)
6. MUSIC BOX DANCER
   (Frank Mills)
7. LADY
   (Little River Band)
8. KNOCK ON WOOD
   (Amii Stewart)
9. SHAKE YOUR GROOVE THING
   (Peaches and Herb)
10. HEAVEN KNOWS
    (Donna Summer with Brooklyn Dreams)

POP ALBUMS

1. SPIRITS HAVING FLOWN
   (The Bee Gees)
2. MINUTE BY MINUTE
   (The Doobie Brothers)
3. BLONDES HAVE MORE FUN
   (Rod Stewart)
4. DIRE STRAITS
   (Dire Straits)
5. CRUISIN'
   (The Village People)
6. 2 HOT!
   (Peaches and Herb)
7. BRIEFCASE FULL OF BLUES
   (The Blues Brothers)
8. 52nd STREET
   (Billy Joel)
9. LIVIN' INSIDE YOUR LOVE
   (George Benson)
10. LOVE TRACKS
    (Gloria Gaynor)

BLACK SINGLES

1. I GOT MY MIND MADE UP (YOU CAN GET IT GIRL)
   (Instant Funk)
2. HE'S THE GREATEST DANCER
   (Sister Sledge)
3. SHAKE YOUR BODY (DOWN TO THE GROUND)
   (The Jacksons)
4. OH HONEY
   (The Delegation)
5. DA YA THINK I'M SEXY?
   (Rod Stewart)
6. DISCO NIGHTS (ROCK FREAK)
   (G.Q.)
7. I WILL SURVIVE
   (Gloria Gaynor)
8. BUSTIN' LOOSE
   (Chuck Brown and the Soul Searchers)
9. I WANT YOUR LOVE
   (Chic)
10. KNOCK ON WOOD
    (Amii Stewart)

BLACK ALBUMS

1. 2 HOT!
   (Peaches and Herb)
2. DESTINY
   (The Jacksons)
3. BUSTIN' OUT OF L SEVEN
   (Rick James)
4. INSTANT FUNK
   (Instant Funk)
5. LIVIN' INSIDE YOUR LOVE
   (George Benson)
6. LOVE TRACKS
   (Gloria Gaynor)
7. WE ARE FAMILY
   (Sister Sledge)
8. BUSTIN' LOOSE
   (Chuck Brown and the Soul Searchers)

---

9. C'EST CHIC
   (Chic)
10. HERE, MY DEAR
    (Marvin Gaye)

JAZZ ALBUMS

1. LIVIN' INSIDE YOUR LOVE
   (George Benson)
2. CARMEL
   (Joe Sample)
3. TOUCH DOWN
   (Bob James)
4. ANGIE
   (Angela Bofill)
5. PATRICE
   (Patrice Rushen)
6. FOLLOW THE RAINBOW
   (George Duke)
7. EXOTIC MYSTERIES
   (Lonnie Liston Smith)
8. REED SEED
   (Grover Washington Jr.)
9. FEETS DON'T FAIL ME NOW
   (Herbie Hancock)
10. SUPER MANN
    (Herbie Mann)

COUNTRY SINGLES

1. I JUST FALL IN LOVE AGAIN
   (Anne Murray)
2. IT'S A CHEATING SITUATION
   (Moe Bandy)
3. SOMEBODY SPECIAL
   (Donna Fargo)
4. (IF LOVING YOU IS WRONG) I DON'T WANT TO BE RIGHT
   (Barbara Mandrell)
5. GOLDEN TEARS
   (Dave and Sugar)
6. ALL I EVER NEED IS YOU
   (Kenny Rogers and Dottie West)
7. TOO FAR GONE
   (Emmylou Harris)
8. TRYIN' TO SATISFY YOU
   (Dottsy)
9. I'VE BEEN WAITING FOR YOU ALL OF MY LIFE
   (Con Hunley)
10. I'M GONNA LOVE YOU
    (Glen Campbell)

COUNTRY ALBUMS

1. THE GAMBLER
   (Kenny Rogers)
2. NEW KIND OF FEELING
   (Anne Murray)
3. WILLIE AND FAMILY LIVE
   (Willie Nelson)
4. TNT
   (Tanya Tucker)
5. STARDUST
   (Willie Nelson)
6. WHEN I DREAM
   (Crystal Gayle)
7. SWEET MEMORIES
   (Willie Nelson)
8. EVERY WHICH WAY BUT LOOSE
   (Original Soundtrack)
9. I'VE ALWAYS BEEN CRAZY
   (Waylon Jennings)
10. JOHN DENVER
    (John Denver)

APRIL 7, 1979

POP SINGLES

1. WHAT A FOOL BELIEVES
   (The Doobie Brothers)

2. TRAGEDY
   (The Bee Gees)
3. I WILL SURVIVE
   (Gloria Gaynor)
4. MUSIC BOX DANCER
   (Frank Mills)
5. KNOCK ON WOOD
   (Amii Stewart)
6. DA YA THINK I'M SEXY?
   (Rod Stewart)
7. LADY
   (Little River Band)
8. YMCA
   (The Village People)
9. SHAKE YOUR GROOVE THING
   (Peaches and Herb)
10. HEAVEN KNOWS
    (Donna Summer with Brooklyn Dreams)

POP ALBUMS

1. SPIRITS HAVING FLOWN
   (The Bee Gees)
2. MINUTE BY MINUTE
   (The Doobie Brothers)
3. DIRE STRAITS
   (Dire Straits)
4. BLONDES HAVE MORE FUN
   (Rod Stewart)
5. 2 HOT!
   (Peaches and Herb)
6. LIVIN' INSIDE YOUR LOVE
   (George Benson)
7. 52nd STREET
   (Billy Joel)
8. BRIEFCASE FULL OF BLUES
   (The Blues Brothers)
9. CRUISIN'
   (The Village People)
10. LOVE TRACKS
    (Gloria Gaynor)

BLACK SINGLES

1. HE'S THE GREATEST DANCER
   (Sister Sledge)
2. SHAKE YOUR BODY (DOWN TO THE GROUND)
   (The Jacksons)
3. I GOT MY MIND MADE UP (YOU CAN GET IT GIRL)
   (Instant Funk)
4. OH HONEY
   (The Delegation)
5. DISCO NIGHTS (ROCK FREAK)
   (G.Q.)
6. I WANT YOUR LOVE
   (Chic)
7. LOVE BALLAD
   (George Benson)
8. KNOCK ON WOOD
   (Amii Stewart)
9. REUNITED
   (Peaches and Herb)
10. DA YA THINK I'M SEXY?
    (Rod Stewart)

BLACK ALBUMS

1. 2 HOT!
   (Peaches and Herb)
2. DESTINY
   (The Jacksons)
3. INSTANT FUNK
   (Instant Funk)
4. LIVIN' INSIDE YOUR LOVE
   (George Benson)
5. BUSTIN' OUT OF L SEVEN
   (Rick James)
6. WE ARE FAMILY
   (Sister Sledge)
7. LOVE TRACKS
   (Gloria Gaynor)

8. KNOCK ON WOOD
   (Amii Stewart)
9. DISCO NIGHTS
   (G.Q.)
10. BUSTIN' LOOSE
    (Chuck Brown and The Soul Searchers)

JAZZ ALBUMS

1. LIVIN' INSIDE YOUR LOVE
   (George Benson)
2. CARMEL
   (Joe Sample)
3. TOUCH DOWN
   (Bob James)
4. ANGIE
   (Angela Bofill)
5. FOLLOW THE RAINBOW
   (George Duke)
6. FEETS DON'T FAIL ME NOW
   (Herbie Hancock)
7. PATRICE
   (Patrice Rushen)
8. TIGER IN THE RAIN
   (Michael Franks)
9. EXOTIC MYSTERIES
   (Lonnie Liston Smith)
10. AN EVENING WITH HERBIE HANCOCK AND CHICK COREA
    (Herbie Hancock and Chick Corea)

COUNTRY SINGLES

1. I JUST FALL IN LOVE AGAIN
   (Anne Murray)
2. IT'S A CHEATING SITUATION
   (Moe Bandy)
3. (IF LOVING YOU IS WRONG) I DON'T WANT TO BE RIGHT
   (Barbara Mandrell)
4. ALL I EVER NEED IS YOU
   (Kenny Rogers and Dottie West)
5. SOMEBODY SPECIAL
   (Donna Fargo)
6. TOO FAR GONE
   (Emmylou Harris)
7. SWEET MEMORIES
   (Willie Nelson)
8. I'VE BEEN WAITING FOR YOU ALL OF MY LIFE
   (Con Hunley)
9. I'M GONNA LOVE YOU
   (Glen Campbell)
10. THEY CALL IT MAKING LOVE
    (Tammy Wynette)

COUNTRY ALBUMS

1. THE GAMBLER
   (Kenny Rogers)
2. NEW KIND OF FEELING
   (Anne Murray)
3. WILLIE AND FAMILY LIVE
   (Willie Nelson)
4. TNT
   (Tanya Tucker)
5. STARDUST
   (Willie Nelson)
6. WHEN I DREAM
   (Crystal Gayle)
7. EVERY WHICH WAY BUT LOOSE
   (Original Soundtrack)
8. JOHN DENVER
   (John Denver)
9. THE OAK RIDGE BOYS HAVE ARRIVED
   (The Oak Ridge Boys)
10. HEARTBREAKER
    (Dolly Parton)

APRIL 14, 1979

POP SINGLES

1. MUSIC BOX DANCER
   (Frank Mills)
2. KNOCK ON WOOD
   (Amii Stewart)
3. TRAGEDY
   (The Bee Gees)
4. WHAT A FOOL BELIEVES
   (The Doobie Brothers)
5. I WILL SURVIVE
   (Gloria Gaynor)
6. HEART OF GLASS
   (Blondie)
7. LADY
   (Little River Band)
8. DA YA THINK I'M SEXY?
   (Rod Stewart)
9. I WANT YOUR LOVE
   (Chic)
10. SHAKE YOUR GROOVE THING
    (Peaches and Herb)

POP ALBUMS

1. SPIRITS HAVING FLOWN
   (The Bee Gees)
2. MINUTE BY MINUTE
   (The Doobie Brothers)
3. DIRE STRAITS
   (Dire Straits)
4. 2 HOT!
   (Peaches and Herb)
5. BLONDES HAVE MORE FUN
   (Rod Stewart)
6. LIVIN' INSIDE YOUR LOVE
   (George Benson)
7. DESOLATION ANGELS
   (Bad Company)
8. 52nd STREET
   (Billy Joel)
9. CRUISIN'
   (The Village People)
10. BREAKFAST IN AMERICA
    (Supertramp)

BLACK SINGLES

1. SHAKE YOUR BODY (DOWN TO THE GROUND)
   (The Jacksons)
2. DISCO NIGHTS (ROCK FREAK)
   (G.Q.)
3. HE'S THE GREATEST DANCER
   (Sister Sledge)
4. I GOT MY MIND MADE UP (YOU CAN GET IT GIRL)
   (Instant Funk)
5. REUNITED
   (Peaches and Herb)
6. I WANT YOUR LOVE
   (Chic)
7. LOVE BALLAD
   (George Benson)
8. KNOCK ON WOOD
   (Amii Stewart)
9. I DON'T WANT NOBODY ELSE (TO DANCE WITH YOU)
   (Narada Michael Walden)
10. OH HONEY
    (The Delegation)

BLACK ALBUMS

1. 2 HOT!
   (Peaches and Herb)
2. LIVIN' INSIDE YOUR LOVE
   (George Benson)

3. WE ARE FAMILY
   (Sister Sledge)
4. INSTANT FUNK
   (Instant Funk)
5. DESTINY
   (The Jacksons)
6. BUSTIN' OUT OF L SEVEN
   (Rick James)
7. DISCO NIGHTS
   (G.Q.)
8. KNOCK ON WOOD
   (Amii Stewart)
9. I LOVE YOU SO
   (Natalie Cole)
10. LOVE TRACKS
    (Gloria Gaynor)

JAZZ ALBUMS

1. LIVIN' INSIDE YOUR LOVE
   (George Benson)
2. FEETS DON'T FAIL ME NOW
   (Herbie Hancock)
3. FOLLOW THE RAINBOW
   (George Duke)
4. CARMEL
   (Joe Sample)
5. TOUCH DOWN
   (Bob James)
6. ANGIE
   (Angela Bofill)
7. TIGER IN THE RAIN
   (Michael Franks)
8. PATRICE
   (Patrice Rushen)
9. MORNING DANCE
   (Spyro Gyra)
10. EXOTIC MYSTERIES
    (Lonnie Liston Smith)

COUNTRY SINGLES

1. IT'S A CHEATING SITUATION
   (Moe Bandy)
2. (IF LOVING YOU IS WRONG) I DON'T WANT
   TO BE RIGHT
   (Barbara Mandrell)
3. ALL I EVER NEED IS YOU
   (Kenny Rogers and Dottie West)
4. I JUST FALL IN LOVE AGAIN
   (Anne Murray)
5. SWEET MEMORIES
   (Willie Nelson)
6. THEY CALL IT MAKING LOVE
   (Tammy Wynette)
7. WHERE DO I PUT HER MEMORY
   (Charley Pride)
8. BACK SIDE OF THIRTY
   (John Conlee)
9. FAREWELL PARTY
   (Gene Watson)
10. WISDOM OF A FOOL
    (Jacky Ward)

COUNTRY ALBUMS

1. THE GAMBLER
   (Kenny Rogers)
2. NEW KIND OF FEELING
   (Anne Murray)
3. WILLIE AND FAMILY LIVE
   (Willie Nelson)
4. STARDUST
   (Willie Nelson)
5. TNT
   (Tanya Tucker)
6. EVERY WHICH WAY BUT LOOSE
   (Original Soundtrack)
7. THE OAK RIDGE BOYS HAVE ARRIVED
   (The Oak Ridge Boys)
8. JOHN DENVER
   (John Denver)
9. CLASSICS
   (Kenny Rogers and Dottie West)

10. OUR MEMORIES OF ELVIS
    (Elvis Presley)

APRIL 21, 1979

POP SINGLES

1. KNOCK ON WOOD
   (Amii Stewart)
2. HEART OF GLASS
   (Blondie)
3. MUSIC BOX DANCER
   (Frank Mills)
4. TRAGEDY
   (The Bee Gees)
5. I WANT YOUR LOVE
   (Chic)
6. I WILL SURVIVE
   (Gloria Gaynor)
7. LADY
   (Little River Band)
8. WHAT A FOOL BELIEVES
   (The Doobie Brothers)
9. IN THE NAVY
   (The Village People)
10. REUNITED
    (Peaches and Herb)

POP ALBUMS

1. MINUTE BY MINUTE
   (The Doobie Brothers)
2. SPIRITS HAVING FLOWN
   (The Bee Gees)
3. 2 HOT!
   (Peaches and Herb)
4. DIRE STRAITS
   (Dire Straits)
5. BREAKFAST IN AMERICA
   (Supertramp)
6. DESOLATION ANGELS
   (Bad Company)
7. BLONDES HAVE MORE FUN
   (Rod Stewart)
8. LIVIN' INSIDE YOUR LOVE
   (George Benson)
9. PARALLEL LINES
   (Blondie)
10. VAN HALEN 2
    (Van Halen)

BLACK SINGLES

1. DISCO NIGHTS (ROCK FREAK)
   (G.Q.)
2. REUNITED
   (Peaches and Herb)
3. SHAKE YOUR BODY (DOWN TO THE
   GROUND)
   (The Jacksons)
4. I GOT MY MIND MADE UP (YOU CAN GET
   IT GIRL)
   (Instant Funk)
5. LOVE BALLAD
   (George Benson)
6. I WANT YOUR LOVE
   (Chic)
7. HE'S THE GREATEST DANCER
   (Sister Sledge)
8. I DON'T WANT NOBODY ELSE (TO DANCE
   WITH YOU)
   (Narada Michael Walden)
9. HOT NUMBER
   (Foxy)
10. IT MUST BE LOVE
    (Alton McClain and Destiny)

BLACK ALBUMS

1. 2 HOT!
   (Peaches and Herb)
2. WE ARE FAMILY
   (Sister Sledge)
3. LIVIN' INSIDE YOUR LOVE
   (George Benson)
4. DESTINY
   (The Jacksons)
5. BUSTIN' OUT OF L SEVEN
   (Rick James)
6. INSTANT FUNK
   (Instant Funk)
7. DISCO NIGHTS
   (G.Q.)
8. I LOVE YOU SO
   (Natalie Cole)
9. KNOCK ON WOOD
   (Amii Stewart)
10. INSPIRATION
    (Maze featuring Frankie Beverly)

JAZZ ALBUMS

1. LIVIN' INSIDE YOUR LOVE
   (George Benson)
2. FEETS DON'T FAIL ME NOW
   (Herbie Hancock)
3. FOLLOW THE RAINBOW
   (George Duke)
4. CARMEL
   (Joe Sample)
5. TOUCH DOWN
   (Bob James)
6. MORNING DANCE
   (Spyro Gyra)
7. TIGER IN THE RAIN
   (Michael Franks)
8. ANGIE
   (Angela Bofill)
9. PARADISE
   (Grover Washington Jr.)
10. LIGHT THE LIGHT
    (Seawind)

COUNTRY SINGLES

1. (IF LOVING YOU IS WRONG) I DON'T WANT
   TO BE RIGHT
   (Barbara Mandrell)
2. ALL I EVER NEED IS YOU
   (Kenny Rogers and Dottie West)
3. WHERE DO I PUT HER MEMORY
   (Charley Pride)
4. THEY CALL IT MAKING LOVE
   (Tammy Wynette)
5. SWEET MEMORIES
   (Willie Nelson)
6. BACK SIDE OF THIRTY
   (John Conlee)
7. FAREWELL PARTY
   (Gene Watson)
8. WISDOM OF A FOOL
   (Jacky Ward)
9. SLOW DANCING
   (Johnny Duncan)
10. IT'S A CHEATING SITUATION
    (Moe Bandy)

COUNTRY ALBUMS

1. THE GAMBLER
   (Kenny Rogers)
2. NEW KIND OF FEELING
   (Anne Murray)
3. WILLIE AND FAMILY LIVE
   (Willie Nelson)
4. CLASSICS
   (Kenny Rogers and Dottie West)
5. STARDUST
   (Willie Nelson)

6. EVERY WHICH WAY BUT LOOSE
   (Original Soundtrack)
7. THE OAK RIDGE BOYS HAVE ARRIVED
   (The Oak Ridge Boys)
8. TNT
   (Tanya Tucker)
9. SWEET MEMORIES
   (Willie Nelson)
10. OUR MEMORIES OF ELVIS
    (Elvis Presley)

APRIL 28, 1979

POP SINGLES

1. HEART OF GLASS
   (Blondie)
2. REUNITED
   (Peaches and Herb)
3. MUSIC BOX DANCER
   (Frank Mills)
4. KNOCK ON WOOD
   (Amii Stewart)
5. I WANT YOUR LOVE
   (Chic)
6. IN THE NAVY
   (The Village People)
7. I WILL SURVIVE
   (Gloria Gaynor)
8. TRAGEDY
   (The Bee Gees)
9. STUMBLIN' IN
   (Suzi Quatro and Chris Norman)
10. TAKE ME HOME
    (Cher)

POP ALBUMS

1. SPIRITS HAVING FLOWN
   (The Bee Gees)
2. MINUTE BY MINUTE
   (The Doobie Brothers)
3. 2 HOT!
   (Peaches and Herb)
4. BREAKFAST IN AMERICA
   (Supertramp)
5. DIRE STRAITS
   (Dire Straits)
6. DESOLATION ANGELS
   (Bad Company)
7. GO WEST
   (The Village People)
8. VAN HALEN 2
   (Van Halen)
9. PARALLEL LINES
   (Blondie)
10. BLONDES HAVE MORE FUN
    (Rod Stewart)

BLACK SINGLES

1. REUNITED
   (Peaches and Herb)
2. DISCO NIGHTS (ROCK FREAK)
   (G.Q.)
3. SHAKE YOUR BODY (DOWN TO THE GROUND)
   (The Jacksons)
4. I GOT MY MIND MADE UP (YOU CAN GET IT GIRL)
   (Instant Funk)
5. LOVE BALLAD
   (George Benson)
6. HOT NUMBER
   (Foxy)
7. HE'S THE GREATEST DANCER
   (Sister Sledge)
8. I DON'T WANT NOBODY ELSE (TO DANCE WITH YOU)
   (Narada Michael Walden)
9. IT MUST BE LOVE
   (Alton McClain and Destiny)

10. IN THE MOOD
    (Tyrone Davis)

BLACK ALBUMS

1. 2 HOT!
   (Peaches and Herb)
2. WE ARE FAMILY
   (Sister Sledge)
3. DISCO NIGHTS
   (G.Q.)
4. LIVIN' INSIDE YOUR LOVE
   (George Benson)
5. BUSTIN' OUT OF L SEVEN
   (Rick James)
6. DESTINY
   (The Jacksons)
7. INSPIRATION
   (Maze featuring Frankie Beverly)
8. INSTANT FUNK
   (Instant Funk)
9. MUSIC BOX
   (Evelyn "Champagne" King)
10. ROCK ON
    (Raydio)

JAZZ ALBUMS

1. LIVIN' INSIDE YOUR LOVE
   (George Benson)
2. MORNING DANCE
   (Spyro Gyra)
3. PARADISE
   (Grover Washington Jr.)
4. CARMEL
   (Joe Sample)
5. FEETS DON'T FAIL ME NOW
   (Herbie Hancock)
6. FOLLOW THE RAINBOW
   (George Duke)
7. TIGER IN THE RAIN
   (Michael Franks)
8. TOUCH DOWN
   (Bob James)
9. ANGIE
   (Angela Bofill)
10. LIGHT THE LIGHT
    (Seawind)

COUNTRY SINGLES

1. ALL I EVER NEED IS YOU
   (Kenny Rogers and Dottie West)
2. WHERE DO I PUT HER MEMORY
   (Charley Pride)
3. BACK SIDE OF THIRTY
   (John Conlee)
4. THEY CALL IT MAKING LOVE
   (Tammy Wynette)
5. FAREWELL PARTY
   (Gene Watson)
6. (IF LOVING YOU IS WRONG) I DON'T WANT TO BE RIGHT
   (Barbara Mandrell)
7. SLOW DANCING
   (Johnny Duncan)
8. WISDOM OF A FOOL
   (Jacky Ward)
9. DON'T TAKE IT AWAY
   (Conway Twitty)
10. LAY DOWN BESIDE ME
    (Don Williams)

COUNTRY ALBUMS

1. THE GAMBLER
   (Kenny Rogers)
2. CLASSICS
   (Kenny Rogers and Dottie West)
3. THE ORIGINALS
   (The Statler Brothers)
4. NEW KIND OF FEELING
   (Anne Murray)

5. WILLIE AND FAMILY LIVE
   (Willie Nelson)
6. THE OAK RIDGE BOYS HAVE ARRIVED
   (The Oak Ridge Boys)
7. TNT
   (Tanya Tucker)
8. STARDUST
   (Willie Nelson)
9. SWEET MEMORIES
   (Willie Nelson)
10. OUTLAW IS JUST A STATE OF MIND
    (Lynn Anderson)

MAY 5, 1979

POP SINGLES

1. REUNITED
   (Peaches and Herb)
2. HEART OF GLASS
   (Blondie)
3. MUSIC BOX DANCER
   (Frank Mills)
4. IN THE NAVY
   (The Village People)
5. KNOCK ON WOOD
   (Amii Stewart)
6. I WANT YOUR LOVE
   (Chic)
7. I WILL SURVIVE
   (Gloria Gaynor)
8. STUMBLIN' IN
   (Suzi Quatro and Chris Norman)
9. TAKE ME HOME
   (Cher)
10. TRAGEDY
    (The Bee Gees)

POP ALBUMS

1. SPIRITS HAVING FLOWN
   (The Bee Gees)
2. MINUTE BY MINUTE
   (The Doobie Brothers)
3. BREAKFAST IN AMERICA
   (Supertramp)
4. 2 HOT!
   (Peaches and Herb)
5. GO WEST
   (The Village People)
6. VAN HALEN 2
   (Van Halen)
7. DESOLATION ANGELS
   (Bad Company)
8. DIRE STRAITS
   (Dire Straits)
9. WE ARE FAMILY
   (Sister Sledge)
10. BLONDES HAVE MORE FUN
    (Rod Stewart)

BLACK SINGLES

1. REUNITED
   (Peaches and Herb)
2. DISCO NIGHTS (ROCK FREAK)
   (G.Q.)
3. SHAKE YOUR BODY (DOWN TO THE GROUND)
   (The Jacksons)
4. HOT NUMBER
   (Foxy)
5. LOVE BALLAD
   (George Benson)
6. IT MUST BE LOVE
   (Alton McClain and Destiny)
7. IN THE MOOD
   (Tyrone Davis)
8. I DON'T WANT NOBODY ELSE (TO DANCE WITH YOU)
   (Narada Michael Walden)

9. I GOT MY MIND MADE UP (YOU CAN GET IT GIRL)
   (Instant Funk)
10. HE'S THE GREATEST DANCER
    (Sister Sledge)

BLACK ALBUMS

1. 2 HOT!
   (Peaches and Herb)
2. WE ARE FAMILY
   (Sister Sledge)
3. DISCO NIGHTS
   (G.Q.)
4. LIVIN' INSIDE YOUR LOVE
   (George Benson)
5. BUSTIN' OUT OF L SEVEN
   (Rick James)
6. INSPIRATION
   (Maze featuring Frankie Beverly)
7. DESTINY
   (The Jacksons)
8. INSTANT FUNK
   (Instant Funk)
9. MUSIC BOX
   (Evelyn "Champagne" King)
10. ROCK ON
    (Raydio)

JAZZ ALBUMS

1. LIVIN' INSIDE YOUR LOVE
   (George Benson)
2. PARADISE
   (Grover Washington Jr.)
3. MORNING DANCE
   (Spyro Gyra)
4. TIGER IN THE RAIN
   (Michael Franks)
5. FEETS DON'T FAIL ME NOW
   (Herbie Hancock)
6. CARMEL
   (Joe Sample)
7. FOLLOW THE RAINBOW
   (George Duke)
8. TOUCH DOWN
   (Bob James)
9. LIGHT THE LIGHT
   (Seawind)
10. NIGHT RIDER
    (Tim Weisberg)

COUNTRY SINGLES

1. WHERE DO I PUT HER MEMORY
   (Charley Pride)
2. BACK SIDE OF THIRTY
   (John Conlee)
3. ALL I EVER NEED IS YOU
   (Kenny Rogers and Dottie West)
4. DON'T TAKE IT AWAY
   (Conway Twitty)
5. FAREWELL PARTY
   (Gene Watson)
6. LAY DOWN BESIDE ME
   (Don Williams)
7. SLOW DANCING
   (Johnny Duncan)
8. DOWN ON THE RIO GRANDE
   (Johnny Rodriguez)
9. LYING IN LOVE WITH YOU
   (Jim Ed Brown and Helen Cornelius)
10. IF I SAID YOU HAD A BEAUTIFUL BODY, WOULD YOU HOLD IT AGAINST ME
    (The Bellamy Brothers)

COUNTRY ALBUMS

1. THE GAMBLER
   (Kenny Rogers)
2. CLASSICS
   (Kenny Rogers and Dottie West)

3. THE ORIGINALS
   (The Statler Brothers)
4. NEW KIND OF FEELING
   (Anne Murray)
5. WILLIE AND FAMILY LIVE
   (Willie Nelson)
6. THE OAK RIDGE BOYS HAVE ARRIVED
   (The Oak Ridge Boys)
7. STARDUST
   (Willie Nelson)
8. TNT
   (Tanya Tucker)
9. GREATEST HITS
   (Waylon Jennings)
10. OUTLAW IS JUST A STATE OF MIND
    (Lynn Anderson)

MAY 12, 1979

POP SINGLES

1. REUNITED
   (Peaches and Herb)
2. IN THE NAVY
   (The Village People)
3. HEART OF GLASS
   (Blondie)
4. MUSIC BOX DANCER
   (Frank Mills)
5. KNOCK ON WOOD
   (Amii Stewart)
6. SHAKE YOUR BODY (DOWN TO THE GROUND)
   (The Jacksons)
7. HOT STUFF
   (Donna Summer)
8. STUMBLIN' IN
   (Suzi Quatro and Chris Norman)
9. TAKE ME HOME
   (Cher)
10. GOODNIGHT TONIGHT
    (Paul McCartney and Wings)

POP ALBUMS

1. BREAKFAST IN AMERICA
   (Supertramp)
2. SPIRITS HAVING FLOWN
   (The Bee Gees)
3. MINUTE BY MINUTE
   (The Doobie Brothers)
4. 2 HOT!
   (Peaches and Herb)
5. GO WEST
   (The Village People)
6. VAN HALEN 2
   (Van Halen)
7. DESOLATION ANGELS
   (Bad Company)
8. WE ARE FAMILY
   (Sister Sledge)
9. DIRE STRAITS
   (Dire Straits)
10. PARALLEL LINES
    (Blondie)

BLACK SINGLES

1. REUNITED
   (Peaches and Herb)
2. DISCO NIGHTS (ROCK FREAK)
   (G.Q.)
3. HOT NUMBER
   (Foxy)
4. SHAKE YOUR BODY (DOWN TO THE GROUND)
   (The Jacksons)
5. IN THE MOOD
   (Tyrone Davis)
6. IT MUST BE LOVE
   (Alton McClain and Destiny)

7. LOVE BALLAD
   (George Benson)
8. YOU CAN'T CHANGE THAT
   (Raydio)
9. FEEL THAT YOU'RE FEELIN'
   (Maze)
10. I WANNA BE WITH YOU (PART 1)
    (Isley Brothers)

BLACK ALBUMS

1. 2 HOT!
   (Peaches and Herb)
2. WE ARE FAMILY
   (Sister Sledge)
3. DISCO NIGHTS
   (G.Q.)
4. BUSTIN' OUT OF L SEVEN
   (Rick James)
5. INSPIRATION
   (Maze featuring Frankie Beverly)
6. LIVIN' INSIDE YOUR LOVE
   (George Benson)
7. DESTINY
   (The Jacksons)
8. ROCK ON
   (Raydio)
9. INSTANT FUNK
   (Instant Funk)
10. THE MUSIC BAND
    (War)

JAZZ ALBUMS

1. LIVIN' INSIDE YOUR LOVE
   (George Benson)
2. PARADISE
   (Grover Washington Jr.)
3. MORNING DANCE
   (Spyro Gyra)
4. CARMEL
   (Joe Sample)
5. TIGER IN THE RAIN
   (Michael Franks)
6. FEETS DON'T FAIL ME NOW
   (Herbie Hancock)
7. FOLLOW THE RAINBOW
   (George Duke)
8. TOUCH DOWN
   (Bob James)
9. LIGHT THE LIGHT
   (Seawind)
10. BRAZILIA
    (John Klemmer)

COUNTRY SINGLES

1. BACK SIDE OF THIRTY
   (John Conlee)
2. DON'T TAKE IT AWAY
   (Conway Twitty)
3. LAY DOWN BESIDE ME
   (Don Williams)
4. WHERE DO I PUT HER MEMORY
   (Charley Pride)
5. IF I SAID YOU HAD A BEAUTIFUL BODY, WOULD YOU HOLD IT AGAINST ME
   (The Bellamy Brothers)
6. LYING IN LOVE WITH YOU
   (Jim Ed Brown and Helen Cornelius)
7. DOWN ON THE RIO GRANDE
   (Johnny Rodriguez)
8. SAIL AWAY
   (The Oak Ridge Boys)
9. FAREWELL PARTY
   (Gene Watson)
10. HOW TO BE A COUNTRY STAR
    (The Statler Brothers)

COUNTRY ALBUMS

1. THE GAMBLER
   (Kenny Rogers)

2. NEW KIND OF FEELING
   (Anne Murray)
3. GREATEST HITS
   (Waylon Jennings)
4. CLASSICS
   (Kenny Rogers and Dottie West)
5. WILLIE AND FAMILY LIVE
   (Willie Nelson)
6. THE ORIGINALS
   (The Statler Brothers)
7. TNT
   (Tanya Tucker)
8. THE OAK RIDGE BOYS HAVE ARRIVED
   (The Oak Ridge Boys)
9. BLUE KENTUCKY GIRL
   (Emmylou Harris)
10. SWEET MEMORIES
    (Willie Nelson)

MAY 19, 1979

POP SINGLES

1. REUNITED
   (Peaches and Herb)
2. IN THE NAVY
   (The Village People)
3. HEART OF GLASS
   (Blondie)
4. HOT STUFF
   (Donna Summer)
5. SHAKE YOUR BODY (DOWN TO THE GROUND)
   (The Jacksons)
6. MUSIC BOX DANCER
   (Frank Mills)
7. GOODNIGHT TONIGHT
   (Paul McCartney and Wings)
8. TAKE ME HOME
   (Cher)
9. KNOCK ON WOOD
   (Amii Stewart)
10. STUMBLIN' IN
    (Suzi Quatro and Chris Norman)

POP ALBUMS

1. BREAKFAST IN AMERICA
   (Supertramp)
2. 2 HOT!
   (Peaches and Herb)
3. DESOLATION ANGELS
   (Bad Company)
4. MINUTE BY MINUTE
   (The Doobie Brothers)
5. SPIRITS HAVING FLOWN
   (The Bee Gees)
6. WE ARE FAMILY
   (Sister Sledge)
7. VAN HALEN 2
   (Van Halen)
8. GO WEST
   (The Village People)
9. BAD GIRLS
   (Donna Summer)
10. PARALLEL LINES
    (Blondie)

BLACK SINGLES

1. REUNITED
   (Peaches and Herb)
2. DISCO NIGHTS (ROCK FREAK)
   (G.Q.)
3. HOT NUMBER
   (Foxy)
4. SHAKE YOUR BODY (DOWN TO THE GROUND)
   (The Jacksons)
5. IN THE MOOD
   (Tyrone Davis)

6. YOU CAN'T CHANGE THAT
   (Raydio)
7. I WANNA BE WITH YOU (PART 1)
   (Isley Brothers)
8. FEEL THAT YOU'RE FEELIN'
   (Maze)
9. AIN'T NO STOPPIN' US NOW
   (McFadden and Whitehead)
10. WE ARE FAMILY
    (Sister Sledge)

BLACK ALBUMS

1. 2 HOT!
   (Peaches and Herb)
2. WE ARE FAMILY
   (Sister Sledge)
3. DISCO NIGHTS
   (G.Q.)
4. BAD GIRLS
   (Donna Summer)
5. INSPIRATION
   (Maze featuring Frankie Beverly)
6. BUSTIN' OUT OF L SEVEN
   (Rick James)
7. ROCK ON
   (Raydio)
8. DESTINY
   (The Jacksons)
9. LIVIN' INSIDE YOUR LOVE
   (George Benson)
10. THE MUSIC BAND
    (War)

JAZZ ALBUMS

1. LIVIN' INSIDE YOUR LOVE
   (George Benson)
2. PARADISE
   (Grover Washington Jr.)
3. MORNING DANCE
   (Spyro Gyra)
4. HEART STRING
   (Earl Klugh)
5. CARMEL
   (Joe Sample)
6. TIGER IN THE RAIN
   (Michael Franks)
7. LIGHT THE LIGHT
   (Seawind)
8. BRAZILIA
   (John Klemmer)
9. FEETS DON'T FAIL ME NOW
   (Herbie Hancock)
10. NEW CHAUTAUQUA
    (Pat Metheny)

COUNTRY SINGLES

1. DON'T TAKE IT AWAY
   (Conway Twitty)
2. IF I SAID YOU HAD A BEAUTIFUL BODY, WOULD YOU HOLD IT AGAINST ME
   (The Bellamy Brothers)
3. LAY DOWN BESIDE ME
   (Don Williams)
4. LYING IN LOVE WITH YOU
   (Jim Ed Brown and Helen Cornelius)
5. SAIL AWAY
   (The Oak Ridge Boys)
6. DOWN ON THE RIO GRANDE
   (Johnny Rodriguez)
7. WHEN I DREAM
   (Crystal Gayle)
8. HOW TO BE A COUNTRY STAR
   (The Statler Brothers)
9. BACK SIDE OF THIRTY
   (John Conlee)
10. ISN'T IT ALWAYS LOVE
    (Lynn Anderson)

COUNTRY ALBUMS

1. THE GAMBLER
   (Kenny Rogers)
2. NEW KIND OF FEELING
   (Anne Murray)
3. GREATEST HITS
   (Waylon Jennings)
4. WILLIE AND FAMILY LIVE
   (Willie Nelson)
5. THE ORIGINALS
   (The Statler Brothers)
6. BLUE KENTUCKY GIRL
   (Emmylou Harris)
7. CLASSICS
   (Kenny Rogers and Dottie West)
8. THE OAK RIDGE BOYS HAVE ARRIVED
   (The Oak Ridge Boys)
9. SWEET MEMORIES
   (Willie Nelson)
10. STARDUST
    (Willie Nelson)

MAY 26, 1979

POP SINGLES

1. REUNITED
   (Peaches and Herb)
2. HOT STUFF
   (Donna Summer)
3. HEART OF GLASS
   (Blondie)
4. IN THE NAVY
   (The Village People)
5. SHAKE YOUR BODY (DOWN TO THE GROUND)
   (The Jacksons)
6. LOVE YOU INSIDE OUT
   (The Bee Gees)
7. GOODNIGHT TONIGHT
   (Paul McCartney and Wings)
8. MUSIC BOX DANCER
   (Frank Mills)
9. KNOCK ON WOOD
   (Amii Stewart)
10. WE ARE FAMILY
    (Sister Sledge)

POP ALBUMS

1. BREAKFAST IN AMERICA
   (Supertramp)
2. 2 HOT!
   (Peaches and Herb)
3. DESOLATION ANGELS
   (Bad Company)
4. BAD GIRLS
   (Donna Summer)
5. SPIRITS HAVING FLOWN
   (The Bee Gees)
6. WE ARE FAMILY
   (Sister Sledge)
7. VAN HALEN 2
   (Van Halen)
8. MINUTE BY MINUTE
   (The Doobie Brothers)
9. RICKIE LEE JONES
   (Rickie Lee Jones)
10. GO WEST
    (The Village People)

BLACK SINGLES

1. REUNITED
   (Peaches and Herb)
2. DISCO NIGHTS (ROCK FREAK)
   (G.Q.)
3. AIN'T NO STOPPIN' US NOW
   (McFadden and Whitehead)

4. I WANNA BE WITH YOU (PART 1)
   (Isley Brothers)
5. WE ARE FAMILY
   (Sister Sledge)
6. YOU CAN'T CHANGE THAT
   (Raydio)
7. HOT STUFF
   (Donna Summer)
8. FEEL THAT YOU'RE FEELIN'
   (Maze)
9. HOT NUMBER
   (Foxy)
10. IN THE MOOD
    (Tyrone Davis)

BLACK ALBUMS

1. WE ARE FAMILY
   (Sister Sledge)
2. 2 HOT!
   (Peaches and Herb)
3. BAD GIRLS
   (Donna Summer)
4. DISCO NIGHTS
   (G.Q.)
5. BUSTIN' OUT OF L SEVEN
   (Rick James)
6. INSPIRATION
   (Maze featuring Frankie Beverly)
7. ROCK ON
   (Raydio)
8. THE MUSIC BAND
   (War)
9. DESTINY
   (The Jacksons)
10. IN THE MOOD WITH TYRONE DAVIS
    (Tyrone Davis)

JAZZ ALBUMS

1. PARADISE
   (Grover Washington Jr.)
2. LIVIN' INSIDE YOUR LOVE
   (George Benson)
3. MORNING DANCE
   (Spyro Gyra)
4. HEART STRING
   (Earl Klugh)
5. CARMEL
   (Joe Sample)
6. BRAZILIA
   (John Klemmer)
7. LIGHT THE LIGHT
   (Seawind)
8. FEETS DON'T FAIL ME NOW
   (Herbie Hancock)
9. NEW CHAUTAUQUA
   (Pat Metheny)
10. TIGER IN THE RAIN
    (Michael Franks)

COUNTRY SINGLES

1. IF I SAID YOU HAD A BEAUTIFUL BODY,
   WOULD YOU HOLD IT AGAINST ME
   (The Bellamy Brothers)
2. LYING IN LOVE WITH YOU
   (Jim Ed Brown and Helen Cornelius)
3. LAY DOWN BESIDE ME
   (Don Williams)
4. SAIL AWAY
   (The Oak Ridge Boys)
5. WHEN I DREAM
   (Crystal Gayle)
6. DON'T TAKE IT AWAY
   (Conway Twitty)
7. HOW TO BE A COUNTRY STAR
   (The Statler Brothers)
8. SHE BELIEVES IN ME
   (Kenny Rogers)
9. DOWN ON THE RIO GRANDE
   (Johnny Rodriguez)
10. RED BANDANA
    (Merle Haggard)

COUNTRY ALBUMS

1. THE GAMBLER
   (Kenny Rogers)
2. GREATEST HITS
   (Waylon Jennings)
3. BLUE KENTUCKY GIRL
   (Emmylou Harris)
4. THE ORIGINALS
   (The Statler Brothers)
5. THE OAK RIDGE BOYS HAVE ARRIVED
   (The Oak Ridge Boys)
6. CLASSICS
   (Kenny Rogers and Dottie West)
7. OUTLAW IS JUST A STATE OF MIND
   (Lynn Anderson)
8. NEW KIND OF FEELING
   (Anne Murray)
9. WILLIE AND FAMILY LIVE
   (Willie Nelson)
10. STARDUST
    (Willie Nelson)

JUNE 2, 1979

POP SINGLES

1. HOT STUFF
   (Donna Summer)
2. REUNITED
   (Peaches and Herb)
3. SHAKE YOUR BODY (DOWN TO THE GROUND)
   (The Jacksons)
4. IN THE NAVY
   (The Village People)
5. LOVE YOU INSIDE OUT
   (The Bee Gees)
6. HEART OF GLASS
   (Blondie)
7. WE ARE FAMILY
   (Sister Sledge)
8. JUST WHEN I NEEDED YOU MOST
   (Randy Vanwarmer)
9. GOODNIGHT TONIGHT
   (Paul McCartney and Wings)
10. KNOCK ON WOOD
    (Amii Stewart)

POP ALBUMS

1. BREAKFAST IN AMERICA
   (Supertramp)
2. BAD GIRLS
   (Donna Summer)
3. 2 HOT!
   (Peaches and Herb)
4. DESOLATION ANGELS
   (Bad Company)
5. WE ARE FAMILY
   (Sister Sledge)
6. RICKIE LEE JONES
   (Rickie Lee Jones)
7. SPIRITS HAVING FLOWN
   (The Bee Gees)
8. VAN HALEN 2
   (Van Halen)
9. MINUTE BY MINUTE
   (The Doobie Brothers)
10. CHEAP TRICK AT BUDOKAN
    (Cheap Trick)

BLACK SINGLES

1. AIN'T NO STOPPIN' US NOW
   (McFadden and Whitehead)
2. REUNITED
   (Peaches and Herb)
3. I WANNA BE WITH YOU (PART 1)
   (Isley Brothers)

4. WE ARE FAMILY
   (Sister Sledge)
5. HOT STUFF
   (Donna Summer)
6. DISCO NIGHTS (ROCK FREAK)
   (G.Q.)
7. RING MY BELL
   (Anita Ward)
8. YOU CAN'T CHANGE THAT
   (Raydio)
9. SHAKE
   (Gap Band)
10. BUSTIN' OUT
    (Rick James)

BLACK ALBUMS

1. WE ARE FAMILY
   (Sister Sledge)
2. BAD GIRLS
   (Donna Summer)
3. 2 HOT!
   (Peaches and Herb)
4. DISCO NIGHTS
   (G.Q.)
5. INSPIRATION
   (Maze featuring Frankie Beverly)
6. ROCK ON
   (Raydio)
7. THE MUSIC BAND
   (War)
8. BUSTIN' OUT OF L SEVEN
   (Rick James)
9. McFADDEN AND WHITEHEAD
   (McFadden and Whitehead)
10. HOT PROPERTY
    (Heatwave)

JAZZ ALBUMS

1. MORNING DANCE
   (Spyro Gyra)
2. PARADISE
   (Grover Washington Jr.)
3. LIVIN' INSIDE YOUR LOVE
   (George Benson)
4. HEART STRING
   (Earl Klugh)
5. CARMEL
   (Joe Sample)
6. BRAZILIA
   (John Klemmer)
7. FEETS DON'T FAIL ME NOW
   (Herbie Hancock)
8. NEW CHAUTAUQUA
   (Pat Metheny)
9. LIGHT THE LIGHT
   (Seawind)
10. LAND OF PASSION
    (Hubert Laws)

COUNTRY SINGLES

1. IF I SAID YOU HAD A BEAUTIFUL BODY,
   WOULD YOU HOLD IT AGAINST ME
   (The Bellamy Brothers)
2. LYING IN LOVE WITH YOU
   (Jim Ed Brown and Helen Cornelius)
3. SAIL AWAY
   (The Oak Ridge Boys)
4. WHEN I DREAM
   (Crystal Gayle)
5. SHE BELIEVES IN ME
   (Kenny Rogers)
6. LAY DOWN BESIDE ME
   (Don Williams)
7. RED BANDANA
   (Merle Haggard)
8. NOBODY LIKES SAD SONGS
   (Ronnie Milsap)
9. YOU FEEL GOOD ALL OVER
   (T. G. Sheppard)
10. HOW TO BE A COUNTRY STAR
    (The Statler Brothers)

COUNTRY ALBUMS

1. GREATEST HITS
   (Waylon Jennings)
2. THE GAMBLER
   (Kenny Rogers)
3. BLUE KENTUCKY GIRL
   (Emmylou Harris)
4. CLASSICS
   (Kenny Rogers and Dottie West)
5. THE OAK RIDGE BOYS HAVE ARRIVED
   (The Oak Ridge Boys)
6. NEW KIND OF FEELING
   (Anne Murray)
7. OUTLAW IS JUST A STATE OF MIND
   (Lynn Anderson)
8. STARDUST
   (Willie Nelson)
9. WILLIE AND FAMILY LIVE
   (Willie Nelson)
10. THE ORIGINALS
    (The Statler Brothers)

JUNE 9, 1979

POP SINGLES

1. HOT STUFF
   (Donna Summer)
2. REUNITED
   (Peaches and Herb)
3. SHAKE YOUR BODY (DOWN TO THE GROUND)
   (The Jacksons)
4. LOVE YOU INSIDE OUT
   (The Bee Gees)
5. WE ARE FAMILY
   (Sister Sledge)
6. JUST WHEN I NEEDED YOU MOST
   (Randy Vanwarmer)
7. IN THE NAVY
   (The Village People)
8. THE LOGICAL SONG
   (Supertramp)
9. YOU TAKE MY BREATH AWAY
   (Rex Smith)
10. HEART OF GLASS
    (Blondie)

POP ALBUMS

1. BREAKFAST IN AMERICA
   (Supertramp)
2. BAD GIRLS
   (Donna Summer)
3. 2 HOT!
   (Peaches and Herb)
4. DESOLATION ANGELS
   (Bad Company)
5. WE ARE FAMILY
   (Sister Sledge)
6. RICKIE LEE JONES
   (Rickie Lee Jones)
7. CHEAP TRICK AT BUDOKAN
   (Cheap Trick)
8. VAN HALEN 2
   (Van Halen)
9. MINUTE BY MINUTE
   (The Doobie Brothers)
10. THE GAMBLER
    (Kenny Rogers)

BLACK SINGLES

1. RING MY BELL
   (Anita Ward)
2. AIN'T NO STOPPIN' US NOW
   (McFadden and Whitehead)
3. I WANNA BE WITH YOU (PART 1)
   (Isley Brothers)
4. WE ARE FAMILY
   (Sister Sledge)
5. HOT STUFF
   (Donna Summer)
6. REUNITED
   (Peaches and Herb)
7. SHAKE
   (Gap Band)
8. DISCO NIGHTS (ROCK FREAK)
   (G.Q.)
9. BUSTIN' OUT
   (Rick James)
10. YOU CAN'T CHANGE THAT
    (Raydio)

BLACK ALBUMS

1. BAD GIRLS
   (Donna Summer)
2. WE ARE FAMILY
   (Sister Sledge)
3. 2 HOT!
   (Peaches and Herb)
4. DISCO NIGHTS
   (G.Q.)
5. INSPIRATION
   (Maze featuring Frankie Beverly)
6. McFADDEN AND WHITEHEAD
   (McFadden and Whitehead)
7. THE MUSIC BAND
   (War)
8. SONGS OF LOVE
   (Anita Ward)
9. ROCK ON
   (Raydio)
10. HOT PROPERTY
    (Heatwave)

JAZZ ALBUMS

1. PARADISE
   (Grover Washington Jr.)
2. LIVIN' INSIDE YOUR LOVE
   (George Benson)
3. MORNING DANCE
   (Spyro Gyra)
4. HEART STRING
   (Earl Klugh)
5. STREET LIFE
   (Crusaders)
6. CARMEL
   (Joe Sample)
7. FEETS DON'T FAIL ME NOW
   (Herbie Hancock)
8. NEW CHAUTAUQUA
   (Pat Metheny)
9. BRAZILIA
   (John Klemmer)
10. JEAN LUC PONTY: LIVE
    (Jean Luc Ponty)

COUNTRY SINGLES

1. SAIL AWAY
   (The Oak Ridge Boys)
2. WHEN I DREAM
   (Crystal Gayle)
3. SHE BELIEVES IN ME
   (Kenny Rogers)
4. IF I SAID YOU HAD A BEAUTIFUL BODY, WOULD YOU HOLD IT AGAINST ME
   (The Bellamy Brothers)
5. RED BANDANA
   (Merle Haggard)
6. NOBODY LIKES SAD SONGS
   (Ronnie Milsap)
7. YOU FEEL GOOD ALL OVER
   (T.G. Sheppard)
8. ME AND MY BROKEN HEART
   (Rex Allen Jr.)
9. ARE YOU SINCERE
   (Elvis Presley)
10. IF LOVE HAD A FACE
    (Razzy Bailey)

COUNTRY ALBUMS

1. THE GAMBLER
   (Kenny Rogers)
2. GREATEST HITS
   (Waylon Jennings)
3. NEW KIND OF FEELING
   (Anne Murray)
4. CLASSICS
   (Kenny Rogers and Dottie West)
5. BLUE KENTUCKY GIRL
   (Emmylou Harris)
6. THE OAK RIDGE BOYS HAVE ARRIVED
   (The Oak Ridge Boys)
7. LOVELINE
   (Eddie Rabbitt)
8. STARDUST
   (Willie Nelson)
9. THE ORIGINALS
   (The Statler Brothers)
10. WILLIE AND FAMILY LIVE
    (Willie Nelson)

JUNE 16, 1979

POP SINGLES

1. HOT STUFF
   (Donna Summer)
2. REUNITED
   (Peaches and Herb)
3. WE ARE FAMILY
   (Sister Sledge)
4. LOVE YOU INSIDE OUT
   (The Bee Gees)
5. JUST WHEN I NEEDED YOU MOST
   (Randy Vanwarmer)
6. YOU TAKE MY BREATH AWAY
   (Rex Smith)
7. THE LOGICAL SONG
   (Supertramp)
8. SHAKE YOUR BODY (DOWN TO THE GROUND)
   (The Jacksons)
9. CHUCK E'S IN LOVE
   (Rickie Lee Jones)
10. SHE BELIEVES IN ME
    (Kenny Rogers)

POP ALBUMS

1. BAD GIRLS
   (Donna Summer)
2. BREAKFAST IN AMERICA
   (Supertramp)
3. RICKIE LEE JONES
   (Rickie Lee Jones)
4. DESOLATION ANGELS
   (Bad Company)
5. CHEAP TRICK AT BUDOKAN
   (Cheap Trick)
6. WE ARE FAMILY
   (Sister Sledge)
7. 2 HOT!
   (Peaches and Herb)
8. VAN HALEN 2
   (Van Halen)
9. MINUTE BY MINUTE
   (The Doobie Brothers)
10. THE GAMBLER
    (Kenny Rogers)

BLACK SINGLES

1. RING MY BELL
   (Anita Ward)
2. AIN'T NO STOPPIN' US NOW
   (McFadden and Whitehead)
3. HOT STUFF
   (Donna Summer)

4. WE ARE FAMILY
   (Sister Sledge)
5. I WANNA BE WITH YOU (PART 1)
   (Isley Brothers)
6. SHAKE
   (Gap Band)
7. REUNITED
   (Peaches and Herb)
8. BOOGIE WONDERLAND
   (Earth, Wind and Fire with The Emotions)
9. BUSTIN' OUT
   (Rick James)
10. LET ME BE GOOD TO YOU
    (Lou Rawls)

BLACK ALBUMS

1. BAD GIRLS
   (Donna Summer)
2. WE ARE FAMILY
   (Sister Sledge)
3. WINNER TAKES ALL
   (Isley Brothers)
4. I AM
   (Earth, Wind and Fire)
5. SONGS OF LOVE
   (Anita Ward)
6. McFADDEN AND WHITEHEAD
   (McFadden and Whitehead)
7. INSPIRATION
   (Maze featuring Frankie Beverly)
8. DISCO NIGHTS
   (G.Q.)
9. 2 HOT!
   (Peaches and Herb)
10. CANDY
    (Con Funk Shun)

JAZZ ALBUMS

1. STREET LIFE
   (Crusaders)
2. PARADISE
   (Grover Washington Jr.)
3. MORNING DANCE
   (Spyro Gyra)
4. HEART STRING
   (Earl Klugh)
5. LIVIN' INSIDE YOUR LOVE
   (George Benson)
6. NEW CHAUTAUQUA
   (Pat Metheny)
7. CARMEL
   (Joe Sample)
8. JEAN LUC PONTY: LIVE
   (Jean Luc Ponty)
9. FEETS DON'T FAIL ME NOW
   (Herbie Hancock)
10. BRAZILIA
    (John Klemmer)

COUNTRY SINGLES

1. SHE BELIEVES IN ME
   (Kenny Rogers)
2. WHEN I DREAM
   (Crystal Gayle)
3. NOBODY LIKES SAD SONGS
   (Ronnie Milsap)
4. YOU FEEL GOOD ALL OVER
   (T.G. Sheppard)
5. RED BANDANA
   (Merle Haggard)
6. SAIL AWAY
   (The Oak Ridge Boys)
7. ME AND MY BROKEN HEART
   (Rex Allen Jr.)
8. IF LOVE HAD A FACE
   (Razzy Bailey)
9. ARE YOU SINCERE
   (Elvis Presley)
10. JUST LIKE REAL PEOPLE
    (The Kendalls)

COUNTRY ALBUMS

1. GREATEST HITS
   (Waylon Jennings)
2. THE GAMBLER
   (Kenny Rogers)
3. NEW KIND OF FEELING
   (Anne Murray)
4. BLUE KENTUCKY GIRL
   (Emmylou Harris)
5. THE ORIGINALS
   (The Statler Brothers)
6. LOVELINE
   (Eddie Rabbitt)
7. CLASSICS
   (Kenny Rogers and Dottie West)
8. TNT
   (Tanya Tucker)
9. WHEN I DREAM
   (Crystal Gayle)
10. JERRY LEE LEWIS
    (Jerry Lee Lewis)

JUNE 23, 1979

POP SINGLES

1. HOT STUFF
   (Donna Summer)
2. REUNITED
   (Peaches and Herb)
3. WE ARE FAMILY
   (Sister Sledge)
4. YOU TAKE MY BREATH AWAY
   (Rex Smith)
5. JUST WHEN I NEEDED YOU MOST
   (Randy Vanwarmer)
6. THE LOGICAL SONG
   (Supertramp)
7. RING MY BELL
   (Anita Ward)
8. CHUCK E'S IN LOVE
   (Rickie Lee Jones)
9. SHE BELIEVES IN ME
   (Kenny Rogers)
10. BAD GIRLS
    (Donna Summer)

POP ALBUMS

1. BREAKFAST IN AMERICA
   (Supertramp)
2. BAD GIRLS
   (Donna Summer)
3. RICKIE LEE JONES
   (Rickie Lee Jones)
4. DESOLATION ANGELS
   (Bad Company)
5. CHEAP TRICK AT BUDOKAN
   (Cheap Trick)
6. WE ARE FAMILY
   (Sister Sledge)
7. 2 HOT!
   (Peaches and Herb)
8. VAN HALEN 2
   (Van Halen)
9. THE GAMBLER
   (Kenny Rogers)
10. MINUTE BY MINUTE
    (The Doobie Brothers)

BLACK SINGLES

1. RING MY BELL
   (Anita Ward)
2. AIN'T NO STOPPIN' US NOW
   (McFadden and Whitehead)
3. HOT STUFF
   (Donna Summer)
4. WE ARE FAMILY
   (Sister Sledge)

5. BOOGIE WONDERLAND
   (Earth, Wind and Fire with The Emotions)
6. SHAKE
   (Gap Band)
7. BAD GIRLS
   (Donna Summer)
8. YOU GONNA MAKE ME LOVE SOMEBODY ELSE
   (The Jones Girls)
9. LET ME BE GOOD TO YOU
   (Lou Rawls)
10. I WANNA BE WITH YOU (PART 1)
    (Isley Brothers)

BLACK ALBUMS

1. I AM
   (Earth, Wind and Fire)
2. BAD GIRLS
   (Donna Summer)
3. WINNER TAKES ALL
   (Isley Brothers)
4. SONGS OF LOVE
   (Anita Ward)
5. WE ARE FAMILY
   (Sister Sledge)
6. McFADDEN AND WHITEHEAD
   (McFadden and Whitehead)
7. TEDDY
   (Teddy Pendergrass)
8. CANDY
   (Con Funk Shun)
9. SWITCH II
   (Switch)
10. DISCO NIGHTS
    (G.Q.)

JAZZ ALBUMS

1. STREET LIFE
   (Crusaders)
2. PARADISE
   (Grover Washington Jr.)
3. MORNING DANCE
   (Spyro Gyra)
4. HEART STRING
   (Earl Klugh)
5. LIVIN' INSIDE YOUR LOVE
   (George Benson)
6. JEAN LUC PONTY: LIVE
   (Jean Luc Ponty)
7. NEW CHAUTAUQUA
   (Pat Metheny)
8. CARMEL
   (Joe Sample)
9. FEVER
   (Roy Ayers)
10. FEETS DON'T FAIL ME NOW
    (Herbie Hancock)

COUNTRY SINGLES

1. SHE BELIEVES IN ME
   (Kenny Rogers)
2. NOBODY LIKES SAD SONGS
   (Ronnie Milsap)
3. YOU FEEL GOOD ALL OVER
   (T.G. Sheppard)
4. WHEN I DREAM
   (Crystal Gayle)
5. AMANDA
   (Waylon Jennings)
6. IF LOVE HAD A FACE
   (Razzy Bailey)
7. ME AND MY BROKEN HEART
   (Rex Allen Jr.)
8. I CAN'T FEEL YOU ANYMORE
   (Loretta Lynn)
9. JUST LIKE REAL PEOPLE
   (The Kendalls)
10. I DON'T LIE
    (Joe Stampley)

COUNTRY ALBUMS

1. THE GAMBLER
   (Kenny Rogers)
2. GREATEST HITS
   (Waylon Jennings)
3. ONE FOR THE ROAD
   (Willie Nelson and Leon Russell)
4. BLUE KENTUCKY GIRL
   (Emmylou Harris)
5. THE ORIGINALS
   (The Statler Brothers)
6. CLASSICS
   (Kenny Rogers and Dottie West)
7. IMAGES
   (Ronnie Milsap)
8. TNT
   (Tanya Tucker)
9. WHEN I DREAM
   (Crystal Gayle)
10. JERRY LEE LEWIS
    (Jerry Lee Lewis)

JUNE 30, 1979

POP SINGLES

1. HOT STUFF
   (Donna Summer)
2. RING MY BELL
   (Anita Ward)
3. BAD GIRLS
   (Donna Summer)
4. YOU TAKE MY BREATH AWAY
   (Rex Smith)
5. WE ARE FAMILY
   (Sister Sledge)
6. THE LOGICAL SONG
   (Supertramp)
7. CHUCK E'S IN LOVE
   (Rickie Lee Jones)
8. SHE BELIEVES IN ME
   (Kenny Rogers)
9. I WANT YOU TO WANT ME
   (Cheap Trick)
10. REUNITED
    (Peaches and Herb)

POP ALBUMS

1. BREAKFAST IN AMERICA
   (Supertramp)
2. BAD GIRLS
   (Donna Summer)
3. CHEAP TRICK AT BUDOKAN
   (Cheap Trick)
4. DESOLATION ANGELS
   (Bad Company)
5. I AM
   (Earth, Wind and Fire)
6. RICKIE LEE JONES
   (Rickie Lee Jones)
7. DYNASTY
   (Kiss)
8. WE ARE FAMILY
   (Sister Sledge)
9. THE GAMBLER
   (Kenny Rogers)
10. 2 HOT!
    (Peaches and Herb)

BLACK SINGLES

1. RING MY BELL
   (Anita Ward)
2. AIN'T NO STOPPING US NOW
   (McFadden and Whitehead)
3. BAD GIRLS
   (Donna Summer)

4. BOOGIE WONDERLAND
   (Earth, Wind and Fire with The Emotions)
5. WE ARE FAMILY
   (Sister Sledge)
6. YOU GONNA MAKE ME LOVE SOMEBODY ELSE
   (The Jones Girls)
7. HOT STUFF
   (Donna Summer)
8. TURN OUT THE LIGHTS
   (Teddy Pendergrass)
9. LET ME BE GOOD TO YOU
   (Lou Rawls)
10. SHAKE
    (The Gap Band)

BLACK ALBUMS

1. I AM
   (Earth, Wind and Fire)
2. BAD GIRLS
   (Donna Summer)
3. WINNER TAKES ALL
   (Isley Brothers)
4. TEDDY
   (Teddy Pendergrass)
5. SONGS OF LOVE
   (Anita Ward)
6. WE ARE FAMILY
   (Sister Sledge)
7. McFADDEN AND WHITEHEAD
   (McFadden and Whitehead)
8. CANDY
   (Con Funk Shun)
9. SWITCH II
   (Switch)
10. DISCO NIGHTS
    (G.Q.)

JAZZ ALBUMS

1. STREET LIFE
   (Crusaders)
2. PARADISE
   (Grover Washington Jr.)
3. MORNING DANCE
   (Spyro Gyra)
4. HEART STRING
   (Earl Klugh)
5. LIVIN' INSIDE YOUR LOVE
   (George Benson)
6. JEAN LUC PONTY: LIVE
   (Jean Luc Ponty)
7. NEW CHAUTAUQUA
   (Pat Metheny)
8. CARMEL
   (Joe Sample)
9. TOGETHER
   (McCoy Tyner)
10. FEVER
    (Roy Ayers)

COUNTRY SINGLES

1. NOBODY LIKES SAD SONGS
   (Ronnie Milsap)
2. SHE BELIEVES IN ME
   (Kenny Rogers)
3. YOU FEEL GOOD ALL OVER
   (T.G. Sheppard)
4. AMANDA
   (Waylon Jennings)
5. I CAN'T FEEL YOU ANYMORE
   (Loretta Lynn)
6. IF LOVE HAD A FACE
   (Razzy Bailey)
7. SHADOWS IN THE MOONLIGHT
   (Anne Murray)
8. I DON'T LIE
   (Joe Stampley)
9. JUST LIKE REAL PEOPLE
   (The Kendalls)
10. IF I GIVE MY HEART TO YOU
    (Margo Smith)

COUNTRY ALBUMS

1. THE GAMBLER
   (Kenny Rogers)
2. GREATEST HITS
   (Waylon Jennings)
3. ONE FOR THE ROAD
   (Willie Nelson and Leon Russell)
4. BLUE KENTUCKY GIRL
   (Emmylou Harris)
5. GREAT BALLS OF FIRE
   (Dolly Parton)
6. CLASSICS
   (Kenny Rogers and Dottie West)
7. IMAGES
   (Ronnie Milsap)
8. STARDUST
   (Willie Nelson)
9. WILLIE AND FAMILY LIVE
   (Willie Nelson)
10. THE ORIGINALS
    (The Statler Brothers)

JULY 7, 1979

POP SINGLES

1. RING MY BELL
   (Anita Ward)
2. HOT STUFF
   (Donna Summer)
3. BAD GIRLS
   (Donna Summer)
4. YOU TAKE MY BREATH AWAY
   (Rex Smith)
5. WE ARE FAMILY
   (Sister Sledge)
6. SHE BELIEVES IN ME
   (Kenny Rogers)
7. I WANT YOU TO WANT ME
   (Cheap Trick)
8. THE LOGICAL SONG
   (Supertramp)
9. CHUCK E'S IN LOVE
   (Rickie Lee Jones)
10. SHINE A LITTLE LOVE
    (Electric Light Orchestra)

POP ALBUMS

1. BREAKFAST IN AMERICA
   (Supertramp)
2. BAD GIRLS
   (Donna Summer)
3. CHEAP TRICK AT BUDOKAN
   (Cheap Trick)
4. I AM
   (Earth, Wind and Fire)
5. DESOLATION ANGELS
   (Bad Company)
6. THE GAMBLER
   (Kenny Rogers)
7. DYNASTY
   (Kiss)
8. RICKIE LEE JONES
   (Rickie Lee Jones)
9. 2 HOT!
   (Peaches and Herb)
10. DISCOVERY
    (Electric Light Orchestra)

BLACK SINGLES

1. RING MY BELL
   (Anita Ward)
2. BAD GIRLS
   (Donna Summer)
3. AIN'T NO STOPPIN' US NOW
   (McFadden and Whitehead)

4. YOU GONNA MAKE ME LOVE SOMEBODY
   ELSE
   (The Jones Girls)
5. TURN OFF THE LIGHTS
   (Teddy Pendergrass)
6. BOOGIE WONDERLAND
   (Earth, Wind and Fire with The Emotions)
7. HOT STUFF
   (Donna Summer)
8. WE ARE FAMILY
   (Sister Sledge)
9. LET ME BE GOOD TO YOU
   (Lou Rawls)
10. CHASE ME
    (Con Funk Shun)

BLACK ALBUMS

1. I AM
   (Earth, Wind and Fire)
2. BAD GIRLS
   (Donna Summer)
3. TEDDY
   (Teddy Pendergrass)
4. WINNER TAKES ALL
   (Isley Brothers)
5. SONGS OF LOVE
   (Anita Ward)
6. McFADDEN AND WHITEHEAD
   (McFadden and Whitehead)
7. CANDY
   (Con Funk Shun)
8. LET ME BE GOOD TO YOU
   (Lou Rawls)
9. SWITCH II
   (Switch)
10. WE ARE FAMILY
    (Sister Sledge)

JAZZ ALBUMS

1. STREET LIFE
   (Crusaders)
2. PARADISE
   (Grover Washington Jr.)
3. MORNING DANCE
   (Spyro Gyra)
4. HEART STRING
   (Earl Klugh)
5. LIVIN' INSIDE YOUR LOVE
   (George Benson)
6. JEAN LUC PONTY: LIVE
   (Jean Luc Ponty)
7. NEW CHAUTAUQUA
   (Pat Metheny)
8. TOGETHER
   (McCoy Tyner)
9. CARMEL
   (Joe Sample)
10. FEEL THE NIGHT
    (Lee Ritenour)

COUNTRY SINGLES

1. AMANDA
   (Waylon Jennings)
2. NOBODY LIKES SAD SONGS
   (Ronnie Milsap)
3. SHADOWS IN THE MOONLIGHT
   (Anne Murray)
4. I CAN'T FEEL YOU ANYMORE
   (Loretta Lynn)
5. SHE BELIEVES IN ME
   (Kenny Rogers)
6. IF I GIVE MY HEART TO YOU
   (Margo Smith)
7. I DON'T LIE
   (Joe Stampley)
8. YOU'RE THE ONLY ONE
   (Dolly Parton)
9. PLAY TOGETHER AGAIN AGAIN
   (Buck Owens with Emmylou Harris)
10. (GHOST) RIDERS IN THE SKY
    (Johnny Cash)

COUNTRY ALBUMS

1. THE GAMBLER
   (Kenny Rogers)
2. GREATEST HITS
   (Waylon Jennings)
3. ONE FOR THE ROAD
   (Willie Nelson and Leon Russell)
4. BLUE KENTUCKY GIRL
   (Emmylou Harris)
5. GREAT BALLS OF FIRE
   (Dolly Parton)
6. CLASSICS
   (Kenny Rogers and Dottie West)
7. THE OAK RIDGE BOYS HAVE ARRIVED
   (The Oak Ridge Boys)
8. STARDUST
   (Willie Nelson)
9. WILLIE AND FAMILY LIVE
   (Willie Nelson)
10. NEW KIND OF FEELING
    (Anne Murray)

JULY 14, 1979

POP SINGLES

1. BAD GIRLS
   (Donna Summer)
2. RING MY BELL
   (Anita Ward)
3. HOT STUFF
   (Donna Summer)
4. I WANT YOU TO WANT ME
   (Cheap Trick)
5. YOU TAKE MY BREATH AWAY
   (Rex Smith)
6. SHE BELIEVES IN ME
   (Kenny Rogers)
7. WE ARE FAMILY
   (Sister Sledge)
8. SHINE A LITTLE LOVE
   (Electric Light Orchestra)
9. THE LOGICAL SONG
   (Supertramp)
10. MAKIN' IT
    (David Naughton)

POP ALBUMS

1. BREAKFAST IN AMERICA
   (Supertramp)
2. BAD GIRLS
   (Donna Summer)
3. CHEAP TRICK AT BUDOKAN
   (Cheap Trick)
4. I AM
   (Earth, Wind and Fire)
5. DISCOVERY
   (Electric Light Orchestra)
6. THE GAMBLER
   (Kenny Rogers)
7. TEDDY
   (Teddy Pendergrass)
8. DESOLATION ANGELS
   (Bad Company)
9. BACK TO THE EGG
   (Paul McCartney and Wings)
10. DYNASTY
    (Kiss)

BLACK SINGLES

1. BAD GIRLS
   (Donna Summer)
2. RING MY BELL
   (Anita Ward)
3. TURN OFF THE LIGHTS
   (Teddy Pendergrass)

4. YOU GONNA MAKE ME LOVE SOMEBODY
   ELSE
   (The Jones Girls)
5. GOOD TIMES
   (Chic)
6. AIN'T NO STOPPIN' US NOW
   (McFadden and Whitehead)
7. BOOGIE WONDERLAND
   (Earth, Wind and Fire with The Emotions)
8. HOT STUFF
   (Donna Summer)
9. CHASE ME
   (Con Funk Shun)
10. LET ME BE GOOD TO YOU
    (Lou Rawls)

BLACK ALBUMS

1. TEDDY
   (Teddy Pendergrass)
2. I AM
   (Earth, Wind and Fire)
3. BAD GIRLS
   (Donna Summer)
4. WINNER TAKES ALL
   (Isley Brothers)
5. SONGS OF LOVE
   (Anita Ward)
6. CANDY
   (Con Funk Shun)
7. McFADDEN AND WHITEHEAD
   (McFadden and Whitehead)
8. LET ME BE GOOD TO YOU
   (Lou Rawls)
9. STREET LIFE
   (Crusaders)
10. THE JONES GIRLS
    (The Jones Girls)

JAZZ ALBUMS

1. STREET LIFE
   (Crusaders)
2. MORNING DANCE
   (Spyro Gyra)
3. HEART STRING
   (Earl Klugh)
4. TOGETHER
   (McCoy Tyner)
5. LIVIN' INSIDE YOUR LOVE
   (George Benson)
6. PARADISE
   (Grover Washington Jr.)
7. NEW CHAUTAUQUA
   (Pat Metheny)
8. JEAN LUC PONTY: LIVE
   (Jean Luc Ponty)
9. FEVER
   (Roy Ayers)
10. FEEL THE NIGHT
    (Lee Ritenour)

COUNTRY SINGLES

1. AMANDA
   (Waylon Jennings)
2. SHADOWS IN THE MOONLIGHT
   (Anne Murray)
3. YOU'RE THE ONLY ONE
   (Dolly Parton)
4. I CAN'T FEEL YOU ANYMORE
   (Loretta Lynn)
5. (GHOST) RIDERS IN THE SKY
   (Johnny Cash)
6. IF I GIVE MY HEART TO YOU
   (Margo Smith)
7. NOBODY LIKES SAD SONGS
   (Ronnie Milsap)
8. PLAY TOGETHER AGAIN AGAIN
   (Buck Owens with Emmylou Harris)
9. SAVE THE LAST DANCE FOR ME
   (Emmylou Harris)
10. SIMPLE LITTLE WORDS
    (Cristy Lane)

COUNTRY ALBUMS

1. THE GAMBLER
   (Kenny Rogers)
2. GREATEST HITS
   (Waylon Jennings)
3. ONE FOR THE ROAD
   (Willie Nelson and Leon Russell)
4. BLUE KENTUCKY GIRL
   (Emmylou Harris)
5. GREAT BALLS OF FIRE
   (Dolly Parton)
6. STARDUST
   (Willie Nelson)
7. THE OAK RIDGE BOYS HAVE ARRIVED
   (The Oak Ridge Boys)
8. CLASSICS
   (Kenny Rogers and Dottie West)
9. WILLIE AND FAMILY LIVE
   (Willie Nelson)
10. NEW KIND OF FEELING
    (Anne Murray)

JULY 21, 1979

POP SINGLES

1. BAD GIRLS
   (Donna Summer)
2. RING MY BELL
   (Anita Ward)
3. HOT STUFF
   (Donna Summer)
4. I WANT YOU TO WANT ME
   (Cheap Trick)
5. SHE BELIEVES IN ME
   (Kenny Rogers)
6. YOU TAKE MY BREATH AWAY
   (Rex Smith)
7. WHEN YOU'RE IN LOVE WITH A
   BEAUTIFUL WOMAN
   (Dr. Hook)
8. SHINE A LITTLE LOVE
   (Electric Light Orchestra)
9. MAKIN' IT
   (David Naughton)
10. GOLD
    (John Stewart)

POP ALBUMS

1. BAD GIRLS
   (Donna Summer)
2. BREAKFAST IN AMERICA
   (Supertramp)
3. CHEAP TRICK AT BUDOKAN
   (Cheap Trick)
4. I AM
   (Earth, Wind and Fire)
5. DISCOVERY
   (Electric Light Orchestra)
6. TEDDY
   (Teddy Pendergrass)
7. BACK TO THE EGG
   (Paul McCartney and Wings)
8. CANDY-O
   (The Cars)
9. DYNASTY
   (Kiss)
10. DESOLATION ANGELS
    (Bad Company)

BLACK SINGLES

1. BAD GIRLS
   (Donna Summer)
2. RING MY BELL
   (Anita Ward)
3. TURN OFF THE LIGHTS
   (Teddy Pendergrass)

4. GOOD TIMES
   (Chic)
5. YOU GONNA MAKE ME LOVE SOMEBODY
   ELSE
   (The Jones Girls)
6. AIN'T NO STOPPIN' US NOW
   (McFadden and Whitehead)
7. BOOGIE WONDERLAND
   (Earth, Wind and Fire with The Emotions)
8. WHAT CHA GONNA DO WITH MY LOVIN'
   (Stephanie Mills)
9. CHASE ME
   (Con Funk Shun)
10. HOT STUFF
    (Donna Summer)

BLACK ALBUMS

1. TEDDY
   (Teddy Pendergrass)
2. I AM
   (Earth, Wind and Fire)
3. BAD GIRLS
   (Donna Summer)
4. WINNER TAKES ALL
   (Isley Brothers)
5. SONGS OF LOVE
   (Anita Ward)
6. CANDY
   (Con Funk Shun)
7. STREET LIFE
   (Crusaders)
8. THE JONES GIRLS
   (The Jones Girls)
9. WHAT CHA GONNA DO WITH MY LOVIN'
   (Stephanie Mills)
10. DEVOTION
    (L.T.D.)

JAZZ ALBUMS

1. STREET LIFE
   (Crusaders)
2. MORNING DANCE
   (Spyro Gyra)
3. HEART STRING
   (Earl Klugh)
4. PARADISE
   (Grover Washington Jr.)
5. AN EVENING OF MAGIC
   (Chuck Mangione)
6. NEW CHAUTAUQUA
   (Pat Metheny)
7. LIVIN' INSIDE YOUR LOVE
   (George Benson)
8. JEAN LUC PONTY: LIVE
   (Jean Luc Ponty)
9. I WANNA PLAY FOR YOU
   (Stanley Clarke)
10. TOGETHER
    (McCoy Tyner)

COUNTRY SINGLES

1. SHADOWS IN THE MOONLIGHT
   (Anne Murray)
2. YOU'RE THE ONLY ONE
   (Dolly Parton)
3. AMANDA
   (Waylon Jennings)
4. (GHOST) RIDERS IN THE SKY
   (Johnny Cash)
5. SAVE THE LAST DANCE FOR ME
   (Emmylou Harris)
6. I CAN'T FEEL YOU ANYMORE
   (Loretta Lynn)
7. SUSPICIONS
   (Eddie Rabbitt)
8. PLAY TOGETHER AGAIN AGAIN
   (Buck Owens with Emmylou Harris)
9. WHEN A LOVE AIN'T RIGHT
   (Charly McClain)
10. REUNITED
    (R.C. Bannon and Louise Mandrell)

COUNTRY ALBUMS

1. THE GAMBLER
   (Kenny Rogers)
2. GREATEST HITS
   (Waylon Jennings)
3. ONE FOR THE ROAD
   (Willie Nelson and Leon Russell)
4. GREAT BALLS OF FIRE
   (Dolly Parton)
5. LOVELINE
   (Eddie Rabbitt)
6. STARDUST
   (Willie Nelson)
7. IMAGES
   (Ronnie Milsap)
8. CLASSICS
   (Kenny Rogers and Dottie West)
9. BLUE KENTUCKY GIRL
   (Emmylou Harris)
10. SERVED LIVE
    (Asleep at the Wheel)

JULY 28, 1979

POP SINGLES

1. BAD GIRLS
   (Donna Summer)
2. RING MY BELL
   (Anita Ward)
3. HOT STUFF
   (Donna Summer)
4. SHE BELIEVES IN ME
   (Kenny Rogers)
5. WHEN YOU'RE IN LOVE WITH A
   BEAUTIFUL WOMAN
   (Dr. Hook)
6. I WANT YOU TO WANT ME
   (Cheap Trick)
7. GOLD
   (John Stewart)
8. I WAS MADE FOR LOVIN' YOU
   (Kiss)
9. MAKIN' IT
   (David Naughton)
10. GOOD TIMES
    (Chic)

POP ALBUMS

1. BAD GIRLS
   (Donna Summer)
2. BREAKFAST IN AMERICA
   (Supertramp)
3. CHEAP TRICK AT BUDOKAN
   (Cheap Trick)
4. I AM
   (Earth, Wind and Fire)
5. TEDDY
   (Teddy Pendergrass)
6. DISCOVERY
   (Electric Light Orchestra)
7. BACK TO THE EGG
   (Paul McCartney and Wings)
8. CANDY-O
   (The Cars)
9. GET THE KNACK
   (The Knack)
10. THE GAMBLER
    (Kenny Rogers)

BLACK SINGLES

1. BAD GIRLS
   (Donna Summer)
2. GOOD TIMES
   (Chic)
3. TURN OFF THE LIGHTS
   (Teddy Pendergrass)

4. RING MY BELL
   (Anita Ward)
5. YOU GONNA MAKE ME LOVE SOMEBODY ELSE
   (The Jones Girls)
6. WHAT CHA GONNA DO WITH MY LOVIN'
   (Stephanie Mills)
7. AIN'T NO STOPPIN' US NOW
   (McFadden and Whitehead)
8. BOOGIE WONDERLAND
   (Earth, Wind and Fire with The Emotions)
9. CHASE ME
   (Con Funk Shun)
10. I'M A SUCKER FOR YOUR LOVE
   (Teena Marie)

BLACK ALBUMS

1. TEDDY
   (Teddy Pendergrass)
2. BAD GIRLS
   (Donna Summer)
3. I AM
   (Earth, Wind and Fire)
4. WINNER TAKES ALL
   (Isley Brothers)
5. SONGS OF LOVE
   (Anita Ward)
6. CANDY
   (Con Funk Shun)
7. STREET LIFE
   (Crusaders)
8. THE JONES GIRLS
   (The Jones Girls)
9. WHAT CHA GONNA DO WITH MY LOVIN'
   (Stephanie Mills)
10. DEVOTION
   (L.T.D.)

JAZZ ALBUMS

1. STREET LIFE
   (Crusaders)
2. MORNING DANCE
   (Spyro Gyra)
3. HEART STRING
   (Earl Klugh)
4. AN EVENING OF MAGIC
   (Chuck Mangione)
5. PARADISE
   (Grover Washington Jr.)
6. NEW CHAUTAUQUA
   (Pat Metheny)
7. LIVIN' INSIDE YOUR LOVE
   (George Benson)
8. I WANNA PLAY FOR YOU
   (Stanley Clarke)
9. FEVER
   (Roy Ayers)
10. MINGUS
   (Joni Mitchell)

COUNTRY SINGLES

1. YOU'RE THE ONLY ONE
   (Dolly Parton)
2. (GHOST) RIDERS IN THE SKY
   (Johnny Cash)
3. SHADOWS IN THE MOONLIGHT
   (Anne Murray)
4. SAVE THE LAST DANCE FOR ME
   (Emmylou Harris)
5. SUSPICIONS
   (Eddie Rabbitt)
6. NO ONE ELSE IN THE WORLD
   (Tammy Wynette)
7. COCA COLA COWBOY
   (Mel Tillis)
8. FAMILY TRADITION
   (Hank Williams Jr.)
9. WHEN A LOVE AIN'T RIGHT
   (Charly McClain)
10. REUNITED
   (R.C. Bannon and Louise Mandrell)

COUNTRY ALBUMS

1. THE GAMBLER
   (Kenny Rogers)
2. GREATEST HITS
   (Waylon Jennings)
3. ONE FOR THE ROAD
   (Willie Nelson and Leon Russell)
4. GREAT BALLS OF FIRE
   (Dolly Parton)
5. LOVELINE
   (Eddie Rabbitt)
6. IMAGES
   (Ronnie Milsap)
7. STARDUST
   (Willie Nelson)
8. BLUE KENTUCKY GIRL
   (Emmylou Harris)
9. CLASSICS
   (Kenny Rogers and Dottie West)
10. SERVED LIVE
   (Asleep at the Wheel)

AUGUST 4, 1979

POP SINGLES

1. BAD GIRLS
   (Donna Summer)
2. RING MY BELL
   (Anita Ward)
3. HOT STUFF
   (Donna Summer)
4. WHEN YOU'RE IN LOVE WITH A BEAUTIFUL WOMAN
   (Dr. Hook)
5. GOLD
   (John Stewart)
6. I WAS MADE FOR LOVIN' YOU
   (Kiss)
7. GOOD TIME
   (Chic)
8. I WANT YOU TO WANT ME
   (Cheap Trick)
9. MAKIN' IT
   (David Naughton)
10. SHE BELIEVES IN ME
   (Kenny Rogers)

POP ALBUMS

1. BAD GIRLS
   (Donna Summer)
2. BREAKFAST IN AMERICA
   (Supertramp)
3. GET THE KNACK
   (The Knack)
4. CHEAP TRICK AT BUDOKAN
   (Cheap Trick)
5. TEDDY
   (Teddy Pendergrass)
6. DISCOVERY
   (Electric Light Orchestra)
7. CANDY-O
   (The Cars)
8. I AM
   (Earth, Wind and Fire)
9. THE GAMBLER
   (Kenny Rogers)
10. BACK TO THE EGG
   (Paul McCartney and Wings)

BLACK SINGLES

1. GOOD TIMES
   (Chic)
2. BAD GIRLS
   (Donna Summer)
3. TURN OFF THE LIGHTS
   (Teddy Pendergrass)

4. RING MY BELL
   (Anita Ward)
5. YOU GONNA MAKE ME LOVE SOMEBODY ELSE
   (The Jones Girls)
6. WHAT CHA GONNA DO WITH MY LOVIN'
   (Stephanie Mills)
7. AIN'T NO STOPPIN' US NOW
   (McFadden and Whitehead)
8. I'M A SUCKER FOR YOUR LOVE
   (Teena Marie)
9. CRANK IT UP (FUNK TOWN) PART 1
   (Peter Brown)
10. CHASE ME
   (Con Funk Shun)

BLACK ALBUMS

1. TEDDY
   (Teddy Pendergrass)
2. I AM
   (Earth, Wind and Fire)
3. BAD GIRLS
   (Donna Summer)
4. WINNER TAKES ALL
   (Isley Brothers)
5. STREET LIFE
   (Crusaders)
6. WHAT CHA GONNA DO WITH MY LOVIN'
   (Stephanie Mills)
7. DEVOTION
   (L.T.D.)
8. THE JONES GIRLS
   (The Jones Girls)
9. CANDY
   (Con Funk Shun)
10. THE BOSS
   (Diana Ross)

JAZZ ALBUMS

1. STREET LIFE
   (Crusaders)
2. MORNING DANCE
   (Spyro Gyra)
3. AN EVENING OF MAGIC
   (Chuck Mangione)
4. I WANNA PLAY FOR YOU
   (Stanley Clarke)
5. HEART STRING
   (Earl Klugh)
6. NEW CHAUTAUQUA
   (Pat Metheny)
7. LIVIN' INSIDE YOUR LOVE
   (George Benson)
8. FEVER
   (Roy Ayers)
9. PARADISE
   (Grover Washington Jr.)
10. MINGUS
   (Joni Mitchell)

COUNTRY SINGLES

1. YOU'RE THE ONLY ONE
   (Dolly Parton)
2. (GHOST) RIDERS IN THE SKY
   (Johnny Cash)
3. SUSPICIONS
   (Eddie Rabbitt)
4. SAVE THE LAST DANCE FOR ME
   (Emmylou Harris)
5. COCA COLA COWBOY
   (Mel Tillis)
6. NO ONE ELSE IN THE WORLD
   (Tammy Wynette)
7. FAMILY TRADITION
   (Hank Williams Jr.)
8. SHADOWS IN THE MOONLIGHT
   (Anne Murray)
9. PICK THE WILDWOOD FLOWER
   (Gene Watson)
10. LIBERATED WOMAN
   (John Wesley Ryles)

COUNTRY ALBUMS

1. THE GAMBLER
   (Kenny Rogers)
2. GREATEST HITS
   (Waylon Jennings)
3. ONE FOR THE ROAD
   (Willie Nelson and Leon Russell)
4. LOVELINE
   (Eddie Rabbitt)
5. GREAT BALLS OF FIRE
   (Dolly Parton)
6. MILLION MILE REFLECTIONS
   (The Charlie Daniels Band)
7. BLUE KENTUCKY GIRL
   (Emmylou Harris)
8. STARDUST
   (Willie Nelson)
9. WE SHOULD BE TOGETHER
   (Crystal Gayle)
10. IMAGES
    (Ronnie Milsap)

AUGUST 11, 1979

POP SINGLES

1. MY SHARONA
   (The Knack)
2. BAD GIRLS
   (Donna Summer)
3. GOOD TIMES
   (Chic)
4. WHEN YOU'RE IN LOVE WITH A BEAUTIFUL WOMAN
   (Dr. Hook)
5. GOLD
   (John Stewart)
6. I WAS MADE FOR LOVIN' YOU
   (Kiss)
7. THE MAIN EVENT/FIGHT
   (Barbra Streisand)
8. RING MY BELL
   (Anita Ward)
9. MAMA CAN'T BUY YOU LOVE
   (Elton John)
10. HOT STUFF
    (Donna Summer)

POP ALBUMS

1. GET THE KNACK
   (The Knack)
2. BAD GIRLS
   (Donna Summer)
3. BREAKFAST IN AMERICA
   (Supertramp)
4. CHEAP TRICK AT BUDOKAN
   (Cheap Trick)
5. CANDY-O
   (The Cars)
6. DISCOVERY
   (Electric Light Orchestra)
7. TEDDY
   (Teddy Pendergrass)
8. I AM
   (Earth, Wind and Fire)
9. MILLION MILE REFLECTIONS
   (The Charlie Daniels Band)
10. DYNASTY
    (Kiss)

BLACK SINGLES

1. GOOD TIMES
   (Chic)
2. BAD GIRLS
   (Donna Summer)
3. TURN OFF THE LIGHTS
   (Teddy Pendergrass)
4. RING MY BELL
   (Anita Ward)
5. YOU GONNA MAKE ME LOVE SOMEBODY ELSE
   (The Jones Girls)
6. WHAT CHA GONNA DO WITH MY LOVIN'
   (Stephanie Mills)
7. AFTER THE LOVE HAS GONE
   (Earth, Wind and Fire)
8. I'M A SUCKER FOR YOUR LOVE
   (Teena Marie)
9. CRANK IT UP (FUNK TOWN) PART 1
   (Peter Brown)
10. FOUND A CURE
    (Nick Ashford and Valerie Simpson)

BLACK ALBUMS

1. TEDDY
   (Teddy Pendergrass)
2. I AM
   (Earth, Wind and Fire)
3. BAD GIRLS
   (Donna Summer)
4. WHAT CHA GONNA DO WITH MY LOVIN'
   (Stephanie Mills)
5. STREET LIFE
   (Crusaders)
6. DEVOTION
   (L.T.D.)
7. WINNER TAKES ALL
   (Isley Brothers)
8. THE JONES GIRLS
   (The Jones Girls)
9. THE BOSS
   (Diana Ross)
10. MINNIE
    (Minnie Riperton)

JAZZ ALBUMS

1. STREET LIFE
   (Crusaders)
2. MORNING DANCE
   (Spyro Gyra)
3. AN EVENING OF MAGIC
   (Chuck Mangione)
4. I WANNA PLAY FOR YOU
   (Stanley Clarke)
5. HEART STRING
   (Earl Klugh)
6. NEW CHAUTAUQUA
   (Pat Metheny)
7. MINGUS
   (Joni Mitchell)
8. LIVIN' INSIDE YOUR LOVE
   (George Benson)
9. FEVER
   (Roy Ayers)
10. PARADISE
    (Grover Washington Jr.)

COUNTRY SINGLES

1. SUSPICIONS
   (Eddie Rabbitt)
2. YOU'RE THE ONLY ONE
   (Dolly Parton)
3. COCA COLA COWBOY
   (Mel Tillis)
4. FAMILY TRADITION
   (Hank Williams Jr.)
5. PICK THE WILDWOOD FLOWER
   (Gene Watson)
6. NO ONE ELSE IN THE WORLD
   (Tammy Wynette)
7. THE DEVIL WENT DOWN TO GEORGIA
   (The Charlie Daniels Band)
8. BARSTOOL MOUNTAIN
   (Moe Bandy)
9. LIBERATED WOMAN
   (John Wesley Ryles)
10. STAY WITH ME
    (Dave and Sugar)

COUNTRY ALBUMS

1. THE GAMBLER
   (Kenny Rogers)
2. GREATEST HITS
   (Waylon Jennings)
3. ONE FOR THE ROAD
   (Willie Nelson and Leon Russell)
4. LOVELINE
   (Eddie Rabbitt)
5. WE SHOULD BE TOGETHER
   (Crystal Gayle)
6. MILLION MILE REFLECTIONS
   (The Charlie Daniels Band)
7. GREAT BALLS OF FIRE
   (Dolly Parton)
8. BLUE KENTUCKY GIRL
   (Emmylou Harris)
9. TEN YEARS OF GOLD
   (Kenny Rogers)
10. IMAGES
    (Ronnie Milsap)

AUGUST 18, 1979

POP SINGLES

1. MY SHARONA
   (The Knack)
2. GOOD TIMES
   (Chic)
3. BAD GIRLS
   (Donna Summer)
4. THE MAIN EVENT/FIGHT
   (Barbra Streisand)
5. I WAS MADE FOR LOVIN' YOU
   (Kiss)
6. WHEN YOU'RE IN LOVE WITH A BEAUTIFUL WOMAN
   (Dr. Hook)
7. MAMA CAN'T BUY YOU LOVE
   (Elton John)
8. GOLD
   (John Stewart)
9. RING MY BELL
   (Anita Ward)
10. AFTER THE LOVE HAS GONE
    (Earth, Wind and Fire)

POP ALBUMS

1. GET THE KNACK
   (The Knack)
2. BAD GIRLS
   (Donna Summer)
3. BREAKFAST IN AMERICA
   (Supertramp)
4. CANDY-O
   (The Cars)
5. CHEAP TRICK AT BUDOKAN
   (Cheap Trick)
6. DISCOVERY
   (Electric Light Orchestra)
7. TEDDY
   (Teddy Pendergrass)
8. I AM
   (Earth, Wind and Fire)
9. MILLION MILE REFLECTIONS
   (The Charlie Daniels Band)
10. DYNASTY
    (Kiss)

BLACK SINGLES

1. GOOD TIMES
   (Chic)
2. AFTER THE LOVE HAS GONE
   (Earth, Wind and Fire)
3. BAD GIRLS
   (Donna Summer)

4. TURN OFF THE LIGHTS
   (Teddy Pendergrass)
5. WHAT CHA GONNA DO WITH MY LOVIN'
   (Stephanie Mills)
6. FOUND A CURE
   (Nick Ashford and Valerie Simpson)
7. YOU GONNA MAKE ME LOVE SOMEBODY
   ELSE
   (The Jones Girls)
8. FIRECRACKER
   (Mass Production)
9. DON'T STOP 'TIL YOU GET ENOUGH
   (Michael Jackson)
10. THE BOSS
    (Diana Ross)

BLACK ALBUMS

1. TEDDY
   (Teddy Pendergrass)
2. I AM
   (Earth, Wind and Fire)
3. BAD GIRLS
   (Donna Summer)
4. WHAT CHA GONNA DO WITH MY LOVIN'
   (Stephanie Mills)
5. MIDNIGHT MAGIC
   (Commodores)
6. STREET LIFE
   (Crusaders)
7. MINNIE
   (Minnie Riperton)
8. THE BOSS
   (Diana Ross)
9. WINNER TAKES ALL
   (Isley Brothers)
10. DEVOTION
    (L.T.D.)

JAZZ ALBUMS

1. STREET LIFE
   (Crusaders)
2. MORNING DANCE
   (Spyro Gyra)
3. AN EVENING OF MAGIC
   (Chuck Mangione)
4. I WANNA PLAY FOR YOU
   (Stanley Clarke)
5. HEART STRING
   (Earl Klugh)
6. NEW CHAUTAUQUA
   (Pat Metheny)
7. MINGUS
   (Joni Mitchell)
8. LUCKY SEVEN
   (Bob James)
9. FEVER
   (Roy Ayers)
10. PARADISE
    (Grover Washington Jr.)

COUNTRY SINGLES

1. COCA COLA COWBOY
   (Mel Tillis)
2. THE DEVIL WENT DOWN TO GEORGIA
   (The Charlie Daniels Band)
3. FAMILY TRADITION
   (Hank Williams Jr.)
4. PICK THE WILDWOOD FLOWER
   (Gene Watson)
5. SUSPICIONS
   (Eddie Rabbitt)
6. STAY WITH ME
   (Dave and Sugar)
7. HEARTBREAK HOTEL
   (Willie Nelson and Leon Russell)
8. BARSTOOL MOUNTAIN
   (Moe Bandy)
9. TILL I CAN MAKE IT ON MY OWN
   (Kenny Rogers and Dottie West)
10. DON'T LET ME CROSS OVER
    (Jim Reeves)

COUNTRY ALBUMS

1. THE GAMBLER
   (Kenny Rogers)
2. GREATEST HITS
   (Waylon Jennings)
3. ONE FOR THE ROAD
   (Willie Nelson and Leon Russell)
4. LOVELINE
   (Eddie Rabbitt)
5. WE SHOULD BE TOGETHER
   (Crystal Gayle)
6. MILLION MILE REFLECTIONS
   (The Charlie Daniels Band)
7. GREAT BALLS OF FIRE
   (Dolly Parton)
8. BLUE KENTUCKY GIRL
   (Emmylou Harris)
9. TEN YEARS OF GOLD
   (Kenny Rogers)
10. STARDUST
    (Willie Nelson)

AUGUST 25, 1979

POP SINGLES

1. MY SHARONA
   (The Knack)
2. GOOD TIMES
   (Chic)
3. THE MAIN EVENT/FIGHT
   (Barbra Streisand)
4. BAD GIRLS
   (Donna Summer)
5. AFTER THE LOVE HAS GONE
   (Earth, Wind and Fire)
6. THE DEVIL WENT DOWN TO GEORGIA
   (The Charlie Daniels Band)
7. MAMA CAN'T BUY YOU LOVE
   (Elton John)
8. LEAD ME ON
   (Maxine Nightingale)
9. I WAS MADE FOR LOVIN' YOU
   (Kiss)
10. RING MY BELL
    (Anita Ward)

POP ALBUMS

1. GET THE KNACK
   (The Knack)
2. BAD GIRLS
   (Donna Summer)
3. BREAKFAST IN AMERICA
   (Supertramp)
4. CANDY-O
   (The Cars)
5. I AM
   (Earth, Wind and Fire)
6. DISCOVERY
   (Electric Light Orchestra)
7. TEDDY
   (Teddy Pendergrass)
8. CHEAP TRICK AT BUDOKAN
   (Cheap Trick)
9. REALITY . . . WHAT A CONCEPT
   (Robin Williams)
10. MILLION MILE REFLECTIONS
    (The Charlie Daniels Band)

BLACK SINGLES

1. GOOD TIMES
   (Chic)
2. AFTER THE LOVE HAS GONE
   (Earth, Wind and Fire)
3. FOUND A CURE
   (Nick Ashford and Valerie Simpson)

4. FIRECRACKER
   (Mass Production)
5. DON'T STOP 'TIL YOU GET ENOUGH
   (Michael Jackson)
6. WHAT CHA GONNA DO WITH MY LOVIN'
   (Stephanie Mills)
7. TURN OFF THE LIGHTS
   (Teddy Pendergrass)
8. BAD GIRLS
   (Donna Summer)
9. THE BOSS
   (Diana Ross)
10. YOU GONNA MAKE ME LOVE SOMEBODY
    ELSE
    (The Jones Girls)

BLACK ALBUMS

1. TEDDY
   (Teddy Pendergrass)
2. I AM
   (Earth, Wind and Fire)
3. MIDNIGHT MAGIC
   (Commodores)
4. WHAT CHA GONNA DO WITH MY LOVIN'
   (Stephanie Mills)
5. BAD GIRLS
   (Donna Summer)
6. STREET LIFE
   (Crusaders)
7. RISQUE
   (Chic)
8. MINNIE
   (Minnie Riperton)
9. THE BOSS
   (Diana Ross)
10. SECRET OMEN
    (Cameo)

JAZZ ALBUMS

1. STREET LIFE
   (Crusaders)
2. MORNING DANCE
   (Spyro Gyra)
3. AN EVENING OF MAGIC
   (Chuck Mangione)
4. I WANNA PLAY FOR YOU
   (Stanley Clarke)
5. LUCKY SEVEN
   (Bob James)
6. MINGUS
   (Joni Mitchell)
7. HEART STRING
   (Earl Klugh)
8. NEW CHAUTAUQUA
   (Pat Metheny)
9. FEVER
   (Roy Ayers)
10. PARADISE
    (Grover Washington Jr.)

COUNTRY SINGLES

1. THE DEVIL WENT DOWN TO GEORGIA
   (The Charlie Daniels Band)
2. COCA COLA COWBOY
   (Mel Tillis)
3. HEARTBREAK HOTEL
   (Willie Nelson and Leon Russell)
4. I MAY NEVER GET TO HEAVEN
   (Conway Twitty)
5. STAY WITH ME
   (Dave and Sugar)
6. TILL I CAN MAKE IT ON MY OWN
   (Kenny Rogers and Dottie West)
7. PICK THE WILDWOOD FLOWER
   (Gene Watson)
8. YOU'RE MY JAMAICA
   (Charley Pride)
9. FAMILY TRADITION
   (Hank Williams Jr.)
10. HERE WE ARE AGAIN
    (The Statler Brothers)

COUNTRY ALBUMS

1. THE GAMBLER
   (Kenny Rogers)
2. GREATEST HITS
   (Waylon Jennings)
3. ONE FOR THE ROAD
   (Willie Nelson and Leon Russell)
4. WE SHOULD BE TOGETHER
   (Crystal Gayle)
5. LOVELINE
   (Eddie Rabbitt)
6. MILLION MILE REFLECTIONS
   (The Charlie Daniels Band)
7. GREAT BALLS OF FIRE
   (Dolly Parton)
8. BLUE KENTUCKY GIRL
   (Emmylou Harris)
9. NEW KIND OF FEELING
   (Anne Murray)
10. IMAGES
    (Ronnie Milsap)

SEPTEMBER 1, 1979

POP SINGLES

1. MY SHARONA
   (The Knack)
2. GOOD TIMES
   (Chic)
3. THE DEVIL WENT DOWN TO GEORGIA
   (The Charlie Daniels Band)
4. AFTER THE LOVE HAS GONE
   (Earth, Wind and Fire)
5. LEAD ME ON
   (Maxine Nightingale)
6. BAD GIRLS
   (Donna Summer)
7. THE MAIN EVENT/FIGHT
   (Barbra Streisand)
8. SAD EYES
   (Robert John)
9. DON'T BRING ME DOWN
   (Electric Light Orchestra)
10. LONESOME LOSER
    (Little River Band)

POP ALBUMS

1. GET THE KNACK
   (The Knack)
2. BREAKFAST IN AMERICA
   (Supertramp)
3. BAD GIRLS
   (Donna Summer)
4. CANDY-O
   (The Cars)
5. I AM
   (Earth, Wind and Fire)
6. DISCOVERY
   (Electric Light Orchestra)
7. CHEAP TRICK AT BUDOKAN
   (Cheap Trick)
8. TEDDY
   (Teddy Pendergrass)
9. REALITY . . . WHAT A CONCEPT
   (Robin Williams)
10. MILLION MILE REFLECTIONS
    (The Charlie Daniels Band)

BLACK SINGLES

1. DON'T STOP 'TIL YOU GET ENOUGH
   (Michael Jackson)
2. GOOD TIMES
   (Chic)
3. FOUND A CURE
   (Nick Ashford and Valerie Simpson)

4. FIRECRACKER
   (Mass Production)
5. AFTER THE LOVE HAS GONE
   (Earth, Wind and Fire)
6. WHAT CHA GONNA DO WITH MY LOVIN'
   (Stephanie Mills)
7. I JUST WANT TO BE
   (Cameo)
8. TURN OFF THE LIGHTS
   (Teddy Pendergrass)
9. THE BOSS
   (Diana Ross)
10. BAD GIRLS
    (Donna Summer)

BLACK ALBUMS

1. TEDDY
   (Teddy Pendergrass)
2. I AM
   (Earth, Wind and Fire)
3. MIDNIGHT MAGIC
   (Commodores)
4. RISQUE
   (Chic)
5. WHAT CHA GONNA DO WITH MY LOVIN'
   (Stephanie Mills)
6. STAY FREE
   (Nick Ashford and Valerie Simpson)
7. OFF THE WALL
   (Michael Jackson)
8. STREET LIFE
   (Crusaders)
9. SECRET OMEN
   (Cameo)
10. BAD GIRLS
    (Donna Summer)

JAZZ ALBUMS

1. STREET LIFE
   (Crusaders)
2. MORNING DANCE
   (Spyro Gyra)
3. LUCKY SEVEN
   (Bob James)
4. AN EVENING OF MAGIC
   (Chuck Mangione)
5. I WANNA PLAY FOR YOU
   (Stanley Clarke)
6. MINGUS
   (Joni Mitchell)
7. HEART STRING
   (Earl Klugh)
8. EUPHORIA
   (Gato Barbieri)
9. NEW CHAUTAUQUA
   (Pat Metheny)
10. PARADISE
    (Grover Washington Jr.)

COUNTRY SINGLES

1. THE DEVIL WENT DOWN TO GEORGIA
   (The Charlie Daniels Band)
2. HEARTBREAK HOTEL
   (Willie Nelson and Leon Russell)
3. I MAY NEVER GET TO HEAVEN
   (Conway Twitty)
4. TILL I CAN MAKE IT ON MY OWN
   (Kenny Rogers and Dottie West)
5. STAY WITH ME
   (Dave and Sugar)
6. YOU'RE MY JAMAICA
   (Charley Pride)
7. COCA COLA COWBOY
   (Mel Tillis)
8. JUST GOOD OL' BOYS
   (Moe Bandy and Joe Stampley)
9. HERE WE ARE AGAIN
   (The Statler Brothers)
10. YOUR KISSES WILL
    (Crystal Gayle)

COUNTRY ALBUMS

1. THE GAMBLER
   (Kenny Rogers)
2. GREATEST HITS
   (Waylon Jennings)
3. ONE FOR THE ROAD
   (Willie Nelson and Leon Russell)
4. MILLION MILE REFLECTIONS
   (The Charlie Daniels Band)
5. LOVELINE
   (Eddie Rabbitt)
6. WE SHOULD BE TOGETHER
   (Crystal Gayle)
7. NEW KIND OF FEELING
   (Anne Murray)
8. GREAT BALLS OF FIRE
   (Dolly Parton)
9. BLUE KENTUCKY GIRL
   (Emmylou Harris)
10. WILLIE AND FAMILY LIVE
    (Willie Nelson)

SEPTEMBER 8, 1979

POP SINGLES

1. MY SHARONA
   (The Knack)
2. SAD EYES
   (Robert John)
3. THE DEVIL WENT DOWN TO GEORGIA
   (The Charlie Daniels Band)
4. AFTER THE LOVE HAS GONE
   (Earth, Wind and Fire)
5. LEAD ME ON
   (Maxine Nightingale)
6. GOOD TIMES
   (Chic)
7. DON'T BRING ME DOWN
   (Electric Light Orchestra)
8. LONESOME LOSER
   (Little River Band)
9. THE MAIN EVENT/FIGHT
   (Barbra Streisand)
10. BAD GIRLS
    (Donna Summer)

POP ALBUMS

1. IN THROUGH THE OUT DOOR
   (Led Zeppelin)
2. BREAKFAST IN AMERICA
   (Supertramp)
3. GET THE KNACK
   (The Knack)
4. CANDY-O
   (The Cars)
5. BAD GIRLS
   (Donna Summer)
6. DISCOVERY
   (Electric Light Orchestra)
7. CHEAP TRICK AT BUDOKAN
   (Cheap Trick)
8. MIDNIGHT MAGIC
   (Commodores)
9. I AM
   (Earth, Wind and Fire)
10. MILLION MILE REFLECTIONS
    (The Charlie Daniels Band)

BLACK SINGLES

1. DON'T STOP 'TIL YOU GET ENOUGH
   (Michael Jackson)
2. FIRECRACKER
   (Mass Production)
3. FOUND A CURE
   (Nick Ashford and Valerie Simpson)

4. GOOD TIMES
   (Chic)
5. AFTER THE LOVE HAS GONE
   (Earth, Wind and Fire)
6. I JUST WANT TO BE
   (Cameo)
7. WHAT CHA GONNA DO WITH MY LOVIN'
   (Stephanie Mills)
8. TURN OFF THE LIGHTS
   (Teddy Pendergrass)
9. THE BOSS
   (Diana Ross)
10. I DO LOVE YOU/MAKE MY DREAMS A
    REALITY
    (G.Q.)

BLACK ALBUMS

1. MIDNIGHT MAGIC
   (Commodores)
2. TEDDY
   (Teddy Pendergrass)
3. RISQUE
   (Chic)
4. OFF THE WALL
   (Michael Jackson)
5. STAY FREE
   (Nick Ashford and Valerie Simpson)
6. I AM
   (Earth, Wind and Fire)
7. WHAT CHA GONNA DO WITH MY LOVIN'
   (Stephanie Mills)
8. STREET LIFE
   (Crusaders)
9. SECRET OMEN
   (Cameo)
10. THE BOSS
    (Diana Ross)

JAZZ ALBUMS

1. STREET LIFE
   (Crusaders)
2. MORNING DANCE
   (Spyro Gyra)
3. LUCKY SEVEN
   (Bob James)
4. I WANNA PLAY FOR YOU
   (Stanley Clarke)
5. AN EVENING OF MAGIC
   (Chuck Mangione)
6. HEART STRING
   (Earl Klugh)
7. MINGUS
   (Joni Mitchell)
8. HIGH GEAR
   (Neil Larsen)
9. WATER SIGN
   (Jeff Lorber Fusion)
10. EUPHORIA
    (Gato Barbieri)

COUNTRY SINGLES

1. I MAY NEVER GET TO HEAVEN
   (Conway Twitty)
2. HEARTBREAK HOTEL
   (Willie Nelson and Leon Russell)
3. YOU'RE MY JAMAICA
   (Charley Pride)
4. TILL I CAN MAKE IT ON MY OWN
   (Kenny Rogers and Dottie West)
5. THE DEVIL WENT DOWN TO GEORGIA
   (The Charlie Daniels Band)
6. JUST GOOD OL' BOYS
   (Moe Bandy and Joe Stampley)
7. YOUR KISSES WILL
   (Crystal Gayle)
8. IT MUST BE LOVE
   (Don Williams)
9. HERE WE ARE AGAIN
   (The Statler Brothers)
10. FOOLS FOR EACH OTHER
    (Johnny Rodriguez)

COUNTRY ALBUMS

1. THE GAMBLER
   (Kenny Rogers)
2. GREATEST HITS
   (Waylon Jennings)
3. MILLION MILE REFLECTIONS
   (The Charlie Daniels Band)
4. ONE FOR THE ROAD
   (Willie Nelson and Leon Russell)
5. STARDUST
   (Willie Nelson)
6. LOVELINE
   (Eddie Rabbitt)
7. NEW KIND OF FEELING
   (Anne Murray)
8. WE SHOULD BE TOGETHER
   (Crystal Gayle)
9. TEN YEARS OF GOLD
   (Kenny Rogers)
10. WILLIE AND FAMILY LIVE
    (Willie Nelson)

SEPTEMBER 15, 1979

POP SINGLES

1. SAD EYES
   (Robert John)
2. MY SHARONA
   (The Knack)
3. DON'T BRING ME DOWN
   (Electric Light Orchestra)
4. LEAD ME ON
   (Maxine Nightingale)
5. THE DEVIL WENT DOWN TO GEORGIA
   (The Charlie Daniels Band)
6. LONESOME LOSER
   (Little River Band)
7. AFTER THE LOVE HAS GONE
   (Earth, Wind and Fire)
8. GOOD TIMES
   (Chic)
9. I'LL NEVER LOVE THIS WAY AGAIN
   (Dionne Warwick)
10. THE MAIN EVENT/FIGHT
    (Barbra Streisand)

POP ALBUMS

1. IN THROUGH THE OUT DOOR
   (Led Zeppelin)
2. GET THE KNACK
   (The Knack)
3. BREAKFAST IN AMERICA
   (Supertramp)
4. CANDY-O
   (The Cars)
5. DISCOVERY
   (Electric Light Orchestra)
6. BAD GIRLS
   (Donna Summer)
7. MIDNIGHT MAGIC
   (Commodores)
8. I AM
   (Earth, Wind and Fire)
9. FIRST UNDER THE WIRE
   (Little River Band)
10. RISQUE
    (Chic)

BLACK SINGLES

1. DON'T STOP 'TIL YOU GET ENOUGH
   (Michael Jackson)
2. FIRECRACKER
   (Mass Production)
3. I JUST WANT TO BE
   (Cameo)

4. FOUND A CURE
   (Nick Ashford and Valerie Simpson)
5. GOOD TIMES
   (Chic)
6. AFTER THE LOVE HAS GONE
   (Earth, Wind and Fire)
7. WHAT CHA GONNA DO WITH MY LOVIN'
   (Stephanie Mills)
8. I DO LOVE YOU/MAKE MY DREAMS A
   REALITY
   (G.Q.)
9. THE BOSS
   (Diana Ross)
10. RISE
    (Herb Alpert)

BLACK ALBUMS

1. MIDNIGHT MAGIC
   (Commodores)
2. OFF THE WALL
   (Michael Jackson)
3. RISQUE
   (Chic)
4. TEDDY
   (Teddy Pendergrass)
5. STAY FREE
   (Nick Ashford and Valerie Simpson)
6. I AM
   (Earth, Wind and Fire)
7. WHAT CHA GONNA DO WITH MY LOVIN'
   (Stephanie Mills)
8. SECRET OMEN
   (Cameo)
9. IDENTIFY YOURSELF
   (The O'Jays)
10. STREET LIFE
    (Crusaders)

JAZZ ALBUMS

1. STREET LIFE
   (Crusaders)
2. MORNING DANCE
   (Spyro Gyra)
3. LUCKY SEVEN
   (Bob James)
4. AN EVENING OF MAGIC
   (Chuck Mangione)
5. I WANNA PLAY FOR YOU
   (Stanley Clarke)
6. MINGUS
   (Joni Mitchell)
7. HEART STRING
   (Earl Klugh)
8. WATER SIGN
   (Jeff Lorber Fusion)
9. HOT
   (Maynard Ferguson)
10. EUPHORIA
    (Gato Barbieri)

COUNTRY SINGLES

1. YOU'RE MY JAMAICA
   (Charley Pride)
2. I MAY NEVER GET TO HEAVEN
   (Conway Twitty)
3. JUST GOOD OL' BOYS
   (Moe Bandy and Joe Stampley)
4. IT MUST BE LOVE
   (Don Williams)
5. TILL I CAN MAKE IT ON MY OWN
   (Kenny Rogers and Dottie West)
6. YOUR KISSES WILL
   (Crystal Gayle)
7. FOOLS
   (Jim Ed Brown and Helen Cornelius)
8. MY SILVER LINING
   (Mickey Gilley)
9. ONLY LOVE CAN BREAK A HEART
   (Kenny Dale)
10. DADDY
    (Donna Fargo)

COUNTRY ALBUMS

1. THE GAMBLER
   (Kenny Rogers)
2. GREATEST HITS
   (Waylon Jennings)
3. MILLION MILE REFLECTIONS
   (The Charlie Daniels Band)
4. ONE FOR THE ROAD
   (Willie Nelson and Leon Russell)
5. STARDUST
   (Willie Nelson)
6. LOVELINE
   (Eddie Rabbitt)
7. WE SHOULD BE TOGETHER
   (Crystal Gayle)
8. LET'S KEEP IT THAT WAY
   (Anne Murray)
9. TEN YEARS OF GOLD
   (Kenny Rogers)
10. CLASSICS
    (Kenny Rogers and Dottie West)

SEPTEMBER 22, 1979

POP SINGLES

1. SAD EYES
   (Robert John)
2. MY SHARONA
   (The Knack)
3. DON'T BRING ME DOWN
   (Electric Light Orchestra)
4. LONESOME LOSER
   (Little River Band)
5. THE DEVIL WENT DOWN TO GEORGIA
   (The Charlie Daniels Band)
6. LEAD ME ON
   (Maxine Nightingale)
7. I'LL NEVER LOVE THIS WAY AGAIN
   (Dionne Warwick)
8. SAIL ON
   (Commodores)
9. GOOD TIMES
   (Chic)
10. BAD CASE OF LOVING YOU (DOCTOR, DOCTOR)
    (Robert Palmer)

POP ALBUMS

1. IN THROUGH THE OUT DOORS
   (Led Zeppelin)
2. GET THE KNACK
   (The Knack)
3. MIDNIGHT MAGIC
   (Commodores)
4. BREAKFAST IN AMERICA
   (Supertramp)
5. DISCOVERY
   (Electric Light Orchestra)
6. CANDY-O
   (The Cars)
7. FIRST UNDER THE WIRE
   (Little River Band)
8. I AM
   (Earth, Wind and Fire)
9. OFF THE WALL
   (Michael Jackson)
10. RISQUE
    (Chic)

BLACK SINGLES

1. DON'T STOP 'TIL YOU GET ENOUGH
   (Michael Jackson)
2. I JUST WANT TO BE
   (Cameo)
3. **FIRECRACKER**
   (Mass Production)

---

4. FOUND A CURE
   (Nick Ashford and Valerie Simpson)
5. GOOD TIMES
   (Chic)
6. SAIL ON
   (Commodores)
7. (NOT JUST) KNEE DEEP—PART 1
   (Funkadelic)
8. I DO LOVE YOU/MAKE MY DREAMS A REALITY
   (G.Q.)
9. RISE
   (Herb Alpert)
10. AFTER THE LOVE HAS GONE
    (Earth, Wind and Fire)

BLACK ALBUMS

1. OFF THE WALL
   (Michael Jackson)
2. MIDNIGHT MAGIC
   (Commodores)
3. RISQUE
   (Chic)
4. STAY FREE
   (Nick Ashford and Valerie Simpson)
5. TEDDY
   (Teddy Pendergrass)
6. I AM
   (Earth, Wind and Fire)
7. IDENTIFY YOURSELF
   (The O'Jays)
8. SECRET OMEN
   (Cameo)
9. WHAT CHA GONNA DO WITH MY LOVIN'
   (Stephanie Mills)
10. THE BOSS
    (Diana Ross)

JAZZ ALBUMS

1. STREET LIFE
   (Crusaders)
2. LUCKY SEVEN
   (Bob James)
3. MORNING DANCE
   (Spyro Gyra)
4. I WANNA PLAY FOR YOU
   (Stanley Clarke)
5. MINGUS
   (Joni Mitchell)
6. AN EVENING OF MAGIC
   (Chuck Mangione)
7. HIGH GEAR
   (Neil Larsen)
8. HEART STRING
   (Earl Klugh)
9. WATER SIGN
   (Jeff Lorber Fusion)
10. EUPHORIA
    (Gato Barbieri)

COUNTRY SINGLES

1. JUST GOOD OL' BOYS
   (Moe Bandy and Joe Stampley)
2. IT MUST BE LOVE
   (Don Williams)
3. YOU'RE MY JAMAICA
   (Charley Pride)
4. FOOLS
   (Jim Ed Brown and Helen Cornelius)
5. BEFORE MY TIME
   (John Conlee)
6. LAST CHEATER'S WALTZ
   (T.G. Sheppard)
7. MY SILVER LINING
   (Mickey Gilley)
8. ONLY LOVE CAN BREAK A HEART
   (Kenny Dale)
9. YOUR KISSES WILL
   (Crystal Gayle)
10. THERE'S A HONKY TONK ANGEL (WHO WILL TAKE ME BACK IN)
    (Elvis Presley)

COUNTRY ALBUMS

1. THE GAMBLER
   (Kenny Rogers)
2. GREATEST HITS
   (Waylon Jennings)
3. MILLION MILE REFLECTIONS
   (The Charlie Daniels Band)
4. ONE FOR THE ROAD
   (Willie Nelson and Leon Russell)
5. STARDUST
   (Willie Nelson)
6. LOVELINE
   (Eddie Rabbitt)
7. WE SHOULD BE TOGETHER
   (Crystal Gayle)
8. LET'S KEEP IT THAT WAY
   (Anne Murray)
9. TEN YEARS OF GOLD
   (Kenny Rogers)
10. CLASSICS
    (Kenny Rogers and Dottie West)

SEPTEMBER 29, 1979

POP SINGLES

1. SAD EYES
   (Robert John)
2. MY SHARONA
   (The Knack)
3. DON'T BRING ME DOWN
   (Electric Light Orchestra)
4. LONESOME LOSER
   (Little River Band)
5. SAIL ON
   (Commodores)
6. I'LL NEVER LOVE THIS WAY AGAIN
   (Dionne Warwick)
7. LEAD ME ON
   (Maxine Nightingale)
8. RISE
   (Herb Alpert)
9. BAD CASE OF LOVING YOU (DOCTOR, DOCTOR)
   (Robert Palmer)
10. THE DEVIL WENT DOWN TO GEORGIA
    (The Charlie Daniels Band)

POP ALBUMS

1. IN THROUGH THE OUT DOOR
   (Led Zeppelin)
2. GET THE KNACK
   (The Knack)
3. MIDNIGHT MAGIC
   (Commodores)
4. BREAKFAST IN AMERICA
   (Supertramp)
5. CANDY-O
   (The Cars)
6. OFF THE WALL
   (Michael Jackson)
7. FIRST UNDER THE WIRE
   (Little River Band)
8. BAD GIRLS
   (Donna Summer)
9. DISCOVERY
   (Electric Light Orchestra)
10. RISQUE
    (Chic)

BLACK SINGLES

1. DON'T STOP 'TIL YOU GET ENOUGH
   (Michael Jackson)
2. I JUST WANT TO BE
   (Cameo)
3. **FIRECRACKER**
   (Mass Production)

4. (NOT JUST) KNEE DEEP—PART 1
   (Funkadelic)
5. FOUND A CURE
   (Nick Ashford and Valerie Simpson)
6. SAIL ON
   (Commodores)
7. I DO LOVE YOU/MAKE MY DREAMS A
   REALITY
   (G.Q.)
8. RISE
   (Herb Alpert)
9. GOOD TIMES
   (Chic)
10. SING A HAPPY SONG
    (The O'Jays)

BLACK ALBUMS

1. OFF THE WALL
   (Michael Jackson)
2. MIDNIGHT MAGIC
   (Commodores)
3. RISQUE
   (Chic)
4. STAY FREE
   (Nick Ashford and Valerie Simpson)
5. IDENTIFY YOURSELF
   (The O'Jays)
6. TEDDY
   (Teddy Pendergrass)
7. SECRET OMEN
   (Cameo)
8. I AM
   (Earth, Wind and Fire)
9. WHAT CHA GONNA DO WITH MY LOVIN'
   (Stephanie Mills)
10. THE BOSS
    (Diana Ross)

JAZZ ALBUMS

1. STREET LIFE
   (Crusaders)
2. MORNING DANCE
   (Spyro Gyra)
3. LUCKY SEVEN
   (Bob James)
4. MINGUS
   (Joni Mitchell)
5. I WANNA PLAY FOR YOU
   (Stanley Clarke)
6. AN EVENING OF MAGIC
   (Chuck Mangione)
7. HIGH GEAR
   (Neil Larsen)
8. HEART STRING
   (Earl Klugh)
9. WATER SIGN
   (Jeff Lorber Fusion)
10. EUPHORIA
    (Gato Barbieri)

COUNTRY SINGLES

1. IT MUST BE LOVE
   (Don Williams)
2. JUST GOOD OL' BOYS
   (Moe Bandy and Joe Stampley)
3. FOOLS
   (Jim Ed Brown and Helen Cornelius)
4. BEFORE MY TIME
   (John Conlee)
5. LAST CHEATER'S WALTZ
   (T.G. Sheppard)
6. YOU'RE MY JAMAICA
   (Charley Pride)
7. THERE'S A HONKY TONK ANGEL (WHO
   WILL TAKE ME BACK IN)
   (Elvis Presley)
8. ONLY LOVE CAN BREAK A HEART
   (Kenny Dale)
9. FOOLED BY A FEELING
   (Barbara Mandrell)
10. DREAM ON
    (The Oak Ridge Boys)

COUNTRY ALBUMS

1. THE GAMBLER
   (Kenny Rogers)
2. GREATEST HITS
   (Waylon Jennings)
3. KENNY
   (Kenny Rogers)
4. MILLION MILE REFLECTIONS
   (The Charlie Daniels Band)
5. ONE FOR THE ROAD
   (Willie Nelson and Leon Russell)
6. JUST FOR THE RECORD
   (Barbara Mandrell)
7. LOVELINE
   (Eddie Rabbitt)
8. STARDUST
   (Willie Nelson)
9. WE SHOULD BE TOGETHER
   (Crystal Gayle)
10. TEN YEARS OF GOLD
    (Kenny Rogers)

OCTOBER 6, 1979

POP SINGLES

1. SAD EYES
   (Robert John)
2. MY SHARONA
   (The Knack)
3. SAIL ON
   (Commodores)
4. LONESOME LOSER
   (Little River Band)
5. I'LL NEVER LOVE THIS WAY AGAIN
   (Dionne Warwick)
6. RISE
   (Herb Alpert)
7. DON'T STOP 'TIL YOU GET ENOUGH
   (Michael Jackson)
8. DON'T BRING ME DOWN
   (Electric Light Orchestra)
9. POP MUZIK
   (M)
10. DRIVERS SEAT
    (Sniff 'n' the Tears)

POP ALBUMS

1. IN THROUGH THE OUT DOOR
   (Led Zeppelin)
2. MIDNIGHT MAGIC
   (Commodores)
3. GET THE KNACK
   (The Knack)
4. OFF THE WALL
   (Michael Jackson)
5. BREAKFAST IN AMERICA
   (Supertramp)
6. HEAD GAMES
   (Foreigner)
7. CANDY-O
   (The Cars)
8. BAD GIRLS
   (Donna Summer)
9. SLOW TRAIN COMING
   (Bob Dylan)
10. FIRST UNDER THE WIRE
    (Little River Band)

BLACK SINGLES

1. DON'T STOP 'TIL YOU GET ENOUGH
   (Michael Jackson)
2. (NOT JUST) KNEE DEEP—PART 1
   (Funkadelic)
3. I JUST WANT TO BE
   (Cameo)
4. FIRECRACKER
   (Mass Production)

5. FOUND A CURE
   (Nick Ashford and Valerie Simpson)
6. LADIES' NIGHT
   (Kool and the Gang)
7. I DO LOVE YOU/MAKE MY DREAMS A
   REALITY
   (G.Q.)
8. RISE
   (Herb Alpert)
9. SAIL ON
   (Commodores)
10. GOOD TIMES
    (Chic)

BLACK ALBUMS

1. OFF THE WALL
   (Michael Jackson)
2. MIDNIGHT MAGIC
   (Commodores)
3. IDENTIFY YOURSELF
   (The O'Jays)
4. STAY FREE
   (Nick Ashford and Valerie Simpson)
5. RISQUE
   (Chic)
6. SECRET OMEN
   (Cameo)
7. TEDDY
   (Teddy Pendergrass)
8. LADIES' NIGHT
   (Kool and the Gang)
9. WHAT CHA GONNA DO WITH MY LOVIN'
   (Stephanie Mills)
10. THE BOSS
    (Diana Ross)

JAZZ ALBUMS

1. STREET LIFE
   (Crusaders)
2. MORNING DANCE
   (Spyro Gyra)
3. LUCKY SEVEN
   (Bob James)
4. MINGUS
   (Joni Mitchell)
5. I WANNA PLAY FOR YOU
   (Stanley Clarke)
6. HIGH GEAR
   (Neil Larsen)
7. WATER SIGN
   (Jeff Lorber Fusion)
8. AN EVENING OF MAGIC
   (Chuck Mangione)
9. 8:30
   (Weather Report)
10. HEART STRING
    (Earl Klugh)

COUNTRY SINGLES

1. LAST CHEATER'S WALTZ
   (T.G. Sheppard)
2. BEFORE MY TIME
   (John Conlee)
3. FOOLS
   (Jim Ed Brown and Helen Cornelius)
4. IT MUST BE LOVE
   (Don Williams)
5. FOOLED BY A FEELING
   (Barbara Mandrell)
6. DREAM ON
   (The Oak Ridge Boys)
7. THERE'S A HONKY TONK ANGEL (WHO
   WILL TAKE ME BACK IN)
   (Elvis Presley)
8. IN NO TIME AT ALL
   (Ronnie Milsap)
9. YOU AIN'T JUST WHISTLIN' DIXIE
   (The Bellamy Brothers)
10. ALL THE GOLD IN CALIFORNIA
    (Larry Gatlin and the Gatlin Brothers Band)

COUNTRY ALBUMS

1. THE GAMBLER
   (Kenny Rogers)
2. GREATEST HITS
   (Waylon Jennings)
3. KENNY
   (Kenny Rogers)
4. MILLION MILE REFLECTIONS
   (The Charlie Daniels Band)
5. ONE FOR THE ROAD
   (Willie Nelson and Leon Russell)
6. JUST FOR THE RECORD
   (Barbara Mandrell)
7. LOVELINE
   (Eddie Rabbitt)
8. STARDUST
   (Willie Nelson)
9. TEN YEARS OF GOLD
   (Kenny Rogers)
10. CLASSICS
    (Kenny Rogers and Dottie West)

OCTOBER 13, 1979

POP SINGLES

1. SAD EYES
   (Robert John)
2. SAIL ON
   (Commodores)
3. RISE
   (Herb Alpert)
4. DON'T STOP 'TIL YOU GET ENOUGH
   (Michael Jackson)
5. MY SHARONA
   (The Knack)
6. I'LL NEVER LOVE THIS WAY AGAIN
   (Dionne Warwick)
7. LONESOME LOSER
   (Little River Band)
8. POP MUZIK
   (M)
9. DON'T BRING ME DOWN
   (Electric Light Orchestra)
10. DRIVERS SEAT
    (Sniff 'n' the Tears)

POP ALBUMS

1. IN THROUGH THE OUT DOOR
   (Led Zeppelin)
2. THE LONG RUN
   (The Eagles)
3. GET THE KNACK
   (The Knack)
4. OFF THE WALL
   (Michael Jackson)
5. MIDNIGHT MAGIC
   (Commodores)
6. HEAD GAMES
   (Foreigner)
7. BREAKFAST IN AMERICA
   (Supertramp)
8. CORNERSTONE
   (Styx)
9. SLOW TRAIN COMING
   (Bob Dylan)
10. CANDY-O
    (The Cars)

BLACK SINGLES

1. (NOT JUST) KNEE DEEP—PART 1
   (Funkadelic)
2. DON'T STOP 'TIL YOU GET ENOUGH
   (Michael Jackson)
3. LADIES' NIGHT
   (Kool and the Gang)

4. I JUST WANT TO BE
   (Cameo)
5. FIRECRACKER
   (Mass Production)
6. I DO LOVE YOU/MAKE MY DREAMS A REALITY
   (G.Q.)
7. FOUND A CURE
   (Nick Ashford and Valerie Simpson)
8. RISE
   (Herb Alpert)
9. SAIL ON
   (Commodores)
10. BREAK MY HEART
    (David Ruffin)

BLACK ALBUMS

1. OFF THE WALL
   (Michael Jackson)
2. MIDNIGHT MAGIC
   (Commodores)
3. IDENTIFY YOURSELF
   (The O'Jays)
4. STAY FREE
   (Nick Ashford and Valerie Simpson)
5. RISQUE
   (Chic)
6. LADIES' NIGHT
   (Kool and the Gang)
7. SECRET OMEN
   (Cameo)
8. UNCLE JAM WANTS YOU
   (Funkadelic)
9. TEDDY
   (Teddy Pendergrass)
10. WHAT CHA GONNA DO WITH MY LOVIN'
    (Stephanie Mills)

JAZZ ALBUMS

1. STREET LIFE
   (Crusaders)
2. LUCKY SEVEN
   (Bob James)
3. MORNING DANCE
   (Spyro Gyra)
4. I WANNA PLAY FOR YOU
   (Stanley Clarke)
5. MINGUS
   (Joni Mitchell)
6. WATER SIGN
   (Jeff Lorber Fusion)
7. 8:30
   (Weather Report)
8. AN EVENING OF MAGIC
   (Chuck Mangione)
9. HEART STRING
   (Earl Klugh)
10. HIGH GEAR
    (Neil Larsen)

COUNTRY SINGLES

1. BEFORE MY TIME
   (John Conlee)
2. LAST CHEATER'S WALTZ
   (T.G. Sheppard)
3. FOOLED BY A FEELING
   (Barbara Mandrell)
4. DREAM ON
   (The Oak Ridge Boys)
5. IN NO TIME AT ALL
   (Ronnie Milsap)
6. ALL THE GOLD IN CALIFORNIA
   (Larry Gatlin and the Gatlin Brothers Band)
7. YOU AIN'T JUST WHISTLIN' DIXIE
   (The Bellamy Brothers)
8. FOOLS
   (Jim Ed Brown and Helen Cornelius)
9. SWEET SUMMER LOVIN'/GREAT BALLS OF FIRE
   (Dolly Parton)
10. HALF THE WAY
    (Crystal Gayle)

COUNTRY ALBUMS

1. THE GAMBLER
   (Kenny Rogers)
2. KENNY
   (Kenny Rogers)
3. GREATEST HITS
   (Waylon Jennings)
4. JUST FOR THE RECORD
   (Barbara Mandrell)
5. MILLION MILE REFLECTIONS
   (The Charlie Daniels Band)
6. ONE FOR THE ROAD
   (Willie Nelson and Leon Russell)
7. MISS THE MISSISSIPPI
   (Crystal Gayle)
8. LOVELINE
   (Eddie Rabbitt)
9. STARDUST
   (Willie Nelson)
10. TEN YEARS OF GOLD
    (Kenny Rogers)

OCTOBER 20, 1979

POP SINGLES

1. SAIL ON
   (Commodores)
2. RISE
   (Herb Alpert)
3. DON'T STOP 'TIL YOU GET ENOUGH
   (Michael Jackson)
4. SAD EYES
   (Robert John)
5. DIM ALL THE LIGHTS
   (Donna Summer)
6. POP MUZIK
   (M)
7. I'LL NEVER LOVE THIS WAY AGAIN
   (Dionne Warwick)
8. MY SHARONA
   (The Knack)
9. LONESOME LOSER
   (Little River Band)
10. YOU DECORATED MY LIFE
    (Kenny Rogers)

POP ALBUMS

1. IN THROUGH THE OUT DOOR
   (Led Zeppelin)
2. THE LONG RUN
   (The Eagles)
3. CORNERSTONE
   (Styx)
4. MIDNIGHT MAGIC
   (Commodores)
5. HEAD GAMES
   (Foreigner)
6. GET THE KNACK
   (The Knack)
7. OFF THE WALL
   (Michael Jackson)
8. DREAM POLICE
   (Cheap Trick)
9. CANDY-O
   (The Cars)
10. SLOW TRAIN COMING
    (Bob Dylan)

BLACK SINGLES

1. (NOT JUST) KNEE DEEP—PART 1
   (Funkadelic)
2. DON'T STOP 'TIL YOU GET ENOUGH
   (Michael Jackson)
3. LADIES' NIGHT
   (Kool and the Gang)

4. I JUST WANT TO BE
   (Cameo)
5. FIRECRACKER
   (Mass Production)
6. I DO LOVE YOU/MAKE MY DREAMS A REALITY
   (G.Q.)
7. FOUND A CURE
   (Nick Ashford and Valerie Simpson)
8. RISE
   (Herb Alpert)
9. SAIL ON
   (Commodores)
10. BREAK MY HEART
    (David Ruffin)

BLACK ALBUMS

1. OFF THE WALL
   (Michael Jackson)
2. MIDNIGHT MAGIC
   (Commodores)
3. UNCLE JAM WANTS YOU
   (Funkadelic)
4. IDENTIFY YOURSELF
   (The O'Jays)
5. LADIES' NIGHT
   (Kool and the Gang)
6. STAY FREE
   (Nick Ashford and Valerie Simpson)
7. SECRET OMEN
   (Cameo)
8. RISQUE
   (Chic)
9. TEDDY
   (Teddy Pendergrass)
10. WHAT CHA GONNA DO WITH MY LOVIN'
    (Stephanie Mills)

JAZZ ALBUMS

1. STREET LIFE
   (Crusaders)
2. MORNING DANCE
   (Spyro Gyra)
3. LUCKY SEVEN
   (Bob James)
4. WATER SIGN
   (Jeff Lorber Fusion)
5. 8:30
   (Weather Report)
6. I WANNA PLAY FOR YOU
   (Stanley Clarke)
7. MINGUS
   (Joni Mitchell)
8. AN EVENING OF MAGIC
   (Chuck Mangione)
9. HEART STRING
   (Earl Klugh)
10. HIGH GEAR
    (Neil Larsen)

COUNTRY SINGLES

1. DREAM ON
   (The Oak Ridge Boys)
2. BEFORE MY TIME
   (John Conlee)
3. FOOLED BY A FEELING
   (Barbara Mandrell)
4. ALL THE GOLD IN CALIFORNIA
   (Larry Gatlin and the Gatlin Brothers Band)
5. IN NO TIME AT ALL
   (Ronnie Milsap)
6. YOU AIN'T JUST WHISTLIN' DIXIE
   (The Bellamy Brothers)
7. SWEET SUMMER LOVIN'/GREAT BALLS OF FIRE
   (Dolly Parton)
8. HALF THE WAY
   (Crystal Gayle)
9. YOU DECORATED MY LIFE
   (Kenny Rogers)

10. I AIN'T GOT NO BUSINESS DOIN' BUSINESS TODAY
    (Razzy Bailey)

COUNTRY ALBUMS

1. KENNY
   (Kenny Rogers)
2. THE GAMBLER
   (Kenny Rogers)
3. GREATEST HITS
   (Waylon Jennings)
4. JUST FOR THE RECORD
   (Barbara Mandrell)
5. MISS THE MISSISSIPPI
   (Crystal Gayle)
6. MILLION MILE REFLECTIONS
   (The Charlie Daniels Band)
7. ONE FOR THE ROAD
   (Willie Nelson and Leon Russell)
8. LOVELINE
   (Eddie Rabbitt)
9. STARDUST
   (Willie Nelson)
10. TEN YEARS OF GOLD
    (Kenny Rogers)

OCTOBER 27, 1979

POP SINGLES

1. RISE
   (Herb Alpert)
2. DON'T STOP 'TIL YOU GET ENOUGH
   (Michael Jackson)
3. DIM ALL THE LIGHTS
   (Donna Summer)
4. POP MUZIK
   (M)
5. SAD EYES
   (Robert John)
6. SAIL ON
   (Commodores)
7. YOU DECORATED MY LIFE
   (Kenny Rogers)
8. HEARTACHE TONIGHT
   (The Eagles)
9. TUSK
   (Fleetwood Mac)
10. GOOD GIRLS DON'T
    (The Knack)

POP ALBUMS

1. THE LONG RUN
   (The Eagles)
2. IN THROUGH THE OUT DOOR
   (Led Zeppelin)
3. CORNERSTONE
   (Styx)
4. MIDNIGHT MAGIC
   (Commodores)
5. HEAD GAMES
   (Foreigner)
6. GET THE KNACK
   (The Knack)
7. OFF THE WALL
   (Michael Jackson)
8. DREAM POLICE
   (Cheap Trick)
9. TUSK
   (Fleetwood Mac)
10. CANDY-O
    (The Cars)

BLACK SINGLES

1. (NOT JUST) KNEE DEEP—PART 1
   (Funkadelic)

2. LADIES' NIGHT
   (Kool and the Gang)
3. DON'T STOP 'TIL YOU GET ENOUGH
   (Michael Jackson)
4. RAPPER'S DELIGHT
   (The Sugarhill Gang)
5. STILL
   (Commodores)
6. I DO LOVE YOU/MAKE MY DREAMS A REALITY
   (G.Q.)
7. RISE
   (Herb Alpert)
8. CRUISIN'
   (Smokey Robinson)
9. SAIL ON
   (Commodores)
10. BREAK MY HEART
    (David Ruffin)

BLACK ALBUMS

1. OFF THE WALL
   (Michael Jackson)
2. UNCLE JAM WANTS YOU
   (Funkadelic)
3. MIDNIGHT MAGIC
   (Commodores)
4. IDENTIFY YOURSELF
   (The O'Jays)
5. LADIES' NIGHT
   (Kool and the Gang)
6. STAY FREE
   (Nick Ashford and Valerie Simpson)
7. SECRET OMEN
   (Cameo)
8. DON'T LET GO
   (Isaac Hayes)
9. RISQUE
   (Chic)
10. TEDDY
    (Teddy Pendergrass)

JAZZ ALBUMS

1. STREET LIFE
   (Crusaders)
2. LUCKY SEVEN
   (Bob James)
3. MORNING DANCE
   (Spyro Gyra)
4. WATER SIGN
   (Jeff Lorber Fusion)
5. 8:30
   (Weather Report)
6. RISE
   (Herb Alpert)
7. I WANNA PLAY FOR YOU
   (Stanley Clarke)
8. MINGUS
   (Joni Mitchell)
9. HEART STRING
   (Earl Klugh)
10. HIGH GEAR
    (Neil Larsen)

COUNTRY SINGLES

1. ALL THE GOLD IN CALIFORNIA
   (Larry Gatlin and the Gatlin Brothers Band)
2. DREAM ON
   (The Oak Ridge Boys)
3. YOU DECORATED MY LIFE
   (Kenny Rogers)
4. HALF THE WAY
   (Crystal Gayle)
5. SWEET SUMMER LOVIN'/GREAT BALLS OF FIRE
   (Dolly Parton)
6. BEFORE MY TIME
   (John Conlee)
7. FOOLED BY A FEELING
   (Barbara Mandrell)

8. SHOULD I COME HOME (OR SHOULD I GO CRAZY)
   (Gene Watson)
9. I AIN'T GOT NO BUSINESS DOIN' BUSINESS TODAY
   (Razzy Bailey)
10. PUT YOUR CLOTHES BACK ON
    (Joe Stampley)

COUNTRY ALBUMS

1. KENNY
   (Kenny Rogers)
2. THE GAMBLER
   (Kenny Rogers)
3. GREATEST HITS
   (Waylon Jennings)
4. MISS THE MISSISSIPPI
   (Crystal Gayle)
5. STARDUST
   (Willie Nelson)
6. MILLION MILE REFLECTIONS
   (The Charlie Daniels Band)
7. TEN YEARS OF GOLD
   (Kenny Rogers)
8. ONE FOR THE ROAD
   (Willie Nelson and Leon Russell)
9. LOVELINE
   (Eddie Rabbitt)
10. JUST FOR THE RECORD
    (Barbara Mandrell)

NOVEMBER 3, 1979

POP SINGLES

1. DON'T STOP 'TIL YOU GET ENOUGH
   (Michael Jackson)
2. DIM ALL THE LIGHTS
   (Donna Summer)
3. HEARTACHE TONIGHT
   (The Eagles)
4. POP MUZIK
   (M)
5. YOU DECORATED MY LIFE
   (Kenny Rogers)
6. RISE
   (Herb Alpert)
7. STILL
   (Commodores)
8. TUSK
   (Fleetwood Mac)
9. BABE
   (Styx)
10. GOOD GIRLS DON'T
    (The Knack)

POP ALBUMS

1. THE LONG RUN
   (The Eagles)
2. IN THROUGH THE OUT DOOR
   (Led Zeppelin)
3. CORNERSTONE
   (Styx)
4. MIDNIGHT MAGIC
   (Commodores)
5. TUSK
   (Fleetwood Mac)
6. HEAD GAMES
   (Foreigner)
7. OFF THE WALL
   (Michael Jackson)
8. DREAM POLICE
   (Cheap Trick)
9. RISE
   (Herb Alpert)
10. GET THE KNACK
    (The Knack)

BLACK SINGLES

1. LADIES' NIGHT
   (Kool and the Gang)
2. RAPPER'S DELIGHT
   (The Sugarhill Gang)
3. (NOT JUST) KNEE DEEP—PART 1
   (Funkadelic)
4. STILL
   (Commodores)
5. DON'T STOP 'TIL YOU GET ENOUGH
   (Michael Jackson)
6. CRUISIN'
   (Smokey Robinson)
7. RISE
   (Herb Alpert)
8. I DO LOVE YOU/MAKE MY DREAMS A REALITY
   (G.Q.)
9. SAIL ON
   (Commodores)
10. BETWEEN YOU BABY AND ME
    (Curtis Mayfield and Linda Clifford)

BLACK ALBUMS

1. OFF THE WALL
   (Michael Jackson)
2. UNCLE JAM WANTS YOU
   (Funkadelic)
3. MIDNIGHT MAGIC
   (Commodores)
4. LADIES' NIGHT
   (Kool and the Gang)
5. IDENTIFY YOURSELF
   (The O'Jays)
6. STAY FREE
   (Nick Ashford and Valerie Simpson)
7. DON'T LET GO
   (Isaac Hayes)
8. SECRET OMEN
   (Cameo)
9. WHERE THERE'S SMOKE
   (Smokey Robinson)
10. RISE
    (Herb Alpert)

JAZZ ALBUMS

1. STREET LIFE
   (Crusaders)
2. MORNING DANCE
   (Spyro Gyra)
3. LUCKY SEVEN
   (Bob James)
4. WATER SIGN
   (Jeff Lorber Fusion)
5. 8:30
   (Weather Report)
6. RISE
   (Herb Alpert)
7. I WANNA PLAY FOR YOU
   (Stanley Clarke)
8. A TASTE FOR PASSION
   (Jean Luc Ponty)
9. ONE ON ONE
   (Bob James and Earl Klugh)
10. HEART STRING
    (Earl Klugh)

COUNTRY SINGLES

1. YOU DECORATED MY LIFE
   (Kenny Rogers)
2. ALL THE GOLD IN CALIFORNIA
   (Larry Gatlin and the Gatlin Brothers Band)
3. HALF THE WAY
   (Crystal Gayle)
4. DREAM ON
   (The Oak Ridge Boys)
5. SWEET SUMMER LOVIN'/GREAT BALLS OF FIRE
   (Dolly Parton)

6. SHOULD I COME HOME (OR SHOULD I GO CRAZY)
   (Gene Watson)
7. COME WITH ME
   (Waylon Jennings)
8. MY OWN KIND OF HAT/HEAVEN WAS A DRINK OF WINE
   (Merle Haggard)
9. PUT YOUR CLOTHES BACK ON
   (Joe Stampley)
10. BLUE KENTUCKY GIRL
    (Emmylou Harris)

COUNTRY ALBUMS

1. KENNY
   (Kenny Rogers)
2. THE GAMBLER
   (Kenny Rogers)
3. GREATEST HITS
   (Waylon Jennings)
4. MISS THE MISSISSIPPI
   (Crystal Gayle)
5. STARDUST
   (Willie Nelson)
6. MILLION MILE REFLECTIONS
   (The Charlie Daniels Band)
7. TEN YEARS OF GOLD
   (Kenny Rogers)
8. STRAIGHT AHEAD
   (Larry Gatlin)
9. ONE FOR THE ROAD
   (Willie Nelson and Leon Russell)
10. JUST FOR THE RECORD
    (Barbara Mandrell)

NOVEMBER 10, 1979

POP SINGLES

1. HEARTACHE TONIGHT
   (The Eagles)
2. DIM ALL THE LIGHTS
   (Donna Summer)
3. BABE
   (Styx)
4. POP MUZIK
   (M)
5. YOU DECORATED MY LIFE
   (Kenny Rogers)
6. STILL
   (Commodores)
7. DON'T STOP 'TIL YOU GET ENOUGH
   (Michael Jackson)
8. TUSK
   (Fleetwood Mac)
9. NO MORE TEARS (ENOUGH IS ENOUGH)
   (Barbra Streisand and Donna Summer)
10. RISE
    (Herb Alpert)

POP ALBUMS

1. THE LONG RUN
   (The Eagles)
2. IN THROUGH THE OUT DOOR
   (Led Zeppelin)
3. CORNERSTONE
   (Styx)
4. MIDNIGHT MAGIC
   (Commodores)
5. TUSK
   (Fleetwood Mac)
6. HEAD GAMES
   (Foreigner)
7. RISE
   (Herb Alpert)
8. OFF THE WALL
   (Michael Jackson)
9. KENNY
   (Kenny Rogers)

10. DREAM POLICE
(Cheap Trick)

BLACK SINGLES

1. LADIES' NIGHT
(Kool and the Gang)
2. RAPPER'S DELIGHT
(The Sugarhill Gang)
3. STILL
(Commodores)
4. (NOT JUST) KNEE DEEP—PART 1
(Funkadelic)
5. CRUISIN'
(Smokey Robinson)
6. DON'T STOP 'TIL YOU GET ENOUGH
(Michael Jackson)
7. I JUST CAN'T CONTROL MYSELF
(Nature's Divine)
8. I WANNA BE YOUR LOVER
(Prince)
9. RISE
(Herb Alpert)
10. DO YOU LOVE WHAT YOU FEEL
(Rufus and Chaka Khan)

BLACK ALBUMS

1. OFF THE WALL
(Michael Jackson)
2. MIDNIGHT MAGIC
(Commodores)
3. UNCLE JAM WANTS YOU
(Funkadelic)
4. LADIES' NIGHT
(Kool and the Gang)
5. IDENTIFY YOURSELF
(The O'Jays)
6. STAY FREE
(Nick Ashford and Valerie Simpson)
7. DON'T LET GO
(Isaac Hayes)
8. FIRE IT UP
(Rick James)
9. WHERE THERE'S SMOKE
(Smokey Robinson)
10. RISE
(Herb Alpert)

JAZZ ALBUMS

1. STREET LIFE
(Crusaders)
2. ONE ON ONE
(Bob James and Earl Klugh)
3. RISE
(Herb Alpert)
4. WATER SIGN
(Jeff Lorber Fusion)
5. MORNING DANCE
(Spyro Gyra)
6. 8:30
(Weather Report)
7. LUCKY SEVEN
(Bob James)
8. A TASTE FOR PASSION
(Jean Luc Ponty)
9. I WANNA PLAY FOR YOU
(Stanley Clarke)
10. HEART STRING
(Earl Klugh)

COUNTRY SINGLES

1. YOU DECORATED MY LIFE
(Kenny Rogers)
2. HALF THE WAY
(Crystal Gayle)
3. ALL THE GOLD IN CALIFORNIA
(Larry Gatlin and the Gatlin Brothers Band)
4. COME WITH ME
(Waylon Jennings)

5. SHOULD I COME HOME (OR SHOULD I GO CRAZY)
(Gene Watson)
6. MY OWN KIND OF HAT/HEAVEN WAS A DRINK OF WINE
(Merle Haggard)
7. BROKEN HEARTED ME
(Anne Murray)
8. BLUE KENTUCKY GIRL
(Emmylou Harris)
9. PUT YOUR CLOTHES BACK ON
(Joe Stampley)
10. BLIND IN LOVE
(Mel Tillis)

COUNTRY ALBUMS

1. KENNY
(Kenny Rogers)
2. THE GAMBLER
(Kenny Rogers)
3. GREATEST HITS
(Waylon Jennings)
4. MISS THE MISSISSIPPI
(Crystal Gayle)
5. MILLION MILE REFLECTIONS
(The Charlie Daniels Band)
6. TEN YEARS OF GOLD
(Kenny Rogers)
7. STRAIGHT AHEAD
(Larry Gatlin)
8. ONE FOR THE ROAD
(Willie Nelson and Leon Russell)
9. STARDUST
(Willie Nelson)
10. JUST FOR THE RECORD
(Barbara Mandrell)

NOVEMBER 17, 1979

POP SINGLES

1. BABE
(Styx)
2. HEARTACHE TONIGHT
(The Eagles)
3. NO MORE TEARS (ENOUGH IS ENOUGH)
(Barbra Streisand and Donna Summer)
4. STILL
(Commodores)
5. POP MUZIK
(M)
6. DIM ALL THE LIGHTS
(Donna Summer)
7. YOU DECORATED MY LIFE
(Kenny Rogers)
8. TUSK
(Fleetwood Mac)
9. DON'T STOP 'TIL YOU GET ENOUGH
(Michael Jackson)
10. RISE
(Herb Alpert)

POP ALBUMS

1. THE LONG RUN
(The Eagles)
2. IN THROUGH THE OUT DOOR
(Led Zeppelin)
3. CORNERSTONE
(Styx)
4. TUSK
(Fleetwood Mac)
5. MIDNIGHT MAGIC
(Commodores)
6. ON THE RADIO—GREATEST HITS VOLUMES I AND II
(Donna Summer)
7. RISE
(Herb Alpert)

8. WET
(Barbra Streisand)
9. KENNY
(Kenny Rogers)
10. ONE VOICE
(Barry Manilow)

BLACK SINGLES

1. LADIES' NIGHT
(Kool and the Gang)
2. RAPPER'S DELIGHT
(The Sugarhill Gang)
3. STILL
(Commodores)
4. CRUISIN'
(Smokey Robinson)
5. (NOT JUST) KNEE DEEP—PART 1
(Funkadelic)
6. I WANNA BE YOUR LOVER
(Prince)
7. I JUST CAN'T CONTROL MYSELF
(Nature's Divine)
8. DO YOU LOVE WHAT YOU FEEL
(Rufus and Chaka Khan)
9. DON'T STOP 'TIL YOU GET ENOUGH
(Michael Jackson)
10. DON'T LET GO
(Isaac Hayes)

BLACK ALBUMS

1. OFF THE WALL
(Michael Jackson)
2. MIDNIGHT MAGIC
(Commodores)
3. LADIES' NIGHT
(Kool and the Gang)
4. UNCLE JAM WANTS YOU
(Funkadelic)
5. IDENTIFY YOURSELF
(The O'Jays)
6. JOURNEY THROUGH THE SECRET LIFE OF PLANTS
(Stevie Wonder)
7. INJOY
(Bar-Kays)
8. FIRE IT UP
(Rick James)
9. DON'T LET GO
(Isaac Hayes)
10. WHERE THERE'S SMOKE
(Smokey Robinson)

JAZZ ALBUMS

1. STREET LIFE
(Crusaders)
2. ONE ON ONE
(Bob James and Earl Klugh)
3. RISE
(Herb Alpert)
4. WATER SIGN
(Jeff Lorber Fusion)
5. A TASTE FOR PASSION
(Jean Luc Ponty)
6. 8:30
(Weather Report)
7. THE WORLD WITHIN
(Stix Hooper)
8. MORNING DANCE
(Spyro Gyra)
9. ANGEL OF THE NIGHT
(Angela Bofill)
10. LUCKY SEVEN
(Bob James)

COUNTRY SINGLES

1. HALF THE WAY
(Crystal Gayle)

2. COME WITH ME
    (Waylon Jennings)
3. YOU DECORATED MY LIFE
    (Kenny Rogers)
4. SHOULD I COME HOME (OR SHOULD I GO
    CRAZY)
    (Gene Watson)
5. BROKEN HEARTED ME
    (Anne Murray)
6. MY OWN KIND OF HAT/HEAVEN WAS A
    DRINK OF WINE
    (Merle Haggard)
7. BLUE KENTUCKY GIRL
    (Emmylou Harris)
8. BLIND IN LOVE
    (Mel Tillis)
9. I CHEATED ME RIGHT OUT OF YOU
    (Moe Bandy)
10. THE LADY IN THE BLUE MERCEDES
    (Johnny Duncan)

COUNTRY ALBUMS

1. KENNY
    (Kenny Rogers)
2. THE GAMBLER
    (Kenny Rogers)
3. GREATEST HITS
    (Waylon Jennings)
4. MISS THE MISSISSIPPI
    (Crystal Gayle)
5. STRAIGHT AHEAD
    (Larry Gatlin)
6. TEN YEARS OF GOLD
    (Kenny Rogers)
7. MILLION MILE REFLECTIONS
    (The Charlie Daniels Band)
8. I'LL ALWAYS LOVE YOU
    (Anne Murray)
9. STARDUST
    (Willie Nelson)
10. LET'S KEEP IT THAT WAY
    (Anne Murray)

NOVEMBER 24, 1979

POP SINGLES

1. NO MORE TEARS (ENOUGH IS ENOUGH)
    (Barbra Streisand and Donna Summer)
2. BABE
    (Styx)
3. STILL
    (Commodores)
4. HEARTACHE TONIGHT
    (The Eagles)
5. POP MUZIK
    (M)
6. DIM ALL THE LIGHTS
    (Donna Summer)
7. YOU DECORATED MY LIFE
    (Kenny Rogers)
8. PLEASE DON'T GO
    (KC and the Sunshine Band)
9. TUSK
    (Fleetwood Mac)
10. SHIPS
    (Barry Manilow)

POP ALBUMS

1. THE LONG RUN
    (The Eagles)
2. ON THE RADIO—GREATEST HITS
    VOLUMES I AND II
    (Donna Summer)
3. CORNERSTONE
    (Styx)
4. TUSK
    (Fleetwood Mac)

5. IN THROUGH THE OUT DOOR
    (Led Zeppelin)
6. MIDNIGHT MAGIC
    (Commodores)
7. WET
    (Barbra Streisand)
8. ONE VOICE
    (Barry Manilow)
9. RISE
    (Herb Alpert)
10. OFF THE WALL
    (Michael Jackson)

BLACK SINGLES

1. RAPPER'S DELIGHT
    (The Sugarhill Gang)
2. LADIES' NIGHT
    (Kool and the Gang)
3. STILL
    (Commodores)
4. CRUISIN'
    (Smokey Robinson)
5. I WANNA BE YOUR LOVER
    (Prince)
6. DO YOU LOVE WHAT YOU FEEL
    (Rufus and Chaka Khan)
7. I JUST CAN'T CONTROL MYSELF
    (Nature's Divine)
8. ROCK WITH YOU/WORKING DAY AND
    NIGHT
    (Michael Jackson)
9. DON'T LET GO
    (Isaac Hayes)
10. MOVE YOUR BOOGIE BODY
    (Bar-Kays)

BLACK ALBUMS

1. OFF THE WALL
    (Michael Jackson)
2. MIDNIGHT MAGIC
    (Commodores)
3. LADIES' NIGHT
    (Kool and the Gang)
4. JOURNEY THROUGH THE SECRET LIFE OF
    PLANTS
    (Stevie Wonder)
5. IDENTIFY YOURSELF
    (The O'Jays)
6. UNCLE JAM WANTS YOU
    (Funkadelic)
7. INJOY
    (Bar-Kays)
8. FIRE IT UP
    (Rick James)
9. MASTERJAM
    (Rufus and Chaka Khan)
10. ON THE RADIO—GREATEST HITS
    VOLUMES I AND II
    (Donna Summer)

JAZZ ALBUMS

1. ONE ON ONE
    (Bob James and Earl Klugh)
2. STREET LIFE
    (Crusaders)
3. RISE
    (Herb Alpert)
4. A TASTE FOR PASSION
    (Jean Luc Ponty)
5. ANGEL OF THE NIGHT
    (Angela Bofill)
6. WATER SIGN
    (Jeff Lorber Fusion)
7. 8:30
    (Weather Report)
8. THE WORLD WITHIN
    (Stix Hooper)
9. MORNING DANCE
    (Spyro Gyra)
10. STREET BEAT
    (Tom Scott)

COUNTRY SINGLES

1. COME WITH ME
    (Waylon Jennings)
2. BROKEN HEARTED ME
    (Anne Murray)
3. HALF THE WAY
    (Crystal Gayle)
4. SHOULD I COME HOME (OR SHOULD I GO
    CRAZY)
    (Gene Watson)
5. BLIND IN LOVE
    (Mel Tillis)
6. I CHEATED ME RIGHT OUT OF YOU
    (Moe Bandy)
7. BLUE KENTUCKY GIRL
    (Emmylou Harris)
8. WHISKEY BENT AND HELL BOUND
    (Hank Williams Jr.)
9. THE LADY IN THE BLUE MERCEDES
    (Johnny Duncan)
10. MY OWN KIND OF HAT/HEAVEN WAS A
    DRINK OF WINE
    (Merle Haggard)

COUNTRY ALBUMS

1. KENNY
    (Kenny Rogers)
2. THE GAMBLER
    (Kenny Rogers)
3. GREATEST HITS
    (Waylon Jennings)
4. MISS THE MISSISSIPPI
    (Crystal Gayle)
5. STRAIGHT AHEAD
    (Larry Gatlin)
6. I'LL ALWAYS LOVE YOU
    (Anne Murray)
7. WHAT GOES AROUND COMES AROUND
    (Waylon Jennings)
8. TEN YEARS OF GOLD
    (Kenny Rogers)
9. WILLIE NELSON SINGS KRISTOFFERSON
    (Willie Nelson)
10. LET'S KEEP IT THAT WAY
    (Anne Murray)

DECEMBER 1, 1979

POP SINGLES

1. NO MORE TEARS (ENOUGH IS ENOUGH)
    (Barbra Streisand and Donna Summer)
2. BABE
    (Styx)
3. STILL
    (Commodores)
4. PLEASE DON'T GO
    (KC and the Sunshine Band)
5. HEARTACHE TONIGHT
    (The Eagles)
6. ESCAPE (THE PINA COLADA SONG)
    (Rupert Holmes)
7. POP MUZIK
    (M)
8. DIM ALL THE LIGHTS
    (Donna Summer)
9. SHIPS
    (Barry Manilow)
10. YOU DECORATED MY LIFE
    (Kenny Rogers)

POP ALBUMS

1. THE LONG RUN
    (The Eagles)
2. ON THE RADIO—GREATEST HITS
    VOLUMES I AND II
    (Donna Summer)

3. CORNERSTONE
   (Styx)
4. MIDNIGHT MAGIC
   (Commodores)
5. IN THROUGH THE OUT DOOR
   (Led Zeppelin)
6. TUSK
   (Fleetwood Mac)
7. WET
   (Barbra Streisand)
8. ONE VOICE
   (Barry Manilow)
9. BEE GEES GREATEST
   (The Bee Gees)
10. OFF THE WALL
    (Michael Jackson)

BLACK SINGLES

1. RAPPER'S DELIGHT
   (The Sugarhill Gang)
2. DO YOU LOVE WHAT YOU FEEL
   (Rufus and Chaka Khan)
3. I WANNA BE YOUR LOVER
   (Prince)
4. STILL
   (Commodores)
5. LADIES' NIGHT
   (Kool and the Gang)
6. ROCK WITH YOU/WORKING DAY AND
   NIGHT
   (Michael Jackson)
7. CRUISIN'
   (Smokey Robinson)
8. MOVE YOUR BOOGIE BODY
   (Bar-Kays)
9. DON'T LET GO
   (Isaac Hayes)
10. SEND ONE YOUR LOVE
    (Stevie Wonder)

BLACK ALBUMS

1. OFF THE WALL
   (Michael Jackson)
2. MIDNIGHT MAGIC
   (Commodores)
3. LADIES' NIGHT
   (Kool and the Gang)
4. JOURNEY THROUGH THE SECRET LIFE OF
   PLANTS
   (Stevie Wonder)
5. MASTERJAM
   (Rufus and Chaka Khan)
6. IDENTIFY YOURSELF
   (The O'Jays)
7. INJOY
   (Bar-Kays)
8. PRINCE
   (Prince)
9. FIRE IT UP
   (Rick James)
10. ON THE RADIO—GREATEST HITS
    VOLUMES I AND II
    (Donna Summer)

JAZZ ALBUMS

1. ONE ON ONE
   (Bob James and Earl Klugh)
2. STREET LIFE
   (Crusaders)
3. RISE
   (Herb Alpert)
4. ANGEL OF THE NIGHT
   (Angela Bofill)
5. A TASTE FOR PASSION
   (Jean Luc Ponty)
6. WATER SIGN
   (Jeff Lorber Fusion)
7. 8:30
   (Weather Report)
8. THE WORLD WITHIN
   (Stix Hooper)

9. MORNING DANCE
   (Spyro Gyra)
10. STREET BEAT
    (Tom Scott)

COUNTRY SINGLES

1. BROKEN HEARTED ME
   (Anne Murray)
2. COME WITH ME
   (Waylon Jennings)
3. BLIND IN LOVE
   (Mel Tillis)
4. I CHEATED ME RIGHT OUT OF YOU
   (Moe Bandy)
5. WHISKEY BENT AND HELL BOUND
   (Hank Williams Jr.)
6. SHOULD I COME HOME (OR SHOULD I GO
   CRAZY)
   (Gene Watson)
7. HALF THE WAY
   (Crystal Gayle)
8. THE LADY IN THE BLUE MERCEDES
   (Johnny Duncan)
9. I'VE GOT A PICTURE OF US IN MY MIND
   (Loretta Lynn)
10. YOU SHOW ME YOUR HEART (AND I'LL
    SHOW YOU MINE)
    (Tom T. Hall)

COUNTRY ALBUMS

1. KENNY
   (Kenny Rogers)
2. THE GAMBLER
   (Kenny Rogers)
3. GREATEST HITS
   (Waylon Jennings)
4. MISS THE MISSISSIPPI
   (Crystal Gayle)
5. I'LL ALWAYS LOVE YOU
   (Anne Murray)
6. WHAT GOES AROUND COMES AROUND
   (Waylon Jennings)
7. WILLIE NELSON SINGS KRISTOFFERSON
   (Willie Nelson)
8. STRAIGHT AHEAD
   (Larry Gatlin)
9. TEN YEARS OF GOLD
   (Kenny Rogers)
10. CLASSIC CRYSTAL
    (Crystal Gayle)

DECEMBER 8, 1979

POP SINGLES

1. NO MORE TEARS (ENOUGH IS ENOUGH)
   (Barbra Streisand and Donna Summer)
2. BABE
   (Styx)
3. PLEASE DON'T GO
   (KC and the Sunshine Band)
4. ESCAPE (THE PINA COLADA SONG)
   (Rupert Holmes)
5. STILL
   (Commodores)
6. HEARTACHE TONIGHT
   (The Eagles)
7. LADIES' NIGHT
   (Kool and the Gang)
8. YOU'RE ONLY LONELY
   (J.D. Souther)
9. DIM ALL THE LIGHTS
   (Donna Summer)
10. TAKE THE LONG WAY HOME
    (Supertramp)

POP ALBUMS

1. THE LONG RUN
   (The Eagles)
2. ON THE RADIO—GREATEST HITS
   VOLUMES I AND II
   (Donna Summer)
3. CORNERSTONE
   (Styx)
4. MIDNIGHT MAGIC
   (Commodores)
5. IN THROUGH THE OUT DOOR
   (Led Zeppelin)
6. WET
   (Barbra Streisand)
7. TUSK
   (Fleetwood Mac)
8. BEE GEES GREATEST
   (The Bee Gees)
9. ONE VOICE
   (Barry Manilow)
10. OFF THE WALL
    (Michael Jackson)

BLACK SINGLES

1. DO YOU LOVE WHAT YOU FEEL
   (Rufus and Chaka Khan)
2. I WANNA BE YOUR LOVER
   (Prince)
3. RAPPER'S DELIGHT
   (The Sugarhill Gang)
4. ROCK WITH YOU/WORKING DAY AND
   NIGHT
   (Michael Jackson)
5. LADIES' NIGHT
   (Kool and the Gang)
6. STILL
   (Commodores)
7. MOVE YOUR BOOGIE BODY
   (Bar-Kays)
8. CRUISIN'
   (Smokey Robinson)
9. SEND ONE YOUR LOVE
   (Stevie Wonder)
10. DON'T LET GO
    (Isaac Hayes)

BLACK ALBUMS

1. OFF THE WALL
   (Michael Jackson)
2. MASTERJAM
   (Rufus and Chaka Khan)
3. MIDNIGHT MAGIC
   (Commodores)
4. JOURNEY THROUGH THE SECRET LIFE OF
   PLANTS
   (Stevie Wonder)
5. PRINCE
   (Prince)
6. LADIES' NIGHT
   (Kool and the Gang)
7. INJOY
   (Bar-Kays)
8. IDENTIFY YOURSELF
   (The O'Jays)
9. ON THE RADIO—GREATEST HITS
   VOLUMES I AND II
   (Donna Summer)
10. WHERE THERE'S SMOKE
    (Smokey Robinson)

JAZZ ALBUMS

1. ONE ON ONE
   (Bob James and Earl Klugh)
2. ANGEL OF THE NIGHT
   (Angela Bofill)
3. STREET LIFE
   (Crusaders)
4. RISE
   (Herb Alpert)

5. A TASTE FOR PASSION
   (Jean Luc Ponty)
6. PIZZAZZ
   (Patrice Rushen)
7. WATER SIGN
   (Jeff Lorber Fusion)
8. 8:30
   (Weather Report)
9. STREET BEAT
   (Tom Scott)
10. MASTER OF THE GAME
    (George Duke)

COUNTRY SINGLES

1. BROKEN HEARTED ME
   (Anne Murray)
2. I CHEATED ME RIGHT OUT OF YOU
   (Moe Bandy)
3. BLIND IN LOVE
   (Mel Tillis)
4. WHISKEY BENT AND HELL BOUND
   (Hank Williams Jr.)
5. HAPPY BIRTHDAY DARLIN'
   (Conway Twitty)
6. I'VE GOT A PICTURE OF US IN MY MIND
   (Loretta Lynn)
7. COME WITH ME
   (Waylon Jennings)
8. MY WORLD BEGINS AND ENDS WITH YOU
   (Dave and Sugar)
9. MISSIN' YOU
   (Charley Pride)
10. YOU SHOW ME YOUR HEART (AND I'LL SHOW YOU MINE)
    (Tom T. Hall)

COUNTRY ALBUMS

1. KENNY
   (Kenny Rogers)
2. THE GAMBLER
   (Kenny Rogers)
3. GREATEST HITS
   (Waylon Jennings)
4. MISS THE MISSISSIPPI
   (Crystal Gayle)
5. I'LL ALWAYS LOVE YOU
   (Anne Murray)
6. WHAT GOES AROUND COMES AROUND
   (Waylon Jennings)
7. WILLIE NELSON SINGS KRISTOFFERSON
   (Willie Nelson)
8. STRAIGHT AHEAD
   (Larry Gatlin)
9. TEN YEARS OF GOLD
   (Kenny Rogers)
10. CLASSIC CRYSTAL
    (Crystal Gayle)

DECEMBER 15, 1979

POP SINGLES

1. BABE
   (Styx)
2. NO MORE TEARS (ENOUGH IS ENOUGH)
   (Barbra Streisand and Donna Summer)
3. PLEASE DON'T GO
   (KC and the Sunshine Band)
4. ESCAPE (THE PINA COLADA SONG)
   (Rupert Holmes)
5. LADIES' NIGHT
   (Kool and the Gang)
6. STILL
   (Commodores)
7. DO THAT TO ME ONE MORE TIME
   (The Captain and Tennille)
8. YOU'RE ONLY LONELY
   (J.D. Souther)
9. HEARTACHE TONIGHT
   (The Eagles)
10. TAKE THE LONG WAY HOME
    (Supertramp)

POP ALBUMS

1. THE LONG RUN
   (The Eagles)
2. ON THE RADIO—GREATEST HITS VOLUMES I AND II
   (Donna Summer)
3. CORNERSTONE
   (Styx)
4. MIDNIGHT MAGIC
   (Commodores)
5. BEE GEES GREATEST
   (The Bee Gees)
6. WET
   (Barbra Streisand)
7. IN THROUGH THE OUT DOOR
   (Led Zeppelin)
8. TUSK
   (Fleetwood Mac)
9. OFF THE WALL
   (Michael Jackson)
10. JOURNEY THROUGH THE SECRET LIFE OF PLANTS
    (Stevie Wonder)

BLACK SINGLES

1. DO YOU LOVE WHAT YOU FEEL
   (Rufus and Chaka Khan)
2. I WANNA BE YOUR LOVER
   (Prince)
3. ROCK WITH YOU/WORKING DAY AND NIGHT
   (Michael Jackson)
4. RAPPER'S DELIGHT
   (The Sugarhill Gang)
5. MOVE YOUR BOOGIE BODY
   (Bar-Kays)
6. LADIES' NIGHT
   (Kool and the Gang)
7. SEND ONE YOUR LOVE
   (Stevie Wonder)
8. CRUISIN'
   (Smokey Robinson)
9. STILL
   (Commodores)
10. DON'T LET GO
    (Isaac Hayes)

BLACK ALBUMS

1. OFF THE WALL
   (Michael Jackson)
2. MASTERJAM
   (Rufus and Chaka Khan)
3. MIDNIGHT MAGIC
   (Commodores)
4. PRINCE
   (Prince)
5. JOURNEY THROUGH THE SECRET LIFE OF PLANTS
   (Stevie Wonder)
6. INJOY
   (Bar-Kays)
7. LADIES' NIGHT
   (Kool and the Gang)
8. WHERE THERE'S SMOKE
   (Smokey Robinson)
9. ON THE RADIO—GREATEST HITS VOLUMES I AND II
   (Donna Summer)
10. IDENTIFY YOURSELF
    (The O'Jays)

JAZZ ALBUMS

1. ONE ON ONE
   (Bob James and Earl Klugh)
2. ANGEL OF THE NIGHT
   (Angela Bofill)
3. MASTER OF THE GAME
   (George Duke)
4. AMERICAN GARAGE
   (Pat Metheny)
5. STREET LIFE
   (Crusaders)
6. RISE
   (Herb Alpert)
7. A TASTE FOR PASSION
   (Jean Luc Ponty)
8. PIZZAZZ
   (Patrice Rushen)
9. STREET BEAT
   (Tom Scott)
10. THE HAWK
    (Dave Valentin)

COUNTRY SINGLES

1. HAPPY BIRTHDAY DARLIN'
   (Conway Twitty)
2. I CHEATED ME RIGHT OUT OF YOU
   (Moe Bandy)
3. WHISKEY BENT AND HELL BOUND
   (Hank Williams Jr.)
4. MISSIN' YOU
   (Charley Pride)
5. I'VE GOT A PICTURE OF US IN MY MIND
   (Loretta Lynn)
6. MY WORLD BEGINS AND ENDS WITH YOU
   (Dave and Sugar)
7. BROKEN HEARTED ME
   (Anne Murray)
8. POUR ME ANOTHER TEQUILA
   (Eddie Rabbitt)
9. TELL ME WHAT IT'S LIKE
   (Brenda Lee)
10. NOTHING AS ORIGINAL AS YOU
    (The Statler Brothers)

COUNTRY ALBUMS

1. KENNY
   (Kenny Rogers)
2. THE GAMBLER
   (Kenny Rogers)
3. GREATEST HITS
   (Waylon Jennings)
4. A CHRISTMAS TOGETHER
   (John Denver and the Muppets)
5. WHAT GOES AROUND COMES AROUND
   (Waylon Jennings)
6. MISS THE MISSISSIPPI
   (Crystal Gayle)
7. WILLIE NELSON SINGS KRISTOFFERSON
   (Willie Nelson)
8. I'LL ALWAYS LOVE YOU
   (Anne Murray)
9. TEN YEARS OF GOLD
   (Kenny Rogers)
10. STRAIGHT AHEAD
    (Larry Gatlin)

DECEMBER 22, 1979

POP SINGLES

1. ESCAPE (THE PINA COLADA SONG)
   (Rupert Holmes)
2. BABE
   (Styx)
3. PLEASE DON'T GO
   (KC and the Sunshine Band)
4. NO MORE TEARS (ENOUGH IS ENOUGH)
   (Barbra Streisand and Donna Summer)
5. LADIES' NIGHT
   (Kool and the Gang)
6. DO THAT TO ME ONE MORE TIME
   (The Captain and Tennille)

7. STILL
   (Commodores)
8. ROCK WITH YOU
   (Michael Jackson)
9. WE DON'T TALK ANYMORE
   (Cliff Richard)
10. HEARTACHE TONIGHT
    (The Eagles)

POP ALBUMS

1. ON THE RADIO—GREATEST HITS
   VOLUMES I AND II
   (Donna Summer)
2. THE LONG RUN
   (The Eagles)
3. BEE GEES GREATEST
   (The Bee Gees)
4. CORNERSTONE
   (Styx)
5. MIDNIGHT MAGIC
   (Commodores)
6. IN THROUGH THE OUT DOOR
   (Led Zeppelin)
7. KENNY
   (Kenny Rogers)
8. TUSK
   (Fleetwood Mac)
9. OFF THE WALL
   (Michael Jackson)
10. JOURNEY THROUGH THE SECRET LIFE
    OF PLANTS
    (Stevie Wonder)

BLACK SINGLES

1. I WANNA BE YOUR LOVER
   (Prince)
2. DO YOU LOVE WHAT YOU FEEL
   (Rufus and Chaka Khan)
3. ROCK WITH YOU/WORKING DAY AND
   NIGHT
   (Michael Jackson)
4. MOVE YOUR BOOGIE BODY
   (Bar-Kays)
5. RAPPER'S DELIGHT
   (The Sugarhill Gang)
6. LADIES' NIGHT
   (Kool and the Gang)
7. SEND ONE YOUR LOVE
   (Stevie Wonder)
8. CRUISIN'
   (Smokey Robinson)
9. PEANUT BUTTER
   (Twennynine featuring Lenny White)
10. STILL
    (Commodores)

BLACK ALBUMS

1. OFF THE WALL
   (Michael Jackson)
2. MASTERJAM
   (Rufus and Chaka Khan)
3. PRINCE
   (Prince)
4. MIDNIGHT MAGIC
   (Commodores)
5. JOURNEY THROUGH THE SECRET LIFE OF
   PLANTS
   (Stevie Wonder)
6. INJOY
   (Bar-Kays)
7. LADIES' NIGHT
   (Kool and the Gang)
8. WHERE THERE'S SMOKE
   (Smokey Robinson)
9. ON THE RADIO—GREATEST HITS
   VOLUMES I AND II
   (Donna Summer)
10. IDENTIFY YOURSELF
    (The O'Jays)

JAZZ ALBUMS

1. ONE ON ONE
   (Bob James and Earl Klugh)
2. ANGEL OF THE NIGHT
   (Angela Bofill)
3. AMERICAN GARAGE
   (Pat Metheny)
4. PIZZAZZ
   (Patrice Rushen)
5. A TASTE FOR PASSION
   (Jean Luc Ponty)
6. MASTER OF THE GAME
   (George Duke)
7. STREET LIFE
   (Crusaders)
8. RISE
   (Herb Alpert)
9. THE HAWK
   (Dave Valentin)
10. WATER SIGN
    (Jeff Lorber Fusion)

COUNTRY SINGLES

1. MISSIN' YOU
   (Charley Pride)
2. HAPPY BIRTHDAY DARLIN'
   (Conway Twitty)
3. POUR ME ANOTHER TEQUILA
   (Eddie Rabbitt)
4. COWARD OF THE COUNTY
   (Kenny Rogers)
5. I'VE GOT A PICTURE OF US IN MY MIND
   (Loretta Lynn)
6. MY WORLD BEGINS AND ENDS WITH YOU
   (Dave and Sugar)
7. TELL BE WHAT IT'S LIKE
   (Brenda Lee)
8. NOTHING AS ORIGINAL AS YOU
   (The Statler Brothers)
9. HELP ME MAKE IT THROUGH THE NIGHT
   (Willie Nelson)
10. I CHEATED ME RIGHT OUT OF YOU
    (Moe Bandy)

COUNTRY ALBUMS

1. KENNY
   (Kenny Rogers)
2. THE GAMBLER
   (Kenny Rogers)
3. A CHRISTMAS TOGETHER
   (John Denver and the Muppets)
4. GREATEST HITS
   (Waylon Jennings)
5. WHAT GOES AROUND COMES AROUND
   (Waylon Jennings)
6. MISS THE MISSISSIPPI
   (Crystal Gayle)
7. WILLIE NELSON SINGS KRISTOFFERSON
   (Willie Nelson)
8. TEN YEARS OF GOLD
   (Kenny Rogers)
9. I'LL ALWAYS LOVE YOU
   (Anne Murray)
10. PRETTY PAPER
    (Willie Nelson)

DECEMBER 29, 1979

POP SINGLES

1. ESCAPE (THE PINA COLADA SONG)
   (Rupert Holmes)
2. PLEASE DON'T GO
   (KC and the Sunshine Band)
3. BABE
   (Styx)

4. COWARD OF THE COUNTY
   (Kenny Rogers)
5. DO THAT TO ME ONE MORE TIME
   (The Captain and Tennille)
6. ROCK WITH YOU
   (Michael Jackson)
7. NO MORE TEARS (ENOUGH IS ENOUGH)
   (Barbra Streisand and Donna Summer)
8. LADIES' NIGHT
   (Kool and the Gang)
9. WE DON'T TALK ANYMORE
   (Cliff Richard)
10. CRUISIN'
    (Smokey Robinson)

POP ALBUMS

1. THE LONG RUN
   (The Eagles)
2. ON THE RADIO—GREATEST HITS
   VOLUMES I AND II
   (Donna Summer)
3. BEE GEES GREATEST
   (The Bee Gees)
4. CORNERSTONE
   (Styx)
5. KENNY
   (Kenny Rogers)
6. IN THROUGH THE OUT DOOR
   (Led Zeppelin)
7. MIDNIGHT MAGIC
   (Commodores)
8. TUSK
   (Fleetwood Mac)
9. OFF THE WALL
   (Michael Jackson)
10. THE WALL
    (Pink Floyd)

BLACK SINGLES

1. I WANNA BE YOUR LOVER
   (Prince)
2. ROCK WITH YOU/WORKING DAY AND
   NIGHT
   (Michael Jackson)
3. DO YOU LOVE WHAT YOU FEEL
   (Rufus and Chaka Khan)
4. MOVE YOUR BOOGIE BODY
   (Bar-Kays)
5. RAPPER'S DELIGHT
   (The Sugarhill Gang)
6. PEANUT BUTTER
   (Twennynine featuring Lenny White)
7. LADIES' NIGHT
   (Kool and the Gang)
8. CRUISIN'
   (Smokey Robinson)
9. SEND ONE YOUR LOVE
   (Stevie Wonder)
10. YOU KNOW HOW TO LOVE ME
    (Phyllis Hyman)

BLACK ALBUMS

1. OFF THE WALL
   (Michael Jackson)
2. MASTERJAM
   (Rufus and Chaka Khan)
3. PRINCE
   (Prince)
4. MIDNIGHT MAGIC
   (Commodores)
5. JOURNEY THROUGH THE SECRET LIFE OF
   PLANTS
   (Stevie Wonder)
6. INJOY
   (Bar-Kays)
7. YOU KNOW HOW TO LOVE ME
   (Phyllis Hyman)
8. WHERE THERE'S SMOKE
   (Smokey Robinson)
9. LADIES' NIGHT
   (Kool and the Gang)

10. IDENTIFY YOURSELF
    (The O'Jays)

JAZZ ALBUMS

1. ONE ON ONE
   (Bob James and Earl Klugh)
2. ANGEL OF THE NIGHT
   (Angela Bofill)
3. AMERICAN GARAGE
   (Pat Metheny)
4. PIZZAZZ
   (Patrice Rushen)
5. STREET LIFE
   (Crusaders)
6. MASTER OF THE GAME
   (George Duke)
7. A TASTE FOR PASSION
   (Jean Luc Ponty)
8. RISE
   (Herb Alpert)
9. THE HAWK
   (Dave Valentin)
10. 8:30
    (Weather Report)

COUNTRY SINGLES

1. COWARD OF THE COUNTY
   (Kenny Rogers)
2. MISSIN' YOU
   (Charley Pride)
3. POUR ME ANOTHER TEQUILA
   (Eddie Rabbitt)
4. HELP ME MAKE IT THROUGH THE NIGHT
   (Willie Nelson)
5. HAPPY BIRTHDAY DARLIN'
   (Conway Twitty)
6. TELL ME WHAT IT'S LIKE
   (Brenda Lee)
7. OH, HOW I MISS YOU TONIGHT
   (Jim Reeves)
8. NOTHING AS ORIGINAL AS YOU
   (The Statler Brothers)
9. YOU KNOW JUST WHAT I'D DO/THE
   SADNESS OF IT ALL
   (Conway Twitty and Loretta Lynn)
10. HOLDING THE BAG
    (Moe Bandy and Joe Stampley)

COUNTRY ALBUMS

1. KENNY
   (Kenny Rogers)
2. THE GAMBLER
   (Kenny Rogers)
3. A CHRISTMAS TOGETHER
   (John Denver and the Muppets)
4. GREATEST HITS
   (Waylon Jennings)
5. TEN YEARS OF GOLD
   (Kenny Rogers)
6. MISS THE MISSISSIPPI
   (Crystal Gayle)
7. WHAT GOES AROUND COMES AROUND
   (Waylon Jennings)
8. WILLIE NELSON SINGS KRISTOFFERSON
   (Willie Nelson)
9. I'LL ALWAYS LOVE YOU
   (Anne Murray)
10. PRETTY PAPER
    (Willie Nelson)

1980

Overall record sales sagged in 1980, but there were a number of albums that were both artistic and commercial achievements. Pink Floyd's *The Wall* was another foreboding album from a band that has made gloom an art form. What distinguished this double album from every other Pink Floyd LP was that it contained a hugely popular single, the catchy "Another Brick in the Wall." Unbelievably, it was danceable, and predictably it took a bitter view of its subject, elementary school, even paraphrasing Charles Dickens. The fact that one actually could play a Pink Floyd record at a dance club suggested one of disco's most positive qualities. Even rock performers who may have rejected disco's image had been encouraged by the general dance-happy atmosphere to create music for both listening and dancing, a welcome departure from the "head" music that comprised most mainstream rock in the 1970s.

Certainly Michael Jackson and producer Quincy Jones capitalized on that dancing urge on *Off the Wall*, a densely arranged celebration of the body's will to move and Jackson's captivating voice. Jackson proved he was no longer a kid star, but a real creative talent who could write, produce, and arrange, as well as sing (e.g., "Don't Stop 'Til You Get Enough"). On *Off The Wall*, Jones utilized an all-star lineup of musicians and writers (Paul McCartney, Stevie Wonder, Rod Temperton) who could work in a variety of styles. Both Jackson and Jones were respected before this album, but its artistic and commercial success magnified that feeling.

Tom Petty and the Heartbreakers' *Damn the Torpedoes* had a very American sound. Unlike so many young U.S. bands, Petty and company weren't inspired by the sounds of punk and new wave from England. The twangy, American rock sound of The Byrds and The Buffalo Springfield influenced their music. Petty's songs were straightforward commentaries on love's lost and found. His conviction and the band's tight playing made above-average listening.

Three women rockers prospered in 1980: Pat Benatar, Deborah Harry of Blondie, and Chrissie Hynde of The Pretenders, all as different as Spandex pants, bleached hair, and leather jackets. The music behind Benatar on *Crimes of Passion* was pop–heavy metal in the Foreigner style with the advantage that Benatar sang and (certainly) looked better than Lou Graham. On *Eat to the Beat*, Harry's miniscule vocal gifts were offset by her sly delivery and a Michael Chapman production that proved new wave was just pop spelled sideways. Chrissie Hynde was the most talented of this trio, her voice and songs suggesting an earthy sexuality and punky aggression that was quite becoming. Along with her three male cohorts in The Pretenders, Hynde made their debut album, which included the single "Brass in Pocket," one of the year's highlights.

ALBUMS: This was an exceptional period for black albums. Kool and the Gang's *Ladies' Night* was a comeback from a mid-decade lull. Replacing the blazing horns and the old ensemble chants were the keyboards of new producer Deodato, and the slinky vocals of young James Taylor, who on stage reminded one of a tall Michael Jackson.

Midnight Magic was the best album the Commodores ever made. For the first time in their history this Tuskegee, Alabama, sextet made full and effective use of studio technology. Instead of the raw, live sound they and producer James Carmichael had favored for several years, *Midnight Magic* had a slick, polished sound that worked beautifully with "Sail On," one of the LP's two #1 singles.

The Whispers' self-titled album, and Shalamar's *Big Fun* introduced a new black pop production sound, the sound of Solar Records. Black concert promoter Dick Griffey scooped up some of Los Angeles's finest young musicians, and led by bassist-writer-producer Leon Sylvers, they created a bouncy, vibrant music that placed busy bass lines, synthesizers, and multi-tracked guitars under the easy vocals of both groups. The Solar sound was a little slight lyrically, but the music percolated and bubbled with an infectious charm.

Sadly, *In Through the Out Door*, a so-so album, was Led Zeppelin's swan song. Later in the year, drummer John Bonham, whose thumping style was so distinctive, died in London of booze and drugs. The surviving members—Jimmy Page, Robert Plant, and John Paul Jones—disbanded after deciding, quite rightly, that it wouldn't be the same without him.

SINGLES: From the streets of Harlem came the syncopated sound of young voices, rhyming over propulsive dance tracks. The style was called "rapping" and it produced two major chart successes: "Rapper's Delight" by The Sugarhill Gang and "The Breaks" by Kurtis Blow. Many felt this was a short-lived fad that after its burst of popularity would go away. However, these million-selling records were just the start of a seemingly unending flow of rap material aimed at an urban teen (black and white) audience. As doo wop was to street-corner singers in the 1950s, rap is to cassette carriers of the 1980s.

Queen had two of the year's more entertaining singles with the neo-rockabilly "Crazy Little Thing Called Love" and the Chic-influenced "Another One Bites the Dust." Diana Ross benefitted from the real Chic sound as Nile Rodgers and Bernard Edwards wrote and performed on "Upside Down" and "I'm Coming Out." Other superstar collaborations of note were Lionel Richie's writing and production of "Lady" for Kenny Rogers and Barry Gibb's similar support of Barbra Streisand on "Woman In Love."

Bette Midler finally had a big single with the theme from the movie *The Rose*. Olivia Newton-John continued to move those records with "Magic" from her horrible roller-disco flick, *Xanadu*. Australia's latest contribution to America's nausea was Air Supply, a wimpy band of balladeers whose "Lost in Love" and "All Out of Love" were abysmal. Christopher Cross, a large Texan with a small voice, made two artful singles, "Sailing" and "Ride Like the Wind," winning a ton of Grammys in the process.

The worst hits of the year were Lipps Inc.'s "Funkytown," the Spinners' "Working My Way Back to You," Teri DeSario with KC's (formerly of the Sunshine Band) "Yes, I'm Ready," Dr. Hook's "Sexy Eyes," and Robbie Dupree's "Steal Away," a Doobie Brothers rip-off.

Singles worth remembering included: Eddie Rabbitt's pop breakthrough, "Drivin' My Life Away," Gerald Austin's brilliant lead vocal on the Manhattan's "Shining Star," the blue-eyed soul of Ambrosia's "Biggest Part of Me," Irene Cara's flamboyant "Fame" from the equally flashy film, Johnny Lee's laid-back country "Looking for Love," Smokey Robinson's romantic comeback single "Cruisin'," and the droll synthesizer pop of Gary Numan's "Cars."

On the record biz side, Warner Brothers-financed Geffen Records signed several major acts including Donna Summer, Elton John, and John Lennon and Yoko Ono. Reflecting America's continuing fascination with Elvis Presley, RCA released an eight-record set of the dead singer's music.

The Blues Brothers film was a tribute to black music disguised as a crazy slapstick comedy with John Belushi and Dan Ackroyd. Though few noticed, The Blues Brothers band, featuring ex-Booker T and the MGs guitarist Steve Cropper and bassist Duck Dunn, was one of the greatest R&B outfits of all time. They cooked even when Belushi's "singing" was criminal. The Beatles' producer George Martin published his autobiography, *All You Need Is Ears*, in which he makes the stunning observation that "the finest record I have ever made" was "Icarus" by the Paul Winter Consort. Rock's second-best-selling book was *No One Gets Out Alive* by Daniel Sugarman and Jerry Hopkins, a biography of the famous lead singer of The Doors, the late Jim Morrison. Morrison is pictured as a sensitive, narcissistic kid who fancied himself a great poet. This was apparently enough to start a Doors cult. There was even talk of John Travolta wanting to play Morrison, an idea so perverse it was probably true.

Bette Midler

Michael Jackson

Whispers   **Joe Walsh**

Christopher Cross

Shalamar

Kurtis Blow

Kool and the Gang

JANUARY 12, 1980

POP SINGLES

1. ESCAPE (THE PINA COLADA SONG)
   (Rupert Holmes)
2. PLEASE DON'T GO
   (KC and the Sunshine Band)
3. BABE
   (Styx)
4. COWARD OF THE COUNTY
   (Kenny Rogers)
5. DO THAT TO ME ONE MORE TIME
   (The Captain and Tennille)
6. ROCK WITH YOU
   (Michael Jackson)
7. NO MORE TEARS (ENOUGH IS ENOUGH)
   (Barbra Streisand and Donna Summer)
8. LADIES' NIGHT
   (Kool and the Gang)
9. WE DON'T TALK ANYMORE
   (Cliff Richard)
10. CRUISIN'
    (Smokey Robinson)

POP ALBUMS

1. THE LONG RUN
   (The Eagles)
2. ON THE RADIO—GREATEST HITS
   VOLUMES I AND II
   (Donna Summer)
3. BEE GEES GREATEST
   (The Bee Gees)
4. CORNERSTONE
   (Styx)
5. KENNY
   (Kenny Rogers)
6. IN THROUGH THE OUT DOOR
   (Led Zeppelin)
7. MIDNIGHT MAGIC
   (Commodores)
8. TUSK
   (Fleetwood Mac)
9. OFF THE WALL
   (Michael Jackson)
10. THE WALL
    (Pink Floyd)

BLACK SINGLES

1. I WANNA BE YOUR LOVER
   (Prince)
2. ROCK WITH YOU/WORKING DAY AND
   NIGHT
   (Michael Jackson)
3. DO YOU LOVE WHAT YOU FEEL
   (Rufus and Chaka Khan)
4. MOVE YOUR BOOGIE BODY
   (Bar-Kays)
5. RAPPER'S DELIGHT
   (The Sugarhill Gang)
6. PEANUT BUTTER
   (Twennynine featuring Lenny White)
7. LADIES' NIGHT
   (Kool and the Gang)
8. CRUISIN'
   (Smokey Robinson)
9. SEND ONE YOUR LOVE
   (Stevie Wonder)
10. YOU KNOW HOW TO LOVE ME
    (Phyllis Hyman)

BLACK ALBUMS

1. OFF THE WALL
   (Michael Jackson)
2. MASTERJAM
   (Rufus and Chaka Khan)
3. PRINCE
   (Prince)

---

4. MIDNIGHT MAGIC
   (Commodores)
5. JOURNEY THROUGH THE SECRET LIFE
   OF PLANTS
   (Stevie Wonder)
6. INJOY
   (Bar-Kays)
7. YOU KNOW HOW TO LOVE ME
   (Phyllis Hyman)
8. WHERE THERE'S SMOKE
   (Smokey Robinson)
9. LADIES' NIGHT
   (Kool and the Gang)
10. IDENTIFY YOURSELF
    (The O'Jays)

JAZZ ALBUMS

1. ONE ON ONE
   (Bob James and Earl Klugh)
2. ANGEL OF THE NIGHT
   (Angela Bofill)
3. AMERICAN GARAGE
   (Pat Metheny)
4. PIZZAZZ
   (Patrice Rushen)
5. STREET LIFE
   (Crusaders)
6. MASTER OF THE GAME
   (George Duke)
7. A TASTE FOR PASSION
   (Jean Luc Ponty)
8. RISE
   (Herb Alpert)
9. THE HAWK
   (Dave Valentin)
10. 8:30
    (Weather Report)

COUNTRY SINGLES

1. COWARD OF THE COUNTY
   (Kenny Rogers)
2. HELP ME MAKE IT THROUGH THE NIGHT
   (Willie Nelson)
3. POUR ME ANOTHER TEQUILA
   (Eddie Rabbitt)
4. MISSIN' YOU
   (Charley Pride)
5. HOLDING THE BAG
   (Moe Bandy and Joe Stampley)
6. YOU KNOW JUST WHAT I'D DO/THE
   SADNESS OF IT ALL
   (Conway Twitty and Loretta Lynn)
7. OH, HOW I MISS YOU TONIGHT
   (Jim Reeves)
8. HAPPY BIRTHDAY DARLIN'
   (Conway Twitty)
9. YOU'D MAKE AN ANGEL WANT TO CHEAT
   (The Kendalls)
10. LEAVING LOUISIANA IN THE BROAD
    DAYLIGHT
    (The Oak Ridge Boys)

COUNTRY ALBUMS

1. KENNY
   (Kenny Rogers)
2. THE GAMBLER
   (Kenny Rogers)
3. A CHRISTMAS TOGETHER
   (John Denver and the Muppets)
4. TEN YEARS OF GOLD
   (Kenny Rogers)
5. GREATEST HITS
   (Waylon Jennings)
6. MISS THE MISSISSIPPI
   (Crystal Gayle)
7. PRETTY PAPER
   (Willie Nelson)
8. WILLIE NELSON SINGS KRISTOFFERSON
   (Willie Nelson)
9. WHAT GOES AROUND COMES AROUND
   (Waylon Jennings)

---

10. I'LL ALWAYS LOVE YOU
    (Anne Murray)

JANUARY 19, 1980

POP SINGLES

1. ROCK WITH YOU
   (Michael Jackson)
2. PLEASE DON'T GO
   (KC and the Sunshine Band)
3. COWARD OF THE COUNTY
   (Kenny Rogers)
4. DO THAT TO ME ONE MORE TIME
   (The Captain and Tennille)
5. ESCAPE (THE PINA COLADA SONG)
   (Rupert Holmes)
6. BABE
   (Styx)
7. THE LONG RUN
   (The Eagles)
8. CRUISIN'
   (Smokey Robinson)
9. LADIES' NIGHT
   (Kool and the Gang)
10. WE DON'T TALK ANYMORE
    (Cliff Richard)

POP ALBUMS

1. THE LONG RUN
   (The Eagles)
2. ON THE RADIO—GREATEST HITS
   VOLUMES I AND II
   (Donna Summer)
3. BEE GEES GREATEST
   (The Bee Gees)
4. CORNERSTONE
   (Styx)
5. KENNY
   (Kenny Rogers)
6. THE WALL
   (Pink Floyd)
7. IN THROUGH THE OUT DOOR
   (Led Zeppelin)
8. MIDNIGHT MAGIC
   (Commodores)
9. TUSK
   (Fleetwood Mac)
10. OFF THE WALL
    (Michael Jackson)

BLACK SINGLES

1. ROCK WITH YOU/WORKING DAY AND
   NIGHT
   (Michael Jackson)
2. I WANNA BE YOUR LOVER
   (Prince)
3. DO YOU LOVE WHAT YOU FEEL
   (Rufus and Chaka Khan)
4. PEANUT BUTTER
   (Twennynine featuring Lenny White)
5. FOREVER MINE
   (The O'Jays)
6. MOVE YOUR BOOGIE BODY
   (Bar-Kays)
7. THE SECOND TIME AROUND
   (Shalamar)
8. RAPPER'S DELIGHT
   (The Sugarhill Gang)
9. YOU KNOW HOW TO LOVE ME
   (Phyllis Hyman)
10. CRUISIN'
    (Smokey Robinson)

BLACK ALBUMS

1. OFF THE WALL
   (Michael Jackson)

2. PRINCE
   (Prince)
3. MASTERJAM
   (Rufus and Chaka Khan)
4. LIVE! COAST TO COAST
   (Teddy Pendergrass)
5. JOURNEY THROUGH THE SECRET LIFE OF PLANTS
   (Stevie Wonder)
6. WHERE THERE'S SMOKE
   (Smokey Robinson)
7. GLORYHALLASTOOPID
   (Parliament)
8. LADIES' NIGHT
   (Kool and the Gang)
9. MIDNIGHT MAGIC
   (Commodores)
10. YOU KNOW HOW TO LOVE ME
    (Phyllis Hyman)

JAZZ ALBUMS

1. ONE ON ONE
   (Bob James and Earl Klugh)
2. ANGEL OF THE NIGHT
   (Angela Bofill)
3. AMERICAN GARAGE
   (Pat Metheny)
4. PIZZAZZ
   (Patrice Rushen)
5. RISE
   (Herb Alpert)
6. STREET LIFE
   (Crusaders)
7. MASTER OF THE GAME
   (George Duke)
8. A TASTE FOR PASSION
   (Jean Luc Ponty)
9. THE HAWK
   (Dave Valentin)
10. WATER SIGN
    (Jeff Lorber Fusion)

COUNTRY SINGLES

1. COWARD OF THE COUNTY
   (Kenny Rogers)
2. HELP ME MAKE IT THROUGH THE NIGHT
   (Willie Nelson)
3. HOLDING THE BAG
   (Moe Bandy and Joe Stampley)
4. LEAVING LOUISIANA IN THE BROAD DAYLIGHT
   (The Oak Ridge Boys)
5. YOU KNOW JUST WHAT I'D DO/THE SADNESS OF IT ALL
   (Conway Twitty and Loretta Lynn)
6. YOU'D MAKE AN ANGEL WANT TO CHEAT
   (The Kendalls)
7. POUR ME ANOTHER TEQUILA
   (Eddie Rabbitt)
8. OH, HOW I MISS YOU TONIGHT
   (Jim Reeves)
9. I'LL BE COMING BACK FOR MORE
   (T.G. Sheppard)
10. LOVE ME OVER AGAIN
    (Don Williams)

COUNTRY ALBUMS

1. KENNY
   (Kenny Rogers)
2. THE GAMBLER
   (Kenny Rogers)
3. GREATEST HITS
   (Waylon Jennings)
4. TEN YEARS OF GOLD
   (Kenny Rogers)
5. MISS THE MISSISSIPPI
   (Crystal Gayle)
6. WHAT GOES AROUND COMES AROUND
   (Waylon Jennings)
7. PRETTY PAPER
   (Willie Nelson)

8. WILLIE NELSON SINGS KRISTOFFERSON
   (Willie Nelson)
9. I'LL ALWAYS LOVE YOU
   (Anne Murray)
10. CLASSIC CRYSTAL
    (Crystal Gayle)

JANUARY 26, 1980

POP SINGLES

1. ROCK WITH YOU
   (Michael Jackson)
2. COWARD OF THE COUNTY
   (Kenny Rogers)
3. DO THAT TO ME ONE MORE TIME
   (The Captain and Tennille)
4. THE LONG RUN
   (The Eagles)
5. PLEASE DON'T GO
   (KC and the Sunshine Band)
6. CRUISIN'
   (Smokey Robinson)
7. BABE
   (Styx)
8. ESCAPE (THE PINA COLADA SONG)
   (Rupert Holmes)
9. LADIES' NIGHT
   (Kool and the Gang)
10. DON'T DO ME LIKE THAT
    (Tom Petty and the Heartbreakers)

POP ALBUMS

1. THE LONG RUN
   (The Eagles)
2. ON THE RADIO—GREATEST HITS VOLUMES I AND II
   (Donna Summer)
3. KENNY
   (Kenny Rogers)
4. CORNERSTONE
   (Styx)
5. THE WALL
   (Pink Floyd)
6. BEE GEES GREATEST
   (The Bee Gees)
7. OFF THE WALL
   (Michael Jackson)
8. IN THROUGH THE OUT DOOR
   (Led Zeppelin)
9. MIDNIGHT MAGIC
   (Commodores)
10. TUSK
    (Fleetwood Mac)

BLACK SINGLES

1. ROCK WITH YOU/WORKING DAY AND NIGHT
   (Michael Jackson)
2. THE SECOND TIME AROUND
   (Shalamar)
3. PEANUT BUTTER
   (Twennynine featuring Lenny White)
4. FOREVER MINE
   (The O'Jays)
5. I WANNA BE YOUR LOVER
   (Prince)
6. DO YOU LOVE WHAT YOU FEEL
   (Rufus and Chaka Khan)
7. JUST A TOUCH OF LOVE
   (Slave)
8. YOU KNOW HOW TO LOVE ME
   (Phyllis Hyman)
9. MOVE YOUR BOOGIE BODY
   (Bar-Kays)
10. HAVEN'T YOU HEARD
    (Patrice Rushen)

BLACK ALBUMS

1. OFF THE WALL
   (Michael Jackson)
2. PRINCE
   (Prince)
3. MASTERJAM
   (Rufus and Chaka Khan)
4. LIVE! COAST TO COAST
   (Teddy Pendergrass)
5. THE WHISPERS
   (Whispers)
6. GLORYHALLASTOOPID
   (Parliament)
7. WHERE THERE'S SMOKE
   (Smokey Robinson)
8. MIDNIGHT MAGIC
   (Commodores)
9. JOURNEY THROUGH THE SECRET LIFE OF PLANTS
   (Stevie Wonder)
10. JUST A TOUCH OF LOVE
    (Slave)

JAZZ ALBUMS

1. ONE ON ONE
   (Bob James and Earl Klugh)
2. ANGEL OF THE NIGHT
   (Angela Bofill)
3. AMERICAN GARAGE
   (Pat Metheny)
4. PIZZAZZ
   (Patrice Rushen)
5. NO STRANGER TO LOVE
   (Roy Ayers)
6. RISE
   (Herb Alpert)
7. BEST OF FRIENDS
   (Twennynine featuring Lenny White)
8. STREET LIFE
   (Crusaders)
9. MASTER OF THE GAME
   (George Duke)
10. STREET BEAT
    (Tom Scott)

COUNTRY SINGLES

1. LEAVING LOUISIANA IN THE BROAD DAYLIGHT
   (The Oak Ridge Boys)
2. COWARD OF THE COUNTY
   (Kenny Rogers)
3. HOLDING THE BAG
   (Moe Bandy and Joe Stampley)
4. I'LL BE COMING BACK FOR MORE
   (T.G. Sheppard)
5. LOVE ME OVER AGAIN
   (Don Williams)
6. YOU'D MAKE AN ANGEL WANT TO CHEAT
   (The Kendalls)
7. HELP ME MAKE IT THROUGH THE NIGHT
   (Willie Nelson)
8. YOU KNOW JUST WHAT I'D DO/THE SADNESS OF IT ALL
   (Conway Twitty and Loretta Lynn)
9. POUR ME ANOTHER TEQUILA
   (Eddie Rabbitt)
10. BLUE HEARTACHE
    (Gail Davies)

COUNTRY ALBUMS

1. KENNY
   (Kenny Rogers)
2. THE GAMBLER
   (Kenny Rogers)
3. GREATEST HITS
   (Waylon Jennings)
4. TEN YEARS OF GOLD
   (Kenny Rogers)

5. MISS THE MISSISSIPPI
   (Crystal Gayle)
6. WHAT GOES AROUND COMES AROUND
   (Waylon Jennings)
7. WILLIE NELSON SINGS KRISTOFFERSON
   (Willie Nelson)
8. I'LL ALWAYS LOVE YOU
   (Anne Murray)
9. STARDUST
   (Willie Nelson)
10. CLASSIC CRYSTAL
    (Crystal Gayle)

FEBRUARY 2, 1980

POP SINGLES

1. COWARD OF THE COUNTY
   (Kenny Rogers)
2. DO THAT TO ME ONE MORE TIME
   (The Captain and Tennille)
3. ROCK WITH YOU
   (Michael Jackson)
4. THE LONG RUN
   (The Eagles)
5. CRUISIN'
   (Smokey Robinson)
6. CRAZY LITTLE THING CALLED LOVE
   (Queen)
7. YES I'M READY
   (Teri Desario with KC)
8. DON'T DO ME LIKE THAT
   (Tom Petty and the Heartbreakers)
9. SARA
   (Fleetwood Mac)
10. ESCAPE (THE PINA COLADA SONG)
    (Rupert Holmes)

POP ALBUMS

1. THE LONG RUN
   (The Eagles)
2. THE WALL
   (Pink Floyd)
3. KENNY
   (Kenny Rogers)
4. OFF THE WALL
   (Michael Jackson)
5. ON THE RADIO—GREATEST HITS
   VOLUMES I AND II
   (Donna Summer)
6. CORNERSTONE
   (Styx)
7. DAMN THE TORPEDOES
   (Tom Petty and the Heartbreakers)
8. IN THROUGH THE OUT DOOR
   (Led Zeppelin)
9. PHOENIX
   (Dan Fogelberg)
10. MIDNIGHT MAGIC
    (Commodores)

BLACK SINGLES

1. THE SECOND TIME AROUND
   (Shalamar)
2. ROCK WITH YOU/WORKING DAY AND
   NIGHT
   (Michael Jackson)
3. PEANUT BUTTER
   (Twennynine featuring Lenny White)
4. FOREVER MINE
   (The O'Jays)
5. I WANNA BE YOUR LOVER
   (Prince)
6. JUST A TOUCH OF LOVE
   (Slave)
7. DO YOU LOVE WHAT YOU FEEL
   (Rufus and Chaka Khan)
8. HAVEN'T YOU HEARD
   (Patrice Rushen)

9. SPECIAL LADY
   (Ray, Goodman and Brown)
10. YOU KNOW HOW TO LOVE ME
    (Phyllis Hyman)

BLACK ALBUMS

1. OFF THE WALL
   (Michael Jackson)
2. PRINCE
   (Prince)
3. THE WHISPERS
   (Whispers)
4. MASTERJAM
   (Rufus and Chaka Khan)
5. GLORYHALLASTOOPID
   (Parliament)
6. LIVE! COAST TO COAST
   (Teddy Pendergrass)
7. JUST A TOUCH OF LOVE
   (Slave)
8. WHERE THERE'S SMOKE
   (Smokey Robinson)
9. YOU KNOW HOW TO LOVE ME
   (Phyllis Hyman)
10. MIDNIGHT MAGIC
    (Commodores)

JAZZ ALBUMS

1. ANGEL OF THE NIGHT
   (Angela Bofill)
2. ONE ON ONE
   (Bob James and Earl Klugh)
3. PIZZAZZ
   (Patrice Rushen)
4. AMERICAN GARAGE
   (Pat Metheny)
5. NO STRANGER TO LOVE
   (Roy Ayers)
6. RISE
   (Herb Alpert)
7. BEST OF FRIENDS
   (Twennynine featuring Lenny White)
8. STREET LIFE
   (Crusaders)
9. MASTER OF THE GAME
   (George Duke)
10. STREET BEAT
    (Tom Scott)

COUNTRY SINGLES

1. LEAVING LOUISIANA IN THE BROAD
   DAYLIGHT
   (The Oak Ridge Boys)
2. I'LL BE COMING BACK FOR MORE
   (T.G. Sheppard)
3. LOVE ME OVER AGAIN
   (Don Williams)
4. COWARD OF THE COUNTY
   (Kenny Rogers)
5. HOLDING THE BAG
   (Moe Bandy and Joe Stampley)
6. BABY, YOU'RE SOMETHING
   (John Conlee)
7. YEARS
   (Barbara Mandrell)
8. BLUE HEARTACHE
   (Gail Davies)
9. YOUR OLD COLD SHOULDER
   (Crystal Gayle)
10. YOU'D MAKE AN ANGEL WANT TO CHEAT
    (The Kendalls)

COUNTRY ALBUMS

1. KENNY
   (Kenny Rogers)
2. THE GAMBLER
   (Kenny Rogers)

3. GREATEST HITS
   (Waylon Jennings)
4. TEN YEARS OF GOLD
   (Kenny Rogers)
5. MISS THE MISSISSIPPI
   (Crystal Gayle)
6. WHAT GOES AROUND COMES AROUND
   (Waylon Jennings)
7. WILLIE NELSON SINGS KRISTOFFERSON
   (Willie Nelson)
8. I'LL ALWAYS LOVE YOU
   (Anne Murray)
9. CLASSIC CRYSTAL
   (Crystal Gayle)
10. STRAIGHT AHEAD
    (Larry Gatlin)

FEBRUARY 9, 1980

POP SINGLES

1. DO THAT TO ME ONE MORE TIME
   (The Captain and Tennille)
2. CRAZY LITTLE THING CALLED LOVE
   (Queen)
3. COWARD OF THE COUNTY
   (Kenny Rogers)
4. YES I'M READY
   (Teri Desario with KC)
5. CRUISIN'
   (Smokey Robinson)
6. ROCK WITH YOU
   (Michael Jackson)
7. SARA
   (Fleetwood Mac)
8. DON'T DO ME LIKE THAT
   (Tom Petty and the Heartbreakers)
9. LONGER
   (Dan Fogelberg)
10. THIS IS IT
    (Kenny Loggins)

POP ALBUMS

1. THE WALL
   (Pink Floyd)
2. OFF THE WALL
   (Michael Jackson)
3. THE LONG RUN
   (The Eagles)
4. ON THE RADIO—GREATEST HITS
   VOLUMES I AND II
   (Donna Summer)
5. DAMN THE TORPEDOES
   (Tom Petty and the Heartbreakers)
6. KENNY
   (Kenny Rogers)
7. PHOENIX
   (Dan Fogelberg)
8. CORNERSTONE
   (Styx)
9. IN THROUGH THE OUT DOOR
   (Led Zeppelin)
10. FREEDOM AT POINT ZERO
    (The Jefferson Starship)

BLACK SINGLES

1. THE SECOND TIME AROUND
   (Shalamar)
2. ROCK WITH YOU/WORKING DAY AND
   NIGHT
   (Michael Jackson)
3. PEANUT BUTTER
   (Twennynine featuring Lenny White)
4. HAVEN'T YOU HEARD
   (Patrice Rushen)
5. JUST A TOUCH OF LOVE
   (Slave)
6. SPECIAL LADY
   (Ray, Goodman and Brown)

7. I WANNA BE YOUR LOVER
   (Prince)
8. FOREVER MINE
   (The O'Jays)
9. DO YOU LOVE WHAT YOU FEEL
   (Rufus and Chaka Khan)
10. I SHOULDA LOVED YA
    (Narada Michael Walden)

BLACK ALBUMS

1. OFF THE WALL
   (Michael Jackson)
2. THE WHISPERS
   (Whispers)
3. PRINCE
   (Prince)
4. MASTERJAM
   (Rufus and Chaka Khan)
5. GLORYHALLASTOOPID
   (Parliament)
6. LIVE! COAST TO COAST
   (Teddy Pendergrass)
7. WHERE THERE'S SMOKE
   (Smokey Robinson)
8. JUST A TOUCH OF LOVE
   (Slave)
9. BIG FUN
   (Shalamar)
10. YOU KNOW HOW TO LOVE ME
    (Phyllis Hyman)

JAZZ ALBUMS

1. ONE ON ONE
   (Bob James and Earl Klugh)
2. ANGEL OF THE NIGHT
   (Angela Bofill)
3. PIZZAZZ
   (Patrice Rushen)
4. AMERICAN GARAGE
   (Pat Metheny)
5. NO STRANGER TO LOVE
   (Roy Ayers)
6. BEST OF FRIENDS
   (Twennynine featuring Lenny White)
7. RISE
   (Herb Alpert)
8. HIROSHIMA
   (Hiroshima)
9. MASTER OF THE GAME
   (George Duke)
10. A TASTE FOR PASSION
    (Jean Luc Ponty)

COUNTRY SINGLES

1. I'LL BE COMING BACK FOR MORE
   (T.G. Sheppard)
2. LOVE ME OVER AGAIN
   (Don Williams)
3. LEAVING LOUISIANA IN THE BROAD
   DAYLIGHT
   (The Oak Ridge Boys)
4. BABY, YOU'RE SOMETHING
   (John Conlee)
5. YEARS
   (Barbara Mandrell)
6. YOUR OLD COLD SHOULDER
   (Crystal Gayle)
7. COWARD OF THE COUNTY
   (Kenny Rogers)
8. BLUE HEARTACHE
   (Gail Davies)
9. DAYDREAM BELIEVER
   (Anne Murray)
10. BACK TO BACK
    (Jeanne Pruett)

COUNTRY ALBUMS

1. KENNY
   (Kenny Rogers)

---

2. THE GAMBLER
   (Kenny Rogers)
3. GREATEST HITS
   (Waylon Jennings)
4. MISS THE MISSISSIPPI
   (Crystal Gayle)
5. TEN YEARS OF GOLD
   (Kenny Rogers)
6. WILLIE NELSON SINGS KRISTOFFERSON
   (Willie Nelson)
7. STRAIGHT AHEAD
   (Larry Gatlin)
8. WHAT GOES AROUND COMES AROUND
   (Waylon Jennings)
9. I'LL ALWAYS LOVE YOU
   (Anne Murray)
10. CLASSIC CRYSTAL
    (Crystal Gayle)

FEBRUARY 16, 1980

POP SINGLES

1. CRAZY LITTLE THING CALLED LOVE
   (Queen)
2. YES I'M READY
   (Teri Desario with KC)
3. COWARD OF THE COUNTY
   (Kenny Rogers)
4. LONGER
   (Dan Fogelberg)
5. CRUISIN'
   (Smokey Robinson)
6. ROCK WITH YOU
   (Michael Jackson)
7. SARA
   (Fleetwood Mac)
8. DO THAT TO ME ONE MORE TIME
   (The Captain and Tennille)
9. ON THE RADIO
   (Donna Summer)
10. THIS IS IT
    (Kenny Loggins)

POP ALBUMS

1. THE WALL
   (Pink Floyd)
2. OFF THE WALL
   (Michael Jackson)
3. THE LONG RUN
   (The Eagles)
4. ON THE RADIO—GREATEST HITS
   VOLUMES I AND II
   (Donna Summer)
5. DAMN THE TORPEDOES
   (Tom Petty and the Heartbreakers)
6. PHOENIX
   (Dan Fogelberg)
7. KENNY
   (Kenny Rogers)
8. CORNERSTONE
   (Styx)
9. IN THROUGH THE OUT DOOR
   (Led Zeppelin)
10. FREEDOM AT POINT ZERO
    (The Jefferson Starship)

BLACK SINGLES

1. THE SECOND TIME AROUND
   (Shalamar)
2. ROCK WITH YOU/WORKING DAY AND
   NIGHT
   (Michael Jackson)
3. SPECIAL LADY
   (Ray, Goodman and Brown)
4. HAVEN'T YOU HEARD
   (Patrice Rushen)
5. JUST A TOUCH OF LOVE
   (Slave)

---

6. AND THE BEAT GOES ON
   (Whispers)
7. PEANUT BUTTER
   (Twennynine featuring Lenny White)
8. I SHOULDA LOVED YA
   (Narada Michael Walden)
9. TOO HOT
   (Kool and the Gang)
10. I WANNA BE YOUR LOVER
    (Prince)

BLACK ALBUMS

1. OFF THE WALL
   (Michael Jackson)
2. THE WHISPERS
   (Whispers)
3. PRINCE
   (Prince)
4. MASTERJAM
   (Rufus and Chaka Khan)
5. GLORYHALLASTOOPID
   (Parliament)
6. LIVE! COAST TO COAST
   (Teddy Pendergrass)
7. JUST A TOUCH OF LOVE
   (Slave)
8. WHERE THERE'S SMOKE
   (Smokey Robinson)
9. PIZZAZZ
   (Patrice Rushen)
10. YOU KNOW HOW TO LOVE ME
    (Phyllis Hyman)

JAZZ ALBUMS

1. ONE ON ONE
   (Bob James and Earl Klugh)
2. ANGEL OF THE NIGHT
   (Angela Bofill)
3. PIZZAZZ
   (Patrice Rushen)
4. BEST OF FRIENDS
   (Twennynine featuring Lenny White)
5. NO STRANGER TO LOVE
   (Roy Ayers)
6. AMERICAN GARAGE
   (Pat Metheny)
7. HIROSHIMA
   (Hiroshima)
8. RISE
   (Herb Alpert)
9. EVERY GENERATION
   (Ronnie Laws)
10. A TASTE FOR PASSION
    (Jean Luc Ponty)

COUNTRY SINGLES

1. LOVE ME OVER AGAIN
   (Don Williams)
2. YEARS
   (Barbara Mandrell)
3. BABY, YOU'RE SOMETHING
   (John Conlee)
4. I'LL BE COMING BACK FOR MORE
   (T.G. Sheppard)
5. DAYDREAM BELIEVER
   (Anne Murray)
6. YOUR OLD COLD SHOULDER
   (Crystal Gayle)
7. I AIN'T LIVING LONG LIKE THIS
   (Waylon Jennings)
8. I CAN'T GET ENOUGH OF YOU
   (Razzy Bailey)
9. NOTHING SURE LOOKED GOOD ON YOU
   (Gene Watson)
10. BACK TO BACK
    (Jeanne Pruett)

COUNTRY ALBUMS

1. KENNY
   (Kenny Rogers)

2. THE GAMBLER
   (Kenny Rogers)
3. GREATEST HITS
   (Waylon Jennings)
4. WILLIE NELSON SINGS KRISTOFFERSON
   (Willie Nelson)
5. TEN YEARS OF GOLD
   (Kenny Rogers)
6. MISS THE MISSISSIPPI
   (Crystal Gayle)
7. STRAIGHT AHEAD
   (Larry Gatlin)
8. THE BEST OF THE STATLER BROTHERS
   RIDES AGAIN, VOL. II
   (The Statler Brothers)
9. CLASSIC CRYSTAL
   (Crystal Gayle)
10. I'LL ALWAYS LOVE YOU
    (Anne Murray)

FEBRUARY 23, 1980

POP SINGLES

1. CRAZY LITTLE THING CALLED LOVE
   (Queen)
2. YES I'M READY
   (Teri Desario with KC)
3. LONGER
   (Dan Fogelberg)
4. ON THE RADIO
   (Donna Summer)
5. COWARD OF THE COUNTY
   (Kenny Rogers)
6. ROCK WITH YOU
   (Michael Jackson)
7. DESIRE
   (Andy Gibb)
8. SEPTEMBER MORN
   (Neil Diamond)
9. DO THAT TO ME ONE MORE TIME
   (The Captain and Tennille)
10. ROMEO'S TUNE
    (Steve Forbert)

POP ALBUMS

1. THE WALL
   (Pink Floyd)
2. OFF THE WALL
   (Michael Jackson)
3. PHOENIX
   (Dan Fogelberg)
4. ON THE RADIO—GREATEST HITS—
   VOLUMES I AND II
   (Donna Summer)
5. DAMN THE TORPEDOES
   (Tom Petty and the Heartbreakers)
6. THE LONG RUN
   (The Eagles)
7. KENNY
   (Kenny Rogers)
8. CORNERSTONE
   (Styx)
9. THE WHISPERS
   (Whispers)
10. SEPTEMBER MORN
    (Neil Diamond)

BLACK SINGLES

1. SPECIAL LADY
   (Ray, Goodman and Brown)
2. AND THE BEAT GOES ON
   (Whispers)
3. THE SECOND TIME AROUND
   (Shalamar)
4. ROCK WITH YOU/WORKING DAY AND
   NIGHT
   (Michael Jackson)

5. HAVEN'T YOU HEARD
   (Patrice Rushen)
6. TOO HOT
   (Kool and the Gang)
7. I SHOULDA LOVED YA
   (Narada Michael Walden)
8. JUST A TOUCH OF LOVE
   (Slave)
9. PEANUT BUTTER
   (Twennynine featuring Lenny White)
10. GOT TO LOVE SOMEBODY
    (Sister Sledge)

BLACK ALBUMS

1. THE WHISPERS
   (Whispers)
2. OFF THE WALL
   (Michael Jackson)
3. RAY, GOODMAN AND BROWN
   (Ray, Goodman and Brown)
4. GLORYHALLASTOOPID
   (Parliament)
5. MASTERJAM
   (Rufus and Chaka Khan)
6. PRINCE
   (Prince)
7. BIG FUN
   (Shalamar)
8. THE GAP BAND II
   (The Gap Band)
9. PIZZAZZ
   (Patrice Rushen)
10. YOU KNOW HOW TO LOVE ME
    (Phyllis Hyman)

JAZZ ALBUMS

1. ONE ON ONE
   (Bob James and Earl Klugh)
2. PIZZAZZ
   (Patrice Rushen)
3. ANGEL OF THE NIGHT
   (Angela Bofill)
4. NO STRANGER TO LOVE
   (Roy Ayers)
5. EVERY GENERATION
   (Ronnie Laws)
6. HIROSHIMA
   (Hiroshima)
7. AMERICAN GARAGE
   (Pat Metheny)
8. BEST OF FRIENDS
   (Twennynine featuring Lenny White)
9. FUN AND GAMES
   (Chuck Mangione)
10. RISE
    (Herb Alpert)

COUNTRY SINGLES

1. YEARS
   (Barbara Mandrell)
2. DAYDREAM BELIEVER
   (Anne Murray)
3. BABY, YOU'RE SOMETHING
   (John Conlee)
4. I AIN'T LIVING LONG LIKE THIS
   (Waylon Jennings)
5. NOTHING SURE LOOKED GOOD ON YOU
   (Gene Watson)
6. I CAN'T GET ENOUGH OF YOU
   (Razzy Bailey)
7. LOVE ME OVER AGAIN
   (Don Williams)
8. MY HEROES HAVE ALWAYS BEEN
   COWBOYS
   (Willie Nelson)
9. WHY DON'T YOU SPEND THE NIGHT
   (Ronnie Milsap)
10. I'LL BE COMING BACK FOR MORE
    (T.G. Sheppard)

COUNTRY ALBUMS

1. KENNY
   (Kenny Rogers)
2. THE GAMBLER
   (Kenny Rogers)
3. GREATEST HITS
   (Waylon Jennings)
4. WILLIE NELSON SINGS KRISTOFFERSON
   (Willie Nelson)
5. THE BEST OF THE STATLER BROTHERS
   RIDES AGAIN, VOL. II
   (The Statler Brothers)
6. TEN YEARS OF GOLD
   (Kenny Rogers)
7. MISS THE MISSISSIPPI
   (Crystal Gayle)
8. CLASSIC CRYSTAL
   (Crystal Gayle)
9. I'LL ALWAYS LOVE YOU
   (Anne Murray)
10. STRAIGHT AHEAD
    (Larry Gatlin)

MARCH 1, 1980

POP SINGLES

1. YES I'M READY
   (Teri Desario with KC)
2. ON THE RADIO
   (Donna Summer)
3. LONGER
   (Dan Fogelberg)
4. CRAZY LITTLE THING CALLED LOVE
   (Queen)
5. DESIRE
   (Andy Gibb)
6. COWARD OF THE COUNTY
   (Kenny Rogers)
7. SEPTEMBER MORN
   (Neil Diamond)
8. WORKING MY WAY BACK TO
   YOU/FORGIVE ME, GIRL (MEDLEY)
   (Spinners)
9. ROCK WITH YOU
   (Michael Jackson)
10. ROMEO'S TUNE
    (Steve Forbert)

POP ALBUMS

1. THE WALL
   (Pink Floyd)
2. OFF THE WALL
   (Michael Jackson)
3. PHOENIX
   (Dan Fogelberg)
4. ON THE RADIO—GREATEST HITS
   VOLUMES I AND II
   (Donna Summer)
5. DAMN THE TORPEDOES
   (Tom Petty and the Heartbreakers)
6. THE LONG RUN
   (The Eagles)
7. THE WHISPERS
   (Whispers)
8. KENNY
   (Kenny Rogers)
9. CORNERSTONE
   (Styx)
10. SEPTEMBER MORN
    (Neil Diamond)

BLACK SINGLES

1. AND THE BEAT GOES ON
   (Whispers)
2. SPECIAL LADY
   (Ray, Goodman and Brown)

3. THE SECOND TIME AROUND
   (Shalamar)
4. TOO HOT
   (Kool and the Gang)
5. ROCK WITH YOU/WORKING DAY AND NIGHT
   (Michael Jackson)
6. HAVEN'T YOU HEARD
   (Patrice Rushen)
7. I SHOULDA LOVED YA
   (Narada Michael Walden)
8. GOT TO LOVE SOMEBODY
   (Sister Sledge)
9. JUST A TOUCH OF LOVE
   (Slave)
10. PEANUT BUTTER
    (Twennynine featuring Lenny White)

BLACK ALBUMS

1. THE WHISPERS
   (Whispers)
2. OFF THE WALL
   (Michael Jackson)
3. RAY, GOODMAN AND BROWN
   (Ray, Goodman and Brown)
4. THE GAP BAND II
   (The Gap Band)
5. GLORYHALLASTOOPID
   (Parliament)
6. PRINCE
   (Prince)
7. BIG FUN
   (Shalamar)
8. MASTERJAM
   (Rufus and Chaka Khan)
9. PIZZAZZ
   (Patrice Rushen)
10. ANGEL OF THE NIGHT
    (Angela Bofill)

JAZZ ALBUMS

1. EVERY GENERATION
   (Ronnie Laws)
2. ONE ON ONE
   (Bob James and Earl Klugh)
3. ANGEL OF THE NIGHT
   (Angela Bofill)
4. FUN AND GAMES
   (Chuck Mangione)
5. PIZZAZZ
   (Patrice Rushen)
6. HIROSHIMA
   (Hiroshima)
7. AMERICAN GARAGE
   (Pat Metheny)
8. NO STRANGER TO LOVE
   (Roy Ayers)
9. BEST OF FRIENDS
   (Twennynine featuring Lenny White)
10. RISE
    (Herb Alpert)

COUNTRY SINGLES

1. DAYDREAM BELIEVER
   (Anne Murray)
2. I AIN'T LIVING LONG LIKE THIS
   (Waylon Jennings)
3. MY HEROES HAVE ALWAYS BEEN COWBOYS
   (Willie Nelson)
4. NOTHING SURE LOOKED GOOD ON YOU
   (Gene Watson)
5. I CAN'T GET ENOUGH OF YOU
   (Razzy Bailey)
6. WHY DON'T YOU SPEND THE NIGHT
   (Ronnie Milsap)
7. YEARS
   (Barbara Mandrell)
8. BABY, YOU'RE SOMETHING
   (John Conlee)

9. THE OLD SIDE OF TOWN/JESUS ON THE RADIO
   (Tom T. Hall)
10. LYING TIME AGAIN/FOOLED AROUND AND FELL IN LOVE
    (Mel Tillis)

COUNTRY ALBUMS

1. KENNY
   (Kenny Rogers)
2. THE GAMBLER
   (Kenny Rogers)
3. GREATEST HITS
   (Waylon Jennings)
4. THE BEST OF THE STATLER BROTHERS RIDES AGAIN, VOL. II
   (The Statler Brothers)
5. WILLIE NELSON SINGS KRISTOFFERSON
   (Willie Nelson)
6. TEN YEARS OF GOLD
   (Kenny Rogers)
7. CLASSIC CRYSTAL
   (Crystal Gayle)
8. MISS THE MISSISSIPPI
   (Crystal Gayle)
9. STRAIGHT AHEAD
   (Larry Gatlin)
10. THE OAK RIDGE BOYS HAVE ARRIVED
    (The Oak Ridge Boys)

MARCH 8, 1980

POP SINGLES

1. ON THE RADIO
   (Donna Summer)
2. LONGER
   (Dan Fogelberg)
3. ANOTHER BRICK IN THE WALL (PART II)
   (Pink Floyd)
4. DESIRE
   (Andy Gibb)
5. CRAZY LITTLE THING CALLED LOVE
   (Queen)
6. WORKING MY WAY BACK TO YOU/FORGIVE ME, GIRL (MEDLEY)
   (Spinners)
7. SEPTEMBER MORN
   (Neil Diamond)
8. YES I'M READY
   (Teri Desario with KC)
9. TOO HOT
   (Kool and the Gang)
10. DAYDREAM BELIEVER
    (Anne Murray)

POP ALBUMS

1. THE WALL
   (Pink Floyd)
2. OFF THE WALL
   (Michael Jackson)
3. PHOENIX
   (Dan Fogelberg)
4. DAMN THE TORPEDOES
   (Tom Petty and the Heartbreakers)
5. ON THE RADIO—GREATEST HITS VOLUMES I AND II
   (Donna Summer)
6. THE LONG RUN
   (The Eagles)
7. THE WHISPERS
   (Whispers)
8. BEBE LE STRANGE
   (Heart)
9. KENNY
   (Kenny Rogers)
10. PERMANENT WAVE
    (Rush)

BLACK SINGLES

1. AND THE BEAT GOES ON
   (Whispers)
2. SPECIAL LADY
   (Ray, Goodman and Brown)
3. TOO HOT
   (Kool and the Gang)
4. THE SECOND TIME AROUND
   (Shalamar)
5. BOUNCE, ROCK, SKATE, ROLL, PART I
   (Vaughan Mason and Crew)
6. STOMP!
   (The Brothers Johnson)
7. GOT TO LOVE SOMEBODY
   (Sister Sledge)
8. I SHOULDA LOVED YA
   (Narada Michael Walden)
9. HAVEN'T YOU HEARD
   (Patrice Rushen)
10. YOU ARE MY HEAVEN
    (Roberta Flack with Donny Hathaway)

BLACK ALBUMS

1. THE WHISPERS
   (Whispers)
2. OFF THE WALL
   (Michael Jackson)
3. RAY, GOODMAN AND BROWN
   (Ray, Goodman and Brown)
4. THE GAP BAND II
   (The Gap Band)
5. LIGHT UP THE NIGHT
   (The Brothers Johnson)
6. PRINCE
   (Prince)
7. GLORYHALLASTOOPID
   (Parliament)
8. LADIES' NIGHT
   (Kool and the Gang)
9. ANGEL OF THE NIGHT
   (Angela Bofill)
10. BIG FUN
    (Shalamar)

JAZZ ALBUMS

1. FUN AND GAMES
   (Chuck Mangione)
2. EVERY GENERATION
   (Ronnie Laws)
3. ANGEL OF THE NIGHT
   (Angela Bofill)
4. ONE ON ONE
   (Bob James and Earl Klugh)
5. PIZZAZZ
   (Patrice Rushen)
6. HIROSHIMA
   (Hiroshima)
7. SKYLARKIN'
   (Grover Washington Jr.)
8. HIDEAWAY
   (David Sanborn)
9. NO STRANGER TO LOVE
   (Roy Ayers)
10. AMERICAN GARAGE
    (Pat Metheny)

COUNTRY SINGLES

1. I AIN'T LIVING LONG LIKE THIS
   (Waylon Jennings)
2. MY HEROES HAVE ALWAYS BEEN COWBOYS
   (Willie Nelson)
3. DAYDREAM BELIEVER
   (Anne Murray)
4. NOTHING SURE LOOKED GOOD ON YOU
   (Gene Watson)
5. WHY DON'T YOU SPEND THE NIGHT
   (Ronnie Milsap)

6. LYING TIME AGAIN/FOOLED AROUND
 AND FELL IN LOVE
 (Mel Tillis)
7. I'D LOVE TO LAY YOU DOWN
 (Conway Twitty)
8. (I'LL EVEN LOVE YOU) BETTER THAN I
 DID THEN
 (The Statler Brothers)
9. THE OLD SIDE OF TOWN/JESUS ON THE
 RADIO
 (Tom T. Hall)
10. MEN
 (Charly McClain)

COUNTRY ALBUMS

1. KENNY
 (Kenny Rogers)
2. THE GAMBLER
 (Kenny Rogers)
3. GREATEST HITS
 (Waylon Jennings)
4. THE BEST OF THE STATLER BROTHERS
 RIDES AGAIN, VOL. II
 (The Statler Brothers)
5. WILLIE NELSON SINGS KRISTOFFERSON
 (Willie Nelson)
6. TEN YEARS OF GOLD
 (Kenny Rogers)
7. STRAIGHT AHEAD
 (Larry Gatlin)
8. STARDUST
 (Willie Nelson)
9. CLASSIC CRYSTAL
 (Crystal Gayle)
10. THE OAK RIDGE BOYS HAVE ARRIVED
 (The Oak Ridge Boys)

MARCH 15, 1980

POP SINGLES

1. ANOTHER BRICK IN THE WALL (PART II)
 (Pink Floyd)
2. LONGER
 (Dan Fogelberg)
3. ON THE RADIO
 (Donna Summer)
4. DESIRE
 (Andy Gibb)
5. CRAZY LITTLE THING CALLED LOVE
 (Queen)
6. WORKING MY WAY BACK TO
 YOU/FORGIVE ME, GIRL (MEDLEY)
 (Spinners)
7. TOO HOT
 (Kool and the Gang)
8. HIM
 (Rupert Holmes)
9. YES I'M READY
 (Teri Desario with KC)
10. SEPTEMBER MORN
 (Neil Diamond)

POP ALBUMS

1. THE WALL
 (Pink Floyd)
2. OFF THE WALL
 (Michael Jackson)
3. DAMN THE TORPEDOES
 (Tom Petty and the Heartbreakers)
4. PHOENIX
 (Dan Fogelberg)
5. ON THE RADIO—GREATEST HITS
 VOLUMES I AND II
 (Donna Summer)
6. BEBE LE STRANGE
 (Heart)
7. THE WHISPERS
 (Whispers)

8. THE LONG RUN
 (The Eagles)
9. FUN AND GAMES
 (Chuck Mangione)
10. PERMANENT WAVE
 (Rush)

BLACK SINGLES

1. AND THE BEAT GOES ON
 (Whispers)
2. SPECIAL LADY
 (Ray, Goodman and Brown)
3. TOO HOT
 (Kool and the Gang)
4. BOUNCE, ROCK, SKATE, ROLL, PART I
 (Vaughan Mason and Crew)
5. STOMP!
 (The Brothers Johnson)
6. THE SECOND TIME AROUND
 (Shalamar)
7. WORKING MY WAY BACK TO
 YOU/FORGIVE ME, GIRL (MEDLEY)
 (Spinners)
8. I SHOULDA LOVED YA
 (Narada Michael Walden)
9. YOU ARE MY HEAVEN
 (Roberta Flack with Donny Hathaway)
10. GOT TO LOVE SOMEBODY
 (Sister Sledge)

BLACK ALBUMS

1. THE WHISPERS
 (Whispers)
2. OFF THE WALL
 (Michael Jackson)
3. RAY, GOODMAN AND BROWN
 (Ray, Goodman and Brown)
4. LIGHT UP THE NIGHT
 (The Brothers Johnson)
5. THE GAP BAND II
 (The Gap Band)
6. ANGEL OF THE NIGHT
 (Angela Bofill)
7. GLORYHALLASTOOPID
 (Parliament)
8. PRINCE
 (Prince)
9. EVERY GENERATION
 (Ronnie Laws)
10. LOVE SOMEBODY TODAY
 (Sister Sledge)

JAZZ ALBUMS

1. FUN AND GAMES
 (Chuck Mangione)
2. EVERY GENERATION
 (Ronnie Laws)
3. ANGEL OF THE NIGHT
 (Angela Bofill)
4. SKYLARKIN'
 (Grover Washington Jr.)
5. PIZZAZZ
 (Patrice Rushen)
6. ONE ON ONE
 (Bob James and Earl Klugh)
7. HIROSHIMA
 (Hiroshima)
8. HIDEAWAY
 (David Sanborn)
9. NO STRANGER TO LOVE
 (Roy Ayers)
10. AMERICAN GARAGE
 (Pat Metheny)

COUNTRY SINGLES

1. MY HEROES HAVE ALWAYS BEEN
 COWBOYS
 (Willie Nelson)

2. WHY DON'T YOU SPEND THE NIGHT
 (Ronnie Milsap)
3. I AIN'T LIVING LONG LIKE THIS
 (Waylon Jennings)
4. I'D LOVE TO LAY YOU DOWN
 (Conway Twitty)
5. LYING TIME AGAIN/FOOLED AROUND
 AND FELL IN LOVE
 (Mel Tillis)
6. (I'LL EVEN LOVE YOU) BETTER THAN I
 DID THEN
 (The Statler Brothers)
7. DAYDREAM BELIEVER
 (Anne Murray)
8. MEN
 (Charly McClain)
9. SUGAR DADDY
 (The Bellamy Brothers)
10. ONE OF A KIND
 (Moe Bandy)

COUNTRY ALBUMS

1. KENNY
 (Kenney Rogers)
2. THE GAMBLER
 (Kenny Rogers)
3. GREATEST HITS
 (Waylon Jennings)
4. THE BEST OF THE STATLER BROTHERS
 RIDES AGAIN, VOL. II
 (The Statler Brothers)
5. TEN YEARS OF GOLD
 (Kenny Rogers)
6. WILLIE NELSON SINGS KRISTOFFERSON
 (Willie Nelson)
7. STRAIGHT AHEAD
 (Larry Gatlin)
8. STARDUST
 (Willie Nelson)
9. THE OAK RIDGE BOYS HAVE ARRIVED
 (The Oak Ridge Boys)
10. ELECTRIC HORSEMAN FEATURING WILLIE
 NELSON
 (Willie Nelson)

MARCH 22, 1980

POP SINGLES

1. ANOTHER BRICK IN THE WALL (PART II)
 (Pink Floyd)
2. WORKING MY WAY BACK TO
 YOU/FORGIVE ME, GIRL (MEDLEY)
 (Spinners)
3. CRAZY LITTLE THING CALLED LOVE
 (Queen)
4. ON THE RADIO
 (Donna Summer)
5. TOO HOT
 (Kool and the Gang)
6. CALL ME
 (Blondie)
7. HIM
 (Rupert Holmes)
8. LONGER
 (Dan Fogelberg)
9. RIDE LIKE THE WIND
 (Christopher Cross)
10. HOW DO I MAKE YOU
 (Linda Ronstadt)

POP ALBUMS

1. THE WALL
 (Pink Floyd)
2. OFF THE WALL
 (Michael Jackson)
3. DAMN THE TORPEDOES
 (Tom Petty and the Heartbreakers)
4. AGAINST THE WIND
 (Bob Seger and The Silver Bullet Band)

5. MAD LOVE
   (Linda Ronstadt)
6. BEBE LE STRANGE
   (Heart)
7. THE WHISPERS
   (Whispers)
8. PHOENIX
   (Dan Fogelberg)
9. FUN AND GAMES
   (Chuck Mangione)
10. THE LONG RUN
   (The Eagles)

BLACK SINGLES

1. AND THE BEAT GOES ON
   (Whispers)
2. SPECIAL LADY
   (Ray, Goodman and Brown)
3. STOMP!
   (The Brothers Johnson)
4. BOUNCE, ROCK, SKATE, ROLL, PART I
   (Vaughan Mason and Crew)
5. TOO HOT
   (Kool and the Gang)
6. WORKING MY WAY BACK TO
   YOU/FORGIVE ME, GIRL (MEDLEY)
   (Spinners)
7. I DON'T BELIEVE YOU WANT TO GET UP
   AND DANCE
   (The Gap Band)
8. YOU ARE MY HEAVEN
   (Roberta Flack with Donny Hathaway)
9. THE SECOND TIME AROUND
   (Shalamar)
10. DON'T PUSH IT, DON'T FORCE IT
   (Leon Haywood)

BLACK ALBUMS

1. THE WHISPERS
   (Whispers)
2. LIGHT UP THE NIGHT
   (The Brothers Johnson)
3. OFF THE WALL
   (Michael Jackson)
4. RAY, GOODMAN AND BROWN
   (Ray, Goodman and Brown)
5. EVERY GENERATION
   (Ronnie Laws)
6. THE GAP BAND II
   (The Gap Band)
7. LOVE SOMEBODY TODAY
   (Sister Sledge)
8. ANGEL OF THE NIGHT
   (Angela Bofill)
9. GLORYHALLASTOOPID
   (Parliament)
10. PRINCE
   (Prince)

JAZZ ALBUMS

1. FUN AND GAMES
   (Chuck Mangione)
2. EVERY GENERATION
   (Ronnie Laws)
3. SKYLARKIN'
   (Grover Washington Jr.)
4. ANGEL OF THE NIGHT
   (Angela Bofill)
5. PIZZAZZ
   (Patrice Rushen)
6. HIROSHIMA
   (Hiroshima)
7. ONE ON ONE
   (Bob James and Earl Klugh)
8. HIDEAWAY
   (David Sanborn)
9. 1980
   (Gil Scott-Heron and Brian Jackson)
10. NO STRANGER TO LOVE
   (Roy Ayers)

COUNTRY SINGLES

1. WHY DON'T YOU SPEND THE NIGHT
   (Ronnie Milsap)
2. I'D LOVE TO LAY YOU DOWN
   (Conway Twitty)
3. MY HEROES HAVE ALWAYS BEEN
   COWBOYS
   (Willie Nelson)
4. (I'LL EVEN LOVE YOU) BETTER THAN I
   DID THEN
   (The Statler Brothers)
5. LYING TIME AGAIN/FOOLED AROUND
   AND FELL IN LOVE
   (Mel Tillis)
6. SUGAR DADDY
   (The Bellamy Brothers)
7. MEN
   (Charly McClain)
8. ONE OF A KIND
   (Moe Bandy)
9. IT'S LIKE WE NEVER SAID GOODBYE
   (Crystal Gayle)
10. HONKY TONK BLUES
   (Charley Pride)

COUNTRY ALBUMS

1. KENNY
   (Kenny Rogers)
2. THE GAMBLER
   (Kenny Rogers)
3. GREATEST HITS
   (Waylon Jennings)
4. THE BEST OF THE STATLER BROTHERS
   RIDES AGAIN, VOL. II
   (The Statler Brothers)
5. TEN YEARS OF GOLD
   (Kenny Rogers)
6. WILLIE NELSON SINGS KRISTOFFERSON
   (Willie Nelson)
7. ELECTRIC HORSEMAN FEATURING WILLIE
   NELSON
   (Willie Nelson)
8. STARDUST
   (Willie Nelson)
9. MISS THE MISSISSIPPI
   (Crystal Gayle)
10. CLASSIC CRYSTAL
   (Crystal Gayle)

MARCH 29, 1980

POP SINGLES

1. ANOTHER BRICK IN THE WALL (PART II)
   (Pink Floyd)
2. WORKING MY WAY BACK TO
   YOU/FORGIVE ME, GIRL (MEDLEY)
   (Spinners)
3. CRAZY LITTLE THING CALLED LOVE
   (Queen)
4. CALL ME
   (Blondie)
5. TOO HOT
   (Kool and the Gang)
6. RIDE LIKE THE WIND
   (Christopher Cross)
7. HIM
   (Rupert Holmes)
8. ON THE RADIO
   (Donna Summer)
9. HOW DO I MAKE YOU
   (Linda Ronstadt)
10. FIRE LAKE
   (Bob Seger)

POP ALBUMS

1. THE WALL
   (Pink Floyd)

2. AGAINST THE WIND
   (Bob Seger and the Silver Bullet Band)
3. OFF THE WALL
   (Michael Jackson)
4. MAD LOVE
   (Linda Ronstadt)
5. DAMN THE TORPEDOES
   (Tom Petty and the Heartbreakers)
6. BEBE LE STRANGE
   (Heart)
7. THE WHISPERS
   (Whispers)
8. GLASS HOUSES
   (Billy Joel)
9. FUN AND GAMES
   (Chuck Mangione)
10. THE LONG RUN
   (The Eagles)

BLACK SINGLES

1. AND THE BEAT GOES ON
   (Whispers)
2. STOMP!
   (The Brothers Johnson)
3. BOUNCE, ROCK, SKATE, ROLL, PART I
   (Vaughan Mason and Crew)
4. SPECIAL LADY
   (Ray, Goodman and Brown)
5. I DON'T BELIEVE YOU WANT TO GET UP
   AND DANCE
   (The Gap Band)
6. WORKING MY WAY BACK TO
   YOU/FORGIVE ME, GIRL (MEDLEY)
   (Spinners)
7. DON'T SAY GOODNIGHT (IT'S TIME FOR
   LOVE)
   (Isley Brothers)
8. YOU ARE MY HEAVEN
   (Roberta Flack with Donny Hathaway)
9. DON'T PUSH IT, DON'T FORCE IT
   (Leon Haywood)
10. TOO HOT
   (Kool and the Gang)

BLACK ALBUMS

1. THE WHISPERS
   (Whispers)
2. LIGHT UP THE NIGHT
   (The Brothers Johnson)
3. OFF THE WALL
   (Michael Jackson)
4. RAY, GOODMAN AND BROWN
   (Ray, Goodman and Brown)
5. EVERY GENERATION
   (Ronnie Laws)
6. THE GAP BAND II
   (The Gap Band)
7. LOVE SOMEBODY TODAY
   (Sister Sledge)
8. ANGEL OF THE NIGHT
   (Angela Bofill)
9. LADIES' NIGHT
   (Kool and the Gang)
10. BIG FUN
   (Shalamar)

JAZZ ALBUMS

1. FUN AND GAMES
   (Chuck Mangione)
2. EVERY GENERATION
   (Ronnie Laws)
3. SKYLARKIN'
   (Grover Washington Jr.)
4. ANGEL OF THE NIGHT
   (Angela Bofill)
5. HIDEAWAY
   (David Sanborn)
6. HIROSHIMA
   (Hiroshima)
7. PIZZAZZ
   (Patrice Rushen)

TOP OF THE CHARTS/1980

8. ONE ON ONE
   (Bob James and Earl Klugh)
9. 1980
   (Gil Scott-Heron and Brian Jackson)
10. CATCHING THE SUN
    (Spyro Gyra)

COUNTRY SINGLES

1. I'D LOVE TO LAY YOU DOWN
   (Conway Twitty)
2. WHY DON'T YOU SPEND THE NIGHT
   (Ronnie Milsap)
3. SUGAR DADDY
   (The Bellamy Brothers)
4. (I'LL EVEN LOVE YOU) BETTER THAN I
   DID THEN
   (The Statler Brothers)
5. IT'S LIKE WE NEVER SAID GOODBYE
   (Crystal Gayle)
6. HONKY TONK BLUES
   (Charley Pride)
7. MEN
   (Charly McClain)
8. ONE OF A KIND
   (Moe Bandy)
9. WOMEN I'VE NEVER HAD
   (Hank Williams Jr.)
10. SHRINER'S CONVENTION
    (Ray Stevens)

COUNTRY ALBUMS

1. KENNY
   (Kenny Rogers)
2. THE GAMBLER
   (Kenny Rogers)
3. GREATEST HITS
   (Waylon Jennings)
4. TOGETHER
   (The Oak Ridge Boys)
5. THE BEST OF THE STATLER BROTHERS
   RIDES AGAIN, VOL. II
   (The Statler Brothers)
6. TEN YEARS OF GOLD
   (Kenny Rogers)
7. ELECTRIC HORSEMAN FEATURING WILLIE
   NELSON
   (Willie Nelson)
8. STARDUST
   (Willie Nelson)
9. CLASSIC CRYSTAL
   (Crystal Gayle)
10. A COUNTRY COLLECTION
    (Anne Murray)

APRIL 5, 1980

POP SINGLES

1. ANOTHER BRICK IN THE WALL (PART II)
   (Pink Floyd)
2. CALL ME
   (Blondie)
3. WORKING MY WAY BACK TO
   YOU/FORGIVE ME, GIRL (MEDLEY)
   (Spinners)
4. RIDE LIKE THE WIND
   (Christopher Cross)
5. CRAZY LITTLE THING CALLED LOVE
   (Queen)
6. TOO HOT
   (Kool and the Gang)
7. HOW DO I MAKE YOU
   (Linda Ronstadt)
8. FIRE LAKE
   (Bob Seger)
9. I CAN'T TELL YOU WHY
   (The Eagles)
10. LOST IN LOVE
    (Air Supply)

POP ALBUMS

1. THE WALL
   (Pink Floyd)
2. AGAINST THE WIND
   (Bob Seger and the Silver Bullet Band)
3. MAD LOVE
   (Linda Ronstadt)
4. OFF THE WALL
   (Michael Jackson)
5. GLASS HOUSES
   (Billy Joel)
6. THE WHISPERS
   (Whispers)
7. DAMN THE TORPEDOES
   (Tom Petty and the Heartbreakers)
8. THE LONG RUN
   (The Eagles)
9. BEBE LE STRANGE
   (Heart)
10. FUN AND GAMES
    (Chuck Mangione)

BLACK SINGLES

1. STOMP!
   (The Brothers Johnson)
2. AND THE BEAT GOES ON
   (Whispers)
3. BOUNCE, ROCK, SKATE, ROLL, PART I
   (Vaughan Mason and Crew)
4. I DON'T BELIEVE YOU WANT TO GET UP
   AND DANCE
   (The Gap Band)
5. SPECIAL LADY
   (Ray, Goodman and Brown)
6. DON'T SAY GOODNIGHT (IT'S TIME FOR
   LOVE)
   (Isley Brothers)
7. DON'T PUSH IT, DON'T FORCE IT
   (Leon Haywood)
8. WORKING MY WAY BACK TO
   YOU/FORGIVE ME, GIRL (MEDLEY)
   (Spinners)
9. YOU ARE MY HEAVEN
   (Roberta Flack with Donny Hathaway)
10. TOO HOT
    (Kool and the Gang)

BLACK ALBUMS

1. THE WHISPERS
   (Whispers)
2. LIGHT UP THE NIGHT
   (The Brothers Johnson)
3. OFF THE WALL
   (Michael Jackson)
4. RAY, GOODMAN AND BROWN
   (Ray, Goodman and Brown)
5. EVERY GENERATION
   (Ronnie Laws)
6. THE GAP BAND II
   (The Gap Band)
7. LOVE SOMEBODY TODAY
   (Sister Sledge)
8. WARM THOUGHTS
   (Smokey Robinson)
9. BIG FUN
   (Shalamar)
10. SKYLARKIN'
    (Grover Washington Jr.)

JAZZ ALBUMS

1. FUN AND GAMES
   (Chuck Mangione)
2. EVERY GENERATION
   (Ronnie Laws)
3. SKYLARKIN'
   (Grover Washington Jr.)
4. ANGEL OF THE NIGHT
   (Angela Bofill)

5. HIDEAWAY
   (David Sanborn)
6. CATCHING THE SUN
   (Spyro Grya)
7. HIROSHIMA
   (Hiroshima)
8. ONE ON ONE
   (Bob James and Earl Klugh)
9. 1980
   (Gil Scott-Heron and Brian Jackson)
10. PIZZAZZ
    (Patrice Rushen)

COUNTRY SINGLES

1. SUGAR DADDY
   (The Bellamy Brothers)
2. I'D LOVE TO LAY YOU DOWN
   (Conway Twitty)
3. IT'S LIKE WE NEVER SAID GOODBYE
   (Crystal Gayle)
4. HONKY TONK BLUES
   (Charley Pride)
5. WHY DON'T YOU SPEND THE NIGHT
   (Ronnie Milsap)
6. (I'LL EVEN LOVE YOU) BETTER THAN I
   DID THEN
   (The Statler Brothers)
7. WOMEN I'VE NEVER HAD
   (Hank Williams Jr.)
8. A LESSON IN LEAVIN'
   (Dottie West)
9. TWO STORY HOUSE
   (George Jones and Tammy Wynette)
10. SHRINER'S CONVENTION
    (Ray Stevens)

COUNTRY ALBUMS

1. KENNY
   (Kenny Rogers)
2. THE GAMBLER
   (Kenny Rogers)
3. GREATEST HITS
   (Waylon Jennings)
4. TOGETHER
   (The Oak Ridge Boys)
5. TEN YEARS OF GOLD
   (Kenny Rogers)
6. ELECTRIC HORSEMAN FEATURING WILLIE
   NELSON
   (Willie Nelson)
7. THE BEST OF THE STATLER BROTHERS
   RIDES AGAIN, VOL. II
   (The Statler Brothers)
8. STARDUST
   (Willie Nelson)
9. AUTOGRAPH
   (John Denver)
10. A COUNTRY COLLECTION
    (Anne Murray)

APRIL 12, 1980

POP SINGLES

1. ANOTHER BRICK IN THE WALL (PART II)
   (Pink Floyd)
2. CALL ME
   (Blondie)
3. RIDE LIKE THE WIND
   (Christopher Cross)
4. WORKING MY WAY BACK TO
   YOU/FORGIVE ME, GIRL (MEDLEY)
   (Spinners)
5. FIRE LAKE
   (Bob Seger)
6. LOST IN LOVE
   (Air Supply)
7. HOW DO I MAKE YOU
   (Linda Ronstadt)

8. I CAN'T TELL YOU WHY
   (The Eagles)
9. CRAZY LITTLE THING CALLED LOVE
   (Queen)
10. SPECIAL LADY
   (Ray, Goodman and Brown)

POP ALBUMS

1. THE WALL
   (Pink Floyd)
2. AGAINST THE WIND
   (Bob Seger and the Silver Bullet Band)
3. MAD LOVE
   (Linda Ronstadt)
4. GLASS HOUSES
   (Billy Joel)
5. OFF THE WALL
   (Michael Jackson)
6. THE WHISPERS
   (Whispers)
7. THE LONG RUN
   (The Eagles)
8. DAMN THE TORPEDOES
   (Tom Petty and the Heartbreakers)
9. LIGHT UP THE NIGHT
   (The Brothers Johnson)
10. BEBE LE STRANGE
   (Heart)

BLACK SINGLES

1. STOMP!
   (The Brothers Johnson)
2. DON'T SAY GOODNIGHT (IT'S TIME FOR LOVE)
   (Isley Brothers)
3. AND THE BEAT GOES ON
   (Whispers)
4. I DON'T BELIEVE YOU WANT TO GET UP AND DANCE
   (The Gap Band)
5. DON'T PUSH IT, DON'T FORCE IT
   (Leon Haywood)
6. BOUNCE, ROCK, SKATE, ROLL, PART I
   (Vaughan Mason and Crew)
7. SPECIAL LADY
   (Ray, Goodman and Brown)
8. WORKING MY WAY BACK TO YOU/FORGIVE ME, GIRL (MEDLEY)
   (Spinners)
9. YOU ARE MY HEAVEN
   (Roberta Flack with Donny Hathaway)
10. TOO HOT
   (Kool and the Gang)

BLACK ALBUMS

1. THE WHISPERS
   (Whispers)
2. LIGHT UP THE NIGHT
   (The Brothers Johnson)
3. OFF THE WALL
   (Michael Jackson)
4. RAY, GOODMAN AND BROWN
   (Ray, Goodman and Brown)
5. THE GAP BAND II
   (The Gap Band)
6. WARM THOUGHTS
   (Smokey Robinson)
7. EVERY GENERATION
   (Ronnie Laws)
8. LOVE SOMEBODY TODAY
   (Sister Sledge)
9. BIG FUN
   (Shalamar)
10. SKYLARKIN'
   (Grover Washington Jr.)

JAZZ ALBUMS

1. FUN AND GAMES
   (Chuck Mangione)

2. SKYLARKIN'
   (Grover Washington Jr.)
3. CATCHING THE SUN
   (Spyro Gyra)
4. EVERY GENERATION
   (Ronnie Laws)
5. HIDEAWAY
   (David Sanborn)
6. DREAM COME TRUE
   (Earl Klugh)
7. HIROSHIMA
   (Hiroshima)
8. 1980
   (Gil Scott-Heron and Brian Jackson)
9. ANGEL OF THE NIGHT
   (Angela Bofill)
10. ONE ON ONE
   (Bob James and Earl Klugh)

COUNTRY SINGLES

1. IT'S LIKE WE NEVER SAID GOODBYE
   (Crystal Gayle)
2. HONKY TONK BLUES
   (Charley Pride)
3. SUGAR DADDY
   (The Bellamy Brothers)
4. I'D LOVE TO LAY YOU DOWN
   (Conway Twitty)
5. A LESSON IN LEAVIN'
   (Dottie West)
6. WOMEN I'VE NEVER HAD
   (Hank Williams Jr.)
7. TWO STORY HOUSE
   (George Jones and Tammy Wynette)
8. BENEATH STILL WATERS
   (Emmylou Harris)
9. ARE YOU ON THE ROAD TO LOVIN' ME AGAIN
   (Debby Boone)
10. THE COWGIRL AND THE DANDY
   (Brenda Lee)

COUNTRY ALBUMS

1. KENNY
   (Kenny Rogers)
2. THE GAMBLER
   (Kenny Rogers)
3. GREATEST HITS
   (Waylon Jennings)
4. TEN YEARS OF GOLD
   (Kenny Rogers)
5. TOGETHER
   (The Oak Ridge Boys)
6. ELECTRIC HORSEMAN FEATURING WILLIE NELSON
   (Willie Nelson)
7. THE BEST OF THE STATLER BROTHERS RIDES AGAIN, VOL. II
   (The Statler Brothers)
8. WILLIE NELSON SINGS KRISTOFFERSON
   (Willie Nelson)
9. AUTOGRAPH
   (John Denver)
10. STARDUST
   (Willie Nelson)

APRIL 19, 1980

POP SINGLES

1. CALL ME
   (Blondie)
2. ANOTHER BRICK IN THE WALL (PART II)
   (Pink Floyd)
3. RIDE LIKE THE WIND
   (Christopher Cross)
4. LOST IN LOVE
   (Air Supply)

5. FIRE LAKE
   (Bob Seger)
6. WORKING MY WAY BACK TO YOU/FORGIVE ME, GIRL (MEDLEY)
   (Spinners)
7. I CAN'T TELL YOU WHY
   (The Eagles)
8. WITH YOU I'M BORN AGAIN
   (Billy Preston and Syreeta)
9. SPECIAL LADY
   (Ray, Goodman and Brown)
10. HOW DO I MAKE YOU
   (Linda Ronstadt)

POP ALBUMS

1. THE WALL
   (Pink Floyd)
2. AGAINST THE WIND
   (Bob Seger and the Silver Bullet Band)
3. GLASS HOUSES
   (Billy Joel)
4. MAD LOVE
   (Linda Ronstadt)
5. OFF THE WALL
   (Michael Jackson)
6. THE LONG RUN
   (The Eagles)
7. THE WHISPERS
   (Whispers)
8. LIGHT UP THE NIGHT
   (The Brothers Johnson)
9. DAMN THE TORPEDOES
   (Tom Petty and the Heartbreakers)
10. DEPARTURE
   (Journey)

BLACK SINGLES

1. DON'T SAY GOODNIGHT (IT'S TIME FOR LOVE)
   (Isley Brothers)
2. STOMP!
   (The Brothers Johnson)
3. DON'T PUSH IT, DON'T FORCE IT
   (Leon Haywood)
4. I DON'T BELIEVE YOU WANT TO GET UP AND DANCE
   (The Gap Band)
5. AND THE BEAT GOES ON
   (Whispers)
6. BOUNCE, ROCK, SKATE, ROLL, PART I
   (Vaughan Mason and Crew)
7. LADY
   (Whispers)
8. LET ME BE THE CLOCK
   (Smokey Robinson)
9. YOU ARE MY HEAVEN
   (Roberta Flack with Donny Hathaway)
10. STANDING OVATION
   (G.Q.)

BLACK ALBUMS

1. GO ALL THE WAY
   (Isley Brothers)
2. LIGHT UP THE NIGHT
   (The Brothers Johnson)
3. THE WHISPERS
   (Whispers)
4. RAY, GOODMAN AND BROWN
   (Ray, Goodman and Brown)
5. THE GAP BAND II
   (The Gap Band)
6. WARM THOUGHTS
   (Smokey Robinson)
7. OFF THE WALL
   (Michael Jackson)
8. ROBERTA FLACK FEATURING DONNY HATHAWAY
   (Roberta Flack and Donny Hathaway)
9. TWO
   (G.Q.)
10. SKYLARKIN'
   (Grover Washington Jr.)

JAZZ ALBUMS

1. SKYLARKIN'
   (Grover Washington Jr.)
2. CATCHING THE SUN
   (Spyro Gyra)
3. EVERY GENERATION
   (Ronnie Laws)
4. FUN AND GAMES
   (Chuck Mangione)
5. DREAM COME TRUE
   (Earl Klugh)
6. HIDEAWAY
   (David Sanborn)
7. HIROSHIMA
   (Hiroshima)
8. 1980
   (Gil Scott-Heron and Brian Jackson)
9. ANGEL OF THE NIGHT
   (Angela Bofill)
10. ONE ON ONE
    (Bob James and Earl Klugh)

COUNTRY SINGLES

1. IT'S LIKE WE NEVER SAID GOODBYE
   (Crystal Gayle)
2. HONKY TONK BLUES
   (Charley Pride)
3. TWO STORY HOUSE
   (George Jones and Tammy Wynette)
4. A LESSON IN LEAVIN'
   (Dottie West)
5. BENEATH STILL WATERS
   (Emmylou Harris)
6. ARE YOU ON THE ROAD TO LOVIN' ME
   AGAIN
   (Debby Boone)
7. SUGAR DADDY
   (The Bellamy Brothers)
8. THE COWGIRL AND THE DANDY
   (Brenda Lee)
9. GONE TOO FAR
   (Eddie Rabbitt)
10. THE WAY I AM
    (Merle Haggard)

COUNTRY ALBUMS

1. KENNY
   (Kenny Rogers)
2. THE GAMBLER
   (Kenny Rogers)
3. GIDEON
   (Kenny Rogers)
4. GREATEST HITS
   (Waylon Jennings)
5. TOGETHER
   (The Oak Ridge Boys)
6. ELECTRIC HORSEMAN FEATURING WILLIE
   NELSON
   (Willie Nelson)
7. TEN YEARS OF GOLD
   (Kenny Rogers)
8. WILLIE NELSON SINGS KRISTOFFERSON
   (Willie Nelson)
9. THE BEST OF THE STATLER BROTHERS
   RIDES AGAIN, VOL. II
   (The Statler Brothers)
10. COAL MINER'S DAUGHTER
    (Original Soundtrack)

APRIL 26, 1980

POP SINGLES

1. CALL ME
   (Blondie)
2. ANOTHER BRICK IN THE WALL (PART II)
   (Pink Floyd)

3. RIDE LIKE THE WIND
   (Christopher Cross)
4. LOST IN LOVE
   (Air Supply)
5. FIRE LAKE
   (Bob Seger)
6. WITH YOU I'M BORN AGAIN
   (Billy Preston and Syreeta)
7. I CAN'T TELL YOU WHY
   (The Eagles)
8. SEXY EYES
   (Dr. Hook)
9. SPECIAL LADY
   (Ray, Goodman and Brown)
10. YOU MAY BE RIGHT
    (Billy Joel)

POP ALBUMS

1. THE WALL
   (Pink Floyd)
2. AGAINST THE WIND
   (Bob Seger and the Silver Bullet Band)
3. GLASS HOUSES
   (Billy Joel)
4. MAD LOVE
   (Linda Ronstadt)
5. OFF THE WALL
   (Michael Jackson)
6. THE LONG RUN
   (The Eagles)
7. WOMEN AND CHILDREN FIRST
   (Van Halen)
8. LIGHT UP THE NIGHT
   (The Brothers Johnson)
9. GIDEON
   (Kenny Rogers)
10. DEPARTURE
    (Journey)

BLACK SINGLES

1. DON'T SAY GOODNIGHT (IT'S TIME FOR
   LOVE)
   (Isley Brothers)
2. STOMP!
   (The Brothers Johnson)
3. DON'T PUSH IT, DON'T FORCE IT
   (Leon Haywood)
4. I DON'T BELIEVE YOU WANT TO GET UP
   AND DANCE
   (The Gap Band)
5. LADY
   (Whispers)
6. LET ME BE THE CLOCK
   (Smokey Robinson)
7. BOUNCE, ROCK, SKATE, ROLL, PART I
   (Vaughan Mason and Crew)
8. GOT TO BE ENOUGH
   (Con Funk Shun)
9. YOU ARE MY HEAVEN
   (Roberta Flack with Donny Hathaway)
10. STANDING OVATION
    (G.Q.)

BLACK ALBUMS

1. GO ALL THE WAY
   (Isley Brothers)
2. LIGHT UP THE NIGHT
   (The Brothers Johnson)
3. THE WHISPERS
   (Whispers)
4. ROBERTA FLACK FEATURING DONNY
   HATHAWAY
   (Roberta Flack and Donny Hathaway)
5. WARM THOUGHTS
   (Smokey Robinson)
6. OFF THE WALL
   (Michael Jackson)
7. LET'S GET SERIOUS
   (Jermaine Jackson)
8. RAY, GOODMAN AND BROWN
   (Ray, Goodman and Brown)

9. THE GAP BAND II
   (The Gap Band)
10. TWO
    (G.Q.)

JAZZ ALBUMS

1. SKYLARKIN'
   (Grover Washington Jr.)
2. CATCHING THE SUN
   (Spyro Gyra)
3. EVERY GENERATION
   (Ronnie Laws)
4. DREAM COME TRUE
   (Earl Klugh)
5. FUN AND GAMES
   (Chuck Mangione)
6. HIDEAWAY
   (David Sanborn)
7. HIROSHIMA
   (Hiroshima)
8. 1980
   (Gil Scott-Heron and Brian Jackson)
9. ANGEL OF THE NIGHT
   (Angela Bofill)
10. ONE ON ONE
    (Bob James and Earl Klugh)

COUNTRY SINGLES

1. HONKY TONK BLUES
   (Charley Pride)
2. TWO STORY HOUSE
   (George Jones and Tammy Wynette)
3. A LESSON IN LEAVIN'
   (Dottie West)
4. BENEATH STILL WATERS
   (Emmylou Harris)
5. ARE YOU ON THE ROAD TO LOVIN' ME
   AGAIN
   (Debby Boone)
6. GONE TOO FAR
   (Eddie Rabbitt)
7. THE WAY I AM
   (Merle Haggard)
8. THE COWGIRL AND THE DANDY
   (Brenda Lee)
9. MORNING COMES TOO EARLY
   (Jim Ed Brown and Helen Cornelius)
10. STARTING OVER AGAIN
    (Dolly Parton)

COUNTRY ALBUMS

1. GIDEON
   (Kenny Rogers)
2. KENNY
   (Kenny Rogers)
3. THE GAMBLER
   (Kenny Rogers)
4. GREATEST HITS
   (Waylon Jennings)
5. TOGETHER
   (The Oak Ridge Boys)
6. TEN YEARS OF GOLD
   (Kenny Rogers)
7. ELECTRIC HORSEMAN FEATURING WILLIE
   NELSON
   (Willie Nelson)
8. COAL MINER'S DAUGHTER
   (Original Soundtrack)
9. SHRINER'S CONVENTION
   (Ray Stevens)
10. WILLIE NELSON SINGS KRISTOFFERSON
    (Willie Nelson)

MAY 3, 1980

POP SINGLES

1. CALL ME
   (Blondie)

2. ANOTHER BRICK IN THE WALL (PART II)
   (Pink Floyd)
3. RIDE LIKE THE WIND
   (Christopher Cross)
4. LOST IN LOVE
   (Air Supply)
5. WITH YOU I'M BORN AGAIN
   (Billy Preston and Syreeta)
6. SEXY EYES
   (Dr. Hook)
7. YOU MAY BE RIGHT
   (Billy Joel)
8. DON'T FALL IN LOVE WITH A DREAMER
   (Kenny Rogers with Kim Carnes)
9. SPECIAL LADY
   (Ray, Goodman and Brown)
10. OFF THE WALL
   (Michael Jackson)

POP ALBUMS

1. THE WALL
   (Pink Floyd)
2. AGAINST THE WIND
   (Bob Seger and the Silver Bullet Band)
3. GLASS HOUSES
   (Billy Joel)
4. MAD LOVE
   (Linda Ronstadt)
5. OFF THE WALL
   (Michael Jackson)
6. WOMEN AND CHILDREN FIRST
   (Van Halen)
7. GO ALL THE WAY
   (Isley Brothers)
8. GIDEON
   (Kenny Rogers)
9. THE LONG RUN
   (The Eagles)
10. DEPARTURE
   (Journey)

BLACK SINGLES

1. DON'T SAY GOODNIGHT (IT'S TIME FOR
   LOVE)
   (Isley Brothers)
2. STOMP!
   (The Brothers Johnson)
3. DON'T PUSH IT, DON'T FORCE IT
   (Leon Haywood)
4. LADY
   (Whispers)
5. LET ME BE THE CLOCK
   (Smokey Robinson)
6. I DON'T BELIEVE YOU WANT TO GET UP
   AND DANCE
   (The Gap Band)
7. GOT TO BE ENOUGH
   (Con Funk Shun)
8. LET'S GET SERIOUS
   (Jermaine Jackson)
9. FUNKYTOWN
   (Lipps Inc.)
10. TWO PLACES AT THE SAME TIME
   (Ray Parker Jr. and Raydio)

JAZZ ALBUMS

1. CATCHING THE SUN
   (Spyro Gyra)
2. SKYLARKIN'
   (Grover Washington Jr.)
3. HIDEAWAY
   (David Sanborn)
4. DREAM COME TRUE
   (Earl Klugh)
5. EVERY GENERATION
   (Ronnie Laws)
6. FUN AND GAMES
   (Chuck Mangione)
7. HIROSHIMA
   (Hiroshima)

8. MONSTER
   (Herbie Hancock)
9. YOU'LL NEVER KNOW
   (Rodney Franklin)
10. 1980
   (Gil Scott-Heron and Brian Jackson)

COUNTRY SINGLES

1. TWO STORY HOUSE
   (George Jones and Tammy Wynette)
2. BENEATH STILL WATERS
   (Emmylou Harris)
3. ARE YOU ON THE ROAD TO LOVIN' ME
   AGAIN
   (Debby Boone)
4. GONE TOO FAR
   (Eddie Rabbitt)
5. THE WAY I AM
   (Merle Haggard)
6. A LESSON IN LEAVIN'
   (Dottie West)
7. MORNING COMES TOO EARLY
   (Jim Ed Brown and Helen Cornelius)
8. STARTING OVER AGAIN
   (Dolly Parton)
9. LET'S GET IT WHILE THE GETTIN'S GOOD
   (Eddy Arnold)
10. TAKING SOMEBODY WITH ME WHEN I
    FALL
   (Larry Gatlin and the Gatlin Brothers Band)

COUNTRY ALBUMS

1. GIDEON
   (Kenny Rogers)
2. KENNY
   (Kenny Rogers)
3. THE GAMBLER
   (Kenny Rogers)
4. GREATEST HITS
   (Waylon Jennings)
5. ELECTRIC HORSEMAN FEATURING WILLIE
   NELSON
   (Willie Nelson)
6. COAL MINER'S DAUGHTER
   (Original Soundtrack)
7. TEN YEARS OF GOLD
   (Kenny Rogers)
8. TOGETHER
   (The Oak Ridge Boys)
9. SHRINER'S CONVENTION
   (Ray Stevens)
10. STARDUST
   (Willie Nelson)

MAY 10, 1980

POP SINGLES

1. CALL ME
   (Blondie)
2. ANOTHER BRICK IN THE WALL (PART II)
   (Pink Floyd)
3. LOST IN LOVE
   (Air Supply)
4. SEXY EYES
   (Dr. Hook)
5. WITH YOU I'M BORN AGAIN
   (Billy Preston and Syreeta)
6. DON'T FALL IN LOVE WITH A DREAMER
   (Kenny Rogers with Kim Carnes)
7. YOU MAY BE RIGHT
   (Billy Joel)
8. BIGGEST PART OF ME
   (Ambrosia)
9. RIDE LIKE THE WIND
   (Christopher Cross)
10. SPECIAL LADY
   (Ray, Goodman and Brown)

POP ALBUMS

1. THE WALL
   (Pink Floyd)
2. AGAINST THE WIND
   (Bob Seger and the Silver Bullet Band)
3. GLASS HOUSES
   (Billy Joel)
4. MAD LOVE
   (Linda Ronstadt)
5. WOMEN AND CHILDREN FIRST
   (Van Halen)
6. OFF THE WALL
   (Michael Jackson)
7. GO ALL THE WAY
   (Isley Brothers)
8. GIDEON
   (Kenny Rogers)
9. LIGHT UP THE NIGHT
   (The Brothers Johnson)
10. CHRISTOPHER CROSS
   (Christopher Cross)

BLACK SINGLES

1. DON'T SAY GOODNIGHT (IT'S TIME FOR
   LOVE)
   (Isley Brothers)
2. FUNKYTOWN
   (Lipps Inc.)
3. LADY
   (Whispers)
4. LET'S GET SERIOUS
   (Jermaine Jackson)
5. LET ME BE THE CLOCK
   (Smokey Robinson)
6. GOT TO BE ENOUGH
   (Con Funk Shun)
7. STOMP!
   (The Brothers Johnson)
8. DON'T PUSH IT, DON'T FORCE IT
   (Leon Haywood)
9. TWO PLACES AT THE SAME TIME
   (Ray Parker Jr. and Raydio)
10. I DON'T BELIEVE YOU WANT TO GET UP
    AND DANCE
   (The Gap Band)

BLACK ALBUMS

1. GO ALL THE WAY
   (Isley Brothers)
2. LIGHT UP THE NIGHT
   (The Brothers Johnson)
3. THE WHISPERS
   (Whispers)
4. ROBERTA FLACK FEATURING DONNY
   HATHAWAY
   (Roberta Flack and Donny Hathaway)
5. LET'S GET SERIOUS
   (Jermaine Jackson)
6. WARM THOUGHTS
   (Smokey Robinson)
7. SPIRIT OF LOVE
   (Con Funk Shun)
8. OFF THE WALL
   (Michael Jackson)
9. MOUTH TO MOUTH
   (Lipps Inc.)
10. TWO PLACES AT THE SAME TIME
   (Ray Parker Jr. and Raydio)

JAZZ ALBUMS

1. SKYLARKIN'
   (Grover Washington Jr.)
2. CATCHING THE SUN
   (Spyro Gyra)
3. HIDEAWAY
   (David Sanborn)
4. DREAM COME TRUE
   (Earl Klugh)

5. EVERY GENERATION
   (Ronnie Laws)
6. FUN AND GAMES
   (Chuck Mangione)
7. MONSTER
   (Herbie Hancock)
8. YOU'LL NEVER KNOW
   (Rodney Franklin)
9. HIROSHIMA
   (Hiroshima)
10. LOVE IS THE ANSWER
    (Lonnie Liston Smith)

COUNTRY SINGLES

1. GONE TOO FAR
   (Eddie Rabbitt)
2. BENEATH STILL WATERS
   (Emmylou Harris)
3. ARE YOU ON THE ROAD TO LOVIN' ME AGAIN
   (Debby Boone)
4. THE WAY I AM
   (Merle Haggard)
5. STARTING OVER AGAIN
   (Dolly Parton)
6. MORNING COMES TOO EARLY
   (Jim Ed Brown and Helen Cornelius)
7. TWO STORY HOUSE
   (George Jones and Tammy Wynette)
8. GOOD OLE BOYS LIKE ME
   (Don Williams)
9. LETS GET IT WHILE THE GETTIN'S GOOD
   (Eddy Arnold)
10. TEMPORARILY YOURS
    (Jeanne Pruett)

COUNTRY ALBUMS

1. GIDEON
   (Kenny Rogers)
2. THE GAMBLER
   (Kenny Rogers)
3. KENNY
   (Kenny Rogers)
4. GREATEST HITS
   (Waylon Jennings)
5. ELECTRIC HORSEMAN FEATURING WILLIE NELSON
   (Willie Nelson)
6. COAL MINER'S DAUGHTER
   (Original Soundtrack)
7. TEN YEARS OF GOLD
   (Kenny Rogers)
8. SHRINER'S CONVENTION
   (Ray Stevens)
9. STARDUST
   (Willie Nelson)
10. MILSAP MAGIC
    (Ronnie Milsap)

MAY 17, 1980

POP SINGLES

1. CALL ME
   (Blondie)
2. ANOTHER BRICK IN THE WALL (PART II)
   (Pink Floyd)
3. SEXY EYES
   (Dr. Hook)
4. LOST IN LOVE
   (Air Supply)
5. DON'T FALL IN LOVE WITH A DREAMER
   (Kenny Rogers)
6. BIGGEST PART OF ME
   (Ambrosia)
7. WITH YOU I'M BORN AGAIN
   (Billy Preston and Syreeta)

8. YOU MAY BE RIGHT
   (Billy Joel)
9. HURT SO BAD
   (Linda Ronstadt)
10. RIDE LIKE THE WIND
    (Christopher Cross)

POP ALBUMS

1. AGAINST THE WIND
   (Bob Seger and the Silver Bullet Band)
2. THE WALL
   (Pink Floyd)
3. GLASS HOUSES
   (Billy Joel)
4. MAD LOVE
   (Linda Ronstadt)
5. WOMEN AND CHILDREN FIRST
   (Van Halen)
6. OFF THE WALL
   (Michael Jackson)
7. GO ALL THE WAY
   (Isley Brothers)
8. GIDEON
   (Kenny Rogers)
9. LIGHT UP THE NIGHT
   (The Brothers Johnson)
10. CHRISTOPHER CROSS
    (Christopher Cross)

BLACK ALBUMS

1. GO ALL THE WAY
   (Isley Brothers)
2. LET'S GET SERIOUS
   (Jermaine Jackson)
3. LIGHT UP THE NIGHT
   (The Brothers Johnson)
4. ROBERTA FLACK FEATURING DONNY HATHAWAY
   (Roberta Flack and Donny Hathaway)
5. SWEET SENSATION
   (Stephanie Mills)
6. THE WHISPERS
   (Whispers)
7. MOUTH TO MOUTH
   (Lipps Inc.)
8. WARM THOUGHTS
   (Smokey Robinson)
9. SPIRIT OF LOVE
   (Con Funk Shun)
10. TWO PLACES AT THE SAME TIME
    (Ray Parker Jr. and Raydio)

JAZZ ALBUMS

1. CATCHING THE SUN
   (Spyro Gyra)
2. SKYLARKIN'
   (Grover Washington Jr.)
3. DREAM COME TRUE
   (Earl Klugh)
4. HIDEAWAY
   (David Sanborn)
5. FUN AND GAMES
   (Chuck Mangione)
6. EVERY GENERATION
   (Ronnie Laws)
7. MONSTER
   (Herbie Hancock)
8. YOU'LL NEVER KNOW
   (Rodney Franklin)
9. ONE BAD HABIT
   (Michael Franks)
10. LOVE IS THE ANSWER
    (Lonnie Liston Smith)

COUNTRY SINGLES

1. THE WAY I AM
   (Merle Haggard)
2. GONE TOO FAR
   (Eddie Rabbitt)

3. GOOD OLE BOYS LIKE ME
   (Don Williams)
4. STARTING OVER AGAIN
   (Dolly Parton)
5. MORNING COMES TOO EARLY
   (Jim Ed Brown and Helen Cornelius)
6. BENEATH STILL WATERS
   (Emmylou Harris)
7. DON'T FALL IN LOVE WITH A DREAMER
   (Kenny Rogers with Kim Carnes)
8. ARE YOU ON THE ROAD TO LOVIN' ME AGAIN
   (Debby Boone)
9. MY HEART/SILENT NIGHT (AFTER THE FIGHT)
   (Ronnie Milsap)
10. TEMPORARILY YOURS
    (Jeanne Pruett)

COUNTRY ALBUMS

1. GIDEON
   (Kenny Rogers)
2. THE GAMBLER
   (Kenny Rogers)
3. KENNY
   (Kenny Rogers)
4. GREATEST HITS
   (Waylon Jennings)
5. COAL MINER'S DAUGHTER
   (Original Soundtrack)
6. ELECTRIC HORSEMAN FEATURING WILLIE NELSON
   (Willie Nelson)
7. TEN YEARS OF GOLD
   (Kenny Rogers)
8. SHRINER'S CONVENTION
   (Ray Stevens)
9. MILSAP MAGIC
   (Ronnie Milsap)
10. TOGETHER
    (The Oak Ridge Boys)

MAY 24, 1980

POP SINGLES

1. CALL ME
   (Blondie)
2. FUNKYTOWN
   (Lipps Inc.)
3. SEXY EYES
   (Dr. Hook)
4. DON'T FALL IN LOVE WITH A DREAMER
   (Kenny Rogers with Kim Carnes)
5. BIGGEST PART OF ME
   (Ambrosia)
6. LOST IN LOVE
   (Air Supply)
7. ANOTHER BRICK IN THE WALL (PART II)
   (Pink Floyd)
8. THE ROSE
   (Bette Midler)
9. HURT SO BAD
   (Linda Ronstadt)
10. CARS
    (Gary Numan)

POP ALBUMS

1. AGAINST THE WIND
   (Bob Seger and the Silver Bullet Band)
2. THE WALL
   (Pink Floyd)
3. GLASS HOUSES
   (Billy Joel)
4. MAD LOVE
   (Linda Ronstadt)
5. WOMEN AND CHILDREN FIRST
   (Van Halen)

6. OFF THE WALL
   (Michael Jackson)
7. GO ALL THE WAY
   (Isley Brothers)
8. GIDEON
   (Kenny Rogers)
9. JUST ONE NIGHT
   (Eric Clapton)
10. CHRISTOPHER CROSS
    (Christopher Cross)

BLACK SINGLES

1. LET'S GET SERIOUS
   (Jermaine Jackson)
2. FUNKYTOWN
   (Lipps Inc.)
3. SWEET SENSATION
   (Stephanie Mills)
4. DON'T SAY GOODNIGHT (IT'S TIME FOR LOVE)
   (Isley Brothers)
5. LADY
   (Whispers)
6. LET ME BE THE CLOCK
   (Smokey Robinson)
7. GOT TO BE ENOUGH
   (Con Funk Shun)
8. SHINING STAR
   (The Manhattans)
9. ALL-NIGHT THING
   (Invisible Man's Band)
10. TWO PLACES AT THE SAME TIME
    (Ray Parker Jr. and Raydio)

BLACK ALBUMS

1. GO ALL THE WAY
   (Isley Brothers)
2. LET'S GET SERIOUS
   (Jermaine Jackson)
3. SWEET SENSATION
   (Stephanie Mills)
4. ROBERTA FLACK FEATURING DONNY HATHAWAY
   (Roberta Flack and Donny Hathaway)
5. LIGHT UP THE NIGHT
   (The Brothers Johnson)
6. MOUTH TO MOUTH
   (Lipps Inc.)
7. THE WHISPERS
   (Whispers)
8. SPIRIT OF LOVE
   (Con Funk Shun)
9. TWO PLACES AT THE SAME TIME
   (Ray Parker Jr. and Raydio)
10. WARM THOUGHTS
    (Smokey Robinson)

JAZZ ALBUMS

1. SKYLARKIN'
   (Grover Washington Jr.)
2. CATCHING THE SUN
   (Spyro Gyra)
3. DREAM COME TRUE
   (Earl Klugh)
4. HIDEAWAY
   (David Sanborn)
5. MONSTER
   (Herbie Hancock)
6. FUN AND GAMES
   (Chuck Mangione)
7. EVERY GENERATION
   (Ronnie Laws)
8. ONE BAD HABIT
   (Michael Franks)
9. YOU'LL NEVER KNOW
   (Rodney Franklin)
10. WIZARD ISLAND
    (Jeff Lorber Fusion)

COUNTRY SINGLES

1. GOOD OLE BOYS LIKE ME
   (Don Williams)
2. THE WAY I AM
   (Merle Haggard)
3. STARTING OVER AGAIN
   (Dolly Parton)
4. DON'T FALL IN LOVE WITH A DREAMER
   (Kenny Rogers with Kim Carnes)
5. GONE TOO FAR
   (Eddie Rabbitt)
6. MY HEART/SILENT NIGHT (AFTER THE FIGHT)
   (Ronnie Milsap)
7. MORNING COMES TOO EARLY
   (Jim Ed Brown and Helen Cornelius)
8. I'M ALREADY BLUE
   (The Kendalls)
9. TEMPORARILY YOURS
   (Jeanne Pruett)
10. SHE JUST STARTED LIKIN' CHEATIN' SONGS
    (John Anderson)

COUNTRY ALBUMS

1. GIDEON
   (Kenny Rogers)
2. THE GAMBLER
   (Kenny Rogers)
3. KENNY
   (Kenny Rogers)
4. GREATEST HITS
   (Waylon Jennings)
5. COAL MINER'S DAUGHTER
   (Original Soundtrack)
6. TEN YEARS OF GOLD
   (Kenny Rogers)
7. ELECTRIC HORSEMAN FEATURING WILLIE NELSON
   (Willie Nelson)
8. MILSAP MAGIC
   (Ronnie Milsap)
9. TOGETHER
   (The Oak Ridge Boys)
10. STARDUST
    (Willie Nelson)

MAY 31, 1980

POP SINGLES

1. FUNKYTOWN
   (Lipps Inc.)
2. BIGGEST PART OF ME
   (Ambrosia)
3. CALL ME
   (Blondie)
4. DON'T FALL IN LOVE WITH A DREAMER
   (Kenny Rogers with Kim Carnes)
5. THE ROSE
   (Bette Midler)
6. SEXY EYES
   (Dr. Hook)
7. ANOTHER BRICK IN THE WALL (PART II)
   (Pink Floyd)
8. CARS
   (Gary Numan)
9. HURT SO BAD
   (Linda Ronstadt)
10. LOST IN LOVE
    (Air Supply)

POP ALBUMS

1. GLASS HOUSES
   (Billy Joel)
2. AGAINST THE WIND
   (Bob Seger and The Silver Bullet Band)

3. THE WALL
   (Pink Floyd)
4. MAD LOVE
   (Linda Ronstadt)
5. GO ALL THE WAY
   (Isley Brothers)
6. WOMEN AND CHILDREN FIRST
   (Van Halen)
7. OFF THE WALL
   (Michael Jackson)
8. GIDEON
   (Kenny Rogers)
9. JUST ONE NIGHT
   (Eric Clapton)
10. CHRISTOPHER CROSS
    (Christopher Cross)

BLACK SINGLES

1. LET'S GET SERIOUS
   (Jermaine Jackson)
2. FUNKYTOWN
   (Lipps Inc.)
3. SWEET SENSATION
   (Stephanie Mills)
4. SHINING STAR
   (The Manhattans)
5. DON'T SAY GOODNIGHT (IT'S TIME FOR LOVE)
   (Isley Brothers)
6. LADY
   (Whispers)
7. TAKE YOUR TIME (DO IT RIGHT) PART I
   (The S.O.S. Band)
8. ALL-NIGHT THING
   (Invisible Man's Band)
9. LANDLORD
   (Gladys Knight and The Pips)
10. GOTTA GET MY HANDS ON SOME MONEY
    (Fatback)

BLACK ALBUMS

1. GO ALL THE WAY
   (Isley Brothers)
2. LET'S GET SERIOUS
   (Jermaine Jackson)
3. SWEET SENSATION
   (Stephanie Mills)
4. ROBERTA FLACK FEATURING DONNY HATHAWAY
   (Roberta Flack and Donny Hathaway)
5. MOUTH TO MOUTH
   (Lipps Inc.)
6. LIGHT UP THE NIGHT
   (The Brothers Johnson)
7. SPIRIT OF LOVE
   (Con Funk Shun)
8. TWO PLACES AT THE SAME TIME
   (Ray Parker Jr. and Raydio)
9. THE WHISPERS
   (Whispers)
10. AFTER MIDNIGHT
    (The Manhattans)

JAZZ ALBUMS

1. SKYLARKIN'
   (Grover Washington Jr.)
2. CATCHING THE SUN
   (Spyro Gyra)
3. DREAM COME TRUE
   (Earl Klugh)
4. WIZARD ISLAND
   (Jeff Lorber Fusion)
5. HIDEAWAY
   (David Sanborn)
6. ONE BAD HABIT
   (Michael Franks)
7. EVERY GENERATION
   (Ronnie Laws)
8. MONSTER
   (Herbie Hancock)

9. YOU'LL NEVER KNOW
   (Rodney Franklin)
10. FUN AND GAMES
    (Chuck Mangione)

COUNTRY SINGLES

1. GOOD OLE BOYS LIKE ME
   (Don Williams)
2. DON'T FALL IN LOVE WITH A DREAMER
   (Kenny Rogers with Kim Carnes)
3. STARTING OVER AGAIN
   (Dolly Parton)
4. MY HEART/SILENT NIGHT (AFTER THE FIGHT)
   (Ronnie Milsap)
5. THE WAY I AM
   (Merle Haggard)
6. I'M ALREADY BLUE
   (The Kendalls)
7. LUCKY ME
   (Anne Murray)
8. TRYING TO LOVE TWO WOMEN
   (The Oak Ridge Boys)
9. GONE TOO FAR
   (Eddie Rabbitt)
10. ONE DAY AT A TIME
    (Cristy Lane)

COUNTRY ALBUMS

1. GIDEON
   (Kenny Rogers)
2. THE GAMBLER
   (Kenny Rogers)
3. GREATEST HITS
   (Waylon Jennings)
4. URBAN COWBOY
   (Original Soundtrack)
5. KENNY
   (Kenny Rogers)
6. COAL MINER'S DAUGHTER
   (Original Soundtrack)
7. SOMEBODY'S WAITING
   (Anne Murray)
8. ELECTRIC HORSEMAN FEATURING WILLIE NELSON
   (Willie Nelson)
9. MILSAP MAGIC
   (Ronnie Milsap)
10. IT'S HARD TO BE HUMBLE
    (Mac Davis)

JUNE 7, 1980

POP SINGLES

1. FUNKYTOWN
   (Lipps Inc.)
2. BIGGEST PART OF ME
   (Ambrosia)
3. THE ROSE
   (Bette Midler)
4. CALL ME
   (Blondie)
5. CARS
   (Gary Numan)
6. DON'T FALL IN LOVE WITH A DREAMER
   (Kenny Rogers with Kim Carnes)
7. COMING UP
   (Paul McCartney)
8. SEXY EYES
   (Dr. Hook)
9. ANOTHER BRICK IN THE WALL (PART II)
   (Pink Floyd)
10. LITTLE JEANNIE
    (Elton John)

POP ALBUMS

1. GLASS HOUSES
   (Billy Joel)

2. AGAINST THE WIND
   (Bob Seger and The Silver Bullet Band)
3. THE WALL
   (Pink Floyd)
4. WOMEN AND CHILDREN FIRST
   (Van Halen)
5. GO ALL THE WAY
   (Isley Brothers)
6. OFF THE WALL
   (Michael Jackson)
7. JUST ONE NIGHT
   (Eric Clapton)
8. GIDEON
   (Kenny Rogers)
9. MAD LOVE
   (Linda Ronstadt)
10. LET'S GET SERIOUS
    (Jermaine Jackson)

BLACK ALBUMS

1. GO ALL THE WAY
   (Isley Brothers)
2. LET'S GET SERIOUS
   (Jermaine Jackson)
3. SWEET SENSATION
   (Stephanie Mills)
4. ROBERTA FLACK FEATURING DONNY HATHAWAY
   (Roberta Flack and Donny Hathaway)
5. MOUTH TO MOUTH
   (Lipps Inc.)
6. SPIRIT OF LOVE
   (Con Funk Shun)
7. LIGHT UP THE NIGHT
   (The Brothers Johnson)
8. TWO PLACES AT THE SAME TIME
   (Ray Parker Jr. and Raydio)
9. AFTER MIDNIGHT
   (The Manhattans)
10. THE WHISPERS
    (Whispers)

JAZZ ALBUMS

1. CATCHING THE SUN
   (Spyro Gyra)
2. SKYLARKIN'
   (Grover Washington Jr.)
3. DREAM COME TRUE
   (Earl Klugh)
4. WIZARD ISLAND
   (Jeff Lorber Fusion)
5. HIDEAWAY
   (David Sanborn)
6. ONE BAD HABIT
   (Michael Franks)
7. MONSTER
   (Herbie Hancock)
8. YOU'LL NEVER KNOW
   (Rodney Franklin)
9. EVERY GENERATION
   (Ronnie Laws)
10. A BRAZILIAN LOVE AFFAIR
    (George Duke)

COUNTRY SINGLES

1. MY HEART/SILENT NIGHT (AFTER THE FIGHT)
   (Ronnie Milsap)
2. DON'T FALL IN LOVE WITH A DREAMER
   (Kenny Rogers with Kim Carnes)
3. TRYING TO LOVE TWO WOMEN
   (The Oak Ridge Boys)
4. LUCKY ME
   (Anne Murray)
5. I'M ALREADY BLUE
   (The Kendalls)
6. GOOD OLE BOYS LIKE ME
   (Don Williams)
7. STARTING OVER AGAIN
   (Dolly Parton)
8. ONE DAY AT A TIME
   (Cristy Lane)

9. SMOOTH SAILIN'
   (T.G. Sheppard)
10. HE STOPPED LOVING HER TODAY
    (George Jones)

COUNTRY ALBUMS

1. GIDEON
   (Kenny Rogers)
2. THE GAMBLER
   (Kenny Rogers)
3. KENNY
   (Kenny Rogers)
4. URBAN COWBOY
   (Original Soundtrack)
5. GREATEST HITS
   (Waylon Jennings)
6. STRAIGHT AHEAD
   (Larry Gatlin)
7. SOMEBODY'S WAITING
   (Anne Murray)
8. COAL MINER'S DAUGHTER
   (Original Soundtrack)
9. ELECTRIC HORSEMAN FEATURING WILLIE NELSON
   (Willie Nelson)
10. IT'S HARD TO BE HUMBLE
    (Mac Davis)

JUNE 14, 1980

POP SINGLES

1. FUNKYTOWN
   (Lipps Inc.)
2. THE ROSE
   (Bette Midler)
3. COMING UP
   (Paul McCartney)
4. BIGGEST PART OF ME
   (Ambrosia)
5. CARS
   (Gary Numan)
6. DON'T FALL IN LOVE WITH A DREAMER
   (Kenny Rogers with Kim Carnes)
7. LITTLE JEANNIE
   (Elton John)
8. CALL ME
   (Blondie)
9. AGAINST THE WIND
   (Bob Seger)
10. STEAL AWAY
    (Robbie Dupree)

POP ALBUMS

1. GLASS HOUSES
   (Billy Joel)
2. AGAINST THE WIND
   (Bob Seger and The Silver Bullet Band)
3. THE WALL
   (Pink Floyd)
4. WOMEN AND CHILDREN FIRST
   (Van Halen)
5. OFF THE WALL
   (Michael Jackson)
6. STAR WARS/THE EMPIRE STRIKES BACK
   (Original Soundtrack)
7. JUST ONE NIGHT
   (Eric Clapton)
8. GO ALL THE WAY
   (Isley Brothers)
9. LET'S GET SERIOUS
   (Jermaine Jackson)
10. SWEET SENSATION
    (Stephanie Mills)

BLACK SINGLES

1. TAKE YOUR TIME (DO IT RIGHT) PART I
   (The S.O.S. Band)

2. LET'S GET SERIOUS
   (Jermaine Jackson)
3. FUNKYTOWN
   (Lipps Inc.)
4. SHINING STAR
   (The Manhattans)
5. LANDLORD
   (Gladys Knight and The Pips)
6. SWEET SENSATION
   (Stephanie Mills)
7. A LOVER'S HOLIDAY
   (Change)
8. GOTTA GET MY HANDS ON SOME MONEY
   (Fatback)
9. BACK TOGETHER AGAIN
   (Roberta Flack with Donny Hathaway)
10. CLOUDS
    (Chaka Khan)

BLACK ALBUMS

1. GO ALL THE WAY
   (Isley Brothers)
2. LET'S GET SERIOUS
   (Jermaine Jackson)
3. SWEET SENSATION
   (Stephanie Mills)
4. MOUTH TO MOUTH
   (Lipps Inc.)
5. ROBERTA FLACK FEATURING DONNY HATHAWAY
   (Roberta Flack and Donny Hathaway)
6. TWO PLACES AT THE SAME TIME
   (Ray Parker Jr. and Raydio)
7. SPIRIT OF LOVE
   (Con Funk Shun)
8. AFTER MIDNIGHT
   (The Manhattans)
9. CAMEOSIS
   (Cameo)
10. HOT BOX
    (Fatback)

JAZZ ALBUMS

1. CATCHING THE SUN
   (Spyro Gyra)
2. SKYLARKIN'
   (Grover Washington Jr.)
3. WIZARD ISLAND
   (Jeff Lorber Fusion)
4. DREAM COME TRUE
   (Earl Klugh)
5. HIDEAWAY
   (David Sanborn)
6. ONE BAD HABIT
   (Michael Franks)
7. MONSTER
   (Herbie Hancock)
8. YOU'LL NEVER KNOW
   (Rodney Franklin)
9. A BRAZILIAN LOVE AFFAIR
   (George Duke)
10. EVERY GENERATION
    (Ronnie Laws)

COUNTRY SINGLES

1. MY HEART/SILENT NIGHT (AFTER THE FIGHT)
   (Ronnie Milsap)
2. TRYING TO LOVE TWO WOMEN
   (The Oak Ridge Boys)
3. DON'T FALL IN LOVE WITH A DREAMER
   (Kenny Rogers with Kim Carnes)
4. LUCKY ME
   (Anne Murray)
5. HE STOPPED LOVING HER TODAY
   (George Jones)
6. ONE DAY AT A TIME
   (Cristy Lane)
7. SMOOTH SAILIN'
   (T.G. Sheppard)

8. I'M ALREADY BLUE
   (The Kendalls)
9. TELL OLE I AIN'T HERE HE BETTER GET ON HOME
   (Moe Bandy and Joe Stampley)
10. YOUR BODY IS AN OUTLAW
    (Mel Tillis)

COUNTRY ALBUMS

1. GIDEON
   (Kenny Rogers)
2. THE GAMBLER
   (Kenny Rogers)
3. KENNY
   (Kenny Rogers)
4. URBAN COWBOY
   (Original Soundtrack)
5. GREATEST HITS
   (Waylon Jennings)
6. STRAIGHT AHEAD
   (Larry Gatlin)
7. COAL MINER'S DAUGHTER
   (Original Soundtrack)
8. ELECTRIC HORSEMAN FEATURING WILLIE NELSON
   (Willie Nelson)
9. ROSES IN THE SNOW
   (Emmylou Harris)
10. DOLLY, DOLLY, DOLLY
    (Dolly Parton)

JUNE 21, 1980

POP SINGLES

1. FUNKYTOWN
   (Lipps Inc.)
2. THE ROSE
   (Bette Midler)
3. COMING UP
   (Paul McCartney)
4. LITTLE JEANNIE
   (Elton John)
5. STEAL AWAY
   (Robbie Dupree)
6. CARS
   (Gary Numan)
7. SHE'S OUT OF MY LIFE
   (Michael Jackson)
8. IT'S STILL ROCK AND ROLL TO ME
   (Billy Joel)
9. AGAINST THE WIND
   (Bob Seger)
10. DON'T FALL IN LOVE WITH A DREAMER
    (Kenny Rogers with Kim Carnes)

POP ALBUMS

1. GLASS HOUSES
   (Billy Joel)
2. AGAINST THE WIND
   (Bob Seger and The Silver Bullet Band)
3. THE WALL
   (Pink Floyd)
4. McCARTNEY II
   (Paul McCartney)
5. OFF THE WALL
   (Michael Jackson)
6. STAR WARS/THE EMPIRE STRIKES BACK
   (Original Soundtrack)
7. JUST ONE NIGHT
   (Eric Clapton)
8. WOMEN AND CHILDREN FIRST
   (Van Halen)
9. LET'S GET SERIOUS
   (Jermaine Jackson)
10. SWEET SENSATION
    (Stephanie Mills)

BLACK SINGLES

1. TAKE YOUR TIME (DO IT RIGHT) PART I
   (The S.O.S. Band)
2. SHINING STAR
   (The Manhattans)
3. LET'S GET SERIOUS
   (Jermaine Jackson)
4. LANDLORD
   (Gladys Knight and The Pips)
5. FUNKYTOWN
   (Lipps Inc.)
6. A LOVER'S HOLIDAY
   (Change)
7. SWEET SENSATION
   (Stephanie Mills)
8. GOTTA GET MY HANDS ON SOME MONEY
   (Fatback)
9. BACK TOGETHER AGAIN
   (Roberta Flack with Donny Hathaway)
10. ONE IN A MILLION
    (Larry Graham)

BLACK ALBUMS

1. LET'S GET SERIOUS
   (Jermaine Jackson)
2. SWEET SENSATION
   (Stephanie Mills)
3. GO ALL THE WAY
   (Isley Brothers)
4. MOUTH TO MOUTH
   (Lipps Inc.)
5. CAMEOSIS
   (Cameo)
6. ROBERTA FLACK FEATURING DONNY HATHAWAY
   (Roberta Flack and Donny Hathaway)
7. AFTER MIDNIGHT
   (The Manhattans)
8. THE GLOW OF LOVE
   (Change)
9. TWO PLACES AT THE SAME TIME
   (Ray Parker Jr. and Raydio)
10. ABOUT LOVE
    (Gladys Knight and The Pips)

JAZZ ALBUMS

1. SKYLARKIN'
   (Grover Washington Jr.)
2. CATCHING THE SUN
   (Spyro Gyra)
3. HIDEAWAY
   (David Sanborn)
4. A BRAZILIAN LOVE AFFAIR
   (George Duke)
5. MONSTER
   (Herbie Hancock)
6. ROCKS, PEBBLES AND SAND
   (Stanley Clarke)
7. WIZARD ISLAND
   (Jeff Lorber Fusion)
8. ONE BAD HABIT
   (Michael Franks)
9. YOU'LL NEVER KNOW
   (Rodney Franklin)
10. THIS TIME
    (Al Jarreau)

COUNTRY SINGLES

1. TRYING TO LOVE TWO WOMEN
   (The Oak Ridge Boys)
2. ONE DAY AT A TIME
   (Cristy Lane)
3. HE STOPPED LOVING HER TODAY
   (George Jones)
4. MY HEART/SILENT NIGHT (AFTER THE FIGHT)
   (Ronnie Milsap)
5. YOUR BODY IS AN OUTLAW
   (Mel Tillis)

6. SMOOTH SAILIN'
   (T.G. Sheppard)
7. MIDNIGHT RIDER
   (Willie Nelson)
8. TELL OLE I AIN'T HERE HE BETTER GET
   ON HOME
   (Moe Bandy and Joe Stampley)
9. FRIDAY NIGHT BLUES
   (John Conlee)
10. HE WAS THERE (WHEN I NEEDED YOU)
    (Tammy Wynette)

COUNTRY ALBUMS

1. GIDEON
   (Kenny Rogers)
2. THE GAMBLER
   (Kenny Rogers)
3. MUSIC MAN
   (Waylon Jennings)
4. URBAN COWBOY
   (Original Soundtrack)
5. GREATEST HITS
   (Waylon Jennings)
6. ROSES IN THE SNOW
   (Emmylou Harris)
7. KENNY
   (Kenny Rogers)
8. COAL MINER'S DAUGHTER
   (Original Soundtrack)
9. STRAIGHT AHEAD
   (Larry Gatlin)
10. DOLLY, DOLLY, DOLLY
    (Dolly Parton)

JUNE 28, 1980

POP SINGLES

1. THE ROSE
   (Bette Midler)
2. FUNKYTOWN
   (Lipps Inc.)
3. COMING UP
   (Paul McCartney)
4. LITTLE JEANNIE
   (Elton John)
5. STEAL AWAY
   (Robbie Dupree)
6. IT'S STILL ROCK AND ROLL TO ME
   (Billy Joel)
7. SHE'S OUT OF MY LIFE
   (Michael Jackson)
8. CUPID/I'VE LOVED YOU FOR A LONG TIME
   (MEDLEY)
   (Spinners)
9. AGAINST THE WIND
   (Bob Seger)
10. LET ME LOVE YOU TONIGHT
    (Pure Prairie League)

POP ALBUMS

1. GLASS HOUSES
   (Billy Joel)
2. AGAINST THE WIND
   (Bob Seger and The Silver Bullet Band)
3. McCARTNEY II
   (Paul McCartney)
4. THE WALL
   (Pink Floyd)
5. OFF THE WALL
   (Michael Jackson)
6. STAR WARS/THE EMPIRE STRIKES BACK
   (Original Soundtrack)
7. JUST ONE NIGHT
   (Eric Clapton)
8. WOMEN AND CHILDREN FIRST
   (Van Halen)
9. LET'S GET SERIOUS
   (Jermaine Jackson)

10. MOUTH TO MOUTH
    (Lipps Inc.)

BLACK SINGLES

1. TAKE YOUR TIME (DO IT RIGHT) PART I
   (The S.O.S. Band)
2. SHINING STAR
   (The Manhattans)
3. LANDLORD
   (Gladys Knight and The Pips)
4. LET'S GET SERIOUS
   (Jermaine Jackson)
5. A LOVER'S HOLIDAY
   (Change)
6. FUNKYTOWN
   (Lipps Inc.)
7. SWEET SENSATION
   (Stephanie Mills)
8. ONE IN A MILLION YOU
   (Larry Graham)
9. GOTTA GET MY HANDS ON SOME MONEY
   (Fatback)
10. CUPID/I'VE LOVED YOU FOR A LONG TIME
    (MEDLEY)
    (Spinners)

BLACK ALBUMS

1. LET'S GET SERIOUS
   (Jermaine Jackson)
2. SWEET SENSATION
   (Stephanie Mills)
3. GO ALL THE WAY
   (Isley Brothers)
4. CAMEOSIS
   (Cameo)
5. MOUTH TO MOUTH
   (Lipps Inc.)
6. DIANA
   (Diana Ross)
7. ABOUT LOVE
   (Gladys Knight and The Pips)
8. ROBERTA FLACK FEATURING DONNY
   HATHAWAY
   (Roberta Flack and Donny Hathaway)
9. THE GLOW OF LOVE
   (Change)
10. AFTER MIDNIGHT
    (The Manhattans)

JAZZ ALBUMS

1. CATCHING THE SUN
   (Spyro Gyra)
2. ROCKS, PEBBLES AND SAND
   (Stanley Clarke)
3. SKYLARKIN'
   (Grover Washington Jr.)
4. HIDEAWAY
   (David Sanborn)
5. YOU'LL NEVER KNOW
   (Rodney Franklin)
6. MONSTER
   (Herbie Hancock)
7. WIZARD ISLAND
   (Jeff Lorber Fusion)
8. THIS TIME
   (Al Jarreau)
9. ONE BAD HABIT
   (Michael Franks)
10. A BRAZILIAN LOVE AFFAIR
    (George Duke)

COUNTRY SINGLES

1. HE STOPPED LOVING HER TODAY
   (George Jones)
2. ONE DAY AT A TIME
   (Cristy Lane)
3. YOUR BODY IS AN OUTLAW
   (Mel Tillis)

4. FRIDAY NIGHT BLUES
   (John Conlee)
5. MIDNIGHT RIDER
   (Willie Nelson)
6. TRYING TO LOVE TWO WOMEN
   (The Oak Ridge Boys)
7. MY HEART/SILENT NIGHT (AFTER THE
   FIGHT)
   (Ronnie Milsap)
8. TELL OLE I AIN'T HERE HE BETTER GET
   ON HOME
   (Moe Bandy and Joe Stampley)
9. YOU WIN AGAIN
   (Charley Pride)
10. HE WAS THERE (WHEN I NEEDED YOU)
    (Tammy Wynette)

COUNTRY ALBUMS

1. GIDEON
   (Kenny Rogers)
2. URBAN COWBOY
   (Original Soundtrack)
3. MUSIC MAN
   (Waylon Jennings)
4. THE GAMBLER
   (Kenny Rogers)
5. GREATEST HITS
   (Waylon Jennings)
6. ROSES IN THE SNOW
   (Emmylou Harris)
7. COAL MINER'S DAUGHTER
   (Original Soundtrack)
8. STRAIGHT AHEAD
   (Larry Gatlin)
9. ELECTRIC HORSEMAN FEATURING WILLIE
   NELSON
   (Willie Nelson)
10. SOMEBODY'S WAITING
    (Anne Murray)

JULY 5, 1980

POP SINGLES

1. THE ROSE
   (Bette Midler)
2. FUNKYTOWN
   (Lipps Inc.)
3. COMING UP
   (Paul McCartney)
4. LITTLE JEANNIE
   (Elton John)
5. IT'S STILL ROCK AND ROLL TO ME
   (Billy Joel)
6. CUPID/I'VE LOVED YOU FOR A LONG TIME
   (MEDLEY)
   (Spinners)
7. STEAL AWAY
   (Robbie Dupree)
8. SHE'S OUT OF MY LIFE
   (Michael Jackson)
9. LET ME LOVE YOU TONIGHT
   (Pure Prairie League)
10. SHINING STAR
    (The Manhattans)

POP ALBUMS

1. GLASS HOUSES
   (Billy Joel)
2. AGAINST THE WIND
   (Bob Seger and The Silver Bullet Band)
3. McCARTNEY II
   (Paul McCartney)
4. URBAN COWBOY
   (Original Soundtrack)
5. THE WALL
   (Pink Floyd)
6. STAR WARS/THE EMPIRE STRIKES BACK
   (Original Soundtrack)

7. JUST ONE NIGHT
   (Eric Clapton)
8. OFF THE WALL
   (Michael Jackson)
9. LET'S GET SERIOUS
   (Jermaine Jackson)
10. MOUTH TO MOUTH
    (Lipps Inc.)

BLACK SINGLES

1. TAKE YOUR TIME (DO IT RIGHT) PART I
   (The S.O.S. Band)
2. LANDLORD
   (Gladys Knight and The Pips)
3. SHINING STAR
   (The Manhattans)
4. ONE IN A MILLION YOU
   (Larry Graham)
5. A LOVER'S HOLIDAY
   (Change)
6. LET'S GET SERIOUS
   (Jermaine Jackson)
7. FUNKYTOWN
   (Lipps Inc.)
8. CUPID/I'VE LOVED YOU FOR A LONG TIME
   (MEDLEY)
   (Spinners)
9. SWEET SENSATION
   (Stephanie Mills)
10. WE'RE GOING OUT TONIGHT
    (Cameo)

BLACK ALBUMS

1. LET'S GET SERIOUS
   (Jermaine Jackson)
2. SWEET SENSATION
   (Stephanie Mills)
3. DIANA
   (Diana Ross)
4. CAMEOSIS
   (Cameo)
5. ABOUT LOVE
   (Gladys Knight and The Pips)
6. GO ALL THE WAY
   (Isley Brothers)
7. AFTER MIDNIGHT
   (The Manhattans)
8. THE GLOW OF LOVE
   (Change)
9. NAUGHTY
   (Chaka Khan)
10. HEROES
    (Commodores)

JAZZ ALBUMS

1. CATCHING THE SUN
   (Spyro Gyra)
2. THIS TIME
   (Al Jarreau)
3. SKYLARKIN'
   (Grover Washington Jr.)
4. ROCKS, PEBBLES AND SAND
   (Stanley Clarke)
5. MONSTER
   (Herbie Hancock)
6. HIDEAWAY
   (David Sanborn)
7. WIZARD ISLAND
   (Jeff Lorber Fusion)
8. YOU'LL NEVER KNOW
   (Rodney Franklin)
9. A BRAZILIAN LOVE AFFAIR
   (George Duke)
10. ONE BAD HABIT
    (Michael Franks)

COUNTRY SINGLES

1. FRIDAY NIGHT BLUES
   (John Conlee)

2. HE STOPPED LOVING HER TODAY
   (George Jones)
3. YOUR BODY IS AN OUTLAW
   (Mel Tillis)
4. MIDNIGHT RIDER
   (Willie Nelson)
5. YOU WIN AGAIN
   (Charley Pride)
6. TRUE LOVE WAYS
   (Mickey Gilley)
7. IT'S TRUE LOVE
   (Conway Twitty and Loretta Lynn)
8. ONE DAY AT A TIME
   (Cristy Lane)
9. BAR ROOM BUDDIES
   (Merle Haggard and Clint Eastwood)
10. THE BLUE SIDE
    (Crystal Gayle)

COUNTRY ALBUMS

1. GIDEON
   (Kenny Rogers)
2. URBAN COWBOY
   (Original Soundtrack)
3. THE GAMBLER
   (Kenny Rogers)
4. MUSIC MAN
   (Waylon Jennings)
5. GREATEST HITS
   (Waylon Jennings)
6. KENNY
   (Kenny Rogers)
7. ROSES IN THE SNOW
   (Emmylou Harris)
8. SAN ANTONIO ROSE
   (Willie Nelson and Ray Price)
9. COAL MINER'S DAUGHTER
   (Original Soundtrack)
10. SOMEBODY'S WAITING
    (Anne Murray)

JULY 12, 1980

POP SINGLES

1. IT'S STILL ROCK AND ROLL TO ME
   (Billy Joel)
2. FUNKYTOWN
   (Lipps Inc.)
3. COMING UP
   (Paul McCartney)
4. THE ROSE
   (Bette Midler)
5. CUPID/I'VE LOVED YOU FOR A LONG TIME
   (MEDLEY)
   (Spinners)
6. SHINING STAR
   (The Manhattans)
7. LITTLE JEANNIE
   (Elton John)
8. LET ME LOVE YOU TONIGHT
   (Pure Prairie League)
9. TIRED OF TOEIN' THE LINE
   (Rocky Burnette)
10. MAGIC
    (Olivia Newton-John)

POP ALBUMS

1. GLASS HOUSES
   (Billy Joel)
2. AGAINST THE WIND
   (Bob Seger and The Silver Bullet Band)
3. McCARTNEY II
   (Paul McCartney)
4. URBAN COWBOY
   (Original Soundtrack)
5. THE WALL
   (Pink Floyd)

6. STAR WARS/THE EMPIRE STRIKES BACK
   (Original Soundtrack)
7. HEROES
   (Commodores)
8. OFF THE WALL
   (Michael Jackson)
9. THE ROSE
   (Original Soundtrack)
10. EMPTY GLASS
    (Pete Townshend)

BLACK SINGLES

1. TAKE YOUR TIME (DO IT RIGHT) PART I
   (The S.O.S. Band)
2. LANDLORD
   (Gladys Knight and The Pips)
3. ONE IN A MILLION YOU
   (Larry Graham)
4. SHINING STAR
   (The Manhattans)
5. A LOVER'S HOLIDAY
   (Change)
6. CUPID/I'VE LOVED YOU FOR A LONG TIME
   (MEDLEY)
   (Spinners)
7. LET'S GET SERIOUS
   (Jermaine Jackson)
8. WE'RE GOING OUT TONIGHT
   (Cameo)
9. SWEET SENSATION
   (Stephanie Mills)
10. FUNKYTOWN
    (Lipps Inc.)

BLACK ALBUMS

1. DIANA
   (Diana Ross)
2. LET'S GET SERIOUS
   (Jermaine Jackson)
3. CAMEOSIS
   (Cameo)
4. S.O.S.
   (The S.O.S. Band)
5. ABOUT LOVE
   (Gladys Knight and The Pips)
6. HEROES
   (Commodores)
7. SWEET SENSATION
   (Stephanie Mills)
8. THE GLOW OF LOVE
   (Change)
9. NAUGHTY
   (Chaka Khan)
10. GO ALL THE WAY
    (Isley Brothers)

JAZZ ALBUMS

1. THIS TIME
   (Al Jarreau)
2. SPLENDIDO HOTEL
   (Al DiMeola)
3. ROCKS, PEBBLES AND SAND
   (Stanley Clarke)
4. WIZARD ISLAND
   (Jeff Lorber Fusion)
5. CATCHING THE SUN
   (Spyro Gyra)
6. YOU'LL NEVER KNOW
   (Rodney Franklin)
7. A BRAZILIAN LOVE AFFAIR
   (George Duke)
8. MONSTER
   (Herbie Hancock)
9. SKYLARKIN'
   (Grover Washington Jr.)
10. RHAPSODY AND BLUES
    (Crusaders)

COUNTRY SINGLES

1. YOU WIN AGAIN
   (Charley Pride)
2. FRIDAY NIGHT BLUES
   (John Conlee)
3. BAR ROOM BUDDIES
   (Merle Haggard and Clint Eastwood)
4. TRUE LOVE WAYS
   (Mickey Gilley)
5. IT'S TRUE LOVE
   (Conway Twitty and Loretta Lynn)
6. HE STOPPED LOVING HER TODAY
   (George Jones)
7. THE BLUE SIDE
   (Crystal Gayle)
8. DANCIN' COWBOYS
   (The Bellamy Brothers)
9. CLYDE
   (Waylon Jennings)
10. TENNESSEE RIVER
    (Alabama)

COUNTRY ALBUMS

1. URBAN COWBOY
   (Original Soundtrack)
2. GIDEON
   (Kenny Rogers)
3. THE GAMBLER
   (Kenny Rogers)
4. MUSIC MAN
   (Waylon Jennings)
5. KENNY
   (Kenny Rogers)
6. GREATEST HITS
   (Waylon Jennings)
7. ROSES IN THE SNOW
   (Emmylou Harris)
8. SAN ANTONIO ROSE
   (Willie Nelson and Ray Price)
9. STARDUST
   (Willie Nelson)
10. COAL MINER'S DAUGHTER
    (Original Soundtrack)

JULY 19, 1980

POP SINGLES

1. IT'S STILL ROCK AND ROLL TO ME
   (Billy Joel)
2. FUNKYTOWN
   (Lipps Inc.)
3. COMING UP
   (Paul McCartney)
4. CUPID/I'VE LOVED YOU FOR A LONG TIME (MEDLEY)
   (Spinners)
5. SHINING STAR
   (The Manhattans)
6. THE ROSE
   (Bette Midler)
7. MAGIC
   (Olivia Newton-John)
8. LET ME LOVE YOU TONIGHT
   (Pure Prairie League)
9. TIRED OF TOEIN' THE LINE
   (Rocky Burnette)
10. LITTLE JEANNIE
    (Elton John)

POP ALBUMS

1. GLASS HOUSES
   (Billy Joel)
2. EMOTIONAL RESCUE
   (The Rolling Stones)
3. URBAN COWBOY
   (Original Soundtrack)

---

4. AGAINST THE WIND
   (Bob Seger and The Silver Bullet Band)
5. McCARTNEY II
   (Paul McCartney)
6. HOLD OUT
   (Jackson Browne)
7. HEROES
   (Commodores)
8. OFF THE WALL
   (Michael Jackson)
9. THE ROSE
   (Original Soundtrack)
10. EMPTY GLASS
    (Pete Townshend)

BLACK SINGLES

1. ONE IN A MILLION YOU
   (Larry Graham)
2. TAKE YOUR TIME (DO IT RIGHT) PART I
   (The S.O.S. Band)
3. LANDLORD
   (Gladys Knight and The Pips)
4. CUPID/I'VE LOVED YOU FOR A LONG TIME (MEDLEY)
   (Spinners)
5. SHINING STAR
   (The Manhattans)
6. A LOVER'S HOLIDAY
   (Change)
7. WE'RE GOING OUT TONIGHT
   (Cameo)
8. LET'S GET SERIOUS
   (Jermaine Jackson)
9. DYNAMITE
   (Stacy Lattisaw)
10. YOU AND ME
    (Rockie Robbins)

BLACK ALBUMS

1. DIANA
   (Diana Ross)
2. S.O.S.
   (The S.O.S. Band)
3. CAMEOSIS
   (Cameo)
4. HEROES
   (Commodores)
5. ABOUT LOVE
   (Gladys Knight and The Pips)
6. ONE IN A MILLION YOU
   (Larry Graham)
7. LET'S GET SERIOUS
   (Jermaine Jackson)
8. SWEET SENSATION
   (Stephanie Mills)
9. NAUGHTY
   (Chaka Khan)
10. THE GLOW OF LOVE
    (Change)

JAZZ ALBUMS

1. THIS TIME
   (Al Jarreau)
2. RHAPSODY AND BLUES
   (Crusaders)
3. SPLENDIDO HOTEL
   (Al DiMeola)
4. "H"
   (Bob James)
5. WIZARD ISLAND
   (Jeff Lorber Fusion)
6. CATCHING THE SUN
   (Spyro Gyra)
7. A BRAZILIAN LOVE AFFAIR
   (George Duke)
8. ROCKS, PEBBLES AND SAND
   (Stanley Clarke)
9. ONE BAD HABIT
   (Michael Franks)
10. INFLATION
    (Stanley Turrentine)

COUNTRY SINGLES

1. BAR ROOM BUDDIES
   (Merle Haggard and Clint Eastwood)
2. YOU WIN AGAIN
   (Charley Pride)
3. TRUE LOVE WAYS
   (Mickey Gilley)
4. IT'S TRUE LOVE
   (Conway Twitty and Loretta Lynn)
5. DANCIN' COWBOYS
   (The Bellamy Brothers)
6. THE BLUE SIDE
   (Crystal Gayle)
7. CLYDE
   (Waylon Jennings)
8. TENNESSEE RIVER
   (Alabama)
9. FRIDAY NIGHT BLUES
   (John Conlee)
10. STAND BY ME
    (Mickey Gilley)

COUNTRY ALBUMS

1. URBAN COWBOY
   (Original Soundtrack)
2. GIDEON
   (Kenny Rogers)
3. THE GAMBLER
   (Kenny Rogers)
4. MUSIC MAN
   (Waylon Jennings)
5. GREATEST HITS
   (Waylon Jennings)
6. KENNY
   (Kenny Rogers)
7. SAN ANTONIO ROSE
   (Willie Nelson and Ray Price)
8. ROSES IN THE SNOW
   (Emmylou Harris)
9. STARDUST
   (Willie Nelson)
10. TEN YEARS OF GOLD
    (Kenny Rogers)

JULY 26, 1980

POP SINGLES

1. IT'S STILL ROCK AND ROLL TO ME
   (Billy Joel)
2. FUNKYTOWN
   (Lipps Inc.)
3. MAGIC
   (Olivia Newton-John)
4. CUPID/I'VE LOVED YOU FOR A LONG TIME (MEDLEY)
   (Spinners)
5. SHINING STAR
   (The Manhattans)
6. COMING UP
   (Paul McCartney)
7. THE ROSE
   (Bette Midler)
8. TIRED OF TOEIN' THE LINE
   (Rocky Burnette)
9. LITTLE JEANNIE
   (Elton John)
10. IN AMERICA
    (The Charlie Daniels Band)

POP ALBUMS

1. GLASS HOUSES
   (Billy Joel)
2. EMOTIONAL RESCUE
   (The Rolling Stones)
3. URBAN COWBOY
   (Original Soundtrack)

4. HOLD OUT
(Jackson Browne)
5. AGAINST THE WIND
(Bob Seger and The Silver Bullet Band)
6. McCARTNEY II
(Paul McCartney)
7. BLUES BROTHERS
(Original Soundtrack)
8. OFF THE WALL
(Michael Jackson)
9. HEROES
(Commodores)
10. S.O.S.
(The S.O.S. Band)

BLACK SINGLES

1. ONE IN A MILLION YOU
(Larry Graham)
2. TAKE YOUR TIME (DO IT RIGHT) PART I
(The S.O.S. Band)
3. THE BREAKS (PART I)
(Kurtis Blow)
4. CUPID/I'VE LOVED YOU FOR A LONG TIME (MEDLEY)
(Spinners)
5. LANDLORD
(Gladys Knight and The Pips)
6. SHINING STAR
(The Manhattans)
7. GIVE ME THE NIGHT
(George Benson)
8. WE'RE GOING OUT TONIGHT
(Cameo)
9. DYNAMITE
(Stacy Lattisaw)
10. A LOVER'S HOLIDAY
(Change)

BLACK ALBUMS

1. DIANA
(Diana Ross)
2. S.O.S.
(The S.O.S. Band)
3. HEROES
(Commodores)
4. CAMEOSIS
(Cameo)
5. ONE IN A MILLION YOU
(Larry Graham)
6. ABOUT LOVE
(Gladys Knight and The Pips)
7. LET'S GET SERIOUS
(Jermaine Jackson)
8. NAUGHTY
(Chaka Khan)
9. THE GLOW OF LOVE
(Change)
10. SWEET SENSATION
(Stephanie Mills)

JAZZ ALBUMS

1. THIS TIME
(Al Jarreau)
2. RHAPSODY AND BLUES
(Crusaders)
3. "H"
(Bob James)
4. CATCHING THE SUN
(Spyro Gyra)
5. SPLENDIDO HOTEL
(Al Di Meola)
6. A BRAZILIAN LOVE AFFAIR
(George Duke)
7. WIZARD ISLAND
(Jeff Lorber Fusion)
8. ROCKS, PEBBLES AND SAND
(Stanley Clarke)
9. ONE BAD HABIT
(Michael Franks)
10. SKYLARKIN'
(Grover Washington Jr.)

COUNTRY SINGLES

1. BAR ROOM BUDDIES
(Merle Haggard and Clint Eastwood)
2. DANCIN' COWBOYS
(The Bellamy Brothers)
3. TRUE LOVE WAYS
(Mickey Gilley)
4. IT'S TRUE LOVE
(Conway Twitty and Loretta Lynn)
5. TENNESSEE RIVER
(Alabama)
6. CLYDE
(Waylon Jennings)
7. STAND BY ME
(Mickey Gilley)
8. YOU WIN AGAIN
(Charley Pride)
9. WAYFARIN' STRANGER
(Emmylou Harris)
10. SAVE YOUR HEART FOR ME
(Jacky Ward)

COUNTRY ALBUMS

1. URBAN COWBOY
(Original Soundtrack)
2. GIDEON
(Kenny Rogers)
3. THE GAMBLER
(Kenny Rogers)
4. GREATEST HITS
(Waylon Jennings)
5. MUSIC MAN
(Waylon Jennings)
6. SAN ANTONIO ROSE
(Willie Nelson and Ray Price)
7. ROSES IN THE SNOW
(Emmylou Harris)
8. KENNY
(Kenny Rogers)
9. TEN YEARS OF GOLD
(Kenny Rogers)
10. STRAIGHT AHEAD
(Larry Gatlin and The Gatlin Brothers Band)

AUGUST 2, 1980

POP SINGLES

1. IT'S STILL ROCK AND ROLL TO ME
(Billy Joel)
2. MAGIC
(Olivia Newton-John)
3. FUNKYTOWN
(Lipps Inc.)
4. CUPID/I'VE LOVED YOU FOR A LONG TIME (MEDLEY)
(Spinners)
5. SHINING STAR
(The Manhattans)
6. TAKE YOUR TIME (DO IT RIGHT) PART I
(The S.O.S. Band)
7. COMING UP
(Paul McCartney)
8. THE ROSE
(Bette Midler)
9. MISUNDERSTANDING
(Genesis)
10. LOVE THE WORLD AWAY
(Kenny Rogers)

POP ALBUMS

1. GLASS HOUSES
(Billy Joel)
2. EMOTIONAL RESCUE
(The Rolling Stones)
3. URBAN COWBOY
(Original Soundtrack)

4. HOLD OUT
(Jackson Browne)
5. AGAINST THE WIND
(Bob Seger and The Silver Bullet Band)
6. BLUES BROTHERS
(Original Soundtrack)
7. THE GAME
(Queen)
8. DIANA
(Diana Ross)
9. HEROES
(Commodores)
10. S.O.S.
(The S.O.S. Band)

BLACK SINGLES

1. ONE IN A MILLION YOU
(Larry Graham)
2. THE BREAKS (PART I)
(Kurtis Blow)
3. TAKE YOUR TIME (DO IT RIGHT) PART I
(The S.O.S. Band)
4. GIVE ME THE NIGHT
(George Benson)
5. CUPID/I'VE LOVED YOU FOR A LONG TIME (MEDLEY)
(Spinners)
6. LANDLORD
(Gladys Knight and The Pips)
7. UPSIDE DOWN
(Diana Ross)
8. BACKSTROKIN'
(Fatback)
9. DYNAMITE
(Stacy Lattisaw)
10. OLD-FASHION LOVE
(Commodores)

BLACK ALBUMS

1. DIANA
(Diana Ross)
2. S.O.S.
(The S.O.S. Band)
3. HEROES
(Commodores)
4. CAMEOSIS
(Cameo)
5. ONE IN A MILLION YOU
(Larry Graham)
6. ABOUT LOVE
(Gladys Knight and The Pips)
7. NAUGHTY
(Chaka Khan)
8. HOT BOX
(Fatback)
9. LET'S GET SERIOUS
(Jermaine Jackson)
10. THE GLOW OF LOVE
(Change)

JAZZ ALBUMS

1. RHAPSODY AND BLUES
(Crusaders)
2. THIS TIME
(Al Jarreau)
3. "H"
(Bob James)
4. ROCKS, PEBBLES AND SAND
(Stanley Clarke)
5. SPLENDIDO HOTEL
(Al DiMeola)
6. CATCHING THE SUN
(Spyro Gyra)
7. WIZARD ISLAND
(Jeff Lorber Fusion)
8. A BRAZILIAN LOVE AFFAIR
(George Duke)
9. SKYLARKIN'
(Grover Washington Jr.)
10. INFLATION
(Stanley Turrentine)

COUNTRY SINGLES

1. DANCIN' COWBOYS
   (The Bellamy Brothers)
2. STAND BY ME
   (Mickey Gilley)
3. TENNESSEE RIVER
   (Alabama)
4. BAR ROOM BUDDIES
   (Merle Haggard and Clint Eastwood)
5. TRUE LOVE WAYS
   (Mickey Gilley)
6. DRIVIN' MY LIFE AWAY
   (Eddie Rabbitt)
7. WAYFARIN' STRANGER
   (Emmylou Harris)
8. SAVE YOUR HEART FOR ME
   (Jacky Ward)
9. CLYDE
   (Waylon Jennings)
10. COWBOYS AND CLOWNS/MISERY LOVES
    COMPANY
    (Ronnie Milsap)

COUNTRY ALBUMS

1. URBAN COWBOY
   (Original Soundtrack)
2. GIDEON
   (Kenny Rogers)
3. GREATEST HITS
   (Waylon Jennings)
4. MUSIC MAN
   (Waylon Jennings)
5. THE GAMBLER
   (Kenny Rogers)
6. ROSES IN THE SNOW
   (Emmylou Harris)
7. SAN ANTONIO ROSE
   (Willie Nelson and Ray Price)
8. HABITS OLD AND NEW
   (Hank Williams Jr.)
9. HORIZON
   (Eddie Rabbitt)
10. KENNY
    (Kenny Rogers)

AUGUST 9, 1980

POP SINGLES

1. MAGIC
   (Olivia Newton-John)
2. IT'S STILL ROCK AND ROLL TO ME
   (Billy Joel)
3. FUNKYTOWN
   (Lipps Inc.)
4. SHINING STAR
   (The Manhattans)
5. TAKE YOUR TIME (DO IT RIGHT) PART I
   (The S.O.S. Band)
6. CUPID/I'VE LOVED YOU FOR A LONG TIME
   (MEDLEY)
   (Spinners)
7. COMING UP
   (Paul McCartney)
8. LOVE THE WORLD AWAY
   (Kenny Rogers)
9. MISUNDERSTANDING
   (Genesis)
10. SAILING
    (Christopher Cross)

POP ALBUMS

1. EMOTIONAL RESCUE
   (The Rolling Stones)
2. GLASS HOUSES
   (Billy Joel)

3. URBAN COWBOY
   (Original Soundtrack)
4. HOLD OUT
   (Jackson Browne)
5. AGAINST THE WIND
   (Bob Seger and The Silver Bullet Band)
6. BLUES BROTHERS
   (Original Soundtrack)
7. THE GAME
   (Queen)
8. DIANA
   (Diana Ross)
9. CHRISTOPHER CROSS
   (Christopher Cross)
10. HEROES
    (Commodores)

BLACK SINGLES

1. ONE IN A MILLION YOU
   (Larry Graham)
2. THE BREAKS (PART I)
   (Kurtis Blow)
3. GIVE ME THE NIGHT
   (George Benson)
4. TAKE YOUR TIME (DO IT RIGHT) PART I
   (The S.O.S. Band)
5. UPSIDE DOWN
   (Diana Ross)
6. BACKSTROKIN'
   (Fatback)
7. OLD-FASHION LOVE
   (Commodores)
8. CUPID/I'VE LOVED YOU FOR A LONG TIME
   (MEDLEY)
   (Spinners)
9. DYNAMITE
   (Stacy Lattisaw)
10. CAN'T WE TRY
    (Teddy Pendergrass)

BLACK ALBUMS

1. DIANA
   (Diana Ross)
2. ONE IN A MILLION YOU
   (Larry Graham)
3. HEROES
   (Commodores)
4. S.O.S.
   (The S.O.S. Band)
5. CAMEOSIS
   (Cameo)
6. NAUGHTY
   (Chaka Khan)
7. REAL PEOPLE
   (Chic)
8. GIVE ME THE NIGHT
   (George Benson)
9. ABOUT LOVE
   (Gladys Knight and The Pips)
10. THIS TIME
    (Al Jarreau)

JAZZ ALBUMS

1. GIVE ME THE NIGHT
   (George Benson)
2. RHAPSODY AND BLUES
   (Crusaders)
3. THIS TIME
   (Al Jarreau)
4. "H"
   (Bob James)
5. SPLENDIDO HOTEL
   (Al DiMeola)
6. ROCKS, PEBBLES AND SAND
   (Stanley Clarke)
7. LOVE APPROACH
   (Tom Browne)
8. CATCHING THE SUN
   (Spyro Gyra)
9. A BRAZILIAN LOVE AFFAIR
   (George Duke)

10. BEYOND
    (Herb Alpert)

COUNTRY SINGLES

1. STAND BY ME
   (Mickey Gilley)
2. TENNESSEE RIVER
   (Alabama)
3. DANCIN' COWBOYS
   (The Bellamy Brothers)
4. DRIVIN' MY LIFE AWAY
   (Eddie Rabbitt)
5. COWBOYS AND CLOWNS/MISERY LOVES
   COMPANY
   (Ronnie Milsap)
6. LOVE THE WORLD AWAY
   (Kenny Rogers)
7. WAYFARIN' STRANGER
   (Emmylou Harris)
8. SAVE YOUR HEART FOR ME
   (Jacky Ward)
9. BAR ROOM BUDDIES
   (Merle Haggard and Clint Eastwood)
10. CRACKERS
    (Barbara Mandrell)

COUNTRY ALBUMS

1. URBAN COWBOY
   (Original Soundtrack)
2. GIDEON
   (Kenny Rogers)
3. GREATEST HITS
   (Waylon Jennings)
4. THE GAMBLER
   (Kenny Rogers)
5. MUSIC MAN
   (Waylon Jennings)
6. ROSES IN THE SNOW
   (Emmylou Harris)
7. HORIZON
   (Eddie Rabbitt)
8. HABITS OLD AND NEW
   (Hank Williams Jr.)
9. SAN ANTONIO ROSE
   (Willie Nelson and Ray Price)
10. KENNY
    (Kenny Rogers)

AUGUST 16, 1980

POP SINGLES

1. MAGIC
   (Olivia Newton-John)
2. IT'S STILL ROCK AND ROLL TO ME
   (Billy Joel)
3. TAKE YOUR TIME (DO IT RIGHT) PART I
   (The S.O.S. Band)
4. SHINING STAR
   (The Manhattans)
5. FUNKYTOWN
   (Lipps Inc.)
6. SAILING
   (Christopher Cross)
7. EMOTIONAL RESCUE
   (The Rolling Stones)
8. LOVE THE WORLD AWAY
   (Kenny Rogers)
9. ALL OUT OF LOVE
   (Air Supply)
10. EMPIRE STRIKES BACK (MEDLEY)
    (Meco)

POP ALBUMS

1. URBAN COWBOY
   (Original Soundtrack)

2. GLASS HOUSES
   (Billy Joel)
3. EMOTIONAL RESCUE
   (The Rolling Stones)
4. HOLD OUT
   (Jackson Browne)
5. AGAINST THE WIND
   (Bob Seger and The Silver Bullet Band)
6. THE GAME
   (Queen)
7. DIANA
   (Diana Ross)
8. BLUES BROTHERS
   (Original Soundtrack)
9. CHRISTOPHER CROSS
   (Christopher Cross)
10. HEROES
    (Commodores)

BLACK SINGLES

1. THE BREAKS (PART I)
   (Kurtis Blow)
2. ONE IN A MILLION YOU
   (Larry Graham)
3. GIVE ME THE NIGHT
   (George Benson)
4. UPSIDE DOWN
   (Diana Ross)
5. BACKSTROKIN'
   (Fatback)
6. OLD-FASHION LOVE
   (Commodores)
7. TAKE YOUR TIME (DO IT RIGHT) PART I
   (The S.O.S. Band)
8. CAN'T WE TRY
   (Teddy Pendergrass)
9. REBELS ARE WE
   (Chic)
10. CUPID/I'VE LOVED YOU FOR A LONG TIME
    (MEDLEY)
    (Spinners)

BLACK ALBUMS

1. DIANA
   (Diana Ross)
2. ONE IN A MILLION YOU
   (Larry Graham)
3. HEROES
   (Commodores)
4. GIVE ME THE NIGHT
   (George Benson)
5. S.O.S.
   (The S.O.S. Band)
6. CAMEOSIS
   (Cameo)
7. REAL PEOPLE
   (Chic)
8. TP
   (Teddy Pendergrass)
9. NAUGHTY
   (Chaka Khan)
10. ABOUT LOVE
    (Gladys Knight and The Pips)

JAZZ ALBUMS

1. GIVE ME THE NIGHT
   (George Benson)
2. RHAPSODY AND BLUES
   (Crusaders)
3. THIS TIME
   (Al Jarreau)
4. "H"
   (Bob James)
5. LOVE APPROACH
   (Tom Browne)
6. BEYOND
   (Herb Alpert)
7. SPLENDIDO HOTEL
   (Al DiMeola)
8. ROCKS, PEBBLES AND SAND
   (Stanley Clarke)
9. MAGNIFICENT MADNESS
   (John Klemmer)
10. CATCHING THE SUN
    (Spyro Gyra)

COUNTRY SINGLES

1. DRIVIN' MY LIFE AWAY
   (Eddie Rabbitt)
2. TENNESSEE RIVER
   (Alabama)
3. COWBOYS AND CLOWNS/MISERY LOVES
   COMPANY
   (Ronnie Milsap)
4. LOVE THE WORLD AWAY
   (Kenny Rogers)
5. STAND BY ME
   (Mickey Gilley)
6. DANCIN' COWBOYS
   (The Bellamy Brothers)
7. CRACKERS
   (Barbara Mandrell)
8. I'VE NEVER SEEN THE LIKES OF YOU
   (Conway Twitty)
9. THAT LOVIN' YOU FEELIN' AGAIN
   (Roy Orbison and Emmylou Harris)
10. (YOU LIFT ME) UP TO HEAVEN
    (Reba McEntire)

COUNTRY ALBUMS

1. URBAN COWBOY
   (Original Soundtrack)
2. GIDEON
   (Kenny Rogers)
3. GREATEST HITS
   (Waylon Jennings)
4. MUSIC MAN
   (Waylon Jennings)
5. HORIZON
   (Eddie Rabbitt)
6. THE GAMBLER
   (Kenny Rogers)
7. ROSES IN THE SNOW
   (Emmylou Harris)
8. SAN ANTONIO ROSE
   (Willie Nelson and Ray Price)
9. FULL MOON
   (The Charlie Daniels Band)
10. HABITS OLD AND NEW
    (Hank Williams Jr.)

AUGUST 23, 1980

POP SINGLES

1. MAGIC
   (Olivia Newton-John)
2. SAILING
   (Christopher Cross)
3. TAKE YOUR TIME (DO IT RIGHT) PART I
   (The S.O.S. Band)
4. ALL OUT OF LOVE
   (Air Supply)
5. EMOTIONAL RESCUE
   (The Rolling Stones)
6. IT'S STILL ROCK AND ROLL TO ME
   (Billy Joel)
7. SHINING STAR
   (The Manhattans)
8. FAME
   (Irene Cara)
9. EMPIRE STRIKES BACK (MEDLEY)
   (Meco)
10. MORE LOVE
    (Kim Carnes)

POP ALBUMS

1. URBAN COWBOY
   (Original Soundtrack)
2. GLASS HOUSES
   (Billy Joel)
3. EMOTIONAL RESCUE
   (The Rolling Stones)
4. HOLD OUT
   (Jackson Browne)
5. THE GAME
   (Queen)
6. DIANA
   (Diana Ross)
7. GIVE ME THE NIGHT
   (George Benson)
8. CHRISTOPHER CROSS
   (Christopher Cross)
9. AGAINST THE WIND
   (Bob Seger and The Silver Bullet Band)
10. BLUES BROTHERS
    (Original Soundtrack)

BLACK SINGLES

1. GIVE ME THE NIGHT
   (George Benson)
2. UPSIDE DOWN
   (Diana Ross)
3. THE BREAKS (PART I)
   (Kurtis Blow)
4. ONE IN A MILLION YOU
   (Larry Graham)
5. BACKSTROKIN'
   (Fatback)
6. OLD-FASHION LOVE
   (Commodores)
7. CAN'T WE TRY
   (Teddy Pendergrass)
8. REBELS ARE WE
   (Chic)
9. TAKE YOUR TIME (DO IT RIGHT) PART I
   (The S.O.S. Band)
10. LOVE DON'T MAKE IT RIGHT
    (Nick Ashford and Valerie Simpson)

BLACK ALBUMS

1. DIANA
   (Diana Ross)
2. ONE IN A MILLION YOU
   (Larry Graham)
3. HEROES
   (Commodores)
4. GIVE ME THE NIGHT
   (George Benson)
5. TP
   (Teddy Pendergrass)
6. S.O.S.
   (The S.O.S. Band)
7. CAMEOSIS
   (Cameo)
8. REAL PEOPLE
   (Chic)
9. NAUGHTY
   (Chaka Khan)
10. JOY AND PAIN
    (Maze featuring Frankie Beverly)

JAZZ ALBUMS

1. GIVE ME THE NIGHT
   (George Benson)
2. THIS TIME
   (Al Jarreau)
3. RHAPSODY AND BLUES
   (Crusaders)
4. LOVE APPROACH
   (Tom Browne)
5. "H"
   (Bob James)
6. WIZARD ISLAND
   (Jeff Lorber Fusion)
7. MAGNIFICENT MADNESS
   (John Klemmer)
8. SPLENDIDO HOTEL
   (Al DiMeola)
9. ROCKS, PEBBLES AND SAND
   (Stanley Clarke)
10. CATCHING THE SUN
    (Spyro Gyra)

COUNTRY SINGLES

1. COWBOYS AND CLOWNS/MISERY LOVES COMPANY
   (Ronnie Milsap)
2. DRIVIN' MY LIFE AWAY
   (Eddie Rabbitt)
3. LOVE THE WORLD AWAY
   (Kenny Rogers)
4. CRACKERS
   (Barbara Mandrell)
5. I'VE NEVER SEEN THE LIKES OF YOU
   (Conway Twitty)
6. THAT LOVIN' YOU FEELIN' AGAIN
   (Roy Orbison and Emmylou Harris)
7. TENNESSEE RIVER
   (Alabama)
8. (YOU LIFT ME) UP TO HEAVEN
   (Reba McEntire)
9. STAND BY ME
   (Mickey Gilley)
10. MISERY AND GIN
    (Merle Haggard)

COUNTRY ALBUMS

1. URBAN COWBOY
   (Original Soundtrack)
2. FULL MOON
   (The Charlie Daniels Band)
3. GIDEON
   (Kenny Rogers)
4. GREATEST HITS
   (Waylon Jennings)
5. HORIZON
   (Eddie Rabbitt)
6. SAN ANTONIO ROSE
   (Willie Nelson and Ray Price)
7. MUSIC MAN
   (Waylon Jennings)
8. THE GAMBLER
   (Kenny Rogers)
9. STARDUST
   (Willie Nelson)
10. ROSES IN THE SNOW
    (Emmylou Harris)

SEPTEMBER 6, 1980

POP SINGLES

1. ALL OUT OF LOVE
   (Air Supply)
2. UPSIDE DOWN
   (Diana Ross)
3. FAME
   (Irene Cara)
4. SAILING
   (Christopher Cross)
5. TAKE YOUR TIME (DO IT RIGHT) PART I
   (The S.O.S. Band)
6. MAGIC
   (Olivia Newton-John)
7. EMOTIONAL RESCUE
   (The Rolling Stones)
8. GIVE ME THE NIGHT
   (George Benson)
9. INTO THE NIGHT
   (Benny Mardones)
10. LOOKIN' FOR LOVE
    (Johnny Lee)

POP ALBUMS

1. URBAN COWBOY
   (Original Soundtrack)
2. GLASS HOUSES
   (Billy Joel)
3. EMOTIONAL RESCUE
   (The Rolling Stones)

---

4. HOLD OUT
   (Jackson Browne)
5. THE GAME
   (Queen)
6. DIANA
   (Diana Ross)
7. GIVE ME THE NIGHT
   (George Benson)
8. CHRISTOPHER CROSS
   (Christopher Cross)
9. XANADU
   (Original Soundtrack)
10. FULL MOON
    (The Charlie Daniels Band)

BLACK SINGLES

1. UPSIDE DOWN
   (Diana Ross)
2. GIVE ME THE NIGHT
   (George Benson)
3. CAN'T WE TRY
   (Teddy Pendergrass)
4. ONE IN A MILLION YOU
   (Larry Graham)
5. THE BREAKS (PART I)
   (Kurtis Blow)
6. GIRL, DON'T LET IT GET YOU DOWN
   (The O'Jays)
7. I'VE JUST BEGUN TO LOVE YOU
   (Dynasty)
8. LOVE DON'T MAKE IT RIGHT
   (Nick Ashford and Valerie Simpson)
9. SHAKE YOUR PANTS
   (Cameo)
10. REBELS ARE WE
    (Chic)

BLACK ALBUMS

1. DIANA
   (Diana Ross)
2. GIVE ME THE NIGHT
   (George Benson)
3. TP
   (Teddy Pendergrass)
4. ONE IN A MILLION YOU
   (Larry Graham)
5. HEROES
   (Commodores)
6. JOY AND PAIN
   (Maze featuring Frankie Beverly)
7. CAMEOSIS
   (Cameo)
8. REAL PEOPLE
   (Chic)
9. S.O.S.
   (The S.O.S. Band)
10. A MUSICAL AFFAIR
    (Nick Ashford and Valerie Simpson)

JAZZ ALBUMS

1. GIVE ME THE NIGHT
   (George Benson)
2. RHAPSODY AND BLUES
   (Crusaders)
3. LOVE APPROACH
   (Tom Browne)
4. THIS TIME
   (Al Jarreau)
5. "H"
   (Bob James)
6. MAGNIFICENT MADNESS
   (John Klemmer)
7. ROUTES
   (Ramsey Lewis)
8. SPLENDIDO HOTEL
   (Al DiMeola)
9. ROCKS, PEBBLES AND SAND
   (Stanley Clarke)
10. WIZARD ISLAND
    (Jeff Lorber Fusion)

COUNTRY SINGLES

1. LOOKIN' FOR LOVE
   (Johnny Lee)
2. MISERY AND GIN
   (Merle Haggard)
3. COWBOYS AND CLOWNS/MISERY LOVES COMPANY
   (Ronnie Milsap)
4. DRIVIN' MY LIFE AWAY
   (Eddie Rabbitt)
5. CRACKERS
   (Barbara Mandrell)
6. CHARLOTTE'S WEB
   (The Statler Brothers)
7. MAKING PLANS
   (Porter Wagoner and Dolly Parton)
8. HEART OF MINE
   (The Oak Ridge Boys)
9. I'VE NEVER SEEN THE LIKES OF YOU
   (Conway Twitty)
10. OLD FLAMES CAN'T HOLD A CANDLE TO YOU
    (Dolly Parton)

COUNTRY ALBUMS

1. URBAN COWBOY
   (Original Soundtrack)
2. FULL MOON
   (The Charlie Daniels Band)
3. GIDEON
   (Kenny Rogers)
4. HORIZON
   (Eddie Rabbitt)
5. GREATEST HITS
   (Waylon Jennings)
6. STARDUST
   (Willie Nelson)
7. MUSIC MAN
   (Waylon Jennings)
8. THE GAMBLER
   (Kenny Rogers)
9. SAN ANTONIO ROSE
   (Willie Nelson and Ray Price)
10. ROSES IN THE SNOW
    (Emmylou Harris)

SEPTEMBER 13, 1980

POP SINGLES

1. ALL OUT OF LOVE
   (Air Supply)
2. UPSIDE DOWN
   (Diana Ross)
3. FAME
   (Irene Cara)
4. SAILING
   (Christopher Cross)
5. TAKE YOUR TIME (DO IT RIGHT) PART I
   (The S.O.S. Band)
6. GIVE ME THE NIGHT
   (George Benson)
7. MAGIC
   (Olivia Newton-John)
8. LOOKIN' FOR LOVE
   (Johnny Lee)
9. EMOTIONAL RESCUE
   (The Rolling Stones)
10. LATE IN THE EVENING
    (Paul Simon)

POP ALBUMS

1. GLASS HOUSES
   (Billy Joel)
2. URBAN COWBOY
   (Original Soundtrack)

3. THE GAME
   (Queen)
4. EMOTIONAL RESCUE
   (The Rolling Stones)
5. XANADU
   (Original Soundtrack)
6. HOLD OUT
   (Jackson Browne)
7. GIVE ME THE NIGHT
   (George Benson)
8. CHRISTOPHER CROSS
   (Christopher Cross)
9. DIANA
   (Diana Ross)
10. FULL MOON
    (The Charlie Daniels Band)

BLACK SINGLES

1. UPSIDE DOWN
   (Diana Ross)
2. GIVE ME THE NIGHT
   (George Benson)
3. CAN'T WE TRY
   (Teddy Pendergrass)
4. ONE IN A MILLION YOU
   (Larry Graham)
5. GIRL, DON'T LET IT GET YOU DOWN
   (The O'Jays)
6. I'VE JUST BEGUN TO LOVE YOU
   (Dynasty)
7. SHAKE YOUR PANTS
   (Cameo)
8. LOVE DON'T MAKE IT RIGHT
   (Nick Ashford and Valerie Simpson)
9. WIDE RECEIVER (PART I)
   (Michael Henderson)
10. THE BREAKS (PART I)
    (Kurtis Blow)

BLACK ALBUMS

1. DIANA
   (Diana Ross)
2. GIVE ME THE NIGHT
   (George Benson)
3. TP
   (Teddy Pendergrass)
4. ONE IN A MILLION YOU
   (Larry Graham)
5. HEROES
   (Commodores)
6. JOY AND PAIN
   (Maze featuring Frankie Beverly)
7. THE YEAR 2000
   (The O'Jays)
8. A MUSICAL AFFAIR
   (Nick Ashford and Valerie Simpson)
9. WIDE RECEIVER
   (Michael Henderson)
10. CAMEOSIS
    (Cameo)

JAZZ ALBUMS

1. GIVE ME THE NIGHT
   (George Benson)
2. LOVE APPROACH
   (Tom Browne)
3. THIS TIME
   (Al Jarreau)
4. RHAPSODY AND BLUES
   (Crusaders)
5. "H"
   (Bob James)
6. MAGNIFICENT MADNESS
   (John Klemmer)
7. ROUTES
   (Ramsey Lewis)
8. SPLENDIDO HOTEL
   (Al DiMeola)
9. BADDEST
   (Grover Washington Jr.)
10. ROCKS, PEBBLES AND SAND
    (Stanley Clarke)

COUNTRY SINGLES

1. LOOKIN' FOR LOVE
   (Johnny Lee)
2. MISERY AND GIN
   (Merle Haggard)
3. CHARLOTTE'S WEB
   (The Statler Brothers)
4. DRIVIN' MY LIFE AWAY
   (Eddie Rabbitt)
5. MAKING PLANS
   (Porter Wagoner and Dolly Parton)
6. HEART OF MINE
   (The Oak Ridge Boys)
7. OLD FLAMES CAN'T HOLD A CANDLE TO YOU
   (Dolly Parton)
8. DO YOU WANNA GO TO HEAVEN
   (T.G. Sheppard)
9. COWBOYS AND CLOWNS/MISERY LOVES COMPANY
   (Ronnie Milsap)
10. LET'S KEEP IT THAT WAY
    (Mac Davis)

COUNTRY ALBUMS

1. URBAN COWBOY
   (Original Soundtrack)
2. FULL MOON
   (The Charlie Daniels Band)
3. HORIZON
   (Eddie Rabbitt)
4. HONEYSUCKLE ROSE
   (Willie Nelson and Family)
5. GIDEON
   (Kenny Rogers)
6. GREATEST HITS
   (Waylon Jennings)
7. MUSIC MAN
   (Waylon Jennings)
8. SAN ANTONIO ROSE
   (Willie Nelson and Ray Price)
9. STARDUST
   (Willie Nelson)
10. THE GAMBLER
    (Kenny Rogers)

SEPTEMBER 20, 1980

POP SINGLES

1. UPSIDE DOWN
   (Diana Ross)
2. ALL OUT OF LOVE
   (Air Supply)
3. FAME
   (Irene Cara)
4. LOOKIN' FOR LOVE
   (Johnny Lee)
5. ANOTHER ONE BITES THE DUST
   (Queen)
6. GIVE ME THE NIGHT
   (George Benson)
7. DRIVIN' MY LIFE AWAY
   (Eddie Rabbitt)
8. MAGIC
   (Olivia Newton-John)
9. HOT ROD HEARTS
   (Robbie Dupree)
10. LATE IN THE EVENING
    (Paul Simon)

POP ALBUMS

1. URBAN COWBOY
   (Original Soundtrack)
2. XANADU
   (Original Soundtrack)

3. THE GAME
   (Queen)
4. GLASS HOUSES
   (Billy Joel)
5. EMOTIONAL RESCUE
   (The Rolling Stones)
6. HOLD OUT
   (Jackson Browne)
7. HONEYSUCKLE ROSE
   (Willie Nelson and Family)
8. CHRISTOPHER CROSS
   (Christopher Cross)
9. PANORAMA
   (The Cars)
10. CRIMES OF PASSION
    (Pat Benatar)

BLACK SINGLES

1. UPSIDE DOWN
   (Diana Ross)
2. GIVE ME THE NIGHT
   (George Benson)
3. CAN'T WE TRY
   (Teddy Pendergrass)
4. GIRL, DON'T LET IT GET YOU DOWN
   (The O'Jays)
5. I'VE JUST BEGUN TO LOVE YOU
   (Dynasty)
6. SHAKE YOUR PANTS
   (Cameo)
7. WIDE RECEIVER (PART I)
   (Michael Henderson)
8. FUNKIN' FOR JAMAICA (N.Y.)
   (Tom Browne)
9. ANOTHER ONE BITES THE DUST
   (Queen)
10. ONE IN A MILLION YOU
    (Larry Graham)

BLACK ALBUMS

1. DIANA
   (Diana Ross)
2. GIVE ME THE NIGHT
   (George Benson)
3. TP
   (Teddy Pendergrass)
4. THE YEAR 2000
   (The O'Jays)
5. JOY AND PAIN
   (Maze featuring Frankie Beverly)
6. WIDE RECEIVER
   (Michael Henderson)
7. LOVE APPROACH
   (Tom Browne)
8. ONE IN A MILLION YOU
   (Larry Graham)
9. A MUSICAL AFFAIR
   (Nick Ashford and Valerie Simpson)
10. HEROES
    (Commodores)

JAZZ ALBUMS

1. GIVE ME THE NIGHT
   (George Benson)
2. LOVE APPROACH
   (Tom Browne)
3. THIS TIME
   (Al Jarreau)
4. RHAPSODY AND BLUES
   (Crusaders)
5. "H"
   (Bob James)
6. MAGNIFICENT MADNESS
   (John Klemmer)
7. ROUTES
   (Ramsey Lewis)
8. BADDEST
   (Grover Washington Jr.)
9. NIGHT CRUISER
   (Eumir Deodato)

10. ROCKS, PEBBLES AND SAND
   (Stanley Clarke)

COUNTRY SINGLES

1. LOOKIN' FOR LOVE
   (Johnny Lee)
2. DO YOU WANNA GO TO HEAVEN
   (T.G. Sheppard)
3. CHARLOTTE'S WEB
   (The Statler Brothers)
4. HEART OF MINE
   (The Oak Ridge Boys)
5. MAKING PLANS
   (Porter Wagoner and Dolly Parton)
6. OLD FLAMES CAN'T HOLD A CANDLE TO
   YOU
   (Dolly Parton)
7. LOVING UP A STORM
   (Razzy Bailey)
8. MISERY AND GIN
   (Merle Haggard)
9. LET'S KEEP IT THAT WAY
   (Mac Davis)
10. FADED LOVE
   (Willie Nelson and Ray Price)

COUNTRY ALBUMS

1. URBAN COWBOY
   (Original Soundtrack)
2. HONEYSUCKLE ROSE
   (Willie Nelson and Family)
3. FULL MOON
   (The Charlie Daniels Band)
4. HORIZON
   (Eddie Rabbitt)
5. GIDEON
   (Kenny Rogers)
6. GREATEST HITS
   (Waylon Jennings)
7. SAN ANTONIO ROSE
   (Willie Nelson and Ray Price)
8. STARDUST
   (Willie Nelson)
9. THE GAMBLER
   (Kenny Rogers)
10. MUSIC MAN
   (Waylon Jennings)

SEPTEMBER 27, 1980

POP SINGLES

1. UPSIDE DOWN
   (Diana Ross)
2. ANOTHER ONE BITES THE DUST
   (Queen)
3. ALL OUT OF LOVE
   (Air Supply)
4. LOOKIN' FOR LOVE
   (Johnny Lee)
5. DRIVIN' MY LIFE AWAY
   (Eddie Rabbitt)
6. GIVE ME THE NIGHT
   (George Benson)
7. HOT ROD HEARTS
   (Robbie Dupree)
8. ALL OVER THE WORLD
   (Electric Light Orchestra)
9. LATE IN THE EVENING
   (Paul Simon)
10. I'M ALRIGHT (THEME FROM
   CADDYSHACK)
   (Kenny Loggins)

POP ALBUMS

1. XANADU
   (Original Soundtrack)

2. THE GAME
   (Queen)
3. URBAN COWBOY
   (Original Soundtrack)
4. GLASS HOUSES
   (Billy Joel)
5. EMOTIONAL RESCUE
   (The Rolling Stones)
6. DIANA
   (Diana Ross)
7. HONEYSUCKLE ROSE
   (Willie Nelson and Family)
8. CHRISTOPHER CROSS
   (Christopher Cross)
9. PANORAMA
   (The Cars)
10. CRIMES OF PASSION
   (Pat Benatar)

BLACK SINGLES

1. FUNKIN' FOR JAMAICA (N.Y.)
   (Tom Browne)
2. ANOTHER ONE BITES THE DUST
   (Queen)
3. UPSIDE DOWN
   (Diana Ross)
4. GIRL, DON'T LET IT GET YOU DOWN
   (The O'Jays)
5. GIVE ME THE NIGHT
   (George Benson)
6. WIDE RECEIVER (PART I)
   (Michael Henderson)
7. MORE BOUNCE TO THE OUNCE (PART I)
   (Zapp)
8. CAN'T WE TRY
   (Teddy Pendergrass)
9. I'VE JUST BEGUN TO LOVE YOU
   (Dynasty)
10. SHAKE YOUR PANTS
   (Cameo)

BLACK ALBUMS

1. DIANA
   (Diana Ross)
2. GIVE ME THE NIGHT
   (George Benson)
3. TP
   (Teddy Pendergrass)
4. THE YEAR 2000
   (The O'Jays)
5. LOVE APPROACH
   (Tom Browne)
6. WIDE RECEIVER
   (Michael Henderson)
7. JOY AND PAIN
   (Maze featuring Frankie Beverly)
8. SHINE ON
   (L.T.D.)
9. ONE IN A MILLION YOU
   (Larry Graham)
10. ZAPP
   (Zapp)

JAZZ ALBUMS

1. GIVE ME THE NIGHT
   (George Benson)
2. LOVE APPROACH
   (Tom Browne)
3. THIS TIME
   (Al Jarreau)
4. "H"
   (Bob James)
5. RHAPSODY AND BLUES
   (Crusaders)
6. MAGNIFICENT MADNESS
   (John Klemmer)
7. ROUTES
   (Ramsey Lewis)
8. BADDEST
   (Grover Washington Jr.)

9. NIGHT CRUSADER
   (Eumir Deodato)
10. HOW TO BEAT THE HIGH COST OF LIVING
   (Original Soundtrack)

COUNTRY SINGLES

1. DO YOU WANNA GO TO HEAVEN
   (T.G. Sheppard)
2. LOOKIN' FOR LOVE
   (Johnny Lee)
3. OLD FLAMES CAN'T HOLD A CANDLE TO
   YOU
   (Dolly Parton)
4. HEART OF MINE
   (The Oak Ridge Boys)
5. LOVING UP A STORM
   (Razzy Bailey)
6. CHARLOTTE'S WEB
   (The Statler Brothers)
7. FADED LOVE
   (Willie Nelson and Ray Price)
8. I BELIEVE IN YOU
   (Don Williams)
9. LET'S KEEP IT THAT WAY
   (Mac Davis)
10. PUT IT OFF UNTIL TOMORROW/GONE
   AWAY
   (The Kendalls)

COUNTRY ALBUMS

1. URBAN COWBOY
   (Original Soundtrack)
2. HONEYSUCKLE ROSE
   (Willie Nelson and Family)
3. FULL MOON
   (The Charlie Daniels Band)
4. HORIZON
   (Eddie Rabbitt)
5. GIDEON
   (Kenny Rogers)
6. GREATEST HITS
   (Waylon Jennings)
7. SAN ANTONIO ROSE
   (Willie Nelson and Ray Price)
8. STARDUST
   (Willie Nelson)
9. THE GAMBLER
   (Kenny Rogers)
10. MUSIC MAN
   (Waylon Jennings)

OCTOBER 4, 1980

POP SINGLES

1. ANOTHER ONE BITES THE DUST
   (Queen)
2. UPSIDE DOWN
   (Diana Ross)
3. WOMAN IN LOVE
   (Barbra Streisand)
4. LOOKIN' FOR LOVE
   (Johnny Lee)
5. DRIVIN' MY LIFE AWAY
   (Eddie Rabbitt)
6. ALL OUT OF LOVE
   (Air Supply)
7. HOT ROD HEARTS
   (Robbie Dupree)
8. ALL OVER THE WORLD
   (Electric Light Orchestra)
9. LATE IN THE EVENING
   (Paul Simon)
10. I'M ALRIGHT (THEME FROM
   CADDYSHACK)
   (Kenny Loggins)

POP ALBUMS

1. THE GAME
   (Queen)
2. XANADU
   (Original Soundtrack)
3. URBAN COWBOY
   (Original Soundtrack)
4. DIANA
   (Diana Ross)
5. HOLD OUT
   (Jackson Browne)
6. GIVE ME THE NIGHT
   (George Benson)
7. HONEYSUCKLE ROSE
   (Willie Nelson and Family)
8. GLASS HOUSES
   (Billy Joel)
9. PANORAMA
   (The Cars)
10. CRIMES OF PASSION
    (Pat Benatar)

BLACK SINGLES

1. ANOTHER ONE BITES THE DUST
   (Queen)
2. MORE BOUNCE TO THE OUNCE (PART I)
   (Zapp)
3. FUNKIN' FOR JAMAICA (N.Y.)
   (Tom Browne)
4. UPSIDE DOWN
   (Diana Ross)
5. WIDE RECEIVER (PART I)
   (Michael Henderson)
6. GIRL, DON'T LET IT GET YOU DOWN
   (The O'Jays)
7. GIVE ME THE NIGHT
   (George Benson)
8. WHERE DID WE GO WRONG
   (L.T.D.)
9. I'VE JUST BEGUN TO LOVE YOU
   (Dynasty)
10. CAN'T WE TRY
    (Teddy Pendergrass)

BLACK ALBUMS

1. DIANA
   (Diana Ross)
2. GIVE ME THE NIGHT
   (George Benson)
3. TP
   (Teddy Pendergrass)
4. LOVE APPROACH
   (Tom Browne)
5. ZAPP
   (Zapp)
6. WIDE RECEIVER
   (Michael Henderson)
7. SHINE ON
   (L.T.D.)
8. JOY AND PAIN
   (Maze featuring Frankie Beverly)
9. THE YEAR 2000
   (The O'Jays)
10. LOVE LIVES FOREVER
    (Minnie Riperton)

JAZZ ALBUMS

1. GIVE ME THE NIGHT
   (George Benson)
2. LOVE APPROACH
   (Tom Browne)
3. THIS TIME
   (Al Jarreau)
4. "H"
   (Bob James)
5. RHAPSODY AND BLUES
   (Crusaders)
6. MAGNIFICENT MADNESS
   (John Klemmer)

7. ROUTES
   (Ramsey Lewis)
8. BADDEST
   (Grover Washington Jr.)
9. NIGHT CRUISER
   (Eumir Deodato)
10. HOW TO BEAT THE HIGH COST OF LIVING
    (Original Soundtrack)

COUNTRY SINGLES

1. DO YOU WANNA GO TO HEAVEN
   (T.G. Sheppard)
2. LOVING UP A STORM
   (Razzy Bailey)
3. OLD FLAMES CAN'T HOLD A CANDLE TO YOU
   (Dolly Parton)
4. FADED LOVE
   (Willie Nelson and Ray Price)
5. I BELIEVE IN YOU
   (Don Williams)
6. LOOKIN' FOR LOVE
   (Johnny Lee)
7. THEME FROM THE DUKES OF HAZZARD (GOOD OLE BOYS)
   (Waylon Jennings)
8. HEART OF MINE
   (The Oak Ridge Boys)
9. YESTERDAY ONCE MORE
   (Moe Bandy)
10. PUT IT OFF UNTIL TOMORROW/GONE AWAY
    (The Kendalls)

COUNTRY ALBUMS

1. URBAN COWBOY
   (Original Soundtrack)
2. HONEYSUCKLE ROSE
   (Willie Nelson and Family)
3. FULL MOON
   (The Charlie Daniels Band)
4. HORIZON
   (Eddie Rabbitt)
5. GREATEST HITS
   (Waylon Jennings)
6. SAN ANTONIO ROSE
   (Willie Nelson and Ray Price)
7. STARDUST
   (Willie Nelson)
8. I BELIEVE IN YOU
   (Don Williams)
9. MUSIC MAN
   (Waylon Jennings)
10. THE GAMBLER
    (Kenny Rogers)

OCTOBER 11, 1980

POP SINGLES

1. ANOTHER ONE BITES THE DUST
   (Queen)
2. UPSIDE DOWN
   (Diana Ross)
3. WOMAN IN LOVE
   (Barbra Streisand)
4. LOOKIN' FOR LOVE
   (Johnny Lee)
5. DRIVIN' MY LIFE AWAY
   (Eddie Rabbitt)
6. ALL OUT OF LOVE
   (Air Supply)
7. XANADU
   (Olivia Newton-John and the Electric Light Orchestra)
8. ALL OVER THE WORLD
   (Electric Light Orchestra)
9. HE'S SO SHY
   (The Pointer Sisters)

10. I'M ALRIGHT (THEME FROM CADDYSHACK)
    (Kenny Loggins)

POP ALBUMS

1. THE GAME
   (Queen)
2. XANADU
   (Original Soundtrack)
3. URBAN COWBOY
   (Original Soundtrack)
4. DIANA
   (Diana Ross)
5. HOLD OUT
   (Jackson Browne)
6. GIVE ME THE NIGHT
   (George Benson)
7. GUILTY
   (Barbra Streisand)
8. HONEYSUCKLE ROSE
   (Willie Nelson and Family)
9. GLASS HOUSES
   (Billy Joel)
10. CRIMES OF PASSION
    (Pat Benatar)

BLACK SINGLES

1. MORE BOUNCE TO THE OUNCE (PART I)
   (Zapp)
2. ANOTHER ONE BITES THE DUST
   (Queen)
3. FUNKIN' FOR JAMAICA (N.Y.)
   (Tom Browne)
4. WIDE RECEIVER (PART I)
   (Michael Henderson)
5. UPSIDE DOWN
   (Diana Ross)
6. GIRL, DON'T LET IT GET YOU DOWN
   (The O'Jays)
7. WHERE DID WE GO WRONG
   (L.T.D.)
8. GIVE ME THE NIGHT
   (George Benson)
9. I'VE JUST BEGUN TO LOVE YOU
   (Dynasty)
10. LET ME BE YOUR ANGEL
    (Stacy Lattisaw)

BLACK ALBUMS

1. DIANA
   (Diana Ross)
2. GIVE ME THE NIGHT
   (George Benson)
3. TP
   (Teddy Pendergrass)
4. ZAPP
   (Zapp)
5. LOVE APPROACH
   (Tom Browne)
6. WIDE RECEIVER
   (Michael Henderson)
7. SHINE ON
   (L.T.D.)
8. JOY AND PAIN
   (Maze featuring Frankie Beverly)
9. THE YEAR 2000
   (The O'Jays)
10. LOVE LIVES FOREVER
    (Minnie Riperton)

JAZZ ALBUMS

1. GIVE ME THE NIGHT
   (George Benson)
2. LOVE APPROACH
   (Tom Browne)
3. THIS TIME
   (Al Jarreau)

4. "H"
   (Bob James)
5. RHAPSODY AND BLUES
   (Crusaders)
6. MAGNIFICENT MADNESS
   (John Klemmer)
7. NIGHT CRUISER
   (Eumir Deodato)
8. LAND OF THE THIRD EYE
   (Dave Valentin)
9. HOW TO BEAT THE HIGH COST OF LIVING
   (Original Soundtrack)
10. BADDEST
    (Grover Washington Jr.)

COUNTRY SINGLES

1. I BELIEVE IN YOU
   (Don Williams)
2. LOVING UP A STORM
   (Razzy Bailey)
3. FADED LOVE
   (Willie Nelson and Ray Price)
4. THEME FROM THE DUKES OF HAZZARD
   (GOOD OLE BOYS)
   (Waylon Jennings)
5. DO YOU WANNA GO TO HEAVEN
   (T.G. Sheppard)
6. ON THE ROAD AGAIN
   (Willie Nelson)
7. OLD FLAMES CAN'T HOLD A CANDLE TO YOU
   (Dolly Parton)
8. I'M NOT READY YET
   (George Jones)
9. YESTERDAY ONCE MORE
   (Moe Bandy)
10. PUT IT OFF UNTIL TOMORROW/GONE AWAY
    (The Kendalls)

COUNTRY ALBUMS

1. URBAN COWBOY
   (Original Soundtrack)
2. HONEYSUCKLE ROSE
   (Willie Nelson and Family)
3. FULL MOON
   (The Charlie Daniels Band)
4. HORIZON
   (Eddie Rabbitt)
5. GREATEST HITS
   (Waylon Jennings)
6. SAN ANTONIO ROSE
   (Willie Nelson and Ray Price)
7. I BELIEVE IN YOU
   (Don Williams)
8. ANNE MURRAY'S GREATEST HITS
   (Anne Murray)
9. STARDUST
   (Willie Nelson)
10. THESE DAYS
    (Crystal Gayle)

OCTOBER 18, 1980

POP SINGLES

1. ANOTHER ONE BITES THE DUST
   (Queen)
2. WOMAN IN LOVE
   (Barbra Streisand)
3. UPSIDE DOWN
   (Diana Ross)
4. XANADU
   (Olivia Newton-John and the Electric Light Orchestra)
5. HE'S SO SHY
   (The Pointer Sisters)

6. ALL OUT OF LOVE
   (Air Supply)
7. JESSE
   (Carly Simon)
8. DRIVIN' MY LIFE AWAY
   (Eddie Rabbitt)
9. REAL LOVE
   (The Doobie Brothers)
10. I'M ALRIGHT (THEME FROM CADDYSHACK)
    (Kenny Loggins)

POP ALBUMS

1. GUILTY
   (Barbra Streisand)
2. THE GAME
   (Queen)
3. ONE STEP CLOSER
   (The Doobie Brothers)
4. DIANA
   (Diana Ross)
5. XANADU
   (Original Soundtrack)
6. URBAN COWBOY
   (Original Soundtrack)
7. CRIMES OF PASSION
   (Pat Benatar)
8. PANORAMA
   (The Cars)
9. BACK IN BLACK
   (AC/DC)
10. GIVE ME THE NIGHT
    (George Benson)

BLACK SINGLES

1. MORE BOUNCE TO THE OUNCE (PART I)
   (Zapp)
2. ANOTHER ONE BITES THE DUST
   (Queen)
3. FUNKIN' FOR JAMAICA (N.Y.)
   (Tom Browne)
4. WIDE RECEIVER (PART I)
   (Michael Henderson)
5. WHERE DID WE GO WRONG
   (L.T.D.)
6. MASTER BLASTER (JAMMIN')
   (Stevie Wonder)
7. LOVELY ONE
   (The Jacksons)
8. GIRL, DON'T LET IT GET YOU DOWN
   (The O'Jays)
9. UPSIDE DOWN
   (Diana Ross)
10. LET ME BE YOUR ANGEL
    (Stacy Lattisaw)

BLACK ALBUMS

1. DIANA
   (Diana Ross)
2. ZAPP
   (Zapp)
3. GIVE ME THE NIGHT
   (George Benson)
4. TP
   (Teddy Pendergrass)
5. LOVE APPROACH
   (Tom Browne)
6. WIDE RECEIVER
   (Michael Henderson)
7. SHINE ON
   (L.T.D.)
8. TRIUMPH
   (The Jacksons)
9. IRONS IN THE FIRE
   (Teena Marie)
10. JOY AND PAIN
    (Maze featuring Frankie Beverly)

JAZZ ALBUMS

1. GIVE ME THE NIGHT
   (George Benson)
2. LOVE APPROACH
   (Tom Browne)
3. THIS TIME
   (Al Jarreau)
4. RHAPSODY AND BLUES
   (Crusaders)
5. "H"
   (Bob James)
6. MAGNIFICENT MADNESS
   (John Klemmer)
7. NIGHT CRUISER
   (Eumir Deodato)
8. THE SWING OF DELIGHT
   (Devadip Carlos Santana)
9. CIVILIZED EVIL
   (Jean Luc Ponty)
10. SEAWIND
    (Seawind)

COUNTRY SINGLES

1. I BELIEVE IN YOU
   (Don Williams)
2. THEME FROM THE DUKES OF HAZZARD
   (GOOD OLE BOYS)
   (Waylon Jennings)
3. ON THE ROAD AGAIN
   (Willie Nelson)
4. LOVING UP A STORM
   (Razzy Bailey)
5. FADED LOVE
   (Willie Nelson and Ray Price)
6. I'M NOT READY YET
   (George Jones)
7. DO YOU WANNA GO TO HEAVEN
   (T.G. Sheppard)
8. OLD HABITS
   (Hank Williams Jr.)
9. PECOS PROMENADE
   (Tanya Tucker)
10. STARTING OVER
    (Tammy Wynette)

COUNTRY ALBUMS

1. URBAN COWBOY
   (Original Soundtrack)
2. HONEYSUCKLE ROSE
   (Willie Nelson and Family)
3. FULL MOON
   (The Charlie Daniels Band)
4. HORIZON
   (Eddie Rabbitt)
5. ANNE MURRAY'S GREATEST HITS
   (Anne Murray)
6. GREATEST HITS
   (Waylon Jennings)
7. SAN ANTONIO ROSE
   (Willie Nelson and Ray Price)
8. I BELIEVE IN YOU
   (Don Williams)
9. STARDUST
   (Willie Nelson)
10. THESE DAYS
    (Crystal Gayle)

OCTOBER 25, 1980

POP SINGLES

1. ANOTHER ONE BITES THE DUST
   (Queen)
2. WOMAN IN LOVE
   (Barbra Streisand)
3. UPSIDE DOWN
   (Diana Ross)

4. XANADU
   (Olivia Newton-John and the Electric Light Orchestra)
5. HE'S SO SHY
   (The Pointer Sisters)
6. THE WANDERER
   (Donna Summer)
7. JESSE
   (Carly Simon)
8. LADY
   (Kenny Rogers)
9. REAL LOVE
   (The Doobie Brothers)
10. ALL OUT OF LOVE
    (Air Supply)

POP ALBUMS

1. GUILTY
   (Barbra Streisand)
2. THE GAME
   (Queen)
3. ONE STEP CLOSER
   (The Doobie Brothers)
4. GREATEST HITS
   (Kenny Rogers)
5. XANADU
   (Original Soundtrack)
6. DIANA
   (Diana Ross)
7. CRIMES OF PASSION
   (Pat Benatar)
8. PANORAMA
   (The Cars)
9. BACK IN BLACK
   (AC/DC)
10. URBAN COWBOY
    (Original Soundtrack)

BLACK SINGLES

1. MORE BOUNCE TO THE OUNCE (PART I)
   (Zapp)
2. ANOTHER ONE BITES THE DUST
   (Queen)
3. MASTER BLASTER (JAMMIN')
   (Stevie Wonder)
4. FUNKIN' FOR JAMAICA (N.Y.)
   (Tom Browne)
5. WHERE DID WE GO WRONG
   (L.T.D.)
6. LOVELY ONE
   (The Jacksons)
7. WIDE RECEIVER (PART I)
   (Michael Henderson)
8. FREEDOM
   (Grandmaster Flash and the Furious 5)
9. GIRL, DON'T LET IT GET YOU DOWN
   (The O'Jays)
10. LET ME BE YOUR ANGEL
    (Stacy Lattisaw)

BLACK ALBUMS

1. DIANA
   (Diana Ross)
2. ZAPP
   (Zapp)
3. GIVE ME THE NIGHT
   (George Benson)
4. TP
   (Teddy Pendergrass)
5. TRIUMPH
   (The Jacksons)
6. LOVE APPROACH
   (Tom Browne)
7. SHINE ON
   (L.T.D.)
8. WIDE RECEIVER
   (Michael Henderson)
9. IRONS IN THE FIRE
   (Teena Marie)
10. THE YEAR 2000
    (The O'Jays)

JAZZ ALBUMS

1. GIVE ME THE NIGHT
   (George Benson)
2. THIS TIME
   (Al Jarreau)
3. RHAPSODY AND BLUES
   (Crusaders)
4. LOVE APPROACH
   (Tom Browne)
5. MAGNIFICENT MADNESS
   (John Klemmer)
6. CIVILIZED EVIL
   (Jean Luc Ponty)
7. SEAWIND
   (Seawind)
8. "H"
   (Bob James)
9. TOUCH OF SILK
   (Eric Gale)
10. NIGHT CRUISER
    (Eumir Deodato)

COUNTRY SINGLES

1. I BELIEVE IN YOU
   (Don Williams)
2. THEME FROM THE DUKES OF HAZZARD (GOOD OLE BOYS)
   (Waylon Jennings)
3. ON THE ROAD AGAIN
   (Willie Nelson)
4. I'M NOT READY YET
   (George Jones)
5. COULD I HAVE THIS DANCE
   (Anne Murray)
6. OLD HABITS
   (Hank Williams Jr.)
7. PECOS PROMENADE
   (Tanya Tucker)
8. LOVING UP A STORM
   (Razzy Bailey)
9. STEPPIN' OUT
   (Mel Tillis)
10. HARD TIMES
    (Lacy J. Dalton)

COUNTRY ALBUMS

1. URBAN COWBOY
   (Original Soundtrack)
2. HONEYSUCKLE ROSE
   (Willie Nelson and Family)
3. ANNE MURRAY'S GREATEST HITS
   (Anne Murray)
4. FULL MOON
   (The Charlie Daniels Band)
5. HORIZON
   (Eddie Rabbitt)
6. KENNY ROGERS' GREATEST HITS
   (Kenny Rogers)
7. I BELIEVE IN YOU
   (Don Williams)
8. SAN ANTONIO ROSE
   (Willie Nelson and Ray Price)
9. THESE DAYS
   (Crystal Gayle)
10. GREATEST HITS
    (Waylon Jennings)

NOVEMBER 1, 1980

POP SINGLES

1. ANOTHER ONE BITES THE DUST
   (Queen)
2. WOMAN IN LOVE
   (Barbra Streisand)
3. LADY
   (Kenny Rogers)

4. UPSIDE DOWN
   (Diana Ross)
5. THE WANDERER
   (Donna Summer)
6. HE'S SO SHY
   (The Pointer Sisters)
7. JESSE
   (Carly Simon)
8. XANADU
   (Olivia Newton-John and the Electric Light Orchestra)
9. REAL LOVE
   (The Doobie Brothers)
10. NEVER KNEW LOVE LIKE THIS BEFORE
    (Stephanie Mills)

POP ALBUMS

1. GUILTY
   (Barbra Streisand)
2. THE RIVER
   (Bruce Springsteen)
3. ONE STEP CLOSER
   (The Doobie Brothers)
4. KENNY ROGERS' GREATEST HITS
   (Kenny Rogers)
5. THE GAME
   (Queen)
6. BACK IN BLACK
   (AC/DC)
7. CRIMES OF PASSION
   (Pat Benatar)
8. XANADU
   (Original Soundtrack)
9. DIANA
   (Diana Ross)
10. TRIUMPH
    (The Jacksons)

BLACK SINGLES

1. MORE BOUNCE TO THE OUNCE (PART I)
   (Zapp)
2. ANOTHER ONE BITES THE DUST
   (Queen)
3. MASTER BLASTER (JAMMIN')
   (Stevie Wonder)
4. LOVELY ONE
   (The Jacksons)
5. WHERE DID WE GO WRONG
   (L.T.D.)
6. FUNKIN' FOR JAMAICA (N.Y.)
   (Tom Browne)
7. WIDE RECEIVER (PART I)
   (Michael Henderson)
8. FREEDOM
   (Grandmaster Flash and the Furious 5)
9. GIRL, DON'T LET IT GET YOU DOWN
   (The O'Jays)
10. LET ME BE YOUR ANGEL
    (Stacy Lattisaw)

BLACK ALBUMS

1. TRIUMPH
   (The Jacksons)
2. TP
   (Teddy Pendergrass)
3. GIVE ME THE NIGHT
   (George Benson)
4. DIANA
   (Diana Ross)
5. ZAPP
   (Zapp)
6. SHINE ON
   (L.T.D.)
7. LOVE APPROACH
   (Tom Browne)
8. WIDE RECEIVER
   (Michael Henderson)
9. IRONS IN THE FIRE
   (Teena Marie)
10. THE YEAR 2000
    (The O'Jays)

JAZZ ALBUMS

1. GIVE ME THE NIGHT
   (George Benson)
2. THIS TIME
   (Al Jarreau)
3. LOVE APPROACH
   (Tom Browne)
4. RHAPSODY AND BLUES
   (Crusaders)
5. CIVILIZED EVIL
   (Jean Luc Ponty)
6. SEAWIND
   (Seawind)
7. NIGHT CRUISER
   (Eumir Deodato)
8. "H"
   (Bob James)
9. TOUCH OF SILK
   (Eric Gale)
10. MAGNIFICENT MADNESS
    (John Klemmer)

COUNTRY SINGLES

1. ON THE ROAD AGAIN
   (Willie Nelson)
2. THEME FROM THE DUKES OF HAZZARD
   (GOOD OLE BOYS)
   (Waylon Jennings)
3. I'M NOT READY YET
   (George Jones)
4. COULD I HAVE THIS DANCE
   (Anne Murray)
5. OLD HABITS
   (Hank Williams Jr.)
6. PECOS PROMENADE
   (Tanya Tucker)
7. STEPPIN' OUT
   (Mel Tillis)
8. HARD TIMES
   (Lacy J. Dalton)
9. SHE CAN'T SAY THAT ANYMORE
   (John Conlee)
10. OVER THE RAINBOW
    (Jerry Lee Lewis)

COUNTRY ALBUMS

1. KENNY ROGERS' GREATEST HITS
   (Kenny Rogers)
2. URBAN COWBOY
   (Original Soundtrack)
3. ANNE MURRAY'S GREATEST HITS
   (Anne Murray)
4. HONEYSUCKLE ROSE
   (Willie Nelson and Family)
5. FULL MOON
   (The Charlie Daniels Band)
6. HORIZON
   (Eddie Rabbitt)
7. I BELIEVE IN YOU
   (Don Williams)
8. THESE DAYS
   (Crystal Gayle)
9. GREATEST HITS
   (Waylon Jennings)
10. SAN ANTONIO ROSE
    (Willie Nelson and Ray Price)

NOVEMBER 8, 1980

POP SINGLES

1. WOMAN IN LOVE
   (Barbra Streisand)
2. ANOTHER ONE BITES THE DUST
   (Queen)

3. LADY
   (Kenny Rogers)
4. THE WANDERER
   (Donna Summer)
5. UPSIDE DOWN
   (Diana Ross)
6. HE'S SO SHY
   (The Pointer Sisters)
7. JESSE
   (Carly Simon)
8. NEVER KNEW LOVE LIKE THIS BEFORE
   (Stephanie Mills)
9. DREAMING
   (Cliff Richard)
10. YOU'VE LOST THAT LOVIN' FEELING
    (Daryl Hall and John Oates)

POP ALBUMS

1. KENNY ROGERS' GREATEST HITS
   (Kenny Rogers)
2. THE RIVER
   (Bruce Springsteen)
3. GUILTY
   (Barbra Streisand)
4. THE GAME
   (Queen)
5. ONE STEP CLOSER
   (The Doobie Brothers)
6. BACK IN BLACK
   (AC/DC)
7. CRIMES OF PASSION
   (Pat Benatar)
8. XANADU
   (Original Soundtrack)
9. HOTTER THAN JULY
   (Stevie Wonder)
10. TRIUMPH
    (The Jacksons)

BLACK SINGLES

1. MASTER BLASTER (JAMMIN')
   (Stevie Wonder)
2. MORE BOUNCE TO THE OUNCE (PART I)
   (Zapp)
3. ANOTHER ONE BITES THE DUST
   (Queen)
4. LOVELY ONE
   (The Jacksons)
5. WHERE DID WE GO WRONG
   (L.T.D.)
6. FUNKIN' FOR JAMAICA (N.Y.)
   (Tom Browne)
7. LOVE T.K.O.
   (Teddy Pendergrass)
8. I NEED YOUR LOVIN'
   (Teena Marie)
9. UPTOWN
   (Prince)
10. WIDE RECEIVER (PART I)
    (Michael Henderson)

BLACK ALBUMS

1. HOTTER THAN JULY
   (Stevie Wonder)
2. TRIUMPH
   (The Jacksons)
3. TP
   (Teddy Pendergrass)
4. ZAPP
   (Zapp)
5. GIVE ME THE NIGHT
   (George Benson)
6. SHINE ON
   (L.T.D.)
7. DIANA
   (Diana Ross)
8. LOVE APPROACH
   (Tom Browne)
9. IRONS IN THE FIRE
   (Teena Marie)
10. WIDE RECEIVER
    (Michael Henderson)

JAZZ ALBUMS

1. GIVE ME THE NIGHT
   (George Benson)
2. LOVE APPROACH
   (Tom Browne)
3. THIS TIME
   (Al Jarreau)
4. CIVILIZED EVIL
   (Jean Luc Ponty)
5. SEAWIND
   (Seawind)
6. CARNAVAL
   (Spyro Gyra)
7. RHAPSODY AND BLUES
   (Crusaders)
8. NIGHT CRUISER
   (Eumir Deodato)
9. FAMILY
   (Hubert Laws)
10. INHERIT THE WIND
    (Wilton Felder)

COUNTRY SINGLES

1. ON THE ROAD AGAIN
   (Willie Nelson)
2. COULD I HAVE THIS DANCE
   (Anne Murray)
3. I'M NOT READY YET
   (George Jones)
4. THEME FROM THE DUKES OF HAZZARD
   (GOOD OLE BOYS)
   (Waylon Jennings)
5. HARD TIMES
   (Lacy J. Dalton)
6. SHE CAN'T SAY THAT ANYMORE
   (John Conlee)
7. STEPPIN' OUT
   (Mel Tillis)
8. IF YOU EVER CHANGE YOUR MIND
   (Crystal Gayle)
9. OVER THE RAINBOW
   (Jerry Lee Lewis)
10. THE BOXER
    (Emmylou Harris)

COUNTRY ALBUMS

1. KENNY ROGERS' GREATEST HITS
   (Kenny Rogers)
2. URBAN COWBOY
   (Original Soundtrack)
3. HONEYSUCKLE ROSE
   (Willie Nelson and Family)
4. ANNE MURRAY'S GREATEST HITS
   (Anne Murray)
5. FULL MOON
   (The Charlie Daniels Band)
6. HORIZON
   (Eddie Rabbitt)
7. I BELIEVE IN YOU
   (Don Williams)
8. THESE DAYS
   (Crystal Gayle)
9. GREATEST HITS
   (Waylon Jennings)
10. SAN ANTONIO ROSE
    (Willie Nelson and Ray Price)

NOVEMBER 15, 1980

POP SINGLES

1. ANOTHER ONE BITES THE DUST
   (Queen)
2. LADY
   (Kenny Rogers)
3. WOMAN IN LOVE
   (Barbra Streisand)

4. THE WANDERER
   (Donna Summer)
5. HE'S SO SHY
   (The Pointer Sisters)
6. JESSE
   (Carly Simon)
7. DREAMING
   (Cliff Richard)
8. NEVER KNEW LOVE LIKE THIS BEFORE
   (Stephanie Mills)
9. LOVELY ONE
   (The Jacksons)
10. YOU'VE LOST THAT LOVIN' FEELING
    (Daryl Hall and John Oates)

POP ALBUMS

1. KENNY ROGERS' GREATEST HITS
   (Kenny Rogers)
2. THE RIVER
   (Bruce Springsteen)
3. GUILTY
   (Barbra Streisand)
4. THE GAME
   (Queen)
5. HOTTER THAN JULY
   (Stevie Wonder)
6. BACK IN BLACK
   (AC/DC)
7. CRIMES OF PASSION
   (Pat Benatar)
8. ONE STEP CLOSER
   (The Doobie Brothers)
9. TRIUMPH
   (The Jacksons)
10. DIANA
    (Diana Ross)

BLACK SINGLES

1. MASTER BLASTER (JAMMIN')
   (Stevie Wonder)
2. MORE BOUNCE TO THE OUNCE (PART I)
   (Zapp)
3. LOVELY ONE
   (The Jacksons)
4. ANOTHER ONE BITES THE DUST
   (Queen)
5. LOVE T.K.O.
   (Teddy Pendergrass)
6. WHERE DID WE GO WRONG
   (L.T.D.)
7. UPTOWN
   (Prince)
8. I NEED YOUR LOVIN'
   (Teena Marie)
9. FUNKIN' FOR JAMAICA (N.Y.)
   (Tom Browne)
10. LOVE X LOVE
    (George Benson)

BLACK ALBUMS

1. HOTTER THAN JULY
   (Stevie Wonder)
2. TRIUMPH
   (The Jacksons)
3. TP
   (Teddy Pendergrass)
4. ZAPP
   (Zapp)
5. GIVE ME THE NIGHT
   (George Benson)
6. SHINE ON
   (L.T.D.)
7. DIANA
   (Diana Ross)
8. CELEBRATE
   (Kool and the Gang)
9. LOVE APPROACH
   (Tom Browne)
10. FEEL ME
    (Cameo)

JAZZ ALBUMS

1. GIVE ME THE NIGHT
   (George Benson)
2. CIVILIZED EVIL
   (Jean Luc Ponty)
3. THIS TIME
   (Al Jarreau)
4. LOVE APPROACH
   (Tom Browne)
5. CARNAVAL
   (Spyro Gyra)
6. WINELIGHT
   (Grover Washington Jr.)
7. SEAWIND
   (Seawind)
8. INHERIT THE WIND
   (Wilton Felder)
9. RHAPSODY AND BLUES
   (Crusaders)
10. FAMILY
    (Hubert Laws)

COUNTRY SINGLES

1. COULD I HAVE THIS DANCE
   (Anne Murray)
2. ON THE ROAD AGAIN
   (Willie Nelson)
3. SHE CAN'T SAY THAT ANYMORE
   (John Conlee)
4. IF YOU EVER CHANGE YOUR MIND
   (Crystal Gayle)
5. HARD TIMES
   (Lacy J. Dalton)
6. LADY
   (Kenny Rogers)
7. I'M NOT READY YET
   (George Jones)
8. SMOKY MOUNTAIN RAIN
   (Ronnie Milsap)
9. THE BOXER
   (Emmylou Harris)
10. THAT'S THE WAY A COWBOY ROCKS AND ROLLS
    (Jacky Ward)

COUNTRY ALBUMS

1. KENNY ROGERS' GREATEST HITS
   (Kenny Rogers)
2. URBAN COWBOY
   (Original Soundtrack)
3. HONEYSUCKLE ROSE
   (Willie Nelson and Family)
4. ANNE MURRAY'S GREATEST HITS
   (Anne Murray)
5. FULL MOON
   (The Charlie Daniels Band)
6. I BELIEVE IN YOU
   (Don Williams)
7. HORIZON
   (Eddie Rabbitt)
8. GREATEST HITS
   (Waylon Jennings)
9. THESE DAYS
   (Crystal Gayle)
10. RONNIE MILSAP'S GREATEST HITS
    (Ronnie Milsap)

NOVEMBER 22, 1980

POP SINGLES

1. LADY
   (Kenny Rogers)
2. ANOTHER ONE BITES THE DUST
   (Queen)
3. WOMAN IN LOVE
   (Barbra Streisand)

4. THE WANDERER
   (Donna Summer)
5. HE'S SO SHY
   (The Pointer Sisters)
6. MORE THAN I CAN SAY
   (Leo Sayer)
7. DREAMING
   (Cliff Richard)
8. JESSE
   (Carly Simon)
9. LOVELY ONE
   (The Jacksons)
10. I'M COMING OUT
    (Diana Ross)

POP ALBUMS

1. KENNY ROGERS' GREATEST HITS
   (Kenny Rogers)
2. GUILTY
   (Barbra Streisand)
3. HOTTER THAN JULY
   (Stevie Wonder)
4. THE GAME
   (Queen)
5. THE RIVER
   (Bruce Springsteen)
6. BACK IN BLACK
   (AC/DC)
7. CRIMES OF PASSION
   (Pat Benatar)
8. ONE STEP CLOSER
   (The Doobie Brothers)
9. TRIUMPH
   (The Jacksons)
10. THE WANDERER
    (Donna Summer)

BLACK SINGLES

1. MASTER BLASTER (JAMMIN')
   (Stevie Wonder)
2. LOVE T.K.O.
   (Teddy Pendergrass)
3. LOVELY ONE
   (The Jacksons)
4. MORE BOUNCE TO THE OUNCE (PART I)
   (Zapp)
5. ANOTHER ONE BITES THE DUST
   (Queen)
6. UPTOWN
   (Prince)
7. WHERE DID WE GO WRONG
   (L.T.D.)
8. CELEBRATION
   (Kool and the Gang)
9. LOVE X LOVE
   (George Benson)
10. I NEED YOUR LOVIN'
    (Teena Marie)

BLACK ALBUMS

1. HOTTER THAN JULY
   (Stevie Wonder)
2. TRIUMPH
   (The Jacksons)
3. TP
   (Teddy Pendergrass)
4. ZAPP
   (Zapp)
5. GIVE ME THE NIGHT
   (George Benson)
6. FACES
   (Earth, Wind and Fire)
7. SHINE ON
   (L.T.D.)
8. CELEBRATE
   (Kool and the Gang)
9. FEEL ME
   (Cameo)
10. DIANA
    (Diana Ross)

JAZZ ALBUMS

1. GIVE ME THE NIGHT
   (George Benson)
2. WINELIGHT
   (Grover Washington Jr.)
3. CARNAVAL
   (Spyro Gyra)
4. CIVILIZED EVIL
   (Jean Luc Ponty)
5. THIS TIME
   (Al Jarreau)
6. LOVE APPROACH
   (Tom Browne)
7. INHERIT THE WIND
   (Wilton Felder)
8. TWENNYNINE WITH LENNY WHITE
   (Lenny White)
9. FAMILY
   (Hubert Laws)
10. SEAWIND
    (Seawind)

COUNTRY SINGLES

1. SHE CAN'T SAY THAT ANYMORE
   (John Conlee)
2. LADY
   (Kenny Rogers)
3. IF YOU EVER CHANGE YOUR MIND
   (Crystal Gayle)
4. COULD I HAVE THIS DANCE
   (Anne Murray)
5. SMOKY MOUNTAIN RAIN
   (Ronnie Milsap)
6. ON THE ROAD AGAIN
   (Willie Nelson)
7. WHY LADY WHY
   (Alabama)
8. YOU ALMOST SLIPPED MY MIND
   (Charley Pride)
9. THAT'S THE WAY A COWBOY ROCKS AND
   ROLLS
   (Jacky Ward)
10. BROKEN TRUST
    (Brenda Lee)

COUNTRY ALBUMS

1. KENNY ROGERS' GREATEST HITS
   (Kenny Rogers)
2. URBAN COWBOY
   (Original Soundtrack)
3. HONEYSUCKLE ROSE
   (Willie Nelson and Family)
4. FULL MOON
   (The Charlie Daniels Band)
5. ANNE MURRAY'S GREATEST HITS
   (Anne Murray)
6. I BELIEVE IN YOU
   (Don Williams)
7. THE OAK RIDGE BOYS' GREATEST HITS
   (The Oak Ridge Boys)
8. GREATEST HITS
   (Waylon Jennings)
9. RONNIE MILSAP'S GREATEST HITS
   (Ronnie Milsap)
10. HORIZON
    (Eddie Rabbitt)

NOVEMBER 29, 1980

POP SINGLES

1. LADY
   (Kenny Rogers)
2. ANOTHER ONE BITES THE DUST
   (Queen)
3. MORE THAN I CAN SAY
   (Leo Sayer)
4. WOMAN IN LOVE
   (Barbra Streisand)
5. THE WANDERER
   (Donna Summer)
6. HE'S SO SHY
   (The Pointer Sisters)
7. HIT ME WITH YOUR BEST SHOT
   (Pat Benatar)
8. JESSE
   (Carly Simon)
9. I'M COMING OUT
   (Diana Ross)
10. NEVER BE THE SAME
    (Christopher Cross)

POP ALBUMS

1. KENNY ROGERS' GREATEST HITS
   (Kenny Rogers)
2. GUILTY
   (Barbra Streisand)
3. HOTTER THAN JULY
   (Stevie Wonder)
4. THE GAME
   (Queen)
5. THE RIVER
   (Bruce Springsteen)
6. BACK IN BLACK
   (AC/DC)
7. CRIMES OF PASSION
   (Pat Benatar)
8. ONE STEP CLOSER
   (The Doobie Brothers)
9. THE WANDERER
   (Donna Summer)
10. TRIUMPH
    (The Jacksons)

BLACK SINGLES

1. MASTER BLASTER (JAMMIN')
   (Stevie Wonder)
2. LOVE T.K.O.
   (Teddy Pendergrass)
3. LOVELY ONE
   (The Jacksons)
4. CELEBRATION
   (Kool and the Gang)
5. MORE BOUNCE TO THE OUNCE (PART I)
   (Zapp)
6. UPTOWN
   (Prince)
7. ANOTHER ONE BITES THE DUST
   (Queen)
8. LOVE X LOVE
   (George Benson)
9. WHERE DID WE GO WRONG
   (L.T.D.)
10. KEEP IT HOT
    (Cameo)

BLACK ALBUMS

1. HOTTER THAN JULY
   (Stevie Wonder)
2. TRIUMPH
   (The Jacksons)
3. TP
   (Teddy Pendergrass)
4. FACES
   (Earth, Wind and Fire)
5. GIVE ME THE NIGHT
   (George Benson)
6. CELEBRATE
   (Kool and the Gang)
7. FEEL ME
   (Cameo)
8. ZAPP
   (Zapp)
9. SHINE ON
   (L.T.D.)
10. DIANA
    (Diana Ross)

JAZZ ALBUMS

1. WINELIGHT
   (Grover Washington Jr.)
2. GIVE ME THE NIGHT
   (George Benson)
3. CARNAVAL
   (Spyro Gyra)
4. THIS TIME
   (Al Jarreau)
5. CIVILIZED EVIL
   (Jean Luc Ponty)
6. TWENNYNINE WITH LENNY WHITE
   (Lenny White)
7. INHERIT THE WIND
   (Wilton Felder)
8. ODORI
   (Hiroshima)
9. FAMILY
   (Hubert Laws)
10. SEAWIND
    (Seawind)

COUNTRY SINGLES

1. LADY
   (Kenny Rogers)
2. SMOKY MOUNTAIN RAIN
   (Ronnie Milsap)
3. IF YOU EVER CHANGE YOUR MIND
   (Crystal Gayle)
4. YOU ALMOST SLIPPED MY MIND
   (Charley Pride)
5. WHY LADY WHY
   (Alabama)
6. SHE CAN'T SAY THAT ANYMORE
   (John Conlee)
7. TAKE ME TO YOUR LOVIN' PLACE
   (Larry Gatlin and The Gatlin Brothers Band)
8. LOVERS LIVE LONGER
   (The Bellamy Brothers)
9. THAT'S ALL THAT MATTERS
   (Mickey Gilley)
10. BROKEN TRUST
    (Brenda Lee)

COUNTRY ALBUMS

1. KENNY ROGERS' GREATEST HITS
   (Kenny Rogers)
2. HONEYSUCKLE ROSE
   (Willie Nelson and Family)
3. URBAN COWBOY
   (Original Soundtrack)
4. ANNE MURRAY'S GREATEST HITS
   (Anne Murray)
5. I BELIEVE IN YOU
   (Don Williams)
6. FULL MOON
   (The Charlie Daniels Band)
7. THE OAK RIDGE BOYS' GREATEST HITS
   (The Oak Ridge Boys)
8. GREATEST HITS
   (Waylon Jennings)
9. RONNIE MILSAP'S GREATEST HITS
   (Ronnie Milsap)
10. HORIZON
    (Eddie Rabbitt)

DECEMBER 13, 1980

POP SINGLES

1. LADY
   (Kenny Rogers)
2. ANOTHER ONE BITES THE DUST
   (Queen)
3. MORE THAN I CAN SAY
   (Leo Sayer)

4. LOVE ON THE ROCKS
   (Neil Diamond)
5. THE WANDERER
   (Donna Summer)
6. (JUST LIKE) STARTING OVER
   (John Lennon)
7. HIT ME WITH YOUR BEST SHOT
   (Pat Benatar)
8. THEME FROM THE DUKES OF HAZZARD
   (GOOD OLE BOYS)
   (Waylon Jennings)
9. GUILTY
   (Barbra Streisand and Barry Gibb)
10. HUNGRY HEART
    (Bruce Springsteen)

POP ALBUMS

1. KENNY ROGERS' GREATEST HITS
   (Kenny Rogers)
2. GUILTY
   (Barbra Streisand)
3. HOTTER THAN JULY
   (Stevie Wonder)
4. THE GAME
   (Queen)
5. BACK IN BLACK
   (AC/DC)
6. CRIMES OF PASSION
   (Pat Benatar)
7. THE RIVER
   (Bruce Springsteen)
8. THE JAZZ SINGER
   (Original Soundtrack)
9. LIVE
   (The Eagles)
10. ZENYATTA MONDATTA
    (The Police)

BLACK SINGLES

1. CELEBRATION
   (Kool and the Gang)
2. MASTER BLASTER (JAMMIN')
   (Stevie Wonder)
3. LOVE T.K.O.
   (Teddy Pendergrass)
4. LOVELY ONE
   (The Jacksons)
5. KEEP IT HOT
   (Cameo)
6. UPTOWN
   (Prince)
7. REMOTE CONTROL
   (The Reddings)
8. LOVE X LOVE
   (George Benson)
9. MORE BOUNCE TO THE OUNCE (PART I)
   (Zapp)
10. ANOTHER ONE BITES THE DUST
    (Queen)

BLACK ALBUMS

1. HOTTER THAN JULY
   (Stevie Wonder)
2. TRIUMPH
   (The Jacksons)
3. FACES
   (Earth, Wind and Fire)
4. TP
   (Teddy Pendergrass)
5. CELEBRATE
   (Kool and the Gang)
6. FEEL ME
   (Cameo)
7. ARETHA
   (Aretha Franklin)
8. GIVE ME THE NIGHT
   (George Benson)
9. ZAPP
   (Zapp)
10. DIRTY MIND
    (Prince)

JAZZ ALBUMS

1. WINELIGHT
   (Grover Washington Jr.)
2. GIVE ME THE NIGHT
   (George Benson)
3. CARNAVAL
   (Spyro Gyra)
4. ODORI
   (Hiroshima)
5. CIVILIZED EVIL
   (Jean Luc Ponty)
6. INHERIT THE WIND
   (Wilton Felder)
7. SEAWIND
   (Seawind)
8. LATE NIGHT GUITAR
   (Earl Klugh)
9. THIS TIME
   (Al Jarreau)
10. MR. HANDS
    (Herbie Hancock)

COUNTRY SINGLES

1. SMOKY MOUNTAIN RAIN
   (Ronnie Milsap)
2. LOVERS LIVE LONGER
   (The Bellamy Brothers)
3. YOU ALMOST SLIPPED MY MIND
   (Charley Pride)
4. THAT'S ALL THAT MATTERS
   (Mickey Gilley)
5. ONE IN A MILLION
   (Johnny Lee)
6. LADY
   (Kenny Rogers)
7. THE BEST OF STRANGERS
   (Barbara Mandrell)
8. TEXAS IN MY REAR VIEW MIRROR
   (Mac Davis)
9. A BRIDGE THAT JUST WON'T BURN
   (Conway Twitty)
10. I THINK I'LL JUST STAY HERE AND DRINK
    (Merle Haggard)

COUNTRY ALBUMS

1. KENNY ROGERS' GREATEST HITS
   (Kenny Rogers)
2. ANNE MURRAY'S GREATEST HITS
   (Anne Murray)
3. HONEYSUCKLE ROSE
   (Willie Nelson and Family)
4. URBAN COWBOY
   (Original Soundtrack)
5. THE OAK RIDGE BOYS' GREATEST HITS
   (The Oak Ridge Boys)
6. I BELIEVE IN YOU
   (Don Williams)
7. HORIZON
   (Eddie Rabbitt)
8. FULL MOON
   (The Charlie Daniels Band)
9. GREATEST HITS
   (Waylon Jennings)
10. RONNIE MILSAP'S GREATEST HITS
    (Ronnie Milsap)

DECEMBER 20, 1980

POP SINGLES

1. LADY
   (Kenny Rogers)
2. ANOTHER ONE BITES THE DUST
   (Queen)
3. MORE THAN I CAN SAY
   (Leo Sayer)

4. LOVE ON THE ROCKS
   (Neil Diamond)
5. (JUST LIKE) STARTING OVER
   (John Lennon)
6. GUILTY
   (Barbra Streisand and Barry Gibb)
7. THEME FROM THE DUKES OF HAZZARD
   (GOOD OLE BOYS)
   (Waylon Jennings)
8. HIT ME WITH YOUR BEST SHOT
   (Pat Benatar)
9. EVERY WOMAN IN THE WORLD
   (Air Supply)
10. HUNGRY HEART
    (Bruce Springsteen)

POP ALBUMS

1. KENNY ROGERS' GREATEST HITS
   (Kenny Rogers)
2. GUILTY
   (Barbra Streisand)
3. HOTTER THAN JULY
   (Stevie Wonder)
4. THE GAME
   (Queen)
5. BACK IN BLACK
   (AC/DC)
6. CRIMES OF PASSION
   (Pat Benatar)
7. THE RIVER
   (Bruce Springsteen)
8. THE JAZZ SINGER
   (Original Soundtrack)
9. LIVE
   (The Eagles)
10. ZENYATTA MONDATTA
    (The Police)

BLACK SINGLES

1. CELEBRATION
   (Kool and the Gang)
2. MASTER BLASTER (JAMMIN')
   (Stevie Wonder)
3. LOVE T.K.O.
   (Teddy Pendergrass)
4. REMOTE CONTROL
   (The Reddings)
5. KEEP IT HOT
   (Cameo)
6. LOVELY ONE
   (The Jacksons)
7. UPTOWN
   (Prince)
8. LOVE X LOVE
   (George Benson)
9. LOOK UP
   (Patrice Rushen)
10. MORE BOUNCE TO THE OUNCE (PART I)
    (Zapp)

BLACK ALBUMS

1. HOTTER THAN JULY
   (Stevie Wonder)
2. TRIUMPH
   (The Jacksons)
3. FACES
   (Earth, Wind and Fire)
4. TP
   (Teddy Pendergrass)
5. CELEBRATE
   (Kool and the Gang)
6. FEEL ME
   (Cameo)
7. ARETHA
   (Aretha Franklin)
8. FANTASTIC VOYAGE
   (Lakeside)
9. WINELIGHT
   (Grover Washington Jr.)
10. GIVE ME THE NIGHT
    (George Benson)

JAZZ ALBUMS

1. WINELIGHT
   (Grover Washington Jr.)
2. GIVE ME THE NIGHT
   (George Benson)
3. CARNAVAL
   (Spyro Gyra)
4. INHERIT THE WIND
   (Wilton Felder)
5. CIVILIZED EVIL
   (Jean Luc Ponty)
6. SEAWIND
   (Seawind)
7. FAMILY
   (Hubert Laws)
8. LATE NIGHT GUITAR
   (Earl Klugh)
9. ODORI
   (Hiroshima)
10. MR. HANDS
    (Herbie Hancock)

COUNTRY SINGLES

1. THAT'S ALL THAT MATTERS
   (Mickey Gilley)
2. LOVERS LIVE LONGER
   (The Bellamy Brothers)
3. ONE IN A MILLION
   (Johnny Lee)
4. SMOKY MOUNTAIN RAIN
   (Ronnie Milsap)
5. I THINK I'LL JUST STAY HERE AND DRINK
   (Merle Haggard)
6. A BRIDGE THAT JUST WON'T BURN
   (Conway Twitty)
7. THE BEST OF STRANGERS
   (Barbara Mandrell)
8. TEXAS IN MY REAR VIEW MIRROR
   (Mac Davis)
9. I LOVE A RAINY NIGHT
   (Eddie Rabbitt)
10. YOU ALMOST SLIPPED MY MIND
    (Charley Pride)

COUNTRY ALBUMS

1. KENNY ROGERS' GREATEST HITS
   (Kenny Rogers)
2. ANNE MURRAY'S GREATEST HITS
   (Anne Murray)
3. HONEYSUCKLE ROSE
   (Willie Nelson and Family)
4. URBAN COWBOY
   (Original Soundtrack)
5. THE OAK RIDGE BOYS' GREATEST HITS
   (The Oak Ridge Boys)
6. I BELIEVE IN YOU
   (Don Williams)
7. HORIZON
   (Eddie Rabbitt)
8. GREATEST HITS
   (Waylon Jennings)
9. RONNIE MILSAP'S GREATEST HITS
   (Ronnie Milsap)
10. FULL MOON
    (The Charlie Daniels Band)

DECEMBER 27, 1980

POP SINGLES

1. (JUST LIKE) STARTING OVER
   (John Lennon)
2. ANOTHER ONE BITES THE DUST
   (Queen)
3. LOVE ON THE ROCKS
   (Neil Diamond)
4. LADY
   (Kenny Rogers)
5. MORE THAN I CAN SAY
   (Leo Sayer)
6. GUILTY
   (Barbra Streisand and Barry Gibb)
7. THEME FROM THE DUKES OF HAZZARD
   (GOOD OLE BOYS)
   (Waylon Jennings)
8. EVERY WOMAN IN THE WORLD
   (Air Supply)
9. HIT ME WITH YOUR BEST SHOT
   (Pat Benatar)
10. HUNGRY HEART
    (Bruce Springsteen)

POP ALBUMS

1. KENNY ROGERS' GREATEST HITS
   (Kenny Rogers)
2. DOUBLE FANTASY
   (John Lennon and Yoko Ono)
3. GUILTY
   (Barbra Streisand)
4. THE GAME
   (Queen)
5. BACK IN BLACK
   (AC/DC)
6. CRIMES OF PASSION
   (Pat Benatar)
7. HOTTER THAN JULY
   (Stevie Wonder)
8. THE RIVER
   (Bruce Springsteen)
9. LIVE
   (The Eagles)
10. THE JAZZ SINGER
    (Original Soundtrack)

BLACK SINGLES

1. CELEBRATION
   (Kool and the Gang)
2. MASTER BLASTER (JAMMIN')
   (Stevie Wonder)
3. LOVE T.K.O.
   (Teddy Pendergrass)
4. REMOTE CONTROL
   (The Reddings)
5. KEEP IT HOT
   (Cameo)
6. UNITED TOGETHER
   (Aretha Franklin)
7. FANTASTIC VOYAGE
   (Lakeside)
8. HEARTBREAK HOTEL
   (The Jacksons)
9. LOOK UP
   (Patrice Rushen)
10. LOVE OVER AND OVER AGAIN
    (Switch)

BLACK ALBUMS

1. HOTTER THAN JULY
   (Stevie Wonder)
2. TRIUMPH
   (The Jacksons)
3. TP
   (Teddy Pendergrass)
4. FACES
   (Earth, Wind and Fire)
5. CELEBRATE
   (Kool and the Gang)
6. FEEL ME
   (Cameo)
7. ARETHA
   (Aretha Franklin)
8. FANTASTIC VOYAGE
   (Lakeside)
9. WINELIGHT
   (Grover Washington Jr.)
10. GIVE ME THE NIGHT
    (George Benson)

JAZZ ALBUMS

1. WINELIGHT
   (Grover Washington Jr.)
2. GIVE ME THE NIGHT
   (George Benson)
3. INHERIT THE WIND
   (Wilton Felder)
4. LATE NIGHT GUITAR
   (Earl Klugh)
5. CARNAVAL
   (Spyro Gyra)
6. CIVILIZED EVIL
   (Jean Luc Ponty)
7. NIGHT PASSAGE
   (Weather Report)
8. SEAWIND
   (Seawind)
9. FAMILY
   (Hubert Laws)
10. THIS TIME
    (Al Jarreau)

COUNTRY SINGLES

1. ONE IN A MILLION
   (Johnny Lee)
2. THAT'S ALL THAT MATTERS
   (Mickey Gilley)
3. I THINK I'LL JUST STAY HERE AND DRINK
   (Merle Haggard)
4. A BRIDGE THAT JUST WON'T BURN
   (Conway Twitty)
5. LOVERS LIVE LONGER
   (The Bellamy Brothers)
6. I LOVE A RAINY NIGHT
   (Eddie Rabbitt)
7. SMOKY MOUNTAIN RAIN
   (Ronnie Milsap)
8. BEAUTIFUL YOU
   (The Oak Ridge Boys)
9. DOWN TO MY LAST BROKEN HEART
   (Janie Fricke)
10. GIVING UP EASY
    (Leon Everette)

COUNTRY ALBUMS

1. KENNY ROGERS' GREATEST HITS
   (Kenny Rogers)
2. ANNE MURRAY'S GREATEST HITS
   (Anne Murray)
3. URBAN COWBOY
   (Original Soundtrack)
4. HONEYSUCKLE ROSE
   (Willie Nelson and Family)
5. THE OAK RIDGE BOYS' GREATEST HITS
   (The Oak Ridge Boys)
6. I BELIEVE IN YOU
   (Don Williams)
7. HORIZON
   (Eddie Rabbitt)
8. GREATEST HITS
   (Waylon Jennings)
9. RONNIE MILSAP'S GREATEST HITS
   (Ronnie Milsap)
10. FULL MOON
    (The Charlie Daniels Band)

1981

John Lennon was murdered in front of his New York City apartment building on December 8, 1980. The effect was as profound as when Elvis Presley died, but in a different way, one that reflected the great difference between the two. Elvis had long ago let himself be controlled by financial and social forces he trusted but didn't understand. The fat, twisted Elvis of his latter years was a by-product of the intellectual and musical laziness affluence sometimes produces. The raw spirit apparent in his Sun and early RCA recordings was dead by the mid-6os and what remained was a commodity, the outer shell of a real man. The commercial carnage that followed his drug-induced demise (for example, Albert Goldman's despicable best-selling biography) was thus as predictable as it was sickening.

Lennon almost was destroyed in the same way by ten-percenters, his own ego, and an image that encompassed only part of the man. But Lennon, displaying admirable inner strength, said "no" to being a Beatle, to being god, and in a way that was characteristic of the '70s went off to rediscover himself by becoming a dedicated house-husband. With the aid of his loving wife, Yoko Ono, Lennon learned to control his own life and make the kind of music he wanted, when he wanted. So while there was some exploitation of Lennon's memory after his death, little of it had the sleazy quality that surrounded Elvis. Yoko Ono wouldn't permit it and his fans respected Lennon as a musician and as a man.

Personality in pop music, the ability to project a distinctive viewpoint and simultaneously write music with popular appeal, is an elusive quality. Steve Winwood, Steely Dan, Bruce Springsteen, Rick James, and Stevie Nicks accomplished this in 1981, making music rich in detail, consistent in tone, and joyous to hear.

Arc of a Diver was a comeback for Winwood, who in recent years had recorded sporadically and with little of the passion that marked his work with Traffic, or earlier with the Spencer Davis Group. This album, recorded at a small house in the English countryside, was charged with his youthful spirit and a maturity many older rock stars find elusive. On the title track and "If You See A Chance, Take It," he sang with marvelous control, phrasing beautifully around the music's perky rhythms.

Due to their own perfectionist standards and legal hassles with MCA Records, Steely Dan's *Gaucho* was several years in the making, but the wait was worth it. Donald Fagan and Walter Becker's lyrics were again inscrutable, while the music continued to fuse jazz chords, R&B rhythms, and complex arrangements of Steely Dan's insidious approach to pop. Unfortunately, Fagan and Becker broke up after *Gaucho*, leaving behind a catalogue of consistently sophisticated music.

Since gracing the covers of *Time* and *Newsweek*, Bruce Springsteen had become everybody's favorite rock 'n' roll hero. His fun, high-spirited concerts, his innocence and openness in interviews, and his working-class identity (after seeing him in the *No Nukes* documentary, film critic Andrew Sarris compared him to John Garfield) made Springsteen seem the embodiment of what was best about rock. *The River* reflected Springsteen's blue-collar concerns, including an obsession with cars (twelve of the LP's twenty songs mention driving). It also contained two exceptional songs: "Point Blank" and "The River," about lost innocence and diminished faith in the future.

While Springsteen chronicled white working-class America, Rick James cursed and celebrated the adventures of a freaky black man (himself) on the autobiographical *Street Songs*. Over music inspired by Parliament, Prince, and Norman Whitfield's "psychedelic" Temptations' productions, James sang about freaky girls, getting high, villainous police, and street life in his home town of Buffalo. "Super Freak" and "Give It To Me Baby" were hits, but "Ghetto Life" and "Fire and Desire" (his duet with Teena Marie) made this the most substantial black album of 1981.

Like a will-o'-the-wisp, Stevie Nicks's music has an ethereal, intangible quality that draws you in. Though her voice is thin, it has an entrancing vulnerability that suits her evocative imagery ("the white winged dove" of "Edge of Seventeen") and flower-child persona. Nicks, first with Fleetwood Mac and on her solo album *Bella Donna*, creates a musical world perfect for her vocal talents and artistic sensibility.

R.E.O. Speedwagon's *Hi Infidelity* and "Keep On Loving You," Styx's *Paradise Theater* and "The Best of Times," and Journey's *Escape* and "Who's Crying Now," constituted the best of a new genre some called "heavy pop." In the past, all three bands were associated with loud, raucous arena rock, but this year gave up hell raising for melodies aimed at adult contemporary radio programmers. This was heavy metal for those who wanted to hum along and it sold tons of records in a depressed marketplace. By year's end the air waves were packed by reformed acid heads all looking to get a piece of the pop pie.

SINGLES: "Bette Davis Eyes" sounded like nothing else on the radio, its weird synthesizer line, grating drums, Kim Carnes's rough, whiskey-soaked vocal, and subtly decadent lyric leaped out and grabbed your attention. Producer Val Garay had created an audacious record that once heard never would be forgotten.

For the most part, the rest of the top singles were light fare with modest talents like Sheena Easton ("Morning Train," "For Your Eyes Only"), Juice Newton ("Queen of Hearts," "Angel of the Morning"), and Joey Scarbury ("Theme from the Greatest American Hero") finding success, hopefully short-lived. "Endless Love" was one of Lionel Richie's worst songs, yet his duet with Diana Ross was Richie's biggest hit. A much more charming contribution from a Motown performer was Smokey Robinson's "Being With You," a soft, summer song that had the wistful spirit of some of his work with the Miracles. Kool and the Gang's "Celebration" was the year's finest pop-dance song. Its mass acceptance was ensured when the networks used it as a welcoming song for the hostages returning from Iran, an instance of the right song for the right event.

The Rolling Stones served notice that there was still some life in Mick Jagger's bones with "Start Me Up," an old-fashioned rocker that heralded a national tour for rock's longest-running circus. Bill Withers, whose career had gone sour due to poor management and his own personal quirks, sang lead and co-wrote Grover Washington Jr.'s "Just the Two of Us," a wonderfully laid-back love song. Three fine singles came from country artists who dabbled in other music forms. Ronnie Milsap's "(There's) No Gettin' Over Me" and Eddie Rabbitt's "Step By Step" were both strong, rhythm and blues songs as good as any performed by blacks in 1981, while Rabbitt's "I Love A Rainy Night" was a creatively arranged rockabilly tune.

There were many significant industry events in 1981. For example, Van Halen lead singer David Lee Roth took out paternity suit insurance policy with Lloyd's of London as protection against accidents on the road. Ozzy Osbourne, late of Black Sabbath, bit the head off a dove at a CBS marketing meeting, so they'd have some idea of what old Ozzy's act was like. They got the message.

Another of music's eccentrics, Miles Davis, returned to the scene with a series of live concerts and a gold album, *The Man With the Horn*. Some disliked his band, some felt he was rusty, but the trumpeter's appearance was unquestionably one of the musical events of the year, and definitely a welcome one.

In a historic move Diana Ross left Motown Records for RCA. It was amazing Berry Gordy let it happen; after all she, more than any other performer, personified Motown's ability to make stars. Ross's desertion symbolized something most inside the record industry had known since the early 1970s—that the magic of Motown was dead and it was now just another record company.

Robert Christgau's Record Guide was a fun, insightful, argumentative look at rock albums of the 1970s by the self-proclaimed "dean" of American rock critics. Each of the short commentaries is full of Christgau's irascible, intellectually demanding prose. Its opening essay provides a fine overview of 1970s' pop music versus 1980s' music.

Diana Ross

Lionel Richie

Styx   **Ronnie Milsap**

The Who

Stacy Lattislaw

Miles Davis

Journey

JANUARY 17, 1981

POP SINGLES

1. (JUST LIKE) STARTING OVER
   (John Lennon)
2. ANOTHER ONE BITES THE DUST
   (Queen)
3. LOVE ON THE ROCKS
   (Neil Diamond)
4. EVERY WOMAN IN THE WORLD
   (Air Supply)
5. MORE THAN I CAN SAY
   (Leo Sayer)
6. GUILTY
   (Barbra Streisand and Barry Gibb)
7. THE TIDE IS HIGH
   (Blondie)
8. LADY
   (Kenny Rogers)
9. HIT ME WITH YOUR BEST SHOT
   (Pat Benatar)
10. PASSION
    (Rod Stewart)

POP ALBUMS

1. KENNY ROGERS' GREATEST HITS
   (Kenny Rogers)
2. DOUBLE FANTASY
   (John Lennon and Yoko Ono)
3. GUILTY
   (Barbra Streisand)
4. BACK IN BLACK
   (AC/DC)
5. CRIMES OF PASSION
   (Pat Benatar)
6. THE JAZZ SINGER
   (Original Soundtrack)
7. THE GAME
   (Queen)
8. HOTTER THAN JULY
   (Stevie Wonder)
9. THE RIVER
   (Bruce Springsteen)
10. LIVE
    (The Eagles)

BLACK SINGLES

1. CELEBRATION
   (Kool and the Gang)
2. FANTASTIC VOYAGE
   (Lakeside)
3. HEARTBREAK HOTEL
   (The Jacksons)
4. UNITED TOGETHER
   (Aretha Franklin)
5. KEEP IT HOT
   (Cameo)
6. REMOTE CONTROL
   (The Reddings)
7. LOVE T.K.O.
   (Teddy Pendergrass)
8. MASTER BLASTER (JAMMIN')
   (Stevie Wonder)
9. LOVE OVER AND OVER AGAIN
   (Switch)
10. TOO TIGHT
    (Con Funk Shun)

BLACK ALBUMS

1. HOTTER THAN JULY
   (Stevie Wonder)
2. TRIUMPH
   (The Jacksons)
3. CELEBRATE
   (Kool and the Gang)
4. FANTASTIC VOYAGE
   (Lakeside)

5. TP
   (Teddy Pendergrass)
6. FACES
   (Earth, Wind and Fire)
7. FEEL ME
   (Cameo)
8. ARETHA
   (Aretha Franklin)
9. GAP BAND III
   (The Gap Band)
10. WINELIGHT
    (Grover Washington Jr.)

JAZZ ALBUMS

1. WINELIGHT
   (Grover Washington Jr.)
2. GIVE ME THE NIGHT
   (George Benson)
3. CARNAVAL
   (Spyro Gyra)
4. LATE NIGHT GUITAR
   (Earl Klugh)
5. INHERIT THE WIND
   (Wilton Felder)
6. NIGHT PASSAGE
   (Weather Report)
7. CIVILIZED EVIL
   (Jean Luc Ponty)
8. FAMILY
   (Hubert Laws)
9. ODORI
   (Hiroshima)
10. SEAWIND
    (Seawind)

COUNTRY SINGLES

1. I LOVE A RAINY NIGHT
   (Eddie Rabbitt)
2. I THINK I'LL JUST STAY HERE AND DRINK
   (Merle Haggard)
3. BEAUTIFUL YOU
   (The Oak Ridge Boys)
4. ONE IN A MILLION
   (Johnny Lee)
5. DOWN TO MY LAST BROKEN HEART
   (Janie Fricke)
6. 9 TO 5
   (Dolly Parton)
7. GIVING UP EASY
   (Leon Everette)
8. IF YOU GO, I'LL FOLLOW YOU
   (Porter Wagoner and Dolly Parton)
9. DON'T FORGET YOURSELF
   (The Statler Brothers)
10. I KEEP COMING BACK/TRUE LIFE
    COUNTRY MUSIC
    (Razzy Bailey)

COUNTRY ALBUMS

1. KENNY ROGERS' GREATEST HITS
   (Kenny Rogers)
2. ANNE MURRAY'S GREATEST HITS
   (Anne Murray)
3. HONEYSUCKLE ROSE
   (Willie Nelson and Family)
4. URBAN COWBOY
   (Original Soundtrack)
5. THE OAK RIDGE BOYS' GREATEST HITS
   (The Oak Ridge Boys)
6. HORIZON
   (Eddie Rabbitt)
7. I BELIEVE IN YOU
   (Don Williams)
8. GREATEST HITS
   (Waylon Jennings)
9. RONNIE MILSAP'S GREATEST HITS
   (Ronnie Milsap)
10. FULL MOON
    (The Charlie Daniels Band)

JANUARY 24, 1981

POP SINGLES

1. (JUST LIKE) STARTING OVER
   (John Lennon)
2. THE TIDE IS HIGH
   (Blondie)
3. EVERY WOMAN IN THE WORLD
   (Air Supply)
4. ANOTHER ONE BITES THE DUST
   (Queen)
5. HIT ME WITH YOUR BEST SHOT
   (Pat Benatar)
6. PASSION
   (Rod Stewart)
7. MORE THAN I CAN SAY
   (Leo Sayer)
8. GUILTY
   (Barbra Streisand and Barry Gibb)
9. CELEBRATION
   (Kool and the Gang)
10. I MADE IT THROUGH THE RAIN
    (Barry Manilow)

POP ALBUMS

1. KENNY ROGERS' GREATEST HITS
   (Kenny Rogers)
2. DOUBLE FANTASY
   (John Lennon and Yoko Ono)
3. GUILTY
   (Barbra Streisand)
4. THE JAZZ SINGER
   (Original Soundtrack)
5. CRIMES OF PASSION
   (Pat Benatar)
6. BACK IN BLACK
   (AC/DC)
7. HOTTER THAN JULY
   (Stevie Wonder)
8. THE GAME
   (Queen)
9. GAUCHO
   (Steely Dan)
10. LIVE
    (The Eagles)

BLACK SINGLES

1. FANTASTIC VOYAGE
   (Lakeside)
2. CELEBRATION
   (Kool and the Gang)
3. HEARTBREAK HOTEL
   (The Jacksons)
4. UNITED TOGETHER
   (Aretha Franklin)
5. KEEP IT HOT
   (Cameo)
6. REMOTE CONTROL
   (The Reddings)
7. LOVE T.K.O.
   (Teddy Pendergrass)
8. LOVE OVER AND OVER AGAIN
   (Switch)
9. TOO TIGHT
   (Con Funk Shun)
10. BURN RUBBER
    (The Gap Band)

BLACK ALBUMS

1. HOTTER THAN JULY
   (Stevie Wonder)
2. TRIUMPH
   (The Jacksons)
3. CELEBRATE
   (Kool and the Gang)
4. FANTASTIC VOYAGE
   (Lakeside)

5. GAP BAND III
   (The Gap Band)
6. FACES
   (Earth, Wind and Fire)
7. FEEL ME
   (Cameo)
8. TP
   (Teddy Pendergrass)
9. ARETHA
   (Aretha Franklin)
10. WINELIGHT
    (Grover Washington Jr.)

JAZZ ALBUMS

1. WINELIGHT
   (Grover Washington Jr.)
2. GIVE ME THE NIGHT
   (George Benson)
3. CARNAVAL
   (Spyro Gyra)
4. LATE NIGHT GUITAR
   (Earl Klugh)
5. NIGHT PASSAGE
   (Weather Report)
6. ODORI
   (Hiroshima)
7. INHERIT THE WIND
   (Wilton Felder)
8. CIVILIZED EVIL
   (Jean Luc Ponty)
9. FAMILY
   (Hubert Laws)
10. SEAWIND
    (Seawind)

COUNTRY SINGLES

1. BEAUTIFUL YOU
   (The Oak Ridge Boys)
2. I LOVE A RAINY NIGHT
   (Eddie Rabbitt)
3. 9 TO 5
   (Dolly Parton)
4. DOWN TO MY LAST BROKEN HEART
   (Janie Fricke)
5. I THINK I'LL JUST STAY HERE AND DRINK
   (Merle Haggard)
6. I KEEP COMING BACK/TRUE LIFE
   COUNTRY MUSIC
   (Razzy Bailey)
7. I FEEL LIKE LOVING YOU AGAIN
   (T.G. Sheppard)
8. GIRLS, WOMEN AND LADIES
   (Ed Bruce)
9. DON'T FORGET YOURSELF
   (The Statler Brothers)
10. 1959
    (John Anderson)

COUNTRY ALBUMS

1. KENNY ROGERS' GREATEST HITS
   (Kenny Rogers)
2. ANNE MURRAY'S GREATEST HITS
   (Anne Murray)
3. HONEYSUCKLE ROSE
   (Willie Nelson and Family)
4. URBAN COWBOY
   (Original Soundtrack)
5. HORIZON
   (Eddie Rabbitt)
6. THE OAK RIDGE BOYS' GREATEST HITS
   (The Oak Ridge Boys)
7. I BELIEVE IN YOU
   (Don Williams)
8. FULL MOON
   (The Charlie Daniels Band)
9. GREATEST HITS
   (Waylon Jennings)
10. RONNIE MILSAP'S GREATEST HITS
    (Ronnie Milsap)

JANUARY 31, 1981

POP SINGLES

1. THE TIDE IS HIGH
   (Blondie)
2. (JUST LIKE) STARTING OVER
   (John Lennon)
3. EVERY WOMAN IN THE WORLD
   (Air Supply)
4. CELEBRATION
   (Kool and the Gang)
5. HIT ME WITH YOUR BEST SHOT
   (Pat Benatar)
6. PASSION
   (Rod Stewart)
7. I LOVE A RAINY NIGHT
   (Eddie Rabbitt)
8. ANOTHER ONE BITES THE DUST
   (Queen)
9. KEEP ON LOVING YOU
   (R.E.O. Speedwagon)
10. 9 TO 5
    (Dolly Parton)

POP ALBUMS

1. KENNY ROGERS' GREATEST HITS
   (Kenny Rogers)
2. DOUBLE FANTASY
   (John Lennon and Yoko Ono)
3. GUILTY
   (Barbra Streisand)
4. THE JAZZ SINGER
   (Original Soundtrack)
5. CRIMES OF PASSION
   (Pat Benatar)
6. BACK IN BLACK
   (AC/DC)
7. HOTTER THAN JULY
   (Stevie Wonder)
8. ZENYATTA MONDATTA
   (The Police)
9. GAUCHO
   (Steely Dan)
10. AUTOAMERICAN
    (Blondie)

BLACK SINGLES

1. FANTASTIC VOYAGE
   (Lakeside)
2. HEARTBREAK HOTEL
   (The Jacksons)
3. CELEBRATION
   (Kool and the Gang)
4. UNITED TOGETHER
   (Aretha Franklin)
5. DON'T STOP THE MUSIC
   (Yarbrough and Peoples)
6. BURN RUBBER
   (The Gap Band)
7. TOO TIGHT
   (Con Funk Shun)
8. LOVE OVER AND OVER AGAIN
   (Switch)
9. I JUST LOVE THE MAN
   (The Jones Girls)
10. BOOGIE BODY LAND
    (Bar-Kays)

BLACK ALBUMS

1. HOTTER THAN JULY
   (Stevie Wonder)
2. FANTASTIC VOYAGE
   (Lakeside)
3. CELEBRATE
   (Kool and the Gang)
4. TRIUMPH
   (The Jacksons)

5. GAP BAND III
   (The Gap Band)
6. THE TWO OF US
   (Yarbrough and Peoples)
7. IMAGINATION
   (Whispers)
8. FACES
   (Earth, Wind and Fire)
9. ARETHA
   (Aretha Franklin)
10. TOUCH
    (Con Funk Shun)

JAZZ ALBUMS

1. WINELIGHT
   (Grover Washington Jr.)
2. LATE NIGHT GUITAR
   (Earl Klugh)
3. GIVE ME THE NIGHT
   (George Benson)
4. NIGHT PASSAGE
   (Weather Report)
5. ODORI
   (Hiroshima)
6. INHERIT THE WIND
   (Wilton Felder)
7. CARNAVAL
   (Spyro Gyra)
8. CIVILIZED EVIL
   (Jean Luc Ponty)
9. SEAWIND
   (Seawind)
10. FAMILY
    (Hubert Laws)

COUNTRY SINGLES

1. 9 TO 5
   (Dolly Parton)
2. BEAUTIFUL YOU
   (The Oak Ridge Boys)
3. I FEEL LIKE LOVING YOU AGAIN
   (T.G. Sheppard)
4. DOWN TO MY LAST BROKEN HEART
   (Janie Fricke)
5. I KEEP COMING BACK/TRUE LIFE
   COUNTRY MUSIC
   (Razzy Bailey)
6. 1959
   (John Anderson)
7. I'LL BE THERE IF YOU EVER WANT ME
   (Gail Davies)
8. GIRLS, WOMEN AND LADIES
   (Ed Bruce)
9. WHO'S CHEATIN' WHO
   (Charly McClain)
10. YOUR MEMORY
    (Steve Wariner)

COUNTRY ALBUMS

1. KENNY ROGERS' GREATEST HITS
   (Kenny Rogers)
2. ANNE MURRAY'S GREATEST HITS
   (Anne Murray)
3. HONEYSUCKLE ROSE
   (Willie Nelson and Family)
4. URBAN COWBOY
   (Original Soundtrack)
5. HORIZON
   (Eddie Rabbitt)
6. THE OAK RIDGE BOYS' GREATEST HITS
   (The Oak Ridge Boys)
7. I BELIEVE IN YOU
   (Don Williams)
8. FULL MOON
   (The Charlie Daniels Band)
9. GREATEST HITS
   (Waylon Jennings)
10. 9 TO 5 AND ODD JOBS
    (Dolly Parton)

FEBRUARY 7, 1981

POP SINGLES

1. THE TIDE IS HIGH
   (Blondie)
2. (JUST LIKE) STARTING OVER
   (John Lennon)
3. 9 TO 5
   (Dolly Parton)
4. CELEBRATION
   (Kool and the Gang)
5. I LOVE A RAINY NIGHT
   (Eddie Rabbitt)
6. PASSION
   (Rod Stewart)
7. KEEP ON LOVING YOU
   (R.E.O. Speedwagon)
8. EVERY WOMAN IN THE WORLD
   (Air Supply)
9. HIT ME WITH YOUR BEST SHOT
   (Pat Benatar)
10. HEY NINETEEN
    (Steely Dan)

POP ALBUMS

1. KENNY ROGERS' GREATEST HITS
   (Kenny Rogers)
2. DOUBLE FANTASY
   (John Lennon and Yoko Ono)
3. THE JAZZ SINGER
   (Original Soundtrack)
4. GUILTY
   (Barbra Streisand)
5. CRIMES OF PASSION
   (Pat Benatar)
6. BACK IN BLACK
   (AC/DC)
7. HOTTER THAN JULY
   (Stevie Wonder)
8. ZENYATTA MONDATTA
   (The Police)
9. GAUCHO
   (Steely Dan)
10. AUTOAMERICAN
    (Blondie)

BLACK SINGLES

1. FANTASTIC VOYAGE
   (Lakeside)
2. HEARTBREAK HOTEL
   (The Jacksons)
3. BURN RUBBER
   (The Gap Band)
4. DON'T STOP THE MUSIC
   (Yarbrough and Peoples)
5. CELEBRATION
   (Kool and the Gang)
6. I JUST LOVE THE MAN
   (The Jones Girls)
7. TOO TIGHT
   (Con Funk Shun)
8. UNITED TOGETHER
   (Aretha Franklin)
9. LOVE OVER AND OVER AGAIN
   (Switch)
10. BOOGIE BODY LAND
    (Bar-Kays)

BLACK ALBUMS

1. HOTTER THAN JULY
   (Stevie Wonder)
2. GAP BAND III
   (The Gap Band)
3. FANTASTIC VOYAGE
   (Lakeside)
4. THE TWO OF US
   (Yarbrough and Peoples)

5. CELEBRATE
   (Kool and the Gang)
6. TRIUMPH
   (The Jacksons)
7. IMAGINATION
   (Whispers)
8. STONE JAM
   (Slave)
9. FEEL ME
   (Cameo)
10. TOUCH
    (Con Funk Shun)

JAZZ ALBUMS

1. WINELIGHT
   (Grover Washington Jr.)
2. LATE NIGHT GUITAR
   (Earl Klugh)
3. GIVE ME THE NIGHT
   (George Benson)
4. CARNAVAL
   (Spyro Gyra)
5. NIGHT PASSAGE
   (Weather Report)
6. VOICES IN THE RAIN
   (Joe Sample)
7. INHERIT THE WIND
   (Wilton Felder)
8. ODORI
   (Hiroshima)
9. POSH
   (Patrice Rushen)
10. REAL EYES
    (Gil Scott-Heron)

COUNTRY SINGLES

1. 9 TO 5
   (Dolly Parton)
2. I FEEL LIKE LOVING YOU AGAIN
   (T.G. Sheppard)
3. I KEEP COMING BACK/TRUE LIFE COUNTRY MUSIC
   (Razzy Bailey)
4. BEAUTIFUL YOU
   (The Oak Ridge Boys)
5. 1959
   (John Anderson)
6. I'LL BE THERE IF YOU EVER WANT ME
   (Gail Davies)
7. WHO'S CHEATIN' WHO
   (Charly McClain)
8. YOUR MEMORY
   (Steve Wariner)
9. SOUTHERN RAINS
   (Mel Tillis)
10. FOLLOWING THE FEELING
    (Moe Bandy and Judy Bailey)

COUNTRY ALBUMS

1. KENNY ROGERS' GREATEST HITS
   (Kenny Rogers)
2. ANNE MURRAY'S GREATEST HITS
   (Anne Murray)
3. HORIZON
   (Eddie Rabbitt)
4. I BELIEVE IN YOU
   (Don Williams)
5. HONEYSUCKLE ROSE
   (Willie Nelson and Family)
6. URBAN COWBOY
   (Original Soundtrack)
7. THE OAK RIDGE BOYS' GREATEST HITS
   (The Oak Ridge Boys)
8. 9 TO 5 AND ODD JOBS
   (Dolly Parton)
9. GREATEST HITS
   (Waylon Jennings)
10. RONNIE MILSAP'S GREATEST HITS
    (Ronnie Milsap)

FEBRUARY 14, 1981

POP SINGLES

1. CELEBRATION
   (Kool and the Gang)
2. 9 TO 5
   (Dolly Parton)
3. I LOVE A RAINY NIGHT
   (Eddie Rabbitt)
4. THE TIDE IS HIGH
   (Blondie)
5. KEEP ON LOVING YOU
   (R.E.O. Speedwagon)
6. PASSION
   (Rod Stewart)
7. (JUST LIKE) STARTING OVER
   (John Lennon)
8. EVERY WOMAN IN THE WORLD
   (Air Supply)
9. HIT ME WITH YOUR BEST SHOT
   (Pat Benatar)
10. HEY NINETEEN
    (Steely Dan)

POP ALBUMS

1. DOUBLE FANTASY
   (John Lennon and Yoko Ono)
2. KENNY ROGERS' GREATEST HITS
   (Kenny Rogers)
3. THE JAZZ SINGER
   (Original Soundtrack)
4. PARADISE THEATER
   (Styx)
5. CRIMES OF PASSION
   (Pat Benatar)
6. GUILTY
   (Barbra Streisand)
7. BACK IN BLACK
   (AC/DC)
8. HI INFIDELITY
   (R.E.O. Speedwagon)
9. HOTTER THAN JULY
   (Stevie Wonder)
10. GAUCHO
    (Steely Dan)

BLACK SINGLES

1. BURN RUBBER
   (The Gap Band)
2. DON'T STOP THE MUSIC
   (Yarbrough and Peoples)
3. FANTASTIC VOYAGE
   (Lakeside)
4. HEARTBREAK HOTEL
   (The Jacksons)
5. I JUST LOVE THE MAN
   (The Jones Girls)
6. CELEBRATION
   (Kool and the Gang)
7. TOO TIGHT
   (Con Funk Shun)
8. I AIN'T GONNA STAND FOR IT
   (Stevie Wonder)
9. TOGETHER
   (Tierra)
10. WATCHING YOU
    (Slave)

BLACK ALBUMS

1. HOTTER THAN JULY
   (Stevie Wonder)
2. GAP BAND III
   (The Gap Band)
3. THE TWO OF US
   (Yarbrough and Peoples)
4. FANTASTIC VOYAGE
   (Lakeside)

5. CELEBRATE
   (Kool and the Gang)
6. IMAGINATION
   (Whispers)
7. TRIUMPH
   (The Jacksons)
8. STONE JAM
   (Slave)
9. IN OUR LIFETIME
   (Marvin Gaye)
10. TOUCH
    (Con Funk Shun)

JAZZ ALBUMS

1. WINELIGHT
   (Grover Washington Jr.)
2. VOICES IN THE RAIN
   (Joe Sample)
3. LATE NIGHT GUITAR
   (Earl Klugh)
4. GIVE ME THE NIGHT
   (George Benson)
5. CARNAVAL
   (Spyro Gyra)
6. NIGHT PASSAGE
   (Weather Report)
7. INHERIT THE WIND
   (Wilton Felder)
8. POSH
   (Patrice Rushen)
9. ODORI
   (Hiroshima)
10. CIVILIZED EVIL
    (Jean Luc Ponty)

COUNTRY SINGLES

1. I FEEL LIKE LOVING YOU AGAIN
   (T.G. Sheppard)
2. WHO'S CHEATING WHO
   (Charly McClain)
3. I KEEP COMING BACK/TRUE LIFE
   COUNTRY MUSIC
   (Razzy Bailey)
4. 1959
   (John Anderson)
5. I'LL BE THERE IF YOU EVER WANT ME
   (Gail Davies)
6. SOUTHERN RAINS
   (Mel Tillis)
7. DON'T YOU EVER GET TIRED OF HURTING
   ME
   (Willie Nelson and Ray Price)
8. YOUR MEMORY
   (Steve Wariner)
9. 9 TO 5
   (Dolly Parton)
10. FOLLOWING THE FEELING
    (Moe Bandy and Judy Bailey)

COUNTRY ALBUMS

1. KENNY ROGERS' GREATEST HITS
   (Kenny Rogers)
2. ANNE MURRAY'S GREATEST HITS
   (Anne Murray)
3. HORIZON
   (Eddie Rabbitt)
4. I BELIEVE IN YOU
   (Don Williams)
5. HONEYSUCKLE ROSE
   (Willie Nelson and Family)
6. 9 TO 5 AND ODD JOBS
   (Dolly Parton)
7. URBAN COWBOY
   (Original Soundtrack)
8. THE OAK RIDGE BOYS' GREATEST HITS
   (The Oak Ridge Boys)
9. RONNIE MILSAP'S GREATEST HITS
   (Ronnie Milsap)
10. GREATEST HITS
    (Waylon Jennings)

FEBRUARY 21, 1981

POP SINGLES

1. 9 TO 5
   (Dolly Parton)
2. CELEBRATION
   (Kool and the Gang)
3. I LOVE A RAINY NIGHT
   (Eddie Rabbitt)
4. KEEP ON LOVING YOU
   (R.E.O. Speedwagon)
5. THE TIDE IS HIGH
   (Blondie)
6. WOMAN
   (John Lennon)
7. THE BEST OF TIMES
   (Styx)
8. PASSION
   (Rod Stewart)
9. SAME OLDE LANG SYNE
   (Dan Fogelberg)
10. (JUST LIKE) STARTING OVER
    (John Lennon)

POP ALBUMS

1. DOUBLE FANTASY
   (John Lennon and Yoko Ono)
2. KENNY ROGERS' GREATEST HITS
   (Kenny Rogers)
3. THE JAZZ SINGER
   (Original Soundtrack)
4. PARADISE THEATER
   (Styx)
5. CRIMES OF PASSION
   (Pat Benatar)
6. HI INFIDELITY
   (R.E.O. Speedwagon)
7. GUILTY
   (Barbra Streisand)
8. BACK IN BLACK
   (AC/DC)
9. HOTTER THAN JULY
   (Stevie Wonder)
10. AUTOAMERICAN
    (Blondie)

BLACK SINGLES

1. DON'T STOP THE MUSIC
   (Yarbrough and Peoples)
2. BURN RUBBER
   (The Gap Band)
3. FANTASTIC VOYAGE
   (Lakeside)
4. IT'S A LOVE THING
   (Whispers)
5. I JUST LOVE THE MAN
   (The Jones Girls)
6. TOGETHER
   (Tierra)
7. CELEBRATION
   (Kool and the Gang)
8. I AIN'T GONNA STAND FOR IT
   (Stevie Wonder)
9. WATCHING YOU
   (Slave)
10. TOO TIGHT
    (Con Funk Shun)

BLACK ALBUMS

1. HOTTER THAN JULY
   (Stevie Wonder)
2. GAP BAND III
   (The Gap Band)
3. THE TWO OF US
   (Yarbrough and Peoples)
4. FANTASTIC VOYAGE
   (Lakeside)

5. IMAGINATION
   (Whispers)
6. CELEBRATE
   (Kool and the Gang)
7. IN OUR LIFETIME
   (Marvin Gaye)
8. STONE JAM
   (Slave)
9. TRIUMPH
   (The Jacksons)
10. TOUCH
    (Con Funk Shun)

JAZZ ALBUMS

1. WINELIGHT
   (Grover Washington Jr.)
2. VOICES IN THE RAIN
   (Joe Sample)
3. LATE NIGHT GUITAR
   (Earl Klugh)
4. GIVE ME THE NIGHT
   (George Benson)
5. CARNAVAL
   (Spyro Gyra)
6. MAGIC
   (Tom Browne)
7. ALL AROUND THE TOWN
   (Bob James)
8. INHERIT THE WIND
   (Wilton Felder)
9. NIGHT PASSAGE
   (Weather Report)
10. ODORI
    (Hiroshima)

COUNTRY SINGLES

1. WHO'S CHEATIN' WHO
   (Charly McClain)
2. SOUTHERN RAINS
   (Mel Tillis)
3. I'LL BE THERE IF YOU EVER WANT ME
   (Gail Davies)
4. 1959
   (John Anderson)
5. I FEEL LIKE LOVING YOU AGAIN
   (T.G. Sheppard)
6. ARE YOU HAPPY BABY
   (Dottie West)
7. DON'T YOU EVER GET TIRED OF HURTING
   ME
   (Willie Nelson and Ray Price)
8. CAN I SEE YOU TONIGHT
   (Tanya Tucker)
9. HILLBILLY GIRL WITH THE BLUES
   (Lacy J. Dalton)
10. ANGEL FLYING TOO CLOSE TO THE
    GROUND
    (Willie Nelson)

COUNTRY ALBUMS

1. KENNY ROGERS' GREATEST HITS
   (Kenny Rogers)
2. HORIZON
   (Eddie Rabbitt)
3. ANNE MURRAY'S GREATEST HITS
   (Anne Murray)
4. 9 TO 5 AND ODD JOBS
   (Dolly Parton)
5. HONEYSUCKLE ROSE
   (Willie Nelson and Family)
6. I BELIEVE IN YOU
   (Don Williams)
7. THE OAK RIDGE BOYS' GREATEST HITS
   (The Oak Ridge Boys)
8. URBAN COWBOY
   (Original Soundtrack)
9. RONNIE MILSAP'S GREATEST HITS
   (Ronnie Milsap)
10. GREATEST HITS
    (Willie Nelson)

FEBRUARY 28, 1981

POP SINGLES

1. 9 TO 5
   (Dolly Parton)
2. CELEBRATION
   (Kool and the Gang)
3. I LOVE A RAINY NIGHT
   (Eddie Rabbitt)
4. KEEP ON LOVING YOU
   (R.E.O. Speedwagon)
5. WOMAN
   (John Lennon)
6. THE TIDE IS HIGH
   (Blondie)
7. THE BEST OF TIMES
   (Styx)
8. HELLO AGAIN (LOVE THEME FROM THE JAZZ SINGER)
   (Neil Diamond)
9. SAME OLDE LANG SYNE
   (Dan Fogelberg)
10. RAPTURE
    (Blondie)

POP ALBUMS

1. HI INFIDELITY
   (R.E.O. Speedwagon)
2. DOUBLE FANTASY
   (John Lennon and Yoko Ono)
3. THE JAZZ SINGER
   (Original Soundtrack)
4. PARADISE THEATER
   (Styx)
5. KENNY ROGERS' GREATEST HITS
   (Kenny Rogers)
6. CRIMES OF PASSION
   (Pat Benatar)
7. GUILTY
   (Barbra Streisand)
8. BACK IN BLACK
   (AC/DC)
9. AUTOAMERICAN
   (Blondie)
10. GAUCHO
    (Steely Dan)

BLACK SINGLES

1. DON'T STOP THE MUSIC
   (Yarbrough and Peoples)
2. BURN RUBBER
   (The Gap Band)
3. IT'S A LOVE THING
   (Whispers)
4. FANTASTIC VOYAGE
   (Lakeside)
5. I JUST LOVE THE MAN
   (The Jones Girls)
6. TOGETHER
   (Tierra)
7. CELEBRATION
   (Kool and the Gang)
8. WATCHING YOU
   (Slave)
9. I AIN'T GONNA STAND FOR IT
   (Stevie Wonder)
10. TOO TIGHT
    (Con Funk Shun)

BLACK ALBUMS

1. GAP BAND III
   (The Gap Band)
2. HOTTER THAN JULY
   (Stevie Wonder)
3. THE TWO OF US
   (Yarbrough and Peoples)
4. FANTASTIC VOYAGE
   (Lakeside)

5. IMAGINATION
   (Whispers)
6. CELEBRATE
   (Kool and the Gang)
7. IN OUR LIFETIME
   (Marvin Gaye)
8. STONE JAM
   (Slave)
9. WINELIGHT
   (Grover Washington Jr.)
10. TOUCH
    (Con Funk Shun)

JAZZ ALBUMS

1. WINELIGHT
   (Grover Washington Jr.)
2. VOICES IN THE RAIN
   (Joe Sample)
3. LATE NIGHT GUITAR
   (Earl Klugh)
4. GIVE ME THE NIGHT
   (George Benson)
5. MAGIC
   (Tom Browne)
6. ALL AROUND THE TOWN
   (Bob James)
7. CARNAVAL
   (Spyro Gyra)
8. INHERIT THE WIND
   (Wilton Felder)
9. NIGHT PASSAGE
   (Weather Report)
10. ODORI
    (Hiroshima)

COUNTRY SINGLES

1. ARE YOU HAPPY BABY
   (Dottie West)
2. SOUTHERN RAINS
   (Mel Tillis)
3. WHO'S CHEATIN' WHO
   (Charly McClain)
4. ANGEL FLYING TOO CLOSE TO THE GROUND
   (Willie Nelson)
5. CAN I SEE YOU TONIGHT
   (Tanya Tucker)
6. I'LL BE THERE IF YOU EVER WANT ME
   (Gail Davies)
7. DO YOU LOVE AS GOOD AS YOU LOOK
   (The Bellamy Brothers)
8. HILLBILLY GIRL WITH THE BLUES
   (Lacy J. Dalton)
9. CUP OF TEA
   (Rex Allen Jr. and Margo Smith)
10. SILENT TREATMENT
    (Earl Thomas Conley)

COUNTRY ALBUMS

1. KENNY ROGERS' GREATEST HITS
   (Kenny Rogers)
2. HORIZON
   (Eddie Rabbitt)
3. 9 TO 5 AND ODD JOBS
   (Dolly Parton)
4. ANNE MURRAY'S GREATEST HITS
   (Anne Murray)
5. RONNIE MILSAP'S GREATEST HITS
   (Ronnie Milsap)
6. I BELIEVE IN YOU
   (Don Williams)
7. THE OAK RIDGE BOYS' GREATEST HITS
   (The Oak Ridge Boys)
8. HONEYSUCKLE ROSE
   (Willie Nelson and Family)
9. URBAN COWBOY
   (Original Soundtrack)
10. ROWDY
    (Hank Williams Jr.)

MARCH 7, 1981

POP SINGLES

1. KEEP ON LOVING YOU
   (R.E.O. Speedwagon)
2. 9 TO 5
   (Dolly Parton)
3. WOMAN
   (John Lennon)
4. CELEBRATION
   (Kool and the Gang)
5. RAPTURE
   (Blondie)
6. THE BEST OF TIMES
   (Styx)
7. I LOVE A RAINY NIGHT
   (Eddie Rabbitt)
8. HELLO AGAIN (LOVE THEME FROM THE JAZZ SINGER)
   (Neil Diamond)
9. CRYING
   (Don McLean)
10. THE TIDE IS HIGH
    (Blondie)

POP ALBUMS

1. HI INFIDELITY
   (R.E.O. Speedwagon)
2. PARADISE THEATER
   (Styx)
3. DOUBLE FANTASY
   (John Lennon and Yoko Ono)
4. THE JAZZ SINGER
   (Original Soundtrack)
5. KENNY ROGERS' GREATEST HITS
   (Kenny Rogers)
6. CRIMES OF PASSION
   (Pat Benatar)
7. GUILTY
   (Barbra Streisand)
8. BACK IN BLACK
   (AC/DC)
9. AUTOAMERICAN
   (Blondie)
10. ZENYATTA MONDATTA
    (The Police)

BLACK SINGLES

1. DON'T STOP THE MUSIC
   (Yarbrough and Peoples)
2. BURN RUBBER
   (The Gap Band)
3. IT'S A LOVE THING
   (Whispers)
4. FANTASTIC VOYAGE
   (Lakeside)
5. WATCHING YOU
   (Slave)
6. TOGETHER
   (Tierra)
7. I JUST LOVE THE MAN
   (The Jones Girls)
8. CELEBRATION
   (Kool and the Gang)
9. THIGHS HIGH (GRIP YOUR HIPS AND MOVE)
   (Tom Browne)
10. ALL AMERICAN GIRLS
    (Sister Sledge)

BLACK ALBUMS

1. GAP BAND III
   (The Gap Band)
2. HOTTER THAN JULY
   (Stevie Wonder)
3. THE TWO OF US
   (Yarbrough and Peoples)

4. FANTASTIC VOYAGE
   (Lakeside)
5. IMAGINATION
   (Whispers)
6. CELEBRATE
   (Kool and the Gang)
7. IN OUR LIFETIME
   (Marvin Gaye)
8. STONE JAM
   (Slave)
9. WINELIGHT
   (Grover Washington Jr.)
10. MAGIC
    (Tom Browne)

JAZZ ALBUMS

1. WINELIGHT
   (Grover Washington Jr.)
2. VOICES IN THE RAIN
   (Joe Sample)
3. MAGIC
   (Tom Browne)
4. ALL AROUND THE TOWN
   (Bob James)
5. GIVE ME THE NIGHT
   (George Benson)
6. CARNAVAL
   (Spyro Gyra)
7. LATE NIGHT GUITAR
   (Earl Klugh)
8. INHERIT THE WIND
   (Wilton Felder)
9. NIGHT PASSAGE
   (Weather Report)
10. ODORI
    (Hiroshima)

COUNTRY SINGLES

1. ANGEL FLYING TOO CLOSE TO THE
   GROUND
   (Willie Nelson)
2. DO YOU LOVE AS GOOD AS YOU LOOK
   (The Bellamy Brothers)
3. ARE YOU HAPPY BABY
   (Dottie West)
4. CAN I SEE YOU TONIGHT
   (Tanya Tucker)
5. GUITAR MAN
   (Elvis Presley)
6. SOUTHERN RAINS
   (Mel Tillis)
7. WANDERING EYES
   (Ronnie McDowell)
8. CUP OF TEA
   (Rex Allen Jr. and Margo Smith)
9. DRIFTER
   (Sylvia)
10. WHAT'S NEW WITH YOU
    (Con Hunley)

COUNTRY ALBUMS

1. KENNY ROGERS' GREATEST HITS
   (Kenny Rogers)
2. HORIZON
   (Eddie Rabbitt)
3. 9 TO 5 AND ODD JOBS
   (Dolly Parton)
4. ANNE MURRAY'S GREATEST HITS
   (Anne Murray)
5. RONNIE MILSAP'S GREATEST HITS
   (Ronnie Milsap)
6. I BELIEVE IN YOU
   (Don Williams)
7. THE OAK RIDGE BOYS' GREATEST HITS
   (The Oak Ridge Boys)
8. HONEYSUCKLE ROSE
   (Willie Nelson and Family)
9. ROWDY
   (Hank Williams Jr.)
10. GREATEST HITS
    (Waylon Jennings)

MARCH 14, 1981

POP SINGLES

1. 9 TO 5
   (Dolly Parton)
2. KEEP ON LOVING YOU
   (R.E.O. Speedwagon)
3. WOMAN
   (John Lennon)
4. CELEBRATION
   (Kool and the Gang)
5. I LOVE A RAINY NIGHT
   (Eddie Rabbitt)
6. THE BEST OF TIMES
   (Styx)
7. RAPTURE
   (Blondie)
8. HELLO AGAIN (LOVE THEME FROM THE
   JAZZ SINGER)
   (Neil Diamond)
9. THE TIDE IS HIGH
   (Blondie)
10. CRYING
    (Don McLean)

POP ALBUMS

1. HI INFIDELITY
   (R.E.O. Speedwagon)
2. PARADISE THEATER
   (Styx)
3. DOUBLE FANTASY
   (John Lennon and Yoko Ono)
4. THE JAZZ SINGER
   (Original Soundtrack)
5. KENNY ROGERS' GREATEST HITS
   (Kenny Rogers)
6. CRIMES OF PASSION
   (Pat Benatar)
7. GUILTY
   (Barbra Streisand)
8. BACK IN BLACK
   (AC/DC)
9. AUTOAMERICAN
   (Blondie)
10. ZENYATTA MONDATTA
    (The Police)

BLACK SINGLES

1. DON'T STOP THE MUSIC
   (Yarbrough and Peoples)
2. BURN RUBBER
   (The Gap Band)
3. IT'S A LOVE THING
   (Whispers)
4. WATCHING YOU
   (Slave)
5. FANTASTIC VOYAGE
   (Lakeside)
6. TOGETHER
   (Tierra)
7. THIGHS HIGH (GRIP YOUR HIPS AND
   MOVE)
   (Tom Browne)
8. ALL AMERICAN GIRLS
   (Sister Sledge)
9. I JUST LOVE THE MAN
   (The Jones Girls)
10. CELEBRATION
    (Kool and the Gang)

BLACK ALBUMS

1. GAP BAND III
   (The Gap Band)
2. THE TWO OF US
   (Yarbrough and Peoples)
3. HOTTER THAN JULY
   (Stevie Wonder)

4. IMAGINATION
   (Whispers)
5. CELEBRATE
   (Kool and the Gang)
6. FANTASTIC VOYAGE
   (Lakeside)
7. IN OUR LIFETIME
   (Marvin Gaye)
8. STONE JAM
   (Slave)
9. WINELIGHT
   (Grover Washington Jr.)
10. MAGIC
    (Tom Browne)

JAZZ ALBUMS

1. WINELIGHT
   (Grover Washington Jr.)
2. MAGIC
   (Tom Browne)
3. VOICES IN THE RAIN
   (Joe Sample)
4. ALL AROUND THE TOWN
   (Bob James)
5. GIVE ME THE NIGHT
   (George Benson)
6. CARNAVAL
   (Spyro Gyra)
7. LATE NIGHT GUITAR
   (Earl Klugh)
8. INHERIT THE WIND
   (Wilton Felder)
9. NIGHT PASSAGE
   (Weather Report)
10. MOUNTAIN DANCE
    (Dave Grusin)

COUNTRY SINGLES

1. DO YOU LOVE AS GOOD AS YOU LOOK
   (The Bellamy Brothers)
2. ANGEL FLYING TOO CLOSE TO THE
   GROUND
   (Willie Nelson)
3. GUITAR MAN
   (Elvis Presley)
4. CAN I SEE YOU TONIGHT
   (Tanya Tucker)
5. ARE YOU HAPPY BABY
   (Dottie West)
6. WANDERING EYES
   (Ronnie McDowell)
7. DRIFTER
   (Sylvia)
8. IF DRINKIN' DON'T KILL ME (HER MEMORY
   WILL)
   (George Jones)
9. THIRTY-NINE AND HOLDING
   (Jerry Lee Lewis)
10. WHAT'S NEW WITH YOU
    (Con Hunley)

COUNTRY ALBUMS

1. KENNY ROGERS' GREATEST HITS
   (Kenny Rogers)
2. 9 TO 5 AND ODD JOBS
   (Dolly Parton)
3. HORIZON
   (Eddie Rabbitt)
4. ANNE MURRAY'S GREATEST HITS
   (Anne Murray)
5. RONNIE MILSAP'S GREATEST HITS
   (Ronnie Milsap)
6. EVANGELINE
   (Emmylou Harris)
7. I BELIEVE IN YOU
   (Don Williams)
8. THE OAK RIDGE BOYS' GREATEST HITS
   (The Oak Ridge Boys)
9. ROWDY
   (Hank Williams Jr.)
10. HONEYSUCKLE ROSE
    (Willie Nelson and Family)

MARCH 21, 1981

POP SINGLES

1. KEEP ON LOVING YOU
   (R.E.O. Speedwagon)
2. 9 TO 5
   (Dolly Parton)
3. WOMAN
   (John Lennon)
4. CELEBRATION
   (Kool and the Gang)
5. RAPTURE
   (Blondie)
6. THE BEST OF TIMES
   (Styx)
7. I LOVE A RAINY NIGHT
   (Eddie Rabbitt)
8. HELLO AGAIN (LOVE THEME FROM THE JAZZ SINGER)
   (Neil Diamond)
9. CRYING
   (Don McLean)
10. THE TIDE IS HIGH
    (Blondie)

POP ALBUMS

1. HI INFIDELITY
   (R.E.O. Speedwagon)
2. PARADISE THEATER
   (Styx)
3. DOUBLE FANTASY
   (John Lennon and Yoko Ono)
4. THE JAZZ SINGER
   (Original Soundtrack)
5. KENNY ROGERS' GREATEST HITS
   (Kenny Rogers)
6. CRIMES OF PASSION
   (Pat Benatar)
7. GUILTY
   (Barbra Streisand)
8. BACK IN BLACK
   (AC/DC)
9. AUTOAMERICAN
   (Blondie)
10. ZENYATTA MONDATTA
    (The Police)

BLACK SINGLES

1. DON'T STOP THE MUSIC
   (Yarbrough and Peoples)
2. IT'S A LOVE THING
   (Whispers)
3. BURN RUBBER
   (The Gap Band)
4. WATCHING YOU
   (Slave)
5. THIGHS HIGH (GRIP YOUR HIPS AND MOVE)
   (Tom Browne)
6. FANTASTIC VOYAGE
   (Lakeside)
7. ALL AMERICAN GIRLS
   (Sister Sledge)
8. BEING WITH YOU
   (Smokey Robinson)
9. TOGETHER
   (Tierra)
10. JUST THE TWO OF US
    (Grover Washington Jr.)

BLACK ALBUMS

1. GAP BAND III
   (The Gap Band)
2. THE TWO OF US
   (Yarbrough and Peoples)
3. HOTTER THAN JULY
   (Stevie Wonder)
4. IMAGINATION
   (Whispers)

5. FANTASTIC VOYAGE
   (Lakeside)
6. IN OUR LIFETIME
   (Marvin Gaye)
7. WINELIGHT
   (Grover Washington Jr.)
8. MAGIC
   (Tom Browne)
9. STONE JAM
   (Slave)
10. THREE FOR LOVE
    (Shalamar)

JAZZ ALBUMS

1. WINELIGHT
   (Grover Washington Jr.)
2. MAGIC
   (Tom Browne)
3. VOICES IN THE RAIN
   (Joe Sample)
4. ALL AROUND THE TOWN
   (Bob James)
5. CARNAVAL
   (Spyro Gyra)
6. GIVE ME THE NIGHT
   (George Benson)
7. LATE NIGHT GUITAR
   (Earl Klugh)
8. MOUNTAIN DANCE
   (Dave Grusin)
9. IT'S JUST THE WAY I FEEL
   (Gene Dunlap)
10. 'NARD
    (Bernard Wright)

COUNTRY SINGLES

1. GUITAR MAN
   (Elvis Presley)
2. ANGEL FLYING TOO CLOSE TO THE GROUND
   (Willie Nelson)
3. DO YOU LOVE AS GOOD AS YOU LOOK
   (The Bellamy Brothers)
4. DRIFTER
   (Sylvia)
5. WANDERING EYES
   (Ronnie McDowell)
6. THIRTY-NINE AND HOLDING
   (Jerry Lee Lewis)
7. YOU'RE THE REASON GOD MADE OKLAHOMA
   (David Frizzell and Shelly West)
8. IF DRINKIN' DON'T KILL ME (HER MEMORY WILL)
   (George Jones)
9. TEXAS WOMAN
   (Hank Williams Jr.)
10. WHAT I HAD WITH YOU
    (John Conlee)

COUNTRY ALBUMS

1. KENNY ROGERS' GREATEST HITS
   (Kenny Rogers)
2. 9 TO 5 AND ODD JOBS
   (Dolly Parton)
3. HORIZON
   (Eddie Rabbitt)
4. ANNE MURRAY'S GREATEST HITS
   (Anne Murray)
5. RONNIE MILSAP'S GREATEST HITS
   (Ronnie Milsap)
6. EVANGELINE
   (Emmylou Harris)
7. THE OAK RIDGE BOYS' GREATEST HITS
   (The Oak Ridge Boys)
8. ROWDY
   (Hank Williams Jr.)
9. I BELIEVE IN YOU
   (Don Williams)
10. HONEYSUCKLE ROSE
    (Willie Nelson and Family)

MARCH 28, 1981

POP SINGLES

1. 9 TO 5
   (Dolly Parton)
2. WOMAN
   (John Lennon)
3. RAPTURE
   (Blondie)
4. CELEBRATION
   (Kool and the Gang)
5. KEEP ON LOVING YOU
   (R.E.O. Speedwagon)
6. THE BEST OF TIMES
   (Styx)
7. KISS ON MY LIST
   (Daryl Hall and John Oates)
8. I LOVE A RAINY NIGHT
   (Eddie Rabbitt)
9. CRYING
   (Don McLean)
10. JUST THE TWO OF US
    (Grover Washington Jr.)

POP ALBUMS

1. HI INFIDELITY
   (R.E.O. Speedwagon)
2. PARADISE THEATER
   (Styx)
3. THE JAZZ SINGER
   (Original Soundtrack)
4. KENNY ROGERS' GREATEST HITS
   (Kenny Rogers)
5. DOUBLE FANTASY
   (John Lennon and Yoko Ono)
6. CRIMES OF PASSION
   (Pat Benatar)
7. GUILTY
   (Barbra Streisand)
8. BACK IN BLACK
   (AC/DC)
9. AUTOAMERICAN
   (Blondie)
10. ZENYATTA MONDATTA
    (The Police)

BLACK SINGLES

1. DON'T STOP THE MUSIC
   (Yarbrough and Peoples)
2. IT'S A LOVE THING
   (Whispers)
3. BURN RUBBER
   (The Gap Band)
4. THIGHS HIGH (GRIP YOUR HIPS AND MOVE)
   (Tom Browne)
5. WATCHING YOU
   (Slave)
6. BEING WITH YOU
   (Smokey Robinson)
7. ALL AMERICAN GIRLS
   (Sister Sledge)
8. JUST THE TWO OF US
   (Grover Washington Jr.)
9. SUKIYAKI
   (A Taste of Honey)
10. BON BON VIE (GIMME THE GOOD LIFE)
    (T.S. Monk)

BLACK ALBUMS

1. GAP BAND III
   (The Gap Band)
2. THE TWO OF US
   (Yarbrough and Peoples)
3. IMAGINATION
   (Whispers)
4. HOTTER THAN JULY
   (Stevie Wonder)

5. IN OUR LIFETIME
   (Marvin Gaye)
6. WINELIGHT
   (Grover Washington Jr.)
7. FANTASTIC VOYAGE
   (Lakeside)
8. BEING WITH YOU
   (Smokey Robinson)
9. THREE FOR LOVE
   (Shalamar)
10. MAGIC
    (Tom Browne)

JAZZ ALBUMS

1. WINELIGHT
   (Grover Washington Jr.)
2. MAGIC
   (Tom Browne)
3. ALL AROUND THE TOWN
   (Bob James)
4. VOICES IN THE RAIN
   (Joe Sample)
5. CARNAVAL
   (Spyro Gyra)
6. MOUNTAIN DANCE
   (Dave Grusin)
7. GIVE ME THE NIGHT
   (George Benson)
8. LATE NIGHT GUITAR
   (Earl Klugh)
9. 'NARD
   (Bernard Wright)
10. IT'S JUST THE WAY I FEEL
    (Gene Dunlap)

COUNTRY SINGLES

1. DRIFTER
   (Sylvia)
2. YOU'RE THE REASON GOD MADE
   OKLAHOMA
   (David Frizzell and Shelly West)
3. TEXAS WOMEN
   (Hank Williams Jr.)
4. THIRTY-NINE AND HOLDING
   (Jerry Lee Lewis)
5. OLD FLAME
   (Alabama)
6. PICKIN' UP STRANGERS
   (Johnny Lee)
7. GUITAR MAN
   (Elvis Presley)
8. IF DRINKIN' DON'T KILL ME (HER MEMORY
   WILL)
   (George Jones)
9. SOMETHIN' ON THE RADIO
   (Jacky Ward)
10. WHAT I HAD WITH YOU
    (John Conlee)

COUNTRY ALBUMS

1. KENNY ROGERS' GREATEST HITS
   (Kenny Rogers)
2. HORIZON
   (Eddie Rabbitt)
3. 9 TO 5 AND ODD JOBS
   (Dolly Parton)
4. ANNE MURRAY'S GREATEST HITS
   (Anne Murray)
5. RONNIE MILSAP'S GREATEST HITS
   (Ronnie Milsap)
6. EVANGELINE
   (Emmylou Harris)
7. SOMEWHERE OVER THE RAINBOW
   (Willie Nelson)
8. ROWDY
   (Hank Williams Jr.)
9. THE OAK RIDGE BOYS' GREATEST HITS
   (The Oak Ridge Boys)
10. FEELS SO RIGHT
    (Alabama)

APRIL 4, 1981

POP SINGLES

1. RAPTURE
   (Blondie)
2. WOMAN
   (John Lennon)
3. 9 TO 5
   (Dolly Parton)
4. CELEBRATION
   (Kool and the Gang)
5. KISS ON MY LIST
   (Daryl Hall and John Oates)
6. KEEP ON LOVING YOU
   (R.E.O. Speedwagon)
7. THE BEST OF TIMES
   (Styx)
8. MORNING TRAIN (NINE TO FIVE)
   (Sheena Easton)
9. JUST THE TWO OF US
   (Grover Washington Jr.)
10. CRYING
    (Don McLean)

POP ALBUMS

1. HI INFIDELITY
   (R.E.O. Speedwagon)
2. PARADISE THEATER
   (Styx)
3. THE JAZZ SINGER
   (Original Soundtrack)
4. KENNY ROGERS' GREATEST HITS
   (Kenny Rogers)
5. DOUBLE FANTASY
   (John Lennon and Yoko Ono)
6. CRIMES OF PASSION
   (Pat Benatar)
7. MOVING PICTURES
   (Rush)
8. GUILTY
   (Barbra Streisand)
9. BACK IN BLACK
   (AC/DC)
10. ARC OF A DIVER
    (Steve Winwood)

BLACK SINGLES

1. DON'T STOP THE MUSIC
   (Yarbrough and Peoples)
2. IT'S A LOVE THING
   (Whispers)
3. BURN RUBBER
   (The Gap Band)
4. THIGHS HIGH (GRIP YOUR HIPS AND
   MOVE)
   (Tom Browne)
5. BEING WITH YOU
   (Smokey Robinson)
6. JUST THE TWO OF US
   (Grover Washington Jr.)
7. SUKIYAKI
   (A Taste of Honey)
8. WATCHING YOU
   (Slave)
9. ALL AMERICAN GIRLS
   (Sister Sledge)
10. BON BON VIE (GIMME THE GOOD LIFE)
    (T.S. Monk)

BLACK ALBUMS

1. GAP BAND III
   (The Gap Band)
2. THE TWO OF US
   (Yarbrough and Peoples)
3. IMAGINATION
   (Whispers)
4. HOTTER THAN JULY
   (Stevie Wonder)

5. GRAND SLAM
   (Isley Brothers)
6. WINELIGHT
   (Grover Washington Jr.)
7. BEING WITH YOU
   (Smokey Robinson)
8. IN OUR LIFETIME
   (Marvin Gaye)
9. MAGIC MAN
   (Robert Winters and Fall)
10. THREE FOR LOVE
    (Shalamar)

JAZZ ALBUMS

1. WINELIGHT
   (Grover Washington Jr.)
2. MAGIC
   (Tom Browne)
3. MOUNTAIN DANCE
   (Dave Grusin)
4. ALL AROUND THE TOWN
   (Bob James)
5. VOICES IN THE RAIN
   (Joe Sample)
6. THE DUDE
   (Quincy Jones)
7. GIVE ME THE NIGHT
   (George Benson)
8. LATE NIGHT GUITAR
   (Earl Klugh)
9. 'NARD
   (Bernard Wright)
10. CARNAVAL
    (Spyro Gyra)

COUNTRY SINGLES

1. YOU'RE THE REASON GOD MADE
   OKLAHOMA
   (David Frizzell and Shelly West)
2. TEXAS WOMEN
   (Hank Williams Jr.)
3. OLD FLAME
   (Alabama)
4. THIRTY-NINE AND HOLDING
   (Jerry Lee Lewis)
5. PICKIN' UP STRANGERS
   (Johnny Lee)
6. DRIFTER
   (Sylvia)
7. LOVIN' WHAT YOUR LOVIN' DOES TO ME
   (Conway Twitty and Loretta Lynn)
8. A HEADACHE TOMORROW (OR A
   HEARTACHE TONIGHT)
   (Mickey Gilley)
9. SOMETHIN' ON THE RADIO
   (Jacky Ward)
10. I'M GONNA LOVE YOU BACK TO LOVIN' ME
    AGAIN
    (Joe Stampley)

COUNTRY ALBUMS

1. KENNY ROGERS' GREATEST HITS
   (Kenny Rogers)
2. GREATEST HITS
   (Willie Nelson)
3. HORIZON
   (Eddie Rabbitt)
4. 9 TO 5 AND ODD JOBS
   (Dolly Parton)
5. RONNIE MILSAP'S GREATEST HITS
   (Ronnie Milsap)
6. ANNE MURRAY'S GREATEST HITS
   (Anne Murray)
7. FEELS SO RIGHT
   (Alabama)
8. EVANGELINE
   (Emmylou Harris)
9. LEATHER AND LACE
   (Waylon Jennings and Jessi Colter)
10. ROWDY
    (Hank Williams Jr.)

APRIL 11, 1981

POP SINGLES

1. RAPTURE
   (Blondie)
2. WOMAN
   (John Lennon)
3. KISS ON MY LIST
   (Daryl Hall and John Oates)
4. MORNING TRAIN (NINE TO FIVE)
   (Sheena Easton)
5. 9 TO 5
   (Dolly Parton)
6. KEEP ON LOVING YOU
   (R.E.O. Speedwagon)
7. CELEBRATION
   (Kool and the Gang)
8. JUST THE TWO OF US
   (Grover Washington Jr.)
9. ANGEL OF THE MORNING
   (Juice Newton)
10. THE BEST OF TIMES
    (Styx)

POP ALBUMS

1. HI INFIDELITY
   (R.E.O. Speedwagon)
2. PARADISE THEATER
   (Styx)
3. THE JAZZ SINGER
   (Original Soundtrack)
4. KENNY ROGERS' GREATEST HITS
   (Kenny Rogers)
5. DOUBLE FANTASY
   (John Lennon and Yoko Ono)
6. FACE DANCES
   (The Who)
7. MOVING PICTURES
   (Rush)
8. CRIMES OF PASSION
   (Pat Benatar)
9. ARC OF A DIVER
   (Steve Winwood)
10. GUILTY
    (Barbra Streisand)

BLACK SINGLES

1. BEING WITH YOU
   (Smokey Robinson)
2. DON'T STOP THE MUSIC
   (Yarbrough and Peoples)
3. BURN RUBBER
   (The Gap Band)
4. IT'S A LOVE THING
   (Whispers)
5. JUST THE TWO OF US
   (Grover Washington Jr.)
6. SUKIYAKI
   (A Taste of Honey)
7. THIGHS HIGH (GRIP YOUR HIPS AND MOVE)
   (Tom Browne)
8. WHEN LOVE CALLS
   (Atlantic Starr)
9. HOW 'BOUT US
   (Champaign)
10. MAGIC MAN
    (Robert Winters and Fall)

BLACK ALBUMS

1. GAP BAND III
   (The Gap Band)
2. THE TWO OF US
   (Yarbrough and Peoples)
3. WINELIGHT
   (Grover Washington Jr.)
4. GRAND SLAM
   (Isley Brothers)

---

5. BEING WITH YOU
   (Smokey Robinson)
6. IMAGINATION
   (Whispers)
7. HOTTER THAN JULY
   (Stevie Wonder)
8. RADIANT
   (Atlantic Starr)
9. MAGIC
   (Tom Browne)
10. THREE FOR LOVE
    (Shalamar)

JAZZ ALBUMS

1. WINELIGHT
   (Grover Washington Jr.)
2. MAGIC
   (Tom Browne)
3. MOUNTAIN DANCE
   (Dave Grusin)
4. VOICES IN THE RAIN
   (Joe Sample)
5. ALL AROUND THE TOWN
   (Bob James)
6. THE DUDE
   (Quincy Jones)
7. 'NARD
   (Bernard Wright)
8. CARNAVAL
   (Spyro Gyra)
9. LATE NIGHT GUITAR
   (Earl Klugh)
10. GIVE ME THE NIGHT
    (George Benson)

COUNTRY SINGLES

1. OLD FLAME
   (Alabama)
2. TEXAS WOMEN
   (Hank Williams Jr.)
3. PICKIN' UP STRANGERS
   (Johnny Lee)
4. YOU'RE THE REASON GOD MADE OKLAHOMA
   (David Frizzell and Shelly West)
5. A HEADACHE TOMORROW (OR A HEARTACHE TONIGHT)
   (Mickey Gilley)
6. LOVIN' WHAT YOUR LOVIN' DOES TO ME
   (Conway Twitty and Loretta Lynn)
7. FALLING AGAIN
   (Don Williams)
8. LOVE IS FAIR/SOMETIME, SOMEWHERE, SOMEHOW
   (Barbara Mandrell)
9. HOOKED ON MUSIC
   (Mac Davis)
10. TAKE IT EASY
    (Crystal Gayle)

COUNTRY ALBUMS

1. KENNY ROGERS' GREATEST HITS
   (Kenny Rogers)
2. SOMEWHERE OVER THE RAINBOW
   (Willie Nelson)
3. HORIZON
   (Eddie Rabbitt)
4. 9 TO 5 AND ODD JOBS
   (Dolly Parton)
5. RONNIE MILSAP'S GREATEST HITS
   (Ronnie Milsap)
6. LEATHER AND LACE
   (Waylon Jennings and Jessi Colter)
7. FEELS SO RIGHT
   (Alabama)
8. ANNE MURRAY'S GREATEST HITS
   (Anne Murray)
9. EVANGELINE
   (Emmylou Harris)
10. ROWDY
    (Hank Williams Jr.)

APRIL 18, 1981

POP SINGLES

1. KISS ON MY LIST
   (Daryl Hall and John Oates)
2. MORNING TRAIN (NINE TO FIVE)
   (Sheena Easton)
3. RAPTURE
   (Blondie)
4. ANGEL OF THE MORNING
   (Juice Newton)
5. 9 TO 5
   (Dolly Parton)
6. JUST THE TWO OF US
   (Grover Washington Jr.)
7. KEEP ON LOVING YOU
   (R.E.O. Speedwagon)
8. BEING WITH YOU
   (Smokey Robinson)
9. WHILE YOU SEE A CHANCE
   (Steve Winwood)
10. WOMAN
    (John Lennon)

POP ALBUMS

1. HI INFIDELITY
   (R.E.O. Speedwagon)
2. PARADISE THEATER
   (Styx)
3. FACE DANCES
   (The Who)
4. KENNY ROGERS' GREATEST HITS
   (Kenny Rogers)
5. MOVING PICTURES
   (Rush)
6. DOUBLE FANTASY
   (John Lennon and Yoko Ono)
7. THE JAZZ SINGER
   (Original Soundtrack)
8. ARC OF A DIVER
   (Steve Winwood)
9. CRIMES OF PASSION
   (Pat Benatar)
10. WINELIGHT
    (Grover Washington Jr.)

BLACK SINGLES

1. BEING WITH YOU
   (Smokey Robinson)
2. JUST THE TWO OF US
   (Grover Washington Jr.)
3. WHEN LOVE CALLS
   (Atlantic Starr)
4. SUKIYAKI
   (A Taste of Honey)
5. IT'S A LOVE THING
   (Whispers)
6. DON'T STOP THE MUSIC
   (Yarbrough and Peoples)
7. HOW 'BOUT US
   (Champaign)
8. BURN RUBBER
   (The Gap Band)
9. AI NO CORRIDA
   (Quincy Jones)
10. MAGIC MAN
    (Robert Winters and Fall)

BLACK ALBUMS

1. GAP BAND III
   (The Gap Band)
2. WINELIGHT
   (Grover Washington Jr.)
3. BEING WITH YOU
   (Smokey Robinson)
4. THE TWO OF US
   (Yarbrough and Peoples)

5. GRAND SLAM
 (Isley Brothers)
6. IMAGINATION
 (Whispers)
7. THE DUDE
 (Quincy Jones)
8. RADIANT
 (Atlantic Starr)
9. MAGIC
 (Tom Browne)
10. THREE FOR LOVE
 (Shalamar)

JAZZ ALBUMS

1. WINELIGHT
 (Grover Washington Jr.)
2. MAGIC
 (Tom Browne)
3. MOUNTAIN DANCE
 (Dave Grusin)
4. VOICES IN THE RAIN
 (Joe Sample)
5. VOYEUR
 (David Sanborn)
6. THE DUDE
 (Quincy Jones)
7. ALL AROUND THE TOWN
 (Bob James)
8. 'NARD
 (Bernard Wright)
9. IT'S JUST THE WAY I FEEL
 (Gene Dunlap)
10. LATE NIGHT GUITAR
 (Earl Klugh)

COUNTRY SINGLES

1. OLD FLAME
 (Alabama)
2. A HEADACHE TOMORROW (OR A HEARTACHE TONIGHT)
 (Mickey Gilley)
3. PICKIN' UP STRANGERS
 (Johnny Lee)
4. TEXAS WOMEN
 (Hank Williams Jr.)
5. FALLING AGAIN
 (Don Williams)
6. HOOKED ON MUSIC
 (Mac Davis)
7. REST YOUR LOVE ON ME/I AM THE DREAMER
 (Conway Twitty)
8. LOVE IS FAIR/SOMETIME, SOMEWHERE, SOMEHOW
 (Barbara Mandrell)
9. LEONARD
 (Merle Haggard)
10. TAKE IT EASY
 (Crystal Gayle)

COUNTRY ALBUMS

1. KENNY ROGERS' GREATEST HITS
 (Kenny Rogers)
2. SOMEWHERE OVER THE RAINBOW
 (Willie Nelson)
3. HORIZON
 (Eddie Rabbitt)
4. 9 TO 5 AND ODD JOBS
 (Dolly Parton)
5. LEATHER AND LACE
 (Waylon Jennings and Jessi Colter)
6. RONNIE MILSAP'S GREATEST HITS
 (Ronnie Milsap)
7. FEELS SO RIGHT
 (Alabama)
8. EVANGELINE
 (Emmylou Harris)
9. ANNE MURRAY'S GREATEST HITS
 (Anne Murray)
10. SOMEBODY'S KNOCKIN'
 (Terri Gibbs)

APRIL 25, 1981

POP SINGLES

1. MORNING TRAIN (NINE TO FIVE)
 (Sheena Easton)
2. KISS ON MY LIST
 (Daryl Hall and John Oates)
3. ANGEL OF THE MORNING
 (Juice Newton)
4. RAPTURE
 (Blondie)
5. JUST THE TWO OF US
 (Grover Washington Jr.)
6. BEING WITH YOU
 (Smokey Robinson)
7. 9 TO 5
 (Dolly Parton)
8. KEEP ON LOVING YOU
 (R.E.O. Speedwagon)
9. WHILE YOU SEE A CHANCE
 (Steve Winwood)
10. SOMEBODY'S KNOCKIN'
 (Terri Gibbs)

POP ALBUMS

1. HI INFIDELITY
 (R.E.O. Speedwagon)
2. PARADISE THEATER
 (Styx)
3. FACE DANCES
 (The Who)
4. MOVING PICTURES
 (Rush)
5. KENNY ROGERS' GREATEST HITS
 (Kenny Rogers)
6. ARC OF A DIVER
 (Steve Winwood)
7. THE JAZZ SINGER
 (Original Soundtrack)
8. WINELIGHT
 (Grover Washington Jr.)
9. DOUBLE FANTASY
 (John Lennon and Yoko Ono)
10. CRIMES OF PASSION
 (Pat Benatar)

BLACK SINGLES

1. BEING WITH YOU
 (Smokey Robinson)
2. JUST THE TWO OF US
 (Grover Washington Jr.)
3. WHEN LOVE CALLS
 (Atlantic Starr)
4. SUKIYAKI
 (A Taste of Honey)
5. AI NO CORRIDA
 (Quincy Jones)
6. HOW 'BOUT US
 (Champaign)
7. IT'S A LOVE THING
 (Whispers)
8. A WOMAN NEEDS LOVE (JUST LIKE YOU DO)
 (Ray Parker Jr. and Raydio)
9. WHAT CHA GONNA DO FOR ME
 (Chaka Khan)
10. MAGIC MAN
 (Robert Winters and Fall)

BLACK ALBUMS

1. GAP BAND III
 (The Gap Band)
2. BEING WITH YOU
 (Smokey Robinson)
3. WINELIGHT
 (Grover Washington Jr.)
4. THE DUDE
 (Quincy Jones)

5. GRAND SLAM
 (Isley Brothers)
6. RADIANT
 (Atlantic Starr)
7. THE TWO OF US
 (Yarbrough and Peoples)
8. IMAGINATION
 (Whispers)
9. THREE FOR LOVE
 (Shalamar)
10. MAGIC
 (Tom Browne)

JAZZ ALBUMS

1. WINELIGHT
 (Grover Washington Jr.)
2. MAGIC
 (Tom Browne)
3. MOUNTAIN DANCE
 (Dave Grusin)
4. VOYEUR
 (David Sanborn)
5. VOICES IN THE RAIN
 (Joe Sample)
6. THE DUDE
 (Quincy Jones)
7. ALL AROUND THE TOWN
 (Bob James)
8. 'NARD
 (Bernard Wright)
9. GALAXIAN
 (Jeff Lorber Fusion)
10. IT'S JUST THE WAY I FEEL
 (Gene Dunlap)

COUNTRY SINGLES

1. A HEADACHE TOMORROW (OR A HEARTACHE TONIGHT)
 (Mickey Gilley)
2. FALLING AGAIN
 (Don Williams)
3. PICKIN' UP STRANGERS
 (Johnny Lee)
4. REST YOUR LOVE ON ME/I AM THE DREAMER
 (Conway Twitty)
5. HOOKED ON MUSIC
 (Mac Davis)
6. OLD FLAME
 (Alabama)
7. I LOVED 'EM EVERY ONE
 (T.G. Sheppard)
8. ROLL ON, MISSISSIPPI
 (Charley Pride)
9. LEONARD
 (Merle Haggard)
10. SEVEN YEAR ACHE
 (Rosanne Cash)

COUNTRY ALBUMS

1. KENNY ROGERS' GREATEST HITS
 (Kenny Rogers)
2. SOMEWHERE OVER THE RAINBOW
 (Willie Nelson)
3. HORIZON
 (Eddie Rabbitt)
4. 9 TO 5 AND ODD JOBS
 (Dolly Parton)
5. LEATHER AND LACE
 (Waylon Jennings and Jessi Colter)
6. FEELS SO RIGHT
 (Alabama)
7. RONNIE MILSAP'S GREATEST HITS
 (Ronnie Milsap)
8. EVANGELINE
 (Emmylou Harris)
9. ANNE MURRAY'S GREATEST HITS
 (Anne Murray)
10. SOMEBODY'S KNOCKIN'
 (Terri Gibbs)

MAY 2, 1981

POP SINGLES

1. MORNING TRAIN (NINE TO FIVE)
   (Sheena Easton)
2. ANGEL OF THE MORNING
   (Juice Newton)
3. KISS ON MY LIST
   (Daryl Hall and John Oates)
4. BEING WITH YOU
   (Smokey Robinson)
5. JUST THE TWO OF US
   (Grover Washington Jr.)
6. RAPTURE
   (Blondie)
7. TAKE IT ON THE RUN
   (R.E.O. Speedwagon)
8. KEEP ON LOVING YOU
   (R.E.O. Speedwagon)
9. WHILE YOU SEE A CHANCE
   (Steve Winwood)
10. SOMEBODY'S KNOCKIN'
    (Terri Gibbs)

POP ALBUMS

1. HI INFIDELITY
   (R.E.O. Speedwagon)
2. PARADISE THEATER
   (Styx)
3. FACE DANCES
   (The Who)
4. MOVING PICTURES
   (Rush)
5. ARC OF A DIVER
   (Steve Winwood)
6. DIRTY DEEDS DONE DIRT CHEAP
   (AC/DC)
7. WINELIGHT
   (Grover Washington Jr.)
8. KENNY ROGERS' GREATEST HITS
   (Kenny Rogers)
9. THE JAZZ SINGER
   (Original Soundtrack)
10. ANOTHER TICKET
    (Eric Clapton)

BLACK SINGLES

1. BEING WITH YOU
   (Smokey Robinson)
2. JUST THE TWO OF US
   (Grover Washington Jr.)
3. WHEN LOVE CALLS
   (Atlantic Starr)
4. SUKIYAKI
   (A Taste of Honey)
5. AI NO CORRIDA
   (Quincy Jones)
6. HOW 'BOUT US
   (Champaign)
7. A WOMAN NEEDS LOVE (JUST LIKE YOU DO)
   (Ray Parker Jr. and Raydio)
8. WHAT CHA GONNA DO FOR ME
   (Chaka Khan)
9. MAGIC MAN
   (Robert Winters and Fall)
10. MAKE THAT MOVE
    (Shalamar)

BLACK ALBUMS

1. BEING WITH YOU
   (Smokey Robinson)
2. WINELIGHT
   (Grover Washington Jr.)
3. GAP BAND III
   (The Gap Band)
4. THE DUDE
   (Quincy Jones)

---

5. GLAND SLAM
   (Isley Brothers)
6. RADIANT
   (Atlantic Starr)
7. A WOMAN NEEDS LOVE
   (Ray Parker Jr. and Raydio)
8. THE TWO OF US
   (Yarbrough and Peoples)
9. THREE FOR LOVE
   (Shalamar)
10. IMAGINATION
    (Whispers)

JAZZ ALBUMS

1. WINELIGHT
   (Grover Washington Jr.)
2. VOYEUR
   (David Sanborn)
3. MAGIC
   (Tom Browne)
4. MOUNTAIN DANCE
   (Dave Grusin)
5. THE CLARKE/DUKE PROJECT
   (Stanley Clarke and George Duke)
6. GALAXIAN
   (Jeff Lorber Fusion)
7. VOICES IN THE RAIN
   (Joe Sample)
8. THE DUDE
   (Quincy Jones)
9. ALL MY REASONS
   (Noel Pointer)
10. ALL AROUND THE TOWN
    (Bob James)

COUNTRY SINGLES

1. FALLING AGAIN
   (Don Williams)
2. REST YOUR LOVE ON ME/I AM THE DREAMER
   (Conway Twitty)
3. I LOVED 'EM EVERY ONE
   (T.G. Sheppard)
4. HOOKED ON MUSIC
   (Mac Davis)
5. A HEADACHE TOMORROW (OR A HEARTACHE TONIGHT)
   (Mickey Gilley)
6. ROLL ON, MISSISSIPPI
   (Charley Pride)
7. SEVEN YEAR ACHE
   (Rosanne Cash)
8. AM I LOSING YOU/HE'LL HAVE TO GO
   (Ronnie Milsap)
9. MISTER SANDMAN
   (Emmylou Harris)
10. PICKIN' UP STRANGERS
    (Johnny Lee)

COUNTRY ALBUMS

1. KENNY ROGERS' GREATEST HITS
   (Kenny Rogers)
2. SOMEWHERE OVER THE RAINBOW
   (Willie Nelson)
3. HORIZON
   (Eddie Rabbitt)
4. FEELS SO RIGHT
   (Alabama)
5. 9 TO 5 AND ODD JOBS
   (Dolly Parton)
6. RONNIE MILSAP'S GREATEST HITS
   (Ronnie Milsap)
7. LEATHER AND LACE
   (Waylon Jennings and Jessi Colter)
8. JUICE
   (Juice Newton)
9. EVANGELINE
   (Emmylou Harris)
10. ANNE MURRAY'S GREATEST HITS
    (Anne Murray)

MAY 9, 1981

POP SINGLES

1. MORNING TRAIN (NINE TO FIVE)
   (Sheena Easton)
2. ANGEL OF THE MORNING
   (Juice Newton)
3. BEING WITH YOU
   (Smokey Robinson)
4. TAKE IT ON THE RUN
   (R.E.O. Speedwagon)
5. JUST THE TWO OF US
   (Grover Washington Jr.)
6. KISS ON MY LIST
   (Daryl Hall and John Oates)
7. BETTE DAVIS EYES
   (Kim Carnes)
8. RAPTURE
   (Blondie)
9. TOO MUCH TIME ON MY HANDS
   (Styx)
10. SOMEBODY'S KNOCKIN'
    (Terri Gibbs)

POP ALBUMS

1. HI INFIDELITY
   (R.E.O. Speedwagon)
2. PARADISE THEATER
   (Styx)
3. FACE DANCES
   (The Who)
4. DIRTY DEEDS DONE DIRT CHEAP
   (AC/DC)
5. ARC OF A DIVER
   (Steve Winwood)
6. MOVING PICTURES
   (Rush)
7. WINELIGHT
   (Grover Washington Jr.)
8. KENNY ROGERS' GREATEST HITS
   (Kenny Rogers)
9. THE JAZZ SINGER
   (Original Soundtrack)
10. ANOTHER TICKET
    (Eric Clapton)

BLACK SINGLES

1. WHEN LOVE CALLS
   (Atlantic Starr)
2. BEING WITH YOU
   (Smokey Robinson)
3. A WOMAN NEEDS LOVE (JUST LIKE YOU DO)
   (Ray Parker Jr. and Raydio)
4. SUKIYAKI
   (A Taste of Honey)
5. WHAT CHA GONNA DO FOR ME
   (Chaka Khan)
6. HOW 'BOUT US
   (Champaign)
7. JUST THE TWO OF US
   (Grover Washington Jr.)
8. AI NO CORRIDA
   (Quincy Jones)
9. MAKE THAT MOVE
   (Shalamar)
10. YEARNING
    (The Gap Band)

BLACK ALBUMS

1. WINELIGHT
   (Grover Washington Jr.)
2. BEING WITH YOU
   (Smokey Robinson)
3. GAP BAND III
   (The Gap Band)
4. THE DUDE
   (Quincy Jones)

5. A WOMAN NEEDS LOVE
   (Ray Parker Jr. and Raydio)
6. RADIANT
   (Atlantic Starr)
7. GRAND SLAM
   (Isley Brothers)
8. THREE FOR LOVE
   (Shalamar)
9. STREET SONGS
   (Rick James)
10. WHAT CHA GONNA DO FOR ME
    (Chaka Khan)

JAZZ ALBUMS

1. WINELIGHT
   (Grover Washington Jr.)
2. VOYEUR
   (David Sanborn)
3. MAGIC
   (Tom Browne)
4. THE CLARKE/DUKE PROJECT
   (Stanley Clarke and George Duke)
5. MOUNTAIN DANCE
   (Dave Grusin)
6. GALAXIAN
   (Jeff Lorber Fusion)
7. VOICES IN THE RAIN
   (Joe Sample)
8. THE DUDE
   (Quincy Jones)
9. ALL MY REASONS
   (Noel Pointer)
10. 'NARD
    (Bernard Wright)

COUNTRY SINGLES

1. I LOVED 'EM EVERY ONE
   (T.G. Sheppard)
2. REST YOUR LOVE ON ME/I AM THE
   DREAMER
   (Conway Twitty)
3. AM I LOSING YOU/HE'LL HAVE TO GO
   (Ronnie Milsap)
4. HOOKED ON MUSIC
   (Mac Davis)
5. ROLL ON, MISSISSIPPI
   (Charley Pride)
6. SEVEN YEAR ACHE
   (Rosanne Cash)
7. FALLING AGAIN
   (Don Williams)
8. HEY JOE (HEY MOE)
   (Moe Bandy and Joe Stampley)
9. MISTER SANDMAN
   (Emmylou Harris)
10. PRIDE
    (Janie Fricke)

COUNTRY ALBUMS

1. KENNY ROGERS' GREATEST HITS
   (Kenny Rogers)
2. SOMEWHERE OVER THE RAINBOW
   (Willie Nelson)
3. FEELS SO RIGHT
   (Alabama)
4. HORIZON
   (Eddie Rabbitt)
5. 9 TO 5 AND ODD JOBS
   (Dolly Parton)
6. JUICE
   (Juice Newton)
7. RONNIE MILSAP'S GREATEST HITS
   (Ronnie Milsap)
8. OUT WHERE THE BRIGHT LIGHTS ARE
   GLOWING
   (Ronnie Milsap)
9. LEATHER AND LACE
   (Waylon Jennings and Jessi Colter)
10. EVANGELINE
    (Emmylou Harris)

MAY 16, 1981

POP SINGLES

1. ANGEL OF THE MORNING
   (Juice Newton)
2. MORNING TRAIN (NINE TO FIVE)
   (Sheena Easton)
3. BEING WITH YOU
   (Smokey Robinson)
4. TAKE IT ON THE RUN
   (R.E.O. Speedwagon)
5. BETTE DAVIS EYES
   (Kim Carnes)
6. KISS ON MY LIST
   (Daryl Hall and John Oates)
7. TOO MUCH TIME ON MY HANDS
   (Styx)
8. JUST THE TWO OF US
   (Grover Washington Jr.)
9. SUKIYAKI
   (A Taste of Honey)
10. WATCHING THE WHEELS
    (John Lennon)

POP ALBUMS

1. HI INFIDELITY
   (R.E.O. Speedwagon)
2. PARADISE THEATER
   (Styx)
3. FACE DANCES
   (The Who)
4. DIRTY DEEDS DONE DIRT CHEAP
   (AC/DC)
5. ARC OF A DIVER
   (Steve Winwood)
6. KENNY ROGERS' GREATEST HITS
   (Kenny Rogers)
7. WINELIGHT
   (Grover Washington Jr.)
8. MOVING PICTURES
   (Rush)
9. THE JAZZ SINGER
   (Original Soundtrack)
10. BEING WITH YOU
    (Smokey Robinson)

BLACK SINGLES

1. WHAT CHA GONNA DO FOR ME
   (Chaka Khan)
2. WHEN LOVE CALLS
   (Atlantic Starr)
3. A WOMAN NEEDS LOVE (JUST LIKE YOU
   DO)
   (Ray Parker Jr. and Raydio)
4. BEING WITH YOU
   (Smokey Robinson)
5. SUKIYAKI
   (A Taste of Honey)
6. YEARNING
   (The Gap Band)
7. MAKE THAT MOVE
   (Shalamar)
8. HOW 'BOUT US
   (Champaign)
9. AI NO CORRIDA
   (Quincy Jones)
10. JUST THE TWO OF US
    (Grover Washington Jr.)

BLACK ALBUMS

1. BEING WITH YOU
   (Smokey Robinson)
2. WINELIGHT
   (Grover Washington Jr.)
3. THE DUDE
   (Quincy Jones)
4. A WOMAN NEEDS LOVE
   (Ray Parker Jr. and Raydio)

5. STREET SONGS
   (Rick James)
6. GAP BAND III
   (The Gap Band)
7. WHAT CHA GONNA DO FOR ME
   (Chaka Khan)
8. GRAND SLAM
   (Isley Brothers)
9. RADIANT
   (Atlantic Starr)
10. THREE FOR LOVE
    (Shalamar)

JAZZ ALBUMS

1. WINELIGHT
   (Grover Washington Jr.)
2. VOYEUR
   (David Sanborn)
3. THE CLARKE/DUKE PROJECT
   (Stanley Clarke and George Duke)
4. MAGIC
   (Tom Browne)
5. GALAXIAN
   (Jeff Lorber Fusion)
6. THE DUDE
   (Quincy Jones)
7. MOUNTAIN DANCE
   (Dave Grusin)
8. 'NARD
   (Bernard Wright)
9. RIT
   (Lee Ritenour)
10. VOICES IN THE RAIN
    (Joe Sample)

COUNTRY SINGLES

1. AM I LOSING YOU/HE'LL HAVE TO GO
   (Ronnie Milsap)
2. I LOVED 'EM EVERY ONE
   (T.G. Sheppard)
3. SEVEN YEAR ACHE
   (Rosanne Cash)
4. ROLL ON, MISSISSIPPI
   (Charley Pride)
5. ELVIRA
   (The Oak Ridge Boys)
6. REST YOUR LOVE ON ME/I AM THE
   DREAMER
   (Conway Twitty)
7. HEY JOE (HEY MOE)
   (Moe Bandy and Joe Stampley)
8. PRIDE
   (Janie Fricke)
9. FRIENDS/ANYWHERE THERE'S A JUKEBOX
   (Razzy Bailey)
10. I'M JUST AN OLD CHUNK OF COAL
    (John Anderson)

COUNTRY ALBUMS

1. KENNY ROGERS' GREATEST HITS
   (Kenny Rogers)
2. FEELS SO RIGHT
   (Alabama)
3. SOMEWHERE OVER THE RAINBOW
   (Willie Nelson)
4. HORIZON
   (Eddie Rabbitt)
5. 9 TO 5 AND ODD JOBS
   (Dolly Parton)
6. JUICE
   (Juice Newton)
7. RONNIE MILSAP'S GREATEST HITS
   (Ronnie Milsap)
8. OUT WHERE THE BRIGHT LIGHTS ARE
   GLOWING
   (Ronnie Milsap)
9. LEATHER AND LACE
   (Waylon Jennings and Jessi Colter)
10. I LOVE 'EM ALL
    (T.G. Sheppard)

MAY 23, 1981

POP SINGLES

1. BETTE DAVIS EYES
   (Kim Carnes)
2. BEING WITH YOU
   (Smokey Robinson)
3. TAKE IT ON THE RUN
   (R.E.O. Speedwagon)
4. MORNING TRAIN (NINE TO FIVE)
   (Sheena Easton)
5. STARS ON 45
   (Stars On)
6. ANGEL OF THE MORNING
   (Juice Newton)
7. A WOMAN NEEDS LOVE (JUST LIKE YOU DO)
   (Ray Parker Jr. and Raydio)
8. SUKIYAKI
   (A Taste of Honey)
9. WATCHING THE WHEELS
   (John Lennon)
10. LIVING INSIDE MYSELF
    (Gino Vannelli)

POP ALBUMS

1. HI INFIDELITY
   (R.E.O. Speedwagon)
2. PARADISE THEATER
   (Styx)
3. DIRTY DEEDS DONE DIRT CHEAP
   (AC/DC)
4. KENNY ROGERS' GREATEST HITS
   (Kenny Rogers)
5. ARC OF A DIVER
   (Steve Winwood)
6. FACE DANCES
   (The Who)
7. WINELIGHT
   (Grover Washington Jr.)
8. MOVING PICTURES
   (Rush)
9. BEING WITH YOU
   (Smokey Robinson)
10. BACK IN BLACK
    (AC/DC)

BLACK SINGLES

1. WHAT CHA GONNA DO FOR ME
   (Chaka Khan)
2. A WOMAN NEEDS LOVE (JUST LIKE YOU DO)
   (Ray Parker Jr. and Raydio)
3. BEING WITH YOU
   (Smokey Robinson)
4. WHEN LOVE CALLS
   (Atlantic Starr)
5. YEARNING
   (The Gap Band)
6. MAKE THAT MOVE
   (Shalamar)
7. SUKIYAKI
   (A Taste of Honey)
8. GIVE IT TO ME BABY
   (Rick James)
9. HOW 'BOUT US
   (Champaign)
10. PARADISE
    (Change)

BLACK ALBUMS

1. THE DUDE
   (Quincy Jones)
2. BEING WITH YOU
   (Smokey Robinson)
3. STREET SONGS
   (Rick James)

4. A WOMAN NEEDS LOVE
   (Ray Parker Jr. and Raydio)
5. WHAT CHA GONNA DO FOR ME
   (Chaka Khan)
6. GAP BAND III
   (The Gap Band)
7. WINELIGHT
   (Grover Washington Jr.)
8. THREE FOR LOVE
   (Shalamar)
9. RADIANT
   (Atlantic Starr)
10. GRAND SLAM
    (Isley Brothers)

JAZZ ALBUMS

1. WINELIGHT
   (Grover Washington Jr.)
2. VOYEUR
   (David Sanborn)
3. THE CLARKE/DUKE PROJECT
   (Stanley Clarke and George Duke)
4. MAGIC
   (Tom Browne)
5. GALAXIAN
   (Jeff Lorber Fusion)
6. THE DUDE
   (Quincy Jones)
7. MOUNTAIN DANCE
   (Dave Grusin)
8. RIT
   (Lee Ritenour)
9. 'NARD
   (Bernard Wright)
10. ALL MY REASONS
    (Noel Pointer)

COUNTRY SINGLES

1. SEVEN YEAR ACHE
   (Rosanne Cash)
2. ELVIRA
   (The Oak Ridge Boys)
3. AM I LOSING YOU/HE'LL HAVE TO GO
   (Ronnie Milsap)
4. I LOVED 'EM EVERY ONE
   (T.G. Sheppard)
5. FRIENDS/ANYWHERE THERE'S A JUKEBOX
   (Razzy Bailey)
6. I'M JUST AN OLD CHUNK OF COAL
   (John Anderson)
7. WHAT ARE WE DOIN' IN LOVE
   (Dottie West)
8. PRIDE
   (Janie Fricke)
9. LOUISIANA SATURDAY NIGHT
   (Mel McDaniel)
10. BUT YOU KNOW I LOVE YOU
    (Dolly Parton)

COUNTRY ALBUMS

1. KENNY ROGERS' GREATEST HITS
   (Kenny Rogers)
2. FEELS SO RIGHT
   (Alabama)
3. SOMEWHERE OVER THE RAINBOW
   (Willie Nelson)
4. HORIZON
   (Eddie Rabbitt)
5. 9 TO 5 AND ODD JOBS
   (Dolly Parton)
6. JUICE
   (Juice Newton)
7. RONNIE MILSAP'S GREATEST HITS
   (Ronnie Milsap)
8. SEVEN YEAR ACHE
   (Rosanne Cash)
9. LEATHER AND LACE
   (Waylon Jennings and Jessi Colter)
10. I LOVE 'EM ALL
    (T.G. Sheppard)

MAY 30, 1981

POP SINGLES

1. BETTE DAVIS EYES
   (Kim Carnes)
2. STARS ON 45
   (Stars On)
3. TAKE IT ON THE RUN
   (R.E.O. Speedwagon)
4. MORNING TRAIN (NINE TO FIVE)
   (Sheena Easton)
5. A WOMAN NEEDS LOVE (JUST LIKE YOU DO)
   (Ray Parker Jr. and Raydio)
6. ANGEL OF THE MORNING
   (Juice Newton)
7. BEING WITH YOU
   (Smokey Robinson)
8. SUKIYAKI
   (A Taste of Honey)
9. WATCHING THE WHEELS
   (John Lennon)
10. LIVING INSIDE MYSELF
    (Gino Vannelli)

POP ALBUMS

1. HI INFIDELITY
   (R.E.O. Speedwagon)
2. PARADISE THEATER
   (Styx)
3. DIRTY DEEDS DONE DIRT CHEAP
   (AC/DC)
4. KENNY ROGERS' GREATEST HITS
   (Kenny Rogers)
5. ARC OF A DIVER
   (Steve Winwood)
6. MOVING PICTURES
   (Rush)
7. WINELIGHT
   (Grover Washington Jr.)
8. FACE DANCES
   (The Who)
9. BEING WITH YOU
   (Smokey Robinson)
10. BACK IN BLACK
    (AC/DC)

BLACK SINGLES

1. A WOMAN NEEDS LOVE (JUST LIKE YOU DO)
   (Ray Parker Jr. and Raydio)
2. WHAT CHA GONNA DO FOR ME
   (Chaka Khan)
3. BEING WITH YOU
   (Smokey Robinson)
4. GIVE IT TO ME BABY
   (Rick James)
5. YEARNING
   (The Gap Band)
6. MAKE THAT MOVE
   (Shalamar)
7. WHEN LOVE CALLS
   (Atlantic Starr)
8. SUKIYAKI
   (A Taste of Honey)
9. PARADISE
   (Change)
10. YOUR LOVE IS ON THE ONE
    (Lakeside)

BLACK ALBUMS

1. THE DUDE
   (Quincy Jones)
2. STREET SONGS
   (Rick James)
3. A WOMAN NEEDS LOVE
   (Ray Parker Jr. and Raydio)

4. WHAT CHA GONNA DO FOR ME
 (Chaka Khan)
5. BEING WITH YOU
 (Smokey Robinson)
6. GAP BAND III
 (The Gap Band)
7. WINELIGHT
 (Grover Washington Jr.)
8. THREE FOR LOVE
 (Shalamar)
9. RADIANT
 (Atlantic Starr)
10. MIRACLES
 (Change)

JAZZ ALBUMS

1. WINELIGHT
 (Grover Washington Jr.)
2. THE CLARKE/DUKE PROJECT
 (Stanley Clarke and George Duke)
3. VOYEUR
 (David Sanborn)
4. MAGIC
 (Tom Browne)
5. GALAXIAN
 (Jeff Lorber Fusion)
6. THE DUDE
 (Quincy Jones)
7. RIT
 (Lee Ritenour)
8. MOUNTAIN DANCE
 (Dave Grusin)
9. 'NARD
 (Bernard Wright)
10. TARANTELLA
 (Chuck Mangione)

COUNTRY SINGLES

1. ELVIRA
 (The Oak Ridge Boys)
2. SEVEN YEAR ACHE
 (Rosanne Cash)
3. FRIENDS/ANYWHERE THERE'S A JUKEBOX
 (Razzy Bailey)
4. I'M JUST AN OLD CHUNK OF COAL
 (John Anderson)
5. WHAT ARE WE DOIN' IN LOVE
 (Dottie West)
6. BUT YOU KNOW I LOVE YOU
 (Dolly Parton)
7. LOUISIANA SATURDAY NIGHT
 (Mel McDaniel)
8. A MILLION OLD GOODBYES
 (Mel Tillis)
9. AM I LOSING YOU/HE'LL HAVE TO GO
 (Ronnie Milsap)
10. BLESSED ARE THE BELIEVERS
 (Anne Murray)

COUNTRY ALBUMS

1. KENNY ROGERS' GREATEST HITS
 (Kenny Rogers)
2. FEELS SO RIGHT
 (Alabama)
3. SOMEWHERE OVER THE RAINBOW
 (Willie Nelson)
4. HORIZON
 (Eddie Rabbitt)
5. JUICE
 (Juice Newton)
6. WHERE DO YOU GO WHEN YOU DREAM
 (Anne Murray)
7. SEVEN YEAR ACHE
 (Rosanne Cash)
8. 9 TO 5 AND ODD JOBS
 (Dolly Parton)
9. OUT WHERE THE BRIGHT LIGHTS ARE GLOWING
 (Ronnie Milsap)
10. EVANGELINE
 (Emmylou Harris)

JUNE 6, 1981

POP SINGLES

1. BETTE DAVIS EYES
 (Kim Carnes)
2. STARS ON 45
 (Stars On)
3. TAKE IT ON THE RUN
 (R.E.O. Speedwagon)
4. MORNING TRAIN (NINE TO FIVE)
 (Sheena Easton)
5. A WOMAN NEEDS LOVE (JUST LIKE YOU DO)
 (Ray Parker Jr. and Raydio)
6. ANGEL OF THE MORNING
 (Juice Newton)
7. BEING WITH YOU
 (Smokey Robinson)
8. SUKIYAKI
 (A Taste of Honey)
9. WATCHING THE WHEELS
 (John Lennon)
10. LIVING INSIDE MYSELF
 (Gino Vannelli)

POP ALBUMS

1. HI INFIDELITY
 (R.E.O. Speedwagon)
2. PARADISE THEATER
 (Styx)
3. DIRTY DEEDS DONE DIRT CHEAP
 (AC/DC)
4. FAIR WARNING
 (Van Halen)
5. KENNY ROGERS' GREATEST HITS
 (Kenny Rogers)
6. MOVING PICTURES
 (Rush)
7. HARD PROMISES
 (Tom Petty and the Heartbreakers)
8. MISTAKEN IDENTITY
 (Kim Carnes)
9. ARC OF A DIVER
 (Steve Winwood)
10. WHAT CHA GONNA DO FOR ME
 (Chaka Khan)

BLACK SINGLES

1. A WOMAN NEEDS LOVE (JUST LIKE YOU DO)
 (Ray Parker Jr. and Raydio)
2. GIVE IT TO ME BABY
 (Rick James)
3. WHAT CHA GONNA DO FOR ME
 (Chaka Khan)
4. BEING WITH YOU
 (Smokey Robinson)
5. YEARNING
 (The Gap Band)
6. MAKE THAT MOVE
 (Shalamar)
7. TWO HEARTS
 (Stephanie Mills)
8. WHEN LOVE CALLS
 (Atlantic Starr)
9. PARADISE
 (Change)
10. YOUR LOVE IS ON THE ONE
 (Lakeside)

BLACK ALBUMS

1. STREET SONGS
 (Rick James)
2. THE DUDE
 (Quincy Jones)
3. A WOMAN NEEDS LOVE
 (Ray Parker Jr. and Raydio)

4. WHAT CHA GONNA DO FOR ME
 (Chaka Khan)
5. BEING WITH YOU
 (Smokey Robinson)
6. GAP BAND III
 (The Gap Band)
7. STEPHANIE
 (Stephanie Mills)
8. THREE FOR LOVE
 (Shalamar)
9. RADIANT
 (Atlantic Starr)
10. WINELIGHT
 (Grover Washington Jr.)

JAZZ ALBUMS

1. WINELIGHT
 (Grover Washington Jr.)
2. THE CLARKE/DUKE PROJECT
 (Stanley Clarke and George Duke)
3. VOYEUR
 (David Sanborn)
4. RIT
 (Lee Ritenour)
5. GALAXIAN
 (Jeff Lorber Fusion)
6. MAGIC
 (Tom Browne)
7. THE DUDE
 (Quincy Jones)
8. FRIDAY NIGHT IN SAN FRANCISCO
 (Al DiMeola, John McLaughlin and Paco DeLucia)
9. 'NARD
 (Bernard Wright)
10. TARANTELLA
 (Chuck Mangione)

COUNTRY SINGLES

1. ELVIRA
 (The Oak Ridge Boys)
2. FRIENDS/ANYWHERE THERE'S A JUKEBOX
 (Razzy Bailey)
3. I'M JUST AN OLD CHUNK OF COAL
 (John Anderson)
4. WHAT ARE WE DOIN' IN LOVE
 (Dottie West)
5. BUT YOU KNOW I LOVE YOU
 (Dolly Parton)
6. LOUISIANA SATURDAY NIGHT
 (Mel McDaniel)
7. A MILLION OLD GOODBYES
 (Mel Tillis)
8. BLESSED ARE THE BELIEVERS
 (Anne Murray)
9. SEVEN YEAR ACHE
 (Rosanne Cash)
10. IT'S A LOVELY, LOVELY WORLD
 (Gail Davies)

COUNTRY ALBUMS

1. KENNY ROGERS' GREATEST HITS
 (Kenny Rogers)
2. FEELS SO RIGHT
 (Alabama)
3. SOMEWHERE OVER THE RAINBOW
 (Willie Nelson)
4. WHERE DO YOU GO WHEN YOU DREAM
 (Anne Murray)
5. HORIZON
 (Eddie Rabbitt)
6. JUICE
 (Juice Newton)
7. SEVEN YEAR ACHE
 (Rosanne Cash)
8. OUT WHERE THE BRIGHT LIGHTS ARE GLOWING
 (Ronnie Milsap)
9. EVANGELINE
 (Emmylou Harris)
10. RONNIE MILSAP'S GREATEST HITS
 (Ronnie Milsap)

JUNE 13, 1981

POP SINGLES

1. STARS ON 45
   (Stars On)
2. BETTE DAVIS EYES
   (Kim Carnes)
3. ALL THOSE YEARS AGO
   (George Harrison)
4. A WOMAN NEEDS LOVE (JUST LIKE YOU DO)
   (Ray Parker Jr. and Raydio)
5. TAKE IT ON THE RUN
   (R.E.O. Speedwagon)
6. ANGEL OF THE MORNING
   (Juice Newton)
7. MORNING TRAIN (NINE TO FIVE)
   (Sheena Easton)
8. SUKIYAKI
   (A Taste of Honey)
9. AMERICA
   (Neil Diamond)
10. BEING WITH YOU
    (Smokey Robinson)

POP ALBUMS

1. HI INFIDELITY
   (R.E.O. Speedwagon)
2. PARADISE THEATER
   (Styx)
3. DIRTY DEEDS DONE DIRT CHEAP
   (AC/DC)
4. FAIR WARNING
   (Van Halen)
5. MISTAKEN IDENTITY
   (Kim Carnes)
6. HARD PROMISES
   (Tom Petty and The Heartbreakers)
7. KENNY ROGERS' GREATEST HITS
   (Kenny Rogers)
8. MOVING PICTURES
   (Rush)
9. ARC OF A DIVER
   (Steve Winwood)
10. WHAT CHA GONNA DO FOR ME
    (Chaka Khan)

BLACK SINGLES

1. GIVE IT TO ME BABY
   (Rick James)
2. A WOMAN NEEDS LOVE (JUST LIKE YOU DO)
   (Ray Parker Jr. and Raydio)
3. WHAT CHA GONNA DO FOR ME
   (Chaka Khan)
4. PULL UP TO THE BUMPER
   (Grace Jones)
5. TWO HEARTS
   (Stephanie Mills)
6. BEING WITH YOU
   (Smokey Robinson)
7. YEARNING
   (The Gap Band)
8. DOUBLE DUTCH BUS
   (Frankie Smith)
9. MAKE THAT MOVE
   (Shalamar)
10. PARADISE
    (Change)

BLACK ALBUMS

1. STREET SONGS
   (Rick James)
2. THE DUDE
   (Quincy Jones)
3. A WOMAN NEEDS LOVE
   (Ray Parker Jr. and Raydio)

4. WHAT CHA GONNA DO FOR ME
   (Chaka Khan)
5. BEING WITH YOU
   (Smokey Robinson)
6. STEPHANIE
   (Stephanie Mills)
7. GAP BAND III
   (The Gap Band)
8. THREE FOR LOVE
   (Shalamar)
9. RADIANT
   (Atlantic Starr)
10. WINELIGHT
    (Grover Washington Jr.)

JAZZ ALBUMS

1. WINELIGHT
   (Grover Washington Jr.)
2. THE CLARKE/DUKE PROJECT
   (Stanley Clarke and George Duke)
3. VOYEUR
   (David Sanborn)
4. RIT
   (Lee Ritenour)
5. GALAXIAN
   (Jeff Lorber Fusion)
6. FRIDAY NIGHT IN SAN FRANCISCO
   (Al DiMeola, John McLaughlin and Paco DeLucia)
7. THE DUDE
   (Quincy Jones)
8. HUSH
   (John Klemmer)
9. TARANTELLA
   (Chuck Mangione)
10. MAGIC
    (Tom Browne)

COUNTRY SINGLES

1. WHAT ARE WE DOIN' IN LOVE
   (Dottie West)
2. FRIENDS/ANYWHERE THERE'S A JUKEBOX
   (Razzy Bailey)
3. I'M JUST AN OLD CHUNK OF COAL
   (John Anderson)
4. BUT YOU KNOW I LOVE YOU
   (Dolly Parton)
5. BLESSED ARE THE BELIEVERS
   (Anne Murray)
6. LOUISIANA SATURDAY NIGHT
   (Mel McDaniel)
7. A MILLION OLD GOODBYES
   (Mel Tillis)
8. IT'S A LOVELY, LOVELY WORLD
   (Gail Davies)
9. WHISPER
   (Lacy J. Dalton)
10. SURROUND ME WITH LOVE
    (Charly McClain)

COUNTRY ALBUMS

1. KENNY ROGERS' GREATEST HITS
   (Kenny Rogers)
2. FEELS SO RIGHT
   (Alabama)
3. SOMEWHERE OVER THE RAINBOW
   (Willie Nelson)
4. WHERE DO YOU GO WHEN YOU DREAM
   (Anne Murray)
5. SEVEN YEAR ACHE
   (Rosanne Cash)
6. JUICE
   (Juice Newton)
7. OUT WHERE THE BRIGHT LIGHTS ARE GLOWING
   (Ronnie Milsap)
8. HORIZON
   (Eddie Rabbitt)
9. 9 TO 5 AND ODD JOBS
   (Dolly Parton)

10. RONNIE MILSAP'S GREATEST HITS
    (Ronnie Milsap)

JUNE 20, 1981

POP SINGLES

1. BETTE DAVIS EYES
   (Kim Carnes)
2. STARS ON 45
   (Stars On)
3. ALL THOSE YEARS AGO
   (George Harrison)
4. A WOMAN NEEDS LOVE (JUST LIKE YOU DO)
   (Ray Parker Jr. and Raydio)
5. THE ONE THAT YOU LOVE
   (Air Supply)
6. TAKE IT ON THE RUN
   (R.E.O. Speedwagon)
7. MORNING TRAIN (NINE TO FIVE)
   (Sheena Easton)
8. SUKIYAKI
   (A Taste of Honey)
9. AMERICA
   (Neil Diamond)
10. I LOVE YOU
    (Climax Blues Band)

POP ALBUMS

1. HI INFIDELITY
   (R.E.O. Speedwagon)
2. PARADISE THEATER
   (Styx)
3. DIRTY DEEDS DONE DIRT CHEAP
   (AC/DC)
4. FAIR WARNING
   (Van Halen)
5. MISTAKEN IDENTITY
   (Kim Carnes)
6. HARD PROMISES
   (Tom Petty and The Heartbreakers)
7. MOVING PICTURES
   (Rush)
8. KENNY ROGERS' GREATEST HITS
   (Kenny Rogers)
9. ZEBOP!
   (Santana)
10. STREET SONGS
    (Rick James)

BLACK SINGLES

1. GIVE IT TO ME BABY
   (Rick James)
2. A WOMAN NEEDS LOVE (JUST LIKE YOU DO)
   (Ray Parker Jr. and Raydio)
3. DOUBLE DUTCH BUS
   (Frankie Smith)
4. PULL UP TO THE BUMPER
   (Grace Jones)
5. TWO HEARTS
   (Stephanie Mills)
6. WHAT CHA GONNA DO FOR ME
   (Chaka Khan)
7. HEARTBEAT
   (Taana Gardner)
8. SWEET BABY
   (Stanley Clarke and George Duke)
9. FREAKY DANCIN'
   (Cameo)
10. YEARNING
    (The Gap Band)

BLACK ALBUMS

1. STREET SONGS
   (Rick James)

2. THE DUDE
   (Quincy Jones)
3. A WOMAN NEEDS LOVE
   (Ray Parker Jr. and Raydio)
4. WHAT CHA GONNA DO FOR ME
   (Chaka Khan)
5. STEPHANIE
   (Stephanie Mills)
6. BEING WITH YOU
   (Smokey Robinson)
7. NIGHTCLUBBING
   (Grace Jones)
8. THREE FOR LOVE
   (Shalamar)
9. GAP BAND III
   (The Gap Band)
10. KNIGHTS OF THE SOUND TABLE
    (Cameo)

JAZZ ALBUMS

1. WINELIGHT
   (Grover Washington Jr.)
2. THE CLARKE/DUKE PROJECT
   (Stanley Clarke and George Duke)
3. RIT
   (Lee Ritenour)
4. THE DUDE
   (Quincy Jones)
5. VOYEUR
   (David Sanborn)
6. GALAXIAN
   (Jeff Lorber Fusion)
7. HUSH
   (John Klemmer)
8. FRIDAY NIGHT IN SAN FRANCISCO
   (Al DiMeola, John McLaughlin and
   Paco DeLucia)
9. TARANTELLA
   (Chuck Mangione)
10. MAGIC
    (Tom Browne)

COUNTRY SINGLES

1. BUT YOU KNOW I LOVE YOU
   (Dolly Parton)
2. BLESSED ARE THE BELIEVERS
   (Anne Murray)
3. WHAT ARE WE DOIN' IN LOVE
   (Dottie West)
4. I'M JUST AN OLD CHUNK OF COAL
   (John Anderson)
5. I WAS COUNTRY WHEN COUNTRY WASN'T
   COOL
   (Barbara Mandrell)
6. BY NOW
   (Steve Wariner)
7. SURROUND ME WITH LOVE
   (Charly McClain)
8. IT'S A LOVELY, LOVELY WORLD
   (Gail Davies)
9. WHISPER
   (Lacy J. Dalton)
10. LOVIN' ARMS/YOU ASKED ME TO
    (Elvis Presley)

COUNTRY ALBUMS

1. KENNY ROGERS' GREATEST HITS
   (Kenny Rogers)
2. FEELS SO RIGHT
   (Alabama)
3. SEVEN YEAR ACHE
   (Rosanne Cash)
4. WHERE DO YOU GO WHEN YOU DREAM
   (Anne Murray)
5. SOMEWHERE OVER THE RAINBOW
   (Willie Nelson)
6. FANCY FREE
   (The Oak Ridge Boys)
7. I LOVE 'EM ALL
   (T.G. Sheppard)

8. OUT WHERE THE BRIGHT LIGHTS ARE
   GLOWING
   (Ronnie Milsap)
9. JUICE
   (Juice Newton)
10. HORIZON
    (Eddie Rabbitt)

JUNE 27, 1981

POP SINGLES

1. BETTE DAVIS EYES
   (Kim Carnes)
2. STARS ON 45
   (Stars On)
3. ALL THOSE YEARS AGO
   (George Harrison)
4. THE ONE THAT YOU LOVE
   (Air Supply)
5. ELVIRA
   (The Oak Ridge Boys)
6. A WOMAN NEEDS LOVE (JUST LIKE YOU
   DO)
   (Ray Parker Jr. and Raydio)
7. JESSIE'S GIRL
   (Rick Springfield)
8. YOU MAKE MY DREAMS
   (Daryl Hall and John Oates)
9. TAKE IT ON THE RUN
   (R.E.O. Speedwagon)
10. I LOVE YOU
    (Climax Blues Band)

POP ALBUMS

1. HI INFIDELITY
   (R.E.O. Speedwagon)
2. PARADISE THEATER
   (Styx)
3. MISTAKEN IDENTITY
   (Kim Carnes)
4. DIRTY DEEDS DONE DIRT CHEAP
   (AC/DC)
5. FAIR WARNING
   (Van Halen)
6. HARD PROMISES
   (Tom Petty and The Heartbreakers)
7. STREET SONGS
   (Rick James)
8. KENNY ROGERS' GREATEST HITS
   (Kenny Rogers)
9. ZEBOP!
   (Santana)
10. STARS ON LONG PLAY
    (Stars On)

BLACK SINGLES

1. GIVE IT TO ME BABY
   (Rick James)
2. DOUBLE DUTCH BUS
   (Frankie Smith)
3. PULL UP TO THE BUMPER
   (Grace Jones)
4. TWO HEARTS
   (Stephanie Mills)
5. A WOMAN NEEDS LOVE (JUST LIKE YOU
   DO)
   (Ray Parker Jr. and Raydio)
6. HEARTBEAT
   (Taana Gardner)
7. FREAKY DANCIN'
   (Cameo)
8. SWEET BABY
   (Stanley Clarke and George Duke)
9. NIGHT (FEEL LIKE GETTING DOWN)
   (Billy Ocean)
10. WHAT CHA GONNA DO FOR ME
    (Chaka Khan)

BLACK ALBUMS

1. STREET SONGS
   (Rick James)
2. THE DUDE
   (Quincy Jones)
3. A WOMAN NEEDS LOVE
   (Ray Parker Jr. and Raydio)
4. WHAT CHA GONNA DO FOR ME
   (Chaka Khan)
5. STEPHANIE
   (Stephanie Mills)
6. KNIGHTS OF THE SOUND TABLE
   (Cameo)
7. NIGHTCLUBBING
   (Grace Jones)
8. IT MUST BE MAGIC
   (Teena Marie)
9. BEING WITH YOU
   (Smokey Robinson)
10. THREE FOR LOVE
    (Shalamar)

JAZZ ALBUMS

1. WINELIGHT
   (Grover Washington Jr.)
2. THE CLARKE/DUKE PROJECT
   (Stanley Clarke and George Duke)
3. RIT
   (Lee Ritenour)
4. VOYEUR
   (David Sanborn)
5. HUSH
   (John Klemmer)
6. THE DUDE
   (Quincy Jones)
7. GALAXIAN
   (Jeff Lerber Fusion)
8. FRIDAY NIGHT IN SAN FRANCISCO
   (Al DiMeola, John McLaughlin and
   Paco DeLucia)
9. AS FALLS WICHITA, SO FALLS WICHITA
   FALLS
   (Pat Metheny and Lyle Mays)
10. TARANTELLA
    (Chuck Mangione)

COUNTRY SINGLES

1. I WAS COUNTRY WHEN COUNTRY WASN'T
   COOL
   (Barbara Mandrell)
2. BLESSED ARE THE BELIEVERS
   (Anne Murray)
3. BUT YOU KNOW I LOVE YOU
   (Dolly Parton)
4. BY NOW
   (Steve Wariner)
5. SURROUND ME WITH LOVE
   (Charly McClain)
6. FEELS SO RIGHT
   (Alabama)
7. THE MATADOR
   (Sylvia)
8. FIRE AND SMOKE
   (Earl Thomas Conley)
9. LOVIN' ARMS/YOU ASKED ME TO
   (Elvis Presley)
10. MY WOMAN LOVES THE DEVIL OUT OF ME
    (Moe Bandy)

COUNTRY ALBUMS

1. KENNY ROGERS' GREATEST HITS
   (Kenny Rogers)
2. FANCY FREE
   (The Oak Ridge Boys)
3. SEVEN YEAR ACHE
   (Rosanne Cash)
4. FEELS SO RIGHT
   (Alabama)

5. WHERE DO YOU GO WHEN YOU DREAM
   (Anne Murray)
6. I LOVE 'EM ALL
   (T.G. Sheppard)
7. SOMEWHERE OVER THE RAINBOW
   (Willie Nelson)
8. OUT WHERE THE BRIGHT LIGHTS ARE GLOWING
   (Ronnie Milsap)
9. RONNIE MILSAP'S GREATEST HITS
   (Ronnie Milsap)
10. HORIZON
    (Eddie Rabbitt)

JULY 4, 1981

POP SINGLES

1. BETTE DAVIS EYES
   (Kim Carnes)
2. THE ONE THAT YOU LOVE
   (Air Supply)
3. ALL THOSE YEARS AGO
   (George Harrison)
4. ELVIRA
   (The Oak Ridge Boys)
5. STARS ON 45
   (Stars On)
6. JESSIE'S GIRL
   (Rick Springfield)
7. YOU MAKE MY DREAMS
   (Daryl Hall and John Oates)
8. THEME FROM THE GREATEST AMERICAN HERO
   (Joey Scarbury)
9. A WOMAN NEEDS LOVE (JUST LIKE YOU DO)
   (Ray Parker Jr. and Raydio)
10. I LOVE YOU
    (Climax Blues Band)

POP ALBUMS

1. HI INFIDELITY
   (R.E.O. Speedwagon)
2. MISTAKEN IDENTITY
   (Kim Carnes)
3. PARADISE THEATER
   (Styx)
4. DIRTY DEEDS DONE DIRT CHEAP
   (AC/DC)
5. LONG DISTANCE VOYAGER
   (The Moody Blues)
6. FAIR WARNING
   (Van Halen)
7. STREET SONGS
   (Rick James)
8. HARD PROMISES
   (Tom Petty and The Heartbreakers)
9. MOVING PICTURES
   (Rush)
10. STARS ON LONG PLAY
    (Stars On)

BLACK SINGLES

1. GIVE IT TO ME BABY
   (Rick James)
2. DOUBLE DUTCH BUS
   (Frankie Smith)
3. PULL UP TO THE BUMPER
   (Grace Jones)
4. TWO HEARTS
   (Stephanie Mills)
5. FREAKY DANCIN'
   (Cameo)
6. HEARTBEAT
   (Taana Gardner)
7. NIGHT (FEEL LIKE GETTING DOWN)
   (Billy Ocean)
8. LOVE ON A TWO WAY STREET
   (Stacy Lattisaw)

9. SWEET BABY
   (Stanley Clarke and George Duke)
10. A WOMAN NEEDS LOVE (JUST LIKE YOU DO)
    (Ray Parker Jr. and Raydio)

BLACK ALBUMS

1. STREET SONGS
   (Rick James)
2. THE DUDE
   (Quincy Jones)
3. KNIGHTS OF THE SOUND TABLE
   (Cameo)
4. WHAT CHA GONNA DO FOR ME
   (Chaka Khan)
5. STEPHANIE
   (Stephanie Mills)
6. IT MUST BE MAGIC
   (Teena Marie)
7. NIGHTCLUBBING
   (Grace Jones)
8. A WOMAN NEEDS LOVE
   (Ray Parker Jr. and Raydio)
9. RADIANT
   (Atlantic Starr)
10. THREE FOR LOVE
    (Shalamar)

JAZZ ALBUMS

1. WINELIGHT
   (Grover Washington Jr.)
2. RIT
   (Lee Ritenour)
3. THE CLARKE/DUKE PROJECT
   (Stanley Clarke and George Duke)
4. VOYEUR
   (David Sanborn)
5. HUSH
   (John Klemmer)
6. THE DUDE
   (Quincy Jones)
7. AS FALLS WICHITA, SO FALLS WICHITA FALLS
   (Pat Metheny and Lyle Mays)
8. TARANTELLA
   (Chuck Mangione)
9. THREE PIECE SUITE
   (Ramsey Lewis)
10. FRIDAY NIGHT IN SAN FRANCISCO
    (Al DiMeola, John McLaughlin and Paco DeLucia)

COUNTRY SINGLES

1. I WAS COUNTRY WHEN COUNTRY WASN'T COOL
   (Barbara Mandrell)
2. FEELS SO RIGHT
   (Alabama)
3. BY NOW
   (Steve Wariner)
4. SURROUND ME WITH LOVE
   (Charly McClain)
5. THE MATADOR
   (Sylvia)
6. LOVIN' HER WAS EASIER
   (Tompall and The Glaser Brothers)
7. FIRE AND SMOKE
   (Earl Thomas Conley)
8. BLESSED ARE THE BELIEVERS
   (Anne Murray)
9. FOOL BY YOUR SIDE
   (Dave and Sugar)
10. MY WOMAN LOVES THE DEVIL OUT OF ME
    (Moe Bandy)

COUNTRY ALBUMS

1. KENNY ROGERS' GREATEST HITS
   (Kenny Rogers)

2. FANCY FREE
   (The Oak Ridge Boys)
3. FEELS SO RIGHT
   (Alabama)
4. WHERE DO YOU GO WHEN YOU DREAM
   (Anne Murray)
5. SEVEN YEAR ACHE
   (Rosanne Cash)
6. I LOVE 'EM ALL
   (T.G. Sheppard)
7. SOMEWHERE OVER THE RAINBOW
   (Willie Nelson)
8. I AM WHAT I AM
   (George Jones)
9. RONNIE MILSAP'S GREATEST HITS
   (Ronnie Milsap)
10. JUICE
    (Juice Newton)

JULY 11, 1981

POP SINGLES

1. THE ONE THAT YOU LOVE
   (Air Supply)
2. BETTE DAVIS EYES
   (Kim Carnes)
3. ALL THOSE YEARS AGO
   (George Harrison)
4. ELVIRA
   (The Oak Ridge Boys)
5. JESSIE'S GIRL
   (Rick Springfield)
6. THEME FROM THE GREATEST AMERICAN HERO
   (Joey Scarbury)
7. YOU MAKE MY DREAMS
   (Daryl Hall and John Oates)
8. STARS ON 45
   (Stars On)
9. I DON'T NEED YOU
   (Kenny Rogers)
10. A WOMAN NEEDS LOVE (JUST LIKE YOU DO)
    (Ray Parker Jr. and Raydio)

POP ALBUMS

1. MISTAKEN IDENTITY
   (Kim Carnes)
2. HI INFIDELITY
   (R.E.O. Speedwagon)
3. PARADISE THEATER
   (Styx)
4. LONG DISTANCE VOYAGER
   (The Moody Blues)
5. DIRTY DEEDS DONE DIRT CHEAP
   (AC/DC)
6. STREET SONGS
   (Rick James)
7. MOVING PICTURES
   (Rush)
8. HARD PROMISES
   (Tom Petty and The Heartbreakers)
9. FAIR WARNING
   (Van Halen)
10. STARS ON LONG PLAY
    (Stars On)

BLACK SINGLES

1. DOUBLE DUTCH BUS
   (Frankie Smith)
2. GIVE IT TO ME BABY
   (Rick James)
3. PULL UP TO THE BUMPER
   (Grace Jones)
4. FREAKY DANCIN'
   (Cameo)
5. LOVE ON A TWO WAY STREET
   (Stacy Lattisaw)

6. HEARTBEAT
   (Taana Gardner)
7. NIGHT (FEEL LIKE GETTING DOWN)
   (Billy Ocean)
8. TWO HEARTS
   (Stephanie Mills)
9. VERY SPECIAL
   (Debra Laws)
10. RUNNING AWAY
    (Maze featuring Frankie Beverly)

BLACK ALBUMS

1. STREET SONGS
   (Rick James)
2. KNIGHTS OF THE SOUND TABLE
   (Cameo)
3. IT MUST BE MAGIC
   (Teena Marie)
4. THE DUDE
   (Quincy Jones)
5. WHAT CHA GONNA DO FOR ME
   (Chaka Khan)
6. STEPHANIE
   (Stephanie Mills)
7. NIGHTCLUBBING
   (Grace Jones)
8. A WOMAN NEEDS LOVE
   (Ray Parker Jr. and Raydio)
9. RADIANT
   (Atlantic Starr)
10. THE CLARKE/DUKE PROJECT
    (Stanley Clarke and George Duke)

JAZZ ALBUMS

1. THE CLARKE/DUKE PROJECT
   (Stanley Clarke and George Duke)
2. WINELIGHT
   (Grover Washington Jr.)
3. RIT
   (Lee Ritenour)
4. VOYEUR
   (David Sanborn)
5. HUSH
   (John Klemmer)
6. AS FALLS WICHITA, SO FALLS WICHITA
   FALLS
   (Pat Metheny and Lyle Mays)
7. THREE PIECE SUITE
   (Ramsey Lewis)
8. FRIDAY NIGHT IN SAN FRANCISCO
   *(Al DiMeola, John McLaughlin and
   Paco DeLucia)*
9. THE DUDE
   (Quincy Jones)
10. TARANTELLA
    (Chuck Mangione)

COUNTRY SINGLES

1. FEELS SO RIGHT
   (Alabama)
2. I WAS COUNTRY WHEN COUNTRY WASN'T
   COOL
   (Barbara Mandrell)
3. LOVIN' HER WAS EASIER
   (Tompall and The Glaser Brothers)
4. SURROUND ME WITH LOVE
   (Charly McClain)
5. THE MATADOR
   (Sylvia)
6. BY NOW
   (Steve Wariner)
7. FOOL BY YOUR SIDE
   (Dave and Sugar)
8. PRISONER OF HOPE
   (Johnny Lee)
9. GOOD OL' GIRLS
   (Sonny Curtis)
10. DON'T BOTHER TO KNOCK
    (Jim Ed Brown and Helen Cornelius)

COUNTRY ALBUMS

1. KENNY ROGERS' GREATEST HITS
   (Kenny Rogers)
2. FANCY FREE
   (The Oak Ridge Boys)
3. FEELS SO RIGHT
   (Alabama)
4. SEVEN YEAR ACHE
   (Rosanne Cash)
5. WHERE DO YOU GO WHEN YOU DREAM
   (Anne Murray)
6. RONNIE MILSAP'S GREATEST HITS
   (Ronnie Milsap)
7. JUICE
   (Juice Newton)
8. I AM WHAT I AM
   (George Jones)
9. SOMEWHERE OVER THE RAINBOW
   (Willie Nelson)
10. OUT WHERE THE BRIGHT LIGHTS ARE
    GLOWING
    (Ronnie Milsap)

JULY 18, 1981

POP SINGLES

1. THEME FROM THE GREATEST AMERICAN
   HERO
   (Joey Scarbury)
2. THE ONE THAT YOU LOVE
   (Air Supply)
3. ELVIRA
   (The Oak Ridge Boys)
4. BETTE DAVIS EYES
   (Kim Carnes)
5. JESSIE'S GIRL
   (Rick Springfield)
6. I DON'T NEED YOU
   (Kenny Rogers)
7. STARS ON 45
   (Stars On)
8. YOU MAKE MY DREAMS
   (Daryl Hall and John Oates)
9. ALL THOSE YEARS AGO
   (George Harrison)
10. BOY FROM NEW YORK CITY
    (Manhattan Transfer)

POP ALBUMS

1. HI INFIDELITY
   (R.E.O. Speedwagon)
2. LONG DISTANCE VOYAGER
   (The Moody Blues)
3. MISTAKEN IDENTITY
   (Kim Carnes)
4. PARADISE THEATER
   (Styx)
5. STREET SONG
   (Rick James)
6. DIRTY DEEDS DONE DIRT CHEAP
   (AC/DC)
7. MOVING PICTURES
   (Rush)
8. HARD PROMISES
   (Tom Petty and The Heartbreakers)
9. SHARE YOUR LOVE
   (Kenny Rogers)
10. FANCY FREE
    (The Oak Ridge Boys)

BLACK SINGLES

1. DOUBLE DUTCH BUS
   (Frankie Smith)
2. GIVE IT TO ME BABY
   (Rick James)
3. LOVE ON A TWO WAY STREET
   (Stacy Lattisaw)
4. FREAKY DANCIN'
   (Cameo)
5. PULL UP TO THE BUMPER
   (Grace Jones)
6. HEARTBEAT
   (Taana Gardner)
7. VERY SPECIAL
   (Debra Laws)
8. NIGHT (FEEL LIKE GETTING DOWN)
   (Billy Ocean)
9. I'M IN LOVE
   (Evelyn King)
10. RUNNING AWAY
    (Maze featuring Frankie Beverly)

BLACK ALBUMS

1. STREET SONGS
   (Rick James)
2. KNIGHTS OF THE SOUND TABLE
   (Cameo)
3. IT MUST BE MAGIC
   (Teena Marie)
4. LIVE IN NEW ORLEANS
   (Maze featuring Frankie Beverly)
5. THE DUDE
   (Quincy Jones)
6. RADIANT
   (Atlantic Starr)
7. STEPHANIE
   (Stephanie Mills)
8. NIGHTCLUBBING
   (Grace Jones)
9. A WOMAN NEEDS LOVE
   (Ray Parker Jr. and Raydio)
10. THE CLARKE/DUKE PROJECT
    (Stanley Clarke and George Duke)

JAZZ ALBUMS

1. THE CLARKE/DUKE PROJECT
   (Stanley Clarke and George Duke)
2. WINELIGHT
   (Grover Washington Jr.)
3. RIT
   (Lee Ritenour)
4. VOYEUR
   (David Sanborn)
5. AS FALLS WICHITA, SO FALLS WICHITA
   FALLS
   (Pat Metheny and Lyle Mays)
6. THREE PIECE SUITE
   (Ramsey Lewis)
7. HUSH
   (John Klemmer)
8. FRIDAY NIGHT IN SAN FRANCISCO
   *(Al DiMeola, John McLaughlin and
   Paco DeLucia)*
9. THE DUDE
   (Quincy Jones)
10. TARANTELLA
    (Chuck Mangione)

COUNTRY SINGLES

1. FEELS SO RIGHT
   (Alabama)
2. LOVIN' HER WAS EASIER
   (Tompall and The Glaser Brothers)
3. I WAS COUNTRY WHEN COUNTRY WASN'T
   COOL
   (Barbara Mandrell)
4. PRISONER OF HOPE
   (Johnny Lee)
5. FOOL BY YOUR SIDE
   (Dave and Sugar)
6. SURROUND ME WITH LOVE
   (Charly McClain)
7. DIXIE ON MY MIND
   (Hank Williams Jr.)
8. TOO MANY LOVERS
   (Crystal Gayle)

9. GOOD OL' GIRLS
   (Sonny Curtis)
10. UNWOUND
    (George Strait)

COUNTRY ALBUMS

1. FANCY FREE
   (The Oak Ridge Boys)
2. KENNY ROGERS' GREATEST HITS
   (Kenny Rogers)
3. FEELS SO RIGHT
   (Alabama)
4. SHARE YOUR LOVE
   (Kenny Rogers)
5. SEVEN YEAR ACHE
   (Rosanne Cash)
6. RONNIE MILSAP'S GREATEST HITS
   (Ronnie Milsap)
7. JUICE
   (Juice Newton)
8. WHERE DO YOU GO WHEN YOU DREAM
   (Anne Murray)
9. OUT WHERE THE BRIGHT LIGHTS ARE
   GLOWING
   (Ronnie Milsap)
10. URBAN CHIPMUNK
    (Chipmunks)

JULY 25, 1981

POP SINGLES

1. THEME FROM THE GREATEST AMERICAN
   HERO
   (Joey Scarbury)
2. THE ONE THAT YOU LOVE
   (Air Supply)
3. ELVIRA
   (The Oak Ridge Boys)
4. JESSIE'S GIRL
   (Rick Springfield)
5. BETTE DAVIS EYES
   (Kim Carnes)
6. I DON'T NEED YOU
   (Kenny Rogers)
7. STARS ON 45
   (Stars On)
8. SLOW HAND
   (The Pointer Sisters)
9. BOY FROM NEW YORK CITY
   (Manhattan Transfer)
10. HEARTS
    (Marty Balin)

POP ALBUMS

1. LONG DISTANCE VOYAGER
   (The Moody Blues)
2. HI INFIDELITY
   (R.E.O. Speedwagon)
3. SHARE YOUR LOVE
   (Kenny Rogers)
4. MISTAKEN IDENTITY
   (Kim Carnes)
5. STREET SONGS
   (Rick James)
6. PARADISE THEATER
   (Styx)
7. DIRTY DEEDS DONE DIRT CHEAP
   (AC/DC)
8. HARD PROMISES
   (Tom Petty and The Heartbreakers)
9. FANCY FREE
   (The Oak Ridge Boys)
10. THE ONE THAT YOU LOVE
    (Air Supply)

BLACK SINGLES

1. DOUBLE DUTCH BUS
   (Frankie Smith)

2. LOVE ON A TWO WAY STREET
   (Stacy Lattisaw)
3. GIVE IT TO ME BABY
   (Rick James)
4. FREAKY DANCIN'
   (Cameo)
5. I'M IN LOVE
   (Evelyn King)
6. VERY SPECIAL
   (Debra Laws)
7. PULL UP TO THE BUMPER
   (Grace Jones)
8. SQUARE BIZ
   (Teena Marie)
9. SHAKE IT UP TONIGHT
   (Cheryl Lynn)
10. RUNNING AWAY
    (Maze featuring Frankie Beverly)

BLACK ALBUMS

1. STREET SONGS
   (Rick James)
2. KNIGHTS OF THE SOUND TABLE
   (Cameo)
3. IT MUST BE MAGIC
   (Teena Marie)
4. LIVE IN NEW ORLEANS
   (Maze featuring Frankie Beverly)
5. THE DUDE
   (Quincy Jones)
6. RADIANT
   (Atlantic Starr)
7. IN THE POCKET
   (Commodores)
8. STEPHANIE
   (Stephanie Mills)
9. I'M IN LOVE
   (Evelyn King)
10. A WOMAN NEEDS LOVE
    (Ray Parker Jr. and Raydio)

JAZZ ALBUMS

1. THE MAN WITH THE HORN
   (Miles Davis)
2. THE CLARKE/DUKE PROJECT
   (Stanley Clarke and George Duke)
3. RIT
   (Lee Ritenour)
4. WINELIGHT
   (Grover Washington Jr.)
5. VOYEUR
   (David Sanborn)
6. HUSH
   (John Klemmer)
7. AS FALLS WICHITA, SO FALLS WICHITA
   FALLS
   (Pat Metheny and Lyle Mays)
8. THREE PIECE SUITE
   (Ramsey Lewis)
9. THE DUDE
   (Quincy Jones)
10. APPLE JUICE
    (Tom Scott)

COUNTRY SINGLES

1. FEELS SO RIGHT
   (Alabama)
2. LOVIN' HER WAS EASIER
   (Tompall and The Glaser Brothers)
3. PRISONER OF HOPE
   (Johnny Lee)
4. DIXIE ON MY MIND
   (Hank Williams Jr.)
5. FOOL BY YOUR SIDE
   (Dave and Sugar)
6. TOO MANY LOVERS
   (Crystal Gayle)
7. UNWOUND
   (George Strait)
8. I DON'T NEED YOU
   (Kenny Rogers)

9. DREAM OF ME
   (Vern Gosdin)
10. THEY COULD PUT ME IN JAIL
    (The Bellamy Brothers)

COUNTRY ALBUMS

1. FANCY FREE
   (The Oak Ridge Boys)
2. SHARE YOUR LOVE
   (Kenny Rogers)
3. KENNY ROGERS' GREATEST HITS
   (Kenny Rogers)
4. FEELS SO RIGHT
   (Alabama)
5. SEVEN YEAR ACHE
   (Rosanne Cash)
6. JUICE
   (Juice Newton)
7. WHERE DO YOU GO WHEN YOU DREAM
   (Anne Murray)
8. OUT WHERE THE BRIGHT LIGHTS ARE
   GLOWING
   (Ronnie Milsap)
9. RONNIE MILSAP'S GREATEST HITS
   (Ronnie Milsap)
10. URBAN CHIPMUNK
    (Chipmunks)

AUGUST 1, 1981

POP SINGLES

1. JESSIE'S GIRL
   (Rick Springfield)
2. THEME FROM THE GREATEST AMERICAN
   HERO
   (Joey Scarbury)
3. THE ONE THAT YOU LOVE
   (Air Supply)
4. ELVIRA
   (The Oak Ridge Boys)
5. I DON'T NEED YOU
   (Kenny Rogers)
6. SLOW HAND
   (The Pointer Sisters)
7. QUEEN OF HEARTS
   (Juice Newton)
8. BETTE DAVIS EYES
   (Kim Carnes)
9. BOY FROM NEW YORK CITY
   (Manhattan Transfer)
10. HEARTS
    (Marty Balin)

POP ALBUMS

1. HI INFIDELITY
   (R.E.O. Speedwagon)
2. LONG DISTANCE VOYAGER
   (The Moody Blues)
3. SHARE YOUR LOVE
   (Kenny Rogers)
4. PRECIOUS TIME
   (Pat Benatar)
5. STREET SONGS
   (Rick James)
6. 4
   (Foreigner)
7. MISTAKEN IDENTITY
   (Kim Carnes)
8. HARD PROMISES
   (Tom Petty and the Heartbreakers)
9. FANCY FREE
   (The Oak Ridge Boys)
10. THE ONE THAT YOU LOVE
    (Air Supply)

BLACK SINGLES

1. DOUBLE DUTCH BUS
   (Frankie Smith)
2. LOVE ON A TWO WAY STREET
   (Stacy Lattisaw)
3. I'M IN LOVE
   (Evelyn King)
4. SQUARE BIZ
   (Teena Marie)
5. FREAKY DANCIN'
   (Cameo)
6. VERY SPECIAL
   (Debra Laws)
7. GIVE IT TO ME BABY
   (Rick James)
8. SHAKE IT UP TONIGHT
   (Cheryl Lynn)
9. LADY (YOU BRING ME UP)
   (Commodores)
10. SHE'S A BAD MAMA JAMA (SHE'S BUILT, SHE'S STACKED)
    (Carl Carlton)

BLACK ALBUMS

1. STREET SONGS
   (Rick James)
2. IT MUST BE MAGIC
   (Teena Marie)
3. LIVE IN NEW ORLEANS
   (Maze featuring Frankie Beverly)
4. IN THE POCKET
   (Commodores)
5. KNIGHTS OF THE SOUND TABLE
   (Cameo)
6. I'M IN LOVE
   (Evelyn King)
7. DIMPLES
   (Richard "Dimples" Fields)
8. WINNERS
   (The Brothers Johnson)
9. THE DUDE
   (Quincy Jones)
10. RADIANT
    (Atlantic Starr)

JAZZ ALBUMS

1. THE MAN WITH THE HORN
   (Miles Davis)
2. THE CLARKE/DUKE PROJECT
   (Stanley Clarke and George Duke)
3. RIT
   (Lee Ritenour)
4. VOYEUR
   (David Sanborn)
5. WINELIGHT
   (Grover Washington Jr.)
6. AS FALLS WICHITA, SO FALLS WICHITA FALLS
   (Pat Metheny and Lyle Mays)
7. HUSH
   (John Klemmer)
8. APPLE JUICE
   (Tom Scott)
9. THE DUDE
   (Quincy Jones)
10. FRIDAY NIGHT IN SAN FRANCISCO
    (Al DiMeola, John McLaughlin and Paco DeLucia)

COUNTRY SINGLES

1. PRISONER OF HOPE
   (Johnny Lee)
2. DIXIE ON MY MIND
   (Hank Williams Jr.)
3. FEELS SO RIGHT
   (Alabama)
4. TOO MANY LOVERS
   (Crystal Gayle)
5. I DON'T NEED YOU
   (Kenny Rogers)
6. UNWOUND
   (George Strait)
7. RAINBOW STEW
   (Merle Haggard)
8. DREAM OF ME
   (Vern Gosdin)
9. I STILL BELIEVE IN WALTZES
   (Conway Twitty and Loretta Lynn)
10. THEY COULD PUT ME IN JAIL
    (The Bellamy Brothers)

COUNTRY ALBUMS

1. SHARE YOUR LOVE
   (Kenny Rogers)
2. FANCY FREE
   (The Oak Ridge Boys)
3. KENNY ROGERS' GREATEST HITS
   (Kenny Rogers)
4. FEELS SO RIGHT
   (Alabama)
5. JUICE
   (Juice Newton)
6. SEVEN YEAR ACHE
   (Rosanne Cash)
7. WHERE DO YOU GO WHEN YOU DREAM
   (Anne Murray)
8. I AM WHAT I AM
   (George Jones)
9. URBAN CHIPMUNK
   (Chipmunks)
10. OUT WHERE THE BRIGHT LIGHTS ARE GLOWING
    (Ronnie Milsap)

AUGUST 8, 1981

POP SINGLES

1. JESSIE'S GIRL
   (Rick Springfield)
2. THEME FROM THE GREATEST AMERICAN HERO
   (Joey Scarbury)
3. THE ONE THAT YOU LOVE
   (Air Supply)
4. SLOW HAND
   (The Pointer Sisters)
5. I DON'T NEED YOU
   (Kenny Rogers)
6. QUEEN OF HEARTS
   (Juice Newton)
7. ELVIRA
   (The Oak Ridge Boys)
8. BOY FROM NEW YORK CITY
   (Manhattan Transfer)
9. ENDLESS LOVE
   (Diana Ross and Lionel Richie)
10. BETTE DAVIS EYES
    (Kim Carnes)

POP ALBUMS

1. PRECIOUS TIME
   (Pat Benatar)
2. 4
   (Foreigner)
3. SHARE YOUR LOVE
   (Kenny Rogers)
4. HI INFIDELITY
   (R.E.O. Speedwagon)
5. LONG DISTANCE VOYAGER
   (The Moody Blues)
6. STREET SONGS
   (Rick James)
7. ESCAPE
   (Journey)
8. HARD PROMISES
   (Tom Petty and the Heartbreakers)
9. THE ONE THAT YOU LOVE
   (Air Supply)
10. DON'T SAY NO
    (Billy Squier)

BLACK SINGLES

1. LOVE ON A TWO WAY STREET
   (Stacy Lattisaw)
2. I'M IN LOVE
   (Evelyn King)
3. SQUARE BIZ
   (Teena Marie)
4. DOUBLE DUTCH BUS
   (Frankie Smith)
5. ENDLESS LOVE
   (Diana Ross and Lionel Richie)
6. SHAKE IT UP TONIGHT
   (Cheryl Lynn)
7. LADY (YOU BRING ME UP)
   (Commodores)
8. SHE'S A BAD MAMA JAMA (SHE'S BUILT, SHE'S STACKED)
   (Carl Carlton)
9. GIVE IT TO ME BABY
   (Rick James)
10. FREAKY DANCIN'
    (Cameo)

BLACK ALBUMS

1. STREET SONGS
   (Rick James)
2. IT MUST BE MAGIC
   (Teena Marie)
3. LIVE IN NEW ORLEANS
   (Maze featuring Frankie Beverly)
4. IN THE POCKET
   (Commodores)
5. I'M IN LOVE
   (Evelyn King)
6. DIMPLES
   (Richard "Dimples" Fields)
7. KNIGHTS OF THE SOUND TABLE
   (Cameo)
8. WINNERS
   (The Brothers Johnson)
9. WITH YOU
   (Stacy Lattisaw)
10. THE CLARKE/DUKE PROJECT
    (Stanley Clarke and George Duke)

JAZZ ALBUMS

1. THE MAN WITH THE HORN
   (Miles Davis)
2. THE CLARKE/DUKE PROJECT
   (Stanley Clarke and George Duke)
3. RIT
   (Lee Ritenour)
4. VOYEUR
   (David Sanborn)
5. AS FALLS WICHITA, SO FALLS WICHITA FALLS
   (Pat Metheny and Lyle Mays)
6. APPLE JUICE
   (Tom Scott)
7. HUSH
   (John Klemmer)
8. THE DUDE
   (Quincy Jones)
9. LIVE IN JAPAN
   (Dave Grusin and the GRP All-Stars)
10. FRIDAY NIGHT IN SAN FRANCISCO
    (Al DiMeola, John McLaughlin and Paco DeLucia)

COUNTRY SINGLES

1. PRISONER OF HOPE
   (Johnny Lee)

2. DIXIE ON MY MIND
   (Hank Williams Jr.)
3. I DON'T NEED YOU
   (Kenny Rogers)
4. TOO MANY LOVERS
   (Crystal Gayle)
5. RAINBOW STEW
   (Merle Haggard)
6. UNWOUND
   (George Strait)
7. I STILL BELIEVE IN WALTZES
   (Conway Twitty and Loretta Lynn)
8. DREAM OF ME
   (Vern Gosdin)
9. DON'T WAIT ON ME
   (The Statler Brothers)
10. (THERE'S) NO GETTIN' OVER ME
    (Ronnie Milsap)

COUNTRY ALBUMS

1. SHARE YOUR LOVE
   (Kenny Rogers)
2. FANCY FREE
   (The Oak Ridge Boys)
3. KENNY ROGERS' GREATEST HITS
   (Kenny Rogers)
4. FEELS SO RIGHT
   (Alabama)
5. JUICE
   (Juice Newton)
6. SEVEN YEAR ACHE
   (Rosanne Cash)
7. I AM WHAT I AM
   (George Jones)
8. YEARS AGO
   (The Statler Brothers)
9. URBAN CHIPMUNK
   (Chipmunks)
10. WHERE DO YOU GO WHEN YOU DREAM
    (Anne Murray)

AUGUST 15, 1981

POP SINGLES

1. ENDLESS LOVE
   (Diana Ross and Lionel Richie)
2. JESSIE'S GIRL
   (Rick Springfield)
3. THEME FROM THE GREATEST AMERICAN HERO
   (Joey Scarbury)
4. SLOW HAND
   (The Pointer Sisters)
5. QUEEN OF HEARTS
   (Juice Newton)
6. THE O' JE THAT YOU LOVE
   (Air Supply)
7. ELVIRA
   (The Oak Ridge Boys)
8. BOY FROM NEW YORK CITY
   (Manhattan Transfer)
9. I DON'T NEED YOU
   (Kenny Rogers)
10. LADY (YOU BRING ME UP)
    (Commodores)

POP ALBUMS

1. PRECIOUS TIME
   (Pat Benatar)
2. 4
   (Foreigner)
3. ESCAPE
   (Journey)
4. HI INFIDELITY
   (R.E.O. Speedwagon)
5. LONG DISTANCE VOYAGER
   (The Moody Blues)

6. SHARE YOUR LOVE
   (Kenny Rogers)
7. STREET SONGS
   (Rick James)
8. DON'T SAY NO
   (Billy Squier)
9. ENDLESS LOVE
   (Original Soundtrack)
10. THE ONE THAT YOU LOVE
    (Air Supply)

BLACK SINGLES

1. I'M IN LOVE
   (Evelyn King)
2. SQUARE BIZ
   (Teena Marie)
3. ENDLESS LOVE
   (Diana Ross and Lionel Richie)
4. LOVE ON A TWO WAY STREET
   (Stacy Lattisaw)
5. SHAKE IT UP TONIGHT
   (Cheryl Lynn)
6. LADY (YOU BRING ME UP)
   (Commodores)
7. SHE'S A BAD MAMA JAMA (SHE'S BUILT, SHE'S STACKED)
   (Carl Carlton)
8. DOUBLE DUTCH BUS
   (Frankie Smith)
9. JUST BE MY LADY
   (Larry Graham)
10. GIVE IT TO ME BABY
    (Rick James)

BLACK ALBUMS

1. STREET SONGS
   (Rick James)
2. IT MUST BE MAGIC
   (Teena Marie)
3. IN THE POCKET
   (Commodores)
4. I'M IN LOVE
   (Evelyn King)
5. DIMPLES
   (Richard "Dimples" Fields)
6. LIVE IN NEW ORLEANS
   (Maze featuring Frankie Beverly)
7. WITH YOU
   (Stacy Lattisaw)
8. WINNERS
   (The Brothers Johnson)
9. BLACK AND WHITE
   (The Pointer Sisters)
10. THE CLARKE/DUKE PROJECT
    (Stanley Clarke and George Duke)

JAZZ ALBUMS

1. THE MAN WITH THE HORN
   (Miles Davis)
2. THE CLARKE/DUKE PROJECT
   (Stanley Clarke and George Duke)
3. RIT
   (Lee Ritenour)
4. VOYEUR
   (David Sanborn)
5. APPLE JUICE
   (Tom Scott)
6. AS FALLS WITCHITA, SO FALLS WITCHITA FALLS
   (Pat Metheny and Lyle Mays)
7. HUSH
   (John Klemmer)
8. THE DUDE
   (Quincy Jones)
9. LIVE IN JAPAN
   (Dave Grusin and the GRP All-Stars)
10. FRIDAY NIGHT IN SAN FRANCISCO
    (Al DiMeola, John McLaughlin and Paco DeLucia)

COUNTRY SINGLES

1. I DON'T NEED YOU
   (Kenny Rogers)
2. PRISONER OF HOPE
   (Johnny Lee)
3. RAINBOW STEW
   (Merle Haggard)
4. I STILL BELIEVE IN WALTZES
   (Conway Twitty and Loretta Lynn)
5. TOO MANY LOVERS
   (Crystal Gayle)
6. (THERE'S) NO GETTIN' OVER ME
   (Ronnie Milsap)
7. DON'T WAIT ON ME
   (The Statler Brothers)
8. DIXIE ON MY MIND
   (Hank Williams Jr.)
9. OLDER WOMEN
   (Ronnie McDowell)
10. IT'S NOW OR NEVER
    (John Schneider)

COUNTRY ALBUMS

1. SHARE YOUR LOVE
   (Kenny Rogers)
2. FANCY FREE
   (The Oak Ridge Boys)
3. KENNY ROGERS' GREATEST HITS
   (Kenny Rogers)
4. FEELS SO RIGHT
   (Alabama)
5. JUICE
   (Juice Newton)
6. SEVEN YEAR ACHE
   (Rosanne Cash)
7. YEARS AGO
   (The Statler Brothers)
8. I AM WHAT I AM
   (George Jones)
9. ESPECIALLY FOR YOU
   (Don Williams)
10. ROWDY
    (Hank Williams Jr.)

AUGUST 22, 1981

POP SINGLES

1. ENDLESS LOVE
   (Diana Ross and Lionel Richie)
2. JESSIE'S GIRL
   (Rick Springfield)
3. THEME FROM THE GREATEST AMERICAN HERO
   (Joey Scarbury)
4. SLOW HAND
   (The Pointer Sisters)
5. QUEEN OF HEARTS
   (Juice Newton)
6. THE ONE THAT YOU LOVE
   (Air Supply)
7. ELVIRA
   (The Oak Ridge Boys)
8. THE STROKE
   (Billy Squier)
9. LADY (YOU BRING ME UP)
   (Commodores)
10. BOY FROM NEW YORK CITY
    (Manhattan Transfer)

POP ALBUMS

1. 4
   (Foreigner)
2. ESCAPE
   (Journey)

3. PRECIOUS TIME
   (Pat Benatar)
4. HI INFIDELITY
   (R.E.O. Speedwagon)
5. LONG DISTANCE VOYAGER
   (The Moody Blues)
6. ENDLESS LOVE
   (Original Soundtrack)
7. BELLA DONNA
   (Stevie Nicks)
8. DON'T SAY NO
   (Billy Squier)
9. STREET SONGS
   (Rick James)
10. SHARE YOUR LOVE
    (Kenny Rogers)

BLACK SINGLES

1. ENDLESS LOVE
   (Diana Ross and Lionel Richie)
2. SQUARE BIZ
   (Teena Marie)
3. I'M IN LOVE
   (Evelyn King)
4. SHE'S A BAD MAMA JAMA (SHE'S BUILT, SHE'S STACKED)
   (Carl Carlton)
5. SHAKE IT UP TONIGHT
   (Cheryl Lynn)
6. LADY (YOU BRING ME UP)
   (Commodores)
7. LOVE ON A TWO WAY STREET
   (Stacy Lattisaw)
8. JUST BE MY LADY
   (Larry Graham)
9. SLOW HAND
   (The Pointer Sisters)
10. DOUBLE DUTCH BUS
    (Frankie Smith)

BLACK ALBUMS

1. STREET SONGS
   (Rick James)
2. IT MUST BE MAGIC
   (Teena Marie)
3. IN THE POCKET
   (Commodores)
4. I'M IN LOVE
   (Evelyn King)
5. DIMPLES
   (Richard "Dimples" Fields)
6. LIVE IN NEW ORLEANS
   (Maze featuring Frankie Beverly)
7. WITH YOU
   (Stacy Lattisaw)
8. BLACK AND WHITE
   (The Pointer Sisters)
9. WINNERS
   (The Brothers Johnson)
10. KNIGHTS OF THE SOUND TABLE
    (Cameo)

JAZZ ALBUMS

1. THE MAN WITH THE HORN
   (Miles Davis)
2. BREAKIN' AWAY
   (Al Jarreau)
3. RIT
   (Lee Ritenour)
4. THE CLARKE/DUKE PROJECT
   (Stanley Clarke and George Duke)
5. AS FALLS WICHITA, SO FALLS WICHITA FALLS
   (Pat Metheny and Lyle Mays)
6. HUSH
   (John Klemmer)
7. APPLE JUICE
   (Tom Scott)
8. VOYEUR
   (David Sanborn)

9. THE DUDE
   (Quincy Jones)
10. FRIDAY NIGHT IN SAN FRANCISCO
    (Al DiMeola, John McLaughlin and Paco DeLucia)

COUNTRY SINGLES

1. I DON'T NEED YOU
   (Kenny Rogers)
2. (THERE'S) NO GETTIN' OVER ME
   (Ronnie Milsap)
3. RAINBOW STEW
   (Merle Haggard)
4. I STILL BELIEVE IN WALTZES
   (Conway Twitty and Loretta Lynn)
5. DON'T WAIT ON ME
   (The Statler Brothers)
6. OLDER WOMEN
   (Ronnie McDowell)
7. MIRACLES
   (Don Williams)
8. YOU DON'T KNOW ME
   (Mickey Gilley)
9. IT'S NOW OR NEVER
   (John Schneider)
10. PRISONER OF HOPE
    (Johnny Lee)

COUNTRY ALBUMS

1. SHARE YOUR LOVE
   (Kenny Rogers)
2. FANCY FREE
   (The Oak Ridge Boys)
3. KENNY ROGERS' GREATEST HITS
   (Kenny Rogers)
4. FEELS SO RIGHT
   (Alabama)
5. JUICE
   (Juice Newton)
6. SEVEN YEAR ACHE
   (Rosanne Cash)
7. I AM WHAT I AM
   (George Jones)
8. YEARS AGO
   (The Statler Brothers)
9. ESPECIALLY FOR YOU
   (Don Williams)
10. ROWDY
    (Hank Williams Jr.)

AUGUST 29, 1981

POP SINGLES

1. ENDLESS LOVE
   (Diana Ross and Lionel Richie)
2. JESSIE'S GIRL
   (Rick Springfield)
3. QUEEN OF HEARTS
   (Juice Newton)
4. SLOW HAND
   (The Pointer Sisters)
5. THEME FROM THE GREATEST AMERICAN HERO
   (Joey Scarbury)
6. THE STROKE
   (Billy Squier)
7. ELVIRA
   (The Oak Ridge Boys)
8. URGENT
   (Foreigner)
9. LADY (YOU BRING ME UP)
   (Commodores)
10. (THERE'S) NO GETTIN' OVER ME
    (Ronnie Milsap)

POP ALBUMS

1. 4
   (Foreigner)
2. ESCAPE
   (Journey)
3. PRECIOUS TIME
   (Pat Benatar)
4. BELLA DONNA
   (Stevie Nicks)
5. HI INFIDELITY
   (R.E.O. Speedwagon)
6. ENDLESS LOVE
   (Original Soundtrack)
7. LONG DISTANCE VOYAGER
   (The Moody Blues)
8. DON'T SAY NO
   (Billy Squier)
9. STREET SONGS
   (Rick James)
10. SHARE YOUR LOVE
    (Kenny Rogers)

BLACK SINGLES

1. ENDLESS LOVE
   (Diana Ross and Lionel Richie)
2. SHE'S A BAD MAMA JAMA (SHE'S BUILT, SHE'S STACKED)
   (Carl Carlton)
3. SQUARE BIZ
   (Teena Marie)
4. I'M IN LOVE
   (Evelyn King)
5. LADY (YOU BRING ME UP)
   (Commodores)
6. JUST BE MY LADY
   (Larry Graham)
7. SLOW HAND
   (The Pointer Sisters)
8. LOVE ON A TWO WAY STREET
   (Stacy Lattisaw)
9. SUPER FREAK (PART 1)
   (Rick James)
10. I'LL DO ANYTHING FOR YOU
    (Denroy Morgan)

BLACK ALBUMS

1. STREET SONGS
   (Rick James)
2. IT MUST BE MAGIC
   (Teena Marie)
3. I'M IN LOVE
   (Evelyn King)
4. DIMPLES
   (Richard "Dimples" Fields)
5. IN THE POCKET
   (Commodores)
6. ENDLESS LOVE
   (Original Soundtrack)
7. LIVE IN NEW ORLEANS
   (Maze featuring Frankie Beverly)
8. CARL CARLTON
   (Carl Carlton)
9. BLACK AND WHITE
   (The Pointer Sisters)
10. WITH YOU
    (Stacy Lattisaw)

JAZZ ALBUMS

1. BREAKIN' AWAY
   (Al Jarreau)
2. THE MAN WITH THE HORN
   (Miles Davis)
3. RIT
   (Lee Ritenour)
4. THE CLARKE/DUKE PROJECT
   (Stanley Clarke and George Duke)
5. AS FALLS WICHITA, SO FALLS WICHITA FALLS
   (Pat Metheny and Lyle Mays)

6. APPLE JUICE
   (Tom Scott)
7. HUSH
   (John Klemmer)
8. VOYEUR
   (David Sanborn)
9. WINELIGHT
   (Grover Washington Jr.)
10. LIVE IN JAPAN
    (Dave Grusin and the GRP All-Stars)

COUNTRY SINGLES

1. (THERE'S) NO GETTIN' OVER ME
   (Ronnie Milsap)
2. OLDER WOMEN
   (Ronnie McDowell)
3. DON'T WAIT ON ME
   (The Statler Brothers)
4. I DON'T NEED YOU
   (Kenny Rogers)
5. MIRACLES
   (Don Williams)
6. YOU DON'T KNOW ME
   (Mickey Gilley)
7. RAINBOW STEW
   (Merle Haggard)
8. TIGHT FITTIN' JEANS
   (Conway Twitty)
9. IT'S NOW OR NEVER
   (John Schneider)
10. I JUST NEED YOU FOR TONIGHT
    (Billy "Crash" Craddock)

COUNTRY ALBUMS

1. SHARE YOUR LOVE
   (Kenny Rogers)
2. FEELS SO RIGHT
   (Alabama)
3. FANCY FREE
   (The Oak Ridge Boys)
4. KENNY ROGERS' GREATEST HITS
   (Kenny Rogers)
5. JUICE
   (Juice Newton)
6. STEP BY STEP
   (Eddie Rabbitt)
7. SOME DAYS ARE DIAMONDS
   (John Denver)
8. I AM WHAT I AM
   (George Jones)
9. YEARS AGO
   (The Statler Brothers)
10. SEVEN YEAR ACHE
    (Rosanne Cash)

SEPTEMBER 5, 1981

POP SINGLES

1. ENDLESS LOVE
   (Diana Ross and Lionel Richie)
2. QUEEN OF HEARTS
   (Juice Newton)
3. JESSIE'S GIRL
   (Rick Springfield)
4. SLOW HAND
   (The Pointer Sisters)
5. URGENT
   (Foreigner)
6. THE STROKE
   (Billy Squier)
7. LADY (YOU BRING ME UP)
   (Commodores)
8. (THERE'S) NO GETTIN' OVER ME
   (Ronnie Milsap)
9. WHO'S CRYING NOW
   (Journey)
10. STOP DRAGGIN' MY HEART AROUND
    (Stevie Nicks with Tom Petty and
    the Heartbreakers)

POP ALBUMS

1. ESCAPE
   (Journey)
2. 4
   (Foreigner)
3. BELLA DONNA
   (Stevie Nicks)
4. PRECIOUS TIME
   (Pat Benatar)
5. HI INFIDELITY
   (R.E.O. Speedwagon)
6. ENDLESS LOVE
   (Original Soundtrack)
7. LONG DISTANCE VOYAGER
   (The Moody Blues)
8. DON'T SAY NO
   (Billy Squier)
9. STREET SONGS
   (Rick James)
10. PIRATES
    (Rickie Lee Jones)

BLACK SINGLES

1. ENDLESS LOVE
   (Diana Ross and Lionel Richie)
2. SHE'S A BAD MAMA JAMA (SHE'S BUILT,
   SHE'S STACKED)
   (Carl Carlton)
3. SQUARE BIZ
   (Teena Marie)
4. I'M IN LOVE
   (Evelyn King)
5. JUST BE MY LADY
   (Larry Graham)
6. SUPER FREAK (PART 1)
   (Rick James)
7. SLOW HAND
   (The Pointer Sisters)
8. I'LL DO ANYTHING FOR YOU
   (Denroy Morgan)
9. LADY (YOU BRING ME UP)
   (Commodores)
10. LOVE ON A TWO WAY STREET
    (Stacy Lattisaw)

BLACK ALBUMS

1. STREET SONGS
   (Rick James)
2. IT MUST BE MAGIC
   (Teena Marie)
3. DIMPLES
   (Richard "Dimples" Fields)
4. I'M IN LOVE
   (Evelyn King)
5. ENDLESS LOVE
   (Original Soundtrack)
6. IN THE POCKET
   (Commodores)
7. CARL CARLTON
   (Carl Carlton)
8. BREAKIN' AWAY
   (Al Jarreau)
9. LIVE IN NEW ORLEANS
   (Maze featuring Frankie Beverly)
10. BLACK AND WHITE
    (The Pointer Sisters)

JAZZ ALBUMS

1. THE MAN WITH THE HORN
   (Miles Davis)
2. BREAKIN' AWAY
   (Al Jarreau)
3. RIT
   (Lee Ritenour)
4. APPLE JUICE
   (Tom Scott)
5. AS FALLS WICHITA, SO FALLS WICHITA
   FALLS
   (Pat Metheny and Lyle Mays)

6. FREE TIME
   (Spyro Gyra)
7. THE CLARKE/DUKE PROJECT
   (Stanley Clarke and George Duke)
8. WINELIGHT
   (Grover Washington Jr.)
9. VOYEUR
   (David Sanborn)
10. THE DUDE
    (Quincy Jones)

COUNTRY SINGLES

1. OLDER WOMEN
   (Ronnie McDowell)
2. (THERE'S) NO GETTIN' OVER ME
   (Ronnie Milsap)
3. DON'T WAIT ON ME
   (The Statler Brothers)
4. MIRACLES
   (Don Williams)
5. YOU DON'T KNOW ME
   (Mickey Gilley)
6. TIGHT FITTIN' JEANS
   (Conway Twitty)
7. I DON'T NEED YOU
   (Kenny Rogers)
8. PARTY TIME
   (T.G. Sheppard)
9. I JUST NEED YOU FOR TONIGHT
   (Billy "Crash" Craddock)
10. YOU'RE THE BEST
    (Kieran Kane)

COUNTRY ALBUMS

1. SHARE YOUR LOVE
   (Kenny Rogers)
2. FEELS SO RIGHT
   (Alabama)
3. FANCY FREE
   (The Oak Ridge Boys)
4. KENNY ROGERS' GREATEST HITS
   (Kenny Rogers)
5. STEP BY STEP
   (Eddie Rabbitt)
6. JUICE
   (Juice Newton)
7. SOME DAYS ARE DIAMONDS
   (John Denver)
8. I AM WHAT I AM
   (George Jones)
9. SEVEN YEAR ACHE
   (Rosanne Cash)
10. YEARS AGO
    (The Statler Brothers)

SEPTEMBER 12, 1981

POP SINGLES

1. ENDLESS LOVE
   (Diana Ross and Lionel Richie)
2. QUEEN OF HEARTS
   (Juice Newton)
3. URGENT
   (Foreigner)
4. SLOW HAND
   (The Pointer Sisters)
5. JESSIE'S GIRL
   (Rick Springfield)
6. WHO'S CRYING NOW
   (Journey)
7. LADY (YOU BRING ME UP)
   (Commodores)
8. (THERE'S) NO GETTIN' OVER ME
   (Ronnie Milsap)
9. STOP DRAGGIN' MY HEART AROUND
   (Stevie Nicks with Tom Petty and
   the Heartbreakers)

10. MEDLEY
(The Beach Boys)

POP ALBUMS

1. ESCAPE
(Journey)
2. 4
(Foreigner)
3. BELLA DONNA
(Stevie Nicks)
4. PRECIOUS TIME
(Pat Benatar)
5. TATTOO YOU
(The Rolling Stones)
6. ENDLESS LOVE
(Original Soundtrack)
7. HI INFIDELITY
(R.E.O. Speedwagon)
8. LONG DISTANCE VOYAGER
(The Moody Blues)
9. DON'T SAY NO
(Billy Squier)
10. PIRATES
(Rickie Lee Jones)

BLACK SINGLES

1. ENDLESS LOVE
(Diana Ross and Lionel Richie)
2. SHE'S A BAD MAMA JAMA (SHE'S BUILT, SHE'S STACKED)
(Carl Carlton)
3. SUPER FREAK (PART 1)
(Rick James)
4. SQUARE BIZ
(Teena Marie)
5. JUST BE MY LADY
(Larry Graham)
6. I'M IN LOVE
(Evelyn King)
7. SLOW HAND
(The Pointer Sisters)
8. I'LL DO ANYTHING FOR YOU
(Denroy Morgan)
9. LADY (YOU BRING ME UP)
(Commodores)
10. SWEAT (TIL YOU GET WET)
(Brick)

BLACK ALBUMS

1. STREET SONGS
(Rick James)
2. IT MUST BE MAGIC
(Teena Marie)
3. DIMPLES
(Richard "Dimples" Fields)
4. I'M IN LOVE
(Evelyn King)
5. ENDLESS LOVE
(Original Soundtrack)
6. IN THE POCKET
(Commodores)
7. CARL CARLTON
(Carl Carlton)
8. BREAKIN' AWAY
(Al Jarreau)
9. BLACK AND WHITE
(The Pointer Sisters)
10. LIVE IN NEW ORLEANS
(Maze featuring Frankie Beverly)

JAZZ ALBUMS

1. BREAKIN' AWAY
(Al Jarreau)
2. FREE TIME
(Spyro Gyra)
3. THE MAN WITH THE HORN
(Miles Davis)

4. RIT
(Lee Ritenour)
5. APPLE JUICE
(Tom Scott)
6. AS FALLS WICHITA, SO FALLS WICHITA FALLS
(Pat Metheny and Lyle Mays)
7. THE CLARKE/DUKE PROJECT
(Stanley Clarke and George Duke)
8. WINELIGHT
(Grover Washington Jr.)
9. VOYEUR
(David Sanborn)
10. THE DUDE
(Quincy Jones)

COUNTRY SINGLES

1. YOU DON'T KNOW ME
(Mickey Gilley)
2. OLDER WOMEN
(Ronnie McDowell)
3. TIGHT FITTIN' JEANS
(Conway Twitty)
4. MIRACLES
(Don Williams)
5. PARTY TIME
(T.G. Sheppard)
6. (THERE'S) NO GETTIN' OVER ME
(Ronnie Milsap)
7. STEP BY STEP
(Eddie Rabbitt)
8. MIDNIGHT HAULER/SCRATCH MY BACK
(Razzy Bailey)
9. DON'T WAIT ON ME
(The Statler Brothers)
10. I JUST NEED YOU FOR TONIGHT
(Billy "Crash" Craddock)

COUNTRY ALBUMS

1. SHARE YOUR LOVE
(Kenny Rogers)
2. FANCY FREE
(The Oak Ridge Boys)
3. FEELS SO RIGHT
(Alabama)
4. KENNY ROGERS' GREATEST HITS
(Kenny Rogers)
5. STEP BY STEP
(Eddie Rabbitt)
6. JUICE
(Juice Newton)
7. I AM WHAT I AM
(George Jones)
8. ESPECIALLY FOR YOU
(Don Williams)
9. YEARS AGO
(The Statler Brothers)
10. SOME DAYS ARE DIAMONDS
(John Denver)

SEPTEMBER 19, 1981

POP SINGLES

1. ENDLESS LOVE
(Diana Ross and Lionel Richie)
2. QUEEN OF HEARTS
(Juice Newton)
3. URGENT
(Foreigner)
4. SLOW HAND
(The Pointer Sisters)
5. WHO'S CRYING NOW
(Journey)
6. STOP DRAGGIN' MY HEART AROUND
(Stevie Nicks with Tom Petty and the Heartbreakers)
7. MEDLEY
(The Beach Boys)

8. STEP BY STEP
(Eddie Rabbitt)
9. (THERE'S) NO GETTIN' OVER ME
(Ronnie Milsap)
10. JESSIE'S GIRL
(Rick Springfield)

POP ALBUMS

1. ESCAPE
(Journey)
2. 4
(Foreigner)
3. BELLA DONNA
(Stevie Nicks)
4. TATTOO YOU
(The Rolling Stones)
5. PRECIOUS TIME
(Pat Benatar)
6. LONG DISTANCE VOYAGER
(The Moody Blues)
7. ENDLESS LOVE
(Original Soundtrack)
8. HI INFIDELITY
(R.E.O. Speedwagon)
9. DON'T SAY NO
(Billy Squier)
10. PIRATES
(Rickie Lee Jones)

BLACK SINGLES

1. ENDLESS LOVE
(Diana Ross and Lionel Richie)
2. SHE'S A BAD MAMA JAMA (SHE'S BUILT, SHE'S STACKED)
(Carl Carlton)
3. SUPER FREAK (PART 1)
(Rick James)
4. SQUARE BIZ
(Teena Marie)
5. JUST BE MY LADY
(Larry Graham)
6. I'M IN LOVE
(Evelyn King)
7. NEVER TOO MUCH
(Luther Vandross)
8. WHEN SHE WAS MY GIRL
(The Four Tops)
9. WE'RE IN THIS LOVE TOGETHER
(Al Jarreau)
10. SWEAT (TIL YOU GET WET)
(Brick)

BLACK ALBUMS

1. STREET SONGS
(Rick James)
2. IT MUST BE MAGIC
(Teena Marie)
3. BREAKIN' AWAY
(Al Jarreau)
4. I'M IN LOVE
(Evelyn King)
5. ENDLESS LOVE
(Original Soundtrack)
6. CARL CARLTON
(Carl Carlton)
7. IN THE POCKET
(Commodores)
8. DIMPLES
(Richard "Dimples" Fields)
9. BLACK AND WHITE
(The Pointer Sisters)
10. LOVE ALL THE HURT AWAY
(Aretha Franklin)

JAZZ ALBUMS

1. BREAKIN' AWAY
(Al Jarreau)

2. FREE TIME
   (Spyro Gyra)
3. THE MAN WITH THE HORN
   (Miles Davis)
4. APPLE JUICE
   (Tom Scott)
5. AS FALLS WICHITA, SO FALLS WICHITA FALLS
   (Pat Metheny and Lyle Mays)
6. SIGN OF THE TIMES
   (Bob James)
7. RIT
   (Lee Ritenour)
8. THE CLARKE/DUKE PROJECT
   (Stanley Clarke and George Duke)
9. WINELIGHT
   (Grover Washington Jr.)
10. CLEAN SWEEP
    (Bobby Broom)

COUNTRY SINGLES

1. YOU DON'T KNOW ME
   (Mickey Gilley)
2. TIGHT FITTIN' JEANS
   (Conway Twitty)
3. PARTY TIME
   (T.G. Sheppard)
4. MIRACLES
   (Don Williams)
5. STEP BY STEP
   (Eddie Rabbitt)
6. MIDNIGHT HAULER/SCRATCH MY BACK
   (Razzy Bailey)
7. OLDER WOMEN
   (Ronnie McDowell)
8. (THERE'S) NO GETTIN' OVER ME
   (Ronnie Milsap)
9. TAKIN' IT EASY
   (Lacy J. Dalton)
10. TODAY ALL OVER AGAIN
    (Reba McEntire)

COUNTRY ALBUMS

1. SHARE YOUR LOVE
   (Kenny Rogers)
2. FANCY FREE
   (The Oak Ridge Boys)
3. FEELS SO RIGHT
   (Alabama)
4. KENNY ROGERS' GREATEST HITS
   (Kenny Rogers)
5. STEP BY STEP
   (Eddie Rabbitt)
6. JUICE
   (Juice Newton)
7. YEARS AGO
   (The Statler Brothers)
8. ESPECIALLY FOR YOU
   (Don Williams)
9. SOME DAYS ARE DIAMONDS
   (John Denver)
10. THE PRESSURE IS ON
    (Hank Williams Jr.)

SEPTEMBER 26, 1981

POP SINGLES

1. ENDLESS LOVE
   (Diana Ross and Lionel Richie)
2. QUEEN OF HEARTS
   (Juice Newton)
3. WHO'S CRYING NOW
   (Journey)
4. URGENT
   (Foreigner)
5. MEDLEY
   (The Beach Boys)

6. STOP DRAGGIN' MY HEART AROUND
   (Stevie Nicks with Tom Petty and The Heartbreakers)
7. STEP BY STEP
   (Eddie Rabbitt)
8. ARTHUR'S THEME (BEST THAT YOU CAN DO)
   (Christopher Cross)
9. SLOW HAND
   (The Pointer Sisters)
10. HOLD ON TIGHT
    (Electric Light Orchestra)

POP ALBUMS

1. TATTOO YOU
   (The Rolling Stones)
2. ESCAPE
   (Journey)
3. BELLA DONNA
   (Stevie Nicks)
4. 4
   (Foreigner)
5. PRECIOUS TIME
   (Pat Benatar)
6. LONG DISTANCE VOYAGER
   (The Moody Blues)
7. THE INNOCENT AGE
   (Dan Fogelberg)
8. DON'T SAY NO
   (Billy Squier)
9. STREET SONGS
   (Rick James)
10. PIRATES
    (Rickie Lee Jones)

BLACK SINGLES

1. SHE'S A BAD MAMA JAMA (SHE'S BUILT, SHE'S STACKED)
   (Carl Carlton)
2. ENDLESS LOVE
   (Diana Ross and Lionel Richie)
3. SUPER FREAK (PART 1)
   (Rick James)
4. NEVER TOO MUCH
   (Luther Vandross)
5. WHEN SHE WAS MY GIRL
   (The Four Tops)
6. SQUARE BIZ
   (Teena Marie)
7. SILLY
   (Deniece Williams)
8. WE'RE IN THIS LOVE TOGETHER
   (Al Jarreau)
9. JUST BE MY LADY
   (Larry Graham)
10. I'M IN LOVE
    (Evelyn King)

BLACK ALBUMS

1. STREET SONGS
   (Rick James)
2. BREAKIN' AWAY
   (Al Jarreau)
3. CARL CARLTON
   (Carl Carlton)
4. I'M IN LOVE
   (Evelyn King)
5. ENDLESS LOVE
   (Original Soundtrack)
6. IT MUST BE MAGIC
   (Teena Marie)
7. IN THE POCKET
   (Commodores)
8. LOVE ALL THE HURT AWAY
   (Aretha Franklin)
9. TONIGHT
   (Four Tops)
10. DIMPLES
    (Richard "Dimples" Fields)

JAZZ ALBUMS

1. BREAKIN' AWAY
   (Al Jarreau)
2. THE MAN WITH THE HORN
   (Miles Davis)
3. FREE TIME
   (Spyro Gyra)
4. SIGN OF THE TIMES
   (Bob James)
5. AS FALLS WICHITA, SO FALLS WICHITA FALLS
   (Pat Metheny and Lyle Mays)
6. APPLE JUICE
   (Tom Scott)
7. RIT
   (Lee Ritenour)
8. THE CLARKE/DUKE PROJECT
   (Stanley Clarke and George Duke)
9. CLEAN SWEEP
   (Bobby Broom)
10. WINELIGHT
    (Grover Washington Jr.)

COUNTRY SINGLES

1. PARTY TIME
   (T.G. Sheppard)
2. TIGHT FITTIN' JEANS
   (Conway Twitty)
3. STEP BY STEP
   (Eddie Rabbitt)
4. MIDNIGHT HAULER/SCRATCH MY BACK
   (Razzy Bailey)
5. YOU DON'T KNOW ME
   (Mickey Gilley)
6. TAKIN' IT EASY
   (Lacy J. Dalton)
7. TODAY ALL OVER AGAIN
   (Reba McEntire)
8. HURRICANE
   (Leon Everette)
9. I'LL NEED SOMEONE TO HOLD ME (WHEN I CRY)
   (Janie Fricke)
10. RIGHT IN THE PALM OF YOUR HAND
    (Mel McDaniel)

COUNTRY ALBUMS

1. SHARE YOUR LOVE
   (Kenny Rogers)
2. FANCY FREE
   (The Oak Ridge Boys)
3. FEELS SO RIGHT
   (Alabama)
4. KENNY ROGERS' GREATEST HITS
   (Kenny Rogers)
5. STEP BY STEP
   (Eddie Rabbitt)
6. JUICE
   (Juice Newton)
7. ESPECIALLY FOR YOU
   (Don Williams)
8. THERE'S NO GETTIN' OVER ME
   (Ronnie Milsap)
9. SOME DAYS ARE DIAMONDS
   (John Denver)
10. THE PRESSURE IS ON
    (Hank Williams Jr.)

OCTOBER 3, 1981

POP SINGLES

1. ENDLESS LOVE
   (Diana Ross and Lionel Richie)
2. QUEEN OF HEARTS
   (Juice Newton)

3. WHO'S CRYING NOW
   (Journey)
4. ARTHUR'S THEME (BEST THAT YOU CAN DO)
   (Christopher Cross)
5. MEDLEY
   (The Beach Boys)
6. URGENT
   (Foreigner)
7. STEP BY STEP
   (Eddie Rabbitt)
8. START ME UP
   (The Rolling Stones)
9. FOR YOUR EYES ONLY
   (Sheena Easton)
10. HOLD ON TIGHT
    (Electric Light Orchestra)

POP ALBUMS

1. TATTOO YOU
   (The Rolling Stones)
2. ESCAPE
   (Journey)
3. 4
   (Foreigner)
4. BELLA DONNA
   (Stevie Nicks)
5. THE INNOCENT AGE
   (Dan Fogelberg)
6. PRECIOUS TIME
   (Pat Benatar)
7. NINE TONIGHT
   (Bob Seger and The Silver Bullet Band)
8. DON'T SAY NO
   (Billy Squier)
9. STREET SONGS
   (Rick James)
10. HEAVY METAL
    (Original Soundtrack)

BLACK SINGLES

1. SHE'S A BAD MAMA JAMA (SHE'S BUILT, SHE'S STACKED)
   (Carl Carlton)
2. ENDLESS LOVE
   (Diana Ross and Lionel Richie)
3. SUPER FREAK (PART 1)
   (Rick James)
4. NEVER TOO MUCH
   (Luther Vandross)
5. WHEN SHE WAS MY GIRL
   (The Four Tops)
6. WE'RE IN THIS LOVE TOGETHER
   (Al Jarreau)
7. SILLY
   (Deniece Williams)
8. SQUARE BIZ
   (Teena Marie)
9. LOVE ALL THE HURT AWAY
   (Aretha Franklin and George Benson)
10. ON THE BEAT
    (B.B. and Q. Band)

BLACK ALBUMS

1. STREET SONGS
   (Rick James)
2. BREAKIN' AWAY
   (Al Jarreau)
3. CARL CARLTON
   (Carl Carlton)
4. NEVER TOO MUCH
   (Luther Vandross)
5. I'M IN LOVE
   (Evelyn King)
6. ENDLESS LOVE
   (Original Soundtrack)
7. TONIGHT
   (The Four Tops)
8. LOVE ALL THE HURT AWAY
   (Aretha Franklin)

9. IN THE POCKET
   (Commodores)
10. IT MUST BE MAGIC
    (Teena Marie)

JAZZ ALBUMS

1. BREAKIN' AWAY
   (Al Jarreau)
2. THE MAN WITH THE HORN
   (Miles Davis)
3. SIGN OF THE TIMES
   (Bob James)
4. FREE TIME
   (Spyro Gyra)
5. LOVE BYRD
   (Donald Byrd and 125th Street, New York City)
6. AS FALLS WICHITA, SO FALLS WICHITA FALLS
   (Pat Metheny and Lyle Mays)
7. APPLE JUICE
   (Tom Scott)
8. THE CLARKE/DUKE PROJECT
   (Stanley Clarke and George Duke)
9. CLEAN SWEEP
   (Bobby Broom)
10. THE DUDE
    (Quincy Jones)

COUNTRY SINGLES

1. STEP BY STEP
   (Eddie Rabbitt)
2. PARTY TIME
   (T.G. Sheppard)
3. MIDNIGHT HAULER/SCRATCH MY BACK
   (Razzy Bailey)
4. TAKIN' IT EASY
   (Lacy J. Dalton)
5. TODAY ALL OVER AGAIN
   (Reba McEntire)
6. HURRICANE
   (Leon Everette)
7. I'LL NEED SOMEONE TO HOLD ME (WHEN I CRY)
   (Janie Fricke)
8. EVERYTHING'S A WALTZ
   (Ed Bruce)
9. RIGHT IN THE PALM OF YOUR HAND
   (Mel McDaniel)
10. I LOVE YOU A THOUSAND WAYS/CHICKEN TRUCK
    (John Anderson)

COUNTRY ALBUMS

1. FEELS SO RIGHT
   (Alabama)
2. STEP BY STEP
   (Eddie Rabbitt)
3. FANCY FREE
   (The Oak Ridge Boys)
4. KENNY ROGERS' GREATEST HITS
   (Kenny Rogers)
5. SHARE YOUR LOVE
   (Kenny Rogers)
6. THERE'S NO GETTIN' OVER ME
   (Ronnie Milsap)
7. SOME DAYS ARE DIAMONDS
   (John Denver)
8. THE PRESSURE IS ON
   (Hank Williams Jr.)
9. JUICE
   (Juice Newton)
10. GREATEST HITS
    (Willie Nelson)

OCTOBER 10, 1981

POP SINGLES

1. ENDLESS LOVE
   (Diana Ross and Lionel Richie)

2. ARTHUR'S THEME (BEST THAT YOU CAN DO)
   (Christopher Cross)
3. WHO'S CRYING NOW
   (Journey)
4. QUEEN OF HEARTS
   (Juice Newton)
5. MEDLEY
   (The Beach Boys)
6. FOR YOUR EYES ONLY
   (Sheena Easton)
7. STEP BY STEP
   (Eddie Rabbitt)
8. START ME UP
   (The Rolling Stones)
9. URGENT
   (Foreigner)
10. HOLD ON TIGHT
    (Electric Light Orchestra)

POP ALBUMS

1. TATTOO YOU
   (The Rolling Stones)
2. ESCAPE
   (Journey)
3. 4
   (Foreigner)
4. BELLA DONNA
   (Stevie Nicks)
5. THE INNOCENT AGE
   (Dan Fogelberg)
6. NINE TONIGHT
   (Bob Seger and The Silver Bullet Band)
7. PRECIOUS TIME
   (Pat Benatar)
8. DON'T SAY NO
   (Billy Squier)
9. STREET SONGS
   (Rick James)
10. HEAVY METAL
    (Original Soundtrack)

BLACK SINGLES

1. ENDLESS LOVE
   (Diana Ross and Lionel Richie)
2. NEVER TOO MUCH
   (Luther Vandross)
3. WHEN SHE WAS MY GIRL
   (The Four Tops)
4. SHE'S A BAD MAMA JAMA (SHE'S BUILT, SHE'S STACKED)
   (Carl Carlton)
5. SUPER FREAK (PART 1)
   (Rick James)
6. WE'RE IN THIS LOVE TOGETHER
   (Al Jarreau)
7. SILLY
   (Deniece Williams)
8. LOVE ALL THE HURT AWAY
   (Aretha Franklin and George Benson)
9. I HEARD IT THROUGH THE GRAPEVINE (PART 1)
   (Roger)
10. ON THE BEAT
    (B.B. and Q. Band)

BLACK ALBUMS

1. STREET SONGS
   (Rick James)
2. BREAKIN' AWAY
   (Al Jarreau)
3. NEVER TOO MUCH
   (Luther Vandross)
4. CARL CARLTON
   (Carl Carlton)
5. IT'S TIME FOR LOVE
   (Teddy Pendergrass)
6. ENDLESS LOVE
   (Original Soundtrack)
7. TONIGHT
   (The Four Tops)

8. I'M IN LOVE
   (Evelyn King)
9. THE MANY FACETS OF ROGER
   (Roger)
10. LOVE ALL THE HURT AWAY
    (Aretha Franklin)

JAZZ ALBUMS

1. BREAKIN' AWAY
   (Al Jarreau)
2. THE MAN WITH THE HORN
   (Miles Davis)
3. SIGN OF THE TIMES
   (Bob James)
4. FREE TIME
   (Spyro Gyra)
5. SOLID GROUND
   (Ronnie Laws)
6. LOVE BYRD
   (Donald Byrd and 125th Street,
   New York City)
7. AS FALLS WICHITA, SO FALLS WICHITA
   FALLS
   (Pat Metheny and Lyle Mays)
8. APPLE JUICE
   (Tom Scott)
9. THE CLARKE/DUKE PROJECT
   (Stanley Clarke and George Duke)
10. THE DUDE
    (Quincy Jones)

COUNTRY SINGLES

1. STEP BY STEP
   (Eddie Rabbitt)
2. TAKIN' IT EASY
   (Lacy J. Dalton)
3. MIDNIGHT HAULER/SCRATCH MY BACK
   (Razzy Bailey)
4. I'LL NEED SOMEONE TO HOLD ME (WHEN
   I CRY)
   (Janie Fricke)
5. TODAY ALL OVER AGAIN
   (Reba McEntire)
6. HURRICANE
   (Leon Everette)
7. NEVER BEEN SO LOVED (IN ALL MY LIFE)
   (Charley Pride)
8. EVERYTHING'S A WALTZ
   (Ed Bruce)
9. PARTY TIME
   (T.G. Sheppard)
10. I LOVE YOU A THOUSAND WAYS/CHICKEN
    TRUCK
    (John Anderson)

COUNTRY ALBUMS

1. FEELS SO RIGHT
   (Alabama)
2. STEP BY STEP
   (Eddie Rabbitt)
3. FANCY FREE
   (The Oak Ridge Boys)
4. THERE'S NO GETTIN' OVER ME
   (Ronnie Milsap)
5. GREATEST HITS
   (Willie Nelson)
6. KENNY ROGERS' GREATEST HITS
   (Kenny Rogers)
7. SHARE YOUR LOVE
   (Kenny Rogers)
8. JUICE
   (Juice Newton)
9. THE PRESSURE IS ON
   (Hank Williams Jr.)
10. BARBARA MANDRELL LIVE
    (Barbara Mandrell)

OCTOBER 17, 1981

POP SINGLES

1. ARTHUR'S THEME (BEST THAT YOU CAN
   DO)
   (Christopher Cross)
2. ENDLESS LOVE
   (Diana Ross and Lionel Richie)
3. FOR YOUR EYES ONLY
   (Sheena Easton)
4. QUEEN OF HEARTS
   (Juice Newton)
5. MEDLEY
   (The Beach Boys)
6. PRIVATE EYES
   (Daryl Hall and John Oates)
7. STEP BY STEP
   (Eddie Rabbitt)
8. START ME UP
   (The Rolling Stones)
9. WHO'S CRYING NOW
   (Journey)
10. I'VE DONE EVERYTHING FOR YOU
    (Rick Springfield)

POP ALBUMS

1. ESCAPE
   (Journey)
2. TATTOO YOU
   (The Rolling Stones)
3. 4
   (Foreigner)
4. NINE TONIGHT
   (Bob Seger and The Silver Bullet Band)
5. THE INNOCENT AGE
   (Dan Fogelberg)
6. BELLA DONNA
   (Stevie Nicks)
7. PRECIOUS TIME
   (Pat Benatar)
8. DON'T SAY NO
   (Billy Squier)
9. HEAVY METAL
   (Original Soundtrack)
10. BREAKIN' AWAY
    (Al Jarreau)

BLACK SINGLES

1. NEVER TOO MUCH
   (Luther Vandross)
2. ENDLESS LOVE
   (Diana Ross and Lionel Richie)
3. WHEN SHE WAS MY GIRL
   (The Four Tops)
4. SHE'S A BAD MAMA JAMA (SHE'S BUILT,
   SHE'S STACKED)
   (Carl Carlton)
5. SUPER FREAK (PART 1)
   (Rick James)
6. I HEARD IT THROUGH THE GRAPEVINE
   (PART 1)
   (Roger)
7. SILLY
   (Deniece Williams)
8. LOVE ALL THE HURT AWAY
   (Aretha Franklin and George Benson)
9. WE'RE IN THIS LOVE TOGETHER
   (Al Jarreau)
10. I'LL DO ANYTHING FOR YOU
    (Denroy Morgan)

BLACK ALBUMS

1. NEVER TOO MUCH
   (Luther Vandross)
2. BREAKIN' AWAY
   (Al Jarreau)

3. STREET SONGS
   (Rick James)
4. IT'S TIME FOR LOVE
   (Teddy Pendergrass)
5. THE MANY FACETS OF ROGER
   (Roger)
6. TONIGHT
   (The Four Tops)
7. CARL CARLTON
   (Carl Carlton)
8. ENDLESS LOVE
   (Original Soundtrack)
9. I'M IN LOVE
   (Evelyn King)
10. TIME
    (Time)

JAZZ ALBUMS

1. BREAKIN' AWAY
   (Al Jarreau)
2. SIGN OF THE TIMES
   (Bob James)
3. FREE TIME
   (Spyro Gyra)
4. SOLID GROUND
   (Ronnie Laws)
5. THE MAN WITH THE HORN
   (Miles Davis)
6. LOVE BYRD
   (Donald Byrd and 125th Street,
   New York City)
7. STANDING TALL
   (Crusaders)
8. MAGIC WINDOWS
   (Herbie Hancock)
9. REFLECTIONS
   (Gil Scott-Heron)
10. EVERY HOME SHOULD HAVE ONE
    (Patti Austin)

COUNTRY SINGLES

1. STEP BY STEP
   (Eddie Rabbitt)
2. TAKIN' IT EASY
   (Lacy J. Dalton)
3. NEVER BEEN SO LOVED (IN ALL MY LIFE)
   (Charley Pride)
4. I'LL NEED SOMEONE TO HOLD ME (WHEN
   I CRY)
   (Janie Fricke)
5. HURRICANE
   (Leon Everette)
6. MIDNIGHT HAULER/SCRATCH MY BACK
   (Razzy Bailey)
7. SLEEPIN' WITH THE RADIO ON
   (Charly McClain)
8. FANCY FREE
   (The Oak Ridge Boys)
9. I LOVE YOU A THOUSAND WAYS/CHICKEN
   TRUCK
   (John Anderson)
10. TEACH ME TO CHEAT
    (The Kendalls)

COUNTRY ALBUMS

1. FANCY FREE
   (The Oak Ridge Boys)
2. FEELS SO RIGHT
   (Alabama)
3. STEP BY STEP
   (Eddie Rabbitt)
4. THERE'S NO GETTIN' OVER ME
   (Ronnie Milsap)
5. GREATEST HITS
   (Willie Nelson)
6. SHARE YOUR LOVE
   (Kenny Rogers)
7. KENNY ROGERS' GREATEST HITS
   (Kenny Rogers)
8. JUICE
   (Juice Newton)

9. THE PRESSURE IS ON
   (Hank Williams Jr.)
10. BARBARA MANDRELL LIVE
   (Barbara Mandrell)

OCTOBER 24, 1981

POP SINGLES

1. ARTHUR'S THEME (BEST THAT YOU CAN DO)
   (Christopher Cross)
2. ENDLESS LOVE
   (Diana Ross and Lionel Richie)
3. FOR YOUR EYES ONLY
   (Sheena Easton)
4. PRIVATE EYES
   (Daryl Hall and John Oates)
5. QUEEN OF HEARTS
   (Juice Newton)
6. MEDLEY
   (The Beach Boys)
7. STEP BY STEP
   (Eddie Rabbitt)
8. START ME UP
   (The Rolling Stones)
9. I'VE DONE EVERYTHING FOR YOU
   (Rick Springfield)
10. THE NIGHT OWLS
   (Little River Band)

POP ALBUMS

1. TATTOO YOU
   (The Rolling Stones)
2. ESCAPE
   (Journey)
3. 4
   (Foreigner)
4. NINE TONIGHT
   (Bob Seger and The Silver Bullet Band)
5. THE INNOCENT AGE
   (Dan Fogelberg)
6. BELLA DONNA
   (Stevie Nicks)
7. PRECIOUS TIME
   (Pat Benatar)
8. SONGS IN THE ATTIC
   (Billy Joel)
9. HEAVY METAL
   (Original Soundtrack)
10. BREAKIN' AWAY
   (Al Jarreau)

BLACK SINGLES

1. NEVER TOO MUCH
   (Luther Vandross)
2. WHEN SHE WAS MY GIRL
   (The Four Tops)
3. ENDLESS LOVE
   (Diana Ross and Lionel Richie)
4. SHE'S A BAD MAMA JAMA (SHE'S BUILT, SHE'S STACKED)
   (Carl Carlton)
5. I HEARD IT THROUGH THE GRAPEVINE (PART I)
   (Roger)
6. SUPER FREAK (PART 1)
   (Rick James)
7. SILLY
   (Deniece Williams)
8. GET IT UP
   (Time)
9. WE'RE IN THIS LOVE TOGETHER
   (Al Jarreau)
10. I'LL DO ANYTHING FOR YOU
   (Denroy Morgan)

BLACK ALBUMS

1. NEVER TOO MUCH
   (Luther Vandross)
2. BREAKIN' AWAY
   (Al Jarreau)
3. THE MANY FACETS OF ROGER
   (Roger)
4. IT'S TIME FOR LOVE
   (Teddy Pendergrass)
5. STREET SONGS
   (Rick James)
6. TONIGHT
   (The Four Tops)
7. SOMETHING SPECIAL
   (Kool and the Gang)
8. TIME
   (Time)
9. SHOWTIME
   (Slave)
10. IN THE POCKET
   (Commodores)

JAZZ ALBUMS

1. BREAKIN' AWAY
   (Al Jarreau)
2. SIGN OF THE TIMES
   (Bob James)
3. FREE TIME
   (Spyro Gyra)
4. SOLID GROUND
   (Ronnie Laws)
5. STANDING TALL
   (Crusaders)
6. THE MAN WITH THE HORN
   (Miles Davis)
7. LOVE BYRD
   (Donald Byrd and 125th Street, New York City)
8. REFLECTIONS
   (Gil Scott-Heron)
9. MAGIC WINDOWS
   (Herbie Hancock)
10. THE DUDE
   (Quincy Jones)

COUNTRY SINGLES

1. NEVER BEEN SO LOVED (IN ALL MY LIFE)
   (Charley Pride)
2. STEP BY STEP
   (Eddie Rabbitt)
3. I'LL NEED SOMEONE TO HOLD ME (WHEN I CRY)
   (Janie Fricke)
4. TAKIN' IT EASY
   (Lacy J. Dalton)
5. SLEEPIN' WITH THE RADIO ON
   (Charly McClain)
6. FANCY FREE
   (The Oak Ridge Boys)
7. MY BABY THINKS HE'S A TRAIN
   (Rosanne Cash)
8. TEACH ME TO CHEAT
   (The Kendalls)
9. GRANDMA'S SONG
   (Gail Davies)
10. WISH YOU WERE HERE
   (Barbara Mandrell)

COUNTRY ALBUMS

1. FEELS SO RIGHT
   (Alabama)
2. STEP BY STEP
   (Eddie Rabbitt)
3. GREATEST HITS
   (Willie Nelson)
4. FANCY FREE
   (The Oak Ridge Boys)
5. SHARE YOUR LOVE
   (Kenny Rogers)

6. THERE'S NO GETTIN' OVER ME
   (Ronnie Milsap)
7. BARBARA MANDRELL LIVE
   (Barbara Mandrell)
8. THE PRESSURE IS ON
   (Hank Williams Jr.)
9. URBAN CHIPMUNK
   (Chipmunks)
10. KENNY ROGERS' GREATEST HITS
   (Kenny Rogers)

OCTOBER 31, 1981

POP SINGLES

1. ARTHUR'S THEME (BEST THAT YOU CAN DO)
   (Christopher Cross)
2. PRIVATE EYES
   (Daryl Hall and John Oates)
3. FOR YOUR EYES ONLY
   (Sheena Easton)
4. ENDLESS LOVE
   (Diana Ross and Lionel Richie)
5. START ME UP
   (The Rolling Stones)
6. I'VE DONE EVERYTHING FOR YOU
   (Rick Springfield)
7. TRYIN' TO LIVE MY LIFE WITHOUT YOU
   (Bob Seger and The Silver Bullet Band)
8. THE NIGHT OWLS
   (Little River Band)
9. STEP BY STEP
   (Eddie Rabbitt)
10. HARD TO SAY
   (Dan Fogelberg)

POP ALBUMS

1. TATTOO YOU
   (The Rolling Stones)
2. 4
   (Foreigner)
3. ESCAPE
   (Journey)
4. NINE TONIGHT
   (Bob Seger and The Silver Bullet Band)
5. THE INNOCENT AGE
   (Dan Fogelberg)
6. BELLA DONNA
   (Stevie Nicks)
7. PRECIOUS TIME
   (Pat Benatar)
8. SONGS IN THE ATTIC
   (Billy Joel)
9. GHOST IN THE MACHINE
   (The Police)
10. BREAKIN' AWAY
   (Al Jarreau)

BLACK SINGLES

1. NEVER TOO MUCH
   (Luther Vandross)
2. WHEN SHE WAS MY GIRL
   (The Four Tops)
3. ENDLESS LOVE
   (Diana Ross and Lionel Richie)
4. TAKE MY HEART
   (Kool and the Gang)
5. I HEARD IT THROUGH THE GRAPEVINE (PART 1)
   (Roger)
6. LET'S GROOVE
   (Earth, Wind and Fire)
7. GET IT UP
   (Time)
8. SHE'S A BAD MAMA JAMA (SHE'S BUILT, SHE'S STACKED)
   (Carl Carlton)

9. SUPER FREAK (PART 1)
   (Rick James)
10. SILLY
   (Deniece Williams)

BLACK ALBUMS

1. NEVER TOO MUCH
   (Luther Vandross)
2. THE MANY FACETS OF ROGER
   (Roger)
3. SOMETHING SPECIAL
   (Kool and the Gang)
4. IT'S TIME FOR LOVE
   (Teddy Pendergrass)
5. BREAKIN' AWAY
   (Al Jarreau)
6. TONIGHT
   (The Four Tops)
7. STREET SONGS
   (Rick James)
8. TIME
   (Time)
9. SHOWTIME
   (Slave)
10. IN THE POCKET
   (Commodores)

JAZZ ALBUMS

1. BREAKIN' AWAY
   (Al Jarreau)
2. SIGN OF THE TIMES
   (Bob James)
3. FREE TIME
   (Spyro Gyra)
4. STANDING TALL
   (Crusaders)
5. SOLID GROUND
   (Ronnie Laws)
6. THE MAN WITH THE HORN
   (Miles Davis)
7. LOVE BYRD
   (Donald Byrd and 125th Street, New York City)
8. REFLECTIONS
   (Gil Scott-Heron)
9. THE DUDE
   (Quincy Jones)
10. MAGIC WINDOWS
   (Herbie Hancock)

COUNTRY SINGLES

1. NEVER BEEN SO LOVED (IN ALL MY LIFE)
   (Charley Pride)
2. FANCY FREE
   (The Oak Ridge Boys)
3. SLEEPIN' WITH THE RADIO ON
   (Charly McClain)
4. WISH YOU WERE HERE
   (Barbara Mandrell)
5. MY BABY THINKS HE'S A TRAIN
   (Rosanne Cash)
6. SHARE YOUR LOVE WITH ME
   (Kenny Rogers)
7. TEACH ME TO CHEAT
   (The Kendalls)
8. GRANDMA'S SONG
   (Gail Davies)
9. I'LL NEED SOMEONE TO HOLD ME (WHEN I CRY)
   (Janie Fricke)
10. ALL MY ROWDY FRIENDS (HAVE SETTLED DOWN)
   (Hank Williams Jr.)

COUNTRY ALBUMS

1. GREATEST HITS
   (Willie Nelson)

2. FEELS SO RIGHT
   (Alabama)
3. SHARE YOUR LOVE
   (Kenny Rogers)
4. FANCY FREE
   (The Oak Ridge Boys)
5. THERE'S NO GETTIN' OVER ME
   (Ronnie Milsap)
6. STEP BY STEP
   (Eddie Rabbitt)
7. BARBARA MANDRELL LIVE
   (Barbara Mandrell)
8. THE PRESSURE IS ON
   (Hank Williams Jr.)
9. KENNY ROGERS' GREATEST HITS
   (Kenny Rogers)
10. URBAN CHIPMUNK
   (Chipmunks)

NOVEMBER 7, 1981

POP SINGLES

1. PRIVATE EYES
   (Daryl Hall and John Oates)
2. ARTHUR'S THEME (BEST THAT YOU CAN DO)
   (Christopher Cross)
3. FOR YOUR EYES ONLY
   (Sheena Easton)
4. ENDLESS LOVE
   (Diana Ross and Lionel Richie)
5. START ME UP
   (The Rolling Stones)
6. I'VE DONE EVERYTHING FOR YOU
   (Rick Springfield)
7. TRYIN' TO LIVE MY LIFE WITHOUT YOU
   (Bob Seger and The Silver Bullet Band)
8. THE NIGHT OWLS
   (Little River Band)
9. HERE I AM (JUST WHEN I THOUGHT I WAS OVER YOU)
   (Air Supply)
10. HARD TO SAY
   (Dan Fogelberg)

POP ALBUMS

1. 4
   (Foreigner)
2. TATTOO YOU
   (The Rolling Stones)
3. ESCAPE
   (Journey)
4. NINE TONIGHT
   (Bob Seger and The Silver Bullet Band)
5. GHOST IN THE MACHINE
   (The Police)
6. BELLA DONNA
   (Stevie Nicks)
7. ABACAB
   (Genesis)
8. SONGS IN THE ATTIC
   (Billy Joel)
9. THE INNOCENT AGE
   (Dan Fogelberg)
10. PRECIOUS TIME
   (Pat Benatar)

BLACK SINGLES

1. NEVER TOO MUCH
   (Luther Vandross)
2. TAKE MY HEART
   (Kool and the Gang)
3. WHEN SHE WAS MY GIRL
   (The Four Tops)
4. LET'S GROOVE
   (Earth, Wind and Fire)
5. I HEARD IT THROUGH THE GRAPEVINE (PART 1)
   (Roger)

6. GET IT UP
   (Time)
7. ENDLESS LOVE
   (Diana Ross and Lionel Richie)
8. CONTROVERSY
   (Prince)
9. SNAP SHOT
   (Slave)
10. SHE'S A BAD MAMA JAMA (SHE'S BUILT, SHE'S STACKED)
   (Carl Carlton)

BLACK ALBUMS

1. NEVER TOO MUCH
   (Luther Vandross)
2. THE MANY FACETS OF ROGER
   (Roger)
3. SOMETHING SPECIAL
   (Kool and the Gang)
4. IT'S TIME FOR LOVE
   (Teddy Pendergrass)
5. BREAKIN' AWAY
   (Al Jarreau)
6. TONIGHT
   (The Four Tops)
7. SHOWTIME
   (Slave)
8. TIME
   (Time)
9. STREET SONGS
   (Rick James)
10. INSIDE YOU
   (Isley Brothers)

JAZZ ALBUMS

1. BREAKIN' AWAY
   (Al Jarreau)
2. FREE TIME
   (Spyro Gyra)
3. STANDING TALL
   (Crusaders)
4. SOLID GROUND
   (Ronnie Laws)
5. SIGN OF THE TIMES
   (Bob James)
6. THE MAN WITH THE HORN
   (Miles Davis)
7. LOVE BYRD
   (Donald Byrd and 125th Street, New York City)
8. REFLECTIONS
   (Gil Scott-Heron)
9. MAGIC WINDOWS
   (Herbie Hancock)
10. TENDER TOGETHER
   (Stanley Turrentine)

COUNTRY SINGLES

1. FANCY FREE
   (The Oak Ridge Boys)
2. WISH YOU WERE HERE
   (Barbara Mandrell)
3. SLEEPIN' WITH THE RADIO ON
   (Charly McClain)
4. SHARE YOUR LOVE WITH ME
   (Kenny Rogers)
5. MY BABY THINKS HE'S A TRAIN
   (Rosanne Cash)
6. ALL MY ROWDY FRIENDS (HAVE SETTLED DOWN)
   (Hank Williams Jr.)
7. TEACH ME TO CHEAT
   (The Kendalls)
8. GRANDMA'S SONG
   (Gail Davies)
9. MISS EMILY'S PICTURE
   (John Conlee)
10. CRYING IN THE RAIN
   (Tammy Wynette)

COUNTRY ALBUMS

1. FEELS SO RIGHT
   (Alabama)
2. GREATEST HITS
   (Willie Nelson)
3. SHARE YOUR LOVE
   (Kenny Rogers)
4. FANCY FREE
   (The Oak Ridge Boys)
5. STEP BY STEP
   (Eddie Rabbitt)
6. KENNY ROGERS' GREATEST HITS
   (Kenny Rogers)
7. THERE'S NO GETTIN' OVER ME
   (Ronnie Milsap)
8. THE PRESSURE IS ON
   (Hank Williams Jr.)
9. URBAN CHIPMUNK
   (Chipmunks)
10. BARBARA MANDRELL LIVE
    (Barbara Mandrell)

NOVEMBER 14, 1981

POP SINGLES

1. PRIVATE EYES
   (Daryl Hall and John Oates)
2. PHYSICAL
   (Olivia Newton-John)
3. ARTHUR'S THEME (BEST THAT YOU CAN DO)
   (Christopher Cross)
4. HERE I AM (JUST WHEN I THOUGHT I WAS OVER YOU)
   (Air Supply)
5. WAITING FOR A GIRL LIKE YOU
   (Foreigner)
6. START ME UP
   (The Rolling Stones)
7. I'VE DONE EVERYTHING FOR YOU
   (Rick Springfield)
8. THE NIGHT OWLS
   (Little River Band)
9. TRYIN' TO LIVE MY LIFE WITHOUT YOU
   (Bob Seger and The Silver Bullet Band)
10. EVERY LITTLE THING SHE DOES IS MAGIC
    (The Police)

POP ALBUMS

1. 4
   (Foreigner)
2. TATTOO YOU
   (The Rolling Stones)
3. ESCAPE
   (Journey)
4. GHOST IN THE MACHINE
   (The Police)
5. NINE TONIGHT
   (Bob Seger and The Silver Bullet Band)
6. BELLA DONNA
   (Stevie Nicks)
7. ABACAB
   (Genesis)
8. RAISE!
   (Earth, Wind and Fire)
9. THE INNOCENT AGE
   (Dan Fogelberg)
10. SONGS IN THE ATTIC
    (Billy Joel)

BLACK SINGLES

1. TAKE MY HEART
   (Kool and the Gang)
2. LET'S GROOVE
   (Earth, Wind and Fire)

3. NEVER TOO MUCH
   (Luther Vandross)
4. I HEARD IT THROUGH THE GRAPEVINE (PART 1)
   (Roger)
5. CONTROVERSY
   (Prince)
6. GET IT UP
   (Time)
7. WHEN SHE WAS MY GIRL
   (The Four Tops)
8. SNAP SHOT
   (Slave)
9. OH NO
   (Commodores)
10. SHE'S A BAD MAMA JAMA (SHE'S BUILT, SHE'S STACKED)
    (Carl Carlton)

BLACK ALBUMS

1. RAISE!
   (Earth, Wind and Fire)
2. SOMETHING SPECIAL
   (Kool and the Gang)
3. NEVER TOO MUCH
   (Luther Vandross)
4. THE MANY FACETS OF ROGER
   (Roger)
5. IT'S TIME FOR LOVE
   (Teddy Pendergrass)
6. BREAKIN' AWAY
   (Al Jarreau)
7. SHOWTIME
   (Slave)
8. TIME
   (Time)
9. CONTROVERSY
   (Prince)
10. INSIDE YOU
    (Isley Brothers)

JAZZ ALBUMS

1. BREAKIN' AWAY
   (Al Jarreau)
2. STANDING TALL
   (Crusaders)
3. SOLID GROUND
   (Ronnie Laws)
4. FREE TIME
   (Spyro Gyra)
5. LOVE BYRD
   (Donald Byrd and 125th Street, New York City)
6. SIGN OF THE TIMES
   (Bob James)
7. THE MAN WITH THE HORN
   (Miles Davis)
8. CRAZY FOR YOU
   (Earl Klugh)
9. MAGIC WINDOWS
   (Herbie Hancock)
10. REFLECTIONS
    (Gil Scott-Heron)

COUNTRY SINGLES

1. WISH YOU WERE HERE
   (Barbara Mandrell)
2. FANCY FREE
   (The Oak Ridge Boys)
3. MY BABY THINKS HE'S A TRAIN
   (Rosanne Cash)
4. SHARE YOUR LOVE WITH ME
   (Kenny Rogers)
5. ALL MY ROWDY FRIENDS (HAVE SETTLED DOWN)
   (Hank Williams Jr.)
6. SLEEPIN' WITH THE RADIO ON
   (Charly McClain)
7. MISS EMILY'S PICTURE
   (John Conlee)

8. IF I NEEDED YOU
   (Emmylou Harris and Don Williams)
9. ONE NIGHT FEVER
   (Mel Tillis)
10. CRYING IN THE RAIN
    (Tammy Wynette)

COUNTRY ALBUMS

1. FEELS SO RIGHT
   (Alabama)
2. GREATEST HITS
   (Willie Nelson)
3. FANCY FREE
   (The Oak Ridge Boys)
4. STEP BY STEP
   (Eddie Rabbitt)
5. SHARE YOUR LOVE
   (Kenny Rogers)
6. KENNY ROGERS' GREATEST HITS
   (Kenny Rogers)
7. THERE'S NO GETTIN' OVER ME
   (Ronnie Milsap)
8. THE PRESSURE IS ON
   (Hank Williams Jr.)
9. BARBARA MANDRELL LIVE
   (Barbara Mandrell)
10. HOLLYWOOD, TENNESSEE
    (Crystal Gayle)

NOVEMBER 21, 1981

POP SINGLES

1. PHYSICAL
   (Olivia Newton-John)
2. PRIVATE EYES
   (Daryl Hall and John Oates)
3. WAITING FOR A GIRL LIKE YOU
   (Foreigner)
4. HERE I AM (JUST WHEN I THOUGHT I WAS OVER YOU)
   (Air Supply)
5. ARTHUR'S THEME (BEST THAT YOU CAN DO)
   (Christopher Cross)
6. START ME UP
   (The Rolling Stones)
7. I'VE DONE EVERYTHING FOR YOU
   (Rick Springfield)
8. THE NIGHT OWLS
   (Little River Band)
9. EVERY LITTLE THING SHE DOES IS MAGIC
   (The Police)
10. OH NO
    (Commodores)

POP ALBUMS

1. 4
   (Foreigner)
2. TATTOO YOU
   (The Rolling Stones)
3. ESCAPE
   (Journey)
4. GHOST IN THE MACHINE
   (The Police)
5. NINE TONIGHT
   (Bob Seger and The Silver Bullet Band)
6. RAISE!
   (Earth, Wind and Fire)
7. ABACAB
   (Genesis)
8. BELLA DONNA
   (Stevie Nicks)
9. THE INNOCENT AGE
   (Dan Fogelberg)
10. SOMETHING SPECIAL
    (Kool and the Gang)

BLACK SINGLES

1. TAKE MY HEART
   (Kool and the Gang)
2. LET'S GROOVE
   (Earth, Wind and Fire)
3. NEVER TOO MUCH
   (Luther Vandross)
4. I HEARD IT THROUGH THE GRAPEVINE
   (PART 1)
   (Roger)
5. CONTROVERSY
   (Prince)
6. SNAP SHOT
   (Slave)
7. WHEN SHE WAS MY GIRL
   (The Four Tops)
8. OH NO
   (Commodores)
9. GET IT UP
   (Time)
10. TURN YOUR LOVE AROUND
    (George Benson)

BLACK ALBUMS

1. RAISE!
   (Earth, Wind and Fire)
2. SOMETHING SPECIAL
   (Kool and the Gang)
3. NEVER TOO MUCH
   (Luther Vandross)
4. THE MANY FACETS OF ROGER
   (Roger)
5. CONTROVERSY
   (Prince)
6. IT'S TIME FOR LOVE
   (Teddy Pendergrass)
7. SHOWTIME
   (Slave)
8. BREAKIN' AWAY
   (Al Jarreau)
9. TIME
   (Time)
10. INSIDE YOU
    (Isley Brothers)

JAZZ ALBUMS

1. BREAKIN' AWAY
   (Al Jarreau)
2. SOLID GROUND
   (Ronnie Laws)
3. STANDING TALL
   (Crusaders)
4. LOVE BYRD
   (Donald Byrd and 125th Street,
   New York City)
5. SIGN OF THE TIMES
   (Bob James)
6. FREE TIME
   (Spyro Gyra)
7. CRAZY FOR YOU
   (Earl Klugh)
8. THE MAN WITH THE HORN
   (Miles Davis)
9. MAGIC WINDOWS
   (Herbie Hancock)
10. REFLECTIONS
    (Gil Scott-Heron)

COUNTRY SINGLES

1. ALL MY ROWDY FRIENDS (HAVE SETTLED
   DOWN)
   (Hank Williams Jr.)
2. WISH YOU WERE HERE
   (Barbara Mandrell)
3. MY BABY THINKS HE'S A TRAIN
   (Rosanne Cash)
4. MY FAVORITE MEMORY
   (Merle Haggard)
5. IF I NEEDED YOU
   (Emmylou Harris and Don Williams)
6. MISS EMILY'S PICTURE
   (John Conlee)
7. ONE NIGHT FEVER
   (Mel Tillis)
8. BET YOUR HEART ON ME
   (Johnny Lee)
9. HEART ON THE MEND
   (Sylvia)
10. IT'S ALL I CAN DO
    (Anne Murray)

COUNTRY ALBUMS

1. FEELS SO RIGHT
   (Alabama)
2. FANCY FREE
   (The Oak Ridge Boys)
3. GREATEST HITS
   (Willie Nelson)
4. STEP BY STEP
   (Eddie Rabbitt)
5. BARBARA MANDRELL LIVE
   (Barbara Mandrell)
6. KENNY ROGERS' GREATEST HITS
   (Kenny Rogers)
7. THERE'S NO GETTIN' OVER ME
   (Ronnie Milsap)
8. THE PRESSURE IS ON
   (Hank Williams Jr.)
9. SHARE YOUR LOVE
   (Kenny Rogers)
10. HOLLYWOOD, TENNESSEE
    (Crystal Gayle)

NOVEMBER 28, 1981

POP SINGLES

1. PHYSICAL
   (Olivia Newton-John)
2. PRIVATE EYES
   (Daryl Hall and John Oates)
3. WAITING FOR A GIRL LIKE YOU
   (Foreigner)
4. HERE I AM (JUST WHEN I THOUGHT I WAS
   OVER YOU)
   (Air Supply)
5. OH NO
   (Commodores)
6. START ME UP
   (The Rolling Stones)
7. ARTHUR'S THEME (BEST THAT YOU CAN
   DO)
   (Christopher Cross)
8. EVERY LITTLE THING SHE DOES IS MAGIC
   (The Police)
9. I'VE DONE EVERYTHING FOR YOU
   (Rick Springfield)
10. YOUNG TURKS
    (Rod Stewart)

POP ALBUMS

1. 4
   (Foreigner)
2. TATTOO YOU
   (The Rolling Stones)
3. ESCAPE
   (Journey)
4. GHOST IN THE MACHINE
   (The Police)
5. NINE TONIGHT
   (Bob Seger and The Silver Bullet Band)
6. RAISE!
   (Earth, Wind and Fire)
7. BELLA DONNA
   (Stevie Nicks)
8. EXIT . . . STAGE LEFT
   (Rush)
9. PHYSICAL
   (Olivia Newton-John)
10. SOMETHING SPECIAL
    (Kool and the Gang)

BLACK SINGLES

1. LET'S GROOVE
   (Earth, Wind and Fire)
2. TAKE MY HEART
   (Kool and the Gang)
3. NEVER TOO MUCH
   (Luther Vandross)
4. CONTROVERSY
   (Prince)
5. SNAP SHOT
   (Slave)
6. I HEARD IT THROUGH THE GRAPEVINE
   (PART 1)
   (Roger)
7. OH NO
   (Commodores)
8. TURN YOUR LOVE AROUND
   (George Benson)
9. GET IT UP
   (Time)
10. WHEN SHE WAS MY GIRL
    (The Four Tops)

BLACK ALBUMS

1. RAISE!
   (Earth, Wind and Fire)
2. SOMETHING SPECIAL
   (Kool and the Gang)
3. NEVER TOO MUCH
   (Luther Vandross)
4. CONTROVERSY
   (Prince)
5. THE MANY FACETS OF ROGER
   (Roger)
6. IT'S TIME FOR LOVE
   (Teddy Pendergrass)
7. SHOWTIME
   (Slave)
8. WHY DO FOOLS FALL IN LOVE
   (Diana Ross)
9. TIME
   (Time)
10. BREAKIN' AWAY
    (Al Jarreau)

JAZZ ALBUMS

1. BREAKIN' AWAY
   (Al Jarreau)
2. SOLID GROUND
   (Ronnie Laws)
3. STANDING TALL
   (Crusaders)
4. LOVE BYRD
   (Donald Byrd and 125th Street,
   New York City)
5. SIGN OF THE TIMES
   (Bob James)
6. THE GEORGE BENSON COLLECTION
   (George Benson)
7. CRAZY FOR YOU
   (Earl Klugh)
8. FREE TIME
   (Spyro Gyra)
9. REFLECTIONS
   (Gil Scott-Heron)
10. THE MAN WITH THE HORN
    (Miles Davis)

COUNTRY SINGLES

1. MY FAVORITE MEMORY
   (Merle Haggard)
2. IF I NEEDED YOU
   (Emmylou Harris and Don Williams)

3. ALL MY ROWDY FRIENDS (HAVE SETTLED DOWN)
   (Hank Williams Jr.)
4. BET YOUR HEART ON ME
   (Johnny Lee)
5. MISS EMILY'S PICTURE
   (John Conlee)
6. STILL DOIN' TIME
   (George Jones)
7. ONE NIGHT FEVER
   (Mel Tillis)
8. YOU MAY SEE ME WALKIN'
   (Ricky Skaggs)
9. HEART ON THE MEND
   (Sylvia)
10. IT'S ALL I CAN DO
    (Anne Murray)

COUNTRY ALBUMS

1. FEELS SO RIGHT
   (Alabama)
2. FANCY FREE
   (The Oak Ridge Boys)
3. GREATEST HITS
   (Willie Nelson)
4. BARBARA MANDRELL LIVE
   (Barbara Mandrell)
5. THE PRESSURE IS ON
   (Hank Williams Jr.)
6. KENNY ROGERS' GREATEST HITS
   (Kenny Rogers)
7. THERE'S NO GETTIN' OVER ME
   (Ronnie Milsap)
8. SHARE YOUR LOVE
   (Kenny Rogers)
9. STEP BY STEP
   (Eddie Rabbitt)
10. BET YOUR HEART ON ME
    (Johnny Lee)

DECEMBER 5, 1981

POP SINGLES

1. PHYSICAL
   (Olivia Newton-John)
2. WAITING FOR A GIRL LIKE YOU
   (Foreigner)
3. PRIVATE EYES
   (Daryl Hall and John Oates)
4. HERE I AM (JUST WHEN I THOUGHT I WAS OVER YOU)
   (Air Supply)
5. OH NO
   (Commodores)
6. START ME UP
   (The Rolling Stones)
7. WHY DO FOOLS FALL IN LOVE
   (Diana Ross)
8. EVERY LITTLE THING SHE DOES IS MAGIC
   (The Police)
9. YOUNG TURKS
   (Rod Stewart)
10. LET'S GROOVE
    (Earth, Wind and Fire)

POP ALBUMS

1. 4
   (Foreigner)
2. TATTOO YOU
   (The Rolling Stones)
3. ESCAPE
   (Journey)
4. GHOST IN THE MACHINE
   (The Police)
5. RAISE!
   (Earth, Wind and Fire)
6. NINE TONIGHT
   (Bob Seger and The Silver Bullet Band)

7. BELLA DONNA
   (Stevie Nicks)
8. EXIT . . . STAGE LEFT
   (Rush)
9. PHYSICAL
   (Olivia Newton-John)
10. SOMETHING SPECIAL
    (Kool and the Gang)

BLACK SINGLES

1. LET'S GROOVE
   (Earth, Wind and Fire)
2. TAKE MY HEART
   (Kool and the Gang)
3. CONTROVERSY
   (Prince)
4. TURN YOUR LOVE AROUND
   (George Benson)
5. SNAP SHOT
   (Slave)
6. NEVER TOO MUCH
   (Luther Vandross)
7. OH NO
   (Commodores)
8. WHY DO FOOLS FALL IN LOVE
   (Diana Ross)
9. GET IT UP
   (Time)
10. I HEARD IT THROUGH THE GRAPEVINE (PART 1)
    (Roger)

BLACK ALBUMS

1. RAISE!
   (Earth, Wind and Fire)
2. SOMETHING SPECIAL
   (Kool and the Gang)
3. NEVER TOO MUCH
   (Luther Vandross)
4. CONTROVERSY
   (Prince)
5. WHY DO FOOLS FALL IN LOVE
   (Diana Ross)
6. IT'S TIME FOR LOVE
   (Teddy Pendergrass)
7. THE MANY FACETS OF ROGER
   (Roger)
8. SHOWTIME
   (Slave)
9. TIME
   (Time)
10. BREAKIN' AWAY
    (Al Jarreau)

JAZZ ALBUMS

1. BREAKIN' AWAY
   (Al Jarreau)
2. SOLID GROUND
   (Ronnie Laws)
3. STANDING TALL
   (Crusaders)
4. THE GEORGE BENSON COLLECTION
   (George Benson)
5. CRAZY FOR YOU
   (Earl Klugh)
6. SIGN OF THE TIMES
   (Bob James)
7. FREE TIME
   (Spyro Gyra)
8. LOVE BYRD
   (Donald Byrd and 125th Street, New York City)
9. REFLECTIONS
   (Gil Scott-Heron)
10. SOMETHING ABOUT YOU
    (Angela Bofill)

COUNTRY SINGLES

1. IF I NEEDED YOU
   (Emmylou Harris and Don Williams)
2. BET YOUR HEART ON ME
   (Johnny Lee)
3. MY FAVORITE MEMORY
   (Merle Haggard)
4. STILL DOIN' TIME
   (George Jones)
5. ALL MY ROWDY FRIENDS (HAVE SETTLED DOWN)
   (Hank Williams Jr.)
6. ALL ROADS LEAD TO YOU
   (Steve Wariner)
7. WHAT ARE WE DOIN' LONESOME
   (Larry Gatlin and the Gatlin Brothers Band)
8. YOU MAY SEE ME WALKIN'
   (Ricky Skaggs)
9. LOVE IN THE FIRST DEGREE
   (Alabama)
10. THE WOMAN IN ME
    (Crystal Gayle)

COUNTRY ALBUMS

1. FEELS SO RIGHT
   (Alabama)
2. FANCY FREE
   (The Oak Ridge Boys)
3. GREATEST HITS
   (Willie Nelson)
4. BARBARA MANDRELL LIVE
   (Barbara Mandrell)
5. THE PRESSURE IS ON
   (Hank Williams Jr.)
6. THERE'S NO GETTIN' OVER ME
   (Ronnie Milsap)
7. KENNY ROGERS' GREATEST HITS
   (Kenny Rogers)
8. STEP BY STEP
   (Eddie Rabbitt)
9. BET YOUR HEART ON ME
   (Johnny Lee)
10. HOLLYWOOD, TENNESSEE
    (Crystal Gayle)

DECEMBER 12, 1981

POP SINGLES

1. PHYSICAL
   (Olivia Newton-John)
2. WAITING FOR A GIRL LIKE YOU
   (Foreigner)
3. PRIVATE EYES
   (Daryl Hall and John Oates)
4. LET'S GROOVE
   (Earth, Wind and Fire)
5. OH NO
   (Commodores)
6. WHY DO FOOLS FALL IN LOVE
   (Diana Ross)
7. YOUNG TURKS
   (Rod Stewart)
8. EVERY LITTLE THING SHE DOES IS MAGIC
   (The Police)
9. DON'T STOP BELIEVIN'
   (Journey)
10. HERE I AM (JUST WHEN I THOUGHT I WAS OVER YOU)
    (Air Supply)

POP ALBUMS

1. 4
   (Foreigner)
2. TATTOO YOU
   (The Rolling Stones)

3. ESCAPE
   (Journey)
4. GHOST IN THE MACHINE
   (The Police)
5. RAISE!
   (Earth, Wind and Fire)
6. FOR THOSE ABOUT TO ROCK WE SALUTE
   YOU
   (AC/DC)
7. PHYSICAL
   (Olivia Newton-John)
8. EXIT . . . STAGE LEFT
   (Rush)
9. BELLA DONNA
   (Stevie Nicks)
10. ON THE WAY TO THE SKY
    (Neil Diamond)

BLACK SINGLES

1. LET'S GROOVE
   (Earth, Wind and Fire)
2. TAKE MY HEART
   (Kool and the Gang)
3. CONTROVERSY
   (Prince)
4. TURN YOUR LOVE AROUND
   (George Benson)
5. WHY DO FOOLS FALL IN LOVE
   (Diana Ross)
6. SNAP SHOT
   (Slave)
7. OH NO
   (Commodores)
8. HIT AND RUN
   (Bar-Kays)
9. NEVER TOO MUCH
   (Luther Vandross)
10. I HEARD IT THROUGH THE GRAPEVINE
    (PART 1)
    (Roger)

BLACK ALBUMS

1. RAISE!
   (Earth, Wind and Fire)
2. SOMETHING SPECIAL
   (Kool and the Gang)
3. WHY DO FOOLS FALL IN LOVE
   (Diana Ross)
4. NEVER TOO MUCH
   (Luther Vandross)
5. CONTROVERSY
   (Prince)
6. IT'S TIME FOR LOVE
   (Teddy Pendergrass)
7. THE MANY FACETS OF ROGER
   (Roger)
8. SHOWTIME
   (Slave)
9. TIME
   (Time)
10. NIGHTCRUISING
    (Bar-Kays)

JAZZ ALBUMS

1. THE GEORGE BENSON COLLECTION
   (George Benson)
2. BREAKIN' AWAY
   (Al Jarreau)
3. SOLID GROUND
   (Ronnie Laws)
4. CRAZY FOR YOU
   (Earl Klugh)
5. COME MORNING
   (Grover Washington Jr.)
6. SIGN OF THE TIMES
   (Bob James)
7. STANDING TALL
   (Crusaders)
8. FREE TIME
   (Spyro Gyra)

9. LOVE BYRD
   (Donald Byrd and 125th Street,
   New York City)
10. REFLECTIONS
    (Gil Scott-Heron)

COUNTRY SINGLES

1. BET YOUR HEART ON ME
   (Johnny Lee)
2. STILL DOIN' TIME
   (George Jones)
3. IF I NEEDED YOU
   (Emmylou Harris and Don Williams)
4. ALL ROADS LEAD TO YOU
   (Steve Wariner)
5. LOVE IN THE FIRST DEGREE
   (Alabama)
6. WHAT ARE WE DOIN' LONESOME
   (Larry Gatlin and the Gatlin Brothers Band)
7. MY FAVORITE MEMORY
   (Merle Haggard)
8. THE WOMAN IN ME
   (Crystal Gayle)
9. YOU'RE MY FAVORITE STAR
   (The Bellamy Brothers)
10. FOURTEEN CARAT MIND
    (Gene Watson)

COUNTRY ALBUMS

1. FEELS SO RIGHT
   (Alabama)
2. FANCY FREE
   (The Oak Ridge Boys)
3. GREATEST HITS
   (Willie Nelson)
4. CHRISTMAS
   (Kenny Rogers)
5. BARBARA MANDRELL LIVE
   (Barbara Mandrell)
6. THERE'S NO GETTIN' OVER ME
   (Ronnie Milsap)
7. THE PRESSURE IS ON
   (Hank Williams Jr.)
8. KENNY ROGERS' GREATEST HITS
   (Kenny Rogers)
9. CHRISTMAS WISHES
   (Anne Murray)
10. STILL THE SAME OLE ME
    (George Jones)

DECEMBER 19, 1981

POP SINGLES

1. PHYSICAL
   (Olivia Newton-John)
2. WAITING FOR A GIRL LIKE YOU
   (Foreigner)
3. LET'S GROOVE
   (Earth, Wind and Fire)
4. PRIVATE EYES
   (Daryl Hall and John Oates)
5. YOUNG TURKS
   (Rod Stewart)
6. WHY DO FOOLS FALL IN LOVE
   (Diana Ross)
7. I CAN'T GO FOR THAT (NO CAN DO)
   (Daryl Hall and John Oates)
8. HARDEN MY HEART
   (Quarterflash)
9. DON'T STOP BELIEVIN'
   (Journey)
10. TROUBLE
    (Lindsey Buckingham)

POP ALBUMS

1. 4
   (Foreigner)

2. ESCAPE
   (Journey)
3. TATTOO YOU
   (The Rolling Stones)
4. FOR THOSE ABOUT TO ROCK WE SALUTE
   YOU
   (AC/DC)
5. RAISE!
   (Earth, Wind and Fire)
6. PHYSICAL
   (Olivia Newton-John)
7. GHOST IN THE MACHINE
   (The Police)
8. EXIT . . . STAGE LEFT
   (Rush)
9. BELLA DONNA
   (Stevie Nicks)
10. ON THE WAY TO THE SKY
    (Neil Diamond)

BLACK SINGLES

1. LET'S GROOVE
   (Earth, Wind and Fire)
2. TAKE MY HEART
   (Kool and the Gang)
3. TURN YOUR LOVE AROUND
   (George Benson)
4. CONTROVERSY
   (Prince)
5. WHY DO FOOLS FALL IN LOVE
   (Diana Ross)
6. CALL ME
   (Skyy)
7. OH NO
   (Commodores)
8. HIT AND RUN
   (Bar-Kays)
9. SNAP SHOT
   (Slave)
10. LET THE FEELING FLOW
    (Peabo Bryson)

BLACK ALBUMS

1. RAISE!
   (Earth, Wind and Fire)
2. SOMETHING SPECIAL
   (Kool and the Gang)
3. WHY DO FOOLS FALL IN LOVE
   (Diana Ross)
4. NEVER TOO MUCH
   (Luther Vandross)
5. CONTROVERSY
   (Prince)
6. IT'S TIME FOR LOVE
   (Teddy Pendergrass)
7. THE MANY FACETS OF ROGER
   (Roger)
8. SHOWTIME
   (Slave)
9. NIGHTCLUBBING
   (Grace Jones)
10. LIVE
    (The Jacksons)

JAZZ ALBUMS

1. THE GEORGE BENSON COLLECTION
   (George Benson)
2. COME MORNING
   (Grover Washington Jr.)
3. BREAKIN' AWAY
   (Al Jarreau)
4. CRAZY FOR YOU
   (Earl Klugh)
5. SOLID GROUND
   (Ronnie Laws)
6. SIGN OF THE TIMES
   (Bob James)
7. STANDING TALL
   (Crusaders)
8. FREE TIME
   (Spyro Gyra)

9. LOVE BYRD
   (Donald Byrd and 125th Street,
   New York City)
10. REFLECTIONS
   (Gil Scott-Heron)

COUNTRY SINGLES

1. STILL DOIN' TIME
   (George Jones)
2. LOVE IN THE FIRST DEGREE
   (Alabama)
3. ALL ROADS LEAD TO YOU
   (Steve Wariner)
4. BET YOUR HEART ON ME
   (Johnny Lee)
5. THE WOMAN IN ME
   (Crystal Gayle)
6. WHAT ARE WE DOIN' LONESOME
   (Larry Gatlin and the Gatlin Brothers Band)
7. FOURTEEN CARAT MIND
   (Gene Watson)
8. YOU'RE MY FAVORITE STAR
   (The Bellamy Brothers)
9. I WOULDN'T HAVE MISSED IT FOR THE
   WORLD
   (Ronnie Milsap)
10. HEADED FOR A HEARTACHE
   (Gary Morris)

COUNTRY ALBUMS

1. CHRISTMAS
   (Kenny Rogers)
2. FEELS SO RIGHT
   (Alabama)
3. FANCY FREE
   (The Oak Ridge Boys)
4. GREATEST HITS
   (Willie Nelson)
5. CHRISTMAS WISHES
   (Anne Murray)
6. THE PRESSURE IS ON
   (Hank Williams Jr.)
7. KENNY ROGERS' GREATEST HITS
   (Kenny Rogers)
8. STILL THE SAME OLE ME
   (George Jones)
9. THERE'S NO GETTIN' OVER ME
   (Ronnie Milsap)
10. BARBARA MANDRELL LIVE
   (Barbara Mandrell)

DECEMBER 26, 1981

POP SINGLES

1. PHYSICAL
   (Olivia Newton-John)
2. WAITING FOR A GIRL LIKE YOU
   (Foreigner)
3. LET'S GROOVE
   (Earth, Wind and Fire)
4. I CAN'T GO FOR THAT (NO CAN DO)
   (Daryl Hall and John Oates)
5. YOUNG TURKS
   (Rod Stewart)
6. WHY DO FOOLS FALL IN LOVE
   (Diana Ross)
7. HARDEN MY HEART
   (Quarterflash)
8. TROUBLE
   (Lindsey Buckingham)
9. DON'T STOP BELIEVIN'
   (Journey)
10. HOOKED ON CLASSICS
   (Louis Clark conducts the Royal Philharmonic
   Orchestra)

POP ALBUMS

1. 4
   (Foreigner)
2. ESCAPE
   (Journey)
3. FOR THOSE ABOUT TO ROCK WE SALUTE
   YOU
   (AC/DC)
4. TATTOO YOU
   (The Rolling Stones)
5. RAISE!
   (Earth, Wind and Fire)
6. PHYSICAL
   (Olivia Newton-John)
7. CHRISTMAS
   (Kenny Rogers)
8. MEMORIES
   (Barbra Streisand)
9. GHOST IN THE MACHINE
   (The Police)
10. ON THE WAY TO THE SKY
   (Neil Diamond)

BLACK SINGLES

1. LET'S GROOVE
   (Earth, Wind and Fire)
2. TAKE MY HEART
   (Kool and the Gang)
3. TURN YOUR LOVE AROUND
   (George Benson)
4. CALL ME
   (Skyy)
5. WHY DO FOOLS FALL IN LOVE
   (Diana Ross)
6. CONTROVERSY
   (Prince)
7. HIT AND RUN
   (Bar-Kays)
8. I CAN'T GO FOR THAT (NO CAN DO)
   (Daryl Hall and John Oates)
9. OH NO
   (Commodores)
10. LET THE FEELING FLOW
   (Peabo Bryson)

BLACK ALBUMS

1. RAISE!
   (Earth, Wind and Fire)
2. SOMETHING SPECIAL
   (Kool and the Gang)
3. WHY DO FOOLS FALL IN LOVE
   (Diana Ross)
4. NEVER TOO MUCH
   (Luther Vandross)
5. CONTROVERSY
   (Prince)
6. NIGHTCRUISING
   (Bar-Kays)
7. IT'S TIME FOR LOVE
   (Teddy Pendergrass)
8. SKYLINE
   (Skyy)
9. LIVE
   (The Jacksons)
10. THE MANY FACETS OF ROGER
   (Roger)

JAZZ ALBUMS

1. THE GEORGE BENSON COLLECTION
   (George Benson)
2. COME MORNING
   (Grover Washington Jr.)
3. BREAKIN' AWAY
   (Al Jarreau)
4. CRAZY FOR YOU
   (Earl Klugh)
5. SOLID GROUND
   (Ronnie Laws)

6. REFLECTIONS
   (Gil Scott-Heron)
7. STANDING TALL
   (Crusaders)
8. SIGN OF THE TIMES
   (Bob James)
9. FREE TIME
   (Spyro Gyra)
10. YOURS TRULY
   (Tom Browne)

COUNTRY SINGLES

1. LOVE IN THE FIRST DEGREE
   (Alabama)
2. THE WOMAN IN ME
   (Crystal Gayle)
3. FOURTEEN CARAT MIND
   (Gene Watson)
4. ALL ROADS LEAD TO YOU
   (Steve Wariner)
5. I WOULDN'T HAVE MISSED IT FOR THE
   WORLD
   (Ronnie Milsap)
6. RED NECKIN' LOVE MAKIN' NIGHT
   (Conway Twitty)
7. HEADED FOR A HEARTACHE
   (Gary Morris)
8. YOU'RE MY FAVORITE STAR
   (The Bellamy Brothers)
9. YEARS AGO
   (The Statler Brothers)
10. RODEO ROMEO
   (Moe Bandy)

COUNTRY ALBUMS

1. CHRISTMAS
   (Kenny Rogers)
2. FEELS SO RIGHT
   (Alabama)
3. CHRISTMAS WISHES
   (Anne Murray)
4. FANCY FREE
   (The Oak Ridge Boys)
5. WILLIE NELSON'S GREATEST HITS (AND
   SOME THAT WILL BE)
   (Willie Nelson)
6. GREATEST HITS
   (Kenny Rogers)
7. STILL THE SAME OLE ME
   (George Jones)
8. THERE'S NO GETTIN' OVER ME
   (Ronnie Milsap)
9. JUICE
   (Juice Newton)
10. THE PRESSURE IS ON
   (Hank Williams Jr.)

AFTERWORD

The following albums, issued between 1970 and 1981, have given me considerable pleasure. They are either works of art, historic documents, or just plain fun. These aren't all my favorites of the period, but rather a representative cross section of what I enjoyed.

1970

LIVE AT THE FILLMORE EAST
  (Allman Brothers Band)
ALL THINGS MUST PASS
  (George Harrison)
BAND OF GYPSYS
  (Jimi Hendrix)
ABRAXAS
  (Santana)
LAYLA
  (Derek and the Dominos)
GREATEST HITS
  (Sly and the Family Stone)
SEX MACHINE
  (James Brown)

1971

STICKY FINGERS
  (The Rolling Stones)
ALL DAY MUSIC
  (War)
THE LOW SPARK OF HIGH HEELED BOYS
  (Traffic)
WHO'S NEXT
  (The Who)

1972

TO BE YOUNG, GIFTED AND BLACK
  (Aretha Franklin)
SUPERFLY
  (Curtis Mayfield)
THE WORLD IS A GHETTO
  (War)
HARVEST
  (Neil Young)
LET'S STAY TOGETHER
  (Al Green)

1973

CALL ME
  (Al Green)
INNERVISIONS
  (Stevie Wonder)
LET'S GET IT ON
  (Marvin Gaye)
THE HARDER THEY COME
  (Jimmy Cliff)
GOODBYE YELLOW BRICK ROAD
  (Elton John)

1974

CAUGHT UP
  (Millie Jackson)
NEW AND IMPROVED
  (Spinners)
FIRE
  (Ohio Players)
DO IT 'TIL YOU'RE SATISFIED
  (B.T. Express)
SHIP AHOY
  (The O'Jays)
WILD AND PEACEFUL
  (Kool and the Gang)

1975

BLOOD ON THE TRACKS
  (Bob Dylan)
BORN TO RUN
  (Bruce Springsteen)
WISH YOU WERE HERE
  (Pink Floyd)
MOTHERSHIP CONNECTION
  (Parliament)
QUIET STORM
  (Smokey Robinson)

1976

SONGS IN THE KEY OF LIFE
  (Stevie Wonder)
SPIRIT
  (Earth, Wind and Fire)
WAKE UP EVERYBODY
  (Harold Melvin and the Blue Notes)
STILL CRAZY AFTER ALL THESE YEARS
  (Paul Simon)
THE PRETENDER
  (Jackson Browne)

1977

HOTEL CALIFORNIA
  (The Eagles)
AJA
  (Steely Dan)
THE STRANGER
  (Billy Joel)
A REAL MOTHER FOR YA
  (Johnny "Guitar" Watson)
HEAVY WEATHER
  (Weather Report)
LITTLE QUEEN
  (Heart)

1978

ICE PICKIN'
  (Albert Collins)
DOUBLE VISION
  (Foreigner)
IS IT STILL GOOD TO YOU
  (Nick Ashford and Valerie Simpson)
PLAYER OF THE YEAR
  (Bootsy's Rubber Band)
STARDUST
  (Willie Nelson)

EXCITABLE BOY
    (Warren Zevon)
DARKNESS ON THE EDGE OF TOWN
    (Bruce Springsteen)

1979

OFF THE WALL
    (Michael Jackson)
WE ARE FAMILY
    (Sister Sledge)
THE BOSS
    (Diana Ross)
BREAKFAST IN AMERICA
    (Super Tramp)
WHATCHA GONNA DO WITH MY LOVIN'
    (Stephanie Mills)
LADIES' NIGHT
    (Kool and the Gang)

1980

DIRTY MIND
    (Prince)
HOTTER THAN JULY
    (Stevie Wonder)
RAP'S GREATEST HITS
    (Grandmaster Flash)
THE GAME
    (Queen)
CAMEOSIS
    (Cameo)
BIG FUN
    (Shalamar)
1980
    (Gil Scott-Heron and Brian Jackson)

1981

GHOST IN THE MACHINE
    (The Police)
STREET SONGS
    (Rick James)
SHOW TIME
    (Slave)
A WOMAN NEEDS LOVE
    (Ray Parker Jr. and Raydio)
IT MUST BE MAGIC
    (Teena Marie)
GAUCHO
    (Steely Dan)
DEUCE
    (Kurtis Blow)